D0904195

JOSEPH BRANT

An Iroquois Book

Joseph Brant, 1786. Painting by Gilbert Stuart. *New York State Historical Association, Cooperstown.*

/1238
[illegible] copy 2

JOSEPH BRANT

1743-1807

MAN OF TWO WORLDS

Isabel Thompson Kelsay

ONTARIO HISTORICAL SOCIETY

SYRACUSE UNIVERSITY PRESS   1984

Copyright © 1984 by Syracuse University Press
Syracuse, New York 13210

All Rights Reserved

First Edition

Winner of the 1981 John Ben Snow Manuscript Prize

Library of Congress Cataloging in Publication Data

Kelsay, Isabel Thompson, 1905–
    Joseph Brant, 1743–1807, man of two worlds.

    (An Iroquois book)
    Bibliography: p.
    Includes index.
    1. Brant, Joseph, 1742–1807.   2. Iroquois Indians—
Biography.   3. United States—History—Revolution,
1775–1783—Participation, Indian.   4. Iroquois
Indians—Government relations.   5. Indians of North
America—Government relations—To 1789.   I. Title.
II. Title: Joseph Brant, 1743–1807.   III. Series.
E99.I7B784   1983   970.004'97   [B]   83-4701
ISBN 0-8156-0182-4

Manufactured in the United States of America

Contents

ILLUSTRATIONS

Isabel Thompson Kelsay was born in Appalachia. In a small local school she fell in love with history and has involved herself with it, in one way or another, ever since.

Dr. Kelsay holds academic degrees from three universities—Tennessee, Wisconsin, and Columbia. She has taught on the Iroquois at the Seminars in American Culture at Cooperstown, New York, and has contributed to *Calendar of North Carolina and Tennessee Papers*, *Dictionary of Canadian Biography*, *New York History*, and *East Tennessee Historical Review*.

Preface

I T HAS BEEN my pleasure to spend thirty years trying to clear up the mystery of Joseph Brant. Brant, though in my opinion the most famous American Indian who ever lived, has been for two centuries a virtual unknown. He has been solemnly described as a Mohawk, an Onondaga, a Cayuga, a Huron, a Shawnee, a Cherokee, and a half-breed Caucasian. He has been acclaimed for his aristocratic lineage and downgraded as nothing but a "common" Indian. Reputable witnesses have placed him all over the map, from London to the banks of the St. Lawrence, from Detroit to the Mohawk, at the same time. If we may believe even half that has been said about him, he was a dauntless hero, a gallant warrior whose compassion for his captives was legendary, a noble defender of Indian rights—also a drunkard, the murderer of his first-born son, and a scoundrel who robbed his own people.

In this biography I have leaned heavily on primary sources. How else, except by a careful reading of contemporary correspondence, journals, records of conferences, petitions, account books, legal documents, and the like, is one to get the feel of an era? How can one discover what Indians were really like in Joseph Brant's day unless one goes to that great collection of eighteenth-century documents known as the Johnson Papers, and reads them word for word? For Sir William Johnson knew Brant's Six Nations, and many other Indians, too, as no other man ever did, or ever will; and he can say volumes in one brief aside. Who but Johnson would be likely to drop the casual remark about his Indian neighbors that "they foamed, and Gnashed their Teeth as is common with them when in a passion"? And what can be known of Joseph Brant himself, trying to penetrate the mists of

British policy, except that he tells it all in his torment and frustration, his broken sentences preserved forever in the Haldimand Papers or the Canadian State Papers?

Because the primary bibliography must run to so great a length, the secondary bibliography, which could be many times longer, is necessarily cut back. In this instance, at least, space is not infinite. I have been able to list only a few secondary titles to cover, or provide background for, Brant's most important activities. Joseph Brant was a very busy man, and his activities were varied and far-reaching. Many authoritative works have had to be left out; oddly enough, some less than authoritative works had to be included. The interested reader, wishing further information, will have little trouble judging which are which.

Except in quotations, which are always exact, I prefer the simplest forms for Indian names as were in common use at the time. Since most Indian names have been spelled differently by English, Irish, Scotch, Dutch, French, Spanish, and German scribes, and even by such Indians as could write, who is to say what is correct? I leave this problem to those who are greater linguists, Algonquian and Iroquoian, than I am, and stick to simplicity. To the Indians themselves Ohio and Allegheny referred to the same river and Degonwadonti and Gonwatsijayenni to the same person. Joseph Brant's Indian name has been written in a variety of ways (and by himself, too), and he has been called Tekanaweta at least twice by a scribe who heard the name that way.

Some readers will think this book teems with footnotes; others will think there are too few. Both sorts, of course, will be annoyed. I have tried to document everything regarding Brant himself, even to the smallest detail; every quotation longer than three or four words; and every opinion or interpretation gleaned from another author. As to background material I have provided footnotes only for something unusually significant or that comes from some unusual source. Much background material is quite ordinary and can be checked by anybody who will read carefully in the old *American Archives*, the old *Documentary History of New York*, the *New York Colonial Documents*, or other well-known printed collections. Publications of Dartmouth College provide details about Eleazar Wheelock's earnest but inept young Indian missionaries, who were the friends and associates of Brant's youth. Finally, a word of warning: the *general*, as well as the *specific*, context of all statements must be considered by the researcher at all times. As in the Bible, support can be found somewhere in some document for almost any opinion provided a particular statement stands, and is considered, alone.

I owe thanks far and wide. This is expecially true regarding the staff of the great Public Archives of Canada, that wonderful depository of manuscripts, where one may work twenty-four hours a day, every day—that is, one may if one can. It has been a long time since I worked in Chicago, and Detroit, and Ann Arbor, and Williamsburg, and Princeton, and New York and Toronto and Albany, and Washington and Boston, but I remember fondly the helpful friends I met in those places. Philadelphia, near my home, has fine libraries, and I have been running back and forth among them for years, while kindly librarians have come and gone.

There was an especially good friend whom I never met whose enduring passion was historical research. He was Canadian born, and he knew all those little Canadian byways an American might never have found, and he sent me copies of significant bits of material which have contributed much to my understanding and knowledge. (I suspect he helped many others, too.) I owe to Dr. Carson E. Johnson, of St. Thomas, Ontario, a friend I never saw, my most sincere thanks for all that aid.

To Dr. Milton W. Hamilton, authority on Sir William Johnson, I also owe sincere thanks for his participation in interesting discussions, and long letters, and the loan of manuscripts I did not even know existed. And to my old friends, Charles and Edna Norgan, who took the time while on vacation to photograph Roche de Bout for me, many thanks, too.

Lastly, to my dear husband, Vernon Kelsay, who was always the first to admit he knew nothing about Indians in general or Joseph Brant in particular, and who has gone these three years on a long journey, my heartfelt gratitude; for he did everything that he possibly could to help me—nor was there ever anyone like him for propping up a poor soul when she got discouraged and fell into a gloom.

Though this is Joseph Brant's own history, I have tried to be even-handed; for he could look two ways, and sometimes he had to *work* at being an Indian even though his heart was always with his people. Many men and women entered Joseph's life. They are of both sides and both races. I have encountered among them few saints and only a few blackened sinners, but a great many who were neither the one nor the other. Some of these people it has been a real privilege to know. One must admire the unconquerable spirit of Margaret Brant who would do *anything* to get to the Plentiful Country; or Philip Schuyler, patriot, who has never yet received his due; and that indomitable Gansevoort family who could urge a loved young son and brother to conquer or die, though the youthful Peter needed no such admonition. And whose heart will not mourn for honest Little Abraham, trudging through the snows on his impossible errand?

Joseph has been a good companion. Traveling in his company was never a bore. Who but Joseph could worry so hard about so many things and the next moment be playing pranks? Or dancing all night? Or ordering gold lace? The pilgrimage has had its excitements, too. There was the time, for instance, when Peter and Margaret first appeared and introduced themselves; when the letter was found that described in detail Joseph's and Peggie's wedding; and when suddenly out of the fog the figures of Catharine and Henry began to take shape and so much that was mysterious became plain.

Media, Pennsylvania   ITK
January 1983

JOSEPH BRANT

1

The World of the Longhouse

CONTROVERSY has long obscured the particulars of Joseph Brant's birth. The time, the place, his parentage, his station in life, have been subjects of earnest debate. Yet one fact always stands out. Those who knew the famed chief best, however contradictory their other testimony, do not deny that he was born in the Longhouse.

The educated Brant, who seldom spoke in the idiom of his people, did not often mention the Longhouse by name. One time that he did was on a hot August day in 1779. It was just before the decisive battle of Newtown. As he lay concealed in the woods, counting out his own scanty forces, awaiting the approach of an enemy whose overwhelming might assured him almost certain defeat, he looked ahead in an agony of anxiety to the near and uncertain future. "Then we shall begin to know," he said, "what is to befal[l] us the People of the Long House." And later, as he made those toilsome journeys, sometimes for months at a time, west, northwest, south and east—to Detroit, to the Maumee River and the Ohio, to Montreal and Quebec, to Albany and Philadelphia, twice across the ocean—he journeyed with one purpose: to reestablish the freedom of his people, to make the fallen Longhouse once more respected and "respectable."

At last, tired and beaten down by circumstances, Brant tried to run away from the Longhouse; and he built a fine residence among white people. It was no use. He could not escape. He would spend the rest of his life traveling the miles between fine new residence and old home.

The Longhouse of Joseph Brant's anxiety and concern was ancient, even then. For centuries the League of the Iroquois (as the

1

Iroquois Village Life c. A.D. 1600. Scale Diorama. The World of the Long-house was Joseph Brant's heritage. *Courtesy of the Rochester Museum and Science Center, Rochester, New York. Photograph by William G. Frank.*

French called them) or the Confederacy of the Five Nations (according to the English) had likened their renowned political union to a house. As early as 1654 one of their chieftains told a French missionary: "We, the five Iroquois Nations, compose but one cabin; we maintain but one fire; and we have, from time immemorial, dwelt under one and the same roof."[1]

That all-encompassing roof, of which the primitive chief spoke with such poetry, covered an imaginary house that was as real to its people as the long bark huts they actually lived in and after which it was modeled. More than 250 miles in length, the imaginary house reached all the way across what is now central New York but what was, then, only a tangled wilderness of beech, maple and elm, and pine and hemlock, in its fastnesses the lair of the black bear and the wolf. One could go out the east door of the Iroquois Longhouse and hear the mighty falls of Cohoes as the Mohawk River thundered down toward the Hudson, and one could see from the west door the riotous, tumbling Genesee. The Longhouse could scarcely have commanded a more strategic location. The only easy way from east to west for the struggling English and Dutch colonies that occupied the Atlantic seaboard lay through its corridor. Everywhere else loomed the forbidding bulk of the Appalachian Mountains.

Five families of Indians inhabited the Longhouse, each in its own rightful place beside the mystic corridor; and each gave its name to a stream or lake in its vicinity. The Mohawks guarded the east door and lived on the river that bears their name. Going gradually westward, the Oneidas, the Onondagas, the Cayugas, and the more numerous Senecas who watched the western door had each a lake; while several of the families could claim both a river and a lake as namesakes. About these rivers and lakes the Indians had burned and hacked clearings in the forest, and in these fertile clearings their women with little effort, and using only stone hoes, raised luxuriant gardens of squashes and beans. Fine cornlands stretched as far as the eye could see.

The five families or "nations" called themselves Kanonsionni, meaning "People of the Longhouse," and they spoke of one another as brethren. About the formation of their Confederacy or League they told a story which had been handed down from their forefathers and which varied somewhat from place to place and from person to person, but all the story-tellers agreed that their union was a union of peace. On this main point they placed great emphasis. The people of the Five Nations, according to unvarying tradition, had chosen to sit down together under the Tree of Peace.

Joseph Brant, who at one time planned to write the history of the Longhouse and who knew its history as well as anyone, gave his version of the founding legend thus: A long time ago, he related, many years before white people came to our country, there lived in a Mohawk village just above the Little Falls, two brothers, who were chiefs of the village. The elder, named Tekanawidagh, kept the east gate; and the younger, named Adergaghtha, watched the western gate. Tekanawidagh was a peaceable man, but Adergaghtha was cruel and had no peace for anyone who came within his reach.

The evil disposition of his brother grieved Tekanawidagh very much, Joseph continued, and finally the good chief resolved to do something about it. He set out for the west to find some allies who might help him obtain peace. First he went to the neighboring

Oneidas and explained his plan of a confederacy to their chief, Otatseghte. The latter fell in with the idea at once and, being the younger
man, politely addressed Tekanawidagh as "father." Tekanawidagh
with matching courtesy suggested that the son take precedence in the
union, but Otatseghte modestly declined the honor. The two chiefs
then decided that they would be equals.

After a while the Mohawk and the Oneida went on together to
Onondaga, the next country. The leader there, T'hadodarhoagh,
stubbornly refused to join them, no matter how much they pleaded.
Not until Tekanawidagh proposed that the Onondaga should keep the
great council fire of the confederacy, was he at last won over by the
distinction and induced to come in.

The chiefs next proceeded to Cayuga Lake, where they met no
opposition. They immediately named the Cayuga chief son, and
brother to the Oneidas. Finally they went on to the far country of the
Senecas, and here they found two leading chiefs who also agreed to
join them. The Senecas, because of their frontier situation, were
assigned the rank of doorkeeper of the confederacy.

All these negotiations took more than four years to accomplish.
Thereafter, as Joseph carefully explained, the five separate nations
considered themselves mutually bound to share one another's fortune,
whether good or bad, and to act toward one another with brotherly
and filial love.[2]

Joseph Brant's story was part legend and part actual history. Sometime in the dim past, probably over a span of many years, a working
union gradually had evolved among the Iroquois Indians of central
New York. By making it possible to substitute a blood price for a blood
feud, this union had promoted peace, slowing down the destructive
quarrels of those primitive people. The Mohawks, Onondagas, and
Senecas actually were, as Brant's legend indicates, the fathers or
senior partners in the Confederacy, and the Oneidas and Cayugas
were the sons or junior partners. The former were also called, at times,
elder brothers, and the latter, younger brothers.

Each of these five nations, while managing its own local affairs,
furnished a fixed quota of civil chiefs to the grand Confederate Council at Onondaga. These chiefs, or sachems, were hereditary in the
sense that they were chosen from certain leading families, descent
being in the female line; and they bore the same official names from
one generation to the next, perpetuating in their persons the names of
the leaders alive at the time of the League's founding. These civil
chiefs held office for life or during good behavior, for the aristocratic
families who appointed them also could remove them. They were not

often removed, however, save for extreme age or serious disability, and they enjoyed considerable prestige among their people. As late as 1794 the observant Mrs. Simcoe, wife of the lieutenant governor of Upper Canada, noted that the Indian leaders were usually attended by apparent inferiors who walked behind them; and only the chiefs, she said, shook hands with the governor.

Interesting though it was, the Five Nations Confederacy was not unique. Other Indians also had political unions, which had evolved probably in similar ways; and their unions also promoted peace. Circumstances of geography, history, and economics were to make of the Iroquois League something set apart.

It was the coming of the white man that worked the great change. In 1609 the Dutch reached the head of navigation on the Hudson River and there, only a short journey from the east door of the Longhouse, founded, a few years later, the settlement that was to become Albany. The Dutch brought with them guns and ammunition and cloth and (to the Indians) wondrous tools of metal. The Indians had bows and arrows and primitive tools of bone and stone, and their clothing was made of skins. They saw what the Dutch had to offer and their own Stone-Age produce no longer satisfied them. Soon they were bartering their peltry for European goods, peltry being the only thing they had that the Dutch wanted.

About the same time other Indians, on the Susquehanna, on the Delaware, in Canada, and, to some extent, in New England, were also exchanging furs and skins with various Swedish, French, and English traders for the coveted firearms, metal, and cloth. So began the famous fur trade that was to alter the course of history. American furs, warm and beautiful, found ready markets in western Europe, in Russia, and even around the world in China. White traders (and they included nearly everybody on the various frontiers) wanted these furs quite as much as the Indians wanted manufactured goods. The demand on both sides seemed inexhaustible, and the trade flourished like the Psalmist's green baytree.

For the Five Nations this feverish trade soon proved disastrous. Fur-bearing animals, notably the beaver, whose pelt was so prized in hatmaking, had never been too plentiful in their country. Incessantly hunted and trapped, these animals grew in ever shorter supply. At the same time the people of the Five Nations were becoming more and more dependent on European manufactures, so soon does man lose an unused skill. Even if they had wished, they could not wholly go back to their old ways. To be comfortable and happy, even to survive, they had to find a new source of furs.

Urgently they looked around, but in every direction they saw other Indians, their competitors in trade, hemming them in. Many of these rivals were of their own Iroquoian linguistic stock, and some were of the neighboring Algonquian stock whose language the Five Nations could not understand and had much difficulty in learning. But kin or strangers, the surrounding Indians stood as obstacles in their search for furs.

The main obstacle, however, existed in the north, in Canada, where the French colonists and their native allies, the Hurons, had monopolized the entire trade of the vast north country and the upper Great Lakes. In the cold northland furs were not only more plentiful than elsewhere but far more desirable. The Five Nations set out to get part of this rich trade. They tried diplomacy; and the Hurons, also an Iroquoian people, seem not to have been averse to a treaty of friendship. There was a possibility that the Confederacy could become middlemen in the trade. At this point the French intervened. Alarmed lest their only article of profitable commerce be drawn away to the Dutch in New Netherland, they took pains to thwart a Huron-Five Nations rapprochement. For the Confederates, frustrated in their hopes of an easy accommodation, there remained only the warpath.[3]

Heretofore the Five Nations had probably done no more fighting than any primitive people and met with no more than ordinary success—that is, they had engaged in petty strife for glory or revenge, and they had experienced enough victories to look forward to others. But now they had to win or starve, and necessity made might. They also possessed a great advantage. They had, with reference to the peoples they must fight, an almost impregnable military position. They bordered the main French trade route of the St. Lawrence and Lake Ontario, and they had easy access down many large and small streams to their enemies of the south and west. If the going got too hard for them, there were always mountains and forests into which they could retreat.

With such a strong motive and with such a decided advantage the warriors of the Confederacy were able to defeat, by the end of the seventeenth century, all the Indians who surrounded them, and had succeeded in making life miserable for the white colonists of New France. The rival Hurons were overcome in 1649, and in the next few years the Petuns to the northward and the Neutrals and Eries who lived in the west went down before a furious onslaught. It took longer to defeat the Mahicans of the Hudson River valley (who were brash enough to claim part of the Longhouse country), but this was finally accomplished, mainly by the Mohawks who lived on their borders, and peace made by 1673. In this warfare the Mohawks got so terrible a reputation that the neighboring New England Indians took to their heels at the sight of a single one of them. "A Mohawk! A Mohawk!" they would cry in panic, and fly like sheep before wolves. About the same time the Senecas at the other end of the Longhouse were fighting a hard war with the Susquehannock Indians who lived on the lower Susquehanna River, in Maryland and what is now Pennsylvania. The Susquehannocks were no mean adversary, but they were finally subdued in 1675. The Senecas, too, acquired a terrible reputation.[4]

As the Five Nations overcame their neighbors, the survivors were often brought under the Tree of Peace and absorbed. This wise and humane policy not only increased the population of the conquerors but also made friends of conquered enemies. Like the real longhouse, the symbolic Longhouse was capable of great extension. New families and new fireplaces could be added to the one, individuals or even whole "nations" to the other. In just this way some of Joseph Brant's own ancestors were brought into the Longhouse. Joseph used to relate a story told him by his mother of how his Wyandot (Huron) grandmother had been captured by Mohawks. The Mohawk warriors found their youthful captive trying to hide on an island in Lake Ontario where she had fled when the fighting reached her village. When the victorious warriors returned home to the Mohawk River, they carried their prisoner along with them. Here Joseph's grandmother was adopted by a Mohawk family, lived out her life, and grew content with her lot.[5]

Other conquered peoples might be assigned land to live upon and so become faithful "Props to the Longhouse." For instance, some scattered Delawares and Shawnees, two Algonquian peoples, the former of whom seem to have been allied to the defeated Susquehannocks, were permitted, along with various other strays, to move into the Susquehanna valley under Five Nations authority. In this way the Iroquois secured the southern entrance to their own country, and for many years they were able to forbid white men to enter by this route.

The bulk of the conquered Delawares and Shawnees eventually moved away to the west where, from the Iroquois point of view, they still remained dependents. These wandering Indians were to make history again and again. Like most subject peoples, they felt aggrieved; but the former had a very personal grievance. It is not clear how it happened (the Delawares claimed they were tricked), but somehow or other, sometime or other, the Delawares acquired the status of "women"—that is, they lost the right to make war or peace on their own. In the picturesque imagery of the Indians, the Five Nations put "petticoats" on them. The thought of these petticoats rankled in the hearts of the Delawares for many years.[6] Try as they might to throw off the hated garments, the effort never seemed to get them anywhere. The Delawares, and the Shawnees, too, continued to nurse their grudges; and the farther away they roamed, the less they behaved like proper dependents. Over and over their distant monitors had to reprove them for their bad conduct.

The last Iroquois conquest, or attempt at conquest, took place in the far west. In the 1680s the Five Nations turned their attention to the Illinois country. Here they met no such resounding success as they were used to. Illinois was too far away and the Iroquois raiders too few. But the Five Nations established a shadowy claim to that area, whose inhabitants they also claimed as dependents or "allies"; and they extended their "empire," in talk at least, to the banks of the Mississippi. These were the great days of Longhouse glory, to be celebrated by the aged, in stories around the fire, for all time to come.

Strangely enough, these great conquerors, even at the height of their fame, were unable to take over any substantial part of the northwest fur trade. Indians far out of their reach continued to serve the French monopoly. The Five Nations still had to content themselves with the produce of their own hunters' labor. Though they had seized vast new hunting grounds, they could never feel quite secure in their conquests. There were always hostile Indians to reckon with, and latterly there were white people who appeared to be looking with hungry eyes at the Longhouse domain. The wisest among the Iroquois felt a growing sense of their own weakness. The Five Nations might be a terror to a far-flung territory, but they were also relatively few in numbers. At their best they seem to have had a population of only about fifteen thousand or so, and, by the late 1600s, even those numbers were growing less. Incessant war was taking its toll. So, too, were disease, famine, and vice, problems which had increased since the white man's advent.

Having achieved no great economic success by warfare, the sachems of the Onondaga Council, about the turn of the new century, carefully reappraised their policy and determined upon peace, especially with their European neighbors. Heretofore they had been friends with the Dutch settlers in New Netherland and then with the English successors of the Dutch, but implacable enemies to the French. This situation suited the English very well, for the English and the French had brought along their old animosities to the new world. The English were also eyeing the lucrative French fur trade as traders of both nationalities began to vie with each other in the vast wilderness to the west. Happily the English sang the praises of their native allies. "The five Indian nations . . . are a bulwark between us @ the French @ all other Indians," boasted Governor Dongan of New York in 1687. Another time he declared they "are a better defence to us, than if they were so many Christians."[7] But the English had an unpleasant surprise coming.

With French and English rivalries growing (for the French and the English had just concluded their first war for control of the continent and were about to embark upon the second), the sachems of the Confederacy saw a way to play off one white power against the other, to their own advantage. It was a brilliant solution to their predicament. If at peace themselves, they reasoned, they could take what furs they had to the better market; and, with so many wants, now, and so little opportunity to supply them, they could obtain gifts to make up the deficiency, from both sides. Peace on their part would also save the Five Nations country from the periodic French invasions which, though not of much military consequence, had been painful. Most important of all, these Indians, who were by no means unaware of their larger interests, hoped to prevent either the French or the English from growing too strong. Already they were beginning to harbor uneasy suspicions of burgeoning white strength. With these thoughts in mind they made a treaty of friendship with the French in 1701 at Montreal and another with the English in Albany a few months later. It was a complete about-face. The Five Nations were to spend the better part of the next century trying to cling to and implement this policy of neutrality in white quarrels.[8]

The English, expert balancers of power themselves, were stunned. At first they imagined that this new aloofness of their Indian friends was all a Jesuit trick. Finally it dawned on them where the trickery lay. Then the unhappy English, or British (for the union with Scotland had been accomplished), acknowledged that their one-time allies were "the most Politic" of peoples and, as fellow craftsmen, grudgingly admired their skill in diplomacy. The French, who had been reeling under Iroquois blows for years, might be supposed to have considered any change as a change for the better. But the French were displeased, too. The behavior of *les sauvages*, fumed French authorities, was "indecent."

The Five Nations held tenaciously to their neutral role. The wily sachems saw to it that they and their people got plenty of presents as they, with an air of artless candor, carried news of British overtures to Canada and news of French overtures to the British. Hungry and ragged these chiefs might often be, for their old skills in maintaining themselves continued to decrease; but whenever they showed up at the fort in Albany or Montreal, they were greeted by a five-gun salute, and while on the premises they were provisioned at the public expense, this being a humble admission that the fort stood by their consent. And when, after the conference with the French or British was over, the chiefs set out for home again, they took with them canoes loaded with blankets, cloth, hoes, guns, kettles, war paint, brass and silver jewelry, food delicacies and rum, and all the other appurtenances of what they considered good living. There would be joy in the Indian country while these supplies lasted.

Fresh from their conquests, the Five Nations had at first no need to assert the value of their friendship. But as the years passed on, and the League's reputation dimmed a little while the white people were growing in numbers and confidence, then, indeed, the chiefs were likely to proclaim themselves a great imperial power. When the speechmaking grew warm, they would assert their dominion over all the lands and peoples from the St. Lawrence and Great Lakes west to the distant Mississippi, and south to the far-off Cherokee (Tennessee) River, and sometimes even from Hudson Bay to the Carolinas. Hordes of allies, so their white audience could infer, awaited their mere call. The Mohawks, who kept the eastern door that directly faced the British, were particularly good at this bluster. What a great people they were! They did not need to raise their whole hand against their enemies. No! Their little finger was enough!

The white people, confused by their own notions of empire and alliances, listened respectfully. This respect was reinforced by the still formidable reputation of the Iroquois warriors. Were not three hundred of them a match for a thousand Frenchmen or as many British? This belief was no uncommon factor in the calculations of the whites. It placed upon the white colonists, especially the British, who had begun to crave land quite as much as, if not more than, the precious furs, a certain prudent restraint. Though they might nibble tentatively at the nearest edges of Longhouse country—a fact of which the local Mohawks were becoming uncomfortably aware—its whole vast extent seemed forever out of their reach.

The Iroquois sachems labored hard to present to the world a façade of strength and unity, and in the main they succeeded. As the eighteenth century wore on, no less a man than Benjamin Franklin could openly admire the Confederacy. The thoughtful Franklin marveled to see so lasting and powerful a union of what he called "ignorant Savages." Indeed, he predicted it would be a most desirable event if the British colonies could create a similar union and, he implied, do as well for themselves as the Indians had done.[9]

But the grand Iroquois façade was not always as strong as it looked. Though the Confederacy had reduced the number of blood feuds among its members, the several nations had never been able to forget all their conflicting interests. Between the Senecas and the Mohawks, in particular, a permanent jealousy subsisted, for each nation liked to consider itself first in the League. On one occasion the Dutch Governor Stuyvesant, in presenting some Senecas with a keg of powder, felt it necessary to urge them not to use it against the Mohawks. When the Senecas and Cayugas were waging their hard-fought war against the Susquehannocks, the Mohawks greeted the latter as their children and told them they might come to live with them. Both the Mohawks and the Onondagas were openly pleased when the French Denonville attacked the Senecas. Some Mohawks who had gone to live in Canada actually guided Denonville's expedition into the Seneca heartland. Over a century later Joseph Brant told some white settlers in the area that his grandfather was one of those guides and pointed out where the battle was fought.[10] Like grandfather, like grandson. Between Joseph, the Mohawk, and certain Seneca leaders of his day there would always be friction.

These unleashed animosities and pulling at cross-purposes show up the main weaknesses of the League. One obvious weakness was the necessity for complete agreement in the Council. The chiefs of the Confederacy could talk and talk, but unanimity was a requirement for action. Unfortunately, even the wisest of the chiefs might reflect the clashing interests of the various nations more than they reflected their mutual ties, and unanimity was hard to come by. But the union had a still graver defect. If the leaders did come to an agreement, their policy, no matter how carefully formulated, bound nobody. The League had no coercive power, no system of enforceable public law. In national affairs there was only moral force; in personal affairs there was only private revenge. Not only the several nations, but even individuals, could do as they chose.

The neutrality established in 1701, therefore, was never completely adhered to. Some of the young fellows *would* take sides. A good fight was sport to those who did not get hurt; and the young warriors, by their mode of hit-and-run raids and almost invisible woods fighting, did not suffer very much. Even mature chiefs, subjected to intense white pressures, might agree to lead a war party against some attractive objective. Yet for fifty-eight years neither the British nor the French could ever persuade more than a handful of the entire Confederacy to break the neutrality. In spite of white subtleties and white bribes the Five Nations stood firm. Their union seemed to grow stronger. Overt hostilities toward one another cooled off. The chiefs could boldly proclaim that a threat to one nation was a threat to all.

Neither the British nor the French were in a position to make threats. The Iroquois were far too important to both sides. For a long time they held the balance of power between the two contenders. In the colonial wars of the eighteenth century no white commander dared to start out on an expedition without a few warriors. As guides and scouts the Indians were a necessity. In woods fighting they had no superiors. As one French official explained it: "They are conversant with the forests and the paths through those vast wildernesses, and follow the trail of men, as of wild beasts; and whether in wet or dry soil, calculate on the autumn leaves, their number pretty nearly as correctly as if they saw them. . . . They act bravely when they please; risk much to secure the scalp of a man they have killed, which they have sometimes taken amidst a storm of musket balls, and are very adroit in surprising their enemies. They would be a great assistance to us, were they willing to serve us faithfully, and we are always in need of some of them."[11] In this estimate the British fully concurred. Whoever gained the most Indians, suspected the warring rivals, would gain the continent.

The British had boasted of their allies and continually tried to win them back. The French were not idle, either. White agents busied themselves in the Indian villages. Traders and even blacksmiths served a political as well as an economic purpose. Missionaries served a double purpose, too, bringing with them a little religion and a leaning toward the one king or the other. In years of relative calm these men of God might slacken their efforts or even disappear; but when a new crisis began to heat up, a new missionary would somehow arrive upon the scene. In the midst of war and war's alarms the cause of Christianity slowly advanced among the Nations. "But with them we must always be the strongest, and be giving them," lamented the French.[12] Yet both contenders did not stint, and both made some headway. Some Mohawks, Joseph Brant's parents among them, early accepted the Anglican faith and fell into the political orbit of the neighboring British. Meanwhile the Senecas who lived close to the French post of Niagara were drawn irresistibly into the French orbit. The people of the other Nations were pulled about, hither and yon.

Some Mohawks preferred the French, too, and wore the crucifixes of the Catholic faith, Joseph Brant's "grandfather" being one such. In the late seventeenth century these Mohawks ("seduced" by Jesuits, as Mohawk sachems charged) had moved off to the St. Lawrence River to live under French protection. The emigrants settled above the Sault St. Louis, or Lachine Rapids, near Montreal. They called their village and mission Caughnawaga, a name, like that of the old home they had left, descriptive of a location "At the rapids." Later some of these Caughnawaga Indians split off and moved upstream to St. Regis Point, forming another pro-French settlement. A third band of Iroquois settlers, among them some of Brant's relations, made their homes at Caneghsadagey, or Lake of the Two Mountains, at the mouth of the Ottawa River near Montreal;[13] and still a fourth village of Five Nations people was established at Oswegatchie (Ogdensburg, New York) in 1749. The French gave the Oswegatchie emigrants a fort as well as a mission—the fort, of course, an eyesore to British New York.

These four pro-French Iroquois settlements, combined with a few Algonquian Indians who also lived in the St. Lawrence valley, spoke of themselves as the Seven Nations of Canada, and they long served as a barrier for the protection of Montreal. Though they had their disputes with the parent Confederacy, they generally acknowledged its overlordship and were mostly friendly. There was a great deal of coming and going on each side of the border, much to the distress of both colonial governments. The white people suspected (probably rightly) that the Canada Indians sometimes allowed their Five Nations relatives to take French captives, while the Indians of the Five Nations permitted their Canadian kin to take British captives. It was well known that these Indians did not like to fight each other, no matter which white power they leaned toward or who persuaded them to go to war. Nevertheless, the more responsible Five Nations leaders disapproved of any breach of the neutrality, and they often urged their wandering people to come home.

A famous example of the British attempt to woo the Confederacy took place in 1710. Peter Schuyler, a member of the New York Indian Commission, persuaded some Mohawks and an allied "River" Indian to go with him to London. The four Anglo-minded Indians caused a great stir at the court of Queen Anne who was waging her war with France at the time. Passed off as an "emperor" and three "kings" (though only one of the travelers was a sachem), these Indians were presented to the queen by Schuyler and his friends to draw the attention of the British to the American theater of war and to impress the Indians themselves with the might of Britain, and thus to intensify local British and Indian military efforts. The ruse succeeded, in a sense. Queen Anne did send an expedition against Canada. As for the four Indians, they became the heroes of a ballad, sat for their portraits, learned to sleep in English beds, and were properly dazzled by all that they saw. They made an eloquent speech to the queen, urging the British to conquer Canada. Their own people, they implied, would leap at the chance to do their part. (Actually, their people did nothing of the kind.) Years afterward, when Joseph Brant himself visited London under much the same circumstances, he told the biographer, James Boswell, that his "grandfather" was one of the Indians honored by Queen Anne.[14] This must have been another of Brant's grandfathers, not the pro-French ancestor who guided Denonville.

Already it was obvious that the Mohawks, because of their geographical situation, would be the first member of the Confederacy to give up all pretensions to neutrality. Each passing year was making it a little more difficult for the Indians who lived at the eastern door of the Longhouse. The white settlers in New York were pressing harder all around them. The result was that in King George's War of 1744–48 several Mohawk war parties went out against Canada. The Mohawk villages were now so hedged in by the local whites that they had scant choice but to act as their allies. This display of weakness did not set well with the other Nations. The Senecas, especially, watched with disgust as the Mohawks wavered. They themselves felt little of the British pressure. The Mohawks, they declared scornfully, had become slaves to the English! They threatened to "kick them from them."

In the meantime, beginning about 1710, the Five Nations got a welcome addition to their numbers. Several bands of Tuscaroras, an Iroquoian people hard beset in their native Carolina, were from time to time admitted into the Longhouse and allowed to sit down under the Tree of Peace. The Oneidas gave them land near one of their own villages; and, while the newcomers did not become full-fledged members of the League, they were numerous enough to be considered by the British and by the Indians themselves as another Nation. After the first quarter of the eighteenth century the Confederacy was more and more styled the *Six* Nations.

With the two rival powers bidding so hard for their favor, the Six Nations chiefs, though the situation of the Confederacy was worsening, were still able to make good use of their boasted neutrality. They managed to get something of value at every meeting with the white people. One chief, at a time of great public alarm, laid it on the line to a British official thus: "Brother [the Indians always addressed the white man as brother or, if appropriate, as father]—as we are verry poorly Cloathed for the Season of the Year, and agst ye approaching Snows & Cold, we hope you will take pitty of us, & not let our Enemies laugh [he really meant, don't let *your* enemies laugh!] should they see us lye perished by the Road, and say these are Bretheren to the English. we also entreat you will give us a little Ammunition, having none to hunt with, w^h is ye reason of our poverty."[15]

Yet the Indians, in their own way, clung to their self-respect. The payments which on any trifling occasion the two rivals might make to a few chiefs to ensure their neutrality or, as it was sometimes hoped, to obtain their aid, the Indians themselves always called presents. Though payments to men were insults under their code, the presents (so desperately needed) were proper and polite, and could be carried home to their families without shame. On these small occasions the Indians brought gifts of their own if they could, venison or perhaps turkeys or fresh fish. The white people were forced to play this game as the Indians wanted it played. The whites also called the payments "presents."

Then there were the formal diplomatic occasions. At such times the Indians, as was their wont, brought important gifts, valuable furs if possible or the heavy, more utilitarian hides. The officer who received these presents was supposed to credit them to his government and put them away in storage. Perhaps he did this. Perhaps he did not. But the Indians who visited the posts, especially in the west, came to believe that they could "cover" (that is, buy or bribe) any white official with a beaver blanket! If the Indians had nothing of value to bring to a diplomatic function, they could always give land. The famed Sir William Johnson (whom we shall meet in time) told his government that he often received unsolicited gifts of land which he could not refuse, but which cost him a great deal in presents and which he did not patent. But generally white officials, whether British or French, did not talk too much about what they received.

On these state occasions the meeting together and the bestowing of the presents became a set and solemn ceremony usually referred to by all participants as "renewing the covenant chain," or "brightening the covenant chain of friendship." The concept of the metal covenant chain, though of Dutch origin, was an idea which appealed to the Indian's lively imagination. "You see how early we made Friendship with You," the chiefs might say in council with the British. "We tied each other in a very strong Chain, that Chain has not yet been broken, We now clean and rub that Chain to make it Brighter and stronger, And we determine on our part that it never shall be broken, and we hope you will take care that neither you or any one else shall break it." Such a valuable chain! What is it worth to you? was the unspoken question. Though the Six Nations orators could not say quite so much to the French, still the polishing of even a relatively new covenant chain did not come cheap. It was clear to all that the chiefs expected something of consequence in return.[16]

The white people always paid up. Indeed, this system of diplomatic gifts had its advocates even among them. It was much favored by the manufacturers of Indian goods, most of whom lived across the sea and had never seen an Indian. It was also favored by the merchants of both countries who dealt in Indian goods. It was not at all favored by the taxpayers, either in the colonies or in Europe, but during wars and threats of wars they had to endure it. The situation contained seeds of trouble. But of taxpayers and their problems the Indians were blessedly unconscious. They had no taxes and no taxpayers, themselves.

In all their negotiations with the Indians both British and French authorities behaved to the Confederacy as though they considered it an independent nation. Neither, of course, actually believed that this was so. But the aid of the Six Nations in war or even the lesser good of their standing aloof from the fighting, made the two white governments strain a point. The Confederates, situated on the flanks of their frontiers, on the main waterway to the west, often squarely in the route of advancing armies, and able, too, to disrupt the fur trade whenever they chose, could be either their best friends or most deadly enemies. But the truth was, both the French and the British considered Indians, whether within or without the Confederacy, as subjects. Both set up claims to each other to lands "our Indians" claimed. In the case of the Confederacy this was a great and valuable territory, well worth fighting for. In spite of the exaggerations of Indian orators, the Six Nations actually did control, in their way, most of New York and what is now southwestern Ontario as well as western Pennsylvania and eastern Ohio; and they did have allies or dependents in all this country whom they could sometimes influence. The Indians, however, did not know what the word "subject" meant. There was no such word in their vocabulary, and the white people did not dare to explain it to them or point out their real status.

As time passed on the Indians always assumed they were just as free as they had been before the white men came. How often would Six Nations orators describe themselves as "free and independent." This was their great illusion. The Six Nations had no standing in international law. For one reason, they were "heathen"—justification enough in the eighteenth century for denying a people nationhood. In the long run, however, the Indian nations simply did not measure up to European requirements for a sovereign state. The British and the French did negotiate with them about prisoners. They also considered the Indians as owners of the soil and made "treaties" with them for its purchase. Their sense of justice required this much, officially at least. Besides, it was too dangerous to do otherwise.

In spite of the conciliatory policies of both white governments, Indian-white relations deteriorated. The attitudes of friendliness at the top did not penetrate very far down into the colonial populations. If the individual Indian, with no laws, feared nothing but private revenge, the individual Briton or Frenchman, with laws aplenty, feared nothing. If the Indians could not control their own people, neither the two imperial governments nor the various colonial governments could do much better. French authorities made strict laws regulating the fur trade and tried to control their traders, at least once sentencing a notorious transgressor to death. Yet the French trade laws were generally flouted. The freer British, whose efforts to regulate the trade were seldom more than half-hearted, had scarcely any semblance of control. British traders went wherever they pleased, and if the rival French were unable to drive them away, they set up shop. Though their goods were usually better than those the Frenchmen offered, their reputations were worse. They paid the Indians as little as possible for pelts and got all the traffic would bear for their cargoes of trade goods, their cheating limited only by their ingenuity. After some flagrant violation of decency the injured Indians would try to revenge themselves—upon the wrongdoer if they could or upon some other trader if the wrongdoer got away. One part or another of the Indian country was in continual uproar.

Though both white governments could fret, French traders carried brandy to the Indians and traders from the British colonies carried up immense cargoes of rum. Liquor was the most profitable article of trade. It was what the Indian eagerly awaited and its transport was comparatively easy. Its outpouring could not be stopped, and it often removed whatever restraint upon behavior either the Indian or the white man might have had.

The ordinary Frenchman, however, when he came in contact with the natives, in trade or otherwise, could get along better with them than the ordinary British settler. The French habitant was friendlier; he often mingled with the Indians in good fellowship and, with a thinly scattered and relatively static population, he was not so ambitious for land. But as French influence in America began to wane, it mattered more to the Indians what the ordinary Briton thought.

"Savages we call them," said that extraordinary Briton, Benjamin Franklin, "because their Manners differ from ours"; and he proceeded to describe the cultural differences between red and white man, all of which he thought redounded to the credit of the former.[17] It did not occur to Franklin—nor, indeed, to anyone else—that there was at least one impressive point of similarity between white settler and Indian. It is notorious that the frontiersman had a rough and ready sense of humor. It is not so well known that the Indians possessed an equally rough humor; and they used it often, especially when they wished to demonstrate their contempt. A party of Oneidas, for instance, had a devastating way of damping the pretensions of a certain famous Mohawk lady,[18] and some young Senecas (though not countenanced by their elders) greeted a peace missive from the American secretary of war with awesome vulgarity.[19] A noted scholar has suggested that certain Algonquians did not intend to describe the enemy whom they called Mohawks—Mohawk being an Algonquian term meaning man-eater—as cannibals, but only as lice![20] And some Mohawk villagers cast into great commotion a whole company of white soldiers who had been quartered on them by telling them they had put lice in the broth.[21] All these were the sort of broad jokes which the white frontiersman could have relished hugely, and might even have perpetrated in similar circumstances if he had thought of them.

There were other points of resemblance between the Indians and their nearest white neighbors which were less appealing. When two cultures meet, something is bound to rub off on both; and that something is not necessarily the best of either. Whites made much of Indian cruelty, and there was hardly a white on the frontier who could not relate some story of someone who had been scalped at sometime or other. Was it not true, added the frontiersman, that Indians make tobacco pouches from human skin? This man quite overlooked the fact that many persons of his own kind could peel off as neat a scalp as any Indian, and sell it, too. The famous Robert Rogers was one who did not hesitate to scalp an enemy and unblushingly report the act;[22] and there were also whites, some of them on the famed Sullivan expedition, who boasted of tobacco pouches or leggings made of Indian skin.[23] But on one occasion an Indian was killed for this evil practice, when it was found, too late, that all he had done was to store his tobacco in an old leather glove! And the Indian, who had once been the soul of hospitality to everyone who passed by, was learning, after observing how white people prospered, to keep more of his food supplies for himself.[24]

British traders, of all people, accused the Indians of lying and cheating; they act "in the dark and underhanded," one such trader charged. And whites in general complained that Indians killed cattle and stole horses and pilfered the very latches off barn doors.[25] The Six Nations man might have countered—and sometimes did—that whites also stole horses, that they broke down his fences, and turned their cattle into his fields, and absconded with the corn his women had put out to dry; and that they were pretty underhanded, too. While the very white who complained that Indian cooks wiped their hands on their hair seems to have ignored the fact that his own cooks were likely to wipe their nose on their sleeve.

Nevertheless, some cultural differences between the two races were so real as to appear insurmountable. That peripatetic observer, the Marquis de Chastellux, looked upon some refugee friend Indians in 1780 and predicted it "impossible for the Americans to consent to have them long for neighbours";[26] and some twenty years later Dr. Edward Walsh, a British soldier-surgeon who had traveled far and wide in Canada, gave it as his opinion that "The Red & white people cannot co-exist in the same place."[27] These were perceptive observations.

The average British settler could not think well of customs which in general did differ materially from his own. Unlike Franklin, this man found nothing to admire in the natives. Having encountered some of them in war, he had come to fear and dislike all of them. He rejected their morals, their way of fighting, what he called their cowardice, their laziness, their religion (or lack of it)—he even abominated their smell, for the bear's grease which the Indian found so comforting as an insect repellent in the woods or as a soothing balm when he got home offended the white man's nostrils. The ordinary British settler also believed an old, old story (once true) that he had heard many times: that Indians roasted and ate their captives. Such an act violated the white's most powerful and ancient taboo; it was not to be endured. But perhaps the Indian's real (and unpardonable) offense was economic. He held on to vast stretches of empty land which, in the settler's eyes, he made no use of—land which the settler himself, his friends and family, could use. And the settler could write. The paper this fellow filled with his complaints and fears can be found in many an archive. If he could not write, he could talk very loud and there was no lack of literate contemporaries willing to take up the pen in his behalf.

Most Indians, on the other hand, could not put their thoughts on paper, and were not so likely to speak up for themselves. When they went to councils with white authorities, they talked business. They talked of land problems or their increasing poverty, or their desire for a blacksmith to mend their tools or a teacher to instruct their children.

They talked about their worries over rum and drunkenness. Once in a while some Six Nations orator would drop a significant remark or an unusually perceptive white official might let fall a few words which reveal a little of what the native American was thinking. He certainly resented insults cast at him in his presence, for he could often understand more English than the speaker gave him credit for.[28]

The Indian particularly resented being called a "savage," though that was the ordinary word for him, used by almost everybody, in the eighteenth century. When he found out what the word meant, it hurt his feelings exceedingly. There were, perhaps, he could admit, far, far to the west, beyond the great Mississippi, beyond the beyond, wild Indians with tails like bears, who still used the bow and arrow— perhaps these were what "you call savages." But *he* was a good man, and his people were good people; and he thought they had some very agreeable ways. Savages they were not. Such thoughts he mentioned sometimes, and so they were obviously on his mind though, unlike the white, he did not put them on paper.[29] Sir William Johnson who knew the Longhouse people better than any white man who ever lived was one who championed the Indians' cause. He did not call them barbarians or savages, either in or out of their presence. Sir William thought it but justice to say that "unless heated by liquor, or inflamed by revenge, their ideas of right and wrong and their practices . . . would, if more known, do them much honour."[30] All his hurt feelings the Indian usually managed to conceal. He was astonishingly long-suffering. But if he did not defend his habits and customs, he knew they were right for him and that they had always served him well, even though it did seem to him as if, latterly, something had gone awry.

The Indians were "heathen," complained the white settler; and, as far as he was concerned, that alone put them beyond the pale. Of course the settler was right in one respect. Most Indians were not yet Christians. (Some never would be.) The three westernmost nations of the Longhouse had not accepted Christianity, and neither had the Confederacy's far allies about the Great Lakes (except a few Jesuit converts), nor had most of the Shawnees and Delawares who had moved out to the Ohio country. These more distant Indians had their spirits of land and water and sky, whom they proudly cherished, and they spurned the white man's religion. The white man's Book, declared some Senecas, was "never made for Indians."[31] But the Mohawks and the Oneidas and the Susquehanna strays begged very early for Christian missionaries and teachers, and when such a one came to labor among them, they treated him with great kindness. They took him to board and shared with him all that they had. Or they built a little house for him, and saw that he had food, when they themselves had food. A cleric who in 1729 came up from Albany only occasionally to preach to the Mohawks said he was met with shouts of joy.[32]

The Indian's idea of courage was very different from that of the white man—unforgivably different, thought the latter. Though the aborigine might risk his life to rescue a wounded comrade, he would not stand and fight to the last survivor. Forlorn stands were not for the red man, and he also refused to face artillery or anything else that put him at great disadvantage. If the whites were not such fools, he thought disgustedly, they would make war "as we do" and save their men. The Indian preferred surprise attacks. The very smallness of his numbers made life doubly precious, with losses so much the more to be avoided. The warrior always proceeded upon the theory that he who fights and runs away may live to fight another day. Even when he was winning, the Indian preferred to fight just once and then go home. The loss of only one man of his party obliged him to return and condole with the bereaved relations. Again it was the fewness of their numbers that made the Indians set such great store by their ceremony of condolence. They had an elaborate formula for wiping away the tears, burying the griefs, and clearing the throats of the bereaved so that they could once more speak and attend to their affairs. Literally nothing of the least importance could be done by the sorrowing family till this condolence had taken place. Few white soldiers could understand the Indian's need to go home, and they damned the departing warriors as the greatest cowards on earth. Even those whites who understood Indians thoroughly still found this custom disconcerting. Sir William Johnson grew very uneasy when the friendly Mohawks left him after the battle of Lake George.

Scalps were highly prized trophies, but they were ordinarily taken from persons thought to be dead. No cruelty was intended. The part removed was not large, and some of these persons, still living, actually recovered and survived to tell their harrowing story. The Indian himself boldly provided on his own head a scalp lock, a section which was decorated with feathers and red paint in time of war and which was easy to grasp and cut off, the rest of the upper head being plucked or shaved. An enemy's scalp, placed in a small hoop, dried and painted red around the edge, was treasured by the warrior for years. It was not only proof of prowess in battle, it was also a friendly gift for a family who had lately lost a loved one. Though the family preferred a prisoner whom they could adopt, they would take the memento with many thanks and hang it up on the crosspole of their hut. It became a constant reminder of the departed. If the departed had been killed in battle, it was also a satisfactory proof that he had been avenged. Scalps, however, soon grew to be of economic value to the Indian, for the two colonial governments paid for these grim trophies in time of war, the French for British scalps and the British for Frenchmen's scalps. Then the Indians, so often poverty-stricken, went to even greater lengths to obtain such valuable spoils—lengths which, strangely enough, horrified the whites.

It had been a long time since the people of the Six Nations had burned their captive enemies. These ceremonial burnings had occurred about the same time the people of Salem were hanging witches and Europeans were torturing and burning heretics. Like so many primitive men, the Iroquois had once believed there was something magical in the heart of a brave adversary. In the old days they had literally eaten their foes, hoping to acquire qualities they admired. The very name, "Mohawk," as we have seen, had been given that nation by their Algonquian enemies among whom it meant "man-eater." The Mohawk Joseph Brant, obviously embarrassed about this, always denied that the name of his nation meant any such thing. The original word, alleged Joseph indignantly, was "Munkwas meaning fish dryed, which the Dutch and English have turned into Mohawk—the cause of this name being given them was the general custom they had of preserving fish in that manner."[33]

Be that as it may, other Iroquois, besides Joseph, were ashamed of what they had once done. As early as 1753, when Brant was only ten years of age, an old Onondaga chief confessed to a missionary that "the Six Nations were a very bad people, for they eat[34] human flesh, but [he hastened to add] only in war time. They had done so with the French"—that is, in the great wars before 1701.[35] No matter how regretful these Indians were, such a custom, though long past, was not something the people of the British colonies were likely to forget. As late as the American Revolution many of the rebels firmly believed the Six Nations were devouring their captives. The dread name of cannibal clung to them for many years. Along with their heathenism, it could justify the murder of Indians if, indeed, justification was needed.

In spite of what their white neighbors believed about them, even in the dark old past the Iroquois had usually chosen to adopt their prisoners and turn them into friends. Though this policy of amalgamation did increase their numbers, the increase was made at the expense of whatever racial homogeneity they may have had. Jesuit priests noted very early that most of the Iroquois were not pure Iroquois at all, but mixed with the bloodstreams of many nations. By the mid-years of the seventeenth century these French missionaries (who penetrated deep into Iroquois country) observed eleven different nations of Indians among the Senecas and seven among the Onondagas.[36] Each of the five original members of the Confederacy, in their incessant warfare of the 1600s, had countless opportunities to acquire recruits, and each nation became a melting pot. There were Mahicans living among the Mohawks; large numbers of Tutelos, Nanticokes, and Delawares among the Oneidas and Cayugas; as well as scatterings of many other peoples throughout the Longhouse; while the Senecas, who lived nearest the Hurons and other conquered nations about Lake Erie, probably attained their position as most populous of the entire five through adoptions.

In a bereaved Iroquois family a captive would take the place of a deceased relative. The newcomer, at least in theory, took the deceased's place in every way; and an adult son of the family might call a young boy father—or even, apparently, mother.[37] If the adopted youth married among the Iroquois, his children acquired the rank, clan, and nationality of their mother and so became full-fledged Mohawks, Onondagas, Senecas, or whatever the case might warrant. Joseph Brant was but one of many who had forebears outside the Six Nations. The famous sachem, Hendrick, one of the Mohawk "kings" who visited Queen Anne, and who enjoyed unusual prestige, had a Mahican father; and that extraordinary female trader, Sally Ainse, and the great Oneida, Skenando, could claim ancestors from out of the west and south.

There also dwelt in the security of the Longhouse and its Tree of Peace a good many white persons who had settled voluntarily among the Six Nations. Some were prisoners of war taken as children, who remembered no other home and were content with their Indian friends; others were runaway servants and army deserters; and the rest were traders who liked the free life. These people were married to Indians and lived as Indians. The white captives refused to go home and often resisted with all their strength when attempts were made at force. There are many stories of the affection and kind treatment such captives received among the Indians, and the latter gave up their white adopted kin with the greatest reluctance. Some sorrowing Shawnees spoke for all Indians as they returned their cherished captives to Fort Pitt: "We have taken as much Care of these Prisoners, as if they were own Flesh, and blood; they are become unacquainted with your Customs, and manners, and therefore, Father we request you will use them tender, and kindly, which will be a means of inducing them to live contentedly with you."[38]

Thus the Six Nations got their modicum of white blood, and in some cases, much more than a modicum. Gideon Hawley, who went to Oquaga as a missionary in 1753, noted that nearly every family of the Oneida and Tuscarora inhabitants of that village had "more or less" white blood in their veins; while James Dean who taught and interpreted at Oneida missions for many years thought that by the end of the Revolution there was not a pure Oneida in existence, many of that nation being mixed with white blood as well as other strains.[39] If this was true of people as remote as the Oneidas, it was certainly true of the Mohawks who lived in the midst of the white frontier, in whose two main villages of Fort Hunter and Canajoharie soldiers were often quartered, and on whose famous river thoroughfare traders and other travelers passed and repassed on business to and from the west. Joseph Brant, whose skin was accounted light in color and whose portraits show this to have been so, probably had somewhere his strain of white blood though he seems to have been unaware of it.

Save for those white friends who were settled in the Indian country, the generality of American colonists gave scant consideration to the needs or the viewpoint of the red man. The Indian was of no consequence to them, except as a nuisance in time of peace and, even when he tried to remain neutral, an object of distrust and fear in time of war. The Indian had no friends among the settlers on the frontier who were the white people he met most often. To be sure, some of his neighbors would pass the time of day with him or engage him in small talk or gossip, but not one was likely to side with him in war or in disputes about land unless he had some ax of his own to grind. Even the missionaries were interested mostly in his soul (for they thought he had one), and in converting him to an uneasy Christianity they always hoped somehow to convert him into less of a nuisance to their own kind. The Indian was all alone with his massive problems. For centuries he had lived by a set of standards that had changed but slowly, and probably never painfully, but now all his ideas were in a state of confusion and upheaval. Change was rushing in upon him, and change hurt.

Though deeply attached to his old customs (and never realizing how many of them he had lost), the Indian could see that there was a way of life that, somehow or other, offered more material good, now, than his own. The nearer he lived to the white frontier, the better he could see this, and the more the perception hurt and baffled him. How fast the white people were increasing! What fine possessions they had! In this strange and uneasy situation how to get presents became the Indian's great object. In war he wanted plunder, too, and young men were the more easily persuaded to involve themselves in the colonial wars in the hope of garnering loot. Presents and plunder had become the indispensable supplements to a meager living. Long gone were the days of native self-sufficiency.

If the Indian was strong and agile, and on his hunting ground most of the time, and if he met with good luck, he could earn forty pounds and up a year by the chase.[40] This was more than many white men could earn, but the whites had not the Indian's vast prodigality nor were they expected to feed everybody who claimed kinship. Indians did not save for the future whatever they desired today, and they divided their stores with any needy friends and relatives, or even strangers, who came along. They also believed that friends and even strangers should share with them in time of necessity, and when they were hungry enough, they did not hesitate to invade neighboring barnyards and pigsties. Since Indians lived, as often as not, in a state of grinding poverty—for hardly a year passed that did not have its long "starving time"—such invasions took place much too frequently to suit the white owners of livestock. As the scuffling and bellowing and squealing broke out in the barnyard, the white people reached for their guns.

Regardless of whether the Indians' native culture was intrinsically better than that of the whites as some say, or whether it was inferior as others say, or merely different as still others maintain, the hard fact remains that the aborigines had to deal with ever-growing numbers of whites, and there were facets in their culture, whether superior, inferior, or different, that placed them at an ever-growing disadvantage.

Perhaps the heaviest burden that the red man had to carry in his confrontation with an alien and hostile culture was his lack of letters. The Indians possessed no alphabet, but only a rudimentary picture-writing which they painted on trees and rocks or wove into the beaded strips of their famous and colorful "wampum." This beaded material, which was the most efficient means of communication the Indian had, and his only annals, had once been all he needed, but was not so serviceable now. Often of great beauty, it consisted of strings and "belts," strung and tied together by the patient fingers of women workers. The beads had once been made of varicolored shells or bits of painted wood, but latterly the women preferred to use beads of European manufacture—though no matter what they worked with, a good belt of wampum was expensive.[41]

When the Indian (or, more likely, a whole village or a group of Indians) had a formal communication to make to someone, he (or their chosen speaker) handed over one of these strings or belts as soon as he had finished speaking. Ordinary strings of wampum could give point to some of his words, but the elaborate and costly belts were needed to guarantee important news; and the longer and wider the belt, the more urgent was the information it conveyed. White beads denoted peace and good news; dark purple ranging to black were reserved for war and bad news. Certain figures worked among the beads showed men and towns and nations and roads and other simple concepts, but all these were open to various interpretations, depending upon their arrangement and the whims of the maker, the ideas of the interpreter, or even the lapse of time since the event pictured. Wampum still served well enough to impart ideas or refresh the memory in dealings with other Indians. It is easy to see, however, that the natives were at a disadvantage with men who could read and write and who had documents which remained immutably the same, or could, if necessary, be quietly tampered with.

Indians were further handicapped in their new circumstances by having less specific ideas of numbers and time than their white adversaries. The Indian counted with notched sticks and beans arranged in patterns or by pointing to the stars or the leaves of trees, and he reckoned time by such vaguenesses as day's journeys and moons and the growth of corn.[42] In all the most important affairs of his life, such as the making of peace or war and the selling of land, no matter how cleverly he made his computations, he could seldom be as precise as men who possessed clocks and calendars and familiarity with arithmetic. Indians almost never got to an appointment on time, a proceeding which proved of great detriment to them.

Though the Indians boasted of exceptionally good memories, there does not seem to be much evidence that this boast was well founded. On the contrary. They were fighting a sanguinary war with the Cherokees and Catawbas in the south and could not remember how or why it had started,[43] they had sold land in their immediate neighborhood and could not remember when or where or to whom,[44] they had forgotten the purport of many of the words in their rituals,[45] and they had been known to stare at a wampum belt and wonder what it meant.[46] Then there was the time Sir William Johnson had to urge the Onondagas not to relay an important message from village to village, but to send it to him directly, to prevent its arriving "quite altered from what it was at first."[47] Unfortunately, also, the Indian was fond of gossip, and his wife liked gossip, too, and their country teemed with rumors and idle stories. Far more than even the most illiterate whites, who could usually get some sort of help from some source and to whom legal processes were not entirely unknown, Indians lived at the mercy of their ignorance and credulity. Vicious white neighbors could throw them into turmoil with boasting and extravagant talk.

The difficulty of dealing with the natives, especially in land matters, soon turned the white man's thoughts to subterfuge. Though it was proper Indian custom to sell land only in a full and open council of the nation or village concerned, white speculators and their agents often ignored the custom. It was almost impossible, they knew, to collect all the Indians together, much less to see that every family got its rightful share of the purchase price. It fell to the sachems to divide the purchase price, and individuals, families, even whole nations, were often dissatisfied with what they received. Thoroughly exasperated, Sir William Johnson on one occasion declared he would himself see a fair division made "since they could not trust one another."[48]

White buyers, by no means saints, were not unwilling to cut a few corners, and never mind the consequences to the Indians. It was easier and cheaper—much, much cheaper—to ply a few of the Indian population with liquor and then, in some clandestine place, get their consent to a sale while their minds were hopelessly befuddled. In such a way, in early 1730, the astute Philip Livingston procured a deed from a few drunken Mohawks to a huge, vaguely-defined tract on the south bank of the Mohawk River which somehow included the site of their own village of Canajoharie. Another questionable deal took place in 1754. At the breaking up of the historic Albany Congress, while the rum was flowing freely, agents of the Susquehannah Company of Connecticut persuaded some drunken Iroquois chiefs to sign away the heretofore jealously guarded country at their southern gateway. This purchase, located in the beautiful Wyoming valley of northeastern Pennsylvania, a place claimed by both Pennsylvania and Connecticut, set the stage for a bloody three-way conflict that was to pit white man against white man and white man against red man for a generation. The Six Nations complained bitterly about both of these deeds, as well as several others of a similar nature, and disavowed them from the beginning. But such disavowals never seemed to do them the least good.

It is a moot point whether white buyers committed such frauds because they did not fully understand Indian customs or because they understood them only too well. The agents who generally carried on these negotiations with the Indians were familiar with the require- ment for a complete council at every sale, even though their principals might not have been. A person like John Henry Lydius who engi- neered the Wyoming purchase, being an adoptee of the Mohawks and thoroughly familiar with Indian customs, knew what he was about. He also knew that to the Indians what they did while drunk did not count.

Even if sober, a heedless young fellow or some old straggler might put his mark on a deed to get a new blanket or a gun. If the white people were foolish enough (he thought) to pay him for land he as an individual did not own and had no right to sell, he was smart enough (he thought) to let them do it.[49] Such a business caused a great outcry among the rest of the Indian community when they found out about it, and the guilty signers might be driven from home or even put to death.[50] Unfortunately the blameless villagers usually lost the disputed tract, or they had to compromise, which meant the same thing. In time the Indians lost much more land than they could afford to do without. An economy based even partly on hunting required a vast extent of territory for hunters to range over. This was the "empty" and "unused" country toward which the eyes of speculators and settlers alike yearned with so steady a passion.

Life in the declining Longhouse was short and precarious. Seldom did man or woman achieve great age. Gideon Hawley noted that among his Oneida and Tuscarora charges none of the men, after he knew them, reached the age of sixty. Hawley also judged that the two oldest Mohawk men he had ever seen were under seventy, though he had seen a woman who appeared older.[51] George Croghan, long a trader and Indian agent, thought this lack of longevity was due to the evil effects of the white man's presence. Croghan, who was acquainted with the most distant allies of the Six Nations, asserted that those Indians who lived farthest from the whites had the greatest number of aged persons.[52] It is true that Europeans did bring tuberculosis and smallpox to the natives, and these diseases, especially the latter, al- most destroyed them. Existing, as they did, on the ragged edge of starvation for several months out of every year—for they got very hungry just between crops—these primitive people who had no natu- ral immunity could develop little resistance to either the slow killer or the pestilence. Tuberculosis was a constant menace, and epidemics of smallpox raged periodically throughout their country.[53]

The white man contributed further to the Indians' troubles by introducing liquor among them—and liquor-induced violence. Though the aborigine had many kinds of juices, he seems never to have discovered fermented drink, but he took to it very quickly. No one thought any the less of a head man of the Senecas who bore the name of The Drunkard and, indeed, it appears that almost any Indian anywhere could have borne that name. Liquor, more than anything else, was the Indians' downfall. In their drunken revels these unfortunate people lost all restraint, fighting and maiming one another, while the few who chanced to be sober fled in terror. A horrified Moravian missionary describes one wild night of drunken revelry at Onondaga in these words: "During the whole night such a dreadful noise was kept up in the town, that it seemed as if evil spirits were let loose. They almost killed each other; some burned themselves and others were beaten to cripples. Oh, what a sad sight it is, to have to see them thus, as if led to the slaughter."[54] Gideon Hawley mentioned that in one five-year period seventeen of his Mohawk acquaintances, mostly young, had died, and twelve of them not by natural causes. At his own little Oquaga mission, of six men dead, half died violently.[55] An Anglican missionary in the Mohawk country reported that in less than six months fifty-five Mohawks had died, chiefly from the effects of liquor.[56]

Time and again Sir William Johnson in his capacity of British superintendent of Indian affairs complained that the Indians would sell their guns or the clothes off their backs for liquor, that they would exchange their newly received presents for it, and go home empty-handed.[57] Nor were the women exempt from the general weakness;[58] mothers and daughters fought and pulled hair, and apparently more than one woman died or was maimed in a drunken brawl. A missionary records in some detail a frenzied quarrel in which a young woman who lived in Sejehowanah's house beat Moses' wife almost to death.[59] It may be that the youngsters got their drams, too, for Johnson often makes such remarks as that "My Neighbors at the Mohawks Castle are almost incessantly Drunk, old & Young."[60] The Indians themselves fully realized their destructive tendencies. Some Tuscaroras begged Johnson to give them some medicine to cure them of their obsession,[61] while the sachems of the entire Six Nations would often pray that liquor be kept out of their villages—and then just as often the same sachems would turn around and beg that it be readmitted. They hated it, but how they loved it![62]

Iroquois social organization, like that of so many primitive peoples, was based on matrilineal clans—that is, descent was reckoned through women, and all the people of a clan were related through some distant female ancestor. In every Iroquois family, therefore, the father was an outsider. As an outsider he had no authority over his own children. Children belonged entirely to their mother, and were always members of their mother's clan. At the same time marriage among the Indians was easy and almost without ceremony; divorce was even easier. The reverse was of course true among whites, especially those of any status or property who desired legitimate heirs. And though some whites could understand the function of clans, female descent was more a subject for coarse humor than for understanding.

Chastity was usually expected of an Indian wife, and her husband might leave her if she committed adultery.[63] There is at least one recorded instance when an Indian killed a white man who seduced his wife.[64] But young Indian girls and unmarried women were free; they might do as they pleased in sexual matters with no resultant stain on their character.[65] Any wandering trader or blacksmith or soldier or, for that matter, any passing Indian could find a complaisant mate for an hour or a year. Sir William Johnson, who did not always set a good example before his charges, had no trouble whatever in producing a copper-colored "Princess of the first Rank" for the entertainment of a visiting dignitary.[66] Young Indian men roved from maid to maid, and nobody minded. Given time, however, the young of both sexes seem to have settled down to the adult business of taking care of a family. Each had age-old tasks. She cooked and sewed and hoed the corn and beans, and he hunted for venison and skins with which to make, or later to exchange for, clothing.

A properly wedded Indian couple customarily lived with the bride's relations. The new husband built a little extension to the crowded cabin of his wife's parents. The cabin got longer and longer as girls grew up and married; and if man and wife could not agree, it was the husband who went home to mother. Often, in each little cubicle, a surprising number of brothers and sisters of the half-blood mingled in their childish games.[67] They were joined by youngsters from the other households, youngsters whom the Europeans called cousins but whom the Indians thought of as closer, for this long, long house was the abode of sisters, all affectionate mothers to all. If some of the young ones happened to be the children of unmarried girls, most were probably the offspring of widows who because of the high death rate among the men may have had three or four or more husbands in succession and several different growing families. In this motley group the ties of kinship were very strong. The trouble was, the strength that the Iroquois family possessed was mainly collateral; it did not pass down from one generation to the next through both parents. The father's line was only of secondary importance. At a time when the Indian child needed all the help he could get, his paternal relatives, though they might look upon him with affection, did not feel so close to him as his mother's kin,[68] and of course acted accordingly.

When at home from the hunt a husband slept till breakfast (provided there was breakfast), and then he might mind the children all day while his wife worked in the field. "You may See half a dozen walking about with Children upon their Backs—lazy and Sordid Wretches," commented an educated young Indian from Long Island, with all the disapproval of a visiting foreigner.[69] This young Indian observer, who had lost all his own native culture, mistook the situation. It was the hunter who had the hard and arduous task, not his wife. The wife did not exert herself unduly in the field. All the women worked together, taking first one row and then the next, and the rich bottom land responded quickly to their light hoes. Field work was a sort of social occasion, with laughter and jokes tossed back and forth. If the husband had tried to interfere with his wife's prerogative, there would have been some name-calling and very likely some words flung at him uncomplimentary to his manhood. Iroquois wives were not meek; they said what they pleased. But after weeks and even months in the woods the hunter was tired and not inclined to argue. For him the path of ancient custom (and least resistance) was good enough.

The hunter did not accumulate much in the way of permanent worldly possessions, and when he died, the few small belongings that he had, his clothing, his gun, a knife or two, perhaps a horse, were taken over by his mother's kin. Nothing was left for his children. There was no such thing as the inheritance of landed property. The individual Indian had no landed property as the white man knew it. The family did have regular places to hunt and plant, which he knew, and he seldom overstepped their bounds—it was too risky.[70] Yet his hunting grounds and his fishing grounds and his agricultural lands and even the spot he lived upon might be sold by irresponsibles right out from under him.

What were his concerns, this man of little expectation, as he padded about with a child on his back or sat for hours in the shade of a tree with his head between his knees? A dog, a horse, a ball game? The high cost of powder and the low price of skins? A rumor that a great army was coming from somewhere or other to destroy him? A rumor that a great army was on its way from somewhere to help him? The rumor that all the Indians were going to unite and push the white people into the sea? Or what a fine thing it would be if he had a keg of rum? Perhaps some Chippewa allies came close to the truth when they assured their white superintendent: "Brother we are peaceably in-clined, & wish to live long, we have no evil thoughts, they are chiefly taken up in thinking of y^t Darling Water made by Man. . . ."[71]

Yet, thanks to missionaries and the slow attrition of native cus-toms, the economic scene was changing. Some Indians were learning to cope with the white man's world. By the time of the Revolutionary War a few Mohawks owned a bit of land in fee simple, and presumably they had deeds to show, even as white people.[72] Long before the Revolution there were Indian men whose names could be found on regular pay rolls. They gave the lie to the canard, spread by Indians themselves, that "Indians cannot work." They worked on the river boats as sailors and polers, they carried heavy goods around waterfalls and rapids, and they hired themselves out as guides and couriers. They labored and they earned what the white people, at least, called wages.[73] Men like these and the families they supported prospered, but their numbers were still relatively few.

It has often been noted that women, in this matrilineal society, were the controlling force. It is true that the women from certain aristocratic families exercised considerable authority. These Iroquois noblewomen made and unmade the League's sachems who served in the great Council at Onondaga, deciding among the merits of various claimants in their family (for certain sachemships belonged to certain families, and to them alone); and if they wished, these ladies could exert a powerful influence for war or peace.[74] Little has come down to us about the women's private councils, but it is clear that the headwo-man or matron of the great family had the final say. The matron really named the sachem, and he, of course, had to be related to her in the female line. In theory she chose the man best qualified for the honor, but as a practical matter she seldom failed to choose her own son, brother, or favorite nephew. Apparently the lady's dictum was not always accepted with good grace. There is evidence that losing candi-dates and their supporters could throw a whole Indian village into turmoil.

Matters of state meant nothing to women from the wrong families.[75] They had no authority in great affairs. Men from common families fared better. They could go to war or undertake some mission of private revenge, and if they conducted themselves bravely, they might acquire a following among their clansmen. They might be elected war chief—a loose but important-sounding title that covered a leader of thirty warriors, or of three or four. But in this aristocracy-ridden society the women of non-noble families could attain nothing of position or power, and their offspring inherited their mother's nothingness. Joseph Brant's Wyandot "grandmother," obviously adopted into some common family, had no distinction to hand down to daughter or grandson.

The Indian, as he strove to deal with his massive problems or, contrariwise, tried to ignore them altogether, wore many faces. Said a young British soldier, of the Mohawks: "They are hospitable, friendly, and civil to an immense degree; in good breeding I think they infinitely surpass the French or any other people that ever I saw, if you will allow good breeding to consist in a constant desire to do ev'rything that will please you, and a strict carefulness to not say or do anything that may offend you."[76] But a missionary to these same folk called them "Swine." "I hate the sight of such Creatures," said he. "Pray for me that I may chearfully exerte my little Strength to reform them."[77] There is an explanation for two such differing viewpoints: the young soldier had a Mohawk "wife" whose family treated him with great consideration and made life easy for him, while the man of the bitter words had seen the terrible massacre at Fort William Henry when wild French Indians from over the lakes ran amuck in blood.

Indians had to be polite to one another, for a man might take umbrage at anything he disliked about another's actions or speech, and kill him on the spot. Or, hoping to escape the vengeance of relatives, he might plan to get drunk and then kill him. Such customs assured careful behavior. A sachem or chief needed to be especially careful. If he offended too many of his people, he might be assassinated; or his own family might choose to put him to death, thus preventing an outsider's doing it and themselves having to exact atonement.[78] But all restraints went up the smoke-hole when rum came in the door. For this reason sober Indians fled the company of drunken ones. Who wanted to get hurt if he could help it, or get caught up in the payment of a costly blood price, or, worse still, to become involved in all the distresses of a blood feud? Not the sober Indian!

The people of the Longhouse were not the noble savage of philosophy and romance. They were people—merely people—with a full assortment of faults and virtues. Kindness they often displayed, and generosity, and sensitivity to another's feelings. In peacetime they were very hospitable to travelers, sharing with them whatever they had of food and lodging. They were mild parents, too, and they loved their offspring tenderly—a fact which always surprised the whites! Yet they could behave with childish unreason,[79] indulging themselves in fits of jealous sulks, and they could act like demons at times. Some European observers found the Indians dull and uncomprehending. But the Onondaga man who was overheard to remark to a companion that "we are cheated by the white people in this world, and if we dont stand clear of them they will cheat us in the other and make Slaves of us" was not uncomprehending.[80] Nor was the Mohawk a dullard who observed to some white officials: "The Governor of Virginia and the Governor of Canada are both Quarrelling about lands which belong to us. And such a Quarrel as this may end in our destruction."[81]

Indians soon noticed the difference between the white man's profession of Christianity and his practice of it. Those who looked a little deeper pointed to the poor broom-making tribes of New England as sad examples of what "learning to pray" had done to a once proud people: Where, now, they asked, was the pride of the Pequots and the Narragansetts? Where were their warriors? Yet these same scoffing Indians were not above pretending a conversion in order to profit by it, and some went more than once to Canada, where Jesuit priests were generous, for this purpose.[82]

On the other hand, some Indians took the white man's religion very seriously. Good Jesuit converts told their beads interminably, to the dire neglect of their hunting, while those who professed Anglicanism cherished their prayer books and looked down their noses at dissenters. Even stranger things happened when the aborigine succumbed to the Puritan ethic. Nobody was more puritanical than the zealous, newly converted, slightly educated, Indian dissenter. If he undertook to preach a sermon, it burned with all the fires of hell, and if he undertook to write a letter, it was one page news and three pages theology.

Christian or not, the individual Indian was as truthful as anybody, and he blushed if caught in a lie. He also worried a great deal about his drinking. If he had had the benefit of missionary teachings, he was afraid he was going to hell. Some poor dependent Nanticokes voiced the anxieties of all mission Indians when they begged the Onondaga Council to limit the flow of liquor into Iroquois villages. They pointed out that rum was the cause of early death among the Indians, and even famine, since very often crops did not get planted on time because of drunkenness. Let none say that when we die everything ends, they warned. "No!" declared the worried Nanticokes, "those that have been drunkards will be sent to the Devil, and what will *he* do with them? He will torment them. In what way? He has a great kettle of boiling water, and will say to such an Indian: 'Come here! You were fond of drinking; now you shall have a great plenty.' He will throw the Indian into the kettle, where he wil[l] be cooking without dying." Then the traveler who reported this anxious plea, went on to say:

"The council, however, could not agree on the subject, and now, as before, there is no end to drinking."[83]

All the Indian wanted was to live happily and at peace, as he imagined he had once lived in that far-off long ago, before the advent of pushing, crowding whites. But though his better judgment told him the halcyon days of his ancestors would never return, he was not a man to exist without joy. He had his moments of light-heartedness and his good times. He had his races, his ball games, his dancing, and his ceremonial feasts. He had his gambling, too, with whole villages playing against each other and risking all their possessions on a fall of dice. He loved gewgaws and adornments. If he could get a gold-laced coat or an officer's hat, he was happy. Indian women took great pleasure in fancy leggings and silver brooches, and they used thimbles by the dozens, not so much as aids to sewing but as decorations for their clothes.

The Indian, humble or aristocratic, was eager to look well. He would spend hours painting his face and decorating his scalp lock, rubbing the paint off or taking the ornaments apart again and again. He fancied varicolored paints put on in streaks, applied to his skin wherever it showed, the object being to inspire fear and awe. These ambitious effects were limited to war and ceremonial occasions; in his usual daily appearances he did not mind looking more like himself. But paint was always one of the fastest-moving articles in trade. What enjoyment this fellow could find in small things! He would double up with guffaws if a companion fell off a log or missed a fair shot or told a ribald story.

When sober, the Indian of Joseph Brant's day had a lurking suspicion that he did not amount to much. He knew that all his glory was behind him.[84] But drunk, he was still a conqueror, still the master of everything he beheld. At such times he could put the white man in his place with a word or two or a single dark look. (This was what the whites called insolence.)[85] In this same mood the Indian might, by apparent accident, fire off his gun uncomfortably close to the white man's head.[86] But in a kindlier mood he could take pity on a palefaced bungler and show him how to build a bark canoe.[87] He had a sure hand, and quick; and what he built would paddle safely across the river or over the lake. There! Let the white man try to equal this! And he could whine and beg till he pried gifts from a reluctant donor, and then, considering them but poor things anyway, proudly throw them down on the trail as he headed for home.[88]

In a battle of wits with a trader the Indian did not always come out second best. Traders did not invariably find him an easy mark, and the merchant who gave him credit often rued the mistake. It seemed reasonable to any Indian that the most recent creditor should be paid first; old creditors might sing for their pay. Nor did the Indian always undervalue his land. Sometimes he wanted even more than it was worth. For some poor, stony ground near Schoharie the Mohawks asked fifty pounds for one hundred acres, a fat price, indeed, to the local farmers to whom that amount represented years of toil and thrift.[89] The native could make some sharp remarks when he had a mind to. A wise Mohawk sachem observed to Sir William Johnson that "we are sorry to see that the white People, who have more Sense than we, will for the sake of getting land, wrong one another.— Since that is the case, what are we Indians to expect from you."[90] Then there were those other times when he spoke in pure poetry. "Should we find ourselves deprived of the Land we looked on as ours," declared a sorrowing Caughnawaga, "we shall be without father or brother neither shall we have any comfort left us."[91]

This was the man of the Six Nations. He could have been called John or Lucas or Peter or Andrew, for if he lived near the white frontier, he usually had a baptismal name. If he was still pagan, he would bear only a name of his people. Translated, his name might mean something like "The Wind that Melts the Snow" or "Leather-lips" or "Stinking Fish," all acceptable as far as he was concerned. White traders, missionaries, soldiers, and goverment agents wrote down these names often in accounts or reports. Almost any Indian got more written notice than most of the whites of his day. His uneasy life, his embarrassments, his mistakes, his impermanent triumphs, his failings, and his frustrations are public property. Seldom does he cut much of a figure. Yet for decades he managed to hold on to the neutrality that was his only real protection. Throughout the greater part of the eighteenth century, this Six Nations man, alternately proud and fawning, often pathetic, suspicious, moody, restless, and, as frontiersmen well knew, sometimes terrible, was able to maintain a balance of power between the quarreling Europeans. As long as the white people fought, he was safe. He was courted and gifted. He knew, however, that some day one of the white powers would weaken and falter. He also knew that he must be alert to recognize when that time had come. As his very life depended on white largess and trade, he must eventually throw in his lot with the dominant force. To place himself at the mercy of the white victor must be his final bitter choice.[92]

For Cornelius and Seth and The Running Deer's Nephew, there was yet another terror to clutch at the heart. In the mid-eighteenth century and for a long time thereafter, the Indian and his white adversary shared one belief in common. Both were convinced that the known parts of America had once teemed with a numerous native population, most of which had already dwindled away. Many a time, in the quiet of the woods, or when he awoke in the darkness of the night, the perceptive Indian could take out this thought and mull it over. It was as an ax poised over his head. But to the white people the same thought appeared more like the pot of gold at the end of the rainbow. White observers, assessing the red man's way of life—and death—had come to the conclusion that his race was doomed to extinction. They freely predicted among themselves that his days on earth were numbered. Nobody, however, expressed much regret, and some actively awaited the event. This the Indian also knew.[93]

Such was the troubled world of Joseph Brant's birth—a world declining, its old culture falling into a shambles,[94] more and more dependent upon unfriendly whites for a livelihood; but with a memory of past glory, and still sufficient of a menace to affect the balance of power between France and Britain in America. Such was the world of the Longhouse in that early spring of 1743 when Joseph Brant was born.

2

Peter and Margaret

Two CLERGYMEN who knew Joseph Brant intimately have told different stories about his origin. The Reverend John Stuart, Anglican missionary to the Mohawks, in whose household Joseph lived for many months, confided to a friend that Joseph's family had no especial standing in their village.[1] But the Reverend Eleazar Wheelock, founder of the Indian charity school where Joseph spent nearly two years, asserted that he came "of a Family of Distinction."[2] Other persons in a position to know the truth have differed as widely. Major Archibald Campbell, commander at Fort Niagara, a place frequented by Brant for two decades, once commented that though the chief aspired to become "a man of the first consequence" among the Indians, "the meaness [sic] of his extraction, will certainly be a strong bar in his way."[3] Yet Sir William Johnson who sent Joseph away to be educated expected him to prove useful among the Indians because of his "connection and residence."[4] It remained for General Philip Schuyler to add the crowning touch of confusion. At the time Schuyler spoke he knew Joseph only slightly, if at all, but he had heard a great deal of gossip, so he said Joseph Brant was Sir William Johnson's half-breed son![5] Like the fabled blind men who felt an elephant and then described the animal in such a variety of ways, all these witnesses told the truth as they saw it, and they were all, to some extent, right.

Joseph himself almost never mentioned his parentage. Once in great agony of spirit he exclaimed "if I have not got so many children I would soon do some thing to drown my unhappiness & Leave more marks behind Me than what my father did."[6] Aside from revealing a black mood, these words are not very helpful. But Joseph did make one clear and explicit statement. In his famous denunciation of imprisonment for debt he declares: "I was, sir, born of Indian parents."[7] This should dispose of Schuyler's gossip, for Joseph's mother lived long after he reached manhood and he had ample opportunity to learn about his father. Among the Loyalists in Canada, and all the people with whom he lived intimately and by whose side he fought, there seems never to have been a whisper that Brant was Johnson's son. Not one British officer seems ever to have suggested that he was a half-breed. In the frontier garrisons they might praise Joseph or condemn him, but then how very often they would conclude their praise or blame by remarking upon what a "regular Indian" he was—as if that explained everything. The question among his associates was not whether Joseph Brant was an Indian, but whether he was an Indian of high or low degree.

The historian, William L. Stone, interviewed Joseph's children in the 1830s when they were in the prime of life and of presumably clear memory, and they told him that the name of Joseph's father was Tehowaghwengaraghkwin.[8] But this name seems to have been all that they knew. For their grandparent they claimed no distinction. No legend of prowess as a warrior or wisdom as a civil chief had passed down to them. If pressed, they would have had to admit that Joseph's father did not bear one of those famous titles, handed down from generation to generation, denoting high rank in the Iroquois Confederacy. Indeed, his name conveys in the Mohawk language no more remarkable idea than that of "A man taking off his snowshoes."[9]

But if Joseph's father bore an undistinguished name, he also, fortunately, bore an uncommon one. In all the Indian records of his period that have been preserved—deeds, records of councils, account books, missionary rolls, reports of Indian agents—the name of Tehowaghwengaraghkwin is mentioned only twice, and both times the same person is obviously meant.

The two references to this person appear in the records of the Reverend Henry Barclay, a young missionary who labored among the Indians on the Mohawk River from 1735 till 1746. In his carefully kept "Register Book, Fort Hunter" young Mr. Barclay noted a few marriages, a few burials, and many baptisms.[10] His troublesome flock cared little whether they were married according to the white man's custom and they preferred their own funeral rites, but they wished, indeed they insisted, that their children be christened. Like all good parents, they wanted their children to have advantages. If sometimes in other villages there lived a missionary of a sterner sort who balked at baptizing an infant unless its parents were in a state of grace—a state which Indians were hardly ever in—parental threats usually forced him to yield. Mr. Barclay was more agreeable. He willingly baptized the babies and even, on occasion, contrived to marry the parents at the same time. Year after year Indian couples trooped into the little chapel at Fort Hunter with their new baby and two or three friends or relatives as sponsors, and then they would troop proudly out carrying their little Paul or David or John, or Mary or Esther.

One of these proud couples, on July 18, 1741, is listed as Peter Tehonwaghkwangeraghkwa and his wife, Margaret. At this time their infant son received the name of Jacob. Next year, on February 6, 1742 (date corrected for Gregorian calendar), a daughter was baptized Christina. This Peter and this Margaret appear to have been the parents of the lad afterward known as Joseph Brant. The name, Tehonwaghkwangeraghkwa, is almost identical with the name of Joseph's father as given to the historian, Stone, by the Brant family, and all available evidence suggests that his mother's name was Margaret.[11] Of the two children, Joseph's elder brother and sister, nothing more has ever been heard. They probably died when infants. Comparatively few Indian babies lived to grow up.

There was at this time at least one other child in the hut of Peter and Margaret, a girl whose Indian name was Degonwadonti, meaning "Several against one."[12] Her Christian name was Mary, and years later, in 1783, she said she was forty-seven years old, thus claiming to be born in 1736.[13] But there is no record of her baptism in that year, so she may not have known the exact date of her birth. The record does show that a Mary, daughter of Margaret and Cannassware, was christened April 13, 1735. If this was our Mary, later the famous Molly Brant, she was Margaret's child by a former husband and so only Joseph's half-sister. Be that as it may, Mary was certainly six or seven years old at this time and Joseph not yet born.

Peter and Margaret by the mere fact of their being mentioned in the Reverend Henry Barclay's Register may be called Christian Indians. Indeed, the Mohawks had been considered Christian for many years. They went faithfully to church on Sunday. There they sang Psalms with gusto and listened as intently to sermons treating of deserts and chariots and lions as if they comprehended every word. But they still believed in their old myths and mingled them indiscriminately with stories from the Bible. They still peopled the woods and fields with spirits, good and bad, and paid great regard to dreams and omens, and were terrified of witches. Harmless, good-hearted creatures generally, their one great vice was drink. Male and female, old and young, they all craved rum; it was their greatest pleasure, and when really thirsty any of them would give everything he possessed for a dram of "that Darling Water." There is no reason to suppose that Joseph's parents were any better, or any worse, than this.

From Mr. Barclay's Register it is also clear that Joseph's parents had no powerful friends or relatives. The Mohawk aristocracy of that day is well known, but not one of them sponsored Peter's and Margaret's children in baptism. All five of their sponsors were nobodies among the Indians, and the conclusion must be that Peter and Margaret themselves were nobodies. It is true that the friendly John Norton, who was Joseph's secretary and confidant for many years, mentions that Joseph's father was said to have been a "great" warrior.[14] But the famed wars of the Iroquois with neighboring and western Indians were over long before Peter was born. He was too young to have fought the French in Queen Anne's War of 1702–13, and he seems, even if still alive, to have been far removed from the main theater of operations during King George's War of 1744–48. Perhaps he occasionally joined some straggling party going against the Cherokees, southern kin with whom his people had an ancient feud, and he may have brought back a few scalps. This would have been enough, in Indian eyes, to make him a "great" warrior.

But a father had little importance in the Indian scheme of things. Regardless of what sort of warrior Peter was, Joseph was still a nobody. If Peter had been the hereditary Tekarihoga, the leading sachem of the Mohawks, it would not have profited his son. Among the Indians hereditary honor passed through the mother, not the father. Unfortunately for Joseph, Margaret had nothing of this kind to pass on to him. There is abundant evidence that throughout his life Joseph Brant's aspirations and capacities for leadership far overmatched his inheritance. It was an almost fatal defect in the world of the Longhouse, and it was to cause him innumerable difficulties.

After the baptism of their baby Christina, in February 1742, the names of Peter and Margaret disappear from the records. The Reverend John Stuart, one of Mr. Barclay's successors who knew Joseph intimately and had many opportunities to talk with him, said Joseph's family drifted off to the Ohio country.[15] This explanation rings true, for the Indians did not hesitate to go great distances on hunting trips. The Ohio journey also accords with family tradition, being one of the stories told to the historian Stone by Brant's children. A sojourn in the Ohio country accords with history, too. The Mohawks had a right to hunt in Ohio and many of them did, indeed, go there, and some of them lived there for long periods. A decade or so later Sir William Johnson, the new Indian superintendent, would be continually urging

the Mohawks and the rest of the Six Nations to bring in their people
from the west where they had grown wild and lawless and were acquiring bad names.

Margaret and Peter could have gone away to hunt. They had to
have pelts to exchange for clothing and tools and household utensils
(and rum), and they had to have meat. There were two big hunts
every year, spring and fall, and it may have been in the spring of 1742
that Joseph Brant's parents left home. Hunger often lent urgency to
such journeys. Winter and spring were the starving time, for the
Indians could seldom save enough food to tide them over to a new
hunt or a new harvest. Their crops were always at the mercy of flood
and cold and insects, and it was the measure of these poor creatures'
daily need that they spoke of heaven as the Plentiful Country. Almost
anything could upset their economy. Grasshoppers, a blight, a drouth,
an early frost, an epidemic, or just a bout of drunkenness at planting or
harvest time—any of these occurrences foretold future hunger and
suffering. Then, too, even under the best of circumstances the preservation of food was difficult. By midwinter the Indians were often
reduced to the greatest extremity. It was then that they eagerly devoured meat and fish in the last stages of decomposition, and acorns
and bark and even the bearskins they slept on.

Narratives of early travelers are full of these annual famines. In the
winter of 1754 the Indians were starving at Onondaga, and in 1767
the Mohawks were "in the utmost distress." At Oneida in February
1768 a missionary lamented: "they now begin to cook some good dried
guts of Dear and what is in it. (Dung if I may So call it.) to Season the
corn; likewise some rotten fish which they have kept Since last fall to
Season their Samps, rottener the better they Say as it will Season
more broth. corn they have plenty yet, but no thing to Season it."[16]
Alas, the next winter there was not even corn or hominy (samps), for
all the Six Nations as far west as Cayuga lost their new crop by early
frosts. And in 1758 the Indians of Canajoharie, Joseph's home village,
had not a meal of anything to share with some passing friends.

The Ohio is nearly a thousand miles long, but when the Mohawks
spoke of it they usually meant its northern headwaters, the Allegheny
River and its creeks and tributaries. Here in the wild mountain fastnesses of what is now northwestern Pennsylvania and contiguous parts
of New York and Ohio dwelt emigrants from all the Six Nations, as
well as Shawnees and Delawares, and a few other assorted peoples.
Indian villages were scattered throughout this rugged country, some
even below what is now Pittsburgh. When white settlers began to

move into the region, the inhabitants of all these villages were lumped together under the name of Mingo, a name of Algonquian derivation which was sometimes particularly applied to the Senecas and which has been said to mean "rascal." White people always dreaded the Mingoes, and there was scarcely a frontiersman anywhere from New York to Virginia who would not have said the name was well deserved.

To this country, then, Peter and Margaret came, sometime after February 6, 1742. They were hunting beaver or searching for food (and probably visiting as they went, for they had relatives among the Cayugas whom they could have visited[17] and they knew their kinsmen would feed them as long as they had anything for themselves), or perhaps they were just roaming around. At any rate, in this Ohio country, according to the account of the Reverend Dr. Stuart and according to family tradition, Joseph Brant was born. John Norton, Joseph's secretary, is more definite. He says that Joseph was born at Cuyahoga,[18] meaning either a village at the mouth of the Cuyahoga River (site of present Cleveland, Ohio) or somewhere along that stream at some small settlement or isolated cabin. The wanderings of Peter and Margaret had taken them far afield.

The date of Joseph's birth was 1743, probably in March.[19] He was called Thayendanegea, a name which denotes "Two sticks of wood bound together,"[20] and which seems to have been pronounced Tai-yen-da-nay-geh. He was a member of the Wolf clan,[21] membership in which came to him through his mother; and he was, so far as it can possibly be ascertained, a Mohawk by birth,[22] again through his mother. John Norton adds a fact which explains the many rumors current in Joseph's lifetime that he was someone other than a Mohawk. Joseph Brant, said Norton, was descended on both sides of his family from Wyandot (Huron) captives taken on the north shore of Lake Ontario and adopted into the Longhouse.[23] It was an ancestry which Jesuit missionaries might have thought preferable to descent from within the Longhouse, for the Hurons were accounted by them the most advanced and intelligent of Indians. To the conquering Mohawks, however, it was a different story. Nevertheless, somewhere along the line there must have been intermarriage between the captives and the Mohawks as well as adoptions.

How much time elapsed after Joseph's birth is not known. But the next thing that happened, Peter Tehowaghwengaraghkwin, the wandering warrior, died. Many years ago an old Mohawk in Canada told the collector-historian, Lyman C. Draper, that Joseph's father died in an epidemic. There was a terrible sickness, he said, and all the people ran away.[24] It could have happened. Epidemics frequently occurred among the Indians, and it is true that they sometimes fled in terror, leaving their sick to die and their dead to bury themselves.

Next, as Dr. Stuart told the story, and as Norton corroborates,[25] poor, lowly Margaret with her two children in tow came straggling back to Canajoharie. She was still young in years though perhaps not very handsome, for Indian women lost their looks early. But she was certainly a woman of spirit, and it is pleasing to note that her life was about to improve.

Once back on the Mohawk, Margaret had something important to do. There had been no minister among the Mingoes in the Ohio country, but now, at home, she could see to it that her son Thayendanegea was decently baptized and provided with a proper Christian name. The Reverend Henry Barclay records the baptism of a Joseph on February 16, 1744.[26] But this date seems almost too early for Margaret's return home, and this particular Joseph was probably an adult since his parents are not listed. It is more likely that Thayendanegea was christened Joseph by some German or Dutch clergyman in the neighborhood after Barclay left Fort Hunter but before the Reverend John Ogilvie came to the mission to replace him. If so, this would fix the date of Margaret's return sometime between February 1746 and February 1750. Again we turn to John Norton for corroboration. Joseph's mother, related Norton, went back to the Mohawk a few years before the outbreak of the last French and Indian War.[27]

Somewhere or other, sometime or other, Margaret acquired, briefly, a second (or was he a third?) husband. His name was Lykas[28] and she may have found him in the Ohio country. Or she may have wedded him back home on the Mohawk. Lykas was of higher status than the deceased Peter, being, it seems, one of the Mohawks' "Principall Men."[29] He has even been listed as a sachem though that may be an error. But Lykas was no luckier than Peter, for by the spring of 1750 Margaret (who in her person exemplifies so many of the woes of Indian women) was a widow again. In May she learned that her new husband, who had gone off with a war party to fight the Catawbas, had been killed on the way by some of the southern Indians.[30]

Widowhood was hard. One's relatives would generally share their food, but there were always small ways to evade this obligation and, indeed, there were many times when relatives had no food to share. And where was clothing coming from for mother and children? Margaret could not hunt deer. She would have had nothing to turn to but the local liquor trade. This trade was open to any enterprising Indian, but it was mostly the Indian women who carried it on. All they had to do was to go to the nearest store and, if they could get credit, carry home a keg of rum on their shoulders. Once back in the village, they sold the liquor.[31] It was a living. If they did well, they could hold back a little for themselves—that is, they could if they could find a place to hide it.

The great ginseng speculation of 1752 was a godsend to women like Margaret. Ginseng, which grew wild on the Mohawk, was bought up in unlimited quantities by merchants suddenly hopeful of amassing fortunes, and then it was sent all the way to London and on to China where it was known to be highly prized. For a little while the roots of the plant, green or dried, commanded a great price, and men, women, and children searched diligently and made more money than they ever dreamed of and could buy fine clothes and plenty to eat.[32] Among the most zealous searchers—for nobody scorned getting rich—was a well-known Mohawk sachem from Fort Hunter, a friend of powerful whites, named Brant. Brant went searching up and down the river, far out of his neighborhood. He was at it all day long, we are told.[33] But the happy craze did not last. Something went awry. Speculators found it was easier to hope for riches than actually to get them, and the furor died down. The ginseng trade turned routine again, and everything was as before.

Not quite. It was about this time that Margaret, who (as we shall see) truly meant to be a good Christian, fell into grievous error. It was an error that the new missionary could not condone. Unfortunately for Margaret, life had to grow worse before it could get better.

3

Canajoharie Castle

C ANAJOHARIE CASTLE, Margaret's old home, was not much of a
place. Its population varied (depending on how many had gone
hunting, fishing, fighting, or roaming) from about 250 to, at most,
around 300. Despite the imposing name, it was no castle. A century
ago it had had a sort of rude palisade, as, indeed, did many Indian
villages in those days. White people soon began to speak of these
fortified places as castles, and the Indians themselves took up the
term; and now, in the mid-eighteenth century, almost any collection
of bark huts might be called a castle. As to the name, "Canajoharie,"
all authorities agree that it refers to a pot or a kettle. Joseph Brant
once said that the word meant "a kettle stuck on a pole,"[1] and he must
have known what he was talking about. But missionries speaking at an
earlier day thought Canajoharie meant "Great Boiling Pot" or "to
wash the cauldron." One rendition was not an inappropriate name for
the village, for the Indians liked to keep a pot always boiling on the
fire, provided, of course, they had something to boil in it. But "to
wash the pot" was not quite so apt for, Indian housekeeping being
somewhat careless, little pot washing got done. However, nobody
complained about such things except an occasional missionary or soldier quartered in the village, both known to be absurdly finical. The
Indians were quite content with their domestic arrangements, and the
local whites, many of whom did not live very differently, saw nothing
to cavil about.

This Indian village of Canajoharie lay on the south side of the
Mohawk River, near the mouth of Nowadaga Creek, on what was
then the western frontier of Albany County in His Britannic Majesty's

province of New York.[2] About fifty miles or so to the eastward, where the navigation of the Mohawk River began, lay the old Dutch trading town of Schenectady. Schenectady contained at this time about three hundred houses, in a goodly number of which lived persons who made their living by trading with the Indians. Sixteen miles farther on to the southeast, through the pine barrens and down the Hudson, lay the old Dutch town of Albany. Albany was the largest town anywhere about and consequently could boast of even more traders. Both Albany and Schenectady had been famed (and damned) for generations past for their great Indian trade. They had men at Oswego up on Lake Ontario whose sole purpose was to intercept Indians traveling with furs to Montreal, and they had men out in the Indian country as far as they dared go—which was very far, indeed, and the only reason they did not go on into the country of the Great Lakes was that the French, who also lived by trade, had got there first. Needless to say, these rival groups of traders did not love each other; and wars had been fought, and would yet be fought, largely for that reason.

Going back up the Mohawk River from Schenectady toward Canajoharie, one passed on the south bank the white settlement of Warrensbush, which was very small, but not too small to shelter a few traders (for at times almost any white settler was a trader of sorts and would swap liquor for peltries). A little farther on up the river, near the mouth of Schoharie Creek, one came to another Indian village named Tiononderoga, but which was almost always called Fort Hunter, from the fort and its dependent white settlement. Fort Hunter had been a defensive place for many years and usually housed a small company of soldiers. Here, too, was the tiny Anglican chapel where both whites and Indians brought their children to be baptized whenever a missionary was in attendance. Young Mr. Barclay was gone now, but the Reverend John Ogilvie came up periodically from Albany. The Indians who lived at Fort Hunter were also Mohawks, and they had about thirty cabins. Their village was known as the Lower Castle, while Canajoharie was called the Upper Castle. These two villages, though about thirty miles apart, were very closely associated, and together with a few Indians at Schoharie they made up the bulk of the so-called Mohawk "Nation."

On the north side of the Mohawk River, not far from Fort Hunter, one found a stout, fortress-like house of stone, wherein dwelt a youngish, good-looking Irishman named William Johnson. Johnson had first come to the Mohawk valley in 1738, and he was, of course, a trader. A fairer trader than most, Johnson also applied himself to a study of the Indians and was not above joining them in some of their frolics, so

most of the Indians liked him most of the time. For the white people
Johnson had a joke and a ready smile, and these qualities, added to
considerable intelligence and more than adequate education, made
him just the sort of man who was bound to do well on a frontier. In his
stone house by the river this affable Irishman kept a store and a
somewhat unusual household.

Nearer home, both to the east and the west, the Canajoharie
Indians could look around at another sort of neighbors. These were
Germans who had fled the Palatinate over a generation before. They
now lived in such places as Stone Arabia and Palatine on the north
bank and in scattered houses on both sides of the river, with outlying
settlements about ten miles to the west in an area called the German
Flats which was the very fringe of the frontier. Once poor and miserable, some of these Germans had become by this time solid, substantial citizens. But others were still very poor and lived in wretched
hovels through which the winds tore and shrieked in winter. Though
they had been in America so long, the Germans still liked to speak
their own language and had somewhat different ways, so they were
looked at askance by the British settlers down the river and by passing
British soldiers and travelers. They were often spoken of as Dutch or
High Dutch and accounted very stupid. Of course the Holland Dutch
in Albany and Schenectady were called Dutch, too—Low Dutch, that
is; and they were accounted stupid, too. But as they had been in the
province for many generations (even longer than the British) and
obviously knew what was what and where to get it, they were stupid in
a more reprehensible way.

What the Mohawk Indians thought about all this, they never got
around to saying. All white people, whether Germans, British, or
Dutch, were whites to the Indians, and it was enough for them just to
try to hold their own against the oncoming horde. Though there were
still almost limitless forests far to the north, the south, and the west,
the Indians of Canajoharie and Fort Hunter could feel the hot breath
of civilization on their necks. They were, in fact, surrounded.

They were surrounded—yes, and day by day they surrendered a
little. For more than a century they had been giving up land. This
they knew well enough. What they did not seem to realize was that
they were also giving up their old way of life. They thought they set
great store by their ancient customs. Yet many of their ancient customs were already lost and forgotten. Others had undergone great
change. The Mohawks were still excellent marksmen, but with guns,
not bows and arrows, and their hunters had to have firearms and
ammunition or starve. Their women no longer cooked in pottery

kettles or scratched the earth with stone hoes; they demanded utensils of brass and metal hoes. Man and woman, old and young, they all preferred cloth to fur or leather, and would unhesitatingly trade three fine deerskins for a coarse piece of wool called a stroud with which to wrap themselves. The time was when they would have thought a dog the finest kind of meat, but now they had a taste for beef and pork and mutton, and many of them tried to keep poultry and a few scrawny cattle. And even their myths, which they thought were very, very old, sounded, at times, strangely Biblical.

In a very real sense these Indians were, except in name, no longer the same people. But for all their changing way of life, they had not yet achieved the status of even the lowest sort of whites. Though they often understood English, they could seldom speak it. Though they might profess Christianity, their oath was not accepted in the courts. Though they still possessed a great deal of land, they had no money. Worst of all, they could not cope with the white man's liquor or the white man's diseases. So, while the white man flourished, their own numbers diminished year by year. From an estimated population of five hundred fighting men in 1660, they could now, in the mid-eighteenth century, muster scarcely half that number.

In outward appearance the two Mohawk villages looked not very different from settlements on any new frontier. In the previous century returning travelers had spoken of the famous bark-covered long-houses which they described as fifty to one hundred paces long and as much as twenty feet high. Such houses were built to accommodate all the branches of one family, from the oldest to the youngest. But now that Mohawk families had shrunk in size, their houses were correspondingly smaller. Present-day travelers generally spoke of seeing cabins, and these cabins were obviously not the great longhouses. Changing customs also played their part in the changing scene. It would seem that now when a young fellow acquired a wife, he did not choose to live with her relatives, as formerly, but preferred to go out and build his own bark hut or log cabin. Indeed, the time was not far off when there would rise, both in Canajoharie and Fort Hunter, a number of small frame houses with floors, chimneys, and even windows. And there would be white people passing by along the road who would cast envious glances at these decent little houses.

What was life like in these two villages? For one thing, it held some very nice social distinctions. All the Mohawks were not born equal. Some families and some persons were accounted much better than others. At the very top of the social ladder of Canajoharie Castle stood a certain Seth Tekarihoga, head chief of the proud Turtle tribe which was descended from the first woman on earth. Seth was an old man now and when he passed on to the Plentiful Country (which he was to do soon, via getting drunk and falling into the fire), he would be succeeded by a young fellow named Johannes, sometimes called Hans or Hance. Johannes was probably Seth's sister's son, since inheritance passed in the female line; and he, too, would some day be called Tekarihoga, for this was one of those great names which were handed down from one generation to another. Among the Mohawks there would always be a Tekarihoga, and Tekarihoga would always be the first man of his people.

Best known to the white people, however, was a forceful chief named Hendrick or Henry, and by them sometimes called "King" Henry. His Indian name was Thayanoge, and the French in Canada called him Tete Blanche after his silver hair. In his youth Hendrick had been one of the visiting Indian notables who had caused such excitement at Queen Anne's court. This great chief was looked upon with mixed emotions by the whites. Governor Clinton of New York had been known to inquire solicitously "how poor old Henrick does," but a Pennsylvania official called him "that vile Indian Henry," and very likely did not care how he did.

But Hendrick had a brother named Abraham, and here all the whites were in perfect agreement. Abraham, they declared, was a good old man. He had every virtue. He was honest. He was sincere. He was prudent. He was a true Christian. In other words it would seem that Abraham was the nearest to a white man that an Indian could ever hope to come!

Abraham's old wife was named Gesina and Hendrick's wife seems to have been called Mary. Each chief had a son named Paulus, but Abraham's son died an untimely death in one of the French wars. When some white people replaced the lost Paulus, first with a French captive and then with a scalp, the old father was full of gratitude for the polite attention. These two families were the first among the Mohawks to acquire a surname. The old men were known as Hendrick and Abraham Peters, or Petersen, probably after their father. Old Abraham could read prayers and make a pretty good discourse on the Sabbath, and Hendrick's son, Paulus, taught school and could write a pretty good letter. But "King" Hendrick was more a politician than a scholar.

Another leading sachem, or civil chief, of Canajoharie was a certain Nicholas or Nickus who was generally called "Old" Nickus, not necessarily because he was so old but simply because he was the oldest Indian of that name. This chief may have been related to the

Petersens.[3] Nickus' wife was an aristocrat, for she and Nickus were the parents of Johannes, the future Tekarihoga. They were also the parents of a girl who was to inherit all her mother's social prestige and who would one day become the Indian wife of the white trader, George Croghan. (This alliance, strangely enough, was to be of enormous importance to the unimportant Joseph Brant.) Nickus had been the first Mohawk to visit the famous mission at Stockbridge, Massachusetts, but they did not think well of him there. "Nicoles," they said disapprovingly, "is no very desirable person." Nickus had also been a prisoner of the French in Canada during King George's War and had come back talking insolently to William Johnson and other white people. But he spoke softly to his lady wife. When urged by Colonel Lydius to join an expedition to Niagara, the proud chief hesitated at first and then, pointing to his wife, suggested that Lydius "ask her Consent."

Brant was a common name among the Mohawks. There were Brants all over the Mohawk country, but, since this was a Christian name and not a surname, all the Brants were not necessarily related. In Canajoharie dwelt a well-known chief called "Old" Brant or, according to one spelling, Aroghiadecka. His wife bore the good Dutch name of Alida. Oddly enough, this couple had a son christened Joseph who, had he lived to adulthood, might have become another Joseph Brant.[4]

At Fort Hunter the leading men were a chief named Abraham Tyorhansere—often called Young Abraham or even Little Abraham to distinguish him from the old Abraham at Canajoharie—and a middle-aged fellow named Brant Canagaraduncka. The latter had been duly married by the Reverend Mr. Barclay to Christina, a noble lady of the Bear tribe, in 1738. They had a young son Nickus or Nicholas, who seemed to be on the verge of acquiring a surname. He was known as Brant's Nickus or Nickus Brant's.[5] There was also in the family a grown, married son named Thomas, probably by some former wife of Brant's. Brant Canagaraduncka was a man to be reckoned with. Besides his prestige as a sachem of the powerful Turtle clan, he also had wealth and more of the white man's education than most Indians. He owned a horse and wagon, some fat cows, and a pretty good house, and he could sign his name.[6] Even more important, from the historical point of view, Brant got along well with the trader, William Johnson. The two were already firm friends.

Also at Fort Hunter lived still another chief Brant whose Indian name was Kaweghnagey. The white people called him Wide-Mouthed Brant, and he had a wife named Lydia and a swarm of what must have been, for Indians, unusually healthy children. This Brant was to die in 1760, but his widow and all his family were thriving up until the eve of the Revolution. They were good, honest Indians, too, for they were permitted to have charge accounts for many years with most of the traders in the neighborhood.[7]

Of such was the Mohawk elite. Their names have been handed down to posterity because they came into contact with white people who mentioned them in letters or documents, or because they themselves may have done a little writing that has survived. Perhaps they signed a deed or a treaty. But most of the Indians were "common" Indians—and *they* hardly counted at all except when going to war. It is no coincidence that the first mention of young Joseph Thayendanegea in any contemporary document would some day come about as a result of his going to war. Joseph was much too common to sign a treaty.

The villages of Canajoharie and Fort Hunter were, like their white counterparts, somewhat given to contention and gossip. Cliques formed. There were arguments over land sales and surveys and fences and kegs of rum and who should be the next sachem. Rumors flew around. Matrons, blue-blooded and plebeian, gathered at the dumps and exchanged such news as only matrons had or could manufacture. Such-and-such a one, they declared, though he pretended to be as godly as the missionary, had been seen coming out of the cornfield drunk. Or such-and-such a one had threatened to take his ax and knock such-and-such a one on the head. Or such a one had left his wife and the poor thing was wailing in her hut. Listen to her! Or another one had sold some land to a Dutchman all by himself and now he's run off to the French. The chiefs are going after him! Or such a one had dreamed he had a silver arm band and was going down to Johnson's to see if he could get his dream fulfilled. Or (proudly) my children found a whole bushel of ginseng roots yesterday.

Toward the end of 1752 or the beginning of 1753 some new gossip erupted in both villages. For Margaret, the widow of Lykas, who had no husband and had not had one for some time, gave birth to a young warrior. She claimed the young warrior's father was the sachem, Brant Canagaraduncka, and Brant did not deny it. And Brant himself a grandfather! How long had his good wife Christina been dead? Not very long, it seems.[8] Who (they may have inquired at Fort Hunter) was Margaret? And what think you of that? There were people, good church people mainly, who shook their heads and clicked their tongues aplenty.

On March 4, 1753, Margaret's child was christened. The Reverend John Ogilvie officiated and duly recorded the baby's name in his

"Register of Indian Children" as "Jacob Son of Marg^t. the Widow of Lykas by Brandt of Canijohare."[9] No more is known of this little Jacob, but he may have lived at least a few months. For on September 9, 1753, Margaret and Brant were married.[10] The ceremony took place at Canajoharie Castle and the Reverend Mr. Ogilvie, very likely with some satisfaction, tied the knot. But they were not pleased down in Fort Hunter. Almost immediately the new bridegroom, who was considered to have ruined himself by the marriage, was forced to leave his old home and move up to Canajoharie.[11]

What was the matter? Though the behavior of Margaret and Brant was not exactly the norm of Mohawk behavior, still it was not so extraordinary as to give cause for such commotion. Both Mr. Barclay and Mr. Ogilvie had christened any number of Mohawk children whose fathers were not identified, but whose mothers were now going calmly about their business, and nothing much said. Evidently Brant and Margaret had violated some rule of conduct which the Indians held important. As they belonged to different clans (an essential in Iroquois marriages), there could have been no trouble in that respect. The likelihood is that Brant had been expected to marry his late wife's sister. This was good Indian custom and, if broken, it would have insulted her family. Nor is it clear whether Brant had observed the prescribed period of mourning for the deceased Christina, and if he had not, this also would have affronted her family. Christina's family was very influential in the Fort Hunter community.[12] There is also some evidence that the unfortunate Christina lost her life in a drunken revelry, and this could have resulted in a blood feud with all kinds of social repercussions.

But censure or no, for Margaret this was a great marriage. In a world where aristocracy wedded aristocracy, as Barclay's Register Book so plainly shows, and where the common Indian had "nothing to Say," Margaret had bettered herself enormously. For her children the future abruptly changed. One, at least, would get an education, and some day both would have plenty to say. Practically, too, Margaret had taken a great step forward. Where, or with whom, she had been living, who knows? What an achievement it must have been, most of the time, just to keep body and soul together! The two children, Joseph and Molly, could have known little else but hunger and want. Now suddenly life was good. Brant was a kind father to them. He was also an industrious Indian and merely by virtue of being a sachem he had various interesting ways of getting his hands on extra income. Shortly after his marriage, for instance, Brant went with Hendrick, Tekarihoga, and some other chiefs to Philadelphia on business for the

Iroquois Confederacy, and came home loaded with presents, among which was a gift for his wife from the government of Pennsylvania.[13] Whenever land was to be sold, a party of young fighters to be sent on the warpath or any other favor required of the Indians, the leading sachems were showered with gifts from the white people. Soon Brant and his family were living in the best house in Canajoharie. The children were seldom hungry any more. And the time was coming when Margaret would be known by traders as far away as Schenectady and Albany.

For the lad Joseph, ten years old, it was enough just to eat his fill. But for the girl Molly, now seventeen or eighteen, who would some day turn into an extraordinary woman, there may have been food for thought as well. Molly was, as the phrase went, a "pretty likely" girl, and once when she was visiting in Albany a white officer saw her and fell in love with her. How serious this romance became is not known, but it is obvious that Molly had her share of admirers.[14]

In the midst of such good fortune, Margaret's heart was not content. Her religion and her church meant a great deal to her, and she wanted to partake of the Holy Communion. But the Reverend Mr. Ogilvie forbade it, and pointed out that Margaret was a sinful woman. She would have to make public confession of her sin before she could be restored to the full fellowship of the church. This was a hard thing to do, but finally Margaret mustered up her courage, and on Sunday, February 17, 1754, "made an Humble Confession in Publick, for the heinous Sin of Adultery, for which Crime she had been put off from the Comunion for a considerable Time past."[15]

The next Sunday, when the Holy Sacrament was celebrated, the winter weather was at its worst and only ten attended church, but a happy-hearted Margaret Brant must have sat in that little congregation. Some day, surely, she would see the Plentiful Country. (And thereafter, so far as anyone knows, Margaret lived a very, very respectable life, though if now and then she hid a small keg in the woods, who was to see it?)

4

The Young Warrior

K ING GEORGE'S WAR of 1744–48 had settled nothing. A few years
after the peace treaty, hostilities were about to break out again.
The French in Canada, who could not exist without the fur trade, and
the British in the colonies to the south, who could live without the
trade but not without western land, glared at each other across their
shifting boundaries.

The Six Nations of Indians continued to hold fast to their official
neutrality. They, too, could not exist without the trade, but they
preferred to do business where they could get the better deal. The
better deal was the sticking point. Though the British offered superior
merchandise and often cheaper prices, French traders had ways of
getting the same merchandise and, to the western nations at least, the
French were more available—and certainly more amiable. For the
Mohawks, however, there was not much choice. They almost had to
take their peltry to Johnson's store or to the traders at Albany and
Schenectady, just as the Senecas almost had to go to Niagara. Loaded
with favors by French officials, many Senecas and Cayugas, too, made
encampments near the French post. Such was the pressure of geography and politics. The two ends of the Confederacy were pulled apart
as by magnets.

When the French began to build a chain of forts to connect Lake
Erie with the Ohio River and ultimately with their province of Louisiana, thus demonstrating their intention to control all the land at the
back of the British colonies, the war for the continent was on again.
At first the struggle did not go well for the British. The French seemed
quite secure in their new posts, and from their stronghold of Fort

Duquesne (present Pittsburgh) they were able to command the very gate to midland America. Here, where the Allegheny and Monongahela Rivers met to form the Ohio, was an almost unbroken waterway to all the country served by the tributaries of the Ohio, north and south, even as far as the Mississippi, and on down that mighty stream to the French port of New Orleans. Like the famed passage through the Longhouse that opened up the great northwest, the forks of the Ohio was a place of immense importance in a wilderness where traffic had to move by raft and boat. Both imperial rivals had coveted this strategic spot at the meeting of the waters, and people from Virginia had tried to occupy it, too, but the French had driven them away.

The Indians thereabouts observed French boldness and French successes, impressed. Long acknowledged as dependents of the Six Nations, these Ohio Indians were mostly Delawares, Shawnees, and the straying Iroquois called Mingoes. They were also, mostly, refugees from the east and northeastward, and they had no very favorable opinion of Virginians, Pennsylvanians, or Yorkers. In fleeing to the Ohio wilderness from former homes near the white settlements, they had designed to live out their lives, unmolested, in their ancient, accustomed ways. But to live under any circumstances at all, they required guns and ammunition, and they also wanted, a little inconsistently perhaps, some of the white man's comforts. French traders were now the only traders who could come into their forests, and Frenchmen pressed for a French alliance. Iroquois policy or no, could these western allies of the Six Nations afford to remain neutral? There was much counciling, much hemming and hawing. The Delawares were in a mood to throw off their petticoats again. They, at least, were not too dismayed at the turn of events. They had plenty of grievances against the British, and it was no trouble at all to find more.

The Six Nations who did not relish seeing forts going up in country they considered theirs, except the few absolutely necessary for trade, warned the French away and admonished their dependents. But the Confederates themselves were divided and confused. Said the Red Head, a great Onondaga sachem, to William Johnson: "Brother Warraghiiyagey . . . . it is not with our Consent, that the French have Commited any Hostilities at Ohio, we dont know what you Christians French, and English together intend we are so hemm'd in by both, that we have hardly a Hunting place left, in a little while, if we find a Bear in a Tree, there will immediately Appear an Owner for the Land to Challenge the Property, and hinder us from killing it which is our livelyhood, we are so Perplexed, between both, that we hardly know what to say or to think."[1]

The coming war could be the final struggle between Frenchmen and Britons. The dreaded time when Indians had to take sides might be approaching. But which of the two great rivals was going to get the upper hand? This the Indians as a weak third party had to know, before abandoning their neutral position. The Iroquois were inclined to think the British would win, and to some extent this coincided with their view of their own interests. If either white power must emerge as a conqueror, a British victory would tend to firm up their old empire, the domain on which they still relied, either directly or indirectly, for furs. The Indians on the Ohio thought differently, and their interests were just the opposite. They wanted to be free. Indeed, they cherished a hope they might finally get free of the Iroquois and perhaps at the same time drive the land-hungry British out of North America. It was an enticing thought. Yet the wiser heads, on the Ohio as well as at Onondaga, suspected there could be no permanent victory for Indians at all. It was to their only real advantage to keep the whites balanced against each other as long as possible. The land that the white people were fighting over was *Indian* land. And whoever got it finally, was not likely to give it back, not even to those Indians who had helped them win the prize.

Such was the state of affairs in the spring of 1755. At this time Margaret and the sachem Brant Canagaraduncka had been husband and wife for a little over a year. Unlike the Red Head, who wavered between the French and the British, Joseph's new stepfather was not perplexed. He had no problem of loyalty or of what to do or think. Thanks to the influence of William Johnson, the friendly Irishman who operated a store across the river from the chief's former home, Brant was heartily pro-British. The affable Johnson had been in the colonies since 1738, and nearly all that time he had assiduously cultivated the Indians, at first, no doubt, for purposes of trade and later for purposes of policy. Chief Brant had long been won over and, indeed, Johnson was by this time firmly installed as the best friend of the whole Mohawk nation.

William Johnson was a very shrewd man. He was also endowed with a gifted tongue and great personal charm. He visited the Indians in their huts, spoke their language, caressed their girls, wore their clothes, and joined in their dances and feasts. He could eat boiled dog and soup enriched with lice without turning a hair. At one and the same time he laid the foundation for chronic ill-health and a unique

William Johnson. Painting by John Wollaston, Jr. Sir William did not like this portrait because of the "narrow hanging Shoulders"; his own, he said, were "verry broad and square." It was Johnson who sent Joseph away to school, and for many years Joseph gave him a son's obedience. *Courtesy of the Albany Institute of History and Art, Albany, New York.*

and brilliant career. By the Indians Johnson was adopted and called Warraghiyagey, or "He who does much business" or "A man who undertakes great things"; and he was recognized throughout the whole province as the persuasive persuader who had persuaded the Mohawks to take part in King George's War. Now with the American colonies on the eve of the last great French and Indian war, he had just received a commission from General Braddock, commander in chief of the British forces, to manage Indian affairs. It was a commission he was to hold, with varying titles and powers, for the rest of his life. Johnson's star was rising fast. It was, indeed, as many historians have noted, a lucky star—but first how very carefully had he polished it and himself set it in the sky.

Johnson, armed with his new authority, immediately invited a general council of the Six Nations to meet at his house in June 1755. There would be presents, of course, for all who would attend. Over a thousand Indians, men, women, and children, responded. They comprised perhaps a fifth of the entire Confederacy. From the west and the south they came, some on foot and some on horseback, and took over the meadows about Mount Johnson. The Mohawks were all there, and a motley group from Oquaga and other settlements down the Susquehanna. A good many Oneidas came who lived east and south of Oneida Lake, and with them the neighboring Tuscaroras. From forty miles farther west came some Onondagas from the region of Onondaga Creek and Lake. From about the same distance farther on came a few Cayugas from the shores of Cayuga Lake. There were even a few people from the far-off Seneca country, though mostly the distant Indians held themselves aloof.

Tension trembled on the air. The Indians were wary, the whites anxious. On June 24 Johnson spoke to the assembled multitude, and boldly threw down the war belt. Hendrick and old Abraham, both heartily pro-British, had helped him prepare his speech. Brant must have known what was in it and Margaret and the children would have been among the crowd to hear it read and interpreted. Although many of the Indians could understand English and Johnson could certainly speak Mohawk, the dignity of the Six Nations demanded an interpreter. Daniel Claus interpreted. Claus was a young German who had lived for some time among the Mohawks, first with Brant and his former wife and then with Hendrick's family, and he was striving to make himself useful to Johnson in Indian affairs. This was his day, too, as well as Johnson's. Both had a rendezvous with the future.

The speech was long and artful. Johnson carefully adhered to the customs of his listeners. He had already condoled with them for the deaths that had occurred since he last saw them and, figuratively speaking, had wiped away their tears so they could attend to business. With every important statement he held up a belt or a string of wampum as confirmation. He reminded the Six Nations of their early friendship with the English. The two peoples, he declared, were bound together as with a silver chain which could neither rust nor decay and whose ends were fixed to the immovable mountains. ("Oyeh!" The Indians shouted their agreement.) But the French, Johnson continued, had always been their cruel enemies, ever ready to burn their villages and murder their people. And now, he pointed out, the French had seized their best hunting grounds on the Ohio. Were they not building forts there? He called upon the Great Spirit above to witness that the English harbored no such ill designs against them. Then he alluded to his own friendship with them:

> If you have any regard for . . . me your Brother and friend . . . who, you know has never deceived you—hearken to my advice [he pleaded]—I love you and speake for your good—*Stand by your Bretheren the English*—dont break your Covenant Chain with them, let not the French boastings or lies deceive you. The English . . . are slow to spill blood, but when they begin, they are like an angry Wolf, and the French will fly before them like Deer. Now is your time, Brothers to chose, which side you will be of; if you are wise you want but little time to determine, but upon this determination depends the future happiness of yourselves, your Wives & children after you.[2]

The speech, artful though it was, was not the most important part of the proceedings. Johnson was also working night and day in private conferences with the sachems and head warriors. There were arguments, promises, and presents. His expense accounts bear eloquent testimony: four pounds to a Tuscarora to buy a cow, pumps and buckles to an Onondaga, a dollar to a Mohawk, tea and sugar to some principal families, and the like. Still the chiefs were hard to convince and would not rush their decision. For several days they deliberated among themselves; then, succumbing to their general weakness, they got drunk. Finally, on June 29, the assembled Indians, sober again, relieved white anxieties and accepted Johnson's war belt. Two days later they divided up the nearly eleven hundred pounds' worth of merchandise which Johnson gave them and headed for home, promising to return. In their packs, as they set off, they had the first payment on more than a century of annual British subsidies.

Perhaps the Indians had meant to return. But on July 9 Major General Braddock suffered his disastrous defeat in the wilds of western Pennsylvania at the hands of a force of French and allied Indians not half the size of his own army. It was the first of the military "miracles" that surprised even the French. The news quickly spread. The Six Nations were paralyzed into inaction. The Indians on the Ohio declared for France, and began to work terror upon the Pennsylvania and Virginia frontiers, gaining for themselves the undying hatred of all the white settlers thereabouts. It was more than three years later, when the fortunes of war began to turn and the French could no longer supply the western Indians, that the Six Nations, strengthened by concessions from Pennsylvania, were able to assert themselves once more over their allies and force them to drop the hatchet. This took place at the famous treaty of Easton in 1758. In the meantime only the Mohawks and a few stragglers from the rest of the Six Nations actually broke the neutrality and went out to fight for their friend, Johnson, in the summer of 1755.

Joseph, only twelve years old, had no choice but to stay at home and yearn for glory. His mother saw to that. But he could watch the exciting preparations in his castle. There was the customary council-ing, with the old chiefs warning the young warriors of danger, and the old women reminding them to obey their leader and not to disgrace their ancestors. Then came the great war dance with a roasted ox and beer for everybody, meat and drink that were symbolic of Frenchmen's flesh and Frenchmen's blood. Afterward the Indians set out in small parties, each war chief with his own little band and some white man along to dole out the supplies and look out for them. John Butler, a young interpreter, whose name would some day become anathema in the valley, accompanied one party. Old Hendrick, heavy with age, rode away, never to return. Daniel Claus rode off, too, a young fellow who seems to have been really fond of his Indian companions.

Near the southern end of Lake George, on September 8, 1755, a gory and decisive battle was fought. By dusk the French were fleeing through the forest or lying dead on the ground, and the Mohawks were howling mournfully over great losses. The victors, those who were still alive and whole, could celebrate an invasion stopped, a French gen-eral captured. As for William Johnson, the trader-turned-soldier, his luck was both ill and good. He lay in his tent with a wound that would plague him the rest of his life, but when he returned home to the Mohawk valley, he would return a baronet of Great Britain. Always, thereafter, he would enjoy the favor of the king. Always, among the Indians, he would speak with the voice of the king.

They called it the Seven Years' War. Each year the Mohawks volunteered for the British. Beleaguered, pressed, and bribed, some were hesitant and some were insolent; but others declared staunchly that they meant to live and die as Englishmen. But each year the greater part of the Six Nations continued neutral, explaining to the French that it was only some hotheads who were fighting. Angrily they sent word to the Mohawks that if they did not stop, they would "kick them from them."

For Joseph the war was still only a distant prospect. These were still the days of boyhood, days to spear salmon, to hunt with his dog, to swim in the creek, to listen wide-eyed to the old warriors as they told legends or bragged of their youthful exploits. Sometimes he would go down the river to the Wasson farm where there were two white boys nearly his own age, cronies of his. Here he could have learnt the few words of English that he knew. There was a little girl in the family who watched the boys at their sports. She, too, was fond of Joseph and described him years later to her grandchildren as a "noble good-hearted boy."[3] Sometime or other Joseph also got a little schooling, though it is not clear whether he went to an Indian school taught by Hendrick's son, Paulus, or to a school with white children.[4] Whichever it was, it was not much of a school and it did not last long.

Joseph saw his first military service in the summer of 1758. He was fifteen years old. Major General Abercromby was preparing to invade Canada, and Joseph joined a force of nearly four hundred Indians under the leadership of the new baronet, Sir William Johnson.[5] Also serving in the expedition were Johnson's deputy, George Croghan, and Indian officers, Daniel Claus and John Butler, and young Guy Johnson, Sir William's nephew, who had come over from Ireland to make his fortune—all men who would one day set their mark on Joseph's life. On July 8 this force of Indians and white officers occupied a hill near the head of Lake Champlain. There, at what the Mohawks called Ticonderoga, they could watch the slaughter in the narrow pass below as General Abercromby, without waiting for his artillery to come up, sent wave after wave of valiant British troops against the tangled French breastworks of felled trees and sharpened branches. There was some futile firing by the Indians; and long after Joseph, in telling the missionary, Stuart, of his first experience in battle, is reported to have said that he "was seized with such a tremor when the firing began that he was obliged to take hold of a small sapling to steady himself—but that after the discharge of a few vollies he recovered the use of his limbs and the composure of his mind, so as to support the character of a brave man, of which he was extremely ambitious."[6]

The Mohawks had come in force and there were a few parties from the other nations besides, and they all saw a few thousand French turn back a British army nearly five times stronger. To the wondering French this was a miracle even greater than Braddock's defeat. When the fighting was over, the Indians set out for home, as they had been used to do from time immemorial. But it was common gossip in the camp that before they left, the indignant Mohawk sachems told the British general that his army had fine limbs but no head and that he was an "old Squah" and had better "go home and make sugar"!

But thinly populated Canada, looking south at an enemy multitude bursting its bounds, could not always expect miracles. In late August the English Colonel Bradstreet captured Fort Frontenac, and the French lost control of Lake Ontario. Again young Joseph was present as a volunteer,[7] and no doubt got his share of an immense plunder. It was the beginning of the end for the French. Everything they had in the west trembled precariously. In the remote reaches of the once friendly Seneca and Cayuga countries this was known as precisely as it was known in Albany and Montreal. These western Indians must begin to look elsewhere for the trade and supplies on which their life depended. It was bitterly obvious now that the entire Six Nations must cast aside their protecting neutrality and acquiesce in the dominance of Britain.

Major General Jeffery Amherst, who succeeded Abercromby as commander in chief, was a better soldier. He planned a far-flung campaign for 1759. It would be the part of Sir William Johnson and his Indians to join the forces of Brigadier General Prideaux and help take Niagara. Here, at the western end of Lake Ontario, was the famed post on which the whole French west, with its vast fur trade and native Indian allies—some so distant that even their names were unknown to the British—depended.

Early in June Johnson and the Mohawks set out. Every able-bodied warrior went along, and in the number, of course, was Joseph Thayendanegea.[8] He did not, as it has been claimed, command six hundred warriors on this campaign. No chief in the entire Six Nations had influence enough to command such a great number of warriors, certainly not sixteen-year-old Joseph who had neither position nor experience. He went as a member of some small band led by his stepfather or, more likely, by one of his kinsmen of the Wolf clan.

The expedition followed the age-old route of the fur traders. Up the Mohawk River they traveled, in long, light, flat-bottomed boats which the French called bateaux and which could be propelled, depending on circumstances, by oars or poles or even sails. At the Little Falls all hands got out to haul or drag or carry both boats and cargoes around the obstruction. At the head of navigation on the Mohawk stood brand-new Fort Stanwix (now Rome, New York). Here began a long portage which people generally referred to as the Great Carrying Place. The portage trail led across country to another navigable

stream, the narrow, winding Wood Creek, which flowed into Oneida
Lake. This was Oneida country, and many Oneidas, most formerly
neutral or even hostile to the British, now flocked to Johnson's banner. The Reverend Mr. Ogilvie, chaplain to the expedition, baptized
some of the warriors' children at the lake. Flowing out of Oneida Lake
was the Oneida River which finally merged with the Seneca River to
form still a third river, the foaming Oswego. Here the going got very
rough, for the Oswego River was swift and rocky and interrupted by a
great waterfall. Experienced pilots were a necessity, and strong backs
as well. At last the weary expedition emerged at the cove of old
Oswego, on Lake Ontario. The journey of less than 140 miles had
taken three weeks.

General Prideaux waited at Oswego with twenty-two hundred
troops. Here, too, in the service of the British was a Swiss soldier of
fortune, one Frederick Haldimand, whose task it was to build the new
fort at Oswego that summer. Joseph may not have seen, much less
have spoken to, Lieutenant Colonel Haldimand; there was, after all,
no reason for a meeting between so high an officer and so lowly a
retainer. If, by chance, they passed each other by one day, the light-
colored, almost naked Indian lad and the dignified, middle-aged soldier in his handsome uniform, the one would have noticed the
uniform and the other would have noticed nothing. Which of them
could have possibly foreseen that fateful decision in the Castle of St.
Louis nearly a quarter of a century hence?

The expedition sailed away on July 1, and on July 7 the siege of
Fort Niagara began. General Prideaux had planned well, and day by
day the trenches of the besiegers burrowed nearer to the fort. Inside, a
frantic French garrison was expending its scant store of ammunition
and provisions, rebuilding shattered embrasures with bales of precious
furs, and awaiting a relief force which was gathering from far-away
Detroit and other French posts in the west. Sir William and his
Indians were also waiting, and every day his scouts and spies went out
into the woods, as only Indians could, to get news of the approaching
relief. Johnson had 945 warriors, among whom were, for the first time,
considerable numbers of Senecas, Cayugas, and Onondagas who had
joined him at Oswego or at camps along the way. Johnson had done
his best to play upon the Indians' hopes and fears, but it had been
hardly necessary. It was the time, they knew, for them to take a stand.
Reluctantly, they did so.

Sir William's lucky star was shining bright. On July 20 General
Prideaux was accidentally killed by a bursting shell from one of his
own guns. Johnson, who held a commission as colonel of Indians from

the king, took command as the next ranking officer. (This was not to the liking of Lieutenant Colonel Haldimand, at Oswego, when he found out about it, but he was too far away to protest effectively.) Four days later the French relief force appeared; it was no match for the besiegers, and after a short but sharp fight it was defeated. On July 25 the garrison of Fort Niagara gave up. With it fell the entire French west.

Johnson wrote to England that the Indians had behaved very well, and he ascribed to them their full share of credit for the victory. This campaign was young Joseph's first real baptism of fire. It may never be known what special service he rendered, but probably he went out on some of the scouts. He must have taken part in the battle. If he was frightened as before, there is no word about it anywhere. Years later he is said to have remarked when talking of music: "I like the harpsichord well, and the organ still better; but I like the drum and trumpet best of all, for they make my heart beat quick."[9] There was plenty of trumpeting at Niagara that summer to quicken a boy's heart.

The Indians went home loaded with spoils. They never liked to linger after a battle, and within a very few days French merchandise gladdened many an Iroquois hearth. Some of the Mohawks returned to Oswego later, for Johnson sent word they might be needed again. The biddable lad, Joseph, was probably among their number. Then came news of the surrender of Quebec. New France lay prostrate. Further fighting could wait, and the warriors could go out that fall to hunt deer instead of men.

Next year the Indians did not behave so well. In the summer of 1760 three British armies converged on Montreal in a mopping-up operation. Sir William Johnson with nearly seven hundred Six Nations volunteers accompanied the army of General Amherst by way of Oswego. On an island in the St. Lawrence, about three miles below the Catholic Iroquois village of Oswegatchie, stood the small French post of Fort Levis. Amherst halted to take this little post, and trouble began. The British, eager to placate the French Canadians, were determined that the Indians should observe the rules of white warfare. This order did not set well with the western Iroquois who had come to get plunder to take back to their families, and prisoners and scalps to replace lost friends. Many of their warriors, disgruntled, went home. Another time an officer swore at an Indian who was passing by his tent, vowing that the white people would soon get rid of them all when the war was over. The Indian happened to understand English and spread the word around, and more warriors took their leave. Only the Mohawks and a very few others remained. On the list of those who loyally stayed with the army and went on to Montreal was Joseph Thayendanegea.[10] After this episode General Amherst, who had never cared much for Indians anyway, cared even less. Since he was to remain on the scene for several years after the war, the general's attitude did not bode well for the future relations of the two races.

On the way down the St. Lawrence Johnson was able to make peace with the Seven Nations of Canada and other domiciled Indians who had always fought for France. Like the recently converted western Iroquois, they had no real choice in the matter since they, too, depended on the white man's trade and supplies. They readily agreed to stop fighting. Several amiable Caughnawagas rowed Sir William to Montreal, and some of the natives even took up arms for the British. For these Indians it was only a change of white allies. They could seldom be induced to fight their own kind, anyway.

Montreal surrendered on September 8, and with it went all of Canada. Soon it would be the British flag which would fly over such distant points as Michilimackinac, Sault Ste. Marie, St. Joseph, Green Bay, and Detroit. Soon the British must face the problem of dealing with far-off strangers such as the Miamis, the Ottawas, the Hurons, and the nations of the Illinois, not to mention the perennially hostile Delawares and Shawnees in the Ohio country, and others whose names were scarcely known. There would be other problems, too. The war was still to be paid for. And though Canada had surrendered, its people were still French and unfriendly. So were the people of Detroit and every trading post in the west, and so were all the traders scattered in all the Indian villages throughout the country of the Great Lakes or, as it was then more commonly called, the upper country. Most serious of all, frontier Americans were now free to cast covetous eyes at the vast and (to them) empty Indian lands. Such bold spirits laughed at danger. They would not be long in trespassing.

Young Joseph went home from Montreal, back to Canajoharie, to the house where his mother and his stepfather were living. It could have made no difference to him that about that time an old man collapsed on the floor in a royal palace, and that a new young king named George III ascended the throne. Next spring Joseph was one of 182 warriors to receive a silver medal for good conduct. On one side of the medal was depicted the city of Montreal, and on the other side was engraved his Indian name, Thayendanegea.[11] This was almost the last of Joseph Thayendanegea. It was easier for white people to say Brant's Joseph or, sometimes, Joseph Brant's. A stepfather or even a father had little importance in the matrilineal world of the Longhouse, but among the white people he was the head of the family; so, thanks to all-pervading white influence, it was coming about that an Indian father would very soon have something of social value to pass on to his children—his name. Joseph would soon be called Joseph Brant,[12] and many of his young friends and neighbors would eventually get their surnames in the same way.

During the war Sir William Johnson had made frequent visits to the Mohawk villages, and when he went to Canajoharie he always put up at Brant's house. Though Brant's house was not exactly Fort Johnson, Sir William and his entourage could lie by the fire in their clothes without too much discomfort. They were no worse off than they would have been in one of the local inns. Sir William and Brant continued to see eye to eye, and indeed Sir William was in high favor with the whole family. Under such circumstances it was to be expected that Joseph's sister Molly should attract his attention, for Molly was young and blooming, and her presence graced the house.

White traders who went out into the Indian country took Indian women for wives as a matter of course; by this action they not only got a wife and a kind of home life away from home, they gained protection and influence, too. If the white man took care of his native wife and children, the other Indians looked upon him kindly. His wife and his wife's family would do their utmost to protect him from danger. So there were traders who remained far out in the Indian country for years. And there was an astonishing number of half-breeds growing up with good old Scotch, Irish, and English names who would one day make those names famous—or infamous.

But ordinary white settlers who lived on the frontier and stayed out of the Indian country took another view. They did not marry the natives or even mate with them often. Indians, they thought, were an inferior race; and though occasionally they treated them with kindness, more often they scorned or feared and hated them. The saying that "the only good Indian is a dead Indian" was already an old one, and it summed up white frontier opinion rather well. Nor had the atrocities of the French and Indian War improved this opinion. No jury on the frontier was likely to convict a white man for the murder of a red man.

Sir William Johnson was a frontiersman, but he had started life as a trader. When he gave up trade in the course of the war to manage Indian affairs, his vital interests remained the same. It was still to his advantage to fraternize with the Indians. He did not hate them. His feelings toward them seem to have run the gamut from a kindly view that they "are really much to be pitied" to an avowed hesitation to make peace between his own northern Indians and the Cherokees in the south because, as he said, "we enjoy the most security when they are divided amongst themselves." Though the Indians very often got on his nerves, he treated them well. Or, at least, it usually seemed to them that he treated them well. He fought their battles with unfailing energy, especially when it suited high policy or when he was pitted against white people whom he disliked. Sir William was a good Indian superintendent. He was also a white man, a subject of the king, a politician, and a land speculator.[13]

This backwoods baronet led an odd sort of personal life, even for the time and place. Three children ran about his estate at Mount, or Fort, Johnson, though he had never had a legal wife. These children were Ann, born 1740, John, born in 1742, and Mary, born in 1744. The children's mother, a German servant girl named Catharine Weissenberg, and her mother had lived in the Johnson household for many years. Catharine seems to have been quiet, undemanding, not much given to spending money, and, of course, unnoticed by anybody of consequence. The tradition is that she died of tuberculosis, an illness which is of long duration. Tradition also has it that Sir William married her on her deathbed, and the meager evidence points in the same direction. The two may have been married by a German minister sometime toward the end of Catharine's life.

Besides the three white children, Sir William had at this time at least two half-breed sons. Both were to be mentioned in his will. One was named William Tagawirunta, though more often referred to as William of Canajoharie. The other, who was older, was called young Brant Kaghneghtago. When he grew up he was called Brant Johnson or, as some would have it, William Brant Johnson. He was born in the early 1740s, and he was undoubtedly a close relation of someone in the Brant house. Indeed, both these boys seem to have lived with the Brants, and by some the elder was taken to be Joseph's half-breed brother, though this was not so.[14] The vague gossip years later that Joseph was a half-breed himself probably stems from his being confused with Brant Johnson.

Catharine Weissenberg, Sir William's wife, died in April 1759. He did not have to look far for a replacement. In Canajoharie, or perhaps already living at Fort Johnson as some sort of servant maid, was Joseph's sister, Molly. Molly was about twenty-three or twenty-four, a good-looking and certainly very intelligent young Indian woman. For a man like Johnson, ambitious, able to look ahead, quite at home with the natives, she also had other attractions. Her stepfather, Brant, a sachem of the lordly Turtle clan which always furnished the Tekarihoga, was a leader among the Mohawks. The latter, of course, as elder brothers or fathers of the Confederacy, were leaders among the Six Nations. The Six Nations, in their turn, still wielded strong influence over populous Indian nations farther west whom they had, in a way, conquered long before. It was those Indians of the west who could get the most valuable furs and whose trade was so much sought after. Through Molly's people of the Six Nations, then, and their influence over the trading Indians, as well as their own value as allies in war, lay the road to political advancement and royal favor. The Six Nations also possessed land, and the acquisition of land by a white man was the one sure way to wealth. Even the poor dwindling Mohawks who had lost so many men in the late war and who were so closed-in and surrounded—even those Indians still possessed land. They still had some rich holdings along the river and vast hunting grounds to the north which figured in the hopes and dreams of many a speculator.

There was, moreover, no lady of a suitable station whom Johnson was inclined to wed, and, indeed, there was probably none inclined to wed him and his manner of living out there on that rude frontier. Johnson had little social contact with the female aristocracy of the province. Yet with Catharine out of the picture, he had neither wife nor housekeeper, an intolerable situation for him. And Molly Brant was already bound to him by the closest of ties, for she was undeniably pregnant with his child. So Molly went to, or stayed on at, Fort Johnson, and one of history's strangest alliances began. It was an alliance that bound the Canajoharie Indians to the Johnson family as with bands of steel; it set its mark on all kinds of people and on entire nations both white and Indian—but on nobody more than on Molly's brother, Joseph.

In August 1759, when Johnson stopped at Oswego on his return from Niagara, he wrote Molly not to come there. It was good advice, for next month her child was born. The child was a boy, and he was named Peter, probably after Molly's father. Though the Reverend John Ogilvie was still preaching to the Mohawks, there is no record that Molly, under the powerful protection of Sir William, was ever required to confess her sins in church. The minister always spoke highly to his sponsors of Sir William. On the subject of Molly he chose to keep quiet.

As for the Indians, they soon looked upon Molly as Sir William's lawful wife. Next year the Mohawks at Canajoharie sent their leading sachem to invite their "Affectionate Brother and Friend" to come up to their castle. Johnson went, and there, on December 22, 1760, in full council the Indians told him of their intention to present him with a tract of land on the north shore of the Mohawk. In a few days a deed was made out to their specifications, and everybody in the castle signed it. Sir William in his turn then gave the signers a present of money, the only polite thing to do. Of this money young Joseph got as his share fifty pounds.[15] The Mohawks had told Sir William they wanted to act "Whilst it is in our power to give you this proof of our friendship, which we fear, will not be long, as our White Brethren are getting all our Lands from us."[16] Their great gift was to survey to eighty thousand acres. If a wedding present, it was a wedding present fit for a king. It was enough, Sir William said, to do him the rest of his life. It was also nearly all the land that the Canajoharie Indians had left that bordered upon the river.

In the early summer of 1761, when the war was virtually over and everywhere people's thoughts were turning to their peacetime plans, a special messenger rode up to the massive door of Sir William's fortress home. The messenger brought with him a letter addressed to the baronet. The letter was from a stranger, and as Sir William read it, he grew thoughtful.

Up in Canajoharie that day eighteen-year-old Joseph could have been fishing for eels or burning stumps or playing ball with other young men and boys. After a long, hard winter when water had actually frozen by the fireplace, it was good to be outdoors in the warm sun. But for Joseph carefree days like this would soon be over. A letter from a man he had never heard of was about to alter the whole course of his life. It was to set his feet upon a new and thorny trail, a trail of accomplishment and of heartbreak, and send him off on a journey that would last a lifetime.

5

The World of Parson Wheelock

T HE LETTER came from Lebanon, Connecticut, and it was signed
by a certain Eleazar Wheelock who wrote that he kept a free
school for Indians. Wheelock said, in part:

> The Hon^le. Comiss^rs. of the Society in Scotland for Propagating
> christian Knowledge have granted a Support for three Boys of the
> Six Nations at the School under my Care in order to their being
> fitted as Soon as may be for Interpreters. or other publick usefulness
> among their Own Nations . . . . the Barer who is one of my Pupils
> waits upon Your Hon^r. to be advised and assisted in the Affair. The
> chusing Such as are Suitable for the Purpose and . . . also y^e. using
> proper Endeavours to Move them to Accept the Offer of An Educa-
> tion now made them, is principally referred to you, as being best
> able to Judge of the Persons, and Influence them in the Affair.[1]

With this letter came another from Major General Phineas Lyman, a Connecticut officer with whom Johnson had served in the
Lake George campaign. Lyman described Wheelock as "a very Worthy
honest Gent^n." and recommended his school in glowing terms. Johnson had of course heard of the Indian school though he had never met
the Reverend Mr. Wheelock. It had been established only a scant
seven years before but, thanks to the untiring efforts of its founder, it
was already rather widely known. (Some notable men were to come
out of this school. One of its graduates, the famed Mohegan preacher,
Samson Occom, was just beginning his mission work. And some day
the school would move to New Hampshire and change its name to

71

Dartmouth College—but this move still lay in the uncharted future.)

Johnson recognized the good opportunity and he knew just the boys to send. Joseph, Molly's brother, should go, and with him two of his young friends of the Wolf clan named Sander and Nickus, both veterans of the recent Montreal campaign and recipients of General Amherst's silver medals. Johnson used his influence and presumably Molly used hers, and the three young fellows set out in July 1761. They were conducted on their journey by David Fowler, Wheelock's messenger, a young Indian who had been living at the school about two years.

The four travelers reached Lebanon on August 1. The Reverend Mr. Wheelock was dismayed to find that his new scholars had ridden their own horses. Horse feed was scarce and expensive that year in Connecticut, and the good clergyman had made no provision for animals. But the boys obviously meant to have means of escape at hand if school should not prove to their liking.

Wheelock was also dismayed at the appearance of his new pupils. One of them, he afterward said, was considerably clothed "Indian-fashion" (this was Joseph, of course), but the other two were almost naked. All three were very dirty and, it must be admitted, lousy. First of all, it was necessary to clean them up. One of them (Joseph again) could speak a few words of English, but the other two spoke only Mohawk. They tried to tell Wheelock their names. He understood Joseph's name well enough, but Sander and Nickus sounded to him like Center and Negyes, so Center and Negyes they remained as long as they stayed at the school.[2]

Lebanon was only a crossroads, not even a village. Wheelock's house was large and commodious, but not large enough for a school. Next door, on its own two-acre plot, stood the school proper—once a dwelling house—and a work shop. These two buildings had been donated to Wheelock for his project by a local philanthropist named Joshua Moor, so the institution was known in the neighborhood as Moor's Indian Charity School. It was to Moor's house that Joseph and his friends were brought; here they were to live and work and begin the arduous process of getting an education.

Only a few other Indian pupils were living at the school just then. There were some Delawares enrolled, a Mohegan, and a Montauk. These Indians ranged in age from mere children to grown young men. Some white boys also lived at the school from time to time. Most of the latter had dedicated themselves to missionary work among the Indians and welcomed the chance to associate with and get to know their future charges. But at least one white boy who partook of the

Reverend Mr. Wheelock's hospitality wished he was somewhere else. Years later he was to write:

> When I first enter^d. this school I was struck with horrer at the sight of these wild indians a sight of one I had never seen before, and it struck me with such horrer that I have never been able intirely to clear myself of it to this day. Some of them were nearly men grown others smaller and some that had just enter^d. the school were about of my own age, These last could not speak a word of english and still had on their indian costume, from my first sight at these indians it gave me such a shock that I determined that I never should be willing to spend my life with such people as they were, But what could I do my Parents had placed me in this school and I dare not leave without their consent. . . .[3]

For Joseph and Sander and Nickus, stared at and homesick and in a strange land, and so unwontedly clean, the first night at school could not have been altogether easy. Lying in their bunks on beds of straw, their thoughts turning this way and that, what a comfort it must have been, before they fell asleep, to think of those three horses!

The boys had to be up and dressed next morning by six when a blast from a conch shell would call them to prayers. The Reverend Mr. Wheelock prayed over his students every morning in the hall of his home. He was a well-built, fine-looking man of fifty with a sonorous voice and dignified bearing, and his prayers, whether the boys understood them or not, were impressive. His sermons were even more impressive, as the trio were to learn when Sunday came and they took their place in their pew in the gallery of the church. A stern Calvinist, Wheelock dwelt long upon such themes as the doctrine of human depravity, the moral impotence of the sinner, the approaching wrath of God, and the immediate duty of repentance and faith. Sometimes he trembled like a leaf. Other times he would let out an involuntary groan. On such occasions, as an admirer once testified, "the pulpit was clothed in thunder; the coruscations of truth were as forked lightning."[4] Never before had the boys from Canajoharie heard anything like this, and on one of them, at least, it produced a strong effect. Young Joseph could understand a little of what was being said, and the son of pious Margaret Brant was not a lad to take lightly the wrath of God. This terrible wrath was surely something to think about at night in his bunk, when the candle was out. Perhaps he even shook a bit, himself.

After morning prayers Wheelock's pupils had their breakfast and a

The Reverend Eleazar Wheelock. Painting by Joseph Steward. The Reverend Mr. Wheelock hoped to make a missionary out of Joseph. At Wheelock's school young Joseph found a new world. *Courtesy of Dartmouth College, Hanover, New Hampshire.*

little free time. Then at nine o'clock there were more prayers and their lessons began. They worked at reading and writing and English or they studied Hebrew, Greek, and Latin, and "the several arts and sciences." They were also taught the importance of civility and good manners, a teaching that Joseph, at least, never forgot. Sometimes they did chores about the farm and learned a little of the white man's agriculture. (This was work which they were likely to resent, and which their families resented, too, if they found out about it.) At noon they all sat down to a dinner of boiled meat and Indian pudding with bread and milk and little sweet cakes. It was good fare and they ate heartily. It was more than most of them had ever seen at home, and no doubt it helped to keep them content. At two o'clock there were more lessons. At five, after another prayer, school was over for the day. Final evening prayers took place in Wheelock's house before dark, and afterward the boys studied.[5]

Parson Wheelock, for all his talk of damnation and hell-fire, was a kindly man and deeply interested in all that concerned his flock. Nevertheless, he could speak feelingly of the many problems connected with the school.

> None know [said he], nor can any, without Experience, well conceive of, the Difficulty of Educating an Indian. They would soon kill themselves with Eating and Sloth, if constant care were not exercised for them at least the first Year—they are used to set upon the Ground, and it is as Natural for them as a seat to our Children—they are not wont to have any Cloaths but what they wear, nor will without much Pains be brot to take Care of any.— They are used to a Sordid Manner of Dress, and love it as well as our Children to be clean.— They are not used to any Regular Government, the sad Consequences of which you may a little guess at—they are used to live from Hand to Mouth (as we Speak) and have no Care for Futurity—they have never been used to the Furniture of an English House, and dont know but that a Wineglass is as strong as an Hand Iron— Our Language when they seem to have got is not their Mother Tongue and they cannot receive nor communicate in that as in their Own.— It is a long time before they will learn the proper Place & use of the Particles. *a, an the, &c.* And they are as unpolished & uncultivated within as without.[6]

It was an eloquent description of some of the more apparent differences between the white man's world and the Indian's world.

Gradually Joseph and his two companions grew accustomed to their new surroundings. Wheelock had thought them a little sulky at first, but kind treatment and acquaintance with the other Indian pupils in the school broke down their reserve; and it was not long until they appeared to feel at home. Probably they soon found out that a wine glass is not as strong as a hand iron. They began to wrestle with *a, an,* and *the,* while their horses grazed peacefully in the fields.

Wheelock had already provided the boys with some clothing more

appropriate to the Connecticut countryside than their Indian leggings
and blankets. Each had received a pair of trousers and a shirt on
arrival. Nickus and Sander were also given jackets. (Joseph would
have had his own.) But Joseph's pants were checked and cost more,
and his shirt was of better quality. Wheelock thought Joseph came "of
a Family of Distinction"—after all, Joseph came better dressed, could
talk a little English, and seemed to have Sir William Johnson's particular regard. To be thus singled out and honored must have pleased
the boy inordinately. But if he realized what a mistake the Reverend
Mr. Wheelock was laboring under, he never got around to setting him
straight. Wheelock was to speak of Joseph's high origin long
afterward, and more than once. Among these gifts Nickus also received a comb and a book. Joseph was given a book, too, but his cost
more. Sander got neither book nor comb; let him use Nickus', just as
he and Nickus had to sleep in the same bed.[7] The unfortunate Sander
appeared to be sickly from the start, and there could have been no
sense in wasting such losable and perishable items as combs and books
on him. The Reverend Mr. Wheelock was a kind-hearted and generous man, but he had had some frustrating experiences with sickly
students.

To induce the boys to leave home, Sir William had promised that
they could return in the fall for a visit. This they told Wheelock
almost at once. When fall came poor Sander was so sick that a physician had to be called and advised Wheelock that he had better send
him home immediately or he would never get there at all. Nickus was
sent along with him, and the two set out on October 23. They never
returned. Sander died and Nickus got married, and so both were
irretrievably lost to education.

But Joseph was healthy and he liked his new world of checked
pants, and learning, and fragile glasses, and cake, and prayers, and
being made much of. He, too, went home, but only for the promised
visit. He left Lebanon on November 4. His traveling companion was a
young fellow only a little older than himself, a white student named
Samuel Kirkland. The two set out harmoniously together, chatting
amiably of this and that. Kirkland, who planned to become a missionary, was trying to learn the Mohawk language, and Joseph, who thoroughly approved of missionaries, was exerting himself to be a good
teacher. (Very likely some day the man Joseph would wish that the boy
Joseph had not been so cooperative!) But Kirkland's immediate task
was to get some more boys for the Charity School, Wheelock having
recently obtained additional funds for this purpose. Kirkland carried
with him a letter in which Wheelock explained the new project to Sir

William Johnson and again asked his aid. In this letter the clergyman reported how well the first lads had behaved and then added some especially kind words about Joseph, whom he described as "a considerate, modest, and manly spirited youth." "I am much pleased with him," continued the good man. "If his Disposition, and Ability, upon further Trial, shall appear as inviting as they seem to be at present, there shall nothing be wanting, within my Power, to his being fitted, in the best Manner for Usefulness."[8] How it would have gratified Joseph to know that he was missionary material, himself!

Joseph had been away almost four months and, when he reached home, it took some time just to get abreast of the news. There had been a "malignant fever" at the castle which took away many of his neighbors, but all his family had escaped. Molly had a new baby, a girl named Elizabeth, born the previous summer. Sir William, whose authority now extended over all the Indians north of the Ohio, had just returned from a long and dangerous journey to Detroit where he had settled affairs and made peace, as he thought, with the many stranger nations of the upper country who had been in the service of the French. And Sir William was planning to move his residence away from the river, near a new little settlement he had made on his own land called Johnstown. Here, some nine miles from Fort Johnson, he would build the mansion known as Johnson Hall. Later, when Joseph got the opportunity to feast his eyes on its great white clapboards arranged like blocks of stone, on its handsome Palladian window, and on its, to him, immense size, he thought it the noblest building he had ever seen. Many visits never dulled his appreciation; he was to admire it always, and thirty-five years afterward, in a strange land, he would be able to recall it in detail.

But there were other changes and other news of not so pleasant a character. The Mohawks of both castles, Joseph learned, had been having continual trouble with white people. This was certainly no new situation, but of late there was more for the Indians to complain about. Down in Fort Hunter they were actually worrying about the ownership of the meadows, or flats, on which their village stood. Many years ago the Fort Hunter Indians in a moment of weakness—or as some declared, drunkenness—had deeded their homesite in trust to the Corporation of Albany. A royal governor had later burned the deed, after much commotion, taking a similar deed in trust to the king, but the Indians still worried about it. The Corporation of Albany was presently making no claims (having the not unreasonable expectation, it was said, that the Indians would one day die out), but from time to time some of the local whites would bring up the matter, either from ignorance or from viciousness, and taunt the Indians about their dangerous situation, assuring them that they were likely to be driven away from their homes at any moment. And the Indians, who knew that strange things could happen whenever white people and land were concerned, grew uneasy and frightened and, as they declared, could scarcely sleep of nights.

In Joseph's own home village there was a similar, but much more immediate, problem. About a generation before, a few of the tribesmen, also persuaded by liquor, had signed a deed in favor of Philip Livingston for a tract of land east of the village. This tract had been surveyed secretly by moonlight, the Indians claimed, instead of in their presence as was proper, and its boundaries had been extended westward until it actually included their own little cabins and planting lands. When the proprietors (for Livingston had had several partners) obtained a patent for this larger tract,[9] the Indians took alarm and began to resist. A fight against this Canajoharie patent had been going on for years, but to no effect, for the patentees numbered some of the richest and most influential people in the province. But of late the dispute swirled around a certain George Klock, a well-to-do farmer of German extraction who lived in the neighborhood, who had recently bought out the claims of the Livingston heirs. Klock, though a man of little education, had a cool head and nerve enough to stand his ground even in the presence of the Indian superintendent. He once told Johnson to go hang himself, and between the two of them no love was lost whatever. As the upper Mohawks had long rented some of the disputed land to white tenants and Klock was threatening to evict the latter, he had the whole community, both white and Indian, in an uproar.

As if worry over their homes and cornfields were not enough for Joseph's people, the Mohawks were also alarmed about their hunting grounds. Twice a year, for six weeks or so, they all went hunting—the young men to hunt and everybody else to take care of the kill—and on the pelts they were able to bring home they depended for a good part of their livelihood. Their nearest hunting lands lay to the north in a wild, unsettled country called Kayaderosseras, situated between the Hudson and Mohawk Rivers. Extensive white settlements in this territory would ruin the Mohawk economy for they would drive the game away. Hitherto this wilderness had been left unspoiled. But of late, and much to the distress of the Indians, there were rumors of settlements in preparation, of surveys and road-building, up there on Kayaderosseras Creek. Such settlements, they heard, were to take place under authority of another of those vague, all-too-fraudulent land patents which had been issued to a group of white people many years before. The Indians claimed indignantly that acreage enough for only three or four farms had been sold and that they had never received payment for that. But the proprietors, in some inscrutable way, had been able to obtain a patent for a vast tract estimated at from 250,000 to 800,000 acres! Even before the rumors of settlements and surveys—indeed, long before—the Mohawks had been complaining about this fraud; they held meetings with Johnson about it regularly, and Johnson was bending every effort, both at home and abroad, to get something done for them. Every responsible royal official, whether in New York or in London, who had anything to do with the matter, wanted to do something. But what? And how? Neither governors, attorney generals, or even the august Lords of Trade, could say. The proprietors of Kayaderosseras, like those of Canajoharie, were both powerful and insistent upon their rights. They would not give up easily.

All these grievances were Mohawk grievances only, and they did not directly concern the rest of the Six Nations. But the latter knew what was going on, and, as the Mohawks later pointed out, if *they* could not get justice "it must alarm all the Nations of Indians, and shew them what a bad Return we have for our Services to the English."[10] If the Mohawks who had lost over a hundred men in the war with France, could not get justice, what Indians could?

The Cayugas, far to the west of the Mohawks, did have a grievance of their own. They owned valuable hunting lands in the province of Pennsylvania, between the Delaware and Susquehanna Rivers. Some people from Connecticut were making claims to this territory by right of an old coast-to-coast charter and another dubious land sale, much to the dismay not only of the Cayugas but of the entire Six Nations who rightly considered it as a sort of back corridor to their own country. The Pennsylvanians, too, were dismayed, for they would have liked to buy the beautiful and fertile land for themselves. Local wars would be fought over this matter and it was to lead to one of the bloodiest massacres of the American Revolution. But it was now just one more grievance for the Indians to mull over and to brood upon—sober or drunk.

But land was just one of the Indians' grievances. In the fall of 1761 red men from the Mohawk country to the Illinois were full of a sense of outrage. So much had been promised them if they would help destroy the French or if they would only make peace. Many of them had helped, and all had accepted the peace, and French power was destroyed. And what had happened? Trade, which had been pictured as becoming cheap and easy, was dearer than ever and none at all allowed except at military posts. The kettles and blankets and gun-powder they had to have were scarcer and harder to get than in wartime, and British traders, they now believed, were far greater ras-cals than the worst French traders had ever been. Sir William Johnson had fixed the profits of the Indian trade at 50 percent at Oswego, 70 percent at Niagara, and 100 percent at Detroit, and this mark-up he considered reasonable. But the Indians who rambled so far with so little to-do could not understand why distance added so much to the price of the goods they must buy. And, of course, traders very often were rascals who abided by no law whatsoever. They watered rum, gave false weights, and cheated the Indian hunter in every way possi-ble. Trade as a way of life was always difficult for the Indian; with his best efforts he often could just barely keep body and soul together. His ancient ways before the white man came had not been so hard. But trade was now the only way of life he understood. It was his only way to earn a living for his family. So when game was plentiful and am-munition on hand, his wife and children had food and clothing; but when game was scarce or no ammunition to be had, all the family went naked and starved.

That fall ammunition was very scarce indeed in Indian huts. Trad-ers had little to sell and nobody had any to give away. When the French and British were rivals for the continent, both gave generously to the natives and courted their favor. An Indian could always go to the nearest fort and get some powder or a little rum or something to fill his belly. The officers and soldiers were friendly. But French forts were no more. In the others the faces were not so friendly. Now that the war was over, the British government had decreed a policy of re-trenchment. Economy was the watchword of the day. The Indians were no longer important. And General Amherst who continued as commander in chief in America, was just the man to carry out this policy. In ten thousand lifetimes Amherst could not have understood the Indian point of view; "it is not My Intention," he informed John-son, "ever to Attempt to gain the Friendship of Indians by presents." So he forbade all gifts to them at the posts, no matter how many miles they had come or how hungry they were; and he limited the sale of powder, thinking that he thereby limited their ability to disturb the white frontier. The general thought he was a just man. He gave orders that the visitors were not to be mistreated, "but I would have the Indians know," he said, "that we will be Masters at these posts." He hoped they would never give him reason to turn upon them, but if they did, he was firmly resolved "to punish the delinquents with Entire

Destruction."[11] And it seemed to him highly unlikely that anybody had ever robbed the Indians of land.

The truth was, Amherst did not like Indians. Every officer and every soldier from the highest to the lowest sensed this, and most of them acted accordingly. They had always scorned the red men as inferior beings. Now this scorn was open. Instead of finding a welcome at the posts as formerly, visiting Indians were cursed, kicked, and beaten. In Canada a domiciled Indian driving a horse and sleigh had to turn out of the road every time he met a few soldiers on foot. Near Fort Brewerton, at the west end of Oneida Lake, the Onondagas were not allowed to fish in what were indisputably their own streams. The soldiers horsewhipped the Indian braves or lunged at them with bayonets and drove the women and children away. At Fort Schuyler on the Mohawk (present Utica) the Indians were not permitted to earn their living hauling goods around the carrying place; and at Niagara the Senecas, glum and discontented, had lost the right to carry goods and furs around the Falls, a right which the French had allowed them from earliest days. How very often the French traders, who were still making the rounds of the villages, reminded them of this and their other troubles. With what relish the French could say I told you so! So the Senecas brooded darkly and carried their woes to the west where they had allies who would listen. And Indians everywhere hated the posts and all that they represented, and time after time their speakers got up in public councils with Sir William Johnson or his agents and demanded that the posts in their country be dismantled and abandoned according to promise. But General Amherst said no—he would keep the posts. When he thought a fort essential at a certain spot, he declared, "I must and will therefore, say what they will, have one at that place."[12]

In the midst of this ferment French patriots were biding their time. As no peace treaty had been signed, the war was not yet officially over. So there were Frenchmen in the west and Frenchmen in Canada and Frenchmen scattered throughout the Indian country, priests and officers as well as traders and soldiers and ordinary citizens, who believed that Canada would be given back to them at the peace treaty. Or, unbelievably optimistic, they expected that a French fleet would one day sail into the St. Lawrence and a French army ascend the Mississippi from New Orleans to reconquer their own. These hopes they confided to the Caughnawaga Indians and others of the Seven Nations of Canada and to the Miamis near Detroit and to the Hurons and Ottawas and Chippewas and Missisaugas of the western Lakes,

and to interested—very interested—Delawares and Shawnees and
Mingoes of the Ohio, and whatever Six Nations people they happened to come across. In the course of this talk they also told the
Indians what they had always told them and what they themselves
often firmly believed, that the British were black-hearted heretics who
had abandoned God and religion, that they carried poisoned rum and
poisoned blankets among the Indians to sicken them with deadly
diseases, and that they were plotting to kill them all off, every one,
and seize their lands. And if there was, perhaps, a tiny kernel of truth
in some of these charges, it but rendered them the more credible to
Indian ears.

Joseph's family and friends had no every-day contacts with such
Frenchmen, but they knew what was going on. Occasionally someone
from one of the castles wandered far from home and brought back
gossip. Or occasionally the Senecas or some other malcontents would
send the Mohawks a black belt painted with red. The latter, in spite of
their own troubles, loyally took no notice of such communications. Or
if they did, they showed only disapproval. More than once they
roundly scolded the Senecas and sent warnings to Sir William about
their plots. Young Joseph himself, just before he went to Wheelock's,
had been the bearer of one such warning.[13]

Joseph's visit home was short. He returned to school in about a
fortnight. He and Samuel Kirkland arrived back in Lebanon on
November 27. They brought with them two Mohawk lads named
Moses and Johannes, and this time Sir William had seen to it that
they left their horses at home. Wheelock breathed a sigh of relief and
speedily bought the boys some new clothes. It was the best way to get
rid of the smell of rancid bear's grease, and livelier things; but
Wheelock did let Joseph keep his pants, which he had apparently
taken good care of. The cost of this new clothing was borne by the
Boston board of the Society in Scotland for Propagating Christian
Knowledge. All three youths were being sponsored by that organization for the ensuing six months, and their board and tuition for that
period were to amount to eight pounds fifteen shillings apiece.[14] Later
they would be supported by a fund set up by Sir Peter Warren, the
naval hero, and administered by the Massachusetts General Assembly. Wheelock obtained funds from many sources for his school. Like
the heads of most institutions of learning, before and since, he spent
much of his time trying to raise money.

The three young Mohawks settled down quietly to their studies
and did not see home again for many months. Moses and Johannes,
though mere children, were preparing to be assistant teachers or, as

Wheelock called them, "ushers." As for Joseph, he must have burned many a midnight candle. He learned to speak English and then to read and write the language surprisingly well. The first letters of his which are extant, while certainly not models of grammar and spelling and penmanship, do show remarkable progress, considering the length of his schooling—less than two years—and his very scant knowledge of English at the start. Sir William Johnson's Canadian agent, Daniel Claus, has said that Joseph accomplished a great deal at Wheelock's.[15] The Reverend John Stuart, when he came on the scene, thought not—but the Reverend Mr. Stuart obviously did not take into consideration Joseph's poor beginnings. To Stuart, Joseph read but "indifferently" from the New Testament, and his writing was not what it should have been.[16] But the miracle was that Joseph in so short a time could read the New Testament at all, or write anything that was legible and made sense.

Wheelock's method of teaching most subjects was modeled after the spelling bee. The boys would stand in line and "turn down" one another according as they answered or missed a question. They always spoke in English. A visitor to the school describes one such session:

in the morning . . . they assemble at Mr. Wheelock's house about five o'clock with their master, who named the chapter in course for the day, and called upon the near Indian, who read three or four verses, till the master said "Proximus," and then the next Indian read some verses, and so on till all the Indians had read the whole chapter. After this, Mr. Wheelock prays, and then each Indian parses a verse or two of the chapter they had read. After this they entered successively on Prosodia, and then on Disputations on some questions propounded by themselves in some of the arts and sciences. And it is really charming to see Indian youths of different tribes and languages in pure English reading the word of God and speaking with exactness and accuracy on points (either chosen by themselves or given out to them) in the several arts and sciences; and especially to see this done with at least a seeming mixture of obedience to God, a filial love and reverence to Mr. Wheelock, and yet with great ambition to excel each other. And indeed in this morning's exercises I saw a youth degraded one lower in the class who before the exercises were finished not only recovered his own place, but was advanced two higher.[17]

Wheelock's method of teaching worked much better than the one they had been using at the famed Stockbridge mission in Massachusetts where the pupils spoke little English. At Stockbridge, it was

said, the "children learn, after a sort, to read; to make such sounds, on
the sight of such marks; but know nothing what they say; and having
neither profit, nor entertainment by what they read, they neglect it
when they leave school, and quickly lose it."[18] But some of Wheelock's
students never lost their proficiency, and Joseph Brant was one of the
number. Intelligent, and sustained by what must have been a powerful
incentive, he learned and he kept what he learned. But such an
unaccustomed and laborious way of life was a grueling experience even
for him, and some of the other boys collapsed under the strain. They
were plagued with all kinds of illnesses, "a nervous Fever, Pleurisies,
Dysenterys, &c.," according to Wheelock; and more than one died
young. There was plenty to eat at Wheelock's and the boys were
inclined to stuff themselves, so the good man feared that his "full
Table" was the cause of the general ill health and prescribed more
exercise—a good enough prescription if only the rickety and under-
nourished young Indians had got to the full table in time.

Wheelock wrote frequently to Sir William to report the boys'
progress. On December 11, 1761, he told of their safe arrival back in
Lebanon and added that they "are now well and Seem well pleased,
and content, and hitherto behave Well in the School; and I see
nothing but that they may well answer the Design proposed." The
boys were not yet out of bed, he started to explain, and know nothing
of this chance to write; and then he crossed it out—perhaps the
remark was too informal.[19] Next spring he wrote again, "Joseph Moses
& Johannes are all well, and have behaved considerably well, and
seem well contented." He enclosed a specimen of their handwriting
and added happily that their progress in reading was fully equal to
their progress in writing. However, without an interpreter he still
found it difficult to make them understand anything but the most
common matters.[20]

In June 1762 Wheelock sent David Fowler, his former messenger,
again to Johnson to try to get some more young Mohawks for his
school. The "Three which I now have are well & behave very Well
and have made laudable Proficiency in reading and Writing," he said
in a letter entrusted to David; and he enclosed another specimen. He
had been thinking, he went on, of sending Samuel Kirkland to New
Jersey College (Princeton) next fall, "And Joseph with him to bed &
board with him of Whom M^r. Kirtland may be learning something of
the Mohawke Language Without any great Interruption to his other
Studies, While Joseph in the Grammer School there May be perfecting himself in the English Tongue and also pursuing other parts of

Useful Learning perhaps fitting for College. Joseph can now read hansomely in the Bible." What did Sir William think of this idea?[21]

In due time David returned with three more boys and Johnson's promise to refer the matter of Joseph's going to New Jersey to Joseph's family.[22] There the matter rested. The Indians were slow to act; family councils and tribal councils took a long time. When they finally did consent, it was too late. As Wheelock heard nothing more from Johnson, Kirkland had to go to New Jersey alone. In September Wheelock again wrote to Sir William that Joseph and the rest of the boys were "well, studious and diligent."[23] This seems to have been his final report for 1762.

Throughout Joseph's stay the school had been growing slowly but steadily. Nine more Indian boys came in 1762 and another lad early the next year. There were also a few girls who were learning housewifery and, one day a week, a little reading and writing. All these students came from New England, New Jersey or New York and were of various ages and nations. Joseph was always glad to see his former classmates in after life and did them many little favors when they came his way.

David Fowler, the young fellow who had first conducted Joseph to Lebanon, was one friend that he was to see often. David went with Samuel Kirkland on a mission to the Oneidas and passed and repassed Joseph's home many times. He was a brother-in-law to the famed Indian preacher Samson Occom and was several years older than Joseph. It was David, the fastidious young Montauk from Long Island, who thought the Oneidas as nasty as hogs and who wrote longingly of Mrs. Wheelock's good bread and milk and little sweet cakes. David's features were not prepossessing or else he must have been somewhat awkward and ungainly. He proposed to three of the girls before he could find a bride or, as he put it, a "rib." When he finally did get married, he and the rib set out on their mission prepared for almost any eventuality—sartorially speaking, at least—leaving the Reverend Mr. Wheelock staring after them, overwhelmed by the knowledge that they had four pairs of new shoes in their saddlebags! But David lived an honorable life and won the name, "Mercury of the Indian Missions," and he and his rib lie today beneath the sod of old Oneida where they labored so long.

Most of the young Indians at Moor's Charity School, like David, had a passion for genteel apparel. Joseph Woolley, another of Joseph Brant's classmates, was such a one. He began his missionary labors at Oquaga, a good-sized Indian village some sixty-eight or seventy miles down the Susquehanna. In this wilderness Woolley tried hard to bring his charges into something approximating the Wheelock ideal of Christian grace. It was rough going. The inhabitants of Oquaga, Six Nations Indians mostly, seem to have been not much impressed with Woolley, the Delaware, who was, after all, not their social equal. Indeed, for almost twenty years now they had seen missionaries come and go, and by any standards at all Woolley must have been the worst. As a missionary, they obviously thought that he left a good deal to be desired. All this was not lost on the poor young fellow who seems somehow to have felt that if he could live like a white man, things might be different. Urgently he wrote to his supervisor, Samuel Kirkland in Oneida, begging for tea and coffee and what he longed for more than anything, a cloth shirt. Kirkland was irritated. Money to buy cloth was scarce. *I* am about to put on a leather shirt like the Indians, he said, and you can do the same. This was unanswerable logic and Woolley could say no more. How could he put into words what he himself only dimly perceived—that the white-skinned Kirkland, let him wear what he would, was still a missionary, but that he, Woolley, in a leather shirt was just another Delaware.

Woolley's cousin, Jacob, had troubles, too, but of a different sort. As a child Jacob had been one of the first students at the Charity School. Eventually he learned a little Latin and Greek, and Wheelock sent him down to the College of New Jersey at Princeton to complete his education. But in 1762 the college authorities sent him back. The youth had "loitered away" his time, they reported sternly. But what Jacob really wanted to study, as he had tried to explain to Wheelock, was not the languages and sciences, but mankind, and how was he going to "get acquainted with Mankind" at Princeton? The rest of that year the graceless Jacob appears to have remained in Lebanon, with Joseph Brant tutoring him in Mohawk. This did not work out well, either, and eventually the Reverend Mr. Wheelock had to admit that Jacob Woolley, not yet twenty, had turned "apostate"—that is, he had taken to drink.

Indeed, drink proved the greatest stumbling block in the pathway of Wheelock's students and caused the good man many a disappointment. The great Samson Occom himself succumbed, but he managed to pull himself together again. Jacob Woolley lost the battle. So did Hezekiah Calvin, who finally landed in prison for forging a pass for a Negro—one gentleman of color trying to help out another, perhaps? But Samuel Ashpo, Joseph Johnson, and several more of Joseph Brant's classmates, though they backslid now and then, lived useful lives. They preached and taught, and several were active in the famous Brothertown movement, helping to resettle some poor eastern Indians among the Oneidas, and some became soldiers of the Revolution. There is not the slightest evidence, however, that drink was any problem for Joseph, though coming from Canajoharie, he could not have been unacquainted with it.

One friend that Joseph made in school was different from the rest. At a place where the white students were just as much on charity as the Indians, young (and prosperous) Mr. Charles Jeffry Smith stuck out like a sore thumb. His father had left him an estate estimated at from three to eight thousand pounds, and instead of going out to raise cain as any normal youth would have done, he elected to live at Wheelock's and help with the teaching. A graduate of Yale, he planned to become a missionary himself eventually, and he, also, turned to Joseph in order to learn Mohawk. (It might almost be said that Joseph was working his way through school.) Joseph, who evidently improved upon close acquaintance, made a good impression during the lessons that followed. Pretty soon the young gentleman was describing him as "a promising Youth, of a sprightly Genius, singular Modesty, and a Serious Turn," and he earnestly declared that he "has so much endeared Himself to me by his Amiable Deportment; his Laudable Thirst after and Progress in Learning."[24] How incredibly serious-minded the two young fellows were as they pored over their language studies together, Joseph but nineteen and Mr. Smith a ripe twenty-two!

The great aim of the Charity School was to Christianize and "civilize" the Indians. This the Reverend Mr. Wheelock hoped to accomplish by educating their youth and sending them back to their own country as missionaries and teachers. With what eloquence he could describe the misery and wretchedness of Indian life:

> Strangers to the sweets of friendship, and all the emoluments of science, immersed amidst scenes of cruelty and blood, they have nothing noble or worthy the rational creature to entertain and feast themselves and one another with, in a social way [he lamented]. Can we think of this wretched state of our fellow men, and feel no compassion moving towards them? Or [he would continue] can we think much of a little expense, to turn such habitations of cruelty into dwelling places of righteousness, and little sanctuaries where the true God may be worshipped in spirit and truth, instead of sacrifices to devils?[25]

Some of his hearers were moved enough to make a donation.

A prerequisite to the success of this ambitious plan was, of course, the conversion of Wheelock's own students. One by one he would take them into his study and inquire with fatherly concern into their spiritual state. And when they felt any religious stirrings in their primitive young breasts (as more and more often they did), they would go to him, and he would exhort and instruct them. At times the poor young creatures would burst into tears, thinking of all their sins; and so Wheelock was able to announce in early 1763 that Joseph Woolley had been converted and that one of the girls has lately "had such Discoveries of the Truth, Reality, and Greatness of things reveald, as were more than Nature could sustain; she fainted under them, and has Sometimes seem'd almost to forget that she was a Tenant of the lower World."[26] Six of his Indians, he reported happily, are real Christians, and among all the rest, not one is without prayer.

No son of good Margaret Brant could have lived through such scenes unmoved, and the Reverend Mr. Wheelock did not fail to notice how Joseph's thoughts were turning. Said he, in a letter to another clergyman: "A young Mohawk, of a Family of Distinction in that Nation (his English name is Joseph) of a Sprightly Genius, a manly and genteel Deportment, and of a Modest courteous and benevolent Temper, I have Reason to think began truly to love our Lord Jesus Christ Several Months ago; and his religious Affections Seem Still agreably increasing."[27] More and more Joseph seemed destined for a missionary career.

The first chance for that career was to come through his friend Charles Jeffry Smith. That young gentleman, who expected to be ordained as a minister in a few months, decided to go to the Mohawk country on his own first mission. He proposed to take Joseph with him as a paid interpreter and helper. Joseph should continue to teach him Mohawk and he, in turn, would instruct Joseph in English and other studies.

The Reverend Mr. Wheelock was all for this plan. It would benefit both parties, he thought; and both he and Mr. Smith wrote Sir William asking for his permission. It would never have occurred to Joseph to take so important a step without Sir William's approval. Indeed, he seemed to look upon Johnson as a sort of second father, and all at school knew it. Wheelock also wished to take Joseph with him on a fund-raising trip to Boston and Portsmouth, and he asked Johnson's consent for this, too.[28]

No one supposed that the consent would not be forthcoming, and there was much preparation for both enterprises. Mr. Smith went to New York on the business of the mission. There was much outfitting to be done, much choosing of cloth and sewing and tailoring, much going to the store.

Then, in May, in the midst of all this excitement, Joseph received a letter. It did not come from Sir William, but from Molly. Wheelock did not see the letter, himself—he supposed it was in Mohawk—but Joseph told him that Molly had directed him to come home, that the family did not like the kind of people he was with!

Wheelock was greatly puzzled. He immediately wrote Sir William asking what to do. Joseph was very uneasy, he said. But he was afraid to send him home alone on foot, and he did not want to send a horse with him because of the difficulty of getting it back (it was hard enough to get letters back and forth, much less horses); and he hoped Joseph could wait till Mr. Smith was ready to go. Joseph, he added, wished to do whatever Johnson thought best.[29]

It was no wonder that Wheelock was puzzled and Joseph worried. What did Molly have on her mind? The Indians were whimsical and easily offended. If Joseph had written the family about his agricultural labors, it would have been enough to cause a summons home. Or did Molly have another, more secret, reason? She knew of some terrible rumors; Joseph might soon be needed in his own country.

The whole Indian world was seething with unrest that spring. Far out in the west, sinister belts of black and red wampum were carried from village to village. Swarthy figures sat around council fires and talked dark schemes and brooded over their grievances. George Croghan, Sir William's western deputy (whose perception was so much better than his spelling), wrote from Fort Pitt that "the Sinecas seem Ripe for some Mischiff, and there Nott being Alowed amunision & Nessarys as they pass an Repass hear . . . Make them very uneasy"; and again he warned that "y^e. french att y^e. Elinoies is Very Busey in Stiring up y^e. Western Nations to do Misthef. . . . and I have Rason to blive from y^e. Sulkeyness of the Indians this Sumer that y^e. french att all our posts are acting as those att y^e. Elinoies."[30] Other stories of French intrigue and Indian discontent were coming from points as far apart as Detroit and Montreal. Dissatisfaction with the peace treaty had also shaken the Indian world. Official news of the peace had not yet come, but rumors were plentiful. Croghan from his vantage point on the remote frontier wrote Johnson that "the Indians . . . are very uneasy in their minds, since they have heard that so much of this Country is ceded to Great Britain . . . as 'till now they always expected *Canada* would be given back to the French on a Peace. they say the French had no Right to give up their Country to the English."[31]

At home on the Mohawk Indian affairs wore no better an aspect than they had eighteen months before. George Klock still kept the Canajoharie neighborhood in turmoil. Besides serving writs of ejectment on white tenants who paid rent to the Indians, he had managed to divide the Indians themselves into quarreling factions by plying a few with drink and getting them to sign a deed in his favor for the disputed land. More than one broken head was the result of this, as Indian fought Indian. Johnson, with the help of royal officials, had taken a title suit against Klock and the Livingstons to court and had been told that a patent was a good title, no matter how obtained. Evidence of fraud was not even admissible at common law, and there were technical reasons why the suit could not be tried in chancery. It was plain that nothing more could be done in the courts. The only hope now lay in appeal to the king.

There was more trouble, too, down on the Susquehanna River, in the province of Pennsylvania. Here some emigrants from Connecticut were actually making settlements in spite of Indian opposition. In May 1763 the Council of the Six Nations appealed to Johnson, and he sent his nephew Guy (who was now both his son-in-law and deputy agent) with an Indian deputation to complain to the Governor of Connecticut. The governor, prodded also by letters from London, had already tried to bring his people back home, but most of them defied his authority. They had found a beautiful valley called Wyoming, and there they were determined to stay.

About this time an Onondaga saw the Great Spirit in a vision. In this vision, he said, the Great Spirit told him that "when He first made the World, He gave this large Island to the Indians for their Use; at the same time He gave other Parts of the World beyond the great Waters to the rest of his creating . . . That He now saw the white People squabbling, and fighting for these Lands which He gave the Indians; and . . . . that He was quite displeas'd, and would, altho their Numbers were ever so great, punish them if They did not desist."[32] But Indians were always dreaming, as everyone knew.

Charles Jeffry Smith returned at last from New York, the business of his mission accomplished. He was ordained as a minister in June.

On June 13 Johannes Tekarihoga, head chief of the Mohawks, hastened to Sir William Johnson with an almost unbelievable story. Belts, he said, had come to Canajoharie from the west, reporting that a French army had ascended the Ohio. The Shawnees, Delawares, and other Indians in that country, he said, had joined the French, and together the Indians and the French had already killed eight hundred men and captured several British forts! Sir William listened patiently.

Could there be anything in such a tale? He had long been uneasy. But he had also heard many an empty Indian rumor.

On July 5 the Reverend Mr. Smith and Joseph set out for the Mohawk country. In their keeping was a letter from Parson Wheelock to Johnson. Wheelock thought Johnson would find Joseph much improved in useful knowledge, and he hoped Joseph would return to school when the mission was finished; "he has much Endeard himself to Me (and I think to every body Else) by his good Behaviour," he assured Johnson.[33]

It was an uneventful journey up the Hudson. The two young men conversed earnestly about their plans. They expected to return to Lebanon in the fall. In the meantime, during the summer, they hoped to do some good among the Indians. In their bestowal, so Charles Jeffry Smith firmly believed, were life's two greatest treasures: learning and a knowledge of God. From such gifts the poor Indians were bound to benefit both in their material and in their spiritual affairs. Joseph agreed wholeheartedly. Now in Mohawk, now in English, the two friends discussed the happy prospect. It was quiet talk, and calm.

They did not know that the world into which they were going was on fire.

6

The Conspiracy of Pontiac

THE STORY that Tekarihoga told Johnson, incredible though it seemed, was no idle rumor. The belts received by the chiefs at Canajoharie Castle had been remarkably accurate. The Indians of the west were indeed in revolt. For a long time they had sullenly sharpened their axes; now they were ready to strike them into English heads. In their plots and stratagems they were helped by the French, sometimes in secret and sometimes openly; and every day they looked for a great French army that was to come to their aid. The French regime they thought of fondly as the good old days and longed to bring it back again. This land was theirs; they would put on it whom they chose. The British, they boasted, had not conquered *them*.

It was on the hated forts that the natives first vented all their pent-up rage. Led by an Ottawa chief named Pontiac (whose name has been attached to the uprising, but who later claimed that the Senecas and their allies had been urging him on for two years), the Ottawas, Hurons, Potawatomies, and Chippewas, after first failing at a surprise attack, began a siege of Detroit on May 9, 1763. Amherst's new blockhouse at Sandusky fell to the fury of the Ottawas and Hurons on May 16. Traders and garrison alike were slain; the fort itself, which the general had insisted he must have, burned to the ground. Fort St. Joseph, in Potawatomi country, was captured on May 25, and the Miami Indians took Fort Miamis at the head of the Maumee River two days later. On June 1 Indians living nearby seized Fort Ouiatenon on the Wabash; and on June 2, a day of indescribable horror, Fort Michilimackinac at the narrows between Lakes Huron and Michigan fell to a surprise attack of the neighboring Chippewas. A trader who managed to escape from Mackinac told how the wildly exulting Indians tore open bodies and drank the blood of their victims. Shortly thereafter Fort Edward Augustus on Green Bay was abandoned by its British garrison. Whatever survivors remained here and there could only guess the fate of their friends at other posts; none of them really knew, that terrible summer, who was alive and who was dead.

The war drew closer to the white frontier when the Delawares, Shawnees, and Mingoes besieged Fort Pitt at the famous forks of the Ohio in southwestern Pennsylvania, and Senecas of the Genesee wreaked their vengeance on Fort Venango eighty miles to the north. The little blockhouse at Venango was put to the torch and its commander slowly roasted to death. But before he died he was forced to write out the reasons the Indians gave for the war: the scarcity of ammunition for hunting and the fear that the English, by building so many forts in their country, meant to take over all their land. Not a white man lived to tell the tale of Venango's fate, but the Mohawks again got the news and reported to Johnson what had happened. A few days later Forts Le Boeuf and Presque Isle, also in northwestern Pennsylvania, fell to the victorious Senecas who were joined, at the latter place, by Indians from Detroit.

Some of this news took weeks to trickle back east, but a Philadelphia newspaper published a report from Fort Pitt on June 9, and New York and Boston were reading the same story a few days later. The two young travelers, Joseph Brant and the Reverend Charles Jeffry Smith, must have heard some rumors as they made their way up the Hudson in early July. But the fort at Detroit and even Fort Pitt were far away. Nobody they met could realize just what was happening. At Albany, on July 10, they stopped to enlist the help of John Macomb, a local merchant, for their missionary enterprise.[1] They found that Sir William Johnson had been there about two weeks before, trying to raise volunteers to defend the frontier. But Albanians were not much interested.

Going on to Schenectady, the two young fellows found their first hint of real alarm. Here men were volunteering for military service. Schenectady was the jumping-off place, the last sizable outpost of civilization. What happened on the frontier and out in the Indian country mattered to the people of Schenectady. It was here, no doubt, that Joseph and his friend began to feel some qualms about the practicability of their mission. They had planned to go on to Oquaga, but Oquaga was perilously close to the country of the hostile Delawares.

Johnson Hall was the next stop. Though the two travelers found Sir William on a sickbed, it did not take him long to set their minds straight. No, they could not go to Oquaga or anywhere else in the Indian country. They would have to stay among the Christian Mohawks. He himself meant to fortify Johnson Hall and apply to Amherst for a military guard. Every day panic-stricken people were flying in from the frontier, and it was all he could do to keep his own tenants from leaving. Bateaux full of refugees were coming down the Mohawk. Nobody was going up. Johnson also told them that as soon as he had heard of the Indian uprising, he had called a council of the Six Nations to meet at German Flats to consider what ought to be done. Joseph would naturally attend with his family. The Reverend Mr. Smith might go along, too, if he wished.

The council met on July 18 with 340 Indians present. The Mohawks, Oneidas, Tuscaroras, Onondagas, and Cayugas had sent delegates, but the Senecas, most populous of all, were conspicuous by their absence. Not one Seneca put in an appearance. Johnson, weak and ill, was more indignant than he dared to show. He was also worried. Without the support of the Six Nations the white people could never hope to hold the vital trade route to the Lakes nor even to maintain their present frontier. Nevertheless, he spoke with much seeming assurance. "I then delivered them a Speech," Johnson later told Amherst, "wherein I represented the behaviour of the Western & other Indians, their unprovoked hostilities and the absurdity of their Attempts to distress a People, who had entirely defeated the united efforts of both the French & them, concluding with recommending it to them to consider y^e. behaviour of these People as a breach of the Covenant, not only with us, but with themselves, & that therefore it was expected they would give us a proof of their Attachment to us by a Strict observance of their Treaties, and by their resentment at the Hostilities committed."[2]

These were bold words that Johnson spoke, especially so in view of the fact that not a month before some of the Mohawks had sat in court in Albany to hear the disposition of a suit against George Klock and what they had heard was that a patent is a sufficient title, no matter how fraudulently obtained. Johnson really wanted the Six Nations to go out to fight the hostile Indians, but he did not think it prudent to mention such an idea just yet. The conference ended with the Indians present promising to try to talk some sense into the heads of the Senecas; they would send deputies to the Senecas immediately, they declared. Little Abraham of Fort Hunter and three others were appointed to go to the Seneca country as peacemakers.

All the rest of that summer the long frontier of Virginia, Maryland, and Pennsylvania was ablaze as parties of warriors painted in fearful red and black roamed up and down the river and creek valleys. Many a lonely cabin went up in flames; many a small settlement was wiped out. Twenty-seven rash Connecticut settlers lingering on at Wyoming were massacred in the fall by the furious Delawares who even swept up into New York, to the borders of Ulster, Orange, and Albany counties, on their raiding expeditions. George Croghan, Sir William Johnson's agent at Fort Pitt, estimated that within four months two thousand white frontiersmen had been killed or captured and thousands more reduced to beggary.

In the far west Pontiac and his followers kept up their stubborn siege of Detroit. Hundreds of Indians camped outside the fort with the idea of intercepting supplies and reinforcements. Captain Dalyell, Amherst's aide-de-camp, an incautious officer who shared the general's contempt for red men, slipped out to attack the Indian encampment, but was ambushed while crossing a stream which has ever afterward borne the name of Bloody Run. Dalyell himself was slain and a great proportion of his troops killed or captured. The water ran red with English blood, and after the battle the victorious Indians cut out Dalyell's heart and rubbed it on the faces of their white prisoners.

In the fall came news of a frightful ambush by the Senecas at the Niagara carrying place. At a dark and gloomy spot on the trail now called the Devil's Hole a convoy of supplies with its military guard was destroyed. Only two white men escaped. Two companies of soldiers trying to go to the aid of their comrades suffered very nearly the same fate. The rebel Indians were actually fighting and winning battles with British regulars! The very thought of such a thing had its own especial horror. Whole frontier settlements pulled up stakes and fled. To the terrified populace every tree had become an Indian.

General Amherst could hardly believe the news as it came in. He had been sure that Indians could not fight; but even if he was wrong, he did not intend to buy their loyalty with presents and favorable treatment. He had instructions from government to use economy, and he meant to follow his instructions. But the British ministry, when they finally heard what was going on, at once thought of a remedy which would cost nothing. They had been considering for some time how best to restrain the American colonies from expanding to the west. It was feared that settlements so far from market could not support themselves by agriculture, that they would eventually go into manufacturing and compete with the mother country. This could not be tolerated. Now there was an additional reason to hold back American frontiersmen; it would gratify the Indians. The ministers hurried their deliberations, and the famous Proclamation of 1763 was born.

The renowned document was signed by King George III on October 7. It established the crest of the Appalachians as the boundary line between the colonies and the Indians and prohibited white people from settling on the other side. It was a perfect solution, of course, to two vexatious problems.

In the meanwhile, Joseph, who had happily looked forward to a summer of missionary work at Oquaga, remained at home with his family in Canajoharie. Occasionally he was given a chance to make himself useful in public service. This was more than he had a right to expect, but Brant, to whom he probably owed the chance, was a sachem with unusual influence. When Little Abraham and his fellow deputies returned from their journey to the Seneca country, Joseph was one of the messengers sent down to inform Sir William. Next day Sir William sent Joseph to Fort Hunter to ask Abraham to come over to Johnson Hall for a private talk. Another Six Nations council was to take place in which Johnson would be formally notified of what had occurred among the Senecas. On August 21 Sir William sent Joseph with a letter to the commanding officer at Fort Stanwix in order to prepare the way for the Indians as they came down the country.[3] Lieutenant Colonel Campbell was instructed to see to it that the Indians got provisions for their journey; this would not only please the Indians, it would also please the local farmers and safeguard their livestock. The Indians of the upper nations who were used to sharing everything among themselves thought it not at all improper to raid barnyards along the way when they got hungry on their travels.

The council opened at Johnson Hall in early September. This time six Seneca deputies attended, and the Six Nations reported that Little Abraham and the other messengers had been able to bring to peace and friendship the first two Seneca castles of Canaderagey and Canadesaga. This left populous Geneseo Castle and the scattered Mingoes or Ohio Senecas still in the war. The Caughnawagas from Canada also attended the council and a motley group of Indians from the upper Susquehanna region, all of whom avowed their friendship for the English. The Caughnawagas offered to go fight the hostile Indians. When Johnson reported the Caughnawaga offer to Amherst, the latter was not pleased. He was planning some punitive expeditions of his own and considered Indian help "rather a dangerous expedient." Was there an Indian alive who could be trusted? He thought not. George Croghan who had an audience with Amherst in New York after the council declared that the general "Did Nott blive there was an Indian in America to be Depended on." Croghan, who shared Johnson's opinions, answered smoothly that he "wold be very Sorrey the Mohockes & others of yᵉ. five Nations who had Lost Many of thire people in his Majestys Service Dureing the Late Warr Should know that was his opinion of them." To this Amherst made no reply.[4]

But Johnson, understanding Indians, still clung to the hope of sending some Iroquois war parties against the hostile Delawares and Shawnees of the upper Ohio country. The Delawares and Shawnees were vulnerable, living nearest to the white settlements, and they had done a great deal of damage on the frontier. The Six Nations would not mind punishing these restive dependents and thus reasserting their authority over them. Johnson could not have been unaware that some hostile Senecas who were intermingled in this region might also get hurt—if so, well and good. He knew that primitive ideas of revenge would make the fight a continuing process, once blood was drawn. The Indians, as he reminded his correspondents, dreaded their own sort much more than they feared white troops. With white people a war could be ended; with other Indians, once hostilities had started, peace was almost impossible. Such wars could drag on for decades. The Iroquois, for instance, had been fighting the Cherokees in the south for so many years that neither party could recall how the war had started. They only knew that each blow had to be revenged. So Johnson did not hesitate to send Indian against Indian; besides being the sort of venture for which they were better fitted than white troops, it will "create a Division among them," he thought, "w'ch will prove a great Check to their Power hereafter."[5]

Two events played into Johnson's hands. In October General Amherst received his long-wished-for permission to return home and left for England the next month. Major General Thomas Gage became the new commander in chief in America. Gage did not despise the capabilities of Indians, and he agreed to Johnson's plan. Gage wanted peace. With the French war over and the natives pacified or put down, he foresaw no more problems. What else was there to disturb the public tranquillity?

In the early winter the Senecas of Geneseo began to throw out peace feelers. They knew that a peace treaty had actually been signed by France and Great Britain giving Canada to Great Britain, and that Pontiac, faced with cold and hunger and deserted by the local French, had given up his long siege of Detroit. And even before Pontiac had succumbed, the Delawares had given up their siege of Fort Pitt. (At one of their parleys with the commander of that post he had thoughtfully presented them with a couple of blankets from the smallpox hospital, and many of them were soon too busy to wage war.) Reading these events aright, three delegates from Geneseo came unblushingly to a council at Johnson Hall in December. The other Six Nations delegates were overjoyed and urged that Johnson make peace immediately. Once more their League had weathered the storm. Johnson, mindful of the atrocities at Venango and Devil's Hole, could scarcely control his resentment. But, though he put off making peace until the hostile Senecas should show a little more contrition, he had to content himself with merely reading them a lecture. Any real punishment was out of the question. However, with Geneseo suing for peace, he knew he could send out an Indian expedition against the other malcontents at once. There could be no difficulty now in the minds of the Six Nations chiefs about having to fight a member of their own Confederacy.

The expedition, as usual, turned out to be mainly Mohawks and Oneidas, those Indians most susceptible to white influence, and a few local whites. It was led by Henry Montour, William Hare, and John Johnston, three of Johnson's Indian department employees who were good woodsmen and who could also be depended upon to keep order and distribute supplies. All the Indians were in small parties, each under its own head warrior. Joseph, now nearly twenty-one, was one of the number, but it is very unlikely that he had any followers of his own. He had neither the age, the social standing, nor yet the experience for leadership in war.

The Mohawk braves boiled their war kettle and held their usual dance before setting out. The noisy festivities lasted all night. The young men, painted in bars and zig-zags of vermilion and lampblack, with feathers in their hair and rattles on their feet, looking fearsome— and to themselves, no doubt, handsome—danced facing each other in two rows. It was vigorous, exhausting exercise. When they sat down to rest, one of the old fellows would jump up, thrust his hatchet into the war post, and tell a tall story of some past exploit. And so on with dancing and singing and boasting till dawn. They ate boiled meat, drank whatever liquor Johnson had provided, and nearly everybody ended up dead drunk. All this was the customary preparation for war. It was unthinkable that the dance should not be held. The Mohawks who went to church and lived like their white neighbors in many ways set great store by their ancient customs, especially when they involved a revel.

On February 9 the party of nearly two hundred set out for the Oneida country where they expected to collect additional warriors. But there was an unexpected delay at Oneida. All the Indians there did not favor the expedition and a few tried to cause trouble. The three leaders, Montour, Hare, and Johnston, wrote back to Sir William that one Oneida warrior was threatening to scalp some white people and that others were making other threats, and they advised Sir William to be on his guard. Presumably these troubles were surmounted in time by white finesse, flattery, and finance, since some Oneidas were finally collected. Another fete was held and off they all went, on February 22. They took the old well-worn trail to Oquaga, across country to the Unadilla River and then down that stream to the Susquehanna. The snow was still three feet deep in the woods, but the expedition was well equipped with snowshoes, and the trip was not hard. Late winter was a good time to travel. The crusted snow and ice made fast going. In a few days Oquaga Mountain loomed into view.

So far as is known Joseph had no relatives in Oquaga nor had he ever gone there as a messenger. When carrying wampum and running errands for Johnson or the Indians of Canajoharie he had traveled mostly up and down the Mohawk. He may have passed through Oquaga on his return from the Ohio country years before as a child but, if so, he could scarcely have remembered it. Perhaps he was having his first glimpse of this Indian village that was to figure so prominently in his life.

Oquaga[6] contained at this time about fifteen or sixteen big, old houses. These were located on the east side of the Susquehanna, but a few stragglers squatted on the west side and formed a sort of suburb. The people were mostly Oneidas with a sprinkling of Tuscaroras and Mohawks. They were prosperous, as Indians went. They had some cattle and poultry, some pretty good gardens and some flourishing fruit trees. Many of them were Christians, as they had been exposed to various forms of Christian doctrine for many years. Oquaga was a place much frequented by missionaries from New England. Indeed, this was the place where Joseph and his friend Charles Jeffry Smith had hoped to go and make their war on ignorance. But Mr. Smith had long ago returned home, and here was Joseph on his way to fight a different sort of war altogether.

At Oquaga the expedition halted while some local warriors prepared to join. This delay gave Joseph a chance to look about. What he saw was a pretty Oneida girl named Neggen Aoghyatonghsera, generally called Peggie but probably christened Margaret.[7] Peggie's father was Isaac, the religious leader of the village. Isaac was a good old man who had read prayers in church for many years and who, though it pained him that his people did not always properly regard the Ten Commandments, still cherished the hope that some day they would become as godly as the people of Boston. As for himself, as he once told Sir William, he was "determined to follow the Words of Jesus

Christ as near as I can."[8] In this laudable purpose he seems to have done better than most people, too; it might be said, indeed, that he was *almost* Bostonian.

Isaac and his family lived in an old-fashioned longhouse into which were also gathered his married daughters and their husbands and children. This crowded abode was a long, barn-like structure made of squared logs and bark. It had an unfloored passage through the center, with raised-up bunks or stalls on either side and a fireplace in the passage for each family unit. These fireplaces were hollowed-out depressions in the earth, the smoke escaping through holes in the roof. With such fireplaces, houses often caught fire and burned to the ground, and people sometimes actually fell into the flames while trying to make their way from one end of the house to the other—the latter danger increasing, of course, in proportion to the walker's state of inebriation. Isaac's house had no windows. It was dark and smoky and, it must be admitted, not very clean.[9] But Joseph was not depressed by the dirt and smoke. True, he was used to a better house at home and he had seen much better in Connecticut, but he had seen worse right on the Mohawk River, and occupied by white people, too.

In all probability this was a happy house. There was always somebody to pick up and soothe a crying baby, and there was as much to eat as Indians could hope to have. Isaac was a most important man in his village. Though it is not known who his wife was, the whole family seems to have been the very cream of Oquaga society. Peggie was, in a manner of speaking, the local heiress. She was a good girl, too—a pronouncement we have on the authority of as stern a Calvinist as ever passed judgment on his fellow-man, the missionary, Theophilus Chamberlain.[10] If Chamberlain said Peggie was good, his statement can be depended upon; she was, without doubt, *good.* And Joseph had sojourned at Wheelock's long enough to appreciate a good girl when he met one (especially if she was pretty).

The Oquaga warriors took an unconscionable time to get themselves ready to leave home. They had to mend their shoes and weapons, lay in a supply of paints, gather together some provisions for their families, attend several councils (smoking their long pipes and, as usual, recapitulating every day all that had been said the day before), and hold the inevitable war dance. This was all good Indian custom, and the expedition, no matter what its need for haste and no matter how the Messrs. Montour, Hare, and Johnston fumed and fretted, could wait.

Late in February an unexpected event relieved the tedium of the delay. A considerable party of Delawares showed up at Oquaga bound on some unexplained mission, and Johnson's three employees suspected that they were going up country, perhaps to the white settlements at Cherry Valley or Schoharie, to do mischief. With the connivance of some of the chiefs of Oquaga, the expedition seized seven of the enemy warriors in the village one night and slipped down to the Delaware camp early next morning and took the rest by surprise. Most of the prisoners were sent up to Johnson in chains though a few young ones were distributed to deserving Oquaga families to replace deceased relatives. Among the prisoners sent to Johnson (and thence on to Albany and New York) was a famous Delaware chief named Captain Bull, a leader who had done much damage on the white frontier and who had been responsible for the late massacre at Wyoming. Captain Bull being so valuable a hostage and surprises and ambushes being their favorite mode of warfare, this action was exactly to the taste of the Six Nations fighters. Indeed, it was considered such a grand coup that all the Oneidas immediately left the expedition as they felt they had now done their duty. After all, Sir William had sent them only one war belt.

The Mohawks (including Joseph, of course) stayed on and waited, and a few Oquaga warriors finally got ready to join them. The expedition set out again on March 21. Their number had dwindled to 140 Indians and a few white persons. Thanks to the long delay in getting started, the spring floods had already begun and traveling was now very difficult. Each swollen creek and river that had to be crossed presented its own special problem. The expedition had a great way to go, too, through wild, almost unknown, country. Their orders from Sir William were to search along the various branches of the Susquehanna and root out the enemy wherever they found him. Rewards of fifty dollars had been promised for the capture of certain notorious enemy leaders. The party's ultimate destination was Canesteo, a hostile village of Shawnees and Delawares and renegade Senecas who had as yet shown no signs of suing for peace. This village, described by Johnson as a "nest of villains," was located on the Canesteo River, in what is now Steuben County, New York, and it was only about forty miles from Geneseo. The Senecas living in Canesteo or wandering about the vicinity, though they had friends on the Genesee, paid no more attention to the dictates of the Onondaga Council than those so-called Mingoes who lived still farther afield, on the Ohio. The Mohawks did not mind going against such people. To them it was really an exercise of authority.

More than two weeks later, on April 7, Montour, Hare, and Johnston, writing from Tioga on their return, reported to Sir William that the expedition had destroyed three good-sized towns and all the small villages and outlying settlements they could find. They had burned 130 large, well-built Indian houses—many with good chimneys, they marveled. They had dug up and carried away a great quantity of corn which the Indians had tried to hide, and had found a large number of cattle suspected to have been stolen from white settlers. The animals which were too poor and scrawny to drive away had had to be destroyed. In the Indian houses were all sorts of implements and gear which had also evidently been stolen on frontier raids. But there were no Indians in any of the towns. (They had been fled for weeks, some to the Genesee, some to the Ohio, some even as far as the Miami country.) Not one enemy could be seen, much less captured. No other troops need come this way, added Johnson's three correspondents. We have driven the enemy far from these parts. They wrote enthusiastically about the region they had just passed through; "it is the Most beautyful Country that I [sic] Ever See for Land and prety Improvements for Indian Settlements."[11] Few white men had ever visited this land before, for the Senecas had generally forbidden them all access to it. It had taken a small army, composed mostly of Indians, to escort white men along the Senecas' Forbidden Path.[12]

Joseph arrived home on the Mohawk on April 20. He was ahead of the main expedition by several days because he had come back in haste to deliver letters to Sir William from the chiefs at Oquaga.[13] Apparently the service to Canesteo was Joseph's sole—or, at least, main—contribution to putting down the Indian uprising known as Pontiac's conspiracy. True, a party of Mohawk warriors went with Bradstreet on his abortive expedition to Detroit in the summer of 1764, and another party set out to accompany Colonel Bouquet on his punitive march through the Ohio country that fall (but got to the meeting place too late) but, if Joseph Brant was one of either number, he accomplished nothing of importance. Yet his military service in his one actual campaign, small though it was and insignificant though he was, was to have its repercussions. Joseph was worthy of nobody's attention now. But some day the Shawnees and the Delawares, the Senecas and the Mingoes would demonstrate that they had long memories.

In late March and early April, while Joseph and the Mohawk warriors were still searching out the enemy on the Susquehanna, another council met at Johnson Hall. Each of the Six Nations was well represented. In all, 468 Indians were present. Delegates from Geneseo came again to sue for peace though at that very moment their people were sheltering Canesteo refugees. The Seneca delegates could look around them and with sullen eyes see the Mohawks in friendly conference with Johnson and his white officers—the Mohawks whom the Senecas had so often accused of speaking with the tongues of Englishmen. But the chiefs from the Genesee spoke words of friendship themselves now—and words of repentance. They were willing to condole with Johnson over the losses the white people had suffered. They even offered to go fight their brothers, the Shawnees, and their nephews, the Delawares.

The Senecas had a reason for this about-face. Back home they had made a bitter discovery. It was the same discovery that hostile Indians all over the west were making: no matter how hard they tried, they could not live without British trade. Many Indians, Pontiac included, had thought that they could go back to the old, simple ways of their ancestors: to the bow and the arrow, to the blanket of deerskin, to the stone hoe and the pottery kettle. They were finding that they could not do this. They had lost their old skills irretrievably. It was far too late for them to try to turn back. Without British ammunition they could actually starve. At the same time British manufacturers and merchants and every trader, big and little, in the colonies, and the many segments of the population that depended upon them, both in America and in England, realized anew the great value of the Indian trade. To give it up would be almost as drastic a change for white society as for the Indians. In their need for each other, which was so much greater, even, than their hate or their contempt, both sides could overlook the recent past. Sir William Johnson, superintendent of northern Indians for the British crown, gave the men from the Genesee peace. We "can swallow you at a Mouthful," he boasted, but he made peace with them. He promised to send them traders and they promised to send him their white captives. In time, though he meted out such punishment as he could where he could, the Shawnees and the Delawares and Pontiac himself would get peace on substantially the same terms. But never again, if he could help it, would Sir William permit a friendly intercourse between the Six Nations and their western allies.

Joseph had left home with the Mohawk expedition on February 9, 1764. By early March an extraordinary rumor had gained wide credit in New England. The Reverend Mr. Wheelock, trying to raise money in Boston for his Indian school, heard to his dismay that Joseph (known in Boston because he had once received his support from there) had put himself at the head of a large party of savages and had gone off to fight against the British! Wheelock did not believe this slanderous rumor, but he found that he could get no appropriation for the school till he disproved it. He immediately wrote Johnson appealing for the truth. The letter went astray, and he received no answer. A short time later he wrote again. Still no answer. That letter, too, had gone astray. Again he wrote, and his third letter finally got to Johnson's hands.[14]

Johnson answered immediately, and what he said was calculated to set Wheelock's mind at rest and satisfy the gentlemen in Boston. This letter was dated April 25, 1764, and it is especially interesting in that it affords the earliest known instance of Joseph Brant's character having been maligned. The slander was, of course, easily refuted, for Johnson merely had to state what he knew. "J—— is just returned," wrote Johnson reassuringly, "from an expedition against the enemy, who have abandoned their towns, of which three were burned, with four villages . . . and vast quantities of corn, &c."[15]

In each of his letters Wheelock had sent his love to Joseph (once to "My dear Joseph") and on each occasion he expressed the hope that Joseph would come back to school. Indeed, he had been expecting him to return for months. But the times were not propitious for such a journey. It was not safe for the young Mohawk to travel so far from home alone or with only a few other boys. He might be very roughly treated or even killed. Ever since the news of the Indian atrocities at the forts had got abroad, more white people than ever before were incensed against Indians as a race, and they often made no discrimination between the innocent and the guilty. The unprovoked murder of several families of inoffensive Christian Indians by a gang of white savages known as the "Paxton Boys" in Pennsylvania in December 1763 is an extreme and shocking example. But Johnson was afraid to let Joseph travel back to school even before that crime occurred. He would have preferred to send Joseph to New York to be educated by the Reverend Henry Barclay, the former missionary who was now a prominent clergyman in that city, and perhaps eventually to King's College (Columbia University), but both men feared the consequences of such a trip.[16] They could foresee that some ignorant or vicious whites would answer atrocity with atrocity, without distinction.

Johnson had noted that Joseph since his return from Wheelock's school appeared "very zealously and devoutly inclined"[17] and he undoubtedly had him marked down as a future missionary. Missionaries were desperately needed among the Indians, but white missionaries were likely to be always scarce. They did not usually want to live in Indian villages, but that would be no problem to another Indian. Joseph would do very well, so Johnson could have reasoned.

About this time another white missionary did appear on the Mohawk, a certain Cornelius Bennett, sent by the Society for the Propagation of the Gospel, the same organization that had sent Barclay and Ogilvie. Johnson helped the young man set up a mission school at Fort Hunter and enrolled Joseph. It looked for a while as though Joseph would be able to continue his education after all.[18] But his schooling was again interrupted—this time by military service—and finally ended by a smallpox epidemic. This epidemic was especially virulent at Johnson Hall in early 1765 and, indeed, may have started there—a present in a roundabout way, perhaps, from the Fort Pitt hospital, for Johnson had some Delaware hostages at his house. Many of the Mohawk Indians died that winter and spring. Molly, Joseph's sister, got the disease and lost her looks. If Joseph was ill, he had a light case, for he was not pock-marked. But when the smallpox appeared in the neighborhood, Cornelius Bennett, the young schoolmaster, fled. Joseph got no more learning except what he could acquire by himself, painfully, little by little, over the years. His career as a missionary died aborning, for he had none of the educational qualifications needed by a candidate for the ministry. (And, in truth, his thoughts were turning now to something more interesting than the ministry.) It would be a very long time before Joseph would venture to write anything without a dictionary by his side.[19] By then his life had flowed on in a far different channel.

But this obscure young Indian was not the only person upon whose destiny Pontiac's short-lived uprising had left an imprint. Its horrors (and its lost hopes) would be remembered by white men (and red men) for decades. On the one hand, there were very few white people left who did not heartily subscribe to the theory that the only good Indian is a dead Indian. It was considered a meritorious thing, at least along the new frontiers of Virginia, Maryland, and Pennsylvania, to kill any Indian any time, young or old, male or female. As people poured over the mountains after the war (in defiance, of course, of the king's recent Proclamation), the murders of Indians increased. Frontier people were a rough breed. Their very lives were a declaration of independence. Though peace was made, they paid it no mind. All too often they fought a war of their own against those whom they were pleased to call "heathen"—and with the heathen's own weapons, the firebrand, the rifle, and the scalping knife. This war of theirs was to go on unabated and, indeed, rising in fury for the next ten years. At times the Indians who bore the brunt of these attacks (mostly Shawnees, Delawares, Mingoes, or Hurons) retaliated and got their revenge as individuals, but there was no more full-scale rebellion. The Indians were remarkably patient. Life under General Gage was easier than under Amherst. They still had hope and they had the trade, and sometimes even the far Indians could get presents. Presents were the great solace.

The Six Nations in general, from their numbers, their warlike reputation, and their strong vantage point along New York's great western waterway, were not in danger of their lives nor even of their property, for there were no frontiersmen bold enough at this time to venture into their country. With the Mohawks who actually lived among white people, it was a different story. Their lives were safe enough (at least there was no concerted effort to exterminate them); they were not "heathen" and their frontier was old and comparatively staid. But the Mohawks still had many grievances to mull over. Their disputes with white people, mainly over land, caused them great worry, and they were fearful of the future. More and more they were coming to realize that if they were ever to get justice, it would have to come to them from outside the colonies. They knew they had no standing in local courts nor could they expect much consideration from their neighbors. But across the sea they had a father, the king (from whom came regular presents now and trade and such good things), and there were great men around him, they believed, who would do his bidding and sometime give them justice.

They had grounds enough for this belief. There was the day, for instance, when their superintendent told them about the royal Proclamation of October 7, 1763. It was late December, that same year, and Johnson had just received the news. Although he had little faith in the efficacy of the measure himself, he was able to report it to a council of 230 Indians at his house with apparent joy and confidence. "I have at this Meeting made the best use in my power of his Majestys Proclamation for the convincing the Indians here of his gracious & favourable disposition to do them Justice," he afterward assured General Gage, "& shall communicate the same to all the rest."[20] He formally proclaimed the edict to the world on Christmas Eve and early in the next year had it printed and copies sent to the various nations of Indians concerned. It was made abundantly clear to them that the king, their father, wished to protect them and all Indians in their just rights.

Next year the Mohawks saw another instance of the king's goodness. On July 10, 1764, with the furies of Pontiac's war still fresh in their minds, the Lords of Trade in London instructed Lieutenant Governor Cadwallader Colden to recommend to the Assembly of New York to pass a bill for vacating the patents of Kayaderosseras and the

Corporation of Albany. This resolution came in the nick of time for in September the Mohawks went on their usual fall hunt and found that some white settlements were going up on Kayaderosseras Creek. They immediately complained to Sir William, and he was glad, indeed, to be able to tell them, the next month, of what the king's great men across the sea had done for them. If the Assembly did not act, he explained, the matter would be laid before Parliament.

The Assembly did not act (nobody really expected that it would, the patentees being who they were), but the patentees in the weakness of their position began to consider compromise, and they organized a committee to settle the dispute. "They rather incline to give up part of their Right," the committee told Johnson, "that they may enjoy the Rest in peace."[21] They asked Johnson's good offices. Numerous meetings ensued, at one of which the new governor, Sir Henry Moore, in accordance with his instructions, came and talked with the Indians and expressed sympathy for their cause and even threatened to get the patent broken in England. Many proposals were discussed, and finally, in 1768, the affair was settled. The Kayaderosseras patentees gave up part of their claim (a survey showed it to be far less than they had been contending for), and paid the Indians for the rest. The Mohawks knew full well where the impetus for the settlement came from. It came straight from their father.

That Pontiac's conspiracy had availed them something, also, probably did not occur to any of them. If Joseph had been twenty years older, he would have thought of it. But in 1768 Joseph Brant was untainted by the slightest cynicism. The young man saw nothing that the others did not see. His loyalty to the crown, as natural to him as breathing, grew, if possible, stronger.

7

A Home on the Mohawk

WHEN JOSEPH BRANT was an elderly gentleman, full of years and dignity, he was asked one time to describe an Indian courtship. According to his answer, this courtship was a very precise affair, well governed by ancient etiquette. It was carried on, he said, by older women relatives of the couple, such as aunts. When a young fellow wished to be married, he confided in his aunts and pointed out the girl of his choice. His aunts thereupon went to her aunts and presented them with a gift, perhaps a fine suit of clothing. If her aunts approved of the match, they asked the girl what she thought about it, and if she consented, they kept the clothes. If they did not like the match, or if the girl did not like it, they sent the present back. The wedding itself, when it took place, was very simple. The bride was conducted to the young man's abode, and all the relatives brought the newlyweds gifts of bread.[1]

This is what Joseph said, but he must have forgotten a few things. The boys at Wheelock's school used to do their own courting, their own letter-writing, gift-giving, and even proposing. Joseph would have seen this going on, or heard the youthful whisperings and the light-hearted jokes, and he was not an old-fashioned boy. The Mohawks were not an old-fashioned people, either. They were quick enough to adopt a new custom that pleased them. So, though Joseph may have had some elderly female relatives who were capable of doing everything that etiquette demanded, it is more than likely that he made his own way down to Oquaga several times in late 1764 or early 1765. It was not a country much settled by white people that he had to go through; the journey was safe enough, if he thought at all of safety. He probably saw his lady love there on these occasions, and they must have had some tender talks; and what more natural than that he should take her a present? A pretty green hat in the latest mode? A silver brooch? Some ribbons for her hair? In such delicate negotiations Joseph was hardly the boy to burden his aunts more than was strictly necessary.

However it happened, Peggie certainly said yes. Joseph was a good-looking young fellow in those days, capable of a wide, infectious smile, not likely to be overlooked by the girls. He was tall, about five feet, eleven inches in height,[2] and his portraits show that he was always clean-shaven, as most Indians were, with dark eyes, and hair that waved slightly toward his cheek. At this time Joseph probably wore his back hair tied in a queue as Sir William and other white men did though in later life he was to choose, self-consciously and deliberately, the ancient warrior's scalp lock and shaved head. Joseph's portraits also show that he was lighter-colored than Indians are generally supposed to be. Indeed, all the Mohawks were lighter-colored (so it is said)—a circumstance easily explained by the fewness of their numbers and the fact that they had been in contact with white traders for at least a century and a quarter. There is not much doubt that Joseph had in his veins some faint strain of white blood which he seems not to have known about—and, for that matter, so did Peggie.[3]

Peggie's prominent and influential family apparently made no objections to the match. To be sure, Joseph's lineage was nothing. He did not come from sachem stock. But Brant was somebody, and who could overlook the protecting arm of Sir William Johnson? The big question was, would Joseph's wife have meat to boil in the kettle? Yes, she would, nearly always, must have been the consensus, and that settled the matter. Joseph was as likely to be a good provider as anybody the family could think of. And they were thinking rather hard of provisions and providers that spring, for it was one of the hungriest springs the Indians had known in years.

Joseph and Peggie were married on Monday, July 22, 1765. It was a modern religious ceremony. There was none of this nonsense about the bride being conducted to the groom's house and people bringing bread. There had not been a Mohawk wedding like that in years, probably. Joseph and Peggie were married by a proper minister, the Reverend Theophilus Chamberlain, a new missionary just sent out to the Indians by Wheelock. As the Reverend Mr. Chamberlain had been only recently ordained and this was the first wedding he ever solemnized, he wrote back to Lebanon describing it in considerable detail.[4] And lucky he did, too, for Joseph would have sadly misled posterity with all that folklore.

The wedding took place in Canajoharie, and both families were present. Samson Occom, the great Indian preacher, was also a guest, but Sir William was not there—he was ill. The bride, said Chamberlain, "is a handsome, Sober, discreet & a religious young woman." He did not say anything in particular about the groom, but who ever does say anything in particular about the groom? Joseph was there, looking a little foolish perhaps but otherwise as he always did. The young clergyman was nervous. This was not only his first wedding ceremony; it was a triple ceremony as well. Young Brant Kaghneghtago (otherwise known as Brant Johnson), Sir William's oldest half-breed son, was being married, too. His bride was a beautiful white girl, a captive who had been sent back to Sir William by some of the western Indians the previous fall. She could speak several Indian languages as well as her native English and was said to be the daughter of a Virginia gentleman.[5] The third couple were, as Chamberlain put it, "common Indians." How pleased Joseph would have been to know that *he* was not considered "common"!

"The marriage," continued Chamberlain, "was attended without a great Deal of Indecency (I mean amongst the Indians) of any Kind. how I conducted upon this unusual occasion you must guess." After the ceremony there was a dinner attended by all the newlyweds, their families, and friends—some of whom were undoubtedly very hungry. Among the viands to be consumed were a whole ox (whether boiled or roasted, Chamberlain does not say), great quantities of boiled corn, and many pies—also a precarious amount of liquor: seven or eight kegs of rum and wine, each keg holding two or three gallons. The two ministers, Chamberlain and Occom, having already dined, stayed at the table with the newly-married couples just long enough to ask a blessing for them, and then set out for Cherry Valley on business. And a good thing, too! When the clergymen returned to Canajoharie on Wednesday, two days later, they found that a really great frolic had taken place and that somehow, in the melee, two guests had been stabbed. The following Friday the Reverend Mr. Occom left Canajoharie and the Reverend Mr. Chamberlain visited two little mission schools he was helping to get started. When he learned from some of the scholars that family prayers were not said in their homes, he tried to remedy the defect by ordering the children to gather every night with him for devotions. This they did. "Jos. Brant," says Chamberlain, "joyns with us." Apparently the bride modestly stayed out of sight.

In the next few months the documents do not mention Joseph at all, so quiet, so unnoteworthy was his life. By this time the Stamp Act troubles had erupted. Joseph knew about them, of course, as did all the Indians. They heard and saw things, and questioned Johnson in some detail. He, in turn, told them what was suitable for them to know. But the Stamp Act did not really bother Joseph. He had no need of stamps. His pretty Peggie did not need stamps. Brant did not need them. Neither did his mother, nor Molly, nor any of the children. Perhaps Sir William required stamps but, if so, he was able to cope with them. Sir William could cope with anything. He could do everything.

Joseph comes back into the news on Christmas Eve. That was the day that he went down to Johnson Hall with Johannes Tekarihoga, titular head of the Mohawks; King Hendrick's son; Brant's son, Nickus (the "Indian prince"); and several other sachems. This was pretty rarefied company for Joseph to be in, but he was, in a way, related to Sir William and, being so well educated in white learning, the council who sent him presumably thought that he was one of those who knew best how to conduct themselves with white people. But Tekarihoga delivered the message for all. Joseph and the others merely stood by as the customary prompters. First Tekarihoga wanted to know from Johnson whether the king had done anything about the Indians' land grievances. Then he got down to what was probably the important matter at hand just then. The Indians, he said, needed a blacksmith in their village to mend their hoes and other implements (though they couldn't pay him), and they very much wished some help in repairing the fences around their cornfields. All this, added Tekarihoga craftily, would make them more self-supporting and less of a burden to government. Johnson assured the group that the king, though he had not yet replied about their complaints, loved all good Indians; and he promised to send them the necessary workmen.[6]

A great event was now in preparation. The crown was about to make final peace with the western Indians and with Pontiac in particular. George Croghan, Sir William's deputy, had journeyed to Detroit the previous summer, laying the groundwork and making much of Pontiac in public—intending thereby to destroy his influence with his people and succeeding rather well. The peace conference was set for the following summer, at Fort Ontario at Oswego. Sir William, who was to make the peace treaty for the king, set out from home in

mid-July. With him went four bateau-loads of provisions and some of
the Indians from Fort Hunter and Canajoharie, as well as a goodly
number of white people. Joseph and Peggie were almost certainly in
the train. Joseph had especial business at Fort Ontario besides the
treaty, and he and Peggie must have traveled in one of the king's
boats.

Johnson and his party took the usual water route up to Lake
Ontario: the Mohawk, Wood Creek, Oneida Lake, Oneida River, and
Oswego River. There was no change in the countryside since Joseph's
trips in '59 and '60 except that all the smaller forts had been abandoned. General Gage had removed the garrisons from Fort Schuyler
(present Utica), the Royal Blockhouse (east end of Oneida Lake),
Fort Brewerton (west end), and Oswego Falls. This was Gage's concession to the Indians and to the government's loud call for economy.
There were no soldiers at these places, but sometimes a sutler had
remained, offering hospitality of a sort for the benefit of travelers. As
had been the case for many years, the white settlements petered out
near the German Flats. There were still no settlers foolhardy enough
to invade Oneida country, much less the country farther west. The
Six Nations remained a bar invincible to the extension of the white
frontier in New York. Only the wolves dared to dispute their sway.
This time it took a mere ten days or so for the travelers to get to
Oswego, since they were traveling light. Oswego was in Onondaga
country, but the Indians did not object to the fort there. It had been
built by their consent as a place of trade.

The conference with Pontiac opened on July 23, 1766. It was held
in a leafy bower which Johnson had had constructed, nothing else
being large enough to hold the crowd. The weather was fine. Lake
Ontario (to the Indians the "beautiful lake") sparkled in the sun, and
cool breezes blew up from the water. Though many other western
chiefs were present—Twightwees (or Miamis), Chippewas, Ottawas,
Hurons, and Potawatomies—it was truly Pontiac's conference. Indeed, there was a rumor all over the west that Pontiac was to receive a
pension of ten shillings per day from the British for his part in the
peacemaking. There were also Frenchmen willing to lay bets that, if
that was true, the British would not have to pay the pension very long.
Probably Pontiac did not know this, but very likely his companions
did.

At any rate, the council turned into a love feast between the white
man and the red man. All differences were publicly settled between
the two, and they took the ax out of each other's head. Pontiac bowed
gracefully to the inevitable. Said he: "Father . . . . it is the will of the

Great Spirit that we should meet here to day and before him and all present I take you by the hand and never will part with it . . . for I perceive that the Great Spirit who has made all these Lands about us will have it so. . . . and [I] promise as long as I live no ill shall ever happen about Detroit, if in my power to prevent it."[7] Answered Sir William: "There remains then nothing now for me to add or do in order to compleat the great work we met for, but to tell you, that I do now strengthen & ratify all my Deputys Transactions with you last year, confirm all that I have now said to you at this congress, and bury in oblivion all past transactions disagreeable to our remembrance . . . so that we may all for the future live together in the strictest friendship & brotherly love & this I desire you to make publick."[8] It was to be the foundation for an even greater alliance, though the two protagonists would never live to see it.

The conference broke up on July 31 and Johnson prepared to return home. He and Pontiac bid each other farewell, and Pontiac, pleased and happy, promised to visit Johnson Hall next year. Man proposes.

Joseph did not go home but remained at Fort Ontario as interpreter for the Indian department.[9] The job of interpreter was a responsible one and also one which was very difficult to fill adequately. Most interpreters were illiterate and often drunken, and garbled messages and speeches so badly that listening Indians could become insulted at words which were actually well-meant. Many a time it had been necessary for Johnson himself to explain some point which the interpreter, none too familiar with his own language, had misunderstood; and missionaries had a difficult time, indeed, trying to explain the intricacies of the white man's God via such persons.

It was Joseph's education and knowledge of English, of course, which made him eligible for this good position. It paid seventy pounds sterling a year, much more, for instance, than schoolteachers, missionaries, and ministers usually received. When distant Indians came to Fort Ontario with their peltry and furs, his duty was to help them and the various traders who did business there, to understand each other. He also interpreted at the conferences which inevitably took place between the resident military and the Indian visitors. He was very busy for the remainder of the summer, but in the fall fewer Indians appeared, and by winter there was little for him to do. He appears not to have liked the job, or more likely the place, too well. By late September he was trying to get Sir William's permission to leave.[10] The weather was getting chilly and Joseph and the commissary whom Sir William had appointed to supervise the trade had been arguing with the military commandant about firewood. Joseph, a married man, did not wish to live in the barracks with the soldiers, and the commandant would not permit the barrackmaster to issue him firewood unless he did. The commissary complained to Johnson and Johnson complained to General Gage.[11] How the dispute ended is not known. But Joseph received his pay up to March 25, 1767, and presumably he stayed at Fort Ontario.[12] His son, Karaguantier, was probably born at Fort Ontario sometime during that stay. The welcome young warrior was eventually christened Isaac. Thus did Peggie and Joseph honor her father.

Joseph and his little family were back on the Mohawk by early March. The accounts of the Indian department were made up semiannually from March 25 to September 24 and from September 24 to March 25. Joseph received his pay for the latter period, but as he had undoubtedly gone to Fort Ontario in August, he must have been permitted to leave his station a little early. At any rate, on March 7, 1767, we find that a certain Henry van Driessen, Jr., of Schenectady is complaining to Johnson that Joseph and the Indians have laid claim to some of his (van Driessen's) lands.[13] This seems to have been one of the minor land disputes that the Indians had from time to time, as distinguished from their major, continuing disputes with the Livingstons and George Klock, with the Corporation of Albany, and, until it was settled in 1768, with the numerous patentees of Kayaderosseras. Nor is this the first time that Joseph has intervened in some such controversy. Even before his marriage the documents mention him in this connection, but the references are so vague that it is impossible to say just what was really going on. Still, it is clear that Joseph, young as he was, was concerning himself with what he considered his people's wrongs, and they, apparently, were permitting him to do so. Already they tacitly recognized in him superior abilities (and, it must be said, superior connections) and if, perhaps, he could do something for them, they were broad-minded enough to let him try.

Joseph's domestic arrangements, now that he was a husband and a father, were not exactly of the old Indian style, but they were not of the newest mode, either. Instead of going to live with Peggie's family, as would have been proper in the old days, he had taken her to live with his own relatives. How we know this makes an interesting story and reveals a little more about his mother. It seems that while Joseph was at Fort Ontario, the missionary Theophilus Chamberlain spent some time at Canajoharie and, as was his habit, he lodged at the home of Joseph's mother and stepfather. Molly, Joseph's sister, had taken an active dislike to Chamberlain and evidently what Molly did not like her mother did not like, either. Chamberlain assumed, of course, that the reason "the old woman" (as he called her) was cool to him was his inability to give her presents, and he may have been right. What other reason could there have been? Chamberlain was an earnest, zealous clergyman; his sermons were full of hell-fire, and he was so eager to see the children take advantage of the new mission schools that he was willing to go personally from house to house (if the parents would but let him) and drive the lazy little wretches to their classes with a horse whip. Chamberlain finally resolved to change his lodgings because of the old woman's attitude, and left one day while she was out. The next time they met, he relates, she "took me by the Throat and bid me come home. She did this in a manner so faint that I easily read from it the meaning of her heart. She very well knows that Joseph will never be pleased at my living out of his house, unless I had one of my own; and his return is shortly expected."[14] So Joseph was living at his mother's, and mother was trying to be polite, even though her heart was not in it. It is really not likely that mother feared what Joseph would say or do. After all, it was her house, and Mohawk matrons, new customs to the contrary, were still pretty independent.

Brant Canagaraduncka died sometime during the mid-1760s,[15] but the rest of the family continued to live in the home place. The place was always full of people, relatives and friends and whatever traveler, white or Indian, happened to be passing that way. It must have been larger than the cellar hole (still in view in 1878) would indicate. The cellar was then estimated at about fourteen by sixteen, and if the house was no bigger, it would have been crammed to the rafters. The house was located between the river and the highway, but nearer to the highway, and on the slope of a long hill that ran down toward the river.[16] The hill was partially wooded and dotted with other Indian houses. On this same hill, after 1769, stood a tiny church, built for the Indians by Sir William Johnson, which still stands today. Joseph's home was to the north of this church. Two miles down the Mohawk was another cluster of Indian houses. Together, these two groups of houses made up the scattered village of Canajoharie. To the west of Joseph's home Nowadaga Creek raced down the hill, boisterous and frothing over the boulders. Near the Mohawk the land leveled out. It was clear of trees, and here on the famous Canajoharie flats the Indians planted their corn. In this same neighborhood there also lived a number of white people who rented land from the Indians. Some of these good whites had been tenants of the Mohawks for many years. The example they set was very important, Joseph had come to believe.

Joseph owned eighty acres of land on the flats in fee simple, just as any white man owned land.[17] How he got the eighty acres nobody knows, but Joseph was industrious and always able to earn some money. The simplest explanation is that he bought the land from the council. Two or three other Indians owned land as the white people did, but most held their land in the Indian way. The Mohawk nation possessed a certain territory with certain well-defined boundaries; this land was subdivided into clan holdings, and then finally into family holdings, so that each family knew its own allotment. Joseph also owned a tract of 512 acres which had been given to him by deed by Sir William Johnson. This land lay across the Mohawk River opposite Canajoharie, and forty acres of it were cleared.[18] Joseph apparently never did own a house. Years later it was Molly who laid claim to the old homestead. However, the dwelling at Canajoharie was always known as Brant's house. At first, of course, people were referring to the elder Brant. Later, they meant Joseph. So the transition of names became complete, from Thayendanegea to Joseph, to Brant's Joseph or Joseph Brant's, to Joseph Brant; and then, as time went on, our hero was often called just Brant.

Joseph and his wife and child lived comfortably. He had accounts at more than one store in the valley, and some old account books furnish a just idea of his standard of living. It was, for the day and place, very good; and there were certainly many white men, all up and down the river, who did not get along so well. Though money was scarce and hard to come by, Joseph was able to charge at Robert Adems' store in Johnstown, between January 1769 and May 1773, nearly one hundred and fifty pounds' worth of goods. Many of these purchases were wearing apparel. His whole family liked finery and wore good clothes, for Joseph bought broadcloth, mohair, thread and fancy buttons, skeins of silk, white linen, calico, blue and red ribbons, blue coating and binding, flowered serge, scarlet coating, white flannel, a woman's hat, a cap, mittens, a pair of men's shoes, a pair of red shoes (for the baby?), not to mention several pieces of jewelry. He also bought a hunting saddle and bridle, a mattress, a length of sheeting, a bed cord, a blanket, a quire of paper, and even an almanac.[19] Nor did this represent all of his spending. He had a good-sized account with, and purchased articles from, Daniel Campbell's well-known store in Schenectady[20] and quite likely he did business with other traders as well. He seems to have paid his bills promptly.

Most of the family's food was not bought at stores, but came, of course, from the farm. Joseph probably raised the usual corn, beans, and squash, and other vegetables long favored by the Indians, as well as wheat, a money crop for which the rich valley lands had already become famous. He also kept cattle, sheep, and hogs. There were apple trees in front of his door[21] and berries by the wayside. He had twelve sugar kettles, large and small, and in March he tapped the maple trees, and Margaret and Peggie boiled the sap down to sugar. There were fish in the creek and river, and Joseph often took his dog and rifle and went hunting for deer or bear. He did not consider this recreation; it was work. The family had enough to eat, and it was a leisurely sort of life they lived, with breakfast over about eleven, dinner over by two, and supper perhaps catch-as-catch-can.[22] But as there was likely to be always food on the fire, Joseph did not go hungry if his business could not wait for such a late breakfast.

Joseph's part of the house was furnished with two beds, a table and twelve chairs, some fireplace implements, and (for every gentleman must have one!) a liquor case. For working the land he had a wagon, a plow and a harrow, and a sleigh for hauling. He also owned a pleasure sleigh and kept seven horses,[23] and in winter he could take part in races on the ice or go sleighing with his wife and child down the frozen river. The Indians delighted in winter games and sports, and sleighing was by far the easiest and most pleasurable way to travel.

Though agriculture and fishing and hunting provided the family's main subsistence, Joseph was a sort of jack-of-all-trades, and he always had a number of little enterprises from which he got some income. He continued to interpret for the Indian department from time to time, wherever he was needed in the Six Nations country,[24] and (but probably only in times of great necessity) he may have worked on the bateaux—hard physical labor, this, which required much lifting and hauling and pulling and standing in water up to the knees or waist.[25] The Adems account book also shows that Joseph kept a little store. For a while he bought large quantities of wampum, paint, and other trade goods, much more than he could have used himself, so he was evidently a merchant in a small way, dispensing necessities to the Indians and taking in a few beavers, some dried corn, or a little cash in return. The fur trade was vast and far-reaching, and there were many Indians who took part in it, at least to some degree, as merchants. Even old women would ride down to Schenectady now and then and bring back liquor to sell to their friends.

Of the streams of guests and boarders that passed through Joseph's home, many were missionaries and schoolmasters sent out by his old preceptor, the Reverend Eleazar Wheelock. Some of these missionaries were white men and some were Indian men or boys. Indeed, some of Wheelock's native schoolmasters were too young to be called schoolmasters; he called them "ushers," and they were almost as young as their own students. These Indian youths boarded around with the families of their students, a few weeks at each place, and they seem to have been not always too popular in Mohawk homes. The Mohawks had a nice sense of what was fitting. They expected their schoolmaster to say a polite "How do you do" when he came in and an equally polite "Farewell" when he left. They thought he ought to take off his hat and not complain about the cooking. Above all, they objected when he began to beat the children; Indian parents invariably took it ill when their offspring came home with hands swollen from too vigorous a caning. It was hard for the schoolmasters, young or older, to explain to them that this was the proper way to teach, that this was the way all white children were taught, too.

But Joseph seems to have had no such trouble with his visitors and boarders. Even with Theophilus Chamberlain there seems to have been no break in friendship, though his mother and Molly disliked him so heartily. For one thing, Joseph's little son Isaac was still too young to go to school and hence to get a beating. Also, Joseph had a good, substantial house, and there the older, more sensible missionaries were glad to come. They made no uncouth remarks about Peggie's or Margaret's cooking—at least none that is on record. Joseph often interpreted for these friends and tried to help them whenever he could, and on more than one occasion they spoke of his kindness. Chamberlain said Joseph was "exceeding kind" to him when he lay ill with dysentery at his house in the summer of 1765.[26] Ralph Wheelock, son of the Reverend Eleazar, also spoke of his helpfulness in 1768.[27] From time to time Joseph was visited by his old friend Charles Jeffry Smith, his former traveling companion Samuel Kirkland, the Indian preacher Samson Occom, Joseph Johnson a former schoolmate, and many others who were on their way hither and yon. "His House," declared one of Wheelock's associates proudly, "is an Asylum for the Missionaries in that Wilderness."[28]

Simple men, these missionary friends of Joseph's, with scarcely a thought as to the rise and fall of earthly kingdoms. Existing on almost no money, fighting cold and hunger and disease, struggling to learn some strange Indian dialect so that they could instruct their stubborn charges, walking by the side of a harsh God and ever worried that they did not merit His approval—such they were; but in no way did they seem extraordinary. And if anyone had suggested that one of them would some day play a vital role in the disruption of an empire, all—and certainly Joseph himelf—would have stared in disbelief.

But, indeed, there was no one on the Mohawk in those days who seemed destined to play a vital role in anything important, barring, of course, Sir William who, as everyone knew, was sickly and getting along in years; and if destiny had further plans for him, destiny had better hurry. Of course, there was still Sir John, Sir William's only white son and heir. Sir John had made the grand tour to England and King George III himself had conferred knighthood on him. He loved his sovereign but he did not love England, and he had fled back home again as soon as possible. He lived at old Fort Johnson now with a rustic sweetheart and their children and, if in this situation he could be called a simple family man, that is what he was. Sir John was no libertine, all the sad, old gossip to the contrary. But he was no conquering hero, either, and obscurity was his evident, and obviously not unrelished, portion.

A mile from Sir John, in Sir William's first modest home in the valley, now remodeled and modernized and equipped with all the latest conveniences, lived Daniel Claus, Sir William's first son-in-law. Daniel, the quiet German, had married the baronet's elder daughter, Ann, in 1762. Daniel was deputy agent to the Canadian Indians, but he was more and more an agent in absentia and left his comfortable Williamsburg only part of the year. With this Sir William seemed satisfied and the Caughnawagas and other Indians to the north not dissatisfied. Daniel Claus loved his family, and he loved to eat; he was overweight and a bit lethargic; playing the fiddle was his solace and the life of a country squire his greatest delight. Destiny could have no special plans for such as he.

A mile still farther down the river at Guy Park lived Guy Johnson, Sir William's nephew and next in command. Guy had married the baronet's younger daughter, Mary, in 1763. Guy and Mary lived in a mansion with spreading flower gardens and a pavilion built over the water. Guy was overweight, too, and somewhat conscious of his importance. He would have been more conscious of his importance if only he had been more important. But a host of friends thought him very jolly, and jolly he was likely to remain until gout and age and good wine sometime took their toll. Guy did not seem to be a likely candidate for the honors of history, either.

About a two-hour horseback ride inland from the old Fort lay Johnson Hall, Sir William's newest and most beautiful home. The mistress of this gleaming mansion continued to be Joseph Brant's sister, Molly, who has sometimes been called "Brown Lady Johnson" though she was never formally married to her lord and master. Surrounded by her ever-increasing brood of children, Molly had the careful respect of all those who hoped to get a land grant from the Mohawks, and this included practically everybody who came visiting

Sir William. If Molly was firmly ensconced in the favor of the whites, she was even more thoroughly entrenched in the favor of the Indians. Molly dispensed largess with a lavish hand, and this was the most direct way to the hearts of any people so poverty-stricken as the Mohawks. The more meals Molly served, the more blankets and shirts she handed out, the more drams she poured, the more small gifts of cash she made to indigent and begging Indians, the more orders on merchants she authorized, the greater her influence grew.[29] In just a few years she had made herself the most powerful woman among the Mohawks. Even Tekarihoga's mother, had she been still alive, could have wielded no greater influence than the humbly-born Molly. Brant's death, when it came, made not a whit of difference; by this time she had more real atuhority than he ever dreamed of. Both she and Sir William were able to get along without him. Joseph's accounts with the local stores pale into insignificance beside Molly's. There was probaby not a tradesman anywhere in the whole long valley or even in Albany whom she did not patronize, and patronize handsomely. As Guy Johnson once so aptly remarked of her, Molly was "pretty large minded." In a competition to determine who was the most expensive lady in the province, Molly, if not the winner, would certainly have been a close runner-up. It must be admitted, Molly Brant was of the stuff of history. She lacked only opportunity.

Close to Johnson Hall lay Sir William's growing settlement of Johnstown. Though only a few years old, it was a thriving little mart of perhaps twenty houses, the terminus of several public roads. It drew its sustenance from a countryside filling up with Sir William's new tenants, families who were laboring earnestly among their recently girdled trees and heaped-up piles of brush. Many of these tenants, by 1773, were Scotch Highlanders, pitifully poor and grateful to an understanding landlord for this new chance in a new country. Their hopes were great, their hearts were high, and they knew Sir William could be depended upon to give them a helping hand during the hard first years. This was what mattered to them most of all. Surely history could have no rendezvous with such simple-hearted creatures.

A few miles southeast of Johnson Hall and about a mile from the river stood a plain frame house reminiscent of old New England. In this house lived Captain John Butler, a plain man of Connecticut birth, and perhaps for that reason a little suspect by some of his good Dutch neighbors. He was a veteran of the French war, an interpreter in the Indian department (but not so well paid as Joseph), an experienced woodsman, a farmer, almost as much a jack-of-all-trades as was Joseph Brant himself. A quiet, modest man, Captain John Butler seemed destined to round out a quiet, modest life. He had a teen-aged son named Walter and several younger children, and he was the sort of father who meant that his son should have more education and better opportunities than life had so far afforded himself. And young Walter (born in 1753) seems to have been nothing averse.

In our search for heroes let us go back up the river to Canajoharie where lived Sir William's two oldest half-breed sons, and, indeed, one or both of them may have lived in the all-encompassing Brant house. William, unhappy and unruly, was sent from home twice to be educated, first with the Reverend Mr. Wheelock in Connecticut and then with the Reverend Thomas Barton in Lancaster, Pennsylvania. The resentful heart of William never quite took to learning. But young Brant Kaghneghtago and his beautiful white wife were more at peace with the world and quietly happy in their growing family of little fair-haired girls. Brant Johnson craved no place in the sun. What it was big William craved he did not know. He was the one to wrestle and fight and read a book and brag about his father and brood over the wrongs of his race, though it was not likely that he would ever be able to do anything about them.

Among all these commonplace people there was perhaps none more common than a plain German farmer-trader who lived in a sturdy house about two miles west of Joseph's home. This man's name was Nicholas Herckheimer, or Herkimer. His family had been poor refugees from the Palatinate, and they and Nicholas were among those who had done well in America. It was a big family, there were many relatives, and most of them lived decently and comfortably. Nicholas was a pipe-smoking, Bible-reading, rough, good fellow. He and Joseph knew each other well. One was just as likely to merit a chapter in the history of his country as the other, which was to say not at all. Who could foresee the great stone shaft which would one day cast its long shadow on the plains of Oriskany? Or who could foresee that other monument of everlasting granite and bronze which would ennoble the square of a city not yet born?

Regretfully it must be said that the Mohawk was not the place to look for heroes. Its people were wholly absorbed in their small daily ordinariness. It was enough just to make a living, to raise children, to work in the fields, to drink flip in the taverns and sit close by the fire in the long, cold winters. But such doings were not the doings of heroes. They were not the stuff of legends.

This was Joseph's life, too, of course, yet he always had one other activity which occupied some of his time. He still concerned himself with the many problems that worried his people. Very likely he could not see that some of these problems were petty and need never have come up at all if the local whites had been less ignorant and the Indians less credulous. The former by gossip and loose talk could easily get the latter into an uproar, and it may have sometimes been done with malice aforethought. But Joseph seems to have taken all these small embroilments much to heart.

Then there were the genuine troubles, too. On January 31, 1765, for instance, Joseph went with Johannes Tekarihoga, head chief of the Mohawks, to Johnson Hall to complain about a certain "Cobus" Maybe, a squatter living on the flats at Canajoharie. Maybe, having plied some Indians with rum, had thrown three of the most inebriated on sleds and set out with them to Albany to get them to execute a deed in his favor. But Joseph and Tekarihoga had caught up with him on the road and seized the drunken Indians and sent them back home. The whole village, they now told Sir William, was much enraged and had determined to drive Maybe off their land by force. Sir William promised to look into the affair and urged the Indians not to do anything rash.[30]

On another occasion Joseph is represented as "teazing" Lieutenant Augustine Prevost for some money that was due the Indians, probably for a land sale. Young Prevost, who was the son-in-law of George Croghan, the Indian agent, lived at the head of Lake Otsego, and is supposed to have been the object of Joseph's profound admiration and, indeed, to have been chosen by him, according to an Indian custom, as a sort of alter ego. But apparently Joseph did not let admiration stand in the way of trying to collect the debts due his people.[31]

All these years the big dispute with George Klock was running on. During the fright that swept over the white population in the early months of Pontiac's war, the various claimants of the Canajoharie patent, in the very real fear that the Mohawks and even the entire Six Nations might go on the warpath, too, were persuaded to put their signatures to a release of that part of the patent the Indians actually occupied. Everybody signed—everybody, that is, except stubborn old George Klock who was already making plans to sell his part of the property, and did sell some of it soon afterward. The old man always steadfastly refused to sign the release, even though on one occasion he was hauled up before the then governor, Sir Henry Moore, for the purpose. Mr. Livingston, he said, had advised him that he did not have to sign. The Canajoharies were so unhappy that many threatened to move away to their allies. A few actually did leave the castle, while the rest begged Sir William to get a law passed confirming them in their property.

Joseph was in the thick of this fight. On July 28, 1772, he and Johannes Tekarihoga formally complained about Klock to Sir William and his house-guest, Governor Tryon (who had come to buy some Mohawk land), and this time Joseph did the talking. Tekarihoga merely announced that the sachems were weary of the affair and had turned it over to their young warriors—a threat in itself. Then Joseph, as spokesman for the warriors, rose and made a long speech. That Joseph had this opportunity to speak supports John Norton's claim that Sir William had used his influence to get him appointed a "chief"[32]—meaning, of course, a chief warrior. This was as high an honor as a common Indian could ever aspire to, being based on merit, and Joseph modestly demurred about accepting it. But Sir William got his way. As a war chief, Joseph would be useful.

In his speech, which was a strong one, Joseph outlined the entire history of the Klock controversy. He did not spare the governor. "Now Brother," he boldly told him, "we rely on your justice for relief, and hope we may obtain it, so as to continue to live peaceably, as we have hitherto done. We are sensible that we are at present but a small number, but nevertheless our connections are powerful, and our alliances many, & should any of these perceive that we who have been so remarkable for our fidelity and attachment to you, are ill used and defrauded, it may alarm them, and be productive of dangerous consequences." At least this is what the interpreter said Joseph said, and it seemed to be a very clear threat.[33] No wonder Joseph spoke so passionately. In the tract that George Klock claimed lay his own little eighty acres. This speech perturbed Governor Tryon, and he promised to try to procure justice for the Indians. Unfortunately, the governor's powers did not extend so far.

The lower Mohawks at Fort Hunter still had their worries, too. They suspected that the Corporation of Albany was getting ready to seize their lands. Their rather baseless fears were continually fanned by ignorant white persons in the neighborhood who delighted in telling them alarming stories of secret surveys and in making predictions as to how soon they would be driven from their homes.

Both castles of Mohawks sent deputies periodically to Sir William to find out what the king's great men in England were going to do about all these things. They put their entire faith in the crown. Johnson soothed them as best he could. The truth was, the king's ministers did wish to give justice to the Indians. But in reality there was little that they could do. Squatters and land-jobbers and dishonest traders and malicious purveyors of gossip and even the murderers of Indians could easily slip through nets spread from London. Nor did it seem likely that the colonial legislatures would ever spread stronger nets of their own. As John Watts, a New York merchant who understood the problem, put it: ". . . I am really concernd at the bad Aspect of Indian Affairs, A Goverment [sic] of such extreme Liberty as Ours is, certainly is not calculated for Connextions with such Allies, Justice is not summary enough, nor power sufficient lodg'd in The publick Officers—"[34]

The names of the Indian deputies sent to the superintendent are seldom listed in the records but, when they are, Joseph's is usually among the number. His closeness to Sir William and Molly would have assured that, even without his own manifest abilities. Many of the Indians could understand a little English; Joseph actually spoke it. This was a great advantage, though Mohawk was still the language of formal meetings. Joseph also knew the ways of white people—or the Indians, seeing his way of life, thought he did. Then, too, he was friendly with Johannes Tekarihoga, and Tekarihoga was certainly the right sort of friend for an able young Mohawk to have. But Joseph could not have gone on missions with Tekarihoga if the council had not sent him. He did not take anything upon himself that the chiefs had not given him to do. For him to have acted outside the council would have been virtually impossible. It would have also been dangerous. The Indians were not used to brooking such forwardness in anybody, and least of all in the young. So when the news came from out of the west—as it did, finally—that Pontiac had been slain, the thought must have occurred to Joseph (for the Mohawks heard all the gossip) that perhaps Pontiac had become, in Indian parlance, "too great a man." But it was not a thought that Joseph would have dwelt much upon. He would not have supposed that it had, or would ever have, anything to do with him.

Ever since the end of the French war Sir William had been one of those talking up a boundary line (something permanent and more definite than the Proclamation line of 1763, and something which the Indians themselves would agree to and be paid for) which should separate the white frontier and the Indian hunting grounds. Since any such line would open new land to white settlement, it should, of course, run as far west as the Indians could possibly be brought to assent to. Johnson had his own reasons for pushing this project, some disclosed and some undisclosed; and, in time, there came to be reasons within reasons.[35] With his great influence and power of gift-giving, it had not taken him long to convince most of the Six Nations chiefs that the boundary line was what they wanted. It was also, they knew, one way they could obtain payment for land across the mountains which Virginia squatters had already appropriated. They seem to have had another idea, too. "Let us . . . make a Line for the benefit of our Children, that they may have lands which can't be taken from them," an Oneida sachem urged his brethren, "and let us in doing that shew the King that we are Generous, and that we will leave Him land enough for his people, then he will regard us, and take better care that his people do not cheat us."[36] It was a hopeful thought.

The Six Nations taken care of (their Ohio allies who had taken part in Pontiac's war had already agreed to a line as a condition of peace), Johnson had only to persuade the British government that the boundary was what it wanted, too. This took longer. The most potent argument he could use with the government was the likelihood of another Indian uprising. So eloquent was he, in letter after letter, that the Lords of Trade, the secretary of state, and other key officials, should have been able to hear the hatchets swishing about their heads, the burning cabins caving in, and, what was even worse, the French plotting to return to Canada, and the Spanish, who now had Louisiana, counting up the profits of the fur trade. In this campaign Sir William was joined by numerous persons, both at home and abroad—persons who had one thing in common; they were all looking with eager eyes toward Indian land. These concerted efforts finally had their intended effect in London, for Pontiac's war had cost the British a great deal of money, and the British public was getting more and more touchy about the vast expense of the American colonies. Perhaps, the ministry began to reason, one great boundary from north to south, permanent and unbreachable, no matter how expensive at first, would be cheapest in the long run. It would protect the fur trade and contain the white colonists, making them serve British industry and the empire, as was proper. This, too, was a hopeful thought—and in early 1768, the government, after years of hemming and hawing, instructed Johnson to go ahead with the purchase. The latter lost no time in sending belts throughout his department summoning the chiefs to meet with him at Fort Stanwix for the long-awaited negotiations.

The great council was set for September 20, but because of travel difficulties and other delays it did not open till October 24. The proceedings, public and private, went on thirteen days. The result was one of the most important treaties ever made between white man and red man. Though, in a sense, it was not to last long, its repercussions were felt for decades. Joseph was among those present at Fort Stanwix (he may even have done some work as an interpreter on the occasion), and he never forgot what he heard.[37] Some three thousand other assorted Indians were also there: Conoys, Nanticokes, and other Indians from about the Susquehanna, Caughnawagas from Canada, Delawares and Shawnees and Mingoes from the Ohio, even Stock-bridge Indians from New England, as well as the entire Six Nations (all who could travel), and they never forgot what they heard, either. The Six Nations were considered the owners of the land in question and only they could sell it, but their restive allies, the Shawnees and Delawares, hunted on it and had been invited by Johnson to come to the council because of their nuisance value (being such close neigh-bors to the Virginia, Maryland, and Pennsylvania frontiers, they had to be appeased, and the only way they could be appeased was to be invited to the festivities and given some presents).

The business of the treaty was, as usual, transacted only with the head men. The common sort of Indians had no part in anything except the eating and the gifts. The Indians were usually hungry and, as Sir William complained, any one of them could consume enough for two white men. It was hard to get enough provisions transported so far out on the frontier for such a multitude; indeed, it had required twenty bateaux just to carry up the great Six Nations "present" or purchase price. But as Sir William so aptly put it, "it cannot be Supposed that Hungry Indians can be kept here, or in any temper without a Bellyfull,"[38] and so by supreme effort he got the cattle and the peas and the salt pork, the flour and the rice and the corn sent up the river.

All kinds of white men also came to Fort Stanwix that fall, the great and the near-great, as well as adventurers and people of the plainer sort (the latter just guessing at what mysterious things were going on), and they all had their own kind of hunger, which may or may not have been reprehensible. Commissioners from Pennsylvania, for instance, completed a purchase of their own from the Six Nations which took in that part of the land to the east of the new boundary line which lay in that province. By this sale the chiefs of the Confed-eracy completely repudiated the old Connecticut Susquehanna pur-chase of 1754 which they always claimed had been obtained by fraud, and left the Yankee settlers of the Wyoming valley in an even more precarious situation than formerly. Two very earnest missionaries sent by Wheelock to plead for land for his school were present, and they almost succeeded in throwing a monkey wrench into the whole vast undertaking. They almost persuaded the Oneidas not to consent to their part of the line. For this Johnson never forgave Wheelock (al-though the latter disavowed what his representatives had done), and it was not long before the Six Nations were removing their children from Wheelock's school, so all-pervading was the superintendent's influence.

On November 5, 1768, the great cession was at last agreed upon. One sachem from each of the Six Nations made his mark (for not one could sign his name) on the document. They gave up an unbelievable extent of territory—a territory which included large parts of the present states of Tennessee, Kentucky, West Virginia, Pennsylvania and New York. The boundary line began on the Ohio River at the mouth of the Tennessee, followed the Ohio up to Fort Pitt, proceeded on up the Allegheny to Kittanning, then directly overland to the west branch of the Susquehanna, continued down that stream and thence by two smaller streams to the east branch of the Susquehanna and up to Owegy and then east to the upper Delaware, went on up the Delaware and back again to the Susquehanna at Unadilla and up the Unadilla to its source, and then finally to a point on Wood Creek near Fort Stanwix. Everything to the south and east of this line, except what the Mohawks still owned, would be white country. The Six Nations had indeed shown the king that they were generous!

This was much more than the British ministry expected or even wanted. They were aware that the Cherokee Indians who lived in the south as well as the Shawnees and others who lived in the Ohio country hunted on some of this land. It was obvious that all these Indians had a sort of counter-claim and might make future trouble. Besides, the government did not like to see the white colonists spread out so far that they would become more unmanageable (and unprofitable) than they already were. But the government was far away, and Sir William Johnson was right there and bold enough to trade upon his great prestige. The cession was what he and his friends wanted and he accepted it. The purchase price—worth, perhaps, fifty thousand dollars—was laid out on exhibit in the square of the fort, the goods hither and yon and the money piled up on a table, and the Six Nations sachems divided it among their people. Next day the assembled Indians set out for home, each with whatever blankets, kettles, knives, brooches, or dollars that had fallen to his lot. Joseph, like the rest, went home with his gifts, asking no questions at all. If he had any uneasy thoughts, he may have been thinking that the Mohawks were now far inside the line of white settlement. True, the Ohio River could be counted as something gained, but it was perhaps too far away for him to consider. Though so much territory had been given up, the Ohio remained indubitably an Indian river, for the line of Fort Stanwix followed its south and east banks—this at least the Six Nations sachems, bemused though they were by persuasion and "private presents," had seen to. The Ohio was theirs forever.

What the Shawnee hunters, whose gifts had been but trifling, were thinking as they trudged homeward, is anybody's guess. The Six Nations had sold their Kentucky hunting ground right out from under them.

In the months of May and June 1769, Joseph Brant guided a party of white people down the Susquehanna as far as Oquaga. It was another way to earn some extra income, and he had probably done the like before and would do it again, but this trip was unique in that Richard Smith, who headed the party, has left a detailed record of the whole journey.[39] After the cession of Fort Stanwix there was much frantic activity in land, and Smith was one of those who had an interest in a new patent. His land lay on the upper Susquehanna, and he set out to inspect it and begin surveys. He traveled up the Hudson and the Mohawk and then across country by wagon to Cherry Valley and Lake Otsego. At the head of Lake Otsego he was entertained by Joseph's friend, Lieutenant Augustine Prevost, who had built a log house there. He first encountered Joseph himself at the foot of the lake where George Croghan, the Indian agent and Prevost's father-in-law, was making a new settlement.

Richard Smith, who was not at all interested in Croghan's domestic arrangements, says not a word about Croghan's Mohawk wife and child who must have been on the scene. But the wife (who was a wife only in the Indian sense) was the sister of Johannes Tekarihoga and a very powerful lady (in the Indian sense), and the child, little ten-year-old Catharine, was undoubtedly the most blue-blooded little girl in the entire Six Nations. Her blue blood, of course, came from her mother, for George Croghan's blood was scarcely worth mentioning, and at any rate the Indians would not have mentioned it, for a father made not a particle of difference to them. And he would make not a particle of difference to us except that we ought to get acquainted with little Catharine, and this is our only opportunity to do so for a long, long time to come.

What Joseph was doing at Croghan's can only be surmised, but the likelihood is that he was trying to collect a debt. Another likelihood is that he was not having much luck. Few people did, at Croghan's. However, he managed to get himself a job as guide for Smith and his party, which was something. Smith does not say what pay Joseph was to receive. He was simply "engaged," but Joseph was sophisticated enough not to consider this an exchange of favors. It was pay, not a present, and it should have been at a good rate, for acting as guide involved much more than merely knowing the way.

Among the surveyors and chainbearers going down with Smith to the patent was a certain Robert Wells, a man who had been long settled at Cherry Valley, a little place between Lake Otsego and the Mohawk. Wells was probably a friend or at least an old acquaintance of Joseph's. He certainly knew just about everybody, white and Indian, along the Mohawk, and he was familiar with Oquaga and knew the Indians down there, too. He knew old Isaac, Joseph's father-in-law, and had even heard old Isaac preach and admonish the citizens of Oquaga for their hard drinking which, as he said, the old man did with tears running down his cheeks. This rather touched Wells, who appears to have been an amiable, good-hearted man. Indeed, the whole Wells family was a nice family and highly respected, and lived no more extraordinary a life than anybody else in the valley, and did not expect to. Joseph and Robert Wells probably found plenty to talk about.

Once Smith got his business attended to at the patent, he again hired Joseph to guide him farther down the Susquehanna to Oquaga, for he had determined to make a grand-circle tour and return to civilization by a different route. This was all right with Joseph as he may have been headed for a visit to his wife's family in the first place, for Peggie and the baby were with him during the entire trip. So it happens that Richard Smith can tell us a little more about Peggie. She wore, he says, either a chintz or a calico dress (like most men, he did not know which), and she had several rows of valuable silver brooches attached to her dress. (Of course, these crude brooches with their heavy fastenings would soon have the blouse in tatters, but this was not a thought that disturbed anybody.) Unlike Theophilus Chamberlain, Smith does not mention Peggie's beauty. But as subsequent events prove, she was not feeling well just then; perhaps that was the reason. Smith says nothing about Joseph's looks, either, except that he was dressed in a suit of blue broadcloth. Joseph's habit of wearing his fine broadcloth in the woods and Peggie's fondness for brooches go far in explaining why they had to spend so much of their income for clothing.

Smith also notes that Indian mothers (and he must mean Peggie, for she was the only Indian mother he seems to have known) have a convenient way of carrying their babies, and he goes on to describe the well-known cradle board. It was a board with bindings of cloth or wampum arranged in a basket-like effect into which the baby was tied securely and the whole slung over the mother's shoulders by a strap.

Smith imagined the baby was uncomfortable. He even thought the baby's face was swollen from being fastened too tight, but he was probably wrong—little Isaac just had a broad, fat, Indian-baby face. Sometimes Peggie hung little Isaac, board and all, upon a limb, and sometimes she leaned him against a tree. At any rate, the toddler, who was now perhaps two and a half years old, could get into no mischief. Peggie seems to have taken good care of him. Indian mothers, says Smith, wash their babies often.

The party traveled down the Susquehanna by water. Several horses had been brought along with the workmen, but the water route was certainly more pleasant for the trails by land were narrow and rough, or swampy. Joseph and another Mohawk guide who attended the travelers built two canoes for the trip. One was made of a hollowed-out pine tree, over thirty-two feet long and very narrow. The other was of bark, very light in weight, about twelve or fourteen feet long and three or four feet wide. Each craft took the better part of two days to make. Everybody had to sit rather low in these canoes, but with this precaution they could be maneuvered easily (if one knew how) except when the stream was very rapid or choked up with logs. Smith relates in a most heartfelt way how they all had to get out and cut away a fallen tree. It was very hard labor.

When the party stopped for the night, Joseph and the other Indian built a shelter. They set four crotched sticks in the ground, placing the two higher in front. They then laid other sticks across these as rafters. Wide sheets of hemlock bark made a sloping roof and enclosed three sides. The front was left open. With a good fire just outside the opening and plenty of bearskins and blankets, the travelers usually slept snug. But at times they had to put on their greatcoats, too, for some nights it was very cold or the rain came pouring down. For supper the party broiled salt pork which they had brought along, or fish which was easily caught in the clear water of the river or even harpooned with a sharp stick. Once Joseph took his dog and rifle and went out and shot a bear, and that evening they all dined upon bear's meat. Several nights Joseph was not feeling well. He was probably suffering from his usual spring bout with the recurring malaria that afflicted him most of his life; many white people had it, too, and they called it chills and fever or the ague. On these occasions he drank sassafras tea and bedded down in the open air. Taking to the open air was a good old Indian remedy for almost anything. A doctor, of course, would have bled him properly. But there was no doctor for many miles around. Such were the perils of the wilderness.

Each morning the party set out upon the river again. The farther down they traveled, the more Indians they saw. Down below the mouth of the Unadilla was real Indian country, land which had been assigned to various allies by the Six Nations or inhabited by Six Nations Indians themselves who had strayed from their own people. Here dwelt Oneidas and Tuscaroras, Nanticokes and Conoys, Tutelos and Delawares. These Susquehanna Indians had a better reputation than the wandering Mingoes who lived farther west. They were not very knowing and they had to scrape along without much benefit of civilization, somewhat in the immemorial Indian way. Unlike the people of Oquaga, they seldom saw a missionary. This was one of their hungry years. Smith conjectured that only their Fort Stanwix money had saved many of them from starvation the past winter. They were wretchedly poor. For clothing they were lucky to have any kind of shirt and blanket. No fine blue broadcloth adorned their backs! Finally the travelers reached Oquaga. Richard Smith went to lodge with the local missionary, the Reverend Ebenezer Moseley, and his interpreter, James Dean; and Joseph and Peggie visited in the home of her father and sisters where little Isaac, no doubt, was made much of. Smith found the houses of Oquaga dark and dismal. They were as open as barns, he wrote, with little furniture and only dirty blankets for beds. The criticism was not unjust. The blankets were dirty, yes; but the baby, at least, was magnificently clean.

Joseph and Peggie Brant's second child was born later in 1769. This child was a daughter. They called her Christina, and she was christened by a German clergyman at Schoharie.[40] Wheelock's missionaries were no longer welcome on the Mohawk. Joseph seldom saw his old schoolmates any more. Though Samuel Kirkland was still living among the Oneidas, he was soon to leave Wheelock's sponsorship. Sir William Johnson could have given many reasons for his break with the founder of the Indian charity school, but the great underlying reason was political. The truth was (and events of every sort were proving it every day), many people in the colonies had begun to survey their world from two opposite positions. Some lived in contentment, never doubting that they enjoyed all the rights of Englishmen, but others, dwelling under identical law, grew restive and suspected that somebody was trying to steal away their liberties. Sir William was of the one persuasion and Wheelock was of the other.

The more Sir William saw of Wheelock's clergymen, the more he wished for a good, safe Anglican missionary. To this end he carried on a long correspondence with the Society for the Propagation of the Gospel in Foreign Parts. A proper missionary, he reminded the Society in October 1766, was needed to take care of the white population as well as the Indians. It was a political necessity to strengthen the Church of England, he pointed out, "as I cannot but think that the Members of that Church are the Surest Supports of the Constitution, and that they are the faithfullest Subjects of the Crown an Argument which may be particularly applied to America Where the Number of the Dissenters and the measures they pursue threaten more than our Religious libertys if not timely prevented . . . ."[41] This was the burden of Johnson's subsequent letters to the Society and to anyone else who might be thought influential. The Mohawks, both at Fort Hunter and Canajoharie, also begged for a minister; and they would have taken any kind they could get provided only Sir William approved. Fort Hunter still had its little, old chapel, built in Queen Anne's time. The Canajoharies yearned for a church, too, and, poor though they were, actually raised one hundred dollars among themselves to get it started. Sir William contributed the rest, and the church was almost finished in 1769. It was just up the hill from Joseph's house—a charming, small edifice that the Indians were to take much pride in.

The long-hoped-for missionary finally arrived in December 1770. He turned out to be an earnest young man, anxious to be of service, only a few years older than Joseph. His name was John Stuart, and he went to live in the little parsonage at Fort Hunter. He had recently received his ordination and, indeed, had made the long voyage back to England for just that purpose. His sponsor was the Society for the Propagation of the Gospel, and, like his predecessors, Barclay and Ogilvie, the Reverend Mr. Stuart came upon the scene at a time of crisis. The SPG had a knack for sending clergymen to the Mohawks at moments most opportune for the empire. Both Barclay and Ogilvie had done useful work among the Indians on the eve of, or during, the last two French wars. In 1770, when Stuart first appeared, the colonies could look back upon five years of political turmoil. Though there was no foreign war in sight, domestic strife was increasing every day. Taxation was a fighting word. This was the year of the "Boston Massacre," with rioting in New York, and smuggling and boycotts nearly everywhere. Merchants, protesting the hated Townshend Acts, had agreed not to import British goods. The Indians, who understood nothing of Non-importation but heard all kinds of rumors, found their own supplies cut very short and begged their superintendent to tell them why. Sir William told them why, in his own way.

The Reverend Mr. Stuart preached his first sermon in the new church at Canajoharie on Christmas day, 1770. He had twenty Indian communicants. He paid a visit to the Brant home, and through him we have a new report on Joseph and Peggie, the first in the eighteen months since Richard Smith had toured the Susquehanna in their company. Stuart found Joseph comfortably settled in a good house, with everything necessary for the use of his family. But all was not well in that house for Joseph's wife, said Stuart, was dying of consumption.[42]

It was probably March 1771, when Peggie passed away. On the 20th of that month Sir William contributed some money "To the Burial of the Chief of Conajohares Wife being a True Friend" and on March 31 another sum "To the Condolence of a principal Indian."[43] Such contributions were required etiquette at Mohawk deaths, and there were times when almost anybody could be a "Chief" or "principal Indian" in Sir William's accounts depending upon whether he was thinking as a white man or as an Indian and, indeed, upon who was drawing up the accounts for him. By this time, too, Joseph may already have been raised to the status of war chief. Joseph bought a little piece of black cloth at Robert Adems' store on March 23 and again on April 22. These bits of cloth could have been for mourning for him and the babies. He would have thought that that was what gentlemen, and all good Christians, did on such occasions.

So Peggie was laid to rest in the old graveyard at Canajoharie. There would have been the Indian equivalent of a wake, with the guests bringing food and firewood and playing games of chance to while the night away, and some of them getting drunk, and the old women wailing, for so strange a mixture of white and Indian customs did the Mohawks practice. Then very likely a painted wooden tomb was raised over Peggie's new-made grave, and after that there was nothing else that Joseph could do, and life went on somehow in the Brant house without her.

Ministers seemed to have an attraction for Joseph, and he for them. Besides the "dissenting" missionaries whom Joseph never broke with, he was a friend of the Reverend Harry Munro, the Anglican minister in Albany.[44] He soon became friends with the new missionary, too. In the spring of 1772 he agreed to go to Fort Hunter to help the Reverend John Stuart translate some portions of the Scripture and the church liturgy into the Mohawk tongue. Since he also acted as Stuart's interpreter while there, the latter was able to start preaching to the Indians regularly. Stuart wished to learn Mohawk and, as Joseph lived at the parsonage, the two young men had the opportunity for many long talks together. Joseph told Stuart about his Ohio birth and his first experience in battle, and about his mother and his stepfather, and anecdotes about things that had happened at school. Peggie's death had affected him deeply. As an Indian, he was well used to death, but it had never come so close before. Into his mind crowded all the questions that invariably haunt the sensitive at such a time. With Stuart's help he found consolation in religion, and once again his heart turned toward mission work and the teaching and betterment of his people.[45]

But Stuart did not think highly of Joseph's educational qualifications. There was so much that the young Indian was ignorant of. For instance, when his friend Lieutenant Augustine Prevost left to join his regiment in the West Indies, Joseph thoughtfully presented him with a complete outfit of handsome furs. Of course this looked absurd to the well educated Stuart who was also perhaps a little piqued, because Joseph had said *nobody* could take Lieutenant Prevost's place in his esteem, and when Stuart offered himself as a substitute, rejected him forthwith.[46] Yet Joseph turned out to be of invaluable aid with the translations, and Stuart later rated him as probably the only person in America equal to such a task.[47] Joseph worked at the parsonage "a considerable time."[48] The SPG, however, had provided an annual salary of only five pounds for an interpreter, and Stuart was unable to supplement this enough from his own small income to pay a living wage. Joseph still had two children to support, and he felt that he had better return to his hunting and his other more profitable enterprises. But he continued to help Stuart with the translations from time to time, and by 1774 the two of them had almost finished preparing for the press the Gospel of St. Mark, an explanation of the catechism, and a short history of the Bible, all in Mohawk.[49]

The Indians had a custom that when a man remained a widower for a year, his late wife's family would provide him with another wife. Something like this may have happened in Joseph's case, for in the winter of 1772–73 he asked the Reverend Mr. Stuart to marry him to Peggie's half-sister. Stuart refused on the ground of the close relationship. Joseph considered this very unreasonable and pointed out to his friend that the children's aunt would be the best mother they could have. Stuart, however, was adamant. He positively could not solemnize such a marriage. But Joseph was equally adamant and he eventually found a German clergyman who was willing to perform the ceremony.[50] There is a tradition that Joseph's second wife was named Susanna.[51] Very little is known of her for sure. Only once did she step out into the clear light of history, but this one revealing moment shows that Susanna, if that was her name, lived as good a life as Joseph could provide. In 1778 we find our hero writing a note to a mercantile firm and he instructs them that they are to "let my Wife have any

thing she may want out of your Store."[52] Many a white wife would
have gladly settled for that!

The situation of the Indian, wherever he came in contact with the
white man, was growing more uneasy year by year. If the formidable
Six Nations had troubles, the troubles of their dependents to the south
and west may be imagined. There was no legend of invincibility to
protect them. As early as September 1771 Sir William Johnson reported to General Gage that the line of Fort Stanwix had been
breached. Squatters had crossed over the Susquehanna and the Ohio
and were building cabins in the Indian country. The great boundary
that was supposed to be inviolate forever had been inviolate for less
than three years. Neither Johnson nor Gage was surprised. Both knew
the character of the frontiersmen, their rashness, their land-hunger.
As far as the frontiersmen could see, the country across the boundary
line was lying there, empty and useless, theirs just for the taking. If
they did not take it right then, they loudly proclaimed that they were
going to when they got good and ready. But whether they actually
moved upon Indian land or only dwelt near its edge, these rash and
ignorant people carried on a sort of running warfare with the local
Shawnees, Delawares, and Mingoes, and whatever other of the "black
dogs" that got in their way. Since they hunted almost as much as the
Indians did, they interfered greatly with the latter's only means of
livelihood. There were murders, and plunderings, too, for the red man
often had movable property that the white man coveted.

Some of the western Indians, especially the Shawnees, had become bitterly dissatisfied with the treaty of Fort Stanwix. It was one
thing to acknowledge the claim of the Six Nations to the wilderness
they hunted upon. This caused them no great inconvenience. But it
was quite another thing to have the wilderness sold and to look across
the Ohio and see surveyors staking out new settlements in what they
considered their own country. Furious now with white mistreatment,
they took their revenge on the innocent and the guilty alike,
whenever and wherever they could. The white people were hogs, they
raged, and they meant to slaughter them. Thus the border troubles
known as Dunmore's War broke out on the frontiers of Virginia and
Pennsylvania in 1774. Governor Dunmore of Virginia was determined
to push into the Indian country and punish the murderous and
marauding red savages. He set about collecting troops.

Alarmed by these warlike proceedings and by a series of particularly atrocious killings on the part of the white savages, and suspecting
that the dependent Shawnees would soon come begging them for

Indian Council at Johnson Hall. Painting by E. L. Henry. Owned by Mr.
John B. Knox. At a gathering like this in 1774 Sir William Johnson held his
last council and died a few hours later. Joseph's life was turned upside down.
Courtesy of the Albany Institute of History and Art, Albany, New York.

military aid, the Six Nations headed for Johnson Hall. Nearly six
hundred strong, they convened there on a blindingly hot July 9. Their
complaints were angry and long, and covered everything from the
recent murders in the Ohio country, the encroachments on Indian
land, and the lack of trade regulations, to the too-great plentitude of
rum in their villages and George Klock's illegal activities. It was
Seneca and Mohawk sachems who voiced all these grievances. This
was important Confederacy business, and young warriors like Joseph
Brant, whether war chiefs or not, had not a word to say about it.

But during these speeches, and on July 11, as Johnson made a
fervent appeal to the Six Nations to sit still and wait for the king's
justice and mopped his perspiring face, Joseph had some angry
thoughts of his own to occupy his mind. In May the Canajoharie
Indians had had a meeting with George Klock or, rather, they had
gone to his house and forced a meeting. They were determined to
make him sign the release of their land. About twenty Mohawks were
in the party. Joseph was there, and so were French Peter who lived in
Joseph's house, Paulus Petersen (old Hendrick's son), the usually
peaceable Brant Johnson, and an Indian whom Klock had secretly

spirited off on a trip to England a few months before and who claimed that Klock had cheated him of his money and other belongings on the return passage. The Indians took justice in their own agelong way, the only way that was really open to them. They gave Klock a beating, took back the money and valuables, and carried off some papers. Klock promised them to sign the release (indeed, he was in no position to refuse), and a day was appointed when the Indians should return. They returned on June 25, bringing with them a justice of the peace who they innocently supposed would make everything legal and proper as far as the white man's law was concerned. But Klock was nowhere to be found. Enraged, the Indians threatened Klock's family and killed some sheep belonging to his sons.[53]

As Johnson continued his speech, doing his utmost to thwart any possible Six Nations-Shawnee alliance for a frontier war, Joseph may or may not have known that George Klock had sworn out a complaint against the Indians only three days before and had named him, Joseph, as the ringleader of the party. Joseph Brant, declared Klock, had struck him down with a pistol, and four of the others had beaten him senseless. He tried to get the whole party indicted.

Now Sir William, who had been ill, finished speaking and was helped to his room. He was looking spent.

The council had been held in the open air, and so Joseph had another opportunity to gaze around him and admire the beauty of Johnson Hall. But it could have been only the most impersonal sort of admiration that he bestowed on this jewel-like dwelling. He knew, of course, that he could never aspire to anything like it. But there was in him the stirring (strange, to most of his people) of what has come to be known as the American dream. It was manifested in all his little enterprises and his ingenuity, his diligence and his very busyness, and in a sort of pride that was working its way to the surface of his personality.

It was about six P.M. when Johnson left the meeting ground. The sun was still high and hot. The Six Nations must council together and frame their reply to Johnson's speech. This was the usual procedure and nobody supposed that any detail would be changed.

But in two more hours everything on the Mohawk fell apart at the seams.

8

Loyalist and Rebel

A T EIGHT O'CLOCK that hot July evening Sir William Johnson was
dead. The event was not unexpected. Johnson had been in
declining health for years. But his death was unexpected just then and
the rumor soon got out among the Indians that he had killed himself.
Confused, miserable, dumfounded though not really surprised, they
ran about or huddled together, knowing only that they had lost their
best friend. All that night, as was their custom, they cried and wailed
and howled, according to their various temperaments or the strength
of their vocal cords or what was expected of them (for the old women
knew it was proper that their grief should be the loudest), and no
doubt many a handsome paint job that had taken hours to put on got
woefully besmeared and tear-stained. What Joseph Brant felt can only
be surmised. At one blow he had lost a friend, a protector, an em-
ployer—almost, as he then thought, a father. For him the night of July
11 was a night of desolation, the days and nights that followed, a time
of deepest mourning.

Guy Johnson, Sir William's nephew and younger son-in-law, took
immediate charge of department business. Shortly after the great funeral and the formal condolences of the Indians, and with scarcely any
trouble at all, he was able to persuade the Six Nations to keep the
peace. The assembled chiefs not only promised not to help the Shawnees against the Virginians but they also agreed to send deputies to
read the riot act to them and to prevent any other western nations
from coming to their aid. This was as much as Sir William himself
could have done. It was enough to confound rather largely all those
critics who were already proclaiming that there was nobody left who

knew how to deal with Indians. A jubilant Guy, sending the colonial secretary, the Earl of Dartmouth, an account of his proceedings, wrote proudly: "I have the honor to acquaint your Lordship that the Congress with the Six Nations (. . . interrupted by the sudden death of Sir Willm Johnson Bar^t) is now happily terminated and such measures resolved on by that Confederacy as will I trust be very soon productive of advantage to the Public, the Indians having dispatched an Embassy composed of some of the principal men of each nation to the Southward charged with such belts and messages as will I persuade myself have considerable effect at this alarming Crisis . . . ."[1]

Later, Guy wrote a friend in London that he had concluded the treaty in a manner "far Exceeding my Expectations." He told his friend a good many details about Indian affairs and then, before he ended the letter, he mentioned that some American delegates were meeting in Philadelphia. He was referring, of course, to the first Continental Congress that had opened on September 5, 1774, to consider the grievances of the colonies against the mother country. I hope, added Guy, that this "will rather be productive of harmony than disunion." It was obvious, however, that he was much more interested in a coming congress of the Six Nations which was to be held at Onondaga in the fall than in anything that the colonial delegates were likely to do in Philadelphia.[2]

Guy Johnson could well rejoice for he appeared to be undoubtedly on his way to becoming the new superintendent of Indian affairs. He had been recommended by Sir William himself as his successor (after his son, Sir John Johnson, had declined the post—indeed, one may gather that Sir John had had enough of Indians to do him the rest of his life). Guy soon received from General Gage the plum of the hoped-for provisional appointment, good until the king's pleasure could be known, and Gage proceeded to add his own recommendation in the young man's behalf. Certainly Guy had been an efficient deputy under Sir William's direction. He had had charge of much of the department correspondence, and he had carried out Sir William's orders faithfully and well. Guy was also a county judge, a lieutenant colonel and adjutant general of the militia, and a representative in the provincial Assembly. Still fat and a little pompous, he was well aware that he was a prominent and busy man, and likely to become more so; and life looked good.

Sir William's passing was bringing other changes. Sir John Johnson (who had also declined to run for the Assembly) moved out of old Fort Johnson. With his bride of a year, a New York heiress named Mary Watts, he took over Johnson Hall and set out to become a simple gentleman-farmer, landlord to a numerous tenantry, and—his only concession to what was expected of him—a major general of the militia. Sir John had settled his former sweetheart and her two children in a house in Schenectady and probably never thought of her with any great regret, though he sent her money and faithfully paid her bills—which he could well afford. For Sir John, too, life looked good.

Joseph's sister, Molly Brant, left Johnson Hall and returned to Canajoharie. Although deprived of Sir William's affection and guidance, Molly was not bereft in other ways. She had an inheritance and all of her eight minor children had their individual inheritances in real and personal property. Miss Molly, as she was often called, descended upon her home village with her brood and two maidservants and two menservants[3] and a great quantity of goods and baggage (among which were a quilted white ballgown styled in the French mode, two pairs of green velvet leggings, two scarlet cloaks, such fripperies as silken hose and gloves, two hundred silver brooches and three hundred silver crosses, eight hats, a picture, a violin and a set of music books—which, of course, she could not read—fine silver, china, all kinds of bedding, twelve chairs, three side-saddles, a wagon, a chaise, a bateau, and plenty of money);[4] and if she settled down in the already bulging Brant house, as tradition says, one can only wonder *how*. Miss Molly had other houses in the neighborhood, and it would seem more sensible to suppose that she went to one of them. At any rate, she was back home and able to live comfortably and, what was of almost equal importance to her, able to entertain her friends and give them a judicious present or two when circumstances required it. Life, perhaps, did not look too bleak to her though she could never speak of the late Sir William without tears.[5]

To Joseph, also, came some changes. Gradually he was given more work to do by both the Indians and Guy Johnson. But contrary to tradition, he never did become Guy's secretary. That was the job of Joseph Chew, a white man. Joseph Brant, the Indian, could not write or spell well enough to fill such an important position. In all likelihood, he still spoke only broken English. But Guy Johnson continued him as one of his interpreters, and his duties were expanded to include all treaties and negotiations.[6]

So Joseph kept on living at Canajoharie. He remained one of the Reverend Mr. Stuart's regular communicants and always showed up at the church whenever the minister came to preach. In spite of Joseph's attention to religion, the minister probably had some mental reservations about him; "there appears in the Conduct of even the best of them something savage and cruel," said he, speaking of the Indians, and then he added significantly, "especially when intoxicated."[7] But Stuart did admit that there was a "sober Part" among the Mohawks, and there is no evidence whatever to show that Joseph did not belong to it. Canajoharie and Fort Hunter, too, were the scenes of many wild outbreaks—one of Wheelock's missionaries had said of the Canajoharie Indians in 1766 that "they are Drunk half their Time"—but tradition has it that Joseph spent a sober boyhood and youth. Joseph's two children were about seven and five now, and Isaac, the elder, was going regularly to school. The schoolmaster at Canajoharie was an Indian and of course not too well-read himself, but better than nothing. Joseph was a firm believer in education, and when a new schoolmaster had to be hired, he recommended to Guy Johnson a qualified young man he knew at Oquaga.[8] His home village must not be without its school.

Twice, that summer of 1774, George Klock tried to get Joseph and the Indians who had assaulted him, and, indeed, the whole village of Canajoharie, indicted.[9] Apparently he did not succeed. On September 6 the Indians held a meeting with some of the local white people and the sachems explained their troubles and asked for help. The white people, already alarmed by the near riots, came to the Indians' aid and sent a memorial to the acting governor (the governor being absent) in which they roundly condemned Klock and his activities.[10] The first man to sign the document was Hendrick Frey, a colonel of the local militia, and the others were all freeholders of the county. This did not stop George Klock. A few weeks later he wrote a letter to the governor and Council of the province denouncing Joseph Brant by name and complaining about the local militia officers. Brant, he said, "asked Mr. Frey if they [the Indians] should Kill George Klock & distroy his Estate, if he would Rase man against them or not and Mr. Frey said he would not Rase man against them."[11]

Though Guy Johnson had eagerly sought the post of superintendent of Indian affairs, there were times when he must have had some secret misgivings. When he said of Sir William that "I am also conscious of my own Inferiority to Succeed a Gentleman of his consummate knowledge in Indian Affairs,"[12] it was probably the simple truth. When he told the Indians that he felt himself "unequal to the load . . . yet . . . I trust that the *Great Spirit* will give me strength,"[13] he but voiced a very human fear of new and painful responsibilities. One quiet summer afternoon, as Samson Occom, the Indian preacher, happened to be passing by Guy Park, he stopped to pay his respects to the colonel. It was just before sunset, that time so universally devoted to introspection and soul-searching. "Sat a little while with him," wrote Occom in his diary, "found him very Solitary on the account of the Death of Sir William Johnson."[14] Never again would Guy hear the clear, firm instructions to write thus, to speak thus, to do thus, to go to such a place. It must have been a lonely and sobering thought. But the sun sets only once a day, and there were many, many other hours in which Colonel Guy could nourish his ambitions.

Immediately after Sir William's death Guy had sent a message throughout the Six Nations country assuring all the Indians there that "the fire still burns, and the *Road* is open to this place."[15] Joseph may have been one of those entrusted with the message for, on July 22, when Samson Occom passed through Canajoharie and stopped for the night at Joseph's house (where else?), he found the young man absent from home.[16] At any rate, the Indians took their new superintendent at his word, and on September 12–18 about 235 of them gathered at Johnstown. Those who had not already condoled with Guy, did so, and then they gave him a fine new name, Uraghquadirha, or "Rays of the Sun Enlightening the Earth." Nobody thought to mention whether the sun was rising or setting, but Guy was well pleased. Afterwards the chiefs got down to their real business. They announced that the Shawnees had come to Onondaga begging for aid against the Virginians and that there was to be a grand meeting of the whole Confederacy to consider what ought to be done.

Guy had already heard this news and was prepared to deal with it. It had been Sir William's policy to make friends with the Indians when he could, to redress their grievances when possible (and practicable), and to give them presents in public and in private—and, indeed, they had been on a regular dole for years—but his first and last rule of conduct had always been to divide, and rule. This was also Guy's policy. He now reminded the Six Nations of what was a very sore point with them: that their allies were not exactly their allies any more, that their dependents were restive and very weary of being dependent. He blamed the Shawnees for the war on the Ohio; "these people whom you conquered," he said, "are endeavouring to raise themselves above you," and mean to "draw you into a quarrel, & abandon you afterwards." They aim, he declared, "at raising themselves on your ruins."[17] It was a clever speech and Guy hammered home his points in telling fashion. Again Sir William could have done no better.

Afterward Guy gave a "handsome present" to the "Principal men" and detained six of them for a private conference about their conduct at the proposed council. This was also in keeping with Sir William's own procedure. The latter had always had a few chiefs on whom he could "depend." For presents or for friendship, or for both, wittingly or unwittingly, these chiefs had helped steer Six Nations policy into acceptable channels—acceptable, that is, to the Indian department and the British government. Brant Canagaraduncka had been one of these compliant chiefs. Joseph, in his small way, in so far as he could have any influence, was headed in the same direction.

The great Council of the Confederacy opened at Onondaga on November 5. Joseph was present, for he had been sent there by Guy Johnson as an official observer.[18] Apparently he conducted himself so circumspectly as to create no jealousy, a feat in itself. Joseph's written report is still preserved.[19] It reads as well as most reports of Indian councils and must have had a thorough going-over by Guy's secretary, Joseph Chew. Joseph Brant's own handiwork could not have been good enough to go to England, where all such documents were filed, in its original state. The content of the report, however, was what mattered, and that pleased Guy Johnson very much. His six chiefs had done all that was required of them. The Council answered the pleas of the Shawnee deputies with a resounding no. The Six Nations refused to help them and advised them to make peace with the white people. The advice came a little late. The greatly outnumbered Shawnees, had the truth been known, having already been chastened by the Virginians at Point Pleasant on the Ohio, had just concluded a humiliating preliminary peace with Governor Dunmore. The permanent peace treaty was set for the next year. The ties between the unhappy Shawnees and the Six Nations were strained to the breaking point.

After Joseph made his report, some of the Six Nations chiefs came down to Guy Park to confer again with the new superintendent. They told Guy Johnson that Joseph had done an exact job, and they had little to add to the Council minutes. Once more the whole body of the Confederacy complained about the encroachments on the Ohio and, in behalf of the Mohawks, about George Klock and the Corporation of Albany. Then they mentioned that the Onondaga conference had been disturbed by some "strange stories." There were all kinds of rumors going about that the king and his colonies were at outs, that the American people were oppressed, that the king no longer had any regard for the Indians. And why, they asked, had so many troops been sent to Boston? They were referring, of course, to the closing of the port of Boston and the general hubbub that was going on throughout

New England and most of the other colonies. The Mohawk was far away from all this, and the Indian country even farther away, but reports of the growing dissensions could not be stilled.

Guy Johnson worked for the government, and he hoped to remain in the government service. He did not approve of uprisings and rebellions and refusals to pay taxes. He had no patience with associations and committees of correspondence. He did not think highly of liberty poles or of the low sort of people who raised them. Most especially he did not like to see news of such goings-on getting to the Indians. Management of the Indians was already difficult enough, he would have said. His appointment was not yet permanent, his own position none too secure. Very probably he expected that the troubles between the colonies and the mother country would eventually be resolved and calm restored. He had talked a little on these subjects to a few favorite chiefs. He had probably talked to Joseph. But to the Six Nations as a whole he offered no explanations. Any trouble between the white people and the king, he said, did not concern the Indians and they were not to bother their heads about it. But of course the king still loved his Indian children and would always look after their welfare. They would get their usual trade and presents. They were not to worry.[20]

If Guy Johnson's attitude was still largely that of a man who lived far remote from the turmoil, General Gage, who had the task of subduing Boston, had already adopted a different viewpoint. To General Guy Carleton, governor and commander in chief in Canada, Gage had written earlier that year: "As I must look forward to the worst, from the apparent Disposition of the People here, I am to ask your Opinion, whether a Body of Canadians and Indians might be collected, and confided in, for the Service in this Country, should matters come to Extremities; and on what Plan, and what Measures would be most efficacious to raise them, and for them to form a Junction with the King's Forces in this Province?"[21]

General Carleton did not appear to be repelled, or even surprised, by this thought. He replied that he was convinced of the fidelity and zeal of the Canadians. News of the passage of the recent French-oriented Quebec Act[22] had been received by them with much joy and gratitude, and he thought formation of a Canadian regiment would complete their happiness. He was less sure of the Indians, however; "the Savages of this Province, I hear, are in very good Humor, a Canadian Battalion would be a great Motive, and go far to influence them, but you know what sort of People they are."[23]

While the two British commanders were discussing the possibility of getting military aid from the Indians, the Indians themselves were certainly not thinking of taking sides. Unlettered, nearly all of them, they were not able to write very much about their innermost thoughts, and what they said has been filtered through white interpreters. Yet many of them seem to have been genuinely dismayed at the turn of events in the rebellious colonies, and not entirely because they felt something was sure to come of it that would cause themselves hurt. As matters got worse and worse with the white people, there were Indians who said they could not hunt, or eat, or sleep, for worrying. "O," wailed one poor woman, "strange *Englishmen* kill one another. I think the world is coming to an end."[24] The Indians might not understand the cry of "no taxation without representation," but some of them thought of the religious implications of the strife at once. "O Britain! O North America!" exclaimed one of Joseph Brant's former school-mates in anguish, "can the heathens Say, Behold and See how those Christians love one another."[25] What Joseph himself thought, we shall probably never know. Under the influence of Guy Johnson, perhaps at first he did not take the white man's troubles too seriously. In the fall of 1774, while Gage and Carleton were writing their letters back and forth, Joseph's thoughts seem to have been about equally divided among the projected trip to the Onondaga Council, the misdeeds of George Klock, and plans to attend Parson Wheelock's next commencement.[26]

These were the days in which the people of New York's new Tryon County[27] were sorting themselves out and taking sides. In a way some had been sorting themselves out all their lives. Now that it was time to choose between long accustomed authority and the new ideas that were taking root all over the country, some people knew immediately just where they stood. Sir John Johnson was one of these persons. Sir John was genuinely bewildered to hear all that talk about liberty. He said he had liberty. Didn't everybody have liberty? Daniel Claus, Sir William's elder son-in-law and deputy to the Indians of Canada for many years, was another man who knew exactly what he stood for. He thought the rebels "stupid," and he suggested as early as October 1774 that his Indian charges "might easily be brought to fall out with them."[28] The Reverend John Stuart, Anglican missionary to the Mohawks, and the Reverend Samuel Kirkland, Presbyterian missionary to the Oneidas, had no hesitations, either. The one was an ardent Loyalist and the other an ardent Whig. Though both these good men thought they were not meddling in politics, their conversation had a distinct political ring. And with what artless innocence they could sermonize about two different deities!

By the beginning of 1775 relations between Samuel Kirkland and Guy Johnson erupted into open conflict. There had been a strain between the two all that previous fall. Kirkland had been living with the Oneidas since 1766 and without money or presents had managed to gain their affections. They were learning agriculture, had opened a smithy and erected two mills, and had even built themselves a church. The only fly in the ointment, from the viewpoint of a few of the Oneidas, was that Kirkland refused to baptize the children of sinners. Though this was the perennial problem of all missionaries, Anglican as well as dissenting, Guy Johnson seized upon it and encouraged some of his chiefs to complain; and Kirkland's conduct was thoroughly aired at a meeting of the Confederacy at Guy Park in January 1775. Joseph Brant and John Butler were both present as interpreters. This was only one of Kirkland's clashes with Guy Johnson. Between the minister and the superintendent was a political gulf, deep and wide. Kirkland was interpreting the doings of the Continental Congress to the Oneidas and, as he expressed it, opening their eyes. This was a shocking thing to Guy Johnson. But even had Guy been more complacent about Kirkland's activities, General Gage had instructed him to get rid of trouble-making missionaries. Be it said for him, he did try.

Joseph became involved in the difficulties with Kirkland—on Guy Johnson's side, of course. Joseph was very much under Guy's influence. Yet when he got a chance to save his old friend's life, he did not hesitate. Sometime that spring, when both Joseph and Kirkland happened to be at Fort Stanwix, the latter was attacked by hostile Indians. One aimed a blow at him, vowing to kill him. Kirkland tried to defend himself with a chair. At this point Joseph intervened. At no little risk to himself he seized the infuriated Indian. According to Kirkland's own account of the fray, these were Joseph's words: "He is our prisoner, said He, & therefore not to be treated ill, We think him ungrateful to our King, He thinks he does his duty towards his country. Let him then be considered as our enemy, but do not kill him while he is our prisoner—" This stilted sort of talk, reported long after the event, sounds more like Kirkland than Joseph. Yet with some such arguments Joseph was able to calm the Indians, and Kirkland made his escape.[29]

By this time there were some very militant Whigs in Joseph's home county of Tryon. They had organized several committees of correspondence and were concerting measures with similar groups in other counties. But those who called themselves Loyalists were not idle. If the Whigs set up a liberty pole, the Loyalists cut it down. If the Whigs gathered in force, the Loyalists tried to gather in more force. If the Whigs adopted a declaration of grievances, the Loyalists adopted a declaration disavowing any grievances. If the Whigs sent off messengers, the Loyalists stopped and searched them. No Whig was inclined to trust any Loyalist, and vice versa. The Whigs watched Guy Johnson narrowly, for according to widespread rumor he was already tampering with the Six Nations and spiriting them up to attack such whites as he disapproved of. Guy Johnson indignantly denied this. But the Whigs were scared. They knew an Indian council was due to meet soon at Guy Park, and they were afraid of what might come of it. They appointed a committee to go to the Indian country to explain the trouble with Great Britain and try to persuade the Indians not to come down to the settlements. They also began to search for and buy up scarce gunpowder.

In the meantime Guy Johnson was as fearful, as given to seeing bogies, as uncertain of the future as any Whig could possibly be. It would have taken him months to dispatch a letter to England (provided he had the opportunity—and he did not) and get back an answer, and on his own he did not know what to do or which way to turn. It was almost impossible now even to carry on a correspondence with General Gage in Boston—who, moreover, had his own troubles, and no more recent orders from London than Guy himself. But General Gage had authority, and the comfort of an authoritative voice was what Guy longed to hear.

Instead, he heard a report that terrified him. On May 14 he received a letter from a British officer in Philadelphia who had been sent there to spy on the doings of the second Continental Congress. This officer warned Guy that a force was coming from New England to arrest him and carry him off to prison.[30] It was now the turn of the Whigs to deny a rumor. The rebel committees in Albany and Tryon counties insisted they knew nothing of any such plot. But they were no more able to reassure Guy than he had been able to reassure them. He hastily fortified his house and armed his friends and retainers. The Mohawks also went on guard at Guy Park, and they sent a runner with a letter to the Oneidas begging for help. The letter was written by Joseph Brant and signed by him, Johannes Tekarihoga, head chief of the Turtle clan, and two other Mohawks—the latter, probably head chiefs of the Bear and Wolf clans. It was a very official communication.

The runner lost the letter on the road, and it fell into the hands of the local Whigs. Translated from the Mohawk, it read thus:

Written at Guy Johnson's, May 1775.

This is your letter, you great ones, or Sachems, Guy Johnson says he will be glad if you get this intelligence, you Oneidas, how it goes with him now, and he is now more certain concerning the intention of the Boston people. Guy Johnson is in great fear of being taken prisoner by the Bostonians. We Mohawks are obliged to watch him constantly. Therefore we send you this intelligence that you shall know it, and Guy Johnson assures himself and depends upon you coming to his assistance, and that you will without fail be of that opinion. He believes not that you will consent to let him suffer. We therefore expect you in a couple of days time. So much at present. We send, but so far to you Oneidas, but afterward perhaps to all the other nations. We conclude and expect that you will have concern about our ruler, Guy Johnson, because we are all united.[31]

As far as the people of Tryon County were concerned, this might have been considered a harmless letter. It was, after all, only an appeal to the Oneidas to range themselves on the side of their superintendent if the New Englanders came to arrest him. But the Whigs feared the worst. Every day they expected an Indian invasion. They thought any force raised against the New Englanders would be used against them, too. They redoubled their search for powder and lead, resolving, as they said, "to be free, or die." A few days passed, with Whigs and Loyalists watching each other, and no Oneidas in sight, and no Bostonians, either.

Amid all these fears a committee of leading Whigs from Albany and Schenectady called upon Guy Johnson to give him further reassurances, and a conference ensued between them and the Mohawk chiefs at Guy Park. Little Abraham, the principal sachem of Fort Hunter, spoke several times. He promised that the Mohawks would be neutral and begged the white people not to molest Guy Johnson. The Indians could not stand idly by, he declared, and see their superintendent carried off and their council fire put out. The Whig leaders, in their turn, gave the Mohawks assurances that they would keep the peace. But the tensions did not lessen. There was no trust anywhere.

Guy Johnson was in an agony of indecision. The full council of the Six Nations was due shortly at his house, but he did not have enough Indian presents on hand for it and could get no more sent up. Some of the goods and ammunition ordered by his agent had already been confiscated at New York. His expresses to the west had been stopped and searched, and he suspected that his communication with the upper Indians would soon be entirely cut off. With all these thoughts churning around in his mind, he finally decided it would be best for him to go to the frontier himself while he was still able, and hold the conference there. He made preparations to set out. For once, the Whigs were pleased. They thanked him for going to the Indians rather than having so many of them come down to Guy Park. This, they said, might ease the fears of the people. It was the first sincerely civil word they had said to him in months. As matters turned out, it was the last civil word they ever would say to him or of him.

While Guy was getting ready to leave for the west, he finally received an order from General Gage. The letter seems to have come a very devious route, for he got it through the ingenuity of John Stedman, a merchant who held the contract for the portage of government goods around Niagara Falls. The letter was written in cipher. General Gage (his soldiers already bested by the minutemen at Concord and Lexington) ordered Guy to take as many Indians as he could gather together to Canada and join the forces of General Carleton for a joint descent upon the rebels of New England.[32] By this time, of course, the entire thirteen colonies were in an uproar.

Guy Johnson was not the one, at such a time, to question the undoubted voice of authority. Quickly he revised his plans. He increased his white retinue, arranged to take his wife and three young children, collected the Mohawks (ostensibly for the conference) and, with all the Indian presents he could assemble, set out. It was the last day of May 1775. As the great flotilla of bateaux proceeded slowly up the river, numbers of good Whigs breathed sighs of relief and children waved from the banks. The grown-ups were so relieved they at first saw nothing odd in the size of the exodus.

Whatever the thoughts of those on board, they, including Guy Johnson himself, could not have supposed that they were leaving home forever. Some, like the Indians, probably did not even know that they were going to Canada. John Butler, long-time interpreter for the Indian department, must have been one of the latter, for though he took his son Walter, a young attorney, he left his wife and still younger children at home. But Daniel Claus knew, for he took his wife and child along, even as Guy Johnson took all his family. It is impossible to say whether Joseph knew where he was really going. His sister Molly stayed at home; perhaps his mother and wife did, too. But sometime or other Joseph's mother went to her relatives among the Cayugas, and his Oneida wife and children to their Oneida relatives at Oquaga. It is likely that they both left Canajoharie soon. But Molly was a strong-minded woman. This was her home. She was not afraid and, though of course she was loyal to the king, the quarrels of white people, she would have said, did not much concern her.

In all, about 120 white persons and ninety Indians left with Guy Johnson that day. Among the latter were Sir William Johnson's unruly half-breed, William, and Peter Johnson, Molly's oldest child. The latter, not quite sixteen years old, had been gently reared and educated. A boyish young fellow, he spoke French well, had studied dancing and fencing, and was fond of playing the violin. Among the white persons were Guy's local employees in the Indian department and thirty Catholic Highlanders, tenants of the Johnson family. The Highlanders went armed and were to serve as guards. Brant Johnson and his white wife elected to remain at home. So, too, did Sir John Johnson. As heir to Johnson Hall and vast holdings in land, Sir John's position was more unassailable than his cousin Guy's. Moreover, he was not so easily frightened. But Sir John had been presented at court and knighted by the king in person. He was genuinely fond of George III and grateful to him. He vowed he would rather have his head cut off than raise his arm against his sovereign. But when urged by Guy and Claus to go with them, he decided against it. He feared that Lady Johnson's health could not endure such a trip. As he had no public responsibilities, he hoped he could weather the storm.

There is a story to the effect that when Joseph Brant left Johnson Hall for the last time he danced his hatchet along the mahogany stair-rail, making his mark as a sign of his protection for all the Indian war parties in the years to come, to behold and heed;[33] and the cuts in the wood can be seen to this day. But this is just one of the legends that have grown up around Joseph. He could not possibly have known what sort of war was coming to the Mohawk valley. Even if he had known, his mark, if he had a mark, would have meant exactly nothing. Joseph had no authority whatsoever among the Six Nations. All the Six Nations Indians knew Johnson Hall, anyway, and neither Sir John nor the Hall needed protection from them.

There is another story that in those troubled times Joseph's old teacher, the Reverend Eleazar Wheelock, wrote him a long letter to sound out his views and try to win him over to the rebel side. Joseph answered and, recalling the many happy hours he had spent at school, reminded his friend of the prayers and family devotions that took place there every day. He never could forget those prayers, he declared, and certainly not the passage so often repeated "that they might be able to live as good *subjects*—to fear God, and HONOR THE KING!"[34] Perhaps this really happened, but there is no proof.

By June 5 the travelers were at Cosby's Manor, far out on the frontier. Here Guy Johnson wrote his last letter to the Whigs of Tryon County. Joseph's appeal to the Oneidas had not been authorized by him, he said, and he was surprised at those people who have, "either through malice or ignorance, misconstrued my intentions, and supposed me capable of setting the *Indians* on the peaceable inhabitants of this Country."[35] The word "peaceable," of course, was the sticking point. There was a wide divergence of opinion between Guy Johnson and the Whigs as to its true meaning.

At Fort Stanwix, the next stop, Guy received a nasty shock. Some Oneidas, coming to greet him, carefully proclaimed their neutrality! But neutrality was not what Guy had been sent out to get. He immediately wrote an urgent request to General Carleton in Canada for two hundred soldiers. The troops, he declared, were needed to encourage the Indians and keep them from listening to designing men. By designing men, he meant, of course, such persons as Samuel Kirkland, Samson Occom, Joseph Johnson, and other dissenting missionaries who were well-known among the Oneidas. Guy's suspicions of the missionaries were just. Samuel Kirkland had already been applied to by the Massachusetts provincial Congress to use his influence to bring the Six Nations into the war on the side of the rebels. But the neutrality of his own Oneidas was the best that Kirkland had been able to accomplish. The greater part of the Oneidas did not want to interfere in what they called a dispute between two brothers. They would not help either side, they declared. Unfortunately, Indian neutrality was not what General Gage had had in mind, either. With this unpleasant thought to contemplate, a disappointed Guy Johnson set sail upon Oneida Lake and then turned to the northwest toward old Oswego.

To the sensitive Joseph the trip must have brought its memories, of the exciting journey to Niagara in 1759, and to Montreal in 1760, with Sir William and the army, and that other journey to Fort Ontario in 1766 with Peggie when they were young and newly married. Nine long years had passed since that last carefree time, almost a third of his life. Joseph was thirty-two years old now, old enough to feel nostalgia for happier days gone by, and that was getting along. He had come to an age when he might suppose the pattern for his life was set. The future rushed toward him faster and faster but already the future merged into the present, and nothing appeared likely to change.

At Fort Ontario, in late June and early July, the long deferred council finally took place. Present were 1,458 Indians (so Guy Johnson said), men, women and children, mostly of the Six Nations, but two Shawnee deputies were there and some Caughnawagas from Canada, and a few Huron chiefs had come from as far away as Detroit. Most of these Indians had come in quest of presents. Ontario, though the northern gateway to the Six Nations country, was not frequented by the Indians and traders very much any more, and the fort, lonely and falling into ruin, was one of those posts dismantled by General

Gage for reasons of economy. Little Abraham of Fort Hunter, who attended the council, later told the Americans in Albany that Guy Johnson had advised the Indians to sit still and mind nothing but peace, and that the Indians had promised they would be neutral.[36] Guy himself told the British government another story. He said that he had given the Indians a hatchet with which they were to cooperate with the king's troops, and that the Indians had accepted his hatchet.[37] To accept the hatchet, of course, meant that the Indians had agreed to go to war.

The truth lay somewhere in between. Both Abraham and Guy had good reason to say what they knew their listeners wanted to hear. Records are very scanty for those early confused days of the war, but it is almost certain that Guy did offer the Indians a hatchet, and it is equally certain that the Indians took up the hatchet with many reservations, if at all. Subsequent events proved that the Six Nations, though they had had to acquiesce in the downfall of New France, had not forgotten the neutrality which had formerly served them so well. With the exception of a few Mohawks, the Confederates could hope to play off the British and Americans against each other as they had once played off the British and French in a like situation. In 1775 it looked to the wiser heads as though this could be done. What the two sullen Shawnee deputies did or said on this occasion is unknown. They could have been in no mood to cooperate with British, Americans, or Six Nations just then.

The Indians divided their presents and began to go home. The western Six Nations, muttering among themselves that the Mohawks were still slaves of the British, left. Most of the lower Mohawks, on sober second thought, also left. These latter Indians had some good frame houses, plenty of cattle, and several owned farms or plots of land in their own name. Little Abraham spoke for them as well as himself when he said he just wanted to be neutral and live in peace. Even part of the Canajoharies, young warriors as well as older men, went home. In the end Guy Johnson was able to take with him to Montreal 220 persons (he said), including both whites and Indians. There were a few lower Mohawk warriors, some Oneidas from Oquaga, and two or three from each of the other nations sent along as observers. The rest were young men from Canajoharie—the latter village, for obvious reasons, being always the friendliest to the Johnson family. Joseph Brant, William the half-breed, and young Peter Johnson, Molly's son, were among those who went on to Canada. Guy Johnson later claimed that though he did not have enough boats to take all the Indians with him who wanted to go, the latter promised to follow when they were needed. It is not at all unlikely that they did promise. Indian diplomats always had been well versed in the art of making promises.

Guy and the white members of the Indian department, the Scotch Highlanders, some other tenants and friends, and the small body of Indian warriors set out from the wooded shores of Oswego on July 11, 1775. It was exactly one year since the death of Sir William Johnson. It was also the day on which the first of the long series of misfortunes that were to befall Guy Johnson, happened. Mary Johnson, Sir William's younger daughter and Guy's wife, died in childbirth just a few hours before the party set out. She had finally succumbed to the rigors of the long journey in the open boats which Sir John had feared his own wife could not endure. Thereafter Guy seldom saw his children since he could not keep them with him. In a very real sense, he lost his entire family that day. It was only the beginning of his losses.

As the cortege wound its way among the rocks and islands and out into the open St. Lawrence, and bobbed down the swirling rapids, a pall lay upon everybody. Many of the travelers had known Mary Johnson from her childhood. Then, too, news from Montreal was not good. General Carleton had not been able to send soldiers to keep the Indians from listening to designing men. He could not spare any soldiers at all. For the benighted rebels had not only had the folly and madness to join battle with the king's troops in New England; they were now poised to invade Canada, and it really looked as though they might succeed! The French peasants utterly refused to fight. Unlike the upper classes, they had not been especially pleased by the Quebec Act and seemed not to care ΐ all whether they became a fourteenth rebel province.

In the meantime there was a great hue and cry upon the Mohawk River when it was found out where Guy Johnson and his followers had gone. Rumors of the direst sort were flying around. Joseph Brant, who had never led a war party, and Walter Butler, who was too young to have seen any warfare whatsoever, were the subjects of the scariest rumor of all. What a very well-founded rumor it was, is revealed by a letter written on July 13 by two subcommittees of the Tryon County committee of safety to their correspondents in Schenectady and Albany:

Mr. Ebenezer Cox informed this Board, that Mr. Peter S. Tygert told this Informant, that he was informed by a person, who we have Reason to think, has it from good authority, that Col. Johnson was ready with 800. or 900. Indians to make an Invasion of this County, that the same Indians were to be under the Command of Joseph

Brand and Walter Butler, and that they were to fall on the Inhabitants below the Little Falls, in order to divide the people in two parts, and were to march yesterday, or the Day before; Capt. Jacob Clock [old George's son!] informed this Board, that this Morning about an hour before day three Indians of Fort Hunter came to his House from Oswego in their Way home, that he was informed by a free Negroman, a serv^t. of him, that they had each a Bag of powder on their horses, that they staid about an hour and then went off.— From these and other concomitant Circumstances, We have but too much Reason to think, it is true, and that all our Enemies in this County will appear in arms against us, as soon as the Indians are nigh to us, which from the above Information we must expect in a few Days—[38]

But even as the Whigs of Tryon County begged their friends in Albany and Schenectady for men and ammunition, "to save this County from Slaughter and Desolation," Joseph Brant and Walter Butler, quite unaware, were moving farther and farther away. With the rest of Guy Johnson's party, they landed at Montreal on July 17.

Whatever Guy had expected, he was not received with open arms. Governor Carleton who, at best, had a distant and reserved bearing, was not the man to receive anyone with open arms and certainly not any member of the Johnson family. Carleton and Sir William had had some sharp run-ins in the past over trade (Carleton had made it his business to take the part of the French traders), and more than likely, also, the austere Carleton had no very good opinion of Sir William personally. At any rate, the meeting between Carleton and Guy Johnson seems to have been a shade cool on the former's part. Guy explained his instructions from General Gage. Carleton recognized the necessity for gaining the Indians' good will, and he advised calling a council in Montreal with as many Canadian Indians as could be assembled and those Mohawks and others who had come along with their superintendent. But regardless of all Gage's instructions, the governor specified that the Indians were not to fight outside the boundary of the province. Guy Johnson was by no means pleased at this ruling, but he hardly dared to argue about it.

The council took place from July 26 to July 29. Nearly seventeen hundred Indians, so Guy Johnson claimed, were present. These were mainly domiciliated Indians such as the Caughnawagas (descendants of the Mohawks) and others of the Seven Nations of Canada, and some Missisaugas from north of Lake Ontario. They had shown little desire, so far, to join in the war, being swayed by some of the same influences that operated on the French Canadians. Like the latter, they did not yet know where their own interest lay.

The records of this Montreal council are lost, but Guy Johnson said he gave the Indians an even "sharper" hatchet than he had given them at Oswego, and that they accepted it. Thus, according to Guy, both the Six Nations and the Canadian Indians agreed to fight for the British. Perhaps this was true for some of the natives present. Yet at this very moment a portion of the Caughnawagas were on their way to treat with the Americans and most of the eastern Six Nations who had not gone to Canada were gathering for a council in Albany. At the same time the upper Six Nations, clinging to their old policy of neutrality, held themselves coolly aloof from both sides.

During this conference both Johnson and Daniel Claus (long Sir William's deputy for Canada) dwelt heavily on the American colonists' greed for land. Was not the line of 1768 already broken? And in disputes over land who had been the Indians' great friend? The king! They also reminded the Indians of the inability of the rebels to supply them with trade goods. This, too, was a most telling point. The Bostonians,[39] they proclaimed, had no blankets, no kettles, no hoes; they could not even manufacture powder, and such Indians as sided with them would surely starve for lack of ammunition.

One other fact is known about this great council in Montreal. For Joseph Brant it became a fact of supreme importance, and he was to refer to it in his speeches and letters again and again. Governor Carleton assured the Mohawks in the audience that they should not lose by their cooperation with the British but that they should get back all the lands and property that they had had to leave behind, when the war was over. Years later Joseph told the story in these words: "Upon our arrival there [Montreal], this conduct was approved of by Sir Guy Carleton, who, in a public Council, desired us to take up the hatchet and defend our country, and that any losses we might sustain by the war, he promised should be replaced."[40] Though we have only the word of Joseph and other Indians for it, such a promise does not appear unreasonable. It must have been given as they said, for Governor Carleton wished to reassure the Mohawks. It was a simple, straightforward promise, the Indians thought, and so, doubtless, did Carleton. Nobody could misunderstand it.

About five hundred of the Indians sat down in various encampments outside Montreal, and it was not long until their services were required. Late in August the much feared rebel invasion of Canada got under way. Though Lake Champlain was full of boats and soldiers, Carleton's orders against using the Indians south of the forty-fifth parallel still held. He permitted small parties of the "savages" to go to St. Johns, a weakly-held fort on the Richelieu River near the outlet of the lake, and to scout in the neighborhood for intelligence. But nothing else.

Some of the Indians took this prohibition a little hard, and Guy Johnson was baffled. Carleton's attitude did not seem to him to comport very much with General Gage's instructions. Indeed, Carleton's attitude is still a mystery. If he was opposed to Indians *per se*, he never did tell Gage about it. He had written letters on February 4, May 31, June 28, and July 27, in all of which he seemed fully to acquiesce in the use of the "savages" in the war.[41] But apparently Carleton had all kinds of mental reservations about Indians as fighters. In the letter of July 27 he made the usual sort of statement about them that British officers were to make throughout the American Revolution. Though he agreed that it was absolutely necessary to win the Indians over, he let Gage know that he did not put much confidence in them. On August 5, reporting on the Montreal council, he said the Indians appeared to be in very good humor and that they had promised to join heartily against the rebels—but what, he added, can be expected from them further than "cutting off a few unfortunate Families, whose Destruction will be but of little avail towards a Decision of the present Contest—"[42] On October 25, while defending himself against rebel charges of cruelty to prisoners, Carleton declared positively to Lord Dartmouth that "I wou'd not even suffer a Savage to pass the Frontier, though often urged to let them loose on the Rebel Provinces, least cruelties might have been committed, & for fear the innocent might have suffered with the guilty."[43]

Carleton did not reveal any such scruples to Guy Johnson. Always he seemed to imply that much would be done with the Indians if only the Canadians could be persuaded to support the war.[44] Guy got the impression that policy forced the general to restrain the warriors. Carleton's main object at this time was to raise a Canadian militia since he had so few regular troops. Yet the French peasants, who were beset by all kinds of fears (including a fear of being sent to Boston, or even to Spain, to fight) and who did not even want to fight to defend their own province, never would be won over if they got the idea that their English governor was going out of his way to commit aggressions on the Americans.

Whatever the reason, the painted and feathered Indians were used only in the province of Quebec. They served in scouting parties and fought several little skirmishes, and on September 6 they defeated the invaders in a small engagement near St. Johns. This slowed up the advance of the conquering Americans to some degree. Though the latter went on to take Chambly, St. Johns, and even Montreal, General Carleton gained a little time to work on the defenses of Quebec, the capital city.

It was a foregone conclusion that Joseph Brant would do his part in this fighting. Was it not what Guy Johnson wanted? Daniel Claus reported that Joseph served "faithfully" throughout the campaign of 1775,[45] and Joseph himself said he did his utmost to defend Canada.[46] Joseph was not lucky enough to distinguish himself in any way though, since he was stationed at St. Johns for a while, he was probably in the important little fight near the fort.[47] It was young Peter Johnson, Molly's son, who had the luck to distinguish himself. It happened thus: On September 25, Ethan Allen, the conqueror of Ticonderoga, making a rash, ill-timed attempt on Montreal, found himself outnumbered by a party of Indians and whites and surrendered his sword to the enemy who looked most like a gentleman. This happened to be sixteen-year-old Peter, and for this exploit the lad was to get an ensign's commission. Governor Tryon of New York suggested he ought to be made a general!

By mid-August some of Guy Johnson's five hundred warriors had begun to drift homeward. The Canadian peasants were still not in a fighting mood. The Indians, explained Guy, were discouraged at the prospect of carrying on a war single-handed. Besides, it was almost time to set out on their fall hunt; they had their families to think of. In mid-September the Caughnawagas of Canada, impressed by the steady advance of the Americans (and their threats) and by the pleas of the Oneidas and other neutrals who had come up from Albany, actually made peace at the camp of the rebel general, Montgomery, who was then investing Fort St. Johns. For this the so-called Seven Nations of Canada received from the Americans a gift of one thousand dollars. Joseph and Daniel Claus were present while the Caughnawagas were discussing this business with the Oneida deputies, and as he saw the tendency of the negotiations Joseph is said to have exclaimed that "it is over with *Johnson*; all the *Indians* will quit him."[48] He was right. All the Indians left St. Johns. Eventually some of the Canajoharie warriors turned up as far away as Niagara.

In the meantime something had happened which gave Guy Johnson more pause than anything the vacillating Caughnawagas might do. It was an event that intimately concerned himself. On September 10 a certain Major John Campbell, who was related to a powerful French-Canadian family, arrived from England bearing, of all things, a commission as superintendent of the Canadian Indians. This commission, which had been in the making for several years, had the approval of General Carleton who had long looked with disfavor on the way Indian affairs in Canada had been conducted or, as he thought, neglected. At one swoop Daniel Claus, deputy employed by the late Sir William since 1760, was out of a job and Guy could feel the ground quaking beneath his own feet. Guy still held only a temporary commission. Promptly Governor Carleton advised him that he had no authority to command Indians in Canada and that he must discharge the white forces he had brought with him from the Mohawk River. As some officer with influence was desperately needed to hold the Six Nations in line, Carleton seems to have thought that Guy should go to Fort Niagara and take charge of Indian affairs there, or that he should even go to live in the Indian country. But Guy Johnson liked easy living too much and had too great an idea of his own importance to bury himself in the Indian country. Within ten days of Major Campbell's appearance on the scene, Guy had decided to go to England and lay his case before Lord Dartmouth, the colonial secretary. From the viewpoint of his own personal welfare he had now made his second major mistake.

A few Mohawks still remained in Canada, and when they heard their superintendent's decision, they saw a chance to lay their own grievances before the king. It seemed a heaven-sent opportunity. A letter had just been received in which Lord Dartmouth (looking forward to calling upon the Indians for military aid) asked for a summary of Indian grievances and promised to do all he could to redress them. The Indians had been complaining for years; now they thought they were in a position to get some definite action. They deputed Joseph Brant to go with Guy to England.[49] Joseph was capable of making a good speech, and he knew the history of all their troubles. Certainly no one could tell the story of George Klock with greater authority. John Hill Oteronyente, a young warrior of good family, who had just come up from Fort Hunter with messages from Sir John Johnson, was persuaded to go along as prompter. This was old Indian custom. In business of importance, two messengers, a speaker and a prompter, were necessary. Guy Johnson was all the more willing to take the Indians with him in that he hoped their presence would further his own plans. He may even have suggested to the Mohawks in the first place that they should send the deputies.

Having made up his mind what to do, Guy dispatched some of his white employees to various stations among the Indians: Lieutenants John Johnston and William Johnston to the Seneca country, Lieuten-

ant Christopher Kreuser to the Missisaugas, and three other lieutenants and four rangers to Fort Niagara. John Butler, the interpreter, was
promoted to the position of deputy agent and put in charge of Indian
affairs at the latter place. Butler did not want to go to the west. He
wanted to go home, but letters from his family convinced him he
could not return to the Mohawk in any safety. The rebels had officers
posted at various places along the route who were to arrest him on
sight. Reluctantly, Butler allowed himself to be persuaded to accept
the unpleasant, but highly necessary, post at Niagara. In doing so he
won the heartfelt gratitude of General Carleton. The latter, now
beleaguered by the rebels on all sides, took the time to give Butler
careful instructions as to his conduct among the Indians. The new
deputy then set out on his long journey, and Carleton never forgot
who it was who helped him in his darkest hour. But for Guy Johnson
and Claus he felt only a cold disdain. In leaving the country they were
deserting their plain duty. In Carleton's lexicon this was the unpardonable offense.

In due time Guy Johnson and party journeyed down to Quebec,
and Joseph got his first glimpse of the city on the rock. Here he saw
calashes dashing about and ladies in scarlet cloaks and some very fine
houses. He also saw some very dirty streets which, of course, he did
not mind. At the inn all the travelers had to sleep together in one big
room, which he did not object to either, for in a sense it must have
reminded him of home. Joseph was used to snores.

It was a large party to be going so far together. There were Daniel
Claus and his wife and child and Guy's three little girls. Young Walter
Butler was going along, too; he bore Carleton's recommendation,
given, no doubt, for his father's sake. Peter Johnson was also among
the number; he bore a recommendation awarded for his great exploit
in the capture of Ethan Allen. Gilbert Tice, erstwhile innkeeper at
Johnstown and one of the new employees in the Indian department,
also carried with him a recommendation to government because he
had been wounded in the fighting. With their recommendations from
Carleton these three hoped to get commissions. Joseph Chew, secretary in the Indian department, went by virtue of his job. The two
Mohawk messengers, Joseph and John; Guy's cousin, John Dease, also
of the Indian department; the department surgeon; and Guy Johnson
himself brought the number to fifteen. There were possibly some
others. The cold northern winter was setting in. Most of Guy's entourage were afraid to go back home, and they had no means of livelihood.
They looked to England as a place where loyalty might be rewarded.

Guy had put as many of these friends as he could on the Indian department pay roll, but there was a limit to that.

On November 11, 1775, this band of expatriates, who had never intended to go so far for so long a time, set sail from Quebec on the ship *Adamant.* Most of them had never seen England, and apprehension and hope struggled equally for possession of their thoughts. For many of them the future was dark, and for some of them there was no future at all. As for Guy Johnson himself, the man whom the Indians called Uraghquadirha or "Rays of the Sun Enlightening the Earth," the sun in reality was setting. But for one of the travelers the sun was just coming up. Joseph Brant's sun was rising on a storm—but it was rising.

9

Joseph Accepts the War Belt

JOSEPH, who had the run of the ship and who was used to bateaux and hollowed-out logs and bark canoes, no doubt thought the *Adamant* a fine vessel. But Ethan Allen, manacled down in the hold, took a more jaundiced view.

> A small place in the vessel, enclosed with white oak plank, was assigned for the prisoners, and for me among the rest [said Allen, in writing about his captivity]. I should imagine that it was not more than twenty feet one way, and twentytwo the other. Into this place we were all, to the number of thirty-four, thrust and handcuffed . . . . where we were denied fresh water, except a small allowance which was very inadequate to our wants—and in consequence of the stench of the place, each of us was soon followed with a diarrhoe and fever, which occasioned an intolerable thirst. When we asked for water, we were most commonly, instead of obtaining it, insulted and derided—and to add to all the horrors of the place, it was so dark that we could not see each other, and were overspread with body lice. We had, notwithstanding these severities, full allowance of salt provisions, and a gill of rum per day—the latter of which was of the utmost service to us, and probably was the means of saving several of our lives.[1]

Actually, the *Adamant* was larger and more spacious than most ships that carried passengers. It was one of the better merchantmen, and its owner, Brook Watson, a rich banker and former lord mayor of London, was on board. For Guy Johnson and his party who had little to do but eat, drink, and amuse themselves, the time ought to have passed pleasantly enough. But they were bitter about the rebellion in general and all rebels in particular, and there is no reason to doubt Ethan Allen's statement that they came down and gave him many a tongue-lashing. Only Daniel Claus, said Allen, refrained from reviling him but, as he makes no mention of the Indians, perhaps they refrained, too.

In about forty days the *Adamant* reached the port of Falmouth in southwestern England. A great crowd was on hand, for Ethan Allen, the conqueror of Ticonderoga, was famous in Europe. People lined the wharf and gaped at him from windows and climbed to roofs to watch. They must have stared also at the two young Indians, considering them a fascinating added attraction. Though the gentlemanly Peter Johnson probably escaped notice, Joseph and John were unmistakable. Their features, their dark skin, and at least part of their garb and equipment betrayed them. There is no record as to how they took this scrutiny, whether they shrank from it or carefully allowed their weapons to show.

Soon after the party arrived in London, Guy Johnson, in behalf of himself and the two Mohawk deputies, requested an interview with the colonial secretary. The latter turned out to be not Lord Dartmouth whom the travelers had expected to meet but a new appointee, Lord George Germain. Germain, though scarcely two months in office, had already become a key figure in the government and, as time went on, he was to accumulate to himself almost the sole management of the war against the colonies. A favorite of George III, and with no little strength of character, the new secretary was to fill a power vacuum in the weak and squabbling North ministry. But Lord George was also arrogant and uncompromising, determined to uphold the full authority of the king and Parliament. He meant to put down the American rebellion and had no qualms whatever as to methods. Lord Dartmouth had finally become willing to enlist the Indians in the struggle. Germain was not only willing; he was eager. To this end he instructed Guy Johnson to put all pertinent information about Indian affairs in writing.

It was a very long communication that Guy addressed to Germain on January 26, 1776.[2] He described the Indians' grievances in detail, and in a separate paper drawn up by his secretary, Joseph Chew, recounted all that he and the Indians had accomplished since they left their homes on the Mohawk.[3] If they had not been able to save Canada, at least they had protracted its fate. Guy had been in London long enough to hear some gossip for he did not hesitate to hint to Germain what impressive successes the Indians might have achieved if only they had met with proper support from the authorities in Canada. This implied censure of General Carleton was the sort of thing which no one in Guy's precarious situation would have dared to utter had he not been very sure that it would be welcomed. And he was right; anything against Carleton whom he heartily disliked, was welcomed by Lord George Germain.

At long last Guy Johnson got down to the matter nearest his heart: the hoped-for appointment as superintendent of Indian affairs. This was the true business he had crossed the ocean for, and he described in much detail the powers and military rank the Indians (who loved him) requested that he should have—all which suggestions he offered "at the desire of the Indians and from a thorough conviction that an attention thereto will produce solid advantage to the Crown." In closing, Guy referred Germain to the two deputies themselves. Said he confidently (for there was nobody to dispute him): "The Indian Chief who accompanied me, with his companion, are persons of character and influence in their country; they can more at large speak on any matters that may be required of them."[4] The implication was clear that the "Chief" could, if he chose, do much more than merely speak.

Guy's carefully thought-out letter brought quick, and delightful, results. On February 29 he had the pleasure of presenting the influential Joseph and John to His Majesty, George III. This interesting event occurred at St. James's palace, and it was duly mentioned in *The London Chronicle*, a newspaper which specialized in gossip and chitchat, under date of March 1. Said the *Chronicle:* "The two Canadian [sic] Chiefs are come to this Court to offer the King their assistance, and also to assure him of their fidelity on all occasions." Needless to say, the chiefs had been "graciously received."[5] A few days later the same gossip sheet reported that the two chiefs were to carry home with them "some curious military accoutrements as presents to some other chiefs in alliance with them."[6] It was speculated that they would return with General John Burgoyne who (the rumor was all over London now) was to supersede General Carleton as commander of the British forces in Canada.

Joseph's presentation at court was not mentioned in any further detail, but Madame Riedesel has described a similar ceremony she attended the next year. Said she:

> I found the castle very ugly, and furnished in old fashioned style. All the ladies and gentlemen were stationed in the audience room. Into this room came the king, preceded by three cavaliers. The queen

George III, Queen Charlotte, and Their Six Eldest Children, 1771. Painting by John Zoffany. In all the vicissitudes of his life Joseph never lost his admiration and affection for George III. Yet it was said that, for political reasons, he refused to kiss the king's hand though he gallantly kissed the hand of the queen. *Courtesy of The Queen's Gallery, Buckingham Palace Road, London. Property of Her Majesty The Queen. Copyright reserved. Photograph by A. C. Cooper Ltd.*

followed him, accompanied by a lady, who carried her train, and a chamberlain. The king went round to the right and the queen to the left. Neither passed by any one without saying something. At the end of the drawing room, they met, made each other a profound bow, and then returned to the place whence they had started. I asked Lady Germaine how I should act, and whether the king, as I had heard, kissed the ladies? "No," she replied, "only Englishwomen and marchionesses; and that all one had to do, was, to remain quietly standing in her place."

But the king did kiss pretty Madame Riedesel (even though she was German and only a baroness), and she blushed. Shortly afterward came the queen, making her return circuit of the room, and she, too, was very friendly. "During this reception," added Madame Riedesel, "I saw all the royal children, with the exception of one that was sick. They were ten in number, and all beautiful as pictures."[7]

With the exception of the kissing and the number of the royal children, who were one less at Joseph's presentation, the two ceremonies must have been about the same. As to the kissing, Joseph would have been expected to kiss the king's hand, but there is a curious tradition that he proudly refused. The newspapers drop no hint of this, but if Joseph did refuse it was probably on the ground that he was the emissary of the Six Nations who were allies of the king but not his subjects. This was certainly a distinction which he would have had firmly in mind. The tradition goes on to say, however, that Joseph gallantly kissed the queen's hand.[8] Yet Joseph was completely won over by the king. He sincerely admired George III. "I have had the honour to be introduced to the King of England—" he once said years later, "a finer man than whom I think it w^d be a truly difficult task to find."[9]

The requested interview with Lord George Germain took place two weeks later. If, after their great day at St. James's, the visitors from America had any real trepidations, they were soon made easy. The usually distant colonial secretary was genial and charming. His acquaintances, could they have seen him, would have been amazed. Lord George did not know much about America and even less about Indians and nothing about "chiefs," but he did know, as he expressed it later, that "The Dread the People of New England &c have of a War with the Savages, proves the Expediency of our holding that Scourge over them."[10] Here, now, in front of him, in the persons of this fat provincial officer and the two swarthy natives, stood the Scourge. Lord George was affability itself.

Joseph, as befitted his great importance as a leader of the savages, was permitted to do most of the talking. After some careful opening remarks about how troubled the Six Nations were about the disturbances at home and how much they had always loved the king and what they had done last year in defense of Canada and how little they had been supported (for on this question Joseph naturally had no original thoughts), he passed on to the subject he innocently considered his real business. This was what *he* had crossed the ocean for.

Brother [so Joseph addressed the noble lord]. The Mohocks our
particular Nation, have on all occasions shewn their zeal and loyalty
to the Great King; yet they have been very badly treated by his
people in that country, the City of Albany laying an unjust claim to
the lands on which our Lower Castle is built, as one Klock and
others do to those of Conijoharrie our Upper Village. We have been
often assured by our late great friend Sr William Johnson who never
deceived us, and we know he was told so that the King and wise men
here would do us justice; but this notwithstanding all our applications has never been done, and it makes us very uneasie.

Joseph then mentioned a minor mistake in the boundary line of 1768
and added a request for missionaries of the Church of England, but he
quickly returned to the subject nearest his heart. "Indeed it is very
hard," he continued, "when we have let the Kings subjects have so
much of our lands for so little value, they should want to cheat us in
this manner of the small spots we have left for our women and children to live on. We are tired out in making complaints & getting no
redress."[11]

Lord George was kindly and reassuring. He all but patted the two
young warriors on their heads as he set out to win their aid. Though he
had no actual war belt to tender, he knew the right words. Joseph later
reported to the Six Nations that "his Lordship reply'd, he was well
acquainted with our Loyal behaviour in Canada and returned us his
most hearty Thanks, and he said respecting the Lands which was
wrongfully taken, he Knew every Circumstance that I related to be
true, but on Account of these Disputes they could not attend to them
but that I might rest assured, as soon as the troubles were over, every
Grievance and Complaint, should be Redress'd & he hop'd the Six
Nations would to fulfill their Engagements with Government as they
had ever done, and in Consequence of which, they might rest assur'd
of every Support England could render Them."[12]

It must have appeared to Joseph an ironclad promise. That it was
also a promise wholly dependent upon England's ability to win the war
caused him no uneasiness. Deeply impressed by the signs of wealth and
power he saw on every hand, the thought never occurred to him that
England might not emerge the victor. But far more sophisticated
persons than Joseph, that spring of 1776, did not question England's
ultimate victory.

As for Lord George Germain, he felt that his meeting with the
Indian ambassadors had accomplished its prime object. He had not
the slightest idea of Joseph Brant's real position nor of how the Six

Nations actually conducted their affairs. "Of the good will and Affection of the Indians," he remarked happily, "there seems to be little doubt, if they are managed with Attention, and proper Persons employed to negociate with them."[13] The London papers soon carried the news of Guy Johnson's appointment as superintendent of Indian affairs with the same powers that Sir William Johnson had had. There was one difference which the papers did not mention: Guy had no authority in Canada. Major Campbell retained charge of the Canadian Indians. Though this left Daniel Claus, Sir William's former deputy in that country and Guy's brother-in-law, out in the cold, Guy was not much disturbed. He had got what he came to England for. He did not realize what a poor impression he had made on the colonial secretary. The truth was, from the very first Lord George Germain considered Guy Johnson incompetent.[14] His appointment had been made for lack of anything better. It was the good will of the Indians themselves, not the efforts of the superintendent, that Germain put his faith in.

Joseph's appearance at court and his endorsement by the ministry quickly conferred on him a sort of social distinction. Several noble and highly-placed gentlemen, as the saying went, "took notice" of him, and then, of course, society in general adopted him. He became a new and strange kind of lion, and it was chic to be seen in his company. Indians always had been a great novelty in London. But now they were not only a novelty, they were worth courting—and certainly so important a chief as Joseph Brant, who, it was rumored, had but to raise up his hand and three thousand warriors would come running, was worth courting. Though Joseph's entry into fashionable circles was no doubt at first promoted by the government, his continued acceptance must have owed something to his own personal qualities. Here again his smattering of education stood him in good stead. The Reverend Eleazar Wheelock, at far-away Dartmouth, exerting himself to the utmost for the rebel cause, might have been a little chagrinned at his pupil's progress, had he known. Joseph was certainly the most presentable Indian who had ever been seen in London.

Joseph even managed to get on good terms with the Whig opposition.[15] One little encounter with the opposition which he himself later told about took place at a masquerade ball. Masquerades were a very popular form of entertainment, lasting all night and sometimes till nine o'clock the next morning. The maskers made merry with dining and dancing and drinking; gallants sometimes got into sudden fights over their wives or someone else's wives or ladies who were nobody's wives; and sometimes the window draperies caught fire or somebody a

Joseph Brant, 1776. Painting by George Romney. Joseph is 33 years old, he is in London, and has already declared for the king. He has no inkling of what lies ahead, and he looks unworried. *Courtesy of The National Gallery of Canada, Ottawa.*

little unsteady fell down the stairs. At such affairs Joseph was a natural success. Masked balls gave him a chance to dress up (a thing he loved), and he looked fearsome, and was happy. Boisterous revelers bothered him not. He had seen and heard far worse in Canajoharie

any time the Indians could get a keg of rum. At one of these masquerades a certain nobleman came up to him and, noting his tomahawk (for Joseph was wearing his Indian finery), asked him in a
meaningful sort of way if he intended to lift it against the Americans.
Joseph, sensing the other's sentiments in favor of the rebels, politely
answered no. Whereupon (according to a British officer to whom he
later told the story) the nobleman "replied, he was glad to hear it, he
hoped all the Indians were of the same way of thinking for the Americans were an injured people, and with a seeming degree of Satisfaction
Kissed his Tomahawk."[16] Such pro-American sentiments, of course,
could not shake the young man who felt sure he knew exactly where
the true interests of the Indians lay.

One of those noblemen who took notice of Joseph was the Earl of
Warwick. It was probably at the earl's desire that Joseph sat for his
portrait to the great English artist, George Romney. There were at
least two sittings in Romney's studio in Cavendish Square, one on
March 29 and another on April 4.[17] The resulting work hung in
Warwick Castle for many years. It shows a three-quarter figure attired
in Indian blanket, plumes, and a silver gorget (but wearing a fine,
ruffled shirt nevertheless!) and holding a tomahawk in his hand. The
countenance is smooth and tranquil and handsome. It betrays no hint
of soul-searching, no slightest inner turmoil. The youthful naivete in
Joseph's face wholly belies his thirty-three years. He appears well-fed,
even a little plump.[18] Though Joseph in the flesh may not have looked
quite so innocuous—for Romney did not probe deeply into character—the picture must have been a good likeness. Joseph himself heartily approved of it, and Lord George Germain later had a box of prints
made as a present for him.[19]

John, Joseph's Mohawk companion, was not permitted to feel
even a twinge of jealousy. His portrait was painted by Mrs. Richardson, an artist well thought of in her day, and the British government
paid the cost of four pounds four. The ministry could not afford to take
the chance of alienating John. Guy Johnson's portrait, with Indians in
the background, symbolic of his important office, was also painted,
though presumably at his own expense. He sat to the expatriate
American, Benjamin West, and certainly got his money's worth.
West made Guy so lithe and handsome that nobody back home on the
Mohawk would have recognized him. But that was all right, for nobody back home ever saw the picture.[20]

In spite of Joseph's social success and his acceptance by the elite,
he continued to live at the common inn where he had stopped when
he first came to London. He had been committed to Gilbert Tice's
care at that time by Guy Johnson (Tice had been a great friend of the

late Sir William and, in fact, Sir William had saved him from debtor's prison), and the two of them, and possibly John, had put up at The Swan with Two Necks, in Lad Lane. Later, when Joseph was given the opportunity to move to better and more permanent quarters, he refused to budge. It seems he had taken a liking to the Swan's proprietor and the servants, and so he spent his entire London stay in the plebeian atmosphere of Lad Lane.[21]

The Swan with Two Necks must have been a very busy place. Like many London inns, it probably was a sort of coach station and travelers' waiting room. In all likelihood it also had its Saturday-night pay tables and its clubs of various kinds. People must have been coming and going all the time. This hubbub was what Joseph was used to; quieter, more elegant lodgings would not have suited him nearly so well. The same was true of John, and as for Tice, he had been an innkeeper himself, in Johnstown. The Swan was their home away from home. No wonder the trio became such fast friends with everybody in the place that they could not be torn away. But Lord George Germain must have thought it very odd.

Though Joseph was still getting his salary as an interpreter and John was on the pay roll, too, their expenses in England had been assumed by the Indian department, and Guy Johnson kept them both regularly supplied with funds. Both bought all kinds of knickknacks and souvenirs and presents for their families back home. Besides these things Joseph was to take back with him jewelry, new clothing, and a fusil and a pistol, all paid for by the British government,[22] as well as a watch and a silken banner, gifts of the king.[23]

From time to time Tice and his two Indian charges went nosing about London. They covered a great deal of ground, saw the sights with tourists from the continent, and probably got footsore as so many sightseers before and after them. They also visited Newmarket (for the races, no doubt), Windsor (the castle), Portsmouth (the navy yard), and similar places of interest. But what impressed Joseph most was the Tower of London.[24] There was nothing like that back home on the Mohawk, not even at Johnson Hall. One fine March morning Joseph was in the crowd that watched the king review some companies of foot guards on Wimbledon Common. The soldiers went through their exercises with great dexterity, forming themselves into squares, then demonstrating platoon and circular firing, and finally ending with a general running fire of pursuit till each man had used up thirty-two rounds of powder. Joseph, who had adorned himself suitably for the occasion in his war paint, was considerably taken aback. He had seen nothing like that at Niagara or down on the Susquehanna. "This may do here," he was heard to exclaim, "but it won't do in America!"[25] It was a trenchant thought but apparently he did not harbor it very long.

On April 18 Joseph and Gilbert Tice attended a subscription ball at Haberdashers' Hall. Here they mingled with a genteel company of ladies and gentlemen from the city and got into conversation with an interesting new acquaintance. The latter, a journalist and bon vivant named James Boswell (whose great *Life of Samuel Johnson* was still fifteen years in the future), took an immediate liking to Tice and scented a newsworthy story in Joseph. On the spur of the moment Boswell decided to write an article about Joseph and asked permission to call on him for an interview.

Two days later Boswell showed up at The Swan with Two Necks ready to drink tea with Joseph and Tice. The interview, which appears to have been as much with Tice as with Joseph, was continued later the same day at another meeting place. Joseph consented to sit for a drawing for a print which was to accompany the article. There was a little more talk at Forbes's on April 22.[26]

James Boswell's impressions of Joseph Brant were published in *The London Magazine* a few months later. Boswell obviously thought Joseph was the head chief of the Mohawks, though he said he did not look it, especially in English dress. He was apparently a little disappointed that Joseph "had not the ferocious dignity of a savage leader"—on the contrary the chief's manners were gentle and quiet, he spoke English very well, and was engaged in a translation of the New Testament into Mohawk. It just goes to prove, added Boswell, that education can tame even the wildest race.

Joseph had been struck with the appearance of England in general, but he had said he "chiefly admired the ladies and the horses." Not only could Joseph give the right answers; he could give them in the right order! Boswell, who liked to collect celebrities, was pleased to hear that Joseph was the grandson of one of the Mohawk chiefs who had created a sensation in England in Queen Anne's time. What Boswell did not know was that one Mohawk word for "grandfather" could mean any of a grandfather's brothers or half-brothers. And if Joseph did, indeed, refer to this less specific kinship, Joseph's English, or Tice's interpretation of Joseph's Mohawk, was hardly equal to explaining the difference.

The Mohawks had made great progress since Queen Anne's day, recorded Boswell. Their very name had once inspired fear and terror. But now, he told his readers, they live in a fixed place, have good houses, cultivate land with industry and skill, are converted Christians, and trade with the British colonies. When the civil war broke out in America, chief Brant, who had been solicited by both sides for help, had been perplexed by the many different arguments. He had finally crossed the sea in order to find out the truth from the king himself. Just how the chief has been convinced of the justice of the British cause, we have not been informed, added Boswell, but it is said he has promised to help government by bringing three thousand men into the field! This was the story that Joseph, Tice, or *somebody* told James Boswell.[27]

Those three thousand warriors were to open for Joseph still another door. On April 26 he was initiated into the Falcon Lodge of Masons, a lodge of the Moderns on Princess Street, Leicester Fields, London. No less a person than George III is said to have presented him with his apron.[28] This was flying high, indeed. There had been a Masonic Lodge in Johnstown since 1766 but nobody had ever thought of admitting Joseph to it, or any other Indian.

But all good things must end. On May 7 the Indian department, as represented by Joseph and John and Guy Johnson and probably some others, had a final interview with Lord George Germain. By this time Joseph was no longer a mere chief; he had been promoted to a sachem, one of the hereditary leaders of the Six Nations! Joseph Chew, Guy Johnson's secretary, took down Joseph's remarks in writing, and this is what he said "Sachem" Thayendanegea told Germain:

Brother.
When we delivered our speech you answered us in few words, that you would take care and have the grievances of the Six Nations on account of their lands, particularly those of the Mohocks and Oughquagas, removed; and all those matters settled to our satisfaction whenever the troubles in America were ended, and that you hoped the Six Nations would continue to behave with that attachment to the King they had always manifested; in which case they might be sure of his Majesty's favour and protection.

Brother. We return you thanks for this promise, which we hope will be performed, and that we shall not be disapointed, as has often been the case, notwithstanding the warm friendship of the Mohocks to his Majesty and his government, who are so immediately concerned, that the same has been often mentioned by the Six Nations and their getting no redress a matter of surprize to all the Indian Nations.

We are not afraid Brother, or have we the least doubt but our brethren the Six Nations will continue firm to their engagements with the King their father. Our Superintendant knows that in order to keep true to their treaties they have at times punished their friends and Allies.

Brother. The troubles that prevail in America and the distance we are from our country, allows us only to say that on our return we shall inform our Chiefs and Warriors what we have seen and heard and join with them in the most prudent measures for assisting to put a stop to those disturbances notwithstanding reports of their generally taking the strongest side. Which was not the case last Summer when we offered to prevent the invasion of Canada and lost several of our people in defending it. The only reason we mentioned the conduct of the Six Nations at that time was, that they might have credit for what they actually did, as we have heard much that affair has been attributed to the Nippissings and other Indians of Canada.

Brother. As we expect soon to depart for our own Country having been long here, we request you, and the great men who take charge of the affairs of government, not to listen to every story that may be told about Indians; but to give ear only to such things as come from our Chiefs and wise men in Council; which will be communicated to you by our Superintendent.[29]

This was, undoubtedly, as near to a lecture on good faith in government as the powerful secretary was likely to hear from anybody. Yet Joseph had made no claim of personal authority nor had he said anything about three thousand warriors. He had said he would report Germain's promise to the Six Nations. This was the correct procedure. Naturally he would do his utmost to get the councilors to declare for Britain. He had wanted to make the best bargain for them that he could. But as far as he was concerned as an individual, he had already accepted the war belt. He had accepted the war belt when he fought last summer in Canada. Anything more he could do was only a formality. Joseph belonged to the Indian department. From the highest to the lowest, the Indian department was loyal. In a very real sense Joseph also belonged to the Johnson family, and certainly the Johnsons were loyal. But over and above these considerations, Joseph was concerned about the welfare of his people. Again and again he would explain his motives for espousing the British cause. When, in later life, he wanted to make a fine speech to impress the Indian superintendent or some other British official, he would speak eloquently of the covenant chain of friendship between his forefathers and theirs, and of how the Mohawks had always cherished it and kept it bright. Those ancient engagements with the king he himself had always held sacred, he said. But Joseph Brant was not always speaking to British officialdom. Sometimes he spoke plainly to his own people as, for instance, about 1804, when he declared, "Every man of us thought, that by fighting for the King, we should ensure to ourselves and children a good inheritance."[30]

Soon after this last interview with Lord George Germain the long visit to London came to an end. Joseph and John set out with Tice to the port of Falmouth, traveling via Exeter, in a coach. And if the coachman roared drunkenly and swayed precariously on his box, as so often happened, it was no more than Joseph was used to, and he would not have been much alarmed. A convoy was assembling at Falmouth. The ship assigned to the trio was a merchantman, a little snow, a brig with a trysail, called the *Lord Hyde*. The little vessel, in deference to the perils of the voyage, had been armed with twelve three-pounders.[31] Already American privateers roamed the Atlantic, preying upon British shipping from Nova Scotia to the West Indies.

At Falmouth the travelers equipped themselves with all kinds of supplies, including still more clothing for Joseph and John.[32] The crossing was not likely to take less than a month and might take a great deal more, and passengers had to be prepared for almost any eventuality.

While the two Mohawks were getting ready to sail, something happened in America which was to produce one of the strangest of the Brant legends. An engagement was fought at a place called the Cedars, about forty miles above Montreal, in May 1776. A party of wild Missisauga Indians from west of Lake Ontario joined in the fray. They fought for the king, and they claimed for their own, to torture and put to death, a certain wounded rebel prisoner, a New Yorker named John McKinstry. Joseph Brant, so the story goes, ransomed Captain McKinstry, giving the Indians instead an ox to feast upon. After the war, it is said, Joseph and McKinstry became great friends. They were both Masons, and Joseph sometimes visited the white veteran at his home in Livingston Manor. Thus the story ran and was vouched for by McKinstry's family to William L. Stone, Joseph Brant's early biographer.[33] And posterity is left with three piquant, unanswered questions: Who did save John McKinstry's life? What forged the bond of friendship between him and Joseph Brant? Or was the whole story, from beginning to end, a myth? Certain it is, that Joseph was in England at the time the battle of the Cedars took place.

Joseph and his friends set sail in early June.[34] Most of the other Indian department travelers (some having met with a modicum of success in England and some not) were again on board: among them, Guy Johnson, his secretary Joseph Chew, and the surgeon, Dr. John Constable. Absent were young Peter Johnson who had obtained a commission as ensign and was to sail with his regiment, and Daniel Claus, the ex-deputy to Canada, who was not yet ready to return. Claus had had no luck in getting another appointment, and he was resolved to wait it out in the British Isles a while longer.

The fleet's destination was New York. Guy Johnson's orders were to remain in New York, that province being nearest to his Indian charges. It was expected that General Howe, the British commander there, would in time advance up the Hudson to join another British army coming down from Canada. Guy was to go along in Howe's expedition and make himself useful in his role as superintendent of the Six Nations. At any rate, this is what Guy always maintained his instructions were, and there is nothing to disprove his claim. But as Lord George Germain later confessed, *he* did not much care where Guy went. As far as he was concerned, he might as well stay in New York as anywhere.[35] Guy, naturally, did not know this. He was happy he had his appointment, happy that his superior talents had been recognized, very happy that the Indians were to be induced to join in the war. Getting the Indians into the war had been his main objective, next to clearing up his own status. The more Indians in the fight, the more important the Indian department; and the more important the Indian department, the more invaluable, even indispensable, would Guy Johnson become. Such are the motives, sometimes, of men.

Now, again, as the party sailed homeward, there was nothing to do but eat and drink, visit the other ships of the convoy when the wind was fair, or stagger about when the gales howled. During foggy nights trumpets were blown to warn off the other vessels, and the men-of-war fired cannons every hour to prevent straggling. On Sundays, if the weather permitted, religious services were held on deck, and the crew, hard-bitten though they were, got down on their knees to pray. All this was normal life at sea that summer of 1776.

The fleet spread out over a great expanse of ocean, making a southward course because of the prevailing winds. At one time Joseph's ship, the *Lord Hyde*, found itself as far south as the twenty-seventh parallel. It was a long passage, and in the final three weeks rebel privateers were a constant harassment. Near Bermuda, about mid-July, the *Lord Hyde* fought a naval engagement. The fight took place in such close quarters that Joseph and John with their new firearms and expert marksmanship were able to distinguish themselves and work some havoc upon the enemy. The little *Lord Hyde* was badly damaged, but the rebel privateer finally gave up the attack. At last, on July 29, 1776, the weary voyage ended and the travelers landed safely at British-held Staten Island.[36] Across the bay lay the rebel-occupied city of New York.

It was a vastly different country and vastly different circumstances to which the travelers returned. The thirteen united colonies had formally declared their independence. The Continental Congress now functioned as a central government, and General George Washington was the man of the hour. But the rebel Americans had not been able to hold on to Canada. Smallpox, the Canadian winter, and the indomitable Guy Carleton had driven them out. The invading General Montgomery had been dead in the swirling snow at Quebec these past seven months. His tattered forces were clinging by the weakest of holds to Fort Ticonderoga at the outlet of Lake George. Never again throughout the war would a regular American army set foot on Canadian soil. There was to be no fourteenth united colony.

During the long period that Joseph had been away and while all these changes had been occurring, many people in America refused to take an active part in the struggle between mother country and colonies. Some of these people did not comprehend the issues. Others simply did not care. The rest were Loyalists, or Tories, as the rebels now called them, who tried to maintain at least a semblance of neutrality. They hoped against hope that the dangerous situation would quiet down. It was supposed that rebellious neighbors would somehow come to their senses. But time wore on and the rebellious neighbors did not oblige. On the contrary, they grew more restless, peremptory, demanding. Suspected Loyalists were increasingly harassed, as one of their number put it, by "Committees, Congresses, & Minute men." They were not permitted to bear arms. They were watched. They were questioned. Their movements were restricted. The pressure to take a stand against Parliament and the king was almost irresistible. It was almost unbearable, too, and sometimes the pressured were prompted to talk back. "We have as good Men among us, as you have, and we will shew you the same," avowed one Peter Bown, standing at the front door of Johnson Hall. And one Thomas Baxter, defying the Tryon County committee of safety, spoke his mind about that august body, describing it as just "a d . . . d club of people." And a certain Lewis Clement, as he fled northward, roundly cursed some neighborhood rebels upon whom he blamed his troubles. "Is it not a pity," he exclaimed, between oaths, "that I being a Man of a good Estate must go and leave the same for the sake of these d . . . d Fondas"![37]

Persons that Joseph knew well, or knew slightly, or had heard of, or had never heard of at all but would sometime know very well, were coming at last to their hard decisions. Sir John Johnson, after a year of struggle with the Tryon County committee of safety, gave up and fled through the wilderness to Canada, taking with him 170 of his loyal Scotch tenants. The committee thought Sir John was corresponding with their enemies and planning an uprising of Indians and Loyal-

ists—which, indeed, he was, though he vowed he was not; and Sir
John thought the rebels were getting ready to march against him—
which, indeed, they were, though they vowed they were not. Sir John
could not understand what the rebellion was all about, and he had
reason to fly, but it was to cost him dearly.

The young half-breed, William Johnson, who had gone off on the
long trek to Canada and who it was reported had been killed in the
action at St. Johns, had unabashedly returned home that fall to Canajoharie, much to the indignation of the local patriots. As William was
not one to blush unseen or to brag unheard, he soon got into trouble.
Before the end of 1775 he killed a man in a tavern brawl and fled the
country, this time for good. Brant Johnson, the quieter half-breed,
was to stick it out till the fall of 1776, and then he, too, would flee,
leaving his not inconsiderable property. Joseph's sister, Molly Brant,
still lived at home with her younger children, and perhaps her
widowed mother, though, again, the latter may have already taken
refuge with her Cayuga relatives. Molly kept in the background and
was not much talked about, but she was watched. By this time, no
doubt, Joseph's wife and children were safe at her father's at Oquaga,
far down the Susquehanna. And out in seething Pittsburgh two men
whom Joseph would come to hate and one whom he would try to
befriend were still treading their wary way as secret Loyalists. Alexander McKee, the late Sir William Johnson's deputy agent for the west,
and Matthew Elliott, trader extraordinary, and one Simon Girty,
interpreter to the western tribes, had not yet unmasked themselves by
the precipitate flight to Detroit.

Families everywhere were torn apart by dissensions. Alexander
McKee's brother turned rebel. Not all of the Girtys stuck to the king.
Most of John Butler's relatives were rebels in Connecticut. And
Joseph's former neighbor, Nicholas Herkimer, now a major general in
the Tryon County militia, had a brother, John Joseph Herkimer,
confined in jail as a suspected—and rightly so—Loyalist. Henry Glen,
patriot leader in Schenectady, pleaded for a Tory brother-in-law in
simple words: "I am unfortunate that I have some near relations differs
with me in sentiment about the times, though I am determined to
stick to the principle I set out upon to the last, let the consequences be
what it will, [yet] . . . I have that humanity and have a feeling for a
sister and four young ones."[38] It was a hard time to be alive.

If white people were in confusion, how much more so the Indians.
And if many white people, during Joseph's long stay in England, were
trying to cling to a neutrality, real or assumed, how much more so his
own people for whom that policy had always been the best defense.

It had been easy for the Indians to claim neutrality while General Montgomery was pushing his way through the heart of Canada, when it was not clear who was going to control the St. Lawrence River and the trade route up the lakes, and when nobody, rebel or British, had the power to force the natives to take a stand. The Caughnawagas of the upper St. Lawrence protested their peaceable intentions to Washington in August 1775 and made a treaty with the Americans at Albany the following winter. About the same time they and other Canadian Indians were busy assuring General Carleton they would hold fast to the ancient covenant chain of friendship with Britain. They held out hope of aid to both contenders, and both contenders were eager to give them presents. But when a powerful British army arrived in Canada in the spring of 1776 and the sick and ragged Yankees began to retreat homeward, the Canadian Indians were left in a precarious situation. They lived in the midst of people who could be, they knew, either generous friends or implacable foes. Eventually, too, they must acknowledge the power of whoever controlled the St. Lawrence. These were the painful facts of their life.

In the meanwhile the Six Nations looked benignly upon the neutrality of their allies and, insofar as their own responsible chiefs were concerned, embraced the same policy for themselves. Their chances of holding neutral appeared somewhat better; they were more numerous than the Canadian Indians and, in general, more isolated from white attacks and influence. As early as June 1775 the Oneidas had declared they would take no part in the white people's family quarrel. Though chiefs from the whole Confederacy listened to Guy Johnson at Oswego in June and General Carleton at Montreal in July, they went down in great numbers to Albany in August to find out what the rebels had to say. As some of the Senecas put it, they wanted to "open our ears to hear truth and to see where we are going."[39] At Albany the chiefs made a peace treaty (but the Mohawks complaining at the same time of their grievances) with General Schuyler and several other newly appointed American commissioners of Indian affairs.[40] They promised the Americans to "sit still and see you fight it out."[41] They kept this promise as well as they could. Little Abraham who lived at Fort Hunter and the sachems at Canajoharie did not always meet with success in controlling their young Mohawks—for the Johnson influence was strong, and the young fellows, as Abraham said, had unsteady minds—but they insisted that they did try.[42] The rest of the Six Nations kept the peace in 1775 and even gave up to Schuyler the great war belt that Guy Johnson had pressed upon some individuals that summer.[43] Nevertheless there were the usual alarms among the frontiersmen that the "savages" were coming down.

This was the situation when John Butler, new deputy agent for the British, reached Niagara. It was November 17, less than a week after Joseph, Guy Johnson, and most of the Indian department had sailed for England. Butler's orders from Carleton were clear and simple: to hold the Indians neutral.[44] At this point Indian policy and British policy seemed to coincide.

Subsequent events, however, proved that there was a difference. The sachems of the Onondaga Council, looking to their own well-being, hoped to play off the British and the Americans against each other. This was the Indian idea of neutrality. But word was to go out from Carleton to the commanders of all the upper posts that, though the Indians were to be kept from fighting at the moment, they must be held in readiness to join in the war when needed. This was British neutrality. It looked toward the preservation of the western posts and, in turn, the fur trade.

John Butler, carrying out his orders, held several councils with the Six Nations at Niagara in the spring of 1776. One of his most telling arguments, just as Guy Johnson's had been, was that the Americans were beggarly rogues who had nothing for themselves and who, consequently, could neither make the Indians presents nor carry on a trade. Some Oneida chiefs who were present reported that Butler had pointed out that Schuyler, the American commissioner, "has no men, guns, cannon and ammunition or cloathing, and should he survive the summer he must perish by the cold next winter for want of blankets." But the king had plenty of everything, both for himself and for the Indians.[45] As the Americans retreated from Canada, these words carried more and more weight. Though they prized their neutrality, the Six Nations could not live without trade goods.

Butler did not have everything his own way. News of what was going on at Niagara leaked back east through both white and Indian spies. The Americans had an agent, too—and a good one. Samuel Kirkland, missionary to the Oneidas, was a devout patriot. As Guy Johnson had already found out, Kirkland's influence over one of the Six Nations was very strong. Kirkland had no Indian "wife" to make his way smooth, no half-breed children, no money for gifts. But he treated his charges kindly and in his solemn, humorless way saw to their welfare. He was as unselfishly devoted to the Indians as any white man could have been, and they responded by giving him their love. Thus Kirkland, the patriot missionary, was able to hold his

Oneidas neutral but leaning toward the Americans. The Continental Congress quickly recognized the value of his services and in the early part of the war took into its pay not only Kirkland himself but his interpreter, James Dean, also a product of Wheelock's school and, like Kirkland, cut off by the war from his salary, and two of Joseph's former Indian schoolmates who also worked sometimes among the Oneidas. General Schuyler and other rebel officials cooperated with these missionaries, bending every effort to supply at least the friendly Oneidas with presents and a trade in the necessities of Indian life which the Americans themselves often went to desperate lengths to obtain.

There was little that John Butler could do about Samuel Kirkland. He sent emissaries to the Oneidas (one being the young half-breed, William Johnson, who had made his way to the Indian country), but these emissaries accomplished nothing. The Oneidas answered Butler's messages softly and placatingly—and stood firm. They went to Niagara to councils and took their share of British rum and goods, but they always came home again; and usually they brought along to Kirkland intelligence of British movements.

The dissident Oneidas were also a serious problem to the Six Nations Confederacy. The chiefs of the Onondaga Council were anxious that the Six Nations present a united front to the white people. Any pressure which they could hope to exert on the Americans or the British must be the united pressure of all. Time and again the chiefs sent for the stubborn ones to appear before them. The latter came and made fair promises, but their conduct continued unsatisfactory. A large party of Cayugas and Onondagas journeyed to Oneida Castle to remonstrate. On home ground the Oneidas scorned to turn away wrath with appeasing speeches. A bitter quarrel developed, and words ran high.[46]

The ruling sachems had their hands full. Some of the young warriors of the other nations were just as uncontrollable as the Oneidas, but they insisted on going off to Canada to fight for the British. They must have British goods, these disobedient young men declared, for the support of their wives and children. Meantime the Canadian allies of the Six Nations were appearing at every general council with new complaints and problems. But what was even worse, the western allies of the Confederacy seldom showed up at all. Out on the Ohio the Six Nations had scarcely any authority left over their old empire. The Shawnees were ill-humored and sulky, the Mingoes doing as they pleased, and the Delawares were again trying to cast off the hated petticoats. In the fall of 1775 the Ohio Indians had joined with the Six Nations in making a treaty of neutrality with the scared and now very conciliatory Americans, at Pittsburgh. Both whites and Indians ratified the Ohio River (the Fort Stanwix line) as the permanent boundary between them. With the main point of contention settled, Dunmore's War formally ended and the Americans got a breathing spell on the frontier. But the Six Nations were to get no respite. The Delawares suddenly asserted their independence in the very faces of the Six Nations deputies, and later Captain White Eyes, an influential Delaware chief, went off to visit the Americans at Philadelphia and spent there in much too friendly a manner the entire winter of 1775–76.

The insubordination of the Delawares was very alarming to the chiefs at Onondaga who feared that the Americans might inveigle the Ohio Indians into letting them march armies against British Detroit. Ohio land was Six Nations land, and these wise sachems did not care to see armies of either side marching through it. They suspected out of sad experience that on whatever land white armies might set foot, especially if they were American armies, that land they would claim as conquered. The Six Nations chiefs were for neutrality on the Ohio, as elsewhere, but they wanted it to be their own brand of neutrality.

Joseph Brant, as he disembarked at Staten Island that July day in 1776, was not aware of all these difficulties. He had not set foot in the Indian country for more than a year. No messages could have reached him in England over the winter. He had no knowledge of what had been going on anywhere in America, least of all among his own people. Joseph had a great deal to learn. Unfortunately, he had not come to the proper place, nor was he in the proper company, for learning what he urgently needed to know.

The new arrivals found Staten Island in a hubbub. General William Howe had established headquarters there and was planning an assault on New York. Much of the island had become one vast cantonment, a welter of soldiers of all ranks, both Hessian and British, and women, children, servants, and camp followers, personal baggage, stores and equipment. Ships anchored in the nearby Narrows sheltered many wealthy royalists and those formerly in authority. Governor Tryon and his staff had been living in the ship *Dutchess of Gordon* for months.

Joseph, Guy Johnson, and the rest of the Indian department had orders to put themselves under General Howe's command. Once New York was subdued, the British forces would proceed up the Hudson River to meet a second British army coming down from Canada, thus cutting the rebellious colonies in two. This plan was common knowledge and everybody spoke of it, including the Americans. It was expected that the Six Nations could be persuaded to join as a third force from the west, and it was the task of Guy Johnson and his department to effect this result. No real difficulties, it was thought, lay ahead. The rebel army was nothing, their general nothing, New York was full of loyal subjects eager to arise and help, and the Indians, every man of them, were Britain's friend.

Joseph and his companions spent little time on Staten Island. They were soon comfortably quartered in the ship *Earl of Suffolk*,[47] awaiting, as did everyone else, the coming of greater armaments and still more troops from England. The expected reinforcement arrived soon afterward, and on August 22, before daybreak, some fifteen thousand of Howe's great army began to move.

Joseph took part with these troops in the ensuing campaign and we are told he proved himself active and brave.[48] Nobody has listed the details of his military service that summer and fall, but presumably he landed with the rest of Howe's forces at Gravesend Bay on Long Island and helped to drive the rebels back to Brooklyn Heights. He was probably with Clinton, Cornwallis, and Percy in the flanking movement at Jamaica Pass. He must have seen the taking of New York on September 15 and perhaps the battle of White Plains on October 28.

Joseph's presumed importance quickly secured for him entree into the best military circles, but his own amiable qualities helped him make the most of his opportunities. No other American Indian ever became so friendly with the great and near-great. Joseph won the esteem of young Lord Rawdon, aide-de-camp to Sir Henry Clinton and son of the Earl of Moira. Many a night he slept in the same tent with Sir Charles Stuart, later the famous General Stuart, son of George III's favorite, the Earl of Bute.[49] He frequently saw Governor Tryon at his quarters in Flatbush, renewing the acquaintance made in 1772 when he had complained to the governor about Mohawk grievances. One meeting with Tryon took place in General Clinton's headquarters where the two held a "particular Conversation" in Clinton's presence[50]—a conversation which probably had something to do with plans to bring the Six Nations into the war. On another occasion Joseph, while walking with Tryon and others in an orchard, chanced to pick a crabapple from a tree. Tasting the fruit and finding it very unpalatable, Joseph screwed up his face and exclaimed, "It's as bitter as a Presbyterian!"[51] For one who had had such a heady sojourn in London, that part of the white world represented by Lebanon, Connecticut, had lost some of its charm.

While with Howe's forces around New York Joseph also attracted the attention of Lord Percy, heir to a dukedom.[52] The two young men, almost the same age, the one born in a bark hut and the other in a ducal palace, struck up a real and lasting friendship. It was the only lasting friendship Joseph ever shared with a white man. He never grew disenchanted with Percy, nor Percy with him, and the two were to carry on an intermittent correspondence for the rest of their lives. Lord Percy was a true product of his century; he was steeped in the writings of Rousseau and Monboddo, and he thought there was something innately virtuous in primitive man. To him, obviously, Joseph Brant was the noble savage. As for Joseph, in the proud Percy he found the perfect gentleman, the true and gallant knight; and Percy's example reinforced his own vague longings in that direction. Back home on the Mohawk, after returning from Wheelock's, Joseph had tried hard to live as he supposed a gentleman should live. In time (was it a little of Percy's influence?) he even assayed the role of the true and gallant knight. Joseph was always practical and generally had good reasons for his conduct. But sometimes good reasons do not explain everything. More than once, in later life, he went out to joust with dragons, even when the jousting was a forlorn hope and the dragons ignored by everyone else. What prompted him to fight that losing battle all those lonely years in behalf of Sally Ainse? Or for Matthew Elliott's right to a fair and legal trial? Or what kept him staunchly loyal to the king after the king's ministers had treated him so shabbily?

Winter came early in 1776, and by the end of October the well-clad British soldiers were already complaining of the cold. They supposed Washington's "tatterdemalions" must be freezing. But though they retained New York and had won nearly all the battles, they had not yet won the war. Washington had kept his army together, tattered breeches or no. In the midst of his and their woes, Washington could permit himself a bit of smugness. He was thinking, on November 7, that Howe "must attempt something on account of his reputation, for what has he done as yet with his great Army?"[53]

But General Howe attempted nothing more. In his book of rules it was too late in the season for fighting. He had already written to Lord George Germain for reinforcements for the coming year. He had not received the Loyalist help he had been led to expect. For this and other reasons one more campaign must be fought. Howe was not discouraged. It had simply happened that a little more effort was needed.

For Joseph Brant, who for seventeen months had been living through such glorious adventures, it was time to return to reality. Joseph still had a message to deliver to his people from the king. He must tell the Six Nations all about his mission to England. By every account, too, their spines needed stiffening. Sir William Howe agreed that Joseph should return to the Indian country and gave him a message of his own. He wished to be remembered to the Six Nations, so Joseph reported later, and "hop'd they would not put the least confidence in the rebbles, as he Knew Them to be A Cowardly Deceitfull People, and he would be glad to see the Chiefs of the Six Nations, the first Opportunity."[54]

Guy Johnson also gave Joseph a message and many instructions. Guy supposed that the armies from Canada and New York would be making their juncture as soon as the weather permitted. That was the plan, and he had heard nothing to the contrary. Joseph was to prepare the Six Nations to cooperate with these military movements. Guy remained in New York, expecting to go to Albany with Howe, and the officers of his department remained with him.[55]

Gilbert Tice, Joseph's mentor and companion in England, was chosen to make the long journey with Joseph. Tice, being a native of New Jersey, probably knew the way across that province, and Joseph himself could find the rest of the way. The two crossed the Hudson River near Kingsbridge on November 16. They were in disguise and for a while they expected to travel only by night. The country near New York was full of rebel scouts and patrols.[56]

Having left the city and its environs behind, the two adventurers pretended to be an Oneida and a militiaman on leave from Washington's army. Up on the Delaware they turned themselves into hunters. Once they encountered a suspicious countryman who asked why they carried pistols if they were only hunting. This was a poser, and they thought for a moment they would have to kill the man to keep him from spreading an alarm. But Joseph quickly replied that pistols were useful for dispatching a wounded bear that might attack them, and so satisfied the questioner. It was a narrow escape for all concerned.[57]

The rest of the journey appears to have been uneventful. The two travelers set out again, this time across country to the Susquehanna. They were aiming for Oquaga, where Joseph's little family was now living.[58]

10

The Divided Longhouse

THE INDEFATIGABLE Samuel Kirkland, at his listening post among the Oneidas, did not miss very much. On December 18 he reported to the rebel authorities in Albany that Joseph Brant and Captain Tice had arrived at Oquaga on their way to Niagara.[1] It would appear, then, that the dangerous journey across country had taken the travelers between three and four weeks.

The joyous reunion with Susanna and the children (and how those two young ones had grown!) and old Isaac and the rest of the family, and the giving of presents, and the shrieks of delight can only be imagined. Later, in solemn council, Joseph delivered his messages from the king and General Howe and Guy Johnson to the Indians of the village. He had so much to tell and the Indians were eager for news.

They were eager for news, yes, but most of them were not eager to join in the war. Like the entire Six Nations, there were a few at Oquaga who favored Britain, a few who favored the rebels, and a much larger number who felt as Fort Hunter's Little Abraham did: they just wanted to live in peace with both sides. But Daniel Claus says that the people of Oquaga agreed "unanimously" to Joseph's propositions.[2] Very likely they did make him some promises. Promises were cheap. However, subsequent events proved that the villagers were not stopped from accepting any presents the rebels could offer or from sending friendly messages to General Schuyler, the rebel Indian commissioner. Schuyler could openly rejoice in the thought that the Indians of Oquaga, as well as the Oneidas, were his real friends. What the Oquagans really wanted was trade, anybody's trade. Already they were feeling the pinch of doing without. The Americans had so little to sell, and the British at Niagara were such a long distance away.

Before he left Oquaga Joseph sent word to those Mohawks still remaining in their old homes that they should come to Niagara to hear what he had to tell them.[3] He was very anxious to get his old neighbors and friends away from the evil influence of the rebels. Then it was time for another leave-taking, and though it was the dead of winter, Joseph and Tice set out for Niagara. They were accompanied on their journey by old Isaac and some other Oquagans who went to trade. Where the Susquehanna forked at Tioga, the party took the trail to the west. This was the old Forbidden Path, the back corridor to the Six Nations and now treacherous with snow and ice. All along here, in spite of the rigors of the season, Joseph did his work thoroughly. Wherever there was a settlement or a house or two, he delivered his messages. With passionate conviction he urged that the Indians, for their own good and the good of their country, must get ready to cooperate with the British army. The people he talked to were friendly and seemed not to disagree with his arguments.[4] But like the people of Oquaga, they really said more than they meant. Then they fed the travelers and sent them on their way with fresh provisions. Such sharing was the way it was when Indians traveled.

The rest of the journey led through the Seneca country. Leaving the Forbidden Path, the party made their way down Seneca Lake to Canadesaga (Geneva), west to Canandaigua, then on to Geneseo, or Genesee Castle, the great town of the Senecas.[5] But in all these places promises to join in the war were to prove even less firm than those of the Susquehanna Indians. The Senecas were grimly committed to neutrality, the sort of neutrality which could wring the most concessions and gifts from both sides. Many of these Indians had never been too friendly to the British, anyway. They would not change easily.

After four days among the Senecas Joseph and his party hurried on to Niagara. They arrived there on December 28. The journey from Oquaga had been very swift. At the fort they found that the commanding officer had recently died and no one had much interim authority in Indian affairs except John Butler. Butler and Joseph knew each other well. Butler was taken aback at the purport of Joseph's messages. They did not coincide at all with General Carleton's careful instructions to *him.* But Joseph was determined to deliver his appeal to the Onondaga Council and throughout as much of the Six Nations country as possible. Butler disapproved and apparently tried to remonstrate with him and explain. This did not set well with Joseph.

General Carleton's wishes did not much matter to him. He thought Butler strangely lukewarm in the royal cause.

Greatly perturbed, Joseph wrote the following letter to the Mohawks and other Iroquois settled down the St. Lawrence at the Lake of the Two Mountains:

> I am just now arrived at Niagara— I acquaint you of this as I intend going down on an Expedition this year— Early in the Spring, and I expect you will let me know if you will come up and join me— I intend to go with the Indians to deliver my brothers the Mohawks, who I imagine are prisoners, I wish to have some of my relations the Indians of your Village to come up, to see what success we will have, as we intend to be in earnest to relieve my brothers the Mohawks from the hands of the Rebels, and you may depend on having your own way of making war. I do not think it right to let my brothers go to war under the command of General Carleton as General Carleton expects & trys to have the Indians under the same command as the regular Troops, but it will be the best method for us to make war our own way. This is my reason for acquainting you, that any of you that wish to come up—may come and join me. This is all I have to say, but I wish to have your answer as soon as possible—[6]

If Joseph got an answer we do not know what it was. His efforts to lead his own relatives in war, which was all that he could ever expect to do, were to come to nothing. General Carleton soon heard of Joseph's plan and exerted his influence against it. He did not intend that even small bodies of Indians should move until British armies were ready to move.[7] But even without Carleton's objections there was little hope of success of such a project. It was a long time till spring, and by then Joseph's clansmen in Canada had probably forgotten all about him and his letter. Besides, they, too, liked the kind of neutrality that could produce gifts.

Offended and resentful, Joseph did not linger at Niagara. Nothing could stop him from carrying his messages to Onondaga. As before, he tried his best to get the chiefs to commit themselves to helping the British. It was the only way that they could protect their homeland, was his solemn warning. Again the chiefs seemed friendly enough.[8] In all these affairs Joseph may have thought that he was proceeding with the utmost secrecy. But even before he reached Onondaga the Indian Commission at Albany knew that Joseph Brant was on the move again.[9]

The young man, who thought he was doing very well, resolved to try his powers of persuasion on the Oneidas. Venturing as close to Samuel Kirkland's bailiwick as he dared, he stopped at a border village peopled by Onondagas and Oneidas. From this place he sent messages to the Oneidas and to some of his wife's clansmen in particular to come to meet him at Niagara. At the same time the Oneidas were also invited to a conference by a rival messenger from Butler. One of Joseph's in-laws, an influential man named Good Peter who lived at Kirkland's headquarters at Canowaraghere, promised Kirkland that he would not go to either meeting. When Joseph tried to hold a council with some Oneidas who came to the village where he was staying, it broke up in a furious quarrel, with most of the latter determined to remain neutral since, as they said, they were friends to both the king and the Americans.[10]

Frustrated, Joseph retraced his steps to Cayuga, where he spent some time with his mother's kin and pondered what to do next. He decided to return to Niagara. Going back through the Seneca country, he found that the Senecas no longer showed him even a semblance of friendliness.[11] This he blamed on John Butler, and perhaps he was right. However, the Senecas had also had time to reflect upon what an upstart Joseph Brant was and what slaves the Mohawks had always been to the English; and some, at least, remembered the war against their nephews, the Delawares, thirteen years before, which Joseph and the Mohawks had taken part in. The Senecas were vengeful and had long memories. Their head warrior, Sayengaraghta, a celebrated old chief much favored by John Butler, did not approve of Joseph Brant at all—this, in spite of the fact that Sayengaraghta had been a great friend of Sir William Johnson. But times were different now.

Arriving at Niagara, Joseph tried to get some gunpowder to carry back to Oquaga. John Butler would let him have only a little and Joseph, more aggrieved than ever, bought some on his credit. Then he set out again to Oquaga and his family.[12] He still had ideas of rescuing the Mohawks and of ultimately going to rejoin General Howe. All these events he wrote faithfully to Guy Johnson though the latter was often afraid to answer for fear his instructions would fall into the hands of the rebels.[13] Becalmed in New York, Guy was trying with no success at all to get some instructions from Howe for himself and the Indians or at least to find out when Howe expected to move his expedition up the Hudson. Thus Joseph was left very much on his own.

Oquaga was one of those Indian towns torn by religious dissension. The clergy whom the people encountered from time to time seemed to have two different Words. This had always been very bewildering. But now that the Word and the war were so intimately entwined, Oquaga was even more confused. Those residents who accepted the Anglican church disliked, and were disliked by, those residents who were called dissenters. The one group tended toward the established government and the other rather thought of themselves as rebels. They were all very sorry, of course, that the white people were fighting and they hoped that they would soon stop. They sorely missed their trade. The lack of powder, a blanket in tatters, a broken gun, a lost knife, was a calamity. When those who favored the rebels went up to the Mohawk country, they found the stores almost empty. General Schuyler, who had charge of Indian affairs for Congress, held councils from time to time and made treaties, but he was strangely stingy. Indians hung about him and thronged his house and cast hints and begged, but they got few gifts. They did not know that Schuyler was almost as empty-handed as they were. "My house is daily crowded wih them," he lamented, "and I have next to nothing wherewith to relieve their distress."[14] In February 1777 Philip Schuyler not only had no ammunition for the Indians; he had none for the northern army which he commanded, and he did not even know where the Continental magazines were, if any! It was a stern fact of life that the rebels had to supply the Oneidas or give up the frontier and the great granary that was the Mohawk valley. For the people of Oquaga and the rest of the Indians along the Susquehanna they had scarcely anything left. The latter were being pushed, inexorably, toward the British at Niagara.

Joseph was back in Oquaga by early spring. The Indians there and in the vicinity were quite ready to consider him as the voice of their superintendent. Whether they would let him lead them in war, however, was another matter. His clansmen might accept his leadership if they thought him a brave warrior; other Indians would expect to have their own relatives as leaders. But a strange thing was about to happen.

In the mountainous areas along the Delaware and, indeed, in that whole rugged country between the Hudson and the east branch of the Susquehanna there lived a surprising number of Loyalists. These Loyalists were not wealthy men intent on protecting their privileges. Actually they were very poor men, mostly tenant farmers, and they had a hard struggle trying to eke out a living from stony ground which they had leased for two or three lives, or longer, from the owners of the great semi-feudal estates in the Catskills or the Helderbergs. Many lived on the Great Hardenbergh Patent which contained over a million acres and others lived on the domain of the Van Rensselaer family which was almost as large. These people—for who knew what dangerous plots such Tories might hatch?—were feared and resented by the rebels from the very beginning of the war. They were watched, spied upon, threatened with tar and feathers, plundered of their small property, and preyed upon in many ways. Sometimes they were actually attacked and even killed by over-zealous rebel scouts and patrols.

When Joseph Brant appeared at Oquaga in the spring of 1777 and raised the king's flag over the village, it seemed to these unhappy Loyalists that here was their deliverance. Brant was someone they had heard of or could easily find out about. Rumor had it that he had been received well in England, and his connection with the great Johnson family was widely known. Brant was, to them at least, an educated man. He would make a strong leader. Almost immediately some of these poor fellows gave up the struggle at home and fled to his protection. In time at least one hundred white Loyalists gathered at his side,[15] coming mostly in the early years of the war, in 1777 and 1778. So began that highly irregular military corps who called themselves Brant's Volunteers.

Some of Brant's Volunteers were killed in action or captured, and some eventually joined more regular corps such as Butler's Rangers or Sir John Johnson's Royal Greens. But fifteen still clung to Joseph in late 1783, long after the fighting had ceased. This is their roster at that time:[16]

> James Middagh [Middaugh], aged 23;
> William Crumb, aged 51 (wife and three children in the colonies);
> Daniel Cole, aged 40 (wife and four children in the colonies);
> Anthony Westbrook, aged 47 (wife and four children in the colonies);
> Alexander Westbrook, aged 16;
> Robert Land, aged 30;
> Henry Hoff [Hough], aged 51;
> John Hoff [Hough], aged 24;
> James Pemberton, aged 23;
> John Sheverland, aged 48;
> John Chisolm [Chisholm], aged 30;
> Rudolp [Rudolph] Johnston, aged 29;
> Loudewick Leley [Ludowick Ziely], aged 26;
> James Park, aged 32;
> Daniel Secord, aged 27.

A year earlier five other persons were still on the list: James Pownall, Jacob Deckert, Adam Ford, Joseph Rake, and Mr. Hand.[17]

From various Loyalist records come a few details about some of these men. James Park, for instance, had lived at the head of the Delaware River and joined Brant in May 1778. He was a Scotchman and had a tiny property. John Chisholm had also lived on the headwaters of the Delaware, in Tryon County. He, too, joined Brant in May 1778. Chisholm was probably a Presbyterian. He had a house and ten acres and personal property, all worth over £82. James Middaugh was also a Presbyterian. John Hough had lived in Albany County, and he owned personal property valued at £26. Robert Land joined Brant in 1777. Joseph sometimes employed Land as his courier or messenger.[18]

In petitions for land grants made many years after the war, two more names of Volunteers turn up, Archibald Thompson and Daniel Rose. Both these men lived on the upper Delaware and joined Brant in May 1778. Both served throughout the war. From another source we also learn that Thompson was a native of Scotland, a recent arrival in America, and that he had a very small property which, of course, he lost.[19]

Two additional names, those of Richard Dingman and George Barnhart, appear in the voluminous records of claims for losses suffered by Loyalists during the war. Richard Dingman was a native-born American who joined Brant in 1777 and served two years with the Volunteers before enlisting with Sir John Johnson. This man was more prosperous than some of his companions. He possessed one hundred acres on the Susquehanna on perpetual lease. He had cleared sixteen acres of his property and he owned a house and barn, three cows, a horse, two sheep, seventeen hogs, and furniture and farming equipment. But the richest member of the Volunteers, so far as is known, was George Barnhart. Barnhart, also a native American, lived in Ulster County, and joined Brant in 1778. Before that time he had been imprisoned by the rebels for giving aid to John Butler. Very likely he had been guilty of selling supplies to some of Butler's men in the Indian department. The enterprising Barnhart had a lease of 180 acres on the Delaware, with more than half of the ground cleared, and a house and a barn. He also held a second lease of eighty acres with ten cleared. And he possessed a third leasehold property of 170 acres which he rented or, as he said, he had put a man on. Besides these leases he also owned nine horses, twenty-eight cattle, forty-four sheep, fifty or sixty hogs, and much furniture, grain and tools which the rebels had confiscated and sold while he was in prison. A witness to Barnhart's claim for compensation says he "was in very good Circumstances. He was the richest man there about except Mr. Burch."[20]

Perhaps the poorest man in Brant's corps was a certain Anthony

Bratt [Bradt?] who petitioned General Haldimand for relief in 1780, declaring he was destitute.[21] This unhappy fellow completes a list of twenty-five Volunteers whose names are definitely known and who served with Joseph most of the war.

Most of Brant's Volunteers seem to have been of English, Scotch, or Irish descent, though a few bore German names. Most came from New York though some may have come from neighboring sections of Jersey or Pennsylvania. These men were not all at the best age for soldiering—indeed, some were entirely too old or too young—and they fought any way they could and got very bad reputations. Because they fought in disguise, they were seldom recognized. Yet sometimes their disguises were penetrated, for certain men such as Daniel Cole, Daniel Secord, and the Houghs were personally known to the rebels and especially notorious for what were conceived to be their misdeeds. These four men, along with Joseph himself, were the most hated and the most sought-for. Any one of the Volunteers, however, would have been hanged without much of a trial if he had been caught. Out in the field more than any other Loyalists in the American war, the Volunteers led harsh and dangerous lives. We were "almost irremittingly on actual Service," declared one of them after the war, and he spoke truly.

Why so many men preferred Joseph Brant's leadership to an easier and more regular service is difficult to explain. The simplest explanation is that they were wild and undisciplined, unwilling to accept a strict regimen. There have always been such men, and the refugee Loyalists had their share of them. "Some of them," exclaimed an officer in exasperation, "refuse to take arms or be under any command—but to go along with the army, the Devil knows what the scoundrels wou'd be at, I have been thirty years a soldier, but never had so much trouble as with those fellows."[22] The devil did not know what such scoundrels would be at, but Joseph Brant did. Joseph let his men fight as Indians. His Volunteers dressed and painted themselves as Indians, and during all the border warfare the rebels naturally assumed that their dreaded Mohawk enemy had a large party of grotesquely painted warriors under his command. Actually, Brant's personal party as a war chief (as distinguished from those who merely happened to be traveling in the same direction) consisted of scarcely more than one-fifth Indians, most, if not all, his clansmen.[23] The rest were white men. It was late in the war before Joseph was able, for a very special reason, to attract a larger number of Indians. It was his whites upon whom he usually depended.

The white men who clung to Joseph were individualists—

nevertheless, they must have seen something reassuring in him. They served without pay, getting only their food and clothing, which Joseph himself procured by scrounging around the country or buying on government credit when they were in the field. At Niagara the Volunteers got regular issues and rations, but still no pay. Yet they could have joined many provincial regiments, and they bore up firmly under a great deal of pressure. Recruiting was fiercely aggressive in those days. Bands of recruiters roamed, secretly or openly, throughout the province of New York, and in Montreal they handed down enlistment papers through the grating to rebel prisoners who, merely by signing, could go free. But whether the rebels were young or old, reliable or unreliable, in sickness or in health, who cared? The levy money was generous. There was intense rivalry among Sir John Johnson, Allan Maclean, John Butler, Major Rogers, Jessup, Peters, and others who were trying to raise and head Loyalist regiments. But most of Joseph's men were sincerely attached to him, and there are instances of some who, when separated from him, went through great hardships in order to rejoin his corps and absolutely refused any other service.

With so many mouths to feed, Joseph soon had to concern himself about the problem of provisions. Oquaga at its best was no source of abundant supplies, and springtime was a very unprofitable season, anyway, to try to obtain food from the Indians. The Indian corn was scarcely up; not even the little wild sand cherries were ripe. In his perplexity Joseph bethought himself of the nearest white settlement. There was bound to be food at Unadilla, a village about twenty miles away, just above the confluence of the Unadilla River and the Susquehanna. Joseph sent a message to the people of Unadilla that he was coming up to see them, and that they should not be alarmed; and on June 2 he and about one hundred of his men arrived. They went to the house of a Loyalist friend, a certain M'Ginnis, and sent for the leading men of the settlement, the Reverend William Johnston and his son, a captain of the local militia. According to a man to whom the old gentleman later told his story, Brant said

> that he and his party were for the King, and that he did not think proper to fall out for every trifle; but as he had a large party, and wanted provision for them, if the people would let him have it, he would pay for it, letting them know at the same time that he would have it at any rate; and after getting cattle, sheep and swine, and other provisions, he told the people that Butler would be along soon, and pay for what he had taken from them; that he then

appeared there in a warlike manner, and intended to bring off his people [from the Mohawk River] in spite of every opposition; and further said, there would be great trouble there soon.

Having obtained some boards from M'Ginnis to build huts for his men, Brant said he would return for them in a few days, and left with the cattle and provisions which he had requisitioned. But before the party went away his white Volunteers told the people of Unadilla that they were "not afraid of the American troops now."[24]

This was the way Joseph and his men usually lived when they were out on their campaigns. On July 6 he was back in Unadilla, and he must have got all the place afforded, for at that time he wrote a note to Persafor Carr, agent for a large estate in the vicinity, and a Loyalist, asking to buy provisions.[25] Carr and a man named John Tunnicliff, also a Loyalist, as well as John Bullock and Robert Gamett of the Butternuts settlement, let him have cattle and cheese and such things, either then or later.[26] Numerous other persons willingly, or with a little push, supplied Joseph and his party with foodstuffs and with horses to ride, from time to time. Most of these persons later had to flee the country, and many of them did receive their promised payment when their bills were verified, in Canada.

Such high-handed doings caused great alarm. After Joseph's appearance at Unadilla many of the rebel sympathizers fled, sure that their property and their lives were in danger. The few who remained sent urgent messages to Harpersfield, to Schoharie, to Albany and whatever other places they could think of, for aid. Philip Schuyler, struggling with Indian affairs and the manifold problems of dealing with the British general, Burgoyne, who was obviously poised for an invasion from Canada, took time out from his more pressing duties to post additional troops along the frontier. He also sent to the Oneidas, urging them to use their influence with Brant to stop his depredations. The Oneidas promptly sent runners hither and yon to try to prevent the Indians from joining Brant. Beyond that they threw up their hands in frustration. What could they do? Brant, they told Schuyler, had long since declared he would never regard anything they should say to him.[27]

Toward the end of June, Nicholas Herkimer, Joseph's former neighbor, made a personal effort to ease the situation. Herkimer had been appointed brigadier general of the Tryon County militia the preceding year. With several hundred of his men he marched down to Unadilla. Brant at his request came up from Oquaga to meet him, and the two held a conference which lasted two days. Herkimer hoped to persuade Joseph to stay out of the war. Each man, however, feared the other and both were wary. Each was backed up by his own party. Brant's corps and the rebel militiamen faced each other from opposite sides of the council ground. According to agreement both parties had left their arms at their respective camps.

There are several accounts of this meeting, none of them by the two principals. Daniel Claus, who probably got some of his information from Joseph himself, says that Joseph had at the time less than two hundred men, that the rebels entreated him to stand neutral, and that he flatly refused. Claus also states that when a rebel colonel hinted that he would be compelled to do as they asked, Brant gave a sign to his party who put themselves in such a warlike posture that the rebels drew in their horns and sneaked off. If Brant's men had had more ammunition, added Claus, they might have given a good account of the whole party.[28]

An old gentleman who in his youth had been one of Herkimer's militiamen declared many years later in a pension application that Brant had between two and three hundred Indians, and that the talks took place under a covered bower with the Indians sitting nearby on seats of boards under the trees. Sometime during the proceedings Colonel Cox (George Klock's son-in-law), who was in Herkimer's party, muttered an explosive "Damn him" and began to curse and swear at Brant. The latter, affronted, signaled to his men who all sprang up and, whooping and yelling, ran for their guns. Whereupon Herkimer took Brant by the arm and told him not to mind what Cox had said, that they were old neighbors and ought not to be spilling each other's blood. "Herkimer talked very nice to him—Brandt was moderate too," asserted the old gentleman.[29]

Another old militiaman declared years later that on the second day Herkimer gave him instructions to shoot Brant on the spot, but that Brant was always too wary for him to accomplish the job![30]

Brant himself said nothing about the meeting; and Herkimer wrote Schuyler shortly afterward that he had promised that the Fort Hunter Indians would be permitted to move up to Canajoharie, and that the Reverend John Stuart, missionary at Fort Hunter, and Mrs. Butler, wife of John Butler, who were virtual prisoners at this time, might go along, too. Schuyler was disapproving. He thought, as far as the two white persons were concerned, that this was an "improper agreement," and that they would only make trouble at Canajoharie.[31] The agreement shows, however, that Joseph's anger at John Butler did not prevent him from trying to help Butler's family.

In the meantime Joseph and his friends were still trying to get some information and, they hoped, some orders from Guy Johnson. He sent Volunteer Robert Land on the dangerous journey to New York City with a letter telling where he and his men were, and asking where they should join Howe's army and when it would be moving north. This was a real puzzler for Guy who, approaching Howe about it, was advised to tell them to join the first army that got to the Hudson River.[32]

But before Robert Land could return, all Joseph's problems were resolved from another direction. General Carleton, prodded by the British government, had finally sent word to John Butler that it was time for the Indians to move. A British army was to mass at Oswego just as the rebels feared. The Indians were now expected to help. Butler sent messages all over the Six Nations country, inviting everyone to a great council at Oswego where there would be many presents. His exact words are not known, but he probably said as little as possible about the war.

Deprived of so much of their trade, the Six Nations Indians were especially hungry for presents. If they did not wish to go to war, they would not go to war—they thought. They even went so far as to assure Schuyler they would meet with him as soon as Butler's council was over.

Joseph and his party, among all the rest, were instructed to go to Oswego immediately.[33] They seem to have taken a northwest path, by way of Onondaga, for they had to avoid Fort Stanwix with its rebel garrison. They had some company on their journey. For many weeks small bands of dissident warriors who could see no sense in neutrality had been gathering on the Susquehanna in hopes of a military movement. They and their various leaders traveled with Joseph and his party, though certainly not under his authority. The whole company probably numbered about three hundred.[34]

By July 23 Joseph had arrived at Oswego. Here, much to his delight, he met his old friend, Daniel Claus. Almost immediately the two of them were in a heart-to-heart consultation.[35] Claus, who knew nothing but the management of Indians, had lingered behind in England hoping to get a suitable post in the department. Though he had no more wanted to bury himself in Niagara in 1775 than had Guy Johnson and though John Butler had gone there so reluctantly, Claus had somehow convinced himself that he had been undermined by Butler. It was true that Carleton did not like him and treated him coolly. It was also true that Claus had not met with much success in England, being now on hand at Oswego merely as an "extra" superintendent of Indians for this one expedition. Yet by no stretch of the imagination were his troubles Butler's fault. But he thought they were, and the two friends poured out their woes to each other. This was to be common practice for all the years of the war whenever they could get together or even write a letter, and such grievances as Joseph could not think of Claus could think of for him. Joseph's antipathy toward Butler was to grow and grow.

Old Oswego, so long abandoned, echoed once more to the bugle's call. In just two days a vast encampment sprang up. Soldiers in red or green busied themselves with a myriad of duties. Here were one hundred men from the 8th regiment; there, one hundred from the 34th regiment—all professionals, disciplined and ready. At another part of the campground stood the tents of Sir John Johnson's new Loyalist corps, the so-called Royal Greens or the King's Royal Regiment of New York. Though the provincials were not so smartly disciplined, they had high hopes and they were full of zeal for the king's cause. Among the late arrivals appeared a company of Hanau Chasseurs, one of Lord George Germain's first regiments of German mercenaries. Making war was their life's work, and they could give a good account of themselves in the European style. Brant's Volunteers, both Indians and whites, had their own camp, and near them were the rest of the warriors who had come up from the Susquehanna as well as some Canadian Indians enlisted by Claus. Hourly expected was a contingent of Six Nations Indians and white officers from Niagara with some other whites and Indians from as far away as Detroit, all these under John Butler and Captain Lernoult, the interim commandant of Niagara. The leader of the entire expedition was Lieutenant Colonel Barry St. Leger, an officer long experienced in America.

This motley force was but one thrust of a long planned triple offensive. Its grand design was to split the rebel territory in two as well as to prevent any attempt which the rebels might have in mind for another invasion of Canada. General Burgoyne, marching southward from Montreal, would proceed by way of Lake Champlain, Lake George, and the Hudson River. His object was Albany, and he was already far advanced on his way. Having captured the famed Fort Ticonderoga at the outlet of Lake George, he was now hacking a path through the wilderness toward the head of the lake. General Howe and a second army sailing north from New York would arrive at Albany via the Hudson River. This was the movement which Joseph and his friends had been awaiting with such impatience. St. Leger, having already rendezvoused the third force at Oswego, was to go from Lake Ontario via the old trade route of Oswego River, Oneida Lake, and the Mohawk. He, too, would head for Albany as soon as he had captured Fort Stanwix. New England and the middle colonies would be separated. George Washington would have to give up the one or the other or divide his little army. For the British invaders the prospects looked rosy indeed.

At length John Butler and his lagging Indians, mostly Senecas, reached Oswego. There was some counciling with the inevitable presents, but the main council was to be held down at Three Rivers where the rest of the Six Nations were to join in a body. Except for the Indians the expeditionary forces were now complete. On July 26 they all set out—all, that is, except Butler who, with his not very zealous cohorts, brought up a distant rear. In the throng was a surprising number of women and children, soldiers' wives and families, Indian women and their progeny, and female camp followers of all sorts. Daniel Claus had brought along his family, and Lady Mary Johnson, Sir John's wife, was present with her children.[36] The distaff side of the Johnsons and the Clauses had eagerly seized upon so fine an opportunity to go home. Once back on the Mohawk, and with the king's arms triumphant, they expected to settle down in security and peace.

At Three Rivers, where the Oneida and Seneca Rivers merged to form the Oswego, most of the Six Nations were waiting. They had had to decide between this council with the British and a council with Schuyler who had sent them an invitation for almost the same time. But they suspected that Schuyler could give them few presents and they were in great want of everything. Their clothing was in tatters and they had no ammunition with which to hunt and support themselves. They went to Three Rivers. Even the Oneidas, who leaned in so friendly a fashion toward the rebels, showed up at Three Rivers. They knew they would get their share of the presents, for the British dared not offend them. But except for the Mohawk warriors who were veterans of the fighting in Canada in 1775 and who had not been home since, most of the Six Nations still steadily proclaimed their neutrality.

Many years later an old Seneca chief described the great council of 1777 which he had attended in his youth. His words were taken from his own lips and written down by an Indian scribe almost as illiterate as he was:

> But when we arrived there at the place appointed, ground for council fire or convention, immediately after arrival the officers come to us to See what wanted for to support the Indians with Provisions and with the flood of Rum, they are some of the amongst the our warriours made use of this indoxicating Drinks, there was Several Bar-

real Delivered to us for us to Drinked for the whit man told us to Drinked as much we want of it all free gratis, and the goods if any of us wishes to get for our own use, go and get them, for and from our father gaven to you, and for the same the above gift, our chiefs began to think that the great Britain government is very Rich and Powerfull to his Dominion to force things and kind to his Nation, all things a bondantly provided for his people and for us to and Seval head of cattle been killed for us to Eat and flour the our female Sect was very well please for the Kindness we Receive from our white Brothers.[37]

To people starved for trade and presents, it was a heady situation. As parched mouths got their rum and empty bellies got their fill, as the naked were clothed and the hunters provided with all the powder they needed, even those Indians who opposed taking part in the war could see that their "Rich and Powerfull" father was going to win. What would be the consequences of his victory to themselves? Their minds filled with indecision as they calculated this and that. All the while John Butler and Claus and the other white officers and even St. Leger himself were urging the warriors to go along with the expedition. Joseph, who was so sure of the king's eventual triumph, redoubled his own efforts. But the Senecas at least were still determined to go back home. Their animosity toward Joseph flared up anew. It was noised about that they had threatened to kill him, and he had to be kept out of their way.[38] At length some white man got a brilliant idea, and Claus claims that it was he. Go with us, he said to the Indians, and see us whip the rebels. Just sit down and smoke your pipes and see what a great show we shall provide. We shall not need your help, he told them loftily.[39] The Indians, even the Senecas, finally decided to go. There was nothing they liked better than to watch a good fight.

The expedition now consisted of about seven hundred white men and eight hundred Indians. The river was full of boats as they all set out once more for Fort Stanwix. Again Butler brought up a distant rear.

The going was not easy. To the provincials it seemed that they were always the ones who stood in the water when obstructions had to be removed or boats and cargo had to be carried around the portages. Why could not the regular soldiers share in this unpleasant work? A provincial officer who broached this thought to St. Leger got a scathing reply. Neither St. Leger nor any other regular thought of provincial troops with anything but scorn, and the affair ended with St. Leger and the complaining officer scarcely on speaking terms.

That was the year that hardly anybody was on speaking terms with hardly anybody. The tension between Joseph and the Senecas and the provincials and the regulars was only part of the story. Discord reached into high places. Burgoyne, who had superseded General Carleton in command of the military operations from Canada, felt uncomfortable with Carleton and he with Burgoyne. Carleton, who had been knighted by the king for stopping the rebel invasion, blamed this loss of command on Lord George Germain, and had already tendered his resignation. In the meantime Sir Guy had as little as possible to do with Claus whom he considered Germain's appointee and whom he had a grudge against anyway. And when Guy Johnson managed to send a letter of instructions to Butler, and Butler asked Carleton what to do about it, the latter sent word that he was to obey *him,* and when he joined Howe, he was to obey *him*—and nobody else, was the clear implication. In the bad feeling between Butler and Claus, Sir John Johnson who had a strong sense of family loyalty, was easily turned against Butler. To make matters worse, sometime or other on the march, Lieutenant Colonel St. Leger, who was a breveted brigadier general for only this one expedition but who yearned for a permanent commission, took to drink. St. Leger loved "milk," declared the Indians, even better than they did!

Yet it cannot be said that the marchers were dejected. They foresaw an easy victory. Butler's Indian spies, who ought to know, had reported that Fort Stanwix was weak and almost defenseless. And Sir John Johnson, who also ought to know, had reported that the whole frontier teemed with Loyalists who were ready to rise up and strike a blow for the king as soon as his army came near. These Loyalists were not only ready, Sir John avowed; they were eager and impatient. Indeed, they could hardly wait. The news that filtered through from the rebel ranks was also heartening. It was well known that the rebels of Tryon County were terrified.

The reports from Tryon County were completely accurate. The rebels were scared to death. They had been greatly alarmed by the gathering of the Indians and Tories on the Susquehanna. Burgoyne's advancing army frightened them still more, and they were demoralized by the fall of their stronghold at Ticonderoga. It seemed to them that Ticonderoga, which had been given up without a struggle, portended their own fate. When Oneida spies reported the coming of St. Leger's force; though it had been long expected, it was the last straw. The frontiersmen saw themselves threatened and besieged and overwhelmed on all sides. They felt sure, as they said, that they were going to "fall a prey to the merciless Savages." They stopped their militia from going to reinforce Fort Stanwix. Every man, they declared, was needed at home. Wildly they called for Continental troops. If they did not get Continental troops, they would have to lay down their arms and surrender to the first British army that appeared. Burgoyne had already issued a proclamation that he would protect those who surrendered, from the Indians. They would take him at his word. They would accept his protection.

A despairing General Herkimer described the situation of his neighbors to Schuyler.

> I can assure you, [he wrote] that some are already busy with moving away, some declare openly that if the Enemy Shall come, they would not leave home, but Stay with their Families, and render themselves over to the Enemy, as they can't help themselves otherwise without Succour— I may say, whole Numbers of Men in each District are So far discouraged, that they think it worthless to fight; and will not obey orders for Battle, if the County is not in Time Succour'd with at least Fifteen hundred Men Continental Troops. . . . A good many of the principal Inhabitants, who were always true to our Cause, are quite discouraged, and by their Conduct others join 'em in Numbers, they mention, that it is their opinion by all the Circumstances, that this River is Sold alike as Fort Ticonderoga— I with a party of well Spirited Friends endeavoured to remonstrate all those weakhearted and false opinions and cowardly Suppositions, and effected but very little; By our Encouragements the Spirits of some seemed to rise and to revive, but when they come afterwards in Discourse with the discouraged, their Spirit immediately sinks again— In this Manner is the present Situation of our County; I have Reason to fear, that upon any alarm or actual Invasion of our Enemies into our County, I shall not be able to raise two hundred Men of the Militia, willing to fight and to obey orders to oppose the Enemy—[40]

The Oneida Indians, who were right in the path of St. Leger's advancing army, had worries and fears of their own. They begged their American friends not to "make a Ticonderoga" of Fort Stanwix. Stand up and fight like men, they urged. General Schuyler, faced with the alarm on the frontier and trying to cope with Burgoyne's invasion as it came down from the north, remarked unhappily that if he had fifty thousand troops they would not suffice for all the calls on him. His whole army consisted of less than three thousand Continentals. His militia of short-termed recruits was coming and going all the time, and none of them knowing much of fighting.

Aware of the despondency among the rebels, St. Leger, who described them contemptuously as a "Confused Rabble," sent a small detachment ahead of his main force to cut off the communication between Fort Stanwix and the Mohawk valley. Before he left the scene of the council at Three Rivers, he ordered Lieutenant Henry Bird and thirty white soldiers to carry out this important operation. A little later he sent two hundred Indians with two white officers and Joseph Brant and a chief named Bull to support Bird.[41] Assuming that the rebels in the fort might want to surrender at once to anybody, St. Leger instructed Bird that he was to wait till the main force arrived. He did not mean to withhold any honor from a young officer, he added, but he thought there were too many Indians in the small detachment who might plunder or butcher the fallen foe.

Lieutenant Bird and Joseph and their force were encamped at the landing at the head of the Mohawk River by August 2. They got there just a little too late to prevent a small reinforcement of men and supplies from reaching the fort.[42] This ill luck Bird blamed on the dilatoriness of some of the Indians and he was probably right—they never liked to hurry themselves. Nor did the fort appear as defenseless as it had been assumed to be. Its four sides looked substantial enough, not at all out of repair, and not to be knocked over with what the Indians called "Pop Guns." St. Leger having neglected to bring along from Canada any heavy artillery, the expedition had only two six-pounders, two three-pounders, and four little coehorns, the effect of which was, as the Indians afterward observed, like "Apples that Children were throwing over a Garden Fence."[43]

There were to be many recriminations on this point later. Claus was to claim that his Indian spies had made truer reports than Butler's, and that neither Carleton nor St. Leger had paid any attention to them. The ill feeling between Claus and Butler completely clouds the issue. But whatever the Indians could or should have reported about the condition and garrison of the fort, they could not have reported anything of consequence about its commander because they did not know him. Yet the commander of Fort Stanwix was all-important. Though this is Joseph Brant's story, some of it belongs, for a time, to this young man.

Colonel Peter Gansevoort had come to Fort Stanwix (or Fort Schuyler, as the rebels had renamed it)[44] the preceding May. He was barely twenty-eight years old and, except for having taken part in the Yankee invasion of Canada, his military experience consisted of parading his militia up Albany's main street. However, he came from an indomitable family, a family of courage and iron will. His father, though obviously a loving father, sent him word that he expected him to conquer or die, and his brother, though a loving brother, said much the same thing. Such admonitions were hardly necessary. When the young man had begged frantically for troops and ammunition and supplies, and very little was forthcoming, he made do with what he had. What he had was trees and sod and fish. Day and night he sent his few men out to labor. He choked up Wood Creek with logs, shored up the fort with sod, and everybody ate fish—and ever so often he would write his worried little fiancee in Albany what a good time he was having, fishing.

Above Fort Stanwix this dauntless young fellow unfurled a flag, the first to bear the stars and stripes in major combat. So far as is known, neither Joseph nor any of the Loyalists or regular soldiers mentioned the flag or observed it with any interest at all. But if they had remarked that it looked as if it was made out of somebody's old shirttail, they would have been right. It was also made, so it is said, of a red petticoat donated by a soldier's wife and an officer's blue cloak.

St. Leger, after getting some of his army around, if not through, Wood Creek, arrived before the fort on August 3 and began his famous siege. For the next few days, in order to bring up the rest of his troops and the stores and equipment, he set his men to work pulling the logs and branches out of the stream. It was backbreaking labor, even harder than throwing them in had been. While the whites worked, the Indians kept up an incessant gunfire, with yelling and whooping, to terrify the garrison. St. Leger then turned his attention to a proclamation which he copied after Burgoyne's. Taking care to mention his "extensive Corps of Indian Allies" but declaring he was "anxious to spare where possible," he invited the people of the settlements to cease their resistance and gather around his banner. The proclamation was bombastic and pretentious throughout, and he must have considered it a veritable masterpiece of persuasion. After Sir John's optimistic predictions St. Leger had no doubt that the Mohawk valley was full of loyal subjects eager to accept his protection. He had only to sit down and await their coming.

On August 5, in the midst of all these plans and labors and frenzied noisemakings, a message arrived in camp for Joseph Brant. The message came from Joseph's sister Molly who, it must be remembered, was still living in Canajoharie where little that the rebels were doing could escape her eyes and ears. Molly warned that General Herkimer and the entire militia of Tryon County were on their way to relieve the fort![45]

This news was certainly not in keeping with what the invaders knew of the state of mind among the rebels. However, when a scout confirmed the information, St. Leger immediately sent Sir John Johnson and a detachment of his regiment and Joseph and the Canadian officers with their Indians and whites to cut off the advancing enemy.[46] John Butler and the hesitating Senecas and other Indians who expected merely to watch set out afterward—but with Butler knowing full well that mere sightseeing was no part of the program.

The rebels of the Mohawk valley had been ready to give up without even a semblance of a fight. What had caused such a sudden turnabout? It seems to have been one of those small, unexpected events that have sometimes influenced the course of history. A girl who lived up on the northern frontier had set out to join her sweetheart who was a Loyalist with Burgoyne's forces. Some Indians, also attached to Burgoyne, had captured her (or were escorting her) and, apparently in some sort of dispute over who should be her guard, had killed her and carried her scalp with its long hair streaming, back with them to the British camp. Persons who claimed to know what happened reported this and that, but even Burgoyne himself admitted the atrocious nature of the deed though denying that it had been premeditated. There were a dozen versions of the story, and the details are still in dispute. But Jane McCrea—that was the girl's name, so it is said—became an instant celebrity. Accounts of her murder ran like wildfire over the countryside, getting a little more adornment with each telling. Jane was killed, by someone or other in some way or other, on July 26. Three days later the chairman of the committee of safety in Albany County wrote to the desponding committee of Tryon County. He pointed out that the victim of the atrocity was strongly attached to the enemy and had gone out in friendship to meet them. "What then can those expect who Tamely submit," he asked, and answered himself, "nothing but Murder and Rapine—"[47]

It was a sobering thought. If Burgoyne could not, or would not, protect his own, then what protection could the rebels expect, either for themselves or for their families, if they surrendered to him? Burgoyne's great proclamation of amnesty suddenly appeared a very weak straw on which to lean. And St. Leger was no better than Burgoyne and his Indians no more reliable.

Nobody had been willing to do anything or to go anywhere. Now, as if with but one thought among them, the supine bestirred themselves. The downhearted felt a mighty wrath. Some eight or nine hundred strong, they rose up, and damning General Herkimer for a coward because he cautioned them to proceed with care, they set out, all helter-skelter, for Fort Stanwix. They swore they were going to "eat the enemy up." They swore they would be quick about it, too. And near the small Oneida village of Oriskany, six miles from the fort, they ran into the ambush. It was early on August 6, 1777, a sultry, dark, and lowering morning.

The road to the fort crossed a marshy ravine, and here, behind some bushes and willows, Sir John Johnson and his forces lay waiting. This disposition of the troops has been attributed to Joseph, but Butler says it was a Seneca plan while Claus and St. Leger say it was Sir John's plan. At any rate, the plan was to lie quiet until the rebels could be completely surrounded. But before all the enemy had crossed the ravine, some of the Indian warriors could contain their impatience no longer. They leaped up shouting their war whoop and firing their guns, and the battle was on.

Neither the Loyalists nor the rebels had had much experience in combat for it had been many years since the last French war. Consequently a good deal of unexpected heroism took place and some unexpected cowardice, too. The rear ranks of the rebels, who were, of course, farthest from the din, broke and fled. Gossip said afterward that one of their adjutants, a man who was suspected of being a trimmer, repeatedly cried aloud in low Dutch, "Run Boys Run or we shall all be kill'd." Gossip also said that the colonels of one rebel battalion crawled into holes and left their men to command themselves.[48] Whether or not this was true, Joseph Brant and his followers pursued the retreating foe with hatchets and spears and probably worked more havoc among them than if they had stood their ground.[49]

Accounts of battles never seem to agree. The rebels usually tell of an action which lasted well into the afternoon. The Loyalists are not so explicit; John Butler reports only that the worst of the fighting lasted about an hour and a half. The main body of the rebels, after the first onslaught, held firm. The attackers were just as steady. Attackers and defenders fought from behind trees, hand to hand, any way they could. A storm came up, and the combatants had to take cover to keep their powder dry. The storm ceased, and the battle began all over again, this time with a little more order. Former neighbors fought each other, and relatives and even brothers, for many frontier families could count members in both armies. General Herkimer's own brother was among the Loyalists, and a father and son, John and Bernard Frey, fought on opposite sides. Among the white men, at least, nearly everybody knew everybody else. All the furies and passions of years of controversy exploded.

Screams and curses and grunts and groans, the sharp report of musketry, the clash of bayonets, rent the air. In a welter of spears,

tomahawks, knives, gun butts and Indian war clubs, whatever instrument death could be dealt with, was used. The watching Senecas were
sucked in, either because their young warriors could not resist a fight
or because in the melee they had to fight to save themselves. Years
later, one of these young warriors, when an old man, declared that in
the heat of that terrible battle "while we [were] doing of it, [it] feels no
more [than] to kill the Beast, and killed most all, the american
army."[50] John Butler wrote to Carleton a few days later that "the
Indians shewed the greatest zeal for His Majesty's Cause, and had they
not been a little too precipitate, scarcely a Rebel of the party had
escaped," and added that their behavior "exceeded anything I could
have expected from them."[51]

The carnage was almost unbelievable. The ground was littered
with the dead and dying. St. Leger reported that four hundred rebels
lay dead on the field, and Butler and Claus, though they could agree
on nothing else, estimated five hundred rebel casualties. The rebels
themselves admitted two hundred dead and a great number missing or
wounded. Five members of the Tryon County committee of safety
were killed, a member of the Assembly and a senator were lost, and
many of their militia officers. General Herkimer was so severely
wounded that he was to die of a leg amputation a few days later. But
while the battle raged, the old man sat beneath a tree, ignoring his
shattered limb, and calmly smoked his pipe and directed the movements of his men. Among the Loyalists fewer white men had fought,
and they suffered only about half a dozen casualties; however, Sir John
Johnson's brother-in-law was badly wounded and two officers of the
Indian department were killed.

The heaviest losses on the Loyalist side fell upon the Indians.
They lost thirty-three men killed and twenty-nine wounded, more
than half of these casualties being among the Senecas and including
several of their chief warriors. Joseph said later that his "poor
Mohawks" also suffered heavily.[52] The young half-breed, William
Johnson, who had been with Joseph's forces down on the Susquehanna, was killed. The tradition is, that as he lay with a broken
leg, a wounded rebel caught sight of him and struck the final blow.

The rebels had been stopped in their tracks, though they retained
possession of the field. St. Leger called this a victory, and perhaps it
was.[53] But his forces did not pursue their victory. They heard sounds of
a skirmish that was going on back at the fort, and left. The Indian
warriors returned to camp howling with rage. Their howls were soon
augmented by the anguished cries of their women, and the din went
on all night. One and all, the Indians clamored for revenge. Such

prisoners as they could get hold of, they clubbed or tortured to death, thrusting their bodies under weeds and brush. St. Leger and his officers could not stop them and certainly Joseph could not, and it is not known whether anybody tried.

Claus's "Stratagem" had worked. The entire Six Nations, and particularly the once reluctant Senecas, were now wholeheartedly in the war. But unfortunately for their peace of mind, the nations were not all in the war on the same side. Some Oneidas had joined Herkimer's militiamen as they marched along and had taken part in the fighting. After the battle the Loyalist Indians in their thirst for revenge destroyed a small Oneida village. The stricken Oneidas to whom revenge was also sweet immediately went down the country and burned some Mohawk dwellings. The Longhouse was divided and distraught. There had not been such bitterness under its roof for generations.

As for Lieutenant Colonel St. Leger, he sat and waited. With only his light artillery, there was still little he could do against the fort, but perhaps he could starve out its garrison. He sent his proclamation and a threatening message (telling of the defeat of the relief forces at Oriskany and saying with what difficulty he restrained his Indians) into the fort. Colonel Peter Gansevoort rejected both proclamation and message. He intended to defend his post, he declared, "to the last Extremity."

General Schuyler got the terrible news of the cutting to pieces of the Tryon County militia at six in the morning on August 8. He knew that without Fort Stanwix the whole Mohawk valley as well as the help of the friendly Oneidas was lost. He made a supreme effort. There was at his side one strength and comfort, General Benedict Arnold, the hero of the Canadian campaign, a man whom he trusted and whom he accounted "Active Sensible and brave." He sent General Arnold and one brigade of Continental soldiers with whatever militia might be left and whatever troops might be spared from the small frontier garrisons to the relief of the fort.

In his progress through Tryon County Arnold encountered no more than the usual impediments due to bad roads and missing bridges. He made his way to Fort Dayton, high up the Mohawk, where the militia was slowly gathering. Here there fell into his hands a simple-minded and half-demented fellow who had been captured in the company of some Loyalist spies and condemned to death. Whereupon Arnold proved that the rebels, too, could work a stratagem.

Holding the simpleton's brother as hostage, Arnold spared his life on condition that he go to the British camp pretending to be an escapee and tell them that a great army was on its way to do them battle. Han Jost Schuyler (for that was the fellow's name) performed his part well. Appearing in the Indian camp and showing clothing riddled with bullet holes, he told of his escape from an army as numerous as the leaves on the trees. The Indians, to whom the feeble-minded were objects of awe, were frightened and depressed. They had never liked to fight more than once without going home, and they had never liked to fight at all when the odds were against them. They thought of their losses. They began to decamp.

St. Leger, seeing half of his army melt away, heard the story of the great force that was coming against him. He heard it from Han Jost, and he heard it from the Indians, and it seemed to grow worse each time he listened to it. There were three thousand rebel troops, he was finally told, and they were only two miles away! The general whose preconceived ideas had already been so rudely shocked apparently had not much difficulty in believing this. It was August 22, and he had sat before Fort Stanwix for nineteen days without accomplishing much. Faced now with such an alarming prospect, together with the defection of his Indians, he realized there was only one thing that he could do. It was a hard course he had to follow, he explained later to Burgoyne, but follow it he must. He must raise the siege. By nightfall that same day he and his whole expedition, including the Johnson and Claus families and all those other Loyalists who had meant to go home, were on the run. In their haste they left provisions, hospital supplies, tents, clothing, money, and even their private papers to be taken over by the exulting, and very surprised, garrison of Fort Stanwix. When St. Leger got back to Oswego, he wrote letters hither and yon, blaming everything on the Indians. Perhaps he was right. It would not be the only time that everything was blamed on the Indians.

Claus says that Joseph and the Seneca chief Sayengaraghta wanted to follow up the victory at Oriskany by taking a detachment down the country against the rebels, but St. Leger would not permit it.[54] He also says that Joseph, not content with the retreat to Oswego, made his way through the woods with some of his men to join General Burgoyne. Claus gave him some money for the trip. Apparently Joseph did not like what he saw at Burgoyne's camp, for he soon returned,[55] and escorted Molly and her family, and perhaps his mother, to their relatives among the Cayugas.[56] Molly, whom the rebels suspected of spying on them, could no longer stay in Canajoharie in any safety.

She departed in such haste that she had to leave behind all her beloved possessions. Years later her family blamed the necessity for her sudden flight on General Herkimer, but the truth was General Herkimer was already dead. Claus says the Oneidas forced Molly to flee, and one of them occupied her house from then on. At any rate Molly felt herself very ill-treated and complained bitterly. What had she done that was improper? Nothing! She set out toward the west determined to carry her woes to the Onondaga Council. They, she was confident, would see to it that she got justice. It did not occur to her that the Onondaga Council might not have the final say.

Most of those Mohawks who had tried to remain quietly at home also had to flee. The fugitives were Fort Hunter Indians, for almost nobody was left in Canajoharie. Spurred on by Oneida attacks and the unfriendliness of the rebel whites, about one hundred of these Indians sought a haven first with Burgoyne and then finally in Canada. Little Abraham and a few others refused to budge. They were stubbornly determined to remain neutral, a position which did not endear them to either side. Abraham, especially, was a man to be pitied. The rebels always distrusted him. The Loyalists, as will be seen, would not even speak to him in ordinary friendship. But throughout the war Abraham clung desperately to his home and refused to make the choice between king and rebel neighbors.

Those in high places were suffering their own particular chagrins. General Burgoyne, bogged down in the wilderness of northern New York and facing a constantly increasing American army, surrendered his whole force on October 17. He had no alternative. General Howe had not even attempted to make the expected junction with him and, indeed, had gone off in the opposite direction, much to the bewilderment of both friend and foe. It was a fatal mixup that required much explanation then and since. It was also a mixup which illustrates as well as anything can, the incredible problem of communications which the British had to contend with in carrying on a war that was three thousand miles away.

The man who received Burgoyne's sword at Saratoga was not General Schuyler who had laid all the groundwork for the occasion, but General Gates who, after much jockeying, had taken over the command of the American forces but a short time before. Thereafter, Schuyler, who might almost have been excused for sulking in his tent, applied himself devotedly to Indian affairs. "My country may justly claim my last services," he had said from a sickbed in 1776. "It shall have them."[57] He remained of the same mind. With the help of Samuel Kirkland he managed to keep the bulk of the Oneida nation in line during the whole war. Joseph Brant who continually tried to pry the Oneidas loose from such a wicked allegiance, was to find Schuyler a worthy foe. Joseph, and particularly his sister Molly, grew to hate Schuyler with a passion.

In the meantime Sir Guy Carleton chafed away another winter in Canada. His long awaited replacement, sailing on a ship that was beset by contrary winds, never got beyond the Gulf of St. Lawrence and had to return to England. Such were the vicissitudes of travel-ing—and governing a province.

At the Onondaga Council that fall Joseph exerted himself to the utmost to put heart into the Indians. Schuyler had sent them a mes-sage after Burgoyne's downfall boasting of what the Americans had done to Britain's best general and inviting them to meet with him and renew the old friendship. He did not blame them for what had hap-pened, he said, but a threat was no less implied. Joseph countered by reminding them of their great losses at Oriskany, as yet unavenged, and of all their previous sufferings at the hands of land-hungry whites.[58] But neither of these was the most cogent argument. The most cogent argument of all was the ships that were plying back and forth on Lake Ontario, bringing supplies and troops and trade goods to Fort Niagara. The Indians could plainly see where their future living was coming from. It was coming from their father the king. What could the rebels offer them? Nothing—the beggarly rebels had noth-ing.

Faced with the facts of their life, the Six Nations remained firm. They dispatched a courier to New York City with a letter to the officer in command. They begged to know when and where they could be most useful. Joseph was named as one of those "ready to wait your Orders."[59] Guy Johnson, who also received a message from the In-dians, could get no information from Sir Henry Clinton, successor to General Howe, as to how to answer it. He then wrote to Howe himself in Philadelphia. Guy thought the savages ought to be let loose to carry on the "Petitte Guerre" in their own way. What Howe thought, no one knows. He always answered Guy's communications without actually answering them.

The Six Nations also sent belts to the Ohio country and as far away as Detroit to arouse their western allies for next season's warfare. Their waning influence may have had some slight effect in favor of the British. But many of the western Indians, after holding neutral for almost two years, were falling into line of their own accord. Already the Mingoes and Shawnees and various other scattered warriors were carrying out raids in Kentucky. They had their own grievances against the Americans, interminable, never-ending: American assaults, American squatters and land speculators, actions of the rash and misguided American militia. The western Indians, also, needed trade and presents, and they had a generous father at Detroit. They had a generous father, moreover, who knew how and when and where to direct their motions. The Six Nations could just as well have saved their wampum.

Joseph spent most of the winter at Niagara. He and Sayengaraghta apparently got on a somewhat friendlier footing for they planned the next campaign together. Sayengaraghta had his eye on the Wyoming settlements whose leaders had been making some threats against the Indians and who held several of their chiefs in prison, and Joseph was interested in reclaiming his own Mohawk valley. The two shared equally in mapping out the strategy.[60]

It seems a remarkably big role for the lowly Joseph to have been permitted by the Senecas to play. Unfortunately we have only Daniel Claus's word for it, for better records are scarce in the half light of the interregnum in the government. The prolific letter and memoir writer, Claus, must be used to supply the deficiency, but the truth is Claus scarcely wrote a line that was not meant to discredit John Butler. In his consuming hatred for the man who had usurped his own rightful place (as he thought), he raised up Joseph and Molly and anybody else he could think of in order to make Butler look small. Butler, according to Claus, never accomplished anything in Indian affairs or in the conduct of the war. Somebody else was always responsible for any successes in those fields. Butler was a nonentity, an ignoramus, a slothful incompetent. He never did anything but spend vast sums of money for which he got nothing in return. Thus Claus's outpourings must always be seasoned with their proper grain of salt.

Butler, who certainly knew what was going on, went a remarkably serene way. A newly commissioned major, he spent the winter organizing the first of those companies of provincial troops, the famous—or infamous—Butler's Rangers who, as their orders and commissions stated, were to act in the field with the Indians. He also kept in the good graces of the commander of Fort Niagara and satisfied him at least in his management of the Indian department there. Carleton still liked and trusted him and would give him a good character to his successor. Butler had more to worry about than Claus's machinations. His wife and children were still virtual prisoners back on the Mohawk and his eldest son, Walter, was actually in irons at Albany. Walter had been captured after the battle of Oriskany while on a secret mission to some Loyalists at German Flats and, but for the intervention of old friends, would have paid with his life for his errors. Walter did not think so much of his blessings as he might have, but was more prone to brood upon his wrongs. Strangely enough, the young man's brooding held ominous implications for Joseph Brant.

Joseph was, of course, completely influenced by Claus. Through Claus he had been able to obtain necessities for himself and his men from merchants at Niagara.[61] So he was not beholden to Butler, and that was the way he wanted it. Claus gave him instructions for his behavior,[62] and very probably he carried them out. But Joseph had other things to worry about, too. His family must be made secure, and sometime or other he got them away from Oquaga. Then there was the problem of the Oneidas. Joseph recognized the fact that his own Mohawks could not hold fast to their loyalty to the king and still keep their old homes. Surrounded by American frontiersmen, they had to give up the one or the other. Joseph should have also realized that the Oneidas could not stay where they were unless they sided with the rebels. They were too close to the American frontier, and the practicalities of the situation coincided with their own sentiments. They would stay with their beloved Kirkland and they would fight alongside their white neighbors. Joseph had not a chance to pry them away, particularly with the efficient Schuyler always on the alert and performing prodigies in keeping them supplied.

The Six Nations would continue to think of themselves as the balance of power in America. This had been their studied policy all through the eighteenth century. They could not imagine that anything had changed. But since Oriskany the bitter truth was that they were no longer free agents. The old Iroquois Confederacy, or Confederacy of the Six Nations (for since the French were gone, Iroquois was not a name much in use), could no longer dispense its favors as it pleased, with canniness and judgment. Ripped asunder, the erstwhile confederates bobbed about, directionless, upon the torrent of the white man's affairs. White people thousands of miles away and kings and ministers they had never seen gave them their impetus. Yet, though they were no longer independent, the thought that they were, died hard. The oratory of the council still sounded brave and free.

Now the snows fell and the harbors froze over, and the St. Lawrence was stilled, and Joseph and Sayengaraghta quietly made their plans. The dissident Oneidas, deaf to all pleas, turned their faces adamantly toward the east, taking with them the poor remnants of the Tuscaroras who lived nearby and whom they had once befriended. Some of the Oneidas had actually joined Gates at Stillwater and participated in the humiliation of Burgoyne. Stunned by such faithlessness to their ages-old union, the Onondaga Council promised themselves that they would fall upon their younger brothers at Canowaraghere, the village where Samuel Kirkland had his mission, and teach them a lesson. In their present anger this was very easy for the chiefs to say.

In mid-December the British held a great council at Niagara with their red allies. In spite of the season nearly three thousand Indians came. While there, they got all they could eat and the promise that all they could drink would be delivered to their villages. John Butler and Colonel Mason Bolton, the new commander of the fort, condoled with the bereaved Senecas, covering the grave of each fallen warrior with scalps and wampum. They made light of Burgoyne's "small disappointment"; the king, they declared, has just begun to fight and will show the rebels no mercy. Presents exchanged hands, amounting to more than thirty-four thousand pounds. "We are determined to make the War our own," declared the gratified Sayengaraghta. Joseph Brant, acting in his official capacity, interpreted.[63] "Joseph . . . has been of great service & deserves every favour I can shew him," said Colonel Bolton.[64]

11

The Monster Brant

URGOYNE's surrender shocked the world. When the news broke in
Britain a stunned public refused at first to believe that an army
of theirs could have been given up en masse and to, as they thought,
so insignificant an enemy. When belief finally forced itself upon the
people, a great hue and cry erupted. In the press, in Parliament, in the
drawing rooms and coffee houses, the inevitable questions rose in
volume. Some great reputations all but collapsed via explanations that
could not explain and excuses that could not excuse. Even Lord
George Germain did not emerge unscathed. Across the channel the
French, who had been awaiting a signal to move, knew that their wait
was over. The rebel colonists had proved themselves in battle. On
February 6, 1778, the French foreign office placed its seal on a treaty
of friendship with the fledgling United States of America. In the long
game of politics France had a score to even.

Early that spring General Schuyler, urged on by Congress, tried to
hold the hoped-for conference with the Six Nations. It was a dismal
failure. Only the Oneidas and Tuscaroras came in strength to the
council place at Johnstown, bringing with them a few stragglers from
the Onondagas and Cayugas. Not a Seneca showed up. On the contrary the Senecas sent a message that they were surprised they should
even be invited to such a council considering that rebel axes were still
sticking in their heads!

In May, when Schuyler first heard the good news of the French
alliance, he tried to turn it to his own purposes. Again he failed.
Among the Six Nations the alliance changed nothing. What the
French did mattered little to them. Those Indians who thirsted for

revenge continued to thirst. Those who got their living by way of the St. Lawrence and the lakes continued in their attachment to the British. Only to the Indians of Canada, the Caughnawagas especially, did news of the French action bring tremors of indecision. The Caughnawagas had not forgotten their old French father. They loved him despite his long absence. A schism developed among them. A chief named Colonel Louis led those who leaned toward the Americans, and managed throughout the war to carry intelligence to Schuyler. Other chiefs followed the urgings of British agent, John Campbell, and remained steady, and sometimes went on little forays to the south. They were small forays, indeed. There was not much fight left in the Caughnawagas.

Joseph Brant was, of course, among those who cared nothing for the French. Toward the end of January he had ordered two silver gorgets with the king's arms engraved on them[1]—this was his answer to Schuyler's invitation to Johnstown. Shortly afterward he returned to Cayuga, taking with him some of his men. He had heard rumors that the rebels were planning an attack on the Indian country, and he wished to do his part in defending his people.[2] The rumors were to turn out to be just rumors. No rebel army appeared.

In the meanwhile Joseph, whose tastes were rather expensive and who had received no pay since he left Guy Johnson, was finding it hard to live on his credit for so long. Although it must have been painful for him to have to do so, he finally applied to John Butler to get on the pay roll at Niagara. Butler's recommendation of Joseph to Carleton was as handsome as if the young man had been his best friend. He wrote:

> Mr. Brant who is I believe known to your Excellency & very deserving of the character of an active and intelligent man & very willing to do every thing in his power for the public good having represented that he has been employed two years past without any allowance & out of hopes of receiving any reward for his past services from Col. Guy Johnson has desired me to lay his situation before your Excellency praying that you would allow him some certain pay for his future support, I humbly hope your Excellency would be pleased to attend to his request as he is very deserving of your favour.[3]

By late April, after the snows had melted, Joseph was again on his way to Oquaga. He was one of the first, either white or Indian, to go out for the new summer campaign. On May 15 Butler reported to

General Carleton that Brant and Lieutenant Frey of the Rangers were already on the New York frontiers and that they had been instructed to try to rescue the remaining Mohawks. Getting these Mohawks out of danger would be preparation for a general attack on that part of the country which Butler said he himself meditated.[4] Joseph also expected to use his knowledge of the trails and the terrain to guide and direct the various war parties which were to harass the back settlements.[5] If the back settlements could be broken up by the Indians and Loyalists, Washington's army might starve. Thus reasoned British strategy. In addition Joseph was to gather supplies against Butler's coming with his army of Rangers and Indians, and to receive whatever Loyalists wished to enlist with either Butler or himself.[6] He still expected eventually to join General Clinton who was supposed to be coming up the Hudson from New York.[7] In those days everybody, except General Clinton, thought General Clinton was coming up the Hudson. Butler who was now parleying with the Indians in the Seneca country looked forward to joining Clinton, too.

The rebels on the frontier knew something of what was going on and were greatly alarmed. They knew Butler had some military movement in view. They also knew Joseph was not far away. James Dean, Kirkland's assistant, reported from Oneida that though intelligence was so varied and contradictory as to make it impossible to determine the real intentions of the Six Nations, it was publicly known that Joseph Brant was collecting his friends on the Susquehanna for an attack on Cherry Valley.[8]

Joseph did not make the expected attack on Cherry Valley. Instead, on May 30, he struck at Cobleskill, to the southeast. He seems to have been looking for provisions and cattle primarily, but his force, which the rebels estimated at at least two hundred, burned ten houses and virtually destroyed the settlement. Contemporary accounts of this action are very confused, but it appears that most of the inhabitants escaped though with only the clothes on their backs. While the cattle were being driven away, the local militia and a few Continentals which had been stationed nearby at Schoharie set out in pursuit. They came up with their quarry at noon; a fight ensued, and most of the rebels were killed. Only a sergeant and four of his men returned to Schoharie. Some of the dead were found horribly mutilated. Joseph had not much control over the passions of his vengeful Indians and vengeful Loyalists. He was able, however, to give the few prisoners taken in the raid the choice of going to Niagara or of being distributed among Indian families. They chose Niagara, of course.[9]

Before he left Cobleskill, Joseph heard a rumor that the rebels of

Cherry Valley were plotting to kill him, and being not far away from that place he set out with a few of his men to investigate. At a point on the road just outside Cherry Valley the party met two young men on horseback. Though subsequent details are murky, it appears that Joseph and his men shot and scalped one youth and captured the other. This affair occurred on June 2,[10] and a rather senseless and stupid affair it seems to have been. Stone, Joseph's early biographer, claims that after the war Joseph admitted his part in this killing, saying he was sorry, that he thought the young man was a Continental officer whereas in reality he was one of his own friends. But Stone takes this story from another early historian and neither says to whom Joseph made such a confession,[11] and British accounts are silent on the subject. A contemporary American spy does bear out part of Stone's contention. He says Joseph was sorry about the killing, that the man was actually a good Loyalist.[12] What confusing times! Certain it is that the rebels ever afterward mourned the dead youth as one of their own.

This incident naturally did nothing to alleviate the uneasiness in Cherry Valley. Rumors about Joseph Brant's evil intentions increased daily. Greatly worried, the people of the settlement offered a reward for some definite information, and a certain Captain McKean volunteered to go down the Susquehanna to reconnoiter. Though McKean did not get very far, in the course of his journey he took it upon himself to write Joseph a letter upbraiding him for his mode of warfare and challenging him to a fair fight, either singly or with an equal number of men. This letter he fastened to a stick and placed in an Indian path, a sure postoffice. If Brant would come to Cherry Valley and have a fair fight, so McKean is said to have written, they "would change him from a *Brant* to a *Goose.*"[13] This challenge and the pun on his name was duly noted by an indignant Joseph in a letter to his Loyalist friend Persafor Carr. Stung, Joseph said: "I heard that Cherry Valley people is very bold, and intended to make nothing of us; they called us wild geese, but I know the contrary." He also declared that "I mean now to fight the cruel rebels as well as I can," and he asked Carr for guns.[14]

Rumors were putting Joseph not only in Cherry Valley but all over the map. Many small parties of Indians and whites were out that summer, but Joseph usually got the credit for any depredation on the frontier. Let an Indian be seen; it was Joseph. Let a cow be stolen or a barn burnt; he did it. His was the name that was on every tongue. On June 5 it was reported he was on his way to attack German Flats.[15] On June 11 the "Infernal Savage" scalped two unarmed men near Fort Stanwix.[16] On June 23 he was said to be headed for Crown Point.[17]

Three days later he was about to join Butler; the two with a force of
one thousand men were going to the Mohawk River.[18] The local
militia and Continental soldiers, too, were ordered hither and yon to
head him off, but they could not get even a glimpse of him.

Actually Joseph was never very far from his base on the Susquehanna. Two of his prime objects he had had to abandon. He could
think of no means of rescuing the Mohawks, particularly since the
remaining Mohawks did not wish to be rescued. Nor did he have force
enough to push his way through a hostile countryside to join Sir Henry
Clinton. But perhaps he could slip through with three or four men. He
was thinking seriously of that.[19] In the meantime, however, he could
concentrate on another of his objects—that of getting recruits for the
royal cause. A week after the Cobleskill raid he was back at work. On
June 7, according to an American spy, he swore in two men to be true
to George III.[20] Brant did not insist on people's joining him, said
another spy, but he promised to protect anybody who did. If they
refused to join him, they refused at their own risk.[21] Many did not
refuse.

In the midst of this activity a message came from John Butler
requesting Joseph to meet him at Tioga. Tioga was about a two-days'
journey from Oquaga, and Joseph was gone eight or nine days.[22] Here
he saw Sayengaraghta again and the vengeance-hungry Senecas. The
latter were still determined on their strike at Wyoming and were busy
preparing canoes and rafts and everything necessary for traveling down
the Susquehanna. Joseph and Butler conferred together, and it was
agreed that Butler should go with the Senecas and Joseph should
return to Oquaga and continue collecting men and provisions against
the time that Butler should join him. They parted then, the one going
down the river and the other going up the river.[23] It was near the end
of June.

On July 3, 1778, the famous "Wyoming massacre" took place. At
first glance it appears strange that the Senecas wished to wreak
vengeance so far from the scene of their injury. Oriskany was a very
long way from the Wyoming valley. But the Indians never made much
distinction between those who had hurt them and those who had not.
The inhabitants of Wyoming were white, and rebels, as those who had
injured them were; and rumor had it, moreover, that they were getting
ready to invade the Indian country. Ill will between the Wyoming
people and the Six Nations was of long standing. For years the Indians
had objected to the presence of these emigrants from Connecticut
who had settled at the very back door to their country, and on land
which they claimed had never been fairly purchased. All winter the

Wyoming Massacre. Painting by Alonzo Chappel. Out of 232 men captured in arms the Indians killed 227. Joseph, who *may* be represented by the Indian in the foreground, got credit for the killings although he was not even present. It brought him the name of "the Monster Brant" in a famous poem by Thomas Campbell in 1809. *Courtesy of the Chicago Historical Society, Chicago, Illinois. No. 5886, X. 38.*

Indians had nursed their anger with incantations and witchcraft. That anger grew to a white-hot fury when three of their number were killed by a white scouting party soon after they entered the valley. John Butler could always say that the people of Wyoming had fired the first shot.

On July 8 John Butler reported the entire destruction of Wyoming to his superior at Fort Niagara. With his army of about five hundred Rangers and Indians he had taken and destroyed eight forts, burned about a thousand dwellings, and killed or driven off about a thousand cattle and great numbers of sheep and swine. He admitted that in the action that preceded the surrender his Indians took 227 scalps but only five prisoners. The Indians were so exasperated with their losses last year near Fort Stanwix, he explained, "that it was with the greatest difficulty I could save the lives of those few." It gave him the "sincerest satisfaction," however, that he could "with great truth assure you, that, in the destruction of this settlement, not a single Person has been hurt of the Inhabitants, but such as were in Arms; to those indeed the Indians gave no Quarter."[24]

The people of Wyoming took a different view of the situation. They called it a massacre. Those who survived fled in terror to the eastward. Some made it to Minisink on the Delaware (present Port Jervis-Milford area). From Minisink, on July 10, it was reported to Governor Clinton of New York that everything there was in the greatest confusion, that women and children by the hundreds and some few men were flocking in from Wyoming "where by the concurent Testimony of numbers the most horrid Sceans of Savage Barbarity has been Exhibited."[25] From the very first news of Wyoming's plight, which had arrived at a frightened Minisink five days earlier, it was stated as fact that Butler and *Brant* commanded the invaders.[26]

The stories of murder and atrocity at Wyoming were never doubted. Wherever there were Indians in battle people were inclined to believe the worst. They were not surprised to hear that women and children had been burned in their houses or that the tongues of cattle had been cut out. The last French and Indian war and Pontiac's war had convinced nearly everybody that all Indians were monsters of cruelty. The Jane McCrea story was still fresh in people's minds. Then, too, some of the prisoners who had been taken at Oriskany had returned, bringing back stories of murder and cannibalism on the retreat of St. Leger's army. For this, the Indians and Tories had only themselves to blame. They liked to torment and tease their captives, brandishing knives and feeling their flesh, and estimating when they would be fat enough to slaughter! A reputable physician captured at Oriskany swore he had been told that on an island in Lake Ontario lay a pile of human bones, all picked clean, where the Indians had devoured a prisoner.

As to Brant's part in the atrocities at Wyoming, nobody had the least doubt that he had been the leading spirit. Obviously some Indian chief had commanded the Indians at the massacre. Of course it was Brant. He was operating on the Susquehanna; he had a large force; and he was the savage everybody knew about and feared most. No inquiries were made as to who had actually seen him at Wyoming or whether anyone there even knew him by sight. It was enough that the terrified refugees thought they were running from Brant.

The atrocity stories were seized upon, and made the most of, by the rebel newspapers. Eventually they also got into the British opposition press, causing another great uproar in Parliament. For many years thereafter historians both in America and Britain solemnly repeated the accounts of the horrors at Wyoming, in many of which, of course, Joseph Brant figured. William Gordon, John Adolphus, Charles Botta, Isaac Weld, and many a lesser light, all condemned this chief "of extraordinary ferocity." One pamphlet, luridly illustrated, showed Brant in scanty Indian dress, flourishing a tomahawk, and with one foot on a corpse, while other Indians in the background were clubbing prisoners or tearing off scalps with their teeth.[27] In 1809 the Scottish poet, Thomas Campbell, wrote his famed narrative poem "Gertrude of Wyoming"—a poem in which flamingoes were made to disport themselves on the palm-studded banks of the Allegheny and Joseph Brant was referred to as "the Monster Brant." A noble Oneida chieftain, one of the characters in the poem, was made to say:

> Accursed Brant! he left of all my tribe
> Nor man, nor child, nor thing of living birth:
> No! not the dog, that watch'd my household hearth,
> Escaped that night of blood, upon our plains![28]

Rumor, poetry, and history to the contrary, Joseph Brant had no part in the tragic events at Wyoming. In late June and early July he was going about his own business in the neighborhood of Oquaga and Unadilla. On July 10 a spy who had left Oquaga just three days before reported to the American authorities that Brant had been to a conference with Butler but had *returned.*[29] (This much the Americans had already heard.)[30] After the return, he said, Brant set out for Lackawack, on Rondout Creek, to collect provisions but was called back after a day's march by news that Unadilla (where some of his friends had gathered) was threatened by the rebels. Brant hastened back to Oquaga and sent all his white Volunteers to Unadilla, and two days later, July 5, he himself followed with all the Indians. Thus it appears that Joseph was still in Oquaga on July 3, the day of the massacre.[31] He seems to have stayed at Unadilla several days, till he found that the rebel threat was only a rumor. On July 9 he wrote, from that place, his well-known letter to his friend Persafor Carr, asking for provisions and guns.[32] Later both Daniel Claus and Guy Johnson referred to the fact that Joseph Brant was not present at Wyoming, interpreting it, however, to suit their own particular requirements. Claus said that Joseph had not approved of Butler's expedition against Wyoming and had gone elsewhere and done something more useful.[33] Guy merely took credit for all that both men had accomplished. He said *he* had sent his deputy, Mr. Butler, to Wyoming and another of his officers, Mr. Brant, to the New York frontier, and that each had brought much credit on himself[34]—and on Guy, too, is the obvious inference.

In the meanwhile, on July 5, John Butler and Sayengaraghta signed a certificate promising safety to the garrison and people of one of the surrendered forts.[35] By July 8 Butler and his army had moved a short distance up the river to Lackawanna[36] where they were apparently resting up from their labors. By July 12 they had reached Tioga where Butler ordered Captain William Caldwell, one of his Rangers, to go to Oquaga and take command of his new recruits who were assembling there. Caldwell was also to harass the countryside and to gather intelligence. Butler was sure Joseph Brant would help in this work, and he sent Brant his regards.[37] Butler never did join forces with Joseph nor did he go to New York or anywhere else he had talked of. He returned to Niagara late in August in very poor health, and he never again led Indians out on an offensive. His health was always his excuse. It was freely bruited about the fort that he was weary of Indian affairs and wished he could get rid of them.

Joseph, left on his own, continued to look for recruits, apparently doing well. This was the summer that he got the greater part of his white Volunteers. He also continued to receive recruits meant for Butler's Rangers. Oquaga and Unadilla were both busy reception centers, for the white rebels had long since fled the latter place and those Indian rebels still at Oquaga were too few to make any difficulty. Most of the Indian rebels on the Susquehanna had left for more satisfactory abodes at Oneida.

The year that followed Oriskany was perhaps the worst time for Loyalists. Neutrality was no longer possible. Pacifism was just as unpopular. By state law all suspicious persons had to take the oath of allegiance or suffer banishment and forfeiture of property. Many swallowed their principles and took the oath, but found that this did not necessarily solve their problems. Those suspected of lukewarmness were still hounded and harassed by their neighbors. Rebel mobs became almost uncontrollable, even by their own duly elected authorities. The committee of Saratoga complained, in February 1778, that a mob abused them for not punishing Tories,

> and since that we are informed that they went round the Town that Day, and when they found a Man, they would ask him if he was sworn and if he said no, then they swore that he was so big a Tory

that the Regulars had no need to swear and he must be whipp'd; and
then they would proceed on to another, and if he confessed he was
sworn and thought the oath binding then he must be flogged, and
made the first flog the other. The next Confessed he was forced to
take the oath of allegiance, But did not intend to keep it; nether had
keep'd it; then they swore he must be flogged for not keeping his
oath Caling him D——— pergurd villion and Could not Be trusted;
and so preceded on in such a Maner, I do begain to mention for the
space of three days, all under the Spureous nam of Liberty—.[38]

After such an experience many a man who did not really wish to leave
home was driven to seek security with the British.

Yet to all those who enlisted in the royal cause because of conviction or because of mistreatment by the rebels must be added a great
number who were coaxed and persuaded by Loyalist recruiters. The
state of New York, being so close to Niagara and the Canadian frontier and the British-held metropolis, offered a fertile field for such
activity. Beaters for the king's forces swarmed over the countryside.
Every Loyalist officer who hoped to raise a regiment sent agents out to
drum up trade. In secret and sometimes openly these agents beguiled
the populace with stories of high pay and royal favors and free land
and the great abundance of everything good within the British lines.
Men whose means of livelihood had been unsettled by the war were
pathetically vulnerable to such persuasion. Only when they got to
Niagara or Montreal did they discover that these stories were mostly
fabrications. Sometimes they slunk home again, only to find that their
houses had been burned, their property confiscated, their families
scattered. Then they fled back to the British and the pay of a Ranger,
or enlisted in one of the Loyalist regiments. Such a magnificent confusion reigned in men's minds that some poor fellows swung back and
forth like a pendulum, returning every now and then home, each time
swearing a new oath and abjuring the old; if peace finally found them
at Niagara they were accounted Loyalists; if in their old homes, they
were accounted rebels!

John Butler had admonished his recruiters not to lie, but they all
knew, as one of them frankly said, that they were "Obliged to Say
more than the Truth." In one way or another Butler enlisted five
hundred men, so he declared later. Sir John Johnson claimed he
enlisted two battalions. Neither revealed whether he had counted
anybody twice. In comparison Joseph's hundred or so appears not very
impressive. It must be remembered, however, that Joseph had no
authority to promise anyone pay.

On July 18 Joseph made his second raid into enemy territory.

Again he was looking for provisions though, of course, not unmindful of the British objective to break up the frontier. Andrewstown (Jordanville) and Springfield, where Joseph struck, were not far apart. The one lay about five miles southeast of German Flats and the other at the head of Lake Otsego. Both, though small settlements, had good stores of grain and cattle. Andrewstown, according to rebel accounts (for these little incursions were too disorganized and unimportant to get into the British dispatches), was totally destroyed. At Springfield fourteen families lost everything except the clothes on their backs. Houses and barns were burned, the cattle driven away. Everything movable was carried off.[39] The British authorities had expected that captured cattle would be driven to Fort Niagara. This expectation turned out to be only wishful thinking. The Loyalists and Indians in the field needed nearly all the cattle they could get to feed themselves. The cattle were driven down to Unadilla, and no farther.

To the Americans these attacks were far from unimportant. Refugees were flying in terror to the Mohawk River and eastward. People who had not been hurt at all were just as terror-stricken as those who had, and joined in the flight or huddled together in hastily built stockades. To make matters worse, it was harvest time for winter wheat, and crops lay rotting in the fields. All was in great confusion, with the militia rushing about, accomplishing nothing. Nobody knew which way the raiders had come nor what route they had taken back. Only later did it come out that Joseph and his men had traveled from Unadilla via Butternuts and the west side of Lake Otsego, places where the rebels did not usually send scouts.[40]

Eight men were killed at Andrewstown and Springfield, and fourteen captured.[41] Two old men were turned loose to go home and reported that Brant had told them German Flats would be next. He and his men had also said "that Fight they would, for they had come on purpose to fight. And burn and Destroy they must."[42] Not till years later did it become generally known that Joseph himself had saved the women and children of Springfield from captivity or death at the hands of his followers.[43] Nothing was mentioned of this in contemporary American correspondence. But even at the time Joseph's Loyalist friends at Niagara and in Canada were saying among themselves that it was his policy not to hurt women and children.[44]

Joseph did not get to German Flats as soon as he thought he would. Raiding was not the best way to procure supplies. It was difficult to drive cattle such long distances; some were invariably lost, and there was always the danger that the pursuing rebels would catch up and there would be more fighting than the Volunteers and Indians could handle. It was much easier to buy provisions from the friendly people on the Susquehanna and Delaware and their tributaries, and Joseph and his men went out often on shopping expeditions. Their bills were sent back to Butler at Fort Niagara all summer long.[45] Absolute necessities which could not be had by local purchase or plunder seem to have been ordered from stores at Niagara and charged to Claus.[46]

Personal problems occupied many of Joseph's thoughts at this time. Without a bit of pay (for there is no evidence that any had yet come through), he was supporting Susanna and the children at Niagara on his credit. Molly, who was also living at Niagara now but often traveling back and forth to the Indian country, was also subsisting her large family on credit, sending some of her children to school in Canada, buying jewelry and trinkets, and maintaining her influence with the Indians by means of presents and entertainment, keeping open house for them on rather a large scale. This was the background for Joseph's letter to a mercantile firm at Niagara requesting that "youll please to advance to the value of thirty pounds to my Sister of any thing in your Store which she may want, and also let my Wife have any thing she may want out of your Store, what my Sister & Wife may want is to be Charged to my private acco[ts]."[47] Living on credit would not have bothered most Indians in the least. It worried Joseph. He had always had so many ways to earn a living. He was not used to debts and money troubles.

Other worries preyed on Joseph's mind, but there are only vague indications as to what they were. Susanna was certainly ill; like Peggie, she was tubercular, and she must have died that fall or winter. Afterward, it would appear that Christina and Isaac were taken to the Indian country for perhaps a year. Isaac, a lonely, moody, unhappy little boy, still too young to go to war, must have missed the excitement of Niagara and resented having to leave. To Isaac, his father, after so many long absences, was almost a stranger.

To make matters worse, Joseph had been expecting some military aid all summer, but none was forthcoming. He had thought all summer long that John Butler would eventually join him for an expedition to the Mohawk. Finally it became obvious that John Butler had returned to Niagara and intended to stay there. If anybody was going against the traitors at German Flats, it would have to be Joseph and his men and the Ranger party under Captain Caldwell. It was about the middle of September when they all gave up on Butler and set out without him.

The party set out up the Unadilla River where they hoped, as before, to pass unnoticed by the rebels. But the latter were now sending scouts out in all directions. Joseph and his men met nine scouts on the way and killed some of them, but others escaped. Thus the traitors of German Flats had ample warning to collect themselves and their property into their two strongholds, Forts Dayton and Herkimer. On September 17, in a driving rain, the raiders arrived. But not a captive could be taken and movables were much scarcer than usual. However, the party got a great number of cattle, some of which had been destined for the garrison of Fort Stanwix. The Loyalists and Indians then destroyed the settlement. They burned sixty-three rebel houses and fifty-seven barns full of grain, killed three men, and headed back to the Susquehanna. Only the church and the houses of a few Loyalist families were left standing amid the ruins.[48] As usual the rebel militia ran around in circles, responding to all kinds of rumors, not knowing which way to go, and making no effective pursuit.

Joseph's depredations had been getting a little too close to the Oneida villages for comfort. Throwing aside whatever small pretense of neutrality they were still trying to maintain (and it was a small pretense, indeed, since there were Oneidas fighting in Washington's army, and Oneidas were regularly spying for the Americans and carrying their news to Fort Stanwix or to Samuel Kirkland and General Schuyler), the Oneidas sent a party of warriors down on the Unadilla to look around and do a bit of destruction on their own. Five unwary Oneidas were captured by the Loyalists. Now began that odd difference between Indian threat and performance which baffled the white people but which the Indians understood perfectly. The Six Nations in their councils had threatened to destroy Oneida, to kill Oneida spies, to give the whole of Oneida no quarter. But now, faced with these guilty Oneida captives, they arranged it so that they could escape! And escape they did, burning, as they went along, some Loyalist houses at Unadilla and Butternuts and even taking a few white prisoners.

In spite of this incident, however, many threats continued to be made against the Oneidas; they were sometimes fired on (but, strangely enough, not hit) by parties of Loyalist Indians, and Joseph made a few threats himself from time to time. The Oneidas said they lived in fear and trembling. Even General Frederick Haldimand, who had succeeded Carleton in Canada, made some threats against them, but he was never able to get the Indians to carry them out; and the white men could not carry them out alone, and would not have dared to do so if they could. In this very strange sort of warfare the Oneidas politely reciprocated. They turned loose their Indian captives, too.

The authorities on both sides of the border were extremely unhappy about such goings-on, but there was not one thing they could do to stop them. The Six Nations were willing to fight in the white man's war, but apparently, so far as they were concerned, it *was* the white man's war.

There is no evidence as to whether or not Joseph freed Indian captives. Unlike his tribesmen, however, he felt it keenly that he was not able to do more for the cause, or so his old friend Claus, who corresponded with Molly, said she told him. "My Bro^r. Joseph," said Molly, "has done; & is doing his best for the King but am only afeard he cant do enough, or as much as his Heart would fain do."[49] Of course the rebels would have said that Joseph had nothing with which to reproach himself. He was much too busy for them. Colonel Bolton had reported to General Haldimand that summer that he had stationed parties of Rangers and Indians all over the frontier; they were scouting on the Delaware as low as Minisink; on Schoharie Creek; on the Susquehanna as low as Wyoming (where some rebels were reassembling); toward German Flats and Cherry Valley; from the Seneca country down to the west branch of the Susquehanna, as far as Juniata; from Carleton Island, at the east end of Lake Ontario, toward Fort Stanwix; and even toward Fort Pitt. These parties made many small depredations. They were not averse to burning single isolated cabins, and the rebels thought Joseph and his "party of infernals" must be wearing seven-league boots to be able to go so far and in so many directions at once. It added much to his terrible reputation. But there is no reason to believe that Joseph Brant destroyed more than one individual house that summer, and even that was done at the instance of local Loyalists who urged him on. They accused James Marr, a man who lived on Butternuts Creek, as a rebel, and Joseph at their behest took Marr prisoner and burned his house and all his effects.[50] Indeed, the local Loyalists, or Tories, were now considered more savage than the Indians. Colonel Alden, commander of the fort at Cherry Valley, speaking of some of these people, declared, "Should much Rather fall into the hands of Brant than either of them."[51]

By the time Joseph returned from German Flats it began to appear that he was finally to get a reinforcement. He heard that John Butler's son Walter, who was certainly not the person whom he most wanted to see, was coming out to join him. Walter, a newly-made captain in the Rangers and only twenty-five years old, had managed to escape from detention at Albany the previous spring. Furious with his jailers and hoping now to get rebel captives to exchange for his mother and the younger members of the family, he was trying to collect the

Senecas for an expedition to the Mohawk. He had expected to go with the party to German Flats, but the Indians were slow in assembling. Some of them, seeing Loyalists fleeing to Niagara, frankly said that the white men were running away and leaving the Indians to fight their war. The warriors may never have assembled in sufficient force if Colonel Hartley who was stationed with a regiment of Continental troops on the Pennsylvania frontier had not come up and burned Tioga and some other Indian villages. The Senecas, enraged at this (to them, unprovoked) attack at their back door, flew to arms. They were sure that the rebels meant to invade their country.

In the meantime Joseph had decided to make another foray. This time he went off in the direction of the Delaware rather than the Mohawk. On October 13 he and his men suddenly appeared at Peenpack, a small settlement on the Neversink River. The people of Peenpack had three little forts, and Joseph took one by storm. The others held out. The party got some prisoners and inflicted a few casualties, but recent heavy rains had made the streams too high to drive away cattle.[52] Joseph had meant to go back and meet Walter Butler at Oquaga. Now he got the news that there was no Oquaga to go back to! The rebels with a determined force of Continentals and militia had come down from Schoharie and, in his absence, had burned both Oquaga and Unadilla. Joseph's absence may, or may not, have been pure coincidence. The rebels thought he had fled from them and perhaps they were right, for Joseph did not have enough men or ammunition to risk battle, and it hardly seems reasonable that he had no inkling the enemy was marching. At any rate, the destruction of these two towns left Joseph and his Volunteers without a home base and many Indians and Loyalists without a home. Seventeen residents of Oquaga who remained steadfastly friendly to the rebels fled to Oneida. The others left for other parts of the Indian country.

Joseph revised his plans and set out for Cochecton on the Delaware.[53] Leaving about twenty of his men at Cochecton, he then went on to join Walter Butler. He met young Butler about October 22 at Owego, near the end of the Forbidden Path. He had been traveling nine days from Peenpack.[54] He was determined to take part in what must be the last campaign of the season.[55] Already it was getting cold and soon there would be snow, making the expedition's footprints easy to follow. The Indians never liked to fight in the snow.

Walter Butler had brought a force of about three hundred Indians and all the Rangers from Niagara, plus a detachment of volunteers (perhaps as many as fifty) from the King's regiment of British regulars.

When Colonel Bolton had heard that the rebels were invading the Indian country, he had sent all the aid he could, knowing that the meager garrison of Fort Niagara could never hold out if the Indians were forced to neutrality. With young Butler, also, were those Rangers who had recently fled from Oquaga and Unadilla. Among the latter were Captain Caldwell and his command who had been on the frontier most of the summer and fall. Joseph had brought his usual complement of whites and Indians, making the whole party 321 Indians and about an equal number of whites.[56] The Indians with Walter Butler were made up of their customary small autonomous parties, but if anyone could be said to command them, it was Sayengaraghta who, according to Joseph, had gained almost complete control over the Loyalist part of the Six Nations.[57]

All these whites and Indians held a council together shortly after they joined. After much consideration they decided to attack Cherry Valley. As usual, an Oneida spy reported the plan to the Americans. On November 6 the commander at Fort Stanwix sent an express to the garrison at Cherry Valley with word of the projected attack. On November 8 Colonel Alden acknowledged the warning.[58] Oneida spies, however, had been crying wolf for a long time. For more than two years the people of Cherry Valley had been getting warning after warning and they had heeded each one, living in dread the whole time. But to get a warning so late in the season when it was well known that Indians never fought so late in the season was too much. Colonel Alden himself was sceptical though he sent out a scouting party to reconnoiter. He promised to give the people ample warning if an attack really was to take place. This was all that was done. Colonel Alden was not a frontiersman. He commanded a Massachusetts regiment.

By October 29 Walter Butler's party of Indians and Loyalists were on their way. On that date Joseph wrote a letter to a friend at Niagara mentioning their plans, but he did not state where they had advanced to. He did state, however, that he and Walter were quarreling. The point of contention was Joseph's white Volunteers. The bit of yellow lace which Joseph's men wore on their hats[59] was to Walter, a somewhat arrogant young man, a great eyesore. Ambitious to raise as many Rangers for his father's corps as possible, he told every recruiter he met that nobody but him had any right to recruit in that area, and he threatened to send at least one recruiter in irons to Niagara. Joseph became so angry at what he considered ill treatment from Walter and the Rangers that he almost left the expedition. His own zeal and good sense, however, and the zeal and good sense of his Indian friends prevailed. The latter begged him to stay, reminding him that he could take his case up with Walter's superiors.[60]

Though this argument persuaded Joseph, ninety of his men fled to the woods. Young Walter, according to Claus, had told them that if they did not join the Rangers they should receive no provisions and even be treated as rebels.[61] Joseph continued with the expedition but was left with practically no command.

By early November the invaders were far up the Susquehanna. They seem to have taken the usual route up the river, on the west side as far as the mouth of Schenevus Creek, then across the river by the ford, and up the east side. On November 9 they discovered the tracks of Colonel Alden's scouting party who had imprudently lain down to sleep beside a blazing campfire. All nine of the party were captured or killed. Not a soul escaped to carry the news back to the settlement.

On the night of November 10 the Loyalists camped on a hill about six miles from Cherry Valley, amid some evergreens. It was cold, raining and snowing by turns. The Indians wanted to wait till daylight to attack, and they got their way. The party ate their parched corn or whatever food they had, cold, and lay down without a fire. The town was sleeping.

The Indians had left home with the purpose of defending their country. Though it turned out that no defense was called for, they had acquired fresh incentives to war. They must take revenge for Colonel Hartley's burning of Tioga and for the destruction of Oquaga. They had found out that one of the officers who signed the capitulation at Wyoming, thereby promising not to fight again, had in fact joined Colonel Hartley in his attack. The Indians did not like, as they said, to fight the same person twice. They were also angry because the rebels called the Wyoming affair a massacre. The warriors did not consider it a massacre to kill prisoners captured in arms. On November 10, as they lay down under their hastily constructed shelters, they harbored many grudges.[62] Something dark was brooding. Walter Butler did not sense it. Joseph Brant did.

At dawn the party set out once more. Rain was still falling. Soon they saw two men cutting wood. Shots rang out from some of the Indians. One man was killed; the other, wounded, fled toward Cherry Valley. The wounded man actually got to Cherry Valley, bringing the final warning to an incredulous Colonel Alden that the enemy was coming in force. The colonel appears to have thought the Indians were only some stragglers, signifying nothing.

Over the hills Walter Butler approached nearer. The town came in sight, one of the finest settlements on the entire frontier and the principal settlement south of the Mohawk. Before the war Cherry Valley had had nearly three hundred inhabitants. Its beautiful cherry orchards were sere and leafless now, but in spring those that were left would bear a glory of blossoms and cover for a while the horror that had happened.

By judicious questioning Butler and his men had learned from the captive scouts just what the arrangements in Cherry Valley were. The invaders knew that Colonel Alden and some of his officers lodged with the Wells family who lived near the fort. Other officers lodged with other families close by. Walter and most of the Rangers planned to attack the fort and head off anybody trying to get inside. The Indians and about fifty whites were to attack the houses and capture or kill the soldiers. If Walter Butler wished to prevent Indian outrages (and he did), his plan was not well calculated to accomplish its purpose. Indeed, nothing in Walter's experience had ever qualified him for this command. General Carleton, who was kindly disposed to all the Butlers, had called him a "promising" young man. But nobody had ever said he knew anything about leading Indians, especially the vengeful Senecas.

Joseph Brant, as he claimed after the war, took a short cut, hurrying over a plowed field. He had several Loyalist friends in the town. One of these was Robert Wells, and he seems to have had some idea that he could save the Wells family. Robert had gone with him and Peggie and the baby on that tour down the Susquehanna back in '69. Was it really so long ago? Joseph hurried faster, but the plowed ground was hard going. The Senecas got there first.[63]

British and American accounts of the massacre at Cherry Valley do not differ very much. On his retreat Walter Butler wrote a long letter of explanation to Colonel Bolton.[64] He managed to write page after page without once mentioning the name of the place he had desolated. He knew nearly everybody in Cherry Valley, or could have known them, for it was an old settlement for a frontier. The sturdy Scotch-Irish pioneers had lived there since long before he was born, and he was born not far away. Though Walter's report was long, it was, in a strange way, almost noncommittal. He told everything, and said nothing.

Walter told how the major and a few other soldiers managed to get into the fort; how the rest of the officers and their guards were either captured or killed by the Indians; how he himself stormed the fort but to no avail; how he stayed near the fort to prevent a sally while the Indians were "dispersed over the Settlement, killing and taking Pris-

oners the Inhabitants, plundering and destroying the Buildings &c";
how he remained in the same position till late in the evening, though
it rained incessantly, and then retired about a mile away where he
spent the night; how the next morning he sent Captain McDonald
with sixty Rangers and Mr. Brant with fifty Indians to complete the
destruction of the "Place" while the other Indians and the weaker
Rangers drove off the cattle, and he himself again watched the fort;
how "The Garrison all the while coop'd within their Breast-Works
remained Spectators of our Depredations which they made no Attempts to interrupt"; how, unable to take the fort, he had to retire and
leave it "the only remaining Building amidst the Ruins of the Place."

> I have much to lament, [he went on] that notwithstanding my ut-
> most Precaution and Endeavours to save the Women and Chil-
> dren, I could not prevent some of them falling unhappy Victims to
> the Fury of the Savages. They have carried off many of the Inhabi-
> tants Prisoners and killed more . . . .
>
> I could not prevail with the Indians to leave the Women and
> Children behind; tho the second Morning of our March Capt John-
> ston (to whose Knowledge of the Indians and Address in managing I
> am much indebted,) and I, got them to permit twelve,[65] who were
> Loyalists, and whom I had concealed the first Day with the humane
> Assistance of Mr Joseph Brant & Capt Jacobs of Ochquaga, to re-
> turn.

He then explained why the Indians had behaved as they did and
what caused them to harbor such terrible grudges. Though he said
nothing in the letter of his shame, his shame burned on every page.

Persons at Niagara who got their information from the Rangers
added further dreadful details in days to come. The merchants, Taylor
& Duffin, wrote Daniel Claus that all the Indians and many of the
Rangers did not know who were Loyalists and who were rebels, and
that thirteen members of the Wells family, though thought to be good
friends to government, were all killed.[66] Another person writing from
Niagara to a friend at Detroit said the Seneca chief, Little Beard, was
responsible for the Wells murders. Some of the American soldiers had
fired back at him and wounded three of his followers so "he put Men
Women & Child[r]en to death." Lieutenant Hare, one of the Rangers,
was able to save the old minister (thought to be another Loyalist) and
his daughter. The lieutenant found the young lady trying to protect
her dead mother from being scalped. The Indians killed all that were
in their way, though "the Evening before the attack the Chiefs promised to observe the same humanity they had with Colo Butler [at

Wyoming] instead of which they exerted the most horrid barbaritys, the bloody seen is almost past discription. I think it hath determin'd Cap^tns Butler & McDonald from ever having any more to do in such a service where Savages make the principle part of the army . . . ."[67] The writer was correct in his prediction. Walter Butler never again went out on such a service.

The rebels were too busy to write very much for a long time after the massacre. Their accounts are short and terse, almost dazed. They said only that more than thirty women and children had been slain, that the town was totally destroyed.[68] Hardly a day went by that additional bodies were not found and brought in for burial. Walter Butler had thought it strange the Americans did not come out to fight; but the troops in the fort numbered far less than the attackers, and most of their officers had been killed or captured. Colonel Alden was one of the first to be killed, and the lieutenant colonel was taken prisoner. The command devolved on the major who with his best exertions could only watch the houses burn and hold on to his post. Those townspeople who had succeeded in getting into the fort or hiding themselves in the woods were left with neither shelter against the winter nor clothing nor bedding nor food. The county militia, summoned for help, could, as usual, accomplish nothing in the way of pursuit, and was soon involved in name-calling and fault-finding. Nobody seems to have had a good word for the unhappy militia. They were "laggards" or "cowards," people thought; they did not even try to do their duty.

The story of the massacre at Cherry Valley, so far as Joseph Brant is concerned, ends in paradox. On November 23, just twelve days after the blow had been struck, J. H. Livingston, a rebel par excellence, wrote to his brother describing the terrible devastation out on the frontier. Somewhere, somehow, Mr. Livingston had picked up a strange piece of gossip. Let him tell it in his own words: "there is an Anecdote of the famous Brant mentioned upon this occasion which deserves to be made public . . . . it is Said when this party Came out, their Orders were Read by young Butler. upon which Brant turned round & wept and then recovering himself told Butler he was going to make war against America but not to Murder and Butcher; that he was an Enemy from principle but he wod never have a hand in massacring the Defenceless Inhabitants upon which the bloody department was committed [to] a Seneca Indian while the noble Brant with another party attacked the fort."[69]

Though this story got no acceptance at the time, and was not even common knowledge, there was at least one deserter from Butler's force who could have told it.[70] It is not precisely true; Brant did not attack the fort, at least not the first day. Yet the rest of Livingston's story *might* be true. There is no doubt that Joseph did try to save the Loyalists at Cherry Valley and, from what old people remembered years later, he also tried to save women and children, as well as other noncombatants, in general. His "Generosity to the Prisoners he took during the War" was certainly known and admitted by the Americans as early as 1784.[71]

But the account of Cherry Valley does not end here. On December 1, before the Indians and Loyalists had been able to return to Niagara, and while they were momently expected, the firm of Taylor & Duffin wrote Claus that an express had come in with the news of the destruction of Cherry Valley. The messenger, a Ranger, had reported that Brant had started back to Niagara with Butler's party, and gone part of the way, but "not being at all satisfied with what had been done at Cherry Valley" had returned to the Mohawk with seven of his Indians to burn Honicle Harkiman's (General Herkimer's) house and get a prisoner.[72] Something like this, apparently, is just what Brant did. On the very same day that J. H. Livingston wrote his letter extolling Joseph's nobility, he made a new irruption near Fort Plank, burned four houses and barns (though not Herkimer's), took three prisoners, and uttered threats that he still would have the river.[73]

Satisfied with what they had done, Brant and his Indians turned their faces once more toward Niagara. Along the way they remembered the plight of the Volunteers who were still hiding in the woods, some of whom would undoubtedly try to return to their homes. With this thought in mind four members of the party (and certainly not without their leader's knowledge) sent word to the rebels about the upper Delaware that if they bothered any of their white brothers that winter, they would "be worst delt with, then your Nighbours the Cheryvalle People was."[74]

In one campaign the break-up of the frontier had almost come to pass. So great was the fear of Brant and of the Indians which it was supposed he led, and so monstrous his (and their) reputation, that those frontiersmen who had anywhere else to go had left or were leaving. It was mournfully predicted among the rebels that soon there would not be a smoking chimney west of Schenectady. Some of the most productive land in the whole thirteen states was being abandoned to the encroaching forest—an irreparable blow to the Continental army which was already hard put to get enough food. The problem occupied minds in the very highest places, in the halls of Congress and at the headquarters of General George Washington. It was a problem which all agreed was worthy of a supreme effort to resolve.

12

The Destruction of the Longhouse

IN HIS first winter in Canada General Frederick Haldimand, Carleton's successor, began the practice of sending out scouts and spies to find out what was going on to the southward. He hoped to learn not only what the rebels were doing but also what his counterpart, Sir Henry Clinton in New York, was doing. Sometimes, because of the common difficulties of communication due to the vast distances by land and sea and the vagaries of the weather, and the uncommon difficulties due to the activities of French naval vessels and American privateers and the watchfulness at American outposts, the commander in chief in Canada did not hear for months whether his side was accomplishing anything, anywhere. He was, naturally, curious. Unfortunately, the spies who went out that first winter did not report that Sir Henry Clinton was doing anything remarkable or that he was getting matters in any forwardness for coming up the Hudson River, but they did say that the rebels were building boats at Schenectady. Why *boats?* worried General Haldimand. And why at *Schenectady?* he wondered. Then came other reports that all the saddlers in Philadelphia were busy making saddles as fast as they could. Saddles? *Boats* and *saddles,* too? The long nights in the Castle of St. Louis seemed made for pondering and worrying.

In the meantime Joseph Brant and Walter Butler, and all the Rangers and most of the Indian department, and throngs of Loyalist refugees and their families, and numerous prisoners, and Molly Brant and her younger children, and many of the Indians were gathered at crowded Niagara and seemed likely to burst the walls. Walter and the Rangers were drilling; the refugees were building huts; the rebel prisoners were being cooperative or uncooperative according to their ideas of what was good and proper; Molly was rendering herself somewhat obnoxious, it is feared; and the Indians were lounging about or getting drunk or helping themselves to the traders' merchandise and cattle, or making impossible demands upon Colonel Bolton who was already driven to distraction by rheumatism and gout. Last winter, he recalled, had been very much like this, and next winter probably would be the same. Colonel Bolton heartily wished he was somewhere else.

Fort Niagara, which lay on the east side of the Niagara River as it fell into Lake Ontario, was a place perpetually out of repair. The pickets which had been put up eight years ago were almost ready to fall down, several parapets had burst, the wharf was in a ruinous state, and on the north water lapped within a few feet of the fort's foundations. To make matters worse, logs for repairs could not be cut less than two miles away and most of the stone had to be brought in from a distance of seven miles. Fort Niagara was also under-garrisoned, having less than 350 troops, some of whom were stationed up the river at two little auxiliary forts, and a few artillerymen; and everybody suffered from malnutrition and scurvy and respiratory complaints and malaria and all kinds of digestive upsets. Dr. McCausland, surgeon to the Eighth, or King's, regiment, was the busiest man in the place. Winter and early spring were the worst times of all. After the long, dreary winter months many of the soldiers could just barely get up off their straw and creep outside to warm themselves a little in the pale spring sunshine.

Those Indians who had not remained in the area all winter usually returned with their families for councils and gifts before the next campaign was due to open. It was unthinkable that there should be no counciling together before going again to war. Besides, last fall's gifts were used up, or lost or broken. The Indians had never learned to repair their guns and tools and jewelry; articles of white manufacture not in good order simply had to be replaced. Whole families began to come in as early as December 30, 1778, and in just one month they had consumed 57,000 rations, adding the specter of starvation to the specters of decay and disease. Colonel Bolton could only issue the required provisions and hope that more could be brought up the lake from Canada before everything in the storehouse was consumed. With Niagara isolated by the winter's ice, this was by no means a certainty. The Indians did not concern themselves with such a dark thought. It never occurred to them that more and more and still more provisions might not be forthcoming. Few Indians ever worried about their own tomorrows, much less the tomorrows of their white allies.

Six councils took place between January 29 and May 8, 1779. As

Butler and Bolton had predicted, nearly three thousand Indians came in from time to time, including 276 Mohawks and 287 former residents of Oquaga who were now living at Niagara, having nowhere else to go. The Six Nations had heard that the rebels were building a fort at Oneida and they felt particularly threatened, although they still insisted that the quarrel was the white man's quarrel. The tribesmen spent their time trying to spirit up their allies; they sent belts and messages to the west and south, to the Seven Nations of Canada, and to the Oneidas. They also sent a letter to Sir Henry Clinton urging him to advance up the Hudson River (they wanted to meet him and take him by the hand, they said) and to General Haldimand urging him to establish a post at Oswego for the protection of their families. They assured Haldimand they were determined not to yield to the rebels "while we have a Man left." In all these councils Sayengaraghta seems to have been the leading spirit. Sayengaraghta was riding high and Joseph Brant was nowhere in evidence. Joseph's only public act that winter seems to have been to send another remonstrance to the Oneidas.[1] Subsequent events show that the Seneca and the Mohawk were again at odds with each other. It must have been this situation that John Butler was thinking about when, in January, he begged the Indians to compose their differences.

Joseph, pouring out his woes to Colonel Bolton, found a sympathetic listener.[2] Bolton thought highly of Joseph Brant because of his humane behavior at Cherry Valley. The commander of Fort Niagara was a good man himself and did not approve of using the aborigines in warfare. He was also a good officer, and used them, as he was instructed. But Colonel Bolton had little authority to remedy Joseph's complaints. For this reason, early in 1779, he gave Joseph permission to go down the country to see General Haldimand. The letter of introduction which he wrote for him on February 12 read, in part: "Mr Brant (the Bearer of this) with his Indians from Capt. Butlers Account as well as every other report made to me beheaved with great humanity to all those who fell into his hands at Cherry Valley. This I am convinced will recommend him to your Excellency's Notice much more than any thing else I cou'd Say in his favour."[3]

February seems a strange time for anybody to have wanted to make the long and painful journey from Niagara to Quebec, but having to be back in time for the next season's fighting, Joseph had no choice. He set out a few days after Bolton wrote the letter of introduction. It took him nearly a month to get as far as Montreal. He has not said anything about the trip other than that it was "tedious"[4]—a real understatement, that. However, Walter Butler who went down to see

Haldimand in March—on Ranger business, and especially on the business of an exchange of prisoners—did describe the journey in detail.[5] Joseph's travels must have been similar, though slower since he had worse weather, and he saw about the same sights. It is significant that Walter and Joseph did not travel together. Each took the long, cold, and perilous trip with someone else. Joseph's companion was Lieutenant Adams, an officer in the Indian department.[6] If anybody else went along, we are not told about it. Some paid laborers, of course, had been hired to man the bateau.

The route followed the north shore of Lake Ontario, or as near as it was possible to follow the shore, considering the ice. Ontario's shore line and harbors were frozen over during the winter, completely stopping all but emergency communication between Canada and the upper posts. There were no such things as inns along here, not even of the rudest sort, and no buildings at all except a trader's cabin and a few huts belonging to the Missisauga Indians. At night the travelers made camp as best they could, in tents. The Indians had a way of digging a deep rounded bowl in the snow, making a fire in the center, and lying more snug on fir branches than might be supposed. This bowl formed a sort of shelter from the wind and cold, the rim being piled higher on the windward side; and very likely, wherever there was deep snow, Joseph pitched his tent in such a place. He always stopped late, and the next day he would be on his way by daylight. Only a heavy wind and high swell would make him interrupt the journey. Walter Butler records on March 10 that some Missisaugas told him that Joseph Brant had left his boat at the head of the lake eleven days before and had continued his journey with two canoes.[7] So, sailing and rowing, Joseph passed along the low, level beaches and some few bluffs, and crossed the mouths of many streams, big and little; he made a portage or two from one point of land to another; passed the site of Toronto; and then passed old Cataraqui with its ruined French fort. From here on lay many small islands where those not in the know could easily get lost. At Carleton Island at the east end of the lake Joseph said farewell to Lieutenant Adams who was leaving him, but he did not try to land to visit the island's new post because of large chunks of floating ice.[8] Oddly enough, throughout this entire journey the rebels back on the Mohawk were marching and countermarching, firmly convinced that Joseph Brant was about to descend on them any minute.[9]

Arriving finally at Montreal, Joseph saw his old friend Daniel Claus again. To Claus had been entrusted the task of superintending the Fort Hunter Mohawks who had fled their homes at the time of Burgoyne's campaign. These Mohawks were now settled at nearby

Lachine, in a village of bark huts. They went out on little excursions against the rebels from time to time while Claus overlooked their activities and took care of their material needs. Until they could return to their own country (a thing they fully intended to do) these Fort Hunter Indians had to live wholly on the charity of the British government. Joseph was able to see some of his old friends. He and Claus met frequently and Joseph got his prejudices and grievances reinforced. Without doubt he also got some new instructions. At this time Claus was bombarding all his friends and acquaintances everywhere with accounts of the shortcomings of Butler & Son.

General Haldimand, informed that Joseph Brant wished to wait upon him, sent Claus and Joseph permission to come to Quebec. At the same time he instructed Sir John Johnson, who was supervising the gathering of intelligence and who was also living in Montreal, to come, too.[10] As the three travelers made their way down over the ice in sleighs, past little white farmhouses and many a wayside cross, and sampling the rude local inns, Haldimand, who was long experienced in the colonial warfare in America, had time to reflect upon Brant's value to the British government. Claus had sung Joseph's praises unremittingly, emphasizing time and again his great influence with the Six Nations. Butler had never stinted in his praise of Joseph, and Bolton thought very highly of him. General Carleton, in briefing his successor, seems also to have spoken well of him.[11] Indeed, General Haldimand had been brought to think that all the successes of the Rangers and Indians of the previous summer "Must be Attributed greatly to the Indian Joseph Briant Whose Attachment to Government, resolution And Personal Exertion, makes him a character of a very distinguished Kind"; and he had already recommended him to Germain for "some particular Mark of the King's favor."[12] Accordingly, the general was prepared to trust Joseph wholeheartedly and to give him almost anything he wanted. In 1759 Joseph, an Indian lad on his way to the siege of Niagara, could not have been an object of interest to the commanding officer at Oswego; twenty years later that same officer, now commander in chief of all of Canada, was eager to lay before him the welcome mat. So great a change had the years wrought.

At the Castle of St. Louis Joseph was received with as much graciousness as a tough-minded old fighter could muster, and he, in turn, appears to have unburdened himself of all his troubles. He could not have gone through what he did, he told Haldimand, if it had not been for Colonel Bolton's kindly support and protection.[13] The general liked Bolton, too, and was glad to hear him praised. Here was a common bond.

The matter of Joseph's salary was quickly taken care of. There is record that he received for the next six months a captain's pay of twelve shillings per day New York currency. In October his pay was raised to ten shillings sterling—an increase of about twenty pounds semi-annually and equivalent to what the white captains received.[14] He was also left with the expectation that he would get a pension after the war.[15] Joseph evidently made some requests in Molly's behalf for her status in Claus's accounts seems to have been regularized and made permanent, and later that year Haldimand invited her to move herself and family down to lower Canada where he promised to take care of her.

Joseph's next thoughts were for his Volunteers. Though they seem never to have received pay, they did get clothing, rations, and medical attention.[16] Haldimand sent them one hundred outfits as soon as the navigation of the lakes opened.[17] In time all the Volunteers took refuge at Niagara. Joseph's Indian followers, numbering twenty-seven at this time, were clothed, along with the other Indians, at Niagara, each chief and principal warrior receiving such niceties as a scarlet blanket and waistcoat, a hat with a feather, a fine ruffled shirt, scarlet leggings with ribbons, a black silk handkerchief, and the usual silver jewelry.[18]

Joseph had brought some letters to the general from the Six Nations, and he was expected to return with an answer.[19] The Six Nations were worrying about the loss of Canajoharie, Fort Hunter, and Oquaga. The Indians from these three villages had been left homeless, and they (and the entire Six Nations as well) wanted some assurance that they would have somewhere to go after the war. This seemed a reasonable request to Haldimand, who was not only a fair and just man but also a man who thought the Indians indispensable to the security of the upper posts, the fur trade, and, indeed, the whole of Canada. Even before he left England he had urged Germain to supply the Indians with plenty of goods; their "assistance . . . is most essential to our success," he had said, "and their attachment to His Majesty at all times to be secured."[20] Haldimand knew what was what. He had not fought through the war with France for nothing.

After having been on the spot for almost a year, Haldimand had not changed his mind. He was willing to promise the Indians almost anything in his power. As far as he was concerned, the Indians need have no fear that they would have nowhere to go, and he sent back to them a letter to that effect.

Some of the Mohawks of the Villages of Conajoharie, Tiyondarago, and Aughwago, [wrote Haldimand] whose settlements there, had been upon account of their steady attachment to the King's service and the Interests of Government Ruined by the Rebels; having informed me, that my Predecessor Sir Guy Carleton, was pleased to promise, as soon as the present Troubles were at an End, the same should be restored at the Expence of Government, to the state they were in before these broke out, and said promise appearing to me Just, I do hereby Ratify the same, and assure them the said Promise, as far as in me lies, shall be faithfully executed, as soon as that happy Time Come.[21]

This was a promise that was to mean more and more to the Six Nations as time went on.

General Haldimand had many problems of his own, and those that concerned the Indians he undoubtedly discussed with Joseph and the two experts on Indian affairs, Claus and Sir John. What were the rebels up to? They were certainly preparing an invasion. Their preparations could not be hidden. But where? Some spies reported that the rebels, as before, would mount an attack into Canada by way of Lakes George and Champlain. Other spies reported the rebels were going to try to take Oswego. Still others said they were aiming for Niagara or Detroit or even for far-away Michilimackinac. Sir Henry Clinton wrote Haldimand that he thought the real object was Detroit, but that there would undoubtedly be a feint toward the Susquehanna in order to immobilize Bulter's Indians and Rangers. Haldimand was inclined to agree with Clinton insofar as he thought the movement toward the Susquehanna would be a feint. Joseph, who was easily alarmed when it came to his own people, had some misgivings, one may be sure. He had always feared some sort of rebel attack on the Six Nations country, and one of the objects of his visit to Quebec was to request the general to establish a post at Oswego for the protection of the Indians.[22] Claus gave his opinion that Detroit, at least, was safe. Sir John could only repeat what his own spies had told him, and his spies could agree no better than Haldimand's or Bolton's.

At this critical juncture General Haldimand was more than ever worried about the Oneidas and the Indians of Canada. The faithless Oneidas were in a position to give considerable support to any rebel invasion toward the Susquehanna or toward Lake Ontario or Niagara. Haldimand proposed making a great effort to win these Indians back. He had in mind a combination of threats and promises which he hoped would accomplish the purpose. Joseph was certainly agreeable to such an attempt; he had exerted himself to the utmost to bring the Oneidas to a proper sense of duty. While Joseph was in the capital Haldimand did send the Oneidas what he said was his "last and final" offer, and he asked Joseph to point out some loyal Indian messengers to entrust it to.[23] Haldimand's message was long and persuasive and very threatening. It had no effect.

The Canadian Indians were a different problem. Though they loudly proclaimed their loyalty, some of them continued to spy for the Americans. They expected to see a French fleet in the St. Lawrence any day and, buoyed up by a proclamation by the French Admiral d'Estaing and a letter from the famed Marquis de Lafayette, they looked forward to a happy reunion with their dear old former father. Officers at various posts in lower Canada reported great discontent among the natives; they were "almost intollerable greedy and importunate," they would not do the least service without being paid ten times its worth, and if refused some request did not hesitate to taunt that they would "get better Treatment soon from the Yankees." Some of the Caughnawagas had tried to get the Six Nations to come over to the rebel side, telling them that Washington and the French fleet had blocked up the English in New York and kept them there "like Pigs in a Pen," that they could cut their throats whenever they pleased. It was difficult to decide what to do about the deceitful Canadians.

A very critical situation had developed the previous year on the Ohio and in the Illinois country where the Virginian, George Rogers Clark, had made an amazing capture of the old French settlements of Kaskaskia, Cahokia, and Vincennes; and Americans from Fort Pitt were pushing closer toward Detroit. Joseph had brought the commander in chief the welcome news that Governor Hamilton of Detroit had succeeded in recapturing Vincennes from Clark.[24] Joseph's information, however, was very out of date, winter communication between Detroit and Niagara being almost non-existent. In reality Hamilton had been captured at Vincennes in February and was already on his way to a rebel prison. Though the Six Nations were willing to exert all their influence, they could not do much about the distant French and French Indians who had welcomed George Rogers Clark to the Illinois.

The greatest problem on Haldimand's mind was the shortage of men and supplies. The inhabited part of Canada seldom had enough of either, much less the outposts. That spring the general could count only sixteen hundred regular British troops below Lake Ontario that were fit for duty. There was a somewhat greater number of German mercenaries but they were unacquainted with woods fighting and very short of officers. Haldimand begged Clinton to send him German officers if any of Burgoyne's Germans had been exchanged. Twice a year provision fleets sailed from England bringing manufactured goods, Indian supplies, salt meat, and flour (for Canadian flour could be used only where it was grown; it would not keep during the long transport up the lakes). By spring the whole of Canada was usually very scarce of food and if the fleet was lost or even late the province had to go on short rations. Similarly if the fall fleet was lost by storms or capture, the winter became a perilous prospect. It was difficult to estimate what might be needed so far ahead, and the commander did not always get what he ordered. Boxes had broken open and casks had leaked their brine. Somebody had not packed properly. Somebody had handled the cargoes too roughly. Other times the commander's requisitions might be lost, and the provisioners in England had to do the best they could to send him what they supposed he might need. And always Yankee privateers hovered near the shipping lanes, catching the unwary, and boldly ventured into the Gulf of St. Lawrence where they made havoc of entire fleets, it being not unusual that a quarter of the ships might be lost. General Haldimand had many anxious moments waiting for news of latecomers.

Even if he had all the troops in the world, Haldimand could not reinforce the upper country if he could not also send supplies. Yet only by herculean efforts could Niagara, Detroit, and Michilimackinac be provisioned. Transport of supplies up the lakes began about April 15 when the ice had melted and had to stop by the end of November when the ice had formed again. This was all too short a period. There were not enough workmen, and Canadians had to be drafted to man the bateaux. The wretched peasants stood waist-deep and even shoulder-deep in the swirling rapids of the St. Lawrence, towing, pushing, pulling; shoving and hauling and straining; in waters of numbing cold where neither poles nor oars nor sails were of any use; often losing boats and cargo, dragging boats over portages, then loading and unloading those larger lake vessels by which the British controlled their watery lanes of commerce. Such transport could be done only at immense expense. The upper posts cost more by far than all the rest of Canada, Haldimand knew. He understood, however, that they must be preserved at any cost, but sometimes he wondered if they were worth it. Howls of pain were already emanating from the government at home. The posts must be maintained (so essential were they to trade), but the general *must* cut expenses. Haldimand tried. He urged the officers at Niagara and Detroit and all the small dependent places to have their soldiers make kitchen gardens, raise cattle, and catch fish, to do all they could to support themselves. He begged the agents of the Indian department to see that the Indians remained in their villages rather than spending so much of their time at the forts, or at least to leave their families behind when they came.

One may be sure that Haldimand tried to impress these urgencies on Joseph's mind, too. Though he may not have realized it, the attempt was not to much purpose. Joseph could not do anything about the Indians. Besides, pleas for economy left him not much moved. He could not take too seriously the difficulties attending the transport. It was his blind spot, just as it was the blind spot of all the Indians. They never thought moving things from place to place was so difficult. *They* did it all the time. Joseph was sorry provisions were so scarce "as you say," but trusted politely that in a little while there would be better news and plenty of everything.[25] Later he told Sir John Johnson that he hoped scalps would be as acceptable in the general's eyes as the raising of corn.[26]

Joseph had made a good impression. "I recommend Brant, to your protection, as a very intelligent and good man," wrote Haldimand to Bolton after Joseph had gone.[27] Haldimand sent Joseph away in the company of his aide-de-camp, Captain Brehm, whom he had ordered on an inspection trip to the west. He instructed Brehm to pay Joseph's expenses on the voyage to Montreal and to buy Molly a present of whatever her brother might think appropriate.[28]

On April 9, in the evening, the two travelers left Quebec.[29] They reached Montreal five days later after what Joseph described as a "very tedious" journey, due probably to unfavorable winds and the strong current. Brehm, warned to be careful of the Oneidas, went on, but Joseph tarried. He said he had some business to attend to.[30] For one thing he probably wished to pick up some clothing which he had ordered from a local seamstress, for Claus paid the bill a short time later.[31] He must have had another conference with Claus for he wrote Haldimand regretting that his "worthy friend," Colonel Claus, had not been given a royal commission, and praising him for all that he had done for him and for the king's service.[32]

By May 8 Joseph had got as far as Carleton Island where he was awaiting the next boat to Niagara.[33] Here he met Walter Butler who was returning from his visit to the commander in chief.[34] Walter had been successful in an attempt to get his mother and family exchanged for some of the Cherry Valley prisoners. Walter had also satisfactorily explained the Cherry Valley affair to Haldimand who, a kindly man in spite of his apparent severity, at first had been inclined to be critical. On the whole Walter had made a favorable impression, too. Haldimand thought him active and useful, and counted much on him, as he said, "to keep back the Rebels." The general praised the young man to Bolton and to Captain Brehm as well as to his father. Only to the Johnson family, when it particularly suited his purpose, did he make any disparaging remarks. It was an uncomfortable situation for Walter which he was sensitive enough to divine and perhaps to see as worse than it really was. He knew that the Johnsons were, so to speak, after his scalp, and he thought Joseph had been influenced to complain about him.[35] If Joseph did complain about him, we have no evidence of it.

In the meantime, far to the south of Carleton Island, something important *was* going on. Haldimand's spies and scouts had not been wrong. The rebels were working and consulting with one another and planning and rushing to and fro. There was the sound of hammers and saws, the sound of blows on anvils. Mill wheels were turning. Women were sewing. Expresses hurried from place to place. In a myriad of ways the rebels were getting themselves in readiness for the greatest military effort they had ever made. They were determined that 1779 should not be like 1778.

It had been a terrible summer and fall, a terrible winter. Wagons and sleighs and bateaux that used to arrive in Albany and Schenectady loaded with flour for sale now came in empty, their drivers and boatmen desperately searching for flour. Schenectady was crowded with hungry refugees. From German Flats and Cherry Valley alone 827 persons who had lost their all were being fed at the public expense. The army must cut its rations for the next campaign. "God Knows where it will End; must it not very Soon Create a famine?" cried one civilian leader, shaken by the suffering he saw.[36]

There was a similar note of desperation among the military. "It is impossible for us to defend the County," they had lamented, "for whenever we march from one place to defend another, the places we leave are attacked, in this distracted situation we . . . intreat you to send us what Assistance you can as soon as possible."[37]

Governor Clinton, when begged for help, could find nothing optimistic to say. "I have done every Thing in my Power . . . to obtain you Succour from the Continental Army," he replied to one such plea, "but when we consider the Extent of the Western Frontier only from Virginia Northward, equally exposed to & infested by the Tories & Savages, you will readily perceive it woud take our whole Army to guard it. This will account for the want of greater Success in my Applications."[38]

Gloom had reached the highest levels. General Washington had said, in answer to one of the governor's appeals for aid: "To defend an extensive frontier against the incursions of Indians and the Banditti under Butler and Brant is next to impossible; but still if you think the addition of another Regiment, ill as I can spare it, or a change of position in the troops that are already upon the Frontier, will answer any good purpose, I will cheerfully comply."[39] But what good were a few more soldiers spread out among far-flung garrisons or a mere change of position of those already there? The invaders could avoid them all with ease. "The garrison of Fort Schuyler [Stanwix] . . . might as well be in the moon," noted one observer, "for the Enemy take Care to leave it at a sufficient Distance."[40]

In truth, everybody had come to the one inescapable conclusion. It was admitted that "we are now brought to this, we must make Peace with the Indians or Early in the Spring, Carry an army up into their Country and Destroy them or Else they will Come Down in the Spring (if they wait so Long) and Destroy our Frontiers."[41] Actually the rebels realized they did not have even this choice. They could not make peace with the Indians so long as the Indians got their living from the British and they themselves could give them nothing. Congress and General Washington and every person of influence up and down the whole frontier knew what had to be done. Indeed, most of these leaders had known for months what had to be done, and had been planning accordingly. There was remarkable unanimity that offense was the only means of defense. The power of the Indians to make war had to be broken. And that General Haldimand from his observation post in far-off Quebec could suppose that the rebels had any other prime object in view shows how little he really knew of the horrors that had been let loose on them. When a man goes out in the morning to the fields or the wood lot to work, to provide food and warmth for his family, not knowing that he will ever return, or, if he does, whether he will find that family alive or his house still standing, the situation becomes so intolerable that any effort will be made to stop it. It was not just the bigger invasions, bad as they were; it was all the little irruptions, too, of three or four skulking warriors, and their constant burnings and scalpings and taking into captivity, and the terrible uncertainty that hovered over everything and everybody.

So the rebels gathered supplies and ammunition and horses; they made saddles and tents and wagons and bateaux. They had something to do, and they did it with a will. Then, maddened by the fears and anxieties of two years, they struck. Onondaga was their first target. Their plan was a well kept secret. They took care not to tell the Oneidas, although they had to pass through Oneida country; and they carefully sent some of the Oneida warriors off on a wild-goose chase in another direction. On April 21, after fording an arm of Onondaga Lake, an army of some 558 men began the work of destruction. The surprised and fleeing Indians offered no resistance. Three villages fell to the torch, and thirty-three prisoners were taken as hostages. The fireplace of the Confederacy was destroyed. The fire that the Indians had decreed must never go out, was extinguished. It had been almost easy. The rebels returned home in high spirits. They had just begun.

Joseph Brant got the bad news of the destruction of Onondaga, at Carleton Island. It was bad news, indeed, for he was told that one of his children had been captured.[42] This was not hard for him to believe, for some of the Cayuga villages lay very close to Onondaga, and in one of those villages he had evidently left Isaac and Christina. Walter Butler wrote that Joseph was greatly distressed about his child.[43] The government boat finally arrived just as Joseph, in a frenzy of anxiety, too impatient to wait longer, was contemplating setting out in a canoe.[44] The two not-so-friendly associates immediately embarked to-gether for Niagara. They arrived on May 14.[45] Here Joseph learned to his very great relief that his children were safe.[46]

Joseph and Walter found Niagara in turmoil. Colonel Bolton knew no more of the rebels' plans than General Haldimand knew, and he was trying to send aid everywhere simultaneously. The attack on Onondaga showed that troops were needed to the east and south. There were great fears for Oswego. There were also alarming reports that the Americans from an advanced post on the Tuscarawas River might be headed toward Detroit. George Rogers Clark was still a very definite threat. He had sent word to Captain Lernoult at Detroit that he was glad to hear that he was strengthening the fortifications there since it would save the Americans expense!

At Bolton's request Walter Butler agreed to go to the Tuscarawas with a reconnoitering party. Joseph, however, refused that service, saying he knew nothing about the area.[47] Joseph probably did not want to awaken any more jealousy on the part of the Senecas. The Tus-carawas was, in a vague sort of way, Seneca country; if anybody should go, it should be Senecas. There was further discussion then as to whether Joseph, and Walter, too, should go to Detroit or, perhaps, to Fort Pitt.[48] Captain Lernoult, who had heard of Joseph's exploits, hoped he would come to Detroit, and wrote that he would give him and his warriors a hearty welcome.[49] The idea of going to Detroit appealed to Joseph, and Walter was left to take a party down toward Fort Pitt. Joseph set out around the Falls with sixty followers late in June. Somewhere along the road a runner caught up with him bring-ing an alarming report (later found to be false) that the Americans were on their way to attack the Cayugas. Joseph hastily returned to Niagara. Then he set out again, in the opposite direction, to the Indian country.[50]

Major John Butler was already in the Indian country, having been ordered out there by Bolton as soon as the attack on Onondaga was known. Ill health or no, John Butler had to go to the aid of the Indians. He had with him about four hundred Rangers and warriors, all that were at Niagara at the time he left. By late June he had proceeded as far as Canadesaga (present Geneva), at the north end of Seneca Lake. Here a new fireplace had been established by the Confederacy, and Butler found the worried Indians holding council and calling upon their Indian allies far and near for aid. They sent messages to Sir John Johnson, too, to come quickly with his troops and take post at Oswego, and to Sir Henry Clinton urging him to advance up the Hudson. They promised Clinton that as soon as the booming of his guns was heard, they would try to cut their way through to him. What Sir Henry thought of this promise, if he ever got it, is not known; it went to him by the hands of two men whom he had sent to Niagara months before to find out if the British still held the upper posts!

The chiefs at Canadesaga were also discussing General Haldimand's latest letter to the Six Nations. Haldimand had reminded them that they were not fighting the king's battle solely but were defending the line of 1768, too. The Americans, he said, aim to take the whole continent from you and the king's people. He also pointed out that the rebels could not give the Indians anything since they had nothing and were "getting poorer every day." Prove yourselves worthy descendants of your brave ancestors, he urged. Defend the conquests of land which your forefathers made and you will regain the same awe and veneration which they enjoyed. Such was Haldimand's answer to those Indians who thought they were fighting the white man's war.

Joseph must have reached Butler's camp about the end of June, and sometime later Walter Butler, who had either never gone on the scout to Fort Pitt or had been called back, showed up, too. Walter, like his father, had to go to the aid of the Indians though, as he said, service of that sort was "far from being agreeable to me." Then they all waited, for they expected the rebels to attack somewhere soon. Every scout and spy reported that two rebel armies were poised, one down the Susquehanna near Wyoming, and one up the Susquehanna at Otsego Lake. Indians who had been in the vicinity of these armies further reported the soldiers were as numerous as the leaves on the trees, but Indians always exaggerate so. How could they be? How could the rebels raise so many men?

Butler and his little force had more immediate worries than the mythical numbers of their enemies. They were trying to live off the

land, but the hunting and fishing were very bad, and they had almost
nothing to eat. They were almost literally starving. The provision fleet
was late again. General Haldimand had not been able to send anything to Niagara, consequently Colonel Bolton could not send anything out in the field. Butler held off as long as he could, till he saw
that some of the men were getting sick. Then he sent most of the party
to Genesee Falls where the fishing was better. Finally he had to beg for
provisions though knowing how scarce they were. All Bolton could
allow him was a little flour and peas and oatmeal, and a very, very
little pork. When the hungry men saw the food brought in they were
so overjoyed to get even that much, that they "ran whooping &
hallooing & skipping about as if they had lost their senses."[51] The
Indians could supply nothing. They, too, were hungry. They were
living, themselves, on roots and greens gathered in the woods, and
using up precious ammunition by firing at every little bird they saw.
Last year's crop was eaten up, this year's not ready to harvest. It was
their annual dilemma. When some of the Indians stole a little calf that
the Rangers had been trying to fatten, the latter were furious. "May
the first morsel choke them!" one Ranger exclaimed. "That such rep-
tiles should enjoy such a delicious bit," was another's anguished cry.[52]

Several parties of whites and Indians went out in search of cattle.
One such party was led by Joseph. With a rebel army at Lake Otsego
he hardly dared to attempt to drive cattle from the Mohawk or from
Schoharie, and there was nothing to be had on the Susquehanna near
the ruins of Oquaga and Unadilla. He elected to try Minisink, down
on the Delaware, which was reputed to be a flourishing settlement. It
was a very long way to go, through some of the roughest country he
had ever traveled. It was his first service of the season except for some
small scouts which he had sent out from Niagara,[53] though as usual
rumors had had him all over the map.[54]

By July 8 Joseph and his party had reached Chemung, an Indian
town on the Chemung River. One Moabary Owen, a double deserter
(once from a rebel regiment and once from Joseph's party), reported to
rebel authorities at Goshen that Joseph had with him about sixty
Indians and twenty-seven white men and that he, Owen, "Heard Said
Brand gave Orders that they Should not Kill any woman or Children,
and if they Knew any person to be a Tory not to Kill them, and any
that would Deliver them Selves up to Take them prisnors, but any
person Running from them to Kill them," and that they expected
more Tories to join them and were threatening to destroy Catskill,
and that an army from Canada was coming to take Fort Stanwix. No

one gave much credence to anything Owen said, but some of it must have been true for he was able to name very accurately about thirteen of Joseph's white Volunteers.[55]

Joseph and his men got to their destination at noon on July 20. This in itself was a disappointment since they had wanted to attack before daybreak. There was no resistance, and they burnt some houses and proceeded to round up the cattle. Then came a second disappointment for most of the cattle were in the woods. A third disappointment was reported by Joseph himself in these words: "We have burnt all the Settlement called Minisink, one Fort excepted, round which we lay before about an Hour, & had one man killed and one wounded. We destroyed several small stockaded Forts, and took four Scalps & three Prisoners, but did not in the least injure Women or Children. The Reason that we could not take more of them, was owing to the many Forts about the Place, into which they were always ready to run like Ground-Hogs."[56]

The invaders left Minisink early the next morning, knowing the neighboring militia would soon be at their heels. The rebel militia was becoming more effective. Men from Orange and Ulster counties and even from New Jersey not only answered the alarm promptly, they were able to locate their quarry, and they sped off in hot pursuit. They were in high spirits, confident, and inclined more to boasting of what they might do than to caution.

The trail led through a howling wilderness. On July 22, two days after the raid, the two parties were close enough together to be aware of each other's presence. They had come about twenty-seven tangled, rock-strewn miles. On the right a mountain rose darkly and on the left was the rippling Delaware. In the distance loomed the far-ranging Catskills. There was not a wilder, lonelier place on the whole frontier, a place where the wolves gathered by night but men were seldom seen.

The militia caught sight of Joseph's men at a ford where they were taking some plunder across the river, the whole party obviously meaning to cross over and head for the Indian country. Some of the Americans set out to intercept Brant at the ford and veered off to the left to get in front of him. They accomplished their design, and the first shots were exchanged.

Joseph was about four hundred yards in the rear of his party. Hearing the shots and sensing the maneuver that had taken place, Joseph with forty men slipped through the underbrush and, getting on the American rear, managed to ambush the ambushers. It was an adroit movement. The American militia was completely surprised. Part of the Americans, mostly those who had come from Goshen, were cut off from their brothers-in-arms. Of those who were not trapped, many ingloriously fled.

Years later Brant, when faulted for the murderous debacle of that day (some called it a massacre), put up a defense of his conduct. He told Samuel Woodruff, an American traveler who visited him in 1797, that he had tried to get the Americans to surrender by telling them his force was enough to destroy them, and had promised them good treatment, but had warned that his Indians, once blood was shed, would be uncontrollable. The Americans, he said, refused his offer, and shot at him, the bullet going through his clothing.[57]

There was, of course, nothing of this exchange noted in Joseph's official report which he made to Colonel Bolton a week later, and nothing of the sort mentioned in contemporary American documents. But an old veteran who had been in the battle related the following many years afterward: "It was now announced to us in english who commands you? Daniel Myers with us answered None of your business. Who are you? Answer Captain Brandt! You lie you are little Han Cole he knew him and he was a tory Show your face and I'll make another hole in it Answer 'Surrender in fifteen minutes and you shall have quarters.' Oaths passed on both sides but the answer was 'we want none of your quarters.' "[58]

The fight raged nearly all day, up and down the leafy shadows of the mountain and in the bright water. Though the Americans numbered about 120 men[59] and Joseph had only about eighty-five, that part of the militia which bore the brunt of the fighting was much weaker in numbers than the Volunteers and Indians. The battle was fought Indian style, every man for himself, behind rocks and trees, and it was one of the hardest fought battles of the war. Joseph's force finally got the upper hand. Both parties had spent nearly all their ammunition, but the rebels ran out just a little sooner, and so lost the day. Very few of the losers were able to save themselves, some being shot while trying to swim the Delaware.

Brant's men took over forty scalps and only one prisoner. The Indians and perhaps the Loyalists, too, were in no mood for the burden of prisoners. The wounded were clubbed and tomahawked even while begging for their lives—a merciful fate, essentially, since they could not have been carried to Niagara and there was no way they could ever get back home. The one prisoner who was not killed, a Captain John Wood, gave the Masonic sign of distress, and for this reason Joseph personally intervened and saved his life. Eventually, when he found out that the man was not really a fellow Mason, he treated him with all the contempt he thought he deserved.[60] On this same occasion, as Joseph himself afterward related, he found a man on the battlefield who was wounded past any hope of recovery. Night was falling and night would bring the wolves. Joseph engaged the wounded man in talk, and then, diverting his attention in this way, he quickly dispatched him with his tomahawk. This was Joseph Brant's idea of humanity.[61] The Reverend Eleazar Wheelock had taught him many things but he had never taught him what to do under such circumstances!

Colonel John Hathorn, who commanded the rebel expedition, has added his own period to all these inhumanities. On July 27 he wrote a long report to Governor George Clinton describing the engagement at the ford in considerable detail. His heart, he said, bled for the unfortunate wounded who fell into the hands of those fiends of hell. "However," he added, "circumstances give me a little consolation. Mr. Roger Townsend, of Goshen, received a wound in his thigh; exceedingly thirsty, making an attempt to go to find some water, was met by an Indian who very friendly took him by the hand and said he was his prisoner and would not hurt him. A well-directed ball from one of our men put the Indian into a dose, and Mr. Townsend ran back into the lines. I hope some little humanity may yet be found in the breasts of the savages."[62]

Joseph Brant left the battlefield of Minisink with the loss of ten men wounded and three killed. Of the wounded six died in a few days. One of these, named Captain John, a Tuscarora, was Joseph's great friend. Joseph deeply mourned his friend, calling him his "trusty chief" and wondering what he would ever do without him.[63] As for the chastened and defeated rebels, so many leading citizens were killed that their neighbors and families at home could not believe it, and thinking they must be prisoners in Canada, made for many months pathetic and vain attempts to get some news of them. It was a sad time for everybody.

Joseph and his party went up the river by way of Cochecton and Cokeose (present Deposit) and then over to the Susquehanna.[64] At the ruins of old Oquaga, on July 29, he wrote an official report of his activities.[65] From Oquaga Joseph sent most of his men to Chemung.[66] His few prisoners he sent up to the Indian country where, according to one of the Rangers, they were cruelly beaten.[67] They probably had to run the Indian gauntlet, an always unpleasant experience, but in the present mood of the Indians they were lucky to escape with their lives. Then Joseph himself went up toward the Mohawk with a small party in order to find out what the rebel army was doing at Lake Otsego.[68] This was dangerous business. By this time Joseph had a price on his head put there by the highest rebel authority, General Washington himself. Just two months before, the general had suggested that some of the captured Onondagas might be persuaded to kidnap Brant or Butler, but obviously anybody else who brought in either could expect to be well rewarded. It will be "a most essential piece of service," said Washington, "which will meet with suitable encouragement."[69]

The details of what Joseph did when he went on this scout are somewhat murky. On August 2 he destroyed a small settlement somewhere near Little Falls which he called Onawatoge. He carried off two prisoners who told him the army at Lake Otsego had boats and provisions and was getting ready to invade the Indian country. When the local militia caught up with him (as they now had a habit of doing), Joseph was wounded slightly in the foot and his coat and breechclout riddled with buckshot, but he held on to his prisoners. One of the prisoners, a man named John House, became lame when the Indians made him march without shoes and pinioned him into a forked stick at night. The Indians then debated whether they should kill him. But when Joseph discovered House was a friend of Butler's, he got him to sign a neutrality oath and turned him loose. The lamed man was soon found by an American scout and taken to Otsego Lake. Here he was questioned by General James Clinton who commanded the army there. House told Clinton about his captivity and asserted that the Indians had killed the other prisoner. Joseph did not mention such a thing in the two letters he wrote about this affair.[70] In later life, however, when the subject came up, he could justify the killing of prisoners. There were times when prisoners could not be taken any farther; moreover, the Indians had no jails in which to keep them. But he did not approve the common practice of torturing prisoners, and he claimed that he had saved several not only from torture but from death. He also thought Indian prisoners were equally likely to be killed by their white captors. So reported General Peter B. Porter, a well-known American, who talked with him after the war.[71]

In view of what spies and deserters and captured rebels had been repeating for so long, Joseph could not doubt that the Indian country was going to be invaded. He set out for Chemung where his men were waiting, knowing that real warfare would erupt soon and much worried for the outcome. John Butler, still encamped at Canadesaga, was inclined to believe that General Clinton would make a triumphant advance up the Hudson and that the American armies would be called in that direction. General Haldimand too could not believe that the Indian country was in any danger. It was impossible, he thought, that the rebels should be massing in such numbers as reported. As late as

August 20 he was telling some Six Nations deputies who had come to
Colonel Campbell for aid and whom he had called down to Quebec to
see for themselves that there was no French fleet in the St. Lawrence,
that their fears of a rebel invasion were groundless. "As to your apprehensions of the Rebels coming to attack your Country," he comforted them, "I cannot have the least thought of it; if they mean any
thing; it is to secure their Frontiers against your incursions and depredations; and in order to enable you to keep them the better at Bay, I
shall give my leave and encourage the seven Nations of Canada to cooperate with and join you in opposing your Enemies, the Rebels."[72]
The worried Indians could scarcely have been offered a more broken-
down staff upon which to lean. But British authorities in Quebec had
no way to know that on that very day three American expeditionary
forces were moving into the Six Nations country for the kill. Armies
under Generals John Sullivan and James Clinton[73] had reached the
outskirts of Chemung, and Colonel Daniel Brodhead, a man whom
the Indians called the "Great Sun," had advanced up the Allegheny
into the heart of lower Seneca-Munsee land.

The Americans had been gathering their strength for months.
Their plans were carefully laid. General Washington himself had seen
to that. By questionnaires sent to experts on Indian affairs, by letters
and by interviews he got all the information he could regarding the
Six Nations and their country. How many men were necessary for an
expedition against the Indians? What route should they take? What
was the best time for an expedition, considering the state of the rivers
and grass for pack horses? How much stores and provisions should be
carried? How much artillery? How many bateaux? Should forts be
built along the way? Where should magazines be established? What
are the natural difficulties of the terrain? What is the strength of the
Indians? Of the garrison at Niagara? What rumors should be spread for
the benefit of the British in Canada? All this information and a great
deal more Washington assimilated and analyzed. Then he wrote out
instructions so simple and clear that almost anybody could have followed them to victory, and he sent them to General John Sullivan of
New Hampshire, his hand-picked leader, the man who had got the
beleaguered American forces safely out of Canada in 1776, and whom
he trusted completely. Washington was more than direct about the
object of the expedition. It was, and he underlined the key words, "to
lay waste all the settlements around . . . that the country may not be
merely *overrun* but *destroyed*."[74]

The expedition was slow in getting started. The rebels had not
much organization as yet, and General Sullivan had to wait a long

time and make many a requisition before he got a reasonably good part of what he felt he needed. But the troops were finally assembled and the supplies were finally collected—American supplies, French supplies, and even British supplies pirated on the high seas.

Sullivan himself headed the army that advanced from the south. By June 23 his troops had hacked their way from Easton on the Delaware to Wyoming on the Susquehanna. The troops had a high resolve and, if anything was needed to reinforce that resolve, they got it at Wyoming. Here they saw the burned-out homes, the weed-grown fields, and the bones of those who had fallen in Butler's raid. They picked up massive Indian war clubs. They heard about every possible kind of atrocity. All the terrible tales that people had been repeating and believing so implicitly for the past twelve months were poured into their ears: that prisoners, even women and children, had been shut up in houses and the houses set on fire; that "the prattling infant, the blooming maid and persons of venerable years" were butchered in cold blood; that one Tory killed and scalped his own brother and another cut off his father's head; that even the cattle in the fields were tortured unmercifully, for, as it was said, "what will not those hell hounds doo us." Exclaimed Samuel Kirkland who had come down from Oneida to act as an army chaplain: "Are these the fruits & effects of thy Clemency O George, thou tyrant of Britain & scourge to mankind! May He, to whom Vengeance belongs, pour forth his righteous Indignation in due time."[75] Kirkland echoed the sentiments of everybody.

At Wyoming the troops celebrated the Fourth of July with the most splendid, the most patriotic, and the most spirited (in more ways than one) ceremonies of which they were capable. After the feasting and singing the entertainment ran to toasts. The celebrants drank thirteen of these (one for each state) to whatever they felt ought to be toasted, everything from "The United States" to "Gen. Washington and the army," and from "The King and Queen of France" to "Civilization, or death to all Savages." As to the latter toast, if someone had taken a vote just then, very likely death would have been the preference.

By the end of the month General Sullivan and his army were finally ready to leave that "place of skulls." On July 31 they set out up the Susquehanna. They numbered about twenty-three hundred rank and file. An unusual number of the officers and men were keeping diaries for they sensed that they were making history.[76]

General James Clinton brought his army down from the north. Near Canajoharie he captured two of John Butler's men, a Ranger and

a member of the Indian department, and had them hanged—
ostensibly for spying but in truth for atrocities at Cherry Valley—and
the tears and pleas of their wives and children who lived nearby
mattered not a whit. Then Clinton dammed up the outlet of Lake
Otsego where the Susquehanna begins as a shallow creek, and when
Sullivan gave the order, broke the dam and rode down a river of
swelling waters. The few Indians still living along the stream fled in
terror. It was August 9 and Clinton had two thousand men, and he
had made his last will and testament. On his way down the river he
burned such Tory and Indian houses as had escaped the fate of Oquaga
and Unadilla.

As Joseph and his small party made their way down to Chemung to
join the rest of the Volunteers and Indians, they had to exercise great
caution and must have done most of their traveling under cover of
night. Both American armies were too close for comfort. How very
close one was, even Joseph himself did not realize, for he had not
heard that Clinton had started down the Susquehanna.[77] Joseph was
ahead of Clinton's army, but not far ahead, and on August 11 some of
Clinton's advance guard saw fresh Indian tracks.

By traveling as fast as they could Joseph and his party soon put
more distance between them and Clinton, but the farther they got
from Clinton the closer they got to Sullivan. Sullivan and his army
had reached Tioga on August 11. The next night most of the troops
marched west, and on August 13 burned the lower part of Chemung,
houses, corn, and all, the inhabitants having fled. From this very
beginning the invaders were amazed at the quality of the corn and
vegetables they saw and the fine country, for this was an unusually
good crop year for the Indians. Joseph had to pass Sullivan's men at
their work of destruction, as he reached the upper end of Chemung on
August 14.[78] His Indians had fired a few shots at the Americans and
there were some casualties. But Sullivan's troops were out in far too
great a force for the few warriors to cope with, and they fled on ahead
while the Americans returned to Tioga to await Clinton.

Small parties of warriors were drifting in slowly from farther out in
the Indian country. By August 19 Joseph could count a force of three
hundred in the neighborhood of Chemung. But this was not nearly
enough. The enemy's many campfires were lighting up the sky at
night, and their morning and evening guns could be clearly heard.
Joseph wrote a carefully cheerful letter to Colonel Bolton and sent it
off by runner. It was almost as though he feared he might discourage
Colonel Bolton. He had had a skirmish on the Mohawk, and had been
wounded but was almost well. He had managed to retain two prisoners

he had taken. The rebels were certainly out in great force and meant to invade the Indian country. The Indians had already had a brush with them and had acquitted themselves well. He expected Butler and Sayengaraghta with the Rangers and Senecas tomorrow. Though most of the warriors with him were in good spirits and even thought they were going to win, he himself, he said, was "a little afraid we shall have hard work to drive the Enemy back, for our Friends are too slow in joining us." He begged Bolton to "drive all the Indians from Niagara, and not suffer a man of them to go to Canada." "If we beat the Rebel Army," he predicted, "they will never invade our Country again."[79]

To his friend Claus, with whom he kept in close touch, Joseph wrote in different terms. To Claus he could unburden himself. All his true feelings and anxieties welled to the surface. The rebels were only eight miles away, and they had thousands to his hundreds. He was sure that they intended nothing less than the extermination of the Indians. There would be a decisive battle almost any day. "Then," he said, lapsing into the ancient figures of speech which sound so strange on his lips, "we shall begin to know what is to befal us the People of the Long House."[80] He was too intelligent not to realize that the prospects were bleak.

Frequent reports from Joseph and others who had gone out to watch the rebel movements had convinced John Butler that the Indian country really was on the point of being invaded. The Americans had not yet been called away to stop Sir Henry Clinton's progress, and it began to look as though Sir Henry, unaccountably, was making no progress. Like Joseph, Butler thought of all the vagrant and idle Indians who were whiling away their time at Niagara. He, too, wrote Bolton urging that all the warriors in the vicinity be sent to him at once. Let them march night and day till they join us, he said; and he hoped "that Such as do not Come, may not be allowed Provisions nor any thing Else, nor be looked upon as Friends, and this we desire you will tell them."[81]

John Butler was ready to set out from Canadesaga on August 16. But the local Senecas refused to stir, causing another day's delay. They insisted on having their traditional feast (from scant supplies) and war dance first (for how else could they hope to win?), and they would not let Butler and his white men start without them. Declared an exasperated Ranger: "Such another tardy Set never was known. The enemy if they had known it might have overrun half their country before they got together."[82]

Next day the party started south except such of the Indians as were too tired from all their festivities and who delayed a little longer. Four days later everybody reached Chucknut, a small village on the Chemung River, where Joseph and his party of whites and Indians, and all the other Indians who had joined him, lay encamped.[83] The camp was about a mile from a larger village called Newtown (present Elmira, New York).

Butler's combined force now consisted of about six hundred.[84] Of these 180 were white men, mostly Rangers and members of the Indian department, with a small detachment from the King's regiment.[85] The remaining 420 included all the Indians and Joseph Brant's white Volunteers.

Sir William Johnson had stated in 1770 that the Senecas alone had about one thousand fighting men and the Cayugas about 260.[86] This being the case, where were the rest of the Indians? It was their own country that was being invaded, yet hundreds of Indian warriors who should have been present at this very critical time were notable by their absence. Some may have been immobilized by Brodhead who was burning the upper Allegheny country. Perhaps a few had wandered so far away that they did not know what was going on. There had been some casualties during the war, mainly at Oriskany. Many distant Senecas, apparently, remained at home, thinking they were out of harm's reach, but other Indians, more fearful, were already fleeing westward with their families. Still others simply refused to leave the safety of Fort Niagara. Out of two hundred warriors at the post, Bolton could persuade only forty-four to leave,[87] and it is uncertain whether, or when, they ever did join Butler. Unfortunately, Bolton does not state how many of the warriors at Niagara were Missisaugas and other Indians not of the Six Nations. The Canadian Missisaugas who spent much time at the fort and to whom Butler had also sent an appeal, never showed up. If Butler had not been desperate, he would have known better than to ask them for aid. Indians of different nations seldom helped one another in war.

The Delawares had promised more than two hundred warriors and they, at least, lived in the Chemung-Susquehanna area, and their own homes were in danger. The Delawares actually supplied less than thirty fighters.[88] Some Cayugas had come early, but their chiefs kept the others at home, presumably to protect the main Cayuga villages.[89] Both the Senecas and the Cayugas had every reason to be present in force at the approaching battle, yet Butler could not even muster four hundred warriors. Were the Indians uninterested in protecting their country? Did their villages and cornfields mean so little? The villages could be rebuilt; the British could feed them. The Indians certainly saw nothing dishonorable in running away; a forlorn last-ditch fight was no part of their practice. Nor had years of presents done anything to strengthen their will.

It has been said that Sullivan forced the Indians to make a stand. The truth is, Sullivan was not able to force even half of them, if their numbers have been stated correctly, to make a stand. But were the Indians, indeed, so numerous? Could Sir William Johnson have been ignorant of something he should have known or did he purposely overstate the numbers of his charges?

After the war Guy Johnson told of a census of the Indians which he had made in 1781 after the attritions of many hard-fought campaigns. He counted at that time 1,572 Senecas and 744 Cayugas and Cayuga dependents.[90] About half of these must have been males, and of these, half may have been too old, too young, or too disabled to fight. This would leave, roughly, about 579 able-bodied fighting men. But even this lesser number was considerably more than the number of warriors who joined Butler. There were also a few members of the eastern Six Nations who fought Sullivan who must be counted in Butler's force, the Canajoharie Mohawks in particular and perhaps some Onondagas intent on revenge, as well as the thirty Delawares who had their own anxieties; but not many outsiders, even of the Confederacy, took part in the battle. To the Indian mind, the saving of the Seneca and Cayuga country was up to the Senecas and the Cayugas. It was not the concern of anybody else. If Guy Johnson's figures can be accepted, it also appears not to have been the concern of a relatively large number of the Senecas and Cayugas as well. But even Guy's lesser figures are more flattering to Indian courage and will (or to the growth of white ideas among them) than Sir William's. Both Guy and Sir William, however, had some reason to overstate the true numbers of the Indians. The mystery remains whether lack of population or Indian character and customs prevented the collection of a more respectable force of warriors to defend their country.

The Delawares, because they wanted to preserve Newtown, had insisted that the ambush be prepared beyond that village. Sayengaraghta and his Senecas backed them up. It was good Indian custom that those most immediately concerned in a decision, should make the decision. John Butler opposed the Delaware plan, but he was overruled. He told Bolton that since he was so outnumbered he had wanted to retreat to a better position and send out strong parties to harass the enemy on the march, from the heights above the path, and keep them in continual alarm. In this idea, he said, he was strongly seconded by Joseph Brant, who labored hard (though to no purpose) to make the Indians understand and give their approval.[91] Under the circumstances Butler's plan was not a bad one. But Butler was a white man, and white men were not enjoying great popularity at the moment; and Joseph Brant was not an Indian of wide influence—indeed, Brant was just as likely to antagonize the Indians as to influence them to his way of thinking. The white people thought of Joseph as an outstanding leader, but the more they "noticed" him, the more the Indians wanted to tear him down. Walter Butler made the sage observation that Brant "has been more notice taken of than has been good for his own interest with his own people."[92] Walter was right. Joseph's getting so much attention paid to him was a fault that Sayengaraghta and the Senecas could not forgive.

For three days, off and on, Butler and his force waited in ambush. They were on a ridge about half a mile in extent, and protected by a bend in the river. On their right was the water, on their left a mountain, and in front of them a creek. Joseph and his men and some Rangers were stationed near the river, Butler with a few Indians, the regulars, and the main body of Rangers in the center, and the rest of the Indians, by far the greatest part, on the left. To the rear lay Newtown. The unsuspecting enemy would be coming along the river path with their entire right flank exposed. As far as the Indians were concerned, this was a fine place for an ambush, but Butler was still not satisfied.

The warriors, such as had turned out, and the white Loyalists were not on the best of terms. The Indians were angry and sullen because General Haldimand had not taken post at Oswego (a thing they much desired) nor did their friends, the British, appear to be sending them any aid. The Loyalists, for their part, found it difficult, even distasteful, to work with Indians. They did not like Indians. They did not understand Indians. They had a contempt for Indians. Necessity alone made the two kinds of men allies. A great deal of mutual antagonism lay behind that line of hastily cut brush and logs.

On the first day there was a false alarm caused by two Delawares shooting at deer on the mountain. Thinking that the enemy was trying to surround them, the Rangers left the breastwork and retired, intending to get ahead of the enemy and gain the heights. When the alarm was over, the Rangers had to return, while the Indians hooted at them and yelled insults.

On the second day Butler tried to get the Indians to move a few miles up the river but, no, they would not. Finally, on the third day, August 29, it was reported for sure that the enemy approached very near. At this time one of the Indians took it upon himself to alter their part of the line, sloping it toward the mountain in such a way as to give the enemy room for a flanking movement on that side. When this was pointed out to the chiefs, they (through "mere sulkiness," noted a Ranger) refused to change the arrangement. About two o'clock, as the first of the enemy appeared and began to fire, Major Butler, Joseph Brant, and the Cayuga chiefs tried vainly to persuade the Indians to move up the hill.[93]

In the meantime the rebel movements had not been swift, but they had been sure. General James Clinton had joined forces with Sullivan on August 22, and the two armies set out together along the old Forbidden Path. They hardly knew where they were going. Out of twenty-five Oneidas who had urged on the expedition and who had volunteered to show the way, only two remained. The Oneidas had begun to realize what very, very serious business they, as members of the Confederacy, were embarked upon. They gave various excuses for decamping. They mentioned Haldimand's threats. An army, they said, was coming down from Canada. They had to go home to protect their wives and children. In reality, they were terror-stricken, and they fled. For guides the rebels finally had to manage with the two remaining Oneidas and a Stockbridge Indian from Massachusetts who probably knew as little about the route as they did. The Forbidden Path was still a *terra incognita* to white men.

Bravely, apparently recklessly, the combined armies made their way up the Chemung River. But these troops were not green militiamen, and they were not reckless. They were disciplined and experienced Continental soldiers, most of them; and they kept going, but always watchfully, stopping only to burn whatever small Indian settlements they found in the area. The careful and steady Sullivan never let down his guard. He refused to be ambushed. On August 29, 1779, his advance riflemen discovered the hidden breastworks behind which Butler and his men waited. One of the riflemen had climbed a tree and glimpsed some brilliantly painted bodies, for it was hot and the warriors were almost naked. The Americans began to fire from behind trees and the creek banks, and their artillery was soon brought up and began to play. Cannon, as always, demoralized the Indians.

With every kind of missile—shells, grapeshot, harrow teeth, iron spikes, etc.—falling all around them, the Indians, as John Butler told the story to Bolton in his official report, thought they were surrounded. Terrified, most of the warriors broke ranks and fled, some of the Senecas not stopping till they got back home to the Genesee! Butler himself, with the Rangers and the few remaining Indians, retreated to the mountain but, as he had feared, soon encountered

Sullivan's men who were trying to outflank his left. After a sharp running fight the Loyalists, greatly outnumbered and exhausted by all their deprivations, fled across the river or along the mountain. They finally huddled for the night about ten miles away. It was very late, and they had been soaked by a sudden shower, and some were ill with the ague. They had had nothing to eat since daybreak, and then only a few ears of corn. All these factors considered, Butler felt he had nothing for which to apologize. "Both Officers and Men," he noted proudly, "behaved with Much Spirit, but the Efforts of Such a hand full were of little avail against the Force they had to oppose."[94]

The conduct of the Indians has been seen only through the eyes of white men. What they themselves might have said about it, no one knows. Joseph Brant did not discuss it in his letters. John Norton, Joseph's white friend, who wrote many years later, merely said that, contrary to Brant's advice, the courage of the warriors had been allowed to cool too long behind their entrenchment; and that he, Brant, favored a less cautious course.[95] Brant could have told Norton this. Some of the Americans thought the Indians behaved well enough under the cannonading. Virtually all the Americans admitted that the Indians they met on the mountain fought bravely. Of these latter Butler declared: "Joseph Brants Conduct through the Whole of this affair does him much honor, he with Kiangarachta and Several Other Chiefs and Indians remained with us to the last."[96] In their flight part of Butler's troops got separated from the main body. There is some evidence that Joseph was one of these and that he spent that dark and lowering night hiding disconsolately in a tree.[97] But there is also evidence that after the battle Joseph took the wounded to a place of safety up the Chemung River.[98] Perhaps he did both.

So befell the famous battle of Newtown. Butler reported five Rangers killed or missing and three wounded, and five Indians killed and nine wounded. The Americans lost somewhat more but not enough to dampen their enthusiasm. The Americans camped that night at the place the Loyalists had occupied the night before, and they immediately set to burning Newtown from whence, of course, all the inhabitants had fled. The path was open before them all the way to Niagara if they had the ability to take it.

When General George Washington heard of Sullivan's success,[99] his reaction was swift and predictable. "The advantages we have already gained over the Indians, in the destruction of so many of their settlements," he wrote to his victorious general, "is very flattering to the expedition. But to make it as conclusive as the state of your provisions and the safety of your army will countenance," he went on,

"I would mention two points which I may not have sufficiently expressed in my general instructions, or if I have, which I wish to repeat." His two points were indeed a repetition, as emphatic as he could make them: "The one is the necessity of pushing the Indians to the greatest practicable distance from their own settlements and our frontiers; to the throwing them wholly on the British enemy. The other is the making the destruction of their settlements so final and complete as to put it out of their power to derive the smallest succor from them in case they should attempt to return this season."[100] If anyone had asked Washington to name his favorite peoples, Indians would have been far down the list. The events of his youth when he had fought the French and their savages, were clear in his mind. To Washington, Indians were enemies, crafty, diabolical, cruel. He had once likened them to "wolves," and in a quarter of a century he had not changed his opinion.

This was one of the most self-righteous armies that ever marched. The hosts of the Crusaders never went forth with greater zeal. When asked, after Newtown, if they would submit to half allowance (for their provisions were already low), the whole army responded with three rousing cheers. Fording rivers, building bridges where they could not ford, bogged down sometimes in mud up to their waists, climbing mountains hand over hand, Sullivan's men painfully, slowly, laboriously, inched along. West they made their way, and then north off the Forbidden Path and into the Seneca country, and then west again. Some days they could march only three miles; on good days they might do as much as sixteen. They pulled ammunition wagons and heavy artillery up heights where 120 men were needed to go to the aid of the straining horses. They fought rattlesnakes and camped in swamps. Cautiously they moved through ravines and sunless woods. They marched sometimes by night when it was so dark they had to stay in touching distance of the man in front and build fires in order to see to build bridges. When horses fell under impossible burdens, the men added all the provisions they could carry to their own heavy packs. Among the impedimenta of some of those packs were the scalps of Indians killed at Newtown and almost certainly two of their skins designed for making leggings.[101]

Steadily the Americans cut through the thick underbrush. The narrow Indian path became a road. What had been a *terra incognita* was reduced to surveys and maps, and entries in dozens of diaries described every detail. Always, whenever the soldiers saw an Indian house or a cornfield, they destroyed it. When they saw an apple orchard or a grove of peach trees, they girdled it. When they came to a town they burned it. All the while the Americans looked for the enemy who fled before them, but they could never quite catch up. So close were pursued and pursuer that Sullivan's men found smoldering campfires and even, at times, corn still boiling in pots. And all the while Joseph Brant and a few of his men dogged the Americans' footsteps and hung on their flanks, hoping to get a prisoner to interrogate about their intentions.[102] Joseph never got the prisoner he wanted, but he was not captured, either, though he was a prize the enemy eagerly sought. They never knew he was so near.

From the hills and woods around, the stricken Indians could see the smoke rising from their homes and hear the crackle of the flames. The women in their anguish, and some of the men, too, so an old woman who had been left behind at Catharine's Town reported to Sullivan, wanted to stay and give themselves up.[103] They wanted to try to make peace. But the warriors forbade it and Butler told them the Americans would scalp them all if they remained. They could go on to Niagara, promised Butler, and be fed and clothed. It was not only a promise, it was an urgent invitation, almost an order. Joseph Brant added his bit.[104] He realized, as did all the wiser heads, that a peace treaty might give back to the Indians their towns, but their trade, which was their life, must remain with the British. It was impossible for the Indians to make peace.

On this occasion Joseph is said to have had his first clash with a young Seneca orator named Red Jacket. Red Jacket, whose tongue was mightier than his sword, was among those who wished to sue for peace. The story comes third-hand, but some part of it may have been true. Red Jacket and his friends sent off a runner to Sullivan's camp telling of the divisions among the Indians and inviting Sullivan to send a flag of truce with certain proposals which would increase those divisions and further the designs of the peace party. Joseph, learning what was afoot but not daring to try to suppress it with force, got some of his men to waylay and kill Sullivan's messenger and take charge of his dispatches. The Americans, who actually thought they had some chance of making peace, never knew what had happened till Joseph told the story to General Peter B. Porter after the war and Porter, so Joseph's biographer says, repeated it to him.[105] The warriors might very well have had some trouble with Red Jacket but there is not the slightest evidence that General Sullivan knew anything about it. The only peace feeler Sullivan received came from some of the Cayugas, via their Oneida friends, and he turned it down. If Joseph's men killed anybody, it was the Indian runner, for at no time did Sullivan send out a flag of truce.

Butler had counciled with the Indians at Catharine's Town on August 31. By September 2 he and his small force had moved twelve miles north along the lake. More than half of his men, he reported, were sick and unfit for service. By this time the rebels had entered Catharine's Town. Butler started to retreat again for his next dispatch comes from Canadesaga on September 3. The Indians were much alarmed, he said, and he feared he would be able to keep only a small body of them together. Nevertheless, he intended to harass the rebels on their march and, if possible, stop them before they got to Canadesaga.

But Sullivan, as Butler said later, was driving a wedge that could not be stopped. The Americans reached Canadesaga on September 7. Butler had been able to make no opposition. Along their way, however, the Americans had found a tree with Joseph Brant's Indian name carved on it. Nearby a sapling was twisted around like a rope and bent down, which signified, according to one diarist, who must have got his information from the Oneida guides, that "if we drove and distressed them yet we would not conquer them."[106]

By this time Butler had retreated beyond the Genesee River to the last Seneca town. He reported to Bolton on September 8 that he had tried to get the Indians to make a stand at Canadesaga but they had refused. Joseph Brant, he said, had stayed behind to reconnoiter and was actually nearby when Sullivan's army, all unsuspecting, entered the deserted town.[107] Joseph seems never to have given up the hope of getting a prisoner to question. He rejoined Butler without the prisoner but with an estimate that Sullivan's army could not be less than three thousand men.[108] In the meantime runners were coming in from the Allegheny telling of the onward progress of Brodhead's expedition. Brodhead, of course, had already accomplished his purpose in the lower Seneca country and was turning homeward, but the terrified runners did not know it.

At this point the chiefs finally decided to collect all the force possible and meet the rebels. Butler again sent to Niagara for help, and he again begged Bolton to send him all the warriors who happened to be at the fort. "The Indians," he continued, "seem in better Spirits, and more determined than I have seen them since they left Chucknut, and if they get any Succour from Niagara, I am in Hopes I shall be able to persuad them to attack the Rebels on their March, at any Rate, I shall do my Endeavour to get them to make a Stand." Joseph and the chiefs, he concluded his message, added their pleas for a few regular troops.[109]

Actually, Bolton who feared that Sullivan was headed for Niagara, had already sent reinforcements of troops and artillery, and they were on their way, as Butler heard the next day. The Indians were very pleased when told of this, Butler wrote Bolton on September 10; and Joseph and Sayengaraghta returned to Genesee Castle to make arrangements for the coming encounter. All the Delawares had arrived at Genesee and were reported to be thirsting for vengeance. The two leaders intended to take advantage of this mood. Joseph and Sayengaraghta, added Butler, were now on very good terms and cooperating with each other in every way. In the crisis they had put aside their enmities. Butler expected that if the rebels continued their advance, he would be meeting them on September 12. On the twelfth, in the morning, he wrote this postscript: "We are just setting out, as the Indians intend to attack them before they reach Genessee."[110]

The next day Butler and his four hundred Rangers and Indians posted themselves on a hill near the south end of Conesus Lake and waited in ambush. Sullivan's army was about a mile and a half away. But by a strange series of accidents Butler and his force ambushed, not Sullivan's main army, but a small scouting party of riflemen who had been sent ahead to reconnoiter. There was a hot skirmish. About thirteen of the party were killed, ten escaped, and four were captured. Among the latter were Lieutenant Thomas Boyd, the leader of the party; Sergeant Michael Parker; and two Indian guides, an Oneida and the Stockbridge. The Stockbridge managed to escape. The Oneida was almost immediately executed by the infuriated Indians. His body, when found later by the Americans, was cut almost to pieces. Boyd and Parker were interrogated by Butler who reported to Bolton that the lieutenant was a very intelligent man. From this questioning Butler learned that Sullivan had nearly five thousand Continental troops, that he had only a month's provisions, and that he meant to come no farther than Genesee.

What happened next Butler does not see fit to mention. He was forced to give up the two officers to the Indians. The Indians, reverting in their fury to an old practice, abandoned all idea of an attack on the main army. They took their prisoners back to Genesee Castle, tied them to trees, and inflicted on them every torture that their frenzied minds could devise. It was one great, ghastly act of revenge. Sullivan's men found the mangled bodies when they reached Genesee the next day. At this time Butler and the Indians had been gone from the town scarcely two hours. Boyd's head, partially skinned, had been carefully placed on a log with the mouth gaping open. Flesh on the sergeant's neck and shoulders had been gnawed off—by dogs, the Americans assumed.

Years later John Norton, the adopted nephew of Joseph Brant, claimed the reason the Indians tortured the two captives was that the rebels had killed an old Tuscarora they found in a deserted town while on their scouting expedition. It is true that Murphy, a famous marksman, did kill an Indian in the town; and the act was quite unnecessary and cruel. Norton also claimed that Brant tried his best to save the two men.[111] Butler said nothing, then or later. The two Butlers, father and son, never wanted to talk about atrocities they had seen.

Sullivan turned his face homeward on September 15. His provisions were just barely enough to get back to Tioga, there was no fodder for the horses, and the nights, and days, too, were growing cold. Months before there had been some half-hearted talk and wishful thinking about the possibility of going on to Niagara. But Washington had no such delusions. The object of the expedition, he had said on August 15, was "only the destruction of some Indian Settlements." Sullivan had fulfilled that object in full measure. He had searched every creek and river, he reported, and explored the whole country. He had destroyed forty towns (counting every cluster of houses as a town) and at least 160,000 bushels of corn and vast quantities of vegetables. In actuality, he had left only two Seneca towns standing, one beyond the Genesee that he did not know about and one fifty miles toward the Allegheny that he could not possibly reach.

On his return Sullivan destroyed what he had not taken the time to destroy before. He sent troops along the west side of Seneca Lake to burn any settlements found there, and over to Cayuga Lake to burn the Cayuga country on both sides, and even to Fort Stanwix and on down the Mohawk with orders to destroy what was left of the Lower Castle at Fort Hunter. This latter assignment fell to Colonel Peter Gansevoort, the young officer who had so distinguished himself at the siege of Fort Stanwix. Again Joseph Brant (who had been to Niagara but had returned)[112] was hanging on the rebels' flanks or in their rear.[113] Long after the war he told the then General Gansevoort that he was so close behind him that "I roasted my venison by the fires that you left."[114]

On September 30 the American army under Sullivan proudly returned to the little fort they had built at Tioga. A short distance away they sent ahead for their colors and their music, superfluities which they had had to leave behind five weeks before. Then with flags flying and drums beating they marched on. When they reached the fort they were saluted with thirteen joyful guns. They had accomplished a near-miracle of logistics. It was the sort of combined, concentrated effort

that was turning rebels into Americans. Furthermore, the whole ad-
venture had put food for thought into many minds. When, later, the
soldiers bragged about their exploits, they never forgot to mention the
fine country they had seen which was inhabited only by "savages"
(that is to say, nobody lived in it), and the corn that grew sixteen feet
high.

General Frederick Haldimand, who had been finally convinced by
a frantic Bolton that the Indian country was really threatened, had
worriedly put together a relief expedition of sorts. It was composed of
whatever men he could spare and provisioned with rations that he
could not spare. The men he could spare were Sir John Johnson's
regiment of Loyalists; some Canadian Indians, perhaps 100 or 150,
who might be supposed interested in the fate of their Six Nations
relatives; small detachments of several British regiments and a few
German mercenaries, besides Butler's corps and the Six Nations warriors who were expected to join; all under Sir John's command. The
whites, not counting the Rangers, numbered about four hundred; the
Indians would be an unknown quantity as usual. Haldimand cautioned
Sir John that he must not quarrel with Joseph over recruits.[115] Then he
cautioned him again that he must get along with Butler (and Butler,
that he must get along with Sir John), and sent him off.

By the time Sir John reached Carleton Island, on September 26,
Sullivan was already safely out of the Seneca country. Sir John, whose
instructions were very broad, had decided to go to Aserodus (Sodus
Bay) and then to Canadesaga with the idea of following Sullivan to
Tioga! Fortunately for him a gale blew his small fleet to Niagara. After
a few days he sailed back to Oswego intending to march by the old fur-
trading route against the rebel Oneidas. The Six Nations warriors and
Rangers, with Joseph Brant, Butler, and the rest of the Indian department, were to meet him at Three Rivers or at Oswego, Butler by water
and Joseph by land, since there were not enough boats for
everybody.[116]

Sir John actually got to Oswego, but at Oswego he met with an
unforeseen obstacle. The Canadian Indians positively refused to attack Oneida. Sir John saw no use in going down to Three Rivers to
meet Joseph and the party of warriors or in waiting for them to come
to Oswego. Instead, having received instructions from Haldimand
regarding winter quarters, he turned and went back home. He had not
wanted very much to go a-fighting, anyway.

General Haldimand was not particularly disappointed. He knew it
was too late in the season to mount a real campaign, and he had not
expected much. Moreover, it was a great relief to him that the rebels

had retreated, and that his provisions had not run out, the provision fleet having arrived when he was down to a five-days' supply. He consoled himself with the thought that he had shown the Indians he could be depended on to come to their aid, that he was, as always, their "Loving and Strong Brother." The Indians, for their part, were surprisingly good-natured about the whole affair. At the moment they really preferred to go to Niagara rather than to fight. They had had enough of fighting for a while. Besides, it was getting colder and colder. They were nearly naked, and they wanted to collect the new winter clothing which Butler had promised.

Joseph, though he had had probably the most strenuous year of his life, would have gladly fought all winter. He burned with indignation. Colonel Bolton could not praise him enough; "Joseph Brant . . . upon all Occasions," he declared, "deserves every thing I can Say in his favour."[117] But Joseph had to return to Niagara without doing anything more. He got back to the fort on November 12.[118] He had been gone a month (for the Indians moved slowly) on what he well knew was nothing but a wild-goose chase. Sir John Johnson was supposed to meet him, but he had not even caught a glimpse of him.

Colonel Bolton had been afraid that the homeless Indians would come flocking in to Niagara for the winter, and he had been afraid that they would not come to Niagara; but on the whole he was more fearful that they would not come than that they would come. After reporting the destruction of the villages and cornfields of the savages, he wrote Haldimand that "I wish Soon to See their Families come in, Otherwise I shall give over all hopes of their assistance any Longer."[119] Yet he also admitted that "I am extremely alarmed, for to support such a multitude I think will be absolutely impossible."[120]

The Indians did come to Niagara. They came on foot and on horseback: men, women, and children, the old and the young, the vigorous and the crippled, the healthy and the sick, many with babies on their backs. There were the newly homeless Senecas and Cayugas, to be added to the Mohawks who had been living at the fort for several years past and the Onondagas who had been living there since spring; and the Tutelos, Oneidas, Tuscaroras, Mahicans, Nanticokes, Conoys, and Delawares, and even a few Shawnees, from the devastated Susquehanna and Allegheny. Bereft of food and shelter and country, they came empty-handed and almost naked. Their sacred fire that had burned so long at Onondaga burned no more. Their Confederacy was shattered and broken. All that they had to look forward to, was behind them.

These wretched refugees arrived at Niagara just in time to give a doleful welcome to, of all persons, their old friend Colonel Guy John-son, superintendent of Indian affairs. Guy had finally prevailed on the reluctant powers-that-were to let him go to his "duty." It had taken him more than a year to get there. He had left New York in September 1778. Storms, gales, contrary winds, a near shipwreck, a long winter at Halifax, a scarcity of shipping the next spring—all had contributed to the inordinate delay. Finally Guy managed to get as far as Quebec. At Quebec General Haldimand gave him his orders. The expense of the upper posts, complained the general, far exceeded the expense of all the rest of Canada combined, including the army, the navy, and the engineering department. This great expense was mostly attribut-able to the Indians. There was a growing clamor at home about it, explained Haldimand, and something must be done to economize. Therefore it was to be Guy's responsibility not only to keep the In-dians faithful, but to cut down the cost of doing so. The enormous consumption of the Indians must be reduced.

Full of promises to do all that was required, Guy set out again. But ill luck still followed him. In the raging St. Lawrence one of his boats overturned, and he lost his papers and records. Before he got to Niagara he began to pay back bills in the department and in three weeks he had written orders on Haldimand for £7,100. It was not an auspicious beginning.

On October 5 Guy Johnson faced a throng of 3,678 refugees. He tried to get the Indians to go out hunting for the winter or to go to their remaining villages or to Carleton Island where it was easier to bring up supplies. Some did as he asked, but most would not. On November 11 there were still 2,628 Indians at the fort and they were soon augmented to three thousand. They had many excuses for re-maining. But the fact that those who went down to Canada would be hostages for the good behavior of the whole probably did not escape the perception of either the British or the Indians.

Such a winter followed as none ever forgot. The tradition of that terrible time lingers to this day. There were Indians living in tents and Indians crowded into the flimsiest of huts, and Indians existing in tiny lean-tos such as they sometimes used on the trail, for logs and bark for building and even stones were very hard to come by. Winters were always severe at Niagara, and the winter of 1779–80 was no exception. Indeed, it was even colder than usual. Mary Jemison recalled that the snow fell five feet deep that year and lay on the ground for a long time, and when it melted in the spring deer were found dead in great numbers and many other animals had perished from cold and hunger.

The Indians suffered as they had never suffered before. When they could get rations, they ate rations and counted themselves very lucky. But every ration cost two shillings and incredible labor, and Colonel Bolton was as saving with the issues as it was possible to be, this side of starvation. Mostly the Indians lived on fish heads and the feet and entrails of meat animals, and they were glad to get hides that stank, and rancid fat and anything maggoty. When the winds howled in the long dark nights, there were no furs to line frail walls and no bearskins to sleep on. If they had had bearskins they could have eaten them.

By December Fort Niagara was locked in by the winter's ice. No news got through from anywhere. Detroit and Montreal and friends and allies were a million miles away. Day by day, alone in their misery, the Indians fought starvation and freezing. What is to become of us? wondered those who still had strength to think. If ever a people needed a Moses to lead them out of captivity, the Six Nations were that people. Unfortunately, the only Moses they had was the one they could not recognize and would not follow.

Joseph Brant had thought, before the battle of Newtown, that he would soon know "what is to befal us the People of the Long House." What had happened must have been infinitely worse than anything he could have imagined. Now, as Joseph looked upon his suffering coun-trymen, he knew that before he could attempt to solve their massive problems, he had to solve his own problem.

It was in that bitter winter that he finally found the solution. He found it in the characteristic way of his family.

13

The Triumvirate

NEARLY ALL of Joseph's friends and relatives, both white and Indian, were crowded into Niagara that winter. Margaret Brant, his mother, was there, having been forced to flee her Cayuga home by Sullivan's advance. Joseph's children were also at the post, and he conferred with Guy Johnson on the possibility of getting a teacher and starting a school.[1] He did not want his young ones to grow up in ignorance. Brant Johnson was living at Niagara, too, and he had somehow managed to gather his family around him. Brant Johnson had served in the Rangers since the founding of the corps but fighting was hardly the profession he would have chosen, had he been free to choose. Nevertheless, he served faithfully, and Butler sometimes picked him to lead scouting parties.

Molly was at Niagara till late November, grieving for her lost "sons," William, and the promising young Peter who had gone with Howe to Philadelphia and had lost his life at Mud Island. Molly had spent two months that summer and fall in Montreal on Haldimand's invitation but had returned, in one breath complaining about her accommodations and in the next declaring she *must* go to her people in their trouble. She stayed just long enough on her return to help herself from the government store and then departed for Carleton Island where she could find better quarters. Colonel Bolton was heartily glad to get rid of her. Butler was not fond of her, either; and some of the Cherry Valley prisoners, when they were finally exchanged, told horrendous stories of Molly's continual hostility toward one of their number and her attempts to induce Butler to give her the man's head to kick about the fort![2] Obviously, the ways of adversity had not sweetened Molly's disposition.

One person was missing who should have been present, Joseph's good old father-in-law. In December Guy Johnson in solemn ceremony replaced Isaac of Oquaga with a scalp and a belt of black wampum. A devout Christian since 1748, the old man had stayed at Oquaga to the bitter end, ministering to his flock. Then, village gone and home gone, he made his way to Niagara and soon died, a minor casualty of the great American Revolution. Under the same circumstances some of Isaac's people had set out for Oneida and the welcoming arms of Samuel Kirkland. Indian families were divided, too.

Those Volunteers who had tried to live in the woods and remain near their loved ones had given up the attempt. Now all the Volunteers were collected at Niagara, and their families were shifting for themselves as best they could. Some of Joseph's white followers had left a wife and small children destitute and friendless back at home. Even Governor Clinton, good rebel though he was, expressed sympathy for the plight of Loyalist families such as these and honestly wished to do something to ameliorate their lot. He had all he could do, however, to ameliorate the lot of those he considered patriots.

Though Niagara was crowded and uncomfortable, all its inhabitants were not starving. The soldiers of the garrison had their usual meals, the Rangers were fed, too, and the Indian department and even the Volunteers got rations. Able-bodied Loyalists not employed by the military could still find work and receive pay (for there was a great scarcity of labor), and anyone who had pay could buy from the traders enough to satisfy basic needs.

Not even all the Indians were hungry. With his good salary Joseph and his family were in no distress. Even had that not been so, Guy Johnson and the Indian department would have taken care of him. Sayengaraghta was one of the lucky ones, too, having just received from Haldimand a pension of one hundred dollars a year. Haldimand thought both Sayengaraghta and Joseph had behaved well and sent them both presents of pistols.[3] At the same time he never did let Joseph know that he had been instructed by Germain to forward to him a royal commission as colonel of the Indians.[4] Though he himself had recommended that something be done for Brant, he was taken aback by the government's generosity. Brant was "zealous," he admitted, but, after all, he had never accomplished anything of real military consequence; and his "small strokes," he wrote Germain, should be put in their proper perspective.[5] The truth was, Haldimand was too wise in the ways of Indians to inflame the jealousy that already subsisted against Joseph. But any notice by the commander in chief guaranteed that the favored person would also be favored by Bolton and Butler as well as the entire Indian department. It was also known by private letters from England that Brant was highly thought of in ministerial circles and much praised by those newspapers that supported the government. Joseph's position, at least as far as the white authorities at Niagara were concerned, was secure. He was certainly in no danger of going hungry.

Guy Johnson had ten or twelve sachems and principal warriors of whom he took especial care. Sayengaraghta could get anything he wanted from the superintendent. So, too, could families like the Montours who had been outstanding even in the days of the French, and the Hills who had always had Sir William's particular regard. Johannes Tekarihoga, the head chief of the Mohawks, and his two nieces, Catharine Adonwentishon and her younger sister, the half-breed daughters of George Croghan, suffered no want. Persons such as these enjoyed a comfortable living while the ordinary Indians were happy to get anything they could put in their mouths. While the latter existed on soup made of fish heads, Tekarihoga and his kind supped on fresh beef and butter, and tea and wine and sugar and sago, and delicacies such as raisins, almonds, and prunes, and essence of peppermint, a preparation which the Indians liked to drink in water. The leading Indians had grown accustomed to, and did not hesitate to demand, better and better goods and provisions. They wanted fine silverware and fine cloth. They scorned cheap lace. Tinsel did not fool them.

Higher and higher soared Guy Johnson's accounts. But Guy's mentor, Sir William, had always taken particular care of the leading families; and Guy, though admonished by Haldimand to cut expenses to the bone, could not unlearn a lesson so well learned. In one period of fifteen months he spent ten thousand pounds for private issues to Indians, exclusive of ordinary presents and provisions. Guy thought, as he said later, he was only doing his duty. To him, cutting expenses did not mean leaving the sachems and head warriors dissatisfied. These leaders were far too important to the work of keeping the entire Six Nations faithful. The upper country, the fur trade, perhaps all of Canada, depended on them.

It was not that Guy supposed Johannes Tekarihoga and the other sachems had great authority over the rest of the Indians. He knew they did not. But he also knew, as Sir William had advised long ago, that counciling with "any more Indians, than the Sachims & Head Warriours . . . is only expensive, and troublesome & not of the least

Service [for] they [the rest] have nothing to Say."[6] What Guy recognized in the chiefs with his largess was their prestige among their tribesmen. The common Indians, the lowborn who had "nothing to Say," deferred to the chiefs and followed their example unless they were completely unworthy, and sometimes even if they were. The Indian idea of worthiness did not coincide with the white idea, anyway. Tekarihoga would have had to be very bad, even from the Indian point of view, to have lost all his influence—was he not descended from the first woman on earth? Did he not light the council fire? Was not his the first place in the council, his the first name intoned on the list of chiefs in the solemn ceremony of condolence? Yes, the Indians all agreed, Tekarihoga was a great man.

In some respects Catharine Croghan enjoyed even more prestige than her uncle. When Johannes died, she would name his successor from among her relatives of the female line, perhaps her mother's brother, her mother's sister's son, her own brother, or, some day, her own son. She might be assisted by relatives in making the decision, but hers was the final word, and the council would ratify her choice. This was her birthright, and it was unassailable. Catharine's Indian name meant "The Trembling World";[7] and it was rather appropriate, for in a sense her world did tremble a little in her presence. Catharine would always exert great influence over whomever she named to the high post of Tekarihoga. He would always listen to her advice. And the great mass of the Indians would always listen to him. Among the Mohawks Tekarihoga was a power. Even among the entire Six Nations none took him lightly.

In this unequal way life went on at Niagara in that bitter winter of 1779–80. Yet amidst the crowding and the discomforts and even the sharpest pangs of hunger, there was one thought that cheered, and it was the same for high and low. The situation, however painful it might be, was only temporary. One and all, everybody expected to go home again. The Indians expected that the victorious British would give them back their old homes one day, as they had promised, with everything intact. Even those who were hungry and numb with cold had a hope, and even an expectation, that some day they would go home.

No less than the Indians, the white Loyalists looked forward to the war's happy outcome. Back east on the Mohawk strangers were living in Johnson Hall and the mansions of Guy Johnson and Daniel Claus and in John Butler's old farmhouse, and in the homes of many a lesser man all over the province, for their owners had been attainted of treason and their property confiscated; nevertheless, white Loyalists in high and low places clung to the same hopes that the Indians cherished. Joseph's friend, Governor Tryon, still lingering on in New York at British headquarters, could speak for all. Describing to Germain how open the city was to attack because of the frozen river, he also assured him that "the friendly part of America keep up their spirits, and are sanguine from the flattering prospects of His Majesty's affairs in all quarters, that the re-union of the Empire will be yet happily established, and those who have been with circumstances of cruelty, drove from their estates and families, restored in peaceful possession of them again."[8] Thus the thought of going home buoyed up Guy Johnson in his handsome house in the compound of Fort Niagara and in like manner cheered the Rangers in their rude barracks across the river, and the Indians and Volunteers and many an unknown Loyalist who were scattered in huts and tents all up and down the river for six miles or more, from the fort itself to the landing where merchants unloaded their boats, and even beyond. One bright day, they told themselves, they would all go home, and they would be happy again, and everything would be just as it once was.

Until that happy event took place life had to go on. People ate and slept and gossiped, and felt jealousy and fear and remorse, and fell in love, and died and were born. Then one day, late in 1779, a girl who had been captured at Cherry Valley and whose relations were the "most inveterate rebels, and implacable Enemies to Loyalists perhaps in the Continent"[9] married (for such are the strange ways of romance) an officer of the hated Indian department. Major John Butler performed the ceremony. There was no clergyman at Niagara—Niagara being in no wise a place of religion—but Butler had been a magistrate back home in better days and, so far as the Loyalists were concerned, nobody had divested him of that office.

This wedding must have been an eye opener to Joseph Brant who had crowded in, with as many others as could get in, to view the rites. Joseph had probably never realized before that anybody but clergymen could solemnize a marriage. The Indians, if they married at all, were married by ministers, never by justices of the peace. Joseph marveled, and acted quickly. It was an opportunity which he could not afford to lose.

Right on the spot Joseph requested—and, it is said, even insisted—that Butler perform a marriage ceremony for him. Butler agreed. And as people craned their necks, Joseph led forth the bride. It was Tekarihoga's niece, Catharine Croghan. There was probably not a white man in the room, including Butler himself, who saw anything odd in this event unless it was the fact that a mere Indian should be so determined to have a formal wedding.

The Cherry Valley prisoners, always talkative, are our only witnesses. Others have mentioned that this marriage took place at Fort Niagara, but only the Cherry Valley people provide any details. Joseph and Catharine, they further reported, had been living together "for some time previous, according to the Indian custom, without marriage."[10] Of course, the white prisoners did not view an Indian union as a marriage, and neither, apparently, did Joseph. But a legal marriage it now became, in the eyes of all, as Butler read the plain words of the service. And Joseph Brant who liked everything in good order must have been very happy for a variety of reasons.

Catharine Adonwentishon was handsome rather than pretty. A tall, robust, big-boned girl, she was a great contrast to the frail Peggie and Susanna. When she got older a traveler could describe the "grandeur of her looks." In age she was called "the old Indian queen." But even in her youth she probably had presence. Catharine's eyes and hair were black, and her cheeks were rosy. Though her complexion was dark in comparison to that of white women, there must have been something in her looks reminiscent of her Irish father. Her hair may have been a little wavy, her cheekbones not quite so high. But whatever her looks, Catharine thought as an Indian. She preferred Indian ways. Though she could understand English, she did not deign to speak it. It was more fitting, she knew, to speak through an interpreter.[11] She could write well enough to sign her name, which she spelled "Katerin," but she obviously did not write very often.[12] She was only twenty years old.[13]

Where had Catharine and her sister come from? Their mother, presumably, was dead. Their father was living outside Philadelphia, old, ill, and not much trusted by anybody. The rebels were sure that George Croghan had gone over to the British. The British were not so sure about him, themselves. But Croghan's era of power and influence had passed. General Haldimand, when asked about him, did not even know who he was. There is some evidence that the two young girls had returned to the Mohawk with their mother from the Ohio country in 1774. Then, again, they may have been among the flotsam and jetsam that turned up at Niagara after the Sullivan campaign. Catharine may or may not have had clear memories of her father and those childhood days at Lake Otsego. Her mother may or may not have left George Croghan years before. But whatever her history, Catharine Croghan was a great match for Joseph Brant.

Mrs. William Johnson Kerr, nee Elizabeth Brant. No portrait of Catharine Brant has been found, but this portrait of her daughter, Elizabeth, probably looks like her, as it answers Patrick Campbell's description very well. *Courtesy of the Metropolitan Toronto Library Board, Toronto.*

Joseph was thirty-six years old at the time of this third and last marriage. A young girl from the Susquehanna, a prisoner that year at Niagara, later described him in these words: "The expression of his face was severe and frightful. He was spare and above the medium height of Indians. His dress was very fine; he wore a broadcloth blanket over his shoulders in the usual Indian style, of the finest make, with a deep, rich, red border. When he showed himself about the fort, he was always in full and careful costume, glittering with brooches, etc."[14] Another captive, a man who saw Brant in 1780, agrees about his "fierce aspect" and fine clothing and also mentions that he was a "likely fellow," tall, well-spoken, and rather spare of build.[15] Obviously Joseph had dignity and a grave mien which the two awed prisoners interpreted according to their very real fears. Also, as he had a lurking sense of humor, Joseph was not above a little play acting to impress them.

It was not long after the wedding, probably, that Joseph gave his bride the ring engraved "Thayendanegea to Catharine" which she treasured so many years.[16] Though not one to wear his emotions on his sleeve, Joseph showed by his lifelong behavior toward her that he loved her tenderly and devotedly. But being Joseph, he could not love her the less because she was the first woman of the Mohawks. As for Catharine, she returned his devotion in full measure. She stood by him in his trials and gave him seven fine children.[17] But should she have cared for him the less because he dressed her in silk and velvet and gave her a good life? A people so poor as the Indians could not afford the luxury of scorning material things. Not one of them but had known want sometime, somewhere. Catharine Adonwentishon, bride of Joseph Brant, never knew it again.

Joseph had a "farm" at the landing (present Lewiston) which he must have bought from somebody or other since we know it was his to sell. There, about six miles up the river from Fort Niagara, he took his new wife and set up housekeeping in his own blockhouse.[18] Probably Catharine did very little of the actual housekeeping. Joseph already had the beginnings of a retinue of Negro slaves whom he had captured or who had run away to join him.[19] If any of these expected an end to their labor, they were mistaken. Their duties may have been somewhat different, but they still had duties; and it was always said of Joseph that he tolerated no nonsense from his slaves.[20] They were well fed and clothed but they worked. In the meantime, other Indians were beginning to settle at the landing, and Joseph who never could keep away from church built a little chapel at his own expense.[21] How astonished the rebels would have been if they could have seen the terrible Brant at home on Sundays!

Joseph's family now consisted of a wife, the two children, his mother, and probably his wife's young sister. The latter married, sometime after the war, Corporal John Elliott of Butler's Rangers and went to live on the Canadian side of Lake Erie where her husband had a grant of land.[22] Joseph's mother may not have lasted the winter and certainly not the war. She put in no claim for losses in 1784. The final mention of her is on January 8, 1780, when Guy Johnson recorded that he gave Joseph's mother and wife "some handsome clothing."[23] After all her ups and downs Margaret Brant departs history clad in fine raiment. She left her son her courage and her indomitable character, and her cherished prayer book. Years later Joseph gave an old Mohawk prayer book to the Moravian missionary, Gottlob Sensemann. There is reason to believe the book was his mother's. It had been carefully cared for and carried on who knows how many painful journeys. It had not been read for Margaret Brant could not read, but it had been cherished.[24]

Joseph's two children were growing up and back in school again.[25] Christina was only ten years old, a docile little girl who gave her father and stepmother no trouble. But Isaac was different. Isaac gave plenty of trouble. Isaac did not take to schooling. Isaac was unruly. And living so near the fort did not improve his behavior. Niagara was, to say the least, an easygoing sort of place. Soldiers and provincials and Indians frolicked and brawled. Drunken revels spilled out of the taverns and disturbed the peace by night and day. Though the brawl- ers probably paid no attention to Isaac, he seems to have paid rapt attention to them. And at far too young an age, for he was only thirteen, Isaac saw some service in the war.[26] He learned to drink. Home did not appeal to him. He hated his stepmother. He was sure that his father was neglecting him and his sister.[27] Perhaps if Catharine had been a humbler woman, he would not have resented her so much or felt such desperate jealousy.

Sometime during the war Catharine's Uncle Johannes died. He may have been the prominent chief who was killed at Newtown, but, on the other hand, he had not been active for a long time previously. The documents, however, are scanty. The times were out of joint, and there was no Sir William to keep the careful records and make the detailed reports which in earlier years had mentioned so many indi- vidual Indians by name. Perhaps Johannes had been ill a long time, his activities curtailed. There is even some evidence that he died shortly after Catharine's marriage, in the winter of the great snows. At any rate, he disappears; and after the war there is a new Tekarihoga.

The successor whom Catharine named (or whom her mother named if she was still alive) was her elder half-brother, Henry. Henry had a different father and he was some six years Catharine's senior.[28] He was a good man, quiet and steady and religious. Faithfully he was to read the prayers in church for many years until age and blindness put a stop to such work.[29] It was Henry's dear wish to see his people devout and God-fearing. If religion could do so much for whites, perhaps it might also do something for Indians.

From the very beginning the three of them, Henry and Catharine and Joseph, joined hands, their resolves fixed on the good of their people. If one thought a plan worthy and likely to further their purpose, the other two thought the plan worthy. What this amounted to, of course, was that the educated and imaginative and energetic Joseph conceived the plans and projects, and the other two helped to carry them out. Joseph by himself could do very little. With Henry and Catharine by his side he could do everything—that is, everything as far as the Mohawks were concerned and much as far as the Six Nations were concerned. Ambitiously he even tried to encompass in his plans all the Indians within his knowledge, but there he failed. There were limits to the influence of Henry and Catharine, and limits even within himself, but it cannot be said that he did not make the effort.

Smoothly and competently these three went to work. It was a triumvirate of affection and mutual good will. If Joseph required a power of attorney, it was Henry Tekarihoga who cheerfully and promptly signed it. When Joseph contended with whites or hostile and dissenting Indians, a stalwart Henry always stood by his side. When Joseph made a treaty or got up a petition, Henry's name led all the rest. Loud and clear rang Henry's approving "Oyeh!" when Joseph made some fiery speech or flourished his tomahawk in the face of the Indian agent at Niagara. And if Joseph tried to gull the superintendent of Indian affairs or carried on some intrigue against the government of Upper Canada, then intrigues and gullings were just what the loyal Henry favored most.

Catharine, the third member of this remarkable trio, signed documents only when she must. Otherwise she remained at home, presiding over her establishment with grace and assurance, dispensing charity, and entertaining friends and strangers almost without number, for Joseph's house was hardly ever without some visitor. But it cannot be supposed that, among the Mohawk women whose attitude was so important in the councils of their nation, she did not exert a potent influence, by her position, by her force of character, and by a little present, every now and then, or a handful of this or that.[30]

Strangely enough, not one white observer ever described the workings of this smooth and successful triumvirate. White people, even those who knew Indians best, could look at these three and see only the commanding figure of Joseph Brant. Henry was no nonentity, but he could have been for all that anyone noticed what he did. The memoir-writing visitors seldom met Henry, anyway. As for Catharine—well, Catharine was Joseph Brant's wife. She was Mrs. Catharine Brant. Catharine got credit for her beauty and hospitality. Joseph got credit for everything else. Henry got credit for nothing. But that, apparently, was the way he was willing that it should be. So long as Joseph lived Henry gave him his loyal support and asked for nothing in return. Among a people so prone to jealousy as the Indians often were, so quick to take offense or to exact revenge, whose leaders were so fiercely competitive that they almost never had a good word to say of one another, and who could seldom be brought to cooperate no matter how great the need, the quiet and self-effacing Henry stands out in stark contrast.[31] Henry was the man the hour demanded, yet it is almost impossible to explain how he got there.

About such things the Indians themselves said nothing, no more than the white people did. Were they to describe in detail the very air they breathed? Perhaps they also did not see anything. Nothing was going on which did any violence to their customs.

Little by little this marriage put power into Joseph's hands, and his own character and ability accomplished the rest. Some fifteen years later awestruck travelers would record that Brant ruled the Mohawks as an absolute monarch. They were very nearly right. Even as early as the first months of 1780 some profound changes in his life were becoming apparent.

14

Revenge!

T HE INDIANS were almost too stunned for a while to think of
revenge. However, there were a number of persons about the fort
whose duty it was to remind them, and that winter a few small war
parties began to go out.

The going, especially in such bitter weather, was not easy. There
was nobody along the way, now, to give them shelter and food, no
tireless female workers to pound corn for them or to wash their shirts
and mend their moccasins. Nor was there a warrior living by the
roadside who might join the party after they left Niagara. If they went
by way of Seneca Lake and the Forbidden Path, as they used to do, all
they saw was the ghosts of towns. The charred ruins whetted their
desire for revenge but offered them no comfort against cold and hunger. Going east through Onondaga was an equally desolate journey.
The garrison of Fort Stanwix had to be by-passed and the more unfriendly Oneida villages as well. Either way the prospect was bleak.
Nevertheless, British authorities thought it absolutely necessary that
the Indians be sent early to war. Of course their going would distress
the rebels. It would also take their minds off their troubles, reduce
their consumption at Niagara, collect intelligence, and who knew (for
the authorities were always optimistic in this respect) but that it might
also support some great plan of Sir Henry Clinton.

Joseph Brant, for one, needed no reminding that revenge was
sweet. He planned that winter to set out as early as possible, and he
had the gratification to know that several hundred warriors were getting ready to join him. On the night of February 8 he and some of his
party held their war dance at Guy Johnson's, but there was not room

for everybody who was going, so the rest had to dance at the Indian camp. Next day Johnson supplied all the warriors with snowshoes, Indian sleds, clothing and provisions.[1] Joseph appears to have been in full charge.

By February 12 Joseph and the vanguard of his party had reached the Cranberry Swamp, a bog which in better weather was only a few hours' march from Niagara. Here Joseph met some old friends whom he had not seen in nearly five years. The Indian grapevine being what it was, nobody was really surprised. Indeed, one of Joseph's objects in coming out ahead of the rest of the warriors was to meet these men, and they may even have expected him. Nevertheless, they could all stare at one another—Joseph and his followers, suspicious and hostile, and the four travelers who had come a long way and who wanted to be friendly. But Joseph refused to fraternize with Little Abraham of Fort Hunter and White Hans (though a relative of his stepfather Brant) and certainly not with his former in-laws, Skenando of Oneida who was a famous rebel, and Peter, one of those who had left Oquaga and gone over to the enemy.

Joseph detained the four and quickly sent off a letter to Guy Johnson. He was afraid the travelers might get a chance to talk privately with some of the Indians at Niagara. "All I would say to you concerning them," Joseph advised Guy, "is, to pretend to be friendly with them at first before those Indians who are going with me to War; I think after we are all gone from Niagara then you may do what you think proper."[2]

Guy sent off a guard to bring in the travelers, and Joseph and his men went on. Joseph's expedition, however, was fated to meet with many difficulties. On February 22 he wrote from the Crossroads that many of his party were ill. Considering the weather, it is to be wondered at that they were not all ill. Three days later Joseph again wrote that illness had delayed his party but that he was going on with the two hundred warriors who were still able to travel.[3]

In the meantime, back at Niagara, Little Abraham was pleading with the Six Nations to lay down their arms and go back to their homes. With Guy Johnson, Butler, and Bolton in charge of the council, Abraham should have saved his breath. The outcome was never in doubt. His belts were thrown back at him. What he wanted was impossible, anyway.

The plucky old man deserved something better from life than he had ever received. Little Abraham had eagerly accepted "civilization," but "civilization" had not accepted him. His white neighbors continually plotted against him; they feared those Indians who called themselves friends; "who can know," they complained, "wheter he be met by an Honest one or a ravinous Creature."[4] Abraham had almost lost his home the previous fall through ill-advised orders of Sullivan, and would have been carried away a prisoner, had not Schuyler and Washington intervened. A true neutral, Abraham wished to try one last appeal to his people, and an exchange of letters between the rebels and authorities at Niagara regarding some prisoners had given him his chance. He begged Schuyler to be allowed to accompany the flag of truce. Schuyler consented, but had little faith in his project. He distrusted him, too. Abraham had honestly thought he had a chance to influence the Six Nations for peace, but he was reviled and scorned and kept closely confined at Niagara. Finally the rebels began to wonder what had become of him but they did not mourn him very much. Little Abraham of Fort Hunter was to die in captivity. Old age and unhappiness and the rigors of a terrible journey took their toll, and far from home a long and honorable life came to an end.

While Little Abraham was pleading his cause at Niagara, some of Joseph's sick died. He decided to split up his party into smaller groups who might find the going easier.[5] About March 8 one division, apparently the largest, was sent on a scout to Oswego.[6] It was feared among the Indians that the rebels had their eyes on Oswego. The other two divisions set out together along the old route of Seneca Lake and the Forbidden Path. At Tioga they separated, one cutting across country toward the Delaware River and Minisink,[7] while Joseph himself, with twenty-four picked Indians and whites,[8] appears to have gone up the Susquehanna and then headed east for Schoharie.[9]

Though there were three forts at Schoharie, Joseph had formed a rather ambitious plan of attacking the place. He believed there were few or no troops in the forts. By April 7 he had reached Harpersfield, a small and now almost deserted settlement near the headwaters of the Delaware. Here he unexpectedly came upon a party of rebel militia who were out making maple sugar. Being only eleven or twelve in number, the rebels did not have a chance. Three were slain and the rest taken prisoners.[10] The prisoners were collected into a hog pen and the Indians debated all night what to do with them. Fifty years later Freegift Patchin, one of the younger captives, dictated a long narrative of his experiences which holds up remarkably well when compared with the few contemporary records available. Patchin said Joseph Brant was for saving their lives but that many of the Indians and Tories wanted to put them to death. Benjamin Becraft, one of

Brant's Volunteers, added Patchin, boasted of how many rebels he had killed and frequently called out to the prisoners that they would all be in hell before morning.[11]

Brant's will finally prevailed, and the next day the prisoners were informed they would be taken to Niagara. They would have to keep up with the marching Indians, the chief told them, or they would be killed. At various times, said Patchin, Brant questioned them about the garrison of the forts. The rebels always told him that Schoharie was defended by three hundred Continental soldiers. The story was not true, but he believed it and gave up all idea of an attack. It would not be the last time that Joseph was taken in by guile.

In the meantime Harpersfield, or what remained of it, was burned, and a few more prisoners were taken. Three women who were captured were turned loose.[12] Joseph then freed Walter Elliot, one of the men, and sent him with a letter in Mohawk to the rebel authorities. He had heard that Loyalist prisoners were being mistreated, and his letter, when translated, was found to contain a threat:

> That you Bostoneans (alias Americans) may be certified of my Conduct, towards all Those whom I have Captured in these Parts, Know that I have taken off with Me, but a Small Number.— Many have I released. Neither were the Weak and helpless subjected to Death; for it is a Shame to destroy those who are defenceless
>
> This has been uniformly my Conduct during the War. I have always been for Saving and releasing— These being my Sentiments, You have exceedingly angered me, by threatning and distressing those who may be Considered as Prisoners. Ye are (or once were) brave men— I shall certainly distroy without distinction does the like Conduct take place in future.[13]

With Joseph's letter Elliot also carried a letter from Captain Alexander Harper, leader of the sugaring party, to his wife, and written or dictated in Joseph's presence, in which he said he was being well treated and was glad (if he must be captured) that he had had the good luck to be captured by Joseph Brant.[14] In view of the fact that Harper was a noted Tory-baiter who had killed in cold blood an uncle of one of Joseph's white friends, this letter was obviously meant as soothing syrup for the chief. No love, however, was lost between captor and captive, and when Joseph got back to Niagara he insisted that Harper be closely confined and never exchanged.[15]

By this time Joseph and his party were suffering greatly from hunger. They lingered near Harpersfield and the headwaters of the Delaware for three days making canoes and wolfing down all the sugar they could hold. There was a heavy snow, and the place was so remote they felt secure. Then they set off down the Delaware in search of provisions, since a few Loyalist families still lived on that river and there was nobody at all to help them in the direction from which they came. Joseph was able to get some corn at one Tory house where the man of the family told him dourly that he had better have taken "more scalps and less prisoners." The Indians counted out the grains of corn to the rebels; it was share and share alike, and when they finished with their cooking pots, they let the prisoners use them. Another time the party found the frozen carcass of a horse and divided it up, head, hoofs, and all. Later, as they neared Niagara and their journey's end, Joseph was able to buy a good horse. It was roasted, and he showed the rebels how to use white wood ashes for salt.

At Cokeose the party left the Delaware and headed through the wilderness for the Susquehanna and the ruins of Oquaga. Here the Indians built rafts and floated downstream. Back at Tioga two warriors showed up who had been of the number Joseph sent to Minisink. They reported that their party, too, had taken some prisoners, but that the latter had managed to get free one night and kill all but two of their captors. Hearing this story, Joseph's Indians crowded around the hapless prisoners, gnashing their teeth and brandishing their tomahawks as if to take instant revenge. This time one of the two newcomers intervened. He had lived near Schoharie before the war and knew all the rebels. He was a harmless, good Indian, said Patchin, and persuaded the others that it was wrong to blame the innocent for somebody else's misdeeds.

Joseph was now so ill with ague that for his sake the whole party stopped to rest every other day. The prisoners had a chance to rest, too, and probably this saved their lives, for they were weak from fatigue and hunger, and found it very hard to keep up with the marching Indians. Somewhere along the way one of their group, an old man, had stumbled and fallen behind. He was killed without much ado, and his body left to the wolves. Freegift Patchin adds that the warrior who did the killing dangled the old man's bald scalp in the faces of his two grandsons. Patchin's story of the killing is probably true. Guy Johnson admits that four from Harpersfield were killed. Presumably they were the three in the sugaring party and the old man along the way.[16]

Joseph found a rattlesnake sunning itself where the snow had melted on the south side of a hill. He killed the snake and made some soup. The hot soup cured his ague. It was a good old Indian remedy. Afterward the hard marching began again.

Approaching near Niagara, Joseph sent word ahead so that the Indian warriors thereabouts might be got out of the way and his prisoners saved from running the gauntlet. The gauntlet was an entertainment which the Indians at home always looked forward to. A prisoner brought into a village had to run between two lines of the inhabitants, being beaten all the way until he reached a goal post. Only the very fleet-footed could escape serious injury, for even the old women and the children were capable of inflicting deep cuts and bruises. Some of the British officers, thus alerted, did get the Indian men away from the fort on some pretext; and Joseph and the prisoners, after the latter had braved the women and children, came in to the usual booming salute of the fort's guns. The party had been out about two and one-half months. They had distressed the rebels, had exacted some part of their revenge, and had saved a great deal of provisions at Niagara.

The people on the frontier had hoped that Sullivan's expedition might bring on peace or at least reduce the number of Indian raids. The Harpersfield episode and some similar attacks which took place about the same time showed them how wrong they were. There was to be no peace. They must spend another summer huddled in forts and blockhouses, their crops uncared for, unharvested, in many cases not even planted. Reluctantly Governor Clinton again ordered out the militia. "How these are to be fed," he worried, "God only knows."[17]

Never before had so large a number of warriors gone out with Joseph Brant and submitted to his leadership. It was a pleasant experience, soothing to whatever pride or vanity or personal ambition he had. Other gratifying experiences awaited him on his return. One came about through the agency of Guy Johnson.

Prodded by Haldimand about the continuing expense of the Indian department and well aware of the hue and cry "at home," Guy had been doing his best all spring to cut down on the outgo. But the difficulties were enormous and might have felled an administrator far wiser than he. The Indians liked presents and, indeed, could not live without them. They also liked presents of the best quality, the common Indians as well as the chiefs, though it must be admitted the latter had a much better chance of satisfying their desires.

All Indians, however, would resort to almost any stratagem to get what they wanted. When warriors came home from war their wives would tear the clothes off their backs so that they could present themselves in a suitable dishabille for the reception of new clothing.

War chiefs felt no qualms in giving out false returns of their parties. Warriors tried to get outfitted more than once; or they got outfitted and then would not go on an expedition, or not go very far. At other times a man and even a whole family might journey down to Montreal or Carleton Island to get gifts from Claus or Colonel Campbell or Captain Fraser and then back to Niagara to get more from Guy Johnson. An Indian with an order on a trader for a necessity could, with the trader's connivance, exchange the necessity for a luxury he fancied but was not supposed to have. Nor were the traders above stimulating an Indian's desire for something he might not have thought of by himself, or of buying it back from him two or three times and making a profit on each transaction. Wartime was the time to get all one could, thought many a trader or soldier or petty official. Then, too, some chicanery in the Indians was overlooked even when nobody planned wrongdoing. Everyone knew that Indian aid was essential, and normal rules had to be relaxed.

To stop some of this expense Haldimand had suggested sending the Indians back to the Genesee. Guy Johnson was more than willing that they should go. He, too, was anxious to see the Indians settled somewhere besides at Niagara—somewhere they could do something toward their own support and, preferably, as far away as possible without limiting their ability to make war. Guy knew that getting them to leave would not be easy. In spite of their terrible winter, when spring came, the Indians looked forward to staying where they were. They liked bustling Niagara. Life there was exciting, rum was easier to get, and they had been promised long ago that they would be supported if the fortunes of war turned against them. Nor had dependency made them fonder of work. All in all, the Indians were well content at the fort once the provision ships began to arrive.

In his dilemma Guy fell upon the idea of dividing the Indians into seven companies, each with its own leader to look after its concerns. In this way he thought he might be able to persuade them, by presents if all else failed, to go away. They could join the two villages that Sullivan had overlooked, one near the Genesee and one toward the Ohio. There was also a good place for a settlement on Cattaraugus Creek, south of Lake Erie (near present Gowanda, New York), which might attract the homeless Ohio Indians and prove a buffer against the rebels at Fort Pitt. Then there was Buffalo Creek at the outlet of Lake Erie, also on its south side—not far away, to be sure, but certainly a settlement there would also protect Niagara.

The leaders whom Guy appointed over the Indians were all white men except one, Joseph Brant. The latter Guy placed over the

Mohawks and the few loyal Oneidas and Mahicans who had been living at Niagara. Joseph, Guy thought, was just as dependable and just as willing and able to execute orders as any of his white officers. He was also amenable to suggestion, not likely to fly off on some strange Indian tangent; and probably Guy could see, if no one else could, that Joseph's status, as far as his people were concerned, had changed for the better. His elevation to a position of leadership was not likely to cause so much jealousy as heretofore.

Joseph's company consisted, on March 24, 1780, when it was first announced, of 91 men, 172 women, and 186 children.[18] By May 26, 20 of the men, 40 of the women, and 26 children had gone to plant at Buffalo Creek.[19] Their numbers fluctuated wildly all year, showing how the Indians came and went. On December 1 Joseph had in charge at Niagara, or perhaps near his home at the landing, 188 men, 276 women, and 233 children. Fifty-three men, 46 women, and 51 children were absent at their new settlements, and two men were still away on service.[20]

Joseph also received, early that fall, a written commission from General Haldimand as captain in the Indian department.[21] Though he had been a captain for a long time, this was his first formal commission; and, so far as is known, he was the only Indian so honored. In rebel eyes, of course, this was a doubtful honor and, commission or no commission, they would probably have hanged him if they could have caught him. Joseph was very fortunate in that he was never captured or had to put them to the test. The commission made little real difference in his military career, for he continued to act informally as a war chief as he had always done.[22]

In the meantime a project was afoot down the country in which Joseph had no part but got just as much opprobrium from the rebels for it as if he had. For a long time Sir John Johnson had been brooding on his inability to complete his regiment, and he finally hit upon a scheme to fill its ranks. He would make a flying raid on the Mohawk, distress the rebels of his old neighborhood, and in passing collect a large number of Loyalist recruits. This operation would also facilitate General Haldimand's taking post at Oswego, an action which had long been contemplated.

Secrecy was of the utmost importance, but Kirkland's Oneidas and other spies got wind of the project. In spite of numerous warnings, however, the rebels were unprepared. They knew there was to be an attack but they did not know when or where. Sir John with an army of 528 whites and Indians was able to sweep down from Lake Champlain and devastate his old neighborhood for twelve miles or so. At day-

break on May 22 the unhappy Mohawk River settlement of Caughnawaga was burned to the ground. Many prominent rebels were killed
or captured, and Sir John collected 143 Loyalists, enough to fill up his
first battalion and even start a second. It was all done very quickly
though at the finish the rebel militia was only a few hours behind as he
retreated.

While Sir John was burning houses and barns on the north shore
of the Mohawk the rumor (apparently started by Sir John himself) got
about that Joseph Brant was to burn the country on the south side.[23]
The rebels knew not which way to fly, and their belief that the savage
Brant was so near magnified their panic.

Actually Joseph was nowhere near the Mohawk. Although he got
back to Niagara from Harpersfield about the first of May, the news of
Sir John's projected raid did not reach the post till May 13. By this
time Joseph appears to have been at or on his way to Carleton Island,
the lake having opened for navigation on May 1. Oneida spies reported that Joseph had gone for "help."[24] They were probably right.
Many Mohawks had wintered on Carleton Island, and Claus's
Mohawks were still living down near Montreal, all of whom could
help Joseph carry out an enterprise he had long had in mind. Captain
Fraser on Carleton Island reports on June 1 that he had seen Joseph a
few days before.[25] Claus does not mention seeing Joseph. He was still
sending him letters of advice, however, the latest in the fall or winter
before the communication was stopped.[26] If Joseph did see Claus he
must have been bewildered by all the conflicting instructions he was
given, for back at Niagara Guy Johnson and Butler were getting along
together very well. Guy did not care enough about his brother-in-law,
Claus, to take up his quarrel, and Butler was a big help in running the
Indian department. Each spoke well of the other. At any rate, Joseph
certainly saw his sister again. Molly had made herself very welcome on
Carleton Island, and Captain Fraser, who did not usually like Indians,
continually sang her praises. Molly cooperated wholeheartedly in
helping Fraser reduce the demands and consumption of the Indians on
the island—but not her own, as Haldimand observed unhappily.
Molly was content again. She chaperoned her girls to parties, began to
think of marrying them off, and apparently never gave a thought to
returning to Niagara.

Joseph's journey was only a short one. By early June he was embarked on a government vessel bound for Niagara and arrived in a
short time without any delay or mishap. At the fort he found a frantic
mother, a prisoner from Pennsylvania named Elizabeth Gilbert, who
begged him to help her get her children out of captivity from among

the Indians. Joseph promised to try to get the children's freedom, and Guy Johnson made the same promise.[27] Even Claus later exerted himself in their behalf. The children were finally released by the reluctant Indians but why, or at whose behest, we are not told.

On June 17 Joseph was still at Niagara, for on that date he attended an Indian council and heard a message of friendship and unity sent by the Shawnees and Delawares of Ohio and another of similar purport sent by the Hurons.[28] The Six Nations and their western allies nearly always had some message of encouragement going back and forth between them. All were now fighting the rebels in one way or another; all officially considered them enemies.

The rebels by their own admission were in a very low state. Washington's army was subsisting on half allowance of meat and sometimes even going without. Officers were living chiefly on bread and water in order that their men might have a little more. The troops had received no pay for five months, what pay they did get was eaten up by depreciation, and a Connecticut brigade had mutinied. The garrison at West Point was worse off, if possible, than Washington's army; and the troops at Fort Stanwix, in Oneida country, with only one month's provisions between them and starvation, were dismayed and disheartened by reports that they would soon be attacked by a force of five thousand men from Canada. When Governor Clinton asked Washington for help he was told that he not only could not spare any troops for the frontier but, even if he could, there would be no way to feed them.

The Oneidas, faced on the one hand by the rebels' disastrous lack of Indian goods and an ever-dwindling trade and on the other by the continual threats from Niagara and Carleton Island, were in a dire predicament. They finally came to a hard decision—a decision which involved a parting of the ways among themselves. On July 2, 1780, some 294 once-rebel Indians came straggling in to Fort Niagara. There were 78 Tuscaroras, 184 Onondagas who had fled to Oneida after their own villages had been destroyed, and 2 Oneida families, relatives of the imprisoned Peter and Skenando. They were a pathetic lot, some shame-faced, some ready to brazen it out, all very much down on their luck.

The refugees were not allowed to eat their fill and loll about the fort. They were told they had to show repentance for the error of their ways by immediately going to war. Such was Guy Johnson's pronouncement. Joseph was present at the council with the newcomers, as were other Loyalist Indians who happened to be at the fort. All the

Loyalists agreed with their superintendent. The refugees must fight their erstwhile friends.[29]

Joseph had long been at odds with the Oneidas. Though some of them were his former in-laws and the blood relatives of his children, he could not tolerate their wrong-headedness. What a great number of tally sticks it would take to count up their sins! They had spied, they had cut off communication between the king's friends in the colonies and Niagara, and they had treacherously struck their own people. They deserved to be destroyed. Indeed, Joseph's recent journey down the lake seems to have concerned a plan of his to attack the Oneidas. Now, if ever, was the time to carry out the plan. It could be combined very readily with an expedition to the Mohawk River. Joseph set out on this twofold objective about July 11. With him were 314 warriors, including 59 of the ex-rebels.[30]

This time Joseph and his party cut across the devastated Six Nations country. They arrived at the Oneida village of Canowaraghere late that month. Finding the place abandoned, they burned everything—houses, Kirkland's church, and the little fort which the rebels had built for their Indian adherents.[31]

The Oneidas, knowing Joseph was coming, had fled with their cattle and effects to the protection of Fort Stanwix. Joseph's party set out after them and reached their camp there on July 26. Many of the Oneidas managed to escape into the fort.[32] The rest were alternately cajoled and threatened until they promised to go to Niagara. Some kept this promise, and by August 24 Guy Johnson was able to report that in all more than five hundred Indians had recanted their former allegiance and joined the royal standard.[33] Like most of Guy Johnson's figures, these numbers seem somewhat inflated.

Next day Joseph and his men attempted to parade before the fort but were driven back by artillery. They then killed whatever horses and cattle they could find outside, and fired at the post for several hours.[34] Fort Stanwix was a thorn in the side of the Six Nations, and Joseph sent an urgent message to General Haldimand that now was the best opportunity to attack it.[35] He did not dare linger much longer for he knew that the militia would soon be coming after him. He set off down the country by a devious route.[36]

On August 2, while most of the rebel militia was heading for Fort Stanwix, Joseph and his men showed up in the lower, and richest, section of Tryon County. They divided into two parties, one to surprise the white settlement at Canajoharie[37] and the other to attack nearby Fort Plank. But some of the Indians, overeager to get prisoners, scattered too soon and alarmed the settlement, and most of the inhabitants were able to escape to the fort. The eight-sided, three-story fort, which was defended by two guns, proved too difficult to handle. The attackers had to content themselves with burning all the houses thereabouts—about one hundred in number—two smaller picketed forts, two mills, and the church—not being an Anglican church, Joseph may by this time have been able to reason, it was not really a church—and destroying grain and cattle. According to Guy Johnson's report sometime later, they killed twenty-nine persons and took forty prisoners, releasing forty women and children; but the rebel Colonel Wemple, who was on the spot, saw dead bodies, including those of children, lying all about. Both reports could have been true; Joseph might have released some women and children, but small Indian parties were all over the settlement, entirely on their own, and could have killed whom they pleased. At any rate, a tract along the river some six miles long and four miles wide had been devastated.[38] This would be very bad news for Washington's hungry army, not to mention the starving and almost mutinous garrison at Fort Stanwix.

After this stroke Joseph and his party went down to Butternuts, a march of about three days. There they divided into seven small parties, some to attack Schoharie, and others to hit Cherry Valley, German Flats, and similar settlements not too far away. Joseph himself went over to Schoharie where on August 9, at a place called Vroman's Land, he destroyed twenty houses (again according to Guy Johnson) and captured or killed twelve men, while releasing seven women and children. All Joseph's other parties appear to have worked considerable havoc, too. The whole county was now in terrible consternation, with people fleeing this way and that.[39]

Before Joseph left the upper Delaware he wrote the rebel authorities another letter. Two of his white Volunteers, Henry Hough and Daniel Cole, had somehow fallen into the hands of the enemy, and he feared for their lives. He sent off the following threat by a woman of the neighborhood: "Sir I understood that my friend Hendrick Huff & Cool is Taken Prisoners near at Esopus, I wou[ld] be glad if you now, be so kind is to let those people know that took them, not to use my friends too hard, for if they will use hard or hurt them—I will certainly pay for it, for we have Several Rebels in our hands makes me mention this for it would be disagreable to me, to hurt any Prisoner Therefore I hope they will not force me."[40] The threat evidently worked for Hough was released or escaped the next spring, and both men were still with Joseph when the war ended.

By the time Joseph got back to Niagara, General Haldimand had heard about his successful attack on the Oneidas. Haldimand was very pleased at the news, for the rebel Indians had been a great source of annoyance to him. He immediately sent off a letter to Guy Johnson with a message for Joseph that "I Shall not forget his attachment and Zealous Services to the King."[41] Haldimand had hoped that all the Oneidas would admit their errors and return to their old allegiance. This was not to be. The rebel Oneidas, reported by spies as about three hundred strong, went down the country and took up their residence at the old Mohawk villages of Canajoharie and Fort Hunter. Most of these soon settled down in huts on the outskirts of Schenectady where they felt safer, and some went eventually to Palmerstown to guard the Saratoga area and help cut off scouting parties from Canada. A few remained at Fort Stanwix. If the British had their "faithful Mohawks," the Americans had their equally faithful Oneidas. For their faithfulness both got somewhat similar rewards.

Joseph enjoyed about three weeks of rest. Although, as usual, he was rumored to be all over the map (and by British spies as well as by the frightened Americans!), he actually remained at Niagara till September 24. On that day, at General Haldimand's particular request,[42] he again set out for war. On very short notice he embarked on a Lake Ontario vessel with volunteers from two companies of regulars and some two hundred hastily gathered Indian warriors, the latter, according to Guy Johnson, "in an unexampled State of Sobriety," and set sail for Oswego. At the same time John Butler and such of his Rangers who were not ill with dysentery or ague set sail in another vessel. After a very stormy passage both boats arrived at their destination somewhat the worse for wear, Butler's on September 29 and Joseph's on October 1. Sir John Johnson and a force from Canada were waiting.[43]

Sir John's May raid on the Mohawk had been so successful that General Haldimand had suddenly decided to try another. This time Haldimand himself initiated the project. The main object was to destroy as much of the enemy's grain crop as possible before it could be sent to Washington or before the rebel farmers themselves could get much good out of it. If a diversion could be raised in favor of Sir Henry Clinton's operations (whatever they were), or if Sir John could engage additional recruits, then so much the better. It was even thought that the proud Oneidas might be humbled, but this was before Haldimand had received the news of what Joseph Brant had done to them.

Haldimand had sent secret instructions to Sir John on August 24. Oddly enough, that was the very day that persistent rumors started on the New York frontier that Sir John and Brant and Butler were coming again, that this time both banks of the Mohawk and even Schoharie were to be completely devastated. The rebels set to work at once to prepare a defense, but not knowing exactly when or exactly where these events were to take place, and their resources being so low, their preparations had to be spread very thin. The frontier people ran to their little forts and blockhouses at every alarm and, almost exhausted by this time, huddled together and awaited the worst. There were many alarms, and the worst was longer in coming than they expected.

Sir John had brought with him to Oswego most of his first battalion (the fledgling second battalion having neither clothes nor arms) and a few regular troops from Canada. These with the arrivals from Niagara made a force of some 657, "the Flowr of our little Army," according to Haldimand. Various parties of whites and Indians who were already out on the frontier would join on the march. Sir John expected to have a command of about eight hundred men when he reached the scene of action.[44] It is doubtful, however, that he ever attained that goal.

The expedition set out by the old trade route up the Oswego River, some troops by land and some by water; but instead of turning east for Fort Stanwix and the Mohawk, they went farther south to Onondaga Lake and then to the eastward, deep into Oneida country. From deserted Oneida there was a good trail to Schoharie, and most of the Loyalists and certainly all the Indians were thoroughly familiar with it. It was easy to bypass the rebel fort since there were so few Oneidas left in the vicinity to spy and tell tales; and in any event the garrison of Fort Stanwix was not strong enough to come out and risk a fight.

It must have been somewhere along here that one of Guy Johnson's "repentant" Oneidas slipped out of Sir John's camp with a mortar shell under his blanket (for Sir John had with him two pieces of artillery), and headed for Fort Stanwix and its commandant, Major Hughes. It was a dangerous journey and a strange burden, but the Oneida knew that Indians were often accused of spreading the false stories of bad birds and causing false alarms; and so, as he must have said to himself as he set out: here, brother Hughes, here is the evidence. If Sir John and Haldimand had ever had a secret plan between them—and they had certainly tried to conceal their object—it was a secret no longer.

After the great raid was over, Sir John wrote a long report to the commander in chief.[45] On October 17, before daybreak, he said, he and his men reached the upper fort at Schoharie (Fultonham). They had meant to slip by quietly, but were discovered by the watchful rebels who fired alarm guns. They then set fire to everything before them for three miles, and in so doing reached the middle fort (Middleburgh). The Indians attacked the fort till Sir John was able to bring up his artillery. Unfortunately, nobody knew how to fire a cannon so that it would hit its target at the proper angle. Fearing he was only losing time and knowing the country was alarmed, Sir John sent a Ranger with a flag to summon the fort to surrender. The only attention the rebels paid to the messenger was to shoot at him. Sir John and his force then moved on, in his own words "burning killing, and destroying every thing within fifty yards of their Forts to the end of the Settlement beyond the third Fort [present Old Stone Fort Museum, Schoharie]," and then camped for the night.

Next day, says Sir John, he started out on the west side of Schoharie Creek, but supposing that the militiamen were hot on his heels (for, of course, the whole district of Schoharie was alarmed, and he knew the Oneida had gone off to warn the rebels at Fort Stanwix), he hastily buried his heavier cannon and all its shells in a swamp, but carried the lighter one on with much difficulty, the road being almost impassable. He sent Joseph Brant and a Ranger captain with about 150 Rangers and Indians to destroy the settlement on the Fort Hunter side of Schoharie Creek. They did this easily since all the inhabitants had fled into the fort. Joseph and the detachment then recrossed the creek and joined the main force. By this time the whole expedition had reached the Mohawk River; "from thence," again in Sir John's own words, "we Marched on laying Waste every thing before us on both sides of the River up to the Nose."[46] At midnight he called it a day, and made camp.

Next morning, October 19, Colonel John Brown, the commanding officer at Stone Arabia, who seems to have expected a large force of militia under General Robert Van Rensselaer to back him up, marched out of little Fort Paris to do battle. Sir John's forces, however, were many times more numerous than Brown's, and the colonel himself and many of his men were slain when the militia failed to appear. Captain Brant was one of those, declared Sir John, who "exerted themselves upon the Occasion in a Manner that did them honour and contributed greatly to our Success." In this action Joseph got another flesh wound in the sole of his foot.

From papers found on Colonel Brown, Sir John learned that General Van Rensselaer and the militia had reached Fort Hunter shortly after he left, and must be very near. He burned Stone Arabia as quickly as possible, while the rebels fired at him from their fort and watched the destruction. Then the raiders set out again up the river, shunning fortified places but burning all the way up to George Klock's, near the Canajoharie ford. Here they took to the woods to avoid some forts that commanded the road.

It was now nearly sunset, and in trying to get back to the highway Sir John and his men found themselves opposed by the militia who had finally come up and had posted themselves behind fences, houses, and trees. After a while the rebels moved back and formed in considerable force under the protection of their fort at Klock's. Sir John's Indians, finding the enemy so strong,[47] fled on their horses in panic across the river. Seeing this, the rebels were encouraged, and advanced under cover of trees and fences, firing heavily. Part of Sir John's forces gave way, and the rebels raised a cheer. Sir John then fired his cannon and that, whether it was aimed properly or not, silenced them. It was now dark, and all was confusion among both pursued and pursuers. In this confusion some of Sir John's troops got separated from the main body. Sir John does not say so, but he was pretty close to a rout for he lost his cannon and much of his baggage.[48]

The invaders headed back to Oneida by various routes, a fact which probably saved them much grief, for the next morning the rebels wasted a good deal of time trying to decide which trail to follow.[49] At Oneida, on October 23, the main body defeated and captured a small scout from Fort Stanwix who had been sent out to destroy their boats at Onondaga Lake. To their great relief they reached the boats the next day, found them intact, and so got safely back to Oswego on October 26.[50]

On November 2 Sir John sent in an additional report. "The Crops at Scoharie, the Mohawk River &c," he exulted, "were never known to be so great since the first Settlement of that Country as they were this year, and as they had sent very little to Market, and we destroyed every grain before us for Near fifty Miles, their loss at the most moderate computation, cannot Amount to less than Six hundred Thousand Bushells of different kinds."[51]

The rebels agreed that great damage had been done, with many persons, both soldiers and civilians, killed or captured. Governor Clinton estimated the property loss as at least two hundred dwellings and 150,000 bushels of wheat. So great was the devastation that he feared to let the whole story get into the newspapers. Colonel William Malcolm of the Continental army who was on the Mohawk immediately afterward noted that "Everything except the soil is destroyed from Fort Hunter to Stone Arabia."[52] As for Schoharie, it was all burned. Hardly more was left than the bleached driftwood in the creek which gave the place its strange Indian name.

Joseph Brant and his warriors could feel, as they set sail again for

Niagara, that they had exacted a fit revenge. They had returned Sullivan's visit. To be sure, Schenectady was still standing though they had meant to destroy it, but they looked forward to another chance. The Indians had been in high spirits all summer. They had been told for months that the rebels were suffering heavy defeats far to the southward. In faraway Carolina and Georgia the king had taken up his great war ax and was busy knocking his rebellious children on their heads. Soon, no doubt, they would return to their proper obedience. The tree of peace would flourish again. Though Joseph did not express himself on the subject, he must have had the same thoughts, for he seems to have been in high spirits, too. Similarly, many white Loyalists had raised their hopes of an early victory. But General Haldimand, waiting for ships to arrive that never arrived and contemplating the actions and inaction of General Clinton and reflecting upon Sir John's recent narrow escape, was not so sure.

The coming winter promised to be not quite so hard for the Indians as the previous winter had been. For one thing, the weather had turned milder. For another, the Indians were somewhat dispersed. Not everybody was camping around the fort. Some had rebuilt their homes and had been able to harvest at least a small crop of corn. But the Indians still came and went from time to time. Guy Johnson had reported on July 26 that he had been able to persuade twelve hundred Indians to go off and establish new homes at Cattaraugus, Chautauqua, and the Genesee. But by October 30 he admitted that more than one-third of the Six Nations was still at Niagara and living principally on rations obtained at the fort. On December 4 he claimed the numbers of the Indians were daily decreasing. However, at the same time he acknowledged that those at the fort were getting reduced allowances, and by February 19, 1781, he had to tell Haldimand that the wants of the Indians "are so alarming that I am really at a loss what to do to relieve them."[53] Still, conditions were not so bad as before.

Haldimand was not displeased with Guy's management of the department although, like Germain, he did not think highly of his abilities. But he had received favorable reports of Guy's diligence from both Bolton and Butler, and he knew that Guy had done his part to inspire the Indians to break up the rebel frontier. But Guy's attention to economy was not all that Haldimand desired. Guy had turned in an incredible requisition for Indian goods for the coming year. The long list included, among many other articles, 12,500 blankets, 8,000 brass kettles, over 16,000 silver ornaments, 25,500 yards of cloth, 10,000 needles, 75 dozen razors, 1,000 hats (including 200 white beaver hats for women), and 20 gross of jew's-harps! In addition Guy was issuing rum to the Indians at the rate of 350 gallons a month, pork at the rate of 35,180 pounds a month, and butter at the rate of 1,710 pounds a month. As these things were not always to be found in the government store, Guy often bought them from local merchants at very high prices. In May 1780, Haldimand had ordered that such purchases be as few as possible. In January 1781, he instructed Guy to buy nothing from local traders except what was indispensably necessary. Economy in the Indian department *must* be achieved. The traders' inflated prices could not be endured.

Once back at Niagara Joseph found a familiar face missing. Colonel Bolton had sailed away on October 31, on the new lake snow, the *Ontario*. He was glad to relieve his pain-racked body of the effects of another Niagara winter, glad to be rid of the accounts, and, above all, glad to be rid of the Indians whom he had always mistrusted. Bolton had favored Joseph even though he was an Indian, but he had also warned Haldimand that even in peacetime the garrison of Niagara should never be weakened while 2,600 unpredictable allies camped so near. On the night after Bolton sailed a terrible storm had roared across the lake. Next day men returning from Sir John's raid found pieces of lifeboats, tables, hen coops, barrels, and all sorts of debris cast up on shore, but no sign of a human being anywhere. So it was that Colonel Bolton, thirty-two soldiers, forty seamen, and Captain Andrews, head of the naval department on the lake, were never seen again—all lost at sea on Lake Ontario. It was a stunning blow. Everybody, white and Indian, felt the loss of so many brave men, the loss of the fine, new vessel, and the loss of precious supplies that might have been brought back from Carleton Island and which it was now too late to transport.

In Bolton's place Joseph found a new commandant, Brigadier General H. Watson Powell, who, he heard, had given the Indians a gracious reception, but who was a stranger to him. Otherwise affairs at the fort were about the same, with Catharine and the family still at the landing, Sayengaraghta at Buffalo Creek and never a hint of discord now, and John Butler (now a lieutenant colonel since he had been able at last to sign up eight companies of recruits) trying to cope with the crowded living conditions of his corps.

Elsewhere, that winter, there was no great change, either. Molly, Joseph heard, was still at Carleton Island where she had her own snug little house and a garden. A young Quaker lady, wife of a British officer, met up with her one day and wrote the following gossipy description: "She has a sensible countenance, and much whiter than the generality of Indians, but her Father was white. She understands

English, but speaks only the Mohawk. Which has something extremely soft and musical in it when spoken by a woman. This Squaw is an expense of three or four thousand a year to the British Government, as I am informed. She has a fine house building at Carleton Island, where several of her daughters live with her, and a great number of dependents. She was now in a travelling dress, a Calico Bedgown, fastened with Silver Brooches and a worsted mantel."[54]

At Haldimand's request Joseph's friend Daniel Claus had been working on a new edition of the Mohawk Prayer Book. He also continued to look after the small affairs of the lower Mohawks, sending them out occasionally on some little scout. As for Sir John Johnson, he was back home in Montreal basking in whatever glory could be had from his late military venture. On the glory of the venture Haldimand blew hot and cold. He described it to Germain as "this arduous Enterprise," and said that he was well pleased with Sir John; but later to Sir Henry Clinton he referred to it slightingly as "this Little Affair." Indeed, there was not very much glory to go around for either Sir John or the rebels. All winter there was much recrimination on both sides of the border. Both the attackers and the defenders were dissatisfied with their own performance. A Ranger officer was court-martialed, and the rebels even court-martialed their general of militia.

On the frontiers of New York affairs had come to their lowest ebb. The supervisors of Tryon County reported, on December 20, 1780, the results of a census which they had taken to determine the extent of the war's damage. Uncultivated farms, they declared, numbered at least twelve hundred, and 354 families had abandoned their farms entirely and had left the county. This, they added, was only a partial count. In some places, such as Cherry Valley, Springfield, and Harpersfield, there was nobody left to make an enumeration. Such were the economic casualties out of a prewar population that has been estimated at perhaps ten thousand. So deserted were the Mohawk valley and once-thriving neighborhoods to the north and south, that Schenectady, which had not been a frontier since the early days of the century, came near again to marking the outermost limit of civilization.

This far-reaching desolation was not all Sir John's doing, or even Brant's. Hundreds of Indian warriors and their white leaders could take part of the credit. Though small war parties had been coming and going since early 1778, no careful record of their numbers was kept until Guy Johnson's arrival at Niagara. In 1780, however, Guy's records begin to show the real extent of Indian involvement in the war. On July 24 he reported that 836 warriors had gone out against the frontiers, some of these having been out two or three times since February. On October 1 the warriors on the frontiers numbered 892. On November 20 Guy reported that during the past campaign his Indians had killed or captured 14 rebel officers and 316 men (there was no mention of women and children or other noncombatants), and had destroyed 714 houses and granaries full of grain, 6 small forts, several mills, and 680 horses and cattle—all this destruction exclusive of what had been accomplished by Indians with Sir John.

By frontiers, Guy meant the back settlements of New York, Pennsylvania, and Virginia, but it was New York that suffered most from Guy's particular charges, the Six Nations. Virginia and Pennsylvania got much of their attention from Detroit and the western Indians. The Six Nations made the war against New York peculiarly their own. Without them, that frontier, after Burgoyne's surrender, would have been relatively quiet. White armies were engaged elsewhere, and the Canadian Indians were not eager to fight an ally of France.

After 1777 the Six Nations Indians constituted the main British offense in the New York area. It was not an offense, however, that many British on the spot could be proud of. The Indians made war in their historic way (indeed, they could not change), through surprise, destruction, annihilation, and sometimes the taking of prisoners, who were just as likely to be noncombatants as not. The few white men with them had to accommodate themselves to this pattern. The whites may not have liked what they were doing, but they had no choice. They followed orders. The orders of Lord George Germain to General Haldimand were very explicit on the subject of breaking up the frontiers, and Haldimand's orders to Niagara, Detroit, Carleton Island, St. Johns, Oswegatchie, and other posts were equally explicit. "Conformable to Your Lordship's Wishes," Haldimand assured Germain toward the end of the war, as the latter once more repeated the familiar instructions, "I have always Sent Detachments upon the Frontiers of the Rebel Provinces to alarm the Country and destroy Supplies—"[55]

So it was, by December 1780, that only one district in all of Tryon County had any grain to spare, and most had not enough to live on till the next harvest. The county could furnish no bread for the hungry Oneidas at Schenectady or even for the garrison at Fort Stanwix, barefoot now and half-naked. Only a few men of the garrison had sufficient clothing to be able to go to Oneida to see if Joseph Brant had left any corn standing. (He had, was the glorious discovery; and what a shout of joy they must have raised on seeing those withered stalks!)

Grain and farm produce had become even costlier than imported articles. As to firewood, getting it sawed cost twenty-six dollars a cord, and who had such a large sum of money? Widows and orphans chopped and sawed their own wood or did without. They did their own farm work, too, just as everybody who could not leave; and all did it "by halfs only," as the supervisors pointed out forlornly, "and under continual fear of the tomahawk and scalping knife."[56]

The rebels believed with passionate intensity that the British were buying scalps. They could believe this all the more readily in that many persons still living knew Indians had been paid for scalps (ten pounds for those of adults and five for children's) in warfare against the French. When Dr. Moses Younglove, returning after his capture at Oriskany, swore in an affidavit that St. Leger had offered twenty dollars apiece for rebel scalps, few of his neighbors found the story hard to credit. Younglove, obviously a victim of some malicious teasing while a prisoner, implicitly believed his own allegation.

The story was, of course, not true. No British officer and gentleman sent the Indians out for scalps in the enlightened era of the American Revolution. What the officers did was to send the Indians out on the warpath. Bringing back scalps was the warriors' own idea—an idea which was very distressing to the white military, especially when the scalps belonged to women and children. British officers actually begged the savages to make war in a civilized way. Said the notorious Governor Hamilton of Detroit (he, whom the American frontiersmen dubbed the "hair buyer") to a party of Indians: "I cannot but praise the behaviour of the Indian nations who have taken hold of their Father's axe and who have acted as men. I hope you'll act the same part and not redden your axe with with [sic] the blood of Women and Children or innocent men. I know that men, kill men and not children. I speak to you who are men."[57] Failing in a call for humanity, Colonel De Peyster tried a more practical appeal. "I am pleased when I see what you call *live meat*," he told the warriors, "because I can speak to it, and get information. *Scalps* serve to show you have seen the enemy, but they are of no use to me, I cannot speak with them."[58] But General Haldimand always emphasized humaneness. When consenting to the sending out of Indian war parties, he instructed one of his officers that they be sent for intelligence or prisoners, "but you must insist upon their containing themselves within the bounds of humanity towards them, otherwise they must not be suffered to go."[59] Haldimand gave similar instructions again and again, and Guy Johnson, John Butler, Captain Fraser, Colonel Bolton, Daniel Claus, and every other officer at any of the posts who had anything to do with sending out Indian war parties, repeated the same urgings.

But when the Indian warriors returned from their expeditions, they got their pay and new clothing and rum and whatever else they fancied in the store. On most occasions the Indians returned bearing scalps. Being simple untutored men, they were incapable of delicate distinctions. They appear to have thought they were being paid for the scalps, and they continued to bring them in throughout the war. The records are very, very scanty. British officers did not talk about scalps any more than they had to, and few Indians could write, and fewer still wrote anything that was preserved. But the Seneca Blacksnake declared (long after the event) that the British told the Indians they would pay for American scalps.[60] And Mary Jemison, who was almost an Indian, asserted (also long after the event) that the British "prom-ised a bounty on every scalp that should be brought in."[61] Joseph Brant, who might have said something, said nothing—that is, he said nothing except what the prisoner Freegift Patchin (a source somewhat suspect and also long after the event) reported. Patchin said that Brant warned him and the other Harpersfield prisoners not to fall by the wayside, "as their scalps were as good for him as their bodies."[62]

At any rate, the rebels believed what they believed. They remem-bered the fate of Jane McCrea. They remembered the massacres at Wyoming and Cherry Valley. They remembered all those incidents of horror which they thought had taken place and some of which had taken place: the mutilation of the dead and dying, the mutilation of dumb beasts, the plundering and pillaging, the stripping of corpses. They did not forget the striking down of prisoners whose only fault was that they were too sick or too old to march.

After Sir John Johnson's great raids of 1780 still more people had still more to remember. For days the smoke of burning houses filled the air. Governor Clinton, just after a final attempt to track down the enemy, noted that all the destruction he saw had been marked by "the greatest barbarity." Stories of atrocities flew about and daily grew more bloody. The murders of women and children were recounted in all their frightful details. Years after the war the people of what had once been Tryon County were still telling how Sir John and his raiders had descended upon them like "a parcel of Wolves"—that "the first notice of their approach, was them in sight; and of their retreat, their being out of reach."[63]

A hatred, white-hot, furious, all-pervading and all-consuming, filled American breasts. Every British officer became a merciless savage. Elevated to a special pantheon of hate were the two Butlers, father and son, and the two Johnsons, Guy and Sir John—and always Brant, the demon, the monster Brant. As for those people who had once thought they hated Indians, they now knew what it was to hate Indians.

The war, some day, somehow, would come to an end. But could there ever be a reconciliation between such foes?

If peace came, would there be peace?

15

On the Ohio

For Joseph Brant there was no pause in the labors of war. Before the end of the year he was already making plans for the campaign of 1781. Thoughts of the rebel Oneidas still rankled. In December he wrote Captain John Deseronto, the leader of Claus's band of lower Mohawks, about a new military project he had in mind. If John would join him early in the spring with a trustworthy party of warriors, they would take revenge against those faithless Indians. John agreed, and set March 20–25 as the time and Carleton Island as the meeting place. General Haldimand heard about the project and interested himself in it. He offered to aid with a party of Loyalists. The Oneidas at Palmerstown were to be the target. Claus commended John for his zeal and sent a long letter of advice to Joseph. About the middle of March Captain John set out for the rendezvous.[1]

Winter communication being what it was, Joseph could not have known what was going on, and he had not the patience (or perhaps Guy Johnson had not the patience) to wait to hear from John. On February 1 Joseph started another way. With about 150 Indians and 30 Rangers under Lieutenant Bradt, a relative of Butler's, he headed east, intending to cut off supplies moving toward Fort Stanwix. The snow was deep, and the party had to march on snowshoes. They arrived just a little too late, for 50 provision sleds and their escort had got safely into the fort the day before. Their disappointment was somewhat softened, however, when they came upon a detachment of woodcutters from the garrison. They killed one of the woodcutters and took 16 prisoners. On March 17 all returned to Niagara[2]—all, that is, except a certain Hewson, one of Joseph's Volunteers. The latter deserted to Fort Stanwix and revealed to the rebels all that he knew about the activities of General Haldimand's spy network. Apparently he knew much too much, for he caused the detection of Haldimand's most important spy. There was great consternation at headquarters.[3]

In the meantime Captain John reached Carleton Island, and waited, and waited, and waited. On April 12 he gave up. He wrote Claus that Joseph had not come to meet him, and he was going on alone.[4] It was just the sort of misadventure that the British military had come to expect of Indians. They may have been a little surprised that Joseph Brant was involved, but of course any Indian would be an Indian.

Back at Niagara Joseph's morale was sagging. His good spirits of the previous year had deserted him. Nothing was working out right, he thought. Going home was still a distant prospect. Though the rebels were almost destroyed, there was no news as yet that they had surrendered. Their behavior was unaccountable. Joseph felt a vague discontent with himself, too. He believed he would have more weight with his people if he were not known to receive pay from the Indian department. He told General Powell he wanted a change. He wished to resign his company. Powell asked him to wait and consider.[5] The long years of war, the hopes unfulfilled, were taking their toll of even such a devoted Loyalist as Joseph Brant.

For an Indian (as they said) Joseph had always been remarkably abstemious; indeed, Claus called him "the most sober quiet & good Natured Ind^n I ever was aquainted with."[6] True, Joseph sometimes bought liquor, but it seems to have been as much for his followers as for himself, some liquor being deemed a necessity for men going out on arduous service. When Joseph was the friend of "dissenting" missionaries, back home on the Mohawk, he had never shocked them with drunken revels as other Indians had done. But that was a long time ago, and he had different associates now and many frustrations. So it happened that on April 6, 1781, the usually temperate and good-natured Joseph got himself involved in a drunken brawl. He was thirty-eight years old, and it is the first instance of drunkenness that has been recorded against him. He had some kind of fight with somebody in the Indian department.

Gossip of the affair got abroad very quickly. In a week Molly heard about it at Carleton Island and wrote a hysterical letter to Claus, claiming that her only brother whom she dearly loved had been almost "murdered" by some of Guy Johnson's men. But what most concerned

her, she added, was how this was going to affect the king's influence
with the Indians! Had not Schuyler warned them that they would be
ill-used and despised by the king's people![7]

A great to-do ensued. Claus reported Molly's complaint to Haldimand at once. Haldimand immediately sent off orders to Niagara.
General Powell was to see that Joseph got justice. He was to do
whatever was necessary to accommodate the matter and take care that
Colonel Johnson "gives that support to Joseph which his services &
attachment to Government really merit."[8] Powell replied that as far as
he could see Johnson did support Joseph.[9] Guy himself later wrote
Claus that Molly's story was untrue. She had been listening to
troublemakers. Joseph, he explained, had got drunk one night and
attacked one of his fellow officers, but when he sobered up, he was
sorry for his misconduct and apologized. Guy added the opinion that
Joseph had been puffed up a little too much for his own good. But in
any case Joseph was no longer at Niagara.[10]

On April 8, two days after the brawl, Guy Johnson sent Joseph to
Detroit.[11] If Joseph was sent away because of drinking, he was not the
first to be removed from Niagara for that reason nor probably the last,
either. Furthermore, he had wanted a change, and this was a change.
Then, too, there was not much work left for him to do on the New
York frontier. Nearly everything had already been destroyed that
could be destroyed. Raiding parties had to go dangerously long distances now and take great risks in order to find any settlement worth
attacking. But the ostensible reason for Joseph's departure, which Guy
gave Haldimand and which was true enough as far as it went, was that
news had come from Detroit that the Virginian, George Rogers Clark,
was preparing another campaign in that area and Joseph was taking
messages and belts to spirit up the western Indians to defend their
country.[12] With Joseph went seventeen young warriors, probably the
greater part of the small Indian party who had stood by him since
Oriskany. Though he told Powell he hoped for some military action in
the west,[13] his white Volunteers seem to have been left behind.

Joseph and his entourage, like everyone on government business,
went to Detroit by boat.[14] Several British vessels plied Lake Erie.
From the landing above Niagara one traveled, on foot or on horseback, up the tortuous portage road to Fort Schlosser, above the falls,
then across the Niagara River to Fort Erie, and from there up the lake
by boat. By April 11 Joseph had reached Fort Erie, for on that day he
wrote a letter to Daniel Claus dated from the fort. He told Claus he
was always thinking of him. Then he said he was sorry to go to
Detroit, and spoke of his "disappoi[n]ted purpose"—meaning the

Oneida expedition which he had planned with Captain John. It troubled him that he had "lied" to John; and he blamed his predicament on Colonel Johnson, whose mind, he added, he could not comprehend. As usual, when writing to his good white friend and though writing in his own tongue, Joseph could not decide which of his two names to use, the Indian name or the Christian name, and so used both.[15] Thayendanegea he might be to the Indians, and Joseph Brant to the whites; but to Claus it seemed right to sign himself "Jos. Thayendanegea," or some variant of the latter, and that was what he always did.

Detroit was an old French post, founded in 1701. It had fallen into British possession after the last French war. Its residents were still mostly French, many of them indifferent to the issues of the present conflict and their loyalty often suspect. General Haldimand did not trust them and worried about their influence over the neighboring Indians with whom they got along so well. The British inhabitants, mainly officials, soldiers, and merchants, who came and went, never could establish that camaraderie with the natives which the French accomplished so easily. Indeed, the British suspected that the Indians would plot with the French against them any day, and they were not far wrong. The Indians liked the French. They only traded with the British.

A great horde of Indians looked to Detroit as their center of commerce. Spread all over the territory which now comprises Illinois, Indiana, Ohio, southern Michigan, and the southwestern part of Ontario, these Indians depended on the white man in ratio to their nearness to the post. It was even more difficult and expensive for the British to transport presents and trade goods to Detroit than to Niagara, but, fortunately, most of the western Indians did not live in such abject dependence as the Six Nations did. True, they also required presents and trade, but their requirements were not quite so nice or so all-encompassing as those of the tribesmen who depended on Niagara. The western Indians lived a little closer to the old ways. They had not yet forgotten everything they once knew. They were a little nearer to self-subsistence. Very old men among them could even remember a time when there had been scarcely any trade at all.

On April 26 Joseph attended his first council at Detroit. Besides himself and his followers there were present six Huron chiefs; nine Ottawa chiefs; two Potawatomies; eight Chippewas; and one Miami; Kayashota, a famed Mingo chief who had also come with encouraging messages from Guy Johnson and the Six Nations; some Shawnee messengers; and a large number of warriors of various nations. Most of these, except the Shawnees and the Mingo, probably lived close to Detroit. To make the council official there were also present four white interpreters, several officers of the garrison, and Major Arent Schuyler De Peyster, commandant of the post. The Shawnee deputies described George Rogers Clark's latest movements and threats and begged the British and the other Indians for aid. Joseph delivered the speech he had been sent to deliver, Kayashota made another speech of the same purport, and Major De Peyster urged all the Indians to unite against the common enemy. Major De Peyster could not promise a great deal of military aid since his garrison was kept busy working on the town's defenses, but he thought the Indians ought to be able to repel Clark with a small force of soldiers and local people. De Peyster and the chiefs after much talk finally decided that the Indians should rendezvous at Sandusky and then proceed against the enemy.[16] Next day, Joseph, obviously not putting too much trust in the warriors, suggested that De Peyster send to Niagara for as many of Butler's Rangers as could be spared.[17]

Sandusky, like most Indian place-names, referred to a vague, inde-terminate area, so-called because of some dominating feature of the landscape. In the case of Sandusky the dominant feature was the Sandusky River, a turgid stream which flowed into Lake Erie about a hundred miles from Detroit. At the mouth of this river and along its lower reaches the trader or soldier or occasional missionary encoun-tered nothing but swamps and soggy plains and tall grasses and crawfish holes. Not a hill was in sight. This part of the Sandusky was not a pretty place, but it was important for trade, being a link in the line of communication with the Ohio. The traveler could go up the river, thence across a low portage to the Scioto, and down the Scioto to Mingo and Shawnee country. Though from time to time a few huts could be seen almost anywhere along the Sandusky, the main settle-ments were Sandusky (sometimes called Lower), about twelve miles from the mouth of the stream (near present Fremont, Ohio), and Upper Sandusky, not far from the site of the present town of the same name. Boats from the lake could get as far as the lower settlement, and here was a fortified British trading post. Both these Indian settlements were inhabited by Wyandots (a branch of the Hurons) with a scatter-ing of Delawares.

It was to Upper Sandusky that Joseph Brant made his way after the council at Detroit on April 26, 1781. He did not linger long at Detroit, for by May 19 he had already been some time at Upper Sandusky. Here he had found Simon Girty, an interpreter in the Indian department, who, with 160 warriors, was waiting for reinforcements to go after Clark. Simon Girty was only a little older than Joseph, and his reputation among the rebels was as bad as, or worse than, Joseph's. Though a white man, Girty was about as much an Indian in his character as Joseph was, having spent some of his formative years as a prisoner among the Senecas. Girty's home was Fort Pitt, from which he had fled to Detroit in 1778. He had three brothers, two of whom, George and James, were Loyalists like himself, but the third, Thomas, had elected to remain at home. Girty's nose was pierced for a ring, and that made him even more menacing and frightening to the rebel frontiersmen who hated him with a passion. But if the rebels hated Simon Girty, he returned the favor.

Joseph had never met Simon Girty and his particular followers before, but he delivered the speech from Guy Johnson and the Six Nations to an audience which no doubt appeared friendly and appreciative. Joseph was certainly not unwelcome on the Sandusky. The rumors of Clark's intentions were growing stronger and stronger, and the local Indians wanted all the help they could get. But Joseph was not exactly welcomed with open arms, either. The Indians knew who he was. They had heard of him. He was almost too great a man for their taste, for the Indians did not like those who seemed to put themselves forward. They had been known to kill such a one. Moreover, this man came from the Six Nations, and he was a Mohawk. Some of these Indians detested the Mohawks, and they did not really like any of the Six Nations even though they were their allies. The two groups, the Six Nations and the western Indians, had been sending messages back and forth during the war, each from time to time asking aid of the other or trying to spirit up the other, as though they were all the greatest friends in the world. But the Hurons and Delawares and the other Indians of the west had long memories of old grievances which went back many years. Right now, however, they were willing to let bygones be bygones. If Joseph, the Mohawk, did not understand this, he would shortly find it out. A mixed welcome was to be his unvarying experience in the west, whenever and wherever he went and whatever his errand. There was something about Joseph Brant as an individual and his people en masse which raised the hackles of the western brethren.

The waiting Indians being scarce of provisions, Joseph wrote to Sandusky to get eight pieces of pork and five gallons of rum for himself. He reported the latest rumors and asked for reinforcements and horses and ammunition. It would not be long, he predicted, till the party met the enemy.[18] Isidore Chesne, interpreter for the Ottawas, and Matthew Elliott, captain in the Indian department, who were collecting the warriors at Sandusky, relayed this news to Major De Peyster the next day. The latter, who had only a thousand men at his disposal, most of whom were Indians and not really at his disposal, and whose powder magazine had just caved in (though he still had in his storehouse fifty-one dozen scalping knives), could do little more than to urge his tawny children to strike the iron while it was hot.

The next two months were spent by Joseph and other officers of the Indian department in collecting warriors from all over the west, and then in trying futilely to hold them together once collected. Some of the young warriors insisted on leaving for the hunt, some *would* go out horse-stealing, others had already lost the new clothing and ammunition sent them from Detroit, and nobody had food. Joseph and George Girty, Simon's brother, moved farther up the Sandusky and then down the Scioto to the Ohio. Coming along behind at various intervals and from various directions (for the leaders had to range far to find the warriors) were Simon Girty and Chesne, some French volunteers, and Captain Thompson with a company of Butler's Rangers who had been long stationed in the west—all headed by Alexander McKee, Guy Johnson's deputy at Detroit. By mid-August Joseph and George Girty had got far in the lead, and were proceeding on down the Ohio. With them were ninety Indians and a few whites.

The rumors were right. George Rogers Clark really did mean to invade the Indian country, but he had been having a great deal of trouble getting his new expedition started. Recruits could not be come by; many men were required in eastern Virginia where Britain's Lord Cornwallis was operating, and the frontier militia were afraid to leave their families alone to bear the brunt of expected Indian attacks. Clark set out down the Ohio from Wheeling with only a few hundred troops, and even they were deserting fast. He was angry and upset. Colonel Archibald Lochry, who had finally managed to collect for Clark some one hundred frontiersmen in western Pennsylvania, set out after him; but he never quite caught up before Clark, trying to thwart desertions by getting his men as far from home as possible, had to move on. Though young Clark had accomplished miracles in the west, and the British rightfully feared him more than anybody else on the frontier, the year 1781 was not to be his year.

On the night of August 18–19 Clark and his main army passed Joseph Brant and the waiting Indians at the mouth of the Great Miami (present Ohio-Indiana border). Joseph could not tell how many soldiers were with Clark, but he knew there were too many for his small force to cope with, and he kept quiet. Three days after Clark had passed, Joseph had the luck to capture an American officer, Major

Charles Cracraft, and six men, who had been left to bring up the rear with stores for Lochry. From them he learned Lochry was coming in a few days. He hastily wrote a letter to McKee who was still on the Scioto trying to assemble the Shawnees, urging him to move forward immediately. While the enemy are scattered, he said, we can easily handle them. But he meant to attack Lochry, he declared, reinforcements or no reinforcements.[19] It is obvious that Joseph considered himself the leader of his party.

On August 24 Colonel Lochry's flotilla hove into sight. Joseph and the Indians and the few whites lay in ambush at the mouth of a creek about eleven miles below the Great Miami. On their right loomed a hill, and a tall canebrake grew on the other side of the river. The numbers of both parties were almost evenly matched. Joseph had never had a better chance to prove his generalship, and he proved it brilliantly. At least the credit for what happened has always been his. Not a man of Lochry's force escaped. Thirty-seven were killed, including Lochry himself and some other officers. The rest were made prisoners. None of Joseph's party was hurt.[20]

By August 29 McKee and his lagging Indians and the two companies of Rangers and French volunteers had finally caught up. There was now on the Ohio in pursuit of Clark a joint British force which some later estimated at about seven hundred men. Though this estimate was probably too large, the Loyalists and Indians do appear to have constituted, in numbers at least, a respectable army. Everyone supposed that Clark would get a reinforcement of Kentucky militia and still try to carry out his plans to invade the Indian country. The pursuers moved on down the Ohio. By September 5 they had reached the mouth of the Kentucky River and were debating whether they should attack Clark, who was at the falls of the Ohio (Louisville). On September 9 the Indians sent off a scout who soon brought in two prisoners. The prisoners reported that Clark had held a council with some Kentucky officials and had decided to make no further attempt against the Indians for the rest of the season. Upon hearing this news most of the warriors decamped. Their clothing was in tatters and they had nothing but green corn to eat. Some present good had been accomplished, they knew; their country was safe for a while longer. This was enough for them, and they began to melt away. With the few men who were left to him, McKee went off to strike a small blow in Kentucky. Joseph and a party of Mingoes dropped a little farther down the Ohio to see if any of their friends would follow. Nobody did.[21]

Joseph had sent off a meticulous account to Detroit, listing all his prisoners, carefully giving their names and rank.[22] The defeat of even part of Clark's army had been a coup of no small importance. Unlike the raids on the Mohawk, this was a military success which nobody could deny. But Joseph was frustrated and discontented. So much more ought to have been accomplished and could have been if all the warriors had been present when Clark's main force passed by. At one of the camps along the Ohio Joseph began to drink heavily. In his cups he boasted of the great victory which he had won and of the numbers of the enemy that he had captured single-handedly. The rest of the story is merely hearsay, and not very good hearsay at that. "You lie!" exclaimed Simon Girty who was probably drunk himself. Perhaps Simon was jealous. Perhaps he thought his brother George deserved some of the credit. A fracas ensued, and Joseph struck Simon across the head with his sword, almost laying him out. Friends had to carry Simon back to the Sandusky where he spent months recovering from the wound, and ever afterward he bore a deep scar on his forehead which he claimed he got in battle and which added to his evil reputation among the rebels. No recognition of this brawl ever got into the official British reports, but there seems to have been plenty of gossip.[23]

Whatever Simon Girty thought, the people at Detroit ascribed the victory over Lochry to Joseph Brant, and he was acclaimed accordingly. De Peyster wrote of Joseph's success to Niagara and Quebec.[24] A friend wrote to Claus,[25] and there were probably other private letters that recounted the affair. Joseph got all the credit for putting an end to whatever intentions George Rogers Clark had had against the Indians and Detroit. Haldimand, when he heard the good news, hoped that "Joseph's persevering and spirited Conduct" would inspire the western Indians to emulate his example. (Had he but known, Brant, the Mohawk, was not the person the western Indians wished to emulate— if, indeed, such independent souls wished to emulate anybody!) Haldimand felt it keenly that Joseph had not had enough force to do more and that the warriors with McKee had been so slow in assembling.[26] Clark had been allowed to keep by default all his previous gains in Illinois and Kentucky. It was a galling thought to the proud old soldier.

Months passed before they found out at Pittsburgh what had happened to Colonel Lochry. On December 3 the commander at Fort Pitt wrote authorities in Philadelphia about the many rumors of a disastrous defeat that were going around. Before he closed his letter he reported that some people in the vicinity were holding meetings "for the purpose of concerting plans to emigrate into the Indian Country— there to establish a Government for themselves."[27] He was not going to try to stop them, he added with weary resignation. It was none of his business. Such news boded no good for the Indians thereabouts, many of whom had been trying to defend their country against the settlers ever since the line of Fort Stanwix had been breached. Thanks to their efforts, the Pennsylvania and Virginia frontiers were a shambles. But even in the midst of war the irresistible force moved onward. If there was any way to stop a determined white settler, it had not yet been found. The fellow thrived on danger. He thumbed his nose at authority. Out there in the wilderness was land, and he meant to have it, Indians or no Indians.

By early October Joseph was back at Detroit. He had come in half-starved as usual, and with an infected leg wound. Gossip said Simon Girty gave him the wound,[28] but General Powell was told that Joseph had accidentally cut himself with his own sword.[29] Such an accident could have happened. Joseph was certainly no expert in handling the sword, and his drinking would have made him even less an expert. A mere scratch could turn very serious when it happened far out in the field and in hot weather. There was nothing to do for open wounds but bathe them in rum. It was feared at first that Joseph would lose his leg.[30] "Poor Brant is very ill yet," reported De Peyster on November 11. The young warriors who had come from Niagara with him were to be sent back home with messages to the Six Nations, but Joseph was too lame to travel. He would have to remain in Detroit for the winter.[31]

Meanwhile, back in the eastern theater of war, nobody was aware that Joseph Brant had transferred his operations elsewhere. All summer long the rebels thought that they were defending themselves against his attacks. In July the son of a clergyman at Schoharie (one of those who seem to have swung back and forth, like a pendulum, from one side to the other) confessed to rebel authorities that he had joined Brant on a recent raid on Currytown. The turncoat swore to many convincing details: that all Brant's men were painted and equipped like Indians, that they were promised ten dollars for every scalp they took, that he counted 190 Indians and about half as many Tories, that after the looting and burning he saw two white children and one black child who had been killed![32] In August one of General Haldimand's own spies reported that Brant and Butler had attacked a fort on the Mohawk and captured Colonel Willett, the commanding officer, and all his garrison.[33] About the same time Haldimand got hold of a rebel newspaper which boasted of Colonel Willett's victory over Brant![34] And in early October, Sir Henry Clinton, wishing to favor Lord

Cornwallis' operations in the south, wrote Joseph a note asking him to make a move against Minisink and the east branch of the Susquehanna as soon as possible.[35]

Though the clergyman's son got a measure of belief from the rebels (in spite of his being a scoundrel), General Haldimand could only reflect upon the undependability of spies and newspapers. The commander in chief knew very well that Joseph had gone to Detroit and, in fact, did not much approve of the trip. Earlier in the season Haldimand had urged that Joseph be recalled, for he thought he could be employed more usefully in his own country.[36] Joseph's services would be particularly needed if the Americans should try to take Oswego, a thing Haldimand always dreaded. Oneida scouting parties were also interfering with the movements of Loyalists and spies on the upper Hudson, and Haldimand thought of Joseph as the proper person to disperse them. He even feared that Joseph was detained in the west against his inclination; "he has really great Merit," he told General Powell, "and altho a bountiful acknowledgement of it May, in Some Measure; have Spoiled him, he Must be encouraged—were any thing to be done from Niagara, his Service Would be indispensably Necessary."[37] Joseph was indeed recalled by Guy Johnson on Haldimand's instructions,[38] but after the news of Lochry's defeat and his own grave illness, no more was said of his returning. By this time the year's campaign was nearly over, anyway. In late November Catharine left the home at the landing and sailed for Detroit to take care of her sick husband.[39]

Friendly Major De Peyster carried Joseph in his accounts, and he collected his salary regularly.[40] But Joseph, like his sister Molly, could spend money with abandon. He drew on Guy Johnson for his living expenses and for some incidentals, too, and seems to have ended the winter in debt.[41] Unfortunately, in a place so far away as Detroit all the good things of life, and the necessities, too, were fearfully dear. The opportunity to get in debt was much greater than at Niagara. But it was always difficult for Joseph not to overextend himself financially, for he and Catharine had a high standard of living. After the war when the numbers of British presents fell off (for Joseph got his share of whatever was handed out), Joseph was always prodded on to new exertions by the demands of his growing, expensive family, and he developed more ingenious ways to augment his income than he had ever thought of in his youth. In time there were few white men who could juggle finances better than Joseph. But if he sometimes robbed Peter to pay Paul, no creditor ever said that he did not settle up eventually.

Detroit, though swollen with sad-eyed refugees who had nowhere else to go and grim-faced prisoners whose only escape route lay through the Indian country, was still a gay place. If Joseph had been in good health, he could have enjoyed himself. The French would always dance, and the British merchants and soldiers were no puritans, having neither church nor preacher and missing neither. There was little fear that the enemy could ever spoil the gaiety. The old post was slowly being strengthened. It had a new fort which, like all the frontier forts, was subject to damage by rainstorms and wintry blasts and required constant repairs. As if that were not trouble enough for the commanding officer, the Indians *would* tie their canoes to the pickets, and the pickets were always tumbling down into the water and floating away. But General Haldimand was sure it would take more men and artillery than the Americans could muster, to take the post by storm. There was no real unease about Detroit in anybody's mind. Occasionally, however, its defenders took some little fright at rebel threats and sent off urgent pleas for aid. But it was their business to take fright, and in spite of their overall sense of security, they kept in readiness for action. There were incessant drillings with all the attendant drumming and fifing every day. Joseph, who was probably quartered near the parade ground, thought this was noble music. But it could drive those who were not used to it almost out of their minds.

Several important councils with the Indians took place at Detroit in the latter part of the year, but Joseph is not listed as attending any of them. Coping with the noxious doses, the purges and bloodlettings, and trying to get up on his injured leg did not leave him much strength for Indian politics. On one occasion, however, some friendly Delawares visited his quarters and presented him with a scalp for each of the Six Nations. The scalps were to be taken back to Niagara to prove that the Delawares had been doing their duty.[42] On another occasion Joseph himself sent for some Huron and Shawnee chiefs and asked them if they would like to see Fort Pitt destroyed. They eagerly answered in the affirmative for, as they said, the bones of their friends lay in piles about that place. Joseph advised them to petition the commander in chief for help in reducing the offending post.[43] A movement was set on foot among the Indians to try to get an expedition started for the purpose. But Haldimand discouraged such plans. There were good reasons he could not help them. Even if he could take Fort Pitt, he could not hold it. Besides, he knew the lateness of the hour. The Indians, however, were not aware of any drawbacks. It tells much about Joseph that he could have seriously proposed such a project.

The political situation at Detroit was even more confused than the situation at Niagara. Like the Indians farther east, the western Indians were not all of one mind. Even those who were generally loyal to the king wavered from time to time. Some wavered when Clark came into the Illinois country or when Governor Hamilton was captured. Some wavered when a proclamation from the French admiral, d'Estaing, was surreptitiously put into their hands. Others wavered when Sullivan and Brodhead made their punitive marches. Many Delawares, especially in the early years of the war, were prone to take sides with the Americans. And some Delawares living on the Tuscarawas branch of the Muskingum River (eastern Ohio) steadfastly refused to fight for or against anybody. Under the influence of Moravian missionaries who had been proselytizing in the area for many years, these peaceable Indians tried to be neutral. Of course they were not well thought of by the adherents of either side, and were accused of helping first one contender and then the other, which, sometimes, they really did. Almost anyone, white or Indian, could obtain provisions or information from the amiable Christian Delawares. It turned out, however, that warriors from the Indian country got most of the food and whites at Pittsburgh got most of the intelligence.

Generally the western Indians were brought to act by the same motives that activated the Indians about Niagara. They were worried about their lands, and British officers never let them forget about their worries. After blood was spilled, they were motivated by thoughts of revenge. But most of all they were motivated by the realities of trade and presents. A certain loyal chief summed it up thus to his wavering brothers: "You see that your wives & your children are in want, you are forced to cover yourselves with animals skins, we, on the contrary, we are glorious to see, our wives, our children, our young men, covered with jewelry. You have neither powder nor shot nor arms, what will you do?"[44]

Like the Six Nations and the Seven Nations of Canada, the western Indians had been long at odds with Indians to the southward, particularly the Cherokees of the lower Appalachians. Nobody knew how the ancient enmity had started, but the Cherokees, often the losers in the warfare, had been willing to cry quits for many years. Urged on by their pleas, the Indian superintendent in the south had asked Sir William Johnson to try to make peace between the warring groups. If the Six Nations would declare a peace, all their dependents would probably do likewise. Some half-hearted attempts were made by Sir William to heal the breach, but he had little enthusiasm for such work. He thought it better for the white settlers if the Indians continued to fight among themselves, and he feared any moves toward a general Indian union. But when the Revolution broke out, British officialdom in the north as well as in the south concluded that it was time for the Indians to close ranks. It was recognized that if all the warriors fought together for the same cause at the same time, their fighting would have far greater effect. The Six Nations, when they needed help in their own country, were brought to easy agreement with this idea, and they sent peace belts to the south via their western allies. Peace embassies went out in 1779, 1780, and 1781, all under western auspices. The Cherokees responded favorably. Delegates came hundreds of miles to sit at council fires with their old enemies and take one another by the arm. Though by late 1781 the situation was still for practical purposes touch-and-go, the Indians appeared to be at last on the road to unity.

Another factor complicated affairs in the west. Fears of foreign influence were rife among the British at Detroit. The French fear was an old one. Fear of the Spaniards wasmore recent. Spain had got control of Louisiana, a vast, unknown territory mostly to the west of the Mississippi, in 1763. Thus the Spanish controlled New Orleans and the post of St. Louis during the entire American Revolution, and after they entered the war against Britain in 1779, they also took over the small British posts on the lower Mississippi. Via the Mississippi and the Ohio they could, and sometimes did, send supplies to the rebels at Pittsburgh. They set up a claim to territory as far east as the Wabash, and invited all the Indians on that river to come and trade with them. So far from their bases, the Spanish were not really very dangerous, but in the midst of warfare on land and on sea, in Europe and in America, the British could not afford to neglect any danger, no matter how small or remote. When Major De Peyster and his officers at Detroit were spending much thought on how to circumvent the French, they also had to spend some thought on how to thwart the Spaniards.

All these ins and outs of Indian and white politics Joseph Brant knew or was coming to know, as the ice clamped its hold on the lakes in late November 1781 and shut off the western posts from the world. The latest news that had come in from the seacoast was reassuring. It had been an unhappy summer for the rebels. The king's great warriors were winning victory after victory in Virginia and the Carolinas. All was well on the other side of the mountains.

16

The Great Betrayal

EARLY IN FEBRUARY 1782, six Oneida warriors arrived in Detroit to
join Joseph. Since these Oneidas were accounted Joseph's "particular friends," they must have been good Loyalists from Oquaga, not
members of that stubborn band who had held out almost to the last
before abandoning the rebels. The young men had been forty-six days
on the long journey across the snow and ice, and they brought letters
from headquarters which had come by the last vessel across Lake
Ontario. According to Major De Peyster, they brought nothing new.[1]
This estimate was true enough. The secret dispatch containing what
was new was lying in the mail depository at Carleton Island. It had just
missed the last boat. All unknowing, Detroit was to have two more
months of business as usual. As yet, the word, "Yorktown," meant
nothing.

By February 25 Joseph was able to attend his first council since his
illness. The visiting Oneidas also attended as representatives of the
Six Nations. This time it was some Indians from the Wabash area who
needed encouragement, and Major De Peyster assured them that "the
English and the Indian Nations are but one," and that they would
have plenty of trade and presents if they remained steadfast. Then it
was Joseph's turn to speak. It had been a long time since Joseph had
received instructions from Guy Johnson, but he knew what to say. It
was the same speech he had been making ever since he came from
Niagara. Its essence was as follows:

> Brethren! We are glad to see you before our father. we who
> address you are of the Six Nations who live on the other side of the

320

Lake, you see here who we depend upon this is our father (the Commandant) who supplies us with our wants . . . it is from him however that we brownskins should take the lead since we make one with him and those who are under him. We invite you Brethren . . . to attend to what your father has said and not listen any more to the Rebels, least that we who have not too much sense may fall out with each other should we not think with our father.[2]

It was the same speech, but it was not quite the same speech. Did there appear to be a hint of sarcasm in Joseph's words? A little bitterness? It was not like him to downgrade himself. Had he been thinking dangerous thoughts during his long winter of inactivity? At Niagara and at Quebec they considered the famous Brant somewhat "spoiled." Joseph had certainly been discontented, at least with himself, before he left Niagara. Nor did it soothe his feelings to find, at Detroit, that the Indians got all the blame because Clark's whole army had not been defeated. This was not Joseph's idea of a just criticism.[3] But whatever impropriety his discontent had led him to now—if any—seems not to have been discerned by De Peyster. De Peyster heard nothing unusual. Indians often said such things. Joseph's Oneida friends, whose ears were more attuned, may have heard something. It was nothing they would have talked about in public.

General Haldimand still wanted Joseph to come home, but now he had an especial reason. All winter long he had heard reports that affairs were going badly in the south, and by mid-February he assumed that it was probably true, as rumored, that Cornwallis had surrendered. That being the case, he knew he had to make a great effort to establish a garrison at Oswego to prevent the Americans from getting there first. With the rebels at Oswego, Niagara could not hold out. The fur trade would be lost, and Canada itself would be in grave danger. Haldimand planned the urgent operation for early spring, just as soon as the ice would permit, and he thought he needed Joseph's help. "I could wish it were possible," he told Powell, "to recall Joseph Brant he would be very usefull on this Occasion, particularly as it is a favorite measure of his— I think you would do well to send off an Express immediately to Him, informing Him that you have something of Importance to Communicate, and desiring he will Return to Niagara with all possible Expedition."[4] Powell replied on March 23 that he was sending off the express at once, but that he had heard there was doubt whether Joseph would ever recover full use of his leg.[5] On April 21 De Peyster wrote Powell that he was sending Joseph down.[6] It had taken more than two months to get the order from Quebec to Detroit even by means of fast expresses. The Americans had a problem of communications, too, but it was not like this.

Joseph was still at Detroit on April 25, but obviously preparing to leave, for he got one of the merchants to advance him £7.10 in cash. With purchases of wine and another cash advance, this made a debt of £40.16 since March 20.[7] Joseph was still living beyond his income. Before he left the alarming rumor of Cornwallis' surrender had reached Detroit. It had probably come, as most rumors came to the post, by way of some prisoner from Fort Pitt. The report also had it that the Six Nations had offered to make peace with the Americans. Though carefully keeping this news from the other Indians, De Peyster, in great consternation about the peace rumor, told Joseph the whole story. Joseph replied, according to the relieved commandant, that "he'll forfeit his life it is not true." If anybody was willing to make peace, thought Joseph, it was only a few neutrals who lived near Fort Pitt.[8] Not long afterward the confirmation of Cornwallis' debacle came from Alexander McKee who was spending the winter in Shawnee country and who was in the best position to get reliable news from the east. The event had taken place months before, on October 19. Cornwallis had surrendered his whole army. It was a cheerless thought to carry home with him, and must have compounded Joseph's dark mood. By April 30 Joseph had not yet arrived at Niagara, communication with Detroit still being closed.[9] By May 14 he was there, and the report of his arrival had already reached Oswego, where Major John Ross, one of Haldimand's favorite officers and a man of some notoriety at the moment, was working furiously to rebuild the old fort.[10]

The atmosphere at Niagara was half gloom and half urgency. With Cornwallis' surrender certain (for confirmations came thick and fast), there was need to move in many directions. Not only must the fort at Oswego be rebuilt and garrisoned, intelligence must be obtained of rebel plans and the triumphant enemy held in check along every part of the frontier. Every precaution must be taken against an attack on any of the upper posts. Joseph shared these anxieties, but he was not quite sure what action he ought to take. In case of an attack he could be very useful at Niagara or even back at Detroit, and General Powell agreed with him for the time being.[11] He also knew he was expected at Oswego where scouting parties were urgently needed, but he hesitated to go because the Indians had quarreled with Major Ross and refused to serve under him. Joseph still wanted to lead an expedition against Fort Pitt and really preferred that service, but he had not heard whether Haldimand would sanction the idea.[12] Moreover, he had personal things to do: to plant his corn and finish his house, and even to make friends again with some of his old enemies.[13] Apparently Sayengaraghta resented Joseph's return. For a year he had been supreme among the Indians, petted and looked up to and catered to by the whites, and he was no longer content to share the sweets of adulation with a rival. Was not Sullivan long gone? Were not the dangers of 1779—and the need to submerge his feelings—long over?

The person who could have quickly resolved Joseph's difficulties was no longer at Niagara. Guy Johnson had been ordered down to Montreal the previous fall. A disgruntled clerk in the trading firm of Taylor & Forsyth, the firm from which Guy had made most of his Indian department purchases, had reported to headquarters that the government was being robbed of vast sums in the conduct of that business. Taylor & Forsyth was in deep trouble, and Guy had been called down, with his books and accounts, as a witness. The case seemed interminable; first a trial, then a judgment against the defendant, then an appeal. Neither Guy nor anyone else could say when he would be able to return to Niagara.

John Butler, who directed the affairs of the Indian department in the superintendent's absence, knew he had no great influence over Joseph Brant, and was too tactful a man to inject himself into the situation. Nor did it much matter to him, anyway. Butler was sick at heart. Some months before, his son Walter, in whom he took so much pride, had been killed. Walter had fallen in Major Ross's unlucky raid on the Mohawk—the last great raid, as it turned out, of the war.

Major John Ross, the same officer who now awaited Joseph at Oswego, had been sent by Haldimand in the fall of 1781 to repeat Sir John Johnson's exploits of the year before. He was to destroy anything the rebels still had left and whatever they had dared to rebuild, and "extirpate" the rebel Oneidas. But 1781 was too late for such a venture. Colonel Marinus Willett, an alert Continental officer, pursued Ross's force of some five hundred whites and Indians with such vigor that the raiders got separated and fled in panic, each trying to save himself any way he could. The Indians, admittedly a poor selection, had been recruited at Niagara on less than a week's notice, and they did not perform as well as Ross expected. He blamed them for the debacle. The Indians swore they would never serve under Ross again. Haldimand, who sided with Ross, blamed Guy Johnson for the Indians' inadequacies. And among the slain was Walter Butler, aged twenty-eight, who died in the new-fallen snow on the banks of West Canada Creek—cut down by an Oneida who had been promised a blanket and who, eleven years later, was still trying to get it. At first the bereaved father refused to believe the terrible news. No, it could not have happened to Walter. Not *Walter!* Afterward he had to believe. His health, never too good, went downhill, and he spent much of 1782 so ill his life was despaired of.

General Powell finally cleared Joseph's pathway and got him off to Oswego at last. Powell induced Major Ross to send the Indians a friendly speech. He also smoothed over the dissension between Joseph and Sayengaraghta, and permitted the latter to go on a mission toward Fort Pitt. It was an important service, and it seems to have mollified the Seneca chief's feelings. It also got him out of the way. Powell was finding both the Seneca and the Mohawk very difficult to manage. Both were proud men, not easy to please. Of Sayengaraghta's pride, John Butler, who held most of the Indians in the palm of his hand, could tell many a story. Once, for instance, Sayengaraghta asked Butler for a gold-laced hat and a fine coat which he said Guy Johnson had promised him. Butler, not having the items on hand, told him that he would give him anything else in the Indian store. Whereupon, as Butler related the incident, Sayengaraghta replied "if the King was grown too poor, and not able to purchase a Hat for him he wou'd do it himself; which he accordingly did, and made his brag of it."[14] There are no anecdotes of this sort about Joseph, but apparently he was becoming just as hard to deal with as Sayengaraghta. Powell said that he had returned from Detroit in a worse mood than when he went away.[15] But it was not gold-laced hats that disturbed Joseph.

On June 14 Joseph finally left for Oswego, taking with him a band of nearly three hundred warriors and ten of his white Volunteers.[16] He left behind his company of Mohawks and Oneidas (for he did not resign their leadership after all), and they and their families continued to come and go between Niagara and their new settlements at Buffalo Creek. The majority being usually at Niagara, they of course contributed their part to the great expense of the Indian department about which there was such an outcry in England. Joseph also left behind the rest of his Volunteers, who were raising corn and vegetables at Buffalo Creek, and for whom, suddenly, there appeared little else to do. Joseph expected to go on service somewhere or other, but mostly with the Indians. His wounded leg was still healing, he had written De Peyster on May 19.[17] Probably it was well by the time he left for Oswego, for he says no more about it.

The trip to Oswego took only four days.[18] Once there, Joseph could see that the work at the newly established post had progressed well. The old fort, which Major Ross had found in a ruinous condition, was already repaired and fairly respectable. Timber had been cut eight miles up the Oswego River, and five blockhouses were being built. Undergrowth had been cleared all the way to the top of the hill. There was an unobstructed view of a vast expanse of Lake Ontario.

Joseph and his warriors were very welcome. Haldimand had written Ross that Joseph was coming; "cultivate him," he advised, "and you will find him, unless much altered, a Zealous, active, useful aid."[19] Ross, an efficient regular officer who did not believe in letting the grass grow under his feet, was more than willing to give Joseph Brant his due. Ross did not understand Indians at all. He thought they ought to be as disciplined as he was, and in just the same way, and he considered their services greatly overrated. He also admitted he could not do without them! He was cordiality itself. Apart·from carrying out Haldimand's instructions to "cultivate" Joseph, he also hoped, by friendly attentions, to erase from Joseph's mind any stories he might have heard from his Indian friends about the late unfortunate raid.

Joseph must have sensed he had the whip hand. The first thing he did was to complain that Butler had not outfitted his men properly for going on service.[20] Ross, who had almost nothing to give away to the Indians, was alarmed. He would have to depend on the warriors both for protection and intelligence, not to mention for any small offensives he might have in view. Ross lost no time in reporting the complaints to Haldimand in Quebec (as Joseph had asked) and to Powell at Niagara.[21] At the latter place Butler promptly produced a long list of arms and accouterments which he had furnished to Joseph's party. They ranged from blankets, leggings, shirts, hats, and shoes to ammunition and weapons and war paint, and from cooking utensils and tobacco to silver jewelry. Joseph had particularly complained of a lack of moccasins. Butler said he gave him five hundred pairs.[22] There was a great deal of correspondence on the subject. Everyone wished to soothe Joseph's hurt feelings, and in the end a special agent from the Indian department was sent to Oswego to take care of the Indians.[23] Haldimand, who admitted Joseph was unreasonable in his demands, thought any actual want of supplies complained of by him could be attributed to a lack of supplies in the store at Niagara.[24] It was Haldimand's secretary who let the cat out of the bag. Captain Robert Mathews had the real explanation of Joseph's conduct. "Entre nous," he told Ross, "there is an old Jealousy between Col: Butler & Joseph— the Latter is a Most Excellent fellow but as he Candidly acknowledges, a thorough Indian, being of a More implacable disposition— The General therefore Wishes that as Little Blame as possible Should appear to fall on Col: Buttler."[25]

Whether the implacability was Joseph's or Daniel Claus's is difficult to say. Joseph had not seen Claus recently and, so far as is

known, had not received a letter from him. But not all the Brant-
Claus correspondence has come down to us. Letters are sometimes
mentioned which have not been found, and Joseph could have had
some letter which set him off. Subsequent events certainly prove that
Joseph, without Claus's advice, could get along very well with Butler.
At any rate, the little storm blew over. Ross reported on June 26 that
Joseph was bearing his disappointment with fortitude.[26]

Having made Butler's shortcomings a public issue on his very first
day, Joseph then fell to work. He took care that his warriors fell to
work beside him. It probably did not involve much persuasion on his
part. For a long time the Indians had pleaded for a garrison at Oswego.
It could have saved them from Sullivan, they thought. It might still
prove useful. So the warriors cut trees and floated logs and dug
trenches. They carried stones up the hill and prepared sod. They did
everything that unskilled labor could do. Nothing seemed too much
effort. Never had men worked so hard and with such apparent good
will. Major Ross looked on in amazement. Indians working! Working?
Indians? It was contrary to all he had ever heard. He could not praise
Joseph Brant enough. "I cannot say too much in his favor," he wrote
Haldimand, "his conduct is surprising he rules the Indians as he
pleases, and they are all rejoiced at seeing this place occupied." Even
the regular soldiers were infected with the warriors' enthusiasm, and
the work went on even faster than before. In another fortnight, Ross
proudly predicted, the fortifications would be raised according to the
plan laid out for him, and in some respects better than the plan.[27]

Ross and Joseph spent many evenings in talk. Ross told Joseph
details of his unsuccessful raid. He explained his own side of the
controversy. Joseph agreed with him that Guy Johnson had not sent
good warriors for the service. Joseph also explained the Indians' side of
the controversy. He knew, for instance, why Indians sometimes went
home early, why they might turn loose prisoners who knew too much.
The two men almost began to understand each other.[28]

Joseph was perturbed about the change of ministry in England. It
had been known for some time that Lord North had fallen, that Lord
George Germain had resigned his office. Joseph's friend General Clinton had left New York, and Sir Guy Carleton, he of the stern mien,
had taken his place as head of the British forces in America. Joseph
thought that these changes did not augur well for his people. The new
ministers, he said, had no sympathy for the Indians, and he told Ross
about the nobleman of the opposition party whom he had met at the
masquerade ball in London. This man, one of those who had come to
power at North's fall, had described the Americans as an injured

people, and he had kissed Joseph's tomahawk when Joseph said he did not intend to raise it against them. From such a one what were the Indians to expect? Joseph asked Ross several probing questions which the latter owned to Haldimand's secretary that he could not answer.[29]

Ross, who knew the war was lost, began to feel sorry for Joseph. He reported to headquarters how economically Joseph measured out the rum and provisions, how careful he was to avoid waste. He told how tactfully he managed his warriors, difficult though it was because of their divisions and jealousies. And, he added, whenever a few extras could be spared for the Indians, Joseph took care to collect them at night and distribute them privately among the needy.[30] Ross never said a word about Joseph's drinking, if indeed there was any word to say. Nor did he try to explain how a man who doled out provisions and managed his comrades with such diplomacy could berate Butler for giving him only five hundred pairs of moccasins. But that was an anomaly that Joseph himself probably could not have explained.

Joseph was eager to go to war again. With the work so forward at Oswego, there was nothing to stop him. He set out on July 5 with 460 warriors and a company of Ross's soldiers.[31] But where to go? Fort Stanwix, relatively near and so long an eyesore to the Indians, had been abandoned by the rebels. It was whispered down in Albany that some of the garrison had set fire to their own post. At any rate, with the Oneidas gone and the frontier so contracted, a fort much nearer civilization would serve just as well. The rebel troops had been removed to Fort Herkimer on the Mohawk, and that is where Joseph decided to go.

One of the white officers kept a journal which records many details about this last expedition.[32] There was much running hither and yon. The enemy was wary and would not come out to fight so superior a force. At Fort Herkimer the raiders captured some cattle and killed eight or nine men. Crossing the river, they attempted a stroke at Fort Dayton, but here even the cattle had been taken inside. Thwarted, they spread out to the nearby settlements. Joseph and the white soldiers then separated, the latter to return to Oswego and the former to try to get some prisoners. The warriors had requests from many bereaved families for prisoners, and Joseph thought something extra was expected of him since his force was larger than usual. Whether the invaders accomplished anything more is doubtful. However, they had already killed those eight or nine men, with the result that eight or nine more families were bereft of a husband, a father, a brother, a son. So passed the terrible Brant's final service of the war. Had he but known, commissioners were already meeting in Paris to fashion a peace. Quite unnecessarily he piled another sheaf on the abundant harvest of hate. The Americans, who had been told by Sir Guy Carleton that he was stopping all offensive operations, were baffled and angry. They would have been astounded to know that the white officer who served with Joseph could compliment him for his "Gallantry, Generosity, and Humanity" in arms. All the Americans saw was another cruel attack when there should have been no attack.

Somewhere along his route Joseph got a message from Ross telling him of a cessation of hostilities and calling him back to Oswego. Ross was very careful to say that the cessation was only temporary. Joseph obeyed the order, "like himself," as Ross said, and brought back his reluctant Indians.[33] Awaiting him was a personal letter from Captain Mathews, Haldimand's secretary, which had been missent to Niagara and which had been a long time on the way. In the course of the letter Mathews assured Joseph that General Haldimand had taken post at Oswego solely because the Indians desired it and solely for their benefit. This was more than Joseph could swallow. Having opened the letter in the presence of several officers of the regiment, he burst out in disbelief in front of them. "My Friend Cap^{tn} Mathews, this wont do," he exclaimed (according to Ross), "it was not for the Reasons you give, it was owing to the news of last winter that the French and Rebels intended Invading Canada otherwise it would not have happened."[34]

If Joseph's followers were unhappy because they had been called back from the warpath, some good news soon lifted their spirits. It was news that was to please Indians near and far, even those who lived so distant from the posts that they could get to Detroit or Niagara or Michilimackinac scarcely once a year. On the St. Lawrence and on the lakes, on the St. Joseph, the Fox, and the Wabash, on the Scioto, the Miami, and the Ohio, every red man and woman who had ever heard of Warraghiyagey, that loving friend of Indians, could smile with anticipation. Sir John Johnson, Warraghiyagey's son, was going to take care of them. Sir John would see that they got justice and all good things.

To the white people the news meant something else. Sir William Johnson's old commission, with all his authority and prestige, had been revived, and Sir John had got the plum. Sir John, who had spent the past winter in England, had returned with a royal appointment as superintendent general and inspector general of Indian affairs. His authority extended over all the northern Indians allied with the crown, including, of course, the Six Nations and their western confederates, as well as the Indians of Canada and the upper lakes. It was a new attempt on the part of government to create order and stop abuses in the Indian department and, above all, to reduce expenses.

Sir John, who had once wanted to avoid anything having to do with the Indians, was more than glad to get the appointment. His estates were gone, his family was large, and he was finding it very difficult to make ends meet. General Haldimand, aware of Sir John's predicament and his probable reception by the natives, and believing him to be the soul of honor (and no doubt influenced by his amiable disposition, for he was his father's son in that respect), and wishing to get the albatross of the Indian department off his own back, had recommended establishment of the new post and named Sir John as the only proper person to fill it. Both the old and the new ministry had approved the appointment, for the Indian department was a great care to them, too. It was a post that Sir John was to fill for forty-six long years, for he was to live to a very advanced age. There were rebels who, knowing of Sir John's one-time aversion to Indians and looking back at the terrible raids of 1780, would have said that this was to be his punishment. In a way, Sir John, already sensitive about his orgies of destruction, could have agreed. He had been tired of Indians for a long, long time.

Early in August the warriors at Oswego decided to send deputies to Montreal to talk with Sir John, and then on to Quebec, if possible, to talk with General Haldimand. They were getting anxious about their prospects; being withheld from war disturbed them. It was obvious to the worried councilors that Joseph Brant was the proper person to go on such an errand. Along with him the warriors sent two chiefs, Captain David, a Mohawk, and a Cayuga.[35] Joseph agreed to carry some letters written by Ross to various persons down the country. "I part with Joseph with great Reluctance," Ross told Captain Mathews, "he is a most excellen[t] fellow."[36]

By August 10 Joseph was conferring with his friend Claus in Montreal, having left the two other deputies at Claus's make-shift village of lower Mohawks.[37] Soon a letter from headquarters informed him that his journey was going to be much longer than he had planned. He was not to visit General Haldimand at Quebec just yet. Instead, he was to accompany Sir John on a tour of the upper posts.[38] The new superintendent had many details to settle before the Indian department could be said to be on a proper footing. It was thought at headquarters that if the Indians were disappointed by any of the changes, Joseph would be a proper mediator between them and Sir John.[39] Perhaps Joseph was a suitable mediator by this time.

Joseph and Sir John had a companion on their journey. With them traveled Lieutenant Colonel Henry Hope, an officer who was to inspect the posts and examine into the military possibilities of an interior, lesser-known route to Michilimackinac which might have to be utilized after the peace if the lake route should be cut off. The three travelers were to make an incredibly quick trip, for the season was far advanced and they had to hurry. Only grave emergency sent them on their way at such a time of the year. With peace so close, the objects of the journey had to be accomplished as soon as possible.

After he returned, Lieutenant Colonel Hope wrote a long report to General Haldimand describing his journey.[40] He told how the three men set out from Montreal on August 21. They had wilderness all the way: up the Ottawa River, then up the Little River to Lake Nipissing, across that lake, then down the French River, and across Lake Huron—in all, a journey of 251 leagues. Thirty-four portages intervened between starting point and destination, and the three helped their laborers carry canoes, baggage, and provisions from one body of water to another. They found the rivers shallow and swift, impossible to navigate except in bark canoes. Lieutenant Colonel Hope concluded regretfully that the route would never serve for transport of an army. Fur traders had long used it, of course. Expresses could use it, and perhaps a very small reinforcement for Michilimackinac or Detroit could be sent that way in an emergency—nothing more.

In exactly one month Sir John, Hope, and Joseph set out on their return. It was already getting cold. This time they could go by the usual lake route, and they enjoyed the comfort of one of the king's sloops. Such transport seemed luxurious indeed after the cramped and open canoes and the hardships of portaging. Late at night, on September 24, they arrived at Detroit. They went to work the next morning. They had no time to dally. Winter would soon be closing in. Forty-eight hours later, Sir John and Hope, their work finished, left on the journey down Lake Erie to Niagara. Only Joseph remained behind.

Sir John had held councils with the Indians at Michilimackinac and Detroit, but Hope does not mention them. His interests lay in another direction. Doubtless Joseph played his part at the councils as well as he could. Now, according to the latest news from the Ohio country, he had a different sort of part to play, more in keeping with his talents. Sir John would have to carry on at Niagara without him.

Joseph, though painfully ill with an ear infection,[41] set out with another companion in another direction. He went with Captain Potts and a small detachment of soldiers to the mouth of the Maumee River (present Toledo).[42] It was a journey of some fifty-four miles by water.

Here, on September 29, a new little post was established. It was a small, roughly built blockhouse, recently constructed to house provisions from the weather and from the depredations of the Indians, and meant as a place of retreat for any small British force that happened to be in the vicinity. It was also a place where supplies were sometimes distributed to the Indians. Mainly, however, it was an outpost covering Detroit from the direction of the important Sandusky-Maumee and Wabash-Maumee portages. From the great security of its situation this little blockhouse was thought by its builder to be defendable by ten men against one hundred.

Joseph did not tarry long at the new blockhouse. On October 2 he set out for Sandusky where, either there or up the river, he expected to join Alexander McKee. McKee and a force of Indians and Rangers were awaiting a rebel attack on the Sandusky villages, and Joseph's services appeared to be urgently needed.[43] The rebels were threatening to exterminate every Indian they met, and their threats were being taken very seriously.

The inflammatory situation had come about in this way: In early March a party of militia from western Pennsylvania, under command of Colonel David Williamson, had pursued some Indian marauders, who had killed a frontier family, to the Tuscarawas River. Here, in the vicinity of Gnadenhutten, former home of Moravian converts, they found a band of the harmless Christian Indians who had returned to get their corn. The Americans accused the Christians of harboring the fugitives, and probably rightly, for these poor creatures would harbor anybody. The result was that some ninety or so men, women, and children, holding up peace wampum and crying out their innocence of the killings, were gathered together and slaughtered by the self-righteous militiamen. The unfortunates, mostly Delawares, had been abhorred and virtually disowned by their nation, but being murdered in this wise, their kinsmen found they were fonder of them than they had realized, and they called aloud for revenge.

The opportunity for vengeance came three months later, when the angry Indians cut off an American expedition and captured Colonel William Crawford, its leader. Though the wrong man, and not responsible for the murders at Gnadenhutten, Colonel Crawford was scalped alive by the vengeful Delawares. Hot coals were heaped on his head, and he was roasted to death by a slow fire—all in the presence of Simon Girty, Matthew Elliott, and other white Loyalists, some of whom were long-time acquaintances of Crawford, and none of whom could do anything to prevent the atrocity. Two other captive officers were also tortured and killed at the same time. Elsewhere as well, the

Indians began to revenge themselves on their prisoners, and they determined not to spare a life in battle. In August, therefore, when Captain William Caldwell of Butler's Rangers, Simon Girty, and a large band of Indians defeated some Kentuckians in an ambush at Blue Licks on the Ohio, the warriors killed a great number of the enemy in the battle. The Americans deemed this a massacre, and vowed to retaliate. They promised, as it was reported, to "kill and burn all before them." Now, in early October, the Indians were massed on the Sandusky River, awaiting an enemy whose enraged threats could not be ignored. As in a series of reflections mirrored over and over, revenge seemed to go backward and forward to infinity.

Joseph found McKee and the warriors at Upper Sandusky, and everybody waited there. The Indians were just as angry as the Kentuckians or the people at Pittsburgh. They well knew—as, indeed, all the Loyalists thought they knew—that the cruel rebels had used poisoned bullets against Burgoyne. They also believed that the rebels killed every Indian prisoner they took. They were sure, too, that James Clinton's soldiers had carried young Indian girls away from Onondaga in '79, to rape and murder them. And last year, when Major Ross was defeated, did not those white savages cut off the hands of captured Rangers? The warriors had been told, by this time, that offensive warfare must stop. But defensive warfare could go on; and everything they did was defensive, they believed. They were defending themselves and their country. Although De Peyster and Powell and their great father, Haldimand, had expressed the highest displeasure at Crawford's fate, the Indians felt no compunctions themselves. Had they not acted with justice and according to their ancient customs?

De Peyster, knowing both the Indians and the American frontiersmen, and trying to honor Haldimand's orders regarding offensive operations, poured out his woes to the latter:

> I have a very difficult card to play at this post and its dependencies, which differs widely from the situation of affairs at Michilimackinac, Niagara, and others, in the upper district of Canada. It is evident, that the back settlers will continue to make war upon the Shawaneese, Delawares, and Wyandotts, even after a truce shall be agreed to, between Great Britain and her revolted colonies; in which case, whilst we continue to support the Indians with troops (which they are calling aloud for), or only with arms, ammunition, and necessaries, we shall incur the odium of encouraging incursions into the back settlements; for it is as evident, that when Indians are on foot, occasioned by the constant alarms they receive from the enemy's entering their country, they will occasionally enter the

settlements, and bring off prisoners and scalps, so that whilst in alliance with a people we are bound to support, a defensive war, will, in spite of human prudence, almost always terminate in an offensive one.[44]

The Indians at Upper Sandusky waited and waited, but nothing happened throughout October. No American army appeared. Finally the warriors began to drift away to their own concerns. Tired out and disgruntled, they felt they had been deceived by somebody or other. The white Rangers, who from ague and sheer hunger looked like "walking spectres," were glad to know the campaign was over. The whites suspected that something unusual was going on in Europe. The fact that the threatening rebels had never appeared strengthened their belief. The American frontier got all the news first. If only they had a knowledgeable prisoner to question—but going out to get prisoners was forbidden. Eventually the distant Indians and most of the whites left the camps on the Sandusky. But all would have said, and they truly believed it, that their side was winning the war in the west. Two important battles had been won in the campaign, and no part of the Pennsylvania and Virginia frontier had been free of depredations. They overlooked the fact that they had not been able to dislodge George Rogers Clark from Illinois and Kentucky.

Joseph was certainly back at Niagara before the middle of November.[45] Of course Sir John had already come and gone, having given orders to the Indian department for stringent economies and new procedures, confirmed appointments and dismissals, and set up rules defining the demarcation between the Indian department and the military—all which had been pointed out to him by authorities in London or at Quebec. Then, because he had just received a letter from General Haldimand which clearly betrayed nervousness about the Indians (for the warriors had left Oswego in an unhappy state of mind, and Haldimand was worried), Sir John assembled the Six Nations at the village at the landing—now formally christened the Loyal Confederate Village—and held a full council. This he did without benefit of the presence of any high-ranking department officer, Butler being very ill and Guy Johnson still absent.

Sir John soothed the Indians and pooh-poohed their fears. There was no firm peace, he told them. The king, he said, had only stopped the bloodshed for a time so that his rebellious children could have an opportunity to reflect on their folly and return to their senses. In the meanwhile, so he assured his hearers, they could confidently rely on the king's favor and protection in all situations, no less in peace than in war. Sir John was very emphatic on this score, just as Haldimand had instructed him to be. Their services, he told the assembled Indians, would never be forgotten. On the whole, as Sir John reported to the worried general, the Indians seemed mollified. Some of them promised to return to Oswego.

The first forebodings of fear for the future clutched at Haldimand's breast. When he had found out for sure that a peace conference was in progress at Paris, he had instructed the military at the upper posts to watch the Indians closely. He well remembered Pontiac's conspiracy and the terrible scenes after the last peace, and he meant to guard against sieges and ambushes and all unpleasant surprises. To Sir Guy Carleton in New York he spelled out his fears and discussed the situation at length:

> Unacquainted with the Terms that may be intended for the Six Nation Indians in the proposals of a Peace with America—I think it necessary as a Commissioner to inform you that my having Restrained them from Hostilities has occasioned a general discontent amongst them. Major Ross who commands Oswego informs me that they have all left that Post in disgust and that he is in daily expectation of being insulted. They are alarmed at the appearance of an accommodation so far short of what our Language, from the beginning has taught them to expect, deprived of their Lands & driven out of their Country they reproached us with their ruin, & project of severe Retaliation from the Hands of the Rebells. Your Excellency is too well acquainted with the Situation and Interests of these People to make it necessary for me to enlarge upon their consequence with respect to the Trade and Safety of this Province, the Expectations their services entitles them to from us, or upon the fatal consequences that might attend our abandoning them to the Intrigues of the Enemy, should they persist in the war, or to their Resentment in case of a Peace, and I persuade myself they will be amply considered by Your Excellency either in a Representation to the King's Ministers or by such arrangement as shall be agreed upon in this Country. Your Excellency will not understand from what I have said of the Six Nations that the King's attention should be confined to them only, many of the Western & Indian Nations in the neighbour hood have suffered equally by shameful encroachments of the Virginians upon their most valuable Hunting Grounds, and have been equally attached and serviceable to the Royal Cause.[46]

To the new ministry in London Haldimand poured out the same fears, summing them up in this wise to the secretary of state: "From an apprehension, Sir, that the Disposition of the Indians, and the indispensible necessity of preserving their affections may not be Sufficiently understood at Home, I think it my duty to assure you that an unremitting attention to a very nice management of that People is inseparable from the safety of this Province, which has been indisputably preserved hitherto in a great measure by their Attachment."[47]

Two days later he had an afterthought: "In case a Peace or Truce should take place during the winter, tho' I apprehend it is unnecessary, yet my anxiety for the good of the Empire makes me observe to you that in making the one or the other, great care should be taken that Niagara & Oswego should be annexed to Canada, or comprehended in the general words, that each of the contending Parties in North America should retain what they possessed at the time. The Possession of these two Forts is essentially necessary to the security as well as the Trade of the Country."[48]

The man on the spot had done his best to sound a warning in the highest echelons of government. It would not be his fault if the highest authorities both in America and Britain did not understand the local situation. Haldimand wrote from Quebec on October 23 and 25, 1782. Five weeks later, on November 30, the preliminary peace was signed in Paris by commissioners who could not possibly have seen his letters. The final peace treaty, however, was still almost a year away.

Sir John had recommended that the Six Nations bring in all their prisoners to Niagara. Four of the nations complied immediately. When Joseph returned, he opposed the idea. He had the old-fashioned notion that prisoners strengthened the Longhouse.[49] It had been true once, of course, but these were hardly prisoners who could be assimilated. Joseph also opposed a reduction in the personnel of the Indian department. He was becoming more difficult every day. He wrote Sir John asking for snowshoes and canoes, as he planned to make an attack in the spring against some Oneidas who were living at Canajoharie.[50] Sir John relayed the request to Haldimand. The latter did not care what Joseph did to the Oneidas, but he warned that he must not touch the white inhabitants.[51]

When the news reached Niagara in early December that George Rogers Clark had struck a Shawnee village near the Ohio, Joseph and indeed all the Indians at the post were beside themselves with anger. The Six Nations held a private council without any white man being present, and decided to send deputies to Detroit to spirit up the Shawnees and to Montreal to await further instructions from Haldimand. The Indians told Brigadier General Allan Maclean, who had recently taken Powell's place at Niagara, that he "may let the great

General know that we shall remain no longer idle and see our Brethren and People destroyed by these cruel Rebels—since the Fate They have met with may be ours next, if we do not go to war to prevent it— We therefore desire that You will request the great General, in our Name, to assist us heartily in sharping our Ax."[52] The chiefs had spoken boldly—but they had spoken timidly, too. Maclean heard that Joseph Brant was disappointed because the council had not chosen to go to war without consulting anybody. However, since the Indians intended to consult the commander in chief, Joseph hoped the latter would have the humanity not to tie their hands. The situation of the Indians, Joseph had said (so it was reported to Maclean), was altogether different from that of the white people.[53]

On Christmas day Joseph tried to explain his sentiments to Sir John Johnson. He wrote his letter alone, without benefit of the secretarial help which he often employed. His English and spelling were not of pedagogical purity, but his meaning was clear enough. His tortured thoughts turned this way and that:

> I have been very uneasy since we had the News of the Shawanese Misfortune who fell in the hands of the white Savages Virginians and did alarmd the five Nations greatly and made them to hold Councils about the Matter & made Speeches to the General but badly translated into English— Wee the Indians wishes to have the blow Return'd on the Enemy as early as possible, but I am afrai[d] it will again [be] but trifling affair when our Speech gets below which is too often the case, which will be very vexatious affair, because we think the Rebels will ruin us at last if we go on as we do one year after another, doing nothing only Destroying the Government goods & they Crying all the while for the great Expences so we are in as it were between two Hells, I am sure you will assist all you can to Let us have an Expedition Early in the Spring Let it be great or small one, let us not hang our heads between our Knees and be looking there— I beg of you dont tell us to go Hunt Deer & find you selves Shoes. because we shall soon forget the War, that Ways for we are gone too far that way already against the Rebels to be doing other things—[54]

So ended the year 1782 for a distracted Joseph Brant. His infected ear still pained him a great deal, but he still looked forward to some stroke against the faithless Oneidas. All winter he worried about the fate of his people. The latter seemed suddenly to stand alone against the rebels. To make matters worse, the usual presents were not forthcoming, having arrived too late from England to be sent to the posts, and the Indians would have to go through the winter without warm clothing. Joseph looked at their rags and decided not to oppose the reduction in personnel in the Indian department. He had the forlorn hope that, in spite of Haldimand's orders against purchases from the local traders, the money saved might be spent on the Indians.[55] After all, the merchants had plenty of clothing for sale.

For some of the white Loyalists Christmas day was not a cheery occasion, either. John Butler, Sir John Johnson and Guy, Daniel Claus, and others who had been conspicuous as leaders in the war, knew that for them there could be no going home when peace came. Their estates were confiscated, their very lives proscribed. They would have to make a future for themselves on an alien soil. Dealing with the triumphant and vengeful rebels was out of the question. But other Loyalists, not so prominent, were rather looking forward to the final peace. Deserters, they knew, were living unmolested in the erstwhile colonies. Of course, deserters had been few of late, ever since General Haldimand had permitted the officers at the posts to send Indians after them to bring back their scalps—still, everybody knew of someone who had managed to return home and settle down in peace. Why should they not do the same? They were so weary of war. The fighting had been so hard and so long. They were glad to have done with it, and they were willing to make the best of a new order. Major Ross at Oswego tried in vain to arouse some of the old martial spirit in his Loyalists, and ended up by distrusting them. He noted in dismay that "the Colony Troops have not that relish for the War they had when carried on offensively; They do not think the King will succeed, and . . . they conclude that the best chance they have now is to make peace with the Rebels. . . . in short, their spirits are low, and I humbly beg leave to observe that the Troops raised from the Colonies are by no means so proper for this Garrison in the present situation of Affairs as British Soldiers—"[56] Obviously it did not occur to Ross nor to the hopeful Loyalists themselves that they had problems which bore any resemblance to those of Joseph Brant.

When General Haldimand heard about the Indians' complaints to Maclean and saw Joseph's Christmas letter (for of course Sir John sent him a copy), he was greatly concerned.[57] He instructed Maclean to discourage any ideas the Indians might have of revenge for Clark's attack on the Shawnees. He knew how difficult it was, he said, to find arguments against so natural an inclination, particularly in a people who "found their Rights, and Even their Existence upon the Principle of Retaliation, and Who Consider themselves, & in fact are a free People," but Maclean must do his best. Maclean was to tell the Indians that the commander in chief condoled with them for their sufferings as if they were his own flesh and blood. And though he could not help them carry on offensive warfare, and earnestly urged them not to do it on their own and not to tarnish their honor by an attack on the innocent (for they could hardly reach the guilty), he again promised to give them every support in protecting and defending their country.[58] And again Haldimand warned the ministry in London that "Policy, as well as gratitude, demands of us an attention to the Sufferings, and future Situation of these Unhappy People involved, on our account, in the miseries of War with an implacable Enemy."[59]

Haldimand's speech and a similar one from Sir John were reported to the Six Nations at a council at Niagara on April 1. Joseph Brant served as interpreter. Next day Sayengaraghta delivered the chiefs' reply. His words were calm enough, for the Indians had found out from Detroit that the rebel attack on the Shawnees had not been so serious or bloody as first reported. Sayengaraghta thanked Haldimand for his tender feelings toward their sufferings and for all his fatherly attentions. He reminded him that the Indians had restrained their young men from going to war or committing any cruelties on the rebels, "and," he added, "if we had the means of publishing to the World the many Acts of Treachery & Cruelty committed by them on our Women & Children, it wou'd appear that the title of Savages wou'd with much greater justice be applied to them than to us." (It always had hurt the Indians' feelings to be called "savages.") Sayengaraghta then ranged far and wide, naming Sir William Johnson as "the greatest and best Friend we ever had or ever heard of" and hoping that the Great Spirit above would enable Sir John to follow his father's example. He blamed nobody for the lack of presents, but he was happy that the presents were finally arriving and that the Indians would no longer be in want. Having heard that peace was nearly concluded, he hoped that "we may not be forgot, but be included with yourselves in such a manner as will be for both our interests—"[60]

On the whole General Maclean thought that the Indians were behaving well. Joseph, he said, had also explained the necessity for remaining quiet to a Delaware party who had recently visited the post. The one fly in Maclean's ointment was Joseph's trying to get the murderer of a local Indian punished. This irked Maclean considerably for, as he said, many Indians had been lying about the fort drunk for the past seven years and nobody hurt till now. The murder had best be forgotten, he implied.[61] And Joseph probably was persuaded to overlook the murder, for the next we hear of him he has gone with a white officer to Sayengaraghta's new village at Buffalo Creek to carry a message from Maclean and Butler. A council was held with the Indians, and Sayengaraghta, who was jittery because of some rumors, requested military aid from Maclean. He also asked Joseph to come with his warriors in case of a rebel attack on the village.[62]

All that winter and spring General Haldimand had kept expresses constantly on the go between Quebec and Detroit. He ordered scouts sent out toward Wyoming, Tioga, Fort Pitt, and the Mohawk. He wished to collect all the intelligence possible, to hear all the stories that were flying about. Perhaps some bit of news would give him some basis for acting; indeed, the general was almost as much at a loss what to do as the meanest of his retainers. He had exerted himself to reinforce and provision the upper posts, for he feared an attack somewhere in their vicinity. He was sure the rebels wanted to extend their frontiers and get the fur trade into their hands before peace was made, and he could point to Clark's late measures on the Ohio and an abortive attempt on Oswego by some Yorkers which seemed to prove his point. And of false alarms, of course, there were a great plenty, both among the Indians and the whites.

The suspense was broken for the general on the night of April 25, 1783, when he received from Carleton the king's proclamation for a cessation of arms and a copy of the preliminary peace treaty which had been signed at Paris nearly five months before. The boundaries between Canada and the victorious Americans were to run through the middle of the lakes. As if this were not bad enough, the treaty did not even mention the Indians! Haldimand decided not to make public the details of the treaty as long as he could avoid it, though he knew that somehow, some way, everybody would know them soon. He hoped he would hear something from England which would mitigate the blow to the Indians. And he instructed the officers at the posts that it was now more necessary than ever to watch the Indians, though without appearing to suspect them. To his friend, the German General Riedesel, he wrote of his great anxiety. "My soul is completely bowed down with grief," he concluded, "at seeing that we (with no absolute necessity), have humbled ourselves so much as to accept such humiliating boundaries. I am heartily ashamed, and wish I was in the interior of Tartary."[63]

Each post commander, as he in his turn received news of the treaty, tried to keep it secret, but to no avail. The awful truth, as Haldimand had feared, was soon out. At Oswego Major Ross noted in wonderment that the news just burst out all over. It was talked of at Niagara even before the general got his announcement from Carleton and at Detroit by the middle of May.

But nowhere did the desponding Indians make the slightest attempt to surprise any post or hurt any Englishman. The year 1783 was not the year 1763. The Indians had grown more "civilized." They were far more dependent on trade and gifts than they had been twenty years ago. And General Haldimand was not General Amherst. He treated them kindly, and they put confidence in his promise to help them if they needed it. Moreover, they still hoped the final peace would bring them better terms. They were heartily sick of the war, too. Even in 1763, except for part of the Senecas, most of the Six Nations had steered clear of Pontiac's schemes. But now the western Indians, who had been leading spirits in the old rebellion, were also disposed to wait and see. Their anger of the previous year subsided. They were willing to let bygones be bygones. Peace seemed a pleasant prospect in the west, too. Only Joseph Brant appeared irreconcilable. He lashed out at Maclean indignantly that "England had Sold the Indians to Congress."[64]

Joseph evidently exerted his own influence and such other influence as he could command, and got himself sent down at once to see Sir John and General Haldimand. He was already gone from Niagara by May 13. He had left in great perturbation of mind. Needless to say, he had also left General Maclean perturbed and upset. Maclean feared the Indians would do something "Very Outrageous" in order to curry favor with Congress and the Americans. Butler had reported to him that the Mohawk chiefs Aaron and David Hill, two friends of Joseph, had become alarmed, too, and were calling for a conference with their western allies. Maclean was going to try to prevent such a conference, at least until Joseph returned. He wrote headquarters advising that Brant be detained in Canada for a while, "for Joseph knows too Much and too Little, tho a good fellow in the main, he is a perfect Indian, and after all the News & intelligence he would Pick up in Canada Some True, & Some false, his returning here, might be attended with bad Consequences." Maclean also thought it very essential that Joseph, when he came back, should come back in a good humor; and he urged that Sir John be sent up immediately to quiet the worried Mohawks. If Joseph and the Mohawks behaved well, perhaps all would behave well.[65]

A few days later Maclean wrote a very long and earnest letter to Haldimand, telling about a conference he had just held with six principal chiefs, and relating all their fears (and his own) in great detail. The Indians found it almost impossible to believe, he said, that the boundaries actually were run as reported, and that Britain had not secured to them their own country. They were all the more unhappy in that some Oneida gossip had come to their ears that General Schuyler and the Americans were threatening to destroy the Six Nations, the Delawares, Hurons, and Shawnees, and all whites who had served with them. And the chiefs declared to Maclean that the Indians would die to the last man in defending their country. The king, they said, had no right to give up to the Yankees what was not his to give.

This new mood of the Indians frightened Maclean; "I would by no means answer for what they may do," he warned, "when they see us evacuate these Posts." He again urged that Joseph Brant be detained in Canada. Brant, he reasoned, "is much better informed and instructed than any other Indians, he is strongly attached to the interest of his Countrymen, for which I do honor him, but he would be so much more sensible of the miserable situation in which we have left this unfortunate People, that I do believe he would do a great deal of mischief here at the Time"; and he added, "I do from my soul Pity these People, and should they commit outrages at giving up these Posts, it would by no means surprize me."[66]

This was the letter which so impressed General Haldimand that he sent on the original to the ministry in London as fast as he could.

Joseph arrived in Montreal on Friday, May 16. He saw Sir John and Claus briefly and in great worry and haste set out for Quebec on the following Monday. With him went John Deseronto, leader of Claus's Fort Hunter Mohawks. Both had told Sir John that they might be willing to remove to the Canadian side of Lake Ontario or even to the St. Lawrence River, and Joseph had specified that some white Loyalists be settled nearby.[67] Even in his distracted state Joseph remembered that the Indians would need set before them an example of some good white farmers.

Two days later, on May 21, 1783, the very day of his arrival, Joseph was making his famous speech to General Haldimand. He had come, he said, to find out the real truth about whether or not the Indians shared in the peace between the king and the Bostonians. And he begged that the king should be reminded of "what we have been when his People first saw us, and what we since have done for him & his Subjects." Passionately he reminded Haldimand that "We the Mohawks were the first Indians that took you by the Hand like Friends and Brothers and invited you to live amongst us, treating you with Kindness upon your Debarkation in small Parties." The rest of the Five Nations approved the Mohawk action; "we were then a great People . . . and you in a manner but a handfull." As you increased, he said, we remained your friends, "joining you from time to time against

Your Enemies, Sacrificing Numbers of our People." We helped you to conquer Canada. Finally we joined you in war against the rebels, and you promised to defend us and our country against all encroachments. You have records which will confirm the truth of these words. And he reminded Haldimand of the great land cession of 1768, and of how, when war broke out, the Indians resisted the snares of the New England priests who tried to alienate them from the king, and how they protected their superintendent and other Loyalists and conducted them to Canada.

> Wherefore, Brother, I am now sent in behalf of all the King's Indian Allies to Receive a decisive Answer from You, and to know, Whether they are included in this Treaty with the Americans as faithful Allies should be, or not? and whether those Lands which the great being above has pointed out for our Ancestors & their Descendants, and placed them there from the beginning, and where the Bones of our Forefathers are Laid is secured to them? or whether the Blood of their grand children is to be mingled with their Bones, thro' the means of our Allies for whom We have often so freely bled?[68]

Haldimand, who expected some instructions from London regarding the Indians since there was nothing in the treaty to guide him, owned to the ministry that he was embarrassed. He did not know what to say. He gave Joseph his stock answer which the Indians had already heard several times, and put him off with the thought that a more specific reply would soon be forthcoming.[69] Then he talked to him about resettling his people in Canada, and Joseph appeared pleased at the idea.[70] Haldimand also gave Joseph a testimonial of his "entire Approbation of his laudable and disinterested Services to the Royal Cause, and of the Personal Esteem I shall always bear him on that account,"[71] and he authorized a pension of one hundred pounds (four hundred dollars) a year for Molly.[72]

Joseph was invited to dinner at the Castle of St. Louis, and it was there, in the midst of the commander's fine English furniture and beautiful spreading gardens, that the Baroness Riedesel saw him. "He conversed well," she said, "possessed polished manners, and was highly esteemed by General Haldimand. . . . He was dressed partly as a military man, and partly as an Indian. He had a manly and intelligent cast of countenance. His character was very gentle."[73] As usual, Joseph was not wearing his feelings on his sleeve.

To convince the Indians of his intention not to abandon them (and also because of Joseph's having mentioned they were in daily expectation of receiving proposals from the United States), Haldimand did what he could without waiting for further orders. He sent Major Samuel Holland, surveyor general of the province, to the old French post of Cataraqui (Kingston) to examine the north side of Lake Ontario with a view to finding a suitable home for those Indians who wished to go to Canada. Joseph was to accompany Holland as far as Cataraqui on his way back to Niagara, and it was fervently hoped that he would return home in a good mood. At the same time Haldimand ordered Sir John to go to Niagara and do what he could to calm the Indians there.[74]

The country that Joseph was to visit with Major Holland was the same country that his Wyandot forefathers had inhabited generations before. There, at the Bay of Quinte, could be seen the remains of a village where his "grandmother" had lived and from which she had fled to the temporary safety of an island before her capture by rampaging Mohawks.[75] At Montreal Joseph fell behind from illness, but eventually he and John Deseronto, who also came along, caught up with Holland and his surveyors. The two Indians, who were joined by some of Claus's Mohawks, went up to Cataraqui Falls and made some journeys of inspection into the woods. It was good land, and they told Holland they would decide where to settle as soon as they examined the whole north shore of the lake. Some of the accompanying Indians were sent to watch the rest of the survey.[76]

Joseph and Captain John went on to Niagara, reaching that post on July 5. General Maclean was happy to see that they seemed in good humor. He gave them rum (without which, he said, nothing could be done), and sent them off to tell the Indians who lived nearby what they had heard from General Haldimand and what they had found on the north side of the lake. They returned on July 9 and in fine spirits, for all the chiefs had given them a good reception. Maclean heaved a great sigh of relief.[77]

Sir John, not very pleased at his assignment and grumbling as much as he dared (for anybody, he said, could do the job as well as he could), showed up at Niagara on July 18. He formally took the hatchet out of the Six Nations' hands (a ceremony they had been waiting for) and delivered to them Haldimand's set speech. A throng of 1,685 Indians crowded around, and all could see the great piles of presents which Sir John had brought.

The councils lasted till July 31, off and on. Sir John condoled, and Sir John reassured. He explained that the placing of the boundary line had nothing to do with whether the Indians retained their lands on

the American side. Those lands had been reserved to the Indians at
the treaty of Fort Stanwix in 1768, and regardless of the outcome of
the war the lands still belonged to them. And the king, he comforted
them, still considers the Indians his faithful allies, and will continue
to promote their happiness by his protection, his encouragement of
trade, and all other benefits in his power. Then Sir John recommended that they bear their losses with fortitude, give up their prisoners, and forgive and forget what is past.

Joseph was present as an officer of the Indian department,[78] but it
was Sayengaraghta who got to the heart of the problem and posed the
important question for the Indians. It is true, he said, "we have been
very uneasy, and with much reason; our fears relative to our Country
having given us great concern, (but should the Americans molest, or
Claim any part of our Country, we shall then ask assistance of the
King our Father who still considers us his faithful Allies, and Children, & will continue to promote our happiness by his protection, and
encouragement)."[79] Then he thanked Sir John for relieving their uneasy minds and promised to comply with his requests. Sir John could
make no further answer. It was the sort of problem and the sort of
question which British authorities preferred to ignore. On the whole,
however, both Sir John and General Maclean thought the Six Nations had behaved "incomparably well." For once they did not inquire
into what Joseph Brant, who had said nothing, was thinking.

Such important transactions must be told to the western Indians as
soon as possible. Sir John had to send them a speech, too, for as yet
they still held the ax in their hands and, to tell the truth, some of the
young braves were still wielding the ax in a sporadic way. The Six
Nations seized at this chance to meet with their allies and to discuss
their mutual peril. They chose their best delegates, some forty or fifty
chiefs and warriors, and proposed to Sir John that they should go to
Sandusky and organize the general confederacy of Indians which had
been under discussion for so long. It was to be a union of thirty-five
nations, with the Six Nations, of course, as the head. It was an
ambitious project, worthy of Joseph Brant, who was undoubtedly the
prime mover.

This project appealed to the British. The Indians needed to be
strong at the moment, and a firm union would be the best protection
for Canada and the fur trade. The authorities made no difficulty at all
and even helped as much as possible by sending a schooner loaded
with presents to Sandusky. There could be no doubt that the proposed
confederacy had the official blessing.

The large Six Nation delegation, of which of course Joseph Brant was a member, went first to Detroit where they transacted some pre-liminary business.[80] Indians could make haste when they thought it necessary, and the delegates were all at Sandusky by August 26. Hordes of other Indians—whole villages, indeed—were daily arriving. Drawn by worries about what was to happen to them and by the lure of presents, men, women, and children came from every direction. There were Delawares and Wyandots from Upper Sandusky, Hurons from Detroit, Shawnees from the Scioto and Mingoes from the upper Ohio, Ottawas from south and east of Saginaw Bay, Chippewas from Lake Huron, and very likely some stray Miamis from the headwaters of the Maumee River. There were also wanderers from almost anywhere where news of the meeting could penetrate, as well as people who bore the name of some isolated village and who had been dignified by the name "nation" even though they actually belonged to the larger groups. Many of these Indians were Algonquians whose language and customs differed from those of the Iroquois and who were likely to be suspicious of Iroquois designs. A large delegation of Creeks and Cherokees from the south was also present, having come, as it hap-pened, in answer to a Six Nations friendship belt of two years before which had been sent as far as Florida and which had received the approval of the British Indian agency at St. Augustine. These dele-gates from the south had been months on the way, and it was a lucky chance that they were on hand at this time. White officers also came from Niagara and Detroit, and Alexander McKee and Matthew El-liott, the two most influential members of the Indian department at Detroit, supervised the proceedings.

The main business was transacted from September 5 to September 8. There were the usual condolences, the usual wiping of eyes so that all might see and understand. Sir John, by a speech which he had sent and which was delivered by Alexander McKee, solemnly buried the hatchet and proclaimed peace. Then he repeated the same assurances he had made at Niagara as to British friendship for the Indians and as to the latter's continued right in their soil. Nearly every important chief now got a chance to say his say; and the burden of all was the defense of their country, for the latest news was grim. American boats were already going down the Ohio to who knew where, and Kentucky people had already been seen north of the river.

Joseph himself made a long speech. He summed up in much detail what the Indians had done for the king during the war. There was a clear implication that it was now time for the king to do something for the Indians. He, too, emphasized the fact that the peace treaty did not legally deprive the Indians of their lands. They still owned everything beyond the Fort Stanwix line, he insisted. Had not Sir John told him this, and General Haldimand, too, for that matter?

Then Joseph proposed the idea of a firm and lasting union of all the Indians. It was the only way the Indians could defend their rights. "Brothers and Nephews," he addressed them, showing them a great belt of wampum: "You the Hurons, Delawares, Shawanese, Mingoes, Ottawas, Chippeweys, Poutteawatamies, Creeks & Cherokees. We the Six Nations with this belt bind your Hearts and minds with ours, that there may be never hereafter a separation between us, let there be Peace or War, it shall never disunite us, for our Interests are alike, nor should anything ever be done but by the voice of the whole as we make but one with you."

The Indians had laid down the hatchet, Joseph continued, but if necessary they would take it up again in defense of their rights.[81] He did not say that the British would take up the hatchet to help them, but it was what he hoped and what all of his people expected.

The Indians readily agreed to the formation of a union. In union was strength—that, all could see. Then some of the chiefs were deputed to go back with Joseph and the other Six Nations delegates to Niagara. At Niagara, on October 6, all the proceedings at Sandusky were solemnly confirmed. The union was an accomplished fact.[82] It was the old Iroquois "empire" in a new guise, and even greater than before, for the old empire, despite Iroquois boasts, had never really included the hostile Creeks and Cherokees. There were Indians who could see this as well as Joseph could, and who were already torn between their interest and their dislike for the Six Nations.

The erstwhile rebels could scarcely wait to drain the cup of victory. For months they had been poised to take over the posts, to deal with the Indians and the Loyalists in a way that they thought proper. They yearned to pay back those vile miscreants for what they had suffered. Then they meant to get on with the business of their freedom—to overrun the wilderness and take their rightful place in the family of nations. The intensity of their impatience was almost overpowering.

The victors knew they got all the news first. When formal notice of the provisional treaty came, Washington apprised the commander at Niagara by letter, since, as he said, General Haldimand could not have told him of it; and he wanted to stop the Indian attacks at once. General Maclean replied in due course, saying the attacks had already been stopped. Later, under instructions from Congress, Washington sent his good friend, Baron von Steuben, to Canada to make arrangements for taking over the posts. To this Haldimand demurred, as he had received no orders on the subject. In the far-off Kentucky country the commander at the falls of the Ohio dispatched a flag of truce to the Shawnees with a view to an exchange of prisoners. Detroit offered no objection. Then some American traders from Schenectady sailed their way past the amazed Ross at Oswego and headed for Niagara to sell rum!

At the same time ominous portents were coming in from the States. The Americans were not repealing their laws against the Loyalists—they were stiffening them, if anything—and newspapers from Boston to Savannah reported meetings and resolutions against those "abominable Wretches," the Tories. Those "Robbers, Murderers, and Incendiaries" were not to be allowed to return home. Major Ross, who had just seen a paper which listed fifty men of his garrison whose little properties had been confiscated, noted the downcast looks around him and admitted in a shamefaced sort of way that his Loyalists were brave and faithful. He could not really distrust them, he said. As for the Indian lands, it was reported that some were already being set aside for disbanded rebel soldiers; and in various places across the Ohio surveyors could be seen plying their trade and squatters actually building cabins.

Though hardly an American now lived who knew the way through the Indian country, Congress sent three intrepid commissioners on a dangerous mission to the upper posts to confer with the Indians about a peace treaty. The commanders at Detroit and Niagara received the official visitors politely. They managed to be both friendly and standoffish while absolutely forbidding any meetings with the Indians in the current uncertain situation. Joseph, however, contrived to get some words in private with Ephraim Douglass, one of the Americans. This did not please General Maclean, but he could do nothing about it. Joseph had the run of the post, and it was Joseph who initiated the meeting. Douglass got a chance to explain his business with the Indians, and he and Joseph "had a good deal of friendly argument," for Joseph insisted that his people would make no peace treaty until their lands were secured to them. Though Maclean would not permit Joseph to take Douglass to the Mohawk village, the American later reported to his superiors that he could see the Indians were "heartily tired of the war and sincerely disposed to Peace."[83]

General Schuyler, who thought it best to try to get along with the Indians rather than to drive them off to Canada to add their strength to that of the British, sent the Six Nations a friendly message in late July. He denied that he had sent them an unfriendly message which had been credited to him by some Oneidas, and he asked them to meet with him in council to discuss a future peace treaty. The Indians answered politely—far too politely, thought Sir John Johnson, who believed the answer might have been different if so many of the chiefs had not been absent at Sandusky; and even General Haldimand thought the reply lacked "Spirit & Energy."

When the delegates got home from Sandusky, the Six Nations sent Schuyler another speech. This speech was written in Mohawk and signed by Joseph Brant. Its tone was considerably firmer. Joseph told Schuyler that "the Six Nations & Confederates have unanimously agreed to live in Peace and Friendship with Congress, provided thier intentions be agreable and leave our possessions undisturbed." He let him know that the Indians intended to insist upon the boundary line of 1768.[84]

At last the long wait was over. Negotiators who knew little of the Indians and cared less, had done their work. They had tried to take care of the interests of the white Loyalists and the merchants, but what did the disposition of a few savages matter? Having given up the country in which the savages lived, they had no more concern for it or them. General Haldimand had hoped that the definitive treaty or some additional instructions from government would provide words of comfort for the Indians. But nobody had paid much attention to Haldimand's anxious letters. Scarcely a voice had been raised in England on the Indians' behalf. The boundary remained as before.

Notification of the final peace treaty signed at Paris on September 3, 1783, reached the Congress of the United States at the end of October. The news spread from the American capital like wildfire. Before the snow fell the Indians had heard the worst. Knowing nothing of the complications of international affairs and baffled at how they could lose a war when, so far as they could see, they had been winning the battles, and when, as Joseph said, they were prepared to go on fighting,[85] they learned they were left alone to settle their destiny as best they could.

Again the Indians had not even been mentioned in the treaty. It was as though they did not exist.

17

Outrageous Fortune

GENERAL HALDIMAND need never have worried. There was no Indian uprising. Years of dependence had done their work. Little fight was left in the Six Nations, and Haldimand soon realized he could gift away such resentments as they had.

A bitter winter, almost as harsh as that of 1779–80, passed, with Haldimand preparing various appeasements and encouraged in his efforts by a letter from the more sympathetic Lord North who was back in the government for a time. North agreed that England must not forsake her Indians. He also felt that all friendly Indians should be encouraged to move to Canada. "It is to be hoped," he said, "that from thence they will be able to carry on their Hunting on their former Grounds, and return with their Furs and Peltry, where the British Traders can meet them, with their wives and children, in security, and being under our protection their attachment to His Majesty may continue, and this Country may enjoy the advantages of their Trade."[1]

Tools and agricultural implements to help the Indians with their new settlements were being sent over from England, and General Haldimand empowered Sir John Johnson to buy land on the north side of Lake Ontario for the future settlers, both white and Indian. Though Joseph claimed the Six Nations were the real owners of the land and none else need be consulted,[2] the Missisaugas (a branch of the Chippewas) were on the spot, and Haldimand thought it best to satisfy them. The purchase went through in the autumn of 1783. Because of the ancient hostility between the Missisaugas and the Six Nations Sir John was very careful not to tell the sellers that the Six Nations meant to occupy some of the newly bought ground. Major Ross was sent from

Oswego to set up a post where old Fort Frontenac had once stood, and by February 1784 mills and other buildings were going up in the new town of Cataraqui. Among these buildings, on the west side of the harbor, on crown lands near the old fort, were a house for Joseph Brant and another for Molly. Molly had requested a house for herself in the town, and Haldimand thought a dwelling nearby would please Joseph. When Joseph was absent on business for the Indians, Molly could take care of his family, Haldimand reasoned.[3]

A very gratified Joseph saw his house going up on February 17, when he passed through Cataraqui on his way down the country to visit the general, and he left in a very good humor.[4] He was going again to confer with Haldimand, having been sent by his people at Niagara. There could have been no doubt among the Mohawks that Joseph was the proper person to go on such an errand. Though David Hill had been sent along, too, Joseph would do the talking. Joseph's influence was steadily rising. He was not only the acting principal war chief at a time when war chiefs were by custom pre-eminent, he was rapidly taking on civilian duties as well. He was becoming a sachem in everything but name. He never claimed the name of the office and, indeed, could not. But he always knew he was carrying out the duties of a sachem.[5]

Arriving in Montreal, Joseph consulted Sir John again, and no doubt his friend Claus, but Guy Johnson, whom he might have looked to for advice, was no longer available. The year before, Joseph and Sir John, too, had done their loyal best to facilitate Guy's return to Niagara,[6] but had achieved nothing. A stern General Haldimand refused to let Guy resume his work with the Indians, placing on his shoulders the ultimate responsibility for the frauds perpetrated by Taylor & Forsyth, whether he profited by them or not. Haldimand obviously suspected that Guy was involved in the frauds. The latter, trying to straighten out his affairs, both public and private, finally gave up accomplishing anything in America and sailed for England in the fall of 1783. In truth, the unfortunate Guy Johnson was never to see the end of the Taylor & Forsyth case.

Joseph immediately made known his business to Sir John. He proposed a settlement for the Mohawks, not on the north shore of Lake Ontario as first decided upon, but much more to the west. The Mohawks now preferred to move to the Grand River, a stream flowing into Lake Erie about forty miles from Buffalo Creek where some Delawares had already located.[7] The reasons for the change in plans were political: The Senecas and other Six Nations Indians who felt they were far enough away from the American frontier not to have to move to Canada, had upbraided the Mohawks for getting them into the war and running out on them and leaving them to their fate. The Senecas thought all the Six Nations would be better off if they stayed closer together, and they offered to let the Mohawks live on their land. Though Joseph and the Mohawks at Niagara refused Seneca land, they could see the justice and the advantage of the Seneca proposal. They were willing to change their plans, and they hoped to persuade Claus's Mohawks to see the situation the same way and go with them to the Grand River. The entire Six Nations would be the stronger.[8]

General Haldimand was glad to acquiesce. Of course the Six Nations, if they remained close together, would be the stronger in any confrontation with the Americans. So, too, would the British gain strength from the increased strength of the Indians and, what was of great importance, they could all the more likely secure the fur trade to themselves. Haldimand promised Joseph all possible help: a grant of land on the Grand River (which he would purchase from the local Missisaugas), tools, seeds, provisions to tide the new emigrants over till they could support themselves, a schoolmaster, a clergyman, a church, even a church bell. Joseph's instructions from the council on all these points had been very explicit, and he had made numerous requests which Haldimand had been pleased to grant. Joseph had also given Haldimand a detailed list of the losses of the Mohawks in the war and had asked that they be recompensed accordingly. The losses came to nearly sixteen thousand pounds New York currency. Haldimand immediately granted the Indians fifteen hundred pounds and promised to refer the rest of the claims to London. Since Parliament was granting recompense for losses to all the Loyalists, he thought the Indians would have no trouble getting their part.[9]

Joseph again broached the subject of whether the Indians could expect British military aid in any war with the Americans over their land, and got from Haldimand the same set answer—that he had no instructions on the matter yet, but that he personally would always remain the friend of the Indians. He again denied that the king had given up the Indians' rights in their land to the Americans.[10]

Baffled, Joseph took up the question with Major Mathews, Haldimand's secretary. Joseph and Mathews were as good friends as two such different men in their different positions could be, and Mathews evidently gave earnest thought to his reply. A candid man, he came as near as he dared to telling Joseph the truth. He, too, denied that the king had ceded the Indian lands to the Americans—meaning, of course, that in the British view they still possessed the right of occupancy—and in a roundabout sort of way he agreed that the Indians ought to defend their right. But if war occurred between the Indians and the Americans, the commander in chief could not help his Indian friends unless they were attacked on the British side of the border. This was the law by which Christians lived. Surely Joseph must realize that.[11]

While still at Montreal waiting for the ice to break, Joseph heard that Schuyler had sent the Indians another message, and that he was wanted back at Niagara as soon as possible.[12] He made all haste and arrived back at the post on May 14. He found his people in much confusion because of Schuyler's message and because of all the rumors and gossip that inevitably swirled around it. The message, which answered Joseph's firm speech of the previous autumn, was equally firm. It upbraided the Six Nations for their part in the war and re-minded them again that they were not mentioned in the peace treaty. Nevertheless, said Schuyler, Congress was willing to give the Indians peace. They were to receive a message from Congress soon regarding terms.[13] Oneida gossip added that the Americans meant to force the Indians to agree to everything they wanted or cut them off from the face of the earth. Under these circumstances Joseph, who had planned to remove at once to the new settlement, decided that all the Indians had better stay where they were. This, he thought, would give courage to the faint-hearted and faltering who feared to deal with the Ameri-cans. He and his Mohawks were not going to abandon their brothers in distress.[14]

Peace or no peace, Joseph felt very bitter at times. Occasionally his bitterness spilled over into what the Indian department thought were new and dangerous areas. While in lower Canada, the St. Regis Indians had complained to him that the local agent was trying to force them to sell land for a Loyalist settlement. Joseph had written Sir John indignantly, advising that the Canadian Indians ought to be treated "in easy manner." Otherwise, he said, "it gives the dam Rebels larger mouths for many things against us and it is very good Example for them, to get all our lands from us, if those Saint Rechis Indians was any any [sic] ways forced a bout lands." Then, being Joseph, and an Indian born, he weakened his indignant posture by asking Sir John to send him a blue-laced coat![15]

About this time an old friend found Joseph greatly changed. The Reverend John Stuart, who had not seen Joseph in nine years, showed up at Niagara in June 1784. Stuart had spent most of the war on parole in Schenectady, enduring much hardship, sending intelligence to Haldimand now and then (though he had sworn he would not), and finally getting off to Canada in 1781, where he became chaplain to Sir

John Johnson's regiment. Now that the war was over, Stuart could resume his missionary work. He visited Captain John Deseronto's new village at the Bay of Quinte (for all Joseph's and Haldimand's persuasions could not induce John to go to the Grand River), and stopped at several white Loyalist settlements where, as he said, he had to start all over again to teach morality and the Scriptures, the people not having seen a clergyman in years. On this tour he also called at the busy town of Niagara (for the post had altogether burst its walls) and was able to renew many acquaintances from Mohawk valley days. June 20 found him preaching at Joseph's church at the landing, where even the windows were filled with eager listeners who could not crowd inside.

As Stuart told it years later to his friend, John Strachan, he was shocked at the change in Joseph Brant. Brant, who had helped so willingly with the translations of the New Testament, who had been so religious, was now cynical about the church! He spoke very freely of persons in the government! He dared to criticize the king! Stuart recoiled in horror. He attributed the disagreeable alteration in Brant's character to the bad company he had met in England. The change in "this miserable man" was the work of freethinkers and the outspoken political opposition who had flattered and caressed him and pandered to his basest desires and set him so wicked an example by ridiculing religion and authority. Nothing else, thought Stuart, could have made the devout and loyal Brant he had once known speak disrespectfully of government and the church.[16] But Stuart was not a man of unusual discernment.

June was a busy time for the Indians at Niagara. Early in the month a messenger came from Governor Clinton and commissioners who represented the state of New York. New York, having already granted some of the Indian lands within its borders to its disbanded soldiers, proposed to make a treaty with the Six Nations. Though it was confusing for the Indians to have to deal with two governmental entities at once, Joseph immediately saw the advantage of playing off Congress against the state.[17] He sensed that Congress and the state had some opposing views, and he was, of course, right. There was a complex legal question involved as to whether New York could lawfully treat with the Indians. The federal government disapproved of New York's action but, being very weak, could do nothing except disapprove. Joseph knew little of legal niceties, but he knew something was wrong between the two governments and he hoped to profit by it. In the meantime he was receiving advice from General Haldimand and the Indian department as to how to conduct himself. He was to take care that no Canadian Indians or anyone else in sympathy

A View of Niagara taken from the Heights near Navy Hall, c. 1783. Water-color by James Peachey. Fort Niagara, when Joseph frequented it, was a very busy place, a settlement both civil and military, with many dwelling houses, places of private business, and shipping. *Courtesy of The Public Archives of Canada, Ottawa. C-2035.*

with the French got to the treaty. He was to refuse to hold the treaty at Albany or far within the American lines. Though he was to make peace, he was to admit to no weakness; indeed, he was to speak very firmly to Schuyler and all the other Americans, whether representatives of Congress or of the state of New York. Above all, he was to see that the Americans got no chance to seduce the Indians from their alliance with Great Britain.[18]

Peter Ryckman, agent of the New York commissioners, had some explicit orders, too. Governor Clinton had instructed him to find out who were the Indian leaders at Niagara. When he discovered who the leaders were, he was to placate and flatter them and make them private promises. "To Captain Brandt," said Clinton, "You will hint that our People in general are pleased with his Generosity to the Prisoners he took during the War, and that he may become a great Man if he conducts himself in such a Manner as will give the Commissioners Occasion to believe that he means to be a sincere Friend."[19]

Though Ryckman was to keep secret the object of his journey by representing himself as having come to collect some private debts, he found that such a secret could not be kept at Niagara. The real reason for his mission was soon out in the open, and he had to hold public councils with the Indians which the British Indian department, perforce, could witness. It was not the most comfortable situation for Ryckman, but he made the best of it, and delivered the Indians an invitation from the New York commissioners for a peace conference at German Flats.

In consequence of this invitation a great council was held at the Loyal Confederate Village at the landing on June 6. Chiefs and warriors of the entire Six Nations were present, and even a few Delawares. Joseph Brant answered for the Indians. After referring to the tone of Schuyler's speeches which he said made peacemaking appear very difficult, and after mentioning that the Indians had heard Virginians were crossing the Ohio (which he said darkly might cause serious consequences), he agreed that the Indians desired peace. He promised that the Six Nations and some of their confederates would meet the New York commission in council as soon as possible, and he suggested that the council fire be removed to Fort Stanwix. He also declared that instead of making peace with one state, "we Expect to make one peace with the whole." He thus put the men of New York on notice that the new Indian confederacy meant to stand together in all negotiations and that it meant to treat with all its old enemies at once.[20]

General Haldimand was pleased at Joseph's proposal to change the meeting place, and the Americans were not displeased. The New York commissioners agreed that Fort Stanwix would be a better place to hold the peace council than German Flats. The people on the Tryon County frontier, they had to admit, "are generally unruly, and don't like to see Indians since the affair of General Herkermer."[21] So it was decided.

General Haldimand was also pleased with the rest of Joseph's proposals and even favored strengthening them.[22] But the Americans, as will be seen, whether New Yorkers or federal commissioners, chose to ignore Joseph's other points. The Americans were not impressed by the Mohawk's assumed attitude of strength and firmness. They knew where the strength lay.

Nothing daunted, Joseph persisted. On July 21 he wrote Henry Glen, one of the New York commissioners, a letter reiterating his stand. Saying he spoke "in behalf of the Confederates," he told Glen that chiefs of the western nations were on their way to attend the treaty, and he asked the New Yorker to notify Congress. He wanted all interested parties, whether federal or state, to appear, he said, "as we wish to settle Matters Finally at this Councel with all Consernd."[23]

It appeared as though Joseph might get his way. Congress was very suspicious of what New York was up to. Both sides wanted to get to the Indians first, and it began to look as though both sides in their anxiety might arrive at the meeting place at the same time. Congress, through newly appointed commissioners, sent the Indians the message that Schuyler had told them to expect. The commissioners of the United States would confer with them at Fort Stanwix on September 20. As a mark of their sincerity the Indians were to bring with them all their prisoners.

Joseph and nine other Six Nations delegates set out from Niagara on August 11. As they set out, he wrote Glen that all the delegates were war chiefs, and not empowered to make a final peace but only to arrange preliminaries. They intended to wait at Oneida till they heard properly authorized deputies from the United States were on their way to Fort Stanwix. After the preliminary arrangements had been made, a more general meeting could take place to establish "an everlasting Peace and Friendship between all the Nations and the United States."[24]

The New Yorkers would have none of this. They insisted, in answer to Joseph's letter of July 21, that the treaty with the state must take place at once, whether representatives of Congress were on hand or not.[25] Governor Clinton, who sent this message over his own signature, had come up from New York City and had been fretting at Albany over the long delay for many days. He and his fellow commissioners and a number of men appointed as associates, as soon as they heard Joseph Brant and the other Indians were nearing Oneida, immediately set out up the Mohawk, carrying with them as many maps of the western country as they could obtain. Several bateau-loads of provisions accompanied them and others had already gone before, for of course they expected to feed the hungry Indian delegates as well as themselves and employees. Before he started, Clinton thoughtfully wrote Peter Ryckman who was going to act as interpreter and who was already on the scene, "If you find that any Jealousy of, or envy to Brant privails, you will try to discover who are most jealous or envious of him, and promote it as much as you prudently can."[26]

By the time Joseph and his companions reached Oneida country, Ryckman was ready to receive them. Ryckman reported that the fact that so few Indian delegates were coming, and even those without full powers, was all a scheme of Brant. Had it not been for Brant, he said, the entire Six Nations would have come down to the treaty. He also reported that Brant was worried lest the Six Nations come anyway. He recounted in detail his own efforts to overturn the chief's schemes.

His efforts had been considerable. Ryckman was doing all he could to cause Joseph trouble.[27]

It was a game that two could play. Joseph, who realized that the state of New York was more intent on getting land than on renewing the covenant chain of friendship with the Indians, managed to drive a little wedge between the state authorities and their old ally, Samuel Kirkland. Kirkland and his Oneidas were now, of course, back at their old homes. Somebody (who could it have been?) told the Oneidas that New York secretly plotted to seize their land and force them to move farther west. This caused the Oneidas to balk at going to the treaty, and Joseph with no little malice informed Ryckman that it was Kirkland who had spilled the secret.[28] The New Yorkers, who did have their eyes on Oneida land, regretfully gave it up for the moment. They assured their Indian friends that their land was safe, and the Oneidas were at length prevailed on to attend the peacemaking. Throughout the proceedings the Oneidas basked happily in the favor of the New York commissioners. Between them and the rest of the Six Nations was a gulf of hostility, deep and wide. Though the war was over, and all the Indians were equally poor and wretched, there was still the distinction of Whigs and Tories among them, and they hated each other accordingly.

As Joseph Brant and his party headed without delay toward the new blockhouse at Fort Stanwix (for Joseph refused to stay in Oneida any longer than he had to),[29] few men have ever been in a more anomalous position for carrying on a successful negotiation. Neither the Americans, the British, the French, or any other white people could have really considered them the representatives of a sovereign power. In the earliest French wars the Six Nations had been strong enough to exercise a sort of quasi-sovereignty. No one had tried to stop them from carrying on independent negotiations for the exchange of prisoners. But as the British colonies grew more powerful, the British claimed to speak for "our" Indians. At the end of King George's War, in 1748, this was a hotly disputed point with the French, who then, since it was to their own interest, professed to believe the Iroquois an independent nation. The stronger British were able to carry their point finally, at least as far as the Mohawks were concerned, and negotiated for the return of Mohawk prisoners, a few of whom languished in jail as much as three years while the dispute was going on. At the end of the last French war, in 1763, there was, of course, no dispute. The French gave up Canada, and with it, the Indians. Similarly, in 1783, the British had abandoned the Indians to the Americans. General Haldimand referred to the Six Nations as "a free people." By this he meant no more than that it was usually impossible to bring an Indian to justice in the ordinary way; the Indians, living distant from white settlements, were not much subject to white laws. He also meant that the Indians owned the land they occupied and hunted upon, and here he was on historically firm ground. The Indians always had been paid for their land cessions. Even when they had been cheated, it was always claimed that they had been paid. No one had asserted that they ought not to be paid. The worst squatter had been wont to claim (and no doubt believed) that he had some sort of agreement with somebody for something.

But as to whether the Six Nations were even a quasi-sovereign power, if they had ever been so, they as losers in a bitter war were so no longer. James Duane, member of Congress from New York and, indeed, chairman of the committee of Congress on Indian affairs, expressed the prevailing opinion very well when he said, "They are used to be called Brethren, Sachems and Warriors of the Six Nations. I hope it will never be repeated. It is sufficient to make them sensible that they are spoken to: without complementing 20 or 30 Mohawks as a nation and a few more Tusceroroes & Onondagoes as distinct nations. It woud be not less absurd than mischievous. They shoud rather be taught that by separating from the Oneidas, and entering into a wicked war, they had weakened and destroyed themselves and that the publick opinion of their importance had long since ceased."[30]

There was another factor which militated against the Indians in a subtle way, and always had hurt them in their dealings with white people. Joseph and his party did not think of bringing their own provisions to the treaty. They expected to be fed at Fort Stanwix by the state of New York and then later by the federal government. White men had always provided for the Indians at treaties and councils, and it made no difference where such meetings were held. Whether at home or abroad, the Indians expected to be fed. It was the way Indian affairs had always been run. But a custom begun in Indian strength had lost its efficacy in Indian weakness. A dependent is seldom in a position to strike a good bargain. It is all the harder to gain something from an adversary if at the same time one depends on him for sustenance. How strange that not one Indian negotiator ever appears to have thought of such a thing! The idea did not occur to Joseph Brant, though he was in general sharp enough. The Indians took what they were given and even asked for more. Nor did they hesitate to complain if all was not to their liking. White people, of course, considered this aspect of Indian affairs a great nuisance, and it always figured in what they paid for land and what they would or would not do.

The first ten days of September were occupied with negotiations, public and private. The New York commissioners demanded their pound of flesh. They must have some land near Oswego and Niagara. They also wanted to establish "boundary lines" between the state and those Indians who lived within the state. This meant, as they were frank enough to say, a land cession. It was only right that the Indians should give up some land to the state, since the people of the state had been so hardly used by them during the war.

Joseph made two public speeches. He was the main expounder of the Indian point of view. In his first speech, on September 7, his remarks were mostly introductory, and he seemed to yield to the New Yorkers' desire to have their treaty take place before that of Congress.[31] The second speech, on September 10, contained the real substance of the reply to the New York demands. It was obvious that Joseph did not intend to enter into any definitive treaty with New York before peace was made with the United States, no matter how conciliatory he might sound.

> Brothers, [he said] We now reply that the request you make for Lands for the above purposes in general, and the manner in which you have made it we as Deputies think reasonable. But we must observe to you, that we are sent in order to make peace, and that we are not authorized, to stipulate any particular cession of Lands, we shall however recommend it to our respective Nations and we beleive they will meet your wishes to specify to you, the Lands they are willing to grant to you. This Business we expect the[y] will treat with you about, as soon as the Treaty with the Commissioners of Congress is ended.

Land about Oswego belonged in this category. Any grant there would be taken care of after the treaty with Congress. As to land at Niagara, it had been ceded to the king long ago.[32] In other words, when General Haldimand surrendered the posts, the land about them would pass at the same time.

The New York commissioners had to be satisfied with this. They left provisions to last till the representatives of Congress should arrive, gave instructions to two spies, and adjourned the conference. Joseph, though seeming to yield, had done what he set out to do. The main treaty would be with Congress, and it would be general as far as the Indians were concerned, for deputies from the newly formed Indian confederacy were waiting at Niagara and would take their proper part in the proceedings. Joseph wrote his friend, Aaron Hill, on September 9, urging him and the rest of the Six Nations and the western delegates to set out for Fort Stanwix immediately. He thought everything seemed likely to be settled in accordance with their wishes. Affairs were really going very well. He anticipated no disputes about land.[33]

Joseph had other reasons to be pleased, too. He had tried to establish friendly relations with George Clinton, and flattered himself that he had succeeded. He made bold to request information about the status of Mohawk land at Canajoharie and even broached the subject of the governor's aid in getting back their confiscated Johnson property for Molly's four eldest children. Clinton assured Joseph that no Indian land had ever been confiscated. He spoke truly. He might also have added that amid such a plethora of long established, good rebel claimants who had already taken over, where was the necessity for confiscation? Though Molly's children's land was a different matter, in that business, too, Clinton promised to act as Joseph's mediator with the state.[34] It seems incredible that Joseph could have been so naive as to take hope at the governor's words. In reality Clinton was as cold as an iceberg to any pretensions of his. The man who had so furiously pursued Sir John Johnson and his Tories and Indians in 1780, and counted up their depredations, and who had sworn that he would "almost submit to any thing or undergo any Trouble" to catch them was hardly the man to oblige Brant and the children of Molly and Sir William.

Joseph also took up these matters privately with commissioner Peter Schuyler and associate commissioner Mathew Visscher, and seems to have got some promises from them, too.[35] None of these promises ever did him the least good, even though Visscher was to write Governor Clinton, "It is evident to me that Brandt ought to be made our Friend, and I am inclined to think it will be no difficult Matter to effect it."[36] If the New Yorkers could play devious games, Joseph could, too. But Clinton was more suspicious than Visscher. Brant was not likely to desert British interests, he thought. However, on the off chance that he could do something trifling and achieve something big, the governor directed state authorities to send Joseph the information and papers he had requested.[37] If Joseph got the information, it was all he ever got from Clinton. For years and years the elder Johnson children would try vainly to get back their land. As for the Canajoharie Indians, they had abandoned theirs, and possession was eleven points of the law. In time the Canajoharies managed to sell some land at Nowadaga Creek and the lower Mohawks sold their claim at Fort Hunter to private buyers,[38] but over a decade would pass before all the Mohawk claims were extinguished by the state.

After the New York commissioners left, Joseph stayed on at Fort Stanwix in order to do his business with the agents of Congress. Another man also lingered behind, and the two, thrown into each other's company, struck up a sort of friendship. Young James Monroe, representative in Congress from Virginia, was on the first leg of a proposed extensive western tour. He had stopped at Fort Stanwix to observe what Governor Clinton and friends were up to and, since the post of Detroit must soon be handed over to the United States, he meant to go on to Detroit, and thence to Fort Pitt, to see with his own eyes some of the western land his state had ceded to the federal government. When a party of New York traders showed up at Fort Stanwix en route west, Monroe made plans to join them.[39]

In the meantime nothing had been heard from the commissioners of Congress. Were they on their way? It was strange that they had sent no word. Joseph was in a great quandary. His inclination pulled him toward Niagara, where Catharine had just given birth to Joseph, Jr., their first-born.[40] The proud father could not have been unaware of the fact that the baby was in line to become some day the Tekarihoga, first sachem of the Mohawks. No doubt that thought added to his joy. But urgent business called Joseph to Quebec. At long last General Haldimand was about to retire to England, and the Indians wanted their land grant put in proper legal form before he left. Most important of all, Joseph was planning to go to England himself, and he would have to get a passage before winter closed in. Daniel Claus was going, too, that fall, to recoup his shattered fortunes, and Joseph expected to go with him. Joseph intended to take along the Mohawk claims for losses. He also meant to find out whether Britain would support the Indians if worse came to worst and war broke out between the Indians and the United States.

The season being so late, Joseph began to think the representatives of Congress had given up their journey for the time. Instead, he surmised, there would be a great general meeting for peacemaking in the spring. If a smaller, less important meeting should be held any time soon, Captain Aaron and his party could carry on. Thus persuaded, Joseph left Fort Stanwix.[41] It was about the middle of September. He left either in company with Monroe and the American traders, or shortly afterward. On the way he met Aaron coming down.

Aaron's party was very small, partly on account of sickness among the Indians and partly because of the chiefs' fears (played upon by some of the agents of the Indian department) of going so far into the

American lines as Fort Stanwix. Of the western delegates only a few Shawnees had come down, the rest having given up and gone home. But under the circumstances Joseph was not unduly alarmed. He promised Aaron that he would have all the American prisoners, slaves or whites, collected and sent down to Fort Stanwix.[42] Aaron, whose party traveled slowly, finally got to Fort Stanwix on October 7, and found the three stern-faced American commissioners, Oliver Wolcott, Arthur Lee, and Richard Butler, already there. Joseph reached Niagara about September 21.[43] He was not at all displeased. If the Americans had appeared in time, he thought, a very satisfactory peace treaty could have been made.[44] If he set about to collect the prisoners, as he had promised, he knew it would be a long-drawn-out process. Obviously, they could not be sent to Fort Stanwix before the great spring meeting.

Joseph's new friend, Monroe, was waiting at Niagara till the traders transported their goods over the portage. Monroe and Joseph had some conversations about Indian affairs, and Joseph thought they agreed very well.[45] How it would have interested Joseph, who always liked to foregather with the great and near-great, could he have known that Monroe would some day become the fifth president of the United States! But it was something he was never to know. Monroe was entertained politely by Lieutenant Colonel De Peyster (formerly Major De Peyster, of Detroit), the new commandant at the post. De Peyster did his best to dissuade the young American from going to Detroit, for he knew it was an expedition upon which his superiors would not look kindly. He also knew it was an expedition fraught with danger. Monroe finally agreed to go to Fort Pitt instead, and he let the traders head west without him. In a few days came a report that some Indians, Delawares or Mahicans, had fired on the party of Americans on the shore of Lake Erie and had killed three and wounded one. Upon hearing this Joseph flew into a great rage. All his efforts at peacemaking would fail dismally if things like this were allowed to happen. He promptly sent ten young warriors after the miscreants, swearing that "he would have them if they were upon the face of the earth, and deliver them up."[46] James Monroe's journey had to be cut short. He decided to return to the States, much to De Peyster's relief.

Joseph could delay no longer. The lakes would soon be closed. He must leave for Quebec. Gathering up Catharine and the new baby and Christina, he set out by lake vessel. Isaac probably did not join the party. Though young, he may have been married by this time and established in his own home. At any rate, he would have been too stubborn to go with his father but still jealous of those who did go. On the vessel with Joseph and his family traveled James Monroe, who was to return home via the St. Lawrence and Lake Champlain.[47] Joseph stopped at Cataraqui just long enough to settle his loved ones in the new house next to Molly's, and hastened on.[48] He expected to be gone for many months.

Joseph arrived at Quebec on October 23, 1784.[49] On October 25 General Haldimand placed his signature on the great land grant to the Six Nations. It was a document which Joseph was to peruse and ponder, over and over, in years to come. The words seemed plain enough:

> Whereas His Majesty having been pleased to direct that in Consideration of the early Attachment to his Cause manifested by the Mohawk Indians and of the loss of their Settlement, which they thereby sustained, that a convenient Tract of Land under his protection, should be chosen as a safe and Comfortable Retreat for them and others of the Six Nations, who have either lost their Settlements within the Territory of the American States, or wish to retire from them to the British; I have at the desire of many of these His Majesty's faithful Allies purchased a Tract of Land from the Indians situated between the Lakes Ontario, Huron, and Erie And I do hereby in His Majesty's name Authorise and permit the said Mohawk Nation, and such other of the Six Nation Indians as wish to settle in that Quarter to take possession of and settle upon the Banks of the River commonly called, Ouse, or Grand River, running into Lake Erie; Allotting to them for that purpose six miles deep from each side of the River beginning at Lake Erie, and Extending in that proportion to the Head of the said River, which them and their posterity are to enjoy for ever.[50]

By this grant Haldimand gave the Six Nations, as he had promised, "the best equivalent I can for the Country they leave."[51] It was one of the general's last official acts. In three weeks he was to sail for England.

General Haldimand did all he could to discourage Joseph's proposed journey to England without actually forbidding it. Haldimand knew very well that nobody in the government was prepared to answer Joseph's embarrassing questions. He offered to take the schedule of Mohawk losses himself to London. He also reminded Joseph of the fifteen hundred pounds which he had already allotted the Mohawks and which, when paid, would alleviate their most pressing needs.[52] Joseph was considering these arguments when some alarming news reached Quebec. Aaron Hill and five other chiefs had been seized as hostages by the Americans at Fort Stanwix, and would be held, it was said, until all the American prisoners were returned.

Joseph did not know what else had happened at Fort Stanwix, but this was enough to make him drop everything and send him hastening back to Cataraqui.[53] Claus would have to go to England alone. The Hills were one of the first families among the Mohawks. They had long been friends to Joseph. The late John Hill Oteronyente had accompanied Joseph to London in 1775. David Hill, Aaron's brother, was even now with Joseph in Quebec. Isaac's wife, or wife-to-be, was a Hill, and Joseph's daughter Christina would eventually marry into the family. Small wonder that Joseph was concerned over Aaron's fate. He entrusted the Mohawk claims to General Haldimand's good offices and wrote Sir John Johnson, who was already in England, begging him to ask the government the great question of whether there would be military help for the Indians in case of war with the Americans.[54] Then he returned to Catharine and his family, but he meant to go back to Niagara as soon as the ice broke. He knew his people needed him. He could at least try to collect the American prisoners and get Aaron and the chiefs freed.

Once back at Cataraqui, Joseph poured out his heart in a letter to James Monroe. He felt great chagrin because it was he who had encouraged Aaron to go to Fort Stanwix. The Mohawks, he said, had already released all their prisoners except one or two children who were too young to go home alone, and they had long advised the other nations to do the same. During the war, he said, we "always favored the prisoners, especially women and children." We have been a generous enemy, he added, and we want to be friends; and if we are prevented from becoming friends with you, it will not be our fault. He suspected Samuel Kirkland and the Oneidas of putting obstacles in the way of friendship. "If I could see you, and talk with you, I could explain myself better than a letter half English half Indian." Obviously Joseph still thought he was on the best of terms with James Monroe, for he mentioned he had hoped to see him again at the great council in the spring, a conference which apparently he still anticipated would take place. He reminded Monroe he had also talked of a projected trip to New Jersey (where Congress was meeting) to see him. "But, my dear sir," he said, "I begin to be backward about going there, since my chief is detained. Perhaps I should be served the same, and be kept from my different sweethearts, which would be too hard for me." It was a feeble attempt at humor, though Joseph was not feeling at all light-hearted. Now, he feared, he would not be able to see Monroe after all, even at the expected spring council, unless there should be some change in the situation. "But believe me this," he concluded, "let the affairs turn out what it will, I should be always very happy to see you. I shall winter here, myself and family; early in the Spring I shall leave this, and go to my new country at Grand River."[55]

Monroe answered this letter with a long one of his own, which Joseph probably did not receive for several months. Monroe tried to justify the taking of hostages at Fort Stanwix, and assured Joseph that he would be safe from insult in the United States and that many of the leaders in Congress, as well as Governor Clinton, would be glad to see him. Then he launched into an impassioned plea for Indian-American friendship. The Indians ought to forsake the British alliance and cast in their lot with the Americans.[56] But that was too great a turnabout for Joseph.

Joseph went down the ice to Montreal in late winter. He hoped to meet some of the New Yorkers with whom he thought he had private agreements, but nobody from New York showed up.[57] He also wished to confer with Lieutenant Governor Henry Hamilton, who was in charge of the civil government of Canada till a permanent governor should arrive from England. Hamilton appears to have thought well of Joseph. "I have a high opinion of Captain Brant's Understanding, and of his knowledge of the dispositions views and interests of the Six Nations, and besides, have a personal regard for him," he said.[58] But Hamilton did not think well enough of Joseph to cause a regular deed to be made out to the Indians for the Grand River land, though Joseph wanted it and thought he was going to get it.[59] When the deed was not forthcoming, Joseph made no protest. He was very busy, and he probably did not realize how important, in the white man's scheme of things, written words can be. Joseph also requested a deed for his house and two hundred acres of adjoining land at Cataraqui,[60] but he did not get that, either, for the house stood on crown land appended to the fort.

Though thoughts of Aaron Hill rankled worse than ever (for the proud Joseph had come to the conclusion that Aaron was held hostage for the return of some slaves, and therefore being compared to a slave),[61] the rest of Joseph's stay at Cataraqui was uneventful. It was the only stay the family ever made together in the new house, and it was the only time they would ever live so close to Molly. It was a good house that Major Ross had built for Joseph, as houses went then, forty feet wide and thirty feet in depth, a story and a half high.[62] Molly, who had just moved from Carleton Island, had a house equally good, also on crown property, and she lived in Cataraqui, or Kingston, as it would soon be called, the rest of her life. She never again mingled in politics, either Indian, American, or British, though she made vain attempts to get back her children's inheritances. Five daughters, still heiresses with their substantial Loyalist claims, married respectable white men. One daughter remained single, and the only surviving son married an Indian girl and was not much heard of. One of Molly's daughters was accounted a beauty, and all were well educated for their day. Molly, in her latter years, was interested only in her family. She died in 1796. At least one of her grandchildren spent much time in Europe, and was heard to murmur now and then against "dirty Indians." Molly's was a topsy-turvy world.

Joseph and family were probably back at Niagara by early April 1785.[63] There was not so much for him to do after all, for the prisoners had been collected, and Aaron and the other hostages would soon be released. But at last he could learn the full details of what had taken place at Fort Stanwix. Aaron and his small party had been completely overborne. Aaron had written to Niagara that their friends should not think hard of anything they might do as they were not free agents. The American commissioners were carrying on with a very high hand, and the Indians, closely watched and surrounded by troops, could scarcely speak to a soul. The Americans told Aaron and his party that the Six Nations were "a subdued people." The king had abandoned them and given away their land. They had nothing. Then the Americans demanded compensation in land for injuries inflicted on them during the war. But how could a people who had no land, pay damages in land? Did Joseph or anyone think of that difficulty? The Americans had not explained it. But in the treaty of October 22, 1784, they had forced Aaron and the other young war chiefs who had expected to arrange no more than a peace, leaving the question of land to the sachems, to give up all Six Nations claims to everything west of Buffalo Creek and the western boundary of Pennsylvania. Nor had the young chiefs been allowed to negotiate for their western allies. The Americans intended to make a separate treaty with them. The new Indian confederacy, they thought, was a "diabolical" idea; they would have nothing to do with it.

There would be no grand conference in the spring between the Americans and all the Indian nations, with his own people taking the lead, as Joseph had optimistically expected. The rout begun by Sullivan in 1779 was complete. The Six Nations had lost the entire west. They were narrowly confined between the new line of 1784 and the old line of 1768. Only a portion of their once proud domain remained to them. It took a stout heart to cherish any dream now of reestablishing the old empire.

Before the American commissioners left Fort Stanwix, representatives of Pennsylvania, more successful than those of New York, bought everything the Six Nations still claimed in that state. For this the Indians were paid five thousand dollars. The land in question being their best hunting ground, they were to be allowed to keep on hunting there. It was a fair purchase. But the commissioners of Congress made no bones that their treaty was not a purchase, although they left the Indians some "goods," value unknown. As for Governor Clinton and the New Yorkers, their frustration would not last too long. They were to get nearly all they wanted, from the Oneidas as well as their former enemies, in a few years. Nor did it matter whether the Indians wished to sell or not.

When the western Indians heard about the treaty of Fort Stanwix, they were furious. They accused the Six Nations of selling them out. What the Six Nations had given up to Congress was land the western Indians actually lived on and from which they got their subsistence. It was land which had been allotted to them long ago by the Six Nations themselves. This wrath fell particularly hard on Cornplanter, a Seneca chief who was just then coming into prominence. Cornplanter, whose English name was Captain Abeel (O'Bail, etc.), and who was half white, had been one of those Senecas who had been convinced against himself in 1777 and who had hung on to his neutrality as long as he could. At Fort Stanwix Cornplanter had appeared to be a sort of pet of the Americans; at least he was the only one of their former enemies to whom they spoke kindly, and he seems to have used his influence to get his followers to bow to the inevitable. For Joseph Brant and many others among the Six Nations, it was also easy to blame Cornplanter for their great trouble. In their first shock they had to blame somebody. The Senecas were torn by dissension, and for a long time the unhappy Cornplanter, trembling in fear for his life, tried vainly to persuade the Americans to abrogate the treaty.

Further news of the activities of the American commissioners reached Niagara as soon as the communication with Detroit opened up. Two of the commissioners, Richard Butler and Arthur Lee, had almost immediately left for Fort Pitt, where they were joined by George Rogers Clark. From Fort Pitt the three journeyed down the Ohio in the dead of winter. At Fort McIntosh, an American post high on a bluff on the north side of the Ohio (Beaver, Pennsylvania), the Americans gathered together the dispirited representatives of the Delawares and Wyandots and a few Ottawas and Chippewas, and used them in the same implacable way they had used the Six Nations. The Indians were a conquered people, they reminded them. They had no land. The king had given it all away. Then the Americans again demanded damages in land. It was the bold face of a bold nation which must have land to give its disbanded soldiers and to pay off the public debt but was too impoverished to make an honest purchase, and which truly thought it had a legitimate grievance against the Indians.

Shortly afterward, on January 21, 1785, and with soldiers of the new United States army at their back, the three American commissioners forced the Indians to give up some three-fourths of what is now the state of Ohio. The Indians were left a reservation bounded by the Cuyahoga, the Maumee, Lake Erie, and a line drawn approximately westward from the site of present Bolivar. This allotment was a generous gift made by a generous conqueror, the Americans told the Indians. The rest of their claims northwest of the Ohio River belonged to the United States. For this great cession the Indians, "in pursuance of the humane and liberal views of Congress," received some "goods," though again nobody called the transaction a purchase.

When the unfortunate signers of the Fort McIntosh treaty got home, they were abused and reviled. Had they not broken their word pledged at Sandusky to cede no land unless sanctioned by the new confederacy? The other western Indians, as well as many of their own people, refused to recognize what they had done. The Shawnees and Mingoes, who lived on some of the ceded land and who also claimed it, and the Miamis, who lived on the Wabash and its tributaries, were aghast. They could expect that the next American treaties would be held with them. All over the west, almost to the Mississippi, anger welled up, deep and abiding. As far as the dissenters were concerned, there had been no treaty at Fort McIntosh. By hurried councils with one another and by belts of wampum sent far and wide, they set about perfecting their union.

Suddenly Congress had a full-fledged problem. The British, who called the Indians allies, also had a problem. Joseph Brant, emerging more and more as the leader of the Mohawks and to some extent of the whole Six Nations, and aspiring to become the leader of the new Indian confederacy, had very great problems. Could he hold his own Mohawks in line in opposition to the Americans? In a practical and everyday way, the land that had been given up at Fort Stanwix meant little to them, for it was mostly land claimed by the Senecas. Could he damp down the jealousies which the Mohawks and the Senecas felt for each other and which he knew the Senecas still felt for him in particular? Could he reconcile the western Indians and both branches of the Six Nations and hold the new confederacy together and maintain all in opposition to the Americans, and yet prevent the young braves from turning to violence? Could he do anything to prevent the outbreak of a war between the Indians and the Americans? He was not so simple-minded as to suppose that the Indians could readily win such a war. And if there was war, what would the British do? More than ever, it was necessary to find out if the Indians could get any military aid from the king. Eagerly Joseph awaited the return of Sir John Johnson from England and the answer to the great question. He did not doubt that Sir John would bring the answer.

All these problems made very indigestible food for thought as Joseph began his removal to the new home on the Grand River. He knew Catharine would do all in her power to help, and Henry, too, but the ideas and the solutions must come from him. Thus the spring and summer of 1785 were spent in revolving great plans and little plans, so that political thoughts became inextricably mingled with thoughts of a new log house, and clearings, and plantings, and a ford across the river, and the proper locations of this and that.

Then, suddenly and unexpectedly, Joseph was confronted with still another problem. It was enough, he felt, to tax the patience of a saint. Some of the neighboring Missisaugas, who had never been fond of the Six Nations and who had sold the land for their new home somewhat hesitantly (hoping, they said, that Brant would keep his young men "in good order"),[64] were having second thoughts. A quarrel had erupted, at first apparently among young people, and then taken up by their elders. On May 30 Joseph urged Colonel De Peyster to intervene. "We cannot tell how it came," he complained, "that these Messisaugas got to be so unreasonable lately, whether it is from the rebels, or from the devil;—it must come from one of the two." He rather thought the trouble was fomented by the rebels, and he said (as he always said) that the rebels had tried to prevent the removal to the Grand River.[65] He was convinced that the Yankees wished to destroy the new settlement and were working in devious ways to do so, never considering how difficult it would have been for any of them to get to and tamper with the Missisaugas. Apparently De Peyster was able to do something to prevent further dissension among the Indians, or the trouble blew over. It was only a tempest in a teapot. But Joseph always maintained that the rebels wanted him and his people to remain in the United States, and he later declared they had offered him personally a payment of £375 a year for life if he would stay.[66] Joseph early convinced General Haldimand that the Americans were eager to welcome him and his people back, and he often brought up the subject in later years when exasperated with Canadian authorities. (But when writing to Americans, he did not refer to the topic; and the Americans themselves said nothing.)

A census of the Six Nations living on the Grand River in 1785 showed that the Mohawks were well in the majority with 448 persons counted. The Cayugas were next, numbering 381. Next in order came the Onondagas with 245; the Oquagas, who were probably Loyalist Oneidas, with 162; the Tuscaroras with 129; and the Senecas, who obviously did not care to live under Mohawk dominance, with only 78. The rest, who had little political importance, were mostly Delawares, Creeks and Cherokees, Tutelos, Nanticokes, and Indians from St. Regis. All in all, 1,843 Indians had settled on the Grand River,[67] but as there was a great deal of coming and going, their numbers varied from time to time. But always, at least in Joseph's lifetime, the Mohawks remained in the majority and were by far the most important. Nevertheless, more than half of the Six Nations still lived in the United States, and of these nearly 1,700 were Senecas and over 600 were Oneidas,[68] neither of whom had any great love for their former compatriots on the Grand River. Joseph, who realized the implications of this fact very well, continued for a long time to urge the lower Mohawks who were settled at Quinte to move in with his people and increase their numbers, but it never did him the least good. Captain John Deseronto preferred to remain the big frog in the little puddle. He and his Mohawks, numbering some two hundred, stayed in their own little settlement, with their own little school and church and their half of the famous Queen Anne silver service from the old mission at Fort Hunter. They never succumbed to Joseph's blandishments.

The engineer from Fort Niagara, on orders from Haldimand, helped the Grand River Indians locate their settlements, and the Indian department provided them with provisions and such tools as saws, axes, grindstones, chisels, files, augers, squares, adzes, and compasses, and even a few tents. In time they got a sawmill and a gristmill in their new home; and a church, which became the oldest Protestant church in what is now Ontario; and a schoolhouse, all of which had been directed by Haldimand before he left. The schoolmaster was to be paid by the government, but to be chosen by the Indians themselves.

The new settlers were spread all up and down the river: Delawares and part of the Cayugas toward its mouth, Mohawks and the rest of the Cayugas farthest up, and the other nations in between. On the outskirts of what is now Brantford arose the main settlement, known as the Mohawk Village, or Ohsweken. This village grew up near a ford in the river where, it is said, Joseph located his own farm and could watch the building of the church close by,[69] Joseph always being a great one for living near churches.

It was a long, narrow tract of land to which these Indians had come, twelve miles wide and of great but indeterminate length, containing, from river mouth to river source, probably close to a million acres; though, of course, it had never been surveyed, and nobody really knew its actual bounds. The river, swiftly flowing in its upper reaches but with less current downstream, and with many tributaries, was navigable for vessels drawing eight or twelve feet for about ten miles up, and for large boats much farther; and its mouth afforded the only harbor on Lake Erie's north shore. The land was very rich, the climate not harsh, and water and wood were plentiful. It was just the sort of place to attract white settlers, though unfortunately held by Indians. At first, before the surrounding countryside filled up with whites, hunting was very good, and meat and pelts were plentiful— and a good thing, too, for without hunting the Indians always said they would have starved. In the meantime the local Onondagas set up a central fireplace for local Grand River councils, and old people tried to reinstate the old customs and rituals, and with about as much success against new ways as old people usually have. The ax rang out, clearings grew in size and numbers, and Fort Stanwix and Fort McIntosh must have seemed, if not to Joseph, at least to some of the Indians, far away.

In those early years after the war thousands of white Loyalists, who were just as poor as the Indians in worldly goods, were also trying to conquer the Canadian wilderness. Their first eager desire to return home had given way to the sad knowledge that, for most, return was impossible. A comparative few did try to go back, and some who had played an inconspicuous part in the war or who had powerful friends, managed to stay. Others met with such hostility on the part of the victorious rebels that they were glad to leave again. They were tarred and feathered or thrown into prison and flogged or threatened with hanging. Getting back their property seemed an impossibility and, even if they could get it back and return among their former neighbors, they realized, as one embittered Loyalist declared, "We must live like Dogs amongst them." Benjamin Becraft, a man known in his old neighborhood to have been with Brant's forces at Harpersfield in 1780, was one who, when peace came, tried to go back to his home at Schoharie. A delegation of his neighbors went to see him. He arose, inquired politely after their health, and offered his hand. Without further ado they seized him and dragged him off to a grove of trees.

After stripping him, they tied him up and gave him fifty lashes. Every ten lashes, they recounted his crimes. Then they untied him and ordered him to leave the country; and, as the contemporary narrator of this story adds with much satisfaction, they never saw him again.[70] Then, of course, there were other Loyalists too proud ever to attempt to return. They did not wish to live in such a place as their once beloved country had turned out to be and swore they "would rather go to Japan than go among the Americans where they Could never live in Peace."[71]

Thousands of the king's fighting men doffed their red or green battle coats and stayed in Canada, and thousands more who had been living in British-controlled territory left the erstwhile colonies when Sir Guy Carleton evacuated New York City in November 1783. From Nova Scotia to the St. Lawrence, to the northeast shore of Lake Ontario, to the Niagara peninsula to Lake Erie to the environs of Detroit, the new immigrants came, with one thought in mind: to set up permanent homes in an alien country. This went on for as much as seven years after the peace; and when the Americans finally decided to let bygones be bygones and permit any Loyalist to return who wished to, there were not many takers.

Near Niagara could be found many of Joseph's old friends—men like Gilbert Tice and Brant Johnson, and other members of the old fighting Indian department or of Butler's Rangers. Joseph saw that some of his particular friends and associates got land on the Grand River, not for a price, but as a gift. About ten miles up the river John Docksteder, a lieutenant in the Indian department, received a fine grant. Henry Nelles, a captain in the same corps, also got a generous grant; so, too, did Lieutenant John Young and a number of other whites who had fought beside the Indians and shared their hardships. Joseph hoped these white friends would teach an agricultural way of life to the Indians by setting them a good example.[72] Some of these same white men also had Indian wives and half-breed children whom he wished to see provided for. Since the land belonged to the Indians and they could do with it as they chose (for neither Joseph nor the Indians could have supposed otherwise), and the men were looked upon as everybody's friends, it could not have been hard for Joseph to influence the council in their behalf. In this way white families came very early to the Grand River.

All this final transplanting themselves to a strange country was not unaccompanied by heartbreak, particularly among those who knew they never could return to their old homes, not even for a visit. Sir John Johnson, often disappointed by policies in London and thinking of what he had lost, noted sadly that he and his family had put themselves in "their" power. John Butler, another who would not have dared to go home regardless of how many anti-Tory laws had been repealed, wistfully sent his "best respects" to some of his old friends, hoping they would accept them as coming from "an honest man who does his duty . . . however disagreeable." Alexander McKee wrote his brother in Pennsylvania that he hoped the blessings of peace would renew "the Amity of Friends" and begged to hear from him; and as late as 1804 Simon Girty, the terror of the frontier, was longing to go home. But Joseph Brant said never a word of regret for the Mohawk valley. Resolutely he turned his face in another direction. Let Molly talk of home; he would not.

The British peacemakers of 1782–83, though forgetful of the Indians, had tried to protect the white Loyalists. Several articles in the peace treaty referred to the Loyalists directly or indirectly. Creditors on either side were to meet with no lawful impediment to the recovery of debts. Congress was to recommend to the various state legislatures restitution of confiscated estates of persons who had not borne arms against the United States. All others were to be permitted to go to the States and remain for a year while trying to get back their property, and terms were spelled out by which they might accomplish this end. There were to be no future prosecutions or confiscations against any person for the part he had taken in the war. Loyalists reading the peace treaty for the first time could have thought that it afforded them reasonable protection.

The Loyalists soon found, however, that not one of the articles in their favor was being carried out by the Americans. Indeed, the latter seemed to think Britain really did not expect them to do as the treaty required. The provisions in behalf of the Loyalists were mostly for appearance's sake, argued the Americans, and they pointed out that Congress, which had negotiated the treaty, had no power to force the state governments to abide by its terms—a fact which the American negotiators had clearly made known to the British negotiators. Nor could it be expected that the state legislatures would act of their own accord, for the distresses and grievances of the war were too fresh in people's minds. Such was the American view of the treaty.

In the meantime several British governments had come and gone since the stunning defeat and surrender at Yorktown, including the government that had made the peace. The new ministry which had come to power in late 1783, that of William Pitt the younger, was having some second thoughts of its own about the peace treaty. Men like Lord Sydney, secretary of state, realized that a great blunder had been made in not taking care of the Indians whose aid Canada would need for a long, long time and whose trade was so valuable.

The ministry had been helped to this conclusion by a deluge of petitions from those who had an interest in the fur trade. These people had property which they must get out of the Indian country or which they must have time to sell, and they had debts they must collect. The petitioners enumerated the thousands of pounds in sterling which were at stake and the thousands of bales of valuable pelts which they wished to save. Always implicit in their statements was the enormous value of the peltry which had come out of the west annually and which was likely to come out for many years in the future. Not only was the direct trader with the Indians affected, but numerous middle-men in Canada as well as workmen of the lowlier sort, and merchants and manufacturers in Britain who supplied the Indians, and even merchants and manufacturers whose hats and processed furs were sold world-wide. It was enough to give any government pause, and the Pitt government paused. They read the letters of General Maclean and others in the frontier posts who feared the Indians would become estranged from Britain or would even precipitate a war which might fall on British citizens as well as on the Americans if the posts were given up; and they heeded the advice of General Haldimand who, always concerned about the trade and the Indians and himself deluged with petitions, thought Britain should proceed as slowly as possible in executing that part of the treaty. American action or inaction toward the Loyalists was the excuse which Haldimand suggested, and by April 1784 Lord Sydney had authorized the indefinite retention of the frontier posts. He did this, he said, because the Americans had not fulfilled their part of the peace treaty.

At first the Americans suspected little of what was going on in British thought, and British authorities deliberately kept them in the dark. After sending agent after agent to Canada to make arrangements for taking over their property and always getting diplomatic and am-biguous answers—for no time had been specified in the treaty as to when the posts should be given up—the Americans finally came to realize that they were not going to get the posts very soon—indeed, perhaps not at all, unless they fought for them, a prospect which in their weakened condition they could not face. Baffled and angry, they had to admit that the British, who had command of the lakes, could do as they chose.

Two other realizations also smote the Americans. The conduct of Indian affairs was going to be very difficult for them. So long as the British kept the posts, they could not deal with the natives as they wished. With British garrisons at Detroit and Niagara and British traders and government agents supplying guns and necessities, the Indians would not be easily intimidated. Yet the new nation, in order to get land, had to intimidate the Indians since it was too poor to pay them and too weak to fight them. The Americans also realized that if they could not organize a stronger government and if they continued to battle among themselves and with Congress (for the dispute between New York and Congress at Fort Stanwix and innumerable boundary and currency disputes were only a few manifestations of the general dissension), they might shortly find themselves again under the British heel—and of course the British realized this, too. It had become a game in which the stakes were very high.

Joseph Brant, back at Niagara for a short visit in June 1785, knew little of these affairs as yet and was in nobody's confidence, but he had a game of his own to play, consistent with his loyalty to the king, and for him the stakes were high, too. From now on almost everything he did was to show some political coloration. On June 25 Joseph and two of the Hill brothers from Grand River delivered in the name of the Six Nations a flattering farewell speech to Colonel De Peyster who was about to leave for England. They thanked De Peyster for all his past kindnesses to them, both at Niagara and Detroit, and wished him a pleasant journey and a gracious reception in England.[73] It was a pretty speech in the best of the white man's tradition. Next day De Peyster responded with equal politeness—and with something extra. He said he was pleased with the address of the chiefs and warriors of the Six Nations, and he wished them "a lasting peace, attended with every other blessing." He also begged his good friend, Thayendanegea, to send belts of white wampum in his name to the two main Shawnee towns and to the Hurons of Sandusky "that they will not forget their promise to continue as firm as the oak, and as deep as the waters, in the cause of the King of Great Britain, and that they will bring up their youth in the same sentiments . . . lest they become an easy prey to their enemies."[74]

Obviously, Joseph still had something to learn in the political line. De Peyster was an experienced and conscientious officer. After some twenty years in the royal service, he was not likely to overlook an opportunity or forget a duty. A very handsome man, too, De Peyster was the second cousin, oddly enough, of General Philip Schuyler of Albany, who was not at all handsome. The two kinsmen had nothing in common but the family nose (which, in Schuyler, had taken a turn for the worse) and a burning desire to uphold his own side in the great dispute. Good and honorable men, both; they heard different drums.

There was a time in the early part of the war when Philip Schuyler came very near being indispensable to his side, but nobody knew it save, perhaps, a few of his intimates—and George Washington. Now both Schuyler and De Peyster were in ill health and about to step down from the stage of Indian affairs. New men were coming in; new voices were being heard. It was a time of great flux and change.

When Joseph came back to Niagara again in August, he showed that he had learned a practical little lesson. Finding that Major Archibald Campbell, who had succeeded De Peyster, was about to write a letter to former Governor Tryon, now in England, Joseph begged Campbell to send Tryon his best respects and the thanks of himself and the Six Nations for all his past kindnesses to them, and to assure him that "their Attachment to the King and the British Nation continues unalterable." The inevitable result followed. Tryon, charmed with such a message from one whom he had not seen for so long, urged Lord Sydney to bring Joseph's declaration to the attention of the king himself.[75]

Joseph's reason for coming back at this time was to attend a council at Niagara with the Six Nations and their western allies, but Major Campbell, the new commander, was so nervous about the near proximity of "so many savages" that he contrived to get the council fire removed to the Loyal Confederate Village at the landing. Joseph did not suspect the major's motive, and probably agreed to the removal because many of the Mohawks were still at the landing. The council seems to have been adjourned from time to time to several other places, for the Indians found it hard to agree. All the Indians were very angry, but Joseph and John Dease, acting agent of the Indian department (John Butler being absent in England and Sir John Johnson not yet returned), advised moderation. The upshot was that the Indians disavowed the treaty of Fort Stanwix (the treaty of Fort McIntosh having already been disavowed at councils in the west) and decided to send a message to Congress asking that Major Peter Schuyler, Colonel James Monroe, and James Dean, the interpreter, meet them at the Seneca settlement at Buffalo Creek to hear their complaints. Joseph signed the message as speaker for the Indians and promised that these men need have no fear they would be detained after the meeting. It was not the practice of his people, he said, to detain those who come to do business with them![76]

Shortly afterward Joseph wrote a letter to the Oneida Skenando, his former in-law and captive, urging him to send the message on through his country and to use his utmost influence with his fellow chiefs to see that *"Congress, your Brothers,"* comply with our request. "There are some things," he added, "that lie deep in our minds."[77]

Joseph sent an account of this council to Colonel Henry Hope, who was soon to succeed Hamilton as lieutenant governor of the province. "I can sincerely assure you, Sir," he said, "that we are heartily inclind to try every mild means with these people before we proceed to Extremities, which nothing but necessity and their persisting to injure us will oblige us to do and then we hope we shall stand Justify'd in the opinion of the world for asserting our rights like Men."[78]

But the world cared little for the rights of a few "savages" in one of its remote corners, and Congress, though urged by the Oneidas to comply with the Indians' request to hear their complaints, had already arranged for a start to the survey and sale of the Ohio country. American soldiers were busy building a fort on the north side of the Ohio near the mouth of the Great Miami, and the American commissioners had sent an ominous invitation to the Shawnees and their neighbors along the Wabash to come to a peace treaty. Brigadier General Barry St. Leger, acting head of the military arm in Canada, who had had little to do with the Indians since his inglorious retreat in 1777, remarked, "I hope Joseph Brants politicks is not the occasion of this bustle between them and the Americans."[79] Admitting he did not understand Indian affairs, St. Leger hoped fervently that Sir John would soon return to his duty and soothe the savage breasts. There was a sinking feeling in Canada that war was about to erupt, and nobody knew what to do about it. And scarcely two thousand soldiers in the province! Some people, like Major Campbell, were indignant as well as worried. He hoped that Congress would not go so far as to bring on a rupture with the Indians; and continued: "I am no Politician, tho sincere well wisher of those who have rendered my Country service; and therefor must say, it would give me uneasiness to see the Indians reduced to any disagreeable extremity, from the consequences of a Quarrel, in which in fact, they were involved, in Steadily supporting the Kings Intrest, against the Rebellious Subjects; I therefor hope that when matters come to be known in England the Nation will not suffer a Brave people to fall a Sacrifice to the Caprice and Resentment of an upstart Power now Swolen beyon the bounds of Discretion."[80]

Thinking that Sir John must arrive soon if he intended to come back before winter set in, Joseph, David Hill, Sayengaraghta, and one of the Cayuga chiefs went down the country in October to meet him. Not finding Sir John at his home in Montreal, Sayengaraghta and the

Cayuga waited for him, while Joseph and David traveled on to Quebec. At Quebec Joseph and David found they had just missed their quarry. Sir John had already embarked on the schooner *Mercury* for Montreal. The two Indians hurried down to the pier and scrambled on board the schooner just in time for an interview. Eagerly they asked Sir John what news he brought. They reminded him of the great question they had asked him to clear up in England. What answer did he have for them?

But their great question remained unanswered. Not a word could Sir John say that they had not heard before.[81]

18

The Emancipation of Joseph Brant

I T WAS Joseph's idea to go to England, but David Hill undoubtedly
acquiesced in it at once. Sir John was horrified. He did not think
Joseph would be very welcome in England. Tactfully, he threw cold
water on the project, but without telling the Indians why. Joseph, he
said, was needed at home to guard against the intrigues and the encroachments of the Americans. Joseph was not impressed by this
argument. Sir John then took another tack. He promised that Joseph,
who was worried about having no job now that the war was over,
should get a temporary pension of half pay for his military services and
that, if the other veterans of the Indian department eventually received pensions, Joseph's pension would become permanent. Joseph
was still not impressed. In desperation Sir John promised to replace
part of the Mohawk losses himself out of the Indian store and to
recommend to the lagging ministry, who had the claims under consideration, a speedy settlement of the rest. This did not bring about
the desired result, either, for Joseph still insisted on going to England.[1]

When Sir John sailed for home, on October 23, he sailed with a
very unquiet mind.

Sir John's was not the only unquiet mind. Henry Hope, the new
lieutenant governor, when informed of Joseph's plan, was equally
horrified. He repeated all the arguments he could think of. He appealed to Joseph's self-interest and he appealed to his honor. When
Joseph still appeared determined to go, Hope changed his tone and
allowed his displeasure to show. When that did not work, the lieutenant governor retreated and promised to get Joseph a passage on the

Madona, which was to sail on November 10. It would be the last sailing of the year. This promise seemed to satisfy Joseph.[2]

There was no thought that David should go to England. The state of their finances forbade so much expense, and David prepared to return to the Grand River. Before he left, there must have been a good many anxious admonitions on Joseph's part and a good many promises on David's part to take care that Catharine and the family did not suffer back home in that new and raw country. Of necessity Joseph and David were both breaking with Six Nations custom. For the first time Joseph would have no Indian companion on an embassy. What would the people at home think? He did not know. He knew only that he must go, and that there was no time to get further instructions or a fellow deputy to share the journey.

Though the lieutenant governor had retreated, he had not surrendered. Colonel Henry Hope was still casting about in his mind for some way to stop the project. Joseph, having done so much traveling in Hope's company, of course knew him well. He surmised what he was thinking. He engaged a passage on a packet which was to sail four days before the *Madona.* Then he told Hope that the *Madona* was not a safe ship and he feared to sail on it. The crew was too small, he said.[3] Hope had to accept the inevitable. He found a returning soldier who had acted with the Indians, to take charge of Joseph, and reluctantly let him go.[4] The packet sailed from Quebec on the morning of November 6.[5] There was a flurry of letter-writing after Joseph left, between Hope and Sir John, and from both to England. Sir John had written to Joseph, detailing many reasons why he should not leave the province. Joseph never saw that letter for many months. He had successfully made his escape.[6]

The passage was vastly different from the passage of ten years before. This time no rebel prisoners moldered in the hold and there was no Ethan Allen to record what went on. But as before, there were numerous Loyalists on board. The Loyalists, now downcast and defeated, were going to England to try to mend their war-torn fortunes. One of these was the former lieutenant governor, Henry Hamilton, who had been so long a prisoner of George Rogers Clark. Another was Captain Richard Houghton, Joseph's appointed overseer. The passage was quicker than before, too. The vessel arrived at the garrison town of Salisbury on December 5. Joseph went off to dine with Colonel De Peyster who was with the garrison, and then immediately set out for London. It was boldly stated in the press that "Colonel Joseph Brant, the celebrated King of the Mohawks" contemplated war with the

Americans, and it was conjectured that "his embassy to the British Court is of great importance."[7]

By December 7 Joseph was in London and had taken lodgings with his old friend Daniel Claus. Claus and his family were living at 18 College Street, Westminster, and it was only natural that Joseph should make arrangements to stay with them.[8] Captain Houghton, who did not neglect his charge, was either there or nearby. Claus kept a little journal of inconsequential events, and from it we learn that Joseph borrowed two shillings sixpence for coach fare on December 22. Where he was going in the coach, Claus does not say.[9]

On January 4, 1786, a little knot of Indian department officers gathered with Joseph in Lord Sydney's office. All had come to London on their own personal business, but this business was official. Guy Johnson was there; it was probably his last official act. Joseph Chew, Guy's secretary, was also there. So, too, was Daniel Claus. Captain Houghton, who was sticking to Joseph as closely as wallpaper, was also present. And John Butler had come, at Joseph's special request! Joseph, whose interview with Lord Sydney was the cause of all this bustle, had insisted that Butler be the one to interpret his speech. It also seems he had not wanted the others to be present, but they came anyway. As far as the men of the Indian department were concerned, this whim of Joseph's had to be a head-shaker and a mind-puzzler. What maggot had got into his brain, they could not say. Had not Joseph hated Butler for years?[10] What they did not know was that Joseph was now prepared to hate or love in accordance with how it affected his people and advanced their cause, and he was canny enough to realize that John Butler was the only member of the department in London who was in solid favor with the government. The taint of the Taylor & Forsyth frauds enveloped Guy Johnson like a miasma, and Claus would always be a foreigner.

With Butler's help (for it was unthinkable that he should speak without an interpreter) Joseph got down to business. Taking up his secondary business first, he spoke to Lord Sydney about the matter of compensation to the Mohawks for their losses in the war. As General Haldimand had already sent in to the government schedules of these losses and as Joseph knew they were already under consideration and that some payment would certainly be made, this first speech was little more than a formality.[11]

It was the second communication that counted. Lord Sydney realized this as well as Joseph did, as he listened to the stream of Mohawk which Butler carefully turned into English.[12] It was substantially the same speech Joseph had made to General Haldimand almost three years before, but brought up to date with an account of recent American encroachments on Indian lands. Joseph reminded Sydney of the important part his people had played in the war and of their unswerving loyalty to the king, and of their astonishment at finding such good allies were not mentioned in the peace treaty. Their omission from the treaty, he said, they could at first hardly believe possible. Since General Haldimand, when applied to (and here Joseph presented Sydney with a copy of his address to Haldimand), had been unable to clear up for the Indians their uncertain situation, and Sir John, upon whose return home they had placed so much hope, had been unable to tell them anything, either, to relieve their uneasiness, he had himself come over the water to find out where they stood. Then he asked the all-important question in so forthright a manner that it could not possibly be ignored.

> It is my Lord the Earnest desire of the Five united nations, and the whole Indian Confederacy, [he said] that I may have an Answer to that Speech and as from our Present Situation, as well as that of the American States, who have Surveyed and laid out great Part of the Lands in our Country, on our Side of the Boundary Line fixed at Fort Stanwix in 1768 . . . (at which time some of the Governors attended in Person . . . so that we had all the Reason to hope that the transaction was binding with Respect to all Parties,) But through their encroaching disposition, we have found they Pay Little Regard to Engagements, and are therefore apprehensive of Imediate Serious Consequences, this we shall avoid to the utmost of our Power, and dearly as we Love our Lands, but Should it Contrary to our wishes happen, we desire to know whether we are to be Considered as his majestys faithfull Allies, and have that Support and Countenance, Such old and true friends Expect.[13]

Joseph also had business in lesser governmental offices. There was the important (to him) matter of his half pay. All the Indian department officers hoped to get half pay for life, as regular military personnel did, and there was a concerted effort among them to achieve this end. Joseph saw no reason why he should not receive the same pension as the others, and he sent in to Evan Nepean, the under secretary who had charge of such affairs, a copy of his captain's commission to support his claim.[14] This claim was of great concern to him. Because of the reduction of the Indian department at the end of the war, he had had no job and consequently no dependable source of income for the past two years.[15]

A month later an incident took place which Joseph did not hear of, but which probably strengthened his hand in some of his negotiations, though it was certainly not meant as a help for him. Joseph never did find out about this occurrence; if he had found out, he would have been both hurt and angry. It happened that Joseph's good friend Daniel Claus got a letter from Patrick Langan, a good friend of his who was secretary of the Indian department in Montreal. Joseph was acquainted with Langan, too, and it seems that he had discussed with him his correspondence with the American, James Monroe. After Joseph defied Sir John and Colonel Hope and made good his escape to England, Langan began to think Joseph's relations with Monroe suspect if not actually subversive, and he wrote Claus a letter casting doubts upon Joseph's loyalty. When Claus got the letter, he immediately sent it on to the ministry.[16] With Joseph's loyalty suddenly in question—it was thought there was some danger he might go over to the Americans—it is likely that he got somewhat tenderer treatment than he might have got if the authorities could have taken him for granted.

Though consumed with impatience, Joseph knew there was a long wait ahead of him. If business proceeded as on his former visit, no decisions would be made and no answers would be forthcoming until the weather moderated and regular Atlantic sailings resumed. Then, doubtless, after arrangements had been completed for his passage home, he would hear his fate. He settled down to wait till spring with what fortitude he could muster.

As it was not in Joseph's nature to sit and pine, he submerged his anxiety in a whirl of sightseeing (for there were always new things to see in London) and social activities. He had a host of acquaintances from ten years before and from his old fighting days to whom he was still a fascinating curiosity, and who sought him out. Embarrassing though he might be to the government, he was still a sort of social lion, a pet of the great and near-great. Joseph also saw and kept company with many of the Loyalists who had thronged to England's shores to get compensation for their losses and who were making affidavits for one another right and left. It was a revelation, he must have thought, to see Claus and Butler swearing to each other's services and credibility. But, then, Joseph had given, and would continue to give, a great deal of evidence for other men, himself. It was the thing to do, under the circumstances they all stood in, and he told Claus he approved of his aiding Butler.[17]

All this running about took money and Joseph was spending, as he so often did, with no thought of tomorrow. The government having made provision for his support while in England and a smaller allowance for Captain Houghton's supervisory activities, Houghton was soon complaining loudly that Joseph was an expensive companion. He told Nepean if he was to keep Joseph company, he must spend guinea for guinea with him and he needed as much spending money as he had in order to do so. Then Houghton mentioned some of their expenses: three guineas per week for lodging and firewood and one guinea per day each for general spending. Either Joseph must be forced to economize or Houghton must have an increased allowance.[18] Houghton probably got the increase, for we hear no more about his complaints. The government did not want Joseph left to wander about alone and get in trouble, or talk to the wrong people, though his talking was difficult to prevent. If the government could pay good money to have certain houses watched—and secret accounts attest to the fact that it did just this—then it would not have begrudged what was necessary to keep so interesting a visitor as Joseph Brant under surveillance for a while.

On February 4 Joseph and Claus and Claus's son, William, went out to see an exhibition of giants and other freaks, and spent some more money.[19] Joseph had a kindly feeling for young Claus, whom he had known from babyhood. At his best William probably was a pleasant, cheerful lad; at his worst he was a no more obnoxious youth than most young gentlemen just out of their teens. A day was surely coming, however, when Joseph could wish in a half-humorous way that he had pushed him under a carriage wheel when he had the chance. Joseph was so often troubled with hindsight about his friends. Of foresight, he had little.

On February 27 Joseph showed up at a masked ball at the Pantheon.[20] This was by no means an aristocratic function. Anybody could get in who had a mask and a guinea for the subscription. It was a very mixed affair, with the nobility, the gentry, the merchant class, the politicians, and the theatrical world rubbing shoulders with one another, dancing, eating, drinking, and making an ungodly noise in a very hot and crowded room. This was an aspect of the white man's world that Joseph could really appreciate. It was gaiety; it was luxury; for a little while it was pure happiness. Wheelock's sermons, dramatic though they were, could never compare. Joseph came as himself—that is, he wore a ruffled shirt and leggings, and a fine blanket which he could carelessly (or carefully) let fall to disclose his weapons. He had placed feathers in his hair, and instead of a mask he work paint.

Circulating about the ballroom were all sorts of characters: Highlanders, Turks, gondoliers, ballad singers, milliners, dancing masters, matchwomen, two more Indian chiefs, a lady dressed as a fortress with popguns decorating her bosom, and a gentleman in the guise of a Freeborn Briton who, though worn down by the weight of customs, excise, and stamp taxes, still contrived to struggle around the floor, lamenting for all to hear that poor old England was undone and abusing all countries except Old England. O'Brien the actor sang some of his own songs; and one of the Turks, if we may believe Brant family tradition, came to grief. Thinking Joseph's red and black streaked complexion was a mask, the Turk made bold to take hold of his nose. Joseph, in a humor for mischief and probably a little tipsy, too, suddenly gave out with his most blood-curdling war whoop. Brandishing his tomahawk around the astonished Turk's head, he scared him half to death and sent ladies shrieking in every direction.[21] Of course it was all in fun. And if Joseph was a little tipsy, so was everybody else.

On another memorable occasion something that Joseph said gave rise to a quite different anecdote. This time he was surrounded by the nobility. One of the noblemen, whose beautiful wife basked in the favor of a Personage and who had himself got some preferment as a result, began to rally Joseph about the strange and savage customs of his people and the difficulty of civilizing them. His Lordship named some of their ridiculous practices. Joseph stood this as long as he could. Then fixing the nobleman with a stern eye, he said the English had some customs which the Indians thought queer, too. And what are they? he was asked. "Why," answered Joseph, "the Indians have heard that it is a practice in England for men who are born chiefs to sell the virtue of their squaws for place, and for money to buy their venison!"[22]

Joseph had such a secure reputation in England as a warrior[23] that he could say what he wished. He usually wished to say something pleasant or witty, however, and his old friends and acquaintances enjoyed his company. Among these friends were Lord Francis Rawdon, of Carolina fame; Charles James Fox, the great Whig orator; and even the Prince of Wales. The prince is said to have entertained Joseph at dinner and to have taken him on some of his rambles about London to places "very queer for a prince to go to," as Joseph used to remark in later life.[24] George III did not hold it against him that he had proudly refused to kiss his hand, and he was a welcome visitor at court.[25] Lord Rawdon gave Joseph his portrait set in gold,[26] Fox presented him with a silver snuffbox,[27] and Evan Nepean (as he told him) commissioned a goldsmith to make him a fine gold watch.[28] Joseph's good friend Lord Percy, who was older and a bit gouty now, would succeed to the duchy of Northumberland a little later in the year. The

Percy family had a great London mansion, Northumberland House, near Charing Cross, and Joseph, still romanticized as the noble savage, enjoyed its hospitality often.

Joseph also saw General Haldimand frequently while in London. The latter, now Sir Frederick Haldimand since his knighthood, was living in the metropolis, going regularly to court, entertaining and being entertained, and enjoying retirement as much as an active man can enjoy retirement. He kept a diary, and in it he recorded many details about Joseph Brant and his affairs. On January 10 Haldimand happened to be calling on the artist, John Francis Rigaud, who was almost a fellow Swiss, since he had spent his early days in Switzerland. Rigaud expressed a desire to paint Joseph's portrait, for of course he, along with everybody else, had heard the famous Brant was in town. That same day Haldimand got busy and had both Joseph and Rigaud to dinner. The three conversed a long time, and Haldimand remarked in his diary that Joseph "appeared to know the interests of his nation, and to be very reasonable." Next day Joseph and Claus took breakfast with Haldimand, and Joseph showed Haldimand a copy of his speech to Lord Sydney. The old general quickly changed his mind about Joseph. He did not like the speech, which he found "weak, shallow and much below what I expected from him." Then he added, "I don't wish to be any longer mixed up with these people." Nor was he. Joseph got no more invitations to dine. The next day, however, Haldimand went again to see Rigaud, and apparently Rigaud was still eager to paint the colorful chief. Haldimand, in spite of his disapproval of Joseph and his speech, seems to have thought it incumbent on him to supervise the whole work. He now began to visit Rigaud very often during Joseph's sittings.

By January 17 the portrait was taking shape, and Haldimand made the artist change a detail which he did not like. Haldimand's interest was now aroused, and he was hoping the finished portrait would be very good. Three days later he was pleased with what he saw, and on January 28 he took General Robertson to see Rigaud's work, and Robertson liked it, too. On February 4 we find Haldimand conferring with Rigaud about getting Joseph's portrait engraved. On February 22 Haldimand took Mr. Dayrolles, another friend, to see the painting, and he, too, admired it.

On March 7 Haldimand again visited Rigaud. He found the artist still working on Joseph's portrait. Rigaud said he would sell the picture for fifty guineas. He also said that Joseph had told him if he did not sell it, he would have it purchased for himself and take it home to America. Perhaps Joseph thought the government would buy it for him or that some of his noble friends would buy it and give it to him.[29] In spite of Haldimand's peevish remarks he appears to have been the person through whom Joseph finally obtained the portrait. Some years later Haldimand sent it to him, along with the portrait of a "friend."[30] The friend was John Hill Oteronyente. The Hill family had wished for years to have Mrs. Richardson's portrait of the deceased John and, indeed, it had been paid for but never delivered.

Rigaud had painted Joseph in the green coat of an Indian department officer with a black shoulder belt buckled with silver. A dark Indian blanket is flung over his left shoulder. Joseph is also wearing a feather headdress with a band ornamented with metal rings. A black ribbon encircles his neck, and a metal gorget hangs below.[31] The mood of this portrait is altogether different from the mood of the Romney portrait of a decade before. No longer does Joseph appear serene or carefree. He looks older, of course, and his features are sharper, his chin heavier. We know trouble and anxiety were gnawing at his thoughts, and his uneasiness shows.

Joseph did not spend all his time sitting for Rigaud or in sightseeing and at dinners and balls. Claus had brought with him to London the manuscript which Stuart and Joseph had prepared before the war for a new edition of the Mohawk Prayer Book. The intention was to get the prayer book published in England and, in fact, it was published there the next year, with suitable engravings and alternate pages in English and Mohawk. Claus had been working on the manuscript off and on for several years and now Joseph was in a position to help him. Together they finished the translations and the corrections, and the Society for the Propagation of the Gospel, under the patronage of the king, took care of the printing.[32] It was through this work, probably, that Joseph met the Bishop of London and the Archbishop of Canterbury. According to family tradition the bishop was very kind to him, and he himself said later that the archbishop in the king's presence offered him any aid in his power in religious matters.[33]

The versatile Joseph was also interested in Indian history. He had the inquiring mind of a true man of his century, and he wanted to delve into ancient Indian customs and arts and religion, and even medicine. Some time or other he had formed the project of writing his own history of the Six Nations. Thinking there might be something in the French archives that would further this work, he planned to go over to Paris before he left for home. He spoke enthusiastically of written records. He hoped he might by the use of French records solve the mystery of the great mounds which he had seen in the Ohio country and which had stimulated his curiosity in 1781–82.[34] When

John Butler told Haldimand of Joseph's plan to go to France, Haldimand remarked laconically, "If it takes place, there is every appearance that he will be more cordially received than he has been here."[35]

On the subject of Joseph's visit to France, there is utter silence in British records; yet apparently he did go. Why was such a visit permitted? The British had always tried to prevent "our" Indians from traveling back and forth to the French colonies, or even from speaking to Frenchmen. They preferred that "our" Indians remain uncontaminated by French influence. Obviously, that preference went double for such a one as Joseph Brant whose loyalty was reported as weakening. But Joseph had an imperious way when he wished to go somewhere, as Colonel Hope and Sir John could testify, and no doubt it was thought that Captain Houghton would keep him out of trouble. At any rate, it appears that Joseph did go to Paris, though he probably did not stay long. Samuel Woodruff, a traveler who interviewed Joseph in 1797, told William L. Stone that Joseph described his trip to Paris to him. His English friends gave him letters of introduction to scholars in France, and the latter helped him with his researches in the archives. The research was not particularly fruitful, though Joseph thought he found something which helped to verify at least one Indian tradition. As Haldimand predicted, Joseph was received with every courtesy, but apparently the French literati did not have time to subvert him.[36]

Busy though he was, and though consumed with worry, too, Lord Percy and Lord Rawdon persuaded Joseph to sit for another portrait. This time the artist was the well-known American, Gilbert Stuart, who would later return home and paint so many of his famous countrymen. Stuart, who had already painted portraits of George III and the Prince of Wales, was in high favor with the court and especially with the followers of William Pitt. Through his elegant London establishment passed most of the notables of the day.

Two portraits of Joseph were actually painted. That commissioned by Rawdon seems to have come first.[37] Joseph is again dressed in his Indian finery, most of which he had already worn while sitting for Rigaud. He is now slightly turned, looking over his left shoulder, so that more of the right side of his face is seen. His headdress of red and white feathers glows all the more against a background of fleecy clouds in a blue sky. He again wears the black ribbon tied around his throat and this time a gorget of shell. Again there is a band of metal rings around his head. A red and black blanket is thrown over a ruffled shirt. Though forty-three years old, he looks strangely young and vulnerable. The dark eyes almost speak. They are so full of pain that they compel the attention of even the most casual observer. This is undoubtedly Joseph Brant just as he was in 1786, after ten years of war and trouble.[38] A very beautiful miniature was made from this portrait, and set in gold, for Christina.[39] Mrs. Catharine Johns, a younger daughter of Brant, always said that this was the best likeness of her father that she had ever seen.[40]

Lord Percy's portrait shows an entirely different pose, but the clothing and ornaments, save for a metal gorget, are nearly the same. Though turned slightly to the right this time, and showing more of the other side of his face, Joseph looks the viewer full in the eyes, just as he did for Rigaud, and he is captured in another uneasy moment. Again his features are etched with sorrow and pain. If he is enjoying his visit to England, he does not show it. If he has any happy expectations, we are not aware of it. He does not look as though he could ever have attended a frivolous masked ball or, in a sportive mood, scared ladies with his upraised tomahawk.[41]

By March 22 Joseph's anxiety had grown to a feverish pitch. His visit to London was almost at an end, but he had heard nothing yet in answer to his questions. His problems were still unresolved. Ignorant of the fact that General Haldimand did not choose to associate with him (for the old soldier could dissemble), he went to him with his worries. He was surprised, he said, that his half pay had not been secured to him since Haldimand himself had led him to expect it. He was also very upset because he had heard nothing from Sydney.[42] We do not know what kind of reply Haldimand made, but next day, apropos of Joseph or perhaps of himself (for Haldimand's own feelings had been hurt by those in power), he wrote in his diary, "The more I know of this country, the more I see that it is the height of folly to trust to the generosity of the nation. Services are forgotten the moment there is no longer need of us."[43]

On March 24 Joseph complained to Haldimand again. This time Haldimand advised him to go to Sir Guy Carleton. The advice worked. Carleton, who had great influence and who, it was reported, was going again to Canada as governor, himself took Joseph to Evan Nepean's office to inquire about his half pay.[44] They found that a difficulty had arisen. Apparently half pay for officers of the Indian department had not yet been determined upon, and Nepean, although polite and affable, did not know how to act in Joseph's case. Joseph was more hurt than ever. On April 5 he proudly told Nepean to forget about the half pay. He had noticed a hesitation about its bestowal, he said, "& where it does not seem clear I should be sorry to accept it therefore I beg of you will say no more about it for was I do get it when doubts about the propriety of it, I should not be happy, for which reason I think it is best to go without it."[45] Though Joseph's grammar was not good, his meaning was clear.

The issue was to hang in abeyance for a year. In 1787 all Indian department officers who had been reduced at the war's end were given half pay, Joseph among them. Sometime, probably before he left London, Joseph got a special pension, granted to a few Indians, of five shillings per day. Both payments were to amount to a little over ninety-one pounds a year.[46] If well managed, they would take care of Joseph's ordinary expenses. They were not enough for extravagant living.

Another subject which bore heavily on Joseph's mind and which he took up with Evan Nepean was that of compensation to the Mohawks for their losses during the war. He himself was in desperate need of this compensation as, indeed, were all the Mohawks. Joseph's personal claims, which included the loss of clothing, jewelry, arms, furniture, farm implements, cattle, horses, cash, and all the land at Canajoharie which he had owned in fee simple, amounted to over £1,112.[47] Molly's claims, which included many luxuries, came to over £1,206. Several other Mohawks also had large claims, but most of the Indians had been poor before the war and could list only the loss of such small items as a beartrap, a brass kettle or two, or a few tools. Joseph heard to his mortification that some of these little claims caused much laughter in government circles.[48] He said afterward the Indians could have claimed the loss of extensive hunting grounds and woodlands north and south of the Mohawk River, and that he, since he had had much to do with making up the schedules of losses, could blame himself for not having included them. Years later this was a deep regret.[49]

Though Sir John and General Haldimand had turned in the Mohawk claims nearly a year ago, nothing had been done about them. In all, the claims amounted to some fifteen thousand pounds, which seemed, even to Joseph, a great sum. Nepean asked Claus and Butler to suggest what payment would satisfy the rest of the Six Nations. Agreeing for once, these two said that six thousand pounds in cash and an equal amount in goods would probably do it. Sir Guy Carleton, when informed of this estimate, said it ought to be doubled. Sir Guy had a very good idea of the value of Indian allies in the defense of Canada, and the situation on the frontier and at the posts was such that he thought a great deal about defense. What the Mohawks finally got was the sum they had asked for, about fifteen thousand pounds. The Senecas and other Indians got what Claus and Butler had suggested. In proportion this was a good deal more than the white Loyalists ever received, for the latter's demands were invariably scaled down. Since the Indians were to be given their regular presents also (and Carleton and Haldimand were in agreement in urging this policy), it would be difficult for them to separate ordinary gifts from compensation or to know which were which. Consequently the Indians were to receive everything from the hands of Sir John (minus what Haldimand had already given them) just as soon as it could be gathered together and sent over to Canada. They were to know that this was bounty straight from the king. To the Indians, it might be compensation for losses; to the British government, it was payment for services, past—and future.

Joseph got his and Molly's compensation on the spot. When he left England he took with him about eight hundred pounds' worth of goods and a bill on Quebec for the rest of the money, some fourteen hundred pounds. He also received a paid-up passage to Canada.[50]

In the meantime there had been a meeting of the Privy Council on the subject of whether to give aid to the Indians in case of a war between them and the Americans. There was nothing to decide except how to word a negative to make it palatable. Lord Sydney was instructed what to say. He spoke verbally to Joseph soon afterward and thought he had satisfied him.[51] A formal, written answer was drafted on April 6.

Joseph was now making his final preparations to leave. He talked with Claus and Guy. Claus suffered from a number of ailments, and Guy was so ill he had to be supported whenever he ventured to walk abroad. Both men were still trying to get their claims adjusted and their accounts straightened out. Both were in very limited financial circumstances and Guy, moreover, was still under the shadow of the great Taylor & Forsyth scandal. Guy hoped to return to Canada, and Claus was considering whether he should or not, but it was the last time Joseph would ever see either.

Joseph gave Claus instructions about the ornaments for his new church on the Grand River. His taste inclined to purple cloth and gold embroidery and gold lettering, and he wanted a silver communion service such as he had seen in the old chapel at Fort Hunter. These sumptuous things, he thought, would strike visiting Indians with awe and respect.[52] He ordered a bell for his church,[53] said his good-bys to Claus and Guy, and set out for the seacoast, laden with letters from people in England to correspondents in Canada, presents from his friends, the gold locket containing his picture, the results of his shopping sprees, and a cage containing two canaries![54]

Somewhere along the way Joseph seems to have received the final answer from Sydney. It came through the hands of a merchant, Alexander Davison. Sydney congratulated the Indians on receiving such a generous financial settlement. On this subject he discoursed at large. Finally, however, he had to get down to the main business. Aquiver with suspense, Joseph came at length to the paragraphs for which he had been waiting three anguished years.

> This liberal Conduct on the part of His Majesty, [Sydney went-on smoothly] He trusts will not leave a doubt upon the Minds of His Indian Allies that he shall at all times be ready to attend to their future Welfare, and that He shall be anxious upon every occasion, wherein their Interests and Happiness may be concerned, to give them such further Testimonies of His Royal favor and countenance, as can, consistently with a due regard to the National Faith, and the honor and dignity of His Crown, be afforded to them.
>
> His Majesty recommends to His Indian Allies to continue United in their Councils, and that their Measures may be conducted with temper and moderation from which added to a peaceable demeanor on their part, they must experience many essential Benefits and be most likely to secure to themselves the possession of those Rights and Privileges which their Ancestors have heretofore enjoyed.[55]

If Sydney had satisfied Joseph with his verbal answer, he had certainly given more encouragement in person than he had put on paper.

In spite of so many weasel words, Joseph managed to grasp the purport of what the minister had written. He was bitterly disappointed for he had hoped against hope, even though he surely had suspected what was coming. Pausing at The Downs, he framed a polite reply, not to Sydney but to Evan Nepean. Then ordering a monkey and a parrot from Davison,[56] he continued on his journey. It seems incredible that Joseph could think of monkeys and parrots on such an occasion, but he always had an extraordinary ability to mingle the ridiculous with the sublime. He could easily mix enticing visions of a gold-laced coat with the gravest affairs of state. He did it time and again. The heavier his heart, it seems, the more he turned to frivolities.

In his letter to Nepean, Joseph gave thanks for the liberal compensation which the Indians had received, and predicted Sydney's message would show all the confederated Indian nations Great Britain's friendship for them. "I should have been more happy," he went on, "if his Lordship letter had also enabled me fully when I return home to have contradicted the reports the Americans have spread among them that great Britain had given to the Americans their Lands & country, and I still hope that when his Lordship reflects on the peace of mind this will restore to the five nations that he will send out by Sir Guy Carleton a Declaration that will afford them Satisfaction on that subject."[57] It was just something to say in a letter that had to be written. In Joseph's breast there was small hope.

A long sea voyage is a time for quiet thinking. It is a time to look backward and a time to look ahead. Joseph was all alone. He had no companion to talk to. There was not even the threat of stalking privateers, as before, to intrude upon his thoughts. He remembered perfectly, so he once said, most Indian transactions since 1760.[58] He could certainly recollect that he, and his family before him, had always done the bidding of the Johnsons. Brant, his stepfather, had been the most compliant of sachems. It was not that Brant had disregarded the interests of his people. It was simply that he had always assumed that what Sir William wanted was best for the Indians. To that end Brant had assented to plans for war and the selling of land, and he truly thought that the king, acting through Sir William, could do no wrong.

Joseph himself had obeyed Sir William as a son obeys a father. Sir William was the best friend the Indians ever had. How many times, at the council fire or in the longhouse, had he heard the chiefs and sachems affirm that belief? Now, perhaps, a little doubt was creeping into his mind. It was a doubt which one day he would acknowledge as a certainty. He had obeyed Guy Johnson, too, and done his bidding when Guy was beset with enemies, and through all the travail of war. He had faithfully tried to help Guy get back to his post at Niagara. But for some time now all the scandals that had been raised were making him wonder if the Indians had consumed the great quantities of supplies ascribed to them. Had they really been so voracious? He had hinted this question to Haldimand before he left Canada.[59] And Claus? Joseph was no fool. He could see who had borne the brunt of Claus's quarrel with Butler.

Did he feel guilty when he thought of the war? There was no denying that he had done his best to involve the Indians in their present disaster, and years later he would try to justify his actions.[60] But in 1786 only a ravaged face, not words, told of inner turmoil. The Oneidas, as he was painfully aware, still had their homeland. Perhaps the Mohawks and others, by careful neutrality, could have held on to theirs as well. When the fighting broke out, all of

Wheelock's young Indian missionaries had cast their lot with the Yankees. Would it have been better if he had done likewise? He did not know, and he never would talk of it. But he could have thought of it, those nights out on the ocean.

Joseph's mind was filling with new resolves which were to guide his conduct for the rest of his life. From now on he would get along with John Butler. He would dissemble to the hypocritical Kirkland—yes, and to George Clinton and General Schuyler and all the rest. He would use their customs against them. He would play upon their fears. But if the hateful Yankees could help him, he would smile upon them, and smile and smile. At the same time, if there were white people in Canada who merited similar treatment, they would get it.

Joseph knew he was expected to transfer the old fealty, the old compliance, to Sir John—Sir John, a man to whom he had never been close. He spurned the idea. Never again would he act as anybody's pliant tool—not Guy Johnson's, not Claus's, not Sir John's—no, not even the king's. At home there was a great work to do. He meant to do it in spite of friend or foe.

Such, as subsequent events so abundantly proved, were Joseph's decisions on that long voyage home. Somewhere out on the Atlantic Joseph Brant became his own man.

19

Rebuilding the Longhouse

JOSEPH'S STOPOVERS in Quebec and Montreal, though short, were enough to produce in the lieutenant governor a whole new range of anxieties and to confirm Patrick Langan in his worst fears. Both men were sure that the ambitious Brant meant only ill to the smooth course of British Indian relations. Said Colonel Hope: "From several conversations with Joseph Brant, during his stay here, wherein I endeavoured to penetrate his intentions and Sentiments, I was sorry to observe that his attachment to Great Britain does not appear to me to have increas'd by his voyage to England, notwithstanding the liberality of Government to the Mohawks, and particularly to himself and Sister—" Then he added hopefully, "But as I believe that he thinks it to be the Interest of the Indians to Keep clear of any Engagements with the Americans, so it is not Probable that he will favor any measure of that Sort."[1]

Patrick Langan, to whose suspicions may be traced the first doubts of Joseph's loyalty, was ready with another critical appraisal for his friend Claus. He pointed out that Joseph Brant had not really possessed full power to treat for the Indians, and that even if he "with all his Subtlety & Craft" should hereafter get such power, "it shou'd not be encouraged by the Minister while the Nation thinks the Indian connections of any consequence, or they keep up an Establishment for Indian affairs, for surely you will agree with me there's no occasion to add to Joseph's vanity, or put any thing in his power that may call forth that restless ambition which you know him to be possessed of."[2]

Joseph's friend, Major Mathews, was also disturbed at the change in him. Mathews reported to Haldimand that Joseph "did not hesitate in all Companies to reprobate the weakness & folly of our Ministers" and that he damned Lord Sydney "for 'a stupid Blockhead.'" "I had whilst at Montreal," declared Mathews, "many conversations with an intimate friend of Joseph's & mine, He assures me that he opened himself to him in a manner that shocked him—very little short of threats to the new [white] Settlements—in short he says that if he speaks the same language to the Indians that he did to Him, there is no saying what the consequences may be—"[3]

Fearing that war, with all its attendant perils for his government, was about to break out between the Indians and the Americans, Colonel Hope called Sir John down to Quebec. He suggested that Sir John go with Joseph to Niagara to deliver Sydney's message to the Indians himself and make the all-important proper explanations (which Joseph could not be trusted to do) or at least to send Butler (who had also just arrived from England) immediately to his post. Sir John appeared to agree to this, and Hope felt greatly relieved. But later he learned that neither Sir John nor Butler had gone anywhere. Joseph had the whole field to himself at Niagara and was able to work what havoc his "poison'd" mind wished. Hope felt that he himself could not be blamed. He could hardly order Sir John to go, he complained to Nepean.[4] He did, however, hurry Butler on, even though he knew he would arrive too late.

The much talked-about Joseph reached Niagara in early July 1786.[5] Here he found that the lieutenant governor's fears of a war between Americans and Indians were well founded. War was indeed on the horizon.

Fresh troubles had broken out while Joseph was in England. Near the beginning of 1786 the American commissioners, Richard Butler, who had officiated at both the treaties of Fort Stanwix and Fort McIntosh, George Rogers Clark, the conqueror of the west, who had also lent his presence at Fort McIntosh, and Samuel H. Parsons, a newcomer to these proceedings, got together some of the Shawnees at a new American fort deep in the Indian country, near the mouth of the Great Miami, and gave them the same harsh treatment that had been meted out to the Indians on the two previous occasions. "We plainly tell you," said Richard Butler, "that this country belongs to the United States—their blood hath defended it, and will forever protect it."[6] The confused and unhappy Shawnees who had come on this excursion against the advice of their British father at Detroit (other western Indians having refused to appear), and who surmised that their brothers in the new Indian confederacy would despise them for their compliance with American demands, tried to protest. They very soon saw that their protests were of no use. The redoubtable Clark set his foot on their wampum belt. Richard Butler told them he would give them eight days' start if they did not sign, and after that they would feel the force of the United States. The now thoroughly cowed Shawnees capitulated. Begging the three commissioners that "as you have every thing in your power, that you will take pity on our women and children,"[7] they extended the line of Fort McIntosh south and west to the Wabash, accepted for themselves a reservation northwest of the Great Miami, and then promptly got very drunk on American liquor. In this wise, on February 1, 1786, while the Great Miami ran thick with ice, the treaty of Fort Finney at one swoop removed the Shawnee barrier and pushed the Americans on through southern Ohio and into what is now Indiana.

It had been a memorable fifteen months of accomplishment. The vast cessions which the Americans had wrested from the Indians—Six Nations, Delawares and Wyandots, and Shawnees—would take care of their exploding population for years to come. Now they had only to bring the Wabash Indians to terms. One more treaty would do it. But Josiah Harmar, chief of the new western army which was to execute the treaties and protect the incoming settlers, did not feel so sure. Harmar had his doubts as to the efficacy of any negotiations with the Indians, past or future, under prevailing conditions. "I am well convinced all their treaties are farcical," said he, "as long as the British possess the posts."[8]

Harmar was right. Relations between the Americans and the Indians rapidly worsened in the spring of 1786. While Joseph Brant awaited the words of Lord Sydney in London, scalping parties of Mingoes, refugee Cherokees living on the Scioto, and Indians from the Wabash harassed the frontiers. Many a settlement in Kentucky and along the Ohio or near Vincennes felt their wrath. Though Colonel Hope in Quebec and Major Ancrum at Detroit and Major Campbell at Niagara scarcely knew what to say to the Indians (for they had received no instructions), British traders and even the lower order of British agents who should have known better, were not so backward. Illiterate and semiliterate Britons living in the Indian towns told the Indians that they expected orders by spring to fight the United States and encouraged them to hope that British military might would soon be on their side. It was easier for the Indians to believe what they wanted to believe than to become reconciled to the idea that they would never receive outright British aid. American frontiersmen came to believe what they perceived that the Indians believed, and soon nearly all Americans thought as a matter of course that it was official

British policy to foment an Indian war on the frontier. The Americans damned the British as perfidious villains.

Dispatches for Hope on the subject of the Indians arrived from England in the same fleet which had brought Joseph home. Lord Sydney was considerably franker to the lieutenant governor than he had been to Joseph, but he was still unable to lay down a hard and fast rule of conduct in case of war between the Indians and the Americans. Said he:

> To afford them open and avowed Assistance, should Hostilities commence, must at all Events in the present State of this Country be avoided; But His Majesty's Ministers at the same time do not think it either consistent with justice or good Policy entirely to abandon them, and leave them to the mercy of the Americans, as from motives of resentment it is not unlikely that they might hereafter be led to interrupt the Peace and Prosperity of the Province of Quebec. It is utterly impracticable for His Majesty's Ministers to prescribe any direct line for your Conduct should matters be driven to the extremity, and much will depend upon your judgment and discretion in the management of a Business so delicate and interesting, in which you must be governed by a variety of Circumstances which cannot at this moment be foreseen.[9]

This was the official British policy, and it was to remain so for nearly a decade. But the generality of Indians did not know it. Spurred on by their friends in the Indian country, they continued to hope for, and even to expect, British military aid. Such was the situation that Joseph found to his horror had developed while he was in England.

Unlike the rest of the Indians, Joseph knew there was to be no British military aid. He also knew the Indians were too weak to fight alone. The best they could do was to put on an appearance of strength and try to win some concessions from the Americans before it was too late. Though the time had come to face reality, Joseph could not bear to lay aside his own cherished dream. He still hoped to rebuild the Longhouse as strong as ever and even to reestablish some semblance of the old Iroquois empire. Perhaps all the Indians from the rising sun to the Mississippi might still sit down together under the Tree of Peace. Was it not a noble thought? Like the sound of the trumpet, it made his heart beat quick. But if it should come about that he could not rebuild the Longhouse to its one-time strength, then at least he might live to see it regain a part of its former influence. From the very first, in pursuance of these aims, Joseph Brant began to work for an accommodation with the Americans on some just principle. Yet for a long time people on both sides of the border believed he was working for war.

He began by doing his utmost to strengthen the union organized at Sandusky in 1783.[10] Many of the Indians hoped for a strong union, too, and there had been councils at Detroit on the subject, and in the Indian towns, and some also at Niagara while he was absent. This news he could take to heart, and it encouraged him to proceed.

He went first to the Grand River with his gifts and all the things he had bought to make the new house more comfortable and to see how the little family was doing. Then he and David Hill returned to Niagara for consultations with Major Campbell.[11] Another council with western deputies was about to meet at Buffalo Creek, for it was at Buffalo Creek that the Onondagas had reestablished the ancient central fireplace of all the Six Nations, both American and British. Joseph was to report to the coming council what he had heard in England. The words he would use and the attitude he would take— these were what kept Lieutenant Governor Hope awake at nights.

Joseph's solitary embassy, though it had violated Indian custom, apparently had not been questioned except by white people. The Indians seemed to know it was no time for them to quibble. Major Campbell predicted dire consequences to Joseph because of the latitude he was giving himself. Campbell thought Joseph was taking upon himself too much, particularly considering his lowly birth, and was heading for trouble. He completely misunderstood Joseph's motives. Said he:

> I cannot help thinking him deep and designing with a stronger attachment to his own Interest than to any Country or People; and I should likewise be induced to add, a very great share of Ambition to become a man of the first consequence among the Nations; tho' his chance of succeeding in this, I should suppose doubtfull; the meaness of his extraction, will certainly be a strong bar in his way among a People possessing Strong Ideas of preeminence in Families and much attached to Hereditary Honours; from these circumstances therefore I should apprehend he may run no small chance of falling a Sacrifice to this last Passion if not managed with considerable address—[12]

The council at Buffalo Creek took place about the middle of July 1786 and was preliminary to a more formal council with British officials which would meet later at Niagara. Since deputies had come from the Wyandots, Chippewas, Ottawas, Potawatomies, Shawnees, Mingoes, and northern Cherokees, Joseph could see to his great joy that the confederacy was holding up. The western Indians wished to make common cause with the Six Nations about the various American treaties they had been forced to sign and all the boundary disputes. As this was only a council among Indians, nothing was put into writing; but the Seneca, Cornplanter, who was present with a message from Congress (though Major Campbell and even Joseph had been very much opposed to his being allowed to attend),[13] later reported to the Americans that Joseph Brant told the Indians that they could expect no military help from the king.[14] Cornplanter also reported he had had some success in persuading several Six Nations chiefs to use their influence for an American-style peace. The main body of the Six Nations, however, still remained firm for the confederacy. Already Joseph and the Seneca, Cornplanter, were headed for a collision.

When the council reconvened at Niagara on July 25, nothing at all was said by Joseph about his embassy to England. The Six Nations were awaiting the arrival of Sir Guy Carleton in Canada, and they officially advised the western Indians to be quiet until Carleton's advice could be heard. Another meeting of the confederacy was set up for the early fall in the Shawnee country.[15] When Lieutenant Governor Hope read the minutes of this council, he was more upset than ever. He wrote Lord Sydney that Brant was going to the west, "where I fear that the poison will be further circulated, and that the Effects of it will very soon be evident."[16]

Joseph did go to the west, although when he left, nothing had been heard from Carleton. He left Niagara about the end of August. At Buffalo Creek he had a brief conference with John Butler, who had just come up from Montreal and who had followed him. Butler reported later that the Indians were so dissatisfied (being in great want of clothing and every other necessity) that Joseph had trouble making up a party of chiefs and warriors to accompany him. Butler soothed the Indians as best he could, though, as he said, "I had nothing to do it with but words"; and next day Joseph and the delegates set sail, first for Fort Erie and then for Detroit.[17] The party arrived at Detroit on September 6.[18] It was the first of Joseph's many journeys to the west in behalf of the Indian confederacy. For almost a decade he would go and come, tirelessly, on one long journey after another. Never did man work harder to realize a vision.

From Detroit Joseph wrote Butler that as soon as he could meet with the local Hurons, he would set out for the Shawnee country. Such news as he had heard from the Indian villages was bad. Most of the western Indians, except part of the Delawares and Hurons, were for fighting the United States. When Kayashota, uncle of Cornplanter, visited the Shawnees and tried to force them by threats to stop their attacks on the American frontier, he had to run for his life. From this and similar news Joseph thought it likely that he and his own party would be treated roughly, too, for the western Indians, fuming over the lack of ammunition, believed the British and the Six Nations were about to leave them in the lurch. The western Indians were just as necessitous as his own people, added Joseph, and he chided Butler because the presents were long overdue. Neither compensation nor anything else had arrived for the Indians, though Joseph suspected there was plenty of goods in store at Montreal. "I wish the English would consider little more serious about this matter," he warned Butler, "otherwise they will at last find themselves too late to do any good to the Indians nor to themselves."[19] Joseph always showed great alarm when the presents were late.

By September 27 Joseph and his party of fifty-seven Six Nations delegates were on their way to the Shawnee town of Wapakoneta (west central Ohio) where they expected to hold council. At this time Joseph told Obidiah Robins, a white man he met at one of the Indian villages, that the Indian country was not a conquered territory and that the Americans had no right to be surveying it. The Indians wished to live in peace, he said, but the Americans must not think they could take any land they pleased.[20] Not long afterward the brother-in-law of Alexander McKee of Detroit told some Moravian missionaries on the Cuyahoga that Brant "was earnest for peace, that the [Indian] nations wanted to have a line fixed and established as far as the land of the free States should extend, and if Congress were contented with this, there would be stable peace among the nations."[21]

In the meantime the Kentucky settlements had been stung into organized reprisals against the western Indians for their continuing attacks. On September 17 General George Rogers Clark with about twelve hundred militia set out from Louisville against the Indians on the Wabash, and on October 1 Colonel Benjamin Logan and nine hundred militia set out from Limestone against the Shawnee towns at the head of the Great Miami. Clark, whose great star was now in its descent, got as far as Vincennes, but his disorderly troops refused to go on to the Wabash towns. But while the Indians were turning their attention to Clark, Logan had everything his own way. His expedition came as a surprise. He burned several Shawnee towns, with all their corn, collected a number of scalps, and captured some thirty women and children. Old Melanthy, head man at one of the towns, who had signed the treaty of Fort Finney and who had always shown friendship for the Americans, was killed by one of Logan's self-righteous volunteers, while holding up his copy of the treaty as witness of his innocence. Among the towns burned was Wapakoneta, where Joseph had come to await the assembling of the council. But luck was with Joseph. He and his deputies were out hunting when Logan's attack took place, and all escaped.[22] Eventually some rather garbled news trickled back to the American frontier that Joseph Brant was instrumental in saving some white people from the revenge of the Indians and getting them sent safely out of the Indian country.[23]

The Shawnee towns being in ashes, the projected council fire of the Indian confederacy was removed to the Huron Village at the mouth of the Detroit River, the next most central place. By November 4 Joseph had returned to Detroit, for it was here that he wrote a letter to Lord Sydney thanking him for a present of a telescope and assuring him that his loyalty was undiminished.[24] By November 19 Joseph had arrived at the Huron Village. Here he patiently waited for the arrival of the Indian delegates who as usual appeared to take their time.[25] Joseph, who could think like a white man, had to resign himself to the delay, although he knew very well that the Indians, who were probably mending shoes and doing similar small chores, did not have all the time they thought they had.

While Joseph was waiting, and while he was traveling to and from the Shawnee country, his actions had been observed and inquired into from Detroit to Quebec. Lieutenant Governor Hope, noting that nearly all Indians in the neighborhood of Detroit had sent out war parties on the American frontier and that they were daily bringing in scalps and prisoners, considered this continuing violence "only to be the prelude to bringing matters to that point, at which Joseph Brant's politics are tending."[26] And Patrick Langan, who had first discovered Joseph's disloyalty, still maintained that "his last Journey to England has neither done him, or His Majesty's Ind^n Interest any service."[27]

As the Indians slowly came in, Joseph talked to them. Langan, who seems never to have missed the latest gossip from his vantage point as Sir John's secretary, reported to his friend Claus that Joseph was very active among the Indians. He frequently harangues them, he said, to prepare their minds for the great meeting, and urges them to unanimity, reminding them they should never lose sight of the fact that they were once the lords of the soil and that all whites are intruders. "Josephs Language," added Langan, "is now very pompous"[28]—all of which Claus faithfully repeated to Evan Nepean.[29]

The meeting got started in late November. Besides the deputies of the Six Nations, there were also present representatives of the Hurons, Delawares, Shawnees, Ottawas, Chippewas, Potawatomies, Twightwees (Miamis), Cherokees (probably those from the Scioto), and various people who lived on the Wabash. Of course not everybody had dared to show up. Some of the Indians who had signed the treaties with the Americans were afraid of being "whipped" by their angry tribesmen.

The Six Nations spoke sternly to the western Indians. Joseph was probably their spokesman though his name is not mentioned in the record. The western Indians were chided for not having come in numbers to the treaty of Fort Stanwix, where all the trouble with the Americans had started. Belts were then given to reestablish and strengthen the union which had been formed at Sandusky—two great black belts with human figures shown hand in hand, and a large white belt with a hand at each end in a position for clasping. The speaker then continued—and if Joseph was not the speaker, these were certainly his sentiments:

> Take but a Cursory view of that large tract of Country, between our present habitations and the Salt water, inhabited by the Christians; and consider the reason why it is not Still Inhabited by our own Colour— It is certain that before Christian Nations Visited this Continent, we were the Sole Lords of the Soil! We were the Lords of the Soil, the great Spirit placed us there! and what is the reason, why we are not Still in possession of our forefathers birth Rights? You may Safely Say because they wanted that Unanimity which we now So Strongly and Repeatedly recommend to you. . . . Therefore let us profit by these things and be unanimous, let us have a Just sense of our own Value and if After that the Great Spirit, wills, that other Colours Should Subdue us, let it be so, we then Cannot reproach our Selves for Misconduct—[30]

This speech swayed the council to action. On December 18 the assembled Indians sent a message to the Congress of the United States. They stoutly denied that they had been conquered. They adamantly denied, too, that they had lost their lands. Then they proposed that a peace treaty be held early in the spring, at some halfway point, and that Congress should treat with all of the Indians there, and not with different Indians at different places. Let the white man and the Indian speak to each other, they said, "in a Style unaccompanied by haughtyness or menaces." Until then, both sides must prevent their people from crossing the Ohio. But if this plan is not carried out, and if fresh ruptures follow, then our united force will be obliged to defend what "the Great Spirit has been pleased to give us, and if we should then be reduced to Misfortunes, the world will Pity us, when they think of the amicable Proposals we made to Prevent the Effusion of unnecessary blood."[31]

This message, with a covering letter from Joseph Brant to Henry Knox, the American secretary of war,[32] was put in the hands of the Shawnees who lived near the Great Miami, and they were instructed to send it on to General Richard Butler. Butler, the American commissioner who had helped negotiate the treaties of Fort Stanwix, Fort McIntosh, and Fort Finney, had recently been named superintendent of the northern department of Indian affairs of the United States. From the Shawnees to the American posts on the Ohio, to Butler, to Congress appeared to be the proper routing of the message, and the Indians assumed that an answer would soon be forthcoming.

On Christmas Eve the same Indians held a council at Detroit with representatives of the British Indian department and with Major Ancrum, the commandant. Through Joseph they related what they had done at the Huron Village to restore peaceful relations with the Americans. Then continued Joseph to his white friends:

> and we Earnestly beg of you to reflect Seriously upon the Consequences and our Critical Situation, It was from an Attachment to your interests that we made Enemies of the Americans, and we are Still involved in hostilities, whilst you are enjoying the blessings of Peace, of which we, your Allies, have not hitherto felt the good Effects—This you must Acknowledge yourselves is a hardship, we again Earnestly require your reflections upon our Situation, you are not ignorant of it, neither are you ignorant of the advantages the Americans would take of us, had they it in their power.
>   . . . as our Affairs with the Americans must absolutely be determined in about five months hence—We will be happy if the English would previous to that period give us a determined Answer, which we may rely on, and by all means freely to Speak their Sentiments, as far as it is consistent with the nature of our alliance—[33]

To this speech Major Ancrum made a noncommittal answer, and Alexander McKee, Sir John Johnson's deputy at Detroit, replied graciously that he would always be happy to give the Indians every aid in his power—consistent with his orders.

To implement their peace proposal the confederated Indians sent a number of their most sensible men as deputies to the south and west, to all the Indian nations who had joined, or who ought to join, the grand union. The deputies were to warn the Indians everywhere to stay on their own ground but to be ready to defend themselves if necessary. Some of these travelers would be gone as long as seventeen months. They visited nearly all their brethren east of the Mississippi, those in the far south as well as in the north.

The Cherokees, Creeks, and other southern Indians were experiencing the same boundary and land troubles as their tribesmen north of the Ohio. White people in Georgia and the Carolinas were as eager for Indian land as New Englanders, Pennsylvanians, and Virginians. The Indians in the south had been equally befuddled by conflicting state and federal treaties, and by rival state and federal authorities, and they were equally dependent on white trade and presents. But like the Indians in the north, the southern Indians thought they had a friendly power to help them oppose the American advance. Spain, who had long owned Louisiana and who had taken over East and West Florida at the recent peace settlement, and whose southern claims extended up to the Tennessee River, essayed to play the same role south of the Ohio that the British played in the north. To safeguard her own possessions Spain encouraged the southern Indians to hold on to their lands, and thereby to act as a buffer for Louisiana and the Floridas against the encroachments of American frontiersmen. New Orleans became a sort of southern Detroit. It was a very tangled situation and, as it progressed, it gave leading Indians and half-breeds and white adventurers below the Ohio a chance to play off the Spanish against the Americans, and vice versa, even as the situation in the north was opening up a chance for Joseph Brant to play off the Americans against the British.

When the far-ranging Indian deputies returned from this welter of intrigue, they reported that they had met with a favorable response. Numerous belts of wampum which they brought back confirmed the good news that Indians south as well as north assented to the idea of a great confederation. By this time Joseph Brant's name was being considered with interest by the Spanish. The Spanish minister to the United States wrote his government that "a certain Brant of the Northern Nations" was one whom "it will be well to win . . . by whatever means we may find necessary."[34] But apparently no overtures from Spain came Joseph's way. The hundreds of miles of hostile territory between New Orleans and Brant were enough to daunt even the most ambitious Spaniards.

While the Indian deputies were going as far as the country of the upper Creeks, the Shawnees who had been entrusted with the message to Congress, seemed in no hurry to send it on its way. For months the important message lay ignored. Perhaps the fatal delay can be attributed to a famine among the western Indians. The Moravian missionaries report of great confusion among the natives, and of Indians fleeing toward the Wabash though "no corn nor means of living to be had, that the children waste away from hunger, and yet all go thither, where many will find their graves."[35] Perhaps some key chief or sachem fell ill. Perhaps someone died. At any rate the peace proposal of December 18, 1786, did not reach General Richard Butler at Fort Pitt till the early summer of 1787. Butler, who was optimistic that Indian relations might soon take a better turn, immediately sent the important packet on across the mountains to New York.[36] Knox, the American secretary of war, received it on July 17. Finally, some seven months after it was written, the message from the Indians was submitted to Congress.[37]

The peace proposal was very late. By mid-1787 new settlements had gone up on the disputed land, surveyors had been laying out additional townships, and so many Indian attacks had taken place (for the young warriors could not be long restrained) and so many reprisals were in the making (for the frontiersmen knew nothing of the Indian peace proposal and would have paid it little mind anyway), that it could be fairly said that war was now raging all along the frontier. If the proposal had ever had a chance to bring about a real peace, it had that chance no longer. Congress had already passed the famed Northwest Ordinance which set up a territorial government for the entire country ceded by Britain north and west of the Ohio. The very country which the Indians proposed to parley about was on its way to being carved up into states!

Shortly before the great confederate council met at the Huron Village Sir Guy Carleton, now Lord Dorchester, whose coming had been so long awaited, arrived at Quebec to take over the government of the remaining British possessions in North America. Lord Dorchester's most immediate problem concerned relations with the Americans and the Indians. He had his instructions about retaining the western posts and for preserving and extending the fur trade, and yet for keeping the peace as far as possible. Lord Dorchester did not mince words. He told Sir John Johnson and the officers at the posts that the Indians were to be warmly clothed and well supplied, but no promises were to be given to them which could not be carried out. On the contrary, the Indians must be made to understand that he had no power to begin a war for their sakes which might involve half the globe in blood and destruction. Furthermore, if war should break out between the Indians and the Americans in spite of British efforts for peace, it must be kept within as narrow bounds as possible.

The Indians did not get Lord Dorchester's message undiluted. The lower sort of agents and traders interpreted official British policy the way they wanted it to be and, indeed, as they may have thought it was. Would Britain stand by and see the Indians destroyed? It was not likely, they agreed. As they were the persons closest to the Indians, they were the persons the Indians believed. They were also the persons the Indians wanted to believe. Apparently, too, the military at the posts and the higher authorities in the Indian department were not so blunt as Dorchester. Though they did not exactly urge the Indians to fight, they rather hoped they would fight—and win. Exclaimed Major Ancrum, at Detroit, after he heard of Logan's burning of the Shawnee towns and of Clark's progress toward the Wabash, "I hope they [the Wabash Indians] will be prepared to give them a better reception than they did at the other Towns."[38] Major Ancrum and officers like him were not influenced entirely by the desire to hold on to the fur trade or by the natural hostility left by a long and bitter war, or even by the realization that the stronger were the Indians the stronger was Canada. Sometimes they felt a measure of genuine concern for the Indians as well.

Occasionally this concern caused the men at the posts to overstep their authority. No doubt they said a few words to the chiefs now and then which did not emanate, in the strictest sense, from Quebec. After the crisis was over, it was officially admitted that the Indians had been "secretly encouraged by the Agents of Government."[39] The British commanders at the posts and the various Indian agents did all they could to promote Indian unity. They also gave the Indians weapons and ammunition. The weapons and ammunition were for hunting, as Lord Dorchester had instructed. Yes, in all humanity the Indians must be permitted to make a living. Could the givers of the gifts help it if the Indians sometimes used their guns against the American frontier? Certainly the officials deplored this new war. They deplored another war just as truly as they had always deplored the taking of scalps.

White people, both Americans and British, had been ever quick to shudder at the horrors of an Indian war. Memories of bloody ambushes, of the unearthly yells of swarming warriors, of surprise attacks in the early dawn, of scalpings and burnings and even cannibalism lurked beneath the surface of every mind. The Indian warriors were indeed ferocious. They were indeed swarming. At least they seemed to appear everywhere at once. They attacked suddenly. They were terrible in their fury. But they were no match for what they had to contend with.

The American frontiersmen were the toughest people on earth. Those who had not been born tough, soon became so. When they said good-by to their old homes and set out to establish new homes in the west, they knew the good-by was final, for scarcely anyone could ever go back. Ahead of them was a journey of unremitting hardship, across mountains and over swamps and down rivers. Their heavy wagons soon converted the old Indian trails into deeply rutted roads, and their flatboats carried families and cattle and furniture past sand bars and over rapids, or got stuck in the shallows and broke up on the rocks. They could hit a snag in the very view of Louisville, and nobody in that roistering new town would bestir himself to come out and help them.

There were frontiersmen who had bought a claim or who received a claim for their war services, but there were others who had no claim at all; where they stopped, they squatted. And they squatted on land in opposition to everybody: the federal government as well as the Indians. Soldiers of the new United States army were sent to dispossess the squatters and pull down their houses, but the dispossessed generally returned. Where else was there to go? In former years such people would have claimed to have bought something; at least before the war they would have thought they had some kind of title. Now they did not claim to have bought anything. The land was there for the taking, they believed, and they were quick to cast passionate aspersions on anybody—Congress, the commissioners of Indian affairs, or the commander of the army—who insisted on such an unreasonable technicality as a legal title. The young leader of a squad of soldiers who had come to evict one Joseph Ross and who read him his instructions, reported that Ross indignantly refused to believe the instructions were genuine. The young officer further reported that Ross declared "Neither did he care from whom they came, for he was determined to hold possession, and if I destroyed his house he would build six more within a week."[40]

Squatter or freeholder, the frontiersman was likely to start his new life desperately poor, subsisting that first winter on little but boundless hope and hominy and water. On his way west he would have ripped the nails and boards from abandoned buildings to get such treasures for his own use, and once he had settled down he delighted to plunder the Indian whenever and wherever he met him. The Indian was envied for his tools and his clothing, and one of the charms of an organized expedition against the "savages" was the chance to plunder whole villages. In due course a horde of towheaded children grew up around the frontiersman's cabin door—children just as tough as he was, for a good many of them survived—their squeals and shouts mingling with the yelps and barks of hungry, mangy dogs, while in the woods and thickets ranged a few razorbacked hogs and a skinny cow or two, symbols of increasing prosperity. And if the well-being of these peripatetic animals depended solely on what they could find in their browsings, it was no matter. Acorns and roots made fine pork according to the frontier taste, and wild onions made milk and butter that one got used to and seldom thought ill of.

The frontiersman bragged a lot, especially of his prowess with a gun, but sometimes he showed himself to be an arrant coward. He had no notion of discipline in fighting and in his disorderliness he lost many a battle. He always worried about the wife and children and crops he had left at home, and his rate of desertions was high. But get him cornered, and he could fight like a demon, often with the aforesaid wife and children doing their best by his side. History is replete with stories such as that of the child who helped his father hold off a party of attacking Indians, of the young girl who ran for a keg of powder amid a hail of bullets, of the family who stationed themselves at the cabin's only two openings, beating back with firewood whatever Indian dared to come in by chimney or door. Then there was the cowardly fellow who fled a fight and was so unmercifully teased by his neighbors that the next time, though disabled by a broken arm, he faced his enemy and fought to the death. And there was Colonel William Crawford, surely the most valiant frontiersman of them all. After Crawford had been tortured to death by the Indians, Simon Girty, who saw it all, reported in awe that, though scalped alive and his head heaped with flaming coals, Crawford never once changed countenance.

The Indian thought if he made it painful enough for the intruding settler, the latter would go away. In similar circumstances the Indian himself would have lost heart and left. But the Indian mistook his enemy. The settler did not go away. Or if he went away, he soon returned. Or some other came in his place. The Indian's great uneasiness grew. He saw boat after boat moving down the Ohio with still more men, women, and children, and he winced. His own numbers which had once been overwhelming were shrinking by a sure attrition. Still, it did not occur to him to question the efficacy of his tactics. He supposed terror, and more terror, was the answer.

Joseph Brant believed he had found a better answer. Fighting was not the solution for a people dwindling in numbers. They would be wiser to keep the peace. And they must hold fast to their union, for in unity lay their only strength. With these thoughts uppermost in his mind Joseph set out for home in early 1787. He was not dissatisfied with his accomplishments at the Huron Village. The western Indians had promised to restrain their young warriors. They had also promised to maintain the union, to do nothing without the common consent. Wisely Joseph did not claim the western country for the Longhouse. No, he said, this land belongs to all, and it must not be disposed of unless all agree. "Upwards of one hundred years ago," as he would later try to explain to a white man, "A Moon of Wampum was placed in this country with four roads leading to the center for the convenience of the Indians from different quarters to come and settle or hunt here. A dish with one spoon was likewise put here with the Moon of Wampum."[41] This was an old Indian metaphor which the Indians broadly applied to all land. The metaphor referred to times of feasting when a great dish was always brought in, with one spoon, and everybody helped himself to meat and broth. So with the land—the land was the dish with one spoon. The western land, so Joseph now conceded, was for the use of all. If only the western Indians would hold fast to this idea and remain united, if only the young warriors could be restrained till the answer came from Congress, the war might yet be won, or at least not totally lost. Such was the hope that Joseph carried home. It was a hope for all Indians as well as a hope for the Longhouse.

On February 10, 1787, John Butler held a council at Niagara with the Six Nations. Though Joseph's name is not mentioned in the minutes, he must have been there, for the subject discussed at the council was taken up by him in a letter to Sir John Johnson a few days later.[42] Butler had asked the Indians whether they would help defend the posts if the Americans attacked. The Indians became indignant. They replied they always had helped, had they not, and why should they be doubted now? Then they pointedly reminded Butler that "we have repeatedly requested your information in case of invasions, which we expected."[43] The remarks were in spirit all Joseph's. Sir John replied to Joseph's letter with a little threat: "Do not suffer an idea to hold a place in your mind, that it will be for your interests to sit still and see the Americans attempt the posts. It is for your sakes chiefly, if not entirely, that we hold them. If you become indifferent about them, they may perhaps be given up; what security would you then have?"[44]

Joseph wrote Major Mathews, Haldimand's former secretary, on the same subject. He thought or, as Mathews reported, *affected* to think that the Americans planned to take the posts by force. Mathews wrote Haldimand that Joseph said the Indians were so disgusted they were seriously considering neutrality in such an event—especially the Senecas, some of whom had gone to Albany to discuss permitting the Americans to build roads through their country.[45]

Mathews answered Joseph at considerable length, and what he said showed that Lord Dorchester had been consulted about Joseph's dangerous leanings. Dorchester again sent word to the Indians that he could not start a war in their behalf. Joseph was willing to believe this—indeed, all his actions were predicated on this hard fact—but the western Indians never lost their incurable hope that it might happen otherwise. Mathews tried to reassure Joseph about the posts and to frighten him a little at the same time. The Indians, he said, "must see it is his Lordship's intention to defend the posts; and that while these are preserved, the Indians must find great security there-from, and consequently the Americans greater difficulty in taking possession of their lands; but should they once become masters of the posts, they will surround the Indians, and accomplish their purpose with little trouble."[46]

The posts were now a matter of the gravest concern. It was vari-ously reported that the Americans were preparing to march against them, or that they were preparing to march against the Indians, or that they were getting ready to set up their own posts in the Indian country, by which they would command not only the Indians but the fur trade as well. Lord Dorchester armed the vessels on the lakes, began a search for additional seamen, set about to count the Canadian militia, and stopped sending mail to England by way of New York. Lord Sydney, when he heard how affairs stood, ordered that the posts be put in a temporary state of defense and that supplies to the Indians be increased. The active aid of the Indians would be needed, he said, if the posts were attacked.

In the midst of this rising furor the Six Nations held one of their private councils at Buffalo Creek. It was about mid-May. Colonel John Butler, who may or may not have been a spectator, reported that Joseph and the chiefs considered the promise made to Congress at the Huron Village binding on them and that they would not stir against the Americans until an answer to their message was forthcoming.[47] Butler obviously thought this attitude on the part of the Indians alarming. He also reported that the Senecas were wavering from their adherence to the king, though he felt sure that Sayengaraghta and some of his followers were as firm as ever in the royal cause. "Brant professes the same," added Major Mathews, who happened to be in

Niagara and who talked to Butler, "but with a certain, either political or saving reserve which is by no means expressive of that decided attachment he has hitherto shown, and which is generally expected from him."[48]

Joseph sent an account of the council at Buffalo Creek to Richard Butler, the American superintendent of Indian affairs. By a strange coincidence Joseph's letter and documents reached Fort Pitt the very same day that the long delayed message from the Huron Village arrived.[49] Richard Butler sent everything on to Congress, but it was far too late. The chiefs had promised no hostilities, and they seem to have been able to keep their promise through April. Then the young warriors grew restive. They could not be controlled. The frontiersmen never had been anything but restive, and they had promised nothing. They also felt themselves far outside the usual restraints of the law. The frontiersmen were not to be controlled any more than the young warriors. By June open warfare had again erupted along the Ohio and in Kentucky.

Such was the situation which confronted Major General Arthur St. Clair, governor of the newly organized Northwest Territory, when he took office. St. Clair, a Revolutionary veteran with years of experience in public life (not all of which was very pertinent to his latest appointment), was one of the wealthiest landowners in the west. A conservative man, with authoritarian leanings, he also had a madcap, pretty daughter who sometimes accompanied him on his travels. Louisa St. Clair was a venturesome miss who might well have been a comfort to a lowlier father when he needed someone to load the matchlock for him between shots at Indians, but to her own father she must have been somewhat of a trial. Strange, however, are the ways of tradition. After a while the dauntless Louisa will gallop her favorite horse right into the story of Joseph Brant. It was the burgeoning war, so it is said, that was to give her this romantic opportunity.

On October 22, 1787, Congress, alarmed by the situation on the frontier and impressed by the message from the Huron Village in which the Indians had so stoutly defended their right to their lands, empowered Governor St. Clair to hold another treaty with them. He was to remove all causes of controversy—but not, however, to abrogate the former treaties unless even more favorable terms could be obtained—to regulate trade, settle boundaries, and do "every thing that is right and proper." Money had already been appropriated to extinguish Indian claims to the lands formerly ceded. The United States now contemplated *payment* to the Indians.

It was a retreat from the untenable position set forth in the treaties of Fort Stanwix, Fort McIntosh, and Fort Finney. For the first time Congress gave up the fiction that the United States, without any purchase whatever, owned all the Indian land by virtue of victory in the war and the peace treaty with Britain. Congress really knew better and had made some slips and admissions along this line from time to time, but this was the first big public retreat. In view of the tenacity of the Indians and their power to punish their enemies and the consequent great expense in maintaining the fiction that they had lost their all, Congress finally drew back. It was well known that the Indians were diminishing in numbers, anyway, and settlement of the west by white people would soon drive away the game and the Indians along with it. Men like Washington and Schuyler and Samuel Kirkland, and Henry Knox, the secretary of war, and, indeed, nearly everyone else, were convinced of the truth of this prognostication.

Knowing that a general meeting with the Indians was in the wind, Richard Butler wrote Joseph Brant in early August asking for a preliminary conference with him and a few Six Nations chiefs as soon as possible.[50] Nothing, however, came of this suggestion. There was no time for a preliminary conference. By the end of the year St. Clair, after a tour of inspection down the Ohio, had invited all the Indians to a treaty to take place the following May. Both Butler and St. Clair promised to attend the treaty. The United States was now preparing to purchase the Indian lands. It seems not to have occurred to the Americans that the Indians would refuse to sell.

Though some of the western Indians had become very uneasy about not hearing from Congress, there is no evidence that Joseph, throughout 1787, suspected his message from the Huron Village had gone astray. Joseph knew messages and replies took a very long time, and he was unusually busy at home. This was the year the Indians finally received their damage payments, and there was much correspondence on the subject. White Loyalists, too, were expecting to be paid for damages sustained during the war, and Joseph attested to many of their claims. His Volunteers, especially, needed his help in proving the extent of their military service.[51] It was a long-drawn-out process. Joseph was also concerned about his pension. Was it for life? he asked Sir John. Sir John replied that the pension was at the king's pleasure, though presumably for life,[52] thus leaving Joseph with a nagging doubt which always worried him.

And while Joseph was so deeply involved in the large issue of reestablishing the power and prestige of the Longhouse, he was also busy with the physical rebuilding of the Longhouse. He continued to hope that the settlement at the Grand River might increase in numbers. He kept his eye on Deseronto's Indians and on the Indians of the Six Nations who had remained in the United States, and never lost a chance to hold out to them inducements to rejoin the rest of their people. He and the chiefs gave formal deeds to the white friends who had moved to the Grand River, and Hendrick (Henry) Nelles and his two sons, Robert and Warner; Adam Young and sons, John, Daniel, and Hendrick; John Docksteder; and Hendrick and John Hough got deeds to the lands they already occupied along the stream. Their farms were to extend three miles back into the country and were never to be alienated. The Indians and their old friends of the war would live side by side in friendly intercourse forever, the one learning from the other, and to the mutual good of both. Fourteen chiefs and sachems signed the deeds and of course Joseph signed, too, but sachem Henry Tekarihoga's name topped all but one.[53] Thanks to hard work and planning, the settlement at the Grand River was looking better. Sir John Johnson after a visit to pay the Indians their "bounty" (which proved how much the king loved them) reported to Claus that the settlement "is a very fine one, they have a Number of good houses, a Neat little Church, and a good School House."[54]

As the year 1787 slid into history several events happened which cast long shadows ahead. General Harmar reported from new Fort Harmar at the mouth of the Muskingum that from June 1 to December 9 one hundred and forty-six boats containing 3,196 persons with all their equipment and cattle had passed down the Ohio in front of his garrison. And General Henry Knox, writing to General Harmar at his far-off command, cautioned him particularly against Joseph Brant. Harmar was to advise his subordinates at all the lonely little outposts in the west to be on guard against Brant and his "confederated" Indians.[55] Arthur St. Clair, the new governor, received from Congress a more general caution that "Every exertion must be made to defeat all confederations and combinations among the tribes."[56] To divide and conquer had become the settled American policy toward the Indians. Sir William Johnson's old rule of conduct went forward in American hands though it had been temporarily abandoned by the British themselves. It suited the British at the moment to encourage Indian unity. It suited the Americans to give Indian unity no countenance whatsoever.

20

The Dish with One Spoon

THE WESTERN INDIANS, not having heard from the Americans, were confused and divided. Many were for peace, but some chose war. Some unhappy Wyandots from Sandusky, for instance, wanted to revenge themselves on the Americans because they had lost a great many of their people in an outbreak of smallpox. All the Indians could agree, however, that another council of the Indian confederacy ought to be held in the spring, and messengers were sent in every direction with belts of invitation.

On March 20, 1788, Joseph wrote Patrick Langan that he expected to attend. He was disgusted with the attitude of that part of the Six Nations who lived on American soil; "most of them," he complained, "have sold themselves to the Devil—I mean to the Yankeys. Whatever they do after this, it must be for the Yankeys—not for the Indians or the English." He had not given up, however, on trying to influence them to remain faithful to the Indian confederacy.[1] Such remarks must have pleased the suspicious Langan very well.

Joseph's concern for his brethren across the border was not new, but it was intensified by something that had happened the preceding year. Late in November 1787 the American part of the Six Nations, led by Cornplanter, had leased for 999 years to a group of powerful speculators, informally called the Lessee Company, everything in New York west of the old line of 1768 which they did not actually occupy. Since the Lessee Company was obviously seeking a legal substitute for an illegal purchase (for only the state could buy Indian land), and since the preemption right to much of the land in question had been given to Massachusetts in a boundary settlement between that state and New York, the government of New York refused to sanction the lease.

The Six Nations in Canada were upset by the vast acreage involved, for they knew British authority frowned upon any grant of land to the Americans, and even the Indians in the United States fell to arguing about how such a thing could have happened. Some accused Cornplanter of taking bribes. The unfortunate Cornplanter, already in trouble with his people, had more likely been fooled by the prestige and wealth of the Lessee Company into thinking that the lease would be legal. At any rate, Joseph leaped into the argument, and so did Governor Clinton and the New York legislature. Presently the Six Nations found themselves expected not only at a council on the Maumee River with the western Indians and a council at the falls of the Muskingum with St. Clair—for the Indians had finally got an answer from the Americans—but also at a council with some Massachusetts people at Buffalo Creek and a council at Fort Stanwix with Governor Clinton, all scheduled to take place at nearly the same time.

Like their western allies, the Six Nations, too, were confused and divided. The problem was the same: land. Thousands of white Americans were pushing for land beyond the old Fort Stanwix line, and the Six Nations, weakened by war, could not withstand the thrust. Their situation, difficult enough, was sometimes exacerbated by their own conduct. Individuals or small groups of chiefs, answerable to nobody, tried to sell land on their own or pretended to sell land on their own and got tangled in all kinds of witless proceedings, harmful to everybody. But even if the Six Nations had been highly organized and fully able to control their people, there would not have been much they could do except to give in. The Indians had once been a formidable barrier to the settlement of western New York. That barrier was crumbling.

Joseph thought he had an opportunity to draw the American part of the Six Nations, which still numbered between four and five thousand, into closer union with the Grand River Indians,[2] making the whole stronger, and he chose to go first to the council at Buffalo Creek. Here, in July 1788, he and most of the Six Nations from both sides of the border met with the Massachusetts people who had the legal right to extinguish the Indian title to everything west of Seneca Lake. The upshot of this council was the famous Phelps and Gorham purchase of some two and a half million acres of Seneca country.

Joseph played as prominent a role as he dared. The Seneca chiefs and sachems would not have looked kindly on his intruding himself too boldly into their affairs. In spite of the legendary dish with one spoon, the Senecas regarded the land in question as theirs and theirs alone; and no Mohawk had a right, they would have said, to intervene in its sale. Oliver Phelps and Nathaniel Gorham had bought some six million acres in western New York (more than half of which they later lost) from the state of Massachusetts, and Phelps was present in person to negotiate an Indian sale. In the end he got all the Indians possessed between Seneca Lake and the Genesee River for a down payment of five thousand dollars and an annuity of five hundred dollars. The rate of payment was higher than the Lessee Company had given, and the rejoicing Senecas, who knew what they sold was already being overrun by squatters, were able to retain for themselves the still empty country west of the Genesee. It was in every way a much better deal than that of the year before.

It was Joseph who, having been chosen with Samuel Kirkland and John Butler to value the land, had insisted on the better price,[3] and he and his friend David Hill were given the credit by those in the know for the success of the negotiations. Brant and David argued and coun-ciled and finally got their way.[4] Kirkland also exerted his influence in favor of the purchase, and so did John Butler, a long-time acquaint-ance of Phelps, and a number of other Loyalists from Niagara, mostly traders and Indian agents. Some of these men had also been mixed up with the Lessee Company. It was a strange combination. When it came to profit in land, however, former Tories and former rebels could usually find some point of agreement. All these white helpers and expediters got land cessions or shares of various sizes and kinds, some of which were to cause a great deal of trouble to their recipients. The trouble, of course, was all in the future. Everybody, for the present, was happy. The Indians were very happy. Though they had had to let the Lessee partners have a large grant to the east of Phelps and Gorham as a compromise, they had been able to extricate themselves from a very difficult position. Joseph wrote in a pleased vein to Gover-nor Clinton that the Six Nations were solving their land problems.[5]

Joseph could well be pleased, for he had won what appeared to be a significant victory for himself, too. His theory of the common ownership of land got some acceptance, even among the not-so-friendly Senecas. On July 8 the entire Six Nations, Canadian as well as American, were permitted to sign the deed to Phelps and Gorham, though it must be admitted that the Americans for their own protec-tion probably insisted upon it. Henry Tekarihoga was the first signer, and Joseph next, with the Senecas signing last of all.[6] The Senecas, in whose eyes the first payment of five thousand dollars loomed very large, meant, of course, to look out for their own interests. They carefully saw to it that the rest of the Six Nations, wherever they lived, should later renounce all claims to the great tract and consequently to the five thousand dollars. For this surrender the Senecas generously allowed the signatory nations to get their "just"—and very small—share of the annuity.[7]

Joseph would not have been so happy about this entire transaction had he known that a rumor had started among the Senecas that he had received a gift of thirty thousand acres from Phelps and Gorham. This rumor finally reached Lord Dorchester, who reported it to Sydney.[8] Though Joseph was distrusted all the more and probably watched even more narrowly, there is not the slightest evidence that the rumor was true. Joseph was probably paid a small fee for helping to value the purchase, but it was a legitimate fee for a legitimate service. He was also promised a fee in land by the Lessee Company which he was never to receive. This fee Joseph must have thought legitimate, since he had no hesitation in mentioning it to Governor Clinton.[9]

The business at Buffalo Creek having been concluded, Joseph sent word to Richard Butler at Fort Pitt that he was coming to his council at the falls of the Muskingum as soon as possible. He begged Butler to be patient till he could arrive and added politely that he was looking forward to meeting him personally.[10] As he could not be in two places at once, he apologized to Governor Clinton for not attending his conference at Fort Stanwix[11] and, with a crowd of Six Nations delegates, immediately set out for the Maumee River and the council with the western Indians. At little Fort Erie Joseph and the rest of the delegates separated. The former went by land along the north shore of the lake, and the others took the more convenient water route. Joseph wanted to visit the Missisaugas, his nearest neighbors. He apparently intended to do a little missionary work for the confederacy as he traveled along. He finally reached Detroit on August 10.[12] He found Detroit prepared for almost any eventuality. If the Americans tried to capture the town, they would attack a fort greatly strengthened and in good repair. If the local French had any ideas about helping the Americans, they would find that six guns were trained on the French part of the town, ready to go into action.

At Detroit Joseph met with some Hurons, Chippewas, Ottawas, Potawatomies, and other Indians who had been waiting for him. He held a council with them and found to his distress that their unanimity had evaporated. There were arguments as to where the confederacy should hold its next council. He finally persuaded the Indians to go on to the Maumee Rapids, as formerly agreed upon, but he suspected that some of them wished first to confer privately with the Americans to take care of their own affairs. Confederacy business could wait. On the other hand, the Miamis wanted to have no council at all with the Americans, but to go to war at once. Joseph hoped he could convince all these people of the error of their ways, but he admitted that if he failed, he would not know what to do next.[13] On September 4 he and his party set out for the council at the Maumee Rapids (above present Toledo). An officer of the Indian department went with them.[14]

Down on the Maumee the confederacy appeared to be even more strained. The Indians came in very slowly, some taking as much as five weeks to make the journey. Before any business could be done, the Shawnees planned to have a feast. The feast would take up two more days. "I have still my doubts whether we will all join or not," Joseph wrote in a pessimistic mood to Patrick Langan, "some being no ways inclined for peaceable methods." He estimated that the Hurons, Chippewas, Ottawas, Potawatomies, and Delawares would join with the Mohawk deputies in favoring moderate measures. Rather than leap headlong into a destructive war, these Indians would give up a small part of their country to the Americans. But the Shawnees, Miamis, and Kickapoos, who lived farther from the reach of American vengeance and who now got the greatest part of their living from plundering the American settlements, would be very willing to declare for war. They would refuse to make any concessions and, indeed, would probably not even go to St. Clair's treaty. It could be the means of the confederacy's breaking up, but Joseph was determined to do his utmost to prevent such a disaster.[15]

In the meantime Governor St. Clair was having a council house built and provisions collected at the falls of the Muskingum (below present Zanesville, Ohio), the place to which he had invited the Indians to parley. But already the Indians were two months late for the meeting. Suddenly, in early July 1788, a war party swooped down the river and attacked the small corps of soldiers who were guarding the treaty premises. One man was killed and two wounded before the warriors were repulsed.

St. Clair had intended to entrust himself to the proceedings with the Indians without military protection. He thought again. The upshot was that he removed the provisions from the falls and sent a sharp remonstrance to the Indians. He also informed the Indians that the meeting place had been changed. The treaty would be held at Fort Harmar, not at the falls. Then he notified the militia of the Pennsylvania and Virginia frontiers to hold themselves in readiness for action. He had heard that many young warriors were among the delegates on the Maumee River, and he thought their presence there not much in keeping with Indian custom. The rumor had also got about that Brant, who talked peace, was really for war and that most of the warriors belonged to his party.[16] At Fort Harmar, where St. Clair waited, nobody knew what to believe. Everyone was uneasy. What were Brant's young fighters up to? Exclaimed one outspoken observer: "Brant is a damn'd Rascal, & by his Influence in the Indian Councils prevents their being with us—but they are not, we are told, unanimous & could this Fellow be deposited with his Ancestors I should enjoy the hope of, at least, a temporary accommodation."[17]

St. Clair was already planning how to conduct the general war with the western tribes that he thought was surely coming and that might even break out at his council. He favored simultaneous expeditions against Ouiatenon, on the Wabash (site of Lafayette, Indiana); the settlements of the Kickapoos, across from Ouiatenon; Terre Haute, home of the Piankashaws, farther down the Wabash; the Miami villages on the Maumee (present Fort Wayne); and, far to the east, Cuyahoga. Could a stroke be made at all those places about the same time, he predicted the Indians would very likely divide themselves in such a way as to make every attack successful; "for you may be assured," he told Knox, the secretary of war, "that their general confederacy, if it exists at all, has not that efficiency which would enable the heads of it to direct its force to a point in the security of which many of the members would not feel themselves much interested, when each had to fear for themselves separately." St. Clair fully understood the Indian weakness which Joseph Brant most deplored. "It is difficult enough," the governor went on, "among nations who have a regular policy and strong governments, where the ideas of union and submission are familiar. With savages it is impossible."[18] St. Clair meant to play upon that weakness unceasingly.

At the Maumee council, where the confederacy had met to determine one policy for all, the Indians, as Joseph had feared, fell to arguing among themselves. Some of the western members of the confederacy had been rethinking their position. The dish with one spoon looked too much like the old Iroquois empire. It was a thought which the western nations could not tolerate long. The Iroquois were their ancient enemies. Confederacy or no confederacy, what right had the Iroquois to meddle in their affairs? What right had Joseph Brant to meddle?[19] Some of the western Indians were for fighting and some were for attending St. Clair's council, and some were for both. Some had one opinion when sober and another when drunk, and then there were others who just wanted to give up and go home.

The widespread gossip about what was going on among the Indians[20] probably did not exaggerate the dissension. Spies reported to the Americans that the Chippewas, who did not like the Mohawks or, indeed, any of the Six Nations, had plenty of company to share their aversion. The Kickapoos and Miamis would agree to nothing that was proposed and would propose nothing themselves. Some Delawares dredged up old gossip that Brant and his Mohawks had offered them up as "broth" to any nation who would undertake to destroy them. The once-proud Delawares, now scarcely more than poor wanderers amidst the swamps, thought again of the hated petticoats and their many grievances. Who were they, in their resentment, to discount a rumor about old enemies? St. Clair, still waiting at Fort Harmar, heard that some of the western Indians had threatened to kill Joseph Brant. He did not know whether Brant was threatened because he advocated war or because he held out for peace. It could be either, the general thought.[21]

St. Clair continued to wait at Fort Harmar for many weeks, and still the rumors eddied about. It was reported that when Brant received St. Clair's notice of the change of meeting place, he threw the letter in the fire, saying it was very bad. He claimed the Americans were trying to persuade the Six Nations to join them in a war against their allies. He cursed and condemned the Americans, and then, drawing the sword he always carried, thrust it into the ground, and told the Indians "there was a sword for them Use it when they pleased." It was also said that if St. Clair had gone to the falls of the Muskingum as first proposed and if he had refused Brant's demands there, "it was likely that the Sword would have been buried in his Body."[22] These tales and many others Indian spies and rumor-mongers and those hostile to the Six Nations or to the idea of a confederacy repeated to the Americans.

The rumors and the gossip about Joseph's warlike stance were far from truth. Subsequent events showed that Joseph, who could read the handwriting on the wall as well as anybody, was actually pleading with the Indians to give up part of their land in the hope that they might retain the rest. He thought they could spare everything east of the Muskingum and its Tuscarawas branch and thence north and east over to Venango. This was territory bound to be settled soon by white people, and it was the least defendable.

By and large, those Indians nearest to the American frontier were willing to accept Joseph's compromise. Those who thought they lived too far away to be hurt, especially those who lived on the Maumee and the Wabash, scorned compromise. The Ohio River, they declared, must remain the boundary between the Indians and the white people. The Ohio had been the boundary since Sir William Johnson made it so in 1768, and they refused to consider any change. They refused even to go to Fort Harmar. They rightly interpreted St. Clair's change of locale to mean that his council would be held under the guns of the fort, and that idea hardened their opposition. Indians had had little luck with councils at American posts. The Indians heard, too, and many believed the rumor, that the Americans meant to give them poisoned rum or blankets contaminated with smallpox. The council was hopelessly divided. There is an old story that about this time someone shot at David Hill, who sided with Joseph. Joseph was furious, for David was his good friend, and he berated the culprit, who claimed the act was an accident, in every language he knew.[23] Amid all these controversies the stock pile of food sent down by the British at Detroit was consumed. Since game was scarce and hunting poor at the rapids of the Maumee, the Indians grew hungrier and hungrier. Many set out for home. It was now late October.

Joseph and his Mohawks started for the Muskingum. They planned at least to meet with St. Clair. They hoped some reasonable agreement could be worked out. Going before Joseph and his party or following at their own leisure were representatives of the nearer Indians who also were willing to treat with the Americans. The knowledge that St. Clair was going to give away presents was enough to get even some hostiles started on the same trail. These were very hungry people. St. Clair himself was well aware of this fact. He also knew that the pangs of hunger fought on his side.

At Upper Sandusky Joseph wrote St. Clair a letter which was probably a protest about the latter's choice of meeting place and a request that the council be held at the falls of the Muskingum as first planned. The falls would be a place much more acceptable to the Indians.[24] This letter was sent to St. Clair by David Hill and Joseph's son Isaac. Probably Joseph used his influence to give Isaac this responsibility, thinking it would be good for him, and David was friend enough to take the youth in tow. The two messengers went on ahead, and both of them made a good impression at Fort Harmar.[25] David always did make a good impression on white people, and Isaac, who could speak English well, for once did nothing outrageous.

Joseph and the rest of his party, making their way down through what is now central Ohio, reached Licking Creek about mid-November. They were now some fifty or sixty miles away from Fort Harmar and close to the falls of the Muskingum. Here messengers arrived from St. Clair. St. Clair refused to comply with Joseph's request.[26] Joseph later said bitterly that the Hurons and Delawares had sent a private message to the American, telling him they would accept whatever terms he proposed. Joseph's position was already undermined.[27]

It was a bad situation, but Joseph and his adherents tried to cope with it. Unfortunately, it was even worse than they thought, for they did not realize how much St. Clair knew of the recent dissensions on the Maumee. Hopefully they sent St. Clair a speech outlining their idea of a proper compromise. The compromise, they declared, was the decision of the Six Nations and the western Indians in council. They repudiated former peace treaties as made with only a few unauthorized Indians, but offered to reopen the question of the boundary. They told St. Clair they would consent to the Muskingum River as the dividing line between whites and Indians. They would give this much land for nothing, they said, but they could neither give nor sell more.[28] The message was sent off. Back came a prompt reply. St. Clair refused to accept their compromise.[29] The Muskingum was too far to the east. The United States could not give up what had been granted at Fort McIntosh and Fort Finney.

Joseph and his Mohawks and all the other Indians at the camp, some of whom had come with him and some of whom had just arrived, councilled together. The Seneca, Cornplanter, who had been down at Fort Harmar with St. Clair, was present. Cornplanter spoke very persuasively and urged the Indians to come with him to the meeting.[30] Joseph opposed. He and his followers constituted the majority of the council, but they could not get unanimity. Joseph finally wrote St. Clair that he could do no more without consulting the confederacy.[31] Then he and the Mohawks and many of the others decamped. On their way back to Lake Erie they met those Indians who were still coming down and persuaded most of them to turn back, too.[32] It was the measure of Joseph's chagrin and disappointment that he told the Shawnees before he finally parted with them that they ought not to send to consult the Six Nations on every little question that came up. Some greater decisions, he added, would not bear putting off. The western Indians should be able to defend themselves against encroachments without consulting anyone. Then he cautioned them against provoking the Americans.[33] It was good, practical advice, given at the expense of Joseph's deepest feelings. There was scarcely anything he liked better than to be consulted.

Sometime before Joseph left the Muskingum, so it is said, Louisa St. Clair suddenly appeared at the Indian camp. A ranger who carried one of St. Clair's letters to Brant reported—it is not clear whether then or long afterward—that the young lady was determined to see the famed chief. She set off alone and, meeting the ranger on the trail, persuaded him to let her deliver her father's letter. At Brant's camp she did not see Joseph, but she did see Joseph's son Isaac. What is more, Isaac saw her, and promptly fell in love with her beauty and daring. Isaac escorted her back home (*he* guarded the brave, he told her) and, according to St. Clair family tradition, asked the general for her hand in marriage. Of course the young Indian's proposal was rejected. Some years later, however, in spite of hurt pride, Isaac, true to his lost love, spared General St. Clair in battle.[34] This does not sound like the bad-tempered Isaac who very likely already had a wife nor is there any evidence that the beautiful Louisa was even at Fort Harmar at the time.

Another version of the romance would have us believe that it was Joseph's youngest son, John, who wanted to marry Louisa St. Clair.[35] This version will not do, either, for John Brant was not yet born in 1788. Many are the legends that have grown up around the Brant name, but the legend of Louisa St. Clair is surely the most fanciful.

Regardless of all that Joseph could do or say, some two hundred Indians went on to Fort Harmar. They were Delawares, Wyandots, Senecas from the Allegheny and the Genesee and other Six Nations Indians who could not escape the American orbit, Ottawas, Potawatomies, Chippewas, and even a wandering Sac or two. Some of them sent St. Clair word that they wanted to hear what their brother had to say, for their hearts were good and they believed his heart was good, too. There were those who felt they could do no other thing and those whose hunger overrode every other thought, and some who hated Joseph Brant and his Mohawks even more than they hated the Americans. But two hundred Indians (and they included women and children) were not many for so important a treaty; and St. Clair, who had felt sure that the Six Nations would hang about all winter just to be fed, had to admit, with no little embarrassment, that his council was sparsely attended. There were no Shawnees, no Miamis or Indians from the Wabash, no Mohawks, and very few of the chiefs of any nation.

Fort Harmar, on the west bank of the Muskingum at its mouth, had been built three years before to protect surveyors and bona-fide settlers and to keep out squatters. It was now headquarters for the main American garrison in the Ohio country, and it overlooked, just across the Muskingum, the burgeoning settlement of Marietta. In one or the other of these places could be found General Harmar who commanded the army of the west and who thought treaties with

Indians were just so much "idle business"; General St. Clair, the territorial governor, who was bound and determined to have a treaty, come what would; and some thirty substantial families from New England who intended to make Marietta in their own image. The two hundred Indians were at a disadvantage from the start, and they knew it.

Throughout the proceedings of the council Joseph Brant was almost as much a living presence as if he were actually there. His name, pronounced in anger, was on every tongue. It was as though the speakers were justifying themselves by attacking Brant. Cornplanter led the assault. Between him and Brant, as the Americans fully realized, was a "mortal and open rivalship and enmity."[36] Indeed, Cornplanter had become Joseph's number-one adversary, for Sayengaraghta had died. Cornplanter accused Joseph of spreading confusion among the Indians at Fort Stanwix in 1784. He was very bitter. "Brothers," he said, "I now tell you that I take Brant & Set him down in his Chair at home and he shall not Stir out of his house, but will keep him there fast, he shall no more run About amongst the Nations disturbing them and causing trouble."[37] Other Indians spoke up, accusing Joseph of misleading them, of withholding information, or of false interpretations of St. Clair's letters. A Wyandot told St. Clair privately that Joseph was getting ready to attack Fort Pitt.[38] It was finally noised about among the Indians that the reason Brant did not attend at Fort Harmar was that St. Clair had bidden him go home, that he had no business there![39]

The council dragged on for nearly a month. Finally getting down to the real matter at issue, Cornplanter reminded St. Clair that the Indians must live by hunting. They could not exist without their land, he said. An old Wyandot chief then told how the Indians had been cheated since the very beginning by the white man. We are poor, helpless people, said the old fellow, and he begged St. Clair to have pity and let the Ohio boundary stand. St. Clair, following the instructions of a government that was ready now to pay for what it took but that could not renounce the taking, answered that the United States would not give up what it had obtained by the previous treaties. The United States wanted peace, he said, but if the Indians wanted war, they should have war. The old Wyandot did not want war. Neither did the other Indians. Most lived too near the frontier to gain anything by fighting. More likely, they knew, war would destroy them. They gave in. It was January 9, 1789, and intensely cold.

Two days later the two treaties of Fort Harmar—often spoken of as one—were signed. "This was the last act of the farce," commented an

American officer.[40] The cessions of Fort Stanwix and Fort McIntosh were confirmed, the first by Cornplanter and his Six Nations followers and the second by the few hungry remnants of the western tribes. The Indians accepted their payments, three thousand dollars to the Six Nations and six thousand dollars to the others, with apparent gratitude. St. Clair, who had done all he could to divide the Indians, even to the making of the two treaties instead of one, reported to Knox on the good consequences of the meeting: "that their confederacy is broken, and that Brant has lost his influence."[41] St. Clair could boast, but it was not he who had divided the Indians. The Indians had accomplished that, themselves.

On his way home, somewhere between Wheeling and Pittsburgh, Cornplanter was fired on by hostile white settlers. And when the Chippewas got back to Detroit and had some conversation with their British friends, they said they thought they had signed nothing but a treaty of peace. They claimed they thought the payments were presents. Obviously they now knew the difference between payments and gifts. Other Indians who had signed the treaty gave various excuses for themselves, and many grew very discontented. By spring some of those who had signed were disavowing the act. They declared that they would fight for their land. If they lost it, they would at least lose it like men. As for those Indians who had not gone to Fort Harmar, they disavowed St. Clair's treaty from the beginning.

Joseph, sore in heart, had returned to the Grand River. His dream of one confederacy, one land for all, seemed far from fulfillment. He had to admit to himself that he had accomplished little for the western Indians and nothing for the glory of the Longhouse. His long journeys, all his labors, had been in vain. The dish with one spoon was broken, perhaps never to be mended. Unhappy thoughts, these—but there was no time for Joseph to puzzle his mind about what he had done wrong. At home he walked straight into another controversy.

A dispute which had been simmering among the Grand River Indians for over a year, and which Joseph had had little opportunity to deal with when it started, had reached the boiling point. Some of the Indians objected to the presence of the white people on their land. Joseph had continued to give large farms to his Volunteers and members of the old Indian department in the hope that their example would educate and inspire his people. There were white families settled now all up and down the river. But some of the Indians were not so eager to perfect themselves in what Joseph called "husbandry and the mechanic arts." They liked their old ways, and they preferred to live remote from whites. Suddenly Joseph and Henry and Catharine and David Hill (for David also helped) had their hands full. Catharine preferred old ways, too, but if Joseph wanted new ways, she would go along. Henry was, as usual, the staunch ally, and Captain David was, as usual, the good friend.

But the trouble was not all white versus Indian or the new mode versus the old or even Fort Hunter Mohawks versus Canajoharie Mohawks as it often appeared to be. Some of it was Joseph Brant himself. There was that about Joseph which could excite the jealousy of other Indians, and he had had too much experience in such situations not to know what was going on at this time. Sayengaraghta and his Seneca followers of the old war days—not to mention the younger Cornplanter and a rising Seneca leader named Red Jacket—and those western Indians who had so recently threatened his life were hostile and unfriendly for more than one reason. All these had their real grievances, but they were also thinking that Joseph Brant had become too great a man. There were now persons on the Grand River, even among Joseph's former friends, who had found something on which to feed jealousy, too; and the usual drunken frolics in home and tavern gave a vent to their feelings.

Sir John Johnson and, eventually, Lord Dorchester were brought into the controversy. While Joseph was absent in the Ohio country, his two main opponents, Isaac and Aaron Hill, took their case to Montreal to a council with Sir John. Sir John, to placate them, promised that the white people should be removed from the Grand River.[42] There is some evidence that Isaac and Aaron went on to Quebec to see Lord Dorchester. At any rate, the latter heard of the dispute with alarm, and he, too, promised to get rid of the offending whites.[43]

Privately Sir John blamed everything on Joseph. The disturbances originated, he said, "in the Ambitious Views of Captain Brant." Brant, having procured the land grant and other benefits for the Indians, "wishes to be considered as the Chief, and to have the rule and direction of the whole Settlement." This, the few Fort Hunter Indians living there naturally oppose, Sir John explained.[44] Major Mathews, taking his cue from Sir John, hit the quick when he reminded Joseph that dissension among his own people on the Grand River "must weaken their interest, and yours in particular, in the great scale of the Indian Confederacy; and how heavy the blame must fall upon whoever shall be considered the promoter of so great a calamity." Then Mathews sent the thrust to the heart by advising Joseph to "exert all your powers in establishing perfect union and friendship among your own nation, and you will convince those at a distance that you are capable and worthy of cementing a general union for good purposes."[45]

Apparently Joseph did try sincerely to mend the rupture. When he returned home and found the ugly situation—for Aaron and Isaac were not only David's brothers but Christina's in-laws as well—there was much counciling among his friends and between his friends and the opposing party. He and his friends seem to have made promises (and apparently carried them out), and he tried all the spring of '89 to settle the controversy and bring back peace to the Grand River. But Aaron and Isaac, who by now were threatening to kill Joseph, were implacable.[46] They ended by returning to Deseronto's settlement at Quinte from whence Joseph had probably persuaded them to come in the first place. It should have been enough to make Joseph think twice about ever again inviting reluctant Fort Hunter Mohawks to the Grand River, but he was so eager to increase the size of his settlement that he never ceased to urge them and almost anybody else to come and join him. Quinte was always a thorn in his flesh. He wrote General Haldimand about his troubles, saying wistfully: "The few who adhere to h¡m [Deseronto] are inconsiderable as a separate body, but if united to us, would be of some note— Misfortunes &ca have allready too much reduced the Numbers of our Nation to admit of Party Spirit and disunion—"[47] These days Joseph was very unhappy. He was hurt at Mathews and all his "friends below" who were so willing to believe ill of him.[48] He became touchy and glowered a great deal. A young lady passing through Niagara on her way to Detroit did not find him at all prepossessing. He was the first and only "savage" with whom she had ever dined at table, she said. The party was large, and she could not hear his conversation, but she was "by no means pleased with his looks."[49]

Nothing came of the official promises to force the white people to leave the Grand River. For many years these people were an irritant to some of the Indians. From time to time disputes arose among the Indians, between whites and Indians, and no doubt even among the whites themselves. Then the disputes would taper off and seem to come to an end. Those who had the power, if there were any such, never tried very hard to remove the white people from the Indian land, possession being eleven points of the law, anyway. And, of course, after a while what happened among the Indians was not nearly so important as it had been in the early years of the province when it had threatened the very peace and well-being of everybody.

After affairs on the Grand River became quieter and while the western Indians were, presumably, making their own decisions, Joseph went once more to the rescue of the American branch of the Six Nations. The great principle of the dish with one spoon as well as concern for the welfare of all his people—not to mention that restless ambition he was purported to have—would not permit him to stay aloof when he was needed. He knew that while he was in the west, the Onondagas had sold all their lands to the state of New York for a lump sum and an annuity, keeping only a small reservation for themselves. Kirkland's faithful Oneidas had done likewise, though they had obtained somewhat more generous terms from their former allies. This had left the Cayugas and the Senecas with land still to sell, and shortly after Joseph got home from the Muskingum, the reluctant Cayugas, persuaded now by poor crops and famine, finally agreed to part with their land. Unfortunately the sales of the Onondagas and Cayugas had been made in contravention to the compromise that had been worked out among the Indians, the Lessee Company, and Phelps and Gorham at Buffalo Creek in July 1788; and in a few months many of the Onondagas and Cayugas, especially those who lived at Buffalo Creek, who had seen little of the purchase money, were dissatisfied with their treaties with New York. They claimed that those Indians who had sold out had not been authorized to do so. At this point Joseph stepped in.

On June 2, 1789, the dissident Indians, with Joseph as one of the signatories, wrote a letter to Governor Clinton from Buffalo Creek, where they were counciling among themselves. They urged that surveys and settlements on all the disputed lands be stopped.[50] At the same time they sent a complaint about New York's actions to the federal government.[51] The letter to Governor Clinton was rather peremptory, and of course that vile Indian, Joseph Brant, got all the credit for it in Clinton's mind.

The indignant Clinton addressed his reply to Captain Joseph Brant and "other Indians." He accused the Indians of selling lands to individuals contrary to New York law (obviously referring to the compromise with the Lessee Company), and gave that as his reason for making additional purchases for the state. He said the treaties were fair, and he forbade the Indians to molest surveyors or settlers. His tone was far from conciliatory. He also informed the Indians that the Lessee Company, who he thought was influencing them, had been forced to give up its recent deeds to the state.[52]

To this Joseph and his friends made a prompt and angry reply. They were sorry that Clinton had paid so little attention to their former letter, for they had tried to explain that he had not negotiated with individuals who were authorized to sell. While the more important chiefs were absent in the Ohio country, Clinton had deliberately held his treaties with a few insignificant Indians whose "Ideas of Advantage are but momentary and never discend [sic] to Posterity, and they are too blind to see the Traps laid to disunite the Nations to which they belong." They reminded Clinton that the Indians held their land in common and a few individuals could not sell it. Denying that they had been influenced by outsiders, they then warned the governor that the surveyors and settlers must proceed no further. Their tone was not conciliatory, either.[53]

By this time everybody was very angry. Clinton, hearing the latest news from the Ohio country, began to think that Brant was trying to create a diversion in favor of the western Indians who had once more gone on the warpath. Still, he could not use force against the Indians even if it were advisable. The state had no adequate force. He must negotiate.[54] He wrote Brant and the rest that their latest letter was so highly exceptionable in every part that he could not answer it in the usual way he liked to address his brothers. Nevertheless, he expected to lay their complaints before the legislature in January, and he thought the legislature would at least authorize a meeting with any chiefs who cared to come to Fort Stanwix when the next annuities were to be paid to the Oneidas, Onondagas, and Cayugas. A full explanation of the land purchases from those tribes would be made then. Clinton promised the Indians that the lands would not be opened to settlement immediately, but he told them the lands must be surveyed. He insisted the surveys not be interrupted. If the Indians committed violence, they must answer for the consequences; and no meeting with them or explanation would take place. The constitution and laws of the state must be maintained, and the state never would admit any right to lands purchased from the Indians without the consent of the legislature. He again accused the Indians of being influenced by the Lessee Company.[55]

Before Joseph had a chance to see this letter, he unburdened himself to Major Mathews, the man whom he always considered his friend. He could scarcely contain his unhappiness. The trouble over the New York land sales and his disappointments in the west seemed equally to agitate his mind. He asked Mathews whether Britain intended to keep the frontier posts, for he had heard rumors that they would soon be given up. He wondered whether the Indian department was to be kept on its old footing. He feared not, for he complained that the Indians were not getting their normal supplies and that they were being mistreated by a new commander at Niagara. Then he went on in his misery (and obviously nobody had helped him compose this letter):

> Dear friend it is a critical times for us here I mean we the Indians. I felt very unhappy often times of late. The most difficult Part for me is of having a many children which concerns me about them very much Particularly when our Indian affairs and Situation stands so unsettled the civilized cruelties I mean the Yankys are taking advantage all the while, and our friends the English seems of geting tired of us. if I have not got so many children I would soon do some thing to drown my unhappiness & Leave more marks behind Me than what my father did, I think you done very right of not having a Wife & Children other ways you would be dam coward like Myself—[56]

For Joseph the year 1789 ended as badly as it had begun. That fall one of the usual frightening rumors that periodically swept through the upper country hit Detroit and Niagara. It was said that the Hurons, Potawatomies, and Chippewas, urged on by some French missionaries, were plotting to attack both the garrison at Detroit and Joseph's settlement at the Grand River. This they planned to do as soon as the navigation was closed and help could not be had from down the lakes.[57] Lieutenant Colonel Harris, who commanded at Niagara and whom Joseph disliked and had already complained of, ordered a strict watch on the Indians. Joseph and David Hill, who had the run of the fort and who always wore their arms when they came in, were stopped at one of the gates by a suspicious sentinel. David was disarmed, but Joseph succeeded in retaining his weapons. Both chiefs were hurt and indignant at the apparent lack of confidence in them.[58] The rumor turned out to have only the flimsiest base. The missionaries were innocent, but it did appear that Deuentite, a Wyandot chief who had signed the treaty of Fort Harmar, was dissatisfied with Joseph and his attempts to organize and carry on the Indian confederation.[59] Joseph could now plainly see that he was distrusted by at least some of the Indians and certainly by many of the British. It was not a thought to lighten his black mood.

The unhappy Onondagas and Cayugas, thoroughly cowed by Governor Clinton's threats, did nothing all spring to stop the surveys of their country. In June 1790, when the annuities were due to be paid, they docilely went down to Fort Stanwix. Here, amid the ruins, they accepted a compromise. Joseph, having had all winter to think things over, realized that a hostile position would avail the Indians nothing.

He, too, at Clinton's invitation,[60] agreed to go to Fort Stanwix.[61] During the council that followed he acted as interpreter, and sometimes as speaker for the Indians,[62] and he smoothed the way for a settlement between them and the state of New York.[63] Joseph believed in making the best of everything. If the Indians could not get what they wanted, then they might as well get what they could, and want what they could get. The explanation Clinton made about the land sales did not explain very much, but he offered the dissenting Onondagas and Cayugas five hundred dollars and one thousand dollars respectively in extra payments. Of course the governor prevailed. The Indians confirmed the former sales, took their money, and went home to their reservations.

Joseph did not hesitate to remind Clinton that he had been promised a tract of land by the Lessee Company. Clinton replied that the state could not confirm anything the Lessees had done, but he gave Joseph a present instead of the land.[64] He and Joseph parted on good terms. Before the two men left Fort Stanwix they discussed the growing troubles in the Ohio country. Joseph admitted that the United States was strong enough to overpower the western Indians and take the lands in dispute, but he thought warfare "was by far the dearest way of securing them."[65] Clinton wrote President Washington, head of the new federal government, that Brant "is a Man of very considerable information, influence and enterprize, and in my humble opinion, his Friendship is worthy of cultivation at some Expense."[66] It was a thought which had already occurred to Washington.

Joseph returned to the Grand River and sent Governor Clinton a polite note thanking him and the other gentlemen who had been at Fort Stanwix for their civilities to him, and he included his regards to all. Joseph was always punctilious in this respect. He essayed a little joke. One of the gentlemen had bought some land on Long Island, a place which the Mohawks had once conquered, and he sent word that he expected a tribute from the new owner.[67] Clinton could be excused if he felt that his relations with the once hostile, and even terrible, Brant were vastly improved.

Before the year 1790 had ended, John Butler was in trouble with his government because of the part he had played in the Phelps and Gorham purchase. It was known that he had received a large tract of land, and it was rumored that he had made a fortune. Actually, he had assigned the land to some American relatives to whom he owed money, but he had a great deal of explaining to do, and he was censured by Lord Dorchester. Joseph, who had been well pleased originally with the Phelps and Gorham purchase, began to feel that he was not so pleased after all. He wrote Sir John Johnson that the sale was not transacted with "either Honor or Justice." He thought the Indians had been swayed too much by Butler and other white men in the Indian department. He said, since the Indians looked to Butler for advice, Butler as their agent should have laid aside his private interests and given them advice for their own good; "however," he added, "I am Sorry to think it has not been the case." He accused Butler of frightening the Indians with a poorly veiled threat that, if they did not sell to Phelps, Phelps would join with the Lessee Company, and the Indians would lose their whole country. Joseph said he was willing to testify to these facts.[68]

In little more than a year Joseph's opinion of the Phelps and Gorham purchase had turned completely around. He believed the growing rumors about Butler and came to his own conclusions. This time nobody put notions into his head. The notions were his own. Daniel Claus had been dead almost three years and Guy Johnson more than two. True, Sir John still lived and harbored a lingering bitterness against Butler, but his influence over Joseph amounted to little. Eventually Joseph got over his hard feelings, and he and Butler went on as before. Joseph did not usually carry grudges and Butler, though hurt to the quick by all the uproar over what he thought was an innocent transaction, was a pragmatic man.

When Joseph left the Ohio country and advised the western Indians to make their own decisions and not come running to the Six Nations with every trifle, he also warned the Indians not to provoke the Americans to organized retaliation. If they did, he cautioned, they would lose their homeland by force. It was a warning which the Indians, especially the young and undisciplined warriors of the Maumee-Wabash country, had not much heeded. Throughout 1789 and on into the next year war parties of Miamis, Shawnees, displaced Cherokees, and others who lived on those rivers, as well as a scattering of youth from other areas, plundered, burned, stole horses, took scalps and prisoners, and killed. They made a profit at the same time they satisfied their thirst for revenge. They aimed many of their expeditions south of the Ohio, against Kentucky, for there were more small settlements and isolated cabins there than elsewhere. Kentucky, which was filling up rapidly, was also the main Shawnee grievance. Kentuckians, not to be outdone and equally undisciplined, carried on counterexpeditions into Indian towns north of the Ohio where they plundered, burned, stole horses, took scalps and prisoners, and killed.

Both whites and Indians exerted themselves to retaliate every wrong, but neither party needed the motivation of revenge to get started. Plunder and horses and even derring-do were motivation enough.

In the early fall of 1789 some of the warring western Indians had come to the great fireplace at Buffalo Creek, ostensibly to get advice, but it is doubtful whether they wanted advice so much as they wanted approval for what they were doing. Joseph and a party of his Mohawks came down from the Grand River to meet them, and a council was held on September 7. The western Indians apologized for those of their number who had broken away from the confederacy and gone to St. Clair's treaty at Fort Harmar, and they declared ingratiatingly that the Ohio lands belonged to all in common—that no particular nation owned them and no particular nation could sell them. They asked for help against the Americans.

They got neither help nor full approval. Joseph was the speaker for all the Six Nations except the Senecas. "You are not to wait for council from us," he said, "after they have encroached upon You. You must look upon Your own strength, and we advise you, that if You can come to any reasonable Terms with those people, it will in our Opinion be best to agree with them." Then he urged them to hold fast to the Indian union and to keep their neighbors informed of what was going on. The Senecas, who had been accused by the westerners of talking too much to the Americans, were even less encouraging. Farmer's Brother, a noted Seneca, defended his own people, saying the king had told them to make peace with the Americans, but he promised that when the king again called upon them, they would rise and show themselves. In the meantime all the Indians should remain united.[69]

The next spring young Isaac Brant was sent by the Six Nations to the Miami chiefs with the message that they should lie still a little longer.[70] This was pure euphemism. The Miamis were not, and had not been, lying still.

The American frontier was screaming for help. The little forts, so far apart, so undermanned, so destitute of supplies, often on short rations, and hungry, were no better protection than their counterparts had been during the Revolution. Scouts did little good, and were expensive. Expeditions sent out by the settlers did little good, and they were expensive, too. A general offensive against the hostile Indians seemed to be the only answer. Let the United States army march out and fight in defense of its suffering citizens. The demand swelled to an uproar.

A new federal government was sitting in Philadelphia, a new

constitution embodied the public hope, and General Washington, the savior of his country, had been elected its first president. Some of the westerners went so far as to think this new and strengthened government would bring them the millennium—that is, everything they wanted of security and even affluence—and they had enthusiastically worked for its adoption. But they became disillusioned quickly when it seemed the new government paid too little attention to their concerns. They grew suspicious and their loyalty became lukewarm when it appeared that the United States was more interested in making a trade treaty with Spain for benefit of the eastern seaboard than it was in getting Spain to open the Mississippi River to free navigation.

Down at New Orleans the jealous Spanish had shut up the great river with an enormous tax, and it was a calamity to the whole length of the American west. Getting free navigation would indeed bring affluence; not getting it meant depression and poverty. It was a long, hard way back to market over the mountains. It was hard for man and beast. It was almost impossible for heavy wagons loaded with grain. Westerners gazed toward the smooth highway of the Mississippi and its feeder rivers, and harbored treasonous thoughts. They would take the law into their own hands. They could declare themselves independent. They would conduct their own foreign relations, carry on their own foreign wars. They could join Spain or fight Spain. Their thoughts turned to France, though now so far removed from their border and now in turmoil itself. They could make a deal with Britain. They could even join the old enemy and send their produce to market through the lakes and down the St. Lawrence. Such were the ideas of desperation; and men like Colonel James Wilkinson were ready to take the advantage, and the great George Rogers Clark, conqueror of the west, was himself about to be involved in strange episodes. Through these scenes canny Britain held on to Niagara and Detroit and Michilimackinac and the other posts and, though very cautious in public, thought privately of getting back what it had lost. British agents and spies, here a Beckwith, here a John Connolly, there a George Welbank, collected intelligence in the capital city or wandered unchecked among Indians and whites. All the while the American frontier, to a man, never ceased to believe that the British incited the Indians to their onslaughts and supplied them with the implements of war. Then what good were treaties with the Indians? While some of the savages came and took presents, their brethren would be out scalping.

The new federal government did not want to make war on the Indians. In many parts of the country it would not be a popular war.

Nor did the new government wish to fight Spain. But the disaster that it desired least of all was war with Britain. The very thought of fighting Britain sent shudders down governmental spines. There was no money for a protracted war. There was so great a distance to traverse to engage the enemy, and the army was new and untried. There were so many urgent but neglected tasks to get on with. Worst of all, there was no other market to go to, to buy what was needed, than Britain.

A few last efforts at peace were made. Major John Doughty was sent to reason with the southern Indians who were making inroads far out of their own country. He and his fifteen men were attacked on the Tennessee, and only five of the party escaped with their lives. A Frenchman from Vincennes was sent by Governor St. Clair to the Miami towns. The Indians there insisted that any deals be made through their confederacy, and St. Clair's agent had to turn back. He had scarcely been gone three days when the Miami Indians, in a gesture of utter disdain, burned a white prisoner.

In Philadelphia the cries of rage and anguish from the frontier were heard at last. It was clear to Congress and the president that they must act, and act soon, lest the country be torn apart. In spite of reluctance and poverty and all the untransacted business of state, in spite, even, of the risk of a British war, the western settlers must be pacified. On June 7, 1790, General Henry Knox, the secretary of war, by direction of the president, authorized General Harmar "to extirpate, utterly," the "banditti" on the western waters. An expedition composed of federal troops and militia would destroy the Indian towns and bring the recalcitrant Miamis and other hostiles to their knees. The expedition was to strike that fall. It was to be a surprise.

General Harmar and Governor St. Clair finally put together an expeditionary force. It was just such an army as could be gathered in those remote parts in the course of a few months. There were 320 federal troops and 1,133 local militia—one battalion of militia from Pennsylvania where the executive, politically opposed to Washington and St. Clair, had not chosen to cooperate, and the rest from Kentucky. As usual the militia and the regulars were not on the best of terms with each other, the militia officers disputed over commands, and as usual the contractors had trouble with the supplies. As usual every militiaman came more or less late, and some of them had not been upon the frontier long enough to know how to handle a gun. Of discipline, there was little.

The government in Philadelphia being eager to allay any trepidations among the British at Detroit or among friendly Indians, Governor St. Clair sent a message to the commander at Detroit that the expedition was not aimed at him, and he sent other messages to the Ottawas, Chippewas, Potawatomies, Wyandots, and Senecas that the expedition was not aimed at them. It was aimed, he said, at the Shawnees, Miamis, and other hostile Indians who had refused to take hold of the chain of friendship at Fort Harmar and whose depredations had become intolerable. The commander at Detroit replied loftily that he was not worried. The friendly Indians made no reply, but awaited the issue with bated breath. They had the uneasy feeling that no matter who got the victory, they were the ones who were about to get the whipping.

In late September the expedition set out from new Fort Washington (Cincinnati)—for so far down the Ohio River had the line of American forts and even settlement been pushed. Nobody could call the expedition a surprise for the eyes of all the west were upon it, and its route soon showed its objective. The expedition headed overland for the Great Miami and thence made its ponderous way across the portage northwest to the Miami of the Lake or the Omee River (now the Maumee), a stream which flows into Lake Erie. It was virtually unknown country, full of brush and briars, obviously flood-washed at times. Near the site of present Fort Wayne, Indiana, where the St. Mary's and St. Joseph Rivers meet to form the Maumee, were some half dozen villages of hostile Miamis, their houses and crops already partially burned by the retreating Indians themselves. Harmar's army finished the burning, and detachments fought scattered engagements with the enemy. These engagements ended with a large proportion of killed and wounded among the Americans but with the Indians relatively unscathed.

The Indians, mostly Shawnees and Miamis, for their medicine men had frightened some others from taking part, fought fiercely. Some had ammunition they had requisitioned from resident traders or obtained from their British friends at the recent annual distribution of presents; some had tomahawks and spears; others possessed only bows and arrows. The American regulars, though few in number, bravely stood their ground; but some of the militia, unnerved at the sight and sound of the painted, yelling Indians, their mounts shying at the bells and flapping ornaments on the Indian horses, threw down their guns and fled. In the meantime the main part of Harmar's army, which took no part in these engagements, was running out of provisions, while heavy October frosts had ruined the grazing for the cattle and horses. The expedition, probably not realizing the purport of its losses, returned in an orderly way to Fort Washington. The Indians did not pursue. They, too, had run out of food.

By November 5 Joseph Brant got some inkling of what had happened and immediately wrote a letter to George Clinton. Though he was no less worried about the course of future events, he must have taken some small, perverse pleasure in the writing of that letter. What he told Clinton was the usual story of ambuscades and the surprise of those who had come to surprise Indians. None of it need have happened, he added, if St. Clair had not claimed so much of their country at one time.[71]

Back east, at the seat of government of the United States, nobody knew what had befallen, for it was a long, weary journey from the Miami towns to Philadelphia. By December 1 Washington had received a disquieting letter from Clinton, and hoped that Brant's news was not true but feared that it was.[72] On December 13 came the long-awaited dispatch from Harmar reporting that the Miami towns, which had been the headquarters of the frontier depredations, were destroyed. The expedition was an "entire success," declared St. Clair in an exuberant dispatch of his own. But it was soon noted that the great success was only a Pyrrhic victory, at best. In the east and in the west the disproportionate losses were pondered over. Presently the more realistic sort of men began calling this latest encounter with the western Indians "Harmar's Defeat." General Harmar, stung by the mounting criticism, demanded a court of inquiry and, after being exonerated, resigned his command.

The Indians did not have to weigh the pros and cons. They knew all along who had won. Their yells, as they approached what was left of their home villages, were the joyful yells of victory.

As the year 1790 closed, Joseph Brant could see only trouble ahead for his grandiose plans for his people. The confederation so carefully nurtured since 1783, was split into three, possibly four, diverse segments. There were those Indians who had gone to Fort McIntosh and Fort Harmar and who were so fearful, they would give the Americans anything they wanted. There were those Indians who feared nothing and would give nothing and who had just won a heartening victory. There were those Indians who, like himself, would prudently give something in the hope of keeping the rest—probably the majority, or at least so Joseph always believed. And then there were others, and some of his Grand River neighbors were among them, who simply did not care. They had their own problems. It was not their ox that was being gored.

At this point Joseph knew only that the Americans were marching into the Miami country. What ought he to do? No Mohawks had taken part in the actions against Harmar, and no other men from the

Six Nations, either, so far as he knew—and if any did, they fought only as individuals and not from the settled policy of their councils. Joseph considered the matter for three days and finally decided to send messengers to get intelligence and to condole with the western Indians for their losses and show them "that we are Steady in our friendship." But this would not be enough, for he well knew that he and his people would soon be getting urgent pleas for military aid. He had to consider very seriously whether he would enter a war in which the Indians had so small a chance of ultimate victory. In his perturbation he asked Sir John Johnson's advice. Sir John was, after all, a representative of the British government, whether he liked him or not. "From my dis-agreeable Situation at present," he wrote Sir John, "when I Know the Enemy are in the Country of our Allies, [I] would wish to have your Opinion and Advice by the Earliest opportunity . . . before I take Any active part."[73] Could he dare hope this late for British intervention? It was a thought which he could not put aside.

21

And the Moon of Wampum

THE COMMANDANT at Detroit, when he told St. Clair that he felt no uneasiness at the approach of Harmar's army, spoke something less than the truth. He was uneasy. He sent Matthew Elliott, second-ranking Indian officer, to the Indian country to watch the American progress from as near a position as he could. He listened eagerly to the intelligence brought in by traders from the Maumee and invited their opinions. Alexander McKee, having gone down to give the Indians their annual presents, reported to headquarters on what information he could gather at the Maumee Rapids.

As the Americans moved forward, excitement mounted in Detroit where rumor had it that an attack on the post was imminent. There was excitement not only in Detroit but at other posts, too. The commanding officer at Niagara was on the lookout for a diversion in support of Harmar. At Oswego they were seeing bogies. There were even fears for Lake Champlain and the St. Lawrence communication. All these fears were exacerbated by the thought that the population of New England alone was four or five times that of Canada.

At Quebec Lord Dorchester, who could believe that the Americans would never be so foolish as to start a war with Great Britain, could also believe that they were aiming at the posts and the fur trade, and he could hold both of these opinions at the same time. Further clouding his peace of mind, temporarily strained relations with Spain over the Nootka Sound controversy made war with that state possible. With a war so near the American frontier, Dorchester thought anything might happen. He went to very great pains to give the Americans no provocation. He censured Sir John Johnson for merely sending a speech to the Indians that conceded they might have to defend their country against an invasion from the south.

In London William Wyndham Grenville, successor to Lord Sydney in the state department, lamented the "excesses" of the Indians. In this he but reflected the views of the Pitt ministry who felt an American-Indian war would create nothing but embarrassment and danger for Britain. When some Creek and Cherokee deputies, therefore, arrived in London looking for aid in their war with the whites of Georgia and the Carolinas, they got no encouragement. The ministry had no intention of giving military aid to the Indians either north or south of the Ohio.

The heads of the British government were eager to settle the matter of the posts. They wanted to keep the fur trade and to control all of it, but they wanted to control it in peace. Indians who went out scalping had little time for hunting. Such Indians might get plunder for themselves, but they had few furs to sell, and it was furs that maintained the trade. General Haldimand, when he urged the keeping of the posts, had also suggested that an Indian buffer zone between American territory and British territory would redound to the benefit of Britain. Haldimand's idea appealed to Pitt and Grenville. With the proper diplomacy, they reasoned, it might be carried out, and much good would flow from it. If both the Indians and the United States could be persuaded to accept British mediation, peace could be made, a buffer zone set up in which no whites would be allowed to settle, the posts given up or dismantled, the trade in furs retained, and everything that could bring on a frontier war with the United States rendered harmless. Nor was it unthinkable that Britain might get back some part of her lost territory. Mr. Oswald, the negotiator in 1783, had not known much about American geography. There were better boundaries between Canada and the United States, from the British viewpoint, much farther south than those established by the peace treaty. Lord Dorchester, agreeing, and hoping to render a great service to his country, was more than willing to act as the mediator. He began at once to set the stage for the great peace effort.

With such an attitude in high places, lower places had to fall into line. The officers on the frontiers, vulnerable in their lonely outposts, deprecated the Indian habit of taking prisoners. They remonstrated with the Indians for their conduct. If prisoners escaped, they freed them. They also bought prisoners from the Indians as often as they could and sent them home. Indian agents and even British traders, who were beginning to see where their true interests lay, did likewise. The passions of the former war were cooling on both sides of the border. In the United States local laws against Tories were being gradually repealed. Nevertheless, when British agents brought some returned prisoners to Pittsburgh, the Americans still thought they had come to spy. Unfortunately the Americans could have been right, for the times, though improving, were not halcyon. Everyone was not behaving just as he ought to behave in every instance. Both sides, of course, remained carefully alert. Warlike rumors never stopped.

In the winter the mail was very slow, and that may have been the reason Sir John Johnson did not answer Joseph's letter of November 8, 1790, till February 22, 1791. On the other hand, Sir John was in a quandary. Joseph had asked for advice on whether he should give active aid to the western Indians. Sir John, in his answer, which was marked "Private," was so noncommittal that he did not even refer to Joseph's question. He used up a good deal of wordage in explaining that the Fort Stanwix line was the proper boundary, and (having been in England recently, where he had conferred with the ministry) he suggested that Britain should offer to mediate between the Indians and the States. He got no closer to the advice Joseph wanted than to vouchsafe: "Upon the whole you understand your own rights better than I do. I shall, therefore, say no more than to recommend coolness and a manly firmness in whatever you may determine on."[1] Joseph was left not knowing whether Sir John had received his letter or not. He continued to wait for more advice.[2] He never got it.

In the meantime the western Indians, jubilant after their humiliation of the Americans, began to press Major Smith, the commander at Detroit, for aid. They were not content merely that the British surgeon should treat their wounded or that extra provisions be sent them or that they should get help in setting up new villages or reestablishing themselves in their old villages. They wanted a promise of definite military aid. Blue Jacket, the Shawnee war chief, who had led the forces against Harmar as much as any war chief could be said to lead any general Indian force, went up to Detroit with a deputation and, scarcely ten days after his victories, put the all-important question to Smith. The chief, once friendly to the Americans, denied that the Indian nations had sanctioned any aggressions against the Yankees. Some "naughty" young men had gone a-scalping without permission, he said; but now that an American army had been sent against them, all the nations were determined to defend their country and the Ohio boundary line. Major Smith hardly knew what to reply. He urged the Indians to stop their depredations, but he could not urge them not to defend their country. He had no authority to give military aid, he finally told them. He would have to write to Quebec for instructions on that subject. Then he begged the Indians to turn their minds once more to hunting and trade. Here the matter rested for the winter, during which the application for aid went down to Lord Dorchester and ultimately to London.

The Americans, since the treaty of Fort Harmar when they had actually paid for the land they took—though they took it willy-nilly— were being moved more and more to treat the Indians with what they considered justice and humanity. It was the one course the Americans had not yet tried, and no doubt a certain amount of frustration over the results of their previous conduct prodded them on. In the summer of 1790 they passed some fair trade laws which even Joseph himself could praise.[3] By the end of that year they were saying—and in the highest places, too—that national honor required that the Indians not only be dealt with justly but even, in some cases, civilized and pro- tected. When Cornplanter came to Philadelphia to plead again for revision of the treaty of Fort Stanwix, President Washington, though explaining that he had no power to alter treaties, saw that some small tracts were returned to the Senecas and promised the chief that his people should be taught agriculture and reading and writing. Knox, Washington's secretary of war, thoroughly agreed with this policy. Not an unkindly man, he had already urged upon Congress negotia- tion and compromise with the warring Indians and better treatment for all the Indians. Like George Clinton on a similar occasion, Secre- tary Knox thought, even if force were available against the hostiles, it would be better not to use it. In a generation or two the aborigines would be reduced to an insignificant number, and in any case they would be easier to handle after Britain gave up the posts. Though it might cost fifteen thousand dollars a year to win their friendship, that was cheaper than warfare.

The United States had now put the finishing touches on its com- plete about-face. Gone was the uncompromising stand that the In- dians had lost their lands in the war. Kindness, conciliation, generosity, humanity: these would be the watchwords, henceforth, of the new American Indian policy. When Joseph Brant, writing to Samuel Kirkland from his Grand River home on March 8, 1791, reprobated the former treatment of the Indians and declared that, so far from their forfeiting their land by their part in the late war, nine- tenths of them had hardly heard of the war,[4] he met with surprising assent. Henry Knox, when told of these arguments, replied, "Colonel Brant is right as to the principle of the boundaries— The idea in future of conquest ought to be relinquished, and fair purchase and optional sale take place."[5]

In line with this new outlook and hoping to pacify the still marauding western Indians, the secretary of war sent Colonel Thomas Proctor, a veteran of the famous Sullivan expedition, on a peacemaking mission to the Maumee-Wabash country. The brave Proctor kept a detailed diary of his activities. He took the difficult route from Reading to Tioga and then along the old Forbidden Path to the Seneca settlements on the upper Allegheny. Here he enlisted the aid of Cornplanter and a party of his Allegheny Senecas, and they accompanied him to a Six Nations council at Buffalo Creek. At Buffalo Creek Proctor hoped to win the support of the Indians living there and persuade some of them to go with him to the west. For the main leg of the journey, across Lake Erie, he planned to secure passage for himself and party on some British vessel.

Proctor spent over three weeks at Buffalo Creek, from April 27 to May 21, sitting around on the grass, counciling with the Indians, and meeting with Indian department officers from Niagara. At first the Six Nations seemed ready to take part in the proposed peacemaking. But unfortunately an agent of the American financier, Robert Morris, was also on the scene trying to buy land, Morris having obtained from Massachusetts certain preemption rights which the hard-pressed Phelps and Gorham had had to give up. The appearance of the land-jobber distracted the attention of the Indians. To make matters worse for Proctor, the British Indian department men pointed out that the western Indians might be very angry with their Six Nations brethren for cooperating with the Americans. There was no need to remind the Buffalo Creek Indians of this aspect of their affairs. They were already afraid of being attacked for their neutral stand. Most of them, including the influential orator, Red Jacket, drew back from Proctor's venture. Finally, when Proctor tried to charter a British vessel for himself and a small party, he was refused. Colonel Andrew Gordon, an officer who had been sent to replace the detested Harris at Fort Niagara—for so much clout did Brant and his protesting Mohawks wield at this critical juncture—found something wrong with Proctor's credentials and insisted that he appeared to be only a private citizen. In this action Gordon won approval all the way to Quebec. Proctor could not be allowed to try to make peace. There was the thought that he might succeed. The peace that the British had in mind, and for which they earnestly strove, could come about only through British mediation.

The Indians at Buffalo Creek and the officials at Niagara had known Proctor was coming, and they knew why. In an obvious move to forestall the American (though they would have gone eventually, anyway, in furtherance of Dorchester's hopes), Joseph and John Butler were sent to Buffalo Creek about ten days ahead. A council was convened and Joseph, who saw no reason why he should not fall in with British desires, dutifully proposed that deputies from the Six Nations should be sent to the west on a peacemaking mission of their own. At the very least, he pointed out, they could find out what was really going on in that quarter. He offered to be one of the number who would make the journey. The Senecas, with unwonted good feeling, promoted probably by presents from Niagara, agreed. Joseph's deputation set out only a few days before Proctor and Cornplanter appeared on the scene. While the Buffalo Creek Indians proceeded to debate what to do, they did so with the knowledge that a peacemaking effort of their own was afoot.[6] To do them justice, the people of the Six Nations who lived on American soil, whether those at the Genesee, the Allegheny, or Buffalo Creek, and certainly those farther east, were very eager for peace. They feared the war and clung desperately to their neutrality. They knew they had nothing to gain by warfare. In truth, they had not much to gain otherwise, except that in peace they could try to resist the irresistible a little longer. This they also probably knew.

After he got to the Miami country, Joseph received an unexpected letter from Colonel Gordon. Gordon told him that the Buffalo Creek Indians had had another message from the Americans. This time St. Clair had invited them to take part in a second grand expedition against the western nations. But the chiefs were not deceived, said Gordon. They saw the matter in its proper light and treated the invitation with the contempt it deserved. He himself professed to be confused. He did not understand how the Americans could be talking both peace and war at the same time. Then he brought up the subject of British mediation between the United States and the western Indians. Peace would have been obtained long before this time, he reasoned, had the British been allowed by the Americans to mediate the dispute. He hoped it still might happen. "I am the more Sanguine in the attainment of my wishes," he concluded, "by your being on the Spot, and that you will call forth the exertion of your influence and abilities on the occasion."[7] Obviously he thought it would help if the Indians demanded British mediation. Colonel Gordon was the highest ranking officer with whom Joseph usually came into contact. His letter was an order.

When writing these words, Colonel Gordon thought his country's mediation was a real possibility. Several years would pass before he and others like him learned better. Yet in Philadelphia and elsewhere, it was already being made clear through various American sources, at least informally, that the United States could never allow British interposition in what they considered an internal matter. Washington and Knox were adamant against it and British agents, sounding this American official and that, reported that the outlook was not en-couraging. Still the British, even in the highest circles, persisted in the belief that they might accomplish their wish. It was their very dear wish, and they refused to give it up. They intended to get their reward out of the peace.

Meanwhile, the Six Nations deputies had arrived at the foot of the Maumee Rapids and had settled down into temporary houses built for them by the Potawatomies. An American prisoner ransomed by the efforts of Alexander McKee spoke respectfully of these little shelters as "clever." Whether he was describing the usual Indian cover of bark and four sticks or something better, it is difficult to say. At any rate, he was sent back home to the Pennsylvania frontier where he made a deposition about his experiences and alleged that "every movement, appearance and declaration seemed hostile to the United States."[8]

As more and more chiefs assembled for the projected council, Joseph soon found that the most warlike, the Shawnees and Miamis, were not much inclined toward peace. Only the Indians living about the lake and the Hurons and Delawares seemed reasonable and "easy advised," and even they, as he noted, were "in high Spirits." Reports were coming in of American movements into the Indian country and one report, of an expedition toward the Wabash, was true enough. Some men from Kentucky and Vincennes had fallen upon several Kickapoo and Wea towns, burned some huts and corn and a trader's goods, and captured some women and children. Though Joseph hoped that the council would agree on "a reasonable Boundary Line," he could still see from these reports that the Indians ought not be left defenseless; "if the English cannot assist the Indians with Arms," he wrote Sir John Johnson, "I hope they will assist them with provision, the Indians can contrive to get Arms & Ammunition some how or other, but the provisions cannot be contrived."[9]

The western chiefs had no intention of contriving anything. What they wanted was military aid. They were well aware that they must have such help from their father if they were to hold their own against the Americans for long. The council opened and soon took a discon-certing turn. Right under the eyes of Alexander McKee, who had come from Detroit to supervise the proceedings and to see that the deliberations stayed in the proper channel, the chiefs decided to send a delegation to Quebec to find out from Lord Dorchester if they could

expect military aid, and how much and what kind. They also determined to ask that a fort be built for them at the mouth of the Maumee.

Joseph, who had heard nothing from Sir John or anybody else to
raise his hopes of British military aid, had to go along with the decision, and apparently with other decisions very disturbing to his peace
of mind. A trader among the Senecas reported that when the western
Indians heard of the Wabash incursion, they handed around the war
hatchet among themselves and then handed it to Brant, and that
Brant saw there was no way to save his life but to accept the hatchet
and take command of the warriors. [10] This was the gossip that swept the
Indian country. Joseph wrote to Sir John Johnson: "My situation is
become such that I cannot withdraw, without incurring the displeasure of all the Nations in this Quarter, therefore find myself obliged by
every Tie of Friendship to join them in defence of their Country." [11]

Joseph was disappointed that he had not met Colonel Proctor at
the Rapids. He had actually expected that the American was coming.
Instead, for some strange reason, it was an army that was coming. He
was afraid, and he ate humble pie before the man whom he never
could like. "I no doubt have often been very troublesome to you," he
went on to Sir John, "in the many requests made for my own Countrymen, and indeed intruded upon your goodness;—the only one that I
have now to make regards my Wife & family, who I hope you will
always befriend as you have heretofore done, and in case of an Accident happening to me, I make no doubt but you'll have the goodness
to make your best endeavours to procure her a pension." [12]

The western Indians were insisting upon all the help they could
get. They brought up the subject of the Moravian converts who had
always shunned war but who were living in the disputed country. They
must help defend the homeland, too, they declared. Joseph, so the
Christians heard, opposed this idea with all his energy. According to
the Indian grapevine, he argued in this fashion:

> Why should we wish to compel them to go to war? They have quite
> a different object; they have something other than we have to think
> of, and of this we know nothing. They have the word of God. About
> this they have to think. By this they wish to live and act. Why
> should we take them from it? Let them be, and disturb them not.
> They have chosen the right way and the best for us all; yes, it were
> to be wished that we would all together make this our chief matter
> and concern. In Pettquotting already they sent us a message, asking
> us to care for them and be thoughtful to show them a place where

they could be safe and out of the way of the present war, where they could hold their worship of God free and undisturbed, but up to this time they have had no answer. Come now, let us stir ourselves, and think about this. It is certainly time. Seek out a place for them somewhere near, but away from us, not here among us, where they can be by themselves alone. The time may come when we shall ourselves be in such need that we shall not know where to bring to safety our wives and children. If then the believing Indians have once a place where they live constantly and safely, we in time of need can take refuge with them, and if not quite with them, they can grant us, or [when we are gone, he was thinking] our wives and children, a place near them, where they can support themselves by planting.

Thus, according to gossip, spoke the skeptic, Brant. Yet Joseph had never mentioned his views to the Christian converts themselves. He had told them only, on the many occasions he had passed by, that they had done well in choosing to remain at peace.[13]

Now was the time that Joseph sorely missed David Hill's support. The well-born David had died the previous fall, perhaps in some epidemic, for David was strong and in his prime. The loss of David, in the councils of war, was irreparable. What David, the war chief (far more renowned among the Indians than Joseph himself), could do, Henry Tekarihoga, the civil chief, could never do. Joseph was on his own. The news was not long in getting back east that Joseph Brant had chosen the warpath. Colonel Gordon did not believe it.[14] Neither did the American, Knox.[15] Nor did Samuel Kirkland.[16] But the American Six Nations were terrified and flocked to Niagara to ask advice. They thought their doom had come. Gordon urged them to be calm.

The western Indians knew they had no time to waste. An American army was expected almost any day, and the deputies were eager to set out immediately for Quebec. Joseph Brant must go along as their spokesman. He was the obvious choice to plead the cause of the Indian confederacy before the king's great man.

Unable to prevent the appeal to Dorchester, McKee and Joseph asked for passage down to Fort Erie on some lake vessel.[17] Major Smith could do nothing but acquiesce. The party left on the *Nancy*,[18] a schooner of sixty-seven tons, which could carry arms. Though only a merchant ship, the *Nancy* was one of that fleet which gave the British command of the lakes and enabled them to hold on to the line of frontier posts from Michilimackinac all the way down the country,

H.M. Schooner *Onondaga*. Sketch by Mrs. Simcoe, from *The Diary of Mrs. John Graves Simcoe*, Toronto, 1911. With such vessels as this the British held control of the Great Lakes for many years after the American Revolutionary War. Joseph was often a passenger on one or another on his journeys to and from the west. *Courtesy of the Metropolitan Toronto Library Board, Toronto.*

much to the frustration of the Americans. Boldly putting out into open water (where a small boat had to hug the shore), the *Nancy* reached Fort Erie in due time, and the party disembarked and crossed to Buffalo Creek. Here they probably held a council, somewhat allaying local Six Nations fears, and then proceeded by land to Niagara, where they arrived about July 20.[19]

At Niagara Joseph and the western deputies found another envoy who had been sent out by the Americans to try to promote peace. This time they had sent an Indian to do their work. The newcomer was a Stockbridge Indian named Captain Hendrick Aupaumut, a chief who lived among the Oneidas and who had been recommended to the secretary of war by Samuel Kirkland. Since the Stockbridge Indians, being of Algonquian not Iroquoian stock, had kept up a friendship in the west from early times and since Captain Hendrick was both intelligent and literate, he was the most suitable Indian the Americans could find for the job.

Captain Hendrick and his small party of like-minded friends mixed among the traveling Indians and tried to calm their fears. He told them "they go wrong way"; they should go for peace to the United States, not to Canada. The westerners said they had heard that the Stockbridge Indians were shut up by the Americans like hogs in a pen. Captain Hendrick answered such stories were lies, that his people were free and independent, that they came and went as they pleased. Captain Hendrick was taken to task by John Butler for coming on such an errand. Molly Brant, up from Kingston (as old Cataraqui was now called) to visit her married daughter, was present at the meeting between the two. Molly had to have her say. She asked why, if Captain Hendrick and his friends were on a mission of peace, they had not brought some women with them. "I suppose she feel like great Sachem," thought the resentful Hendrick, and he told her that bringing women was not customary among his people. Joseph, Hendrick claimed, advised the western Indians not to talk to "these Yankees." Hendrick also accused Joseph of sending word to the Grand River to stop the party until his return from Quebec. Very likely Joseph did just that, for Captain Hendrick was stopped on his journey. He could get no farther than the Grand River.[20] Like Colonel Proctor, he found his mission impossible to carry out.

Joseph and his fellow deputies had left Niagara about the end of July,[21] crossing Lake Ontario in another vessel of the fleet. They had seen growing new white settlements nearly all the way down the lakes. To the thoughtful—and Joseph was always thoughtful—presages of change appeared on every hand. At Kingston the Indians disembarked again. Here they were supplied with government bateaux which they could manage for themselves, and so they continued their journey.[22]

The deputation met with Lord Dorchester on four occasions. On August 14 Joseph spoke twice and made his main points, some of which he had made many times before to many another official. He knew his arguments by heart. He reminded Dorchester that the Indians had always been true and faithful friends to the British, that they had always given military help when their help was needed. He asked for a fort at the Maumee Rapids—apparently the Indians had decided against the river's mouth—for the Indians' protection (and that of Detroit, too, he carefully added), and he asked for aid against the Americans. These requests he made in private. In public he pointed out to Lord Dorchester the boundary which he said the Indians were willing to settle for. It was the line of the Muskingum (though described in more detail than before) which Joseph and his followers had been urging since 1788, and he had finally managed to get the whole confederacy to agree with him. This much of a victory he had won. It was his idea that with this line secure the Indians could make a stable peace with the Americans. If the Americans were not willing to accept the Muskingum as a compromise, then it was obvious to him that they wanted all the land the Indians had.[23]

There was little that the reserved but kindly Lord Dorchester could say in reply. He was on the eve of departure for England, and the deputation from the Indian confederacy was an embarrassment he could have done without. To be asked for military aid against the United States was not what he had bargained for when he thought to mediate peace. The Indians, as well as the Americans, appeared not to understand their roles. His reply to the deputies contained nothing new. Joseph had heard similar words from Sir John Johnson and officers at the posts for years. The king, said Dorchester, was the Indians' great and good friend, and he would always protect them. He had not given away the Indians' land at the peace; the Indian *land* was not his to give. Though Lord Dorchester was himself powerless to make war against the Americans unless attacked by them, he was going home; and he would give the king an exact account of the Indians' situation. But it would give him great pleasure, he added, to hear while away that peace had been reestablished between the Indians and Americans; and he recommended that the Indians never lose sight of this object. "Could I be instrumental in bringing this good work about," he told them, "my pleasure would be still greater." He made much of the fact that Prince Edward, son of the king, happened to be present at the conference and was to be second in command of the army in Canada. The prince and the lieutenant governor, Major General Clarke, would take care of the Indians as usual after he was gone.[24]

With this reply the western chiefs had to be content. On August 18 Lord Dorchester sailed away. It was freely predicted in Canada that he would never return.

The Americans soon heard of Lord Dorchester's speech. To them it appeared to contain something friendly, and they were pleased.

Joseph and the deputies did not leave immediately. They stayed a month in Quebec and Montreal, with Joseph very probably sounding out this person and that, talking with all the officials he could lay hold of and questioning everybody who had influence, and certainly everybody of importance in the Indian department. With all the talking, all the anxious questions, he heard nothing new. There was nothing definite. He must have been reminded of his childhood and of the times when he had tried to catch eels with his bare hands. Finally giving up, Joseph and his party headed back up the lakes. By October 17 the westerners had reached the mouth of the Detroit River, where they borrowed two canoes from the Moravian missionaries and set out for the Miami country. Joseph was expected to follow them by land, meaning, apparently, to make a short stop at his Grand River home. In Detroit and farther west the Indians, and whites, too, eagerly awaited his arrival. It was thought that he would bring important news. That he might have no news at all was not suspected.[25]

During all of 1791 the American frontier reeled from the blows of the young warriors. As early as January 5 Secretary Knox declared that eight counties in Virginia, eight counties in Kentucky, all of western Pennsylvania, and many settlements farther south were in need of help against the Indians. In February it was reported from Washington County, Pennsylvania, that one war party, after killing a family on the right bank of the Ohio, called to the people on the other side to come over and bury their dead, that it would be their turn next. In March, at Marietta, men could go out to work in the fields only in large parties, armed, and with sentinels always posted. By the end of that month people had abandoned farms, stock, and all their belongings for fifty miles along the Allegheny River. New fortifications were going up in those places where the settlers felt numerous enough to stay and bid the Indians defiance, but even in the more populous Pittsburgh there was general alarm. A returning trader reported that the Indians had agreed to take no more prisoners but to kill all in their power. This was not a statement that anyone was inclined to doubt.

Volunteer patrols went out against the Indians and did some wanton killing, as likely as not, among friendly and inoffensive Indians. Some larger expeditions were mounted, and some damage was done as far west as the Wabash. It was not enough damage to deter the warriors, though it had been enough to alarm Joseph and the Indians at the foot of the Maumee Rapids in June, and send them to Quebec. What the Americans on the frontier wanted was an expedition paid for by the federal government and big enough to overwhelm the savages. The frontiersmen clung to their homes and their fertile valleys. Dreams of this rich country had supported them through seven years of revolution. They would not be thwarted now. Complaints and petitions poured into Philadelphia, many of them signed by free-holders who had the vote. Knox could see that, as he said, both justice and policy dictated that another army which would be more successful than Harmar's must be sent west. By spring, preparations were under way. This second army was to be commanded by General Arthur St. Clair himself. St. Clair, it was expected, would chastise the hostile Indians and build forts along his route for the future protection of the frontier.

Colonel Gordon to the contrary, the Americans could talk peace and war at the same time, and mean both. In the months they were planning St. Clair's expedition, they were also sending out Colonel Proctor and Captain Hendrick Aupaumut. The new expeditionary force and the two unsuccessful peace missions were both sincere at-tempts by the Americans to extricate themselves from a very painful situation. For many reasons they preferred a peaceful solution to their problem to a warlike solution. They were thinking along the lines of payment to the Indians for the indispensable land. They were not yet thinking of compromise on the amount of land to be bought. Cer-tainly they were not thinking of a Muskingum boundary. Their situa-tion was not yet that painful.

Colonel Timothy Pickering, a third American emissary, headed a mission which in itself partook of both war and peace—another puz-zler for Colonel Gordon. Though a man who possessed no prior knowledge of Indians, Colonel Pickering had had beginner's luck the year before in appeasing the Senecas for the murder of some of their people by trigger-happy frontiersmen. He was now instructed by his government to try to get the military cooperation, or at least the neutrality, of the entire Six Nations. It was thought that the Six Nations warriors were spoiling to fight on one side or the other and that the only problem, so far as the young Indians were concerned, was how to get a party of them through the frontier to join St. Clair's army without their being set upon by the whites.

Colonel Pickering held a council at historic Newtown in June and July 1791 with as many of the Six Nations as he could induce to appear by promises of presents. Deputies numbering 1,050 from every nation except the Mohawks came to the rendezvous on the Chemung River. Here they reaffirmed their neutrality. This was as much as Pickering could get, and he began to think he was fortunate to get that, as he listened to some sharp talk by Red Jacket and other Senecas. The Six Nations still had some remnant of their one-time reputation, and there was a desperate fear among the Americans that their warriors would join the hostile nations en masse.

Before the council was over Colonel Pickering invited the more

influential chiefs to visit Philadelphia in order to prepare the way for
the introduction of the arts and sciences among their people. At least,
this was the reason he gave them and, being a kindly, honest man who
wanted to be well thought of even by Indians (as he said), he believed
in it utterly; but he also knew that a visit to the American seat of
government would impress the Six Nations with American strength
and perhaps induce their cooperation. Pickering could not extend an
invitation to Joseph Brant since Joseph was not there, but he had been
told to treat him with great consideration if he appeared and to try to
attach him to the United States. He also had authority to offer
pensions to a few of the chiefs if he thought proper.[26]

Though the Americans did not trust Joseph Brant very much,[27]
they had had their eyes on him for a long time.[28] There had been some
correspondence back and forth between the secretary of war and Governor Clinton about getting Brant to Philadelphia and about obtaining Brant's help,[29] for it was supposed that Brant had great influence
with the western Indians; and Secretary Knox said frankly that money
was no object in inducing Brant to come; whatever was necessary
would be paid.[30] Samuel Kirkland, perhaps inspired by some random
remark of Joseph which he misconstrued or by gossip in the Indian
country, somehow got the idea in the summer of 1791 that he was to
meet Brant at Oneida or at Albany and escort him to Philadelphia.
Kirkland waited at both places, then had to give up, for no Brant
appeared.[31] Joseph was at the Maumee Rapids then, with no idea at all
of going to Philadelphia. Indeed, he and the western deputies were
about to depart for Quebec.

With more failures than successes in their peace attempts, the
United States had to go on with preparations for war. The preparations were necessarily slow and never done on schedule. The
difficulties of communication over vast distances, the uncertainties
and hazards of sending out expresses, even the lowness or highness of
the waters of the Ohio retarded the collection of supplies. In the
meantime recruiting in the east did not go well. By August 6 St. Clair
had heard nothing of how his provisions were to be transported. By
the end of that month it was obvious to him that militia would be
required to supplement the new levies. In early September he set out
in person to gather the militia. He was trying to prepare a massive
campaign against the Indians according to his orders, although he had
always advocated small coordinate attacks in many directions as more
effective in combating them. It was just good common sense, he
thought, not to give the Indians a chance to unite. Finally, by October 9, St. Clair and his largely untrained army were on their way to

the Miami towns. They had too little of almost everything they needed. It was very late in the season to be attempting a military campaign, but, of course, an army of over two thousand made the affair "pretty certain."

Joseph Brant, nursing his disappointment, got back to the Grand River in early October. He found Captain Hendrick Aupaumut patiently waiting. Captain Hendrick had not given up on his mission. He hoped that, together, he and Brant could go to the west and perhaps, even yet, bring about a peace. It was still worth trying, he thought. Hopefully, he asked Brant if he was going to Detroit. Joseph, who knew that the entire west was looking for his arrival with British military aid tucked securely under his arm, felt tired and sore and beaten down. He answered shortly, no. Captain Hendrick offered to accompany him to the west, but he still refused. With much talk he tried to discourage Captain Hendrick from going any farther himself, and advised him never to do anything for the United States. They are strong; let them do for themselves, he said. Disheartened, Captain Hendrick left the Grand River and went home.[32]

St. Clair's army, having dwindled in a month, through desertions and the expiration of enlistments, from twenty-three hundred to seventeen hundred effectives, was now, as one officer defined it, "crawling through the Indian Country." Two small forts had been built on the way, named Fort Hamilton and Fort Jefferson respectively, and a road was being cut through the brush. This work of construction necessarily delayed the march, especially since tools proved inadequate and most of the troops knew as little about felling trees and hoisting logs as they did about soldiering. The season coming on very cold, frost destroyed the green forage; and horses and cattle weakened and died. Bread was scarce, pay seldom forthcoming, and the men, more and more disgruntled, continued every day to desert. St. Clair became ill and had to be lifted on and off his horse and, growing worse as he went on, finally had to travel on a litter. Richard Butler, second in command, was also ill. Cold rains, hail, and snow further discouraged the raw levies.

The Indians, who had been gathering at the foot of the Maumee Rapids to hear what Joseph Brant and their other returned deputies could tell them about the prospects of British aid, knew that St. Clair was marching toward the Miami towns. They waited, but Brant and the deputies did not appear. Baffled and angry, they moved off up the river to the endangered towns, and then south and east to meet the enemy. Somewhere along the way the deputies, but not Brant, joined them. They found out they would have no British aid.[33]

The Indians numbered about 1,040 when they left the head of the Maumee. They were mainly Shawnees and Miamis, though they had the help of small straggling parties from every direction. The divided Delawares contributed some warriors; there were probably some Mingoes from the Auglaize River, perhaps a few Wyandots from over the lake (for the Wyandots of Sandusky were mostly peaceable), and even some Chippewas and Ottawas and Potawatomies, divided as they were, with many of them opposing the war. There were also some Creeks and Cherokees, part of them said to be from the far south, though the Americans had managed to make a peace treaty with an influential Creek chief named Alexander McGillivray in 1790 and another with the Cherokees the past summer. The Wea and Kickapoo Indians, whose settlements on the Wabash had been surprised and whose women and children had been captured earlier in the year by an expedition from Kentucky, did not join the hostile force; they were intent on making peace and, indeed, a few of them had gone over to the Americans. There was only one small party from the Six Nations, mostly Cayugas, and estimated variously as eleven, thirty, and thirty-six. If the whole Indian force had a leader, it was the Miami war chief, Little Turtle, a man accounted by the British as sensible and intelligent.

Before sunup, on November 4, the combined force of Indians had surrounded the American camp. The camp was pitched near the present Ohio-Indiana border (Fort Recovery, Ohio) on a branch of the Wabash, but the Americans did not know where they actually were. They knew only that they were coming close to the Miami villages and that their orders were to establish an American post there. They expected to fight a battle somewhere, soon.

The surprised American troops, numbering only about fourteen hundred, one regiment being out to protect a convoy of supplies from deserters, tried to fight back; and, indeed, some fought bravely. The action lasted several hours. It was no use. The Indians, advancing almost invisibly from tree to tree, took deadly aim, apparently singling out officers. When the American artillery was cut off and silenced, the Indians contracted their lines and the dazed Americans were exposed to heavy cross fire. Raw troops huddled together, "perfectly ungovernable," according to one surviving officer. A Seneca warrior later said that he ran up to the crowd and tomahawked men till his arm got sick. The ground was soon covered with the dead and wounded.

Sometime after nine o'clock all was over. The Americans fled back the way they had come, littering their new road for miles with their wildly flung-down equipment. The Indians did not pursue far, but turned their attention to the spoil that was nearby on the ground. It was a terrible defeat. Almost half the American army was lost.

On the field of battle the Indians soon found Richard Butler, American superintendent of Indian affairs for the northern district. Richard Butler had been early wounded. Many of the Indians knew him well. In his person he represented to the victorious warriors all the treaties that they hated, all the councils where they had been forced to submit, all their fears for the future, and all their sufferings. Butler, dead or alive, and in their power, also represented to them just then a cause triumphant.

The news of St. Clair's defeat reached the mouth of the Detroit River in eight days. Not long afterward Joseph Brant, at his home at the Grand River, received a present and a message. The present was the scalp of Richard Butler. The message came from the western Indians, and it was very bitter.[34] Samuel Kirkland, who had ways of finding out confidential Indian matters through his Oneida friends, heard that the Shawnees upbraided Brant in a secret council at Buffalo Creek. Even third-hand the cutting words of the Shawnees reflect not only the grudge against Joseph Brant and the resentment at what they considered his desertion, but all the aching loss of their Kentucky hunting grounds which the Six Nations had sold out from under them nearly a quarter of a century before. "You chief Mohawk!" railed the Shawnees, "what are you doing? Time was when you roused us to war, and told us that, if all the Indians would join with the King, they should be a happy people, and become independent. In a very short time, you changed your voice, and went to sleep, and left us in the lurch. You Mohawk chief! you have ruined us, and you shall share with us. Know it is not good for you to lie still any longer. Arise, and bestir yourself."[35]

Before the year was out Samuel Kirkland also heard that Joseph Brant had fallen so dangerously ill that for a time he was not expected to live.[36]

22

Philadelphia and the Glaize

B Y THE END of December Joseph was able to get himself to Niagara, perhaps to see the regimental physician. He was also able to think of his correspondence, and he dictated a letter to Joseph Chew, new secretary of the Indian department, a man whom he had known since the days on the Mohawk. He told Chew about St. Clair's defeat, relating, apparently, as many details as he had learned. Only an extract of this letter has been preserved, and in that extract Joseph says nothing about his own troubles.[1]

None of his contemporaries has told us the nature of Joseph's illness. No one has said that he had a "gout in the stomach," the ailment which finally carried off Daniel Claus. If he suffered from any of the alarming symptoms which now afflicted the aging John Butler, nobody mentioned it. Joseph always had recurring malaria—as did nearly everyone else—but it was probably not that chronic ailment that had brought him so low; and we are left wondering what could have been so serious but also relatively quick to recover from. Whatever it was, Joseph seems to have suffered from it from time to time for the rest of his life.

By mid-January 1792 Joseph was still at Niagara, now in company with four of the Cayugas who had fought against St. Clair and from whom he had ransomed a prisoner. While on this visit to the post he spent eight days with Benjamin Barton, a young American surveyor and speculator from the Genesee. He promised Barton (so Barton says) that he would go to Philadelphia, provided President Washington sent him a formal, written invitation. Barton, who was preparing to go to Philadelphia himself, was to return with the invitation. This plan was to be a secret between Brant and Barton.[2] The plan was so secret that nobody ever heard of it again but, obviously, something of the nature was brewing in Joseph's mind. He could not forget his troubles with the western Indians. Samuel Kirkland had even heard that Joseph was in a mood to place himself under the protection of Congress.[3] At any rate, Joseph, who was home again by January 19,[4] was seriously considering a Philadelphia trip.

In the meantime the Americans, who never gave up, were busy. Knowing nothing about Joseph's grave illness till he had already recovered, they began to shower him with invitations from almost every direction. On December 19, 1791, Timothy Pickering wrote a letter to the chiefs whom he had already invited to Philadelphia, told them of the arrangements for their journey (Samuel Kirkland and two interpreters would attend them), said he would be happy to see Brant and suggested that Brant should come with them.[5] Pickering, who was not acquainted with Joseph, had sent him just the sort of invitation he would never accept. To give Pickering credit, he had been talking with Knox, and the manner of the invitation was Knox's idea.[6] Knox also wrote Kirkland that he, too, should invite Brant to Philadelphia and that he was to assure him of safe conduct and a welcome reception. He instructed Kirkland to meet the party of chiefs at Geneseo and bring them south by way of Tioga and eastern Pennsylvania. By this time Knox had heard the bad news of St. Clair's defeat, and he was anxious to find out how the Six Nations were taking it. The ostensible reason for the trip, however, was still the "civilization" of the Indians.[7]

About this same time Governor Clinton also invited Joseph to come to New York, promising him a cordial and friendly reception. Recalling Joseph's little joke of the year before, he reminded him that he had better collect his tribute from the man on Long Island before it lapsed. Clinton thought the seashore would be good for Joseph's health. The visit would be serviceable to him in other respects, too, he said.[8] Obviously Clinton's invitation had something to do with land affairs, and Joseph was probably not the one to whom the visit would be most serviceable.

Samuel Kirkland, in response to Knox's instructions, wrote Joseph on January 3, 1792. It was a long and glowing letter, full of talk about civilizing the Indians and about Joseph's own superior merits and the opportunities for good work among his people. He urged Joseph to accept Pickering's invitation and accompany the other chiefs to Philadelphia. He referred to what happened at Fort Stanwix (meaning the time that Joseph had saved his life) and pledged his life for Joseph's safety.[9] The pledge was necessary, for Kirkland knew—and so did Joseph—that there were still many areas below the border where Joseph Brant was not welcome and where it was dangerous for him to show his face. About three weeks after Kirkland had sent off this invitation, he went to Geneseo to meet the party of Six Nations chiefs. He hoped Joseph would be among them and would make the journey or, at least, that he would come for a conference so that a trip at some other time could be planned.

Joseph did not show up at Geneseo. In fact, very few of the chiefs showed up. There was a singular lack of enthusiasm among the Indians for this journey to Philadelphia. Most of the Six Nations chiefs were fearful for their own safety, not so much from the local whites but because of the western Indians who they knew were very displeased that so few Six Nations warriors had helped them in the late battle. Going to Philadelphia to confer with the Americans would certainly not remedy matters. The Six Nations had a great fear of the western Indians. Once it had been otherwise. Finding Joseph not at the meeting place, Kirkland wrote him again.[10]

When Joseph got Pickering's and Kirkland's letters, he reacted angrily. Did they actually think he would let himself be led through the country with a crowd of Indians like a herd of cattle with people running out to gape all along the way? This was the manner in which Indians were usually conducted anywhere. Joseph was old enough to remember the journey of his stepfather and Hendrick to Philadelphia in 1754–55 and how people had run out of their houses to stare at them. He had doubtless heard the story often enough and, indeed, as a child, he may have ridden behind on one of the horses and experienced the stares at first hand. Joseph sent off a polite letter to Kirkland which upset that worthy completely. He told Kirkland he did not like the manner of the invitation. He wanted a formal, personal invitation, and he did not wish to travel with chiefs with whose sentiments he could not agree.[11] From Kirkland's very conciliatory reply it is obvious that he could read between the lines.

"Suffice it [to] say," wrote Kirkland apologetically, "it was not in my idea, that you should be crowded into the company of all the old Chiefs & dragged along with them promiscuously thro' the proposed tour to Philadelphia—No, Sir, the respect I have for your character & h[a]ppi[ness] would have spurned at the thought." There was more in this vein, with Kirkland again referring to Joseph's having saved his life.[12] Kirkland was doing his very best to persuade Joseph to make the trip.

For a man who had had so severe an illness, Joseph did a great deal of traveling. By January 31 he was back again at Niagara. He found that those Buffalo Creek Indians who had not gone to meet Kirkland at Geneseo were there discussing Pickering's invitation and all their nervous fears. Joseph arrived in time to interpret at a council they held with Colonel Gordon and John Butler. The Buffalo Creek chiefs asked Colonel Gordon whether they should accept Pickering's invitation. Gordon told them he thought there was something more in the invitation than appeared on the surface. He thought it would be imprudent to go to Philadelphia, but that they should do as they pleased. Then Joseph told the Indians that he, too, thought the invitation had a hidden meaning. Thus discouraged, the chiefs said they would not go, and promised to send to Geneseo to stop any of their people from going until they could council further among themselves.[13] After this conference Joseph again went home.[14]

By this time so many letters were flying back and forth regarding the trip to Philadelphia that it is difficult to sort them out. The Americans were eagerly awaiting the arrival of the Six Nations chiefs. They were even more eagerly awaiting Joseph Brant's arrival, together with the others if possible, separately if it had to be. Knox sent presents to Cornplanter and his friends to hurry them on. He had heard that they had been threatened by the "bad" Indians, and he offered to build a fort for them or let them move nearer to Fort Pitt. The choice would be theirs. "Speak," said he, "for we wish to consider you and your people as part of ourselves." He put a bold face on St. Clair's defeat. We have not been disheartened by our defeat, he said, and we hope you have not, though of course we lament the blood that has been shed in a war which we wished to avoid. "But the number of men we have lost," he confidently asserted, "we can easily replace; and, therefore, although the continuance of the war will be troublesome, yet, in the long run, we must conquer."[15]

Two days later Knox wrote Kirkland urging him to find out what was going on at an important council at Buffalo Creek which he had heard was to take place soon. Kirkland was to spare no pains or expense in getting the information, even to going himself to Buffalo Creek. "I hope earnestly," added Knox, "that you will succeed in bringing the chiefs to this city with you. I consider this as highly important at this time. I know, when the Indians are persuaded of the good intentions of the United States to them, that they will use their highest exertions for peace."[16] Knox was convinced that American intentions were of the best.

Knox finally heard from Kirkland what was holding up Brant. He immediately sent Kirkland the special invitation which Joseph demanded, and instructed him to spare no pains to induce him to come. He was to arrange with Brant a satisfactory mode of travel "which ought to be as flattering to him as may be."[17] The other chiefs could come under the care of someone else.

Washington had carefully gone over the draft of Knox's letter to Brant. The letter which was finally sent contained the best thoughts of both.[18] It was long, and it piled flattery upon flattery. Knox assured Joseph "that the President of the United States will be highly gratified by receiving and conversing with a chief of such eminence as you are, on a subject so interesting and important to the human race." The president had the purest disposition to promote the welfare of the Indians, Knox went on, but proper occasions were still wanting to impress the hostile Indians with the truth of this assertion. "He considers your mind more enlightened than theirs, and he has hopes that your heart is filled with a true desire to serve the essential interests of your countrymen."[19]

Knox dropped any reference to the "civilization" of the Indians— and a good thing he did it, too; for it would not have fooled Joseph for a moment, Joseph having scornfully said he already knew how to sow and plant, and the subject was not interesting to him.[20] Instead of that pretext, Knox told Joseph something nearer the truth: that the United States was fighting a war of necessity and not a war for the purpose of getting more land than was already ceded by treaty with the Indians. We wish to end the war, he said, because it will destroy the Indians. The business of peace is the main business we wish to take up with you, he admitted, and he urged Brant to come without delay.[21]

Kirkland sent this letter on to Niagara with a request that Colonel Gordon send it to Brant at the Grand River. Through the messenger Gordon got wind of the letter's contents. He immediately wrote Joseph a letter of his own. He did not think Philadelphia was the proper place to negotiate peace, for the western Indians would not be there; and they would be jealous of anything done by the Six Nations alone. If the Americans wish to make peace, he said, let them call a council of all the Indians, and let British commissioners be present along with those of the United States. He himself was eager for peace, but he reminded Joseph that the two of them had often agreed that the Americans, from past conduct, did not appear to have peace seriously in view. Judging from their present method of going about it, he thought they still had not seen the error of their ways. Closing his letter, he said: "I have thus, my dear Friend, been induced to give you my *private* opinion on the present occasion, and I am fully persuaded you will pursue a line of conduct that will deserve the approbation of your Brethren and friends." In a postscript he added that some of the Senecas from Buffalo Creek had finally gone to Philadelphia on Pickering's invitation and that they had caused much uneasiness in their village by doing so.[22]

Joseph got the two letters and immediately sent off his answer to Knox. He could not go just yet. He wished to send to the Miami country to get the approval of the western Indians. "Visiting you, as an individual," he said, "would be by no means tending to the accomplishing any good end; as those meetings must show, that have hitherto been held with people not deputized by the nations, in general, to transact business. I should, therefore, wish to visit you vested with some power that will enable me to speak with certainty to what I may assert, and not assert what I, at the same time, must well know would be by no means approved of. This has been too much the case, of late years, and, in my opinion, principally the cause of the present disturbances." He expected his messengers would return from the west in about thirty days with the approval of the Indians there and possibly "with such powers as will give energy to what I may do." If Knox wished him to come then, he would make the journey. Joseph had been impressed by one of Colonel Gordon's objections, but he did not intend to be wholly deterred by him. He intended to do as he pleased.[23]

By his messengers to the west Joseph sent a letter to Alexander McKee at Detroit. He explained to McKee what had been going on, asked him to send the messengers on, and requested his advice about his problem. He thought a visit to Philadelphia would do some good, and he assured McKee the Five Nations (omitting the Oneidas, of course) were still firm in their alliance with the western confederacy. Although the American part of the Five Nations had attended several American councils, they had told him "it was not through friendship—but policy, to amuse them, and that they never have been sincere in any transactions with them, & have no interest but that of these people of their own colour, all of whom they look upon as relations [a]nd engaged in one general cause, aiming at what is the Interest [of] the Confederacy in General." He told McKee the young Seneca warriors were ready to help their western friends. He even said he thought Cornplanter was changing his opinions and wished to move away from where he was living. He hoped the western Indians would regain their unanimity, for without unanimity, he said, "all our exertions will prove nought."[24] What he said to McKee was probably the very same message he was sending to the Miami country. Joseph was doing his best to soothe his accusers in the west who thought him not hearty enough in their cause.

In the meantime Cornplanter and forty-eight Seneca chiefs had already arrived in Philadelphia with Kirkland and were putting on an imposing display of friendship. Whatever these chiefs thought privately, their position as a buffer between the western Indians and the Americans forced them to try to placate both sides in the controversy. The Americans were growing desperate and, for their part, wished to placate the chiefs, for they had a great favor to ask. They gave the Indians fifteen hundred dollars in goods and domestic animals and agreed that a like amount should be paid annually. They also appointed a superintendent to look after them, for since the war they had had no agent of their own; and Arthur St. Clair, now superintendent for the northern department, was too far away to do them the least good. Their new agent was General Israel Chapin, a distinguished pioneer of the Genesee country. In their turn Cornplanter and his associates agreed to go to the west and try to bring about a peace. There was to be a council in the Miami country in the fall. They promised to attend there and do their best.

Joseph's messengers returned from their western mission about mid-May.[25] At no time did he claim that the western Indians sent him the powers that he wanted or even that they heartily approved a trip to Philadelphia, and this omission seems odd. Yet the hostile Indians probably did not forbid the trip, for Joseph, when he heard from Knox that he would still be welcome,[26] finally consented to make the journey.

Joseph hastened to write Alexander McKee why he was going; for though McKee had passed through Niagara on an important official journey down the lakes, he had not seen him nor had McKee sent him any worthwhile advice. Joseph's letter reveals his inmost feelings and all his perplexities. He explains that

weighing the situation of the Indians and the evasive answers we received from the Officers of Government, when applied to for assistance, I have thought it advisable upon mature reflection, to accept of the last [invitation], and am . . . on my way; my situation at present truly disagreeable—those employed by Government, dissuading me from going without being able, officially to promise us protection, in my opinion, candidly speaking, things are come to that crisis that steps ought to be immediately taken to secure ourselves from the insults and ravages of the Americans, if Great Britain wishes us to defend our Country, why not tell us so in plain language. If the reverse, let it be mentioned, then we will Know how to Act, and be enabled to take such steps as will secure us and our posterity. There is now a field open for our accomodation with the Americans, and which, as far as we consistently can, ought for our own Interest, and the happiness of our Women & Children endeavour to accomplish.

If their demands are such as we cannot comply with, then the best of a Bad bargain must be made, Carrying on a Defensive war, defending our real property, may probably incite the pity of Great Britain [for Joseph was ever hopeful], and make them Explain themselves on this Subject, which I have never as yet been able to prevail upon them to do.

My taking this jaunt to the American seat of Government, will enable me to form an Idea of their intentions, and how far a Peace is likely to take place, as they wish to Consult with me on different Subjects. I shall on this one be no way backward of freely telling the Steps I think necessary to be taken by them, if they are inclined for peace, relinquishing the Idea of having the Muskingum [Fort Harmar] treaty fulfilled, is in my opinion the principle obstacle that prevents an accomodation, the Interests of the Indians has ever and I hope Ever shall be my greatest aim, in accomplishing of which I have never Spared time or trouble, my present step I hope will be a more convincing proof thereof, and Government, I have little doubt but will approve of it, as it is nearly our last effort. The Americans have paved the way for peace, in so doing they'll probably resign pretensions, which they would by no means do were we the Solicitors.

Saying any particular to you about our situation is needless, as you are as well acquainted therewith, as I can describe. I must therefore again solicit you to Know your opinion, and that of Great Britain respecting us, you are now where you may learn it [Joseph addressed his letter to Montreal]— Our Conduct in any wise being disapproved of, would hurt me much, but when I reflect on the Questions, I have frequently asked of the Great leading men, to which they have always declined answering me pointedly, This I hope will now bring the business to an Issue, and we may Know, whether to prosecute the War or to make a peace, one of which must be the Case.[27]

Joseph had already left home when he wrote this letter. He had set out under the positive discouragement of Joseph Chew of the Indian department in Montreal—speaking, of course, for the cautious Sir John Johnson—and the dismay of Colonel Gordon who feared to interfere further, not knowing what was desired in Quebec or London.[28] Only the aged and ill John Butler gave Joseph his blessing, thinking the American mission might in some way benefit the Indians.[29]

Joseph did not travel alone. Israel Chapin had been assigned four hundred dollars for Joseph's journey, and he had sent a certain Dr. Deodat Allen to accompany him as well as his own son, Israel Chapin, Jr. Dr. Allen was the guide who was to take care of all the unpleasant details such as procuring horses and boats, paying for lodging and meals, and coping with anything unusual. Joseph also brought along a servant and, but only as far as Canandaigua, young Isaac who wanted to buy a horse. For Joseph this was to be a royal tour without responsibility.[30]

Given the choice of going by land or going by water as far as the mouth of the Genesee (Rochester), Joseph chose the latter.[31] It was probably the easier route, for Joseph liked his comforts when he could get them. But whether by land or water he could have found nothing along the way resembling an inn. Contemporary travelers speak of the region between Buffalo Creek and the Genesee as an unbroken wilderness where they had to camp out at night. A few white men, mostly former captives who had been adopted by their captors, had been permitted, just after the war, to build lonely cabins deep in the Indian country, but none was west of the Genesee and, by 1792, Indian land sales had stranded such men well within the white frontier. However, the notorious Ebenezer Allen, a man of evil reputation but an acquaintance of Joseph, was living at the mouth of the Genesee with several wives, and operated a mill there. Joseph and his party probably lodged with Allen and his menage at least one night. After the party crossed the Genesee they could stop at Gilbert Berry's tavern near Honeoye Creek. Being so close to the Indian country, Berry was, of course, a trader.

After the crossing of the Genesee many white settlements were springing up. Robert Morris, successor to Phelps and Gorham, had sold a vast acreage to a London capitalist; and agents of both were busy luring settlers to places like Canandaigua and Geneva (old Canadesaga) and elsewhere along the old Indian (and Sullivan) trail. New Englanders by the hundreds were flocking to this country. Not knowing too much about Joseph Brant—for Joseph's wartime activities had never extended beyond the Hudson—the new settlers exhibited toward him more curiosity than anger. Even the veterans of Sullivan's expedition, who were numerous among the pioneers, had not suffered very much at the hands of Joseph Brant. But though the settlers were not unfriendly, there were highwaymen to guard against on the lonelier stretches of road, and the road itself was so bad in places that there was more walking the horses than riding them. Though a royal tour, it was still not an easy journey.

At thriving little Canandaigua, near the north end of Canandaigua Lake, where there were about thirty houses and where several prominent families had settled down, civilized society began. Here lived the new Indian agent, Israel Chapin, and his fashionable wife and daughters, and Jasper Parrish, a former captive who had just been appointed official interpreter for the American Indian department. Joseph was at General Chapin's home by the first of June, and he stayed there, resting and enjoying the local society, for several days.[32] Chapin was, according to a contemporary traveler, "an agreeable facetious man" and, in spite of his prominence, "plain, homely, as any farmer."[33] Chapin welcomed Joseph with great cordiality and, after a few hints from him, bought a horse for Isaac, thinking that as he had already spent so much, he might as well spend thirty dollars more if it would get the chief to Philadelphia in good spirits.[34] At Canandaigua Joseph also saw Captain Hendrick Aupaumut who was passing through on a mission to the west with another American peace offer. Joseph told Hendrick that he ought to let the British carry the American message as they could get there faster. Hendrick, offended, did not bother to reply.[35]

Continuing on his journey, Joseph gave the Oneida reservation (for the Oneidas had already come to that) short shrift. He had never forgiven the Oneidas, and he was not eager to visit with Samuel Kirkland though the latter was again at home. He could write long letters to Kirkland, and Kirkland wrote equally long letters to him; but he thought of the missionary as "that deep dark Presbiterian"[36] and had just as lief keep some space between himself and the Yankee man of God. He proceeded to the Mohawk River as fast as he could. Here the dangerous part of his travels began, though the dangers were not always obvious except in the black looks cast in his direction. People who dwelt on the Mohawk still hated the monster, Brant, and had not forgotten his wartime depredations. Joseph was frankly scared.[37] It took all his courage to continue the journey. He was not free to go where he chose, and at least once, for safety, he had to lodge with a relative of General Schuyler where nobody would dare to disturb him.[38] Of course he found the Mohawk valley greatly changed. No burned-out buildings remained. Everything looked sleek and prosperous; the pastures were full of cattle, and the fields full of grain.

The rest of the journey was not so nerve-racking. The travelers proceeded by water whenever they could, and the sail down the Hudson must have been pleasant. Stopping in New York, Joseph called upon the merchant Richard Varick, one of Governor Clinton's friends, whom he had met in dealings over Indian land. Joseph asked Varick to see that his American visit was not unduly noted in the press. He knew that his political position in Canada and among the western brothers could be made very uncomfortable if he seemed to receive too much attention from the former and present enemy. Varick, hoping that Joseph would be able to exert as much influence as possible for peace, obliged him by sending only the briefest and simplest announcements of his visit to various newspapers.[39] It turned out that the newspapers did, indeed, say little about Joseph's visit.

Before he left New York, Joseph, always an inveterate shopper, ordered a blue cashmere coat and overalls for himself which cost some twelve pounds, and executed a commission for clothing for his friend, Samuel Street of Niagara, with the same tailor.[40] Apparently the Americans paid for Joseph's own purchases.

The ride across Jersey was uneventful, and Joseph and his party arrived in Philadelphia, the busy American capital, on June 20.[41] It had been a quick trip, almost furtive. Joseph had not lingered anywhere along the way except at Chapin's.

American officials were overjoyed to see the powerful (they thought) chief whose visit they had so long anticipated and whose influence (they hoped) would soon be exerted in their behalf. Peace with the western Indians was now of the first importance to the Americans. Besides all the obvious and continuing reasons for desiring peace, Secretary Knox and men like him believed that if the war went on unabated, the Indians would be destroyed and the good name of the United States would be destroyed with them. They knew the world considered the Indians an oppressed race, and they preferred not to see American conduct toward them classed with that of the Spanish conquerors in Mexico and Peru. According to Knox, Washington not only wished to be at peace with the Indians, but to stand their guardian and protector against all injustice. This was Knox's view, too, and that of Pickering and many other Americans of rank and influence. So far had American policy turned around.

Whatever additional leverage was needed, public opinion supplied. The country as a whole strongly opposed the Indian war. In the north and east especially, pacifism had become violent. The capital city itself was riddled with anti-war militance. During the Revolution pacifists had fled to Canada and embraced the British enemy. Though the present pacifists did not go so far as to give up comfortable lives and fly to the Indian country, they did embrace the Indians as passionately as possible from a distance. They had less and less sympathy for the problems of the frontier. And of course the frontier was dangerously discontented and had less and less sympathy for the problems and opinions of the seaboard. The frontiersman, who had to carry his gun even to church and who had to work his fields with a gun slung across his back, and ever ready, was not much concerned as to whether the Indians got justice.

Under such circumstances American authorities were leaving no stone unturned in their desperate search for an acceptable end to the war. General Rufus Putnam, stationed at far-off Fort Washington, and the Moravian missionary, John Heckewelder, were authorized to undertake a peace mission to the Wabash; and two other American agents, Captain Alexander Trueman and Colonel Hardin, had already gone by different routes on a similar journey to the Miamis. By early summer the reports of the two latter were eagerly awaited. Captain Hendrick Aupaumut had been sent on another attempt to confer with the hostile Indians. It was this venture on which Hendrick was embarked when Joseph met him at Canandaigua. If Cornplanter and his Six Nations party could effect nothing with the hostiles, reasoned Knox, perhaps Hendrick, who was more acceptable to them, could do better. Knox also hoped to persuade Joseph Brant to undertake a similar mission.[42]

Given the discontent on the frontier, the Americans had no other choice but to prepare for war at the same time they continued their search for peace. Out in Pittsburgh the famed "Mad" Anthony Wayne, recently appointed commander of the western army in place of St. Clair, was preparing another invasion of the Indian country. Anthony Wayne was no amiable Harmar and no ailing, ineffectual St. Clair. The Revolution had given him a great military reputation, and he was determined to keep it and, if possible, to enhance it. Though eager for action, General Wayne proceeded carefully. Not for him the haste of his predecessors. He insisted on getting the needed troops and supplies—and generally got them. He was a stern disciplinarian. He sent after deserters, had them brought back and branded on the forehead with the word "Coward," and put them to work at the most menial services about the camp. Strict in everything pertaining to training, he would not permit drunkenness; and traders and their liquor were unwelcome in his vicinity. He did not spare the ammunition, and soon made marksmen out of raw recruits. He had no patience with contractors who did not deliver, no patience with Indians and their forked tongues, and certainly no patience with the British who he thought were at the bottom of all the troubles with the savages. He wished ardently that he might get the order to march against Detroit.

Such was the tense situation among the Americans when Joseph arrived in Philadelphia. The very next day, at noon, he had a meeting with President Washington. We do not know what Washington told Joseph, but we do know what he told his friend Gouverneur Morris in a private letter written just before the meeting. "We are essaying every means, in our power," he said to Morris, "to undeceive these hostile tribes with respect to the disposition of this Country towards them; and to convince them that we neither seek their extirpation nor the occupancy of their Lands (as they are taught to believe) except such of the latter as has been obtained by fair treaty, and purchase bona fide made, and recognized by them in more instances than one. If they will not after this explanation (if we can get at them to make it) listen to the voice of peace, the sword must decide the dispute . . . ."

Washington then mentioned how difficult it had been to get the Six Nations chiefs to come to Philadelphia, but that they had finally come and given assurances of their friendship and even made promises to do what they could to stop the war. "With difficulty *still* greater," he continued, "I have brought the celebrated Captn. Joseph Brant to this City, with a view to impress him also with the equitable intentions of this government towards *all* the Nations of his colour." Conscious of such good intentions, Washington believed that if only the Indians would listen, they would understand that the president and government of the United States meant them no ill. Obviously he hoped that Joseph Brant could make them listen.[43]

Joseph, with all his personal difficulties with his people, certainly doubted, when the matter was brought up (though he would never have admitted such a doubt), that his influence extended so far. Back home in Canada, Joseph's former pastor John Stuart doubted, too, and said that he feared the Americans would overrate Brant's interest with the Indians.[44] Stuart, who had known Joseph for so many years, knew all about the chief's problems of leadership.

Joseph met with Secretary Knox several times. Each time Knox urged the merits of the Fort Harmar boundary. Joseph argued for a new boundary,[45] which to him meant the line of the Muskingum River which he and the western Indians had agreed on and which they had described to Lord Dorchester the previous year. The sellers at Fort Harmar, Joseph insisted, had had no right to sell. Knox did not give up easily; indeed, he could not, for he knew some of the Fort Harmar lands were already settled by Americans.

Near the end of Joseph's visit Knox sent him a written summation of the American position. There were six proposals which Knox hoped Brant would himself carry to the warring Indians:

1. The United States is willing to bury the hatchet and forget the past.

2. The United States wants no lands except those ceded by treaties freely made.

3. A map is enclosed which shows the American estimate of the extent of lands ceded at Fort Harmar.

4. If compensation was inadequate or if others have claims to those lands, just compensation will be made.

5. This compensation will be given annually in Indian goods.

6. The United States will teach the Indians, if they so wish, to raise bread and cattle.

For these purposes, added Knox, a treaty is necessary. It can be made at Philadelphia or by American commissioners in the Indian country. All parties must be represented, and hostilities on both sides must cease.

Knox then reminded Joseph that he had seen the power of the United States and that in a long war the Indians must be "utterly ruined." The president, he went on, was anxious to avoid so great an evil, and he hoped that when the Indians understand that all their lands not fairly ceded are to remain their own, they will accede to a treaty "which will secure them the blessings of the earth." Though he was well aware of the labor and trouble involved in making peace, Knox hoped that from Brant's interest in the welfare of the Indians, he would zealously cooperate in accomplishing so benevolent an object.[46]

Joseph knew that in even coming to Philadelphia he was walking precariously on a tightrope not only so far as the Indians were concerned, but the British, too. Without further ado he took Knox's communication to George Hammond, Britain's new young minister plenipotentiary to the United States, and told him what he thought the British government ought to know. Hammond reported to Lord Grenville that Brant believed the majority of the warring Indians would not agree to the American proposals, but that he feared the Americans might be able to split the Indian confederacy by the lure of annual payments. He named the Wyandots, the Delawares, and the Shawnees as most susceptible to such a lure. Brant also said, Hammond reported, that the proposals were "far from meeting his approbation personally."[47]

Other subjects had entered into Knox's conversations with Joseph, but of these Knox had said not a word in his formal paper. There were political secrets which the United States government did not care to publish. Neither Washington nor Knox felt that it was necessary to reveal everything that went on in diplomatic negotiations. All that was said publicly of these delicate matters, Joseph said; and even his story comes second-hand. Apparently Knox had not asked Joseph's help with very much tact. Knox knew little about Indians from his own experience, but he had been told by Pickering that all the chiefs were corrupt and open to bribes. Accordingly he pressed upon Brant considerable sums of money and other gifts and assured him (as Joseph had shown some uneasiness on the subject) that if the British government should object to his visit to the American capital and stop its bounty, the American government would receive him and his people under its protection. All these offers Joseph rejected, said Hammond, except fifty guineas to defray the expenses of his journey. Before parting from Hammond, Joseph promised to take no steps in the business without the approval of the Canadian government. He said he had engaged to perform nothing more than to communicate the American propositions to an Indian council which was shortly to meet at the foot of the Maumee Rapids. On the whole, Hammond concluded, Brant's behavior while in Philadelphia appears to have been "very guarded and proper."[48]

What were the gifts that Knox had offered to Joseph? In later life, in moments of exasperation, Joseph never hesitated to remind the British how much he had given up for their sakes. He told Lieutenant Governor John Graves Simcoe that he had been offered a township for himself, as much land as he chose for his Indians, and a guinea a day for himself for life.[49] Once in chiding his own people for their lack of consideration for him, he said that "At Philadelphia the Americans spoke in a very friendly manner to me, and made me large offers of presents for myself and family if I would prevent any farther attacks from the Indians. But I positively refused to accept of any thing from them, lest I should injure your good name as the Six Nation Indians."[50] To the Count de Puisaye, a French refugee and friend, he declared that he was offered a payment of one thousand guineas and double his British half pay and pension merely on condition that he would try to bring about a peace with the western Indians. Having refused that, he was then offered the preemption right to land in the amount of twenty thousand pounds United States currency and an annuity of fifteen hundred dollars. This, too, he considered "as inconsistent with the principles of honor to receive, as by accepting of any of these offers, they might expect me to act contrary to his Majesty's interest and the honor of our nations; and from the repeated assurances of his Majesty's representatives, I had full confidence his bounty would never fail."[51]

One cannot escape an impression that among all the reasons for Joseph's proper behavior was the thought that a bird in the hand is worth two in the bush. As to the amount of the American offers, they were not far out of line with gifts that the United States government had made to Alexander McGillivray, powerful Creek leader, in 1790. In secret articles in the treaty that year with the Creeks McGillivray got a pension of eighteen hundred dollars per year, a commission as brigadier general, and certain trade concessions for his people.

Joseph's uneasy visit to the American capital lasted only a week. Philadelphia was a commercial and cultural capital, too, and if Joseph had never beheld London, he might have been overpowered by the sights and sounds of so prosperous and busy a metropolis. The city outshone New York or anything Canada could offer. Though president and Mrs. Washington set a formal and dignified style in official entertaining, the fashionable and the new rich did not always profit by their example. Philadelphia society, in spite of its Quaker background and in spite of the Washingtons, was hectic in its pace, often licentious in its conduct, and lavish in its mode of living. There were so many drawing rooms and balls and routs and card parties and dinners that they could scarcely be kept up with, and society grew breathless in the pursuit of such pleasures. Though Joseph's visit was not stressed in the newspapers, the people of Philadelphia were probably just as eager to see him as ever Londoners had been. Thomas Jefferson spoke of the arrival of "the famous Mohawk chief Capt Brandt,"[52] and one may be sure that the secretary of state managed to get a meeting with the celebrity. Joseph came away with the feeling that he had been well treated, and his social life undoubtedly flourished.[53] Secretary Knox himself was a famed host, and he would not have failed to "notice" the influential chieftain with whom he held such important daytime talks. Nor would the great financier, Robert Morris, with his keen interest in speculation in New York land, have overlooked such a one as Brant. Joseph could have had no cause for ennui in the long summer evenings, and he was encouraged to think he would always find a welcome among the Americans. But he dared not linger. On June 28 the busy visit came to an end,[54] and Joseph, his servant, and his two companions set out on horseback for New York. Knox had provided another four hundred dollars for the trip back to the Grand River.[55]

On the whole Secretary Knox was satisfied. The eight hundred dollars had been well spent. Brant, he wrote Wayne, "seems to be strongly impressed with the justice and moderation of the views of the United States," and he obviously thought that Brant's promised embassy to the coming council at the Maumee River had a good chance of producing a peace.[56] To Governor Clinton, Knox wrote that Brant "appears to be a judicious and sensible man," and he thought his journey would be "beneficial to the United States." As Brant had urged the claims of some Cayugas regarding their reservation in New York, Knox passed on the question to Clinton who he hoped would take care of it; and he reminded Clinton that some of the Cayugas were "a little ticklish," and that they had had a war party at St. Clair's defeat.[57] Writing again to Wayne, he urged him to refrain from anything that might increase hostilities in the west or give the western Indians a bad impression or add to the tensions with the British. "I should hope," he said, "that considerable dependence may be placed on Captain Brant— He is well acquainted with the subject, and if his faithfulness in the cause he has undertaken be equal to his intelligence he will probably effect a treaty."[58] Such was Knox's optimism.

In the meantime Joseph continued on his way back home. Stopping in New York, he took lodgings at a hotel on Broadway, and here the only mishap of his journey occurred. One Dygert, a resident of German Flats, who had lost several members of his family at Oriskany, had followed him from the Mohawk valley and was awaiting his return from Philadelphia. Dygert, nursing a long desire for vengeance, intended to kill the monster Brant. Joseph knew of Dygert's pursuit and feared he might be taken unawares. He mentioned his fears to two of his visitors, Colonel Marinus Willett and Colonel Morgan Lewis, whom he had met in battle years before. Glancing out the window, he exclaimed, "There is Dygert now!" Colonel Willett immediately went outside and cornered the man, who did not deny what he was up to. "Do you know," asked Willett, "that if you kill that savage, you will be hanged?" "Who," replied Dygert, "would hang me for killing an Indian?" "You will see," rejoined Willett; "if you execute your purpose, you may depend upon it you will be hanged up immediately." This was news to the ignorant countryman, and upon hearing it from so impressive a source, he gave up and went home.[59]

Since Joseph was called upon at his hotel by a number of prominent visitors, the story of the aborted assassination soon got out. Samuel Ogden wrote Knox that Brant left New York "with his feelings very much wounded." Ogden, a man interested in New York wild lands, suggested that the government prosecute the aggressor in federal court. The honor of the government was at stake, thought Ogden, and the affair ought not to go unnoticed.[60] Though prosecution did not take place, it is likely that the vengeful Mr. Dygert, on his way back to the Mohawk, became the recipient of further tongue lashings from Schuyler or Clinton. Joseph Brant was at this critical time far too valuable a personage to be allowed to nurse wounded feelings unassuaged.

Joseph went home the way he came, and again he did not stop to see Samuel Kirkland. Kirkland was put out. Writing to Oliver Phelps on July 21, he remarked that nobody in the United States had been more friendly to Brant than he had been, yet Brant "must act the Indian sometimes, with all the civility he is master of."[61] The long relationship (one cannot call it a friendship) between Brant and Kirkland was coming to an end. It would not be long before Brant's attention turned exclusively to the Grand River, and Kirkland busied himself with plans for the education and "civilization" of the Indians. Neither man needed the other any more, and Kirkland was no longer necessary to the United States government as an intermediary. The correspondence dropped off. Joseph had been impatient with Kirkland now and again. When Kirkland wrote him in early 1791 asking for his opinions on the prospect for peace and requesting a long reply, Joseph hoped that the very wordy missive he sent off in return would give Kirkland "his Bellyful of it."[62] Captain Hendrick Aupaumut said Kirkland had "too much Charity" for Brant.[63] Kirkland did not have as much charity for Brant as Captain Hendrick thought he did. In the long run Kirkland did not have much charity for Captain Hendrick, either, thinking him corrupted by Brant,[64] and soon grow disillusioned with him. Kirkland liked mainly Cornplanter and the Oneida, Good Peter, both of whom appeared to him very pious and therefore the proper kind of Indian.

Joseph was probably ill when he passed the Oneida reservation. He was very ill, according to Israel Chapin, when he stopped a short time at Chapin's at Canandaigua. The long journey, the trouble in New York, the worries about how the Indians and the British might regard his Philadelphia mission had helped to undermine a constitution no longer so strong as it once was. But Joseph was anxious to go on as fast as possible, and asked Chapin if Dr. Allen might accompany him to Niagara. Chapin consented, and the traveling was resumed.[65]

The little party reached Niagara after what Joseph called a "tedious" journey, on July 24.[66] Joseph expected universal disapprobation of what he had done. Disapproval there was,[67] but it was not universal. Joseph soon got a letter from Joseph Chew which must have heartened him. Through Chew, Sir John Johnson sent his affectionate regards, saying that he had seen an account of his conduct in Philadelphia which was much to his credit. Already, too, Sir John had heard about the Dygert affair.[68] Evidently George Hammond, or somebody, had been busy. But Joseph continued to feel he must be very wary; "my situation since my Visit to Philadelphia obliges me to weigh matters more maturely than heretofore, my Enemies making a handle thereof the least improper word that might drop from me would be taken notice of," he wrote Governor Clinton in the early fall.[69]

Before leaving Niagara Joseph wrote to sound Alexander McKee as to whether his presence would be acceptable at the Maumee Rapids. He was afraid that reports among the western Indians of his activities in the United States may have succeeded in ruining his reputation with them and arousing their enmity.[70] His fears were so strong that he decided to postpone his journey till he heard from McKee, and he asked Chew to send on some pistols that he had ordered from England, as he might need them.[71]

Alexander McKee got Joseph's letter and wrote to reassure him on September 4. It is not clear when McKee's reply reached Joseph, but McKee urged him to come on. McKee had nothing good to say about the American peace proposals; "you must be perfectly sensible," he added, "that after two successful general engagements, in which a great deal of blood has been spilt, the Indians will not quietly give up by negotiation what they have been contending for with their lives since the commencement of these troubles."[72] On September 11 McKee wrote again. He had by this time heard that Joseph was ill (the latter apparently having not mentioned it in his letter), and he hoped that Joseph was sufficiently recovered to be able to travel, for he thought his presence very necessary. McKee wrote both letters from the Maumee Rapids, and it was obvious that he had some strong reason for wanting Joseph to come there at once. Certainly he had always been able to count on Joseph. McKee seemed to have unusual interest in what was, after all, only a private Indian council.

Sometime after August 1 Joseph and Dr. Allen must have set out for Fort Erie. Apparently they—or at least Joseph—intended to go to the Grand River for a brief stay. But at Fort Erie Dr. Allen fell ill of a fever, and Joseph's own ailment, which may have been of the same nature, grew worse.[73] To keep his promise to Knox, Joseph contrived to send his son Isaac to the Maumee with the American peace proposals. Isaac and six Mohawks passed through the new Moravian mission at Fairfield on the Thames (Moraviantown, Ontario) on August 17. The Moravian missionaries and their Christian Indian flock who had wandered, and sometimes been driven, all over the Ohio country from the Muskingum River to Sandusky to the environs of Detroit, had settled at last in Canada. They lent Isaac and his companions a canoe.[74]

In early September Joseph returned from Fort Erie to Niagara in a sedan chair. We have this on the authority of an American prisoner who had been ransomed from the Indians at Detroit and sent back home by way of Niagara. The prisoner, one William May, a deserter from the United States army and possibly a consummate liar as well (for he had certainly told the British some extraordinary stories), swore before Anthony Wayne on October 11 that he saw Brant two days after the latter's return to the post and that he did not look like a sick man. He also told Wayne that the people at Niagara thought Brant was afraid to go to the Maumee Rapids.[75] Joseph himself said on September 10 that he was recovering from his illness and that he meant to leave for the west soon. But he said he was going to the Grand River first, and this lends credence to the belief that he had not yet been home. If he was getting better, of course he must have looked better.[76]

In the meantime all Knox's other Indian peacemakers had gone on to the Maumee. Captain Hendrick Aupaumut arrived long before the main council opened and attempted some private negotiations with small groups of early comers. Cornplanter and his party arrived on September 11. Most of the white peacemakers had not been so fortunate. The news was that three, including Trueman and Hardin, had already been murdered on the way by suspicious Indian hunters. General Putnam and the Reverend John Heckewelder were luckier. They managed to get to the Wabash and by the end of September actually persuaded some of the less belligerent Wabash Indians to come to Philadelphia to make peace.[77] Knox was overjoyed at such success. He thought Putnam's treaty would probably detach eight hundred warriors from the enemy Indians. At the same time he thought he might even be able to make a peace treaty with the hostiles; "if we can fairly gain an audience," he told Wayne, "I have but little doubt that we shall convince them of their true Interest."[78] Gaining the audience was the difficulty. Word had finally come that all the white peace messengers headed for the Maumee area had been killed. Peace depended entirely on what the Indian messengers could do.

The council, supposed to open at the rapids, was moved up the Maumee to the confluence of the Auglaize River (Defiance, Ohio). Here were two Shawnee villages, a Delaware village, some displaced Cherokees from the south, and the dwellings of some newly arrived Miamis who had fled their towns on the upper Maumee. Another village of Delawares was situated a few miles away. From the Glaize, as the forks were often called, the Indians could more easily watch General Wayne's movements. It was reported Wayne had built a new fort, named after St. Clair, between Fort Hamilton and Fort Jefferson, and that he was throwing in supplies and reinforcements all along the line. The Indians were much alarmed. The Moravian missionaries could report that the Indians were anxiously awaiting Brant and whatever news he might bring them from Philadelphia.[79]

Isaac Brant had arrived on September 13 and, according to Captain Hendrick, proved nothing less than an "Emmissary of the Devil." The young man told the assembled Indians that he and his party had come to help them in war and that his father warned they were not to pay attention to any peace proposals brought by Hendrick. He also told them his father said that "I have myself seen Washington, and see his heart and bowels; and he declared that he claims from the mouth of Miamie to the head of it—thence to the head of Wabash river, and down the same to the mouth of it; and that he did take up dust, and did declare that he would not restore so much dust to the Indians, but he is willing to have peace with the Indians." If the listening Indians took the mouth of the "Miamie" to mean the mouth of the Maumee instead of the mouth of the Great Miami, as they apparently did, this was a great deal more land than the Americans had treaties for or claimed.[80] Nor did Isaac mention the promise of additional American payments. However, as the Indians wanted their land, not annuities, this omission probably did not matter. According to Captain Hendrick, Isaac did great harm. Hendrick persisted in speaking of the youth as Brant's nephew, giving him the Algonquian-sounding name of Tawalooth.[81] Hendrick did not know Joseph well, and probably had no acquaintance at all with his family. The two, the Algonquian Hendrick and the Iroquoian Brant, did not even have a common language; without an interpreter they had to speak English together.

If the Indians were not angry at Brant, as McKee claimed, they were certainly angry at Cornplanter and his people. Since the invasions of Harmar and St. Clair the American members of the Six Nations had been considered almost as traitors to their kind. Where were their numerous warriors when most needed? What had they done to help the confederacy which they had been so eager to found? These were questions to which the western Indians, in the ensuing council, demanded answers. Said a Delaware chief accusingly: "I remember when we last met 4 years ago you told us, and all Nations agreed to it, that if any one of us were struck, we should consider it as if the whole of the Nations had received a Blow and that the whole should join in revenging it, think well of this Uncles of the 6 Nations."[82]

The council at the Glaize was to last from September 30 to October 9. The anger which marked its beginning was not easily assuaged.

The Shawnees scornfully asked Cornplanter's party what it was they had brought under their arms, referring, of course, to the messages sent by Knox; and they wanted to know why they had been visiting the Americans so often and what they had been discussing with them for the past several years. At one time the Shawnees were so sarcastic that Red Jacket, who spoke for Cornplanter's party, and who was explaining that they had been trying to do something for the good of all, found himself in a quandary. He had to pause and confer with his people about how he should proceed.

Red Jacket was no great warrior—indeed, he was called the Cow Killer in some derision—but he was the finest orator in the entire Six Nations, British or American. At this council he was at his eloquent best. He spoke for five hours and, unlike many speakers who were at a loss for words, did not have to fill up his discourse with polite nothings or vacuous compliments to his brothers or fulsome references to the glory of the Six Nations. He had probably rehearsed his main speech, as he so often did, and he spoke words of substance. It was very plain that the war party among the western Indians was riding high. Red Jacket chided the hotheads. Not so willing to accept white civilization as Cornplanter, he nevertheless spoke words of peace. Like Cornplanter, he could see nothing for the Indians in war. "Brothers," said Red Jacket at one point, "You were very fortunate that the great Spirit above was so kind as to assist you to throw the Americans twice on their back when they came against your villages, your women & children. Now Brothers, we know that the Americans have held out their hands to offer you peace. Don't be too proud Spirited and reject it, the great Spirit should be angry with you, but let us go on in the best manner we can to make peace with them."[83]

The hostile Indians had a ready answer. They denied that their victories had made them overproud. "We are not proud spirited, nor do we attribute our great good fortune these last 2 years, to our own strength alone, but to the great Spirit who governs all things on this Earth & who looks on us with as much or perhaps more compassion than those of a fairer complexion."[84]

Though Red Jacket did his best to get acceptance for the American peace proposals, as at least a basis for further talk, the war party won. The latter could point to all the sorry history of past relations between Indians and whites. They were mindful of what the Six Nations and the white people had done to them at Fort Stanwix in 1768 and again in 1784. The Shawnees, in particular, remembered the battle of Point Pleasant with bitterness and the treaty they had been forced to sign which gave up their ancient Kentucky hunting ground. Perhaps they had just heard that their Kentucky had been admitted into the American union as the fifteenth state. There had been time for the rankling news to get out. The admission had taken place on June 1.

Those who scorned compromise had also seen the official papers that had fallen into the hands of the victorious warriors at St. Clair's defeat. These papers included Knox's orders to St. Clair. The angry chiefs had seen the papers, but they could not read them. They had handed them over to their British friends—Simon Girty, for one— and they had heard them interpreted by various persons in various ways. St. Clair had been ordered to build a fort at the old Miami towns at the head of the Maumee. Somehow the Indians got the idea that he was to build two other forts as well: at the Glaize and at the mouth of the Maumee on Lake Erie. The Indians also believed that they were to be driven out of their remaining country, away from the lake, and across the Mississippi—though Knox had plainly stated that peaceable tribes were to be allowed to stay where they were and that the United States, while willing to extend the present boundary as far as the Mississippi if it could be "tenderly managed," preferred peace to great extensions of territory. The Indians believed, too, as the Shawnee speaker reported, that if any of their nations offered their hands in peace, St. Clair was to "give them Hoes in their hands to plant corn for him & his people & make them labour like their beasts, their oxen & their Packhorses."[85] Not one word had been said about agricultural labor in St. Clair's original orders or in any subsequent orders, but the Indians firmly believed they were to be put to this demeaning work.

These terms were too hard and too shameful for a twice victorious people—especially a victorious people who had just been assured of help by a party of Creeks and Cherokees who had come up from the south; who knew they could put almost daily pressure on nearer Indians, on the Wabash or the Illinois, for help; and who still firmly believed that in the long run they would have British aid.

The decision of the council reflected all these ideas, mistaken though most of them were. The Indians sent a message to the Americans that they would make peace only under the following conditions: The boundary between the Americans and the Indians must be the Ohio. The Indians did not want more money or goods; they wanted their country restored. To this end the Americans must remove all their forts north and west of the Ohio. If the Americans agreed to peace on these terms, the Indians would meet them in May at Sandusky. The Americans must bring their maps and records of former Indian treaties. The British must be represented, too, and they were to bring their maps and records. The Indians expected that all their troubles would end through the mediation of their British father. Their father would see that they received justice. Had they not always been able to depend on him? The British were also requested to provide supplies for the coming meeting. Matters were so patched up between the western Indians and Cornplanter's would-be neutrals that the latter agreed to hold fast to the confederacy and its decisions, and promised to send the ultimatum on to the Americans. The historic council broke up on October 9.[86]

Joseph Brant, finally able to travel, passed by the Moravian mission on September 29.[87] A few days later, on the way up the Maumee, he met Alexander McKee and a party of white men coming down from the Glaize. Among the whites were Prideaux Selby, an agent from the Indian department at Detroit; William Johnston, an agent from Niagara; and a British officer with important connections, Captain Joseph Bunbury, from Niagara.[88] No white man except the vengeful Simon Girty, whom the Indians considered one of themselves, had been allowed to attend the council, but McKee and his companions, together with Matthew Elliott, had been busy at the Glaize during the sessions distributing the annual presents. The British minister in Philadelphia later admitted that McKee had been able to get the Indians to protract the council. The future would show that that was not the only decision McKee had influenced.

Joseph reached the Glaize on the evening of October 11, but many of the Indians had already left for home. Next day Joseph told the Indians still on the ground what had happened at Philadelphia.[89] That same day a large party of Shawnee and Wyandot warriors divided the ammunition which McKee had given them, and set out for war. Some Delawares and a few Mohawks followed to see the action. Joseph remonstrated, but to no purpose.[90] After about two days Joseph gave up and left, but not before he had accused Captain Hendrick of trying to sow dissension among the Indians.[91] Then McKee's son, so Hendrick states, brought a letter from Detroit which reported that the Americans were poisoning liquor at their advanced posts, intending to let it fall into the hands of the warriors.

When Joseph got back to the foot of the rapids, he was invited to a council by some Indians who had followed McKee down for presents. They spoke to Joseph in a friendly manner and urged him to meet them at Sandusky in the spring. They reiterated the determination that the Ohio must be the boundary. Joseph promised to come to Sandusky and warned them against Washington. Washington, he said, "speaks very smooth, will tell you fair stories, and at the same time want to ruin us." He advised the Indians to take care not to be deceived, and urged them to remain united.[92] William Johnston, the agent from Niagara, reported that Brant appeared unhappy at what had occurred at the Glaize.[93]

On November 8 Joseph, returning home, reached the Moravian mission on the Thames and spent the night there. He told some of the Indian converts that he feared peace would not take place—that every Indian who could carry a gun, even the Christians, might have to turn out and fight before the war was over.[94]

The previous year Joseph had earnestly said to Kirkland: "It has been my constant study since the peace between Great Britain and the United States to unite the Indians together and make such a peace between them and the States as would remove all prejudices and enable us to sit quietly down on our Seats free from apprehensions and jealousy and if not become more respectable at least not more contemptible."[95] The confederacy embodied his dearest hopes, but he feared it had made a disastrous decision. The future for the Indians and the Longhouse looked bleak. War and threats of war were not the answer. The answer was compromise. Worriedly Joseph still clung to the idea of the Muskingum boundary.

Joseph had no way of knowing as yet that every move the Indians had made at the Glaize conformed by remarkable coincidence to the wishes of British authority.

23

"My Wish Ever Was for Peace"

To UNDERSTAND what had gone wrong at the Glaize, it is necessary to take a backward view. The Loyalists had scarcely settled themselves in new homes to the west of Quebec when they began to petition for their own government and the protection of English law. Accordingly, in May 1791, Upper Canada was set off from French-speaking Lower Canada, with the Ottawa River as the dividing line. Lord Dorchester remained governor of both provinces, but a lieutenant governor was to serve under him in each. Sir Alured Clarke, the acting governor while Dorchester was in England, headed Lower Canada. Colonel John Graves Simcoe received the appointment as lieutenant governor of Upper Canada.

John Graves Simcoe was a veteran of the American war. He had commanded a famous Loyalist regiment, the Queen's Rangers, during most of the war, and he had operated from north to south, from Boston to Yorktown. From this extensive experience he felt he could recognize the grave weaknesses of many of the American leaders. He described Washington as "among the most treacherous of Mankind," and the men of Washington's administration as "totally destitute of Public or Private Morality."[1] He also felt that for the good of both Britain and Canada these leaders must be superseded, and he was eager to do his part in working the change. A man of untrammeled imagination, he believed that the Americans would welcome a prince of the German house of Brunswick as their king or permanent president!

But if the American government remained in the hands of Washington and his ilk, Simcoe was convinced that Canada was in great danger. The protection of Canada from the United States was to become the paramount object of his administration. He developed large ideas for the advancement of his province of Upper Canada, wishing to see it strong enough to defend itself against American aggression. In the pursuit of his objectives he was likely to forget that there were limits to his powers. He did not like to consult Lord Dorchester. He could even forget to consult the ministry. To become ambassador to the United States had been his first choice of office, a choice that he found hard to relinquish. He would have liked to add to the duties of lieutenant governor some of those of ambassador, and saw nothing strange in the amalgam, and was even willing to take on the additional responsibility without additional salary. Above all, Simcoe wished to mediate between the Americans and the western Indians, and he agreed fully with the idea that there must be an Indian barrier between Canada and the United States. He, like the ministry in London, clung to this idea long after its time had passed.

The new lieutenant governor arrived in Canada in the late fall of 1791, not long after Dorchester's departure. Immediately he found a situation well suited to his talents, not much restraint on his activities, and an aid whom he could like and trust. At Quebec, in the spring of 1792, and again in Montreal, he met Alexander McKee who was making one of his infrequent trips down the country.

Alexander McKee was well thought of by almost everyone on his side of the border, whether settler, soldier, civil servant, or Indian agent. Lord Dorchester and the officers at Detroit praised him highly, for his accounts were invariably in order, his requisitions reasonable, and he always acted the gentleman. But his greatest value to his government lay in the extraordinary influence which he wielded over the western Indians, especially the Shawnees. Indeed, there was a good deal of gossip that McKee was half Shawnee. His British associates, however, never mentioned such an idea, nor did they treat him as a half-breed. They treated him as one of themselves, and there are at least two letters extant in which he seems to classify himself as among the whites. Joseph Brant in several letters clearly classifies him as white. McKee did have a Shawnee wife (no little reason for his influence), and his son was part Shawnee. His own father was Thomas McKee, long a trader on the Pennsylvania frontier. His mother could have been a white captive of the Shawnees. Perhaps this accounts for the confusion about his identity.

Lieutenant Governor Simcoe naturally seized the opportunity to confer with such an officer as Alexander McKee. There was much for Simcoe to question, to discuss, and to learn. His province of Upper

Canada bordered on the country of the warring American Indians and also included most of the Canadian Indian population, and nobody knew all these Indians better than Alexander McKee who had lived so many years at Detroit and, before the war, at Fort Pitt.

McKee and Simcoe took to each other at once. Presently the two men were poring over maps, and peace treaties as far back as 1713, and old Indian treaties, especially Sir William Johnson's Fort Stanwix treaty of 1768 which forbade white settlement beyond the Ohio. Also at hand were the recent peace treaty between the United States and Great Britain and Simcoe's latest instructions from London. At Quebec acting Governor Clarke and Sir John Johnson added their views, but the main conferees were Simcoe and McKee.

The conferences took place against a political background which was daily growing more complex and frightening. The general European wars which were not to end till Waterloo in 1815 were just beginning. In less than a year Britain would be at war with Revolutionary France, and for almost a quarter of a century no public policy could be set afoot without due consideration of its effect on the great conflict.

Against such a background Colonel Simcoe had been instructed to give the United States no reason to increase its already towering mistrust of Britain. The Americans must not be allowed to think that Britain was helping the hostile Indians. The Pitt ministry, which had its hands full in Europe, wanted no war in America—indeed, could not afford such a war, for American trade was far more valuable than even the vaunted fur trade, and would have to be chosen if Britain could not retain both. At the same time the Indians must be kept friendly to the king, and hopeful; if disillusioned with their British father, they might turn their anger against Canada. Nobody was forgetting Pontiac or the influence of hostile French Canadians on malleable Indian minds.

The protection of a friendly Indian barrier between Canada and the United States was more ardently hoped for than ever. The old Fort Stanwix line of 1768, extended to the east and northeast so as to take in all of Lake Ontario and the St. Lawrence with a safe amount of contiguous country, was the boundary line which Britain wished to see established between the Indians and the Americans. There was only one way to get such a boundary for the Indians: through British mediation of the Indian war. This plan still seemed feasible to the British government, and George Hammond was instructed to propose it to the Americans as soon as he found a favorable opportunity. All Canadian officialdom, from Lord Dorchester down, was to cooperate toward this desirable end. In the meantime Lieutenant Governor Simcoe was to begin a search for every possible way to substantiate claims of the Indians to such lands as the ministry thought they should retain. At points along the boundary, particularly along Lakes Ontario and Champlain, where there were no Indian claimants under British influence, suitable Indians must be found who could be encouraged to set up claims.

Other considerations also entered into the discussions of Simcoe and McKee. There was the dangerous tendency of the Americans to settle as near the border as they could, especially in the Genesee country where British control of the lakes might be threatened. There was the possibility that a victorious Anthony Wayne might go on to attack Detroit, an attack which Simcoe knew would put Wayne in line for the presidency and make him Washington's successor—an event which, as far as Simcoe was concerned, was exchanging the frying pan for the fire. Then there was the uncertain fate of the fur trade. Petitions of merchants impossible to be ignored, reminded the government that £250,000 represented the annual value of furs exchanged for British goods, and importuned for still additional time to settle their affairs before the border posts were given up.

Simcoe and McKee found that they agreed very well. McKee got his instructions, but with him it was to be a case of warm cooperation rather than a mere carrying out of orders. Neither man ever stated the specific agreement or the specific orders given to McKee, but they did send George Hammond a memorandum listing five points which they thought important:

1. An Indian Territory should separate Britain [Canada] and the United States.

2. The posts of Niagara, Oswego, and Detroit should be demolished, and the area of the posts included in the Indian Territory.

3. Michilimackinac to be evacuated.

4 and 5. Britain to give up the Genesee country provided the Americans would give up Detroit and the Maumee River up to the rapids. Detroit and all settlements in the latter area to be subject to British law.[2]

Parts of McKee's orders can also be inferred from the later correspondence of himself and Simcoe or the correspondence of Hammond and Clarke. For instance, McKee was to help find Indian claimants for land which Britain wished to include in the Indian Territory.[3] Simcoe warned McKee "that in no case are the Indians to expect our Interference by any other Means than Mediation" and that he must try to counteract anything the traders might say to the contrary.[4] Simcoe dreaded the grave effects of letting the Indians make peace with the United States independent of British intervention. If the Indians were allowed to make a peace of their own, he feared, the Americans might later induce them to invade Canada.[5]

The conferences between Simcoe and McKee took place in May and June of 1792. Afterward McKee returned to Detroit. In late July Simcoe arrived at his new post and soon set up his headquarters at an old barracks called Navy Hall, across the river from Fort Niagara. Instructions that had come in from England after the winter's lull remained the same. Nothing had changed in London. Nothing had changed in the United States, either. Hamilton, Jefferson, and Washington were still adamantly opposed to British intervention in their Indian war. So final were the American objections after Hammond's private feelers that he suggested to Simcoe that Britain's best chance lay in getting the Indians themselves to ask for mediation. Simcoe made haste to write McKee. His clear instructions were that at the coming council at the Glaize the Indians must appear to ask voluntarily for British mediation of the war. Apparently he thought McKee would meet with no difficulty.[6]

That fall, while the Glaize council was going on, McKee, as we have seen, went to the council ground to supervise the distribution of the annual presents and "extras." The inevitable outcome was that the Indians insisted on the Ohio boundary (if they had not, there would have been little to mediate), and they asked for British mediation of the war. Simcoe promptly wrote McKee a confidential letter signifying his hearty approval of the manner in which he had acted "at the late Council."[7] And Joseph Brant returned home baffled and worried, not knowing what had gone wrong or what had caused the unconciliatory attitude of the Indians.

The Indians were prone to say that Brant knew as much as any white man.[8] That belief was the secret of whatever influence Joseph possessed outside his own nation. But the Indians were wrong. Joseph did not know as much as some white men. With scarcely two years of formal education he had not had time to learn everything about the white man's world. And though he never gave up the effort to learn more, there were occasions when he could be hoodwinked by the proper persons rather easily. Unhappily for his dreams of Longhouse glory and for his grandiose plans for helping his people, the Glaize council of 1792 was one of those occasions.

In spite of his great disappointment Joseph used his good offices to forward the messages of peace back and forth between the Indians and the American government.[9] The American branch of the Six Nations helped in this work, though the Senecas were again not on good terms with Joseph or their Canadian kin.[10] Joseph could take heart once more. He was pleased at what seemed to be a new American attitude and thought "every thing has the best appearance."[11] He wrote McKee: "I am of opinion this is the best time to obtain a good Peace, and if lost, may not be easily regained." Trustingly, he told McKee that he might tell the western Indians whatever he thought proper in his name![12]

Joseph did not err in thinking that the time had come for making peace. Though Secretary Knox responded in general terms to the message from the Glaize, his response was favorable. The president of the United States, he noted, hoped there would be a full and complete representation at the coming council of all the Indian nations concerned, so that the long awaited peace would be known and observed by all. Knox also added that American war parties were being called in, and he urged the Indians to stop their war parties, too. Obviously the Americans were very tired of the war and were prepared at last to make genuine concessions.

There was a small misunderstanding about the place of the coming negotiations, for the Americans seem not to have known the difference between Sandusky and the Maumee Rapids. The exact place was finally straightened out, though Simcoe was inclined to view the misunderstanding with suspicion. Simcoe also refused to allow the United States to send provisions to Sandusky or even to buy them in Canada. He insisted that the British government must supply the provisions. That had always been the custom, he declared, no matter for what reason the Indians met; and he unearthed the old concept, not much thought about for years, that in provisioning Indian councils the British acknowledged that they held the posts by permission of the native owners of the soil. As Simcoe well knew, whoever fed the Indians was in a very good position to control their decisions. John Butler, who expected to go to Sandusky, backed Simcoe's stand. He and McKee must have provisions for the chiefs, he said, during their frequent applications for advice.[13] Brant, as Simcoe told Hammond, agreed. The Indians would feel less independent if supplied by the United States. This would not promote peace.[14] So it was settled, and the Americans had to accept the discomfiture.

More than discomfiture—indeed, an actual rout—was in store for Simcoe himself. In early 1793, while details of the peace council were being worked out, the lieutenant governor finally saw his best hopes crushed. From Hammond in Philadelphia he learned that the Americans would not tolerate British interposition in their affairs no matter who requested it. Simcoe had to send word to the western Indians that he could not meet them at Sandusky. He assured them, however, that Butler and McKee would be there with copies of relevant documents and treaties, though unable to act as mediators.

Now thoroughly alarmed, Simcoe set out, on February 4, on a hurried, 250-mile journey over the frozen wilderness to Detroit, traveling on snowshoes most of the way. It was ostensibly a trip of inspection, but he wrote McKee that he was coming mainly to see him. He wanted to talk over the very "prudent" conduct that McKee must follow at the meeting with the Americans. Since the king's mediation had never been formally offered, McKee must be very "reserved" about this subject[15]—and about other subjects, too, as we shall see.

On the way west Simcoe visited Joseph at the Grand River, and Joseph joined the lieutenant governor and his retinue of soldiers and Indians on their journey.[16] Halfway to Detroit Joseph had the "misfortune," as he said, of having to turn back in order to attend a Six Nations council which had been called in his absence at Buffalo Creek.[17] Simcoe went on to his destination and conferred with McKee. And late that same month those western Indians who could be assembled in the dead of winter met and answered Knox's message. They voiced their disappointment that Knox had not been more specific about the boundary. Still insisting on the Ohio, they spoke bluntly of past American shortcomings. Next, they determined to hold a council of the Indian confederacy at the Maumee Rapids before going to meet the Americans at Sandusky. Then they sent a message to the Five Nations (pointedly omitting the Oneidas) urging them and all their brothers to attend this private council. They also sent word to Simcoe that they intended to pay attention to his good advice.[18] The various messages that they sent out were carefully written down by somebody, though not a soul among the western Indians could write with so much ease and accuracy, if, indeed, any of them could write at all.

In March the Americans named three commissioners to negotiate the peace. If worse came to worst and if they could do no better, the commissioners had power to give up everything across the Ohio that the United States had secured by former Indian treaties except a few places just north of the river that had already been legally settled—namely the areas around Marietta and Gallipolis and Cincinnati and a tract across from Louisville granted the soldiers of George Rogers Clark. If the Indians would sell anything else or confirm the treaty of Fort Harmar, the Americans were prepared to pay handsomely. If not, the Indians would retain the unoccupied territory, including the sites of the advanced American posts built by Harmar and St. Clair.[19] By request of the Indians six American Quakers were permitted to attend the peacemaking and help with the negotiations, though not in an official capacity.

General Wayne, on the point of moving down the Ohio to Fort Washington, was warned not to go near the advanced posts or into the Indian country. All militia parties were to be likewise restrained for it was thought that the very lives of the commissioners were at stake. Nobody was forgetting the murders of Trueman and Hardin. Wayne made the required promises to sit still, but dourly remarked that he wished he could go to the council with 2,500 "Commissioners" unaccompanied by a single Quaker!

Toward the end of May three eminent Americans, the newly appointed negotiators, arrived at Niagara on their way west. They were Beverly Randolph, former governor of Virginia; Timothy Pickering, postmaster general and successful Indian diplomat; and General Benjamin Lincoln, distinguished veteran of the Revolution, who also had experience in Indian diplomacy. Congress and the president had done their best to get the right men for the job. Lieutenant Governor Simcoe welcomed the Americans politely, assured them of his eagerness for peace—and, indeed, there was nothing he wanted so much as the right kind of peace—and invited them to stay at his house at Newark (Niagara-on-the-Lake) on the Canadian side. Simcoe did not want their company, and they did not want his; but the invitation, reluctant though it was, was in the nature of a command, and the Americans could not but yield, uncomfortable as everyone was likely to be. At Navy Hall, Simcoe's house, the Americans were to spend six embarrassed weeks. They were told that McKee would send word when the Indians had finished their preliminary council on the Maumee and were ready to receive them at Sandusky. As the British still had control of the lakes and the Americans must cross Lake Erie in a British vessel, they could not travel freely; and they knew it.

The commissioners spent some of their time in viewing Niagara Falls and making a journey to Buffalo Creek. At Buffalo Creek they conferred with the local Indians, mainly Senecas. In doing so they caused Simcoe much anguish. He was afraid they would succeed in seducing those Indians both from the western confederacy and from British interests. Simcoe thought he had converted Cornplanter to his point of view (Cornplanter having averred his loyalty to the king), and very much feared that the Americans would unconvert him. At this time Cornplanter was running a dark and devious course, doing the best he could in his painful situation. On June 4 the king's birthday was celebrated at Newark. There were toasts and the firing of guns and a ball in honor of the occasion, and it was the Americans' turn to suffer.

All the while Simcoe was sizing up his unwelcome guests. He concluded that they possessed much of that "low Craft" which passes for wisdom among people as uneducated as those of the United States. The youngest commissioner, Beverly Randolph, he dismissed as "able" but "of the rakish or Virginian cast of character." Simcoe's heartiest detestation was reserved for Pickering, "a violent, low, philosophic, cunning New Englander." Only General Lincoln he found "very civil," almost, one may suppose, a gentleman.[20] In thus making himself endurable to Simcoe General Lincoln must have been a consummate diplomat. He was also a writer of clear and interesting prose. His record of his journey to Niagara and the subsequent events of his mission makes a fascinating story.[21]

A few weeks before the American commissioners appeared at Niagara a new complication had entered an already complex situation. The dismaying news had come that Britain and France were at war. Spain, which in 1791 was an enemy to Britain, was now a helpful friend. The Americans had immediately declared their neutrality toward all combatants. Simcoe was pretty sure this was a sham. He knew where their hearts really were. Their hearts were with their old ally, France. Now it seemed to him that Upper Canada was in the greatest peril from enemies both near and far. An Indian buffer state was even more desirable than before. He was more than ever determined to bring it about, and he thought that after all his careful planning success was within his grasp. He was not without hope, he said, that the proceedings of the western confederacy "will be so managed as to assure to the Indians the greatest part of that Territory which His Majesty's Ministers seem desirous should intervene between Canada and the United States."[22]

While the impatient American commissioners were cooling their heels amid the swamps at Navy Hall, what were the western Indians doing? What was Joseph Brant doing?

It had been easy enough for Joseph to get himself sent as a delegate to the preliminary Indian council at the Maumee Rapids, for Simcoe (who had been told of Joseph's good behavior at Philadelphia) had succeeded in reconciling him and the Senecas—again. A Six Nations council at Buffalo Creek gave him the authority to go.[23] Joseph had some definite ideas about the western council. He did not think Captain Hendrick Aupaumut or any "yanky Indian" should be allowed there. He believed that without unity the Indians could accomplish nothing, and he was very displeased to hear that somewhere out in the woods some Indian friends of the Americans had killed a party of hostile Delawares. Joseph hoped the murderers were not Senecas. He said angrily "nothing hurts me so much is [as] to see that some [of] the Indians should still [be] so curset blind is [as] to act against their own interest of killing their frinds for the yankys."[24] Needless to say, these emotional words, composed at the Grand River, were not transmitted through a secretary but written by Joseph himself.

As to the important business of making peace, Joseph still favored reasonable compromise. He thought he could get the Indians to agree to the Muskingum boundary which he had suggested to St. Clair in 1788 and which had been given in to Lord Dorchester in 1791 as what the Indians wanted, though he was willing to allow the Americans the few places they actually inhabited across that line. The Muskingum was the least the Indians could settle for, he thought. In this he actually reflected Simcoe's views and those of the ministry in London: the Muskingum would be acceptable if no better line could be obtained. Joseph also wished to have it agreed that *no* Indian nation, not even the Senecas, could sell their land without the consent of the general confederacy. The land belonged to everybody in common, and everybody should consent to its sale.[25] He still cherished the ancient idea of the dish with one spoon from which all were to eat. There was no Mohawk land, no Seneca land, no Wyandot land, no Miami land, no Shawnee land. In Joseph's mind there was only Indian land. Simcoe, one of the few white persons who ever came close to understanding Brant, knew what Indian unity meant to him; the Indian confederacy, he noted, "is the first wish of his Heart."[26] Another time Simcoe observed that the "independence of the Indians is his primary object" and that "his views are extensive."[27] Joseph had neither given up on the reestablishment of Longhouse glory nor his efforts for the good of all Indians, purposes still in his mind one and the same. Yet Simcoe could expect him to go to the council on the Maumee and do his utmost to cooperate with British plans.[28] But what did McKee think? Apparently McKee was not so sanguine.

Before the opening of the council Simcoe wrote final instructions for the guidance of Butler and McKee. They were to explain the American offers and to influence the Indians to accede if the offers were for their benefit or to reject if the offers were injurious to their real interests. They must proceed with the utmost caution (for they would be watched), so that nothing they did or said would cause the Americans to think British agents prevented peace. They were to give their advice privately, as usual, to some of the chiefs. If a public meeting should be necessary, they could express any disapproval by silence. They were to have as little contact with the American commissioners as possible, explaining that anything more than the civilities would arouse Indian suspicions. If no peace should be made, they must, above all, see that no injury was done to the Americans. He concluded by hoping a safe and solid peace would be established.[29] Through his secretary, Major Littlehales, Simcoe also instructed two interpreters whom he was sending to the west that they should influence the Indians under their guidance "to adopt such measures as Col. McKee shall from time to time direct as necessary for their common benefit and preservation."[30] Presently it was noised about Detroit that a third province was to be established between that place and the Ohio and that Sir John Johnson (now in England) had received the appointment as governor.

Joseph and his party of seventy Grand River men, all in canoes, arrived at Detroit in mid-May. Here Joseph began to keep a journal of a sort, for he realized the great importance of the coming negotiations. He and his party reached the foot of the rapids of the Maumee, a rocky point called Roche de Bout, about May 22. Nobody was there except, of course, Alexander McKee, who had a house there. Joseph sent messages hither and yon to hurry up the proceedings, and presently some people began to show up. They did not appear to be very friendly. Joseph charged them with unfriendliness to him, and they denied it. After a while more people came (some of the warriors were just getting in from their hunt, while others had been detained by drunkenness), but for some mysterious reason the main council did not begin. For several weeks only small private meetings were held.[31]

The great council, when it finally got going, never became part of a record. This time nobody wrote down the proceedings. No official account was ever forwarded to Simcoe or to headquarters at Quebec or across the sea to London. Yet Alexander McKee was present the entire time. Most of the time Simon Girty was also present. Matthew Elliott, assistant agent of Indian affairs since 1790, came and went; so, too, did other members of the Indian department and various British army and naval officers. But nobody took up his pen to write and, of course, the Indians could not.

Without an official record, we must follow Joseph's account. While he was trying to get the Indians to assemble, he was told by the Mingoes that "many evil Reports were circulated against me by the Shawonese, Saying I was a Traitor, & that I only came there to receive Money, and that they would have nothing to do with me."[32]

This was hard for Joseph to take since he was often spending his own money and using his own credit to carry on his work.[33] The Indians were still angry that Joseph had not been with them at St. Clair's defeat. They had always suspected his motives, and they were now glad to believe that he had become an American agent. If McKee did nothing to reinforce these opinions, he certainly did nothing to combat them. The bad reports continued.

By June 9, when some Delaware and Shawnee leaders arrived, the Indians had not yet performed the ceremony of condolence or even welcomed Joseph to their fireplace. By June 15 several other nations had arrived. Joseph decided to take the initiative though such action was contrary to custom. He called a council and performed the good offices himself. Then he asked the Indians to explain their suspicions. Two chiefs, a Shawnee and a Wyandot, replied. They advised Joseph to pay no attention to the evil rumors but to attend to the business "which Concerns every thing that is dear to us." Joseph replied by warning them against spies, referring to Hendrick Aupaumut who was known to have arrived at Detroit. In so doing he was right, for Hendrick had indeed been instructed by Colonel Pickering as to what he should say and how he should act in the best interests of the Americans. As earnestly as he could Joseph continued:

> Brothers
>   We have had various Meetings with the Americans, but none of Such importance as this Will be, it therefore Stands us in Need to give it the Most Serious Attention, and requires the greatest Prudence & unanimity amongst ourselves for upon the event of it Depends the future ease and happiness of ourselves & our Posterity, let us therefore Cooly consider our true Interest, and Disregarding every other object, Pursue that, which is the only means of rendering real Service to our Country. I therefore request your Serious attention to the great Object of this Treaty, which if you Suffer now to escape may not offer again.[34]

In spite of this apparently friendly meeting, the gossip against Joseph went on. Many nights, he says, the Shawnees, Delawares, and Miamis held private councils to which he and his Six Nations party were not invited. Yet still no public business was done.[35]

Finally, about July 1, Alexander McKee asked Joseph in confidence if he thought delegates should be sent to the commissioners at Niagara to find out if they had the power to make a new boundary. (Apparently McKee did not mention a specific line.)

Joseph agreed that this inquiry was a good idea, but suggested that principal chiefs not be sent. If the American answer was unfavorable, the Indian leaders, by remaining in the west, would have more time to prepare their people for war. Now, at last, the principal chiefs came to consult with Joseph and his party and proposed that a delegation should go to Niagara. (They, too, seem to have said nothing about the Ohio.) Joseph himself was chosen one of the deputies—whether by the Indians or by McKee is not clear—and they all set out in great haste. According to Joseph, the haste was so great that no speaker had been appointed.[36]

John Butler returned to Niagara with the deputies. He could not get along with McKee and, as he said afterward, he differed with him in opinion, for he thought it was the most favorable opportunity the Indians would ever have for making an advantageous peace and saving the greatest part of their country.[37] Butler had buried his wife on May 31. His health was growing worse. He was despondent and never went back to the Maumee. His long services for the crown were drawing to a close.

While the Indian deputies were on their way down the Maumee and across Lake Erie, Pickering, Randolph, and Lincoln had finally been allowed to leave Niagara and go as far as the mouth of the Detroit River, Detroit itself being forbidden to them. The three commissioners had already reached Fort Erie on their journey, but the vessel which was to transport them across the lake had to wait for a favorable wind.

On July 5 Joseph and the other deputies, fifty men including himself and Simon Girty, arrived at Fort Erie.[38] They met with the Americans and suggested that a conference should be held in Lieutenant Governor Simcoe's presence. The Americans agreed and returned with the Indians to Niagara.

A white traveler who had considerable contact with Joseph at this time (dining with him, talking with him, and sleeping in the same room) described him as

> shrewd, sensible and intelligent. He speaks English well, and with fluency. . . .
>
> His deportment at table is perfectly that of a gentleman, and I have seen many instances where his manners and address, from their correctness and suavity, were entitled to peculiar regard.
>
> It appears to me to be unfair to object to him a few excesses into which he was on the point of entering when inebriated with wine. Those who expect that human nature can be thus easily changed, ought themselves to be models of perfection.

The true point of prudence, in my opinion, would have been to have substituted other convivial pleasures before the seat of reason was disturbed by intemperance.

Captain Brandt is a man of middle size, and appears in age to be bordering on fifty; but hale, vigorous and active. His countenance is far from prepossessing; it may, however, be a trait in high respect among his tribe—that it is calculated to strike terror into his enemies. . . . We had much conversation in the early part of the night, which confirmed the opinion I had previously entertained of the strength of his mind, and the culture of his understanding.[39]

So much for Joseph Brant in the summer of 1793, his intellect, his appearance, his manners, and his vices. It was probably a fair comment, giving him the benefit of the doubt.

The council between the American commissioners and the Indian delegates was held in Simcoe's presence in the new Freemason's Hall at Newark on July 7. It was a sweltering hot day in the lake country, in some places as much as 102° in the shade. Joseph spoke for the Indians. They had heard reports that General Wayne was advancing beyond Fort Jefferson, and they were alarmed. They did not want to go to Sandusky to meet the Americans under such circumstances. Then Joseph, declaring that the deputies represent "the Indian nations who own the lands north of the Ohio as their common property," asked the commissioners if they were "properly authorized to run and establish a new boundary line between the lands of the United States and the lands of the Indian nations." He said nothing about the Ohio.[40] The other Indian delegates, whose duty it was to refresh his mind if he omitted anything important, seem to have made no protest.

Next day the commissioners gave their answer. They assured the delegation that Washington had forbidden all hostilities against the Indians, and they showed them proclamations of General Wayne and the governors of Pennsylvania and Virginia to the same effect. They declared that they did, indeed, have authority to run a new boundary line, that the location of the line was to be discussed at Sandusky; and they thought some concessions would be required of both sides. They asked whether all the nations who owned the lands had assembled and were prepared to go to Sandusky, and they inquired who and how many they were.[41]

On July 9 Joseph replied for the Indians. He thought the prospects for peace were good. All the trouble had arisen in the past, he said, because the United States had not spoken to the Indians "unitedly."

But now, he added, that you have the opportunity to speak to us all together, an agreement will be binding and lasting. He then invited the Americans to come to the place appointed for the meeting. When he left the Maumee, he said, twelve nations of Indians were there and more coming in daily. The names which he submitted included most of the members of the confederacy.[42]

The council being over, both the Indians and the commissioners set out for the west. About this time several circumstances were reported by various persons on both sides of the controversy. According to Pickering the Quakers reported that Lieutenant Governor Simcoe had worked himself into a passion when discussing with them the posts and Indian affairs, and that he had predicted no peace would be made.[43] An Indian from the Grand River told the commissioners that Simcoe had advised the Indians to make peace but not to give up any land. (Simcoe denied this; when questioned, he said he had not been asked for advice on the subject.)[44] Gottlob Sensemann, a Moravian missionary, reported that Brant disclosed to him that Simcoe had locked the Indian delegates up in a room of his house and warned them against relinquishing any part of their country.[45] Sensemann told another missionary that Brant approved the conduct of the commissioners and judged "they certainly would effect a Peace with the Indians, were they left to act for themselves."[46] Some merchants from Detroit reported to the same missionary that the Indians dared not act as they wished, but only as they were told.[47]

Lieutenant Governor Simcoe was also hearing some gossip that did not please him. He learned that Brant had been overheard telling Butler that "He was pledged to Congress to give it as his opinion to the Council that the Indian Nations should give up part of the territory on the Northern side of the Ohio."[48] Brant had told Simcoe himself that the Shawnees agreed to give up some land actually settled by the Americans.[49] But Simcoe had heard nothing of the sort from McKee; McKee wrote that the Indians were still demanding the Ohio boundary.[50] The Ohio was of course the *preliminary* demand the Indians were to make; *afterward* they could recede. Simcoe disliked to see his plans go awry in any detail and, while Joseph was at Niagara, he tried to stiffen Joseph's backbone. As he said, he "endeavoured more strongly to fix upon Brandt's mind the necessity of that Union, which I trust in the result will be the safeguard of the Indian Nations, and highly beneficial to Great Britain."[51] Though Brant had behaved so well in Philadelphia, Simcoe was not so sure that he could trust him. "I believe," he said, "that He considers the Indian Interests as the first Object—that as a second, tho' very inferior one, He prefers the British, in a certain degree, to the people of the States."[52] It was the truest estimate of Joseph Brant ever made by anybody. Since Brant put the Indians first, Simcoe made up his mind that Brant's influence must be curtailed.[53]

By July 21 the American commissioners had reached the mouth of the Detroit River where they were entertained (constrained was more the word, they thought) in Matthew Elliott's house, the Quakers had been permitted to go as far as Detroit where they reported the Indians were locked outside the gates at night, and Captain Hendrick Aupaumut had managed to get to the Maumee. There was now a great assemblage of Indians at the Maumee Rapids (well over one thousand, perhaps as many as fifteen hundred), including 166 of the American Six Nations (though some Oneidas had been stopped), a large delegation from the Seven Nations of Canada, and a delegation of Creeks and Cherokees up from the south under British agent, George Welbank, who reported that Indian-white warfare was going on on the frontiers of Georgia and that the Spanish were also doing what they could to encourage a general Indian confederacy. Alexander McKee was still at his house at the rapids, apparently with no intention of leaving, busily supervising the distribution of supplies.

By July 21 Joseph and the delegates were back at Roche de Bout with the information that the Americans were fully empowered to make a new boundary. If they thought this was welcome news to all the assembled Indians, they soon realized their mistake. Many of the Indians, especially the Shawnees, the Delawares, the Hurons or Wyandots, and the Miamis, became very angry. Buckongehala, a great Delaware war chief, exploded with censure. According to Joseph, the Indians had changed their minds while he and the deputies were away. They accused the deputies of being drunk at Niagara and of not having delivered their speech properly. (According to Hendrick Aupaumut and Joseph himself, they were angry because *Brant* had delivered the speech.) After a week of private councils and much murmuring among themselves, the dissidents declared that the American reply was inadequate. They appointed another delegation and instructed them to ask the Americans if they were prepared to make the Ohio the boundary. If not, they would not meet with them. Lieutenant Selby of the Indian department at Detroit wrote out the ultimatum, and a chief from each of ten nations signed.[54] Some Indians who signed claimed later that this was not their doing and that on hearing of it their women wept. But McKee had told them that they would not get so much as a needleful of thread from the Americans if they gave in to them, and they believed him—"our dependence," as they said, "was on them [the British]."[55]

Joseph and both branches of the Six Nations refused to sign. "We look upon ourselves as equally concerned in the welfare of this country," said Joseph, "and we are part of the confederacy but we have been kept in the dark. . . . It cannot be supposed that we will implicitly agree to what is daily doing by a few people."[56] Other Indians, as we have seen, signed reluctantly and only through the pressure of want. The great Indian confederacy had finally broken up on the shoals of self-interest. Though Joseph could speak eloquently of the dish with one spoon, those who did not eat from it, especially the Chippewas, Potawatomies, and Ottawas, north of the lakes, and those who were closest to American vengeance, namely the Six Nations of New York and Pennsylvania, hesitated to involve themselves in war over it. The enthusiasm of such people for armed combat was very limited. Whatever McKee was doing, he had been able to influence to a high zeal only those Indians who thought they might gain something by war, people like the Shawnees and Delawares, for example, who had nowhere else to go and in whose breasts rankled old wrongs and whose warriors were very mindful of two fine victories. Such people were rumored to be making threats, and the American commissioners sometimes felt in no wise sure of their personal safety.

Joseph wrote to Lieutenant Governor Simcoe in much distress. He was afraid there would be no peace. Excuse me, he said, for speaking freely, "but the present situation of the Indians and my own feelings prompt me to do everything in my power for what I look upon to be inseparable from my own." He then asked Simcoe to help the Indians with his advice about a boundary.[57] Simcoe replied that since the Americans had not asked him to mediate, he had not studied the subject and so could give no advice. He declared the Indians best understood their own interest. He left the boundary up to them![58]

A few days later Joseph wrote a letter full of complaints to McKee. He had wasted three months of his time, and he could not understand why private councils were taking place to which he and the Six Nations were not invited, but he declared he was willing to go to war if the Americans would not give a just peace.[59] In the latter respect Joseph was speaking more for himself than his people; the Grand River Indians had no more interest in the American war than the rest of the Canadian Indians. Did they eat from the dish with one spoon? Though Joseph would have said yes, his people were not convinced. Large numbers of local zealots did not accompany him on his missions.

The new delegation, headed by the intransigent Buckongehala, faced the American commissioners at Matthew Elliott's on July 30 and made their demand for the Ohio boundary as the condition for further negotiation. Commented one of the Quakers, "This demand appeared a new matter, probably suggested by some designing enemy to peace."[60]

The commissioners considered the Indian speech overnight and explained why it was impossible to give up land which had already been sold, settled, and improved, and which, at the time it was bought at Fort Harmar, the Americans believed they had bought fairly. Though the commissioners hoped to get the treaty of Fort Harmar confirmed (and for this they would pay a sum greater than had ever been paid before for a land cession, and a proportionately large annuity), they were willing to give up everything except the tracts along the Ohio already settled—for which, and for any other land the Indians would agree to sell, they would still pay handsomely. But the Indians must make some concessions, too. The Americans could not evict purchasers and settlers from where they had already bought or settled, and they begged to be allowed to discuss the question of a new boundary line at Sandusky. Again, as at Fort Harmar, and far more publicly, they conceded that the United States had not obtained any Indian land by conquest and that the Indians owned their lands despite the treaty of 1783 with Britain. They admitted that the king had given away only his right to purchase from the Indians. He could not give away what he did not own.[61]

But Buckongehala and his men were not satisfied. Previous treaties, they declared, were not "complete," for they had been negotiated with only a few chiefs; and they denied that any of their lands had been sold. Said their speaker, on August 1:

> Brothers, many years ago we all know that the Ohio was made the boundary; it was settled by Sir William Johnson. This side is ours; we look upon it as our property.
>
> Brothers, you mention General Washington. He and you know you have houses and people on our lands. You say you cannot move them off; and we cannot give up our lands.
>
> Brothers, we are sorry that we cannot come to an agreement. The line has been fixed long ago.
>
> Brothers, we do not say much. There has been much mischief on both sides. We came here upon peace, and thought you did the same. We shall talk to our head warriors; you may return whence you came, and tell Washington.[62]

These harsh words were interpreted by Simon Girty. Girty, with his wild shaggy hair, dark visage, and short, flat nose, the great scar on his forehead only partially hidden by the handkerchief he wore as a hat, and indulging, as he often did, in the more grotesque forms of Indian ornamentation, cut a shocking figure. Even the Moravian missionaries, presumably hardened to such sights, were taken aback at Girty's appearance. His very aspect made the threatening words more threatening.

The council was about to break up. Suddenly Matthew Elliott, who had been to the rapids of the Maumee where of course he had seen McKee, and who had returned with the delegation, interrupted. He reminded a departing Shawnee chief that "the last part of the speech was wrong." The Shawnee came back and, according to Lincoln, "said it was wrong." Girty insisted he had interpreted the speaker's words correctly. Some explanation took place which resulted in a change. Then Girty added: "Brothers, Instead of going home, we wish you to remain here for an answer from us. We have your speech in our breasts, and shall consult our head warriors."[63]

By August 5 the deputies were back at Roche de Bout, and the Americans still at Elliott's. There was no unity among the Indians. Apparently not one nation could wholly agree within itself. The most peaceable nation had its advocates of war, and the most intransigent had some advocates of compromise. Some individuals were for the Ohio boundary, and some, like Joseph, were for the Muskingum. Some were for settling the boundary first, and others, like Joseph, were for going to meet the commissioners first. Petty jealousies were everywhere rampant. There were Indians from the upper St. Lawrence who refused even to speak to the Six Nations, and would not go anywhere in their company. The handsome Shawnee, Blue Jacket, and Little Turtle, the Miami chief, were at loggerheads over who was the greater man. Cornplanter clung to his usual neutral position (though he undoubtedly wanted the Ohio boundary), and Red Jacket was so afraid he might be blamed for any war that developed that he had remained at home, sending the commissioners a message of apology. The southern Creeks and Cherokees had been assured by the Shawnee deputies who summoned them to the council that Britain would intervene in the war in behalf of the Indians. Though Joseph thought this not very likely,[64] it had always seemed to him that it was in Britain's interest to see that the Indians were not destroyed; and he could sometimes hope against hope.[65] Simcoe, knowing Joseph's feelings, grew more and more suspicious that Brant was trying to involve the empire in a war with the United States.[66] Alexander McKee, having such positive orders, was angry at the Shawnees for bringing up the subject of military aid.

In the public councils that followed Joseph pleaded for the Muskingum boundary, contending that the Ohio "was by no means fair."[67] McKee could not always be present, but he had his sources of information about what went on. From a chief "of undoubted Credit" he heard that Brant said "for years He had made it his business to become acquainted with the Politicks of Great Britain and the United States; that they were both actuated by a regard to self Interest; that the United States were now the great power on the Continent, and that if they laid aside their resentment and offered terms of Peace to the Indian Nations, it was their business to embrace that Offer—that Great Britain was neither able nor willing to assist them nor would even supply them with ammunition to carry on the War which they were fomenting."[68]

Some Shawnees, Delawares, and Hurons were won over by Joseph's arguments. They admitted that he knew the white people better than they did and that he was a better judge of their affairs. They said they were ready to accept the Muskingum. It was a short-won victory. After this council, so Joseph heard, McKee held a private meeting with the same chiefs at midnight. Next day the chiefs had again changed their minds. They intended to demand the Ohio. More argument erupted in council, and Buckongehala arose and, pointing at McKee, said (according to Joseph), that is the person who advises us to insist on the Ohio.[69]

Soon afterward Joseph and the Six Nations moved about eight or ten miles down the Maumee to Swan Creek, meaning to go home or even to meet the commissioners, if they came. Being called back to the rapids for one last council, Joseph wished the confederacy success in the coming warfare, and promised some friendly, like-minded Indians to continue to try to promote peace on the basis of the Muskingum line. When this final council was over, a Shawnee chief, after singing the war song, encouraged the assembled warriors to defend their country, saying "their Father the English would assist them and Pointed to Col McKee."[70]

Alexander McKee, later explaining the failure of the Indians to make peace, wrote Simcoe that he did his utmost to persuade the Indians to agree on the Muskingum since the Six Nations could not be brought to agree on the Ohio.[71] Perhaps McKee did finally try to get the Indians to accept the Muskingum. But having been advising them for the past year to demand the Ohio, he had made too good a job of it; and many of the warriors were in too high a mood to accept his change of plan. To the Six Nations—meaning, of course, to Joseph—went much of the blame. Said Simcoe, "His [Brant's] Character is very problematical, his Conduct has been very unsatisfactory to Colonel McKee."[72] It was also Simcoe's belief that the western Indians considered Joseph a traitor,[73] and apparently he was right. McKee's drunken son called Joseph "a Yankee rascal" (and then denied it),[74] and George Welbank told an American interpreter that when the hatchet was passed around, all took it "but Brandt the Damn^d Rascal, who should have been the first man, as he had had so many favours from the King, but it would no more be the case."[75]

For twelve days, while the quarrels raged at the rapids and heavily laden sloops brought furs down from Mackinac, Messrs. Randolph, Lincoln, and Pickering waited with what patience they could at the mouth of the Detroit River. The schooner *Dunmore* that was to take them to Sandusky, lay quietly at anchor. The Americans, on tenterhooks for an answer from the Indians, requested the captain to take them as far as the Maumee Bay or River where they would be some thirty-five miles closer to the Indians and might get messages back and forth faster. The captain, and higher British officers, when applied to, refused. They said they had orders from Lieutenant Governor Simcoe to carry the Americans to the mouth of the Detroit River and then, when the Indians were ready to receive them, to Sandusky, and to nowhere else. The commissioners wrote to the Indians telling them of their great desire for peace; but if there was to be no peace, it was time they went home. They also wrote McKee begging for help.[76]

On August 16 another Indian delegation finally arrived at Elliott's. They brought the long-awaited answer from Roche de Bout. The speech did not sound, as one missionary commented, like Indians. It was as uncompromising a message (not to say insolent, thought the clergyman) as the most ardent warrior (or the most adamant British officer) could have wished. The Indians again repudiated all previous treaties with the United States, saying that the Indians who signed them not only had had no authority to sign but that they had signed through fear. "Brothers," they continued, "money to us is of no value, and to most of us unknown; and as no consideration whatever can induce us to sell our lands, on which we get sustenance for our women and children, we hope we may be allowed to point out a mode by which your settlers may be easily removed, and peace thereby obtained." Then they suggested that the United States should give the settlers the money and annuities! And if the United States would add the great sums necessary for raising armies to take the country by force, there should be more than enough to induce the settlers to leave! "Brothers," the Indians said adamantly, "you have talked to us about concessions. It appears strange that you should expect any from us, who have only been defending our just rights against your invasions. We want peace. Restore to us our country, and we shall be enemies no longer." They then declared it was no concern of theirs what sort of agreements the king and the United States had made; if they wished to sell any of their lands, they would sell whenever and to whomever they chose. They finally reminded their hearers that they had once possessed a great country. "Look back," they said, "and view the lands from which we have been driven to this spot. We can retreat no farther, because the country behind hardly affords food for its present inhabitants; and we have therefore resolved to leave our bones in this small space, to which we are now consigned." The Ohio boundary was the great issue. If you will not consent to it, any meeting with you will be "altogether unnecessary."

This uncompromising speech was signed by sixteen nations: the Wyandots, Seven Nations of Canada, Delawares, Shawnees, Miamis, Ottawas, Chippewas, Senecas of the Glaize, Potawatomies, Conoys, Munsees, Nanticokes, Mahicans, Missisaugas, Creeks, and Cherokees.[77] Many of these nations are known to have had their dissenters. It is very likely that all had some who dissented.

What could the American commissioners say? Though they were willing, indeed very eager, to negotiate everything else, it was impossible for them to agree to the Ohio River as the boundary. They could not give up the settled lands along the Ohio. So the conference ended. Next day the commissioners started back to Fort Erie. There was no difficulty now about the sailing of the *Dunmore.*

The commissioners never saw Lieutenant Governor Simcoe again. When they passed through Niagara, he was at York (Toronto) overseeing the building of a capital for Upper Canada that would be impervious to American attack. Simcoe was not too perturbed about the continuance of the Indian war to his southwest. He had always thought, and still thought, that such another defeat as St. Clair had suffered would make the Americans more amenable to British intervention.[78] A letter from McKee must have been a comfort for the immediate future. "Those Nations," said McKee, "who have not already sold their possessions will now enjoy without dispute all the lands belonging to them respectively; and these lands will form an extensive Barrier between the British & American Territory."[79]

McKee closed his letter thus: "However conscious I may be of having used no improper influence in the Councils of the Confederacy, so as to prevent the attainment of peace, which I again assure your Excellency, would have afforded me a most sensible gratification; I nevertheless expect from the malevolent, disappointed & all ill disposed, to be blamed for the Opinions which the Indians have adopted for their Resolution which put an end to the Negociation I shall not, however, lament on account of their Animadversions while I continue to be honored with your Excellency's Approbation of my conduct."[80]

McKee was right on both counts. Joseph, who was certainly "ill disposed" so far as McKee was concerned, to the end of his life blamed him (and Simcoe) for failure of the peace negotiations of 1793 and, when he grew angry, never hesitated to remind government officials of the ruined opportunity for peace. And Simcoe always remained McKee's friend. He could never say enough in his praise of McKee, and almost immediately recommended him for appointment to the Executive Council of Upper Canada.

By September 1 Joseph was back at Niagara. Next day he wrote Simcoe that "the Advice of some Whites was too much attended to" at the late council, but that he still hoped for an honorable peace on the basis of the Muskingum boundary. As soon as all the Indians returned, there would be a general Six Nations council at Buffalo Creek—presumably to discuss what had happened and what they could do about it. Joseph was sorry there was no time to consult first with the lieutenant governor.[81]

Before the new council could be held, Joseph got word from home that several of his children were seriously ill. (He and Catharine now had a good-sized family of young ones.) All fatherly anxiety, Joseph, though he feared he might miss the council, headed for the Grand River.[82] It was what he always did when Catharine called, no matter how important the business he was engaged in.

The children got the better of their illness, and by early October Joseph was back again at Niagara. He had missed nothing, for the Indians had been very slow in assembling. Finally, with both Chapin and Butler also present, the council opened, as usual, at the Onondaga village at Buffalo Creek. Joseph made the main speech. He was not yet ready to complain openly about McKee in the presence of Americans. Loyalty, and probably prudence, held him back. Dissension had broken out among the Indians on the Maumee, he explained, when the Creeks brought news of more American encroachments in the Creek country. This was probably the reason no peace had been made. Then he offered for himself, the Six Nations, and all who agreed with him, his own peace proposal. It was, of course, the Muskingum boundary (but extended at the insistence of Cornplanter and other Seneca chiefs to follow the Genesee down to its mouth); and he was willing to let the Americans keep those places beyond this boundary which they had already settled. He thought he could get the whole Indian confederacy to agree to this line.[83]

It was such a solution to their problems as the Americans would have been glad to discuss two months before and, except for the Genesee, to accept; but they could not take the proposal seriously. Since Brant had not been able to get all the Indians to agree to the Muskingum in August, why, they must have asked themselves, did he think they could be brought to agree in October? What had changed? Nothing, so far as President Washington and the secretary of war could see. Knox, in answer, suggested that a council of all the Indians, including the hostiles, be held at Venango (away from British influence?) in the spring.[84] This answer disappointed Joseph. He called it "but half an answer,"[85] and regarded it as an American rejection of peace. "Other" steps, he concluded, must be taken. Obviously he meant war.[86] As for the Americans, they were more united now in prosecuting the war. General Wayne could prepare to fight to the finish.

Shortly after this offer was made to the Americans and before Knox's answer was received, Lieutenant Governor Simcoe conferred at length with Joseph who came to the camp at the new capital. Joseph told Simcoe he did not expect that the boundary offered to Congress would be accepted. A rejection, he said, would reunite the Indian confederacy, and all might still be well. Simcoe asked Joseph why he had proposed the Muskingum at the Maumee council when he had gone there with the idea of first demanding the Ohio. Joseph replied that he had found that the Potawatomies, having received a message from Vincennes—whether from the local French or local Indians, he did not say—were absolutely determined on peace, and that many other Indians agreed with them, and therefore he had thought it best to change his own demand in order to hold the dissidents in line. Simcoe seems to have been not greatly impressed with this reason.[87] He knew something of Joseph's political plans for the Indian confederacy, thought such plans "as dangerous as they are difficult to prevent," and meant to do all he could to thwart them.[88]

That fall war between the British and the Americans seemed more and more likely to erupt as an adjunct to the great struggle in Europe. There was much trouble on the high seas where the British were stopping American ships, interfering with American trade to France and its colonies, and impressing American sailors. A large segment of the American public, including Jefferson, the secretary of state, sympathized with revolutionary France and could not forget how France had helped them during their own revolution. Border clashes occurred near Lake Champlain; New York frontiersmen, angry because they could not freely navigate Lake Ontario, had violent disputes with British soldiers near Oswego; and Pennsylvania was preparing to occupy Presque Isle (Erie) which, because of its good harbor, appeared to threaten British control of the Great Lakes. Spain, now trying to extend the Indian confederation along the whole Spanish-American frontier, continued to stir up trouble in the south between Indians and whites. There was as much fear of war in London as in Philadelphia; the conflict seemed to be coming, though neither government wanted it. Knox warned Wayne to commit no aggression against either Spain or Britain, and Henry Dundas, new colonial secretary, urged that nothing be done in Canada to provoke or justify American hostilities.

In September 1793, Lord Dorchester returned to Quebec, and soon became fully convinced that war could not be avoided. It would be one of the few times that Simcoe and Dorchester saw eye to eye, and both worked frantically to improve Canada's military position vis-à-vis the Americans. In February 1794, Dorchester created a great stir on both sides of the border by telling a deputation of Canadian Indians who brought him inquiries from the western Indians regarding the status of their boundary dispute with the United States, that there seemed no hope for British intervention for a peaceful settlement and that, moreover, war was likely to break out between Britain and the United States before the year was out. If victorious in the coming war, then the Indians and British might settle the boundary to their own taste. This speech, though delivered to the Indians in private, soon leaked out. Some people in the United States, knowing Dorchester had recently returned from England, considered his words almost a declaration of war. Hearing about the speech, the western Indians found fresh courage, and even Cornplanter and his people grew bold. When the news reached Joseph, he was down with another of his short but violent attacks of illness (the surgeon from Niagara had been sent to him, and for a few weeks his life was again despaired of),[89] but illness could not prevent him, too, from taking heart. Joseph had wanted British aid so desperately—according to Simcoe, it was a subject he talked about constantly[90]—and he had hoped against hope that eventually it must come. He could breathe a sigh of relief. It seemed that the long-sought help soon would be forthcoming.[91]

By late March Joseph, now recovered of his illness, heard more good news when Simcoe stopped briefly at the Grand River on his way to the west.[92] The lieutenant governor, on Dorchester's orders, was

headed for the Maumee to rebuild an old wartime fort below Roche de
Bout as an outpost for the defense of Detroit. The post, called Fort
Miamis, was soon in good order, and a detachment of British soldiers
moved in. The Indians, who had long wanted such a post, assumed,
and indeed were told, that the stronghold was put there expressly for
their protection. Under such circumstances nothing could come of
Knox's suggestion for a general conference at Venango. The Indians,
greatly buoyed up by the prospect of help, awaited the outcome of the
approaching war between Britain (and their own warriors) and the
United States.

In the spring of 1794 Joseph and Cornplanter—with some help
from Simcoe—grew more and more concerned about Pennsylvania's
proposed occupation of Presque Isle, a place far within the boundary
line that they wanted. As Presque Isle sat athwart the old Lakeshore
Path, so long the route of Indian embassies, white Pennsylvanians
settled at that important point would very effectually cut off communication between the Six Nations and their western allies. This
must not be allowed to happen, the two chiefs agreed. Cornplanter,
always bedeviled by his people for his land sales and eager to get the
new boundary which would place him in a better light, began to deny
that that country (the so-called Erie Triangle) had been purchased
fairly; and he denounced the treaties of Fort Stanwix and Fort Harmar, where he had assented to the original Indian sales both to the
United States and Pennsylvania. Joseph made common cause with his
Seneca enemy and wrote Cornplanter a letter discussing their mutual
problems.[93] Unfortunately Cornplanter construed Joseph's letter as a
reprimand,[94] and the old Seneca-Mohawk dissensions, which Simcoe
thought he had settled, flared up again.

Once more the tireless lieutenant governor became the pacifier.
By this time Simcoe hoped (in case of a successful war) to annex all
the new American settlements in his vicinity—those on the upper
Allegheny as well as those on the Genesee—and even frustrated,
sullen Kentucky, which he expected to revolt almost any time. He
could easily foresee that Americans at Presque Isle would build boats
and armaments on Lake Erie, a proceeding which could ruin every
plan he had. To thwart the Americans he must have Six Nations
help. He contrived again to reconcile the two chiefs (and the Senecas
and the Mohawks) by promising Cornplanter a pension and giving
presents to other leaders, while to Joseph he promised a council house
for the Mohawks and a gunboat on the Grand River. He also seems to
have promised that, when he returned to England, he would do his
utmost to get a pension for Joseph's widow if the chief died in the

king's service.[95] Without this intervention, said Simcoe, the reconciliation never would have taken place—certainly Brant never would have become reconciled to the Senecas. For his pains Simcoe received in solemn council the name of the legendary founder of the Six Nations. It was a very great honor.[96]

Simcoe played on the fears of Joseph and Cornplanter by every means that he could think of, and in the summer of 1794 the Americans found to their horror that they were about to become embroiled in still another Indian war. Two warlike councils were held by the Indians at Buffalo Creek, one on June 18 and another on July 4, where threats were made against the people of the United States. Cornplanter began to make veiled threats of his own to such Americans as he met; and Joseph wrote a threatening letter to Israel Chapin, predicting that if the Americans "go on striving to carry everything before them by force the consequences may be dreadful."[97] Some of the American part of the Six Nations moved closer to Niagara to sit at the foot of British power. Joseph could talk seriously of stockpiling ammunition and supplies and of collecting his warriors for a descent on northwestern Pennsylvania.[98] But when a party of warriors and chiefs set out to Presque Isle to warn the Americans away, taking with them the British agent William Johnston and forcing along a most reluctant Israel Chapin, they found that President Washington had prevailed on Governor Mifflin of Pennsylvania to stop his state's activities at Presque Isle. Eventually Lieutenant Governor Simcoe could make the claim that *he* had stopped the Americans. It was no idle boast.

As for Joseph, he got his council house and probably his gunboat and saw no harm in the getting. President Washington, who suspected Simcoe of evil designs, and who was never deterred by previous failure, was quite willing to try some countermachinations. He instructed Knox to instruct Chapin "to buy Captn. B——t off at almost any price."[99] There were those who believed Chapin did just that, very privately of course,[100] but if so, Chapin got nothing for his money. The cynics were wrong. Nobody could buy Joseph. He would take what he could get from his own government. But what his government got in return was only what he would have given anyway. No more. No less. He appears, however, to have accepted nothing of value from any other government.

In the meantime the United States had sent John Jay to England to try to negotiate another treaty of peace. Jay arrived in the early summer of 1794, and at once made a favorable impression. Negotiations for the new treaty commenced. Though both the British and American governments were sincere in seeking an end to the tension between them (for the British were not doing well in Europe, and the Americans were not doing well at home), the negotiations were of necessity somewhat protracted; for they had to encompass every dispute from the present troubles on the high seas to the question of the frontier posts and the unexecuted portions of the treaty of 1783. The knowledge that these negotiations were going on several thousand miles away while war appeared so imminent in America posed some delicate problems for people in the field such as Wayne and his army and the personnel of British border garrisons, who, wholly in the dark about what progress was being made, had to appear at the same time both vigorously partisan and restrained, to pay finical attention to what concerned the national honor and simultaneously to try to keep the peace.

By mid-June more than two thousand Indians, encouraged by belts as red as blood and relying on their British and even their Spanish friends, had embodied themselves on the Maumee and the Auglaize. Eagerly they awaited Wayne's coming. But patience was no part of the Indian make-up and, while Wayne delayed, the usual departures of warriors satisfied after small forays against the enemy, took place. In late June and early July a large party of Indians made their one strong attack at Fort Recovery (built earlier in the year on St. Clair's old battleground), but the little that they accomplished did not atone for their losses. Afterward many warriors who had taken part in the attack left for home, according to their custom. But home might be far away, and some of the fighters did not return to their gathering places. The slow attrition of numbers continued for weeks. Like the unquenchable bleeding from a mortal wound which foretells the end, the Indians were already defeated by their own customs.

"Mad" Anthony Wayne still belied his nickname. In late July, after meticulous preparation, he moved from Fort Greenville to the Glaize. Like Sullivan, he avoided ambush. Like Sullivan, he found deserted villages where the Indians had fled before him. Unlike Sullivan, he did not immediately burn all he saw, but, instead, sent captives out with messages of peace. At the Glaize, with his eyes on the British garrison at Detroit, Wayne built a fort which he called Defiance. Then he moved down the Maumee to Roche de Bout. On the left bank of the river, just above Simcoe's new Fort Miamis, a great mass of decaying tree trunks lay in the woods where a tornado had once struck. This was to become the famed battlefield of Fallen Timbers.

On the humid morning of August 20 Wayne advanced, cautiously feeling his way. Having had no reply to his peace overtures, he did not know whether he would be met by a flag of truce or bullets. The hoped-for flag of truce did not materialize; the bullets did. The Indian warriors, to an undetermined number, lay hidden in the woods and the tall grass. The warriors fired first and the battle was on. Some thirteen hundred Indians were still gathered in the vicinity, but the greater part had gone down to the fort to get provisions from McKee. Some of the warriors ran back breathlessly and joined in the fighting. However, McKee later claimed that no more than four hundred Indians ever took part. In little more than an hour, both Indian and white defenders (for the Indians had the aid of some sixty old-time Loyalists from Detroit) were routed. The Indians, flushed from their hiding places, took flight, while the whites covered their retreat. The Indians ran to the British fort—*their* fort. They found the doors closed against them. On down the river they sped to Swan Creek. Forlorn hopes were not for them. There was always the thought that they could return and fight again.

The victorious Americans were left in possession of the field. They burned trading houses, huts, cornfields, hay. McKee's own house went up in the flames. Wayne and Major Campbell at Fort Miamis exchanged tart notes, but neither precipitated a military confrontation. Detroit, with gates shut and shops closed, tremblingly awaited the assault which its commander had said he could not withstand. But in a few days Wayne turned and went back up the river, this time destroying everything before him. The crisis was over. Peace between Britain and the United States had been preserved, but the Indians were crushed. They had seen some of their best chiefs slain. They could not hope to fight again.

Those Indians who still had homes, such as those from Michilimackinac and Lake Huron, left. The few Cherokees who had lived so long north of the Ohio, set out for the Tennessee. Those who had lost their villages on the Auglaize and the Maumee thought fleetingly of the Spanish country, of the Mississippi and even the Missouri; while a few straggled in to the Moravian mission where on Christmas Eve they fell on their knees and prayed. But McKee was able to persuade the greatest part of the dispossessed to settle down at Swan Creek. They could not be permitted to go to the south or west. At any time they might be needed for the defense of Canada. How McKee soothed the disillusioned warriors, he does not say, but he gave them such enormous quantities of provisions and goods that the garrison at Detroit had to look to the stores of local traders to escape starvation.

Matthew Elliott, whose position in the Indian department did not prevent him from taking part in trade, claimed years later that he alone saved the garrison that winter.

In the meanwhile Lieutenant Governor Simcoe, knowing that Wayne had advanced to the Glaize and hoping to inspirit the Indians, was gathering a small army to go to the aid of Detroit. On August 17 he wrote McKee that Brant was at Niagara, "anxious for our instantly collecting to attack (with the Indians) Wayne's Army."[101] Six days later Simcoe was awaiting the arrival of troop transports so that he could sail from Fort Erie. By this time he had talked a great deal with Brant, and he said that the chief was determined to join the western Indians with every man he could muster, Brant's own words being that "our fate depends upon the repulse of Wayne."[102] On August 27 Simcoe was still awaiting the transports and wrote that he was going to "hurry" Brant.[103] Next day Simcoe heard of Wayne's victory and wrote the news in great haste to Joseph who had gone home to gather his warriors.[104] By August 31 Simcoe had learned of Wayne's retreat. He breathed a sigh of relief and decided not to take his army to Detroit.

By this time Joseph was on his way west with the warriors he had collected. Obviously he meant to fight. But why was he so late? He said afterward that the western Indians had sent him no word of their perilous situation,[105] but that was not a very good excuse. Though Wayne advanced fast once he started, Joseph must have known what was going on and how urgently the confederates needed help. Undoubtedly he was waiting for Simcoe and the promised army. He was determined that British troops should do their part of the fighting, and he lingered a little too long, waiting for them. Then, too, Joseph was no longer a young and impetuous warrior. He was fifty-one. He was not in good health. However much the whites might call him a "regular" Indian, the description was not wholly merited. Unlike most of his people, Joseph thought of the morrow. He worried about the future. What would Catharine and the children do if he were killed? How would they live? He had been trying desperately to get a pension for them. Depending on relatives would never do. A Mohawk widow and children might not starve, but their situation would be wretched. His own childhood memories could testify to that.

On September 10 Joseph and his party of warriors (another Mohawk party having gone on ahead) passed by the Moravian mission. He exchanged gunfire salutes with the Christian converts, bought a canoe for his sick, and hastened on the same day. To people at the mission he said he went to war unwillingly, but that he must go, for the war was designed to exterminate the Indians.[106]

Joseph and ninety-seven of his people were in Detroit on September 16. He told the commandant he would not have come had he not expected to meet Simcoe.[107]

By September 25 Joseph had reached the Huron Village at the mouth of the Detroit River, opposite Elliott's. This was the place where, in 1786, the confederacy had sent out its first ringing challenge to the Americans. Joseph had had plenty of friends among the local Hurons then. But now no one paid him any heed. Nobody condoled with him. Nobody offered him food or a shelter to rest in. Disconsolately Joseph wandered about, not knowing what to do. He sent to Detroit for wampum, hoping to placate the sullen Hurons with the proper belts and strings.[108] How he needed David Hill! How he must have missed him!

Giving up finally, Joseph went on to meet Simcoe according to their plan. On September 30 he arrived at the camp at Swan Creek. The lieutenant governor was already there. Next day Joseph went with Simcoe, McKee, and Elliott to visit Fort Miamis and view the late mournful battlefield. The party dined at the fort and returned to Swan Creek next morning. The dispossessed Indians, glutted with gifts, seemed to bear no ill will toward Simcoe. On the contrary, they had shown "great joy" at his appearance, and made a grand spectacle of themselves by marching along the riverbank, shooting off their guns.[109]

On October 2 Joseph set out again for Detroit in company with Simcoe and McKee and a party of Indians and whites. It was a hard two-day journey, but not unpleasant, for the weather was fine. All traveled on horseback, fording creeks and sometimes shooting at wild turkeys by the way. They passed through unbroken wilderness except for a few huts of wandering Chippewas. Along the River Raisin, however, there was a large settlement, mostly French of course, and the people not the friendliest. After four days at Detroit where Simcoe inspected defenses and conferred with Lieutenant Colonel England, the party embarked on the *Ottawa* for the trip down the Detroit River to the Huron Village. Indians of many nations, expecting a council, had gathered there.[110]

Four more days, October 11–14, passed while Simcoe tried to reanimate the warriors and patch up their confederacy. For the first time the local Hurons noted Joseph's presence among them. The

Detroit Waterfront in 1794. Watercolor known as the "Lady Astor" picture. Joseph visited Detroit many times between 1781 and 1795 while he was fighting in the west and trying to hold his confederation together. *Courtesy of the Burton Historical Collection, Detroit Public Library. Photograph by Nemo Warr.*

Indians pointedly inquired why they had had no help in their eleven years of fighting, the inquiry apparently meant as much for Joseph as for Simcoe. Joseph replied as principal speaker for the Six Nations. Simcoe says that Joseph ignored the question that was addressed to him and concentrated on what concerned British shortcomings. He, too, wanted to know when the Indians could expect British help. Simcoe answered by minimizing Wayne's victory; it was but a "trifling advantage" over part of the Indians. Yet Wayne had dared to make threats against the king. "Let him come," said Simcoe. Of course the king would fulfill all his engagements with the Indians. His arms were ready to receive them and his territory was open to them. Simcoe then urged them to remain united and not to separate. They must be ready for any emergency.[111] Again Joseph must have felt that he was trying to catch eels with his bare hands—but, then, in fact he had been somewhat slippery himself.

Joseph returned home with Simcoe on the *Ottawa*, arriving at Fort Erie on October 17.[112] He returned in very low spirits about the prospects of the defeated Indians and angry at the way the Hurons had treated him.[113] When he got back to Niagara, he heard nothing to cheer him up. The Presque Isle affair seemed likely to end in total defeat for the Indians.

By the middle of October all the American Six Nations, even those who lived most isolated, had heard of Wayne's victory. Cornplanter's people were in their council house when the news came that the British had locked the retreating warriors out of Fort Miamis. A young white man who happened to be present reported that a dead silence fell upon the room. Then an old man proposed that the meeting adjourn.

Timothy Pickering and Israel Chapin had been urging the Indians to come to a council at Canandaigua where the dispute might be amicably settled. The Indians had held back, insisting that any peace meeting must take place at their fireplace at Buffalo Creek. This had been Simcoe's wish—Joseph's, too.[114] Buffalo Creek meetings could be easily supervised.

Learning of the unhappy events of August 20, the Senecas and their adherents finally gave in. Hundreds of them, including Cornplanter and Red Jacket and most of the chiefs at Buffalo Creek, many of whom were at odds with the luckless Cornplanter, blaming him for their troubles, set out for Canandaigua. The British agent William Johnston got there about the same time, bringing a letter from Joseph urging the Indians to stand firm in their demand for the Muskingum boundary. Pickering promptly ordered Johnston to leave. He refused to sit in council with a British spy.[115] Though this led to some unfriendly correspondence between Joseph and Pickering in which Joseph claimed that the Six Nations were a free people and ought to be able to have anyone they wanted present at the council,[116] the Presque Isle affair was soon settled. In the snows of late October and early November the Six Nations gave up all pretense to the Muskingum boundary. Wayne's victory and British abandonment of the Indians had left them no choice. In the treaty of November 11, 1794, they relinquished their claim to the Erie Triangle and even agreed to let the United States build through their country a road from Fort Schlosser to Lake Erie. For this they received ten thousand dollars in goods and an annuity of three thousand dollars. Though Joseph had done his utmost to prevent the cave-in, after all was over he quietly accepted the inevitable. He commented if the Indians were satisfied, he was.[117] He thought, however, that the western Indians should have been consulted. And he insisted that his Mohawks get part of the money, since the land in question was owned in common.[118] Pickering would not admit this argument, but did suggest to his superiors that the Mohawks be given a little present.[119]

The Presque Isle debacle made Joseph more determined than ever to get the kind of peace he wanted. Having received an apology from the western Indians (who were now desperate for help and advice— any help and any advice),[120] he redoubled his efforts in behalf of the Muskingum boundary. During the winter of 1794–95 and throughout the ensuing spring he sent message after message to the western Indians, urging them to stay away from Wayne's camp. He was sure the confederacy could get better terms by remaining united and aloof. Deserters told him that Wayne's army was distressed for lack of provisions and that his military position was deteriorating. Joseph believed these reports and thought them very significant. Even a small attack, he concluded, would dislodge Wayne from his advanced posts; and he urged the Indians to do nothing about a peace treaty until they had held another general council and had agreed upon common action. Joseph also knew of the negotiations that were going on in London, and he hoped the king would not forget the Indians a second time. Every bit of information he had, suggested to him that the Indians would lose nothing by holding out. Through a woman friend in Detroit, one of his Oneida in-laws who had strayed far from her family, he kept the Indians abreast of current news, sent them his best advice, and attempted to win them over to a course of watchful waiting.[121]

While Joseph was trying to stiffen the resolution of the western Indians, he was also trying to persuade the Americans to agree to his compromise. He wrote Pickering a long letter explaining the good that would come from the Muskingum boundary and promising to get the boundary accepted by all the Indians, and telling at last the story of how the Indians had been influenced against their own best interests in 1793.[122] As for himself, he declared, *"my wish ever was for Peace."*[123] The thoughts were Joseph's, but the words were polished far beyond Joseph's capacity. The letter was very likely the work of the cultivated and intelligent John Norton, a young man who in the course of trade was already well known to the Mohawks and who was to be Joseph's secretary and confidant for the rest of his life. Joseph had finally found an educated friend whom he could trust, who would not tell everything he knew about Indian affairs to the first British official he met.

Joseph made a long, cold journey in mid-winter to confer with Israel Chapin and try to win him over to his idea of a good peace. While with Chapin he quietly gave him the long letter for Pickering's perusal.[124] Secrecy seemed necessary. Though officials in Canada approved anything Joseph could do to keep the Indians out of Wayne's clutches (for their thoughts were still set on the idea of British mediation of the war), he knew they would never approve of Joseph Brant's acting as mediator—nor would they approve of his giving out his version of the events of 1793. Chapin wrote Pickering that Brant was "big with hopes & Expectations of Bringing about an Amicable settlement of hostilities between the United States & the Western Indians."[125]

Joseph told Chapin the Indians were sorry for their treatment of the American commissioners, that they felt they could not treat with Wayne whose talk was part good and part bad and who made many threats; but they did wish to treat with President Washington and would welcome a proposal from him to open negotiations. All this seemed reasonable to Chapin, and he offered his good services to get the negotiations started. To Secretary Knox, Chapin wrote that Brant "is as well disposed to the Interest of the United States as to the British.— He acts on the great Scale of political Friendship. The Rights of the Indians is his favourite pursuit & violently opposes Every Infringement, whether by the British or the United States."[126]

While Joseph was conferring with Chapin on the Genesee, neither man knew the real situation in the far west. As the winter wore on, Joseph found out what was going on there, but largely rejected the unpalatable information. Sally Ainse, Joseph's friend in Detroit, tried to tell him of happenings in her vicinity. Small parties of Indians, she wrote, on February 5, 1795, were sneaking off to Wayne every day and, when they returned, they had no good to say of Simcoe, the British Indian department, or Brant. Thirty Indians had recently gone to the American camp from Swan Creek under leadership of Blue Jacket. The Potawatomies and Hurons of Sandusky had gone, too. She was certain that all the Indians who lived exposed to the Americans would soon make their peace with Wayne.[127] Sally Ainse was right. Throughout the west resistance was crumbling. It was clear that the Americans had won. Indians who had favored war knew they were beaten. Those who had favored peace saw the prospect of at last getting their way. And Simcoe heard to his outrage that traders from Detroit were actually engaged in supplying the American posts!

Joseph would not listen to the bad news about his western friends. What Sally Ainse told him he could not and would not believe. He consoled himself with the thought that "several" of the Indians were being "enticed" by disloyal French traders. All spring he stubbornly looked forward to the general council which the Indians had promised to hold at the Huron Village when any disagreements among them would be smoothed out. He set out to the council at the appointed time, full of hope that the confederacy would hold together and that all would go well.[128]

Joseph arrived at the Huron Village shortly after the middle of June. The principal chiefs did not meet him. Blue Jacket, Little Turtle, Agushua of the Ottawas (Pontiac's successor), Massas the Chippewa, and all the most important men, over eleven hundred in number, had gone to Fort Greenville. The great council with Wayne that was to last all summer was already in progress. Joseph found the Indians who had been left behind—most of whom were of the common sort, anyway—too drunk to do any business with him. The long-awaited council to decide upon a course of united action did not even get started.[129]

Joseph had intended to go to the treaty with Wayne, if there was to be a treaty. But after his disappointment at the Huron Village, he turned back.[130] The Moravian missionaries told an astonishing story. They claimed Brant was afraid to meet the Delawares at the treaty. At the last council the Six Nations had formally taken the petticoats off the Delawares and finally made them men. But the Delawares were no longer so eager to become men, as it would only cause them to be embroiled in more warfare. The Delawares had also heard rumors that the Mohawks had again offered them to the Chippewas for broth. Hence they were very angry. They were waiting for Joseph Brant at Fort Greenville, and Brant thought it best to avoid them![131]

The truth was, Joseph did not wish to go where he had no standing. It was plain that any influence he had ever had with the western Indians was over and done with. Simcoe had been right in concluding that the western Indians thought of Brant as a traitor to their cause. This was a fact of his life that Joseph now had to recognize. With no influence on the Indians, he would certainly have no standing with General Wayne. For the proud Joseph, this would be an intolerable situation. He decided to go home.

On August 3, 1795, the western Indians signed the treaty of Fort Greenville. They put themselves under the protection of the Americans and gave them the right of preemption of all their lands. They confirmed what had been done at Fort Harmar, finally giving up eastern and southern Ohio and part of present Indiana as well as sixteen enclaves in country still remaining to them. As a cession it was more than the Americans had expected to get and more than Wayne had been instructed to obtain. When some of the signers returned to Detroit and listened to the treaty as read to them by their British friends, they declared they had never heard of several of the articles before. But the Indians were tired of fighting. They were very weary of fighting alone. The treaty stood.

Jay's treaty with Britain was signed in November 1794, and in the next year Thomas Pinckney succeeded in getting a settlement with Spain which was to cool off the southern frontier for a while. In 1796 Great Britain gave up all the border posts on the American side of the international boundary. Anthony Wayne marched into Detroit. He confessed himself a little disappointed in the place.

When the provisions of Jay's treaty became public, it was found to offer no more security for Indian territory than the treaty of 1783—which is to say, none. It was "the second time," commented Joseph bitterly, "the poor Indians have been left in the lurch."[132] However, the government of Canada bought a tract twelve miles square on what is now the Sydenham River as a home for dispossessed Indians, and some of them, mainly loyal Shawnees and Ottawas, after wandering about, not knowing what to do, settled there. The ministry in London advised that the Indians be given a "little excess" of presents. The European scene was very uncertain, and their aid would be required if war broke out with Spain.

For months after his return from the Huron Village Joseph felt so low-spirited he was not even up to writing his thoughts to a presumed friend, for, as he said sadly, "the distressed condition of the poor Indians in general especially those in that quarter [the west], prevented me from saying anything as it seemed entirely at an end and gone too far ever to think of repairing the damage." He was so discouraged he had decided to say no more on public affairs.[133] But after a while Joseph's mind returned to its normal state of optimism. He found he could still dream dreams, though the dreams would never be so extensive as before. He was still willing to fight against odds, but he had to accept the fact that the Longhouse would never again flourish as in its heyday. It would be forever contained in a restricted compass. Joseph was seen no more at Detroit or on the Maumee. Isaac Weld, a contemporary traveler, reported that Brant did not dare to return to the west.[134] The fact was, there was no reason Joseph should return to the west. There was nothing in the west for him.

Sir John Johnson, who spent months and even years in England away from his Indian charges, returned to Canada in 1796 from one of his long overseas trips. He was in an ill humor, for the business of getting more recompense for his losses had not gone well. Perhaps it was his ill humor that impelled him to say a scandalous thing (as his secretary reported): that "Brant was Perfectly right in his opinion about treating with the American commissioners in 1793—and if his Advice had been taken the Indians would have had a Better Boundary and Saved great Part of that country they have now Lost."[135]

Eventually there was some criticism in the House of Lords of Lieutenant Governor Simcoe's proceedings in 1793, and Simcoe felt obliged to defend himself for his conduct toward the American commissioners. "It is only necessary for me to observe," said he, "that so various were the Artifices of the United States, & so successful had their emissaries been, in sowing jealousies & apprehensions among the Indians, that it is reasonable to believe had the Commissioners been once admitted to a personal Conference at their Council fire, they would have obtained whatever their prudence or their Avarice might have inclined them to have demanded."[136] It must have occurred to the suspicious Simcoe that the Americans, no matter how artful, could get a great deal more after a victorious war than through peaceful negotiation. Simcoe staked the Indians' all on the chance that Wayne would go the way of Harmar and St. Clair. The Indians lost.

Joseph Brant never forgot. Resentment gnawed at him the rest of his life. In later years it seemed as though he actually picked quarrels with Canadian authorities. Appearances were not deceiving. Joseph did pick quarrels with those in power, quarrel after quarrel. He had a generous spirit, and he liked to right wrongs. He enjoyed helping people, and helping people often involved a fight with the government. His bitterness added point to all the warfare. But there was often more in Joseph's knight-errantry than sympathy for the downtrodden and his own lacerated feelings. The contentions and the quarrels with the government were not random. The wrangling often had a deeper motive. Joseph was now convinced that the Indians must take responsibility for their own lives. The disastrous events of 1793–95 had shown him that the freedom which he and they had always taken for granted was slipping away. He must reverse this decay. He came out of the west determined to get British recognition of the independence of his people. In many devious ways he set out to accomplish his purpose.

24

Brant's Town

THROUGHOUT the Indian country, scattered here and there, were settlements that bore the name of their principal inhabitant, usually though not invariably, a sachem or some great war chief. In the Ohio country could be found Buckongehala's Town, Blue Jacket's Town, Snake's Town, Pipe's Town, or even Girty's Town which was named after a white trader, one of the Loyalist Girty brothers. The Huron Village at the mouth of the Detroit River was often called Brown's Town, after its white adopted chief, Adam Brown. In the Genesee region were Big Tree's Town and Little Beard's Town, and on the upper Allegheny lay Cornplanter's Town and New Arrow's Town. And in the old Seneca country General Sullivan had found Catharine's Town whose leading inhabitant was a woman, the famous "French" Catharine.

Ohsweken, or Little—or New—Oswego, even from the first, seldom bore its Indian name, but was generally called the Mohawk Village; and that is what Joseph himelf called the place where he lived. But in a few years Alexander McKee and Lieutenant Governor Simcoe and the Moravian missionaries and other knowledgeable persons began to speak of the Mohawk settlement on the Grand as Brant's Town or Brant's Village. Joseph actually received letters addressed to him at Brant's Town, and the ford across the river at his farm was invariably called Brant's Ford. The Grand River, out of respect to the predominant Mohawks or, more likely, out of pure nostalgia for the old home, was sometimes called the Mohawk. These names seemed perfectly natural to the people of the area, white or Indian.

Brant's Town was situated on the east side of the Grand River,

The Mohawk Village, Grand River, 1793. Sketch by Mrs. John Graves Simcoe. Joseph has the best house in the village. A flag flies before it. *Courtesy of the Archives of Ontario, Toronto.*

some forty miles upstream, and on the north side of a great bend where the river made a sharp turn, first east and then, back on itself, to the westward. Here from a high gravel ridge the new Indian settlers could look beyond their cornfields and then over a great extent of their valley. Far out of their sight, the river, sometimes deep and placid, sometimes shallow and swift, curved in a generally southeast direction toward Lake Erie and the harbor where big lake vessels often rode at anchor. It was a goodly land, thought Joseph, well worth fighting for—if fighting ever became necessary.

The wife of Lieutenant Governor Simcoe, a talented amateur artist, copied a sketch of Brant's Town which had been made in early 1793 by Lieutenant Robert Pilkington of her husband's staff. Lieutenant Pilkington had made his sketch from a vantage point a little distance below the gravel ridge. In the foreground of Mrs. Simcoe's copy is the river's edge, and on top of the ridge some dozen cabins are scattered about, rather mistily defined but square and oddly tall, considering that most of them had only one room. To the right can be seen the church, partially hidden by some small buildings though its steeple is clearly in view. To the left we note a much larger building with a second story and a wing and a porch, and a fence around the whole—the only good fence in the picture. A flag flies grandly before this building which has been thought to have been the council house. But as Joseph did not manage to inveigle a council house out of the artist's husband till late in 1793, and as work on it was just beginning in 1794 and not even finished in 1798, a good guess would be that the large building with the proud flag was Joseph's own dwelling, Joseph being such a one who would have had a flag flying in front of his house if a flag was to be had. Then, too, this large house is south of the church, the direction in which Joseph is supposed to have lived.[1]

Five years later, in 1798, two passing Moravian missionaries give us a word-picture of Brant's Town. They described it as a large and sprawling settlement and Joseph's house as a handsome two-story house, built like the houses of white people. Brant's house, they commented, was a palace compared to the other dwellings. The missionaries stopped in the settlement long enough to buy corn for their horses and, just as they were leaving, Joseph ran out with a letter for a neighbor down the river. "He is very polite," said the missionaries, "has a dignified & pleasing aspect, dresses well after the Indian manner, and speaks the English language with great fluency."[2] The clergymen were not the best judges of who spoke fluent English, for they seldom heard their Indians speak any English; but they were good judges of Indian looks, and it is noteworthy that they were pleased with Joseph's appearance. Not all white people were similarly pleased—few whites could admire a shaved head and a scalp lock. Perhaps the two Moravians had seen so much of Simon Girty that the less fearsome-looking Joseph provided a happy contrast.

We are indebted, not to Mrs. Simcoe, but to James Peachey, for a picture showing another aspect of Brant's Town. Peachey (the same soldier-artist who sent a portrait of Catharine Brant to General Haldimand) visited the Grand River Indians in the early days of the settlement and made an engaging sketch of the school. His picture, engraved in 1786 for a little Mohawk primer prepared by Daniel Claus, shows the children at their lessons in the schoolhouse.[3] The room is heavily beamed, its floorboards wide, and the one window that can be seen has twelve small panes. The Indian teacher, probably the same Paulus who had taught on the Mohawk, his blanket cast aside, sits regally in his chair. By his side is a table with inkstand and quills and a book, and what appears to be a switch for the unruly. The class is a large one, of both boys and girls, most holding books, some standing and some sitting on benches. The children are barefoot and

A Class of Mohawk Children. Engraved by James Peachey. The school at the Grand River, taken from Daniel Claus's A *Primer for the Use of the Mohawk Children*, London, 1786. *Courtesy of the Metropolitan Toronto Library Board, Toronto. T16552.*

dressed in the English style, though some of the boys wear scalp locks to show that they are already young warriors. Later there would come a white teacher, one Moses Mount, who is listed regularly in Indian department accounts. This man, who told Patrick Campbell he had sixty-six pupils whom he taught English and arithmetic, was to grow old in the service. He died in 1799, when Joseph began the search for a new teacher and an effort to get the teacher a better salary.[4] Since the schoolhouse was also an adult meeting place before the new council house could be built, it seems to have been the scene of some drunken frolics, and by 1794 was reported to have had nearly all its windows smashed, and not by the children, either. There are bills for frequent repairs of the school or church. It seems as though some structure was always in need of repair at the Grand River, if, indeed, it had not burned down and needed complete rebuilding.

Every traveler of note who lingered in Brant's Town seems to have lodged in Joseph's house. It was like those hospitable old days on the Mohawk except that the travelers were of a different stripe from the solemn young dissenters Joseph used to entertain. Sir John Johnson came sometimes, and Lieutenant Governor Simcoe when he had business with the Indians, as well as many other officials, both civil and military, and even some curiosity-seeking Americans who wanted to interview the Indian celebrity. All were welcome in Joseph's house.

The Reverend John Stuart, who lived at Kingston but who still had charge of the Mohawks, was a visitor in 1788. Joseph and four other Mohawks accompanied Stuart from Kingston across Lake Ontario to its head, and then escorted him overland about twenty-five miles to their village, all traveling on horseback. On a Sunday in mid-June the minister preached in the new church and baptized sixty-five persons and married three couples. He commented on the pleasant situation of the village and was very favorably impressed with the church building. None of the white settlements had a church as yet, and Stuart could appreciate an edifice which he described as "about 60 feet in length & 45 in breadth,—built with squared logs and boarded on the outside and painted—with a handsome steeple & bell, a pulpit, reading-desk, & Communion-table, with convenient pews." There was also a small organ, and Stuart had brought with him a large share of Queen Anne's silver from the old church at Fort Hunter. Joseph and fifteen Mohawks escorted the minister back to Niagara and begged that he would visit them as often as possible.[5] Actually this was Stuart's last, as well as his first, visit to the Grand River. Something untoward several times occurred to prevent another visit, and the busy clergyman, no longer a young man, could not look forward with much enthusiasm to such a long, arduous (and expensive) journey.

In 1792 the Reverend Robert Addison, who was now stationed at Niagara, promised Stuart to go in his stead. Addison performed his visit the next year and baptized nineteen persons. Joseph acted as interpreter.[6] Addison went again in 1795 and baptized fifteen persons. Joseph had asked that Addison be given an extra stipend for visiting the village three or four times a year. He thought the Indians would prefer that to a resident missionary. Stuart tartly commented that they "are afraid of the restraint which the continued residence of a Clergyman would necessarily lay them under," and he added that "occasional visits are to be considered more as matters of form than productive of any lasting good effect."[7] This was hardly a fair comment as Joseph had already tried to get Stuart himself to go to live on the Grand River.[8] Mr. Addison, however, was more charitable and was sorry he could not visit "with those devout Indians as much as they deserve."[9]

A different sort of visitor was Lord Edward Fitzgerald. That energetic young nobleman had a good time in Brant's Town where he was adopted as a chief. He was much smitten with the Indians and spoke "in raptures" of their hospitality.[10] "If you only stop an hour they have a dance for you," he wrote his mother. "They are delightful people; the ladies charming and with manners that I like very much, they are so natural. Notwithstanding the life they lead, which would make most women rough and masculine, they are as soft, meek and modest as the best brought up girls. At the same time they are coquettes au possible." Lord Edward planned a long western tour, and Joseph and a party of Mohawks escorted him part of the way along Lake Erie. Of Joseph the young man said, "We have taken very much to one another."[11]

But it is the famed traveler, Patrick Campbell, who has left us the most complete account of a visit to Brant's Town.[12] Campbell braved the journey to the Grand River in the dead of winter. It was not so rash an act as might be supposed, for traveling in a sleigh was easier than by horseback or bateau, and there were not the hordes of ravenous insects and mosquitoes that drew the blood of man and beast in warmer seasons. Journeying through deep virgin snow, Campbell arrived at Joseph's house about nightfall on February 11, 1792. Gossip had already apprised him of Joseph's personal situation. "This renowned warrior," he had been told, "is not of any royal or conspicuous progenitors, but by his ability in war, and political conduct in peace, has raised himself to the highest dignity of his nation, and his alliance and friendship is now courted by sovereign and foreign states." Campbell was, of course, referring to the pressing invitations Joseph had received to visit the American capital.

Joseph welcomed Campbell and his party with "European" politeness, and Campbell was much impressed with his host's good manners. But when Catharine came into the room, richly dressed in silk and embroidered lace, Campbell lost his heart. He admired "the elegance of her person, grandeur of her looks and deportment, her large mild black eyes, [and the] symmetry and harmony of her expressive features"; indeed, he thought her far handsomer than two fair young white ladies who happened to be present, though they were very pretty—she "so far surpassed them," he said, "as not to admit of the smallest comparison." He could not so much as look at them, he added, "without marking the difference."

Tea was on the table when Campbell arrived, and he was quick to note the handsome china and other elegant appurtenances of the meal. After tea, music was played on a hand organ by a young Indian and a young white man alternately. Supper was served in equal style accompanied by rum, brandy, and Madeira and port wine. Joseph who had been seriously ill, as we know, apologized for retiring early, and not long afterward all were abed. Campbell, weary from the long, cold journey, could appreciate the fine sheets and blankets and the comfortable bed with which he was accommodated.

Dinner the next day was another lavish meal, with handsomely attired Negro slaves waiting on the table. Port and Madeira flowed "pretty freely," and Joseph proposed a number of toasts, first to the king and queen and others of the royal family, and then to "the brave fellows who drubbed the Yankies on the 4th of last November," meaning, of course, St. Clair's defeat. Afterward the visitors were entertained with dancing. The young braves, dressed in their most colorful apparel, showed off their traditional war dances, with Joseph beating the drum and singing. Being asked to speak, Campbell thanked the dancers for their agile performance. He told them he had fought in many parts of Europe and killed many men, and now that he was in America he did not doubt but he "would fight with them yet, particularly if the Yankies attacked us." The young men laughed heartily when these words were interpreted to them. They were the sort of words that they liked to hear. Such unsubstantial promises had encouraged them for many years and would certainly encourage them for several more to come. Less warlike dances followed, and even Scottish reels, in which Joseph and the visitors and some Mohawk damsels also participated. They danced till nearly daylight. Campbell thought he had never spent such an enjoyable evening in all his life. He admits he got tipsy. Although he had brought along plenty of liquor of his own with which he meant to treat the company, Joseph insisted that he drink his. One young Indian appeared somewhat inebriated. Joseph sternly reprimanded him, telling him he would have to leave the room if he could not behave better! It was the mark of Joseph's ascendancy that he could get away with this. Brant's Town was Brant's town.

During his stay Campbell was told many anecdotes by Joseph and shown many curiosities that he had accumulated in England. Once the two got into a discussion of religion. Joseph brought up the sub-ject. He asked if Indians who had never heard the gospel could get into heaven. Campbell was sure they could. Joseph then brought up the subject of the Virgin Mary and her husband Joseph, and spoke of Christ in such a way that showed some scandalous doubts. Campbell quickly closed the discussion. Joseph's remarks, he said, showed the great difficulty of converting "these people" from their early preju-dices.

Campbell's visit to Brant's Town lasted just two days. When he took his leave Joseph and Catharine got into their sleigh and accom-panied him the first ten miles or so on his return journey. They stopped then at another Indian home which was very comfortable but not in the class with Joseph's. Joseph produced some meat and drink which he had brought from home, and Campbell and his host and hostess ate their farewell meal together. They never met again. A year later Campbell published his book of travels and told about the memo-rable excursion to the Grand River. In all that he wrote there was not a word of the self-effacing Henry Tekarihoga, though the latter must have been present some of the time.

Campbell mentions that the Brants had a fine family of children. One, about eight years old, he singled out as self-reliant and adventur-ous, already a good little hunter. The boy looked like his mother. Joseph said he was glad of that. This child was the eldest of Joseph's second family, obviously Joseph, Jr., born about the time of the treaty of Fort Stanwix in 1784. Besides young Joseph, the Brants also had by 1792 Jacob, born about 1786, who probably looked like his grand-father Croghan,[13] and Catharine, born in 1791 or very early 1792.[14] Later came John, the youngest son, born September 27, 1794,[15] then Mary and Margaret (or Margaret and Mary),[16] and last of all Elizabeth, the youngest of the family, born a few years after John.[17] John and Elizabeth showed the least of their Indian heritage. In per-sonality they were more Joseph's children than Catharine's. Elizabeth probably looked like her mother,[18] but there the resemblance stopped.

John would turn out to be a very able young man. The white world very nearly claimed these two.

Joseph's first family also lived in Brant's Town. Christina married the respected and amiable Aaron Hill, son of Joseph's great friend, David. Aaron was an educated young man, very active in the church. He was often called Dr. Hill since he dispensed the medicines for his people. When David Hill died Joseph tried hard to get the father's inherited honors and position for Aaron who well deserved them. Even Joseph could not accomplish this; the inheritance, according to Indian tradition, went, inexorably, through the female line to Aaron's cousin, the son of an aunt who was David's sister. Young Aaron kept his family in prosperity. He and Christina had several children, and Christina developed into an excellent housekeeper. Her home was very clean, according to a traveler who saw it.[19]

Isaac Karaguantier, the firebrand, married Mary Hill and had several "lovely" children. Joseph had tried to keep Isaac out of trouble by employing him on Indian business and sometimes as his secretary. But Isaac was probably irredeemable. He caused a riot at Detroit in 1793 and made himself unwelcome there. He was sullen and morose in the presence of white people and is said to have liked to shoot at the horses of whites. He is also said to have assaulted a young man riding along the highway, maiming his victim and killing the man's horse, causing Joseph to have to pay a large sum in damages. Isaac finally got into serious trouble in 1795 when he killed a white man in cold blood, a crime well authenticated in contemporary documents. The victim, a deserter from Wayne's army, had settled on the Grand River where he plied his trade of saddlemaker. One story says the man had been slow in making Isaac a saddle. Another story says Isaac had no excuse at all for the murder. Joseph was very distressed, and is quoted as saying he hoped the authorities would demand Isaac for trial. But the provincial authorities were also distressed. They had heard gossip that Joseph would refuse to give up his son, and that he boldly proclaimed that he had more influence over the Grand River militia than the government had. In the end nothing was done. The authorities finally concluded that the victim was only a vagabond. They saw no real reason to trouble themselves. They even played with the idea (usually so unacceptable) that the Indians were independent; let them deal with the problem.[20]

Joseph had two other relatives—probably only clansmen—who had murdered a white man at the Grand River a few years before, in 1791. There was a big to-do then also about whether the accused would be given up for trial—they never were—and Colonel Gordon stopped the delivery of the usual presents and provisions for a time. This punitive action upset Joseph who generally preferred the ancient way of covering the deceased's grave with wampum, and some coolness sprang up between him and the colonel. The latter's action was countermanded at Quebec, and afterward he tried to get back into Joseph's good graces. Whether he succeeded is not clear.[21]

Most of Joseph's close relatives were never involved in such trouble. Molly's daughters had married respectable white men, and Joseph got along well with his nephews-in-law, particularly Robert Kerr and John Ferguson. There must have been some visiting back and forth between the families; and Joseph tried to get Kerr, who was a physician, an official appointment to live among the Mohawks.[22] There were also harmonious relations with Brant Johnson and his daughters, all of whom received Indian land. One of the girls married the lawyer, Alexander Stewart, to whom Joseph entrusted much legal business. John Elliott, Catharine's white brother-in-law, was no stranger to the Grand River, either, and there is some evidence the John Elliotts and the Joseph Brants saw each other often. The Elliott home, somewhere on the north shore of Lake Erie, could not have been so very far from Brant's Town. Except for Isaac, Joseph was as fortunate in his family and relations as most of his contemporaries, white or Indian.

Joseph had various ways of supporting his Grand River home. There was the income from his half pay and special pension which broke the back of his expenses, though he was never free from the worry that the latter might be terminated. This worry insured at least a modicum of good behavior (as British officialdom called it) on his part. This was especially true after 1796 when a pension was promised to Catharine in the event of his death in the king's service.[23] There would always be a point beyond which Joseph dared not harass the government. His large and growing family, Catharine's predilection for silks and velvets, his own predilection for fine liquors and the gentlemanly life, added to the very high prices of everything on the frontier, even common necessities, dictated prudence. He could not do without his regular cash income.

Joseph had a good farm, did extensive farming, and, indeed, asserted he knew all about planting and sowing. Here was his basic subsistence, and the times were such that he could usually sell his surplus. Agents came often to the Grand River to buy up wheat and flour and Indian corn. Nature helped, too, for there was plenty of fish in the river and venison in the forests. Of course the Brants kept cattle, sheep, and hogs; and Joseph, unlike most Indians, knew enough to feed his stock regularly. Catharine, who was said to be industrious though she had no need to perform household chores, chose to go up to the sugar camps when the sap rose and help to make the family's sugar. For her it was probably a sort of holiday. On such occasions Catharine, no doubt thinking of her own life, might proclaim her philosophy: that none can tell what the future holds.[24] Similarly, although it was not strictly necessary, Joseph probably did some hunting for pelts. Once he and a party of Indians were seen with their dogs trying to catch a mink.[25] That time he failed, but there must have been many other times he did not fail. Perhaps this was a holiday, too, for him, but fatalism formed no part of his philosophy of life. Joseph was not the one to submit meekly to the dictations of fate.

When the Indian department dispensed the annual presents, Joseph got his part; and his part was usually of much better quality than what was given to common Indians. He also got presents, almost anything he demanded, at any time during the year. Indeed, he was accused of knowing his way about the Indian store a little too well,[26] but nothing was ever done about that situation. The government was as wary of Brant as Brant was of the government. If Joseph feared for his pension, the government feared for the safety of the white settlements. After thirty years Pontiac was still a name to inspire terror. The question was: might Brant become a second Pontiac? In such uncertainty Brant's peccadilloes, his "capriciousness," and his expense could be borne.

Joseph also got numerous gifts from individuals—such objects as double-barreled pistols, a gun that fired fifteen times without reloading, a silver-hilted dagger, books, ornaments, and medals, luxuries for Catharine, a horse, and many other things that were valuable or unique. Somebody always hoped to curry Joseph's favor, and in time his house became a kind of museum. But whether the gifts ever did the givers much good is problematical. Nor did Joseph hesitate to return any present that did not come up to expectation. Evan Nepean, for instance, had promised him a gold watch. But when the watch finally arrived, Joseph, not easily fooled, suspected the works were only gilt. He sent the gift back. If he was promised a gold watch, he wanted a *gold* watch and, moreover, he wanted a watch that was gold all the way through. He sent word to Nepean, with tongue in cheek no doubt, that the artisan had deceived him.[27]

Fragments of correspondence about debts and payments can be found. Joseph may say he expects to be paid by someone at such a time, and then he will in turn satisfy a creditor. Apparently he contrived to pay most of his debts punctually, though he bought far and wide, and always the best quality available. He could get credit in New York and Albany and along the Mohawk as well as in Detroit and Montreal. He bought an immense amount of liquor for himself and guests.[28] Perhaps he sold some of it, but if so, only to whites. If his Indians wanted a drink, they did not get it from him, but had to roam up and down the Niagara River begging their drams from passers-by. Joseph disapproved of the Indian propensity to drink to excess, and he would not permit those whites who lived on the Grand River to carry on the liquor trade. His prohibition was evidently much more efficacious than that which the weak government tried from time to time to enforce.[29] Yet brother-in-law John Elliott, who was in trade, would go to the Grand River to get liquor, and where could he have expected to get it, except from Joseph? Later, when taverns and stills sprang up willy-nilly, and the government got interested in excise taxes, Joseph seems to have thought better of his stand on liquor, and claimed for the Indians the taxes engendered on their land.[30]

In spite of all his activities, his travels, and his numerous visitors, not to mention the plots and stratagems of which he was suspected, Joseph's life on the Grand River fell into a certain basic routine. In the spring there was agricultural work. It was demanding, it was hard labor, and it must be done at the right time, and probably not always by slaves and hired hands. At this season there were also public duties to attend to. In the late spring or early summer Joseph would take his people to be inoculated for the dread smallpox, with Dr. Kerr officiating. This did not happen every year or always only in the spring, but it took place often enough to check that terrible contagion. At such a time government officials were very accommodating, placed the sick Indians in comfortable shelter and fed them well, and Joseph thanked them kindly. Indeed, there were times when Joseph appeared to be very grateful, and this served to mitigate those occasions when he appeared bursting with ingratitude.[31]

Every year on the first of May Joseph invited a throng of guests and presided at a great festival, a celebration which seems to have included some of the aspects of an ancient Indian celebration, some of the aspects of the white man's country fair, and some of the aspects of Sir William Johnson's old-fashioned militia days. The Indians came from miles away and camped by the riverside. They sang their songs of love and gallantry and their stirring and prayerful war songs, and the young men showed off their dancing: the various war dances, the calumet, buffalo, feather, serpent, and other dances, not every one of which, thought some visitors critically, bore much resemblance to its name. There were ball games, too, and races, and wrestling, and probably gambling, for the Indians had a passion for gambling, and did not hesitate to risk everything they owned. In the meantime the Grand River militia, both white and Indian, was drawn up and put through its exercises by Captain Brant, and there were such a number of excellent marksmen and such smart maneuvering as to afford the captain a swell of pride and to frighten some of the visiting whites who thought that unreliable chief had a little too much power over the local military. At the proper time food and drink were piled high on tables, and everybody helped himself. On one occasion Joseph, always the man to look out for the fair sex, had to chide a greedy fellow publicly who was not minding his manners. "Reynolds," he is reported to have told him, "I beg to say that the ladies here are also fond of ham & eggs." Afterward there were toasts to the king and reaffirmations of loyalty, and then the memorable spring celebration came to its end.[32]

Spring and summer were also the time for sitting out on the grass and holding councils, the time to eat one's fill of stawberries and cherries, the time to try to sell a slave (for the provincial government, Joseph seems to have thought, made a ridiculous fuss about the keeping of slaves),[33] and, above all, the time to play ball in the sunshine, not for just a day, but for days on end. Rivalry among villages and even among the various nations was so strong that it took much diplomacy to avoid acrimony and disputes, even disastrous quarrels; and councils to soothe somebody's injured feelings had to be held long and often.[34]

In the fall it was time to take in the harvest and go hunting. There was salmon fishing at the River Credit, an activity that seems to have lured Joseph from home every fall.[35] This was also a time to get a pony for the boys to ride,[36] and the time to attend a wedding, such as the October wedding which was held at his own home for Margaret Klein, his servant girl and one-time captive, and Jean Baptiste Rousseau, popular merchant and innkeeper.[37] Most importantly, fall was the time to go for the annual presents, first to Niagara and then later to Fort George or the head of Lake Ontario. At the annual distribution the Indians got everything from cloth, blankets, shoes, hats, and jewelry to guns, ammunition, knives, kettles, and paint—the best quality and the greatest quantity, as was proper, to the head men and their families.

Then it was winter again and well-earned leisure. Joseph liked to travel when crusted snow made the going easy, and often went on snowshoes to Niagara, and much farther, as when, one bitter-cold January, he helped to escort some white children part way to New York.[38] But on such days Joseph also liked to linger by the fireplace in snug warmth, and think and plan. Then he might work on his history of the Six Nations, a project long in view, though additional research was necessary before completion.[39] He planned more Biblical translations, and even considered learning Greek so that he could read the New Testament in the original and do better translating than he had been able to do when working with Stuart and Claus,[40] though planning was as far as this latter idea ever got. Winter was also a good time (as was any other time leisure permitted) to answer some of the many queries which his fame caused him to receive. Someone wanted to know, for instance, whether Indians had beards. Yes, he told him, though long plucking and shaving had made their beards rather sparse.[41] And when questioned by the Reverend Elkanah Holmes of the New York Missionary Society, Joseph gave a long account of the founding of the Six Nations and described many Indian customs, thus providing an early and authentic glimpse of his people and their traditions for the enlightenment of succeeding generations.[42] For this and other instances of friendship to Holmes, Joseph received a letter of thanks from the Missionary Society and a book of sermons.[43]

About 1789 someone inquired of Joseph whether he thought civilization was more conducive to happiness than a state of nature. Which were happier: his Indians or the more civilized white people? Joseph wrote a long letter (obviously with the aid of a secretary) in reply. He believed that life had well qualified him to deal with such a question.

> I was, sir, [he explained] born of Indian parents, and lived while a child, among those you are pleased to call savages; I was afterwards sent to live among the white people, and educated at one of your schools; since which period, I have been honoured, much beyond my deserts, by an acquaintance with a number of principal characters both in Europe and America. After all this experience, and after every exertion to divest myself of prejudice, I am obliged to give my opinion in favour of my own people. . . . I will not enlarge on an idea so singular in civilized life, and perhaps disagreeable to you; and will only observe, that among us, we have no law but that written on the heart of every rational creature by the immediate finger of the great Spirit of the universe himself. We have no prisons—we have no pompous parade of courts; and yet judges are as highly esteemed among us, as they are among you, and their decisions as highly revered; property, to say the least, is as well guarded, and crimes are as impartially punished. We have among us no splendid villains, above the controul of that law, which influences our decisions; in a word, we have no robbery under the colour of law—daring wickedness here is never suffered to triumph over helpless innocence—the estates of widows and orphans are never devoured by enterprising sharpers. Our sachems, and our warriors, eat their own bread, and

not the bread of wretchedness. No person, among us, desires any other reward for performing a brave and worthy action, than the consciousness of serving his nation. Our wise men are called fathers—they are truly deserving the character; they are always accessible—I will not say to the meanest of our people—for we have none mean, but such as render themselves so by their vices.

. . . We do not hunger and thirst after those superfluities of life, that are the ruin of thousands of families among you. Our ornaments, in general, are simple, and easily obtained. Envy and covetousness, those worms that destroy the fair flower of human happiness, are unknown in this climate.

The palaces and prisons among you, [Joseph continued, warming up to his subject] form a most dreadful contrast. Go to the former places, and you will see, perhaps, a deformed piece of earth swelled with pride, and assuming airs, that become none but the Spirit above. Go to one of your prisons—here description utterly fails!—certainly the sight of an Indian torture, is not half so painful to a well informed mind. Kill them [the prisoners], if you please—kill them, too, by torture; but let the torture last no longer than a day. . . . Those you call savages, relent—the most furious of our tormentors exhausts his rage in a few hours, and dispatches the unhappy victim with a sudden stroke.

Then Joseph penned—or more probably dictated—his famous peroration on imprisonment for debt:

But for what are many of your prisoners confined? For debt! Astonishing! and will you ever again call the Indian nations cruel?— Liberty, to a rational creature, as much exceeds property, as the light of the sun does that of the most twinkling star: but you put them on a level, to the everlasting disgrace of civilization. . . . And I seriously declare, that I had rather die by the most severe tortures ever inflicted by any savage nation on the continent, than languish in one of your prisons for a single year. Great Maker of the world! and do you call yourselves christians? . . . Does then the religion of him whom you call your Saviour, inspire this conduct, and lead to this practice? Surely no. It was a sentence that once struck my mind with some force, that "a bruised reed he never broke." Cease then, while these practices continue among you, to call yourselves christians, lest you publish to the world your hypocrisy. Cease to call other nations savage, when you are tenfold more the children of cruelty, than they.[44]

It must have done Joseph a great deal of good to get these sentiments off his chest, though a careful reader will note he was not wholly candid in all he said about life among the Indians. But, then, after 1783 Joseph did not like white people very much.

In these days Joseph was doing his best, for political reasons, to encourage certain harmless old Indian customs. Among his people he carefully emphasized his own Indian heritage. Self-consciously he shaved his head and wore the scalp lock on top, and painted his face on suitable occasions. He urged his Mohawks to do the same and they willingly complied.[45] Long years later son-in-law Aaron Hill was still touching his face with bits of color before he read the Sunday service. A traveler tells a revealing little anecdote. He met Joseph Brant one morning on the American side of the border, dressed in fine western attire. But as the day's travel was about to take him back into the Indian country and so on toward home, he changed his clothes and put on his Indian gear and had a passing Indian paint his face. He obviously preferred, as the traveler remarked, to appear among his own people like one of them.[46] Yet this was the same Brant who, when his boys were out wrestling and playing ball in the early morning, and whooping and yelling, is said to have remarked ruefully, "They will be Indians in spite of all I can do."[47]

This was also the same Joseph Brant who took so much pride in his Biblical translations that he sent them as gifts wherever he thought they might be appreciated, and who, in 1789, got a vote of thanks from the Corporation of Harvard College for one such gift.[48] And this was the selfsame Brant who, with some white associates, founded one of the earliest Masonic Lodges in Upper Canada. This was Lodge No. 11, founded in 1797 at Brant's Town. Joseph became its Worshipful Master and, scalp lock and all, seems to have functioned in that capacity at least till 1801 and perhaps longer.[49]

Any season was a time for Joseph to think about the Indian department and what changes were likely to come about and how they might affect his people. He meant to see that any changes were changes for the better and not for the worse. Joseph brooded about the Indian department constantly, its officers, its policies, and whether it was spending sufficient money.[50] He was ready enough to give his advice on these matters, when asked; and ready to give it when not asked, too. So determined was Joseph to stick his thumb into every Indian department pie that Lieutenant Governor Simcoe completely misunderstood his motives. The lieutenant governor accused him of "improper influence" on the Grand River Indians; Brant, said Simcoe, "always aims to appear to them, to be the distributor of the Kings bounty." To Simcoe this was a situation not to be tolerated.[51]

The Indian department was growing into a behemoth, with agents and sub-agents, secretaries and surgeons, storekeepers, interpreters, clerks, and numerous other employees, each with a vested interest in certain districts and operations. Thievery and corruption were rampant. Sir John Johnson was too often an absentee superintendent to be effective and, according to his critics, not very bright, but, according to his friends, smarter than he appeared to be, though handicapped by an excessive desire for popularity and by the "incredible" number of Indians who claimed kinship to him. At Niagara John Butler was too feeble to carry on his full range of duties and always hampered by his lack of education so that he had as much trouble writing letters or getting them written for him as ever Joseph had. Over all, Lord Dorchester and Lieutenant Governor Simcoe were at constant loggerheads on how and by whom the department should be run—as, indeed, they were at loggerheads on nearly everything. Secretary Joseph Chew, successor to the suspicious Patrick Langan at Montreal, corresponded with Joseph on a friendly basis. Sir John Johnson and Joseph were on a more wary footing with each other, though they could be cordial enough when sharing their common dislike of Simcoe or in resenting some change in the department which adversely affected each.[52] But Sir John made no bones about Joseph's being constantly "a little overcome,"[53] and Joseph spoke very ill of Sir John and, according to Simcoe, accused him of running a private store—but, as Simcoe added thoughtfully, Brant spoke ill of everyone.[54] After 1793 Joseph certainly spoke ill of McKee. But even the critical Joseph could see that John Butler had fully earned the good will of the Indians. Butler did his best for all of them, though it seemed that his favorites lived at Buffalo Creek. Joseph seems not to have resented this little bit of favoritism. Indeed, he would have been only too glad to welcome some of Butler's favorites to Brant's Town.

Joseph still longed to make the Grand River a "respectable," even an important, settlement. Reluctantly he had had to give up on the Bay of Quinte Mohawks. They too clearly wanted little to do with him. But there were hundreds of brothers just across the American border, and Joseph soon turned a speculative eye in their direction. Senecas, Cayugas, Onondagas, Tuscaroras, even Hendrick Aupaumut's "yanky" Indians—everybody, apparently, except the hated Oneidas—got invitations to settle on the Grand River.[55] But after the first general exodus from old homes in the United States, few additional settlers came.

Joseph might have had more success in attracting immigrants to his valley if the American branch of the Six Nations had been less satisfied. But satisfied they were. They had sold most of their lands and were enjoying annuities of money and goods which, in those early days, seemed quite adequate, even munificent. During some of the war scares on the American side of the border there were movements as though Joseph might get some new adherents at last. But Lord Dorchester set his foot down. He did not want the Americans to move over to the Grand River. Provisions might turn scarce, and there was enough trouble, he said, among dissident elements who already lived there.[56] Joseph had to confine his attention to local people. He encouraged more of his white friends to settle with him and saw that they got larger grants than the government gave other Loyalists—a cause of no little heartburning to Lieutenant Governor Simcoe when he came on the scene. In these arrangements Joseph had the staunch support of Henry Tekarihoga who willingly signed the deeds. Henry's "Interest" was "of the first consequence," and he could influence other chiefs and sachems to follow his example. Joseph continued to act as a sachem in this business, but he must have been under no illusions as to why he was able to do so. "Even during Brant's life time," said a man who had been thoroughly familiar with the situation, "Tyhorihoga was acknowledged the first Chief & Sachem, tho' the former from his education & knowledge of European manners, had the management of all their land concerns."[57] If further support was needed, Catharine, too, possessed the prestige of birth, and could influence the women who always had plenty to say in such matters.

The Grand River soon acquired a heterogeneous population. There were Indians called Six Nations who had scarcely any Iroquois blood. There were many Delawares, some of whom had come to the mouth of the river even before General Haldimand had issued his grant. Besides Joseph's white friends from his war days and those squatters who claimed to have bought land from individual Indians, there were white captives who refused to go home—such persons as the Klein girls, a girl named Sarah Anderson, and a man named Abraham Kuhn from the Ohio country. There were deserters from Wayne's army such as the ex-soldier murdered by Isaac, and there was the adventurer, Ebenezer Allen, who had fled his mill on the Genesee for reasons best known to himself. There was also Joseph's confidant, John Norton, for whom Joseph got an appointment as interpreter[58] and who, in spite of his Scotch blood, had his nose bored and his ears cut and liked to claim (for he was young, and it was a romantic gesture toward his Indian friends) that he was all Indian. There were the blacksmith, the miller, and the schoolmaster, three white men. Molly's children and Brant Johnson's children had their various tracts on the Grand River, though only Molly's son George ever actually lived there. The surveyor, Augustus Jones, who had married Tekarihoga's daughter in a church ceremony, also got a grant. And if Joseph had had his way, the Moravian missionaries and their converts would have joined him, too. He had done his best to persuade them,[59] but they settled on the Thames River instead, deeming that location, no doubt, more conducive to the religious life—as, indeed, it was.

Joseph got along very well with the Grand River whites. He liked to take their children on his knee and sing to them his guttural Mohawk lullabies, and he was always playing pranks. One family of white friends, the Solomon Joneses, lived down at the mouth of the river, where Joseph is said to have kept a fleet of five hundred canoes. He had much business in the neighborhood and often looked in on his friends. Once as Mrs. Jones was stooping over the fireplace minding her cooking, with her small child playing nearby, Joseph slipped in and took them by surprise. He seized the good woman by the hair, brandished his tomahawk, and let out a ferocious war whoop. Mrs. Jones refused to be intimidated. Obviously this had happened many times before. "Is that you Brant?" she calmly asked, without even turning around. The child never forgot the incident. He told it in vivid detail to his own son who related it, many years later, to the historian, Lyman C. Draper.[60]

Some six hundred likely prospects as immigrants were the Missisauga Indians who lived on the River Credit, not far west of York. White travelers who saw the Missisaugas wandering about thought them miserable specimens of their race, but to Joseph they were possible friends and adherents and their numbers impressive. They were not so hostile as the parent Chippewas who had just as lief invade the Grand River settlement as join it. Somehow or other Joseph managed to make friends with the Missisauga chief, Wabakenin. Though Wabakenin and his people did not settle on the Grand River—they had plenty of good land of their own, and they were not the settling kind, anyway—they began to dress like Mohawks and to wear the Mohawk scalp lock. Joseph became their adviser and, as he said, their "guardian,"[61] for the Missisaugas had land to sell, and they knew Joseph could deal with white buyers better than they could. The first buyer, however, was not a white man. It was Joseph himself.

Back in 1790 Joseph had been promised the usual allotment of land for a Loyalist captain[62]—three thousand acres for himself and fifty acres apiece for his wife and children. He particularly wanted a certain tract on Burlington Bay at the head of Lake Ontario which was claimed by the Missisaugas. He waited patiently a few years for the government to extinguish the Indian title. Nothing happening,

Joseph finally decided to help himself. He counciled with the now friendly Missisaugas and bought his own land. He had chosen very wisely. His purchase was a fine piece of ground in a very strategic location right on the road between York and Niagara. Any white man would have been delighted to own it.

When Lieutenant Governor Simcoe heard of this transaction between Brant and the Missisaugas, he was scandalized and affronted. That Indians of different nations should make such a deal between themselves, absolutely ignoring the king, smacked far too much of Indian independence. He would not allow it.[63] He insisted that everything must be redone in the proper channels according to British law. But first he tried to persuade Joseph that this was the wrong location for him—some other site would suit him better. Joseph refused to be persuaded. He knew what would suit him.[64] Reluctantly Simcoe gave in. He instructed the Indian department to buy the land for the king. The Missisaugas agreed and took their pay of three hundred dollars in goods. Then the tract, surveyed to the proper 3,450 acres, was reconveyed to Joseph.[65] Joseph did not like this proceeding by half, but it was the only way he could obtain his purchase. Then, thinking this was his land that he had bought and paid for, he reapplied for a military grant. This new application was denied.[66]

What Joseph meant to do with the tract at the head of Lake Ontario, when he first applied for it, is anybody's guess. He had a good house and a good farm on the Grand River and was apparently satisfied with his situation. But people were making big profits in the buying and selling of wild land. Perhaps Joseph thought to speculate a little. He had certainly had stranger thoughts. He did not foresee the drastic change in his life which would come about as the result of this acquisition.

Amid Joseph's incessant travels and his many commitments at home and abroad, he did not forget the matter of Mohawk land claims in New York. It was years before all the legal tangles could be unwound, but in 1789 and the early 1790s Joseph managed to get for his people payments of some £516 for lands they still owned at old Canajoharie. The payments, consisting of flour, cattle, biscuits, and pork, including transportation costs, and cash, were made by Jelles Fonda in behalf of himself and a company of buyers, and came at a time when the Indians were in great need.[67] At this time Joseph also negotiated for the sale of the 512 acres he had got from Sir William Johnson.[68] He also witnessed a deed to the state of New York, and probably helped to negotiate the sale, for all the claims of the Fort Hunter Mohawks to land south of the Mohawk River. Payment for these claims amounted to seven hundred pounds.[69] It was not till March 29, 1797, that all Mohawk claims in the state of New York were settled by a treaty at Albany between commissioners for the state and Joseph, agent for the Grand River Mohawks, and John Deseronto, agent for the Quinte Mohawks. By this treaty the Mohawks were awarded one thousand dollars, and Joseph and John got six hundred dollars for their expenses and work.[70] Joseph, at least, had done a great deal of work, which letters throughout the years attest, and no doubt deserved the payment.

With so much business in New York Joseph kept up his friendship with Israel Chapin and with Israel Chapin, Jr., who succeeded his father when the latter died in 1795. Joseph had liked Israel Chapin; he got along well with him, and after his death he told young Chapin that he wished "we may be all as well prepared for that tremenduous moment as the good old man was."[71]

On his journeys across the border Joseph met many persons of importance though he seldom ventured east of Canandaigua. At the latter place Joseph made the acquaintance of Thomas Morris, son of Robert Morris, famed financier of the Revolution. The elder Morris, rashly speculating in land all over the country, and already sinking into bankruptcy, had bought most of the Phelps and Gorham claims east of the Genesee River as well as the preemption rights to some four million acres west of the Genesee which Phelps and Gorham had had to give up. The Morrises, both father and son, were trying desperately to extinguish the Seneca title to the west Genesee land, in order to pave the way for resale and payment of their debts. They were under the impression that Joseph Brant had great influence with the Senecas and treated him accordingly. Once, as Thomas Morris later told Joseph's biographer Stone, Joseph, with Cornplanter, Red Jacket, and other Seneca leaders, was entertained at his Canandaigua house at dinner. Over the dinner table Joseph, a good conversationalist when he wished, laughingly told the story how a certain chief whose brave words inspired men to battle (meaning Red Jacket, as everyone knew) had killed the warriors' cows while the warriors themselves were out fighting. That day Joseph assured himself of Red Jacket's undying enmity if, indeed, he did not already possess it.[72] In spite of this injudicious performance the Morrises, who finally were able to buy up most of the Seneca title at the treaty of Big Tree, in September 1797, were prepared to pay Joseph a substantial bribe for his influence in their behalf. Joseph did use what influence he had, for he thought it would be a good thing for the Senecas to have additional annuities for their support. He probably did accept the bribe, too, though he was so busy with affairs at home that he did not even show up at the treaty. The Morrises also paid him thirty guineas for his old improvement at the landing on the Niagara River where he had lived during the war. It was another instance of Joseph's shrewdly taking what he could get for something he would have done anyway. [73]

Joseph must have been greatly impressed with what he saw at the Thomas Morris house, for when he invited Morris and Israel Chapin, Jr., to visit him at the Grand River, he apologized for the accommodations there, explaining he could not offer much since he lived in the woods. [74] It seems to have been the only time he ever apologized for the inadequacies of his establishment, and perhaps it started him to thinking that he ought to have something better. Morris would have accepted the invitation except that he found out it would cause jealousy at Buffalo Creek if he visited Brant. Since the treaty of Big Tree had not yet been brought off, Seneca jealousy was the last thing he could afford. He did not go to the Grand River. [75]

One of the Americans Joseph kept in touch with was Oliver Phelps. Phelps, ever the buoyant speculator in spite of grievous losses, had acquired a share in the Connecticut Western Reserve. When Connecticut ceded its western claims to the federal government in 1786, it had retained a tract of about 3,500,000 acres along Lake Erie from the western line of Pennsylvania to Sandusky Bay. Though preemption rights to the extreme western portion of this huge Reserve were granted to New London, Fairfield, Norwalk, and other Connecticut towns as compensation for property destroyed in the Revolution, preemption rights to the rest, some three million acres, were sold, in 1795, to a syndicate called the Connecticut Land Company. Joseph saw his opportunity and immediately set up a claim in behalf of his part of the Six Nations to all the Reserve east of the Cuyahoga River. He was having trouble in Upper Canada over some land sales he wished to effect, and that made him all the more eager to get some American land to sell. [76]

Using Oliver Phelps and Israel Chapin, Jr., as go-betweens, Joseph had little trouble in persuading the Connecticut people, notably Moses Cleaveland and two co-directors, that the Grand River Six Nations were the Indians whose title they must extinguish. It was a very weak claim that Joseph had set up, for his Indians, along with the other Six Nations, had surrendered all the land west of Buffalo Creek at Fort Stanwix in 1784. However, as the Six Nations had had ancient settlements on the lower Cuyahoga (one, it will be recalled, being Joseph's birthplace), Joseph insisted that his Indians still possessed a "particular right" to all that territory. How this right belonged to the Canadian Indians and not to the American part he did not explain, but he was probably thinking of the fact that nobody from the Grand River had signed the confirmation made at Fort Harmar in 1789.[77] At any rate he continued to press claims against the Connecticut Company and made sufficient of a nuisance of himself to get a settlement of fifteen hundred dollars at a council at Buffalo Creek in 1796. Unfortunately the Senecas jumped in with a demand for part of the award, and there was also some interference from a Detroit merchant named John Askin who had acquired the Wyandot title.[78] Payment to Joseph's people was to take over nine years. The Connecticut speculators did not want trouble with the Indians—any Indians—and were willing enough to pay, but they did not know whom to pay. Various phases of the controversy lasted till 1805 when Joseph seems finally to have been able to bring off the affair to his satisfaction and get all the money and goods that he thought were due. It was not, however, the last he heard of the Seneca claim.[79]

When Joseph exerted himself so much and could render such service to whole nations, not to mention the many individuals whom he helped from time to time, it was no wonder that in spite of the widespread jealousy of him, he succeeded in retaining the confidence of his people. Trusting, too, in the unvarying support of Henry and Catharine, he did not hesitate to carry on much Grand River business at his own discretion. The Moravian missionaries could say of him in 1798 that he is "one of those extraordinary characters, who by dint of superior genius, know how to avail themselves of circumstances, so as to raise themselves into eminence, among an uncivilized or unwary people. . . . Though no chief [sachem] among his nation, and incapable of becoming one, on account of the meanness of his descent, yet he possesses a vast ascendency in it. . . . Nothing of moment is resolved on, or undertaken, among all the six nations in Canada, contrary to, or without his consent. His authority is supreme, and they all pay him uncommon respect."[80]

Joseph obviously meant to continue on his path of benevolent despotism despite the fact that, as he very well knew, one chief could not wear a better coat without exciting jealousy in the others.[81] There was the time, and not too long ago (as he also knew), that Captain Cornelius Sturgeon, autocratic Onondaga chief, who was accused of aping white ways, had created so much discord in his nation that he had been put to death by another Onondaga, forcing the Sturgeon family to exact revenge if the murderer's family could not pay the blood price. Whether Joseph read that item in the newspapers[82] or heard it via the grapevine, he understood its significance well enough, but it was unlikely that he took it to heart. It was a shame, he would have said, that Captain Cornelius had become too great a man, and something ought to have been done by his relations before outsiders acted. But Joseph would not have seen the least comparison between himself and Captain Cornelius. What *he* was doing was all for the public good. Everyone must see and appreciate that.

The years at Brant's Town never saw the end of Joseph's struggle to uphold his people's rights. Like a juggler with a handful of balls in the air, he could carry on half a dozen controversies at once. In 1795 he leaped into a public dispute on the side of Sally Ainse, his Detroit friend, whom he described as "one of ourselves." Sally's trouble involved a large and valuable tract of land on the east side of Lake St. Clair, at the mouth of the Thames River. Like Joseph, who had got a private grant from some friendly Missisaugas who were not of his nation, Sally had obtained a private grant from some friendly Chippewas who, of course, were not of her nation. These Indian grants, called deeds of gift, had been common in the Detroit area for many years. Such informal deeds, however, were illegal. By law Indian land could be purchased only by the king, not by individuals. The land board at Detroit, in whose jurisdiction the Thames land was, may have thought that Indians of different nations could no more make such deals with each other than they could with whites. Then again, the land board may not have known about Sally's claim, which antedated government purchase of the area. At any rate, the board began to grant away Sally's land to various white persons. The grantees began to make settlements. Sally complained loudly. She was a smart trader; she lived by her wits; and she was by no means backward in raising her voice in defense of her rights.

Lieutenant Governor Simcoe, though eager to see the Thames valley settled, responded sympathetically to Sally's complaints. Simcoe did not insist that Sally, like Joseph, go through regular legal channels. Her grant was older than Joseph's and, unlike Joseph, she was not politically dangerous. Simcoe met with his Executive Council. The Council resolved that Sally Ainse be put in possession of her property at once. Unfortunately for Sally, her land on the Thames, unlike Joseph's at the head of Lake Ontario, was filling up rapidly with settlers. Settlers were not deer and turkeys; they could not be hunted down or disregarded. This was a fact the government of the United States had already found out and that the government of Upper Canada was about to learn. The resolution of the Executive Council and all Simcoe's assurances had little effect on Sally's situation. For some reason Sally could not obtain her land. She continued to complain.

At this point Joseph, who had heard about his friend's predicament, tried to come to her rescue. For years, in speeches and in letters, he protested to all who would listen. Simcoe and others in authority repeatedly declared to him they wished to do Sally Ainse full justice. Finally Simcoe's secretary let fall the reason for the government's dilatoriness. It was due, he said, to our customs and regulations. The attorney general showed Joseph a "ticket" from the land board which he declared could not be ignored. At length the Executive Council decided that Sally had no valid claim although her deed had been duly registered at Detroit. The Chippewas had sold the Thames tract twice. The second purchaser, being the king, took precedence. Sally remained landless, and Joseph saw all his well-meant efforts come to zero. If there was a lesson to be learnt from this affair, Joseph was too stubborn to learn it. [83]

The controversy involving Davenport Phelps turned out a disappointment, too. Was Joseph merely trying to help a friend who had too large a family and too small an income? Or in his crafty way, did he think to enhance the status of his people by winning for them the right to nominate a clergyman of their own choice? Or was the affair of Phelps a religious issue to Joseph and nothing more? Joseph was not irreligious, no matter what people thought of him. He was concerned about death and the after-life. He often prefaced a description of his plans with the pious words, "God willing." He always managed to live near a church, and acted as interpreter when Stuart and Addison came on their rare visits. But Joseph had his doubts, and some of them were the doubts of all Indians who observed the ways of white Christians. "I have read your bible formerly, and should have thought it divine," said he, "if the practice of the most zealous professor had corresponded with his professions." [84] There were also some stories in the Bible which Joseph found difficult to swallow. He liked to discuss his doubts and sometimes insisted on discussing them with the wrong persons. A Patrick Campbell could not have been comfortable talking theology with anybody, and certainly not with an Indian, and most assuredly not with a doubting Indian. The Reverend John Stuart had no use for doubting Indians, either. They have given Joseph the reputation of one who does not accept Holy Writ.

Nevertheless, Joseph did worry about the spiritual life of his people. He knew they had never recovered from the war and the long years without religious instruction. Though some of the Mohawks went to church and behaved decorously during the services, and though the women sang sweetly on Sundays, things went on in Brant's

Town and all up and down the river that Joseph could not approve of. In spite of his efforts to stop the flow of liquor, there was much drunkenness. Fights broke out between drunken Indians, and sometimes somebody ended up stabbed or beaten to death. Joseph always spoke of such accidents with grave concern. He must have known the Grand River was getting a bad name. One of his own Mohawks told the Moravian missionaries that there was no difference between Brant's people and savages.

It was about this time that Joseph began to consider the case of Davenport Phelps. Davenport Phelps was the son-in-law of Eleazar Wheelock, Joseph's former teacher. He was an educated man, affable and winning, and he had brought his large family to British Niagara in 1792. He set up as a lawyer. Perhaps he was not a very good lawyer, or just too much of a rebel to be generally accepted, for he did not prosper in that Loyalist stronghold. Joseph became friendly with Phelps, and he concluded that it would be a good thing if Phelps turned missionary and came to live with the Indians at Brant's Town. It would be a decent livelihood for Phelps, and the Indians would benefit from his instruction. Joseph found that all Phelps had to do was to pass the examination for the ministry and be ordained. Phelps protested that he had not kept up with his classical studies, for of course it was necessary that a missionary to the Indians be well primed with Latin and Greek. Joseph thought Phelps too modest about his attainments. On December 15, 1797, Joseph wrote Sir John Johnson about the matter of Phelps's ordination. Sir John wrote the Anglican bishop of Quebec, one Jacob Mountain. Mountain thought the whole idea most irregular and wrote Peter Russell, acting administrator of the government of Upper Canada (Simcoe being on leave of absence), about Joseph's proposal.

Peter Russell, a very cautious man, made some inquiries into Davenport Phelps's character and history. What he found out he did not like. Phelps had come from the United States, and he had served in the American militia. He also seemed to be a political firebrand for he had once led some farmers on a march to the courthouse to support an accused seditionist. Above all things, Russell thought, if there was to be a resident missionary at the Grand River, he must be a missionary of the right political hue. This was very important to the infant province of Upper Canada in view of the great war in Europe and the near presence of so many Americans and Frenchmen whose views might be hostile. Russell could not favor Phelps's ordination. Informed of these details in confidence (for Russell had his reasons at this time for not wishing Joseph to know his opinion), Mountain, who had at least considered the matter, drew back. He agreed wholeheartedly that the Indians must not be given a "Spiritual instructor who would be disposed to unsettle their notions of loyalty & obedience." He concluded that Phelps was not only unsafe as a missionary to the Grand River but not even fit for ordination.

As in the affair of Sally Ainse, the controversy over Davenport Phelps dragged on and on. Joseph was determined to have his missionary, and all the Canadian authorities, religious and secular, were equally determined that he should not. Joseph promised in desperation that the Indians and local whites would subscribe Phelps's salary, and he reminded Russell that no less a person than the archbishop of Canterbury had promised to help the Indians in religious matters when they applied to him. Joseph refused to believe that Phelps had engaged in seditious conduct and demanded proof of the allegations. In the meantime the matter was referred to the government in London; and the Duke of Portland, who had succeeded Dundas as secretary in charge of colonial affairs, approved the course of Russell and the bishop. It was very important, he said, that the choice of a missionary "should be entirely independent of them [the Indians], and that they and the Clergymen should know and feel, that they neither have been, nor ever will be, consulted on the Subject." Joseph realized he was up against a stone wall. "Very well," he is said to have threatened, "then I shall turn Methodist." He might even accept a Catholic priest!

If Joseph made such threats, he made them only in anger. He had been a good Church of England man for too many years to change, but he did decide to try to get Phelps ordained in the United States. He applied to Israel Chapin, Jr., and to Aaron Burr, a man whom he had met on his American journeys, for aid. Chapin tried to help. Whether Burr helped is not known, but Phelps, who by this time was very eager to adopt the religious life, did receive Episcopal ordination in New York, first as a deacon and later as a priest. Phelps returned to Canada and preached and farmed for a while near the head of Lake Ontario. He never went to the Grand River, though Joseph is said to have offered him land there. But Phelps had no heart for speculation. He did not want land, and he finally ended up as an Episcopal missionary in western New York, where he worked for many years. Brant's Town remained without a resident clergyman. As Joseph had sadly remarked, no clergyman wanted to go to that "rude and distant quarter."[85]

Another controversy was not of Joseph's making. This dispute was thrust upon him, and certainly at first it had nothing to do with his "politicks." The trouble concerned the Caughnawagas, those Six Nations people, mostly Mohawks, who had gone over to the French long before the last great French war and whose descendants still lived on the upper St. Lawrence, some six hundred near Montreal and perhaps four hundred at St. Regis, both on the south side of the river. These Indians were from time to time caught up in the Six Nations orbit, but they did not always view matters in the same light as their American or even their Canadian kin. There was often some little hard feeling manifesting itself among the various brothers. As for Joseph, he was not too fond of the Caughnawagas. Had they not spied for the Americans during the late war? And as for the Caughnawagas, they belonged to those legions of people who were generally not too fond of Joseph Brant.

It will be remembered that before the British gave up the border posts, Lieutenant Governor Simcoe and the Indian department were searching for some friendly Indians who would claim the land to the south of Lake Ontario and the upper St. Lawrence, which could be erected into a barrier between Canada and the United States. The Caughnawagas, as the local Indian agents knew, were likely prospects as claimants. The Caughnawagas lived near the territory desired as an Indian barrier, they had had vague claims to some of it for many years, and if the 1783 boundary was to be moved southward, it would have to be moved past one of their settlements. The Caughnawagas obviously did not understand perfectly what was required of them, for though they restated claims to the country far to their south, they also claimed land on the north, or wrong, side of the St. Lawrence as far as Kingston and some on the south side which was clearly Canadian soil! As these lands were the abode of many hundreds, if not several thousands, of good Loyalists, officialdom in both Upper and Lower Canada was considerably taken aback. In his famous speech to the Seven Nations of Canada which caused so much American umbrage Lord Dorchester took occasion to remind his hearers that part of the lands they claimed had been settled by Loyalists even before he had returned to Canada in 1786. Nevertheless he promised to look into the matter.[86] Lord Dorchester's reaction was the mildest. Lieutenant Governor Simcoe could only exclaim in surprise.[87] And when Alexander McKee, who had come down the lakes on business, heard that the Caughnawagas were claiming Canadian land, he inquired how they could claim all that country since, when they moved away from the Mohawk River, they had had to petition the French for land to settle upon.[88]

However much their Canadian pretensions were frowned on, nobody discouraged the Caughnawagas from pressing their American claims. Like the western Indians, they may even have hoped for British aid in doing so. As long ago as the old French regime they had argued they had a right to land far below the St. Lawrence. Urged on and supported by French authorities, they cited the ancient concept of the dish with one spoon, and asserted that they were co-owners of Mohawk, Oneida, and Onondaga hunting grounds. This particular application of the theory of common ownership, however, did not set well with the Mohawks, Oneidas, and Onondagas, and these three nations had vigorously rejected it as early as 1765 and probably long before. Whatever right the Caughnawagas had to American land had been disputed by their Indian neighbors for many years. It was so vague a right as to appear almost meaningless.[89] Nevertheless, when Caughnawaga delegates traveled to Albany in the winter of 1794–95, they gave their claim specific boundaries—roughly, about half of northern New York, from the headwaters of the Hudson to the headwaters of Canada Creek and the Black and Oswegatchie Rivers—and they complained that Americans were settling illegally on this land.[90] When they went to their present abodes, they declared, they never left their premises. The nervous Americans were so eager to placate all Indians just then that the state gave the Caughnawaga delegates a royal welcome and appointed commissioners to confer with them.[91]

A second meeting took place between the New York commissioners and the Caughnawaga delegation in New York in the fall of 1795. By this time General Wayne had already negotiated the treaty of Greenville, and the situation in the west had calmed down. It was not so necessary now for Americans to appease Indians. The New York commissioners told the Caughnawaga delegates that they had never heard of their claim before. The land claimed by the Caughnawagas, said the New Yorkers, was Mohawk land. The Mohawks had never given that land to the Caughnawagas, they added, and they listed various sales which the Mohawks had made in the area before the Revolution. Some of that country, they asserted, especially the country bordering Lake Champlain, must have been given up to the French, since the French had long ago granted it out. The New Yorkers then offered the Indians a mere three thousand dollars for their claim. The Indians refused the offer and returned home.[92]

Angered by their disappointment—for they believed the Six Nations were growing rich from sales of land, and they had hoped to do likewise—the Caughnawagas turned on Joseph Brant and his Mohawks as the cause of their undoing. They accused the Mohawks of selling their land and demanded to be given the purchase money.

Joseph was bewildered. He could not understand the accusation. However, he was very busy just then, and he did nothing about it, thinking the whole affair would soon blow over.[93]

Events moved swiftly. In a few months it became clear that, Jay's treaty having been ratified, the British were about to give up the border posts and would soon retire to their side of the lakes. Dejectedly the Caughnawagas returned to New York, aiming to do the best they could.

Their third meeting with the New York commissioners was held in late spring 1796. All winter the New Yorkers had cudgeled their brains, and they had come up with an additional argument to support their cause. They based their denial of the Caughnawaga claim on the two 999-year Lessee Company deeds of November 1787 and July 1788. These deeds, even though disallowed by the state, said the New Yorkers, proved that the Six Nations considered the land in question theirs and not the Caughnawagas'. The point at issue in the deeds was a northeast line starting a little west of Fort Stanwix and running to an unnamed spot on the Canadian border. The meaning of this line depended on its angle, and the New Yorkers gave it as wide an interpretation as they dared. The original deed, they pointed out, had been witnessed by Colonel Louis of St. Regis, famed Revolutionary spy, who was now one of the Caughnawaga delegates! Though Joseph Brant and his Mohawks had had nothing at all to do with the first deed, the New Yorkers noted that the second deed, a compromise among the Indians, the Lessee people, and Phelps and Gorham, had been signed by Brant as a witness. The commissioners made much of these signatures. Would these men have witnessed a sale of land which they knew the sellers had no right to sell? No, declared the New Yorkers, and they adamantly refused to recognize the Caughnawaga claim.

The luckless Caughnawagas, confronted by such unyielding resistance and conscious, no doubt, of both the weakness of their numbers and the weakness of their claim, retired to a new position. They would be content, they said, to keep for themselves a reservation about fifty miles long and twenty miles wide along the St. Lawrence, including the settlement of St. Regis, and then to sell the rest of their claim for an annual payment of three thousand dollars. It was such a reservation that would have made no mean barrier in country which Lieutenant Governor Simcoe had recently denominated the most important part of the American-Canadian boundary. It was also a reservation which New York would not accept.

The Caughnawagas, knowing they had no help, now or ever, reduced their hoped-for reserve by two-thirds and their annuity to £480. The commissioners refused this offer, too, but promised to give the Indian deputies reasonable expenses and the usual presents. The deputies finally capitulated and took what they could get. Before the three New York commissioners and a representative sent by President Washington the unhappy Indians, their dreams of wealth gone, gave up all their claims against the state of New York except a small reservation six miles square at St. Régis. They received in return a one-time payment of approximately £1,233 and an annuity of some £213.[94] The Caughnawagas signed the agreement on May 31, 1796, and again left for home. Their breasts were full of resentment—not at Colonel Louis, not at the New Yorkers, not at the Six Nations, not at the Lessee Company, not at Phelps and Gorham, and certainly not at Simcoe and his Indian department or the British ministry in London. They aimed all their resentment at Joseph Brant.

For more than three years the angry Caughnawagas demanded of Joseph their money. Joseph told them he had no money. He thought that the Caughnawagas did possess hunting grounds in New York, north of the Mohawk lands, though not so much, he said, as they had described. He placed the dividing line at the watershed between the Mohawk and St. Lawrence Rivers and the western limit at Carleton Island.[95] At first he feared some of his people might have been up to old tricks—that is, that some unauthorized individuals had actually sold land they had no right to sell. He investigated and was thankful to find no basis to his fears.[96] He did not think that the compromise deed he had witnessed referred to any territory that the Caughnawagas could possibly claim. It did not even include Oneida land, he said, much less Caughnawaga land.[97] Joseph seems not to have considered whether witnesses to a document were responsible for its contents or whether they merely witnessed signatures, but he did know that neither he nor his Mohawks had ever sold any land in New York that was not theirs. All they had sold, before May 1796, had been small parcels on the Mohawk River about which there could be no controversy.

Joseph asked the Caughnawagas to come to Buffalo Creek, which was still the fireplace of all the Six Nations, to settle the matter. The Caughnawagas refused. They said he and the Mohawks must come to Caughnawaga. He refused. Since the Caughnawagas were the accusers, they should come before a Six Nations council and present their proof. That, he said, was the custom.[98] The affair came to a standstill.

The Caughnawagas went to Oneida to enlist supporters. They also called on friends in the west to come to their aid.[99]

Joseph tried to get documentary evidence from New York that he and the Mohawks had sold no Caughnawaga land. He repeatedly wrote his friends, Thomas Morris and Israel Chapin, Jr., about this problem, and in 1799 he sent a delegation to Albany, headed by the able John Norton. John Norton, too, met with little success. George Clinton and John Jay, who followed Clinton as governor, were wary about involving themselves in a dispute among Indians, but Clinton finally wrote a letter which Joseph could use in his defense, and Jay opened state records for copying.[100]

By 1798 the Caughnawagas were threatening war. Joseph suspected, he said, that they were being agitated by French agents. The authorities in Canada, formerly thinking the affair but a trifle, took alarm. They called on Sir John Johnson to intervene.[101] Sir John finally got Joseph and a great body of the Six Nations, whom, of course, the government supported coming, going, and on the spot, to attend a council at Caughnawaga. The end—or what Joseph supposed was the end—turned out surprisingly tame. The Caughnawagas declared they had not made the accusations of themselves but only because of what the New York commissioners had told them. They admitted they had been listening to bad birds. Nevertheless they insisted that all parties should go to New York to find out the truth.[102]

The Caughnawagas never did find out enough truth to satisfy them. Ten months after they surrendered all their claims to the state of New York, the Mohawks, as we have seen, went to Albany and gave up all their claims against that state, accepting an even smaller payment than the Caughnawagas had received. Governor Jay gave the Caughnawagas a copy of the new Mohawk treaty,[103] and it eventually caused them much anguish. In time the Caughnawagas could blame all their troubles on that Mohawk treaty of 1797. They never got over their confusion, and they never forgave Joseph Brant for "selling" their land.

Joseph worried a great deal about this problem, and he spent an unconscionable amount of time trying to straighten it out. But straighten it out he could not. Finally he had to give up. A far more momentous problem had already presented itself. Joseph was now engaged in the great fight of his life. All his other troubles paled into insignificance.

25

This Land Is Ours

T HE WORRY and uneasiness began in 1788, and they could not be
stilled. It was a terrible year. Crops had failed, and all that winter
and the next spring people had no bread. It was said that in Detroit
the French were eating grass and that already, by July 1789, five
children had starved to death. Boats came down Lake Erie in search of
corn and flour and returned home empty. At Niagara they were killing
and eating their horses. White Loyalists suffered, but Indians suffered
the most, for their agriculture, generally without plows or men's work,
was not so productive as that of the whites. Lord Dorchester could not
send up provisions to the Grand River, for Quebec was in great want,
too, but he did give the new settlement a seine. Famine prevailed on
both sides of the border. One of Samuel Kirkland's Indians walked 120
miles to get a bushel and a peck of corn, and another Indian told
Kirkland that his family had not tasted bread or meat for many days.
They had had nothing to eat, he said, but herbs and sometimes small
fish, and he was so weak he could not hoe his corn. "I have been
travelling all day among white people," he went on, "but they can't
give me anything. I have two shillings in money, but they won't look
at it."[1]

As if hunger and deprivation were not enough, Joseph became
aware that some of his people were drifting away. Slowly the Grand
River was losing population. Individuals and families were always
coming and going from one side of the border to the other, but now
there was more going than coming.[2] He knew why. Among the Indians rights went with residence. Any Indian could cross the border
and join his brethren in the United States and share in all that they

had. And the Indians in the United States had more than those at the Grand River. The American Six Nations were selling most of their land. Though in one way it was a heartbreaking thing for Joseph to watch, he knew it was a necessity, and he believed that his American kin were wisely providing for their future. Their annuities would go on forever. They would always have something coming in, and the foolish, eyes blinded by liquor and gewgaws, could never spend everything at once. Joseph did not think the annuities paltry. Nor did he denounce the selling prices as inadequate. On the contrary. Year by year he kept up with what the Americans were receiving, and in time he would be speaking wistfully of the "great income" which the Senecas, especially, had assured themselves.[3]

It was enough to make any man think, and Joseph thought. The Indians were so vulnerable to life's misfortunes. The death or disabling of a breadwinner, strange turns in the weather, a horde of locusts—all these disasters seemed to hurt them more than they hurt whites. They had not learned from their white neighbors all that he had hoped. The old ways were gone. Sadly Joseph had to admit that. The long, narrow strip of land along the Grand River, the gift of General Haldimand which had seemed so generous, was too confined for hunting. More and more the Grand River land was hemmed in by white settlements, and the game was fast disappearing. Hunting no longer provided a decent subsistence. The fur trade was receding farther away. Remote Indians whose names he scarcely knew were now the important factors in the trade. Agriculture would soon be the mainstay of Canada. What could his people do? There were the presents, the expense of which caused so much discontent in high places, but the presents did not include a full allowance of necessities, lest they injure trade and the traders complain. The presents did not even take care of the helpless, the old men, the women, and children.[4] Joseph was so used to begging for necessaries for his people that the begging had become second nature. Did it ever occur to him that the political independence which he valued so highly was not likely to endure through an ever-increasing reliance on gifts for a livelihood? If so, he never mentioned it. He considered the presents as payments for past services, and always clung to this idea. Yet it would be no less than a galling experience for him when, in 1793, at the height of his disagreements with McKee, he would have to beg McKee three times to come to his aid with provisions and transport for his sick.[5]

But by 1790 Joseph was thinking only of the good fortune of the American Six Nations. He could find some cheer in the fact that the Grand River Indians also had salable land, even though it was true that they did not have so much as they had abandoned when they came to Canada. Still, instead of giving away their land as they had usually done or leasing it for a pittance to those who had some claim on them, could they not sell or lease enough of what was left to provide themselves with a good living? If his people had such security, would not the wanderers come back and perhaps bring friends with them?[6] The Grand River might yet be "respectable."

To think, with Joseph, was to act. First the Indians must find out exactly how much land they possessed and exactly where it was located. A council was held, and all agreed to that. But it was not Joseph who made the first official request for a survey. Others were better qualified by birth for such business. David was alive then, and he and Aaron (who had come back from Quinte) wrote to Sir John Johnson. They asked for a survey so that the Indians could learn their exact boundaries. This was needed, they said, because friends in the United States were coming over to join them.[7]

No white man objected to a survey—it was desired by the whites in neighboring townships as well as the Indians—and Augustus Jones and a party of workmen were sent, so the Indians supposed, to take the course of the Grand River. The work was completed early in 1791 and Jones's plan laid before the Nassau District land board in whose jurisdiction the business lay. Joseph, Henry Tekarihoga, and other leading chiefs met with the land board and agreed that the middle line of their grant should not follow the exact windings of the river, but that it should be drawn from an easterly bend near the river's mouth straight to the Mohawk Village. The Indians would have six miles on each side of this straight line.[8] Unfortunately the original plan which Joseph and the chiefs signed seems to have been lost. It is clear, however, that the river was not surveyed to its head; but the Indians agreed to the survey, no doubt thinking it was all right as far as it went.[9]

A severe disappointment was in store for the Indians. Little had been known about the interior of the country in 1784, and Jones's survey uncovered flaws in the description of Haldimand's grant. The Indians were to be told that their land did not continue so far as they had thought. They could not claim all the way to the headwaters of the river no matter how the grant was described, for Haldimand's original purchase from the Missisaugas did not extend that far north. In other words, the king had not owned (that is, he had not previously bought from the Missisaugas) all that Haldimand's grant specified.[10]

Joseph and the Indians were always indignant about this error. They thought it as much subterfuge as error, and they were never reconciled to it. However, they would never be permitted to keep any land above Jones's top survey line, or what later came to be known as Nichol Township.[11] Joseph could not forget his original contention at the time of Haldimand's purchase that no purchase from the Missisaugas was really necessary. The land, he still thought, had never belonged to those Indians. It was part of the old Six Nations "empire." This was what he thought, but he kept silent, for the Missisaugas were becoming more and more his friends.[12] He did not argue the point, and for many years he hoped for another royal purchase from those friendly people which would make his grant good.

The next step, for the Indians did not hear of the flaw in their grant at once, was to get a proper deed for the Grand River land. Joseph was sophisticated enough to know that something more was needed than Haldimand's mere license of occupation. He had tried to get a deed shortly after General Haldimand left Canada in such hurry and bustle that, as Joseph supposed, he had not had time to put his grant in the proper form. That winter Joseph had discussed the matter with Lieutenant Governor Henry Hamilton, Haldimand's temporary successor, and got the promise of a deed in early 1785.[13]

The promised deed was never forthcoming. Joseph grew so busy at home and in the west that he raised no complaint. For a few years the deed was not uppermost in his mind. It could wait. Then the Six Nations across the border began selling land, the Grand River population began to diminish, and Joseph thought of making a few land sales, himself. Lord Dorchester was approached about the deed. On June 22, 1789, Dorchester declared his thoughts on the subject to Sir John Johnson. "The Lands were promised to the Six-Nations & their posterity," he said. "They as a people are to have the free use and possession of them; and to them they shall be confirmed and secured in a distinct and permanent manner." Lord Dorchester wanted the Indians to be fully satisfied about their grant, but he seems not to have been thinking of a deed in fee simple. He said nothing about a right of alienation. The lands were to be secured "to the Six Nations and their posterity forever." Apparently only that.[14]

Nothing was heard from the Indian department or anyone else regarding the desired "Writings," and in 1790 David and Aaron requested a deed from Sir John at the same time they wrote to request the survey.[15] It turned out that the deed was not so easily obtained as the survey. Yet Joseph continued hopeful, and he even set up some conditions for the deed. He wanted such an instrument as Haldimand had promised, not one which contained many restraints, "otherways," he said, in early 1791, "we shall look upon it not much better than a

Yankee deed or grant to their Indian friends."[16] It was the most cutting thing which Joseph could think of to say.

That same year, 1791, witnessed the creation of Upper and Lower Canada. Then, in the fall, Lieutenant Governor John Graves Simcoe arrived at Quebec on his way west. It was not long till Joseph began to hear some reports that horrified him. It seems that Simcoe and the Nassau land board, according to the reports, were discussing the curtailment of his grant! This was the first time Joseph was apprised of the possibility of a curtailment, and he thought it was Simcoe, rather than the Nassau land board, who was at the bottom of it.[17] Greatly alarmed, he wrote the new lieutenant governor about his concern, and the latter sent him written assurances that he was willing to provide a deed.[18]

Joseph was so indignant that he could not have greeted Simcoe with anything but false friendliness when the latter showed up at Niagara. Simcoe came well recommended to Joseph. The Duke of Northumberland had written from England that he was an intimate friend of his, that he was "brave, humane, sensible, and honest." "In short," added the duke, "he is worthy to be a Mohawk." Joseph was not so sure about that although Simcoe came bearing gifts: a dollar, a brace of pistols from the duke, and other things. "Love him at first for my sake," the duke had urged, "and you will soon come to love him for his own."[19] Well, Joseph would see what happened when the matter of the deed came up.

Simcoe had arrived in Upper Canada, knowing very little about the Haldimand grant. He had not known the grant was so large or that it extended from the mouth of the river to its source. When Joseph produced the very document in council, Simcoe was amazed. He at once assured the Indians that he wished to construe Haldimand's promise in a liberal manner. This assurance, he thought, both justice and policy demanded. During the early months of his government war between the Americans and the British was more than a possibility. It was no time to anger Indians.[20] Apparently Simcoe and Joseph then came to "a proper understanding" (as Joseph later termed it) on the matter of the grant's extent. Whether the understanding was placed on the (now) lost map with the signatures or whether it was only verbal, we do not know. Nor does Joseph say explicitly that the understanding was with Simcoe. He said it took place shortly *after* the formation of the Upper Canada government and *after* the Indians had learned of "an attempt . . . to curtail our land." If so, the understanding would have had to be with Simcoe. What Joseph considered "a proper understanding" we also do not know, but we may be sure it was *not* to give up the upper part of the river. Joseph always looked forward to another purchase from the Missisaugas, and he never would have consented to less.[21] If we may judge from his subsequent actions and his words, he always expected that when the rest of the land was needed, it would be bought for him.

Joseph was in and out of Newark many times in Simcoe's first year on the business of the deed. On one of these occasions, when Joseph explained why the deed was so necessary, Simcoe remonstrated with him, saying the Indians would only lease their lands to landjobbers and render the king's benevolence to them ineffectual. They would find themselves, as in the past, at the mercy of speculators. Joseph replied, Simcoe wrote, that the Indians "were not always to be fools because they had once been such."[22] If Simcoe could not persuade Joseph to forgo land sales, he then tried to persuade him to sell only to the king. There were certain tracts the king could use.[23] In the mean-time Simcoe was talking to Cornplanter. He told Cornplanter that the Haldimand grant had been made not merely to Joseph and the Mohawks but to all the Six Nations, even those who lived in the United States. Cornplanter and the Senecas got the idea that they had a valid interest in what took place on the Grand River.[24]

In early December 1792, Joseph dined at Navy Hall with the lieutenant governor and his wife. Though the lieutenant governor had been pleased by the report of the chief's good behavior in Philadel-phia, by this time he was not so pleased with other aspects of his behavior. Little Mrs. Simcoe, who certainly knew enough from her husband to color her opinion, tells us that Joseph was richly dressed in an English coat, with a handsome crimson silk blanket with gold fringe and a fur cap, and wearing the perfume of a sweet-grass neck-lace; but she was not favorably impressed with his appearance. She thought his countenance "expressive of art or cunning."[25] The lack of good feeling was mutual. Joseph did not like, and never would like, Simcoe.

Simcoe presented his deed to the Indians at a council at Newark on January 14, 1793. Joseph had promised that every Indian who understood English should be there, and no doubt he saw to it that they were.[26] The deed was drawn up according to Augustus Jones's survey. Simcoe had made a new purchase (for five shillings) from the Missisaugas, but all it did was to correct the northwest line of Hal-dimand's original purchase so that it conformed to the survey—a minor matter. Apparently nothing had been said to the Missisaugas about extending the purchase to the source of the Grand River.[27]

Simcoe's deed was objectionable to the Indians in other respects. They were expressly forbidden to alienate the land in any way except among themselves or to the king. Anyone else who might buy or lease any of the land was subject to removal as an intruder. Joseph saw his hands thoroughly tied, his hopes dashed.[28] But he had enough influence, so Simcoe said resentfully, to get the Indians to reject the deed at once, "and with circumstances in his behaviour that were highly offensive and improper."[29] Not long afterward Simcoe heard that there was a great tumult at the Grand River, that the chief women had met in council and had charged their warriors to defend their land.[30] The fine hand of Catharine was not usually so evident.

Joseph's pride had been dealt a severe blow. He was "totally dispirited," he said, and he intimated to McKee (this was in early 1793 before the break between the two men) that his loyalty was shaken. He thought the situation of the Indians as mere occupiers of the soil almost unbearable.[31]

But the hectic events of the next two years did not leave Joseph much time for repining or for attacking the intolerable situation. These were the days when he was trying to work out a reasonable peace between the Indian confederation and the United States, and he was absent from home on many long journeys. The trouble over the Grand River lands quieted down. This suited Lieutenant Governor Simcoe very well. He was doing, as he said, "my utmost to procrastinate any decision on them."[32] He expected the imminent return of Sir John Johnson from abroad. Perhaps Sir John's presence would prove a soothing influence. Simcoe, too, was busy. He was bracing himself and Upper Canada against the inevitable American conflict: building roads, establishing his new capital, looking for the right kind of immigrants to settle in the province—loyal immigrants who, he hoped, would strengthen the some ten thousand whites in their weak and widely scattered districts. The Indians must not be agitated *now*.

In early 1794 Simcoe heard to his great disappointment that Brant had returned to the fray. The unruly chief had held another council at the Grand River.[33] Appearances to the contrary, he had not forgotten about the deed. There was good reason for Joseph's concern. The winter of 1793–94 had been uncommonly mild. In harbors which should have been frozen over scarcely any ice could be seen. Even when cold finally descended, so little snow accumulated that the hungry Indians could not track deer. By February 1794, their usual hunts ruined, they were in an almost starving condition.

Not knowing what to do about the deed, Simcoe, in spite of Brant's renewed complaints, still did nothing. War's alarms were

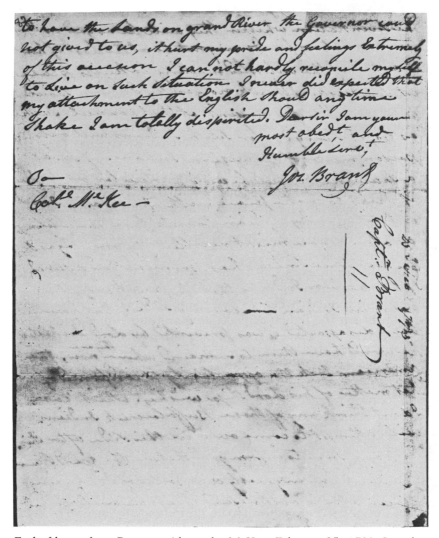

End of letter from Brant to Alexander McKee, February 25, 1793. Joseph is
"totally dispirited" about the Indians' land. Joseph's handwriting is about as
good as anybody's, but his grammar is pretty bad. Most of the time Joseph
managed to find someone to write letters for him. *Courtesy of The Public
Archives of Canada, Ottawa.*

keeping him fully occupied, anyway. Later in 1794 Joseph and many
of his warriors were absent at harvest time and consequently had a
poor crop. Distress at the Grand River continued on into 1795. Joseph

tried to get some extra presents for his people, but there was not enough in the Indian store to take care of all the needy.[34] It was now vitally necessary to sell some land. The Indians had to have a money income. They could not subsist as they once did.

Joseph seized the bull by the horns. On March 2, 1795, a tract twelve miles square at the second fork of the Grand River, a little above Dundas Street, Simcoe's new east-west road, and above the last Indian settlement, was sold to Philip Stedman of Fort Erie. Stedman was an old-time Loyalist whom the Indians had known for many years. The deed to this great tract was signed by the sachems and chief warriors of the various nations, but they thoughtfully reserved one thousand acres out of it as a gift to their Captain Joseph Brant. (No doubt Joseph and the Indians considered this gift as just payment for his many services.) The consideration named in the deed was some £10,250 which was recited as paid in hand—though subsequent events proved that was not so. This was the tract later known as Block 1.[35] Joseph and Stedman managed to get the deed recorded by William Jarvis, provincial secretary and Joseph's fellow Mason.[36]

As a buyer Philip Stedman was unexceptionable. However, Simcoe had wanted some of this wild land to expedite his new communication between Lake Ontario and the Thames River. Also, this was a far greater tract than under present government regulations was ever likely to fall into the hands of one individual, and a good many people besides Simcoe and lesser officials were scandalized. Look what this Indian was doing! Everyone knew, of course, that Brant was the prime mover in the affair.

It was Joseph's belief that his people owned their Grand River land just as surely as they had once owned their Mohawk River land. The one, he understood, had been given in lieu of the other.[37] As we have seen, he had always contended that the Indians were an independent people. They were allies of Britain, not subjects. *Why should they not do what they wished with their own property?* He saw that this was now the great overriding question; upon its answer all his hopes and plans for the Grand River settlements depended. Even a small Longhouse could enjoy freedom. Joseph's anger and bitterness had been growing for many months. He was weary of the lieutenant governor's temporizing. He determined to bring the great question of independence to an immediate issue. He determined to establish the legal status of the Indians once and for all and in so doing, of course, to force his views on the British government. Shortly after the Stedman sale he held an auction and sold two or three more huge blocks of country, this time to the highest bidder. This was the procedure Simcoe had advised in the case the Indians should be allowed to sell, but any sort of sale without specific government permission, Joseph knew, Simcoe would condemn utterly.[38]

Joseph's records for this period, if he kept any, are unavailable, but later records show that Block 2 was knocked down to Richard Beasley, trader, miller, and innkeeper, who had a business at the head of Lake Ontario, and two associates, Joseph's friend, Jean Baptiste Rousseau, and James Wilson; and Block 3 went to William Wallace, of whose previous association with Joseph less is known. There is some mystery and controversy as to who bought Block 4 or, indeed, whether it was sold at all at this time. These three great tracts of land, each containing tens of thousands of acres, were situated on the north side of Dundas Street, which crossed the Grand River a little above Brant's Town, and, with Stedman's, they comprised everything which, by Jones's survey of 1791, the Indians were acknowledged to own on the upper river. The Indians, according to Joseph, were not using this northern property and wished to dispose of it in such a way as to assure themselves an annual income.[39]

Much censure followed this drastic action. Joseph Chew, whom Joseph had always considered his friend, was among those who deplored what he had done. Stung, Joseph indignantly inquired of Chew's son, who was in the Indian department at Newark, and who reported it to the older man, "I see your father . . . says he shall be sorry if we should have disposed of any of our land, Why dont he give me his reasons for it why should he be sorry[?]"[40] Of course a swirl of rumors floated across the border. Israel Chapin, Jr., heard that Joseph had declared if Simcoe "presists [sic] in his imposisions [sic] he will Join some other people that will use him better—" It was also gossiped that Joseph was getting ready to build on the American side of the Niagara River and that he had his eye on various tracts across the border. At this time, with Indian affairs still unsettled in the west, Chapin was obviously hopeful that the rumors were true.[41]

In August Joseph and a great throng of Grand River Indians came down to Fort Erie to a general Six Nations council which Simcoe was holding in order to circumvent some of Pickering's doings. At this council Joseph and his supporters were so importunate about their lands that Simcoe, who wanted no other business to intrude just then, agreed to go to the Grand River to discuss their grievances.[42] Accordingly, in the fall, Simcoe made the journey to the Grand River. Here, at another council, he heard the Indians' complaints, and promised, probably reluctantly, to submit the whole question of their lands to Lord Dorchester.[43]

Simcoe, who had already been subject to various indispositions, went home from the Grand River very ill. He was disheartened. In his administration of Upper Canada little had come about as he wished. His policies for settling the province had gone awry, and Dorchester seemed to delight in opposing him at every turn. And in spite of his success in thwarting the Americans in 1793, he had no further hope of annexing the American west now that Spain had opened the Mississippi to their traffic. By the end of 1795 he was applying for a leave of absence. Ill health was his reason. He looked yellow as saffron, some-one said.

Though Joseph could take throngs of supporters to a council with Simcoe, it must not be supposed that everything he and the sachems were doing was approved by everybody on the Grand River. There had always been some Indians who did not welcome whites in their vicin-ity. From the very beginning some of the Indians did not get along well with the old white Loyalists who lived among them, and they did not look forward to seeing more whites come in. No matter how often Joseph urged them, they were not interested in learning about agricul-ture and the mechanic arts. There were also Indians who, when they observed surveyors at work, feared their own holdings might be sur-veyed and divided up into individual plots; such people preferred the old way of holding land in common. There had been for years other divisions among the Grand River Indians—young versus old, for in-stance, or Fort Hunter Mohawks against Canajoharie Mohawks, or one clan or one nation against some other, or even one chief against some other chief; and at times Joseph had had to take sides in order to settle matters, and someone was invariably offended. There were also people on the Grand River who simply did not like Joseph Brant. The feeling was something more than honest disagreement with his policies. It did not require a great stretch of memory to recall Brant's real status among them. Many people could easily think back fifteen years. Brant's great rise was something to ponder on. Such ponderings led to resentment and jealousy, and jealousy naturally led to the conclusion that Joseph Brant was becoming too great a man.

After Lieutenant Governor Simcoe left the Grand River in Octo-ber 1795, the local Indians went over to the head of Lake Ontario where, since Dundas Street had been opened up, they were in the habit of meeting the boats and collecting their annual presents. There were two respectable inns in the vicinity, one kept by Richard Beas-ley, with a little tavern of Beasley's close by, and a large government inn some miles nearer the main lake built for the benefit of travelers. There were also a number of huts where liquor could be had, at least temporarily, while the Indians were gathered. Many of the Indians were drinking heavily. One day in early November Joseph entered one of these drinking places, maybe Beasley's, maybe the government inn, but more likely one of the smaller houses. The house appears to have had two rooms. Joseph remained in one room. His son Isaac was in the other.

Somehow a fight erupted between father and son. The evidence is never better than second-hand, and some of it is the rankest hearsay, and none of it comes from Joseph himself, but according to all accounts Joseph was not the aggressor. William Johnson Chew, son of Joseph Chew, had been helping to distribute the annual largess, and he, though apparently not present at the actual scene, was certainly not far off. Chew wrote his father:

> When at the Head of the Lake Capt. Brant's son Isaac got drunk and abused his father in the most shameful manner, making use of the most opprobious [sic] epithets that can be imagined, and on Capt. Brant's going into the room where he was made a stroke at him with a knife, which Capt. Brant warded off with his hand, at the same time wounded his son on the head with a Dirke they were almost instantly parted by people present, but the wound which Isaac received terminated his existence two days after at the Grand River, where he made out to get. Capt. Brant was badly hurt in the hand. It is almost unnecessary to mention that the fatal issue of this contest renders him very unhappy.[44]

Hearsay adds many details, often contradictory, to fill in the story. It was said Isaac was making a great din, and that his father told him to be quiet, whereupon Isaac raved and cursed, and Joseph tried to put him out. Or Isaac had been threatening his father's life, and when his father walked by him, and went into a back room and shut the door, Isaac broke open the door. Or that Isaac had heard rumors, a few hours before, that Joseph and the chiefs had sold some Indian land and appropriated part of the proceeds to themselves. All accounts agree the fracas occurred near the door, that Brant struck in self defense, and that Isaac got a scalp wound which did not look dangerous. But Isaac would not allow the wound to be dressed and tore off the bandages as often as they were put on. Or that an old Indian dressed it with a "composition of strong adhesive Qualities." While Isaac lay dying, he sent three times for his father who had not yet reached home; and after his death a loaded pistol being found under his pillow, it was supposed he still meant to kill his parent.[45]

Nobody appears to have blamed Joseph. Simcoe thought it fortunate that Isaac fell the victim of his own atrocity. Simcoe thought Isaac "dangerous."[46] McKee, who knew what Joseph was saying about him and could have had no especial fondness for him, hoped the matter would be carried no further.[47] Stone, Joseph's biographer, who says he made great efforts to find out the truth from witnesses, puts no blame on Joseph.[48] Joseph promptly surrendered his commission, but Dorchester refused to accept it.[49] It was generally agreed that the unfortunate father deeply regretted the death and the way it happened, and John Norton says he "expressed great Contrition" to him.[50] But Joseph was always reserved about his private affairs. To Israel Chapin, Jr., a few days later, he gave as an excuse for not being able to keep an appointment with him at Fort Erie that, an "unfortunate accident" having happened in his family, he was obliged to return home at once.[51] Joseph was never brought to trial.

It is clear, as the Reverend John Stuart says, that Isaac had allied himself with the Grand River malcontents.[52] That being the case, even Joseph would have admitted that if strangers were meditating the killing of an unpopular leader, someone in his family ought to attend to it before anyone else could. And Joseph would have admitted that drunkenness was an excuse for anything. Nobody in Upper Canada was greatly concerned about Isaac's demise. Joseph took care of Isaac's young family and later obtained some military land for them.[53] Only across the border, through Kirkland's Oneidas, the notion got abroad that the monster, Brant, had actually murdered his own son. Most of the Americans who heard this version of the story, considering Joseph's reputation among them, probably believed it.[54]

In early 1796 Lord Dorchester sent Simcoe a deed which he thought could be presented to the Grand River Indians. This deed, which had been prepared by the attorney general of Lower Canada, gave the Indians authority to lease or sell their land provided it was first offered to the king. This, it was thought, would protect both the Indians and the crown. Simcoe, who had not been eager to refer the matter to Dorchester in the first place, resented this document a little, for, as he said, he had his own law officers and did not need advice from Lower Canada. Simcoe's own attorney general, John White, found a great deal of fault with Dorchester's deed. White thought the deed would not do at all since the Indians claimed to be allies, not subjects, and therefore must be considered aliens. No problems of this nature were to come up, however, for as it turned out, the Indians—meaning Joseph Brant—rejected the new deed immediately, Joseph even traveling to Montreal to register his objections at the headquarters of the Indian department.

Joseph said he did not mind making the first offer to the king, but he did object to the fact that the *Six* Nations were named as owners. He thought the Indians actually living on the Grand River should be named sole owners, for the phrase, "Six Nations," also included all those of that designation living across the border, even the detested Oneidas. (Joseph preferred to ignore the Oneidas altogether, and invariably called his Loyalist Oneidas, Oquagas.) Joseph also objected to a reversionary right in the king if the Indian owners failed to perform their obligations under the deed; he feared they might unwittingly transgress or that some of the American Six Nations might transgress (for it seemed as though this was possible under the deed), and the Grand River Indians, innocent of wrongdoing, perhaps lose everything. All in all, Joseph thought the deed too "complicated," and he refused it. Now the Indians and the government of Upper Canada had come to another stalemate.[55]

Joseph dropped a hint to the younger Chew that he was going to take matters into his own hands.[56] To Simcoe he said if the two sample deeds were the best that could be given him, then he would content himself with General Haldimand's grant.[57] Lord Dorchester made no objection to this; if the Indians preferred the Haldimand title, it was all right with him—no other should be forced upon them.[58]

Since Simcoe could see that Dorchester was inclined to favor the Indians as much as possible, he promised Joseph that the attorney general would draw up the necessary deeds for Joseph's buyers as soon as the tracts in question had been surveyed and surrendered to the king.[59] Joseph had to put his reliance on this promise. Yet he was uneasy, for he heard that Simcoe and some of his partisans in and out of the government were conspiring with the American branch of the Senecas to claim ownership in the Grand River lands.[60] This was an application of the dish with one spoon that Joseph could not like. He had been ready enough to argue that the entire Six Nations, having conquered the west by their joint efforts, had a claim to the west. But the Haldimand grant fell into another category. He had obtained that land for those who chose to live there. When the Senecas, or any other Indians (except possibly the Oneidas), moved over to the Grand River, then and only then, they might share in the land or its income. Did the Senecas share their good income with the Grand River people? No, they did not. Joseph had certainly once argued that the Grand River was a part of the Six Nations empire, conquered long ago. However, in deference to the Missisaugas, he had pushed this idea to the back of his mind. He did not intend to bring it out again, outmoded as it was, merely to favor the American Senecas. Furthermore, these Senecas, as Israel Chapin, Jr., for one, could testify, had in public council given up all right of interfering in the Grand River lands. This was the position Joseph was ready to defend.[61]

The surveying began in early June, and Joseph had an opportunity to consult several times with the surveyors. He wanted the surveyors to go over his northern property and try to reconcile the Haldimand grant with the previous Missisauga purchase. This was not, and indeed could not be, done. There was no getting around the necessity of making another purchase of the Missisaugas if the grant was to be taken to the source of the river.[62] In this connection, it should be noted that Lord Dorchester, in sending his deed to Simcoe, asked by what authority the Indian lands at the Grand River had been curtailed in their limits. General Haldimand's grant might be extended, he said, but never contracted.[63] Simcoe answered that he agreed with this sentiment, but that the original survey of the lands appeared to have been done with the Indians' entire approval and with no desire by anyone to limit them.[64]

Perhaps an additional purchase might have been arranged with the friendly Missisaugas but, unfortunately for the Grand River Indians, Dorchester sailed for England in early July. Dorchester's pride had been stung by what he considered an official reprimand for the strong speech against the Americans in 1794. Moreover, he liked Simcoe no better than Simcoe liked him, and he found it increasingly distasteful to work with him. Discontented and unhappy about the whole situation, it was time, he felt, to give up his office and go home. His great services to Canada, his long sojourn in America, were ended. It was a final parting of the ways. Whatever of favor Joseph and the Indians might hope to get from on high, it would never again have its source in the delicate honor of my Lord Dorchester.

Not long afterward Lieutenant Governor Simcoe, too, left for England. It was expected that he would eventually return to Upper Canada, and an administrator was appointed to carry on during his absence. Simcoe was under the impression that all necessary government documents and correspondence had been left for the guidance of his temporary successor. He was mistaken. Very little had been left. The elderly administrator, a man named Peter Russell, was almost wholly in the dark about such important affairs as Indian relations. Nor was he the sort of man who would be disposed to take the initiative in that doubtful sphere. Joseph and the Indians could hope for no especial favors from the timid Russell even had he been inclined to grant them.

Shortly before the departure of Dorchester and just as the Americans were about to take over Fort Niagara, the Grand River people lost their nearest old friend. On May 13, 1796, John Butler, that gentle man, who had been ailing so long but who had always done whatever he could to help his Indian charges, died. Butler was the last link with the old home in New York, for Sir John Johnson, absent so much and never a real intimate, hardly counted. Joseph himself performed the sad condolence. He spoke the solemn words of the Indian ceremony and covered the grave with a great belt of black wampum that the deceased might rest in peace. "His memory," he declared, "will ever be dear to us."[65]

Next day Joseph recommended that William Claus, Daniel Claus's young son, who was stationed in Canada with his regiment, should fill Butler's vacant place at British Niagara.[66] Young Claus soon got the appointment, for many influential whites, as well as Joseph and the Indians, thought his family deserved some good from the hands of government. Joseph naturally assumed that the elevation of Daniel Claus's son would insure the smoothest of Indian relations.[67] Joseph did not know William Claus as well as he thought he did.

Another event occurred that summer that caused Joseph much concern—and later some careful reflection. In August Wabakenin, Joseph's Missisauga friend, came to an untimely end. It happened at York where the Missisaugas had been camping and fishing. They had sold some of their catch and bought liquor. Wabakenin, a little overcome by his potations, had gone to sleep under an upturned canoe. That evening Wabakenin's sister had a rendezvous with a soldier. As the love-smitten soldier led the maiden out of the camp, Wabakenin's wife, not knowing the girl went willingly, set up an outcry. The whites are going to kill your sister, she screamed to the chief. The latter, dazed with sleep and drink, leaped up, struck his head against the canoe, and went staggering after the couple. The soldier, having already given his inamorata a dollar and some rum, took offense at this pursuit. A scuffle ensued, and the soldier, evidently a big, strong fellow, gave poor Wabakenin such a blow as to knock him senseless. Next day the chief died.

There was a great uproar among the Missisaugas. They held a council at Niagara with the commandant of Fort George and complained bitterly, for Wabakenin was held in high respect by his people. What to do? The worried whites knew the chief also had many influential relatives among the Chippewas and other Indians about the lakes who, it was feared, might take some bloody revenge for his death. The new administrator, Peter Russell, was especially upset. All sorts of warlike rumors were going on in the west just then or, as might almost be said, as usual. It must be remembered that the war in Europe had not abated, and who knew what the French or Spanish, or both, might be plotting on the Mississippi? The Indians *must* be kept in good humor. Presents to Wabakenin's family and a fine public funeral might not suffice on this occasion. It was decided to try the soldier for murder. He was indicted, a proper trial was set in motion and would have proceeded, no doubt, to some judgment if any of the Indian witnesses who had been summoned, but who understood nothing of indictments and trials, had appeared. In this nebulous manner the sad affair of Wabakenin's death came to an end.[68]

Now the unfortunate Missisaugas were left with nobody but an ignorant, drunken chief (the worthy Wabakenin's rightful successor) at the head of their affairs. Aghast at their predicament, they begged Joseph Brant anew to take them under his wing. They particularly needed his help in land matters. So for the second time Joseph promised the Missisaugas that he would do what he could for them.[69] Joseph may not have known that additional arms had been ordered for the local militia, but a person of much less discernment than he could have easily perceived that thoughts of an Indian uprising were still able to terrify white people. It was obvious that the new administration of Upper Canada was in a highly nervous state. The death of Wabakenin had exacerbated fears caused by withdrawal of British troops from the frontier posts.[70]

That fall Joseph began to plague the authorities (as they thought) to get his land sales confirmed. He did not intend to let them forget Simcoe's promise that when the surveys had been completed and the various tracts turned over to the king, the purchasers would get their deeds from the crown.[71] Administrator Russell, who would have had to sign the deeds, was not sure his friend, Simcoe, had made any promises at all to Brant, and he attempted to temporize. Russell was not a decisive man, except as regards being indecisive, and he wanted to get some instructions from the Duke of Portland or even from the absent Simcoe before he proceeded. He had been brought over to Canada by Simcoe who had known him years before when, as one of the secretaries to Sir Henry Clinton in the latter's more irresolute moments, he had performed in a highly satisfactory manner. He was too old now, he thought, to get much gratification from this latest appointment. He also feared sometimes he might die from the rigors of the Canadian winter. But as a man who had himself a great affinity for land (was it not the main means of wealth in this country?), he firmly believed Joseph Brant was getting ready to sell this very desirable commodity not only to undeserving persons but to ravenous Americans who would emigrate in such numbers as to be able to snatch all Upper Canada away from the king.[72]

Joseph blandly ignored the administrator's efforts to gain time and redoubled his importunities. It was obvious that he could not be put off much longer. On October 23 Russell capitulated to the extent that he promised he should get his deeds but that the Executive Council must concur in whatever was done. He requested the chief to put his proposals in writing.[73] Joseph was more than willing and, being in Niagara at the time, answered Russell's communication the very next day. The Indians' lawyer, he told him on October 24, would deliver the surveys and the names of the buyers. He himself would obtain a regular power of attorney from the chiefs to complete the business. He thanked Russell politely.[74]

Joseph did not let the grass grow under his feet. The description of the land in question was dated the next day, October 25. It mentioned an approximate 310,391 acres which were to be sold, and the names of the buyers were listed as Philip Stedman; Richard Beasley, St. John B. [Jean Baptiste] Rousseau, and James Wilson; James [William] Wallace; and J. D. [Y.] Cozens.[75] All were British subjects. Russell had to acknowledge that he could not find fault with Joseph's buyers. He was agreeably surprised, for the gossip had frightened him.[76]

Joseph, both then and since, has often been described as wanting to sell, or as selling, large tracts to Americans. In this respect he has been unjustly accused. As early as 1791 he showed himself strongly opposed to the introduction of former rebels into Canadian territory.[77] He has also been faulted for once negotiating with William De Berczy for the sale of some Grand River land, though De Berczy came to him with Simcoe's recommendation (this was before Simcoe had fully thought out what permitting the Indians to sell land might mean), and he was a native German who with a party of Germans had been living in the United States where he and they were having many difficulties. And if the impoverished De Berczy had some support for a short time from a company of American speculators, that was not Joseph's fault nor, under the circumstances, his business to inquire. Apparently De Berczy, a sort of jack-of-all-trades, could not meet Joseph's price, but he did paint a portrait of him and his dog while visiting him at the Grand River.[78] Joseph has also been accused of selling thousands of acres to the younger Israel Chapin. He never did.[79]

Joseph got his power of attorney from the Six Nations on November 2, 1796. It was an impressive document, signed by thirty-five civil and war chiefs, among them, of course, the leading sachem Henry

Joseph Brant, 1797 [1794?]. Painting by William Berczy. Joseph stands on the bank of the Grand River. In these days Joseph is very much the Indian. *Courtesy of The National Gallery of Canada, Ottawa.*

Tekarihoga, and witnessed by three well-known white men, John Norton, Robert Kerr, and John Young. The document had been written by the Indians' white lawyer, Alexander Stewart, a man soon to be married to a daughter of Brant Johnson. Joseph got the power to surrender certain described land to the king which was to be regranted to the persons he nominated, and he was to receive in his own name or in the names of his nominees security for the payment of debts due, as well as to receive money and give receipts, all such money to be used to purchase an annuity for the Indians. In this document Stewart had mistakenly described Joseph as "our Brother Sachem and Chief Warrior." This description must have been read in council, and apparently nobody objected.[80] The signing chiefs knew Joseph was acting as a sachem and that it was necessary that he should. Who else could do that sort of work? The Indians were too eager to get their annuity to be upset by a technicality.

Russell sent Joseph's proposals to the Duke of Portland and asked for instructions. He informed Joseph what he had done and also explained that because of the lateness of the season the Executive Council could not meet before spring. The disappointed Joseph was still perfectly polite. He told Russell he would try to get some help from Sir John Johnson and, if Sir John could do nothing, he was prepared to go to England to see Simcoe and the king's ministers.[81] Naturally any idea of Brant's going to England alarmed Russell.

No matter how polite Joseph had been to the Honorable Peter Russell, he was losing his patience. He knew evasive tactics when he saw them, and he unburdened himself to William Claus, the new Indian agent, whom he considered a friend. His speech, which had been written in October but could not be delivered till late November, created as great a stir as Lord Dorchester's against the Americans, though of course only in Upper Canada. Recounting all his grievances (and Joseph had a good memory for grievances), he ended by exclaiming, "What must we now think of General Haldimand's great Assurances, and friendly promises to us? must we look upon them as false? must we have the same opinion of all Lord Dorchester has said, as also Governor Simcoe's innumerable promises? surely our Father their Master never intended that we were to be trifled with in this manner. I repeat it again that it is not what we deserve." So many broken promises, he went on, would shake the white man's loyalty. The implication was plain that the Indians' loyalty, though still unshaken, could not survive indefinitely under such treatment.[82]

Russell did not get the report of this speech till January 1797. He was greatly perturbed and berated the Indian department for waiting so long in sending it to him. The speech, he thought, was an insult to government, and he feared it would inflame the minds of Brant's young warriors—then who knew what might happen? He invited the "powerful" chief to a meeting before as many of the Executive Council as could be hastily collected. Joseph was somewhat apologetic at the meeting, saying he was hurt because Russell had told him Haldimand did not realize the value of the lands he gave the Indians. It was then Russell's turn to apologize. On the whole the meeting was unsatisfactory to both parties. Russell, in describing it, wrote the Duke of Portland that it might be a good idea if the Indians were allowed to sell their lands provided it could be done in such a way as not to injure them. If their money could be put in trust and out of their power to spend the principal (and so of eventually becoming completely dependent on the bounty of government), then selling the land would be a good thing. So much Indian land in the midst of flourishing white settlements made the exercise of police authority very difficult, Russell said. [83]

To his friend Simcoe, Russell wrote that Brant was selling several townships to an American (naming a man who was not on Joseph's list), and had already received a good deal of money in part payment, "so that," he added, "we may soon expect to see an inundation of Americans pouring in upon us." He thought if Joseph felt bold enough "to insult Government when he had only his Mohawks to back him, how much more so will he feel when strengthened by a number of Aliens whose interest it will be to support him." At least two of Joseph's buyers were said to be on the verge of making great profits out of their bargains. In Russell's view, apparently, this made the chief's sales all the more reprehensible. [84]

After his meeting with Russell and the Executive Council Joseph wrote some explanatory notes on the margin of his much talked-about speech and sent them to Russell by the younger Chew. [85] Joseph's explanations, which were about as impatient as his original speech, did not mollify Russell. The administrator still thought the speech dangerous—and all the more so, because of warnings from Philadelphia that there were many French plots afoot, not only against the United States but apparently against Canada as well. Russell had just received his first news of the machinations of the French minister, Adet, who was doing his utmost by threats and stratagems to undermine American neutrality and American execution of the Jay treaty. Adet's moves had everyone by the ears in late 1796 and 1797, and Russell had good reason for alarm over the effects of French influence among the Indians. [86]

In the meantime Joseph did write Sir John Johnson, who had recently arrived from England, to see if he could do anything to advance the Indians' land business. Sir John answered that he could not (though he had tried), and that Joseph must wait for Russell's instructions from the ministry. However, Sir John, still balked in efforts to get a better settlement for his Loyalist claims, was in no good mood with those in power. He had just as lief favor the Indians as not. He told Joseph that he thoroughly agreed with him that the Indians ought to be permitted to sell some land and get an annuity for their support. It never took much to raise Joseph's spirits, and this was such an encouragement as to send them soaring.[87]

Joseph had threatened to go to England. This was only bravado for he did not have the money to go to England and did not know anyone likely to finance the trip for him. Then he thought of something else he could do which would probably serve his purpose and take much less time as well as money. He would go to Philadelphia and complain to the British minister. No doubt the British minister, as direct representative of the king, could set the Canadian authorities straight on the proper way to treat their Indian allies. As to who would pay his expenses, Joseph had an idea Thomas Morris would pay his expenses. He was right. Thomas Morris did just that.[88] Morris expected to have the aid of the influential Brant at his coming treaty with the Senecas. Brant would be very useful at Big Tree. How could Thomas Morris foresee that the great chief would not even put in an appearance at Big Tree?

Joseph set out for Philadelphia on January 29, 1797.[89] The easy water route was out of the question in winter except for sleighs on the Grand River, but when snow blanketed the rough roads and trails, land travel was at its best. After crossing the Niagara River the route to the American settlements still ran through a white wilderness of more than sixty miles, where the traveler had to carry saddlebags of food for himself and horse. At Canandaigua civilization began. Here Joseph was joined in his journey by Cornplanter, and the two old adversaries left Chapin's house together on February 6.[90] Thomas Morris paid the expenses of both, but each went to the American capital on a different mission. Cornplanter's mission obviously concerned his Allegheny Senecas and the sale of Seneca land to Morris. Joseph told young Chapin he meant to try to get an annuity from the United States for his Mohawks—evidently tying the annuity in Chapin's mind to intervention by Congress in the Connecticut Land Company affair—but Joseph's real mission, as we know, was with the British minister. Chapin thought the friendly chief told him all his secrets. He did not.[91] It is surprising to see Joseph and Cornplanter hobnobbing. However, they were not such enemies as they had been. Both felt more hostility now to Red Jacket than they felt for each other.

Several white gentlemen joined the two Indian gentlemen at

Canandaigua, and the party proceeded down the Mohawk (where Joseph could never feel quite safe) to Albany and then along the usual route to Philadelphia. The travelers did not tarry, and Joseph arrived in Philadelphia long before the month was out.[92] He had thoughtfully provided himself with two letters of introduction to Robert Liston, the new British minister, for George Hammond, whom he had seen in 1792, had left the country. One of these introductions came from Captain James Green, military secretary at Quebec, and the other from Major David Shank, commandant at Fort George on the British side of the Niagara River.[93]

Before Joseph made any attempt to present his credentials to Robert Liston, he settled down at an inn and began to talk. Maybe he got drunk—but maybe he was perfectly sober. At any rate Liston soon heard some very alarming gossip through persons who frequented the inn. The horrified diplomat heard that Brant "talked with great resentment of the Treatment he had met with from the King's Government of Canada, and threatened, *if he did not obtain redress through me* [Liston], that he would offer his Services to the French Minister Adet, and march his Mohawks to assist in effecting a Revolution, & overturning the British Government in the Province." Liston did not know how accurate this gossip was, but after he had seen Joseph he began to think it "not impossible" that he had used such language.[94]

Robert Liston was a diplomat, experienced and polished, much older than the departed George Hammond. When Joseph showed up at his house, the genial Liston heard him out with great tact and encouraged him to tell everything that was on his mind.[95] At first Joseph told his usual story, that the Grand River land was no longer suited for hunting and that the Indians were not suited to agriculture. If the whites could sell land, he asked Liston reasonably, why should not the Indians? Simcoe had promised him that they might. Then Joseph opened up and made some astounding charges. He accused the authorities in Upper Canada (and Liston understood he meant Peter Russell and Russell's friends in the government) of blocking the Grand River land sales because they wanted to get the land for themselves!

Joseph went into so many details about this business that Liston was at first too embarrassed even to repeat them to General Robert Prescott, Lord Dorchester's successor at Quebec, or to the ministry in London, but eventually he realized he must relate all that the chief had said. The Grand River lands, Joseph had declared, lay so near the new capital of Upper Canada that Russell could make a fortune by purchasing them for himself and his friends.[96] That summer, when Liston finally got the courage to reveal all these charges to General

Prescott, the latter replied that he feared there might be some truth in them.[97]

Liston did all that a good diplomat could in his conference, or conferences, with Joseph. He soothed him and promised he would try to help him. The chief seemed to him "so determined, so able, and so artful" that he thought he had better appear to go along with whatever he wished.[98] Though at first hesitant about telling everything, Liston did try to help or at least to clear up any misunderstanding which was poisoning the atmosphere in Upper Canada. He sent off a flurry of dispatches to both Lower and Upper Canada and to England.[99] Liston was very fearful of what French influence might accomplish, not only among the Indians, but on the Canadian and American frontiers in general, and among the French inhabitants throughout Canada.

Joseph did not remain long in Philadelphia. However, while he was there, he was entertained by a number of prominent men, though none was of the administration; for he took care to associate only with the French party in that brilliant but divided capital.[100] On the evening before he left he attended a dinner given by Aaron Burr, pro-French senator from New York, at which Adet and the French savant-traveler, Count Volney, were present. Burr recalled years later that Brant appeared taciturn at first and only opened up and expressed an opinion when the talk got around to the best way of civilizing the Indians. Joseph recommended intermarriage and amalgamation as the only way to accomplish this purpose. After the ice was broken Joseph became his usual talkative, sociable self, and Burr remembered that he was grave and humorous by turns, sometimes setting the table in a roar of laughter.[101] Burr was very interested in Joseph, whom he called "the King of the Mohawks." He sent letters to his daughter, Theodosia, and his ward, Natalie Delage, at home in New York City, advising them to arrange a breakfast party for the celebrated chief, and suggesting that they send his daughter, "the princess," some presents. The polished and courtly Burr spoke glowingly to the two young ladies of Brant's education and social presence.[102]

For the Federalists in Philadelphia Joseph had no time. He kept clear of all those who were trying to implement Jay's treaty, men who, regardless of their antecedents, were now thought of as pro-British. James McHenry, secretary of war, had been told of the chief's coming and repeatedly invited him to a conference. He did not go. McHenry also made an appointment for him to see President Washington. The invitation was a real honor, for the outgoing president (soon to be succeeded by John Adams and much occupied with plans to return to Mount Vernon) was winding up his administration at a time of grave

Joseph Brant, 1797. Painting by Charles Willson Peale. Joseph looks very self-satisfied; he knows he has just carried out a great coup. *Courtesy of the Independence National Historical Park Collection, Philadelphia.*

crisis, and could not receive all who wanted to pay their respects. Joseph did not keep the appointment with Washington.[103] It was a strange way to get an annuity for the Mohawks.

Joseph found time, however, to sit for a portrait by Charles Willson Peale.[104] This painting, which was to be added to Peale's famous portrait gallery and museum, would undoubtedly do much to maintain attendance at the large establishment near Third and Lombard Streets. Either Peale was singularly unperceptive during Joseph's sittings or else Joseph felt so confident of the outcome of his Philadelphia visit that he relaxed into a state of benign amiability. His expression shows no worry, no fear, no pain. He is certainly not the same person whom Gilbert Stuart saw in such anguish eleven years before. In Peale's version of him Joseph permits himself a little smile. We see the head and shoulders only and the usual dark hair, dark eyes and brows, and rather light complexion. There are the dramatic Indian accouterments, for this was a time to be the complete Indian: a scalp lock matted with red paint and decorated with a white feather, a band of metal rings around a shaved head with red and white flowers and greenery over the left ear, two streaks of red paint on his upper left cheek and another streak at the outer corner of his right eye, a red and black striped blanket with gold fringe thrown over his left shoulder, a white shirt printed with a small scattered design, a half-moon gorget of brass or gold hung on a blue ribbon around his neck, and a wide (probably silver) armband on his upper right arm. Though his forehead is furrowed Joseph does not show his nearly fifty-four years. He looks intelligent—and very, very bland. Or is it smug? Such a look might well have overspread the face of a smart tomcat who, with his own paw, had just upset the cream-pot and was about to enjoy its contents.[105]

26

Triumph!

JOSEPH LEFT Philadelphia on February 28. He was not accompanied on his return home by either Cornplanter or his white escort.[1] Somewhere in Jersey he almost came to blows with a man whom he disgustedly called a "Yankee colonel." His antagonist was probably someone who still resented the chief's well-known wartime atrocities.[2]

Joseph continued on to New York and took up his quarters at Batten's Hotel at the corner of John and Nassau Streets.[3] Here, in high good humor despite the Jersey unpleasantness, he held a sort of court and received a throng of visitors—eminent men in whose cultivated minds there was little room for thoughts of old atrocities. Among his visitors were Dr. Dingley and the celebrated scientist and educator, Dr. Joseph Priestley, the Honorable Jeromus Johnson of New York, and the Reverend Dr. Samuel Miller, a divine who was almost as interested in Indian customs and history as in theology.[4] Years later the Honorable Jeromus Johnson remembered that Joseph was very communicative. He talked of his visits to London, his life at the Grand River, his many possessions there and his happy black slaves; and he invited his hearers to visit him. He also spoke of his part in the Revolution, saying he now regretted it, and promised that he would never again take up the tomahawk against the United States.[5]

Long afterward the Reverend Dr. Miller also wrote some comments on Joseph's visit to New York in 1797. He told William L. Stone that Brant was "a remarkable man."

My personal intercourse with him [said Miller] was not considerable;
but it was quite sufficient to impress me with most respectful sentiments of his intellectual character, his personal dignity, and his
capacity to appear well in any society. I met with him repeatedly;—
was with him at a dining party—and listened to his conversation in
various situations—some of them rather trying; and was surprised at
the simple, easy, polished, and even court-like manners which he
was capable of assuming; though, at the same time, I was assured
that he was capable of being as great a savage as any individual of his
nation. I remember, on one occasion, that when some very imperti-
nent and unseasonable questions were addressed to him by a gentleman who ought to have known better, he evaded them with perfect
civility, and at the same time with an adroitness and address which
showed that he was fitted to be no mean diplomatist.[6]

If this praise appears somewhat extravagant, it must be remembered
that, as no Indians were present at these gatherings, Joseph did not
have to put on his Indian costume and regalia. No red streaks adorned
his face. He did not require an interpreter, but spoke English; and his
English was at least "tolerable."[7] Moreover, the true savant can forgive
much in a "savage" that he could not possibly overlook in some untutored person of his own kind.

That precocious child, little Miss Theodosia Burr, did as her father
suggested and invited the king of the Mohawks to dine. She chose as
her other guests some of the most distinguished gentlemen in the city,
Bishop Moore, for instance, and Drs. Bard and Hosack. Apparently
the affair went very well, and Brant exerted himself to please. As the
young lady jokingly told her father, from all the stories she had heard,
she scarcely knew what dishes would gratify her guest of honor. She
had even thought, she said, of trying to get a human head from the
hospital and of serving it up like a boar's head in a medieval hall![8]

Joseph had intended to travel by way of Connecticut and visit
Oliver Phelps at Suffield on his way back, but thought better of it as he
had no one to accompany him.[9] He returned up the Hudson, a route
which he knew. It was probably on this return journey that he walked
around a little church near Croton and stood at a window long enough
to watch the service. General Philip Van Cortlandt, leaving the
church, inquired who the well-dressed stranger was. Upon hearing
that it was the famous Brant, the general drove to the inn where
Joseph was staying and took him home with him to Van Cortlandt
manor house. Here over dinner the two old soldiers refought their
campaigns on the upper Delaware in 1778–79 and, as old soldiers will,

reminisced with the utmost amity of those dear, long-gone days when they were trying to kill each other.[10]

Joseph arrived at Albany, that old city of high Dutch roofs and elderly Dutchmen who still had their memories of a great fur trade, on March 9. Here he said what he had from the first, apparently, planned to say. He wrote Oliver Phelps, explaining why he had not come through Connecticut to visit him, and then went on to remark that his reception in Philadelphia "was such as I told you I did expect. that my stay there would be very short."[11] Obviously Joseph was eager to let it be known to all that he was not on good terms with anybody in the American capital who could be considered on the British side.

Joseph was not neglected in Albany. He met some of the most prominent inhabitants and reminisced of old times with General Peter Gansevoort, the hero of Fort Stanwix.[12] He then rode over to Hartford on his Connecticut Land Company business, for now it really was time to try to get that annuity for the Mohawks. Joseph was also received well in New England.[13] Somewhere along the way he bought a fine horse, took it back to Albany where it sickened and died, and then had to borrow money to buy another. He did not forget to pay the loan when he finally reached home.[14]

At Albany, John Wells whose whole family was destroyed at Cherry Valley was not so pleased to hear of Brant's visit, and made some threats which were relayed to the tight-lipped chief. Some other men had equally good memories and made similar threats, and Governor Jay was forced to send a bodyguard with Joseph through the Mohawk valley as far as German Flats, after which it was thought he might proceed safely alone.[15] So Joseph traveled on, ignoring Kirkland and the Oneidas again, and somewhere meeting up with Israel Chapin, Jr., who was going down himself to Philadelphia. To Chapin Joseph complained that no attention had been paid him as on his former trip to the American capital, and he added significantly that if Indians were ignored except when their services were needed, it was likely to cause bad feelings and prompt them to hostilities. Still, he did not appear to be angry.[16] When Joseph got home to the Grand River, he wrote Chapin a sarcastic letter about the poor treatment he had received from members of the government.[17] From all his remarks, both verbal and written, it appeared that if anybody was trying to cultivate his good will, it was not the pro-British contingent of Americans.

Joseph had returned by way of Buffalo Creek where he exerted himself a little in behalf of Thomas Morris' coming treaty with the Senecas. Gratitude called for this much—besides, it would be better for the Senecas to make the sale. April 18 found him finally at British Niagara where he wrote Morris regarding the latter's land business, and again invited him (and also Charles Williamson, agent for the famous Holland Land Company, who had bought a great tract from the Morrises) to visit him at the Grand River. The Senecas, he thought, would not be suspicious. He had no news, he added, except that the French in Lower Canada were ready to cut the throats of the British![18] Shortly afterward a man who was surveying on the Grand River reported to the authorities that an Indian of his party who had just returned from Brant's Town brought the news that Brant, when he got home, told his people to sit still for the time being, that they might have to join the French yet![19]

Repercussions from Joseph's Philadelphia visit were now being felt on both sides of the border. Secretary James McHenry, who had soon learned from tavern gossip that this influential chief had taken offense at his treatment by the Washington administration, was horrified now that there was so much trouble with France. Regardless of Wayne's treaty with the western Indians, which had seemed for a time to dissolve the menace on the frontier, Americans could no longer feel secure about the Indians. McHenry was deeply distressed about what hostile schemes Brant might be hatching. The worried secretary could not understand why Brant had taken offense, but he wrote Israel Chapin, Jr. (who had evidently confirmed the gossip when in Philadelphia, and who had now returned home) to try to arrange matters with the chief and find out what he was up to. McHenry sent Chapin four hundred dollars with which to do this. It was not good policy, he thought, to offer a crude bribe to Brant (though Chapin might give him a small present and assure him of American friendship); but there must be some means of getting at him through his friends.[20] Chapin replied that he thought he could do what was required.[21] What he did we do not know. Perhaps he realized then that there was no necessity to do very much, for he had just received a letter from Joseph which explained that he had gone to see the British minister on Grand River land business, and which asked him to forward a packet to the minister who had promised help. Chapin sent an abstract of Joseph's letter to McHenry to quiet his fears about Brant. But he may not have been able to quiet all McHenry's fears, for Joseph had added in his letter, almost as an afterthought, "We have no news but only flying reports that the French are endeavoring to insinuate themselves amongst the Indians to prevail on them to Act both against the British & Americans.—"[22]

Joseph had excited even greater fear in Canada than in the United

States. By the time he got home from the American capital letters were flying back and forth among Liston, Prescott, and Russell, and of course to England. Liston said tactfully he knew only what Brant had told him, a story which he found hard to believe; Prescott, obviously upset, sent a copy of Liston's letter on to Russell; and Russell was astonished and insulted that Brant should have questioned his motives and those of his friends.[23] Instructions from far-away England could not be known soon, and it seemed vitally necessary that those on the spot should act immediately to ward off the threatened danger. This was especially true in that the head of the government in Upper Canada had just been given additional powers over Indian relations in his province.

Wherever in America the influence of Britain and France was felt, there were the rumors of impending danger. From Philadelphia to Georgia, to Detroit, across the Detroit River to Amherstburg, to both Niagaras, to Quebec, to New England, it was believed that the French were coming in force. And the French would be helped by the Spaniards, for France and Spain had become friends; and Britain and Spain, in a wild gyration of policy and alliance, were now at war with each other. No rumor was too irrational for credence. The British population of Canada, supposing Spain about to transfer Louisiana to France, fearfully awaited an army of French and Spanish that was on its way up the Mississippi. This army would of course be augmented by Indians on both sides of the border who were assumed to be disaffected (for everyone knew the Indians had reason for disaffection); and the whole British-American west might go down to defeat. It was also firmly believed that Lower Canada and the St. Lawrence were in even greater danger from yet another French attack, this time from the sea or through Vermont, to be augmented by disgruntled French Canadians. The British of Canada did not for one moment suppose they had much hope of sending an expedition down the Mississippi to attack New Orleans, but they were quite willing to believe that an expedition could be sent up from New Orleans to attack them. And as arms and ammunition were being accumulated in both Canadas, so the Spanish in far-off New Orleans, fearful on their part of a combined British-American assault, also armed for defense and unwittingly fed the rumors. Dire prophecies were made to Liston in Philadelphia by frightened American officials who distrusted their own frontier people, and equally frightened officials in Canada who distrusted French Canadians and Indians poured forth the same fears wherever they went.

All these rumors were rooted in the realities of the political situation in Europe and America and undoubted French excesses both at home and abroad, and so had some reasonable basis. No one person could have started them. Joseph Brant could not have started them, but they were ready made for his purpose, and he did not hesitate to seize upon them. Joseph could warn William Claus on May 26 that the Shawnees and Ottawas had sent to tell him "that an evil message has come up the Otowa river, and from Mackinac relating to the French and the Spaniards on the Mississippi."[24] Matthew Elliott, long in the Indian department at Detroit, unintentionally added fuel to Joseph's flames by reporting from new Fort Malden (Amherstburg) that it is "beyond a doubt" that the French and Spanish are moving up the Mississippi.[25] Under such frightening conditions Administrator Russell, who had almost no regular soldiers in his entire province, declared he would have to ignore Joseph Brant's outrageous proceedings and act as if they had not occurred.[26] He was in even more of a quandary than before, for he had heard that Simcoe, whom he had expected to return, had been given an appointment elsewhere and might never return. The awful responsibility which he had confidently expected to relinquish was growing heavier and heavier, and there was no relinquishment in sight.

June 1797 was a busy month for Joseph. Since Russell had had to go to York for the meeting of Parliament on June 1, he invited Joseph to come to the new capital and consult with him and his Executive Council. He said he had always believed the Indians' desires should be complied with, subject to certain regulations which would secure them a permanent income (which he thought Joseph would accede to); and if the answer from England did not arrive soon, he and the Council would adjust all matters to Joseph's satisfaction.[27]

Joseph was pleased but a little wary. He told the surveyor general he was "fearful from experience" that many members of the Executive Council "would not exert themselves to be Generous to us." What would satisfy the Indians, he said (and of course Joseph knew that all his correspondence with any official was sent on to Russell), was "to be on the same footing with Government we were before the War"—that is, free and independent. And he thought if the Indians did not get what they wanted, the covenant chain was in danger of becoming rusted.[28] To the administrator he replied he did not mind waiting till the king's pleasure could be known. Nevertheless, he would come to York as soon as possible. There were other pressing matters he had to attend to first.[29] He referred mainly to the Caughnawaga trouble which was occupying a great deal of his time just then and which he thought could not be put off. Russell answered he wished to render the chain of

friendship brighter than ever, and asked Joseph for an explicit statement of his desires. He again invited him to come to York. This
second invitation was dated June 21.[30]

Joseph surprised Russell by appearing at his headquarters in York
on June 23. Russell asked him for a written statement of the Indians'
wishes about their land, a list of the townships to be sold, the names of
the purchasers, the price to be paid, the amount of money to be
deposited, and the amount of the expected annuity. Russell promised
to lay this statement before the Council, and with the Council's
concurrence he assured Joseph he would order the attorney general to
prepare the surrender that the Indians were to sign and the deeds
which were to be given to the purchasers. When all this had been
accomplished he would invite the Six Nations to meet him in council
at Niagara so that everything might be done publicly and in a manner
which could not be questioned as to its legality. Joseph seemed pleased
with Russell's reception of him (Russell thought), and left headquarters to get all his papers prepared. "This is the most Consequential Act
of my Administration," said Russell, "& fills my mind with apprehension. But sanctioned by the Commander in Chiefs [Prescott's] pressing
desire, the opinion of Mr. Liston, and the advice of the Council I
hope I shall be deemed covered from His Majesty's Censure for not
waiting for His Commands in this very pressing Exigence."[31]

Joseph got his statement ready in three days,[32] and Russell laid it
before the Executive Council on June 29. The Council had to decide
whether the Six Nations should be permitted to dispose of their lands
and whether the question should be settled before instructions came
from England. Before the day was over the Council, whether inclined
to be generous to the Indians or not, came to the unanimous conclusion that "under the present alarming aspect of affairs . . . which call
for the most conciliatory Conduct on the part of this Government to
all the Indian Nations in alliance with us," the wishes of the Six
Nations should be complied with. There was no necessity to wait to
hear from England.[33] This was not the decision which Russell had
hoped for. Of course he did not want to bring on an Indian war, but he
did hate to see all that fine land go to those particular purchasers—and
not even with the king's consent.

Russell thought Joseph's purchasers should pay the usual transfer
fees to the province. Joseph indignantly opposed this idea (for where
did that leave the question of Indian independence?), and a heated
controversy ensued. Again Joseph warned the covenant chain was in
danger of being broken.[34] Before the controversy could be settled,
word finally came from England, the long-awaited dispatch having

survived all the vicissitudes of war on the high seas. The Duke of
Portland wrote that the Six Nations, by the terms of their grant, had
no power of alienation, and he considered this prohibition wise and
foresighted. Since the Grand River leads directly into the heart of the
province, he continued, such an important tract should never become
the property of others without the king's special assent. Russell was
instructed to find out the amount of the annuity the Indians expected
to get from their sales so that the government might consider sub-
stituting an annuity in lieu of the lands.[35] This was the message Russell
wanted to hear, but it had come very late. It was already mid-July.
Was this too late?

Russell hastened to the Council on July 16 (by this time everyone
was back in Niagara) with two more questions. Did Brant's dissatisfaction over the transfer fees release the administrator from carrying out
his promise to the Indians? Did Portland's letter take the entire matter
out of Russell's hands? What Russell hoped for was to be forbidden to
proceed.[36] But the Council did not cooperate. It was the opinion of
every member that Russell had not been released from his promise. As
to Portland's letter, the Council did not think it imperative on Russell
literally to obey it; indeed, the Council was "unanimously of opinion
that in the present very alarming situation of the Province, when we
have every reason to expect an immediate invasion by the French &
Spaniards, aided by the numerous tribes of Indians which surround us,
the Executive Government is fully at liberty to act in such manner as
Emergencies may require." The opinion given on June 29 remained
unchanged. The Council also advised Russell to comply with the
wishes of the Grand River Indians "to the fullest extent, without any
Condition, restriction or reservation whatever." This settled the matter of the transfer fees. Then the Council ended its deliberations by
urging Russell to put the province in as good a posture of defense as
possible.[37] Such prodding was hardly necessary. Russell had been trying to arm ever since the death of Wabakenin.

As soon as Russell heard from Portland, and before he had put his
questions to the Executive Council, he invited the Grand River Indians to meet him, with Joseph coming a little ahead, to hear about
the king's parental regard for them.[38] When Joseph put in a hasty
appearance (of course he arrived after the Council meeting, and Russell was now going contrary to the Council's wishes), Russell told him
about Portland's letter. The sales were not to be confirmed, he explained, but the king was going to give the Indians an annuity equal to
what they were expecting from their purchasers. Joseph was furious.

The Indians, when they got the land, he said, understood that it was theirs to do with as they pleased. They understood they held it just as they had held their former lands on the Mohawk. Much talk followed, conciliatory on Russell's part, but with Joseph remaining adamant. Russell then offered to repay Brant's purchasers the money they had already advanced. Joseph angrily refused this offer. The bargains were closed, he said, and there was no other way to satisfy the purchasers. And if Russell had nothing else to propose, he had better meet the chiefs in council and tell them himself of the king's will. For his part he would take no further trouble in the business. In a rage he took up his hat and started to leave the room.

Let Russell tell the rest of the story as he told it to Portland a few days later. "I confess, my Lord, that I felt very unpleasantly at this Moment. I was well aware that this Man was deeply committed; that he had great Influence not only with his own Tribe, but with the rest of the five Nations, and most of the neighboring Indians; and that he was very capable of doing much mischief."[39] Many fears ran through Russell's mind, prompted not only by Brant's intransigence and the Council's urgings, but also by Matthew Elliott's warning which had just come to hand about the certainty of an invasion from the Mississippi.

There was nothing for Russell to do but to give in. The council with the Six Nations took place at Niagara on July 24–26, and there in a most public and solemn manner Russell again promised to confirm the Grand River sales. (And there were those who thought they saw far too many young warriors among Brant's Indian delegates—as many as three hundred of them, it was estimated,[40] while the entire population of little British Niagara, men, women, and children, and including the garrison of Fort George, scarcely exceeded that number.) Joseph in his answering speech announced that the Indians were satisfied *so far*. But he instructed Russell to tell the king the Indians wished to have such title for the rest of their lands "as will enable us to hold an Inheritable and Assignable Estate in them, having the power in ourselves to receive and grant Titles." This was no more, he declared, than what had been promised them and the principal inducement for their settling there. Russell agreed to consult the king about future sales. Reluctantly he also gave up the transfer fees.[41] Looking on at the council, but taking no part in the Grand River land business, were Red Jacket and a large number of Senecas from the United States. These people were concerned about the new rules in the British Indian department (for they got gifts from the British, too), and they sent a delegation down to Lower Canada for additional informa-tion about the changes.[42] The rest of the Senecas, as later events show, returned home full of thought.

Though Joseph wrote Thomas Morris on July 30 that he was con-tent with what had taken place at the meeting with Russell,[43] weeks and months of frustration soon followed. Joseph's early life on the Mohawk, his meager education, had not fitted him for all the business he had to undertake. Governmental regulations which must be com-plied with in every detail gave him much trouble. He had to provide the authorities with at least two more statements of intention, with lists of purchasers, survey maps, and accounts of moneys involved. There seemed to be endless letters to write, and nobody in his village to help except the ailing schoolmaster who already had enough to do, or someone like Augustus Jones who might be working in the vicin-ity,[44] or John Norton who visited from time to time but whose post was at Niagara and who had to live there. Even Joseph's older sons, schooled at Niagara, were probably better educated than he was; but eleven-, twelve-, or thirteen-year-olds could scarcely write acceptable business letters. Then there were the endless journeys, to York or to Niagara or to the head of Lake Ontario, in heat or cold, in high water or low, in snow or mud, past swamps and across portages. When he could not go by canoe or sledge, then he must go on horseback over roads which could only be described as execrable, where logs of many shapes and sizes had been laid corduroy fashion across the mire, but which did not greatly help the progress of man or beast, and over bridges which were equally bad, or through fording places when there was no bridge at all.

Joseph often conferred with surveyors, the surveyor general as well as those out in the field, and sometimes he walked beside the latter on the job.[45] He had to write to or confer with his purchasers and furnish them with survey data and other information.[46] The purchaser of Block 4, Joshua Cozens, was unable to make any sort of deposit, but Joseph amiably carried him for months on his lists.[47] A new tract, later called Block 6, was added at the request of John Docksteder who wished to procure a regular deed for himself so that he could legally sell his Grand River land to a buyer he had found. Docksteder's land had been a gift from the chiefs years before, and the Indians did not expect to receive anything from him or his assigns. Nevertheless, Joseph undertook the trouble of putting his white friend's grant in order, and he added to it a large piece of Indian land which he apparently also meant to sell to Docksteder's buyer.[48] There were also lawyers to be advised with, and at exorbitant expense. The traveler,

Isaac Weld, mentions that he met a lawyer (probably Alexander Stewart) on a Lake Ontario vessel who bewailed the fact that by not being at Niagara at a certain time to meet Brant, he (the lawyer) had missed one hundred pounds in fees. And Weld talked with this man in 1796, a year before Joseph's main press of business.[49]

Joseph had to find the money for these great legal fees, perhaps through advances from his buyers, for there was scarcely any other way; and he had to pay his own traveling expenses, for which he always said he was not reimbursed—of course the government was not providing him with transportation or food or lodging nowadays. He also had to find some way to pay for further surveys of the Grand River property, lines which were run between the whites and the Indians, for instance, or lines between the planting grounds of various nations. Augustus Jones (who had an Indian wife and children) did much of this work and received for his efforts a 999-year lease of 4,800 acres at a rent of one peppercorn annually.[50] If Joseph was engaged in fraud at his people's expense, as it was later charged by some who generally had their own axes to grind, one can only wonder how he managed it. Probably the only fault that can really be charged to him is that his record-keeping was poor.[51]

Fortunately for his peace of mind, Joseph got some heartwarming news in the midst of his innumerable difficulties. The Grand River settlements were *gaining* population. People who hoped for a share in the coming annuities were now moving over from the Bay of Quinte.[52] Joseph could feel more sure than ever that he was doing the right thing.

General Prescott was glad that the Six Nations land business was settled, though at first thought he wished it had been settled in a more liberal way—meaning, apparently, that he wished the Indians had been given complete control of their lands, to sell, lease, or keep, as they chose, any time in the future.[53] Robert Liston was glad the business was settled, too, for there was too much chance of an Indian uprising if Brant remained dissatisfied. Liston continued to correspond with all the parties involved. He tried to soothe Joseph's fears about the future disposal of Grand River land, though he wrote the ministry he would have been less equivocal to the chief had the political situation been less dangerous.[54] Administrator Russell was at least resigned to the settlement and glad the peril was over, though he could not help dragging his feet a little.

As for the Duke of Portland, he realized that Brant must have his way this time, though the government could not countenance similar liberality in the future. Portland ordered Russell, as new head of the

Indian department in Upper Canada, to see that the Indians were not permitted to work together. He wished to avoid all confederations, all special friendships among the Indian nations. It was the only way to render them harmless until the province acquired a more numerous white population. The various nations were not even to receive their presents at the same place.[55]

These new instructions from London came at a crucial moment. The government of Upper Canada had wished to buy a large tract of Missisauga land which lay between York and the head of Lake Ontario, a strategic location needed for the benefit of travelers going to and from the capital. The government expected to pay about two pence an acre. The perplexed Missisaugas went to their good friend, Brant, for advice. Joseph told them, in effect, to hold out for more money. This they did, and ended up asking the staggering price of three shillings four pence sterling an acre![56] This was far more than the government could pay. Portland's words, therefore, about the desirability of preventing Indian nations from becoming too friendly with one another fell on fertile ground. Joseph would live to rue his advice to the Missisaugas.

After Russell had given in to the Indians, warlike rumors continued to whirl about. On July 31, for instance, Robert Liston wrote from Philadelphia that the American secretary of war warned that French agents had been busy among the Mohawks, and not without success; and on August 9 Israel Chapin, Jr., informed his government that the Spanish, so he heard from the west, were giving the Indians large presents of arms and ammunition.

But amidst all the wild alarms of war a few wisps of calm truth began to emerge. These bits of truth, unfortunately, got entangled in a garrison intrigue at British Fort Malden and in the resulting charges and countercharges between the new commander at the fort and the resident western Indian department. The charges and a little of the truth were aired on August 23 when Captain Hector McLean, the new commander, reported that all seemed tranquil on the Mississippi, boldly adding that "Those having the direction of the Indian Dept. in this vicinity seem most eagerly to seize at every idle tale, which they never fail to magnify & exaggerate to answer their own private views."[57] And though there were still such stories as that a Spanish armed galley had got as far up the Mississippi as Prairie du Chien or that the Spanish were collected in force high up that river, this same Captain McLean, on September 24, reported that most of the Spanish at the post of St. Louis had hastily gone down the Mississippi; and he charged that ideas of Indian hostility were probably urged by the

Indian department to promote their corrupt schemes. McLean gave the local Indians some liquor and told them he had come to protect them against their agent, Matthew Elliott, whom he accused of many frauds.

Captain McLean and Matthew Elliott were now quarreling bitterly. The two appear to have disliked each other on sight, and the rumors of impending disaster gave McLean a weapon to use against Elliott. Though each man accused the other of spreading false accounts of Indian hostility, McLean's accusations carried more weight; for Elliott complained to his immediate supervisor, McKee, but McLean complained to Russell and Prescott. On November 10 McLean noted that the Indians had been spoiled by being given everything they wanted. "A certain artful Indian Chief in the vicinity of Niagara [meaning Brant, of course]" had been stimulated, he charged, by "Persons equally interested" to persist in unreasonable demands.[58] This was talk that governmental authorities down the lakes could understand, and late in 1797 Russell, on Prescott's advice, dismissed Elliott from the service for overnumbering the Indians in his jurisdiction and for other frauds which McLean had enumerated. It now appeared that the terrors of 1797 would be tempered with a little doubt in 1798.

But the rumors of French and Spanish invasions were no more to be placed at Elliott's door or at the door of the Indian department than they could be blamed on Joseph Brant. Nor could all the revelation of truth be attributed to Captain McLean. Some truthful disclosures came from the Indians themselves. The Ottawas near St. Joseph, for instance, plaintively denied that they had sent out bad belts, but no one seemed to be listening.

Near the end of the year a very curious rumor got started. While Joseph was doing everything he could to make it appear that he *might* be amenable to hostile suggestions and to frighten authorities in Canada into fearful suspicions of what he and his warriors were up to, an American in England who was deeply implicated in the so-called Blount conspiracy (involving a United States senator and a plot against Spanish territory) confessed to the American minister that Brant was to have helped an army of frontiersmen invade Louisiana and capture the silver mines on the Red River![59] This story, had Joseph been apprised of it, would have disconcerted him no little.

If Joseph had known about Matthew Elliott's troubles, he would have leaped to his defense immediately, for he considered him (with not much reason) a friend. However, it was winter and news traveled slowly. Joseph did not yet know of Elliott's dismissal. And of course

Joseph was not planning a descent on Louisiana. Nothing could have been farther from his thoughts than Senator Blount of Tennessee and his plots against Spain.

Far from contemplating an attack on the Red River mines Joseph, in late 1797, was trying to tie up the last loose ends of his land business. Since he was an alien (as it was explained to him), he could not receive mortgages or other securities in his own name, regardless of his power of attorney. British subjects must be appointed as trustees to act for the Indians in these matters.[60] Joseph did not take his exclusion ill. As the Indians were independent, he did not claim to be a subject. He named D. W. Smith, the surveyor general and son of a former commander at Niagara; Alexander Stewart, Brant Johnson's son-in-law and the Indians' lawyer; and John Ferguson, a white man who had married one of Molly's daughters; as trustees.[61] It was found that Ferguson could not legally serve because he did not live in the district. Joseph then named William Claus in Ferguson's stead. Administrator Russell was very pleased at so judicious a selection as Claus.[62] Joseph was doing the best he could to protect his people. He tried to arrange that the Indians should get all their annuities at the same time,[63] and he refrained from naming more than three trustees to save expense.[64] Russell had advised him to name officers of the government, since offices never die, but apparently Joseph distrusted this advice.[65] Indeed, he did not thoroughly understand what the trustees were to do nor how the trust would descend, and he had to ask to have these details explained to him.[66]

Late that fall lawyer Stewart advanced the idea that the women of the Grand River should sign the document of surrender to the king. Joseph was taken aback. His power of attorney had come through proper channels—that is, from the women's councils as well as from the men. But now because of Stewart's ill-advised proposal he needed some further support. Catharine and Henry went to work (for there is no other way to explain what happened), and the women met with the chiefs and declared they would not sign for Stewart.[67] So the matter ended.

While this business was being taken care of, Joseph got the disappointing news from Liston that the ministry did not believe the Haldimand grant gave the Indians any general power to sell land.[68] He became very angry. He complained to Sir John Johnson and to Captain Green, the military secretary at Quebec, and of course to Liston himself about all the obstacles that were being put in his path. To Sir John he explained what he wanted: to hold the Grand River land just as the land on the Mohawk River had been held, to sell such parts as his people did not need, but to keep enough for the whole Five Nations should they wish to settle with their brethren. Not to be able to sell would be fatal to his people's future. He had never swerved from his loyalty to the king, always considering the king's interests "as connected with that of the Indians." After the war his people had refused a chance to go elsewhere, he said, referring to the Seneca offer of a homeland, and he blamed himself for the refusal. "What I most lament," he raged, "is that my sincere attachment has ruined the Interests of my Nation unless an alteration takes place."[69]

To Green and Liston Joseph spoke in a similar vein. To the former he said the ministry apparently intended to forbid the Indians "any other use of the lands than that of sitting down or walking on them," meaning, he thought, "to tie us down in such a manner, as to have us entirely at their disposal for what services they may in future want from us, and that in case we should be worried out & obliged to remove, the lands would then fall to them with our improvements & labour." They might think, he went on, that because I have half pay I should not talk so much, "but am I for this entirely to forsake the interests of my people, that put their dependance on me?"[70] To Liston Joseph added: "We have Sir, however great Consolation and confidence in the King's Care and Affection for Us, Our hearts are still united to his Interests, but we are sorry to conceive that we have too much reason to complain of the administration of his Government here, so far as it respects the Territory of the five Nations." He was considering the idea, he continued, of going to Philadelphia again or even going to England, for he could not rest easy with affairs as they were.[71]

Russell got wind of all these complaints, as well as the earlier complaints made to Liston, in February. He denied putting obstacles in Brant's way. If the business moved too slowly, he said crossly, it was Brant's own fault.[72] Why, he asked Joseph, did he complain about *him?* Joseph denied any discontent with Russell's administration. He laid all the blame for his troubles on Simcoe. The questions and explanations dragged on for months, with Joseph always insisting he had nothing against Russell, but only against Simcoe; though that is not the way Liston had understood the matter. It was Simcoe, Joseph charged, who, disappointed of getting Grand River land at one shilling per acre, had tried to block his every effort to sell to others; and he accused the lieutenant governor of machinations in England against him and the Indians.[73] Joseph was at least half right. Simcoe was very busy in England advising what should be done in Indian affairs. His advice naturally had other objects than the well-being of the Indians.

York, 1803. Watercolor by Dr. E. Walsh, 49th Regiment. Scene of Joseph's great triumph. *Courtesy of the University of Michigan, Ann Arbor.*

The great day finally came. The last bargain had been agreed upon, the last purchaser soothed; the last conference with this or that official had been accomplished, the last council with the Indians— men, women, the various nations—was over; the last journey had been made, the last legal advice obtained, the last letter written. All the surveys were now done, all the maps were drawn, and all those seemingly endless statements and lists had been signed and delivered.

On February 5, 1798, Joseph met with Administrator Russell and the attorney general and a quorum of the Executive Council in the Council chamber at York. It was Joseph's proudest moment. He produced his power of attorney and declared he had come in behalf of the Five Nations to execute the instrument of surrender for part of the Haldimand grant. The instrument was voted, accepted. Joseph then stepped forward to Russell and surrendered to him 352,707 acres which he prayed the king would grant in certain portions to Philip Stedman (Block 1); Richard Beasley, James Wilson, and St. John B. Rousseau (Block 2); William Wallace (Block 3); William Jarvis

(Block 5); and Benjamin Canby (Block 6). Russell accepted the surrender and in the king's name consented to reconvey the lands to the named persons, the latter being subjects of the king and freeholders in the province of Upper Canada. The attorney general produced five deeds of grant. The portly Russell (with a little inward sigh, perhaps) signed the five deeds, stipulating that they not be delivered to the purchasers unless the trustees certified they had made the proper security for the considerations and annuities.[74] The only change in the list of purchasers as first given out by Joseph was the omission of the name of Joshua Cozens whose share (Block 4) would be granted to James Wilson a few months later,[75] and the addition of the names of William Jarvis, Joseph's brother Mason and secretary of the province, who had purchased a fifth block of the Indian land which was now removed from Block 6, and Benjamin Canby, John Docksteder's new assignee for Block 6. Jarvis got some 30,800 acres near the mouth of the Grand River on its east side (Dunnville being now in this area), while Canby's, or Docksteder's, land, which had been sold for the benefit of Docksteder's Indian children, and which had been increased (by gift from the Indians, apparently) from its original size to a great tract of 19,000 acres, also lay on the east side of the river, above Jarvis'.

The six immense blocks of land which were now cut off from the original Haldimand grant were to become known as the townships of South Dumfries, Brant County, and North Dumfries, Waterloo County (Stedman's Block 1); Waterloo Township, Waterloo County (Beasley's and associates' Block 2); Woolwich Township, Waterloo County, and Pilkington Township, Wellington County (Wallace's Block 3); Nichol Township, Wellington County (Wilson's Block 4); most of Moulton Township, Haldimand County (Jarvis' Block 5); and most of Canborough Township, Haldimand County (Canby's Block 6).[76] From northernmost Block 4 down to the mouth of the river the land was fertile, with a climate excellent for agriculture. It was, said Russell mournfully, "the finest in the Province."

All Joseph's surrenders, with the exception of the Canby (Docksteder) tract which would be of no benefit to the Grand River Indians in general, and the Wilson (Cozens) tract, still to be disposed of, sold for about £39,867 provincial currency, or from two to six shillings per acre.[77] It was the best price, according to John Norton, ever paid to Indians for wild land up to that time.[78] When the Cozens tract was finally sold, Joseph hoped, with six percent interest coming in on the various mortgages, to get an annuity for his people of more than five thousand pounds.[79]

There were many persons of influence in Upper Canada, besides
Peter Russell, who were not happy with Joseph Brant's land sales.
They firmly believed that Brant was disposing of even more land, and
to American speculators, at that. Chief Justice Elmsley, one of the
councilors not present on February 5, accepted this gossip as fact; and
he asserted what many others of his kind truly believed regarding the
land of Upper Canada: "Can lands be in any hands better than in
those of the officers of Government, in a country in which the influence of extensive property is so much wanted to give effect to the
Laws, & keep the turbulent in good order? & in whose hands can they
be more safely placed than in ours, who depend so entirely upon the
King, & the Mother Country."[80] Land was the key to wealth and
position now. Furs had fallen into second place. In agriculture, people
could see, lay the future of the province. Nevertheless the chief justice
was just as eager to prevent an Indian-French invasion as anyone else,
and he was one of those who had unanimously consented to Brant's
sales the previous summer. But he had not negotiated with Joseph to
buy any of the Indian land. Brant's prices were such that prudent men
would think twice about them.

It was a very cold day, that February 5, and little York was a
wretched place where one was lucky to find a tent for shelter, but to
Joseph Brant the raw little settlement had become the place of
triumph. Never did homecoming warrior feel more like raising his
voice in a victory yell. Though a victory yell was not for the "civilized"
Joseph—and certainly not in York—he knew he had accumulated a
prodigious number of scalps. The successful strategy was his alone. He
had planned and worked and schemed. He had used whatever
weapons came to hand. Now, through his efforts the people of the
Longhouse could rejoice in getting back some part, at least, of their
ancient freedom. And the war was not over. Joseph looked forward to
future victories. Not only should his people have money of their own,
they should buy and sell and ultimately do all else in the independent
manner of their ancestors.

27

Too Great a Man

Aᴛ ʟᴀsᴛ Joseph had time to ponder about his own situation. He knew very well what Isaac's attack on him portended. It meant that Isaac and his co-conspirators had marked Joseph Brant as too great a man. It also meant that some other executioner might try to complete Isaac's unfinished work. Tension still ran high on the Grand River, for there was strong resistance to the introduction of new customs which Joseph and the sachems were trying to effect, as well as resistance to their new land policies. Though the faultfinding was by a minority, it was vehement. Old and young, warriors and civil chiefs glared at each other, sometimes almost literally at each other's throats. Killings, especially when the liquor flowed, were not uncommon.[1]

What should he do? He must be watchful, certainly, as he had been since that fatal day. He must still look out for his people, for they were helpless without him; but he could not live with them any longer. There was the 3,450-acre tract at the head of Lake Ontario which he had obtained from the Missisaugas and which he had not sold. It was more than enough for a good farm and homestead. He began to plan.

By mid-summer of 1798 Joseph had made arrangements with a carpenter to frame "my little houses at the Beach," but finding he was unable to get boards, decided to make do with logs.[2] The next year a fire destroyed one or both of the houses.[3] As he had to go to Quebec on a variety of Indian business, Joseph took the opportunity to get some free building material for himself from the government. He also managed to get the expenses of his stay in the city, and returned home

Home of Capt. Brant at the Head of Lake Ontario, 1804. Watercolor by Dr. E. Walsh, 49th Regiment. Joseph's new home was often called a "mansion," but he never forgot, and could not keep away from, the Grand River. *Courtesy of the University of Michigan, Ann Arbor.*

in "high good humor."[4] He was soon making plans to rebuild. This time he was able to obtain the necessary boards, but the building proceeded very slowly. His lumber had to be spoken for, then sawed, and then dried, and finally transported to the site. One house, of a story and a half, was to measure twenty by twenty-five feet. The larger house, two stories high, was first projected as thirty-five feet by twenty-five, and then changed to thirty-six by twenty-two.[5] The government gift was only a start. Joseph himself paid for all the lumber,[6] and from November 3, 1799, to July 15, 1802, was continually buying from Jean Baptiste Rousseau's store at nearby Ancaster such things as putty, nails, iron, shingles, and more boards. As late as April 29, 1804, he was still buying shingles, perhaps for outbuildings.[7] The state of Joseph's finances (never too healthy) had forced him to proceed even more slowly than was normal.

By June 1802, Joseph and the family had probably moved from the Grand River to Burlington Bay, for he began to write letters from that place then. By March 14, 1803, they were undoubtedly living at the head of Lake Ontario, for on that date he and Catharine signed a deed which mentions their residence. It appears that Joseph and Catharine paid their carpenter with 211 acres of their land on the lake at that time.[8] John Norton says that Joseph's new house was "commodious," and that he placed about one hundred acres of his land under cultivation and planted a fine orchard.[9]

In May 1804, Dr. Edward Walsh of the 49th regiment, working apparently from a distance of several hundred feet away, made a sketch of the new Brant house.[10] The smaller house which Joseph had planned is not visible in the picture. It was probably back of the main structure and used as a kitchen and servants' quarters. From a distance, and with no comparable building nearby, Joseph's house looks like Johnson Hall, though it was actually not half as large. Of course Joseph's house was not nearly so grand as Johnson Hall, either; but it had a portico and a Palladian window, and it is easy to see what its owner was trying to accomplish and where he was getting his ideas. Joseph would never forget stately Johnson Hall. He did not have the means to build a replica, but he had done the best he could, and his new house was imposing for the time and the place, when most settlers still lived in tiny log cabins. By and by people began to refer to Joseph's house as the "Brant mansion"—a description which must have pleased him exceedingly.

Dr. Walsh's sketch shows a substantial frame building situated on top of a gentle slope, with many trees close by and in the background. Joseph had chosen a very beautiful location, for there is the water of an inlet in the foreground and grass grows down to the water's edge. We see four windows across the lower front of the Brant house (two on each side of the door), and four more, besides the Palladian window, upstairs. Shutters are only vaguely indicated. A broad fascia adorns the front of the structure above the upper windows, and a chimney rises at each end. The ends of the house appear to be constructed of heavy squared timbers, but the front could be clapboard or even plaster. In the right foreground of the picture and across the narrow stretch of water part of a log cabin can be seen with a bit of rail fence which appears to enclose a pen, perhaps for some of Joseph's farm animals, though none is in view. In the mid-foreground are two Indians, a woman seated and a man standing, probably poor, wandering Missisaugas, with their dog. The man grasps a pipe-tomahawk in his right hand, and he is staring intently at the house. Never, he must be thinking, did an Indian have such a house!

From various other sources we know Joseph's house was situated on

the north side of Burlington Bay (present Burlington, Ontario), over-
looking the historic beach of white drift sand which divided Lake
Ontario from the bay; that the large, new King's Head Inn which
Simcoe had had built for the benefit of travelers was near the south
shore of the bay, facing it; and that Richard Beasley's trading post,
with his mill and inn, was at the head of the bay, close enough for
Joseph to see his friend and business associate frequently.[11] The surveyor, Augustus Jones, lived reasonably near; so, too, Jean Baptiste
Rousseau; but the country was so far from filled up that everywhere
magnificent, unspoiled scenery still met the eye. York was about forty
miles around the lake to the northeast, and Niagara was about the
same distance along the lake to the southeast; and as late as 1819 the
Brant house could be picked out on the Niagara road from as far away
as five miles.[12] Nearby on the curving white beach (more than half of
which Joseph owned) the Indians gathered for their presents and often
met in council. Joseph wrote many letters dated from "The Beach,"
"Head of the Lake," and "Burlington Bay," and whether he differ-
entiated these various addresses is not clear. The road which had been
cut across country to the Grand River was about eight miles to the
southwest; to get to it there seems to have been a trail back of Joseph's
house. Indeed, there was no lack of Indian trails to any place of
consequence. Though Joseph had moved away, he still meant to keep
a fatherly eye on the people at the Grand River, and his new home
was well situated for such watchfulness.

Peter Russell owned a tract of ground in the vicinity which he
described to a friend in glowing terms. Whatever Russell said about his
land Joseph could also have said about his. Russell considered his
property a suitable site for a gentleman's country residence. It looked
more like a park than wild land, he said. It was near excellent mills
and good stores, and from it one could be conveyed in one's own
private barge to Niagara, York, or any settlement on Lake Ontario.
Near one's front door wild fowl abounded; delicious salmon, black
bass, muskellunge, trout, and pickerel could be caught in the waters of
the nearby bay, while turkeys, pheasants, hares, and woodcocks flourished in great plenty in the rear. Everywhere there was good grass for
cattle. It was a place where one could surely find contentment and
lead a life of ease.[13]

Now, at last, Joseph was settled on his gentleman's estate, and the
worrisome Indians were left behind. Yet he still shaved his head and
wore his customary scalp lock. And if there was nothing outside his
house to remind him of his heritage, there was something of the sort
on the inside. How the interior of the Brant mansion was arranged in

Joseph's day we do not know, but in his son's day, about a decade and a half later, it was described by one of those inquisitive travelers who were always pestering the Brants. First, one entered a "spacious" hall, said the traveler, then a "parlour." (The parlor was on the right, reported another traveler.) "It was a room well furnished with a carpet, pier and chimney glases [sic], mahogany tables, fashionable chairs, a guitar, a neat hanging book-case, in which, among other volumes, we perceived a church of England prayer-book, translated into the Mohawk tongue, and several small elementary works." Later, not seeing the Indian "trophies" which he expected, the traveler asked where they were. He was told that they had all been given away to the numerous visitors who had wished for them. Not one was left.[14] So we know that Joseph had brought along to his gentleman's residence mementos of his Grand River home. . . . Then there was the dagger which hung in his bedroom. Joseph Brant, Jr., told a scholar that whenever his father lay upon his bed and looked at it hanging there, he wept.[15]

Meanwhile, neither the four years of building nor the actual change of residence made much difference in Joseph's busy routine. At the turn of the century there were the usual varied demands upon his time. He performed a condolence for Ann Johnson Claus, William Claus's mother;[16] he caused a mill to be built at the Grand River to replace the old one which had been destroyed by fire;[17] and he was still busy with the stubborn Caughnawagas. He tried to help the Nanticokes who had land claims in Maryland and some Munsees with similar claims in New York near Minisink.[18] The business with the Connecticut Land Company dragged on and on from old house to new house.

As money began to come in from his land sales, Joseph was able to purchase many things for the Indians—for the "public," as he said, and he maintained a special account at Rousseau's store for these purchases. The Indians could now enjoy such luxuries as meals and drinks and new shoes when traveling, quantities of beef and flour, and feed for their horses; and they could even obtain cash when needed.[19] It was a happy time, for the Indians were getting these fine things by their own—or his own—efforts. They were beholden to nobody for them. Joseph also paid the blacksmith, the schoolteacher, the physician, the surveyor, and the lawyer, and he bought large quantities of provisions from other merchants besides Rousseau.[20] In the summer of 1799 the Indians were in great want at the Grand River, and Joseph donated five thousand "weight" of flour, this gift apparently from himself.[21] And when James Wilson, one of his buyers, suffered a severe loss by fire, he generously subscribed £600 toward his friend's relief. It was a great sum, and the press commented very favorably on such a munificent gesture.[22] This must have been Indian money, not Joseph's own; and it was also more than the Indians could afford, but Joseph, like his sister Molly before him, had large ideas. Of course, he still had an eye toward anything he could get that was free, and in 1799 he managed to obtain a government bateau for his people, water travel being so much easier for them than land travel.[23]

But money could not buy everything—or, rather, it sometimes bought too much. Itinerant traders were bringing great quantities of liquor to the Grand River. The schisms and fights were exacerbated by drunkenness, and often the fights originated in drunken revels. The better part of the Indians, young men as well as chiefs, grew concerned.[24] The women were worried, too, and in May 1802 the women from all the settlements up and down the river met and deplored the general drunkenness. They apologized humbly for their part in the trouble among the people. They had often been a bad influence on their male relatives, they admitted, and they promised to comport themselves better in the future. They begged that the outpouring of liquor be stopped before it reached their country. Joseph deplored drunkenness, too. He answered them kindly and promised to do what he could, although he knew that what he could do now depended more on the provincial government than on him.[25] For himself, he had to be careful what he attempted. Yet this meeting was undoubtedly Catharine's effort to contribute to Joseph's peace of mind.

Catharine would do anything for Joseph, even to living at a place uncongenial to her. She would have preferred to stay in the old home, where there were matrons to talk to in her husband's frequent absences, and perhaps more help with the children, for Joseph was no help at all. Captain Brant was not one to walk to and fro in front of the house with a baby on his back, even if at home. And, no doubt, inexplicably to Catharine, now that Joseph was away from the Grand River, he was continually going back there to attend to something. New ways and a new life were not for Catharine. If she learned to make biscuits and "pyes," and to prepare good English roast beef because Joseph liked it, she still had a hankering herself for hominy boiled in rich brown venison broth and she still liked to nibble at a lump of bear's fat on a cold winter day. Catharine found little comfort at Burlington Bay.

In January 1799, when Joseph was still making his plans to leave the Indians, Matthew Elliott showed up at the Grand River house with his tale of woe: the trouble with Captain McLean at Fort Malden, the constant harassment, McLean's false charges against him, and his peremptory dismissal from his post in the Indian department. Four times, he said, he had tried to get an inquiry into his conduct.[26] Joseph was ready with his sympathy. The dark-browed Elliott was his friend and a friend to the Indians, and he never once associated him with McKee's doings in 1793 although he had been second in command to McKee. Though it was the dead of an especially bitter winter, and York for most purposes cut off from the outside world, Joseph willingly accompanied Elliott to the snowed-in capital, and both men appealed to Peter Russell for help. Russell was favorably impressed with Elliott's air of candor (Elliott being one who was usually liked or disliked almost immediately), but said he had no power to order an investigation of the case. Joseph took Russell aside and told him that Elliott was so beloved by the Indians that his dismissal had caused great uneasiness among them and that the Shawnees, in particular, had planned to send a deputation to the king about it, but that he, Brant, had prevented their doing so.[27] Through Russell, Elliott sent a petition to General Prescott begging an inquiry into his affairs, and both Elliott and Joseph, having little faith in what Prescott would do, wrote Simcoe. Apparently Joseph depended on Simcoe's own personal knowledge of Elliott's services to the crown rather than to any characteristic generosity which he thought the man possessed.

The nervous Russell, who was still hearing rumors about the French, asked Elliott if there was any truth in them. Elliott thought there was great truth in them and thoroughly frightened the administrator again[28]—much to Joseph's private glee, who, for his own reasons, still had an interest in those rumors.

Joseph's letter to Simcoe was a very strong plea in Matthew Elliott's behalf. If Elliott is guilty, Joseph argued, a trial would establish his guilt; if innocent, he ought not be denied the means of proving his innocence. Why, he asked, should Elliott be dismissed without a hearing when even a corporal is entitled to that indulgence?[29] As Joseph was never one to stint his efforts in defense of a friend, after he had struggled home through the snowdrifts he wrote Sir John Johnson to the same purpose.[30] The Executive Council, as fearful as Russell, also favored an investigation of the affair (because of Elliott's influence with the western Indians, of course), but London had already sided with Prescott and McLean. General Prescott gave Elliott such a tongue lashing in the presence of Sir John that it caused Sir John great embarrassment just to have to stand by and hear it.[31] This was another of those seemingly hopeless causes in which Joseph Brant so often involved himself. Matthew Elliott would grow old and his services be needed in another war before his persistent appeals brought him relief.

In the meantime Joseph's hopes of a little confederation with the Missisaugas had got him into trouble. The government, both at home and abroad, was determined to frustrate such a dangerous union of Indians, and Joseph's advice to the Missisaugas to hold on to their land on Lake Ontario till they could get a good price reinforced this determination. Very soon Administrator Russell appointed a special agent for the Missisaugas, and he let them know that they should henceforth receive their presents at the River Credit. The River Credit being a stream about halfway between the head of the lake, where the Six Nations got their presents, and York, Russell's new ruling made it more difficult for the two sets of Indians to fraternize. Lieutenant James Givens, the new agent for the Missisaugas, was given explicit instructions to do all he could to prevent the Indians' getting together at any other time. In this action Russell had the full support of Simcoe, in England, and the ministry.[32]

To Russell's disappointment, Givens, a young man who spoke the Missisauga language fluently but who was not equally experienced in Indian management, did not foresee that the cunning Brant would invite the Missisaugas to his next gala May Day celebration to renew their friendship with him and his people.[33] The Missisaugas, very pleased at this polite attention from their friends, came a little ahead of time, and on April 30, 1798, held a council with the Grand River Indians. Very formally, with wampum and by means of a written document to which they signed their marks, and before Richard Beasley who was a justice of the peace; Rousseau, the interpreter; Stewart, the lawyer; and Augustus Jones, the surveyor, they begged Joseph Brant to take charge of their affairs. They promised not to dispose of any of their lands or transact any other business with white people without his assent, and they promised to approve whatever he might do as their agent.[34] Joseph told William Claus that he was sure the formality of these proceedings cleared himself of any blame.[35]

If Joseph really believed he would be considered blameless, he was wrong. Russell was extremely displeased. He wrote Joseph that it surprised him to see that the Missisaugas supposed they needed any other protector when they were already under the protection of the king! He denied that he wanted their land unless they gave it up freely and were perfectly satisfied with the price.[36] He had already apprised the ministry that the purchase of the needed tract between York and the head of the lake must be put off for the time being—but that it would not be lost sight of.[37]

After much thought Joseph had set the price for the Missisauga land at two shillings an acre. This was considerably less than the Indians themselves had demanded the previous year, but still too much for Russell, especially since Joseph did not want to sell all the lake frontage. If the mouths of the creeks were settled, complained Joseph, it would spoil the fishing.[38] The wily chief knew very well that Russell would not want land three miles back from the lake. But Joseph did not wish to sell any Missisauga land; the Missisaugas were more nearly in a primitive state than his own people, and he did not think it just that the government should take their land from them at a shilling an acre "only to give away to Individuals to make money of."[39] The Missisaugas needed all their land, and Joseph was firmly convinced the government had marked the land for speculators.

The great dispute between the Mohawks and the Caughnawagas was at its height just then, and young Givens took the opportunity to try to frighten the Missisaugas out of their Mohawk alliance. If the Caughnawagas should decide to make war against the Mohawks, he warned, they would have to march through Missisauga country. And if they saw the Missisaugas decked out in the Mohawk style with shaved heads and scalp locks, they might naturally mistake them for Mohawks and kill them, too! This forecast did, indeed, frighten the Missisaugas who had aspired to imitate and look like their admired friends. The now thoroughly worried Missisaugas complained to Brant that they were afraid to separate and go on their usual fall hunt. Joseph assured them there was no war with the Caughnawagas and that he would never leave his allies in the lurch if there was, and that he was certain such lies did not come from the king but from someone with an evil heart. He advised the Missisaugas to stay on good terms with the government and to go on about their business as usual.[40]

Russell attempted to smooth over this new controversy by sending Givens to visit Joseph at the Grand River (where he still was). Givens smilingly bore many explanations which Joseph appeared to receive in a friendly manner.[41] Joseph was always friendly to guests, but in this case his friendliness was no more genuine than Givens' explanations. Not long afterward Joseph wrote Russell that if the Indians were not allowed to act together according to their ancient customs, then they could no longer look upon themselves as the same people and there-fore, he added significantly, "no great advantages can be expected from our exertions."[42] Joseph meant, of course, that no great advantages could be expected from their exertions in a war to defend Upper Canada from invasion. Russell was still beset by continuing rumors of a French and Indian attack from the Mississippi, and Joseph knew that he was, or should be, considering how to obtain the help of the local Indians. Joseph knew this very well, for he was still doing all he could (in another connection) to keep those rumors going.

Such was the situation when Count Joseph de Puisaye showed up at the Grand River. De Puisaye was a French royalist who had cooperated with the British for several years in the great war in Europe and who had brought some of his homeless officers and men and their families to make a settlement in Upper Canada. He had the blessing of the British government in this attempt, and both the Duke of Portland and Simcoe wrote letters to Canada in his behalf. He and his people were to be given land in the same proportion as the old Loyalists and they were to receive the same help in provisions and other necessities. There was one proviso: these French emigrants must be settled as far from the French people in Lower Canada and the French near Detroit as possible. The new French were not to be allowed to fraternize with the old French. Who knew what plots they might hatch? Accordingly de Puisaye was granted some land above York in a region without a decent road or water transportation and requiring much manual labor to make it productive or even habitable. Some of de Puisaye's people were strong enough to undergo such rigors. Some were not. Among the latter were several members of the old French nobility, including two noble ladies, a marquise and a viscountess.

Joseph made it his business to have some business up in that forlorn neighborhood, and in January 1799 he met de Puisaye and invited him to visit him.[43] De Puisaye promptly accepted the invitation and spent a few days with Joseph the next month. Joseph was very favorably impressed with the tall and handsome French aristocrat.[44] To be sure, some people thought he looked a little like Simcoe, but Joseph could overlook that in view of his sufferings in behalf of his king. Joseph had no good opinion of the French Revolution, and he had been known to remark that the Indians would never butcher their king and queen in the inhuman manner of the French. That, he told Timothy Pickering, is *"worse than what is called Savage."*[45]

While de Puisaye was with Joseph, Joseph came up with the idea that the Missisaugas should give the French refugees some better land than the government of Upper Canada had given them. He thought de Puisaye ought to have five miles along Lake Ontario adjoining his own land. Letting the refugees have that property would be a good deed done to a deserving people, and it would be a means of improving the communication between Niagara and York, if the communication really needed improving. Then there would be no necessity for the Missisaugas to yield up any more of their holdings and no real necessity for the authorities to try to get anything further from them. So Joseph reasoned, and he offered de Puisaye a tract going back into the country far enough to take in 69,120 acres, right on the way to York. It was to be a gift.[46]

Brant's five-mile gift was part of the thirty-six-mile tract between Burlington Bay and York which Russell had tried to buy the previous fall. The Executive Council leaped at the idea that the Indians might now be willing to part with some of that land on better terms. The Council instructed Russell to buy as much as he could as soon as possible. No part of that tract, however, could be confirmed to de Puisaye without the formality of a royal purchase first and then a royal grant.[47] To this proceeding Joseph had to agree, although he did not like it. A prior royal purchase had been the only way he could obtain his own land on the lake from the Missisaugas. Joseph now set the price to be paid his allies at one shilling three pence per acre, and he was canny enough to insist that the purchase be made for de Puisaye and no one else.[48]

The fat fell into the fire. Joseph's price was still too great, thought the authorities, for thereafter all Indian land could be expected to cost at least that much. They also balked at the proviso in de Puisaye's favor. This would set a bad precedent. It would give the Indians too much say-so as to who should get their land in future sales. It could not be tolerated, said Russell and Prescott, and the Executive Council agreed.[49] When Joseph heard of this decision, he fell into such a fury that he refused to dine with Russell and asked Givens how long Russell *"was to remain a great man."* Nevertheless, Russell said he did not doubt Brant's loyalty.[50]

Russell passed the remark that the Indians ought to be more obliging to the government in view of all the presents they received.[51] Joseph answered him indignantly that the presents were rewards for past services.[52] When informed of Brant's interpretation of the annual subsidies, the Duke of Portland spoke grimly. The presents the Indians got from the king were not payments for past services, he declared. It was the contrary that was true, he said, and he pointed out that "the continuance of the King's Bounty to them entirely and absolutely depends on their using their best Endeavours to promote as far as in them lies, the King's Interests, and the views of His Government within the Province." Portland had little faith in Brant's loyalty. Brant was not to be allowed to consolidate Indian interests. He must not be permitted to form alliances of Indians. Nothing could be worse for Britain's own interests. The Indians must be kept "as separate and disunited as possible."[53]

A stalemate developed, with Joseph pushing for the sale in de Puisaye's behalf, and claiming that the price was actually too low, since land in the province had increased greatly in value since previous Indian sales.[54] This was only too true, for land values had soared since the first sales. However, the idea that *Indians* should expect to profit by the great increase was totally unacceptable to all the white people involved. They believed that it was white labor and white improvements, present or prospective, that gave land its increasing value, and Joseph's argument beat itself in vain against the wall of this prejudice. However much the Count de Puisaye pleaded for his compatriots, Russell firmly told him he would never get the Missisauga tract; he had better content himself with what he had.[55] De Puisaye had to accept the verdict.

The French emigrants struggled along in desolation, and with poverty and unwonted labors, until in the early 1800s those who were able to leave, left. De Puisaye himself abandoned hope more quickly than Joseph's other proteges. In 1802 he returned to England and at length died there. By 1806 only a few of the unlucky French royalists remained in Upper Canada.[56]

This was another contest that Joseph totally lost. As Portland had remarked somewhat petulantly, he wondered that Brant could accomplish anything when the Indian agents with all their superior advantages (meaning all their largess) were opposed.[57] Portland was right; Brant could not win a competition with the Indian department. Joseph had to give up both the sale and the little confederation with the Missisaugas. He was told that the sale was off and that he never would be allowed to act as agent for the Missisaugas.[58] He professed himself surprised that Indian nations should not be permitted to form alliances. It had once been encouraged, he said sadly.[59] Joseph could not bring himself to accept the fact that there was a deal of difference between 1783 and 1803. Reluctantly, though, he had to give up the agency which he appears to have actively carried on in various small ways for several years.[60] In 1805 the Missisaugas sold their land along the lake, but it was not with Brant's help and not at Brant's price.[61]

Of course Joseph knew he was in no good odor with the authorities either in Upper Canada or in England when in the late summer or early fall of 1800 he received a very friendly letter from D. W. Smith, one of his trustees. Smith knew Joseph's circumstances, which were straitened as usual, and he wrote suggesting that Joseph should petition the British ministry to provide for the education of his sons.[62] The two older boys, Joseph, Jr., about sixteen, and Jacob, about fourteen, had been enrolled in a school at Niagara as early as 1795, and they had apparently gone as far as they could under the tutelage of Richard Cockrel, the young surveyor-schoolmaster. These two boys were already better educated than their father; they could write, unaided, far better letters than he could write. John, the youngest son, was only six years old, and he could remain with Cockrel or even at the Grand River school for some years yet. It was the two older boys who were the problem.

Joseph was pleased at Smith's suggestion in behalf of his sons, and he was willing that his friends should initiate the required petition. As for himself, he said proudly, he could not do such a thing. He had met so much opposition from the government in obtaining "what I only considered as our rights" that he could not flatter himself with any prospect of obtaining such a favor, and so he declined to ask it from fear of having his feelings further wounded by a refusal.[63]

Joseph's friends did nothing about the petition or, if they did, they had no success. But thus reminded of his children's needs, Joseph thought back to his own school days of almost forty years before. The Reverend Eleazar Wheelock was long dead and his school for Indians removed from Lebanon, Connecticut, to Hanover, New Hampshire; but James, a son of Wheelock, had lived for a while in Upper Canada, and he had once offered to take charge of the education of Joseph, Jr. Joseph got in touch with James Wheelock and, as a consequence, he was able to get free board and tuition for both of his boys at the old Charity School,[64] which was now an adjunct to Wheelock's Dartmouth College, a school set up for white youths.

Details were quickly arranged, and Joseph's two boys soon set out for Hanover. They traveled east under the care of Colonel Benjamin Sumner, a man who had been spending some time among the Indians on the Grand River. The lads reached their destination on October 25, 1800, and were immediately received into the home of James Wheelock.[65] Sumner brought the pleasing news to Hanover that the Six Nations, especially the Mohawks, had made great advances in their manner of living, and he attributed it to the influence of Brant and others who had been educated by the elder Wheelock.[66] John Wheelock, another son of Eleazar, was president of both the Indian and the white school. Joseph sent word to him through Colonel Sumner, begging him to see to his sons' moral and religious upbringing as well as their general education.[67]

Many letters were soon passing back and forth between Joseph, and James and John Wheelock. Joseph wanted his sons to be exhorted to attend to their studies and "behave in a becoming manner." They were to act according to the customs of the locality, even as to their apparel and the cutting of their hair. The Wheelocks were urged again to look after the boys' spiritual as well as worldly concerns; and Joseph assured John that he was their friend as long as he lived, that he revered the memory of their father and had profited enormously by his instruction. The two Wheelocks soon reported to Joseph that his children were making "laudable progress," that they were attentive to their studies, that they had amiable dispositions and manly deportment. James Wheelock thought the occasions they would require "exhorting" would be very rare. John Wheelock hoped that Joseph's sons would be a great source of comfort and assistance "in the sublime business of enlightening and meliorating your nations." Joseph had promised the boys they should remain at the school only a year, but when he heard they were doing so well, he hoped they could be persuaded to stay longer. He sent them one hundred pounds for pocket money. (Apparently Joseph thought his sons shared his large ideas.)

In September 1801, Joseph, Jr., insisted on going home for a visit. One year of uninterrupted instruction was enough for the homesick youth, although he was considered the more serious-minded of the two brothers. Joseph, Jr., returned to New Hampshire after his visit, but his heart was not in further schooling, and he said his final good-by to the Wheelocks on January 15, 1802, apologized for leaving them, and was back home by March 10. He claimed he and his brother Jacob were in perpetual disagreement, and gave that as his reason for leaving school. Jacob did not remain behind very long, but left school in April. The lad was ill, and became worse on the journey home, and almost died. The Wheelocks thought Jacob might return soon, but it was many months before he did. He continued sickly at home, and his mother and some of the younger children grew very ill, too. In those days there were always fevers at the Grand River during the hot season, and this may explain the illnesses. Jacob finally returned to school in December, riding horseback; and his father sternly ordered the horse to be sold, "as an attentive scholar has no time to ride about." Joseph knew something about the unfortunate juxtaposition of horses and scholars from personal experience. Jacob appears not to have remained at school very long this second time, for by May 1803 he was back at home again and dining at Rousseau's.[68] In October 1804 Joseph reported that Jacob's left hand had been shattered by the bursting of a gun, and that he was about to marry a Mohawk girl.[69] Joseph, Jr., and Jacob were intelligent youths, but they never attained to the standard which their younger brother John would reach. They were not like their father. More like their mother, they knew when they had had enough civilization.

Such a man as Joseph Brant who was so eager to have his children instructed in "Piety" (as he told the Wheelocks) could not approve the Handsome Lake phenomenon. In Joseph's day there arose among the Indians more than one spiritual leader, or seer, who tried to turn them out of the white man's road and back again to their ancient way of life. In his youth the seer of greatest note was an eloquent Delaware called The Prophet. Pontiac became The Prophet's most famous convert. In Joseph's later life the seer was a man named Handsome Lake, a Seneca, half-brother to Cornplanter. In 1799 Handsome Lake began to see visions and to talk with gods who told him the Creator was displeased with the Indians for abandoning their old customs. Soon Handsome Lake was moving about and preaching a sort of gospel of happiness through self-sufficiency and stern morality and a return to the old rites and ceremonies, but with a new idea of heaven and hell which sounds almost Biblical. It was a message that appealed to an unhappy and declining people who had nothing to console themselves with—for there were those among them who buried their face in their blanket and wept tears of despair when they thought of what the war had done to them. Before long Indians from Sandusky to Onondaga had taken hold of this new-old religion with revived hope.

Handsome Lake never got to the Grand River, but the hard circumstances that brought forth his movement were equally painful to Joseph's people. The Grand River had need of comfort, too, and it produced its own spiritual leader. Even before the wondering Seneca had beheld his first messenger from the Creator a young Mohawk of blameless character fell into a lengthy trance and dreamed his own dreams. Indeed, the old gods called to him nearly a year before they called to Handsome Lake; and it would seem that what the young Mohawk saw and dreamt could hardly be distinguished from what the elderly Seneca saw and dreamt. The young Mohawk also preached a going back to traditional ways and a renewal of the ancient rites.[70]

Joseph dreamed dreams, too, but his visions were of a different sort, and not merely of late, for he had seen them since his youth. He would have his people keep whatever they had that contributed to their well-being, but he would also have them come to terms with the worthier parts of the white man's culture. Though Joseph did not think well of the "pompous parade of courts" among the whites or of prisons, and certainly not of imprisonment for debt; and although he hated "sharpers" who cheated widows and orphans; and condemned the great inequalities between rich and poor, aristocrat and plebeian; he thought very well indeed of reading and writing and the science of numbers. His people should have no jails but they should have schools. They should have no "sharpers" but they must learn the mechanic arts. They should possess the best of two worlds. Then life would be happier for them than ever it was in the old days. This was Joseph's continuing dream.

That day in the dead of winter when Joseph made the discovery that some of his people had raised up one of the old idols, he was infuriated. The "idol"—actually a sacrifice—appears to have been a white dog, once the main feature of the Indians' great annual rite of thanksgiving and purification. There had been no white dog hung up on the Grand River for years or perhaps never, at least among the Mohawks; but now here it was, at the very entrance to Brant's Town, neatly strangled (without a drop of blood to show for the killing), and painted in handsome colors, and beribboned, and hung up on a pole for all to see. In a towering rage Joseph ordered the thing torn down.[71]

After a while he had some second thoughts. Joseph was no fool. The attempt on his life and the conspiracies against him which had forced him to leave his Grand River home were not entirely due to disapproval of his land policies or to disapproval of his placing whites among the Indians or even to his high pretensions and low birth. Common sense told Joseph he had been a ceaseless irritant to many of his people. He had built a school and urged them to see that their children acquired education. He had tried to get the warriors to pay more attention to agriculture and less to hunting, and to produce a surplus of grain to sell when the agents from down the country came among them, and not sell what their families might need, as they were prone to do. He wanted those young men to use the plow as white farmers did and get the women out of the fields. He also wanted them to feed their cattle regularly and to learn how to repair their tools. And he had urged all his people to accept Christianity and to attend church and to observe life's great events such as birth, marriage, and death according to Christian practices. He had set the example himself, except for his mode of dress which showed that he was still one of *them.* He sent his children to white schools, and he lived like a white man. . . . And so had Captain Cornelius Sturgeon. . . . It was a sobering thought. For Captain Cornelius Sturgeon was dead, killed by his own people these many years past.

Joseph compromised. The Indians should have their white dog festival, but it was not to supersede the practice of Christianity.[72] Apparently, too, he thought the rites should be transferred from winter to spring. From Dr. Edward Walsh, the soldier-artist who created the picture of Brant's new home and who at this time had the responsibility of inoculating the Indians for smallpox, we know that Joseph's way prevailed. Dr. Walsh attended the annual fair in May 1804, and he describes what he saw in considerable detail. By that time a ceremony involving a dog was an important part of the celebration—perhaps the most important part.[73] And Joseph could relax and hope that the professors of the new, ancient religion would be satisfied for another year.

Around the turn of the new century when the roads got better (by 1798 there was actually a stage between Fort Erie and Queenston) Joseph used to sally forth in his coach and four, with a liveried coachman at the reins and a liveried guard sitting up beside him and outriders in livery, for Joseph knew how a gentleman ought to travel. Tradition says that white settlers along the route would run out of their cabins to stare in awe when he drove by, for they were simple folk and this was a sight worth staring at. And if the children chased after the grand equipage, shouting and waving, keeping it in view as long as they could, who could blame them? Not Joseph. With a delighted grin he was probably beckoning them on.[74]

Where was this great man going, who could set the countryside all agape? If it was fair day, he was going to a white dog festival, nimble politician that he was.

28

The Last War

COLONEL BENJAMIN SUMNER and other visitors who had known the Six Nations in earlier days, as well as some who had not known them at all—especially the latter, who expected to see savages and consequently were pleasantly surprised—thought the Grand River Indians had made great strides toward "civilization." Travelers could point to substantial houses (a few), neat fences (enough to cause comment), good crops (sometimes), well-fed cattle (here and there), attentive behavior in church (by small congregations), baptisms (as many as twenty, some years), and Christian marriage ceremonies (the Reverend Mr. Addison usually married a few couples on his infrequent visits). This was great progress, most observers agreed. And, in truth, the Indians had not been static. Though a long war had slowed down their advance, continuing encounters with white traders and white soldiers and white settlers and an occasional white missionary had assured continual change. The Indians could not live like Indians any more, nor did they try. But all of them had not adapted to those white customs of the worthier sort as fully as Joseph desired.

Joseph was disappointed. He had complained to Liston in 1797 that the Indians were not inclined to the life of cultivators and it was impossible for him to bring them to it,[1] and in 1800 he could lament that at least two-thirds of his people were unacquainted with agriculture.[2] Living near white farmers had not helped them as much as he had hoped. Improvement in agricultural methods and in their attitude toward agricultural labor had not progressed as he had intended. Too many women, jealous of their consequence as the tillers of their society, were still scratching the earth with hoes, and loath to give up the practice. Too many young men who should have been plowing fine, straight furrows preferred to go out weeks or even months at a time on hunts. Those great strides toward civilization which travelers admired were neither long enough nor fast enough for Joseph. Making haste slowly was a concept that did not appeal to him. In his view the Indian settlements ought to look as handsome and enjoy as much prosperity as the neighboring white townships, and the sooner he could make this happen, the better. And Joseph, though so often a victim to his own craving for drink, would always hate liquor and what liquor could do to Indians. He called it "Stinking Rum," and worried incessantly over the fact that his people needed repeated admonitions on the score of drunkenness.

Suddenly it seemed that nothing was working out right. A few months after his great triumph (and while still living at the Grand River), Joseph had realized his financial affairs were in a mess. Since the Indians were to have thousands of pounds in annual revenue from their land sales, he had not hesitated to spend for them whatever was needed. But after a while he was pulled up short. Where were the thousands of pounds? The interest on the Grand River sales was due quarterly, the first payments in early May 1798. Though Joseph's records, whatever they were, have not come down to us, we know that the sales he had fought for so hard were not bringing in what they ought. By the third week of May Joseph was getting worried. His usual amiability was wearing thin. He decided to give the delinquents till June 20 to settle up.[3] Such a threat proved him an optimist. Apparently nobody but Beasley (Block 2) tried to settle up in full, and Joseph had to help him. Beasley and Rousseau owned a mill jointly, and Joseph lent Rousseau one thousand pounds to buy out Beasley's share of the mill so that Beasley could pay the Indians what he owed. And if Rousseau returned five hundred pounds and interest in three years, then Joseph agreed to consider the debt discharged.[4] Joseph had to do this in order to get anything. Something, he reasoned, was better than nothing.

Who else was in arrears? Certainly Stedman of Block 1 and the Wallaces of Block 3 (wholly or partially), and, of course, Jarvis of Block 5 who had had devastating financial reverses and whose interest payments, if any, were very small. Stedman was trying hard to sell his land, even traveling across the border to do so, but without success. Stedman's problem was everybody's problem. Joseph's buyers were speculators. They had expected a quick resale and a quick profit, neither of which was forthcoming. They had paid high prices; they could not get still higher prices immediately. And they were not in a position to hold on for very long. They had, as the saying goes, bitten off more than they could chew.

The sales of two other blocks, 4 and 6, had been confirmed. But James Wilson, the new buyer of Block 4 (now that Cozens, Joseph's first prospect, had failed him), had just made his purchase. No interest was to be expected from Wilson yet. As for Block 6, it was really not Joseph's concern, except that he was trying to help his friend Docksteder create an estate for his Indian children. Docksteder's tract had been listed among the Indian sales to assure the legality of its title. It will be remembered that the Indians had at first planned to sell some adjoining land of their own to Docksteder's prospective buyer, but the project had fallen through; and the Indian land had been later cut off and sold to Jarvis as Block 5. As the Indians had no further share in Block 6, Docksteder's loss or gain was not their affair.[5] Docksteder's business was his own business, and nobody else's. It was certainly not Joseph's, though his good nature in trying to look out for his friend continued unabated. For this reason and because the six sales were allowed by the government at the same time, the misfortunes of the Docksteder transaction have always been—though unfairly—laid on Joseph's shoulders.

From the start Joseph had intended to sell additional land—whatever the Indians did not need—and during the course of 1798 he did not lose sight of his original plan. Joseph knew his people were not free if they could not sell their own property. They *must* be free. Furthermore, the failure of some of his purchasers to fulfill their obligations strengthened Joseph's determination to make more sales. Additional Six Nations people were coming in from the United States and the Bay of Quinte,[6] and they had to be provided for. How better could they be provided for and encouraged to remain at the Grand River than by his selling more land—of course to less disappointing buyers? There was no other way to get additional income. The Indians had a great deal of unused land among their various settlements. They also had, as Joseph firmly believed, huge amounts of land extending from the uppermost tract allowed to be sold (Block 4) to the source of the Grand River. There might be four to six more salable tracts in all. The Haldimand grant read to the "source" of the river, and Joseph did not intend to let anyone forget it. In the early fall of 1798 he applied to Peter Russell for a survey of the upper river.[7] Russell, still bedeviled by rumors of invasion and knowing that he must have Six Nations help in the event of war, promised to send Augustus Jones to do the work.[8] Apparently Jones did make some kind of survey which ran to over 104,000 acres.[9] Still, there was no progress toward getting further sales confirmed. The ministry in London was adamant against further sales. Russell had already promised the Duke of Portland that no more Grand River sales ever would be permitted without the king's express sanction.[10]

Joseph had been threatening to go to England. The threat did not have as much effect as he had hoped. He was told that he could go,[11] for it was known that the ministry had no objections. But the idea did not really appeal to Joseph as much as it might have done when he was younger. Age and sporadic attacks of painful illness and the thought of such vast expense had dampened his enthusiasm for "jaunts" across the ocean. It was easier and much cheaper to see what warlike rumors could do. Joseph renewed the program of constant harassment by rumor that had already served him so well. Indeed, he had never really laid aside that program. He did not have to start rumors; they were already floating about. But when he heard a frightening bit of gossip, he promptly passed it on, and it never grew less with the repetition.

When applied to, Joseph was quite willing to verify any of the rumors. He had heard, he conceded, that Indians in the vicinity of the Fox and Wisconsin Rivers had sent out bunches of black and white wampum to Indians to the eastward, declaring that their father of France was again on his feet as long promised; and he added that some of the Missisaugas were expecting French help to avenge the murder of Wabakenin.[12] Russell, more uneasy than he liked to admit, urged Alexander McKee to find out what was going on on the Fox and Wisconsin Rivers[13] and, though he professed not to be alarmed, asked General Prescott for additional troops to defend York which was so open to western attack.[14]

When Russell did not hear from McKee, who was actually too ill to write, he asked Joseph to find out what was going on to the westward, and he promised him a lieutenant colonelcy in the Indian department in case of war. Joseph tartly reminded the administrator that since McKee had interfered with the peace talks in 1793 and destroyed his union with the western Indians, he had not heard from them and did not know what was happening among them. However, relenting a little, he said he would try to find out if the alarming rumors were true. As to the lieutenant colonelcy, he added haughtily, that rank was "very common." He thought the number of men who would follow him in war would entitle him to the rank of a full colonel.[15] Then Joseph dropped a well considered rumor of his own: that there was undoubtedly criminal correspondence between some pro-French western Indians and the Caughnawagas. He was sure the Caughnawagas had hostile designs against the whites and were using their dispute with the Mohawks as a blind to conceal their real purpose.[16] General Prescott found this story hard to believe, but he promised that Russell should have more troops at York by spring.

McKee finally answered two of Russell's letters. Annoyed by Hector McLean's charges against the Indian department and against his friend, Elliott, he did not say there was no danger. But he did not say there was, either.[17] So ended the year 1798. There were frightening rumors about French and Spanish designs, and many people believed them. Russell could no longer confidently assert that he was not alarmed. Still, he was coming to the conclusion that he had been gulled once.

Joseph sent two of his young warriors to the west to find out what was happening there, and he suggested that Russell recommend to Portland that the Indians be empowered to do what they wished with their land. If that question was settled to their satisfaction, he added significantly, "we can thus have no farther hesitation in joining heartily on any danger approaching the country."[18] By late January 1799, the young men were back, bringing with them, so Joseph said, reports of great ferment among the Indians on the Mississippi. He related details of plots in many places. "Your Honor may judge as you think proper," he told Russell, "as for my part I think the French are busy among the Indians, and they will (if possible) Invade the Country."[19]

On the same day Russell received Brant's letter he also got the dismaying news of the death of Alexander McKee. Three months of trying to strengthen garrisons, repair forts, station armed vessels, collect supplies, and drill the militia followed, though Russell was still a little dubious about some of the invasion reports. General Prescott, also dubious but worried about the loss of McKee, sent Sir John Johnson on a western tour to soothe the Indians and make such discoveries as it was thought only Sir John could accomplish. Both Prescott and Russell found it strange that no warning of French and Spanish plots had come from friendly American posts in the west.

Finally there was a rush of good news from all directions. Spies sent out by McKee just before his death found nothing wrong. Other spies sent out later by order of Russell found nothing wrong. The western Indians themselves declared nothing was wrong. The American secretary of state assured Liston that an invasion by a large force from the Mississippi was impossible. Hector McLean derided the whole idea of invasion as a scare promoted by the Indian department for ulterior purposes. And Sir John returned from a long trek on snowshoes with the news that he had found all the alarms groundless. Joseph said he was happy to hear that that was so. Then he detailed all the mistreatment to which the Indians had been subjected since the end of the late war, and gave it as good reason for their rising up in resentment if they could get any outside help, if only in arms and ammunition, from anybody. In the course of his recital he turned his mind back to Sir William Johnson who he said was no better friend to the Indians than Amherst—just a better politician.[20] So spoke a disillusioned Joseph Brant. He had come a long way since the old days at Canajoharie.

By this time authorities in Canada had satisfied themselves that Brant was using the usual invasion rumors, and perhaps inventing others, for his own purposes. Prescott, in Quebec, supposed that Brant was merely trying to increase his importance in the eyes of the people of Upper Canada.[21] But Russell, on the spot, told the Duke of Portland he feared Brant "has Objects in Contemplation beyond my present power of discovering."[22] To a friend he declared he had "certain Proofs of the whole Story being fabricated here to answer private purposes."[23] Joseph dismissed the growing suspicions against him with the scornful remark that Russell was "Jealous, and afeard of the most trifling thing that I do."[24]

In spite of all his efforts Joseph could get no satisfactory answer regarding future land sales. Indeed, he got no answer at all. And when Lieutenant Governor Peter Hunter who had been sent, finally, to take Simcoe's place, paid a visit to Niagara (being also commander of the forces in place of a departing Prescott, his headquarters was at Quebec), he told Joseph in the plainest terms that he could not be allowed to act as agent for the Missisaugas.[25] The disappointed Joseph again related the story of the Grand River land troubles in a council with the new lieutenant governor.[26] Hunter promised to take the Indians' grievances under advisement. He would have to confer with Sir John Johnson before he made his decision, he said. Joseph, hearing nothing for several months, begged Sir John's help.[27] Sir John met him halfway. He recommended the Indians be allowed to sell what they could not use, but that it should be put out of their power to alienate the remainder.[28] As the year 1799 ended, it was the western Indians who were alarmed. Some terrified Shawnees told the Americans at Cincinnati that they had heard an army of whites (from somewhere or other) was about to descend upon them!

In the spring of 1800 Lieutenant Governor Hunter returned to Upper Canada as he had promised. He gave Joseph no encouragement about future land sales. It was another impasse. What to do? Though there were now some rumors that the United States was turning against Britain, and Joseph could have been tempted to use them, he knew he had carried that jar to the well once too often. He said no more about invasion rumors. Instead, in desperation he wrote the aged Lord Dorchester begging for help in placing an appeal before the king. He told his story again: that hunting was ruined and that most of the Indians did not understand farming. It is "absolutely necessary for Our subsistence," said he, that we sell or lease part of our country. "Two or Three Townships we have been allowed to be sure to make Sale of," he went on, "but with a verry bad grace indeed was this indulgence granted us. and I am sorry to say that afterwards malicious, false, ill grounded reports indeed were circulated, such as that we had frightened Mr President Russell into compliance with our wishes. this I Positively deny and say that no People were more firmly attached at the time, to the interest of His Majesty than the Five Nation Indians inhabiting the Grand River—"[29] It was a strange mixture of truth and untruth that Joseph unfolded to Dorchester. He had done his best to persuade, but he knew many months would pass before he could expect an answer, favorable or unfavorable, to his petition. He could not depend upon the petition. He must go on searching for a way out of his financial predicament.

His mind turning this way and that, the idea had already occurred to Joseph that if he could not sell his own land, he might buy some land somewhere and sell it at a profit. At first he seems to have had his eye on a fine tract of Chippewa land near Lake Huron, but those particular Chippewa owners, who did not like him, turned him down.[30] Then Joseph bethought himself of the Detroit merchant, John Askin, and his purchase of Indian lands, a few years before, to the west of Cuyahoga. In early 1796, when Joseph first heard of Askin's maneuvers among the western Indians, he had strongly disapproved; but now, goaded by necessity, he wrote Askin about a possible purchase from him in that neighborhood. He told Askin that he was considering settling some of his people south of Lake Erie, and he sent Augustus Jones, who probably expected to share in the deal, out to Detroit to get information about Askin's title.[31]

Next Joseph wrote to Thomas Morris in New York, carefully telling him (confidentially) what he planned and asking him to find out whether the United States government would be kindly disposed toward a new Six Nations settlement on American soil as it would require American protection. He had evidently decided Askin's title needed strengthening, for he mentioned that he intended to make a purchase from the western Indians—though they would *give* him land—so as to feel secure. He meant to collect some of his wandering people from the Sandusky and the Maumee and even from the Grand

River, he said, and hinted that he, himself, might go along with them to a new home.[32] As Joseph was then and there building his fine new residence at the head of Lake Ontario, he said all these things with his tongue very much in his cheek. Joseph had not the remotest idea of leaving Upper Canada, but buying land to make a settlement had a better sound to it than buying land to sell and make a profit. By the end of 1800 he had reached that point where a few lies, more or less, bothered him little.

The affairs of the Grand River Indians were slipping from bad to worse.[33] Russell could not understand why they wanted to sell more land since, as he heard, they had been so badly disappointed in the returns from what they had already sold.[34] By 1801 the business of each tract was in an almost hopeless tangle. Philip Stedman, buyer of Block 1, had died in a debtor's prison in New York. He had left no will, and the trustees (two of them, at least, for Smith was in and out of the country a great deal) were trying to locate his heirs and assigns. Stedman had not even executed a mortgage, so lax had the trustees been in taking care of Indian business. William Wallace of Block 3 was still alive and not in jail, but seemingly no more able than the defunct Stedman to honor the terms of his contract. The ownership of Block 4 had fallen into dispute, Joseph's first prospective buyer, Joshua Y. Cozens, having come forward to assert a claim. Jarvis of Block 5 had made a payment to principal and was willing to give up that part of the tract which he could not finance, but there was a dispute as to how much he had paid, and his interest was in arrears. Jarvis appears to have disappointed Joseph more than any of the others,[35] perhaps because he had expected more from a man in public office. It is as well to draw a veil over the affairs of Block 6. If Joseph could not untangle his own business, he certainly could not unsnarl Docksteder's which was in equally bad array.

The future of Block 2 appeared more hopeful. Richard Beasley was the most responsible and affluent of Joseph's customers. Beasley, having executed a proper bond and mortgage, had been making annual payments (though not so large or so prompt as Joseph might have desired), and he wished to return to the Indians the acreage that he and his associates could not pay for, and execute new mortgages for the rest of the tract. For this Joseph intended to bypass the trustees who, he seems to have thought, were not always performing satisfactorily.[36]

To divide up Block 2 appeared a simple matter to Joseph, and he instructed Cockrel, the schoolmaster-surveyor, to draw up the new mortgages. Two of the trustees, Stewart and Smith (who was now in

the country), promptly objected. Cockrel's mortgages were too loose,
they said.[37] William Claus also objected; and Claus not only opposed
the new mortgages, he also advanced the idea that the office of trustee
was perpetual—that is, that the office legally passed to the trustees'
heirs. Joseph was taken aback. He thought there was no authority at
all for Claus's new claim, and he declared the Indians had never
intended to extend power to the trustees' heirs who might be incompetent.[38] Joseph was perhaps slightly mollified when Smith, the friendliest of the trustees, after writing Claus and talking with Stewart, told
him he as the Indians' agent had as much right to receive the various
payments in his name as the trustees had.[39] After this reassurance
Joseph felt it was lawful for him to accept whatever installments,
either to interest or principal, that might be proffered him; and he did
collect some money from time to time. Beasley, for one, preferred to
deal with Joseph, and he made most of his payments to his Indian
friend.

There was still no news from England. Joseph had not heard from
his petition to the king. Nothing had come from Lord Dorchester or
the ministry about the right to sell additional land. Apparently the
Indians were not to be treated as the king's valued allies, but only as
subjects. And what poverty-stricken subjects they were, only Joseph
really knew. He continued to make leases to various individuals, some
for 999 years, but what came in from such small business was but a
drop in the bucket of need.

Desperate for more income, Joseph continued to negotiate for land
on the southwestern shore of Lake Erie. In the late spring or early
summer of 1801 he made a hasty trip to Detroit to see John Askin
(though Askin warned him it was not the proper time to come) and to
try to make a deal with some of the local Indians.[40] Nothing was to
come of this trip but trouble. However, Joseph, always ready to see the
bright side, was so far encouraged as to write Governor Clinton the
same request he had written Thomas Morris. Would Clinton find out
for him whether a settlement of Six Nations Indians on American soil
would be acceptable to the United States government?[41] Clinton
promised he would comply with Joseph's request,[42] and he did put the
question to the secretary of state, who got in touch with President
Jefferson. The latter thought the secretary of war was the proper
person to consult, but whether anyone consulted him is not clear.[43] It
was not an important question to the Americans.

This was the summer that Joseph decided he really would go to
England and began to make plans, and then he hesitated and finally
gave up the journey.[44] And this was the same summer that young

Theodosia Burr Alston, bearing a letter from Governor Clinton in case Joseph had forgotten her, came to Niagara with her new husband on their honeymoon. Joseph had not forgotten Theodosia. Though distracted by all his problems, he could still act the genial host, and entertained the young couple at the Grand River with the usual singing and dancing and feasting.[45] When Theodosia got back home, her father laughingly told her that she had made a conquest of "King Brandt," who had written him two letters full of compliments for her. "It would have been quite in style," he went on, "if he had scalped your husband and made you Queen of the Mohawks." He said nothing about a plot.[46] But the very name of Aaron Burr, that wild democrat known to be under French influence, was enough to raise the hackles of people in Upper Canada. Coupled with that of the fearsome Brant, it was to upset the equilibrium of judges and legislators and others in high places. Evil rumors which started from Theodosia's visit to the Grand River needed but a few months to spread and multiply.

The incorrigible juggler in Joseph was still juggling business affairs like spinning balls. At the turn of the century he was attending to so many concerns at the same time that the beginning of one always coincided with the end or the middle of others equally important. There was a continual overlapping of business that must be done, most of which had some bearing on the good of his people. In 1801 Joseph was still doing his utmost to get Davenport Phelps ordained. He was also winding up the Connecticut Land Company business, negotiating with John Askin and the western Indians for American land, and watching the Indian department with a wary eye. He was still trying to encourage the Christian religion and to discourage the consumption of liquor. He continued to urge his people to send their children to school and to adopt white agricultural methods. He was also trying to finish and move into his new house and to take care of the education of his own children. He was doing all he could to promote the union with the Missisaugas. He hoped to calm the dissensions at the Grand River, to untangle Indian finances (and his own), to get additional land sales confirmed by the government, and to see that the Grand River Indians obtained firm title to everything included in the Haldimand grant. Above all, he meant to see that the independence of his Indians was acknowledged, that the Longhouse might emerge for the future respectable and respected. Even the petty business of finding someone to write a letter took up time. Amid all Joseph's heavy burdens, this was a constant small harassment.

That fall Joseph was still determined to divide Beasley's tract so that Beasley might keep what he could pay for and return the rest. He also had in view a similar division for Jarvis' tract. William Claus, who had moved up into McKee's position of deputy superintendent general of Indian affairs (immediately under Sir John Johnson), was vehemently opposed, though why this was so Joseph could not conceive. It apparently did not occur to him what the stumbling block was. But if a great deal of land was returned to Brant, he would be free (would he not?) to sell it to someone else. To *someone else?* To *whom?* That was the question that would vex the authorities. In such a case it would also vex William Claus.

William Claus was an essentially timid young man who had long ago learned a lesson. He had learned it in his boyhood, by observation of the plight his father had thoughtlessly got himself into. Claus had observed that it is never well to go off and leave your employment if your superiors wish you to stay put. He had also learned that one should do what one is told, and do it cheerfully and at once. But if one has not been told what to do, then it is best to follow the line one judges most likely to please. Such were the precepts that William Claus lived by. Consequently he was liked by those in power, and he was already on the rise. When Joseph met up with William, who seemed of late inexplicably perverse and stubborn, even a little unfriendly, he was to meet up with both the immovable object and the irresistible force. Joseph had not yet found this out.

In October 1801 Joseph and the Grand River Indians went over to the head of Lake Ontario where they were to hold council with Claus and get their annual presents. Claus had just heard some very bad gossip about Joseph's doings in the west.[47] Joseph himself was harried and distraught. He had come early with some of his followers, probably to discuss the division of Blocks 2 and 5. The discussion did not go well, and he and Claus had a heated argument. Both said things they were soon sorry for. Such old, old friends they were. Joseph loved children; he could have dandled the baby, William, on his knee. Next day Claus, who had had time to cool off, sent for Joseph. The two met behind Claus's tent. Before Claus could apologize, Joseph spoke up and begged forgiveness. The unseemly quarrel between old friends was made up.[48]

Controversies at the Grand River had been growing stronger as the Indians' expectations of a great income diminished. The council which followed his quarrel with Claus was one of the lowest points of Joseph's career. His enemies, who were mostly young warriors (encouraged by a few hostile whites, he thought), were present in force. Yielding, finally, to their loud complaints about his bad management, he had to promise to give up his agency on the next May Day and let a committee of twelve chiefs take over in his stead.[49] This outcome could not have been unexpected. Mournfully Joseph had already decided to act only in a "private" line,[50] and the story was now actually going the rounds that Brant was winding up all his affairs, public and private, and that he meant to go to the Mississippi to join the Spanish![51]

About this same time Joseph suffered another blow. Constantly in his thoughts was the great tract of land between the uppermost block which he had sold and the source of the river. This tract with its thousands of acres comprised no small part of Haldimand's grant, and the Indians, in such need of income, could ill afford to lose it. As he was still on a very friendly footing with the Missisaugas, Joseph decided that, if the government would not buy that land for the Six Nations, he would make the purchase himself. He spoke of this plan to Sir John Johnson. Sir John, referring to the troubles at the Grand River, advised Joseph to abandon that notion at once. He warned Joseph that the government was determined not to sanction the Six Nations claim but on the contrary would protect the Missisaugas in their property. He also advised Joseph not to concern himself in Missisauga affairs.[52] Joseph was hurt. He had no intention of defrauding his friends. He wanted to *buy* the rest of the Haldimand grant, and he could have done so easily. He replied to Sir John's advice with obvious resentment. Though he promised to give up his special relationship with the Missisaugas, he intended to meet anybody he pleased at general Confederacy councils. "When called for," said he, "I think it my duty to meet the Indian nations abroad, and cannot at present think of desisting from this ancient and useful custom, until these nations shall be made acquainted with the tenor of your advice, and I become excused by them from attending their councils."[53]

Sir John, whose temper had not been improved by all his own troubles and frustrations, did not answer. Joseph wrote again in the same vein. He also denied that the trouble at the Grand River was so bad as Sir John had pictured, and such as it was he blamed on some Fort Hunter Mohawks, with no real chief among them. The real chiefs, he said, had unanimously approved his conduct as agent in land matters. He thought Sir John's advice regarding councils with other nations was "a threat in disguise," which he did not suppose Sir John himself had originated but in actuality had softened to save his feelings.[54] Again there was no reply from Sir John. So ended many years of correspondence. Henceforward there was no pretension of amity between the two old associates.

The close of 1801 found Joseph trying to refute jokes going around

Queenston and Niagara that he had frightened Peter Russell into confirming the land sales of 1798. He wrote Russell two letters in one day on this touchy subject. His arguments in support of his denials were very reasonable and his indignation properly obvious.[55]

Joseph would never be trusted again. Russell had considered him basically loyal, and probably still thought so; but he also firmly believed that "ambition and desire of wealth" were the chief's "ruling Passions."[56] There were many in and outside the government who could easily concur with the latter estimate but not with the former. Russell, they would have said, was too liberal in his feelings toward Brant.

When, after Joseph's visit to Detroit, stories began to trickle in that he had been up to no good and that he had made a seditious speech to the western Indians, there had been no lack of persons ready to believe the worst. William Claus was one such, and the bad rumors had induced in him the mood which had helped to bring on the quarrel between the two. There was a flurry of letters between Claus and the Indian department at Amherstburg to find out the facts, and testimony from both whites and Indians was taken. A Chippewa chief named Makons (Makounce), who feared and disliked the Six Nations, and who was a sort of pet of the Indian department, had much to say; and, indeed, it was Makons who had started the story about Joseph in the first place. Joseph denied all wrongdoing, but suggested bitterly that some people might be surprised that he claimed the right to free speech.[57] Claus thought Joseph's situation very serious, and the far-flung inquiries went on.

Apparently Joseph, on his sojourn in the west, had not only had his eye on American land but was still trying to buy some Canadian land in the vicinity of Lake Huron. For these reasons he had to make an effort to repair the old confederacy with the western Indians. Gathering around him some Chippewas, Ottawas, and Potawatomies, he told them a few plain truths. The plainest of the plain truths was that, if they had listened to him in 1793 instead of listening to British officers at the posts, they would have been able to retain a large part of the country which they had subsequently lost. Then, according to the testimony of Makons, Joseph went on to say—and either Joseph was drunk, his wampum was misinterpreted, or Makons was deliberately lying—that the British government had shown great ingratitude to those who had rendered it the greatest services; that he himself had been laid aside as "useless" and left with not a cornfield for his family's support; and that he had traveled among the whites and had become well acquainted with their general policy toward Indians. Finally, as it was reported at Amherstburg, Joseph threw aside all restraint. Declaring that he was a greater man than all the British officers, the commander in chief not excepted, he urged his hearers to go to Buffalo Creek and agree to what should be proposed there. What was to be proposed he did not make clear, but it seems to have had something to do with reconciling the western Indians to the Six Nations.[58] Whatever it was, it did not sound well to British authorities.

As Joseph enjoyed no popularity among the western Indians, he got no land on either side of the border. And the reports, true or not, of what he had said did nothing to enhance his reputation anywhere. His reputation was growing worse all the time. Jealousy on the part of both whites and Indians, caused by the belief that much money was flowing through his hands (and sometimes sticking to them, as people thought) was enough to produce an almost universal heartburn.

Joseph probably never knew of another story that was going around to his detriment. It was a frightening tale that was circulated very quietly in certain places, and it depended for its air of authenticity on the fact that Joseph Brant was not the only one in Upper Canada who was disgruntled about land. There were many people—some British subjects, some not—who had never been able to get as much land as they wished or who, getting it, had lost it for nonperformance of their contracts. Such people might not hesitate at revolution to achieve their ends. It was whispered that Aaron Burr, that master of intrigue, had used his son-in-law as an agent between conspirators on both sides of the border. A force from the United States, so the story ran, was to invade Upper Canada; it would be joined by those who had grievances against the government, and Brant and his Indians were to help or at least remain neutral. Upper Canada and Lower Canada, too, would be annexed to the United States, and all those people who nursed grievances, including the Indians, were to be requited. Peter Russell did not believe this story, but Chief Justice Elmsley and at least one of the district judges did. Joseph Brant was acquiring more enemies in high places every day.[59]

From a practical point of view the Longhouse had been divided into two parts for nearly twenty years. Since most of the populous Senecas had elected to remain in the United States, the American part was the more numerous. For this reason Joseph had never questioned the idea that the main fireplace of the Six Nations was with the Onondagas settled at Buffalo Creek, and he had faithfully attended general councils there. But when he heard some of the Onondagas from the American side wished to remove to the Grand River and bring with them their ancient central fireplace, he did his utmost to encourage the measure.[60] It was easy for Joseph to dream new dreams; he could already see his Grand River settlements as the powerful heart of the entire Confederacy. Meticulously Joseph advised Governor Clinton of the Onondaga plan, for he thought Clinton had an interest in the movements of New York Indians; and he had a favor to ask of Clinton. He wanted a statement attesting to the vast extent of the hunting grounds of the Canajoharie Mohawks which had been unsold at the beginning of the late war and in lieu of which they had been given Grand River lands. The governor need have no fear of any further Mohawk claims on the state of New York, he went on; he merely wished to use the statement to reinforce the validity of his people's claims in Upper Canada. But no matter what arguments Joseph presented, Governor Clinton was not inclined to favor either project. He had no desire to involve himself in Indian disputes and certainly not in Indian disputes with the government of Upper Canada. He apparently kept as many Onondagas at home as he could, and Joseph got no statement.[61]

In April 1802, when Count Joseph de Puisaye finally gave up and returned to England, Joseph sent another petition to the king by de Puisaye's hand.[62] He also wrote Lord Dorchester again and his friend, the Duke of Northumberland.[63] A similar letter to the Earl of Moira has been preserved. Without the needed statement from Governor Clinton Joseph could only estimate the extent of the lost Mohawk hunting grounds. The lost tract, he thought, contained over two million acres, and the Grand River tract had been given to the Indians in its stead. "Latterly," he said, "it has made us uneasy to find our title seemingly disputable—and also not to be able to have our Grant confirmed by the legal *deed*, as is the other grants to Loyalists; but I yet have that confidence in the equity and honor of the British Government, that I flatter myself should His Majesty be acquainted with our situation, he would not fail to have justice rendered us." For further details he referred the earl to de Puisaye.[64] Unfortunately de Puisaye was a man of no great influence, and the British government, regardless of any efforts the Frenchman might make, was very, very busy with much greater affairs. Joseph would get no help through this avenue.

In the meantime, in February 1802, the principal chiefs at the Grand River had reiterated their trust in Joseph Brant as their agent.[65] Next month, in spite of the vote of confidence, Joseph, who had apparently had his fill of trouble and who, it will be recalled, was about to move away, was still saying he was going to resign his post on

May 1.[66] But before that date came around Henry Tekarihoga and fifteen other chiefs had succeeded in persuading him to change his mind. He agreed to remain at the head of their land affairs but stipulated that twenty-four chiefs be selected from the various nations who should have the final say.[67]

Joseph continued in the forefront of public business the rest of the year, and little was heard of the twenty-four chiefs. In July he again inquired of the trustees, through D. W. Smith, who was home once more, whether it was legal for him to accept payments of interest in behalf of the Indians. Smith did not consult the other trustees this time, but he again gave his opinion that Joseph could receive payments both to interest and principal. For the second time Joseph was reassured that he was pursuing the right course.[68] Then in November the ax fell. A proclamation by Lieutenant Governor Hunter in Council forbidding the Indians even to lease their land, and in any amounts, large or small, was nailed up in public places. Past as well as future leases would not be recognized![69] Now what was Joseph to do? Must the Indians go forever begging up and down the Niagara road? Did no one care what happened to them? This was "worse than Slavery," stormed Joseph.[70]

In the winter, after Joseph and the chiefs had considered their position and Joseph's agency had been reconfirmed, Joseph went to York to see the lieutenant governor. He took with him John Norton, who had resigned his official post as interpreter and who was now living with the Indians at the Grand River. Joseph and Norton could not get a meeting with the lieutenant governor. His secretary, Major Green, told them that no communications from the Indians could be received except through the agent for Indian affairs—that is, through William Claus. But Claus, they thought, had become so unfriendly that nothing could be expected by his interposition. They discussed the matter with the new chief justice, Henry Allcock, and complained of the trustees and the government. Allcock gave them a little encouragement. He told them that Lieutenant Governor Hunter was considering their affairs and they might hear his decision in two months. With this Joseph and Norton had to give up and go home. It was now February 1803. They waited considerably more than the two months before they heard anything further.[71]

On June 14 Lieutenant Governor Hunter ordered the Executive Council to conduct a formal investigation into the Indians' land affairs and recommend what action ought to be taken. The investigation was done mainly by Chief Justice Allcock, and a report was submitted to the lieutenant governor on June 24.[72] The report was as comprehensive as the short time of ten days would allow. It took up, one by one, each of the six tracts of land that the Indians had sold.

No new information had been uncovered about Stedman or his heirs, but a certain Elisha Welles, who thought he could get a release from the heirs, if any, was willing to take Block 1 on the same terms. It was advised that Welles's offer be accepted. As to Block 2, some six hundred pounds in interest had been paid and distributed among the Indians, but the rest of the interest was in arrears. It was advised that the trustees sue Beasley, Wilson, and Rousseau for the back interest. No grant had been made of Block 4, but the reason why had not been discovered. Wallace (Block 3) and Jarvis (Block 5) must be forced to execute their contracts or give up all claims. If the latter, these blocks should be returned to the Indians, but in the meantime it was recommended that Blocks 1, 3, and 5 be impounded by the Executive Council. It was also advised that it be made clear to the Indians that all these contracts had been negotiated by their agent, Brant, and not by the government of Upper Canada. Block 6, though in a different category, was also investigated. It appeared that Benjamin Canby, Docksteder's purchaser, had obtained his grant without giving any security whatever—how, it was not quite clear, but apparently by some misrepresentation made to Secretary Jarvis. It was advised, then, that Canby be forced to give security and pay his arrears of interest.

Lieutenant Governor Hunter, an efficient executive who wished to do right by the Indians, approved Allcock's report. The report, however, did not contain all pertinent information. The Indians' affairs were much more confused than the chief justice had discovered. The Indians thought they had resold Block 1 (or that Elisha Welles had resold it) to an American named Peter Hogeboom, and they were accepting money from him.[73] Beasley and associates were still trying to clear up their debts, and the Indians still wished to divide Block 2 and give a deed for part. They were very determined that Beasley be treated fairly. He had paid too much, said Joseph, for one individual to lose or for the Indians to gain from such an unfortunate person.[74] Besides, Beasley had already sold part of his mortgaged tract to some Mennonite immigrants from Pennsylvania who appeared, commented Joseph, "honest & industrious" people, and he was determined to protect them.[75] Wallace, of Block 3, whom Allcock had declared completely in arrears, had actually made many payments, according to Joseph.[76] As to Secretary Jarvis and Block 5, the Indians did not care what happened to him. They would like to get that tract of land back. By this time Captain John Docksteder had died, but Joseph was still trying to help his half-breed children. Joseph admitted the law of estates was too intricate for him—he knew nothing of such business, he owned—but he begged the chief justice to point out some way to name an executor to provide for the children and see that creditors were honestly paid.[77]

Out of all these complications two facts clearly emerge: first, Joseph did not possess sufficient education to carry on such difficult business; and, second, he and the trustees were working at cross-purposes, for both parties were collecting the various revenues. Joseph, secure in his power of attorney from the Indians and the authority, as he thought, to accept money, was not only accepting money but managing it. In his situation this was a necessity. He had been forced to borrow at times, and at other times he had lent money at interest, probably more than is known.[78] Whatever the trustees were doing in the way of management, if anything, there seems to have been little consultation among them, each apparently relying upon the others. And whatever consultation there was between the trustees and Joseph he had to initiate. Moreover, Stewart and Joseph were now at daggers' points; Claus was carefully doling out justice to the Indians according to his concept of what the government wanted—and many in the government, with their friends, were as land-mad as any speculator and, in fact, were speculators, as Claus well knew—and the friendly and erudite Smith was away in England most of the time, unknowing and for all practical purposes mostly unapproachable. All the while Joseph, in his ignorance, was wondering how vacancies on the board of trustees were to be filled up and whether the government had the exclusive right to confirm further Indian land sales, such as the sale of Block 4 or of any land that might be returned, or whether, as Claus contended, only the trustees could make such confirmations.[79] Administering the Indians' land affairs was a job for an acute legal mind, and Joseph, unhappily, had no training in the law.

In August 1803 a great council was held at Niagara. Most of the Indians were there, and Claus, and the officers from Fort George. Joseph complained bitterly about the prohibition of leasing. It was based, he was told, on the Proclamation of 1763, and applied to all Indians. But Joseph knew that Indians in Lower Canada were leasing their lands, and he thought an old law, promulgated so many years before, in an entirely different situation and in another country, was of no import. Besides, he knew the Indians of Canajoharie and Fort Hunter had continued to make leases after 1763, proclamation or no proclamation, and nobody said them nay. "Should we be deprived of

Leasing our Lands, how are we to Subsist" was Joseph's despairing question. On that subject Claus had no answer to make; "but I would advise you," he said, "not to expect that there will be any more Sales allowed of, and as to Leases, that is quite out of the question, it cannot be allowed of."[80]

In November Joseph was again begging Governor Clinton of New York to give him a certificate stating the extent of the hunting grounds which the Canajoharie Mohawks and the Indians of Oquaga had formerly possessed. We have no demand on New York, he reiterated, but wish to show the British government how much more we gave up than what we now possess as compensation.[81] Again Governor Clinton appears to have made no answer.

In this same month the young Scottish philanthropist, Lord Selkirk, who was intent on establishing colonies of his poverty-stricken countrymen in Upper Canada, traveled through New York's Genesee country and on through Upper Canada to York and Montreal. On the way he heard a great deal of ugly gossip about Joseph Brant; he "seems," said the young man, "to be generally considered as a complete rogue." He described Joseph's land sales and said that according to report Brant was to receive a "personal douceur" of one-tenth of the various tracts. He also heard that the purchasers had no capital "& seem to have reckoned on juggling away the payment of the interest with Brant's assistance till they should be able to sell enough to make it a good bargain." But General Hunter had intervened, he added, and insisted on compelling regular and punctual payments. One of the purchasers, according to the gossip (he must have meant Beasley), has ruined himself by paying interest to Brant instead of to the trustees. The purchasers, continued the young nobleman, cannot sell until they can give security for performance of their contracts. Lord Selkirk then summed up what nearly everybody believed in these words: "In the affair of the Grand R. Lands, Brant has contrived to get a good deal of Cash into his own hands & perhaps has divided a share of the plunder with a few leading men who have supported & carried thro' his measures in the Councils— The young men & others who have got nothing sometimes clamour, but have no influence in the Councils, & are put off or pacified by the help of the women.—" Gossip had put the worst possible construction not only on Joseph's activities but also on Henry's and Catharine's help.[82] The jealous public, both white and Indian, thought Brant was rolling in wealth, all of which he had got dishonestly.

A short period of peace in Europe had been followed by more war. John Norton, ever the romantic, decided to go to England and offer his services to the British government. Joseph wanted to go, too, but did not have the money. There was a secret meeting of Joseph's supporters at Brant's Town. They gave Norton instructions to try to get the confirmation of the Haldimand grant in England. Some of the chiefs slipped away with Norton to Niagara, and Joseph came down from the head of the lake. Joseph entreated Norton to do his best and gave him letters to the Duke of Northumberland, the Earl of Moira, Evan Nepean, and others.[83] It was now February 1804. Norton crossed the border and headed for New York City. There he could get passage to England despite the wintry weather. At Albany Norton met Lord Selkirk, who was carefully traveling almost the same route a second time, trying to learn how new settlements could be successfully set up. Lord Selkirk readily suspected Norton was going on a mission for the Indians.[84] Norton went on to New York, and Lord Selkirk headed again for Upper Canada.

Joseph, demoted to supporting actor, could only watch and wait and take care of affairs at home. The Indians still thought they had some kind of deal with Elisha Welles regarding Block 1, and Joseph wrote him that the chiefs would not want him to suffer if unforeseen events caused some trivial delay in the performance of his promise.[85] In another matter Joseph and Henry and the other chiefs proposed to Claus that they give Dr. Oliver Tiffany a grant of land in settlement of a £125 bill run up in the past seven years since, as they were so straitened for money, they had no other means of payment. Of course, they suggested hopefully, they were willing that the government should pay the bill.[86] The chiefs also asked Claus his opinion on whether they should record all their public transactions in writing for posterity. Claus frowned upon that idea. He thought nothing should be written down between Indian and Indian since it never had been done, and he advised that they adhere to their old customs. He also urged them to cast away all discords and jealousies. Unity, he said, was their best defense against enemies.[87]

On May 18, 1804, the Executive Council again reported to Lieutenant Governor Hunter on the Grand River lands and made some sweeping recommendations. Again the report was Chief Justice Allcock's work. It had been found that Richard Beasley had managed to buy out his partners and was now ready to settle the affairs of Block 2. There was some controversy about how much Beasley had paid, and a council would have to be held to determine that matter. At the same time Beasley's Mennonites were to be allowed to keep their purchase provided they paid all sums due on it by May 15, 1805. At last the Indians could expect a regular income, for the money due them, if the

ministry agreed, was to be invested in England in three percent government annuities, the interest to be distributed to them yearly. The
Council also advised that Sir John Johnson be added to the board of
trustees, for Smith seemed to be permanently living abroad.[88]

The recommendations of the Executive Council were accepted by
the lieutenant governor, and a council of the Grand River Indians was
convened at Brant's Town in late June to consider Beasley's and
Brant's accounts. The accounts, meticulously set out, were unanimously accepted by a throng of sober and sobered Indians who obviously realized the importance of what they were doing. Sir John was
admitted as a trustee, and compensation in land was requested for the
Wallaces. Henry Tekarihoga's name led the list of signing chiefs, but
although four principal women signed, Catharine's name was not
among them. Catharine and Joseph sat quietly on the side lines. This
was a very proper assemblage, and it was attended by several officers
from Fort George. Lieutenant Colonel Brock himself attested to the
regularity of the proceedings.[89] But in spite of the regularity and the
unanimity there seem to have been some heartburnings here and
there.[90]

Joseph was cheered with the way Indian affairs were shaping up,
and he had great hopes of Norton in England. In a charitable mood
engendered by his hopes and the proceedings at the Grand River he
attended another council with Claus on September 29. The presents
were distributed, and there was no controversy. Joseph was biding his
time. He dined with Claus and some other officers, and, as Claus
observed in his diary, Brant "was a little in liquor but was Very much
inclined to be civil."[91]

Unfortunately for Joseph, though he was thinking charitable
thoughts about people, people were not thinking charitable thoughts
about him. Lord Selkirk had finally made his way up to Burlington
Bay. Joseph met the young nobleman at Hatt's store at Ancaster, and
the two had a long discussion. Lord Selkirk was too much imbued with
hostile gossip to change his mind about Joseph, though the Hatt
brothers who kept the store were Joseph's friends and tried to change
his mind for him. Much of the trouble came, said the storekeepers,
because Claus had such a personal enmity to the chief. Selkirk was not
convinced. He still believed Brant was appropriating Indian money to
himself, but having met Brant, he could be philosophical about the
frauds. After all, Brant was an Indian; his manner was "quite Indian,"
and "it is not very likely that it [the money] would be of real use if paid
up to the Indians—the less money they get the better for themselves—"
In the midst of this conversation Joseph denied that he had sent John

Norton on a mission for the Grand River Indians. Joseph, according
to plan, always denied this. Then he added that Norton was coming
back, though he did not know when.[92]

What was Norton doing while Joseph was denying any interest in
his activities? Norton was doing very well, fully justifying Joseph's
confidence in him. The various letters of introduction smoothed his
way. The Duke of Northumberland was willing to exert all his influence in behalf of his Mohawk friends. And Northumberland had a
great deal of influence—in his own right in the House of Lords and in
the right of a bounty of rotten boroughs in the Commons. He could
see that John Norton was an even more remarkable savage than
Joseph Brant. Norton dressed as an Indian, wore a ring in his nose,
and claimed that he was a chief. He actually was a chief—an adopted
chief, but sometimes he forgot to mention that point. He was just as
likely to say he was an Indian, and his sunbronzed skin was dark
enough for him to get away with the claim.

On June 2 Norton called on the Earl of Moira with Joseph's letter
of introduction. The earl received him hospitably. Moira had often
had letters from Joseph Brant, and he recognized Brant's signature.
Norton explained in great detail in an eloquent memorial just what he
was trying to do, and why. Moira regretfully told him he had no
authority in that field, but he sent Norton to the Earl of Camden, who
did. Camden was favorably impressed with the young man. So, too,
was Alexander Davison, a powerful merchant, who asked John King,
one of the undersecretaries, to give Norton, "a Mohawk Indian," what
assistance he could regarding the land the Six Nations occupied.
Norton also managed to enlist the aid of the aged Lord Dorchester.
The affair was going unbelievably well.

On August 2, 1804, the Earl of Camden sent a copy of Norton's
petition to Lieutenant Governor Hunter. "I am to desire," said he,
"that you will particularly examine into the nature of any difficulties
and inconveniences they [the Six Nations] may experience and afford
such redress as they shall appear entitled to." It was obvious that
Norton was on the verge of success. Camden continued: "You will
transmit to me the fullest information upon this subject and take care
to prevent any encroachment upon the Land and Privileges assigned
to these People."[93]

In Upper Canada there was consternation. If the Haldimand grant
was confirmed, it would be confirmed in its entirety, from the mouth
of the Grand River to its source. The upper portion of the grant would
have to be bought from the Missisaugas (who certainly would not
refuse to sell), and given over to the Six Nations. There were already

people in Canada who prophesied that this must eventually be done,[94] and if the grant was confirmed in England, there would be no doubt about it. And the grant might well be confirmed. The Duke of Port-land was no longer in charge of colonial affairs. The Indians appeared to have an excellent chance of getting full title to all the land they claimed above Block 4, as well as lower down the river. They could then be expected to sell it to anybody they chose. It was known to be very fine land, too.

Lieutenant Governor Hunter did not think well of such a pros-pect. Judge Allcock's reports had given him a very poor opinion of Indian land sales, and it seemed to him Norton had gone off in an underhanded way. Hunter got in touch with William Claus. Claus was ordered to convene the Six Nations and get their views on Norton and his mission.[95] The Indians were to be given an opportunity of dis-avowing Norton and all his proceedings.

Claus says that he did not have to call the Six Nations to council, but that they came forward of their own accord. Yet he also says he felt it his duty to tell them that this white man was in England and, under the guise of being a Mohawk chief, was representing the Six Nations without their knowledge or consent. The necessity to speak up was especially clear, said Claus, since Brant himself denied Norton had any public mission in England. "Whether therefore he [Norton] was doing right or wrong, it was my duty," Claus later defended himself to the Indians, "to inform you of all that came to my knowledge, and," he added virtuously, "that duty I shall ever perform."[96]

The principal chiefs at the Grand River, who were Joseph's friends and associates and who knew what Norton was trying to do, refused to attend Claus's council. But Joseph's enemies and some of the common people did attend. The council was first convened across the border, at Buffalo Creek, where councils involving the entire Six Nations, American as well as Canadian, were customarily held. At least a few chiefs were present from all the American Six Nations, with Red Jacket and the Senecas very much in evidence. Only Cornplanter was conspicuously absent from the Seneca delegation, his hostility to Red Jacket having outgrown his hostility to Brant; and, indeed, Corn-planter figures no more in Joseph's life. John Johnston, a former employee of the British Indian department who was living at Buffalo Creek, took a prominent part in the proceedings. John Norton was quickly repudiated, and Joseph Brant was deposed for "misconduct" from whatever positions he was supposed to hold. New chiefs were raised in place of those who did not attend, and then the whole council adjourned to British territory and resumed work at Newark.

Several officers from American Fort Niagara later certified that about forty Senecas, including Red Jacket and other well-known chiefs, a number of whom were American pensioners, came to Fort Niagara on their way to Upper Canada and, while detained by ice in the river, declared both publicly and privately that they were going into Upper Canada "for the express purpose of breaking Captain Brant."[97]

The council crossed over to the British side as soon as the weather moderated. It was now early April 1805. The American chiefs and Joseph's Grand River opponents, with the newly raised Grand River chiefs, met with Claus and British officers from Fort George and related what had taken place at Buffalo Creek. The recital was evidently satisfactory, and an account of Joseph Brant's deposition was sent to England.[98] Claus also continued to pursue the old Makons affair, apparently with the idea of adding it to the list of Joseph's misdeeds.[99]

In the meantime John Norton had met with a setback. He had left Canada without a copy of the Haldimand grant, and a copy could not be found in England. Though D. W. Smith and Lord Dorchester could attest to the grant's general purport, and the latter did not object to an extension of its terms, a copy of the grant was necessary. A request was sent off to Canada for a copy. By this time John Norton's funds were running low. Having no military commission as yet, he had to ask for an allowance to tide him over. He was told he had better get passage for Quebec before the winter set in. This he was very reluctant to do until he could hear the outcome of his mission. To add to his discomfiture Chief Justice Allcock arrived in England bringing his two reports of Brant's land sales, and Allcock did not hide the fact that he thought the Grand River Indians had only the right of occupancy, with no right to lease their land, much less to sell it. At length the news came from across the Atlantic that Brant had been deposed by his own people and Norton's mission completely repudiated. Much was made of the fact that Norton had left the Grand River in secret.

The outcome was now no longer in doubt. Though Norton could write letters and offer explanations and present petitions and haunt the offices of the great, he got no further encouragement. Nor did anything come of his military aspirations. It was as though a blight had settled down upon him. "What I asked for the Six Nations," said he despairingly, "was no more than justice, and although it might thwart the speculating schemes of avaricious individuals, if granted, yet it would not fail to strengthen the interests of Great Britain in that quarter." It was no use. The blight stayed. Sadly Norton took passage for home. He arrived too late in the season to get a boat up Lake Ontario. He set out walking. Somewhere he managed to obtain a horse, and on foot and on horseback Joseph's desponding emissary finally got back to the Grand River with his story of hope unfulfilled. Almost two years had gone by since Norton had slipped away from Upper Canada with Joseph's letters of introduction and the well wishes of friendly chiefs.[100]

While Norton was undergoing so many disappointments in England, Joseph was trying to overcome the effect of the council that had brought about his "deposition." He got a certificate from the American officers at Fort Niagara as to the plan of the Senecas to "break" him and still another certificate from Israel Chapin, Jr., attesting to his general good character and loyalty to Britain.[101] But the great war in Europe had now taken such a turn—or, rather, the American elections had taken such a turn—that statements of American officials could not be so well received in Canada as they might have been a few years earlier. Joseph had first tried to tell his side of the controversy to at least one British officer, but no help came from that quarter.[102] The officers at Fort George, most of whom had been present at the council between Claus and the Senecas, had become very circumspect in their dealings with the troublesome Brant.

Joseph pointed out indignantly that the Senecas and others of the American Six Nations had no right to meddle in the private affairs of the Grand River, and they certainly had no right to meddle in Grand River business from a council fire kindled at Buffalo Creek.[103] Since the war Joseph had always recognized those Onondagas who had fled to Buffalo Creek as heirs to the ancient right of keeping the central council fire of the Confederacy, and he had gone regularly to their fireplace when American and British Six Nations met together to discuss general concerns. He had attended at Buffalo Creek many times during the troubles in the northwest, meeting with deputies from the western Indians there and trying to inspirit his American brethren to hold fast to the western alliance. Once, in Simcoe's time, when exasperated at his kinsmen, he had threatened never to attend one of their councils again.[104] But it was only a threat, and he went back often; and he had urged the Caughnawagas to bring their grievances to the great fireplace for discussion and settlement. Of course Joseph would have been only too glad to welcome the many American Onondagas to the Grand River but, as we have seen, he had been balked in that hope.[105] But those Onondagas who did live at the Grand River, though fewer in number, had always kept a council fire for local concerns, and Joseph believed that his position and the Grand River lands were strictly local business for local transaction at the local fireplace and in no way the concern of any of the American Six Nations. It was his contention that Indians who did not live at the Grand River had no right to a voice in Grand River affairs.

William Claus contended otherwise. When Henry Tekarihoga and Joseph's other friends reiterated their confidence in him and berated Claus for holding hostile council with chiefs who were actually American pensioners,[106] Claus pointed out that Senecas from the United States had attended the council at Niagara in 1797 when some new chiefs were raised up and Grand River land sales were discussed. He did not point out that the Senecas were on their way to Quebec that year nor that they had come to Niagara only out of concern for their presents.[107] Joseph had the better of this argument; Claus had presents—and power. Nevertheless, with the support of the principal chiefs Joseph continued as agent for the Grand River lands. Defiantly he continued to make leases in spite of the government ban.[108] And after trying unsuccessfully to persuade the American Senecas and others that they had no right to interfere in Grand River land business,[109] he appears to have gone no more to Buffalo Creek. It was the beginning of a permanent split between the two branches of the Six Nations.

On October 18, 1805, Joseph took the time to make his will, the first so far as is known, although he had had severe attacks of illness and had been in many dangerous situations. He provided for his children and Isaac's children, giving them land at the Grand River or at the head of the lake, but most of all he took good care of his "beloved Wife Catharine." Catharine would never have to depend on her offspring for financial help. She was left with such a power over family property that the children would of necessity have to cultivate her good graces, for Joseph gave her all his personal estate for her sole disposal; the valuable seven-hundred-acre farm where they lived, for her lifetime, to be disposed of by will to any or all of their children; and one third of the rents and profits of the big farm at the Grand River for life. Catharine and old friends, Augustus Jones and Ralfe Clench, were named executors, and Joshua Pell and Alexander Stewart (with whom Joseph had made up his quarrel) and Stewart's wife, Jemima (daughter of Brant Johnson), witnessed the will.[110]

For an Indian to make a will was an unheard-of act. But, then, Joseph had valuable real estate to pass on, and in matters of property he could forget he was a "regular Indian." If Joseph had obtained shares of land from his buyers, as was charged, the chicanery did not show up in his will. As he was generally in need of money, there could not have been much cash in his personal estate, and his landed property was such as he had obtained openly and honorably. Nor had he ever sold land (sales he could not have kept secret), and, indeed, nobody has ever accused him of selling any of his ill-gotten real estate. And as Joseph had sold the Indians' Grand River land at very high prices, it hardly seems reasonable that, as many believed, he could have received kickbacks for selling it too low!

About this time or possibly the year before, Joseph is said to have had a violent encounter with a man who later wrote an unfriendly biographical sketch of him. No matter how much he hated "Stinking Rum," Joseph was drinking rather freely in these cheerless days, and of course his drinking was public knowledge. There is a tradition to the effect that a young Scottish clergyman from Cornwall named John Strachan (a Presbyterian turned Episcopalian), who sometimes preached at York, made some critical comments on Joseph's vice in one of his sermons. Joseph heard about this, and in his rage got very drunk and went in search of the clergyman. He swore (so the story runs) that he would make "the ——— Scotch turncoat apologise wherever he found him, even if it were in church." He actually found the young cleric on a street in York and knocked him down and threatened to scalp him if he did not take back the offensive words. The clergyman retracted everything, for if Joseph was elderly, he was big; and if Strachan was young, he was also a little man and no match for the enraged old chief. Afterward Joseph told some friends he only meant to scare the fellow.[111] Regardless of the truth of this story, for some reason Joseph quit his drinking, at least for a while.[112] Many years later Strachan wrote the famous article about Brant, from reminiscences given him by John Stuart, which was not entirely flattering. But it was not likely that Stuart's memories of Brant were very flattering, either, and on the whole Strachan's article in the *Christian Recorder* in 1819 was not more biased than might have been expected.

When John Norton finally returned in late 1805 and told his story, naming the Duke of Northumberland as one who had greatly befriended him (and who may have given him financial aid, for how else had Norton been able to subsist?), Joseph wrote the duke to thank him for his kindness.[113] On January 24, 1806, he again wrote the duke saying he had hoped much from the arrival of a new lieutenant governor (Sir Francis Gore, who had succeeded the recently deceased Hunter), but that he now feared the lieutenant governor had been prejudiced against the Indians by officials who had "an insatiable avarice for lands"; for he (Gore) had already refused to hear from the Indians except through Claus, their "implacable enemy." Therefore another attempt to get the Haldimand grant confirmed must be made in England.[114]

Back came a reply as fast as three thousand miles of ocean would permit. Said the duke: "I am happy to find that the interest I took in the affairs of the Five Nations has been acceptable to their Board, as I am [referring to an adoption by the Mohawks years before] by being one of their community. They may rest assured I shall always be happy to assist them to the utmost of my power." Although Norton failed, the duke said, it was not for want of zeal. But there were some new ministers in office now, and he thought they would listen to the wishes of the Five Nations, and with suitable safeguards do as they desired. He advised that Joseph himself or Norton or some other chief, properly authorized, should come to England to finally settle the business.[115] Then the nobleman added something very characteristic of him which Joseph could only have read with a wry smile.

"There are a number of well-meaning persons here," said this earnest disciple of Rousseau, "who are very desirous of forming a society to better (as they call it,) the condition of our nation, by converting us from hunters and warriors into husbandmen. Let me strongly recommend it to you, and the rest of our chiefs, not to listen to such a proposition. . . . Nine hundred or a thousand warriors, enured to hardship by hunting, are a most respectable and independent body; but what would the same number of men become who were merely husbandmen?"

Some who propose this plan, continued the duke to his Mohawk friend, are not so well-meaning. They would instruct us in agriculture, but their real object is to get our land. "I wish to see the Christian religion, sobriety, and good morals, prevail among our nation; but let us continue free and independent as the air that blows upon us; let us continue hunters and warriors, capable of enforcing respect, and doing ourselves justice; but let us never submit to become the tillers of land, hewers of wood, and drawers of water, by the false and interested advice of those who, from being our pretended friends, would soon become our imperious masters."[116]

Alas, Joseph knew the Mohawks did not have nine hundred or a thousand warriors, and neither did all the Indians of the Grand River. It was the white people of Upper Canada who had the warriors, and their numbers continually increased. No amount of hunting, even was there game, could guarantee independence to the Indians. Under present conditions it would not even assure them a living. Joseph shuddered to contemplate how close the "imperious masters" had really come.

Early in the year Joseph had attempted once more to see what could be accomplished in Upper Canada. On February 14, 1806, he sent a petition to the Assembly, a procedure as yet untried. He told his usual story: the Indians' services in the war, the grant by Haldimand as recompense, the later attempt by the Upper Canada government to cut off a large part of the grant. He then described Claus's use of the American Senecas and his fomenting of dissensions on the Grand River, and said he despaired of any relief through the Indian department. He thought the Grand River property was of little consequence to Britain, but if it was considered too large a compensation for the Indians' services and losses, then "in God's name," he entreated, "let them confirm the one half."

Brant's petition was read in the Assembly on February 22 and debated, and the House voted to consider it early in the next session.[117] It would be a wait of many, many months, but Joseph was used to waiting.

At last Joseph and the Indians heard the good news that they were going to get a part of their long-deferred income. The news was definite. Richard Beasley had finally been able to straighten out the affairs of Block 2 though it had taken the combined efforts of himself and his Mennonite settlers, Joseph, the Executive Council of Upper Canada, Claus, Stewart, Allcock, Sir John Johnson (who declined to be a trustee), and even the British ministry, to bring about this desired result. Over nine thousand pounds of Block 2 money had been invested in British government annuities, and the Grand River Indians were to receive the income.[118] If the sales of the other blocks could be brought to a similar happy conclusion, Joseph knew the protests against him would die down, and Indians from the other side of the border would come flocking in again. The Grand River settlement might yet achieve respectability. It might even achieve independence and affluence.

Unfortunately the tangled affairs of the other blocks did not appear close to unravelment. Block 1 had acquired still another American claimant, one Daniel Penfield, but there were rumors of fraud and forgery in connection with the Penfield claim, rumors all the more to be given credence in that relations with the United States had worsened. There were now three claimants to Block 1, besides a sister of the deceased Stedman whose rights had to be considered. The Wallaces of Block 3, still in arrears, had given up all but seven thousand acres. (For some reason Claus did not object to this division, as he had objected to a division of Beasley's Block 2.) The remaining Wallace lands had been sold or parceled out to Joseph (five thousand acres given him by the chiefs for his services), to William Claus's deceased mother (ten thousand acres in memory, apparently, of her father, Sir William Johnson), and Capt. Robert Pilkington (a purchase of fifteen thousand acres) who planned an ambitious settlement in the wilderness. The rest of the Block 3 land, including Pilkington's share, would soon go to another band of Mennonites. William Jarvis was still in trouble over Block 5 and claimed to have paid more than anybody, either Brant or the trustees, admitted receiving. Block 4 had finally found a buyer, Thomas Clark of Queenston, who, it was thought, was solvent and responsible, though other claimants, in the background, had not given up.[119] The Docksteder tract appeared to be a total loss. The trustees did not concern themselves about it. Nobody but Joseph worried about the Docksteder orphans who, as he said, having acquired the "Superfluous Wants of Europeans," were of course needy.[120]

In July 1806, forty Grand River chiefs held an important public council about their land affairs at Fort George. These were friends of Joseph, and he was the main speaker. Full confidence was expressed in Norton, no confidence in Claus, and it was asked that some other medium be appointed for transacting their business as they were disappointed in the performance of the trustees. Joseph reiterated the argument that Grand River affairs could be decided only at the Onondaga council fire on the Grand River. He went on to accuse Claus of mishandling thirty-eight thousand dollars of Indian money, and he asked that some other person be appointed deputy superintendent. This speech was delivered in the presence of several officers of the garrison; and Judge Robert Thorpe, a powerful but suspect politician; William Weekes, an Irish legislator, also suspect; and the missionary, the Reverend Robert Addison, these latter three being just now, for various reasons, thorns in the side of the government of Upper Canada. Joseph had obviously chosen his audience with forethought. (Sometime during these proceedings a very angry Claus got up and left the council.) After Joseph had spoken, his Indian friends declared they were perfectly satisfied with all his transactions, that they did not object if he used some of their interest money when he was traveling on public business. Admiringly they referred to him as "our leading Chief Col: Brant [who] has stood foremost in our affairs."[121]

Joseph had from time to time considered going to England; he was certainly advised more than once by Henry Tekarihoga and the friendly chiefs to go,[122] and once he had actually started and then turned back.[123] Money was a problem; the Indians never subscribed travel funds as such, and his own purse was thin; and, moreover, he

Joseph Brant, 1806. Painting by Ezra Ames. Joseph is old and has little to smile about, but he has not yet given up hope. *Courtesy of the New York State Historical Association, Cooperstown.*

was always afraid of what might happen on the Grand River if he absented himself too long. But after the Duke of Northumberland's urgent letter, Joseph made definite plans to make the journey, money or no, and finally set out in early August. He made his way across the state of New York, through country that was considerably changed since 1797, with more and bigger settlements and more and better roads (*expensive* turnpikes) and more and better inns (but *expensive*), and people too busy to resent his appearance among them. If he had hopes of getting financial aid from Thomas Morris, he was disappointed. If he thought to get aid from anyone else, or to collect a debt, or to sell something (but what?), he was also doomed to disappointment. And though he could travel on the Indians' money, Indian money was in woefully short supply.

Toward the end of August Joseph was in Albany, a guest of the James Caldwell family. The Caldwells—Mr. Caldwell was Joseph's agent in Albany—received him kindly. Here William, Caldwell's son, suggested that Joseph have his portrait painted, as the town now had the services of a fine artist. Joseph protested he had brought no Indian regalia, for of course he must be painted as an Indian. The lady of the house thought that deficiency was easily remedied. She went out and bought some figured calico, and an Indian shirt was quickly stitched together. With the addition of a few beads and an earring, Joseph was able to look as he ought, and he sat for his portrait.[124]

The artist was Ezra Ames, a New Englander who was equally facile at painting signs and wagons and fire buckets and clock faces, as well as portraits, and he did an admirable job. We see Joseph in his old age, a little corpulent, but still a "regular Indian." He has the authentic scalp lock, and besides the Indian shirt and the beads, he wears a dark scarf or neckcloth, and something which could be an Indian blanket is draped over his left arm and shoulder and caught up on his right. The portrait is somewhat somber, but Joseph smiles faintly.[125] It may be thought wonderful that Joseph could still smile. But he had come through the Mohawk country without unpleasantness. His hosts were hospitable and kind. They did not hold it against him that he had fought kinsmen of theirs thirty years before. They did not accuse him of stealing anything. Though desperately unhappy, Joseph smiled. On August 27 William Caldwell paid the artist his fee of thirty dollars and obtained both the portrait and a frame.[126] It was an excellent bargain. There were some who pronounced this painting the best likeness of Brant they ever saw.[127]

Albany was as far as Joseph got.[128] He had no money to go on. He turned back to Burlington Bay and his family and Catharine, his never-failing helpmate. The visit to England would have to be postponed. But perhaps something—for Joseph still hoped—might come of his petition to the Assembly. Or perhaps he could think of something else to try that was not so costly as a trip across the sea.

On the way back home Joseph had to pass through old Canajoharie where there was a little grave that war and time had very likely obliterated, but he knew where it was. With no enemies in pursuit, he could have visited it. But did he? Joseph had long ago turned his back on memories. In all the years that had passed no one, so far as we know, had ever heard him mourn his old home—a situation almost unique among the Loyalists. And Joseph was a certified Loyalist, a United Empire Loyalist. His name—after he requested it—went on the famous list that year.[129]

Joseph returned to more controversy. He and Claus went at each other tooth and nail. Every claimant of every block claimed to have paid something to somebody. Such vagueness and uncertainty made good grounds for suspicion. Claus answered Joseph's charges of peculation with some veiled charges of his own. He hoped, he said, that others could explain what they had done with Indian money as well as he could. He listed what he had received, and how he had spent it, and what he had sent to England. His lists of figures were loud and clear. More subdued—too low and subdued, the Indians thought— were his explanations of his dealings with the American Senecas in 1805.[130] Joseph had mentioned Claus's fine, new house in connection with missing Indian money.[131] Joseph's charges now appeared outrageous, and nobody believed them. John Norton admitted that Joseph had some misconceptions about Claus's handling of Indian finances. Norton thought Claus had actually taken good care of the Indians' money.[132] Judge Allcock, now back in America, wondered how anybody could fault Claus, and Claus continued to enjoy the confidence of those in power.

One last council for the year 1806 was held at the Onondaga fireplace on the Grand River in November. Joseph and Henry Tekarihoga and Norton and their friends were there. They discussed their business affairs and decided that they preferred to invest their money in England. Though interest was higher at home, it was thought that the money was safer under the king's supervision. Joseph changed his mind over the winter. Norton did not. Living so far apart the two had fewer chances to discuss the difference of opinion, and they may not have discussed it at all. At any rate, in April 1807, Joseph spoke up in favor of Canadian investments. Claus set about making the most of the small dispute.[133] It could be an entering wedge between the two friends. Claus disliked Norton even more than he disliked Joseph, and was determined to drive the former out of the Indians' councils since it was impossible to remove the latter. He had a modicum of success. There was a coolness between chief and adopted chief, at least on Joseph's part, for several months. Joseph disagreed with Norton on certain proposals for selling land as well as on investments, and he claimed he had signed the November speech on Norton's recommendation without reading it.[134]

The estrangement could not have lasted long. By mid-August Judge Robert Thorpe, with whom Joseph had become very friendly, promised to try to reconcile the chief to the idea of sending Indian funds to England (it would strengthen British-Indian ties),[135] and apparently he succeeded. Joseph very naturally perceived Thorpe, fiery opponent of Lieutenant Governor Gore, as a supporter of the Indian cause and a friend to the underdog in general, and Thorpe did have influence with him. Furthermore Joseph had reached that time in life when he wished to make peace with all the old friends with whom he had quarreled,[136] and Norton certainly had been an old and valued friend.

Again there was talk of a trip to England.[137] Again Joseph prepared to go, getting his wardrobe in order.[138] Then again he had to back out. There was not sufficient money. He wrote the Duke of Northumberland sending him powers to act for the Indians.[139] He knew Northumberland was influential and willing. Perhaps something could be done without his own actual presence. Joseph, being Joseph, found it impossible to give up his cherished plan of getting the Haldimand grant confirmed.

Now that some income was coming in, or about to come in, from the Beasley sale, Joseph worked hard to bring the other sales to a like happy ending. He thought Penfield's claim to Block 1 should be countenanced, and repeatedly he and Tekarihoga and their followers petitioned the trustees in the American's favor.[140] It was no use. Tensions were rising between Britain and the United States over British searches and seizures on the high seas, and by the summer of 1807 war seemed imminent. By fall Upper Canada was arming again. The western Indians were reminded of the debt they owed their father, and the French bogey awoke from its doze. Under such conditions Penfield was a man suspect. A more politically acceptable buyer must be found. Two other unsold tracts were more fortunate. Some Mennonites with ready money had taken over the unsold part of Block 3, and Jarvis, suitably reimbursed for what he had spent, had finally given up his claim to Block 5. Lord Selkirk stepped forward. Selkirk was someone on whom Claus and the government and Joseph and the Indians could unite. It looked as though the sales of 1798 might finally confer some benefit on the sellers.[141] But no—not yet. The dividends from the Beasley tract proved so very slow in coming and the Indians grew so very discontented that the government, frightened at a possible loss of red allies, thought it wise to furnish an estimated dividend to set their minds at rest.[142]

It was nearly ten years since Joseph had sold those five tracts with such high hopes. The sweet taste of triumph was long gone. Only the bitterness of failure remained. A dream was dying.

29

"Have Pity on the Poor Indians"

W HEN JOSEPH took stock, he realized that his people were still in
no hurry to emulate that part of the white culture that he
urged upon them. The necessity of adjustment to the white way of life
did not seem to enter into their thoughts. Christianity was making
little progress. There had been more Christian Indians in Ogilvie's
and Barclay's flocks fifty or even seventy years ago than anyone could
count now. The Reverend Mr. Addison was able to make the journey
to his Grand River congregation only twice a year. Then he might
baptize as few as ten or as many as nineteen children or marry perhaps
three couples. These were Mohawk converts; but in 1804 some Tuscaroras offered for baptism, in 1806 a Cayuga couple was married, and
in 1807 several Onondagas requested to be baptized. It did seem to the
missionary, of necessity an optimist, that prospects for Christianity
were not quite so bleak as they had been. Joseph was not sufficiently
impressed to mention this little improvement.

As to education, Joseph had seen to it that Brant's Town got a new
schoolmaster (one William Hesse taught reading and writing now),
but some of the Indians were not sure that schooling improved their
offspring, and they even thought the children had better manners
without schooling. There were parents who did not send their children to school very willingly, and some did not send them at all. And
for those who learned to read, where were the books to be read? There
were only a few books (primers and prayer books) among the Indians
now that Joseph had taken away his own modest collection.

John Norton in a burst of enthusiasm judged the Indians were
drinking less, yet he also admitted it was impossible to keep liquor

away from the Grand River settlements. Joseph said nothing. He was always opposed to drunkenness—but if he himself had become abstemious, it may have been only because he had less company to entertain and therefore less temptation. In 1806 we hear of just one visitor to his home,[1] though there must have been others; and in 1807 no one is particularly mentioned, though there must have been some guests who came to the "mansion." But no traveler could visit Brant's home now with the excuse he wanted to observe Indians. There were no Indians at the head of the lake to observe except Joseph's family, and Catharine, acutely aware of the way they lived, may have thought sadly there were no Indians there at all.

John Norton also thought he saw some improvement in the Indians' agriculture, at least among certain individuals. He reported that several Mohawks raised three or four hundred bushels of wheat annually. These same industrious farmers, he observed, seemed to be the persons who, when the hunting season came around, were also the best hunters. Many of the Indians were raising cattle, too, but, Norton had to admit, not too successfully. Like the Germans, they took the young calves away from their mothers but, unlike the Germans, they did not feed the little animals regularly. They were not very regular in their own meals, said Norton, much less in those of their livestock. Again Joseph said nothing. Obviously he saw no improvement worth his mentioning. Perhaps the only good thing he could see was that the Indians had not, as yet, fulfilled the whites' predictions of disappearing from the face of the earth. At least they still lived.[2]

The year 1807 continued in painful suspense. There was little for Joseph to do, now, except to wait, and he was so tired of waiting. Nothing had been heard from the Assembly, and of course nothing could be expected yet from the Duke of Northumberland. Joseph had no inkling that the short-lived Grenville ministry, in office from January 1806 to March 1807, was not inalterably opposed to his being allowed to sell more land though they said nothing about giving him his deed.[3] But on March 31, 1807, the Duke of Portland, whose views were well known, came back into office, this time as prime minister. Joseph certainly would have known there was no hope from the Duke of Portland.

As war clouds rolled up, there were some strange stirrings here and there. In September 1807 Joseph's old antagonist, Captain Hendrick Aupaumut, set out to renew peace and friendship with the Indians of the Indiana Territory. Captain Hendrick seemed to be in a forgiving and forgetting mood. Writing Joseph from Buffalo Creek, he commiserated him about his land troubles. "And for my part," said he, "I will never live on a land which can be taken away from me without my consent." He hoped Joseph would succeed in his efforts to get his grant confirmed, and he sent him his blessing.[4] Though Joseph may have suspected that Captain Hendrick had been sent by the Americans on some secret mission among the western Indians and that he had some hidden motive for writing the friendly message, he did not raise an alarm. The time was past for alarms.

In the fall of 1807 Joseph was helping to put the finishing touches to Lord Selkirk's deed for Block 5, and he was negotiating with Selkirk's agent for two smaller tracts in the same vicinity. The negotiations were disrupted when the chief fell ill.[5]

Joseph's illness was, so anyone could have predicted, just another of his customary short, painful attacks. For sixteen years he had been ill off and on, the most recent attack apparently in 1804.[6] Had he resumed his drinking? And did it affect his health? The Reverend Robert Addison who depended on him as an interpreter but who did not see him often, thought he had, and implies that his drinking was killing him.[7] John Norton, too, seems to imply that Joseph was drinking heavily again.[8] At any rate Joseph was very ill and in much pain. He was sicker than anyone realized.

Two neighbors, Augustus Bates, who kept the government hostelry at the south end of the beach, and Asahel Davis, who lived next door to Joseph, came in often to see him. They found that he was bearing his sufferings patiently. He was able to talk to them, and brought up religious subjects as he had done many a time. He said nothing shocking. He never had said anything shocking in their presence. Years later these two friendly neighbors made a formal statement that they believed Joseph Brant lived and died in the faith of the Christian religion.[9]

Sick or well, Joseph was still the same man. Whatever random and feverish thoughts came crowding into his brain had to be the thoughts of a lifetime: ". . . my wish ever was for Peace . . . . we are an independent People . . . . it was the British that prevented the Treaty . . . . The establishment and enlargement of civilization and Christianity among the natives must be most earnestly desired . . . . born of Indian parents . . . . even supposing us to be faithless, what could be apprehended of dangerous consequence from us, considering the smallness of our numbers and our situation? . . . Those you call savages."

Yes, Joseph was the same man: ". . . the English might have lost all America had it not been for the friendship & Assistance of the Indians

. . . . at the peace they were left in the lurch to fight alone . . . . Stinking Rum . . . . An unfortunate accident . . . . Every man of us thought, that by fighting for the King, we should ensure to ourselves and children a good inheritance . . . . my beloved Wife Catharine."

They were the thoughts of a lifetime: ". . . justice is all I wish for . . . . it seems natural to Whites, to look on lands in the possession of Indians with an aching heart, and never to rest 'till they have planned them out of them . . . . the Interests of the Indians has ever and I hope Ever shall be my greatest aim . . . . and remain a free people . . . . God willing."

Anguished thoughts that would not go away: ". . . the Gates were shut against them . . . . without being united we are nothing . . . . should we be deprived of making the most of our Landed Property, many must starve, many must go Naked . . . . many of our Nations perfect strangers to Farming . . . . we came to a proper understanding . . . . we want nothing more than what we enjoyed before the American War, the land we then lived on was our own and we could do what we pleased with it . . . . I am totally dispirited . . . . Then we shall begin to know what is to befal us the People of the Long House."

Joseph lay in an English bed in an English room, and fine English blankets covered him over, but a pipe-tomahawk he had given Catharine, and the dagger, were in plain view.

John Norton watched by the bedside. Joseph stirred and roused himself. "Have pity on the poor Indians," he charged his trusted friend; "if you can get any influence with the great, endeavor to do them all the good you can." These, according to William L. Stone's careful findings, were the last words that anyone remembered him to have said.[10]

On November 24, 1807, Joseph died.[11] His stormy sixty-four years and eight months had ended in exile, and there would be a grave in alien earth. But when the news of his death was brought back to his old home, willing hands tolled the bell of the little Mohawk church all the day and throughout the night for a desolate twenty-four hours.[12]

There were those at the Grand River who knew where Joseph Brant belonged.

Epilogue

HOW THE MONSTER BRANT BECAME
THE NOBLE SAVAGE
AND HOW JOSEPH FINALLY WENT HOME

JOSEPH's petition died with him. Catharine got her pension and went back to Brant's Town, where, together, she and Henry Tekarihoga tried for many years to carry out Joseph's policies. And for many years there were wild dissensions on the Grand River as Brant party and anti-Brant party fought their continuing battles.

Eventually young John grew up and took a leading part in the War of 1812 on the Niagara frontier, though the Grand River Indians in general, from bitter experience, betrayed no great enthusiasm for joining the fight. At the close of the war John took Elizabeth, his youngest sister, back to the house at Burlington Bay. It was the home these two remembered best. Catharine frowned upon the move. For her, home had to be Brant's Town.

John was eager to clear his father's name, and in 1819 he got his first chance. That year the Reverend John Strachan, already a power in church and state, started a new little journal called *The Christian Recorder* and published in it his biographical article, "Life of Capt. Brant." The gist of this article had been drawn from conversations with Strachan's missionary friend, Stuart (no great friend to Joseph), and perhaps colored by some prejudice of his own, for he pictured Brant as a drunkard and a man of scant loyalty to either church or king. The twenty-five-year-old John Brant took indignant exception to this libel on his father. A correspondence followed between the young Indian and the clergyman. Strachan's facts, though many, had been grossly misinterpreted, and John was able to show that the offensive statements were not rooted in truth, but in a twisted version of the truth. Explanations ensued on both sides, and the Reverend Dr. Strachan's conduct was "most honorable."[1] Apparently Strachan apologized, though no apology got into print, for the little *Christian Recorder* soon became defunct. Nevertheless John Brant had made a start on a general vindication of his father.

A few years after the war the government of Upper Canada bought

653

from the Missisaugas all the country from Block 4 up to the source of the Grand River, and allotted it to white settlers. When the chiefs of the Six Nations protested that this land was a part of their grant, Sir Peregrine Maitland, the then lieutenant governor, told the Indians in no uncertain terms that the land had not been bought for them.[2] The Indians—or Henry and Catharine—sent John to England to advance their claim to the whole of the Haldimand grant. John made the trip in 1821–22 with the usual results. He was feted and petted, but he did not get what he went after.

While in England John remembered the Scottish poet Thomas Campbell, whose poem, "Gertrude of Wyoming," had been published in 1809, when John was only fifteen. The term, "the Monster Brant," still rankled in the young man's heart. He sent the poet a mass of documentary evidence which proved Joseph Brant was not even at Wyoming and never the monster depicted. The poet was convinced, and he was apologetic. Said he:

> I rose from perusing the papers you submitted to me certainly with an altered impression of his character. I find that the unfavourable accounts of him were erroneous . . . . The evidence afforded induces me to believe that he often strove to mitigate the cruelty of Indian warfare. Lastly, you affirm that he was not within many miles of the spot when the battle which decided the fate of Wyoming took place, and from your offer of reference to living witnesses I cannot but admit the assertion. Had I learnt all this of your father when I was writing my poem, he should not have figured in it as the hero of mischief.[3]

The wording of the poem was never changed, but John accomplished something more in the clearing of his father's name, for Thomas Campbell's apology was published in London in *The New Monthly Magazine* for 1822, where all who would, might read it.

Help for John Brant came from an unexpected source. In the United States the old frontiers had stabilized as new frontiers had been pushed farther and farther west. Old Indiana Territory had become a state, Illinois was now a state, even distant Missouri had been admitted into the union. Whites would soon be fighting Indians far across the Mississippi. Back in New York and Pennsylvania, on the Mohawk, the Susquehanna, and the Delaware, where hatred of Joseph Brant was strongest, people rested from subduing a wilderness. Many had the leisure to read books, and some took up their pens to write books.

In 1831 a different Campbell, one William W. Campbell, son and grandson of Cherry Valley captives, published his *Annals of Tryon County; or, The Border Warfare of New-York during the Revolution.* This Campbell, a native of Cherry Valley, had been raised on its folklore. With great care he gathered together the stories of his boyhood. They were the stories and reminiscences of people whose travels had never taken them very far from home, who had not related what they knew to anybody but homefolk. From Campbell's *Annals* Americans learned for the first time of Joseph Brant's efforts to save the people of Cherry Valley and his humanity toward women and children at nearby Springfield—a story that many old Loyalists knew well, but which could not but surprise the descendants of hard-bitten rebels. William W. Campbell also republished in an appendix to his book the whole story of "Gertrude of Wyoming" and the poet Campbell, and the latter's apology to Brant's son. The apology, known for nine years in England, now became known in the United States. Americans were not ungenerous, they were fond of a romantic tale, and many willingly expunged the atrocities of Wyoming and Cherry Valley from Joseph Brant's record. It was enough to rejoice the heart of John Brant before he died so untimely the next year.

A still more important book, a detailed biography of Joseph Brant, was on its way. William L. Stone, famous biographer and historian, began to collect records of the Revolutionary era. He went far beyond William W. Campbell who had researched mainly on home ground. He visited Six Nations reservations and heard what aged Indians had to say about Joseph Brant, and then went on to Upper Canada to visit Brant's children. He saw the Burlington Bay "mansion" with his own eyes and met Elizabeth and her husband and little family, and in doing so he obtained most of the correspondence that Joseph had left behind.[4]

Back home Stone interviewed or corresponded with aged veterans of the Revolution and former prisoners of war or their sons and daughters or friends and neighbors and, indeed, anybody who could dredge up some memory or legend of Brant, however vague and wispy. He heard how Brant had sent a captured baby back home to its grieving mother (at Fort Hunter, in 1780, was it not?); how he had painted his mark on schoolgirls' clothing and saved them from death or capture (at a little log school, it was thought, somewhere on the upper Delaware); how he had saved this or that prisoner from the torture of the Indian gauntlet (at some Indian town); that he had connived at the escape of frail captives who could not keep up with his marching warriors (somewhere on some trail); and, indeed, that he never failed to show compassion and humanity—sometimes, alas, at places where he could not possibly have been.

Out of all this material Stone wrote his *Life of Joseph Brant-Thayendanegea* and published it in two bulky volumes in 1838. In this impressive work he declared that he had searched in vain and found no instance of wanton cruelty at the hands of Brant or by his permission. Stone was a popular author; his writings held much appeal for the people of his day. Through William L. Stone the public perception of Joseph Brant was almost turned around.

A generation later Lyman C. Draper, the great collector of historical data, did for scholars what Stone had done for the reading public. Using Stone's methods, though on a much larger scale and for many years, he gathered together in two series of three and twenty-two volumes respectively[5] every scrap of information he could find about Joseph Brant, finally bequeathing the whole, with other massive collections on early western history, to the State Historical Society of Wisconsin. Indefatigable researcher that he was, Draper pursued every clue to its end. He unearthed the rest of Brant's private correspondence (whatever Stone and autograph hunters had left); assembled pamphlets and newspaper clippings from hither and yon, anti-Brant as well as pro-Brant; collected court records and diaries and account books; gathered together the vagaries of aged raconteurs and even the recollections of descendants a hundred years away from the events they described. Whether momentous or trivial, Draper preserved everything. Like Stone, he found no actual witness of anything to Brant's dishonor.

And so, inevitably, hatred and suspicion of Joseph Brant turned to an almost general admiration. The "Monster Brant" was no longer a monster. As early as 1879—oddly enough, at the centennial celebration of the battle of Newtown—Brant was publicly eulogized as

> A chieftain of majestic mien,
> With kingly front and warrior eye,
> With soul to dare and to endure,
> To hold, with purpose firm and sure,
> The cause of people and of home.

From that moment to the present there have been few dissenting voices, either in Canada or the United States, in regard to the essentially noble character of Joseph Brant. Brant, says one historian, combined the role of a "British gentleman-officer and an Iroquois warrior-diplomat." His acts, declare others, were "the acts of a noble, generous

In 1886, nearly eight decades after his death, this great monument of granite and bronze was erected to the memory of Joseph Brant at Brantford, Ontario. *Courtesy of the Brantford Regional Chamber of Commerce.*

man"; he was "a loyal subject, a man of noble action, and a dauntless hero"; he was "the apostle of clemency." If Brant was William Johnson's son, says another, "he was a son to be proud of." If greatness consists of "courage, sagacity and honesty," adds still another, then Brant is "the most distinguished Amerind in American history." And on and on, and much to Joseph's delight, could he have known: Brant "carried the sword in one hand and the prayer book (his own Mohawk translation) in the other"; he had "few rivals for daring leadership"; he was as near to the ideal of the "noble red man" as we are ever likely to see. He was "the most civilized savage of his time."

Joseph would not have liked that word "savage." But "noble"? Ah, that was different. Joseph loved compliments. Besides, the praise was well merited (mostly), he would have thought. He always did declare he had done his utmost to mitigate the horrors of war. And he had worked all his life (had he not?) for the good of his people. One can almost see him smiling that gentle smile that Charles Willson Peale painted so long ago.

In time factionalism died down on the Grand River or at least the Brants were no longer the issue. Henry Tekarihoga, aged and blind, died in 1830. Catharine, whose right it was, named her favorite son, John, as the next Tekarihoga. Two years later John died in a cholera epidemic. He was only thirty-eight, but he had already had a worthy career in several fields. Now, out of all her daughters' male progeny there was only a child left whom Catharine chose to honor. This was Elizabeth's young son, and he was hardly more than an infant. There would be a long regency headed by his mother. Catharine herself died November 24, 1837, thirty years to the day after her beloved Joseph. Elizabeth died in her early middle age. There was none left to urge the Grand River to change its ways. There was none left to irritate and prod.

After a while the people of the Grand River (many of whom were becoming excellent plowmen and who, with a good income from their investments, would soon be able to do without presents, and whom almost nobody looked upon as "savage") took prideful thought of their great man who lay so many miles away. By the side of the little, old Mohawk church they set about to prepare a proper resting place for him. Then, in November 1850, they gave Joseph his second, finer funeral. Youthful pallbearers were sent across country, uphill and downhill, through woods and swamps, to Burlington Bay. And on the shoulders of strong, young grandsons of men he had known, Joseph Thayendanegea was carried, by relays, back home.[6]

Notes

When a source is first cited, its title is given in full. Later citations may be shortened to standard abbreviations, but the full title can always be found in the Bibliography. Main standard abbreviations used in this work are: *Johnson Papers*, for *The Papers of Sir William Johnson; Michigan Historical Collections*, for *Collections of Michigan Pioneer and Historical Society; New York Colonial Documents*, for *Documents Relative to the Colonial History of the State of New-York; Russell Correspondence*, for *The Correspondence of the Honourable Peter Russell with Allied Documents* . . . ; and *Simcoe Papers*, for *The Correspondence of Lieut. Governor John Graves Simcoe*. Full titles of the above publications, for instance, with complete publication data, may be located under Published Primary Sources.

CHAPTER 1—THE WORLD OF THE LONGHOUSE

1. *The Jesuit Relations and Allied Documents: 1610–1791*, ed. by Reuben Gold Thwaites, 73 vols. (Cleveland, 1896–1901), 41: 87.

2. The Rev. Elkanah Holmes, January 1801, interview with Col. [Joseph] Brant, Samuel Miller Papers, no. 1. MS. at New-York Historical Society. Joseph's story, which is in the form of answers to questions put by Holmes, is one of the earliest accounts extant of the formation of the Confederacy. It is, of course, a Mohawk account. Other versions of the legend usually name the famed Hiawatha as co-founder of the union. See "A Glimpse of Iroquois Culture History through the Eyes of Joseph Brant and John Norton," ed. by Douglas W. Boyce, *Proceedings of the American Philosophical Society* 117 (1973): 286–94.

3. The economic problems of the Five Nations are set forth in great detail in George T. Hunt, *The Wars of the Iroquois* (Madison, Wis., 1940). Though this work offers a very persuasive thesis, economic motives cannot explain all the Iroquois warfare. In Joseph Brant's eyes, obviously, the wars were for glory and for bringing distant peoples under the Tree of Peace.

4. Modern scholarship doubts that some of these triumphs were so triumphant (even in the Indian way) as history has been led to believe. For instance the boundary between the Mohawks and the Mahicans was not finally settled till 1768. Nevertheless, the Iroquois reaped a harvest of hate and fear among many of their enemies that is usually accorded only to those who have been too successful, militarily. The real point, as far as Joseph Brant is concerned, is that the Indians of his day firmly believed in the one-time glory of the Longhouse, the whites generally accepted it as fact, and Brant himself not only believed in it but did his utmost to reestablish it.

5. Maj. John Norton (Teyoninhokarawen), Journal of A Voyage, down the Ohio [1809] . . . and An Account of the Five Nations, &c from an Early Period, To the Conclusion of the late War Between Great Britain & America [1816], 1: 256, 269. MS. in archives of Duke of Northumberland, Alnwick Castle. Microfilm, Library of Congress. See *The Journal of Major John Norton 1816*, ed. by Carl F. Klinck and James J. Talman (Toronto, 1970).

6. The word *woman* had a much lower connotation among the white settlers than among the Indians—hence the more the Delawares came to know white people, the more they hated their female status. Paul A. W. Wallace, *Indians in Pennsylvania* (Harrisburg, 1961), p. 57.

7. Gov. Tho. Dongan, Feb. 22, Sept. 8, 1687, to Board of Trade, *The Documentary History of the State of New-York,* ed. by E. B. O'Callaghan, 4 vols. (Albany, 1849–51), 1: 154, 256.

8. See Anthony F. C. Wallace, "Origins of Iroquois Neutrality: The Grand Settlement of 1701," *Pennsylvania History* 24, no. 3 (July 1957): 223–35.

9. Benjamin Franklin, Mar. 20, 1750–1, to James Parker, *The Writings of Benjamin Franklin,* ed. by Albert Henry Smyth, 10 vols. (New York and London, 1905–07), 3: 42.

10. Orsamus H. Marshall, "Narrative of the Expedition of the Marquis De Nonville, against the Senecas, in 1687," *Collections of the New-York Historical Society,* Second Series 2 (1849): 159. No one knows which grandfather Joseph meant or if, indeed, he meant grandfather at all in the sense in which white people understood the word. There was a specific Mohawk word for an actual grandparent and a less specific word for certain elders, but we do not know how Joseph spoke or whom he had in mind.

11. M. Boisherbert, November 1747, report on Indians, *Documents Relative to the Colonial History of the State of New-York,* ed. by E. B. O'Callaghan and B. Fernow, 15 vols. (Albany, 1853–87), 10: 87.

12. *Ibid.*

13. In 1776 we shall find Brant writing a letter to his relatives at Lake of the Two Mountains. Some years before he also had relatives among the Caughnawagas.

14. *Private Papers of James Boswell from Malahide Castle,* ed. by Geoffrey Scott and Frederick A. Pottle, 18 vols. (Mount Vernon, N.Y., 1928–34), 11: 257.

15. Council, Nov. 14, 1763, *The Papers of Sir William Johnson,* ed. by James Sullivan, Alexander C. Flick, and Milton W. Hamilton, 14 vols. (Albany, 1921–65), 10: 933–34. Even after the last colonial war had ended, Six Nations chiefs were still able to unnerve the British with a French bogey.

16. The *Johnson Papers* are full of references to the covenant chain. See also Francis Jennings, "The Constitutional Evolution of the Covenant Chain," *Proceedings of the American Philosophical Society* 115 (1971): 88–96.

17. Remarks Concerning the Savages of North America, [1784], *Writings of Franklin,* ed. by Smyth, 10: 97–105.

18. Journal of Indian Affairs, Mar. 13, 1764, *Johnson Papers.* 11: 110.

19. "John Adlum on the Allegheny: Memoirs for the Year 1794," ed. by Donald H. Kent and Merle H. Deardorff, pt. 1, in *The Pennsylvania Magazine of History and Biography* 84, no. 3 (July 1960): 304–05.

20. Paul A. W. Wallace, *Indians in Pennsylvania,* p. 11.

21. Warren Johnson, Journal, Nov. 25, 1760, and Feb. 26, 1761, *Johnson Papers,* 13: 191, 204.

22. Robt. Rodgers, Oct. 22, 1755, to William Johnson, *ibid.,* 2: 226.

23. Warren Johnson, Journal, Jan. 11, 1761, *ibid.,* 13: 198. See also chapter 12, note 101.

24. "The Opinions of George Croghan on the American Indian," [1773], *The Pennsylvania Magazine of History and Biography* 71 (1947): 156.

25. Perhaps such stealing was defensive. There is no evidence that Indians stole very much from other Indians. Among themselves they held theft in contempt.

26. Marquis de Chastellux, *Travels in North-America, in the Years 1780, 1781, and 1782*, tr. from the French by an English Gentleman, 2 vols. (London, 1787), 1: 403–04.

27. Walsh Papers, "Indians," MG19, F10, Public Archives of Canada.

28. Wm. Johnson, Sept. 3, 1757, to Earl of Loudoun, *Johnson Papers*, 9: 828.

29. Joseph Brant, as we shall see, did put such thoughts on paper.

30. Johnson, Feb. 28, 1771, to Arthur Lee, *Documentary History of New York*, 4: 434.

31. Samuel Kirkland, Journal, April 7, 1765, p. 54, Kirkland MSS., Hamilton College, Clinton, N.Y. Lately published in *The Journals of Samuel Kirkland: 18th-Century Missionary to the Iroquois, Government Agent, Father of Hamilton College*, ed. by Walter Pilkington (Clinton, N.Y., 1980).

32. Jon. Miln, Nov. 3, 1729, to SPG, MSS. of the Society for the Propagation of the Gospel in Foreign Parts, Series B, vol. 1, pt. 1, p. 158, transcripts, Library of Congress.

33. Holmes, January 1801, interview with Brant, Miller Papers, no. 1.

34. *I. e.*, "ate" or "had eaten"—an obsolete past form.

35. Diary of David Zeisberger and Henry Frey, Sept. 29 and 30, 1753, *Moravian Journals relating to Central New York, 1745–66*, ed. by Wm. M. Beauchamp (Syracuse, 1916), p. 190.

36. Hunt, *Wars of Iroquois*, pp. 7, 158–59.

37. *Observations on the Inhabitants, Climate, Soil, Rivers, Productions, Animals, and other matters worthy of Notice. Made By Mr. John Bartram, In his Travels from Pensilvania to Onondago, Oswego and the Lake Ontario, In Canada* (London, 1751), pp. 78–79. See also Indian Proceedings, May 22, 1757, *Johnson Papers*, 9: 767, in which Johnson, urging an Indian to get a prisoner to replace a deceased mother, never mentions age or sex. In the Journal of Indian Affairs, Mar. 13, 1764, *ibid.*, 11: 110, Johnson says he gave the Oneidas 8 women and a child to replace "any" of their friends. Such a custom seems to have been not uncommon among Iroquoians, north or south. Among the Cherokees there was a man who went by the name of The Badger's Mother, an adoptee, obviously, in place of The Badger's female parent.

38. Council, May 10, 1765, *Johnson Papers*, 11: 728.

39. Gideon Hawley, Jan. 29, 1794, petition to Senate and house of Representatives, Hawley MSS., vol. 3, Congregational Library of the American Congregational Association, Boston; and "The report of a committee of the board of correspondents of the Scots Society for propagating Christian knowledge, who visited the Oneida and Mohekunuh Indians in 1796," *Collections of the Massachusetts Historical Society, for the Year M, DCC, XCVIII* (Boston, reprinted 1835): 13–14.

40. Warren Johnson, Journal, Nov. 25, 1760, *Johnson Papers*, 13: 188.

41. Wampum had many other uses, too. It served as jewelry and ornamentation, as a medium of exchange, and even, at times, as a replacement for a deceased relative.

42. Journal of Indian Affairs, Jan. 29, 1764, *Johnson Papers*, 11: 33; Council, July 31, 1764, *ibid.*, p. 309; Journal of Indian Affairs, April 27, 1765, *ibid.*, pp. 708, 710; Johnson, Feb. 28, 1771, to Arthur Lee, *Documentary History of New York*, 4: 437; Council, Feb. 27, 1756, *Johnson Papers*, 9: 387–88; William Williams, Mar. 14, 1756, to Johnson, *ibid.*, p. 405; Holmes, interview with Brant, Jan. 1801, Miller Papers, no. 1. When the Indians wanted to describe a larger number of men than they could conveniently indicate by sticks, they would say "a great band" or something similar.

43. Norton, Journal, etc., 1: 190; 2: 674–76.

44. Johnson, Dec. 29, 1760, to Alexander Colden, *Johnson Papers*, 3: 292–93.

45. "Opinions of George Croghan on American Indian," 1773, p. 158.

46. Daniel Claus, Journal, July 6, 1773, *Johnson Papers*, 13: 619.

47. Council, Sept. 8, 1753, *ibid.*, 9: 113.

48. Journal of Indian Affairs, Dec. 16, 1768, *ibid.*, 12: 671.

49. Johnson, June 1, 1763, notes on Klock business, *ibid.*, 10: 997.

50. Johnson, May 24, 1765, to Lords of Trade, *New York Colonial Documents*, 7: 713.

51. Hawley, Dec. 31, 1770, to Lieut. Governour Hutchinson, "Hutchinson Papers," *Collections of the Massachusetts Historical Society*, Third Series 1 (reprinted 1846): 151.

52. "Opinions of George Croghan on American Indian," 1773, p. 155.

53. John Duffy, *Epidemics in Colonial America* (Baton Rouge, 1953), pp. 11, 244–45.

54. Diary of Zeisberger and Frey, Sept. 11, 1753, *Moravian Journals*, p. 188.

55. Journal, [1757?], Hawley MSS. vol. 2.

56. Ernest Hawkins, *Historical Notices of the Missions of the Church of England in the North American Colonies* (London, 1845), p. 288.

57. Johnson, Sept. 17, 1756, to Earl of Loudoun, *Johnson Papers*, 9: 531; Johnson, May 17, 1758, to Maj. Gen. Abercromby, *ibid.*, pp. 905–06; Johnson, Feb. 22, 1759, to Maj. Gen. Amherst, *ibid.*, 10: 102–3; Johnson, Aug. 14, 1770, to Earl of Hillsborough, *Documentary History of New York*, 2: 976. Even in Canada, many years after the American Revolution, this same complaint was made by British authorities and others.

58. Mrs. Anne Grant, *Memoirs of an American Lady*, 2 vols. in one (Boston, 1809), 1: 121. Also, when crops did not get planted or harvested on time because of drunkenness (which happened frequently), it shows that the *women* were drunk, for this was their work. The missionary, Samuel Kirkland, frequently mentions female drunkenness.

59. The Rev. John Ogilvie, A Journal of Time spent at the Mohawk with some Occurrences, pp. 12–13, MS. at New York State Library.

60. Johnson, Sept. 30, 1758, to Maj. Gen. Abercromby, *Johnson Papers*, 10: 17.

61. Journal of Indian Affairs, Feb. 25, 1767, *ibid.*, 12: 273.

62. Council, Nov. 23, 1756, *New York Colonial Documents*, 7: 243; Journal of Indian Affairs, Dec. 12, 1758, *Johnson Papers*, 10: 73; Johnson, Mar. 6, 1766, to Ralph Burton, *ibid.*, 5: 55.

63. "Opinions of George Croghan on American Indian," 1773, p. 156; Holmes, Jan. 1801, interview with Brant, Miller Papers, no. 1.

64. Johnson, July 20, 1765, to Genrl. Gage, *Johnson Papers*, 11: 862.

65. "Opinions of George Croghan on American Indian," 1773, p. 156.

66. Johnson, April 2, 1762, to Goldsbrow Banyar, extract, *Johnson Papers*, 13: 277.

67. In eighteenth century documents dealing with Indian affairs there are numerous references to relatives of the half-blood. They seem almost to have constituted the norm.

68. Norton, Journal, etc., 1: 259.

69. David Fowler, June 24, 1765, to the Rev. Eleazar Wheelock, Kirkland MSS.

70. Johnson, Oct. 30, 1764, to Lords of Trade, *New York Colonial Documents*, 7: 672; Canada Traders, Sept. 20, 1766, memorial to Committee of Merchants for American Affairs, *Johnson Papers*, 12: 189.

71. Council, July 9–14, 1764, *Johnson Papers*, 4: 479.

72. Estimate of losses in real and personal estate of Six Nations as valued in 1775, State Papers, Canada, Q24, pt. 2: 299–324, Public Archives of Canada. Little Abraham of Fort Hunter who never went to Canada probably owned land, too.

73. For instance: Account of Persons employd. in the Battoe Service Under David Schuyler Jur, Schenectady, *Johnson Papers*, 3: 631–33; Johnson, Account of Indian Expenses, *ibid.*, pp. 175–76.

74. Council, Sept. 13, 1763, *ibid.*, 10: 849; Council, Oct. 21, 1763, *ibid.*, p. 903; Council, May 10, 1756, *New York Colonial Documents*, 7: 103; Council, May 26, 1756, *ibid.*, pp. 115–16; Diamond Jenness, *The Indians of Canada* (Fifth Edition, Ottawa, 1960), pp. 136–37; William Nelson Fenton, "A Calendar of Manuscript Materials relating to the History of the Six Nations or Iroquois Indians in Depositories outside of Philadelphia, 1750–1850," *The American Philosophical Society Library Bulletin 1953*, p. 591.

75. Jenness, *Indians of Canada*, pp. 136–37.

76. Charles Lee, June 18, 1756, to sister, *The Lee Papers*, in *Collections of the New-York Historical Society*, 4 vols. (New York, 1872–75), 1: 4.

77. Theophilus Chamberlain, July 10 and 17, 1765, to the Rev. Eleazar Wheelock, Dartmouth College MSS. This and all subsequent quotations from these manuscripts are reproduced by permission of the Trustees of Dartmouth College.

78. Johnson, Feb. 28, 1771, to Arthur Lee, *Documentary History of New York*, 4: 433; Johnson, Oct. 24, 1762, to George Croghan, *Johnson Papers*, 3: 914; Thomas McKee, Nov. 2, 1762, to Johnson, *ibid.*, p. 924; Wallace, *Indians in Pennsylvania*, p. 175. See also chapter 24, note 82.

79. Johnson, April 22, 1756, to William Shirley, *Johnson Papers*, 9: 439.

80. Conrad Weiser, journal to Onondaga, 1750, p. 13, MS. at Historical Society of Pennsylvania.

81. Council, July 2, 1754, *Documentary History of New York*, 2: 580.

82. Weiser, journal to Onondaga, 1750, pp. 11–12.

83. Diary of Charles Frederick and David Zeisberger, July 24, 1754, *Moravian Journals*, pp. 199–200.

84. Council, July 9, 1754, *Documentary History of New York*, 2: 603; Journal of Indian Affairs, May 30, 1756, *Johnson Papers*, 9: 467; Journal of Indian Affairs, April 9, 1767, *ibid.*, 12: 304.

85. Johnson, Sept. 4, 1755, to James De Lancey, *Johnson Papers*, 2: 7; Johnson, Sept. 22, 1767, to Earl of Shelburne, *New York Colonial Documents*, 7: 959–60.

86. Gideon Hawley, July 31, 1794, to the Rev. Dr. Thacher, Narrative of journey to Oquaga, 1753, *Documentary History of New York*, 3: 1044.

87. Diary of Zeisberger and Frey, July 28, 1753, *Moravian Journals*, p. 180.

88. Thomas McKee, Nov. 1, 1762, to Johnson, *Johnson Papers*, 3: 921.

89. Johnson, Sept. 22, 1766, to Banyar, *ibid.*, 12: 192.

90. Journal of Indian affairs, April 9, 1767, *ibid.*, p. 304.

91. Council, July 8, 1799, "Indian Affairs," *Collections of Michigan Pioneer and Historical Society* 20 (1892): 645.

92. Peter Wraxall, Jan. 9, 1755/6, "Some Thoughts upon The British Indian Interest in North America, more particularly as it relates to The Northern Confederacy commonly called The Six Nations," *New York Colonial Documents*, 7: 18; Johnson, Sept. 22, 1767, to Earl of Shelburne, *ibid.*, p. 958; John Thornton Kirkland, "Answer to the foregoing Queries, respecting Indians," *Collections of the Massachusetts Historical Society*, 1 Series 4 (1795): 74; Howard H. Peckham, *Pontiac and the Indian Uprising* (Princeton, N.J., 1947), p. 53.

93. Johnson, Oct. 30, 1764, to Lords of Trade, *New York Colonial Documents*, 7: 671–72; John Thornton Kirkland, "Answer to Queries on Indians," p. 74.

94. Council, May 28, 1756, *Johnson Papers*, 9: 464; S. Kirtland [Kirkland], Feb. 21, 1766, to Johnson, *ibid.*, 12: 27; Johnson, Feb. 28, 1771, to Arthur Lee, *Documentary History of New York*, 4: 431–32; "Opinions of George Croghan on American Indian," p. 158.

CHAPTER 2—PETER AND MARGARET

1. [The Rev. John Strachan], "Life of Capt. Brant," *The Christian Recorder*, Kingston, Upper Canada, May 1819.

2. Eleazar Wheelock, *A plain and faithful Narrative of the Original Design, Rise, Progress and present State of the Indian Charity-School at Lebanon, in Connecticut* (Boston, 1763), p. 40.

3. Maj. [Archibald] Campbell, July 19, 1786, to Henry Hope, extract, State Papers, Canada, Q26, pt. 2: 521.

4. Johnson, Nov. 13, 1763, to Lords of Trade, *New York Colonial Documents*, 7: 580.

5. Philip Schuyler, July 5, 1777, to Gen. Washington, extract, "Proceedings of a General Court Martial . . . for the Trial of Major General Schuyler, October 1, 1778," *Collections of the New-York Historical Society for the Year 1879*, p. 138.

6. Jos. Brant, Sept. 23, 1789, to Maj. Robert Mathews, State Papers, Canada, Q43, pt. 2: 785.

7. *The American Museum, or, Universal Magazine*, Philadelphia 6 (Sept. 1789): 226. See also William L. Stone, *Life of Joseph Brant-Thayendanegea*, 2 vols. (New York, 1838), 2: 481. Joseph's son, John Brant, presented documentary evidence of his father's unmixed Indian parentage to the Scottish poet, Campbell. "Letter to the Mohawk Chief Ahyonwaeghs, Commonly Called John Brant, Esq. of the Grand River, Upper Canada. From Thomas Campbell," *The New Monthly Magazine and Literary Journal* 4 (London, 1822): 98.

8. Stone, *Life of Brant*, 1: 18.

9. H. B. Johnson, Oct. 17, 1877, to Lyman C. Draper, Brant MSS., 14F36, State Historical Society of Wisconsin.

10. MS. at The New-York Historical Society.

11. A Margaret later became the wife of a sachem named Brant, who appears to be the stepfather from whom, as we shall see, both the Rev. John Stuart and John Norton, Joseph's long-time friend, say Joseph got his surname. In corroboration of their story, Henry van Driessen, Jr., a man with whom the Indians had a land dispute, refers to Joseph as "son to Brants wife." *Calendar of the Sir William Johnson Manuscripts in the New York State Library*, compiled by Richard E. Day (Albany, 1909), p. 347. A Margaret Brant is also mentioned in traders' accounts against Sir William Johnson in such a way as to imply a close connection. See chapter 3 for further details.

12. John Deserontyon, Dec. 3, 1778, to Col. Daniel Claus, Brant MSS., 5F11; I. Bearfoot, June 22, 1889, to Lyman C. Draper, *ibid.*, 13F134.

13. Capt. Malcolm Fraser, Nov. 26, 1783, Return of Loyalists . . . on Carleton Island, Haldimand Papers, British Museum, London, Additional MSS. 21,787, pt. 7: 344. (See Bibliography for an explanatory note about the Haldimand Papers.) Presumably Molly herself furnished the information about her age.

14. Norton, Journal, etc., 2: 699.

15. Strachan, "Life of Capt. Brant," *Christian Recorder*, May 1819.

16. Joseph Johnson, Feb. 10, 1768, to the Rev. Eleazar Wheelock, *The Letters of Eleazar Wheelock's Indians*, ed. by James Dow McCallum, *Dartmouth College Manuscript Series*, No. 1 (Hanover, N.H., 1932), p. 128.

17. Daniel Claus, Aug. 30, 1779, to Gen. Frederick Haldimand, Claus Papers, 2: 132, Public Archives of Canada.

18. Journal, etc., 2: 699.

19. The date is fixed thus: Brant said he began his military service at the age of fifteen. Petition, Feb. 1, 1796, to Lieut. Gov. John G. Simcoe, "Petitions for Grants of Land, 1792–6," ed. by Brig. Gen. E. A. Cruikshank, *Ontario Historical Society Papers and Records* 24 (1927): 30. Sir John Johnson gives the date of Brant's first military service as 1758; and Sir John would have known, as he was himself on that campaign. Return of Officers of Indian Department Recommended for Half Pay, n.d., Haldimand Papers, B167, pt. 2: 406, Public Archives of Canada. Brant died Nov. 24, 1807, aged sixty-four years and eight months—this age apparently furnished by the Brant family. Stone, *Life of Brant*, 2: 498–99.

20. Stone, *Life of Brant*, 1: 1. On occasion Brant also signed his Indian name "T'hanendanegea," "Thayendanegen," "Thayendanega," and other slight variations. Stone's version of the name and its meaning is used because it probably came from the Brant family. Stone also had the opportunity to go through Brant's personal papers before they were stolen and dispersed by autograph hunters.

21. Journal of Jelles Fonda, 1760, Fonda Family Papers, The New-York Historical Society. The Mohawks had two other clans, also—the Bear and the Turtle.

22. He was repeatedly mentioned as a Mohawk by Sir William Johnson. Guy Johnson, Daniel Claus, John Norton, and everybody else who knew him well also regarded him as a Mohawk.

23. Norton, Journal, etc., 1: 256.

24. Draper, Sept. 26, 1879, interview with John Smoke Johnson, Brant MSS., 13F26.

25. It should be noted here that the Strachan-Stuart account and the Norton account were entirely independent of each other. Norton wrote first, in 1816, and his manuscript lay unknown for almost a century and a half in the private archives of the Dukes of Northumberland. Stuart, who died in 1811, had told his story to Strachan; and Strachan published his article in 1819.

26. Corrected date.

27. Journal, etc., 2: 699.

28. See chapter 3.

29. Johnson, May 24, 1750, to George Clinton, *Johnson Papers*, 9: 61.

30. *Ibid.*

31. Johnson, Sept. 27, 1756, to Earl of Loudoun, *ibid.*, pp. 545–46; Johnson, July 5, 1758, to Genrl. Abercromby, *ibid.*, 2: 871; Council, June 19, 1757, *New York Colonial Documents*, 7: 264; *David Zeisberger's History of Northern American Indians*, ed. by Archer Butler Hulbert and William Nathaniel Schwarze (Columbus, Ohio, 1910), pp. 117–18.

32. The Rev. John Aemilius Wernig, Sept. 14, 1752, to patron, *Ecclesiastical Records: State of New York*, ed. by Hugh Hastings and E. T. Corwin, 7 vols. (Albany, 1901–16), 5: 3287.

33. Dan. Claus, Aug. 23, 1752, to Conrad Weiser, quoted in Paul A. W. Wallace, *Conrad Weiser, 1696–1760: Friend of Colonist and Mohawk* (Philadelphia and London, 1945), p. 338.

CHAPTER 3—CANAJOHARIE CASTLE

1. Holmes, Jan. 1801, interview with Brant, Miller Papers, no. 1.
2. Now Indian Castle, town of Danube, Herkimer County, N.Y.—not to be confused with modern Canajoharie, which lies to the eastward. All Indian villages, especially in the early days, were moved about from time to time; but by the mid-eighteenth century the Mohawks were permanently settled. By the time of the Revolution the name, Canajoharie, also included a wide area of white settlements up and down the river from the Castle.
3. Daniel Claus says he was a brother, but Sir William Johnson never mentions such a relationship.
4. There was also a white lad born in the neighborhood named Joseph Brant, a son of settler John Michael Brant. What became of this third Joseph nobody seems to know.
5. Stone seems to have thought Brant's Nickus, Old Brant, and Old Nickus were one and the same. From these three he concocted the mythical Nickus Brant, whom he called Joseph's stepfather. But the young fellow, Brant's Nickus, died in 1768, while Old Brant was alive as late as the 1770s. Old Brant and Old Nickus were definitely two different persons. The signatures of both may be found on the same documents.
6. At the Historical Society of Pennsylvania, Peters MSS., 3: 61, is a letter in mixed German and English, written by Daniel Claus, Aug. 23, 1752, to Conrad Weiser. Appended is a postscript in Mohawk, also written by Claus but signed with an awkward "hanakaradon." Since this was Claus's version of Brant's Indian name (there were several other versions; Stuart, for instance, recalled it as Carrihogo), he very likely taught it to Brant. Young Claus, a future son-in-law of Sir William Johnson, was boarding at this time in Brant's household in order to learn the Mohawk language. Brant soon forgot his signature, for he signed later documents with a mark. See chapter 2, note 33.
7. Information about all these Indians has been compiled from a wide variety of sources, the best of which are Barclay's Register Book, the Rev. John Ogilvie's records and journals, the published *Papers of Sir William Johnson*, the MSS. of the Society for the Propagation of the Gospel in Foreign Parts, and various account books at the New-York Historical Society and the New York State Library.
8. She was certainly alive in June 1751, when Daniel Claus and Sammy Weiser, son of Conrad Weiser, went to board with the Brants. Paul A. W. Wallace, *Conrad Weiser, 1696–1760: Friend of Colonist and Mohawk*, p. 326. The elder Weiser took his son away in 1753, finding Brant "debauchd."
9. The Rev. John Ogilvie, A Register of Indian Children Begun Apr. 22d. 1750, 2c., MS. at New York State Library. The phrase, "of Canijohare," refers to Margaret, not Brant. It is interesting to note that Margaret named two of her children Jacob. It may have been her father's name.
10. The Rev. John Ogilvie, An Acct. of Marriages among the Indians, 4c., MS. at New York State Library.
11. Dan. Claus, Jan. 10, 1754, to Governor Hamilton, *Pennsylvania Archives*, First Series, ed. by Samuel Hazard, 12 vols. (Philadelphia, 1852–56), 2: 116.
12. Her son, Nickus Brant's, was born of sachem stock. He was referred to as "ye Indian prince" in a contemporary document.
13. Richard Peters, Account of Proprietors of Pennsylvania, Charges on account

of Connecticut Deed, Feb. 15, 1755, Penn MSS., Indian Affairs, 3: 59, The Historical Society of Pennsylvania.

14. Colonel Claus, Memoirs, Claus Papers, p. 23. This narrative was written years after the event, but Claus probably would have remembered such a love affair clearly. In one respect his memory did fail. Molly was not returning from Philadelphia when it occurred. She did not go to Philadelphia, but she would almost certainly have been in Albany with her family during the Albany Congress of 1754.

15. The Rev. John Ogilvie, A Journal of Time spent at the Mohawk with some Occurrences, p. 4, MS. at New York State Library.

CHAPTER 4—THE YOUNG WARRIOR

1. Council, Sept. 10, 1753, *Johnson Papers*, 9: 117.

2. Council, June 24, 1755, *New York Colonial Documents*, 6: 972.

3. Jeff N. Clyde, Feb. 11, 1878, to Lyman C. Draper, Brant MSS., 5F74.

4. Col. Danl. Claus, September 1778, Annecdotes of the Mohawk Chief Captn. Joseph Brant alias Tayendanegea, Claus Papers (2 vols.), 2: 53, Library of Congress; G. M. Cleland, Aug. 30, 1878, to Draper, Brant MSS., 4F105.

5. See note 19, chapter 2. Both Stuart and Norton thought Joseph had been at Lake George in 1755. This mistake was probably due to the fact that Abercromby's army operated in the same general area.

6. Strachan, "Life of Capt. Brant," *Christian Recorder*, May 1819.

7. Norton, Journal, etc., 2: 700.

8. Sir John Johnson, n.d., Return, Haldimand Papers, B167, pt. 2: 406.

9. "Letter to the Mohawk Chief Ahyonwaeghs," *The* (London) *New Monthly Magazine and Literary Journal* 4 (1822): 98.

10. Journal of Jelles Fonda, 1760, Fonda Family Papers.

11. Jeff. Amherst, Feb. 1, 1761, to Johnson, *Johnson Papers*, 3: 317–18; also April 17, 1761, *ibid.*, p. 378; and List of Indians, Mar./April 1761, *ibid.*, 10: 252.

12. Strachan, "Life of Capt. Brant"; also Norton, Journal, etc., 2: 699.

13. Milton W. Hamilton's *Sir William Johnson: Colonial American, 1715–1763* is a new, definitive, biography of Johnson. A second volume is currently expected.

14. In 1781 Molly spoke of Joseph as her "only" brother; letter, April 12, 1781, to Claus, extract in Haldimand Papers, Additional MSS. 21,774, pt. 4: 180. Yet Brant Johnson was very much alive then, and Molly would have made no distinction between a brother of the half and the whole blood.

15. Council, August 1803, quoted and summarized in Stone, *Life of Brant*, 2: 403.

16. Johnson, Oct. 8, 1764, to Lords of Trade, *New York Colonial Documents*, 7: 659.

CHAPTER 5—THE WORLD OF PARSON WHEELOCK

1. Eleazar Wheelock, May 27, 1761, to Johnson, *Johnson Papers*, 10: 272.

2. Wheelock tells the story of the boys' arrival in his *A plain and faithful Narrative*, pp. 39–41.

3. Jedidiah Phelps, Sept. 5, 1842, narrative at age of 90, p. 2, MS. in Burton Historical Collection, Detroit Public Library.

4. David M'Clure and Elijah Parish, Memoirs of the Rev. Eleazar Wheelock, D. D. (Newburyport, Mass., 1811), p. 120.

5. Wheelock, A plain and faithful Narrative, p. 36.

6. Wheelock, July 4, 1761, to George Whitefield, extract in Letters of Wheelock's Indians, Introduction, p. 17.

7. Wheelock, Aug. 4–8, 1761, An Accompt of Things Deliver'd to 3 Mohawk Lads, (viz:) Joseph, Niccus, & Center, Dartmouth College MSS.

8. Wheelock, Nov. 2, 1761, to Johnson, Johnson Papers, 3: 556–57.

9. In the early eighteenth century, land patents were comparatively easy to get and not much inquired into by royal officials because of the lucrative fees involved and other opportunities for profit. Later came many restrictions, but few that could not be evaded. In any case it was always necessary to extinguish the Indian title first, and the Indian deed and the subsequent patent were supposed to describe the same parcel of land. They were supposed to—but often did not.

10. Journal of Indian Affairs, Sept. 20, 1764, Johnson Papers, 11: 360.

11. Amherst, June 11, 1761, to Johnson; July 6, 1762; and Aug. 9, 1761, ibid., 10: 284; 3: 825; and 3: 514.

12. Amherst, Aug. 9, 1761, to Johnson, ibid., 3: 516. The Johnson Papers of this era are full of incidents of the mistreatment of Indians.

13. A warning sent by the Canajoharie chiefs. Johnson, Diary of Journey to Detroit, July 13, 1761, William L. Stone, The Life and Times of Sir William Johnson, Bart., 2 vols. (Albany, 1865), 2, Appendix no. 4, pp. 431–32.

14. Wheelock, Account, Nov. 28, 1761–May 28, 1762, Dartmouth College MSS.

15. Claus, Sept. 1778, Annecdotes of the Mohawk Chief Captn. Joseph Brant alias Tayendanegea, Claus Papers, 2: 53, Library of Congress.

16. Strachan, "Life of Capt. Brant," Christian Recorder, May 1819.

17. John Smith, May 18, 1764, letter quoted in W. De Loss Love, Samson Occom and the Christian Indians of New England (Boston and Chicago, 1899), p. 80.

18. "A Letter from Rev. Jonathan Edwards, to Hon. Thomas Hubbard, Esq. of Boston [Aug. 31, 1751], Relating to the Indian School at Stockbridge," Collections of the Massachusetts Historical Society, First Series 10 (1809): 150.

19. Johnson Papers, 10: 344–45.

20. April 30, 1762, ibid., p. 440.

21. June 27, 1762, ibid., pp. 469–70.

22. Johnson, July 21, 1762, to Wheelock, ibid., 3: 832.

23. Sept. 8, 1762, Documentary History of New York, 4: 316.

24. Charles Jeffry Smith, Jan. 18, 1763, to Johnson, ibid., p. 325.

25. Sermon, June 1763, extract quoted in M'Clure and Parish, Memoirs of Wheelock, pp. 29–30.

26. Letter, Feb. 24, 1763, to Rev'd. A. Gifford, Letters of Wheelock's Indians, p. 70.

27. Ibid.

28. Wheelock, Jan. 20–April 10, 1763, to Johnson, Documentary History of New York, 4: 322–24.

29. May 16, 1763, ibid., pp. 330–31.

30. Mar. 31, 1762, to Johnson, Johnson Papers, 3: 663; and Oct. 5, 1762, to Amherst, ibid., 10: 543.

31. April 24, 1763, *ibid.*, 10: 659–60.

32. Council, Sept. 10, 1762, *ibid.*, pp. 505–06.

33. July 5, 1763, *ibid.*, p. 729.

CHAPTER 6—THE CONSPIRACY OF PONTIAC

1. John Macomb, July 10, 1763, to Johnson, *Calendar of Sir William Johnson Manuscripts*, p. 173.

2. July 24, 1763, *Johnson Papers*, 10: 754.

3. Journal of Indian Affairs, Aug. 19–21, 1763, *ibid.*, pp. 800–01.

4. Croghan, Sept. 28, 1763, to Johnson, *ibid.*, pp. 826–27. By this time the Mohawks had only 160 men in their whole nation.

5. Letter, Feb. 11, 1764, to Governor of Montreal, *ibid.*, 11: 54.

6. In what is now Broome County, N.Y.

7. Tradition says her name was Margaret, but we shall call her Peggie, to differentiate her from Joseph's mother.

8. Council, Feb. 4, 1764, *Johnson Papers*, 11: 42.

9. An observant traveler saw Oquaga in 1769. All the houses were alike, he said; but it is Isaac's house that he evidently visited and seems to describe. Richard Smith, *A Tour of Four Great Rivers, the Hudson, Mohawk, Susquehanna and Delaware in 1769*, ed. by Francis W. Halsey (New York, 1906), pp. 65–66.

10. Chamberlain, July 29, 1765, to Wheelock, Dartmouth College MSS.

11. *Johnson Papers*, 4: 393.

12. Many letters in *Johnson Papers*, vols. 2, 4, and 11, and *New York Colonial Documents*, vol. 7, relate to this expedition to Canesteo.

13. Journal of Indian Affairs, April 20, 1764, *Johnson Papers*, 11: 159.

14. Letters, Mar. 14, 1764, *ibid.*, p. 102; Mar. 26, 1764, *ibid.*, 4: 379–80; and April 17, 1764, *ibid.*, 11: 133–34.

15. *Ibid.*, 11: 161.

16. Barclay, Oct. 5, 1763, to Johnson, *ibid.*, 13: 300.

17. Nov. 13, 1763, to Lords of Trade, *New York Colonial Documents*, 7: 580.

18. Johnson, Nov. 24, 1763, to Barclay, *Johnson Papers*, 10: 935–36.

19. Strachan, "Life of Capt. Brant," *Christian Recorder*, May 1819.

20. Dec. 23, 1763, *Johnson Papers*, 10: 973.

21. July 22, 1765, *ibid.*, 11: 865.

CHAPTER 7—A HOME ON THE MOHAWK

1. Holmes, January 1801, interview with Brant, Miller Papers, no. 1.

2. A man who visited Brant in 1797 described him thus to his biographer. Stone, *Life of Brant*, 2: 449.

3. Gideon Hawley, a missionary stationed at Oquaga in the mid-1750s, thought almost every family in that village had some white blood. Yet Oquaga, compared to the Mohawk castles, was very far off the beaten track.

4. July 29, 1765, to Wheelock, Dartmouth College MSS.

5. More than a century later, old people in Canada were telling the historian, Lyman C. Draper, this romantic story. Draper noted it down, but must have had some

mental reservations about its value. Chamberlain's letter confirms the tradition almost word for word!

6. Journal of Indian Affairs, Dec. 24–25, 1765, *Johnson Papers*, 11: 984–86.

7. Council, July 25, 1766, *New York Colonial Documents*, 7: 858.

8. Council, July 29, 1766, *ibid.*, p. 865.

9. Chamberlain, Aug. 9, 1766, to Wheelock, Dartmouth College MSS. The records of a council at Ontario, Oct. 15–16, 1766, list Joseph Brant as the interpreter. *Johnson Papers*, 12: 209.

10. Normand MacLeod, Sept. 25, 1766, to Johnson, *Calendar of Johnson Manuscripts*, p. 329.

11. MacLeod, Sept. 9, 1766, to Johnson, *Johnson Papers*, 12: 175; Johnson, Oct. 4, 1766, to Gage, *ibid.*, p. 204.

12. Draper, notes from Johnson Papers, Brant MSS., 15F86. Interpreters stationed at different places were paid at different rates; Joseph's pay was the going rate for Fort Ontario.

13. *Calendar of Johnson Manuscripts*, p. 347. In this connection van Driessen says an odd thing; he describes Joseph as "ye Indian son to Brants wife," a description which seems to imply that Brant's wife also had a non-Indian son. But as Joseph had no living brothers, van Driessen was probably thinking of the half-breed, Brant Johnson, whom he may have supposed to be the son of Joseph's mother.

14. Oct. 4, 1766, to Wheelock, Dartmouth College MSS.

15. He is not mentioned in the *Johnson Papers* after 1764.

16. W. L. Greene, Jan. 4, 1878, to Draper, Brant MSS., 2F43.

17. Estimate of the Losses sustained by the Mohawk Indians . . . in the late Rebellion in America . . . certified by Capt. Jos. Brant, April 22, 1784, and by John Johnson and Dan. Claus, Sept. 28, 1784, State Papers, Canada, Q24, pt. 2: 318.

18. *Ibid.*; also Jelles Fonda, June 16, 1790, to Brant, Miscellaneous MSS., New-York Historical Society.

19. Robert Adems, Day Book, privately owned MS., microfilm at New York State Library.

20. Daniel Campbell, Account Books, 1756–99 (5 vols.), 5: 152, MS. at New York State Library.

21. William L. Stone saw these old trees in 1835 or '36 and found them still bearing. *Life of Brant*, 1: 182; 2: 431.

22. This was the daily routine, according to Theophilus Chamberlain, July 10 and 17, 1765, to Wheelock, Dartmouth College MSS. Indians did not generally rise early.

23. Estimate of Losses sustained by the Mohawk Indians, State Papers, Canada, Q24, pt. 2: 318.

24. Sir John Johnson, Return of Officers . . . of the Northern Departmt. . . . previous to the late Rebellion in America, Dec. 10, 1783, *ibid.*, Q23: 99.

25. A Joseph worked on the bateaux, but there was more than one man by that name among the Indians; and Joseph Brant would certainly have preferred more intellectual work.

26. July 17, 1765, to Wheelock, Dartmouth College MSS.

27. Journal, Mar. 18, 1768, quoted in Stone, *Life of Brant*, 1: 25–26.

28. [Nathaniel Whitaker], *A Brief Narrative of the Indian Charity-School in Lebanon in Connecticut, New England: Founded and Carried on by That Faithful Servant of God The Rev. Mr Eleazar Wheelock* (Second Edition, London, 1767), p. 32.

29. There are sufficient references in the *Johnson Papers* and in numerous account books that have been preserved, to show what was going on. All of Molly's purchases from various tradesmen were by no means for the exclusive use of the Johnson household. Sir William did a good deal of the ordering for the household himself.

30. Journal of Indian Affairs, Jan. 31, 1765, *Johnson Papers*, 11: 555–56. This dispute went on and on, there being no power in Sir William or even in the governor to remove Jacobus Maybe and his mulatto grandmother, tavern-keeper Eve Pickard, from the Canajoharie flats. After Maybe and some of his friends threatened to burn down the whole Indian castle, the Indians actually did burn Maybe's house but he rebuilt it.

31. Prevost, June 22, 1771, to Johnson, *ibid.*, 8: 156; Strachan, "Life of Capt. Brant," *Christian Recorder*, May 1819.

32. Norton, Journal, etc., 2: 700.

33. Council, July 28, 1772, *New York Colonial Documents*, 8: 304–06.

34. Oct. 29, 1767, to Johnson, *Johnson Papers*, 5: 768.

35. For some of the background of the great cession of 1768, see Nicholas B. Wainwright, *George Croghan: Wilderness Diplomat* (Chapel Hill, N.C., 1959), chapter 11.

36. Council, May 5, 1765, *New York Colonial Documents*, 7: 728.

37. Joseph was definitely present. David Avery, Oct. 10, 1768, to Wheelock, Dartmouth College MSS. In later life Brant referred again and again, both in his letters and his speeches, to what took place at Fort Stanwix in '68. The Indians clung passionately for many years to the idea of the boundary as laid down at that time.

38. Oct. 16, 1768, to John Glen, *Johnson Papers*, 12: 608.

39. Smith, *Tour of Four Great Rivers*, ed. by Halsey.

40. William E. Roscoe, *History of Schoharie County, New York* (Syracuse, 1882), pp. 359–60.

41. Oct. 8, 1766, to the Rev. Dr. D. Burton, *Johnson Papers*, 5: 388.

42. Strachan, "Life of Capt. Brant," *Christian Recorder*, May 1819.

43. Account against Crown, *Johnson Papers*, 12: 900, 920.

44. Harry Munro, June 25, 1771, to Johnson, *Documentary History of New York*, 4: 452.

45. John Stuart, July 20, 1772, to SPG, MSS. of the Society for the Propagation of the Gospel in Foreign Parts, Series B, 2, pt. 2, no. 199: 685–86, British Transcripts, Library of Congress; also Strachan, "Life of Capt. Brant," *Christian Recorder*, May 1819.

46. Strachan, "Life of Capt. Brant," *Christian Recorder*, May 1819.

47. Stuart, Oct. 27, 1775, to SPG, SPG MSS., Series B, 2, pt. 2, no. 203: 700, British Transcripts.

48. Strachan, "Life of Capt. Brant," *Christian Recorder*, May 1819.

49. *Ibid.*; Stuart, Aug. 9, 1774, to the Rev. Dr. Hinde, SPG MSS., Series B, 2, pt. 2, no. 201: 693, British Transcripts. Some of these translations were eventually published in England in 1787 as part of a new edition of the Mohawk Prayer Book.

50. Strachan, "Life of Capt. Brant," *Christian Recorder*, May 1819.

51. J. Ojijatekha Brant-Sero, "Some Descendants of Joseph Brant," *Ontario Historical Society Papers and Records* 1 (1899): 113.

52. Aug. 4, 1778, to Messrs. Taylor & Duffin, Claus Papers, 2: 43, Library of Congress. Tradition says Susanna died soon after the marriage, but there is not the

slightest hint in any manuscript that this was so. She could have been very ill by this time, and perhaps died shortly afterward. As Joseph had so little influence among the Indians in 1778, it seems unlikely that this "Wife" was the influential Catharine.

53. Johnson, May 27, 1774, to John Blackburn, *Johnson Papers*, 8: 1160; Council, July 11, 1774, *New York Colonial Documents*, 8: 478; Klock, deposition, July 8, 1774, Brant MSS., 2F53; G. Johnson, Aug. 2, 1774, to Lieut. Gov. Colden, *Johnson Papers*, 8: 1192–93.

CHAPTER 8—LOYALIST AND REBEL

1. July 26, 1774, *New York Colonial Documents*, 8: 472–73.

2. Sept. 12, 1774, to Blackburn, *Johnson Papers*, 8: 1198–1200.

3. [One of Molly Brant's younger daughters], Mar. 15, 1841, narrative, Brant MSS., 15F226.

4. Estimate of Losses sustained by Mohawk Indians, State Papers, Canada, Q24, pt. 2: 315–17.

5. Claus, Aug. 30, 1779, to Gen. Haldimand, Claus Papers, 2: 132.

6. Col. Guy Johnson, Oct. 4, 1776, Return of officers, British Headquarters Papers, 95, no. 10209.

7. July 20, 1772, to SPG, SPG MSS., Series B, 2, pt. 2, no. 199: 685, transcript.

8. Col. Guy Johnson, Minutes, Jan. 6, 1775, Indian Records, Series Two, 11: 35.

9. G. Johnson, Sept. 17, 1774, to Lieut. Gov. Colden, *Johnson Papers*, 8: 1201.

10. Hendrick Frey and others, Sept. 29, 1774, memorial to Cadwallader Colden, Charles F. Gunther Collection. See also Draper, note, Brant MSS., 2F51.

11. Nov. 4, 1774, Brant MSS., 2F60.

12. July 12, 1774, to Lieut. Gen. Gage, *Johnson Papers*, 12: 1123.

13. Council, July 12, 1774, *New York Colonial Documents*, 8: 479.

14. Quoted in Harold Blodgett, *Samson Occom*, Dartmouth College Manuscript Series Number Three (Hanover, N.H., 1935), p. 155.

15. Council, July 12, 1774, *New York Colonial Documents*, 8: 479.

16. Occom, Diary, quoted in Blodgett, *Samson Occom*, p. 155.

17. Council, Sept. 17, 1774, *New York Colonial Documents*, 8: 502–03.

18. Johnson, Minutes, Oct. 4, 15, and Nov. 17, 1774, Indian Records, Series Two, 11: 4, 7, 13.

19. *New York Colonial Documents*, 8: 524–27.

20. Council, Dec. 1–4, 1774, *ibid.*, pp. 519–24; Johnson, Dec. 14, 1774, to Earl of Dartmouth, *ibid.*, pp. 515–16.

21. Sept. 4, 1774, extract, *Documents Relating to the Constitutional History of Canada, 1791–1818*, ed. by Arthur G. Doughty and Duncan A. McArthur (Ottawa, 1914), p. 410.

22. Act passed on the eve of the Revolution to please the French Canadians. It recognized French civil law and the Roman Catholic religion in Quebec and extended the boundary of that province to include the Indian country north and west of the Ohio. This act was generally interpreted by the rebellious American colonies as a slap at them as it presaged their containment east of the mountains.

23. Sept. 20, 1774, extract, *Documents Relating to the Constitutional History of Canada, 1791–1818*, p. 411.

24. Henry Young Brown, May 16, 1775, to Massachusetts Congress, *American Archives*, published by M. St. Clair Clarke and Peter Force, Fourth and Fifth Series, 9 vols. (Washington, 1837–1853), Fourth Series, 2: 621.

25. Joseph Johnson, July 8, 1774, to Sir William Johnson, *Johnson Papers*, 12: 1118.

26. Joseph Johnson, Oct. 17, 1774, to Wheelock, Dartmouth College MSS.

27. Joseph's home county; set off from Albany County in 1772, with Johnstown as the county seat. It was a frontier and on the eve of the Revolution contained the furthermost western settlements in the province.

28. Oct. 21, 1774, to Gen. Haldimand, Claus Papers, 1: 171.

29. Dr. John Eliot [Elliott], "Brandt Indian Warrior—of ye Mohawk nation—Anecdotes respecting him from the mouth of Mr Kirkland—," MS. at Massachusetts Historical Society. See also Kirkland, Feb. 16, 1792, to Brant, Kirkland MSS.

30. Johnson, Jan. 11, 1783, to Haldimand, Haldimand Papers, B106: 206. Joseph Chew, Jan. 26, 1776, Extracts from the Records of Indian transactions . . . during the Year 1775, *New York Colonial Documents*, 8: 658.

31. *The Minute Book of the Committee of Safety of Tryon County, the Old New York Frontier*, ed. by Samuel Ludlow Frey (New York, 1905), note 26, pp. 115–16. The fragmentary Papers of the Tryon County, N.Y., Committee of Safety, 1774–1778, at the New-York Historical Society, contain a copy of this letter which lists the signers and mentions Joseph Brant as Guy Johnson's "secretary"—the latter, probably an error in translation. Very likely Joseph merely said he was writing on Guy's authority.

32. Gage, June 3, 1775, to Carleton, Gage Papers, American Series, vol. 129; Johnson, Mar. 28, 1776, to Lords Commissioners of the Treasury, British Headquarters Papers, 2, no. 147.

33. This legend comes in several different versions. W. Max Reid, *The Mohawk Valley* (New York and London, 1901), p. 202; Jeptha R. Simms, *The Frontiersmen of New York*, 2 vols. (Albany, 1882–83), 1: 249–50; and Rufus A. Grider, Oct. 31, 1886, to Draper, Brant MSS., 10F14.

34. Stone, *Life of Brant*, 1:152–53.

35. *American Archives*, Fourth Series, 2: 911.

36. Council, Aug. 31, 1775, *New York Colonial Documents*, 8: 621–22.

37. Oct. 12, 1775, to Dartmouth, *ibid.*, p. 636.

38. *Minute Book of Tryon County Committee of Safety*, pp. 40–42.

39. Throughout the war and for many years thereafter the rebels were often spoken of as Bostonians by the Indians and Loyalists.

40. Speech, n.d., to William Claus, quoted in Stone, *Life of Brant*, 2, Appendix no. 15. See also speech, Aug. 1803, to William Claus and others, *ibid.*, p. 402; and Haldimand, April 7, 1779, to Mohawks, Claus Papers, 2: 89–90.

41. Gage Papers, American Series, vols. 125, 129, 130, and 132, respectively.

42. *Ibid.*, vol. 133.

43. State Papers, Canada, Q11: 270.

44. Joseph Chew, Jan. 26, 1776, Extracts from Indian Records during 1775, *New York Colonial Documents*, 8: 659, 661–62; Johnson, Oct. 12, 1775, to Dartmouth, *ibid.*, p. 636.

45. Anecdotes of . . . Brant, Sept. 1778, Claus Papers, 2: 54, Library of Congress.

46. Speech, Dec. 1776, to Six Nations, State Papers, Canada, Q56, pt. 2: 520.

47. *Private Papers of James Boswell*, ed. by Scott and Pottle, 11: 258.

48. Gen. Philip Schuyler, Information from Ticonderoga, Sept. 24, 1775, *American Archives*, Fourth Series, 3: 798.

49. They deputed "a faithfull young Chief" who was, of course, Joseph Brant. Joseph Chew, Jan. 26, 1776, Extracts from Indian Records during 1775, *New York Colonial Documents*, 8: 662. As we shall see, the word "Chief" was used advisedly.

CHAPTER 9—JOSEPH ACCEPTS THE WAR BELT

1. Ethan Allen, *Allen's Captivity, Being a Narrative of Colonel Ethan Allen, Containing His Voyages, Travels, &c., Interspersed with Political Observations* (Boston, 1845), pp. 42, 44–45.

2. *New York Colonial Documents*, 8: 654–57.

3. *Ibid.*, pp. 658–62.

4. *Ibid.*, p. 657.

5. *The London Chronicle*, 39, no. 3001: 209.

6. *Ibid.*, p. 223.

7. Mrs. General [Baroness] Riedesel, *Letters and Journals Relating to the War of the American Revolution*, tr. and ed. by William L. Stone (Albany, 1867), pp. 59–60.

8. Stone, *Life of Brant*, 2: 251.

9. Feb. 4, 1792, to Samuel Kirkland, Kirkland MSS.

10. Aug. 23, 1776, to Gen. John Burgoyne, Sackville-Germain Papers.

11. Thayendanegea, Mar. 14, 1776, speech to Lord George Germain, *New York Colonial Documents*, 8: 671.

12. Speech, Dec. 1776, State Papers, Canada, Q56, pt. 2: 521.

13. Mar. 28, 1776, to Burgoyne, extract in Sackville-Germain Papers.

14. Germain, Aug. 8, 1780, to Gov. Haldimand, Haldimand Papers, B44: 49.

15. Claus, Sept. 1778, Anecdotes of . . . Brant, Claus Papers, 2: 54, Library of Congress.

16. Maj. John Ross, June 26, 1782, to Capt. R. Mathews, Haldimand Papers, B124: 8–9.

17. Romney's Diaries, 1776–1795, in Humphry Ward and W. Roberts, *Romney: A Biographical and Critical Essay with a Catalogue Raisonné of his Works*, 2 vols. (London and New York, 1904), 1: 81.

18. Now owned by the National Gallery of Canada, Ottawa.

19. Germain, April 16, 1779, to Haldimand, Haldimand Papers, B43: 117.

20. In the Mellon Collection, National Gallery of Art, Washington. The portrait of an "Ojibbeway Chief" which hangs in the Yale University Art Gallery, and which is attributed to Benjamin West and thought to be Joseph Brant is, in this author's opinion, not Joseph Brant at all. There is no evidence that Joseph sat to West and there is no resemblance to the Romney picture except for the half-moon gorget which was a very common trinket. Also, Joseph was not an Ojibwa. One must admit, however, that the Ojibbeway Chief looks more like Joseph than Guy's portrait resembles Guy!

21. *The London Magazine*, July 1776, p. 339.

22. Draper, notes from Johnson Papers, Brant MSS., 15F87–88.

23. Mrs. John Rose Holden, *The Brant Family*, Third edition (Wentworth Historical Society, n.d.), pp. 32–34.

24. Claus, Sept. 1778, Anecdotes of . . . Brant, Claus Papers, 2: 54, Library of Congress.

25. *The London Chronicle*, 39, no. 3009: 274. The Indian who made this remark is not named, but he must have been Joseph. There is no evidence that John could speak English.

26. *Private Papers of James Boswell*, 11: 257–58, 261–62.

27. "An Account of the Chief of the Mohock Indians, who lately visited England. (With an exact Likeness.)," *The London Magazine*, July 1776, p. 339. The "exact Likeness" composes the frontispiece. Joseph, holding up a knife and wearing Indian regalia, is moon-faced and wooden-looking.

28. Masonic certificate of Joseph Brant, Royal Ontario Museum, University of Toronto; John Ross Robertson, *The History of Freemasonry in Canada*, 2 vols. (Toronto, 1899), 1: 688.

29. *New York Colonial Documents*, 8: 678.

30. Quoted in Stone, *Life of Brant*, 2: 420.

31. Draper, notes from Johnson Papers, Brant MSS., 15F87–88; G. Johnson, Aug. 9, 1776, to Germain, *New York Colonial Documents*, 8: 682.

32. Draper, notes from Johnson Papers, Brant MSS., 15F87–88.

33. Stone, *Life of Brant*, 1: 155–56 and 2: 490–91.

34. G. Johnson, Aug. 9, 1776, to Claus, Claus Papers, 1: 216, Library of Congress.

35. Aug. 8, 1780, to Haldimand, Haldimand Papers, B44: 49.

36. G. Johnson, Aug. 9, 1776, to Germain, *New York Colonial Documents*, 8: 681–82; Johnson, Aug. 9, 1776, to Claus, Claus Papers, 1: 216, Library of Congress.

37. *Minute Book of Tryon County Committee of Safety*, pp. 58–59, 63.

38. Nov. 17, 1776, to Maj. Gen. Schuyler, *American Archives*, Fifth Series, 3: 743.

39. "Life [autobiography] of governor Blacksnake," Brant MSS., 16F116.

40. In July 1775 the Continental Congress set up three Indian departments: Northern, for the Six Nations and Indians to the north of them; Southern, for the Cherokees and Indians to the south; and Middle, for all the rest. Commissioners were appointed for each department to treat with the Indians in the name of the United Colonies in order to preserve peace and friendship and "to prevent their taking any part in the present commotions."

41. Council, Aug. 31, 1775, *New York Colonial Documents*, 8: 622.

42. *Minutes of Tryon County Committee of Safety*, Sept. 13 and Oct. 27, 1775, pp. 72–73, 86–88; also Council, Schenectady, Jan. 16, 1776, quoted in Stone, *Life of Brant*, 1: 127; and Council, German Flats, Aug. 13, 1776, *American Archives*, Fifth Series, 1: 1046.

43. Philip Schuyler, Dec. 14, 1775, to John Hancock, *American Archives*, Fourth Series, 4: 260.

44. Lt. Col. John Butler, May 1785, Narrative of Services in America, Haldimand Papers, B215: 197.

45. S. Kirkland, for Oneida Chiefs, May 22, 1776, to Schuyler, *New York Colonial Documents*, 8: 689.

46. James Dean, Mar. 10, 1776, to Schuyler, Schuyler Papers, Box 28, no. 457; and Kirkland, Mar. 11, 1776, to Schuyler, Kirkland MSS.

47. Draper, notes from Johnson Papers, Brant MSS., 15F88.

48. Claus, [1780?], Observations of J: Brants Distinguished Genius & Character from other Indians, Claus Papers, 2: 208.

49. John Brant, Joseph's son, produced evidence to this effect to the Scottish poet, Thomas Campbell. "Letter to the Mohawk Chief Ahyonwaeghs," *The* (London) *New Monthly Magazine and Literary Journal* 4 (1822): 99.

50. H. Clinton, Oct. 3, 1781, to Joseph Brant, British Headquarters Papers, 30, no. 3531: 90.

51. Anecdote told by Sir John Johnson's brother-in-law, who was present. Stone, *Life of Brant*, 1: 170.

52. Claus, Observations, Claus Papers, 2: 208.

53. To Gov. Livingston, *American Archives*, Fifth Series, 3: 556.

54. Brant, Dec. 1776, speech to Six Nations, State Papers, Canada, Q56, pt. 2: 521–22.

55. G. Johnson, Nov. 25, 1776, to Germain, *New York Colonial Documents*, 8: 687–88.

56. G. Johnson, July 20, 1779, Review of proceedings from end of 1775 till arrival at Quebec, Haldimand Papers, Add. MSS. 21,767, pt. 1: 13; Claus, Observations, Claus Papers, 2: 208–09.

57. Norton, Journal, etc., 2: 701–02.

58. *Ibid.*, p. 701.

CHAPTER 10—THE DIVIDED LONGHOUSE

1. Schuyler, Jan. 5, 1776 [should be 1777], to Kirkland, Kirkland MSS.; J. Trumbull, Jr., Dec. 30, 1776, to Gov. Trumbull, *American Archives*, Fifth Series, 3: 1500.

2. Claus, Observations, Claus Papers, 2: 209.

3. J. Trumbull, Jr., Dec. 30, 1776, to Gov. Trumbull, *American Archives*, Fifth Series, 3: 1500.

4. Claus, Observations, Claus Papers, 2: 209–10.

5. Claus, Anecdotes of Brant, Claus Papers, 2: 55, Library of Congress.

6. Dec. 28, 1776, Haldimand Papers, B39: 360–61.

7. Edward Foy, Feb. 9, 1777, to Capt. Fraser, *ibid.*, p. 362; Carleton, Feb. 9, 1777, to Butler, *ibid.*, pp. 358–59; R. B. Lernoult, April 11, 1777, to Carleton, extract, State Papers, Canada, Q13: 152–54.

8. Claus, Observations, Claus Papers, 2: 210.

9. Schuyler, [dated 1776 by editor; should be early 1777], to [New York Convention?], *Calendar of Historical Manuscripts, Relating to the War of the Revolution, in the Office of the Secretary of State, Albany, N.Y.*, 2 vols. (Albany, 1868), 1: 581.

10. Claus, Observations, Claus Papers, 2: 210–11; Kirkland, Jan. 24 [29?], 1777, to ———, Kirkland MSS.

11. Claus, Observations, Claus Papers, 2: 211; Claus, April 19, 1781, to Haldimand, *ibid.*, 3: 15.

12. Claus, Observations, *ibid.*, 2: 211.

13. Johnson, April 4, 1777, to Robert Mackenzie, British Headquarters Papers, 5, no. 475: 1; Johnson, July 7, 1777, to Germain, *New York Colonial Documents*, 8: 713; Johnson, July 20, 1779, Review of proceedings from end of 1775, Haldimand Papers, Add. MSS. 21,767, pt. 1: 13–14; Johnson, Dec. 19, 1782, to Haldimand, *ibid.*, B108: 96.

14. Jan. 7, 1777, to Congress, extract in "Proceedings of a General Court Martial . . . for the Trial of Major General Schuyler, October 1, 1778," *Collections of the New-York Historical Society for the Year 1879*, p. 60.

15. In 1779 the British in Canada sent them one hundred suits of clothes. Haldimand, May 20, 1779, to Claus, Haldimand Papers, Add. MSS. 21,774, pt. 1: 51.

16. Butler, Dec. 1, 1783, Return of Loyalists in Indian Department, *ibid.*, Add. MSS. 21,765, pt. 8: 376.

17. List of Capt. Brant's Volunteers at and near Niagara, Sept. 4, 1782, *ibid.*, B110: 93.

18. Brant, Aug. 29, 1787, certificate, Calendar of Original Memorials, Vouchers, Etc., 1: 134, American Loyalists Papers, New York Public Library; "Petitions for Grants of Land, 1792–6," ed. by Cruikshank, *Ontario Historical Society Papers and Records*, 24: 116; James Park, Aug. 29, n.d., claim, *Second Report of the Bureau of Archives for the Province of Ontario*, ed. by Alexander Fraser, 2 vols. (Toronto, 1905), 2: 979; Janet Carnochan, *Inscriptions and Graves in the Niagara Peninsula*, Niagara Historical Society No. 19, Second edition (Welland, 1910), pp. 52, 54; John Chisholm, memorial, American Loyalists Papers, 22: 89, 91; John Hough, Dec. 10, 1787, determination, *ibid.*, 30: 313; G. Johnson, July 20, 1779, Review of proceedings from end of 1775, Haldimand Papers, Add. MSS. 21,767, pt. 1: 13.

19. "Petitions for Grants of Land, 1792–6," *Ontario Historical Society Papers and Records*, 24: 116; Archibald Thompson, Aug. 29, n.d., claim, *Second Report of Bureau of Archives for Ontario*, 2: 979.

20. Richd. Dingman, Mar. 3, 1788, claim, *Second Report of Bureau of Archives for Ontario*, 1: 471; Geo. Barnhart, Jan. 29, n.d., claim, *ibid.*, 2: 1101–02.

21. R. Mathews, Mar. 13, 1780, to Maj. MacAlpine, Haldimand Papers, B163: 27.

22. Maj. Jas. Gray, April 20, 1777, to Capt. Foy, *ibid.*, Add. MSS. 21,818, pt. 1: 26–27.

23. Claus, Oct. 13, 1778, to Haldimand, *ibid.*, Add. MSS. 21,774, pt. 1: 5. As late as 1781 only seventeen warriors accompanied Brant to the Ohio country. G. Johnson, April 20, 1781, Return of Indian war parties, *ibid.*, B109: 146.

24. Col. John Harper, June 12, 1777, to Committee of Schoharie, in "Proceedings . . . for the Trial of Major General Schuyler," *Collections of the New-York Historical Society for the Year 1879*, pp. 103–04.

25. MS. at Schenectady County Historical Society.

26. Christopher Pearson, Nov. 1778, deposition, *Public Papers of George Clinton, First Governor of New York*, published by the State of New York, 10 vols. (New York and Albany, 1899–1914), 5: 417–18; George Cannotts, Mar. 26, 1779, affidavit, *ibid.*, p. 418.

27. James Dean, June 25, 1777, to Schuyler, "Proceedings . . . for the Trial of Major General Schuyler," p. 118.

28. Claus, Anecdotes of Brant, Claus Papers, 2: 56, Library of Congress.

29. John Dusler, Feb. 12, 1833, declaration, Brant MSS., 3F40–41.

30. Stone, *Life of Brant*, 1: 184–85.

31. Schuyler, July 4, 1777, to Herkimer, "Proceedings . . . for the Trial of Major General Schuyler," pp. 134–35; Schuyler, July 21, 1777, to Council of Safety of New York, extract, *ibid.*, p. 176.

32. Johnson, July 7, 1777, to Germain, *New York Colonial Documents*, 8: 713–14; Johnson, July 20, 1779, Review of proceedings from end of 1775, Haldimand Papers, Add. MSS. 21,767, pt. 1: 13.

33. Butler, July 28, 1777, to Carleton, State Papers, Canada, Q14: 145.

34. Claus, Oct. 16, 1777, to William Knox, *New York Colonial Documents*, 8: 719. Guy Johnson told Germain in his letter of July 7 that about seven hundred Indians were assembled on the Susquehanna, and that there would be even more when it was time for them to join the army! The gathering Indians, though their numbers were really not large, had been causing the rebels much anxiety.

35. *Ibid.*

36. Lady Johnson's internment and hair-raising escape from the rebels read more like romance than history.

37. "Life of governor Blacksnake," Brant MSS., 16F123. The old man seems to have confused several councils into one, but the emotions were the same.

38. Claus, Mar. 8, 1787, to Evan Nepean, C.O. 42, 19: 86, Public Archives of Canada.

39. *Ibid.* Claus only mentions a "Stratagem." Mary Jemison, famous white captive who lived among the Indians and who was present at the council, related years later what was said but not by whom. James E. Seaver, *Life of Mary Jemison,* Fourth edition (New York, Auburn, and Rochester, 1856), p. 116. The official records of this council have been lost.

40. Letter, July 15, 1777, Schuyler Papers, Box 33, no. 918.

41. Barry St. Leger, Aug. 2, 1777, to Lieut. Bird, Military Papers of Gen. Peter Gansevoort, Jr., vol. 3, New York Public Library; St. Leger, Aug. 27, 1777, to Gen. Burgoyne, in Lieutenant-General Burgoyne, *A State of the Expedition from Canada, as Laid Before the House of Commons* (London, 1780), Appendix, p. xliii.

42. St. Leger, Aug. 27, 1777, to Burgoyne, in Burgoyne, *State of the Expedition from Canada,* Appendix, p. xliii; Bird, Aug. 2, 1777, to St. Leger, Gansevoort Papers, vol. 3.

43. Council, Feb. 19, 1780, Haldimand Papers, Add. MSS. 21,787, pt. 3: 112.

44. As the name reverted to Fort Stanwix after the war, this is the name that we shall continue to use.

45. Claus, Oct. 16, 1777, to Knox, *New York Colonial Documents,* 8: 721.

46. St. Leger, Aug. 27, 1777, to Burgoyne, in Burgoyne, *State of the Expedition from Canada,* Appendix, p. lxiv [should be xliv].

47. Gansevoort Papers, vol. 3.

48. Will'm Wills, chairman Tryon County [committee], Feb. 10, 1778, to Gov. George Clinton, *Public Papers of George Clinton,* 2: 742.

49. Claus, Anecdotes of Brant, Claus Papers, 2: 58, Library of Congress.

50. "Life of governor Blacksnake," Brant MSS., 16F136.

51. Aug. 15, 1777, State Papers, Canada, Q14: 154.

52. Stone, *Life of Brant,* 1: 244.

53. Brant is said to have admitted years later that the Americans won this battle. *Ibid.,* p. 240.

54. Claus, Anecdotes of Brant, Claus Papers, 2: 58, Library of Congress.

55. *Ibid.;* also Claus, Dec. 2, 1777, Account vs. Government, Haldimand Papers, B114: 322.

56. Claus, Mar. 8, 1787, to Nepean, C.O. 42, 19: 88–89.

57. Jan. 22, 1776, to John Hancock, *American Archives,* Fourth Series, 4: 803.

58. Claus, Anecdotes of Brant, Claus Papers, 2: 58–59, Library of Congress.

59. Mason Bolton and John Butler, Nov. 23, 1777, to Gen. Clinton, etc., *New York Colonial Documents,* 8: 741.

60. Claus, Anecdotes of Brant, Claus Papers, 2: 59, Library of Congress.

61. Brant, April 15, 1779, to Haldimand, Haldimand Papers, B109: 22.

62. Claus, Nov. 12, 1777, to Guy Johnson, extract in Sir Henry Clinton Papers, William L. Clements Library, Ann Arbor, Mich.

63. Council, [Dec. 1777], Haldimand Papers, Add. MSS. 21,779, pt. 4: 192.

64. Dec. 14, 1777, to Adj. Gen. Foy, no. 3, "Haldimand Papers," *Michigan Historical Collections,* 19: 337.

CHAPTER 11—THE MONSTER BRANT

1. Letter, Jan. 23, 1778, to Claus, Claus Papers, 2: 1–2, Library of Congress.

2. *Ibid.*; also Butler, Feb. 2, 1778, to Carleton, "Haldimand Papers," *Michigan Historical Collections*, 19: 342.

3. Feb. 2, 1778, "Haldimand Papers," *Michigan Historical Collections*, 19: 342.

4. No. 10, Haldimand Papers, Add. MSS. 21,756, pt. 1.

5. Butler, Sept. 17, 1778, to [Haldimand], no. 12, *ibid.*

6. Deposition of Barney Kelley, in Col. Peter Pellinger [Bellinger], June 26, 1778, to Abm. Ten Broeck, *Public Papers of George Clinton*, 3: 506.

7. Taylor & Duffin, Oct. 26, 1778, to Claus, Claus Papers, 25: 42, Public Archives of Canada.

8. May 25, 1778, to Schuyler, *Public Papers of George Clinton*, 3: 356.

9. This account is pieced together as well as possible from the following sources, all American: William Dietz and others, May 30, 1778, to Gen. Stark, *ibid.*, p. 377; Chrisr. Yates, May 30, 1778, to Col. Wempel, *ibid.*, p. 378; Col. Jacob Klock, May 31, 1778, to Brig. Gen. Abraham Ten Broeck, *ibid.*, p. 382; Klock, June 5, 1778, to Gov. Clinton, *ibid.*, p. 403; Abm. Wempel, June 6, 1778, to Ten Broeck, *ibid.*, pp. 413–14; Col. Peter Bellinger, June 26, 1778, to Ten Broeck, *ibid.*, p. 506; William McKendry, "Journal," May 30, 1778, *Proceedings of the Massachusetts Historical Society*, Second Series 2 (May 1886): 444; Richd. Varick, June 3, 1778, to Col. Gansevoort, Brant MSS., 5F182.

10. Jacob Klock, June 5, 1778, to Clinton, *Public Papers of George Clinton*, 3: 403; Col. Peter Bellinger, June 26, 1778, to Ten Broeck, *ibid.*, p. 506.

11. Stone, *Life of Brant*, 1: 190–91; William W. Campbell, *Annals of Tryon County; or, The Border Warfare of New-York during the Revolution* (New York, 1831), pp. 102–03.

12. Bellinger, June 26, 1778, to Ten Broeck, *Public Papers of George Clinton*, 3: 506.

13. Campbell, *Annals of Tryon County*, pp. 104–05.

14. Letter, July 9, 1778, quoted *ibid.*, pp. 105–06.

15. Jacob Klock to Gov. Clinton, *Public Papers of George Clinton*, 3: 402.

16. J. Gregg to Clinton, *ibid.*, p. 450.

17. Brig. Gen. John Stark to Capt. Willm. H. Ballard, *ibid.*, 5: 413.

18. Bellinger, June 26, 1778, to Ten Broeck, *ibid.*, 3: 506.

19. Taylor & Duffin, Oct. 26, 1778, to Claus, Claus Papers, 25: 42.

20. Narrative, June 16, 1778, *Public Papers of George Clinton*, 3: 462.

21. Statement of Robert Jones, in Henry Wisner, July 10, 1778, to Clinton, *ibid.*, pp. 542–43.

22. *Ibid.*, p. 543; also Bellinger, June 26, 1778, to Ten Broeck, *ibid.*, p. 505.

23. Wisner, July 10, 1778, to Clinton, *ibid.*, p. 543.

24. Letter to Lieut. Col. Mason Bolton, Sir Henry Clinton Papers.

25. Benj. Tusten, Jr., and others, letter, *Public Papers of George Clinton*, 3: 540.

26. Henry Wisner and others, July 5, 1778, to Clinton, *ibid.*, pp. 522–23.

27. Josiah Priest, *Stories of Early Settlers in the Wilderness* (Albany, 1837), frontispiece.

28. William L. Stone, *The Poetry and History of Wyoming* (New York and London, 1841), p. 40.

29. Wisner, July 10, 1778, to Clinton, *Public Papers of George Clinton*, 3: 543.

30. Bellinger, June 26, 1778, to Ten Broeck, *ibid.*, pp. 505–06.

31. Wisner, July 10, 1778, to Clinton, *ibid.*, p. 543.

32. Quoted in Campbell, *Annals of Tryon County*, pp. 105–06.

33. Mar. 8, 1787, to Nepean, C.O. 42, 19: 89.

34. Sept. 10, 1778, to Germain, *New York Colonial Documents*, 8: 752.

35. *Public Papers of George Clinton*, 3: 520–21.

36. Butler, July 8, 1778, to Bolton, Sir Henry Clinton Papers.

37. Butler, July 12, 1778, to Caldwell, Haldimand Papers, B111: 8–9.

38. John Younglove, Chairman, Feb. 26, 1778, to Committee of Albany, *Public Papers of George Clinton*, 2: 855.

39. Jacob Ford [?], July 18, 1778, to Ten Broeck, *ibid.*, 3: 555–57; Jacob Klock, July 19, 1778, to Ten Broeck, *ibid.*, p. 559; Klock, June [should be July] 22, 1778, to Clinton, *ibid.*, pp. 475–76; Bellinger and others, July 22, 1778, to Clinton, *ibid.*, pp. 581–82; Return of Springfield, April 13, 1779, *ibid.*, 4: 722–23.

40. Testimony of captured Tories, Aug. 12, 1778, *ibid.*, 5: 414–16.

41. Klock, [July] 22, 1778, to Clinton, *ibid.*, 3: 475.

42. Bellinger and others, July 22, 1778, to Clinton, *ibid.*, pp. 581–82.

43. Campbell, *Annals of Tryon County*, p. 104; Stone, *Life of Brant*, 1: 312; notes by J. R. Simms, Brant MSS., 4F61; Daniel Franklin, May 27, 1878, to Lyman C. Draper, *ibid.*, 4F72.

44. Taylor & Duffin, Oct. 26, 1778, to Claus, Claus Papers, 25: 42, Public Archives of Canada; Claus, Anecdotes of Brant, *ibid.*, 2: 60–61, Library of Congress.

45. Butler, Sept. 24, 1778, to Haldimand, no. 13, Haldimand Papers, Add. MSS. 21,756, pt. 1.

46. Abstract of Daniel Claus's Indian expenses, Nov. 1, 1777–June 25, 1779, *ibid.*, Add. MSS. 21,774, pt. 2: 56.

47. Aug. 4, 1778, to Taylor & Duffin, Claus Papers, 2: 43, Library of Congress.

48. This time there are accounts from both sides, and they agree substantially. Wm. Caldwell, Sept. 21, 1778, to Butler, Haldimand Papers, Add. MSS. 21,765, pt. 1: 42; and Bellinger, Sept. 16, 1778, to Klock, *Public Papers of George Clinton*, 4: 39; Fredk. Fisher, Sept. 18, 1778, to Wemple, *ibid.*, p. 47; Bellinger, Sept. 19, 1778, to Clinton, *ibid.*, pp. 47–48; Ten Broeck, Sept. 24, 1778, to Clinton, *ibid.*, pp. 80–83; Bellinger, Sept. 20, 1778, to Henry Glen, Single Acquisitions, no. 11147, New York State Library. Sometime before the attack on German Flats Joseph Brant wrote a letter to his old enemy, Col. Jacob Klock, but the letter has been lost. Ten Broeck, Sept. 13, 1778, to Clinton, with footnote, *Public Papers of George Clinton*, 4: 31.

49. Claus, Sept. 15, 1778, to Haldimand, Haldimand Papers, Add. MSS. 21,774, pt. 1: 2.

50. Christopher Pearson, Nov. 1778, deposition, *Public Papers of George Clinton*, 5: 418.

51. Aug. 12, 1778, to Gen. Stark, *ibid.*, p. 416.

52. Taylor & Duffin, Nov. 15, 1778, to Claus, Claus Papers, 2: 67; Lieut. Col. Joh's Hardenbergh, Jr., Oct. 16, 1778, to Clinton, *Public Papers of George Clinton*, 4: 166.

53. Clinton, Oct. 27, 1778, to Col. Van Cortlandt, *Public Papers of George Clinton*, 4: 210.

54. Information of Joseph Showers, Feb. 12, 1779, Pittsburgh and Northwest Virginia MSS., 3NN126–127, State Historical Society of Wisconsin.

55. Taylor & Duffin, Nov. 15, 1778, to Claus, Claus Papers, 2: 67.

56. John Butler, Sept. 17, 1778, to Haldimand, no. 12, Haldimand Papers, Add. MSS. 21,756, pt. 1; Bolton, Oct. 12, 1778, to Haldimand, no. 19, *ibid.*, pt. 2;

Bolton, Nov. 11, 1778, to Haldimand, no. 23, "Haldimand Papers," *Michigan Historical Collections*, 19: 364; Capt. Walter Butler, Nov. 17, 1778, to Bolton, Haldimand Papers, Add. MSS. 21,760, pt. 2: 77; Gen. Edward Hand, Nov. 19, 1778, to Jasper Yeates, Pittsburgh and Northwest Virginia MSS., 3NN30.

57. Bolton, April 8, 1778, to Carleton, no. 6, Haldimand Papers, Add. MSS. 21,756, pt. 2.

58. Ten Broeck, Nov. 13, 1778, to Clinton, *Public Papers of George Clinton*, 4: 267; Campbell, *Annals of Tryon County*, p. 108.

59. George Cannotts, Mar. 26, 1779, affidavit, *Public Papers of George Clinton*, 5: 418.

60. Taylor & Duffin, Nov. 15, 1778, to Claus, Claus Papers, 2: 67.

61. Mar. 17, 1779, to Haldimand, Haldimand Papers, Add. MSS. 21,774, pt. 1: 29.

62. Capt. Walter Butler, Feb. 18, 1779, to Brig. Gen. James Clinton, *ibid.*, Add. MSS. 21,765, pt. 2: 83–84.

63. Campbell, *Annals of Tryon County*, Appendix, p. 16.

64. Nov. 17, 1778, Haldimand Papers, Add. MSS. 21,760, pt. 2: 77–80. Following details come from this letter.

65. A peculiar error—actually many more prisoners were returned, one official American list running as high as forty-five and a British list naming forty-nine. These persons Walter Butler wanted exchanged for an equal number of Loyalist prisoners held by the Americans.

66. Dec. 1, 1778, Claus Papers, 25: 71.

67. Edward Pollard, Jan. 9, 1779, to Geo. Forsith, George Rogers Clark Papers, 49J18, State Historical Society of Wisconsin.

68. Danl. Whiting, Nov. 14, 1778, to Col. William Butler, Brant MSS., 20F19.

69. Single Acquisitions, no. 40, New York State Library.

70. Hand, Nov. 19, 1778, to Yeates, Pittsburgh and Northwest Virginia MSS., 3NN30.

71. Geo. Clinton, April 12, 1784, instructions to Peter Ryckman, *Proceedings of the Commissioners of Indian Affairs, Appointed by Law for the Extinguishment of Indian Titles in the State of New York*, ed. by Franklin B. Hough, 2 vols. (Albany, 1861), 1: 12.

72. Claus Papers, 25: 71.

73. Jacob Klock, Nov. 23, 1778, to Frederick Vischer [Fisher], Brant MSS., 20F23; also William Harper, Dec. 2, 1778, to Clinton, *Public Papers of George Clinton*, 4: 414.

74. Capt. William Johnson, Joseph Ceskwrora, Capt. John, and William George, Dec. 13, 1778, to Col. John Cantine, *Public Papers of George Clinton*, 4: 364.

CHAPTER 12—THE DESTRUCTION OF THE LONGHOUSE

1. Stone, *Life of Brant*, 1: 401.

2. Haldimand, April 8, 1779, to Bolton, no. 9, Haldimand Papers, Add. MSS. 21,756, pt. 3.

3. Letter, no. 29, *ibid.*, pt. 2.

4. Claus, Mar. 17, 1779, to Haldimand, *ibid.*, Add. MSS. 21,774, pt. 1: 29.

5. Journal, Mar. 8–16, 1779, *ibid.*, Add. MSS. 21,765, pt. 2: 85–88.

6. Claus, Mar. 17, 1779, to Haldimand, *ibid.*, Add. MSS. 21,774, pt. 1: 29.

7. Journal, *ibid.*, Add. MSS. 21,765, pt. 2: 85.

8. Claus, Mar. 17, 1779, to Haldimand, *ibid.*, Add. MSS. 21,774, pt. 1: 29.

9. Stone, *Life of Brant*, 1: 400–04. Rumors of an impending Indian attack seem to have been deliberately started at Niagara. P. Langan, April 6, 1779, to Claus, Claus Papers, 26: 77.

10. Mar. 20, 1779, to Claus, Haldimand Papers, Add. MSS. 21,774, pt. 1: 31.

11. Sir John Johnson, July 2, 1778, to Claus, Claus Papers, 2: 37, Library of Congress.

12. Oct. 24, 1778, Haldimand Papers, B54: 52.

13. Haldimand, April 8, 1779, to Bolton, no. 9, *ibid.*, Add. MSS. 21,756, pt. 3.

14. Indian department, pay rolls, Mar. 24–Sept. 25, 1779, and Sept. 24, 1779–Mar. 25, 1780, *ibid.*, B109: 27, 53.

15. Brant, April 5, 1786, to Evan Nepean, State Papers, Canada, Q26, pt. 1: 71.

16. R. McCausland, surgeon to 8th regiment, April 2, 1781, to Brig. Gen. Powell, Haldimand Papers, Add. MSS. 21,761, pt. 1: 30.

17. Haldimand, May 20, 1779, to Claus, *ibid.*, Add. MSS. 21,774, pt. 1: 51.

18. Return of Indians who received clothing, etc., at Niagara, Nov. 1778–Mar. 1779, *ibid.*, B109: 17–18.

19. Claus, Mar. 17, 1779, to Haldimand, *ibid.*, Add. MSS. 21,774, pt. 1: 29–30.

20. Sept. 20, 1777, *ibid.*, B42: 1–2.

21. April 7, 1779, Claus Papers, 2: 89–90.

22. Haldimand, April 2, 1779, to Indians, Haldimand Papers, Add. MSS. 21,779, pt. 1: 29; and Haldimand, May 1780, to Six Nations, *ibid.*, pt. 2: 89.

23. April 8, 1779, to Lieut. Col. Campbell, *ibid.*, B113: 13.

24. Claus, Mar. 17, 1779, to Haldimand, *ibid.*, Add. MSS. 21,774, pt. 1: 29.

25. April 15, 1779, *ibid.*, B109: 21.

26. Johnson, May 20, 1779, to Haldimand, *ibid.*, Add. MSS. 21,818, pt. 2: 74.

27. May 23, 1779, *ibid.*, Add. MSS. 21,764, pt. 1: 17.

28. Instructions, April 9, 1779, "Haldimand Papers," *Michigan Historical Collections*, 19: 392; also letter, April 8, 1779, to Butler, no. 3, Haldimand Papers, Add. MSS. 21,756, pt. 2.

29. Instructions, April 9, 1779, "Haldimand Papers," *Michigan Historical Collections*, 19: 392.

30. April 15, 1779, to Haldimand, Haldimand Papers, B109: 21; D. Brehm, April 16, 1779, to Haldimand, *ibid.*, B99: 27–28.

31. Claus Papers, 21, pt. 2, notebook 7: 32.

32. April 15, 1779, Haldimand Papers, B109: 21–22.

33. Brant, May 8, 1779, to Claus, *ibid.*, Add. MSS. 21,774, pt. 1: 45.

34. Walter Butler, May 10, 1779, to Haldimand, *ibid.*, Add. MSS. 21,787, pt. 1: 39.

35. Letter, April 28, 1779, to Capt. La Matre [Le Maistre], War Office Papers: Field Officers Letters, 1775–1805, M326: 2, Public Archives of Canada.

36. Abm. Yates, Jr., Jan. 9, 1779, to Clinton, *Public Papers of George Clinton*, 4: 478.

37. Col. Jacob Klock, June 6, 1778, to Gen. Ten Broeck, *ibid.*, 3: 414–15.

38. July 21, 1778, to Ten Broeck, *ibid.*, p. 573.

39. Sept. 25, 1778, *The Writings of George Washington from the Original Manu-*

93. Johnson, Oct. 30, 1764, to Lords of Trade, *New York Colonial Documents*, 7: 671–72; John Thornton Kirkland, "Answer to Queries on Indians," p. 74.

94. Council, May 28, 1756, *Johnson Papers*, 9: 464; S. Kirtland [Kirkland], Feb. 21, 1766, to Johnson, *ibid.*, 12: 27; Johnson, Feb. 28, 1771, to Arthur Lee, *Documentary History of New York*, 4: 431–32; "Opinions of George Croghan on American Indian," p. 158.

CHAPTER 2—PETER AND MARGARET

1. [The Rev. John Strachan], "Life of Capt. Brant," *The Christian Recorder*, Kingston, Upper Canada, May 1819.

2. Eleazar Wheelock, *A plain and faithful Narrative of the Original Design, Rise, Progress and present State of the Indian Charity-School at Lebanon, in Connecticut* (Boston, 1763), p. 40.

3. Maj. [Archibald] Campbell, July 19, 1786, to Henry Hope, extract, State Papers, Canada, Q26, pt. 2: 521.

4. Johnson, Nov. 13, 1763, to Lords of Trade, *New York Colonial Documents*, 7: 580.

5. Philip Schuyler, July 5, 1777, to Gen. Washington, extract, "Proceedings of a General Court Martial . . . for the Trial of Major General Schuyler, October 1, 1778," *Collections of the New-York Historical Society for the Year 1879*, p. 138.

6. Jos. Brant, Sept. 23, 1789, to Maj. Robert Mathews, State Papers, Canada, Q43, pt. 2: 785.

7. *The American Museum, or, Universal Magazine*, Philadelphia 6 (Sept. 1789): 226. See also William L. Stone, *Life of Joseph Brant-Thayendanegea*, 2 vols. (New York, 1838), 2: 481. Joseph's son, John Brant, presented documentary evidence of his father's unmixed Indian parentage to the Scottish poet, Campbell. "Letter to the Mohawk Chief Ahyonwaeghs, Commonly Called John Brant, Esq. of the Grand River, Upper Canada. From Thomas Campbell," *The New Monthly Magazine and Literary Journal* 4 (London, 1822): 98.

8. Stone, *Life of Brant*, 1: 18.

9. H. B. Johnson, Oct. 17, 1877, to Lyman C. Draper, Brant MSS., 14F36, State Historical Society of Wisconsin.

10. MS. at The New-York Historical Society.

11. A Margaret later became the wife of a sachem named Brant, who appears to be the stepfather from whom, as we shall see, both the Rev. John Stuart and John Norton, Joseph's long-time friend, say Joseph got his surname. In corroboration of their story, Henry van Driessen, Jr., a man with whom the Indians had a land dispute, refers to Joseph as "son to Brants wife." *Calendar of the Sir William Johnson Manuscripts in the New York State Library*, compiled by Richard E. Day (Albany, 1909), p. 347. A Margaret Brant is also mentioned in traders' accounts against Sir William Johnson in such a way as to imply a close connection. See chapter 3 for further details.

12. John Deserontyon, Dec. 3, 1778, to Col. Daniel Claus, Brant MSS., 5F11; I. Bearfoot, June 22, 1889, to Lyman C. Draper, *ibid.*, 13F134.

13. Capt. Malcolm Fraser, Nov. 26, 1783, Return of Loyalists . . . on Carleton Island, Haldimand Papers, British Museum, London, Additional MSS. 21,787, pt. 7: 344. (See Bibliography for an explanatory note about the Haldimand Papers.) Presumably Molly herself furnished the information about her age.

14. Norton, Journal, etc., 2: 699.

72. Estimate of losses in real and personal estate of Six Nations as valued in 1775, State Papers, Canada, Q24, pt. 2: 299–324, Public Archives of Canada. Little Abraham of Fort Hunter who never went to Canada probably owned land, too.

73. For instance: Account of Persons employd. in the Battoe Service Under David Schuyler Jur, Schenectady, *Johnson Papers*, 3: 631–33; Johnson, Account of Indian Expenses, *ibid.*, pp. 175–76.

74. Council, Sept. 13, 1763, *ibid.*, 10: 849; Council, Oct. 21, 1763, *ibid.*, p. 903; Council, May 10, 1756, *New York Colonial Documents*, 7: 103; Council, May 26, 1756, *ibid.*, pp. 115–16; Diamond Jenness, *The Indians of Canada* (Fifth Edition, Ottawa, 1960), pp. 136–37; William Nelson Fenton, "A Calendar of Manuscript Materials relating to the History of the Six Nations or Iroquois Indians in Depositories outside of Philadelphia, 1750–1850," *The American Philosophical Society Library Bulletin 1953*, p. 591.

75. Jenness, *Indians of Canada*, pp. 136–37.

76. Charles Lee, June 18, 1756, to sister, *The Lee Papers*, in *Collections of the New-York Historical Society*, 4 vols. (New York, 1872–75), 1: 4.

77. Theophilus Chamberlain, July 10 and 17, 1765, to the Rev. Eleazar Wheelock, Dartmouth College MSS. This and all subsequent quotations from these manuscripts are reproduced by permission of the Trustees of Dartmouth College.

78. Johnson, Feb. 28, 1771, to Arthur Lee, *Documentary History of New York*, 4: 433; Johnson, Oct. 24, 1762, to George Croghan, *Johnson Papers*, 3: 914; Thomas McKee, Nov. 2, 1762, to Johnson, *ibid.*, p. 924; Wallace, *Indians in Pennsylvania*, p. 175. See also chapter 24, note 82.

79. Johnson, April 22, 1756, to William Shirley, *Johnson Papers*, 9: 439.

80. Conrad Weiser, journal to Onondaga, 1750, p. 13, MS. at Historical Society of Pennsylvania.

81. Council, July 2, 1754, *Documentary History of New York*, 2: 580.

82. Weiser, journal to Onondaga, 1750, pp. 11–12.

83. Diary of Charles Frederick and David Zeisberger, July 24, 1754, *Moravian Journals*, pp. 199–200.

84. Council, July 9, 1754, *Documentary History of New York*, 2: 603; Journal of Indian Affairs, May 30, 1756, *Johnson Papers*, 9: 467; Journal of Indian Affairs, April 9, 1767, *ibid.*, 12: 304.

85. Johnson, Sept. 4, 1755, to James De Lancey, *Johnson Papers*, 2: 7; Johnson, Sept. 22, 1767, to Earl of Shelburne, *New York Colonial Documents*, 7: 959–60.

86. Gideon Hawley, July 31, 1794, to the Rev. Dr. Thacher, Narrative of journey to Oquaga, 1753, *Documentary History of New York*, 3: 1044.

87. Diary of Zeisberger and Frey, July 28, 1753, *Moravian Journals*, p. 180.

88. Thomas McKee, Nov. 1, 1762, to Johnson, *Johnson Papers*, 3: 921.

89. Johnson, Sept. 22, 1766, to Banyar, *ibid.*, 12: 192.

90. Journal of Indian affairs, April 9, 1767, *ibid.*, p. 304.

91. Council, July 8, 1799, "Indian Affairs," *Collections of Michigan Pioneer and Historical Society* 20 (1892): 645.

92. Peter Wraxall, Jan. 9, 1755/6, "Some Thoughts upon The British Indian Interest in North America, more particularly as it relates to The Northern Confederacy commonly called The Six Nations," *New York Colonial Documents*, 7: 18; Johnson, Sept. 22, 1767, to Earl of Shelburne, *ibid.*, p. 958; John Thornton Kirkland, "Answer to the foregoing Queries, respecting Indians," *Collections of the Massachusetts Historical Society*, 1 Series 4 (1795): 74; Howard H. Peckham, *Pontiac and the Indian Uprising* (Princeton, N.J., 1947), p. 53.

detailed account of events before and during the battle of Newtown from the viewpoint of the Rangers.

94. Aug. 31–Sept. 2, 1779, British Headquarters Papers, 18, no. 2238: 2–3.

95. Journal, etc., 2: 718.

96. Aug. 31–Sept. 2, 1779, to Bolton, British Headquarters Papers, 18, no. 2238: 3.

97. Cartwright, Journal, Aug. 29, 1779, Brant MSS., 6F48; Stone, *Life of Brant,* 1: 244.

98. Sullivan, Sept. 30, 1779, to John Jay, *Journals of Sullivan Expedition,* ed. by Cook, p. 298.

99. Sullivan's official report of the battle of Newtown, made to Washington, Aug. 30, 1779, may be found *ibid.,* pp. 473–76.

100. Sept. 15, 1779, *ibid.,* p. 383.

101. Lieut. William Barton, Journal, Aug. 30, 1779, *ibid.,* p. 8; Sergt. Thomas Roberts, Journal, Aug. 31, 1779, *ibid.,* p. 244; Lieut. Rudolphus Van Hovenburgh, Journal, Aug. 30, 1779, *ibid.,* p. 279; Intelligence of John Jones, Feb. 15, 1780, *New York Colonial Documents,* 8: 785.

102. Haldimand, Oct. 3, 1779, to Germain, Haldimand Papers, B54: 194.

103. Lieut. John Jenkins, Journal, Sept. 2, 1779, *Journals of Sullivan Expedition,* p. 173; Capt. Daniel Livermore, Journal, Sept. 1, 1779, *ibid.,* p. 186; Dr. Jabez Campfield, Journal, Sept. 1, 1779, *ibid.,* pp. 56–57; Maj. Jeremiah Fogg, Journal, Sept. 2, 1779, *ibid.,* p. 96; Lieut. Col. Adam Hubley, Journal, Sept. 2, 1779, *ibid.,* p. 158. A white woman captive who had escaped or been left behind at Genesee Castle told the same story.

104. Capt. Daniel Livermore, Journal, Sept. 1, 1779, *ibid.,* p. 186.

105. Stone, *Life of Brant,* 2: 35.

106. Lieut. Samuel M. Shute, Journal, Sept. 3, 1779, *Journals of Sullivan Expedition,* p. 271.

107. British Headquarters Papers, 18, no. 2247: 2.

108. Butler, Sept. 8, 1779, to Bolton, *ibid.*

109. *Ibid.,* pp. 2–3.

110. Haldimand Papers, Add. MSS. 21,760, pt. 5: 214–15.

111. Journal, etc., 2: 716.

112. Bolton, Sept. 16–17, 1779, to Haldimand, extract, British Headquarters Papers, 19, no. 2308: 3.

113. Bolton, Sept. 22, 1779, to Maj. Nairne, Haldimand Papers, Add. MSS. 21,760, pt. 5: 220; Bolton, Oct. 2, 1779, to Haldimand, no. 41, *ibid.,* Add. MSS. 21,756, pt. 2. Joseph was gone about two weeks on this scout.

114. Stone, *Life of Brant,* 2: 460. A remark overheard by Gansevoort's son and related to Stone.

115. Sept. 9, 1779, Haldimand Papers, Add. MSS. 21,819, pt. 1: 43.

116. John Johnson, Oct. 15, 1779, to Haldimand, *ibid.,* Add. MSS. 21,818, pt. 3: 117; Bolton, Oct. 21, 1779, to Haldimand, *ibid.,* Add. MSS. 21,760, pt. 5: 239; G. Johnson, Nov. 11, 1779, to Germain, *New York Colonial Documents,* 8: 779.

117. Sept. 16–17, 1779, to Haldimand, extract, British Headquarters Papers, 19, no. 2308: 3.

118. G. Johnson, Nov. 12, 1779, to Haldimand, Haldimand Papers, Add. MSS. 21,767, pt. 1: 52.

119. Sept. 16–17, 1779, extract, British Headquarters Papers, 19, no. 2308: 3.

120. Oct. 2, 1779, no. 41, Haldimand Papers, Add. MSS. 21,756, pt. 2.

CHAPTER 13—THE TRIUMVIRATE

1. Johnson, Minutes, Dec. 17, 1779, Indian Records, Series Two, 12: 97.

2. Campbell, *Annals of Tryon County*, p. 182. Bolton actually did send this prisoner down to Montreal for fear of what the Indians might do to him. His action lends some credence to the story of Molly's behavior. Bolton, Sept. 16, 1779, to Haldimand, Haldimand Papers, Add. MSS. 21,760, pt. 5: 219.

3. Bolton, Dec. 4, 1779, to Haldimand, Haldimand Papers, Add. MSS. 21,760, pt. 6: 263.

4. April 16, 1779, *ibid.*, B43: 116–17. Germain also sent some prints of Joseph's portrait by Romney to be distributed among the Indians in his honor. There is no record that Haldimand actually distributed these.

5. Oct. 24, 1779, *ibid.*, B54: 205–06.

6. Dec. 20, 1750, to Gov. Clinton, *Johnson Papers*, 1: 315.

7. Draper, Oct. 6–8, 1879, interview with Mrs. Catharine Hill, granddaughter of Capt. Joseph Brant, Brant MSS., 13F94. Another aged Indian, less closely related, spelled Catharine's name as Ahdohwahgeseon and said it meant "Trembling Ground."

8. Feb. 26, 1780, *New York Colonial Documents*, 8: 781.

9. R. Mathews, Aug. 31, 1780, to Brig. Gen. Maclean, Haldimand Papers, B131: 68.

10. Campbell, *Annals of Tryon County*, Appendix, pp. 16–17.

11. P. Campbell, *Travels in the Interior Inhabited Parts of North America in the Years 1791 and 1792* (Edinburgh, 1793), pp. 190–91. Ensign James Peachey of the 60th regiment sent a drawing of Catharine to Haldimand in 1789. It has not been found.

12. Jos. and Katerin Brant, Mar. 14, 1803, deed to Robert Wilson, Miscellaneous MSS., New-York Historical Society.

13. Stone, *Life of Brant*, 2: 500.

14. Mrs. Jane Whitaker, narrative, extract in clipping from *Daily National Democrat*, July 26, 1853, Brant MSS., 4F53.

15. Charles G. Dewitt, "A Revolutionary Incident," quoting from narrative of Capt. Jeremiah Snyder, clipping from *The* (Saugerties, N.Y.) *Telegraph*, Jan. 3, 1878, Brant Miscellanies, 2G93.

16. Wm. C. Bryant, "Joseph Brant, Thayendanegea, and His Posterity," *The American Historical Record*, 2, no. 19 (July 1873): 295.

17. Stone, *Life of Brant*, 2: 463.

18. Elizabeth Newman, Sept. 4, 1781, petition to Gov. George Clinton, *Public Papers of George Clinton*, 7: 299; Brant, June 12, 1798, to Thomas Morris, copy of privately owned MS. seen through courtesy of Dr. Milton W. Hamilton; also C. L. Ward, narrative, Feb. 22, 1855, Brant MSS., 4F172.

19. Campbell, *Travels in America in 1791–92*, pp. 194–95; Roy F. Fleming, "Negro Slaves with the United Empire Loyalists in Upper Canada," *Ontario History* 45, no. 1 (Winter 1953): 29.

20. Isaac Weld, Jr., *Travels through the States of North America, and the Provinces of Upper and Lower Canada, during the Years 1795, 1796, and 1797* (London, 1799), p. 407.

21. Ward, narrative, Feb. 22, 1855, Brant MSS., 4F172.

22. List of loyalists . . . in Rangers, Nov. 30, 1783, Haldimand Papers, Add. MSS. 21,765, pt. 7: 355; *The John Askin Papers, 1747–1820*, ed. by Milo M. Quaife, 2 vols. (n.p., 1928–31), 1: 258, n. 51; Diary of Indian Church in Fairfield Canada, Jan.

25, 1801, MS. at Moravian Archives, Bethlehem, Pa.; Brant, July 23, 1801, to James Wheelock, Simon Gratz Collection, Historical Society of Pennsylvania; Margaret Pearson Bothwell, "The Astonishing Croghans," *The Western Pennsylvania Historical Magazine* 48, no. 2 (April 1965): 121.

23. Minutes, Indian Records, Series Two, 12: 107.

24. Bro. Mortimer, July 13, 1799, to C. G. Reichel, Ettwein Papers, no. 1539, MS. at Moravian Archives. A well-known scholar told this author years ago that he had seen a prayer book inscribed by Brant, "This is my mother's Bible"; but he could not remember where he saw it. The book is *not* at the Moravian Archives, and has not been found.

25. Johnson, Minutes, Dec. 17, 1779, Indian Records, Series Two, 12: 97.

26. Council minutes, Dec. 22, 1797, State Papers, Upper Canada, Q290, pt. 2: 322.

27. According to testimony of aged Indians, who also said Isaac's jealousy was unjustified. Stone, *Life of Brant*, 2: 464.

28. Draper, Sept. 26, 1879, interview with Sarah Lottridge, granddaughter of Joseph Brant, Brant MSS., 13F30; Draper, Sept. 28, 1879, interview with Mrs. David Jacket Hill, granddaughter of Henry Tekarihoga, *ibid.*, 13F32–33. Most of the old Mohawks interviewed by Draper said Catharine and Henry were sister and brother; one said, cousin. All agreed that Henry was the older of the two; some said, much older.

29. Wm. C. Bryant, Oct. 11, 1877, interview with chief John S. Johnson, Brant MSS., 15F19.

30. Lieut. Gov. Francis Gore in a letter to Viscount Castlereagh, Mar. 1, 1809, acknowledges Mrs. Brant's "considerable influence with the Five Nations." State Papers, Upper Canada, Q312, pt. 1: 18–19.

31. Consider Brant and Sayengaraghta, Brant and Cornplanter, Brant and Red Jacket, Cornplanter and Red Jacket, and, out in the west, Blue Jacket and Little Turtle, each determined to dominate his rival and to be "the greater man."

CHAPTER 14—REVENGE!

1. Johnson, Indian Records, Series Two, 12: 146.

2. *Ibid.*, pp. 150–51; council, Feb. 12–18, 1780, Haldimand Papers, Add. MSS. 21,779, pt. 2: 73; Schuyler, Jan. 13, 1786, to ———, Single Acquisition, no. 13128, New York State Library.

3. Johnson, Indian Records, Series Two, 12: 180, 183.

4. Freeholders and Inhabitants of Tryon County, Aug. 4, 1779, petition to Clinton, *Public Papers of George Clinton*, 5: 178.

5. Johnson, May 3, 1780, to Haldimand, Haldimand Papers, Add. MSS. 21,767, pt. 2: 61–62.

6. Johnson, Oct. 19, 1779–Mar. 24, 1780, account with Thomas Robison, *ibid.*, B109: 42.

7. Josiah Priest, *The Captivity and Sufferings of Gen. Freegift Patchin of Blenheim, Schoharie County, Among the Indians, under Brant, The Noted Chief, During the Border Warfare in the time of the American Revolution* (Albany, 1833), pp. 13–14.

8. Johnson, July 1, 1780, Return of Indian parties sent on service, Feb. 12–June 1780, Haldimand Papers, B109: 80.

9. This was the usual route, and probably the one that Joseph took. As we shall see, he returned another way.

10. Walter Elliot, April 12, 1780, examination, *Public Papers of George Clinton,* 5: 632–33.

11. Priest, *Captivity and Sufferings of Gen. Freegift Patchin,* pp. 7–9. Unless otherwise noted, this narrative is the source for details of the affair at Harpersfield.

12. Johnson, July 1, 1780, Return, Haldimand Papers, B109: 80.

13. April 10, 1780, to Americans, Brant MSS., 3F88. There are several versions of this letter, all of the same purport.

14. April 8, 1780, *Public Papers of George Clinton,* 5: 579–80.

15. John Dease, n.d. [probably July 1780], to Bolton, Haldimand Papers, Add. MSS. 21,760, pt. 8: 414.

16. Return, July 1, 1780, *ibid.,* B109: 80.

17. Mar. 29, 1780, to Abm. Yates, Jr., *Public Papers of George Clinton,* 5: 572.

18. Johnson, Return of Indian Department, Haldimand Papers, B109: 51.

19. Johnson, Return of Indians gone out to plant, *ibid.,* p. 77.

20. Johnson, General state of Indian Department, *ibid.,* p. 97.

21. Commission, n.d., *ibid.,* B85, pt. 1: 60; Haldimand, Sept. 29, 1780, to Guy Johnson, *ibid.,* Add. MSS. 21,767, pt. 3: 131.

22. Brant, Nov. 1801, to Sir John Johnson, quoted in Stone, *Life of Brant,* 2: 408.

23. Col. Jacob J. Klock, May 23, 1780, to Gen. Ten Broeck, *Public Papers of George Clinton,* 5: 740; Klock, May 23, 1780, to Clinton, *ibid.,* p. 741; Maj. Myndert M. Wemple, May 23, 1780, to Col. Van Schaick, *ibid.,* p. 742; John Tayler, May 23, 1780, to Clinton, *ibid.,* pp. 744–45; etc.

24. Cor's. Van Dyck, July 3, 1780, to Van Schaick, *ibid.,* p. 914; Clinton, July 8, 1780, to Col. Johnson, *ibid.,* p. 950.

25. To Capt. Mathews, Haldimand Papers, Add. MSS. 21,787, pt. 3: 139.

26. Claus, Dec. 9, 1779, to Haldimand, *ibid.,* Add. MSS. 21,774, pt. 2: 86.

27. *A Narrative of the Captivity and Sufferings of Benjamin Gilbert and His Family; Who were Surprised by the Indians, and Taken from Their Farms, on the Frontiers of Pennsylvania. In the Spring, 1780* (Philadelphia and London, 1790), pp. 37–38.

28. Haldimand Papers, Add. MSS. 21,779, pt. 2: 91–94.

29. Council, July 3, 6, 1780, *ibid.,* pt. 3: 96–98.

30. Johnson, July 11, 1780, Return of Indians gone to war under Capt. Joseph Brant, *ibid.,* Add. MSS. 21,760, pt. 7: 333. In a later return Johnson lists an even larger number of warriors.

31. Lieut. Jos. Clement, Aug. 14, 1780, to Guy Johnson, *ibid.,* Add. MSS. 21,767, pt. 3: 109.

32. Johnson, Aug. 11, 1780, to Haldimand, *ibid.,* pt. 2: 104.

33. Jacob Reed, Dec. 6, 1780, statement to Lieut. Col. Weissenfels, *Public Papers of George Clinton,* 6: 482; Haldimand, Oct. 25, 1780, to Germain, Haldimand Papers, B54: 390; Johnson, Aug. 24, 1780, to Haldimand, *ibid.,* Add. MSS. 21,767, pt. 3:119.

34. Jno. Graham, July 27, 1780, to V. Schaick, *Public Papers of George Clinton,* 6: 59.

35. Johnson, Aug. 14, 1780, to Haldimand, Haldimand Papers, Add. MSS. 21,767, pt. 3: 111.

36. Bolton, Aug. 8, 1780, to Haldimand, *ibid.,* Add. MSS. 21,760, pt. 7: 344; Johnson, Aug. 11, 1780, to Haldimand, *ibid.,* Add. MSS. 21,767, pt. 2: 104.

37. Though all the Indians had left Canajoharie, the surrounding district still had a white population.

38. Lieut. Jos. Clement, Aug. 14, 1780, to Johnson, Haldimand Papers, Add. MSS. 21,767, pt. 3: 109; Johnson, Return of prisoners and killed by parties under Captain Brant, in August 1780, *ibid.*, B109: 84; Ab'm. Wemple, Aug. 2, 1780, to Ten Broeck, *Public Papers of George Clinton*, 6: 80–81; Gen. Van Rensselaer, Aug. 6, 1780, to Clinton, *ibid.*, pp. 107–08; Saml. Clyde, Aug. 8, 1780, to Clinton, *ibid.*, pp. 88–89. It is impossible to say with certainty what happened in many of these raids, since British and American military reports seldom agree.

39. Lieut. Jos. Clement, Aug. 14, 1780, to Johnson, Haldimand Papers, Add. MSS. 21,767, pt. 3: 109; Johnson, Aug. 24, 1780, to Haldimand, *ibid.*, p. 119; Johnson, Return of prisoners and killed by parties under Captain Brant, in August, 1780, *ibid.*, B109: 84; Clinton, Aug. 10, 1780, to Cols. Van Bergen and Pawling, *Public Papers of George Clinton*, 6: 93–94; Lieut. Ephraim Vroman, List of persons with Brant on the Delaware, Aug. 11, 1780, and taken on 9th, *ibid.*, p. 136.

40. Aug. 11, 1780, to Col. Peter Vroman, Brant MSS., 10F34. See also Vroman, Aug. 24, 1780, to Clinton, *Public Papers of George Clinton*, 6: 135.

41. Sept. 1, 1780, Haldimand Papers, Add. MSS. 21,767, pt. 3: 125.

42. Sept. 1, 1780, to Bolton, no. 30, *ibid.*, Add. MSS. 21,756, pt. 3.

43. Guy Johnson, Oct. 1, 1780, to Haldimand, *ibid.*, Add. MSS. 21,767, pt. 3: 137; John Dease, Oct. 2, 1780, to Claus, Claus Papers, 2: 255–56; John Johnson, Oct. 1, 1780, to Haldimand, Haldimand Papers, Add. MSS. 21,818, pt. 4: 195.

44. Dease, Oct. 2, 1780, to Claus, Claus Papers, 2: 255–56.

45. Oct. 31, 1780, to Haldimand, Haldimand Papers, Add. MSS. 21,818, pt. 5: 205–07. Unless otherwise noted, the details of the raid are derived from this source.

46. The Noses are hills or outcroppings of high rocks which narrow the Mohawk east of old Canajoharie.

47. Gen. Van Rensselaer had about nine hundred men. Letter, Oct. 19, 1780, to Clinton, *Public Papers of George Clinton*, 6: 320.

48. George Clinton, Oct. 30, 1780, to Washington, *ibid.*, 6: 352.

49. Evidence at Court of Enquiry on conduct of Brig. Gen. Robert Van Rensselaer, Mar. 14, 1781, *ibid.*, p. 699.

50. American sources are numerous and do not disagree very much with the general account of his march as related by Sir John. Many of these sources, which add much detail, are to be found in the *Public Papers of George Clinton*, vol. 6.

51. To Haldimand, Haldimand Papers, Add. MSS. 21,818, pt. 5: 209.

52. Oct. 20, 1780, to Henry Glen, "The Glen Letters," ed. by Throop Wilder, *New York History* 26 (1945): 331.

53. Haldimand Papers, Add. MSS. 21,767, pt. 4: 165.

54. Matilda Schieffelin, Dec. 4, 1780, to father, *The New York Genealogical and Biographical Record* 72, no. 2 (April 1941): 122. In 1794 Mrs. Simcoe records Molly as speaking English "well."

55. Oct. 22, 1781, no. 97, Haldimand Papers, Add. MSS. 21,715, Selections.

56. Memorial, Dec. 20, 1780, quoted in Franklin B. Hough, *The Northern Invasion of October 1780* (New York, 1866), p. 212.

57. Council, July 1, 1778, "Haldimand Papers," *Michigan Historical Collections*, 9: 456.

58. Council, April 12, 1781, in J. Watts de Peyster, *Appendix, Explanatory Notes, &c., &c., &c., to "Miscellanies by an Officer"* (New York, 1888), p. ix.

59. Jan. 21, 1779, to Maj. Carleton, Haldimand Papers, B66: 98.

60. "Life of governor Blacksnake," Brant MSS., 16F125.

61. Seaver, *Life of Mary Jemison*, p. 114.

62. Priest, *Captivity and Sufferings of Gen. Freegift Patchin*, p. 9.

63. Campbell, *Travels in America in 1791–92*, p. 274.

CHAPTER 15—ON THE OHIO

1. Claus, Feb. 26, 1781, to Capt. Mathews, Haldimand Papers, Add. MSS. 21,774, pt. 4: 170–71; Mathews, Mar. 1, 1781, to Claus, Claus Papers, 3: 5–7; Haldimand, Mar. 1, 1781, to Capt. Robertson, Haldimand Papers, Add. MSS. 21,780, pt. 3: 118; Haldimand, Mar. 1, 1781, to Maj. Ross, *ibid.*, Add. MSS. 21,788, pt. 2: 120; Claus, Mar. 3, 1781, to Thayendanegea, extract in *Orderly Book of Sir John Johnson during the Oriskany Campaign, 1776–1777*, ed. by William L. Stone (Albany, 1882), note 1, pp. 68–69; Claus, Mar. 19, 1781, to Mathews, Haldimand Papers, Add. MSS. 21,774, pt. 4: 174.

2. Guy Johnson, Feb. 19, 1781, Return of Indian War Parties on service, Haldimand Papers, Add. MSS. 21,767, pt. 4: 163; H. Watson Powell, Feb. 19, 1781, to Haldimand, *ibid.*, Add. MSS. 21,761, pt. 1: 9; Lieut. Andw. Bradt, Mar. 8, 1781, Account . . . for provisions for . . . party to Fort Stanwix, *ibid.*, p. 17; Johnson, April 8, 1781, to Haldimand, *ibid.*, Add. MSS. 21,767, pt. 4: 169.

3. Haldimand, April 12, 1781, to Sir John Johnson, private, *ibid.*, Add. MSS. 21,819, pt. 3: 184.

4. Extract, "Haldimand Papers," *Michigan Historical Collections*, 19: 617–18.

5. Powell, May 15, 1781, to Haldimand, Haldimand Papers, Add. MSS. 21,761, pt. 2: 72.

6. April 19, 1781, to Haldimand, Claus Papers, 3: 15.

7. April 12, 1781, Haldimand Papers, Add. MSS. 21,774, pt. 4: 180.

8. April 23, 1781, "Haldimand Papers," *Michigan Historical Collections*, 19: 627.

9. May 15, 1781, Haldimand Papers, Add. MSS. 21,761, pt. 2: 72.

10. July 3, 1781, Claus Papers, 26: 257–58.

11. Johnson, April 20, 1781, Return of Indian war parties, Haldimand Papers, B109: 146.

12. April 8, 1781, *ibid.*, Add. MSS. 21,767, pt. 4: 169.

13. Powell, Aug. 16, 1781, to Haldimand, *ibid.*, Add. MSS. 21,761, pt. 3: 144.

14. Council, April 26, 1781, "Haldimand Papers," *Michigan Historical Collections*, 10: 473.

15. Claus Papers, 3: 13–14; English translation, *ibid.*, vol. 24.

16. Council, April 26, 1781, "Haldimand Papers," *Michigan Historical Collections*, 10: 472–76.

17. De Peyster, April 25–27, 1781, to Powell, *ibid.*, 19: 630.

18. May 19, 1781, *ibid.*, pp. 634–35.

19. Aug. 21, 1781, to McKee or Thompson, *ibid.*, pp. 655–56.

20. Thompson and McKee, Aug. 29, 1781, to De Peyster, British Headquarters Papers, 30, no. 3531: 75; John Macomb, Sept. 14, 1781, to Claus, "Haldimand Papers," *Michigan Historical Collections*, 10: 512–13; McKee, Sept. 26, 1781, to De Peyster, *ibid.*, p. 516.

21. G. Johnson, Sept. 18, 1781, to Haldimand, Haldimand Papers, Add. MSS. 21,767, pt. 5: 226; Thompson, Sept. 26, 1781, to De Peyster, "Haldimand Papers,"

Michigan Historical Collections, 10: 515–16; McKee, Sept. 26, 1781, to De Peyster, *ibid.,* pp. 516–17.

22. Macomb, Sept. 14, 1781, to Claus, "Haldimand Papers," *Michigan Historical Collections,* 10: 512.

23. Consul Willshire Butterfield, *History of the Girtys* (Cincinnati, 1890), pp. 130–31. Since Girty was able to interpret at an Indian council in Detroit on Oct. 21, part of this story was obviously exaggerated by the gossips.

24. Johnson, Sept. 18, 1781, to Haldimand, Haldimand Papers, Add. MSS. 21,767, pt. 5: 226; Haldimand, Oct. 23, 1781, to Germain, "Haldimand Papers," *Michigan Historical Collections,* 10: 530.

25. Macomb, Sept. 14, 1781, "Haldimand Papers," *Michigan Historical Collections,* 10: 512–13.

26. Oct. 6, 1781, to De Peyster, *ibid.,* p. 524.

27. Wm. Irvine to President of Pennsylvania Council, *Pennsylvania Archives,* First Series, 9: 458.

28. Butterfield, *History of the Girtys,* p. 135.

29. Powell, Oct. 20, 1781, to Haldimand, "Haldimand Papers," *Michigan Historical Collections,* 19: 667.

30. *Ibid.*

31. De Peyster, Nov. 11, 1781, to McKee, in J. Watts de Peyster, *Appendix, Explanatory Notes, &c.,* p. xxx.

32. William Sommer, affidavit, July 15, 1781, *Public Papers of George Clinton,* 7: 81.

33. Lieut. Jones, information, Aug. 14, 1781, Haldimand Papers, B176: 216.

34. Haldimand, Sept. 5, 1781, to Powell, *ibid.,* Add. MSS. 21,764, pt. 4: 214.

35. Oct. 3, 1781, British Headquarters Papers, 30, no. 3531: 90.

36. R. Mathews, July 30, 1781, to Claus, Haldimand Papers, Add. MSS. 21,774, pt. 4: 210.

37. Letter (secret), July 23, 1781, *ibid.,* Add. MSS. 21,764, pt. 4: 208–09.

38. Powell, Aug. 16, 1781, to Haldimand, *ibid.,* Add. MSS. 21,761, pt. 3:144.

39. Powell, Dec 6, 1781, to Haldimand, *ibid.,* pt. 5: 216.

40. Mathews, Aug. 18, 1782, to Guy Johnson, *ibid.,* B108: 66.

41. Johnson, Aug. 18, 1782, to Mathews, *ibid.,* pp. 62–63.

42. Council, Nov. 9, 1781, "Haldimand Papers," *Michigan Historical Collections,* 10: 538.

43. Council, Nov. 16, 1781, Haldimand Papers, Add. MSS. 21,779, pt. 3: 105.

44. Council, Feb. 25, 1781, "Haldimand Papers," *Michigan Historical Collections,* 19: 595.

CHAPTER 16—THE GREAT BETRAYAL

1. De Peyster, Feb. 6, 1782, to [McKee?], in De Peyster, *Appendix, Explanatory Notes, &c.,* p. xxxi.

2. "Haldimand Papers," *Michigan Historical Collections,* 10: 552.

3. Guy Johnson, Dec. 2, 1781, to Haldimand, Haldimand Papers, Add. MSS. 21,767, pt. 5: 264.

4. Feb. 18, 1782, no. 13, *ibid.,* Add. MSS. 21,756, pt. 3.

5. No. 5, *ibid.,* pt. 2.

6. Extract, "Haldimand Papers," *Michigan Historical Collections,* 20: 7.

7. Thomas Smith, Ledger, 1779–1800, p. 272, Thomas Smith Papers, Burton Historical Collection, Detroit Public Library.

8. April 3, 1782, to McKee, in De Peyster, *Appendix, Explanatory Notes, &c.*, pp. xxxi–xxxii.

9. Powell to Haldimand, Haldimand Papers, Add. MSS. 21,762, pt. 1: 29.

10. Ross to Haldimand, *ibid.*, Add. MSS. 21,785, pt. 1: 18.

11. Ross, May 14, 1782, to Haldimand, *ibid.*

12. Brant, May 19, 1782, to De Peyster, in De Peyster, *Appendix, Explanatory Notes, &c.*, p. x.

13. Powell, June 27, 1782, to Haldimand, Haldimand Papers, Add. MSS. 21,762, pt. 2: 94.

14. Dec. 1781, to Guy Johnson, extract, *ibid.*, Add. MSS. 21,767, pt. 5:273.

15. June 27, 1782, to Haldimand, *ibid.*, Add. MSS. 21,762, pt. 2: 95.

16. Butler, June 12, 1782, to Mathews, *ibid.*, Add. MSS. 21,765, pt. 6: 280; Butler, June 14, 1782, Return of Indian presents . . . to Capt. Brant's party, *ibid.*, p. 282; Lieut. John Young, June 21, 1782, Return . . . at Oswego, *ibid.*, p. 283.

17. De Peyster, *Appendix, Explanatory Notes, &c.*, p. x.

18. Ross, June 27, 1782, to Haldimand, Haldimand Papers, B124: 7.

19. May 31, 1782, *ibid.*, Add. MSS. 21,785, pt. 1: 23.

20. June 18, 1782, to Ross, *ibid.*, p. 32.

21. Haldimand, July 1, 1782, to Powell, *ibid.*, Add. MSS. 21,764, pt. 6: 301; Powell, June 27, 1782, to Haldimand, *ibid.*, Add. MSS. 21,762, pt. 2: 94.

22. Butler, June 14, 1782, Return of Indian presents . . . to Capt. Brant's party, *ibid.*, Add. MSS. 21,765, pt. 6: 282; Butler, June 29, 1782, to Mathews, *ibid.*, p. 286.

23. Powell, June 29, 1782, to Haldimand, *ibid.*, Add. MSS. 21,762, pt. 2: 98.

24. July 1, 1782, to Powell, *ibid.*, Add. MSS. 21,764, pt. 6: 301; July 11, 1782, to Powell, *ibid.*, pp. 312–13.

25. July 1, 1782, *ibid.*, Add. MSS. 21,785, pt. 1: 40.

26. To Mathews, *ibid.*, B124: 8.

27. June 27, 1782, *ibid.*, pp. 6–7.

28. Ross, June 26, 1782, to Mathews, *ibid.*, p. 9.

29. *Ibid.*, pp. 8–9.

30. Ross, July 7, 1782, to Mathews, *ibid.*, p. 10.

31. *Ibid.*

32. Capt. George Singleton, journal, July 5–15, 1782, *ibid.*, Add. MSS. 21,785, pt. 3: 148.

33. Ross, Aug. 3, 1782, to Haldimand, *ibid.*, B124: 13.

34. Ross, Aug. 3, 1782, to Mathews, *ibid.*, Add. MSS. 21,785, pt. 2: 54–55.

35. Though there is no evidence of the warriors' holding such a council, Joseph and the two chiefs would not have gone without authority.

36. Aug. 3, 1782, Haldimand Papers, Add. MSS. 21,785, pt. 2: 55.

37. Claus, Aug. 12, 1782, to Mathews, *ibid.*, B114: 259.

38. Mathews, Aug. 15, 1782, to Claus, Claus Papers, 3:151–52.

39. Mathews, Sept. 9, 1782, to Ross, Haldimand Papers, B124: 78.

40. Oct. 19, 1782, "Haldimand Papers," *Michigan Historical Collections*, 10: 656–59.

41. Brant, Dec. 25, 1782, to Sir John Johnson, Haldimand Papers, B115: 47.

42. De Peyster, Sept. 27, 1782, to McKee, "Haldimand Papers," *Michigan Historical Collections*, 10: 648–49.

43. Wm. Potts, Oct. 8, 1782, to McKee, Claus Papers, 3: 175; De Peyster, Sept. 27, 1782, to McKee, in De Peyster, *Appendix, Explanatory Notes, &c.*, p. xxxvi.

44. Sept. 29, 1782, in De Peyster, *Appendix, Explanatory Notes, &c.*, p. xi.

45. By Nov. 20 Sir John, then at Montreal, knew Joseph had returned. Letter to Haldimand, Haldimand Papers, B115: 26.

46. Sept. 18, 1782, "Haldimand Papers and Indian Affairs," *Michigan Historical Collections*, 20: 57–58.

47. Oct. 23, 1782, to Hon. Thomas Townshend, *ibid.*, 10: 663.

48. Letter, private, *ibid.*, pp. 668–69.

49. Sir John Johnson, Nov. 20, 1782, to Haldimand, Haldimand Papers, B115: 26.

50. *Ibid.*; Johnson, Nov. 28, 1782, to Haldimand, *ibid.*, p. 37.

51. Dec. 5, 1782, to Johnson, *ibid.*, p. 39.

52. Council, Dec. 11, 1782, extract, British Headquarters Papers, 56, no. 6385: 1.

53. Maclean, Dec. 16, 1782, to Haldimand, Haldimand Papers, Add. MSS. 21,756, pt. 3.

54. Dec. 25, 1782, to Sir John Johnson, extract, *ibid.*, B115: 47.

55. *Ibid.*, pp. 47–48.

56. Nov. 13, 1782, to Maclean, extract, *ibid.*, Add. MSS. 21,762, pt. 5: 212.

57. Feb. 6, 1783, to Johnson, *ibid.*, B115: 72–73.

58. Feb. 7, 1783, to Maclean, *ibid.*, Add. MSS. 21,756, pt. 4.

59. Feb. 14, 1783, to Thomas Townshend, no. 27, *ibid.*, B56: 51.

60. *Ibid.*, Add. MSS. 21,779, pt. 3: 111–12.

61. April 20, 1783, to Haldimand, *ibid.*, Add. MSS. 21,763, pt. 1: 48–49.

62. Capts. Powell and Brant, April 23, 1783, journal, *ibid.*, pt. 2: 60.

63. April 26, 1783, in *Memoirs, and Letters and Journals, of Major General Riedesel, During His Residence in America*, tr. and ed. by William L. Stone, 2 vols. (Albany, 1868), 2: 168–69.

64. Maclean, May 13, 1783, to Mathews, Haldimand Papers, Add. MSS. 21,763, pt. 2: 108.

65. *Ibid.*; and of same date, to Haldimand, *ibid.*, pt. 3: 110–11.

66. May 18, 1783, "Haldimand Papers and Indian Affairs," *Michigan Historical Collections*, 20: 117–21.

67. Johnson, May 19, 1783, to Haldimand, Haldimand Papers, B115: 105.

68. State Papers, Canada, Q21: 236–42.

69. June 2, 1783, to Lord North, Haldimand Papers, B56: 66–67; answer to a speech by Captain Brant for the 6 Nations, May 27, 1783, Claus Papers, 3: 243–44.

70. Mathews, May 29, 1783, to Johnson, Haldimand Papers, B115: 118.

71. Testimonial, May 23, 1783, C.O. 42, 18: 7.

72. May 27, 1783, to Brant, Haldimand Papers, Add. MSS. 21,765, pt. 7: 330.

73. Baroness Riedesel, *Letters and Journals*, ed. by Stone, pp. 200–01.

74. Haldimand, May 23, 1783, to Maclean, Haldimand Papers, Add. MSS. 21,756, pt. 4; Haldimand, May 26, 1783, to Johnson, "Haldimand Papers and Indian Affairs," *Michigan Historical Collections*, 20: 123–24.

75. Norton, Journal, etc., 1: 256, 269.

76. Maj. Samuel Holland, June 26, 1783, to Haldimand, Haldimand Papers, B124: 34, 36.

77. Maclean, July 10, 1783, to Haldimand, *ibid.*, Add. MSS. 21,763, pt. 4: 184.

78. Council, July 31, 1783, State Papers, Canada, Q21: 451.

79. Council, July 24, 1783, *ibid.*, p. 442.

80. Johnson, Aug. 11, 1783, to Haldimand, "Haldimand Papers and Indian Affairs," *Michigan Historical Collections*, 20: 164.

81. Council, Aug. 26–Sept. 8, 1783, *ibid.*, pp. 174–83.

82. C.O. 42, 15: 53–55.

83. Maclean, July 17, 1783, to Haldimand, "Haldimand Papers and Indian Affairs," *Michigan Historical Collections*, 20: 147; Ephraim Douglass, Aug. 18, 1783, to Maj. Gen. Benjamin Lincoln, Secretary at War, *Pennsylvania Archives*, First Series, 10: 88–90.

84. Council, Oct. 22, 1783, Haldimand Papers, Add. MSS. 21,779, pt. 4: 147–48. This is the official translation of the speech which was probably made by John Butler. Two other translations are extant, one made by the Rev. I. Bearfoot for Draper (Brant MSS., 10F182), and the other probably made by Samuel Kirkland for Schuyler (quoted in "Joseph Brant or Thayeadanegea," *The American Historical Record* 2, no. 20 (Aug. 1873): 355–56. These translations vary in details and even in dates, but mean substantially the same.

85. Council, Sept. 7, 1783, "Haldimand Papers and Indian Affairs," *Michigan Historical Collections*, 20: 179.

CHAPTER 17—OUTRAGEOUS FORTUNE

1. Aug. 8, 1783, Haldimand Papers, Add. MSS. 21,705, pt. 4: 154–55.

2. Claus, July 17, 1783, to Mathews, Claus Papers, 3: 237.

3. Mathews, Sept. 10, 1783, to Ross, Haldimand Papers, Add. MSS. 21,786, pt. 1: 32; Haldimand, Sept. 11, 1783, to John Collins, *ibid.*, p. 34; Haldimand, Nov. 13, 1783, to Ross, *ibid.*, pt. 2: 77.

4. Ross, Feb. 17, 1784, to Mathews, *ibid.*, pt. 2: 91; Mathews, Mar. 4, 1784, *ibid.*, B63: 113.

5. Brant, Nov. 1801, to Sir John Johnson, quoted in Stone, *Life of Brant*, 2: 408.

6. G. Johnson, May 31, 1783, to Sir John Johnson, Haldimand Papers, B115: 120; John Johnson, June 2, 1783, to Haldimand, *ibid.*, p. 122.

7. John Johnson, Mar. 11, 1784, to Haldimand, *ibid.*, p. 234.

8. De Peyster, June 28, 1784, to Haldimand, *ibid.*, Add. MSS. 21,763, pt. 6: 327; Brant, 1795, speech to Gov. Simcoe, Brant MSS., 21F66; Stone, *Life of Brant*, 2: 238.

9. Haldimand, Mar. 15, 1784, to Sir John Johnson, Haldimand Papers, B63: 129; Haldimand, memorandum, [about Mar. 23, 1784], *ibid.*, B169: 131–34; Haldimand, April 12, 1784, to Sir John Johnson, *ibid.*, B63: 206; Mathews, Nov. 8, 1784, to the Rev. John Stuart, *ibid.*, B61: 172.

10. Haldimand, Mar. 24, 1784, to Six Nations, *ibid.*, Add. MSS. 21,779, pt. 4: 158; April 12, 1784, to Sir John Johnson, *ibid.*, B63: 204–05.

11. April 12, 1784, *ibid.*, B65: 9–12.

12. Council, Mar. 7, 1784, *ibid.*, Add. MSS. 21,779, pt. 4: 154; Mathews, April 12, 1784, to Lieut. Col. Robert Hoyes, *ibid.*, B63: 202.

13. Speech, Jan. 1784, *ibid.*, Add. MSS. 21,779, pt. 4: 149–52.

14. Brant, June 5, 1784, to Mathews, *ibid.*, Add. MSS. 21,765, pt. 8: 395.

15. May 4, 1784, *ibid.*, B115: 254–55.

16. Strachan, "Life of Capt. Brant," *Christian Recorder*, June 1819.

17. Brant, June 5, 1784, to Mathews, Haldimand Papers, Add. MSS. 21,765, pt. 8: 395–96.

18. Haldimand, April 1, 1784, to Sir John Johnson, *ibid.*, B65: 6–8; Haldimand,

April 12, 1784, to Johnson, *ibid.*, B63: 204–06; Haldimand, memorandum, summer 1784, *ibid.*, B208: 24.

19. Instructions, April 12, 1784, *Proceedings of the Commissioners of Indian Affairs, Appointed . . . for the Extinguishment of Indian Titles in . . . New York,* ed. by Hough, 1: 12.

20. *Public Papers of George Clinton,* 8: 323–25.

21. Abraham Cuyler and Henry Glen, June 28, 1784, to Clinton, *Proceedings of* [N.Y.] *Commissioners of Indian Affairs,* 1: 17.

22. July 15, 1784, to Johnson, Haldimand Papers, B64: 53–54.

23. Brant MSS., 11F7.

24. *Proceedings of* [N.Y.] *Commissioners of Indian Affairs,* 1: 26–27.

25. Clinton, Aug. 14, 1784, to Brant, *Public Papers of George Clinton,* 8: 334–35.

26. Instructions, Aug. 14, 1784, *ibid.,* p. 335.

27. Aug. 23, 1784, to Glen, *ibid.,* pp. 341–42.

28. *Ibid.,* p. 342; Jelles Fonda, Aug. 31, 1784, to Clinton, *ibid.,* p. 348.

29. Ryckman, Aug. 23, 1784, to Glen, *ibid.,* p. 341.

30. Views on Indian question, 1784, *ibid.,* p. 332.

31. *Ibid.,* pp. 365–69.

32. *Ibid.,* pp. 375–77.

33. Haldimand Papers, Add. MSS. 21,763, pt. 7: 346.

34. Brant, June 18, 1789, to Clinton, quoted in William Ketchum, *An Authentic and Comprehensive History of Buffalo,* 2 vols. (Buffalo, 1864–65), 1: 386; also Brant, Sept. 28, 1784, to Clinton, Brant MSS., 11F15.

35. Brant, Jan. 13, 1785, to Mathew Visscher, quoted in Wm. C. Bryant, "Joseph Brant, Thayendanegea, and His Posterity," *American Historical Record,* 2: 291; Brant, Mar. 23, 1785, to Maj. Peter Schuyler, Brant MSS., 15F199.

36. May 27, 1785, *Proceedings of* [N.Y.] *Commissioners of Indian Affairs,* 1: 76.

37. May 28, 1785, to Peter Schuyler, *ibid.,* pp. 81–82.

38. Jelles Fonda, June 16, 1790, to Brant, Miscellaneous MSS., New-York Historical Society.

39. *The Autobiography of James Monroe,* ed. by Stuart Gerry Brown with the assistance of Donald G. Baker (Syracuse, 1959), pp. 38–39.

40. Brant, Sept. 28, 1784, to Commissioners of United States for Indn. Affairs, Haldimand Papers, Add. MSS. 21,779, pt. 4: 183; James Monroe, Feb. 5, 1785, to Brant, State Papers, Canada, Q24, pt. 1: 229.

41. Brant, Sept. 28, 1784, to Commissioners of U.S., Haldimand Papers, Add. MSS. 21,779, pt. 4: 183.

42. Council, Oct. 12, 1784, *The Olden Time; A Monthly Publication, Devoted to the Preservation of Documents and Other Authentic Information in Relation to the Early Explorations, and the Settlement and Improvement of the Country around the Head of the Ohio,* ed. by Neville B. Craig, 2 vols. (Pittsburgh, 1846–47), 2: 416.

43. John Dease, Sept. 18, 1784, to Sir John Johnson, Haldimand Papers, Add. MSS. 21,763, pt. 7: 348.

44. Sept. 28, 1784, to Commissioners of U.S., *ibid.,* Add. MSS. 21,779, pt. 4: 183.

45. *Ibid.*

46. Council, Oct. 14, 1784, *Olden Time,* 2: 417; Isaac Arnold, declaration, Oct. 18, 1784, copy from *South Carolina Gazette,* Nov. 13, 1784, Brant MSS., 10F54–55.

47. *Autobiography of James Monroe,* ed. by Brown and Baker, p. 40.

48. Brant, Nov. 29, 1784, to Monroe, quoted in Stone, *Life of Brant*, 2: 247.

49. Haldimand, Oct. 24, 1784, to Lord Sydney, Haldimand Papers, B58: 15.

50. State Papers, Upper Canada, Q283: 33–34.

51. April 12, 1784, to Sir John Johnson, Haldimand Papers, B63: 205.

52. Haldimand, June 21, 1785, to Lord Sydney, State Papers, Canada, Q24, pt. 2: 297.

53. Brant, Jan. 13, 1785, to Mathew Visscher, quoted in Wm. C. Bryant, "Joseph Brant, Thayendanegea, and His Posterity," *American Historical Record*, 2: 291.

54. Haldimand, June 21, 1785, to Sydney, State Papers, Canada, Q24, pt. 2: 297; Brant, Nov. 6, 1784, memorandum for Sir John Johnson, Edward E. Ayer Collection, Newberry Library, Chicago.

55. Nov. 29, 1784, quoted in Stone, *Life of Brant*, 2: 245–47.

56. Feb. 5, 1785, State Papers, Canada, Q24, pt. 1: 227–29.

57. Brant, Jan. 13, 1785, to Visscher, quoted in Bryant, "Joseph Brant, Thayendanegea, and His Posterity," *American Historical Record*, 2: 291; Brant, Mar. 23, 1785, to Maj. Peter Schuyler, Brant MSS., 15F199.

58. Nov. 21, 1784, to P. Langan, C.O. 42, 16: 106.

59. Brant, Mar. 22, 1785, to Lieut. Gov. Hamilton, British Transcripts, Library of Congress.

60. *Ibid.*

61. Brant, Mar. 23, 1785, to Maj. Peter Schuyler, Brant MSS., 15F199.

62. Ross, June 14, 1784, report, Haldimand Papers, Add. MSS. 21,786, pt. 2: 101. The house has long since been torn down.

63. Brant, Mar. 22, 1785, to Hamilton, British Transcripts, Library of Congress.

64. Council, May 22, 1784, State Papers, Canada, Q23: 351.

65. Letter, in De Peyster, *Appendix, Explanatory Notes, &c.*, p. xv.

66. Note, [about Jan. 30, 1797], on speech to William Claus, State Papers, Upper Canada, Q283: 83. Joseph gives no reason for the offer; but, since he says it was made in 1785, the implication is that it was tendered to get him to stay.

67. *The Valley of the Six Nations: A Collection of Documents on the Indian Lands of the Grand River*, ed. by Charles M. Johnston (Toronto, 1964), p. 52.

68. *Ibid.*, Introduction, note 15, p. xli.

69. Augusta I. Grant Gilkison, "Reminiscences of Earlier Years in Brant," *Ontario Historical Society Papers and Records* 12 (1914): 81, 84.

70. Priest, *Captivity and Sufferings of Gen. Freegift Patchin*, pp. 27–30.

71. Maclean, May 3, 1783, to Haldimand, Haldimand Papers, Add. MSS. 21,763, pt. 2: 77.

72. Brant, June 9, 1802, declaration, D. W. Smith Collection, B7: 313, Metropolitan Toronto Library; Five Nations, Sept. 3, 1806, speech to William Claus, Ayer Collection, Newberry Library; Map of Grand River Indian lands, 1821, *Valley of Six Nations*, facing p. 128; the Rev. Robert Lugger, Plan of Grand River, 1828, *ibid.*, Introduction, facing p. lxxxvi.

73. De Peyster, *Appendix, Explanatory Notes, &c.*, pp. xv–xvi.

74. *Ibid.*, p. xvi.

75. Tryon, Oct. 22, 1785, to Sydney, C.O. 42, 16: 272.

76. Council, Aug. 2–3, 1785, State Papers, Canada, Q25: 136–44; Maj. A. Campbell, Aug. 6, 1785, to St. Leger, *ibid.*, p. 147; John Dease, Sept. 16, 1785, to Lieut. Gov. Hamilton, *ibid.*, p. 183; Brant, Aug. 1785, to Congress, Kirkland MSS., Hamilton College.

77. Aug. 26, 1785, Kirkland MSS.

78. Aug. 22, 1785, C.O. 42, 17: 110.

79. Aug. 15, 1785, to Hamilton, State Papers, Canada, Q25: 134–35.

80. Sept. 29, 1785, to Hamilton, British Transcripts, Library of Congress.

81. Lieut. Gov. Henry Hope, Oct. 30, 1785, to Johnson, C.O. 42, 17: 153; Johnson, Nov. 7, 1785, to Evan Nepean, *ibid.*, p. 141; Brant, Jan. 4, 1786, speech to Sydney, State Papers, Canada, Q26, pt. 1: 2–3; P. Langan, June 29, 1786, to Claus, Claus Papers, 4: 108.

CHAPTER 18—THE EMANCIPATION OF JOSEPH BRANT

1. Johnson, Nov. 6, 1785, to Lieut. Gov. Henry Hope, C.O. 42, 17: 150–51; Johnson, Nov. 7, 1785, to Nepean, *ibid.*, pp. 141–42.

2. Oct. 30, 1785, to Johnson, *ibid.*, pp. 153–54; also Nov. 9, 1785, to Johnson, quoted in Theodorus Bailey Myers, "Some Tracings from the Footprints of the Tories or Loyalists in America," *Orderly Book of Sir John Johnson*, ed. by Stone, pp. 195–96.

3. Hope, Nov. 9, 1785, to Johnson, quoted in Myers, "Some Tracings . . . of the Tories . . . in America," *Orderly Book of Sir John Johnson*, p. 195.

4. Hope, Nov. 5, 1785, to Nepean, private, C.O. 42, 17: 136.

5. Hope, Nov. 9, 1785, to Nepean, private, *ibid.*, p. 148.

6. See preceding notes. An excerpt of Sir John's letter to Joseph, Nov. 6, 1785, is quoted in Stone, *Life of Brant*, 2: 248–49.

7. Letter from Salisbury, Dec. 12, 1785, published in London, quoted *ibid.*, p. 249.

8. Claus Papers, 21, pt. 2, diary 10.

9. *Ibid.*

10. P. Langan, June 29, 1786, to Claus, *ibid.*, 4: 109.

11. State Papers, Canada, Q26, pt. 1: 11–12; also Sydney, April 6, 1786, to Hope, *ibid.*, p. 73.

12. *Ibid.*, p. 73.

13. *Ibid.*, pp. 1–3.

14. Capt. Richd. Houghton, Jan. 23, 1786, to Nepean, C.O. 42, 18: 6.

15. John Johnson, [about 1785], Return, Haldimand Papers, B167, pt. 2: 406.

16. Langan, Dec. 15, 1785, to Claus, State Papers, Canada, Q26, pt. 1: 31–32; Claus, Feb. 4, 1786, to Nepean, *ibid.*, p. 30.

17. Claus Papers, 21, pt. 2, diary 10, Mar. 1786.

18. Jan. 23, 1786, C.O. 42, 18: 5–6. Joseph got fifteen shillings a day; Houghton, only ten.

19. Claus Papers, 21, pt. 2, diary 10.

20. *The* (London) *Gazetteer and New Daily Advertiser*, Mar. 1, 1786, describes this affair in great detail.

21. Stone, *Life of Brant*, 2: 259–60.

22. *Ibid.*, pp. 258–59.

23. John Blackburn, Mar. 27, 1779, to Claus, Claus Papers, 2: 83. See also Germain, July 8, 1779, to Haldimand, Haldimand Papers, B43: 155–56.

24. These friendships are attested by Joseph's early biographer, Stone, who got his information from Brant's family and American friends, and by the Scotch poet, Thomas Campbell, who got his information from John Brant, Joseph's son. Stone, *Life of Brant*, 2: 250–51, 258; and "Letter to the Mohawk Chief Ahyonwaeghs," *The* (London) *New Monthly Magazine and Literary Journal* 4 (1822): 98.

25. Stone, *Life of Brant*, 2: 251. The refusal to kiss the king's hand is said to have taken place when Joseph was presented at court—that is, in 1776. However, Joseph certainly had a greater sense of his own importance ten years later than he had had in 1776, and the episode may have happened on this second visit to London. It was much talked about in Joseph's lifetime.

26. Stone, *Life of Brant*, 2: 250.

27. *Ibid.*, p. 251.

28. Brant, Aug. 14, 1789, to Haldimand, Haldimand Papers, B77: 230.

29. "Private Diary of Gen. Haldimand," in Douglas Brymner, *Report on Canadian Archives, 1889* (Ottawa, 1890), pp. 127, 129, 131, 135, 139, 145, 151.

30. *Ibid.*, p. 273. The date of this entry is uncertain, but it could be Mar. 23, 1790. If so, Joseph had to wait a long time to get his picture.

31. Milton W. Hamilton has researched the matter of this portrait exhaustively. See his "Joseph Brant Painted by Rigaud," *New York History* 40, no. 3 (July 1959): 247–54. The original portrait was probably destroyed by fire. The New York State Education Department owns what is very likely a 19th century copy. The Hamilton article is illustrated by a black and white photograph of this copy.

32. Stone, *Life of Brant*, 2: 260. This was the fourth edition of the Mohawk Prayer Book, and the first in both languages.

33. Campbell, "Letter to the Mohawk Chief Ahyonwaeghs," *The* (London) *New Monthly Magazine and Literary Journal* 4 (1822): 98; Stone, *Life of Brant*, 2: 433; Brant, May 8, 1798, to Peter Russell, extract, State Papers, Upper Canada, Q284: 187.

34. Brant, Mar. 8, 1791, to Kirkland, Pickering Papers, 61: 207–08, Massachusetts Historical Society; Brant, Feb. 9, 1801, to the Rev. Samuel Miller, quoted in Stone, *Life of Brant*, 2: 440; Campbell, "Letter to . . . Ahyonwaeghs," *New Monthly Magazine*, 4: 98; Stone, *Life of Brant*, 2: 484–86.

35. "Private Diary of Gen. Haldimand," Jan. 20, 1786, in Brymner, *Report on Canadian Archives, 1889*, p. 131.

36. Stone, *Life of Brant*, 2: 486.

37. Charles Merrill Mount, *Gilbert Stuart* (New York, 1964), p. 116.

38. The original painting made for Lord Rawdon is now in possession of the New York State Historical Association, Cooperstown, N.Y. See frontispiece.

39. Stone, *Life of Brant*, 2: 464. Some say the miniature was made for Catharine.

40. Wm. C. Bryant, Sept. 17, 1877, to Draper, Brant MSS., 15F16.

41. This painting is owned by the present Duke of Northumberland. A photograph in black and white may be seen in *Gilbert Stuart: An Illustrated Descriptive List of His Works Compiled by Lawrence Park with an Account of His Life by John Hill Morgan and an Appreciation by Royal Cortissoz*, 4 vols. (New York, 1926), 4: 516.

42. "Private Diary of Gen. Haldimand," p. 157.

43. *Ibid.*, p. 159.

44. *Ibid.*

45. State Papers, Canada, Q26, pt. 1: 71–72.

46. Lieut. Gov. Francis Gore, April 23, 1807, List of Half Pay Officers . . . in . . . Upper Canada, State Papers, Upper Canada, Q306: 157; John Johnson, Return of persons holding . . . pensions in Indian Department in Upper and Lower Canada, Military Papers "Indian," C253: 39, Public Archives of Canada. See also Brant MSS., 21F19.

47. Estimate of Losses sustained by the Mohawk Indians, State Papers, Canada, Q24, pt. 2: 318.

48. Brant, n.d., to Sir John Johnson, Brant MSS., 12F60.

49. *Ibid.*; also Brant, Nov. 15, 1803, to Gov. Geo. Clinton, *ibid.*, 15F224; and Stone, *Life of Brant*, 2: 403.

50. "Private Diary of Gen. Haldimand," April 10, 1786, p. 167. Haldimand's words are subject to more than one interpretation, but he also says "every thing" was granted to Joseph. See also Sydney, April 6, 1786, to Hope, State Papers, Canada, Q26, pt. 1: 74. The Nepean Papers, Secret Service Payments, 1782–1791, under date Mar. 31, 1786, list only the cash, Sydney Papers, William L. Clements Library.

51. "Private Diary of Gen. Haldimand," Mar. 25, 1786, p. 161.

52. Claus, April 24, 1787, to Nepean, Claus Papers, 4: 161–62. Joseph's church did not get a new communion service, but divided the old one with the Bay of Quinte Mohawks.

53. Draper, note, Brant MSS., 13F40.

54. Claus Papers, 21, pt. 2, diary 10, April 13, 1786.

55. April 6, 1786, State Papers, Canada, Q26, pt. 1: 81.

56. Brant, April 11, 1786, to Nepean, *ibid.*, p. 88.

57. *Ibid.*, p. 87.

58. Brant, Nov. 1801, to Sir John Johnson, quoted in Stone, *Life of Brant*, 2: 408.

59. Brant, May 21, 1783, speech to Haldimand, State Papers, Canada, Q21: 242.

60. Brant, about 1804, speech to Indians, quoted in Stone, *Life of Brant*, 2: 420.

CHAPTER 19—REBUILDING THE LONGHOUSE

1. June 26, 1786, to Sydney, State Papers, Canada, Q26, pt. 2: 313.

2. June 29, 1786, Claus Papers, 4: 108–09.

3. Aug. 9, 1786, Haldimand Papers, B76: 184–85.

4. Letter, private, June 28, 1786, C.O. 42, 18: 91–92.

5. Campbell, July 19, 1786, to Hope, State Papers, Canada, Q26, pt. 2: 521.

6. Richard Butler, Journal, Jan. 30, 1786, *Olden Time*, ed. by Neville B. Craig, 2: 524.

7. *Ibid.*

8. May 7, 1786, to Gen. Henry Knox, *Military Journal of Major Ebenezer Denny*, ed. by William H. Denny, in *Publications of the Historical Society of Pennsylvania* 7 (1860): 207–492, Appendix no. 1, p. 419.

9. April 6, 1786, State Papers, Canada, Q26, pt. 1: 75–76.

10. Brant, Aug. 4, 1793, to Lieut. Col. Alexander McKee, Brant MSS., 11F205.

11. Campbell, July 19, 1786, to Hope, State Papers, Canada, Q26, pt. 2: 521.

12. *Ibid.*, p. 522.

13. *Ibid.*, p. 521.

14. Council, Sept. 10, 1786, Harmar Papers, William L. Clements Library.

15. State Papers, Canada, Q26, pt. 2: 527–33.

16. Aug. 17, 1786, *ibid.*, pp. 525–26.

17. Oct. 5, 1786, to Hope, *ibid.*, pp. 594–95.

18. Brant, Sept. 10, 1786, to Butler, *ibid.*, p. 596.

19. *Ibid.*, pp. 596–99.

20. Obidiah Robins, Sept. 29, 1786, to Gen. Richard Butler, Harmar Papers.

21. *Diary of David Zeisberger, A Moravian Missionary among the Indians of Ohio,* tr. and ed. by Eugene F. Bliss, 2 vols. (Cincinnati, 1885), 1: 303.

22. Maj. W. Ancrum, Oct. 13, 15, 20, 1786, to ———, State Papers, Canada, Q56, pt. 3: 652–53; Mathews, Dec. 9, 1786, to Haldimand, Haldimand Papers, B76: 231.

23. Extract of letter from Pittsburgh, Nov. 8, 1786, *The Pennsylvania Gazette,* Dec. 13, 1786.

24. Michigan MSS., William L. Clements Library.

25. McKee, Nov. 20, 1786, to Brant, MG19, F6: 1, Public Archives of Canada.

26. Sept. 8, 1786, to Nepean, private, C.O. 42, 18: 110.

27. Dec. 14, 1786, to Claus, Claus Papers, 4: 134.

28. *Ibid.,* pp. 133–34.

29. Feb. 3, 1787, State Papers, Canada, Q28: 298–99.

30. Frontier Wars MSS., 23U39–46, State Historical Society of Wisconsin, microfilm at Princeton University Library.

31. State Papers, Canada, Q27, pt. 1: 69–75.

32. Brant's letter not found.

33. State Papers, Canada, Q27, pt. 1: 78–80.

34. Diego Gardoqui, Oct. 24, 1788, to Conde de Floridablanca, Confidential No. 21, "Papers from the Spanish Archives Relating to Tennessee and the Old Southwest, 1783–1800," tr. and ed. by D. C. Corbitt and Roberta Corbitt, *The East Tennessee Historical Society's Publications,* no. 18 (1946): 137.

35. *Diary of David Zeisberger,* ed. by Bliss, 1: 344.

36. Butler, Aug. 4, 1787, to Brant, Brant MSS., 20F56.

37. Henry Knox, July 23, 1787, to Brant, quoted in Stone, *Life of Brant,* 2: 266–67.

38. Oct. 13, 15, 20, 1786, to ———, State Papers, Canada, Q56, pt. 3: 653.

39. Extract of a Statement of the Province of Upper Canada Sent with the Approbation of Lieut. General Hunter to Field Marshal His Royal Highness the Duke of Kent Commander in Chief of British N. America, in the Year 1800, in "Papers on War of 1812," *Michigan Historical Collections,* 15: 9.

40. Ensign John Armstrong, April 12, 1785, to Col. Josiah Harmar, *Ohio in the Time of the Confederation,* ed. by Archer Butler Hulbert (Cleveland, 1918), p. 107.

41. Aug. 4, 1793, to McKee, Brant MSS., 11F205. The significance of the moon (a gorget) is not so readily apparent.

42. Joseph's letter has not been found, but it is mentioned in Johnson's reply.

43. State Papers, Canada, Q27, pt. 1: 103–07.

44. Mar. 22, 1787, quoted in Stone, *Life of Brant,* 2: 268.

45. May 9, 1787, "Indian Affairs," *Michigan Historical Collections,* 20: 283–84.

46. May 29 [28?], 1787, quoted in Stone, *Life of Brant,* 2: 271.

47. Maj. R. Mathews, Diary, May 30, 1787, p. 7, MS. copy at Metropolitan Toronto Library.

48. *Ibid.,* May 27, 1787, p. 5.

49. Richard Butler, Aug. 4, 1787, to Brant, Brant MSS., 20F56.

50. *Ibid.*

51. For example: Brant, Aug. 29, 1787, certificate, Calendar of Original Memorials, Vouchers, Etc., 1: 134, American Loyalists Papers, New York Public Library.

52. June 27, 1787, Brant MSS., 20F55.

53. Deed from Six Nations Inhabiting Grand River, Feb. 26, 1787, *Valley of Six Nations*, ed. by Charles M. Johnston, pp. 70–71.

54. Oct. 19, 1787, Claus Papers, 4: 167.

55. Harmar, Dec. 6, 1787, to Maj. Wyllys, *Military Journal of Major Ebenezer Denny*, Appendix no. 1, p. 425.

56. Charles Thomson, Secretary, Oct. 26, 1787, Instructions to Governor of Northwest Territory, *American State Papers, Indian Affairs,* 2 vols. (Washington, 1832–34), 1: 9.

CHAPTER 20—THE DISH WITH ONE SPOON

1. Quoted in Stone, *Life of Brant,* 2: 275.

2. Brant, July 9, 1788, to Clinton, Brant MSS., 11F74.

3. Samuel Kirkland, deposition, May 5, 1792, *The American Museum, or, Universal Magazine,* 11: 243.

4. Butler, Aug. 3, 1788, to Sir John Johnson, extract, Frontier Wars MSS., 23U65–66.

5. July 9, 1788, Brant MSS., 11F74.

6. *American State Papers, Indian Affairs,* 1: 210–11.

7. Brant and eleven other chiefs, quitclaim, Aug. 4, 1789, O'Reilly Papers. These are called the O'Reilly Papers, according to The New-York Historical Society which owns them; but, strangely enough, the man who collected them spelled his name "O'Rielly."

8. Oct. 14, 1788, State Papers, Canada, Q38: 141.

9. July 21, 1790, Brant MSS., 15F206; Clinton, Sept. 1, 1790, to Brant, *Proceedings of [N.Y.] Commissioners of Indian Affairs,* 2: 462.

10. July 8, 1788, in William Henry Smith, *The Life and Public Services of Arthur St. Clair . . . with His Correspondence and Other Papers,* 2 vols. (Cincinnati, 1882), 2: 60–61.

11. July 9, 1788, Brant MSS., 11F74.

12. Brant, Aug. 28, 1788, to Sir John Johnson, quoted in Stone, *Life of Brant,* 2: 276; Gov. Arthur St. Clair, Sept. 14, 1788, to Knox, in Smith, *Life of St. Clair with Correspondence,* 2: 88.

13. Aug. 28, 1788, to Johnson, quoted in Stone, *Life of Brant,* 2: 276.

14. Dorchester, Oct. 14, 1788, to Sydney, State Papers, Canada, Q38: 143.

15. Oct. 7, 1788, quoted in Stone, *Life of Brant,* 2: 278–79.

16. St. Clair, Sept. 14, 1788, to Knox, in Smith, *Life of St. Clair with Correspondence,* 2: 88; St. Clair, Oct. 26, 1788, to Knox, *ibid.,* pp. 93–94.

17. W. Sargent, Oct. 20, 1788, to Knox, Knox MSS., 22: 169, Massachusetts Historical Society.

18. Sept. 14, 1788, in Smith, *Life of St. Clair with Correspondence,* 2: 89.

19. Capt. Hendrick Aupaumut, Narrative of Journey to Niagara & Grand River In July, August, Sept. & Oct. 1791, Pickering Papers, 59: 12A.

20. St. Clair, Nov. 4, 1788, to Knox, in Smith, *Life of St. Clair with Correspondence,* 2: 95–96; St. Clair, Nov. 6, 1788, to Charles Thomson, Secretary of Congress, *ibid.,* p. 97; ex-Gov. William Walker, Dec. 7, 1870, to Draper, Brant MSS., 11F58–60; *Diary of David Zeisberger,* ed. by Bliss, Feb. 4, 1789, vol. 2: 7; also *ibid.,* June 13, 1787, vol. 1: 351 and Oct. 19, 1781, vol. 1: 25.

21. Oct. 26, 1788, to Knox, in Smith, *Life of St. Clair with Correspondence*, 2: 93–94.

22. Council, Fort Harmar, Dec. 16, 1788, Frontier Wars MSS., 23U94.

23. Ex-Gov. William Walker, Dec. 7, 1870, to Draper, Brant MSS., 11F58–59.

24. St. Clair, Nov. 4, 1788, to Knox, in Smith, *Life of St. Clair with Correspondence*, 2: 95. Joseph's letter has not been found.

25. "A Short Account of Br. Joh. Heckewelders Journey to the Muskingum, from Sept. 10 to Dec. 23, 1788," Nov. 7, 1788, quoted in *Thirty Thousand Miles with John Heckewelder*, ed. by Paul A. W. Wallace (University of Pittsburgh Press, 1958), p. 228.

26. Chiefs of Six Nations and Western Confederacy, Nov. 19, 1788, to St. Clair, Frontier Wars MSS., 23U66.

27. Brant, Journal of Proceedings at General Council held at Foot of Rapids of Miamis, Aug. 9, 1793, Records of Superintendent General's Office, 1791–1828, R.G. 10: 8, Public Archives of Canada.

28. Speech, Nov. 19, 1788, Frontier Wars MSS., 23U66–69.

29. St. Clair, Dec. 3, 1788, to Knox, in Smith, *Life of St. Clair with Correspondence*, 2: 99.

30. Solomon Drowne, Dec. 9, 1788, to Mrs. Drowne, "Original Documents," *Magazine of American History* 9, no. 4 (April 1883): 287.

31. Dec. 8, 1788, Frontier Wars MSS., 23U74.

32. St. Clair, Dec. 13, 1788, to Knox, in Smith, *Life of St. Clair with Correspondence*, 2: 106; council, Dec. 16, 1788, Frontier Wars MSS., 23U93.

33. Council, Sept. 7, 1789, Frontier Wars MSS., 23U173–176.

34. John F. Meginness, *The Family of General Arthur St. Clair*, reprinted from Dr. Egle's Notes and Queries (Harrisburg, Pa., 1897), pp. 24–26.

35. Frazer Ells Wilson, *Arthur St. Clair, Rugged Ruler of the Old Northwest* (Richmond, 1944), pp. 238–42.

36. St. Clair, Oct. 26, 1788, to Knox, in Smith, *Life of St. Clair with Correspondence*, 2: 94. St. Clair spoke of Cornstalk. Obviously he meant Cornplanter.

37. Council, Dec. 19, 1788, Frontier Wars MSS., 23U102, 106.

38. Council, Dec. 15–16, 1788, *ibid.*, 23U89, 93–95.

39. *Diary of David Zeisberger*, ed. by Bliss, Jan. 8, 1789, vol. 2: 3.

40. *Military Journal of Major Ebenezer Denny*, p. 334.

41. Jan. 18, 1789, in Smith, *Life of St. Clair with Correspondence*, 2: 109.

42. Statement, Sept. 20, 1788, *Valley of Six Nations*, p. 72.

43. Council, Sept. 2–10, 1800, *ibid.*, p. 54; also Dorchester, June 22, 1789, to Johnson, Indian Records, Series Two, 15: 108.

44. Jan. 28, 1790, to Dorchester, State Papers, Canada, Q46, pt. 2: 407–08.

45. Jan. 3, 1789, quoted in Stone, *Life of Brant*, 2: 282–83.

46. James Peachey, June 11, 1789, to Haldimand, Haldimand Papers, B77: 183; Dorchester, June 22, 1789, to Johnson, Indian Records, Series Two, 15: 108; Butler, Mar. 2, 1790, to Johnson, State Papers, Canada, Q46, pt. 2: 412–13; Stone, *Life of Brant*, 2: 284.

47. Aug. 14, 1789, Haldimand Papers, B77: 229–30.

48. Mar. 8, 1789, to Mathews, quoted in Stone, *Life of Brant*, 2: 281.

49. Ann Powell, journal, [May or June], 1789, quoted in Frank H. Severance, *Studies of the Niagara Frontier* (Buffalo, 1911), p. 227.

50. Indian Records, Series Two, 15: 104.

51. *Ibid.*, pp. 105–06.

52. July 14, 1789, *Proceedings of* [N.Y.] *Commissioners of Indian Affairs*, 2: 335–38.

53. July 30, 1789, *ibid.*, pp. 340–42.

54. Sept. 19, 1789, to Maj. Hardenbergh, *ibid.*, p. 455.

55. Sept. 19, 1789, Brant MSS., 15F204–205.

56. Sept. 23, 1789, State Papers, Canada, Q43, pt. 2: 784–85.

57. Sir John Johnson, Nov. 4, 1789, to Brant, quoted in Stone, *Life of Brant*, 2: 285; Dorchester, Nov. 10, 1789, to W. W. Grenville, State Papers, Canada, Q43, pt. 2: 658.

58. Johnson, Jan. 28, 1790, to Dorchester, State Papers, Canada, Q46, pt. 2: 406–07.

59. Dorchester, Mar. 8, 1790, to Grenville, secret, *ibid.*, Q44, pt. 1: 121–22.

60. Clinton, April 8, 1790, to Brant, *Proceedings of* [N.Y.] *Commissioners of Indian Affairs*, 2: 371.

61. May 26, 1790, to Clinton, *ibid.*, pp. 384–85.

62. Council, June 18, 1790, *ibid.*, pp. 405, 414.

63. Brant, Mar. 4, 1791, to Clinton, *ibid.*, p. 469.

64. Brant, July 21, 1790, to Clinton, Brant MSS., 15F206; Clinton, Sept. 1, 1790, to Brant, *Proceedings of* [N.Y.] *Commissioners of Indian Affairs*, 2: 462.

65. Brant, Mar. 4, 1791, to Clinton, *Proceedings of* [N.Y.] *Commissioners of Indian Affairs*, 2: 470.

66. Nov. 26, 1790, *ibid.*, p. 465.

67. July 21, 1790, Brant MSS., 15F206–207; see also note 1, *Proceedings of* [N.Y.] *Commissioners of Indian Affairs*, 2: 461.

68. Aug. 28, 1790, to Johnson, State Papers, Canada, Q46, pt. 2: 496–97.

69. Frontier Wars MSS., 23U172–179.

70. Miamis chiefs to Alexander McKee and Six Nations, received May 3, 1790, Claus Papers, 4: 213. Isaac is mentioned as Brant's "nephew." Obviously he was his son. Brant was still trying to put Isaac forward.

71. Draper, note from Clinton Papers, Brant MSS., 15F207–208.

72. Washington, Dec. 1, 1790, to Clinton, *Writings of Washington*, ed. by Fitzpatrick, 31: 160–61.

73. Nov. 8, 1790, State Papers, Canada, Q50, pt. 1: 59–60.

CHAPTER 21—AND THE MOON OF WAMPUM

1. Brant MSS., 15F89.

2. Brant, Mar. 7, 1791, to McKee, extract quoted in Stone, *Life of Brant*, 2: 298.

3. Feb. 25, 1791, to Richard Butler, Pickering Papers, 61: 197. Brant had also written to Knox on Feb. 20, probably to the same purport. Knox, May 18, 1791, to Col. Timothy Pickering, *American State Papers, Indian Affairs*, 1: 166. This earlier letter is missing.

4. Pickering Papers, 61: 209.

5. May 11, 1791, to Kirkland, Kirkland MSS.

6. Council, April 19–20, 1791, State Papers, Canada, Q50, pt. 1: 167–71. See also Col. Thomas Proctor, Diary, April 28, 1791, *Pennsylvania Archives*, Second Series, ed. by John B. Linn and Wm. H. Egle, 18 vols. (Harrisburg, 1874–1890), 4: 585; McKee, April 1, 1791, to Sir John Johnson, State Papers, Canada, Q50, pt. 1:

150–51; Knox, June 28, 1791, to Schuyler, Schuyler Papers, no. 1017; McKee, July 1, 1791, speech to Indians, "Haldimand Papers and Indian Affairs," *Michigan Historical Collections*, 20: 310–11; and Dorchester, Aug. 1, 1791, to Johnson and Maj. Smith, State Papers, Canada, Q52: 254–55.

7. June 11, 1791, State Papers, Canada, Q51, pt. 2: 777–78.

8. Thomas Rhea, July 2, 1791, deposition, *Pennsylvania Archives*, Second Series, 4: 669–72.

9. June 23, 1791, extract, State Papers, Canada, Q52: 251.

10. Capt. Dq. De Bartzchi, July 5, 1791, to Capt. Jacob Slough, Richard Butler Papers, Burton Historical Collection, Detroit Public Library.

11. June 4, 1791, extract, State Papers, Canada, Q51, pt. 2: 782.

12. *Ibid.*, pp. 782–83.

13. *Diary of David Zeisberger*, ed. by Bliss, Sept. 12, 1791, vol. 2: 214–15.

14. Council, June 29, 1791, State Papers, Canada, Q52: 188–89.

15. July 21, 1791, to Maj. Gen. Richard Butler, *ibid.*, Lower Canada, Q58, pt. 1: 180–81.

16. June 24, 1791, to the Rev. Thacher, Kirkland MSS.

17. McKee, July 5, 1791, to Maj. Smith, State Papers, Canada, Q52: 252–53; Brant, July 9, 1791, to Smith, *ibid.*, pp. 253–54.

18. *Diary of David Zeisberger*, ed. by Bliss, July 12, 1791, vol. 2: 201.

19. Narrative of Captain Hendrick's Journey to Niagara & Grand River in July, August, Sept. & Oct. 1791, Pickering Papers, 59: 8.

20. *Ibid.*, pp. 8–11.

21. *Ibid.*, p. 10.

22. Joseph Chew, April 7, 1794, to Thomas Aston Coffin, "Haldimand Papers and Indian Affairs," *Michigan Historical Collections*, 20: 338.

23. State Papers, Canada, Q52: 268–70; also Brant, speech to Dorchester, Aug. 17, 1791, *ibid.*, pp. 267–68.

24. Speech to deputies of confederated Indian nations, Aug. 15, 1791, *ibid.*, pp. 260–66.

25. *Diary of David Zeisberger*, ed. by Bliss, Oct. 13, 16–17, 1791, vol. 2: 222.

26. Knox, May 2 and June 13, 1791, to Pickering, *American State Papers, Indian Affairs*, 1: 166, 167.

27. Knox, June 13, 1791, to Pickering, *ibid.*, pp. 166–67; Knox, May 11, 1791, to Governor of New York, *ibid.*, p. 168.

28. Samuel Kirkland, June 7, 1791, to the Rev. Willard, Kirkland MSS.

29. Knox, April 12, 1791, to Clinton, *American State Papers, Indian Affairs*, 1: 167; Clinton, April 27, 1791, to Knox, *ibid.*, pp. 167–68; Knox, May 11, 1791, to Clinton, *ibid.*, p. 168.

30. Knox, April 12, 1791, to Clinton, *ibid.*, p. 167.

31. Kirkland, June 7, 1791, to Willard, Kirkland MSS.; Kirkland, June 8 [18?], 1791, to the Rev. Peter Thacher, Dartmouth College MSS.; Kirkland, June 24, 1791, to Thacher, Kirkland MSS.

32. Narrative of Captain Hendrick's Journey to Niagara & Grand River, July–Oct. 1791, Pickering Papers, 59: 10A.

33. McKee, Nov. 1, 1791, to Sir John Johnson, State Papers, Lower Canada, Q58, pt. 1: 47–48.

34. Letter from Niagara, Nov. 24, 1791, to ———, extract, *ibid.*, Canada, Q57, pt. 1: 179; Kirkland, Dec. 28, 1791, to Knox, Kirkland MSS.

35. Quoted in Lothrop, *Life of Kirkland*, Appendix, p. 367.

36. Dec. 28, 1791, to Knox, Kirkland MSS.

CHAPTER 22—PHILADELPHIA AND THE GLAIZE

1. Dec. 30, 1791, State Papers, Lower Canada, Q58, pt. 1: 227–28.
2. Benj. Barton, Jan. 19, 1792, to Col. Samuel Ogden, Knox MSS., 30: 88.
3. Dec. 28, 1791, to Knox, Kirkland MSS.
4. Brant, Jan. 19, 1792, to Chew, extract, State Papers, Lower Canada, Q59, pt. 2: 346.
5. *Ibid.*, pp. 342–45.
6. Knox, Dec. 20, 1791, to Pickering, Pickering Papers, 61: 307.
7. Dec. 20, 1791, *American State Papers, Indian Affairs*, 1: 226.
8. Dec. 23, 1791, Brant MSS., 15F211–212.
9. State Papers, Lower Canada, Q59, pt. 2: 347–52.
10. Jan. 25, 1792, *ibid.*, pp. 353–54.
11. Feb. 4, 1792, Kirkland MSS.
12. Feb. 16, 1792, *ibid.*
13. Council, Jan. 31, Feb. 3, 1792, State Papers, Lower Canada, Q59, pt. 2: 335–41; Pickering, Mar. 21, 1792, to Washington, Pickering Papers, 62: 12.
14. Gordon, Feb. 5, 1792, to Maj. Gen. Clarke, extract, State Papers, Lower Canada, Q59, pt. 2: 334.
15. Jan. 7, 1792, *American State Papers, Indian Affairs*, 1: 226.
16. *Ibid.*
17. Feb. 25, 1792, *ibid.*, p. 228.
18. Washington, Feb. 25, 1792, to Secretary of War, *Writings of Washington*, ed. by Fitzpatrick, 31: 484–85.
19. Feb. 25, 1792, *American State Papers, Indian Affairs*, 1: 228.
20. Captain Hendrick's Narrative of his journey to Niagara & Grand River in February 1792, Pickering Papers, 59: [18A]–19. Page number in brackets denotes difficulty in reading microfilm.
21. Feb. 25, 1792, *American State Papers, Indian Affairs*, 1: 228.
22. Mar. 20, 1792, State Papers, Lower Canada, Q59, pt. 2: 365–68.
23. Mar. 27, 1792, *American State Papers, Indian Affairs*, 1: 244–45.
24. Mar. 27, 1792, Claus Papers, 5: 3–4.
25. Brant, May 21, 1792, to Gordon, State Papers, Lower Canada, Q59, pt. 2: 412–13.
26. April 23, 1792, *American State Papers, Indian Affairs*, 1: 230.
27. May 23, 1792, State Papers, Lower Canada, Q59, pt. 2: 408–11.
28. Stone, *Life of Brant*, 2: 326–27; Gordon, May 30, 1792, to Francis Le Maistre, extract, State Papers, Lower Canada, Q59, pt. 2: 412.
29. Brant, May 22, 1792, to Gordon, State Papers, Lower Canada, Q59, pt. 2: 413.
30. Knox, April 23, 1792, to Gen. Israel Chapin, *American State Papers, Indian Affairs*, 1: 231; Chapin, May 8, 1792, to Brant, Brant MSS., 20F65; Knox, June 27, 1792, to Israel Chapin, Jr., *American State Papers, Indian Affairs*, 1: 237.
31. Chapin, May 8, 1792, to Brant, Brant MSS., 20F65; Chapin, June 2, 1792, to Knox, O'Reilly Papers, vol. 8.
32. Israel Chapin, June 2, 1792, to Pickering, Pickering Papers, 62: 49; Kirkland, June 5, 1792, to Pickering, *ibid.*, p. [52A?].
33. Campbell, *Travels in America in 1791–92*, p. 249.
34. Chapin, June 2, 1792, to Knox, O'Reilly Papers, vol. 8.
35. "A Narrative of An Embassy to the Western Indians, from the Original

Manuscript of Hendrick Aupaumut, with Prefatory Remarks by Dr. B. H. Coates," *Memoirs of the Historical Society of Pennsylvania* 2 (1827): 78.

36. Brant, Mar. 24, 1791, to [Sir John Johnson?], State Papers, Canada, Q50, pt. 1: 153.

37. Chapin, June 2, 1792, to Knox, O'Reilly Papers, vol. 8.

38. Stone, *Life of Brant,* 2: 327.

39. R. Varick, June 19, 1792, to Knox, HM 22867, Henry E. Huntington Library, San Marino, Cal.

40. Wm. Mathews, Tailor, June 19, 1792, account with Capt. Joseph Brant, O'Reilly Papers, 8, no. 22.

41. Knox, June 27, 1792, to Chapin, *American State Papers, Indian Affairs,* 1: 237.

42. June 22, 1792, to Maj. Gen. Anthony Wayne, no. 3, *Anthony Wayne, A Name in Arms, Soldier, Diplomat, Defender of Expansion Westward of a Nation: The Wayne-Knox-Pickering-McHenry Correspondence,* ed. by Richard C. Knopf (Pittsburgh, 1960), p. 22.

43. June 21, 1792, *Writings of Washington,* ed. by Fitzpatrick, 32: 62–63.

44. July 17, 1792, to the Rev. Dr. White, *The Correspondence of Lieut. Governor John Graves Simcoe,* ed. by Brigadier General E. A. Cruikshank, 5 vols. (Toronto, 1923–31), 1: 180.

45. Brant, July 26, 1792, to Knox, *American State Papers, Indian Affairs,* 1: 245. See also Brant, July 26, 1792, to Clinton, Brant MSS., 15F213, and Brant, Aug. 1, 1792, to Joseph Chew, State Papers, Lower Canada, Q61, pt. 1: 167.

46. June 27, 1792, Hammond-Simcoe Correspondence, William L. Clements Library, Ann Arbor, Mich.

47. July 3, 1792, extract, *ibid.*

48. *Ibid.*

49. J. Graves Simcoe, Dec. 6, 1793, to Dorchester, *Simcoe Papers,* ed. by Cruikshank, 2: 116.

50. Speech, 1806, quoted in Stone, *Life of Brant,* 2: 419.

51. N.d., quoted *ibid.,* pp. 328–29.

52. June 22, 1792, to Adam Lindsay, Jefferson Papers, Coolidge Collection, Massachusetts Historical Society.

53. Chapin, Aug. 14, 1792, to Knox, extract, *American State Papers, Indian Affairs,* 1: 242.

54. Knox, June 29, 1792, to Wayne, no. 4, *Anthony Wayne, A Name in Arms,* ed. by Knopf, p. 25.

55. Knox, June 27, 1792, to Israel Chapin, Jr., *American State Papers, Indian Affairs,* 1: 237.

56. June 29, 1792, no. 4, *Anthony Wayne, A Name in Arms,* p. 25.

57. June 27, 1792, *American State Papers, Indian Affairs,* 1: 237.

58. Aug. 7, 1792, no. 11, *Anthony Wayne, A Name in Arms,* p. 60.

59. Stone, *Life of Brant,* 2: 329–30. The aged Morgan Lewis himself told this story to Stone, and it was confirmed by a person who had heard about it from Brant.

60. July 18, 1792, Knox MSS., 32: 10.

61. Kirkland MSS.

62. Mar. 24, 1791, to [Sir John Johnson?], State Papers, Canada, Q50, pt. 1: 153.

63. Feb. 18, 1792, to Pickering, Pickering Papers, 62: 4.

64. May 31, 1792, to Pickering, Kirkland MSS.

65. Chapin, Aug. 14, 1792, to Knox, extract, *American State Papers, Indian Affairs*, 1: 242.

66. July 26, 1792, to Clinton, Brant MSS., 15F213.

67. Israel Chapin, Jr., Oct. 28, 1805, certificate, quoted in Stone, *Life of Brant*, 2, Appendix no. 12, pp. 33–34.

68. July 31, 1792, Claus Papers, 5: 25.

69. Sept. 10, 1792, Brant MSS., 11F110.

70. Stone, *Life of Brant*, 2: 333.

71. Aug. 1, 1792, extract, State Papers, Lower Canada, Q61, pt. 1: 168.

72. Quoted in Stone, *Life of Brant*, 2: 333–34.

73. Chapin, Aug. 14, 1792, to Knox, *American State Papers, Indian Affairs*, 1: 242. See also Brant, Sept. 10, 1792, to Clinton, Brant MSS., 11F110.

74. *Diary of David Zeisberger*, ed. by Bliss, 2: 276.

75. Deposition, *American State Papers, Indian Affairs*, 1: 244.

76. To Clinton, Brant MSS., 11F110.

77. The Wabash delegates came, and a great proportion of them promptly died of smallpox.

78. Nov. 9, 1792, no. 25, *Anthony Wayne, A Name in Arms*, p. 132.

79. *Diary of David Zeisberger*, ed. by Bliss, July 30, Aug. 9, 1792, vol. 2: 273, 275.

80. There were three Miami Rivers. The Great Miami and the Little Miami emptied into the Ohio near Cincinnati. The Miami of the Lake, now called the Maumee, emptied into Lake Erie. By the treaty of Fort Finney the Americans claimed the mouth of the Great Miami, up that river, and across to the Wabash. By the treaty of Fort Harmar they also claimed most of the east side of the Great Miami. The Americans did not claim the mouth of the Maumee.

81. "Narrative of An Embassy to the Western Indians from Original Manuscript of Hendrick Aupaumut," *Memoirs of Historical Society of Pennsylvania*, 2: 112–13.

82. Council, Oct. 2, 1792, *Simcoe Papers*, ed. by Cruikshank, 1: 220.

83. Council, Oct. 4, 1792, *ibid.*, p. 222.

84. Council, Oct. 7, 1792, *ibid.*, p. 227.

85. *Ibid.* Compare Knox's actual orders to St. Clair, Mar. 21, 1791, *American State Papers, Indian Affairs*, 1: 171–74.

86. For the official report of the Glaize council, see *Simcoe Papers*, 1: 218–29. Aupaumut's version is in *Memoirs of Historical Society of Pennsylvania*, 2: 115–21. See also William Johns[t]on, Journal of proceedings, Aug. 29–Oct. 14, 1792, State Papers, Upper Canada, Q279, pt. 1: 62–71.

87. *Diary of David Zeisberger*, ed. by Bliss, 2: 282.

88. William Johns[t]on, Journal of proceedings, Oct. 7 [9?], 1792, State Papers, Upper Canada, Q279, pt. 1: 70.

89. Aupaumut, "Narrative," *Memoirs of Historical Society of Pennsylvania*, 2: 122.

90. This is what he told Chapin. Chapin, Jan. 27, 1793, to Gen. Philip Schuyler, Ontario County Historical Society, Canandaigua, N.Y. Aupaumut also mentions this war party.

91. Questions to and answers by Hendrick Aupaumut, Feb. 5, 1793, Pickering Papers, 59: [41?]. Parts illegible.

92. Council, Oct. 28, 1792, *Simcoe Papers*, 1: 242–43.

93. Journal of proceedings, Oct. 13 [15?], 1792, State Papers, Upper Canada, Q279, pt. 1: 70.

94. *Diary of David Zeisberger*, ed. by Bliss, 2: 286–87; John Heckewelder, June

17–23, 1793, to Commissioners, Pickering Papers, 59: 185.
    95. Mar. 8, 1791, Pickering Papers, 61: 207–08.

CHAPTER 23—"MY WISH EVER WAS FOR PEACE"

    1. Dec. 20, 1794, to Duke of Portland, *Simcoe Papers*, 3: 233; and June 21, 1792, to Henry Dundas, *ibid.*, 1: 172.
    2. *Ibid.*, 1: 173–74.
    3. Simcoe, June 21, 1792, to Dundas, no. 10, *ibid.*, p. 172.
    4. Sept. 24, 1792, Claus Papers, 5: 41.
    5. Sept. 27, 1792, to Hammond, *Simcoe Papers*, 1: 216.
    6. Aug. 30, 1792, *ibid.*, pp. 207–09.
    7. Nov. 10, 1792, Claus Papers, 5: 57.
    8. Pickering, Mar. 21, 1792, to Washington, Pickering Papers, 62: 12.
    9. Brant, Mar. 26, 1793, to Chapin, O'Reilly Papers, 9, no. 26.
    10. Simcoe, Sept. 27, 1792, to Hammond, *Simcoe Papers*, 1: 217.
    11. Brant, Mar. 26, 1793, to Chapin, O'Reilly Papers, 9, no. 26.
    12. Mar. 23, 1793, Claus Papers, 5: 96.
    13. Simcoe, Jan. 21, 1793, to Hammond, *Simcoe Papers*, 1: 277.
    14. *Ibid.*, pp. 277–78.
    15. Jan. 1793, Claus Papers, 5: 73.
    16. *The Diary of Mrs. John Graves Simcoe, Wife of the First Lieutenant-Governor of the Province of Upper Canada, 1792–6*, ed. by J. Ross Robertson (Toronto, 1911), Feb. 4, 12, 1793, p. 148.
    17. Feb. 25, 1793, to McKee, Claus Papers, 5: 80; Maj. Littlehales, "Journal to Detroit from Niagara in 1793," excerpts copied by the Rev. Dr. Henry Scadding from *Canadian Literary Magazine*, May 1833, Brant MSS., 11F137.
    18. Indians, Feb. 27, 1793, to Washington, "Indian Affairs," *Michigan Historical Collections*, 20: 314–15; Confederate Nations, Feb. 27, 1793, to Five Nations, Claus Papers, 5: 87–89; Confederate Indians, Feb. 27, 1793, to Simcoe, *ibid.*, p. 84.
    19. Knox, April 26, 1793, instructions to Commissioners appointed for treating with the Indians Northwest of the Ohio, *American State Papers, Indian Affairs*, 1: 340–42.
    20. June 14 and July 26, 1793, to Clarke, *Simcoe Papers*, 1: 354, 400.
    21. Gen. Benjamin Lincoln, "Journal of a Treaty Held in 1793, with the Indian Tribes North-West of the Ohio, by Commissioners of the United States," *Collections of the Massachusetts Historical Society* 5, Third Series (Boston, 1836): 109–76.
    22. April 21, 1793, to Clarke, *Simcoe Papers*, 1: 317.
    23. Simcoe, April 29, 1793, to McKee, Records of Superintendent General's Office, RG10: 8.
    24. Feb. 25, 1793, to McKee, Claus Papers, 5: 79–81.
    25. Grenville, Mar. 17, 1792, to Hammond, *Instructions to the British Ministers to the United States, 1791–1812*, ed. by Bernard Mayo (Da Capo Press Reprint Edition, 1971), p. 26; Simcoe, April 29, 1793, to McKee, *Simcoe Papers*, 1: 323.
    26. Jan. 1793, to McKee, Claus Papers, 5:74.
    27. April 1, 1793, to Clarke, *Simcoe Papers*, 1: 308–09.
    28. Simcoe, April 29, 1793, to McKee, Records of Supt. General's Office, RG10: 8.
    29. June 22, 1793, Claus Papers, 5: 157–60.

30. Instructions, June 1793, to Walter Butler Sheehan and William Johns[t]on, *Simcoe Papers*, 1: 368.

31. Brant, May 17, 1793, to McKee, "Papers on Indians and Military Posts, 1762–1799," *Michigan Historical Collections*, 12: 49; Brant, Journal of Proceedings at General Council held at the Foot of the Rapids of the Miamis, May 17, 22, 24, June 3, 9, 15, July 1, 1793, Records of Supt. General's Office, RG10: 8.

32. Journal, June 3, 1793, Records of Supt. General's Office, RG10: 8.

33. Joseph Chew, Aug. 11, 1794, to Thomas Aston Coffin, Military Papers "Indian," C247: 217; Chew, Mar. 26, 1795, to Coffin, *ibid.*, C248: 50–51.

34. Journal, Records of Supt. General's Office, RG10: 8.

35. *Ibid.*, June 15–July 1, 1793.

36. Journal, July 1, 1793, *ibid.*

37. Mar. 1, 1795, to Joseph Chew, extract, *Simcoe Papers*, 3: 313; Simcoe, Mar. 3, 1794, to Dorchester, *ibid.*, 2: 174.

38. Pickering, diary, July 5, 1793, Pickering Papers, 59: 317.

39. Draper, extracts from MS. in Library of Parliament of Canada entitled "Canadian Letters, Descriptive of a Tour thro' the Provinces of Lower & Upper Canada in the course of the years 1792 & 1793," Brant MSS., 11F190–193.

40. Lincoln, "Journal," pp. 130–31.

41. *Ibid.*, pp. 131–33.

42. *Ibid.*, pp. 134–35.

43. Pickering, memorandum, [1793?], Pickering Papers, 59: 257.

44. Pickering, memorandum, June 7, 1793, *ibid.*, 60: 147A; Simcoe, June 7, 1793, to Commissioners, *ibid.*, pp. [148A?]–149.

45. Pickering, memorandum, [1793?], *ibid.*, 59: 257A.

46. *Thirty Thousand Miles with John Heckewelder*, ed. by Wallace, July 26, 1793, p. 315.

47. *Ibid.*, July 28, 1793.

48. Simcoe, July 10, 1793, to Clarke, *Simcoe Papers*, 1: 383.

49. *Ibid.*

50. July 1, 1793, *ibid.*, p. 374.

51. July 10, 1793, to Clarke, *ibid.*, p. 383.

52. Sept. 20, 1793, to Dundas, no. 18, *ibid.*, 2: 59.

53. *Ibid.*

54. Brant, Journal, July 23–28, 1793, Records of Supt. General's Office, RG10: 8; H. A., Aug. 6, 1793, to Pickering, Pickering Papers, 59: 203–203A; Lincoln, "Journal," July 30, 1793, p. 143.

55. Halliday Jackson, *Civilization of the Indian Natives* (Philadelphia and New York, 1830), pp. 24–25. Jackson had lived among the Indians and tells of an interview in 1798 between some chiefs and Quakers.

56. Aug. 4, 1793, to McKee, Brant MSS., 11F205.

57. July 28, 1793, *Simcoe Papers*, 1: 403.

58. Aug. 8, 1793, *ibid.*, 2: 4–5.

59. Aug. 4, 1793, Brant MSS., 11F205.

60. "Jacob Lindley's Account, Of a Journey to attend the Indian Treaty, proposed to be held at Sandusky, in the year 1793; interspersed with various observations, remarks, and circumstances, that occurred on this interesting occasion," *Friends' Miscellany*, ed. by John and Isaac Comly, 12 vols. (Philadelphia, 1831–39), 2: 135.

61. Lincoln, "Journal," pp. 145–49.

62. *Ibid.*, pp. 149–50.

63. *Ibid.*, p. 150. Brant heard of this incident and mentioned it in his Journal, and so did John Heckewelder, who was present at Elliott's on Aug. 1.

64. Sept. 26, 1793, to Joseph Chew, State Papers, Lower Canada, Q66: 207.

65. Simcoe, Sept. 27, 1792, to Hammond, *Simcoe Papers,* 1: 216–17.

66. Nov. 10, 1793, to Dorchester, *ibid.,* 2: 102–03.

67. Brant, Sept. 26, 1793, to Chew, State Papers, Lower Canada, Q66: 206.

68. Simcoe, Sept. 20, 1793, to Dundas, no. 18, *Simcoe Papers,* 2: 59.

69. Brant, Journal, Aug. 9–13, 1793, Records of Supt. General's Office, RG10: 8.

70. *Ibid.,* [after Aug. 13, 1793]. This statement was attested by Nicholas Rosecrantz in a letter to Wayne. See note 74 below.

71. Aug. 22, 1793, *Simcoe Papers,* 2: 34.

72. Sept. 8, 1793, to Hammond, Hammond-Simcoe Correspondence.

73. *Ibid.*

74. Nichos. Rosecrantz, Sept. 23, 1793, to Wayne, Wayne MSS., Historical Society of Pennsylvania.

75. *Ibid.*

76. Lincoln, "Journal," Aug. 12–13, 1793, pp. 156–58.

77. *Ibid.,* pp. 163–67.

78. Sept. 27, 1792, to Hammond, *Simcoe Papers,* 1: 214; and Sept. 8, 1793, Hammond-Simcoe Correspondence.

79. Aug. 22, 1793, *Simcoe Papers,* 2: 35.

80. *Ibid.*

81. Sept. 2, 1793, *ibid.,* p. 47.

82. Brant, Sept. 28, 1793, to Chapin, Wayne MSS., 29: 84.

83. Council, Oct. 10, 1793, State Papers, Lower Canada, Q67: 30–32; Simcoe, Line proposed by Six Nations . . . at Buffalo Creek, 1793, *Simcoe Papers,* 2: 86.

84. Knox, Dec. 24, 1793, to Chapin, O'Reilly Papers, 9, no. 74.

85. Council, Feb. 9, 1794, State Papers, Upper Canada, Q280, pt. 1: 220.

86. May 8, 1794, to McKee, *Simcoe Papers,* 5: 86–87.

87. Simcoe, Nov. 10, 1793, to Dundas, *ibid.,* 2: 100; Simcoe, Nov. 10, 1793, to Dorchester, *ibid.,* p. 103.

88. Simcoe, Sept. 20, 1793, to Dundas, no. 18, *ibid.,* pp. 59, 62; Simcoe, Dec. 22, 1795, to Dorchester, *ibid.,* 4: 165.

89. Simcoe, Mar. 14, 1794, to Dorchester, *ibid.,* 2: 180.

90. Nov. 10, 1793, to Dorchester, *ibid.,* pp. 102–03.

91. Simcoe, June 21, 1794, to Dundas, no. 24, *ibid.,* p. 285.

92. Simcoe, Mar. 26, 1794, to Dorchester, *ibid.,* p. 194.

93. May 30, 1794, Brant MSS., 11F148.

94. Extract of a letter from Fort Franklin [Venango], June 12, 1794, printed in *New York Daily Gazette,* July 1, 1794, *Simcoe Papers,* 2: 261; Simcoe, June 15, 1794, to Dorchester, *ibid.,* p. 266.

95. Simcoe, July 10, 1794, to Dorchester, *ibid.,* p. 316; Simcoe, June 15, 1794, to Dorchester, *ibid.,* p. 266; Simcoe, Nov. 8, 1795, to Duke of Portland, no. 31, *ibid.,* 4: 133.

96. June 21, 1794, to Dundas, no. 24, *ibid.,* 2: 286.

97. June 9, 1794, State Papers, Lower Canada, Q68: 149.

98. July 19, 1794, to Col. John Smith, for Simcoe, quoted in Stone, *Life of Brant,* 2: 379–80.

99. April 4, 1794, to Sec. of War, *Writings of Washington*, ed. by Fitzpatrick, 33: 314.

100. Pickering, Mar. 10, 1796, to James McHenry, Pickering Papers, 2: 241. Joseph later said that in 1794 he was offered, and refused, 11,000 acres of land. Note, [about Jan. 30, 1797], on margin of speech to William Claus, State Papers, Upper Canada, Q283: 83.

101. *Simcoe Papers*, 2: 386.

102. Aug. 23, 1794, to Dorchester, *ibid.*, p. 411.

103. To Lieut. Col. Richard England, *ibid.*, 3: 7.

104. Quoted in Stone, *Life of Brant*, 2: 390–91.

105. Jan. 14, 1795, to McKee, *Simcoe Papers*, 3: 258.

106. *Diary of David Zeisberger*, ed. by Bliss, 2: 373–74.

107. R. G. England, Sept. 16, 1794, to Simcoe, *Simcoe Papers*, 3: 95.

108. Brant, Sept. 28, 1794, to England, *ibid.*, pp. 106–07.

109. William Mayne, journal on expedition to Detroit, etc., Sept. 26, 30, Oct. 1, 1794, *ibid.*, pp. 74, 76.

110. *Ibid.*, Oct. 2–9, 1794, pp. 76–78.

111. *Ibid.*, Oct. 10–13, 1794, p. 78; council, Oct. 11–14, 1794, State Papers, Upper Canada, Q281, pt. 1: 207–16; Simcoe, reply to Indians, Oct. 13, 1794, *Simcoe Papers*, 3: 122–25; Simcoe, Oct. 24, 1794, to Duke of Portland, no. 5, *ibid.*, p. 147; Simcoe, Oct. 24, 1794, to Dorchester, *ibid.*, p. 149.

112. Mayne, journal, Oct. 15–17, 1794, *Simcoe Papers*, 3: 78.

113. Wm. Johnson Chew, Oct. 24, 1794, to Joseph Chew, extract, "Indian Affairs," *Michigan Historical Collections*, 20: 380; Agushua and others, Oct. 27, 1794, to Brant, Brant MSS., 20F74.

114. Simcoe, Oct. 24, 1794, to Portland, no. 5, *Simcoe Papers*, 3: 148.

115. Capt. O'Beale [Cornplanter], Oct. 25, 1794, to Brant, *ibid.*, p. 154; Wm. Johns[t]on, report, Oct. 25–26, 1794, State Papers, Lower Canada, Q71, pt. 1: 113–26—this man, an interpreter in the British Indian department, though often called Johnson, was one of the Johnston family who served under Sir William Johnson for many years before the Revolution.

116. Brant, Nov. 5, 1794, to Pickering, Pickering Papers, 60: 214–[215A?].

117. Chapin, Feb. 9, 1795, to Pickering, *ibid.*, 62: 213.

118. Dec. 30, 1794, to Pickering, quoted in Myers, "Some Tracings . . . of the Tories . . . in America," note 37, in *Orderly Book of Sir John Johnson*, ed. by Stone, p. 199.

119. Nov. 20, 1794, to Brant, O'Reilly Papers, 10, no. 89.

120. Agushua and others, Oct. 27, 1794, to Brant, Brant MSS., 20F74.

121. Sally Ainse, Jan. 26, 1795, to Ottawas, *Simcoe Papers*, 3: 274; Ainse, Feb. 5, 1795, to Brant, *ibid.*, pp. 287–88; Brant, Feb. 24, 1795, to Joseph Chew, "Indian Affairs," *Michigan Historical Collections*, 20: 395–96; Brant, Mar. 17, 1795, to Chew, *ibid.*, pp. 396–97; E. B. Littlehales, Mar. 29, 1795, to Francis Le Maistre, *ibid.*, pp. 397–99; Brant, Mar. 5, 1795, to Chew, Military Papers "Indian," C248: 44–45.

122. Dec. 30, 1794, quoted in Myers, "Some Tracings . . . of the Tories . . . in America," note 37, in *Orderly Book of Sir John Johnson*, ed. by Stone, pp. 197–200.

123. *Ibid.*, p. 197.

124. Chapin, Feb. 9, 1795, to Pickering, Pickering Papers, 62: 213.

125. *Ibid.*, p. 212.

126. Feb. 9, 1795, *ibid.*, pp. 210–11.

127. *Simcoe Papers*, 3: 287–88.

128. Brant, Mar. 17, 1795, to Joseph Chew, "Indian Affairs," *Michigan Historical Collections,* 20: 396–97; Brant, June 28, 1795, to Butler, "Papers on Indians and Military Posts, 1762–1799," *ibid.,* 12: 173.

129. Brant, June 28, 1795, to Butler, "Papers on Indians and Military Posts, 1762–1799," *ibid.,* 12: 173; Brant, July 23, 1795, to Butler, "Indian Affairs," *ibid.,* 20: 408–09; Elliott, July 13, 1795, to McKee, extract, *Simcoe Papers,* 4: 44.

130. Elliott, July 13, 1795, to McKee, extract, *Simcoe Papers,* 4: 44.

131. *Diary of David Zeisberger,* ed. by Bliss, Aug. 16, 1795, vol. 2: 415–16. See also *ibid.,* Nov. 2, 1794, pp. 380–81 and June 15, 1795, pp. 409–10.

132. Jan. 19, 1796, to Joseph Chew, "Indian Affairs," *Michigan Historical Collections,* 20: 434.

133. *Ibid.*

134. *Travels through . . . North America . . . 1795 . . . 1797,* p. 408.

135. Joseph Chew, Oct. 17, 1796, to McKee, private, *The Correspondence of the Honourable Peter Russell with Allied Documents relating to His Administration of the Government of Upper Canada during the Official Term of Lieut.-Governor J. G. Simcoe while on Leave of Absence,* ed. by Brig.-Gen. E. A. Cruikshank and A. F. Hunter, 3 vols. (Toronto, 1932–36), 1: 70–71.

136. July 3, 1794, to Dundas, no. 26, State Papers, Upper Canada, Q280, pt. 1: 201–05.

CHAPTER 24—BRANT'S TOWN

1. Original Simcoe sketch in Ontario Archives. See *Valley of Six Nations,* Plate III, for a reproduction, and compare with various maps in this same work which show the church in relation to the river. The large house with the flag is obviously south of the church. Mrs. Simcoe made another sketch on birch bark which was presented to George III, this second sketch being in the British Museum. See reproduction, in Edwin C. Guillet, *Pioneer Travel in Upper Canada* (Canadian University Paperbooks Edition, 1969), facing p. 120. The two sketches are slightly different. The whereabouts of Pilkington's original, or originals, is unknown.

2. Diary of the brethren John Heckewelder and Benjamin Mortimer, on their journey from Bethlehem in Pennsylvania to Fairfield in Upper Canada, from the 30th April to the 22d May 1798, May 18, 1798, MS. at Moravian Archives.

3. *A Primer for the Use of the Mohawk Children,* London, 1786.

4. James Green, June 27, 1799, to Sir John Johnson, *Russell Correspondence,* 3: 250; Johnson, Oct. 14, 1799, to Green, "Indian Affairs," *Michigan Historical Collections,* 20: 668.

5. *Valley of Six Nations,* quoting SPG Journal, July 2, 1788, pp. 236–37.

6. "The Rev. Robert Addison: Extracts from the Reports and (Manuscript) Journals of the Society for the Propagation of the Gospel in Foreign Parts," ed. by Prof. A. H. Young, *Ontario Historical Society Papers and Records* 19 (1922): 175.

7. *Valley of Six Nations,* quoting SPG Journal, Oct. 10, 1793, p. 238.

8. Stone, *Life of Brant,* 2: 287.

9. *Valley of Six Nations,* quoting SPG Journal, Aug. 27, 1795, p. 238.

10. Ann Powell, Journal, 1789, quoted in Severance, *Studies of Niagara Frontier,* p. 233.

11. Clipping of paper read before Minnesota Historical Society, Jan. 1883, *The* (St. Paul) *Pioneer Press,* Jan. 3, 1883, Brant MSS., 11F78.

12. Campbell, *Travels in America in 1791–92*, pp. 185–204, 209–11.

13. Joseph and Jacob are always mentioned together as being about the same age. Jacob had blue eyes, according to William Allen, the historian, who owned a portrait of him many years ago. Allen, Mar. 22, 1851, to Draper, Brant MSS., 1F17.

14. Draper, copy of obituary in *Brantford Courier*, Feb. 2, 1867, *ibid.*, 13F38.

15. Stone, *Life of Brant*, 2: 501. Portrait, *ibid.*, facing p. 500.

16. Both mentioned in Brant's will, but there is no hint as to their ages.

17. She was spoken of as a "girl" and a "young lady" in 1819.

18. Portrait in John Ross Robertson Collection, Metropolitan Toronto Library.

19. Information about Christina and Aaron comes from Draper, Sept. 24–26, 1879, interview with Mrs. Charlotte Smith, granddaughter of Joseph Brant, Brant MSS., 13F20; Draper, Sept. 28, 1879, interview with Mrs. Lydia Martin, granddaughter of Capt. Isaac Hill, *ibid.*, 13F33; Oliver Phelps, Oct. 11, 1793, to Pickering, Pickering Papers, 59: 25; Campbell, *Travels in America in 1791–92*, pp. 193–94; Lieut. Francis Hall, *Travels in Canada, and the United States, in 1816 and 1817* (London, 1818), p. 223.

20. For information about Isaac see Brant-Sero, "Some Descendants of Joseph Brant," *Ontario Historical Society Papers and Records* 1 (1899): 113; Draper, Sept. 29, 1879, interview with Mrs. Mary Sickles, granddaughter of Isaac Brant, Brant MSS., 13F41; Stone, *Life of Brant*, 2: 464–65; R. J. England, Aug. 18, 1793, to McKee, "Papers on Indians and Military Posts, 1762–1799," *Michigan Historical Collections*, 12: 76; Elliott, June 5, 1793, to McKee, *ibid.*, p. 55; England, June 10, 1793, to McKee, Records of Supt. General's Office, RG10: 8; Strachan, "Life of Capt. Brant," *Christian Recorder*, June 1819; Peter Russell, April 5, 1795, to Simcoe, *Simcoe Papers*, 3: 342; W. J. Chew, April 11, 1795, to Joseph Chew, *ibid.*, p. 344; Butler, April 8, 1795, to Joseph Chew, extract, Military Papers "Indian," C248: 35; Simcoe, July 9, 1795, to Dorchester, *Simcoe Papers*, 4: 38; Wm. Dummer Powell, Jan. 3, 1787 [should be 1797], memorandum to Russell, State Papers, Upper Canada, Q283: 94–96; Diary of Heckewelder and Mortimer, on journey from Bethlehem, Pa., to Fairfield, May 18, 1798.

21. Joseph Chew, Nov. 25, 1791, to Brant, Brant MSS., 20F64; Simcoe, Mar. 10, 1792, to Dundas, *Simcoe Papers*, 1: 119; Simcoe, Dec. 6, 1793, to Dorchester, *ibid.*, 2: 115; Simcoe, July 9, 1795, to Dorchester, *ibid.*, 4: 38; Gordon, Oct. 3, 1793, to Brant, Brant MSS., 20F71.

22. James Green, June 27, 1799, to Sir John Johnson, *Russell Correspondence*, 3: 250.

23. Portland, Mar. 3, 1796, to Simcoe, no. 11, *Simcoe Papers*, 4: 207; Simcoe, June 20, 1796, to Portland, no. 42, *ibid.*, p. 311.

24. Charlotte Smith, Nov. 23, 1877, to Draper, Brant MSS., 14F63.

25. Littlehales, "Journal to Detroit from Niagara in 1793," excerpts copied from *Canadian Literary Magazine*, May 1833, *ibid.*, 11F137.

26. The following is merely a small sampling of the evidence regarding Brant and the number and quality of his "presents." Simcoe, April 1, 1793, to Clarke, *Simcoe Papers*, 1: 309; Butler, Dec. 30, 1795, requisition for Capt. Brant, Claus Papers, 7: 129; James Green, June 27, 1799, to Sir John Johnson, *Russell Correspondence*, 3: 250–51; Simcoe, Jan. 30, 1795, to Dorchester, no. 38, *Simcoe Papers*, 3: 278–79.

27. Aug. 14, 1789, to Haldimand, Haldimand Papers, B77: 230; Sir John Johnson, Aug. 21, 1795, to Nepean, State Papers, Lower Canada, Q74, pt. 2: 397.

28. If the Account Book of trader, Jean Baptiste Rousseau, at the Ontario Archives, Toronto, is a criterion.

29. Diary of Heckewelder and Mortimer, from Bethlehem, Pa., to Fairfield, May 18, 1798.

30. Brant, July 4, 1805, to ———, Brant MSS., 21F26.

31. Brant, May 28, 1797, to Peter Russell, State Papers, Upper Canada, Q283: 168; Maj. David Shank, June 3, 1797, to Capt. Green, Military Papers "Indian," C250: 529–30; Edward Walsh, narrative of Canada of 1804, MG19, F10, no. 18, Public Archives of Canada; Brant, May 11, 1807, to William Hatton, Frank Yeigh Papers, Ontario Archives.

32. Stone, *Life of Brant*, 2: 444–45; *Upper Canada Gazette*, May 12, 1798, copied by Draper, Brant MSS., 13F83–84; Sir John Johnson, June 3, 1799, to Gen. Robert Prescott, State Papers, Lower Canada, Q82: 322; Walsh, narrative of Canada of 1804, MG19, F10, no. 18; Brant, June 28, 1804, abstract of disbursements for 6 Nations, State Papers, Upper Canada, Q301: 126; Draper, Oct. 10, 1879, interview with Mrs. Margaret Ball, Brant MSS., 13F104.

33. Simcoe, May 7, 1792, to Phineas Bond, *Simcoe Papers*, 1: 153; Brant, Mar. 26, 1793, to Chapin, O'Reilly Papers, 9, no. 26; Brant, April 21, 1793, to Chapin, *ibid.*, no. 30.

34. Stone, *Life of Brant*, 2: 445–49.

35. Brant, Oct. 14, 1798, to Russell, Brant MSS., 20F101.

36. Brant, Nov. 9, 1795, to Israel Chapin, Jr., O'Reilly Papers, 11, no. 49.

37. Rousseau Collection, no. 10, Ontario Archives.

38. Catherine Hamilton, Feb. 25, 1795, to John Askin, Sr., *Askin Papers*, 1: 541.

39. Joseph Willard, July 20, 1789, to Brant, quoted in Stone, *Life of Brant*, 2: 288; Brant, Mar. 8, 1791, to Kirkland, Pickering Papers, 61: 207.

40. Weld, *Travels*, p. 408; Stone, *Life of Brant*, 2: 489.

41. April 19, 1783, to Richard M'Causland, quoted in Stone, *Life of Brant*, 2: 479–80.

42. Miller Papers, no. 1.

43. The Rev. John M. Mason, Secretary, June 16, 1801, to Brant, quoted in Stone, *Life of Brant*, 2: 439–40.

44. *American Museum* 6 (Sept. 1789): 226–27; Stone, *Life of Brant*, 2: 481.

45. Weld, *Travels*, p. 409; Diary of Heckewelder and Mortimer, from Bethlehem, Pa., to Fairfield, May 18, 1798; Wm. C. Bryant, Oct. 11, 1877, interview with chief John S. Johnson, Brant MSS., 15F19.

46. Reminiscences of Wm. Hencher, 2nd., quoted in O. Turner, *History of the Pioneer Settlement of Phelps & Gorham's Purchase, and Morris' Reserve* (Rochester, 1852), p. 413.

47. M. R. Hulce, narrative, [some years before July 8, 1878], Brant MSS., 17F71.

48. Vote of thanks, June 5, 1789, quoted in Stone, *Life of Brant*, 2, Appendix no. 6, pp. xi–xii.

49. Robertson, *History of Freemasonry in Canada*, 1: 690–93.

50. Documentation here would be almost endless. Some examples are: Brant, Sept. 23, 1789, to Mathews, State Papers, Canada, Q43, pt. 2: 784; Russell, Sept. 28, 1798, to Brant, *Russell Correspondence*, 2: 271; Brant, Feb. 14, 1799, to Sir John Johnson, Brant MSS., 20F105.

51. Mar. 9, 1795, to Dorchester, *Documents Relating to the Constitutional History of Canada, 1791–1818*, ed. by Doughty and McArthur, p. 181.

52. For example: Johnson, July 6, 1797, to William Claus, Claus Papers, 8: 3–4, 6.

53. Dec. 11, 1799, to Claus, *ibid.*, p. 113.

54. April 1, 1793, to Clarke, *Simcoe Papers*, 1: 309.

55. Brant, Nov. 8, 1790, to Johnson, State Papers, Canada, Q50, pt. 1: 59; Brant, Aug. 14, 1791, speech to Dorchester, *ibid.*, Q52: 270; Aupaumut, Narrative of journey to Niagara & Grand River in February 1792, Pickering Papers, 59: 19; Brant, Feb. 25, 1793, to McKee, Claus Papers, 5: 81; Joseph Chew, May 5, 1796, to Coffin, Military Papers "Indian," C249: 81; Brant, Sept. 30, 1801, to Gov. Clinton, Brant MSS., 15F221; Brant, Mar. 11, 1802, to Clinton, *ibid.*, 15F223.

56. Brant, Feb. 25, 1793, to McKee, Claus Papers, 5: 81; Dorchester, May 20, 1790, to Johnson, State Papers, Canada, Q46, pt. 2: 432–33; Johnson, May 24, 1790, to Dorchester, *ibid.*, p. 435; Dorchester, May 31, 1790, to Johnson, *ibid.*, p. 441.

57. Alexander McDonell, Nov. 28, 1808, to Lord Selkirk, *Valley of Six Nations*, p. 176.

58. Joseph Chew, Sept. 19, 1796, to Capt. James Green, Military Papers "Indian," C249: 340; Chew, April 10, 1797, to Green, *ibid.*, C250: 478.

59. Diary of congregation at Fairfield in Upper Canada, from 31 May to 13 Aug. 1798, June 11, Box 161, F5, MS. at Moravian Archives.

60. Andrew Jones, Mar. 15, 1879, to Draper, Brant MSS., 4F127. See also O. Follett, July 20, 1875, to Draper, *ibid.*, 12F55.

61. Brant, n.d., speech to Gen. Peter Hunter, *ibid.*, 21F77.

62. E. B. Littlehales, Oct. 18, 1795, to D. W. Smith, *Simcoe Papers*, 5: 151; Simcoe, May 10, 1795, to McKee, *ibid.*, p. 141; Dorchester, Jan. 24, 1796, to Simcoe, *ibid.*, 4: 180.

63. Simcoe, Oct. 9, 1795, to Dorchester, no. 70, *ibid.*, 4: 101–02.

64. Simcoe, May 10, 1795, to McKee, *ibid.*, 5: 141.

65. M. Elliott and W. J. Chew, Sept. 12, 1796, agreement with Missisaugas, Military Papers "Indian," C249: 418; D. W. Smith, Aug. 3, 1797, description of land for Capt. Brant, *Russell Correspondence*, 1: 240–41; Abstract of title to Brant Farm, from Register, County of Halton, Ontario, quoted in Holden, *Brant Family*, pp. 20–21.

66. Littlehales, Feb. 6, 1796, to Brant, *Simcoe Papers*, 4: 191.

67. Jelles Fonda, Ledger no. 10, July 27, 1789–July 9, 1792, pp. 264–65, MS. at New York State Historical Association, Cooperstown, N.Y.; Brant and Canajoharie Indians, July 27, 1789, account with Jelles Fonda, Simon Gratz Collection, Historical Society of Pennsylvania; Brant, for Canajoharies, Aug. 14, 1789, to Fonda, Single Acquisition, New York State Library; Fonda, June 16, 1790, to Brant, Miscellaneous MSS., New-York Historical Society.

68. Fonda, June 16, 1790, to Brant, Miscellaneous MSS., New-York Historical Society.

69. Fort Hunter Mohawks, July 9, 1789, deed to state of New York, Single Acquisition, no. 13269, New York State Library.

70. *American State Papers, Indian Affairs*, 1: 636.

71. April 22, 1795, O'Reilly Papers, 11, no. 13.

72. Stone, *Life of Brant*, 2: 416. Another version says Cornplanter told the story and that Brant laughed heartily.

73. Brant, July 30, 1797, to Thomas Morris, Brant MSS., 12F39; Robt. Morris, Aug. 1, 1797, to Thomas Morris and Charles Williamson, O'Reilly Papers, 15, no. 51; Chapin, Sept. 16, 1797, to Jas. McHenry, *ibid.*, no. 71; Brant, Oct. 3, 1797, to Thomas Morris, Edward E. Ayer Collection.

74. July 11, 1796, to Chapin, O'Reilly Papers, 12, no. 22.

75. Thomas Morris, May 29, 1797, to Robert Morris, *ibid.*, 15, no. 46.

76. Brant, Jan. 19, 1796, to Chapin, *ibid.*, 12, no. 3.

77. May 17, 1796, to Chapin, *ibid.*, no. 13.

78. Moses Cleaveland, Samuel Mather, Jr., and Henry Champion, Jan. 29, 1798, to Chapin, *ibid.*, 13, no. 2; Brant, Jan. 11, 1799, to Phelps, Brant MSS., 11F103; Brant, Mar. 15, 1796, to Chapin, *ibid.*, 12F27; Brant, April 3, 1796, to Capt. D. W. Smith, *Russell Correspondence*, 1: 2; A. Jones, Jan. 12, 1801, to John Askin, *Askin Papers*, 2: 325.

79. Brant, Jan. 11, 1799, to Chapin, O'Reilly Papers, 13, no. 36; Brant, Jan. 22, 1800, to Phelps, Brant MSS., 11F105; Brant, Dec. 27, 1800, to Phelps, *ibid.*, 12F51; Cleaveland, July 22, 1801, to Chapin, O'Reilly Papers, 14, no. 11; Brant, Feb. 20, 1802, to Phelps, Ontario County, N.Y., Historical Society; Brant, Aug. 17, 1802, to Phelps, Brant MSS., 12F52; Brant, Mar. 21, 1803, to Phelps, *ibid.*, 12F53; Brant, July 5, 1803, to Phelps, *ibid.*, 12F54; Brant, Nov. 28, 1804, to Chapin, O'Reilly Papers, 14, no. 44.

80. Diary of Heckewelder and Mortimer, from Bethlehem, Pa., to Fairfield, May 18, 1798.

81. Brant, Aug. 1, 1792, to Joseph Chew, extract, State Papers, Lower Canada, Q61, pt. 1: 168.

82. Extract of a letter from Chemung, July 16, 1787, to a man in Baltimore, *The Pennsylvania Gazette*, Aug. 29, 1787.

83. For details of the Sally Ainse controversy, see note 1, *Simcoe Papers*, 4: 356; Littlehales, Nov. 3, 1793, to D. W. Smith, Acting Surveyor General, *ibid.*, pp. 356–57; Brant, June 28, 1795, to Butler, "Papers on Indians and Military Posts, 1762–1799," *Michigan Historical Collections*, 12: 173; J. White, Dec. 28, 1795, to Simcoe, *Simcoe Papers*, 4: 166–67; Littlehales, Feb. 15, 1796, to Smith, *ibid.*, p. 196; note 1, *ibid.*; Brant, for Five Nations, April 3, 1796, to Simcoe, Brant MSS., 12F30; Brant, April 3, 1796, to Smith, *Russell Correspondence*, 1: 2; Littlehales, April 8, 1796, to Brant, *Simcoe Papers*, 4: 238; Joseph Chew, Sept. 26, 1796, to McKee, Claus Papers, 7: 310–11; Brant, Nov. 24, 1796, speech to William Claus, with marginal note, State Papers, Upper Canada, Q283: 82; Minutes of Executive Council, Aug. 12, 1797, *Russell Correspondence*, 1: 245–46; Minutes of Executive Council, April 9, 1798, *ibid.*, 2: 137; Louis Goulet, "Phases of the Sally Ainse Dispute," *Papers and Addresses of the Kent Historical Society* 5 (1921): 92–95.

84. Letter to a friend in New York, *American Museum* 6 (Sept. 1789): 227.

85. For details about the Phelps affair see Stone, *Life of Brant*, 2: 436; *ibid.*, pp. 433–34; Brant, Dec. 15, 1797, to Sir John Johnson, *Valley of Six Nations*, pp. 238–39; Bishop of Quebec, Jan. 11, 1798, to Johnson, Brant MSS., 20F77; Bishop of Quebec, Jan. 11, 1798, to President Russell, State Papers, Upper Canada, Q284: 181–82; Russell, Feb. 22, 1798, to Bishop of Quebec, confidential, *ibid.*, pp. 183–85; Brant, May 8, 1798, to Russell, extract, *ibid.*, pp. 187–88; Russell, May 14, 1798, to Brant, *ibid.*, pp. 189–90; Bishop of Quebec, June 12, 1798, to Russell, private, no. 4, *Russell Correspondence*, 2: 180–81; Portland, Jan. 24, 1799, to Russell, State Papers, Upper Canada, Q286, pt. 1: 2; Brant, [late 1799], to Chief Justice, quoted in Stone, *Life of Brant*, 2: 434–35; "Rev. Robert Addison," ed. by Young, *Ontario Historical Society Papers and Records* 19 (1922): 178, with note *; Chapin, July 1800, to Bishop of New York, Brant MSS., 21F4; Brant, May 7, 1800, to Aaron Burr, quoted in Matthew L. Davis, *Memoirs of Aaron Burr, with Miscellaneous Selections from His Correspondence*, 2 vols. (New York, 1836–37), from Reprint Series: *The Era of the American Revolution*, ed. by Leonard W. Levy (New York, 1971), pp. 164–66; Stone, *Life of Brant*, 2: 438–39.

86. Speech, Feb. 10, 1794, State Papers, Lower Canada, Q67: 116–17.

87. Jan. 30, 1795, to Dorchester, no. 38, *Simcoe Papers*, 3: 278.

88. July 28, 1795, to Capt. James Green, *ibid.*, 4: 51–52.

89. Claus, Aug. 30, 1765, to Sir Wm. Johnson, extract, *Johnson Papers*, 11: 918–19. The Caughnawagas set great store by the idea of the dish with one spoon. Apparently their Canadian claims had the same origin. Council, Aug. 13, 1796, "Indian Affairs," *Michigan Historical Collections*, 20: 464–66.

90. Clinton, Dec. 1, 1799, to Brant, quoted in Stone, *Life of Brant*, 2, Appendix no. 11, p. xxxii. Clinton remembered the Caughnawagas' first visit as somewhat earlier than it actually was.

91. Joseph Chew, April 15, 1795, to Thomas Aston Coffin, *Simcoe Papers*, 3: 345.

92. Council, Sept. 28, 30–Oct. 2, 1795, Military Papers "Indian," C248: 367–76. See also Clinton, Dec. 1, 1799, to Brant, quoted in Stone, *Life of Brant*, 2, Appendix no. 11, pp. xxxi–xxxii.

93. Brant, April 5, 1798, to ———, "Indian Affairs," *Michigan Historical Collections*, 20: 599.

94. The treaty and all the negotiations are in *American State Papers, Indian Affairs*, 1: 616–20.

95. Sept. 4, 1799, to George Clinton, Dreer Collection of Letters of Officers serving in America before the Revolution, MS. at Historical Society of Pennsylvania; Brant, Nov. 22, 1796, to Chapin, Jr., O'Reilly Papers, 12, no. 44.

96. Sept. 4, 1799, to Clinton, Dreer Collection.

97. Aug. 31, 1798, to Chapin, O'Reilly Papers, 13, no. 25.

98. John Johnson, July 4, 1798, to Wm. Claus, Claus Papers, 8: 67–68; council, Aug. 26, 1798, *Russell Correspondence*, 2: 263–64.

99. Brant, April 5, 1798, to ———, "Indian Affairs," *Michigan Historical Collections*, 20: 599–600; Brant, May 14, 1798, to Wm. Claus, *Russell Correspondence*, 2: 152.

100. Brant, June 7, 1798, to Chapin, O'Reilly Papers, 13, no. 10; Brant, Jan. 11, 1799, to Chapin, *ibid.*, no. 36; Brant, April 4, 1799, to Morris, quoted in Stone, *Life of Brant*, 2: 412–13; John Jay, June 18, 1798, to Chapin, O'Reilly Papers, 13, no. 11; Clinton, Dec. 1, 1799, to Brant, quoted in Stone, *Life of Brant*, 2, Appendix no. 11, pp. xxxi–xxxii.

101. Peter Russell, Mar. 21, 1798, to Gen. Prescott, no. 49, *Russell Correspondence*, 2: 124; Brant, May 14, 1798, to Wm. Claus, *ibid.*, p. 152; Prescott, June 7, 1798, to Russell, no. 35, *ibid.*, p. 166.

102. Council, July 5–10, 1799, "Indian Affairs," *Michigan Historical Collections*, 20: 643–48.

103. Jay, June 18, 1798, to Chapin, O'Reilly Papers, 13, no. 11.

CHAPTER 25—THIS LAND IS OURS

1. Kirkland, Journal, June 25, 1789, p. 10, Kirkland MSS.

2. A return of Grand River Indians who received presents, Oct. 26, 1795, lists 1,445 in all, of whom 266 are Mohawks. Military Papers "Indian," C248: 355. This represents a loss of 398 in the general population and 182 among the Mohawks in ten years. All contemporary estimates also record a loss of Grand River population, and

the tenor of Brant's correspondence shows he was painfully aware of what was going on.

3. Speech, 1795, to Simcoe, Brant MSS., 21F66; letter, Jan. 19, 1796, to Joseph Chew, "Indian Affairs," *Michigan Historical Collections*, 20: 434–35; also Mar. 21, 1803, to Oliver Phelps, Brant MSS., 12F53.

4. Every speech and letter of Brant that concerned Grand River lands mentioned, from the early 1790s on, some or all of these hard facts.

5. Aug. 18, 19, and 22, 1793, to McKee, *Simcoe Papers*, 5: 69–70.

6. Mar. 5, 1795, to Joseph Chew, Military Papers "Indian," C248: 46; Littlehales, Mar. 29, 1795, to Francis Le Maistre, "Indian Affairs," *Michigan Historical Collections*, 20: 397–98.

7. April 15, 1790, State Papers, Canada, Q46, pt. 2: 438–39.

8. Minutes of Nassau District land board, Feb. 1, 1791, extract, *Valley of Six Nations*, pp. 56–57.

9. Introduction, *ibid.*, pp. xxxix–xl; *ibid.*, p. 57, note 33.

10. According to law, the crown, when making a purchase from Indians, had to get a survey at the same time to which the Indians agreed. Haldimand, April 26, 1784, to Lieut. Gov. Hay, "Haldimand Papers," *Michigan Historical Collections*, 11: 409–10. Haldimand may have thought the law did not apply when the purchase was made of Indians for the use of other Indians.

11. Brant, n.d., speech to Gen. Peter Hunter, Brant MSS., 21F77; council, July 4, 1819, *Valley of Six Nations*, pp. 66–67; Lord Bathurst, Sept. 28, 1821, to Six Nations, *ibid.*, pp. 68–69; Introduction, *ibid.*, pp. xxxix–xl.

12. He must have broken his silence to John Norton. Norton for Six Nations, June 26, 1805, to Privy Council, State Papers, Upper Canada, Q299: 330.

13. See chapter 17, note 59.

14. Indian Records, Series Two, 15: 108.

15. April 15, 1790, State Papers, Canada, Q46, pt. 2: 438.

16. Mar. 24, 1791, to Johnson, *ibid.*, Q50, pt. 1: 155.

17. Brant, n.d., speech to Hunter, Brant MSS., 21F77; Brant, Dec. 10, 1797, to Capt. Green, Military Papers "Indian," C250: 384.

18. Simcoe, Dec. 6, 1793, to Dorchester, *Simcoe Papers*, 2: 114.

19. Sept. 3, 1791, quoted in Stone, *Life of Brant*, 2: 337; Joseph Chew, Nov. 25, 1791, to Brant, Brant MSS., 20F64.

20. Simcoe, Sept. 20, 1793, to Dundas, no. 18, *Simcoe Papers*, 2: 58–59; Simcoe, Dec. 6, 1793, to Dorchester, *ibid.*, p. 116.

21. Council, July 28, 1806, *Valley of Six Nations*, p. 105.

22. Dec. 6, 1793, to Dorchester, *Simcoe Papers*, 2: 114.

23. *Ibid.*, pp. 115–16.

24. *Ibid.*, p. 115.

25. *Diary of Mrs. Simcoe*, Dec. 9, 1792, p. 141.

26. Brant, Dec. 26, 1792, to Butler, Brant MSS., 20F67.

27. Wabakanyne and others, Dec. 7, 1792, deed to king, Indian Affairs Records, Eastern Treaty 3, RG10, Public Archives of Canada.

28. *Valley of Six Nations*, pp. 73–74.

29. Sept. 20, 1793, to Dundas, no. 18, *Simcoe Papers*, 2: 59.

30. Simcoe, Dec. 6, 1793, to Dorchester, *ibid.*, p. 115.

31. Feb. 25, 1793, Claus Papers, 5: 81–82.

32. Mar. 3, 1794, to Dorchester, *Simcoe Papers*, 2: 174.

33. *Ibid.*

34. Simcoe, Jan. 13, 1794, to Dorchester, *ibid.*, p. 131; *Diary of Mrs. Simcoe*, Mar. 5, 1794, p. 216; Brant, Feb. 24, 1795, to Joseph Chew, "Indian Affairs," *Michigan Historical Collections*, 20: 396; Brant, Mar. 5, 1795, to Chew, Military Papers "Indian," C248: 45–46; Simcoe, Mar. 15, 1795, to Dorchester, no. 48, *Simcoe Papers*, 3: 325–26; Chew, Mar. 26, 1795, to Thomas Aston Coffin, Military Papers "Indian," C248: 49.

35. *Valley of Six Nations*, pp. 147–48.

36. Peter Russell, April 5, 1795, to Simcoe, *Simcoe Papers*, 3: 342.

37. June 28, 1795, to Butler, "Papers on Indians and Military Posts, 1762–1799," *Michigan Historical Collections*, 12: 173; Oct. 10, 1800, to Dorchester, Military Papers "Indian," C253: 229; speech, Oct. 28, 1800, Brant MSS., 21F7.

38. Brant, n.d., speech to Hunter, Brant MSS., 21F77; Brant, Nov. 24, 1796, speech for Five Nations, State Papers, Lower Canada, Q78: 172; Brant, Dec. 10, 1797, to Capt. Green, Military Papers "Indian," C250: 384.

39. Oct. 24, 1796, to Russell, State Papers, Upper Canada, Q283: 40; June 27 [probably 26], 1797, to Russell, *ibid.*, p. 176; speech, Oct. 28, 1800, Brant MSS., 21F7.

40. Wm. J. Chew, Nov. 26, 1795, to Joseph Chew, extract, Military Papers "Indian," C248: 404.

41. Chapin, June 13, 1795, to Pickering, O'Reilly Papers, 11, no. 26.

42. Littlehales, Aug. 17, 1795, to Brant, *Simcoe Papers*, 4: 67; council, Aug. 29, 1795, *ibid.*, pp. 87–88; Simcoe, Oct. 9, 1795, to Dorchester, no. 70, *ibid.*, p. 101.

43. Brant, Jan. 19, 1796, to Joseph Chew, "Indian Affairs," *Michigan Historical Collections*, 20: 434.

44. Nov. 23, 1795, *ibid.*, pp. 428–29.

45. Norton, Journal, etc., 2: 735–36; Draper, Aug. [probably Oct.] 1, 1879, interview with Allen Cleghorn, Brant MSS., 13F59–60; Wm. C. Bryant, Dec. 14, 1877, to Draper, *ibid.*, 15F23; Draper, Sept. 24–26, 1879, interview with Mrs. Charlotte Smith, granddaughter of Joseph Brant, *ibid.*, 13F20–21; Weld, *Travels*, pp. 408–09.

46. Dec. 22, 1795, to Dorchester, no. 80, *Simcoe Papers*, 4: 164.

47. Jan. 29, 1796, to Joseph Chew, extract, "Papers on Indians and Military Posts, 1762–1799," *Michigan Historical Collections*, 12: 195.

48. Stone, *Life of Brant*, 2: 463, 465–67.

49. *Ibid.*, p. 466; Draper, Aug. [probably Oct.] 1, 1879, interview with Allen Cleghorn, Brant MSS., 13F60.

50. Norton, Journal, etc., 2: 736.

51. Nov. 9, 1795, O'Reilly Papers, 11, no. 49.

52. Strachan, "Life of Capt. Brant," *Christian Recorder*, June 1819.

53. Stone, *Life of Brant*, 2: 467; Council minutes, July 6, 1798, State Papers, Upper Canada, Q290, pt. 2: 558.

54. Stone, *Life of Brant*, 2: 466, 463.

55. J. Sewell, Att. Gen., Jan. 25, 1796, to Dorchester, *Simcoe Papers*, 4: 184; Simcoe, Mar. 2, 1796, to Brant, *ibid.*, p. 206; Brant for Five Nations, April 3, 1796, to Simcoe, Brant MSS., 12F29–30; Brant, n.d., speech to Hunter, *ibid.*, 21F77; Simcoe, 1796, proposed deed to Six Nations, Military Papers "Indian," C249: 87–88; Wm. J. Chew, April 29, 1796, to Joseph Chew, extract, *ibid.*, pp. 83–84; Joseph Chew, May 5, 1796, to Coffin, *ibid.*, p. 81; John White, Att. Gen., Sept. 26, 1796, to Russell, State Papers, Upper Canada, Q283: 18–20; Joseph Chew, Sept. 26, 1796, to McKee, Claus Papers, 7: 309–10.

56. W. J. Chew, May 14, 1796, to Joseph Chew, "Indian Affairs," *Michigan Historical Collections*, 20: 443.

57. For Five Nations, April 3, 1796, Brant MSS., 12F29.

58. May 26, 1796, to Simcoe, no. 52, *Simcoe Papers*, 4: 277.

59. Russell, Oct. 23, 1796, to Brant, State Papers, Upper Canada, Q283: 38–39; Brant, Dec. 10, 1797, to Sir John Johnson, *Valley of Six Nations*, p. 94; Wm. Dummer Powell, Nov. 1, 1797, statement about Missisauga lands purchased for 6 Nations, State Papers, Upper Canada, Q284: 71.

60. Brant, May 17, 1796, to Joseph Chew, "Indian Affairs," *Michigan Historical Collections*, 20: 447; Brant, May 26, 1796, to Maj. Macdonell, *Simcoe Papers*, 4: 278; Brant, June 6, 1796, to Littlehales, *ibid.*, pp. 292–93.

61. Brant, May 17, 1796, to Israel Chapin, Jr., O'Reilly Papers, 12, no. 13.

62. Thomas Welch, June 6–Aug. 12, 1796, survey diary, *Valley of Six Nations*, pp. 120–25; Brant, July 26, 1796, to Capt. David Smith, *Russell Correspondence*, 1: 17.

63. E. B. Littlehales, extracts from Dorchester, Feb. 1796, to Simcoe, Brant MSS., 20F81; Dorchester, Feb. 15, 1796, to Joseph Chew, extract, State Papers, Upper Canada, Q283: 37.

64. Simcoe, Feb. 28, 1796, to Dorchester, no. 80, *Simcoe Papers*, 4: 204.

65. Brant for Six Nations, May 16, 1796, *ibid.*, pp. 265–66.

66. Hereafter "Niagara" refers to Newark or British Niagara unless otherwise stated.

67. May 17, 1796, to Joseph Chew, "Indian Affairs," *Michigan Historical Collections*, 20: 448.

68. Council, Sept. 9, 1796, Military Papers "Indian," C249: 373; Russell, Sept. 28, 1796, to Simcoe, *Russell Correspondence*, 1: 49–50; Russell, Dec. 31, 1796, to Simcoe, no. 4, *ibid.*, p. 117; Russell, June 30, 1797, to Prescott, no. 18, *ibid.*, pp. 202–03.

69. Brant, Mar. 25, 1798, to Claus, Military Papers "Indian," C251: 113.

70. Russell, Aug. 29, 1796, to Prescott, no. 4, *Russell Correspondence*, 1: 33; Russell, April 18, 1797, to Prescott, *ibid.*, pp. 164–65; Prescott, May 11, 1797, to Russell, no. 7, *ibid.*, p. 174.

71. Russell, Nov. 15, 1796, to Littlehales, *ibid.*, p. 85.

72. Russell, Sept. 22, 1796, to Simcoe, State Papers, Upper Canada, Q282, pt. 2: 583–85; Russell, Sept. 28, 1796, to Portland, *ibid.*, Q283: 12–14.

73. *Ibid.*, Q283: 38–39.

74. *Ibid.*, pp. 40–41.

75. *Ibid.*, pp. 42–43.

76. Nov. 14, 1796, to Portland, *ibid.*, p. 30.

77. Mar. 4, 1791, to Sir John Johnson, extract, State Papers, Canada, Q50, pt. 1: 123.

78. Wm. Dummer Powell, Nov. 1, 1797, statement, *ibid.*, Upper Canada, Q284: 69–70. One result of Joseph's brief association with De Berczy was two more portraits of him, for De Berczy often painted professionally and is accounted good for the time and place. One portrait, supposed to have been painted at York in 1792 (obviously an error, for York was not founded in 1792 and De Berczy did not come to Canada till 1794), shows the head and shoulders only, with scalp lock, military coat, and dark scarf. The second portrait, probably done in 1794 and far more interesting, is full length. Joseph stands on the banks of the Grand River, dressed in Indian clothing, with his gun and dog. He points, perhaps toward Brant's Town, with his right hand.

The dog looks well-cared for. The first portrait is in the archives of the Seminary of Quebec; the second, in the National Gallery of Canada. The second is reproduced in color for the frontispiece of *Valley of the Six Nations*.

79. Joseph's sales are public matters, and the name of Chapin is *never* listed among the purchasers. Joseph, however, did encourage Chapin to buy a tract from Stedman. Letters, Nov. 22, 1796, to Chapin, O'Reilly Papers, 15, no. 43; and June 16, 1797, *ibid.*, 12, no. 55. Obviously Brant had changed his mind regarding American settlers on Canadian land since 1791. It does not appear that Chapin ever took advantage of Stedman's offers.

80. State Papers, Upper Canada, Q283: 44–49.

81. Brant, Nov. 13, 1796, to Russell, Brant MSS., 20F82; Russell, Nov. 14, 1796, to Portland, State Papers, Upper Canada, Q283: 29–31.

82. Speech for Five Nations, Nov. 24, 1796, State Papers, Lower Canada, Q78: 180–81. Brant's slightly different personal copy, Brant MSS., 12F33, is dated as of Oct. 22.

83. Jan. 28, 1797, State Papers, Upper Canada, Q283: 57–71.

84. Jan. 30, 1797, no. 6, *Russell Correspondence*, 1: 136–37.

85. Marginal notes and explanation, Jan. 30, 1797, State Papers, Upper Canada, Q283: 72–84.

86. Rob. Liston, Nov. 28, 1796, to Prescott, no. 2, confidential, *Russell Correspondence*, 1: 99; Russell, Jan. 30, 1797, to Simcoe, no. 6, *ibid.*, p. 137.

87. Johnson, Dec. 30, 1796, to Brant, Brant MSS., 20F84.

88. Brant, Nov. 22, 1796, to Chapin, Jr., O'Reilly Papers, 15, no. 43.

89. Russell, Jan. 30, 1797, to Simcoe, no. 6, *Russell Correspondence*, 1: 136.

90. Chapin, Jr., Feb. 6, 1797, to Jas. McHenry, O'Reilly Papers, 15, no. 8.

91. *Ibid.*; Chapin, Jr., June 29, 1797, to McHenry, *ibid.*, no. 45.

92. Brant, Mar. 9, 1797, to Oliver Phelps, Brant MSS., 11F102.

93. Rob. Liston, Mar. 28, 1797, to Capt. Green, "Papers on Indians and Military Posts, 1762–1799," *Michigan Historical Collections*, 12: 260; Liston, April 8, 1797, to Prescott, State Papers, Upper Canada, Q283: 187.

94. April 8, 1797, to Prescott, State Papers, Upper Canada, Q283: 187.

95. *Ibid.*, p. 188; Mar. 28, 1797, to Green, "Papers on Indians and Military Posts, 1762–1799," *Michigan Historical Collections*, 12: 260.

96. Liston, July 31, 1797, to Prescott, secret and confidential, State Papers, Lower Canada, Q79, pt. 1: 208–09; Liston, July 19, 1797, to Grenville, *ibid.*, Upper Canada, Q283: 335–36.

97. Aug. 31, 1797, *ibid.*, Lower Canada, Q79, pt. 1: 211.

98. Liston, Mar. 28, 1797, to Green, "Papers on Indians and Military Posts, 1762–1799," *Michigan Historical Collections*, 12: 260; Liston, April 8, 1797, to Prescott, State Papers, Upper Canada, Q283: 187–88.

99. *Ibid.*, [both]. See also Maj. David Shank, May 27, 1797, to Green, Military Papers "Indian," C250: 518, and Portland, June 7, 1798, to Russell, most secret, State Papers, Upper Canada, Q284: 126.

100. Stone, *Life of Brant*, 2: 454.

101. *Ibid.*, p. 455. Burr remembered Talleyrand as among those present—an impossibility, since the latter was then in France.

102. Feb. 28, 1797, to Theodosia Burr, quoted in Stone, *Life of Brant*, 2: 455–56; Feb. 28, 1797, to Natalie Delage, Brant MSS., 12F35.

103. McHenry, June 8, 1797, to Chapin, Jr., secret and confidential, O'Reilly Papers, 12, no. 54.

104. Charles Coleman Sellers, *Portraits and Miniatures by Charles Willson Peale* (Philadelphia, 1952), p. 41.

105. At Portrait Gallery, Independence National Historical Park, Philadelphia. This picture has called forth much philosophical comment in the course of the years, for it has always seemed to demand an explanation.

CHAPTER 26—TRIUMPH!

1. A. Burr, Feb. 28, 1797, to Natalie Delage, Brant MSS., 12F35; Brant, Mar. 9, 1797, to Oliver Phelps, *ibid.*, 11F102.

2. Brant, July 2, 1797, to Chapin, Jr., O'Reilly Papers, 12, no. 57.

3. Jeromus Johnson, Dec. 1, 1837, to Stone, quoted in Stone, *Life of Brant*, 2, Appendix no. 16, p. xliv.

4. *Ibid.*, pp. 453, 457.

5. Johnson, Dec. 1, 1837, to Stone, quoted *ibid.*, Appendix no. 16, pp. xliv–xlv.

6. Quoted *ibid.*, p. 457.

7. Dr. Richard M'Causland, "Particulars relative to the Nature and Customs of the Indians of North-America," *The European Magazine and London Review* 9 (1786): 399.

8. From Stone's conversations with Burr. Stone, *Life of Brant*, 2: 456–57.

9. Brant, Mar. 9, 1797, to Phelps, Brant MSS., 11F102.

10. Catharine E. Van Cortlandt, "An Original Portrait of Joseph Brant," *The American Historical Record* 2, no. 19 (July 1873): 319.

11. Mar. 9, 1797, Brant MSS., 11F102.

12. From conversations of Stone with Gansevoort's son. Stone, *Life of Brant*, 2: 460.

13. Brant, Mar. 9, 1797, to Phelps, Brant MSS., 11F102; Brant, July 2, 1797, to Chapin, Jr., O'Reilly Papers, 12, no. 57.

14. From conversation with man who made loan. Stone, *Life of Brant*, 2: 458.

15. According to a man who was present. *Ibid.*, p. 459. See also Brant, July 2, 1797, to Chapin, Jr., O'Reilly Papers, 12, no. 57.

16. Chapin, June 29, 1797, to McHenry, O'Reilly Papers, 15, no. 45.

17. July 2, 1797, *ibid.*, 12, no. 57.

18. Brant MSS., 12F38.

19. Thomas Welch, Deputy Surveyor, June 12, 1797, to D. W. Smith, Acting Surveyor General, extract, State Papers, Upper Canada, Q283: 201.

20. June 8, 1797, secret and confidential, O'Reilly Papers, 12, no. 54.

21. June 29, 1797, *ibid.*, 15, no. 45.

22. June 16, 1797, *ibid.*, 12, no. 55.

23. Liston, April 8, 1797, to Prescott, State Papers, Upper Canada, Q283: 187–88; Russell, May 30, 1797, to Prescott, no. 15, *Russell Correspondence*, 1: 180–81.

24. Extract, Military Papers "Indian," C250: 528.

25. June 23, 1797, to Sir John Johnson, *Russell Correspondence*, 1: 194. See also Geo. Ironside, May 9, 1797, to Prideaux Selby, *ibid.*, p. 172; and Elliott, June 23, 1797, to Russell, *ibid.*, p. 213.

26. May 30, 1797, to Prescott, no. 15, *ibid.*, p. 180.

27. June 10, 1797, to Brant, State Papers, Upper Canada, Q283: 169–70.

28. June 18, 1797, to D. W. Smith, *Russell Correspondence*, 1: 189.

29. June 19, 1797, State Papers, Upper Canada, Q283: 171–72.

30. *Ibid.*, pp. 173–74.

31. June 23, 1797, to D. W. Smith, *Russell Correspondence*, 1: 195.

32. Brant, June 27 [should be 26], 1797, to Russell, State Papers, Upper Canada, Q283: 175–76; Russell, June 26, 1797, to Brant, *ibid.*, pp. 177–78.

33. Minutes of Executive Council, June 29, 1797, *ibid.*, pp. 190–94.

34. Russell, July 3, 1797, to Brant, *ibid.*, p. 179; Brant, July 10, 1797, to Russell, *ibid.*, pp. 180–81; Brant, July 10, 1797, to Smith, *ibid.*, pp. 181–82.

35. Mar. 10, 1797, to Russell, *ibid.*, pp. 51–52.

36. Russell, July 21, 1797, to Portland, *ibid.*, p. 156; Russell, Sept. 13, 1797, to Simcoe, no. 9, *Russell Correspondence*, 1: 279.

37. Minutes of Executive Council, July 16, 1797, State Papers, Upper Canada, Q283: 196–99.

38. July 15, 1797, to Brant, private, *ibid.*, pp. 184–85.

39. July 21, 1797, *ibid.*, pp. 153–64.

40. Powell, Nov. 1, 1797, statement, *ibid.*, Q284: 72.

41. Council, July 24–26, 1797, *ibid.*, Q283: 221–32, 234.

42. Russell, July 29, 1797, to Portland, *ibid.*, pp. 219–20; Russell, July 30, 1797, to Prescott, no. 22, *Russell Correspondence*, 1: 230.

43. Brant MSS., 12F39.

44. Jones did some writing for Brant on Aug. 28. Jones, survey diary, *Valley of Six Nations*, p. 126.

45. Jones, survey diary, Aug. 7–14, 26, Sept. 1, 1797, *ibid.*, pp. 125–26.

46. Examples: letters, Oct. 17, 1796, and Oct. 4, 1797, to D. W. Smith, *Russell Correspondence*, 1: 71 and 294.

47. Brant, July 22, 1797, statement, State Papers, Upper Canada, Q283: 200; Brant, May 21, 1798, to Smith, *Russell Correspondence*, 2: 155.

48. Brant, July 22, 1797, statement, State Papers, Upper Canada, Q283: 200; Brant, June 9, 1802, declaration, D. W. Smith Collection.

49. Weld, *Travels*, p. 407.

50. Brant, Agt., Oct. 4, 1797, lease to A. Jones, Samuel Street Papers, Ontario Archives.

51. Norton, Journal, etc., 2: 736–37.

52. *Valley of Six Nations*, quoting SPG Journal, Oct. 9, 1797, p. 89.

53. Aug. 31, 1797, to Liston, State Papers, Lower Canada, Q79, pt. 1: 211.

54. Sept. 27, 1797, to Brant, Brant MSS., 12F40; Oct. 3, 1797, to Russell, no. 2, *Russell Correspondence*, 1: 293; April 3, 1798, to Brant, *ibid.*, 2: 171; April 4, 1798, to Grenville, *ibid.*, p. 168.

55. Sept. 11, 1797, to Russell, secret and confidential, State Papers, Upper Canada, Q283: 135–36; Nov. 4, 1797, to Russell, *ibid.*, pp. 260–62.

56. Powell, statement, Nov. 1, 1797, *ibid.*, Q284: 69, 73–75; Brant, Oct. 14, 1798, to Russell, Brant MSS., 20F101.

57. To Capt. Green, "Indian Affairs," *Michigan Historical Collections*, 20: 529.

58. Some . . . Remarks relating to the Indian Department to be submitted to . . . the Commander in Chief, *ibid.*, p. 574.

59. Isabel Thompson, "The Blount Conspiracy," *The East Tennessee Historical Society's Publications*, no. 2 (1930): 19–20.

60. Council, n.d., Brant MSS., 21F68.

61. Oct. 4, 1797, to Russell, State Papers, Upper Canada, Q283: 293.

62. Dec. 15, 1797, to Russell, Brant MSS., 20F93; Russell, Dec. 19, 1797, to Brant, *Russell Correspondence*, 2: 89.

63. Brant, Dec. 15, 1797, to Russell, Brant MSS., 20F93.
64. *Ibid.*
65. Russell, Oct. 4, 1797, to Brant, State Papers, Upper Canada, Q283: 295.
66. Dec. 15, 1797, to Smith, *Russell Correspondence,* 2: 42.
67. *Ibid.;* Russell, Dec. 31, 1797, to Claus, extract, *ibid.,* p. 90; Brant, Dec. 15, 1797, to Russell, Brant MSS., 20F93; Brant, Feb. 26, 1798, to Russell, *ibid.,* 20F94.
68. Liston, Sept. 27, 1797, to Brant, Brant MSS., 12F40.
69. Dec. 10, 1797, *Valley of Six Nations,* pp. 93–94.
70. Dec. 10, 1797, to Green, Military Papers "Indian," C250: 382–84.
71. Dec. 29, 1797, *Russell Correspondence,* 2: 170–71.
72. Feb. 19, 1798, to Prescott, no. 46, *ibid.,* p. 85.
73. Brant, Feb. 26, 1798, to Russell, Brant MSS., 20F94; Brant, Feb. 27, 1798, to Smith, *Russell Correspondence,* 2: 104–05; Brant, Dec. 10, 1797, to Sir John Johnson, *Valley of Six Nations,* p. 94; Brant, Oct. 14, 1798, to Russell, Brant MSS., 20F101.
74. Minutes of Executive Council, State Papers, Upper Canada, Q284: 81–87.
75. Minutes of Executive Council, June 25, 1798, *Russell Correspondence,* 2: 193.
76. *Valley of Six Nations,* note 1, p. 127.
77. Russell, Jan. 31, 1799, to Hugh Hood Farmer, *Russell Correspondence,* 3: 71.
78. Journal, etc., 2: 737.
79. Brant, July 22, 1797, statement, State Papers, Upper Canada, Q283: 200.
80. J. Elmsley, Feb. 18, 1798, to Smith, *Russell Correspondence,* 2: 84.

CHAPTER 27—TOO GREAT A MAN

1. Norton, Journal, etc., 2: 738; Strachan, "Life of Capt. Brant," *Christian Recorder,* June 1819; Claus, Feb. 9, 1800, to Brant, Brant MSS., 21F1; Brant, Mar. 10, 1800, to I. [?] Selby, *ibid.,* 21F2; Brant, June 30, 1800, to Sir John Johnson, quoted in Stone, *Life of Brant,* 2: 441–42; *Lord Selkirk's Diary, 1803–1804,* ed. by Patrick C. T. White (Toronto, 1958), Nov. 20, 1803, p. 161.
2. Brant, July 14, 1798, to Capt. Robert Nelles, Nelles Papers.
3. All we know is that Brant's "house" accidentally burned. James Green, June 27, 1799, to Sir John Johnson, *Russell Correspondence,* 3: 250–51. It could not have been the Grand River house that burned, as he continued to live there throughout 1799.
4. *Ibid.* See also Estimate of cost of nails, hinges, locks, window glass & putty required for Capt. Brant, July 1, 1799, Military Papers "Indian," C252: 139.
5. Brant, Mar. 9, 1800, to Robert Nelles, Nelles Papers; Robert Knox, May 26, 1800, to Nelles, *ibid.*
6. Brant, Aug. 24, 1802, to John Clement, *ibid.;* Brant, Oct. 10, 1803, to Nelles, *ibid.*
7. Rousseau, Account Book, Nov. 3, 1799; Mar, 8, July 26, 1800; Jan. 15, Mar. 31 [?], Nov. 19, 1801; July 15, 1802; April 29, 1804.
8. Deed to Robert Wilson, Miscellaneous MSS., New-York Historical Society.
9. Journal, etc., 2: 738.
10. From "Sketches Made in Upper Canada, 1803–6," originals in William L. Clements Library, Ann Arbor, Mich.
11. D. W. Smith, Aug. 3, 1797, description of land to be purchased for Brant,

Russell Correspondence, 1: 240–41; Plan of a certain Tract . . . formerly called Captain Brant's . . . . By Adrian Marlet, Prov. Dy. Surveyor, in Holden, *The Brant Family,* facing p. 20; *Diary of Mrs. Simcoe,* June 11, 1795, pp. 320–24, including note and Mrs. Simcoe's picture of King's Head Inn; Elma E. Gray and Leslie Robb Gray, *Wilderness Christians* (Ithaca, N.Y., 1956), p. 250.

12. James Buchanan, *Sketches of the History, Manners, and Customs, of the North American Indians,* 2 vols. (New York, 1824), 1: 33.

13. Russell, Feb. 2, 1803, to Henry Hood Farmer, *Russell Correspondence,* 3: 301–02.

14. Buchanan, *Sketches of North American Indians,* 1: 33, 36.

15. Stone, *Life of Brant,* 2: 467.

16. *Ibid.,* pp. 451–52.

17. Brant, April 21, 1803, contract to Manuel Overfield, Claus Papers, 9: 131; council, Mar. 10, 1809, *ibid.,* pp. 271–72.

18. Brant, Feb. 9, 1801, to the Rev. Samuel Miller, quoted in Stone, *Life of Brant,* 2: 441.

19. Rousseau, Account Book, Dec. 22, 1800; Nov. 19, 1801; July 4, Aug. 10, and Dec. 21, 1803.

20. Brant, Abstract of disbursements for 6 Nations, June 28, 1804, State Papers, Upper Canada, Q301: 125–27.

21. Claus, June 17, 1799, to Russell, *Russell Correspondence,* 3: 236.

22. *Upper Canada Gazette,* Jan. 26, 1799, copy by Draper, Brant MSS., 13F84–85.

23. John Chew, July 15, 1799, to Green, Military Papers "Indian," C252: 174.

24. Claus, Feb. 20, 1800, to Chief Justice John Elmsley, State Papers, Upper Canada, Q290, pt. 1: 206–07.

25. Council, May 2 [22?], 1802, Brant MSS., 21F16.

26. Brant, Jan. 22, 1799, to Simcoe, State Papers, Canada, Q57, pt. 2: 474.

27. Russell, Feb. 1, 1799, to Prescott, no. 75, *Russell Correspondence,* 3: 82–83.

28. *Ibid.* See also Russell, Feb. 1, 1799, to Sir John Johnson, Russell Papers, Ontario Archives.

29. Jan. 22, 1799, State Papers, Canada, Q57, pt. 2: 475–76.

30. Feb. 14, 1799, Brant MSS., 20F105.

31. Johnson, Dec. 13, 1799, to Brant, *ibid.,* 20F115.

32. Russell, June 25, 1797, to Lieut. James Givens, *Russell Correspondence,* 1: 231–32; Simcoe, Sept. 7, 1797, to John King, secret & confidential, C.O. 42, 22: 312–13; Russell, Mar, 21, 1798, to Portland, no. 28, State Papers, Upper Canada, Q284: 143–46.

33. Wabanip [Wabaniss], May 17, 1798, speech to Maj. Shank, *Russell Correspondence,* 2: 187–88.

34. Wabaniss, head chief of Missisaugas, April 30, 1798 (signed May 2), speech to Brant, Brant MSS., 20F96.

35. May 8, 1798, extract, *Russell Correspondence,* 2: 187.

36. July 29, 1798, *ibid.,* p. 234.

37. Mar. 21, 1798, to Portland, no. 28, State Papers, Upper Canada, Q284: 145.

38. April 5, 1798, to Claus, Military Papers "Indian," C251: 108.

39. July 24, 1798, to Givens, *Russell Correspondence,* 2: 233.

40. Council, Sept. 18, 1798, Brant MSS., 20F100; Russell, Sept. 20, 1798, to Prescott, no. 64, *Russell Correspondence,* 2: 261.

41. Russell, Sept. 28, 1798, to Givens, most secret, *Russell Correspondence*, 2: 271–72; Russell, Oct. 12, 1798, to Prescott, no. 66, *ibid.*, pp. 278–79.

42. Dec. 15, 1798, Brant MSS., 20F103.

43. A. Jones, Jan. 28, 1799, to D. W. Smith, *Russell Correspondence*, 3: 68–69.

44. Brant, Feb. 14, 1799, to Sir John Johnson, Brant MSS., 20F105.

45. Dec 30, 1794, to Pickering, quoted in Myers, "Some Tracings . . . of the Tories . . . in America," note 37, *Orderly Book of Sir John Johnson*, ed. by Stone, p. 200.

46. Brant, April 10, 1799, to Russell, State Papers, Upper Canada, Q286, pt. 1: 107–08; Russell, May 26, 1799, to Prescott, *ibid.*, pp. 141, 143.

47. Minutes of Executive Council, Feb 27–28, 1799, *ibid.*, Q288: 232–33.

48. Brant, May 10, 1799, to Sir John Johnson, *ibid.*, Q286, pt. 1: 139.

49. Russell, May 26, 1799, to Prescott, *ibid.*, pp. 141–44; Prescott, June 13, 1799, to Russell, no. 52, *Russell Correspondence*, 3: 232; Minutes of Executive Council, June 11, 1799, *ibid.*, pp. 226–27.

50. Russell, June 22, 1799, to Prescott, confidential, State Papers, Upper Canada, Q286, pt. 1: 185; Russell, June 22, 1799, to Portland, *ibid.*, p. 175.

51. May 26, 1799, to Portland, *ibid.*, p. 135; and May 26–June 11, 1799, to Count Joseph de Puisaye, *ibid.*, pp. 187–88.

52. June 11, 1799, to Russell, *ibid.*, p. 183.

53. Oct 4, 1799, to Lieut. Gen. Peter Hunter, *ibid.*, pp. 228–29.

54. June 11, 1799, to Russell, *ibid.*, p. 182.

55. May 26–June 11, 1799, *ibid.*, pp. 187–89.

56. Lieut. Gov. Francis Gore, Oct 1, 1806, to Hon. William Windham, *ibid.*, Q305: 46. See also Janet Carnochan, "The Count De Puisaye," *Ontario Historical Society Papers and Records* 5 (1904): 36–52.

57. Dec. 6, 1798, to Prescott, State Papers, Lower Canada, Q81, pt. 2: 518–19.

58. Peter Hunter, Mar. 8, 1800, to Portland, *ibid.*, Upper Canada, Q287, pt. 1: 111–12.

59. Nov. 1801, to Johnson, quoted in Stone, *Life of Brant*, 2: 408.

60. Chippewas, May 21, 1800, deed to Nicholas Boyer and children, Claus Papers, 8:121; Hannah Jarvis, July 9, 1803, to Brant, Brant MSS., 21F21.

61. Lillian F. Gates, *Land Policies of Upper Canada, Canadian Studies in History and Government, No. 9* (Canada, 1968), p. 50.

62. Brant, Sept. 20, 1800, to D. W. Smith, D. W. Smith Collection, B7: 259.

63. *Ibid.*, pp. 259–60.

64. Stone, *Life of Brant*, 2: 468–69; Brant, Oct. 3, 1800, to James Wheelock, quoted *ibid.*, p. 469.

65. *Ibid.*, p. 470; Jas. Wheelock, Oct. 25, 1800, agreement with John Wheelock, Dartmouth College MSS.; John Wheelock, Feb. 25, 1811, to the Rev. Jedidiah Morse, *ibid.*

66. Stone, *Life of Brant*, 2: 470; M'Clure and Parish, *Memoirs of Wheelock*, p. 97; Benjamin Sumner, Oct 24, 1800, to John Wheelock, Dartmouth College MSS.; John Wheelock, May 1, 1801, to William, Earl of Dartmouth, *ibid.*

67. Sumner, Oct. 24, 1800, to John Wheelock, Dartmouth College MSS.

68. For details about the schooling of Joseph, Jr., and Jacob in New Hampshire see Brant, Feb. 9, 1801, to John Wheelock, *ibid.*; Brant, July 23, 1801, to John Wheelock, *ibid.*; John Wheelock, July 10, 1802, to the Rev. Peter Thacher, *ibid.*; John Wheelock, Feb. 25, 1811, to the Rev. Jedidiah Morse, *ibid.*; Brant, Feb. 9, 1801, to James Wheelock, quoted in Stone, *Life of Brant*, 2: 471–72; James Wheelock,

May 1, 1801, to Brant, quoted *ibid.*, p. 472; John Wheelock, May 6, 1801, to Brant, quoted *ibid.*, p. 473; James Wheelock, Sept. 19, 1801, to Brant, quoted *ibid.*, pp. 474–75; James Wheelock, April 19, 1802, to Brant, quoted *ibid.*, p. 477; Brant, Dec. 17, 1802, to James Wheelock, quoted *ibid.*, p. 478; Brant, July 23, 1801, to James Wheelock, Simon Gratz Collection; Joseph Brant, Jr., Jan. 15, 1802, to John Wheelock, *ibid.*; Brant, Mar. 10, 1802, to James Wheelock, Miscellaneous MSS., New-York Historical Society; Rousseau, Account Book, May 4, 1803.

69. Stone, *Life of Brant*, 2: 478.

70. Kirkland, journal, Feb. 26, 1800, quoted in *Valley of Six Nations*, p. 242; Anthony F. C. Wallace, *The Death and Rebirth of the Seneca* (New York, 1970), p. 207.

71. Jean H. Waldie, "Indians Gave Six Nations Land," quoting and paraphrasing speech of the Rev. Peter Jones, Nov. 1850, *Brantford Expositor*, Nov. 23, 1956. See also Wallace, *Death and Rebirth of Seneca*, p. 207. There are many accounts of the white dog festival: among the earlier, William W. Campbell, *Annals of Tryon County*, pp. 178–79; *ibid.*, Appendix K, pp. 75–76; and Seaver, *Life of Mary Jemison*, pp. 224–28.

72. Kirkland, journal, Feb. 26, 1800, quoted in *Valley of Six Nations*, p. 242; Wallace, *Death and Rebirth of Seneca*, p. 207.

73. Edward Walsh, narrative of Canada of 1804, "Indians," MG19, F10, no. 18 [?], Public Archives of Canada. The practice continued in varying forms. As late as 1826 the Onondagas, Senecas, and Cayugas were sacrificing a dog at the time of planting corn. The Rev. John West, *A Journal of a Mission to the Indians of the British Provinces of New Brunswick and Nova Scotia, and the Mohawks on the Ouse or Grand River, Upper Canada*, extract quoted in *Valley of Six Nations*, p. 255.

74. *The* (Toronto) *Weekly Globe*, Jan. 19, 1877, Brant Miscellanies (3 vols.), 2G105, State Historical Society of Wisconsin; microfilm at Princeton University.

CHAPTER 28—THE LAST WAR

1. Liston, Oct. 3, 1797, to Russell, no. 2, *Russell Correspondence*, 1: 293.

2. Oct. 10, 1800, to Dorchester, Military Papers "Indian," C253: 228.

3. May 21, 1798, to Smith, *Russell Correspondence*, 2: 155.

4. *Wentworth Bygones*, Publications of Head-of-the-Lake Historical Society, 1960, no. 2: 39; Rousseau, bond, June 20, 1798, to Brant, Rousseau Collection, no. 33, Ontario Archives.

5. See chapter 26, note 48, and the account of the final settlement of Feb. 5, 1798.

6. Diary of Br. & Sr. Zeisberger and Br. Benjm. Mortimer, on their journey from Fairfield in Upper Canada, to Schonbrun on the river Muskingum, Aug. 28, 1798, B171, Folder 1, MS. at Moravian Archives; Stuart, Oct. 11, 1798, to S P G, *Valley of Six Nations*, p. 66.

7. Sept. 11, 1798, Brant MSS., 20F99.

8. Sept. 28, 1798, *Russell Correspondence*, 2: 271.

9. Alexander McDonell, Nov. 28, 1808, to Lord Selkirk, *Valley of Six Nations*, p. 177.

10. June 15, 1798, State Papers, Upper Canada, Q284: 159.

11. Russell, Sept. 28, 1798, to Brant, *Russell Correspondence*, 2: 270.

12. Russell, Oct. 12, 1798, to Prescott, no. 66, *ibid.*, pp. 278–79.

13. Russell, Oct. 13, 1798, to McKee, *ibid.*, pp. 280–81.

14. Russell, Oct. 12, 1798, to Prescott, no. 66, *ibid.*, p. 279.

15. Dec. 15, 1798, Brant MSS., 20F103.

16. *Ibid.* See also Russell, Oct. 15, 1798, to Simcoe, C.O. 42, 22: 319; Russell, Nov. 2, 1798, to Prescott, State Papers, Upper Canada, Q286, pt. 1: 36.

17. Dec. 23, 1798, *Russell Correspondence,* 3: 41–42.

18. N.d., Brant MSS., 21F57.

19. Jan. 27, 1799, *Russell Correspondence,* 3: 69.

20. April 10, 1799, to Russell, State Papers, Upper Canada, Q286, pt. 1: 105–07.

21. Mar. 5, 1799, to Portland, *ibid.,* Lower Canada, Q82: 240.

22. April 25, 1799, *ibid.,* Upper Canada, Q286, pt. 1: 94.

23. May 29, 1799, to Col. Edward Willey, *Russell Correspondence,* 3: 216.

24. Mar. 20, 1799, to Johnson, MG19, F6: 6, Public Archives of Canada.

25. Peter Hunter, Mar. 8, 1800, to Portland, State Papers, Upper Canada, Q287, pt. 1: 111.

26. Brant, Aug. 1799, speech to Hunter, Brant MSS., 21F77.

27. Nov. 18, 1799, Military Papers "Indian," C252: 351–52.

28. Dec. 5, 1799, to Green, *ibid.,* pp. 357–58.

29. Oct. 10, 1800, *ibid.,* C253: 228–30.

30. Extract of a Statement of the Province of Upper Canada Sent . . . to . . . Duke of Kent . . . in the Year 1800, in "Papers on War of 1812," *Michigan Historical Collections,* 15: 17.

31. Aug. 30, 1800, to John Askin, *Askin Papers,* 2: 311–12; Askin, Oct. 26, 1800, *ibid.,* p. 320.

32. Dec. 26, 1800, quoted in Stone, *Life of Brant,* 2: 405.

33. For a general discussion of the outcome of Joseph Brant's land sales see *Valley of Six Nations,* Introduction, pp. 1v–lxvi, and appended documents.

34. Feb. 11, 1799, to Liston, confidential, *Russell Correspondence,* 3: 103.

35. Brant, April 18, 1799, to Smith, D. W. Smith Collection, B7: 253–54; Brant, Sept. 19, 1800, to Smith, Brant MSS., 21F6; Smith, Dec. 7, 1800, to Brant, *ibid.,* 21F8; Brant, Dec. 22, 1800, to Smith, D. W. Smith Collection, B7: 275. Everything considered, Jarvis was more unlucky than irresponsible or dishonest. Joseph did not know this.

36. Brant, Feb. 10, 1801, to Smith, D. W. Smith Collection, B7: 291.

37. Smith, Feb. 18, 1801, to Brant, *ibid.,* pp. 293–94.

38. Brant, Sept. 20, 1800, to Smith, *ibid.,* pp. 260–61.

39. Nov. 1, 1800, *ibid.,* pp. 267–68.

40. Askin, April 17, 1801, to Brant, *Askin Papers,* 2: 333.

41. July 23, 1801, Brant MSS., 15F219.

42. Aug. 28, 1801, *ibid.,* 15F220.

43. Th. Jefferson, Sept. 18, 1801, to Secretary of State, Jefferson Papers, Coolidge Collection.

44. Brant, July 23, 1801, to John Wheelock, Dartmouth College MSS.; Brant, Oct. 22, 1801, to Jas. Wheelock, quoted in Stone, *Life of Brant,* 2: 475; N [?]. Le Favre, Nov. 12, 1801, to Brant, Brant MSS., 21F11.

45. Stone, *Life of Brant,* 2: 457.

46. A. Burr, Nov. 3, 1801, to Theodosia, *Correspondence of Aaron Burr and His Daughter Theodosia,* ed. by Mark Van Doren (New York, 1929), p. 69.

47. Claus, Sept. 3, 1801, to Capt. Thomas McKee, Claus Papers, 8: 173–74.

48. Claus, diary 12, Oct. 10–11, 1801, *ibid.*, 21, pt. 2: 6–7.

49. *Ibid.*, Oct. 12, 1801, pp. 8–9. See also Minutes of Executive Council, Sept. 30, 1801, and Oct. 20, 1801, State Papers, Upper Canada, Q295: 22, 26–27.

50. 1801, to Sir John Johnson, Brant MSS., 12F60.

51. Claus, Sept. 14, 1801, to Selby, Claus Papers, 8: 176.

52. Sept. 1, 1801, summarized and quoted in Stone, *Life of Brant*, 2: 405–06.

53. Sept. 10, 1801, Brant MSS., 12F61.

54. Nov. 1801, quoted in Stone, *Life of Brant*, 2: 407–08.

55. Letters, Nov. 24, 1801, Brant MSS., 21F3 and 21F2.

56. Feb. 11, 1799, to Liston, confidential, *Russell Correspondence*, 3: 103.

57. Dec. 18, 1801, to Claus, Claus Papers, 8: 185–86.

58. T. McKee and Chas. Lereaume, speech ascribed to Capt. Brant last spring [1801], Military Papers "Indian," C254: 18–19. For further details about the Makons affairs see James Green, Oct. 22, 1801, to Claus, Claus Papers, 8: 188; Claus, [late Dec. 1801], to Brant, *ibid.*, p. 187; Claus, Feb. 12, 1802, to Selby, *ibid.*, pp. 189–90; Brant, Mar. 8, 1802, to Mr. Schiefflin, Brant MSS., 12F66; Lieut. Col. S [?]. Smith, Mar. 16, 1802, to Green, Military Papers "Indian," C254: 17; Claus, July 22, 1804, to Selby, Claus Papers, 9: 40–41; T. McKee, Jan. 3, 1805, to Selby, *ibid.*, pp. 71–72; Claus, Feb. 1, 1805, to Selby, *ibid.*, pp. 76–77.

59. Gates, *Land Policies of Upper Canada*, pp. 32, 44–45. See also Asa Danforth, Feb. 17, 1801, to Timothy Green, Miscellaneous MSS., New-York Historical Society; and John Elmsley, Feb. 1, 1802, to Hunter, Elmsley Letter-Book, Elmsley Papers, Metropolitan Toronto Library.

60. Brant, Sept. 30, 1801, to Clinton, Brant MSS., 15F221; Brant, Mar. 11, 1802, to Clinton, *ibid.*, 15F223.

61. Brant, Feb. 16, 1802, to Clinton, *ibid.*, 15F222; Brant, Mar. 11, 1802, to Clinton, *ibid.*, 15F223.

62. Stone, *Life of Brant*, 2: 403–04.

63. *Ibid.*, p. 404.

64. April 13, 1802, Brant MSS., 12F67.

65. Aaron Hill, for Grand River chiefs, Feb. 6, 1802, to Sir John Johnson, extract quoted in Stone, *Life of Brant*, 2; Appendix no. 10, pp. xxx–xxxi.

66. Mar. 6, 1802, to Claus, Brant MSS., 12F62.

67. Council, Feb. 9, 1803, *ibid.*, 21F72.

68. Smith, July 19, 1802, to Brant, D. W. Smith Collection, B7: 327–28.

69. Military Papers "Indian," C254: 95.

70. Speech for Six Nations, Aug. 17, 1803, to Claus, State Papers, Upper Canada, Q301: 95.

71. Tekarihoga and 15 other chiefs, Feb. 9, 1803, speech, Brant MSS., 21F72; Norton, July 20, 1805, to Earl Camden, State Papers, Upper Canada, Q303: 127–28; Norton, Feb. 12, 1807, to Five Nations, Edward E. Ayer Collection.

72. Minutes of Executive Council, June 24, 1803, State Papers, Upper Canada, Q298, pt. 1: 97–106.

73. Council, Feb. 9, 1803, Brant MSS., 12F69; Peter Hogeboom, April 8, 1811, to Jones, *Valley of Six Nations*, pp. 151–52.

74. Council, Aug. 17, 1803, State Papers, Upper Canada, Q301: 90–91. See also Aaron Hill, Jr. [?], for the Chiefs, July 3, 1803, to Alexander Stewart, *ibid.*, pp. 83–84.

75. Mar. 6, 1802, to Smith, D. W. Smith Collection, B7: 309–10.

76. Council, Aug. 17, 1803, State Papers, Upper Canada, Q301: 91.

77. June 17, 1803, *Valley of Six Nations,* pp. 179–80.

78. Claus, Sept. 23, 1806, to Six Nations of Grand River, State Papers, Upper Canada, Q309, pt. 2: 440–41.

79. Oct. 6, 1802, to Russell, Brant MSS., 21F17.

80. Council, Aug. 17, 1803, State Papers, Upper Canada, Q301: 87–99.

81. Nov. 15, 1803, Brant MSS., 15F224.

82. *Lord Selkirk's Diary,* Nov. 20, 1803, pp. 148, 161. Other gossip had Joseph first getting paid by the buyers for undervaluing the blocks of land at four shillings an acre and then getting a one-seventh share in each block, for which the purchaser was to pay him the difference between the undervalue and the real value of six shillings three pence, a difference which amounted to thousands of pounds for the lining of Joseph's pockets. Francis Gore, Sept. 4, 1809, to Lord Castlereagh, *Valley of Six Nations,* pp. 112–13.

83. Norton, Feb. 12, 1807, to Five Nations, Edward E. Ayer Collection; Brant, Feb. 20, 1804, to Earl of Moira, State Papers, Upper Canada, Q299: 217; Moira, June 2, 1804, to Earl Camden, *ibid.,* p. 216; Norton, July 20, 1805, to Camden, *ibid.,* Q303: 126–30; Five Nations, Sept. 3, 1806, speech to Claus, Edward E. Ayer Collection.

84. *Lord Selkirk's Diary,* Feb. 26, 1804, p. 243.

85. Jan. 1, 1804, Brant MSS., 21F22.

86. Council, Feb. 8, 1804, Claus Papers, 9: 3–4.

87. Feb. 20, 1804, to Grand River chiefs, Brant MSS., 21F23.

88. Minutes of Executive Council, May 18, 1804, State Papers, Upper Canada, Q299: 155–63.

89. Council, June 29–30, 1804, *ibid.,* Q301: 121–36; Lt. Col. Isaac Brock, July 2, 1804, to Lt. Col. Green, Military Papers "Indian," C254: 195; Claus, July 4, 1804, to Chief Justice Allcock, State Papers, Upper Canada, Q301: 120–21; Beasley's account, June 28, 1804, *ibid.,* pp. 124–25; Brant's account, June 28, 1804, *ibid.,* pp. 125–27.

90. Claus, May 29, 1804, to Allcock, *Valley of Six Nations,* p. 160.

91. Diary 12, Oct. 1, 1804, Claus Papers, 21, pt. 2: 22.

92. *Lord Selkirk's Diary,* May 30, 1804, pp. 300, 303–04.

93. State Papers, Upper Canada, Q299: 53.

94. Alexander McDonell, Nov. 28, 1808, to Selkirk, *Valley of Six Nations,* p. 177.

95. Viscount Castlereagh, April 8, 1809, to Sir James Craig, *ibid.,* p. 280.

96. Speech to Six Nations, Sept. 23, 1806, State Papers, Upper Canada, Q309, pt. 2: 448–49.

97. Chiefs of Six Nations, Mar. 30, 1805, to Capt. Jasper Parrish, Brant MSS., 12F73; John Johnston, April 15, 1805, to Parrish, *ibid.,* 12F74; Capt. W. Leonard and three other American officers, Oct. 20, 1805, certificate, quoted in Stone, *Life of Brant,* 2, Appendix no. 13, p. xxxiv; Israel Chapin, Jr., Oct. 28, 1805, certificate, *ibid.,* Appendix no. 12, pp. xxxiii–xxxiv. See also *ibid.,* p. 415, and O. H. Marshall, Nov. 6, 1877, to Draper, Brant MSS., 12F72.

98. From Joseph's side: Norton, Nov. 26, 1805, to Robert Barclay, Edward E. Ayer Collection; Brant, 1805, to Duke of Northumberland, fragment, quoted in Stone, *Life of Brant,* 2: 417–18; Brant, [1805], to ———, fragment, Brant MSS., 12F75; Henry Tekarihoga, May 1, 1805, speech to chiefs, MG19, F10, no. 7, Public Archives of Canada; Five Nations, Sept. 3, 1806, speech to Claus, Edward E. Ayer Collection; council, July 28, 1806, *Valley of Six Nations,* pp. 106–07. From Claus's

side: Claus, Sept. 23, 1806, to Six Nations of Grand River, State Papers, Upper Canada, Q309, pt. 2: 447–50; Castlereagh, April 8, 1809, to Sir James Craig, *Valley of Six Nations*, p. 280.

99. Claus, July 22, 1804, to Selby, Claus Papers, 9: 40–41; T. McKee, Jan. 3, 1805, to Selby, *ibid.*, pp. 71–72; Claus, Feb. 1, 1805, to Selby, *ibid.*, pp. 76–77.

100. There is much documentary evidence relating to Norton's failure in England—for instance, Norton, Sept. 10, 1804, to Edward Cooke, State Papers, Upper Canada, Q299: 326–27; Hunter, Sept. 15, 1804, to Camden, *ibid.*, p. 142; Norton, Sept. 18, 1804, to Camden, *ibid.*, pp. 336–40; Smith, May 10, 1805, to Norton, extract, *ibid.*, Q303: 104; Norton, May 11, 1805, to Cooke, *ibid.*, pp. 95–97; Norton, May 28, 1805, to Cooke, *ibid.*, pp. 102–03; Norton, June 22, 1805, to Cooke, *ibid.*, pp. 113–15; Norton, June 26, 1805, to Camden, *ibid.*, p. 117; Norton, June 26, 1805, to Privy Council, *ibid.*, Q299: 329–35; Norton, July 16, 1805, to Cooke, *ibid.*, Q303: 120–21; Norton, July 20, 1805, to Camden, *ibid.*, pp. 125–30; Norton, July 23, 1805, to Castlereagh, *ibid.*, pp. 132–38; Sir Steph. Cottrell, July 24, 1805, to Cooke, *ibid.*, p. 139; Norton, Nov. 26, 1805, to Robert Barclay, Edward E. Ayer Collection; H. Allcock, Mar. 14, 1806, to Sir George Shee, State Papers, Upper Canada, Q305: 107–12; Allcock, Sept. 17, 1806, to Lieut. Gov. Gore, Claus Papers, 9: 148–50.

101. Capt. W. Leonard and others, Oct. 20, 1805, certificate, quoted in Stone, *Life of Brant*, 2, Appendix no. 13, p. xxxiv; Chapin, Jr., Oct. 28, 1805, certificate, *ibid.*, Appendix no. 12, pp. xxxiii–xxxiv.

102. May 3, 1805, to Dr. Edward Walsh, MG19, F10, no. 5, Public Archives of Canada.

103. Speech, May 1, 1805, to Chiefs and Sachems of Grand River, *ibid.*, no. 6; speech, n.d., to Claus, Brant MSS., 21F63; letter, [1805], to ———, fragment, *ibid.*, 12F75; speech, 1806, to Claus, quoted in Stone, *Life of Brant*, 2, Appendix no. 15, pp. xli–xliii; council, July 28, 1806, *Valley of Six Nations*, pp. 106–08.

104. May 17, 1796, to Israel Chapin, Jr., O'Reilly Papers, 12: no. 13.

105. See notes 60 and 61, above.

106. Henry Tekarihoga, May 1, 1805, speech at annual meeting, MG19, F10, no. 7, Public Archives of Canada; Claus, Sept. 23, 1806, speech to Six Nations of Grand River, State Papers, Upper Canada, Q309, pt. 2: 445–47.

107. Claus, Sept. 23, 1806, speech to Six Nations of Grand River, State Papers, Upper Canada, Q309, pt. 2: 449–50.

108. Brant made many leases after leasing was forbidden. For examples see Benaijah Mallory, Mar. 20, 1812, to Claus, *Valley of Six Nations*, pp. 115–16; William Renwick Riddell, *Upper Canada Sketches* (Toronto, 1922), pp. 81–84.

109. Council, July 28, 1806, *Valley of Six Nations*, pp. 107–08.

110. "The Probated Wills of Men Prominent in the Public Affairs of Early Upper Canada," ed. by A. F. Hunter, *Ontario Historical Society Papers and Records* 23 (Toronto, 1926): 341–44.

111. J. Chas. Dent, May 17, 1877, to Draper, Brant MSS., 1F102; Dent, May 28, 1877, to Draper, *ibid.*, 1F103.

112. Norton, Aug. 12, 1806, to the Rev. John Owen, Edward E. Ayer Collection.

113. Late 1805, fragment, quoted in Stone, *Life of Brant*, 2: 417–18.

114. Quoted *ibid.*, pp. 424–25.

115. May 5, 1806, to Brant, quoted *ibid.*, pp. 426–27.

116. Quoted *ibid.*, pp. 427–28.

117. *Records of Niagara in the days of Commodore Grant and Lieut.-Governor Gore,*

1805–1811, ed. by Brig. General E. A. Cruikshank, *Niagara Historical Society*, no. 42 (1931): 24–25.

118. Allcock, April 5, 1806, to Sir Geo. Shee, State Papers, Upper Canada, Q305: 126.

119. Minutes of Executive Council, Feb. 26 and April 14, 1807, *ibid.*, Q309, pt. 2: 410–18 and 472–73.

120. Brant and others, Nov. 9, 1806, to Gore, *ibid.*, p. 458.

121. Council, July 28, 1806, *Valley of Six Nations*, pp. 107–09.

122. Power of attorney, Feb. 18, 1805, to Joseph Brant, Claus Papers, 9: 93–95; Brant, June 26, 1807, to Duke of Northumberland, quoted in Stone, *Life of Brant*, 2: 429.

123. Letter, [1805], to ———, fragment, Brant MSS., 12F75.

124. Catharine E. Van Cortlandt, "An Original Portrait of Joseph Brant," *The American Historical Record* 2, no. 19 (July 1873): 318.

125. The Ames portrait of Brant is owned by the New York State Historical Association, Cooperstown, N.Y.

126. Receipt, New York State Historical Association.

127. Stone, *Life of Brant*, 1, Introduction, pp. xxviii–xxix.

128. *Ibid.*, 2: 428; Brant, Jan. 24, 1807, to Judge Thorpe, State Papers, Upper Canada, Q310: 48.

129. Minutes of Executive Council, July 9, 1806, *ibid.*, Q309, pt. 1: 220–21.

130. Speech, Sept. 23, 1806, to Six Nations of Grand River, *ibid.*, pt. 2: 437–54; Norton, Oct. 20, 1806, to Robert Barclay, Edward E. Ayer Collection.

131. Speech, 1806, to hostile Indians, quoted in Stone, *Life of Brant*, 2: 419.

132. Oct. 20, 1806, to Barclay, Edward E. Ayer Collection.

133. Brant and others, Nov. 9, 1806, to Gore, State Papers, Upper Canada, Q309, pt. 2: 454–65; Norton and others, Mar. 25, 1807, to Gore, *ibid.*, p. 467; Brant, April 14, 1807, to Gore, *ibid.*, pp. 468–70; Claus, [late April or May, 1807], to Indians, Claus Papers, 9: 145–46.

134. Alexander McDonell, Mar. 18, 1808, to Selkirk, *Valley of Six Nations*, p. 171; Brant, April 14, 1807, to Gore, State Papers, Upper Canada, Q309, pt. 2: 468–70; Brant, July 2, 1807, to Claus, *ibid.*, Q310: 263.

135. Robert Thorpe, Aug. 14, 1807, to ———, State Papers, Upper Canada, Q310: 259–60.

136. Sir John Johnson, Dec. 16, 1807, to Claus, Claus Papers, 9: 166.

137. Brant, Jan. 24, 1807, to Thorpe, State Papers, Upper Canada, Q310: 48–49.

138. Draper, Oct. 10, 1879, interview with Mrs. Margaret Ball, Brant MSS., 13F101.

139. June 26, 1807, quoted in Stone, *Life of Brant*, 2: 429.

140. Brant, July 2, 1807, to Claus, State Papers, Upper Canada, Q310: 262, 264–65.

141. Minutes of Executive Council, June 25, 1807, *ibid.*, Q309, pt. 2: 493–98.

142. Gore, Oct. 13, 1807, to Castlereagh, *ibid.*, Q310: 13–14.

CHAPTER 29—"HAVE PITY ON THE POOR INDIANS"

1. Simms, *Frontiersmen of New York*, 1: 316; 2: 307, note*.

2. Brant did not live to see the beginnings of the renascence of the Indians. John Norton did.

3. Wm. Harrison, April 1, 1806, to Shee, State Papers, Upper Canada, Q305: 121–23.

4. Sept. 5, 1807, Brant MSS., 12F78–79.

5. Alexander McDonell, Nov. 16, 1807, to Selkirk, *Valley of Six Nations*, pp. 169–70; McDonell, Mar. 18, 1808, to Selkirk, *ibid.*, p. 170.

6. "The Rev. Robert Addison: Extracts from Reports and Journals of S. P. G.," *Ontario Historical Society Papers and Records* 19 (1922): 180.

7. *Ibid.*, p. 181. One of Brant's last visitors told Jeptha R. Simms that Brant's final illness was brought on by drunkenness. Simms, *Frontiersmen of New York*, 1: 316; 2: 307, note *.

8. Norton, Journal, etc., 2: 734–35.

9. Statement, Aug. 15, 1837, quoted in Stone, *Life of Brant*, 2, Appendix 20, p. lvii.

10. *Ibid.*, p. 499.

11. *Ibid.*, pp. 498–99.

12. The (Brantford) *Weekly Expositor*, Oct. 15 [22?], 1886, Brant Miscellanies, 2G6; Jean H. Waldie, "Indians Gave Six Nations Land," quoting and paraphrasing speech of the Rev. Peter Jones, Nov. 1850, *Brantford Expositor*, Nov. 23, 1956.

EPILOGUE—HOW THE MONSTER BRANT BECAME THE NOBLE SAVAGE
AND HOW JOSEPH FINALLY WENT HOME

1. According to a letter of William Johnson Kerr, Joseph Brant's son-in-law, to Stone. *Life of Brant*, 2: 523.

2. George Hillier, Mar. 31, 1819, to Alexander McDonell, *Valley of Six Nations*, p. 66.

3. "Letter to the Mohawk Chief Ahyonwaeghs," The (London) *New Monthly Magazine and Literary Journal* 4 (1822): 98.

4. Much of it now lost.

5. The Brant Miscellanies and the Brant Manuscripts.

6. W. C. Bryant, June 4, 1889, to Draper, Brant MSS., 13F130; Jean H. Waldie, "Joseph Brant Thrice Wed, Father of Nine," *Brantford Expositor*, May 18, 1950; Jean H. Waldie, "Brant Stood Staunchly By the Angelican Church," *ibid.*, July 13, 1950; Jean H. Waldie, "Replica of Indian Chief Brant's Home Recalls Hospitable Welcome Given All in Early Days," *London Free Press*, June 26, 1954; Jean H. Waldie, "Indians Gave Six Nations Land," *Brantford Expositor*, Nov. 23, 1956.

There is also some evidence that Brant's body was removed to the Grand River long before 1850, and that the "second funeral" marked the occasion when the old wooden tomb was replaced by a new stone tomb. Stone, *Life of Brant*, 2: 499; The (Toronto) *Weekly Globe*, Jan. 19, 1877, Brant Miscellanies, 2G106; The (Brantford) *Weekly Expositor*, Oct. 15 [22?], 1886, *ibid.*, 2G7.

Select Bibliography

UNPUBLISHED PRIMARY SOURCES

(Listed under author's last name, or, if not possible, under the subject's last name or the first major word in the title.)

Robert Adems. Day Book. Privately owned. Microfilm at New York State Library.

American Loyalists Papers. Audit Office Transcripts. 60 vols. New York Public Library.

Edward E. Ayer Collection. Newberry Library, Chicago. MSS. relating to John Norton, Six Nations, etc.

Henry Barclay. Register Book, Fort Hunter 1734/5. MS. actually goes to 1745/6. New-York Historical Society.

Brandt Indian Warrior—of ye Mohawk nation—Anecdotes respecting him from the mouth of Mr Kirkland—Dr. John Eliot's, For N. E. Biog. Dictionary [never printed]. Massachusetts Historical Society.

Brant Miscellanies. 3 vols. Draper Collection, State Historical Society of Wisconsin.

Brant MSS. 22 vols. Draper Collection, State Historical Society of Wisconsin.

British Headquarters Papers. 107 vols. Archives Department, Colonial Williamsburg. Calendared in *Report on American Manuscripts in the Royal Institution of Great Britain,* published by Historical Manuscripts Commission. 4 vols. London, Dublin, and Hereford, 1904–09.

Richard Butler Papers. Burton Historical Collection, Detroit Public Library.

Daniel Campbell. Account Books, 1756–99. 5 vols. New York State Library.

George Rogers Clark Papers. 65 vols. Draper Collection, State Historical Society of Wisconsin. 46J and 49J used.

Claus Papers. 35 vols. Public Archives of Canada. The 2 vols. of photostats in the Library of Congress will be referred to when used.

Sir Henry Clinton Papers. William L. Clements Library, Ann Arbor, Mich.

Colonial Office Papers, Canada. Transcripts, Public Archives of Canada. Calendared in Arthur G. Doughty. *Report of the Public Archives for the Year 1921.* Ottawa, 1922. C.O. 42, vols. 15–19 and 22 used.

Dartmouth College MSS. Reproduced by permission of the Trustees of Dartmouth College.

Diary of the brethren John Heckewelder and Benjamin Mortimer, on their journey from Bethlehem in Pennsylvania to Fairfield in Upper Canada, from the 30th April to the 22d. May 1798. B172, F1. Moravian Archives, Bethlehem, Pa.

Diary of the congregation at Fairfield in Upper Canada, from the 31 May to the 13 Augst. 1798. Moravian Archives.

Diary of the Indian Church in Fairfield Canada, 1801. Moravian Archives.

Dreer Collection of Letters of Officers serving in America before the Revolution. Historical Society of Pennsylvania.

John Elmsley. Letter-book. Metropolitan Toronto Library.

Fonda Family Papers. New-York Historical Society.

Jelles Fonda. Ledger No. 10. New York State Historical Association, Cooperstown, N.Y.

Frontier Wars MSS. 24 vols. Draper Collection, State Historical Society of Wisconsin.

Gage Papers, American Series. William L. Clements Library. Some published in *The Correspondence of General Thomas Gage with the Secretaries of State, and with the War Office and the Treasury, 1763–1775.* Compiled and edited by Clarence Edwin Carter. Vol. 2. New Haven and London, 1933.

Simon Gratz Collection. Historical Society of Pennsylvania.

Charles F. Gunther Collection. Chicago Historical Society.

Haldimand Papers. 232 vols., many vols. in two or more parts. British Museum Additional MSS. Photostats of some at Library of Congress, with same catalog numbers as English originals. Transcripts of all at Public Archives of Canada, numbered Series B. Calendared in Douglas Brymner. *Report on Canadian Archives, 1884–89.* 6 vols. Ottawa, 1885–90. Photostats used when possible. Any unnumbered page is referred to by number of facing page.

Hammond-Simcoe Correspondence. William L. Clements Library.

Gen. Josiah Harmar Papers. William L. Clements Library.

Gideon Hawley MSS. 4 vols. Congregational Library of the American Congregational Association, Boston.

Indian Records, Series Two. Vols. 11, 12, and 15 used. Public Archives of Canada.

Jefferson Papers, Coolidge Collection. Massachusetts Historical Society. A few letters used.

Kirkland MSS. Library of Hamilton College, Clinton, N.Y.

Henry Knox MSS. Massachusetts Historical Society. Vols. 22, 30, 31, and 32 used.

Maj. R. Mathews, 53rd Regt. Diary, Feb. 6–June 18, 1787. Metropolitan Toronto Library.

Military Papers of Gen. Peter Gansevoort, Jr. Gansevoort-Lansing Collection. New York Public Library.

Military Papers "Indian." Public Archives of Canada. Vols. 247–55 used.

Samuel Miller Papers. New-York Historical Society. Publication of Brant interview mentioned in chapter 1, note 2.

Miscellaneous MSS. New-York Historical Society.

Nelles Papers. Ontario Archives, Toronto.

Maj. John Norton (Teyoninhokarawen). Journal of A Voyage, down the Ohio; From the Grand River, Upper Canada;—Visit To the Country of the Cherokees:—Through the States of Kentucky and Tennessee: and An Account of the Five Nations, &c from an Early Period, To the Conclusion of the late War Between Great Britain & America. 2 vols. Publication reported in chapter 1, note 5.

The Rev. John Ogilvie. An Acct. of Marriages among the Indians. New York State Library.

The Rev. John Ogilvie. A Journal of Time spent at the Mohawk with some Occurrences. New York State Library.

The Rev. John Ogilvie. A Register of Indian Children Begun Apr. 22d. 1750. New York State Library.

Henry O'Reilly [or O'Rielly] Papers. New-York Historical Society.

Papers of the Continental Congress, 1774–89. National Archives Film M-247. Many available elsewhere in published or unpublished form.

Penn MSS. Historical Society of Pennsylvania.

Peters MSS. Historical Society of Pennsylvania.

Jedidiah Phelps. East Barre, Sept. 5, 1842, narrative at age of 90. Burton Historical Collection, Detroit Public Library.

Pickering Papers. Massachusetts Historical Society. Vols. 59–62 used.

Pittsburgh and Northwest Virginia MSS. 10 vols. Draper Collection, State Historical Society of Wisconsin. Vol. 3 used.

Records of the Superintendent General's Office, 1791–1828. 14 vols. Public Archives of Canada.

Jean Baptiste Rousseau. Account Book. Ontario Archives.

Russell Papers. Ontario Archives.

Sackville-Germain Papers. William L. Clements Library.

Schuyler Papers. 49 boxes and 17 vols. New York Public Library.

Single Acquisitions. New York State Library.

D. W. Smith Collection. 24 vols. Metropolitan Toronto Library.

Thomas Smith Papers. Burton Historical Collection, Detroit Public Library.

MSS. of the Society for the Propagation of the Gospel in Foreign Parts. Transcripts and microfilm. Library of Congress.

State Papers, Canada, Lower Canada, and Upper Canada. Transcripts. 310 vols. Public Archives of Canada. Calendared in Douglas Brymner. Report on Canadian Archives, 1890–92. 3 vols. Ottawa, 1891–93.

Samuel Street Papers. Ontario Archives.

Papers of Tryon County, N.Y., Committee of Safety, 1774–78. New-York Historical Society.

Dr. Edward Walsh Papers. Public Archives of Canada.

E. Walsh, M. D., 49th Regt. Sketches Made in Upper Canada, 1803–6. Paintings. William L. Clements Library.

War Office Papers: Field Officers Letters, 1775–1805. Transcripts. Public Archives of Canada.

Wayne MSS. Historical Society of Pennsylvania.
Conrad Weiser. Journal to Onontago in the Year 1750. Historical Society of
　　Pennsylvania.
Frank Yeigh Papers. Ontario Archives.

PUBLISHED PRIMARY SOURCES

(All published sources, primary or secondary, are listed under author's last
name, or, if no author is recorded, under the first major word of the title of
the book, collection, newspaper, article, or manuscript. Titles of articles are
enclosed in quotation marks, but titles of other published sources are
italicized.)

Ethan Allen. *Allen's Captivity, Being a Narrative of Colonel Ethan Allen, Con-
　　taining His Voyages, Travels, &c., Interspersed with Political Observations.*
　　Boston, 1845.
American Archives. Published by M. St. Clair Clarke and Peter Force, Fourth
　　Series. 6 vols. Washington, 1837–46.
American Archives. Published by M. St. Clair Clarke and Peter Force, Fifth
　　Series. 3 vols. Washington, 1848–53.
American State Papers, Indian Affairs. 2 vols. Washington, 1832–34.
Thomas Anburey. *Travels through the Interior Parts of America.* Edited by
　　Maj.-Gen. William Harding Carter. 2 vols. Boston and New York,
　　1923.
*Anthony Wayne, A Name in Arms, Soldier, Diplomat, Defender of Expansion
　　Westward of a Nation: The Wayne-Knox-Pickering-McHenry Correspon-
　　dence.* Transcribed and edited by Richard C. Knopf. Pittsburgh, 1960.
The Autobiography of James Monroe. Edited by Stuart Gerry Brown, with the
　　assistance of Donald G. Baker. Syracuse, 1959.
James Buchanan. *Sketches of the History, Manners, and Customs, of the North
　　American Indians.* 2 vols. New-York, 1824.
Lieutenant-General Burgoyne. *A State of the Expedition from Canada, as Laid
　　Before the House of Commons.* London, 1780.
*Calendar of Historical Manuscripts, Relating to the War of the Revolution, in the
　　Office of the Secretary of State, Albany, N.Y.* 2 vols. Albany, 1868.
　　Printed documents.
Calendar of the Sir William Johnson Manuscripts in the New York State Library.
　　Compiled by Richard E. Day. Albany, 1909. All that is left of Johnson
　　MSS. lost in fire of 1911.
P. Campbell. *Travels in the Interior Inhabited Parts of North America in the Years
　　1791 and 1792.* Edinburgh, 1793.
Janet Carnochan. *Inscriptions and Graves in the Niagara Peninsula.* Niagara
　　Historical Society No. 19, Second Edition. Welland, 1910.

Marquis de Chastellux. *Travels in North-America, in the Years 1780, 1781, and 1782*. Translated from the French by an English gentleman, Second Edition. 2 vols. London, 1787.

Daniel Claus. "Narrative of His Relations with Sir William Johnson and Experiences in the Lake George Fight." *Society of Colonial Wars in the State of New York*, No. 9 (June 1904): 1–21.

[Cadwallader Colden]. *The History of the Five Indian Nations Depending on the Province of New-York in America*. New-York, 1727.

Collections of Michigan Pioneer and Historical Society. Name varies slightly from year to year. "Haldimand Papers" in 9 (1886): 343–658; 10 (1888): 210–672; 11 (1888): 319–656; "Papers on Indians and Military Posts, 1762–1799," in 12 (1888): 1–315; "Papers on War of 1812" in 15 (1890): 1–63; "Bouquet and Haldimand Papers," etc., in 19 (1892): 1–675; "Haldimand Papers and Indian Affairs" in 20 (1892): 1–673; "Colonial Office Records and Indian Affairs" in 23 (1895): 1–680; "Colonial Office Records," etc., in 25 (1896): 1–698. Copies of papers in Public Archives of Canada relating to Michigan and Great Lakes area.

Correspondence of Aaron Burr and His Daughter Theodosia. Edited by Mark Van Doren. New York, 1929.

The Correspondence of the Honourable Peter Russell with Allied Documents relating to His Administration of the Government of Upper Canada during the Official Term of Lieut.-Governor J. G. Simcoe while on Leave of Absence. Edited by Brig.-Gen. E. A. Cruikshank and A. F. Hunter. 3 vols. Toronto, 1932–36.

The Correspondence of Lieut. Governor John Graves Simcoe. Edited by Brigadier General E. A. Cruikshank. 5 vols. Toronto, 1923–31.

David Zeisberger's History of Northern American Indians. Edited by Archer Butler Hulbert and William Nathaniel Schwarze. Columbus, Ohio, 1910.

Matthew L. Davis. *Memoirs of Aaron Burr, with Miscellaneous Selections from His Correspondence*. 2 vols. New-York, 1836–37. Reprint Series: *The Era of the American Revolution*. Edited by Leonard W. Levy. New York, 1971.

Arent Schuyler de Peyster. *Miscellanies*. Edited by J. Watts de Peyster. Dumfries, 1813.

J. Watts de Peyster. *Appendix, Explanatory Notes, &c., &c., &c., to "Miscellanies by an Officer."* New York, 1888.

Diary of David Zeisberger, A Moravian Missionary among the Indians of Ohio. Translated and edited by Eugene F. Bliss. 2 vols. Cincinnati, 1885.

The Diary of Mrs. John Graves Simcoe, Wife of the First Lieutenant-Governor of the Province of Upper Canada, 1792–6. Edited by J. Ross Robertson. Toronto, 1911.

The Documentary History of the State of New-York. Edited by E. B. O'Callaghan. 4 vols. Albany, 1849–51.

Documents Relating to the Constitutional History of Canada, 1791–1818. Edited by Arthur G. Doughty and Duncan A. McArthur. Ottawa, 1914.

Documents Relative to the Colonial History of the State of New-York. Edited by E. B. O'Callaghan and B. Fernow. 15 vols. Albany, 1853–87.

The European Magazine, and London Review 9 (1786).

The (London) *Gazetteer and New Daily Advertiser,* 1786.

"The Glen Letters." Edited by Throop Wilder. *New York History* 26 (1945): 322–31.

[Mrs. Anne Grant]. *Memoirs of an American Lady.* 2 vols. in one. Boston, 1809.

Lieut. Francis Hall. *Travels in Canada, and the United States, in 1816 and 1817.* London, 1818.

Instructions to the British Ministers to the United States, 1791–1812. Edited by Bernard Mayo. Vol. 3 of the *Annual Report of the American Historical Association for the Year 1936.* Da Capo Press Reprint Edition, 1971.

The Iroquois Book of Rites. Edited by Horatio Hale. Philadelphia, 1883.

Halliday Jackson. *Civilization of the Indian Natives.* Philadelphia and New York, 1830.

"Jacob Lindley's Account, Of a Journey to attend the Indian Treaty, proposed to be held at Sandusky, in the year 1793; interspersed with various observations, remarks, and circumstances, that occurred on this interesting occasion." *Friends' Miscellany,* edited by John and Isaac Comly. 12 vols. Philadelphia, 1831–39. Vol. 2, pp. 49–156.

The Jesuit Relations and Allied Documents: 1610–1791. Edited by Reuben Gold Thwaites. 73 vols. Cleveland, 1896–1901.

"John Adlum on the Allegheny: Memoirs for the Year 1794." Edited by Donald H. Kent and Merle H. Deardorff, 2 parts. *The Pennsylvania Magazine of History and Biography* 84, nos. 3–4 (July–Oct. 1960): 265–324, 435–80.

The John Askin Papers, 1747–1820. Edited by Milo M. Quaife. 2 vols., n.p., 1928–31.

"Joseph Moore's Journal Of a tour to Detroit, in order to attend a Treaty, proposed to be held with the Indians at Sandusky." *Friends' Miscellany,* edited by John and Isaac Comly. 12 vols. Philadelphia, 1831–39. Vol. 6, pp. 289–343.

"Journal of Lieutenant Tjerck Beekman, 1779." Edited by James R. Gibson, Jr. *Magazine of American History* 20, no. 2 (Aug. 1888): 128–36.

"Journal of William McKendry." *Proceedings of the Massachusetts Historical Society,* Second Series 2 (May 1886): 442–78.

Journals of the Military Expedition of Major General John Sullivan against the Six Nations of Indians in 1779 with Records of Centennial Celebrations. Edited by Frederick Cook. Auburn, N.Y., 1887.

Journals of the Provincial Congress, Provincial Convention, Committee of Safety and Council of Safety of the State of New-York, 1775–1777. 2 vols. Albany, 1842.

John Thornton Kirkland. "Answer to the foregoing Queries, respecting Indians." *Collections of the Massachusetts Historical Society,* First Series 4 (1795): 67–74.

The [Charles] *Lee Papers.* 4 vols. *Collections of the New-York Historical Society.* New York, 1872–75.

"A Letter from Rev. Jonathan Edwards, to Hon. Thomas Hubbard, Esq. of Boston, Relating to the Indian School at Stockbridge." *Collections of the Massachusetts Historical Society,* First Series 10 (1809): 142–54.

"Letter to the Mohawk Chief Ahyonwaeghs, Commonly Called John Brant, Esq. of the Grand River, Upper Canada. From Thomas Campbell." *The New Monthly Magazine and Literary Journal,* London 4 (1822): 97–101.

The Letters of Eleazar Wheelock's Indians. Edited by James Dow McCallum. *Dartmouth College Manuscript Series,* No. 1. Hanover, N.H., 1932.

General [Benjamin] Lincoln. "Journal of a Treaty Held in 1793, with the Indian Tribes North-West of the Ohio, by Commissioners of the United States." *Collections of the Massachusetts Historical Society,* Third Series 5 (1836): 109–76.

The London Chronicle, 1776.

The London Magazine, 1776.

Lord Selkirk's Diary, 1803–1804. Edited by Patrick C. T. White. *The Publications of the Champlain Society,* 35. Toronto, 1958.

George Henry Loskiel. *History of the Mission of the United Brethren among the Indians in North America.* 3 vols. in one. London, 1794.

Orsamus H. Marshall. "Narrative of the Expedition of the Marquis De Nonville, against the Senecas, in 1687." *Collections of the New-York Historical Society,* Second Series 2 (1849): 149–92.

David M'Clure and Elijah Parish. *Memoirs of the Rev. Eleazar Wheelock, D. D.* Newburyport, Mass., 1811.

Memoirs, and Letters and Journals, of Major General Riedesel, During His Residence in America. Translated and edited by William L. Stone. 2 vols. Albany, 1868.

Military Journal of Major Ebenezer Denny. Edited by William H. Denny. *Publications of the Historical Society of Pennsylvania* 7 (1860): 207–492.

The Minute Book of the Committee of Safety of Tryon County, the Old New York Frontier. Edited by Samuel Ludlow Frey. New York, 1905.

Missionary Explorers Among the American Indians. Edited by Mary Gay Humphreys. New York, 1913.

Moravian Journals relating to Central New York, 1745–66. Edited by Wm. M. Beauchamp. Syracuse, 1916.

A Narrative of the Captivity and Sufferings of Benjamin Gilbert and His Family; Who were Surprised by the Indians, and Taken from Their Farms, on the Frontiers of Pennsylvania. In the Spring, 1780. Philadelphia printed, London reprinted, 1790.

"A Narrative of An Embassy to the Western Indians, from the Original Manuscript of Hendrick Aupaumut, with Prefatory Remarks by Dr. B. H. Coates." *Memoirs of the Historical Society of Pennsylvania* 2 (1827): 61–131.

"Narrative of Events in the History and Settlement of Western New York, in the Personal Recollections of Thomas Morris, Esq." *The Historical Maga-zine*, Second Series 5 (June 1869): 368–88.

Julian Ursyn Niemcewicz. *Under Their Vine and Fig Tree: Travels through America in 1797–1799, 1805 with some further account of life in New Jersey.* Translated and edited by Metchie J. E. Budka. Elizabeth, N.J., 1965.

Ohio in the Time of the Confederation. Edited by Archer Butler Hulbert. *Marietta College Historical Collections,* vol. 3. Cleveland, 1918.

The Olden Time; A Monthly Publication, Devoted to the Preservation of Docu-ments and Other Authentic Information in Relation to the Early Explorations, and the Settlement and Improvement of the Country around the Head of the Ohio. Edited by Neville B. Craig. 2 vols. Pittsburgh, 1846–47.

"The Opinions of George Croghan on the American Indian." *The Pennsylva-nia Magazine of History and Biography* 71 (1947): 152–59.

The Order Book of Capt. Leonard Bleeker, Major of Brigade in the Early Part of the Expedition under Gen. James Clinton, against the Indian Settlements of Western New York, in the Campaign of 1779. Edited by F. B. H. New York, 1865.

Orderly Book of Sir John Johnson during the Oriskany Campaign, 1776–1777. Edited by William L. Stone. Albany, 1882.

The Papers of Sir William Johnson. Edited by James Sullivan, Alexander C. Flick, and Milton W. Hamilton. 14 vols. Albany, 1921–65.

Pennsylvania Archives, First Series. Edited by Samuel Hazard. 12 vols. Philadelphia, 1852–56; and Second Series. Edited by John B. Linn and Wm. H. Egle. 18 vols. Harrisburg, 1874–90.

The Pennsylvania Gazette. Philadelphia, 1786–87.

"Petitions for Grants of Land, 1792–6." Edited by Brig.-Gen. E. A. Cruik-shank. *Ontario Historical Society Papers and Records* 24 (1927): 17–144.

M. Pouchot. *Memoir upon the Late War in North America, between the French and English, 1755–60.* Translated and edited by Franklin B. Hough. 2 vols. Roxbury, Mass., 1866.

Josiah Priest. *The Captivity and Sufferings of Gen. Freegift Patchin of Blenheim, Schoharie County, Among the Indians, under Brant, The Noted Chief, Dur-ing the Border Warfare in the time of the American Revolution.* Albany, 1833.

"Private Diary of Gen. Haldimand." In Douglas Brymner, *Report on Canadian Archives, 1889* (Ottawa, 1890): 123–299.

Private Papers of James Boswell from Malahide Castle. Edited by Geoffrey Scott and Frederick A. Pottle. 18 vols. Mount Vernon, N.Y., 1928–34.

"The Probated Wills of Men Prominent in the Public Affairs of Early Upper Canada." Edited by A. F. Hunter. *Ontario Historical Society Papers and Records* 23 (1926): 328–59.

Proceedings of the Commissioners of Indian Affairs, Appointed by Law for the Extinguishment of Indian Titles in the State of New York. Edited by Frank-lin B. Hough. 2 vols. Albany, 1861.

"Proceedings of a General Court Martial . . . for the Trial of Major General

Schuyler, October 1, 1778." *Collections of the New-York Historical Society for the Year 1879* (New York, 1880): 1–211.

Public Papers of George Clinton, First Governor of New York. Published by the State of New York. 10 vols. New York and Albany, 1899–1914.

Records of Niagara in the days of Commodore Grant and Lieut.-Governor Gore, 1805–1811. Edited by Brig. General E. A. Cruikshank. *Niagara Historical Society* No. 42, 1931.

"The Rev. Robert Addison: Extracts from the Reports and (Manuscript) Journals of the Society for the Propagation of the Gospel in Foreign Parts." Edited by Professor A. H. Young. *Ontario Historical Society Papers and Records* 19 (1922): 171–91.

The Revolution on the Upper Ohio, 1775–1777. Edited by Reuben Gold Thwaites and Louise Phelps Kellogg. Madison, Wis., 1908.

Mrs. General [Baroness] Riedesel. *Letters and Journals Relating to the War of the American Revolution.* Translated and edited by William L. Stone. Albany, 1867.

James E. Seaver. *Life of Mary Jemison.* Fourth Edition. New York, Auburn, and Rochester, 1856.

Richard Smith. *A Tour of Four Great Rivers, the Hudson, Mohawk, Susquehanna and Delaware in 1769.* Edited by Francis W. Halsey. New York, 1906.

William Henry Smith. *The Life and Public Services of Arthur St. Clair . . . with His Correspondence and Other Papers.* 2 vols. Cincinnati, 1882.

[The Rev. John Strachan]. "Life of Capt. Brant." *The Christian Recorder.* Kingston, Upper Canada, May–June, 1819.

Thirty Thousand Miles with John Heckewelder. Edited by Paul A. W. Wallace. University of Pittsburgh Press, 1958.

The Valley of the Six Nations: A Collection of Documents on the Indian Lands of the Grand River. Edited by Charles M. Johnston. Toronto, 1964.

"Wayne's Western Campaign: The Wayne-Knox Correspondence, 1793–1794." Parts 1–2. Edited by Richard C. Knopf. *The Pennsylvania Magazine of History and Biography* 78, nos. 3–4 (July–Oct. 1954): 298–341; 424–55.

Isaac Weld, Junior. *Travels through the States of North America, and the Provinces of Upper and Lower Canada, during the Years 1795, 1796, and 1797.* London, 1799.

Eleazar Wheelock. *A plain and faithful Narrative of the Original Design, Rise, Progress and present State of the Indian Charity-School at Lebanon, in Connecticut.* Boston, 1763.

[Nathaniel Whitaker]. *A Brief Narrative of the Indian Charity-School in Lebanon in Connecticut, New England: Founded and carried on by That Faithful Servant of God The Rev. Mr Eleazar Wheelock.* Second Edition. London, 1767.

"William Berczy's Williamsburg Documents." Edited by A. J. H. Richardson and Helen I. Cowan. *The Rochester Historical Society Publications* 20 (1942): 141–265.

The Writings of Benjamin Franklin. Edited by Albert Henry Smyth. 10 vols. New York and London, 1905–07.

The Writings of George Washington from the Original Manuscript Sources, 1745–1799. Edited by John C. Fitzpatrick. 39 vols. Washington, 1931–44.

SECONDARY SOURCES AND SUGGESTED BACKGROUND READING

Clarence Walworth Alvord. *The Mississippi Valley in British Politics.* 2 vols. Cleveland, 1917.

William M. Beauchamp. *A History of the New York Iroquois.* Albany, 1905.

Wm. M. Beauchamp. *Iroquois Folk Lore.* Syracuse, 1922.

W. M. Beauchamp. *The Iroquois Trail, or Foot-Prints of the Six Nations, in Customs, Traditions, and History, in Which Are Included David Cusick's Sketches of Ancient History of the Six Nations.* Fayetteville, N.Y., 1892.

Samuel Flagg Bemis. *Jay's Treaty: A Study in Commerce and Diplomacy.* New York, 1923.

Carl Berger. *Broadsides and Bayonets.* Philadelphia, 1961.

Harold Blodgett. *Samson Occom.* Dartmouth College Manuscript Series Number Three. Hanover, N.H., 1935.

Theodore Bolton and Irwin F. Cortelyou. *Ezra Ames of Albany: Portrait Painter, Craftsman, Royal Arch Mason, Banker, 1768–1836.* New York, 1955.

Beverley W. Bond, Jr. *The Foundations of Ohio.* Columbus, 1941.

Richmond P. Bond. *Queen Anne's American Kings.* Oxford, 1952.

Margaret Pearson Bothwell. "The Astonishing Croghans." *The Western Pennsylvania Historical Magazine* 48, no. 2 (April, 1965): 119–44.

A. G. Bradley. *Colonial Americans in Exile.* New York, 1932.

J. Ojijatekha Brant-Sero. "Some Descendants of Joseph Brant." *Ontario Historical Society Papers and Records* 1 (1899): 113–17.

W. H. Breithaupt. "Dundas Street and Other Early Upper Canada Roads." *Ontario Historical Society Papers and Records* 21 (1924): 5–10.

Gerald Saxon Brown. *The American Secretary: The Colonial Policy of Lord George Germain, 1775–1778.* Ann Arbor, Mich., 1963.

Wallace Brown. *The King's Friends.* Providence, R.I., 1965.

Wm. C. Bryant. "Joseph Brant, Thayendanegea, and His Posterity." *The American Historical Record* 2, no. 19 (July 1873): 289–96.

A. L. Burt. *The United States, Great Britain, and British North America from the Revolution to the Establishment of Peace after the War of 1812.* New Haven, Toronto, and London, 1940.

Consul Willshire Butterfield. *History of the Girtys.* Cincinnati, 1890.

North Callahan. *Henry Knox, General Washington's General.* New York and Toronto, 1958.

William W. Campbell. *Annals of Tryon County; or, The Border Warfare of New-York during the Revolution.* New York, 1831.

Janet Carnochan. "The Count De Puisaye." *Ontario Historical Society Papers and Records* 5 (1904): 36–52.

Philip Carrington. *The Anglican Church in Canada.* Toronto, 1963.

Isaac A. Chapman. *A Sketch of the History of Wyoming.* Wilkesbarre, Pa., 1830.

Barbara A. Chernow. " Robert Morris: Genesee Land Speculator." *New York History* 58, no. 2 (April 1977): 195–220.

Gerald M. Craig. *The United States and Canada.* Cambridge, Mass., 1968.

Gerald M. Craig. *Upper Canada: The Formative Years, 1784–1841.* Toronto, 1963.

Ernest Cruikshank. *The Story of Butler's Rangers and the Settlement of Niagara.* Welland, Ont., 1893.

Randolph C. Downes. *Council Fires on the Upper Ohio.* Pittsburgh, 1940.

John Duffy. *Epidemics in Colonial America.* Baton Rouge, 1953.

Seymour Dunbar. *A History of Travel in America.* New York, 1937.

David M. Ellis, James A. Frost, Harold C. Syrett, and Harry J. Carman. *A Short History of New York State.* Ithaca, N.Y., 1957.

William N. Fenton. "Problems Arising from the Historic Northeastern Position of the Iroquois." *Smithsonian Miscellaneous Collections* 100 (Washington, 1940): 159–251.

Charles G. Fenwick. *International Law.* New York and London, 1924.

Roy F. Fleming. "Negro Slaves with the United Empire Loyalists in Upper Canada." *Ontario History* 45, no. 1 (Winter 1953): 27–30.

Alexander Clarence Flick. *Loyalism in New York during the American Revolution.* New York and London, 1901.

40 Miles of American Heroism: A guide to General Herkimer's historic line of march, August 3–6, 1777. Utica National Insurance Group, [1976].

Edith M. Fox. *Land Speculation in the Mohawk Country.* Ithaca, N.Y., 1949.

Lillian F. Gates. *Land Policies of Upper Canada,* in *Canadian Studies in History and Government, No. 9.* University of Toronto Press, 1968.

M. Dorothy George. *London Life in the XVIIIth Century.* New York, 1925.

Don R. Gerlach. *Philip Schuyler and the American Revolution in New York, 1733–1777.* Lincoln, Neb., 1964.

Don R. Gerlach. *Philip Schuyler and the Growth of New York, 1733–1804.* Albany, 1968.

Gilbert Stuart: An Illustrated Descriptive List of His Works Compiled by Lawrence Park with an Account of His Life by John Hill Morgan and an Appreciation by Royal Cortissoz. 4 vols. New York, 1926.

Augusta I. Grant Gilkison. "Reminiscences of Earlier Years in Brant." *Ontario Historical Society Papers and Records* 12: 81–88.

Louis Goulet. "Phases of the Sally Ainse Dispute." *Papers and Addresses of the Kent Historical Society* 5 (1921): 92–95.

Louis E. Graham. "Fort McIntosh." *Western Pennsylvania Historical Magazine* 15 (1932): 93–119.

Elma E. Gray and Leslie Robb Gray. *Wilderness Christians.* Ithaca, N.Y., 1956.

Barbara Graymont. *The Iroquois in the American Revolution*. Syracuse, 1972.

Barbara Graymont. "New York State Indian Policy after the Revolution." *New York History* 57 (Oct. 1976): 438–74.

William Elliot Griffis. *Sir William Johnson and The Six Nations*. New York, 1891.

Edwin C. Guillet. *Pioneer Days in Upper Canada*. Toronto and Buffalo, reprinted 1975.

Edwin C. Guillet. *Pioneer Travel in Upper Canada*. Toronto: Canadian University Paperbooks Edition, reprinted 1969.

William T. Hagan. *American Indians*. Chicago, 1961.

Francis Whiting Halsey. *The Old New York Frontier*. New York, 1901.

Philip M. Hamer. "The British in Canada and the Southern Indians, 1790–1794." *The East Tennessee Historical Society's Publications* 2 (1930): 107–34.

Edward P. Hamilton. *The French and Indian Wars*. New York, 1962.

Milton W. Hamilton. "Joseph Brant—'The Most Painted Indian.'" *New York History* 39, no. 2 (April 1958): 119–32.

Milton W. Hamilton. "Joseph Brant Painted by Rigaud." *New York History* 40, no. 3 (July 1959): 247–54.

Milton W. Hamilton. *Sir William Johnson: Colonial American, 1715–1763*. Port Washington, N.Y., and London, 1976.

Charles A. Hanna. *The Wilderness Trail*. 2 vols. New York and London, 1911.

Ernest Hawkins. *Historical Notices of the Missions of the Church of England in the North American Colonies*. London, 1845.

Rev. Orlo D. Hine and Nathaniel H. Morgan. *Early Lebanon*. Hartford, Conn., 1880.

James Austin Holden. "Influence of Death of Jane McCrea on Burgoyne Campaign." *Proceedings of the New York State Historical Association* 12 (1913): 249–310.

Mrs. John Rose Holden. *The Brant Family*. Third Edition. Wentworth Historical Society, n.d.

Reginald Horsman. "American Indian Policy in the Old Northwest, 1783–1812." *The William and Mary Quarterly*. Series 3, vol. 18 (1961): 35–53.

Reginald Horsman. *Matthew Elliott, British Indian Agent*. Detroit, 1964.

Archer Butler Hulbert. "The Indian Thoroughfares of Ohio." *Ohio Archaeological and Historical Publications* 8 (July 1899–April 1900): 264–95.

George T. Hunt. *The Wars of the Iroquois*. Madison, Wis., 1940.

Harold A. Innis. *The Fur Trade in Canada*. New Haven and London, 1930.

Wilbur R. Jacobs. *Dispossessing the American Indian: Indians and Whites on the Colonial Frontier*. New York, 1972.

Cornelius J. Jaenen. *Friend and Foe: Aspects of French-Amerindian Cultural Contact in the Sixteenth and Seventeenth Centuries*. New York, 1976.

James Alton James. *The Life of George Rogers Clark*. Chicago, 1928.

Derek Jarrett. *Pitt The Younger*. New York, 1974.

Diamond Jenness. *The Indians of Canada.* Fifth Edition. Ottawa, 1960.

Francis Jennings. "The Constitutional Evolution of the Covenant Chain." *Proceedings of the American Philosophical Society* 115 (1971): 88–96.

Charles M. Johnston. "Joseph Brant, the Grand River Lands and the Northwest Crisis." *Ontario History* 55, no. 4 (1963): 267–82.

Charles M. Johnston. "An Outline of Early Settlement in the Grand River Valley." *Ontario History* 54, no. 1 (1962): 43–67.

Thomas Jones. *History of New York during the Revolutionary War.* Edited by Edward Floyd de Lancey. 2 vols. New York, 1879.

"Joseph Brant or Thayeadanegea." *The American Historical Record* 2, no. 20 (Aug. 1873): 354–56.

William Ketchum. *An Authentic and Comprehensive History of Buffalo.* 2 vols. Buffalo, 1864–65.

Gustave Lanctot. *Canada and the American Revolution, 1774–1783.* Cambridge, Mass., 1967.

Gustave Lanctot. *A History of Canada.* 3 vols. Cambridge, Mass., 1963–65.

The Life and Times of Sa-Go-Ye-Wat-Ha, or Red Jacket, by the Late William L. Stone; with a Memoir of the Author, by His Son. Albany, 1866.

Samuel K. Lothrop. *Life of Samuel Kirkland,* in *The Library of American Biography.* Edited by Jared Sparks. Second Series, vol. 15. Boston, 1864.

W. De Loss Love. *Samson Occom and the Christian Indians of New England.* Boston and Chicago, 1899.

Solomon Lutnick. *The American Revolution and the British Press 1775–1783.* Columbia, Mo., 1967.

James Macauley. *The Natural, Statistical, and Civil History of the State of New-York.* 3 vols. New York and Albany, 1829.

William Christie Macleod. *The American Indian Frontier.* New York, 1928.

John K. Mahon. "Anglo-American Methods of Indian Warfare, 1676–1794." *The Mississippi Valley Historical Review* 45, no. 2 (Sept. 1958): 254–75.

Jean N. McIlwraith. *Sir Frederick Haldimand.* Toronto, 1906.

S. R. Mealing. "The Enthusiasms of John Graves Simcoe." *Canadian Historical Association Report.* 1958, pp. 50–62.

John F. Meginness. *The Family of General Arthur St. Clair.* Reprinted from Dr. Egle's Notes and Queries. Harrisburg, Pa., 1897.

Charles Miner. *History of Wyoming, in a Series of Letters, from Charles Miner, to His Son William Penn Miner, Esq.* Philadelphia, 1845.

Walter H. Mohr. *Federal Indian Relations 1774–1788.* Philadelphia and London, 1933.

Malcolm Montgomery. "The Legal Status of the Six Nations Indians in Canada." *Ontario History* 55, no. 2 (June 1963): 93–105.

Lewis H. Morgan. *Ancient Society.* Edited by Leslie A. White. Cambridge, Mass., 1964.

Lewis H. Morgan. *League of the Ho-Dé-No-Sau-Nee, or Iroquois.* Rochester, 1851.

J. L. Morris. *Indians of Ontario.* Department of Lands and Forests, Toronto, 1943.

Richard B. Morris. *The Peacemakers: The Great Powers and American Independence.* New York, 1965.

Charles Merrill Mount. *Gilbert Stuart.* New York, 1964.

Hilda Neatby. *Quebec: The Revolutionary Age, 1760–1791.* Toronto, 1966.

William H. Nelson. *The American Tory.* Oxford, 1961.

Mary Beth Norton. *The British-Americans; The Loyalist Exiles in England, 1774–1789.* Boston and Toronto, 1972.

[William E. Palmer]. *Memoir of the Distinguished Mohawk Indian Chief, Sachem and Warrior, Capt. Joseph Brant.* Brantford, Ont., 1872.

Arthur C. Parker. *An Analytical History of the Seneca Indians.* Canandaigua, N.Y., 1926.

Parker on the Iroquois. Edited by William N. Fenton. Syracuse, N.Y., 1968.

Samuel Parrish. *Some Chapters in the History of the Friendly Association for Regaining and Preserving Peace with the Indians by Pacific Measures.* Philadelphia, 1877.

C. F. Pascoe. *Two Hundred Years of the S. P. G.* London, 1901.

George Peck. *Wyoming.* New York, 1858.

Howard H. Peckham. *Pontiac and the Indian Uprising.* Princeton, N.J., 1947.

Paul Chrisler Phillips and J. W. Smurr. *The Fur Trade.* 2 vols. Norman, Okla., 1961.

Josiah Priest. *Stories of the Revolution.* Albany, 1838.

D. B. Read. *The Life and Times of Gen. John Graves Simcoe . . . together with Some Account of Major André and Capt. Brant.* Toronto, 1890.

W. Max Reid. *The Mohawk Valley.* New York and London, 1901.

William Renwick Riddell. *The Life of William Dummer Powell, First Judge at Detroit and Fifth Chief Justice of Upper Canada.* Lansing, Mich., 1924.

William Renwick Riddell. *Upper Canada Sketches.* Toronto, 1922.

Charles R. Ritcheson. *Aftermath of Revolution: British Policy Toward the United States 1783–1795.* Dallas, 1969.

John Ross Robertson. *The History of Freemasonry in Canada.* 2 vols. Toronto, 1899.

William E. Roscoe. *History of Schoharie County, New York.* Syracuse, 1882.

Eugene H. Roseboom and Francis P. Weisenburger. *A History of Ohio.* Columbus, 1953.

E. M. Ruttenber. *Indian Geographical Names.* [Newburgh, N.Y.], 1906.

Charles Coleman Sellers. *Portraits and Miniatures by Charles Willson Peale.* Philadelphia, 1952.

Ellen Churchill Semple. *American History and Its Geographic Conditions.* Boston and New York, 1903.

Frank H. Severance. *An Old Frontier of France.* 2 vols. New York, 1917.

Frank H. Severance. *Old Trails on the Niagara Frontier.* Buffalo, 1899.

Frank H. Severance. *Studies of the Niagara Frontier.* Buffalo, 1911.

Jeptha R. Simms. *The Frontiersmen of New York.* 2 vols. Albany, 1882–83.

Jeptha R. Simms. *History of Schoharie County, and Border Wars of New York.* Albany, 1845.

George S. Snyderman. "Behind the Tree of Peace." *Pennsylvania Archaeologist* 18, nos. 3–4 (Fall 1948): 3–93.

Jack M. Sosin. *The Revolutionary Frontier 1763–1783.* New York, Chicago, San Francisco, Toronto, and London, 1967.

Jack M. Sosin. *Whitehall and the Wilderness: The Middle West in British Colonial Policy, 1760–1775.* Lincoln, Neb., 1961.

Frank Gouldsmith Speck. *The Iroquois: a Study in Cultural Evolution.* In *Cranbrook Institute of Science Bulletin No. 23,* Second Edition. April 1955.

Charles Worthen Spencer. "The Land System of Colonial New York." *Proceedings of the New York State Historical Association* 16 (1916): 150–64.

William L. Stone. *Life of Joseph Brant-Thayendanegea.* 2 vols. New-York, 1838.

William L. Stone. *The Life and Times of Sir William Johnson, Bart.* 2 vols. Albany, 1865.

William L. Stone. *The Poetry and History of Wyoming.* New-York and London, 1841.

Symposium on Local Diversity in Iroquois Culture. Edited by William N. Fenton. Smithsonian Institution, Bureau of American Ethnology, Bulletin 149. Washington, 1951.

Ralph S. Tarr. *The Physical Geography of New York State.* New York and London, 1902.

B. B. Thatcher. *Indian Biography.* 2 vols. New-York, 1832.

Elisabeth Tooker. "The Iroquois White Dog Sacrifice in the Latter Part of the Eighteenth Century." *Ethnohistory* 12, no. 2 (Spring 1965): 129–40.

Allen W. Trelease. *Indian Affairs in Colonial New York: The Seventeenth Century.* Ithaca, N.Y., 1960.

Allen W. Trelease. "The Iroquois and the Western Fur Trade: A Problem in Interpretation." *The Mississippi Valley Historical Review* 49, no. 1 (June 1962): 32–51.

O. Turner. *History of the Pioneer Settlement of Phelps & Gorham's Purchase, and Morris' Reserve.* Rochester, 1852.

O. Turner. *Pioneer History of the Holland Purchase of Western New York . . . .* Buffalo, 1849.

Alan Valentine. *Lord George Germain.* Oxford, 1962.

Catharine E. Van Cortlandt. "An Original Portrait of Joseph Brant." *The American Historical Record* 2, no. 19 (July 1873): 318–19.

Claude Halstead Van Tyne. *The Loyalists in the American Revolution.* New York and London, 1902.

Albert T. Volwiler. *George Croghan and the Westward Movement, 1741–1782.* Cleveland, 1926.

John J. Vrooman. *Forts and Firesides of the Mohawk Country, New York.* Philadelphia, 1943.

Nicholas B. Wainwright. *George Croghan, Wilderness Diplomat.* Chapel Hill, N.C., 1959.

Jean H. Waldie. "Joseph Brant Thrice Wed, Father of Nine." *Brantford*

Expositor, May 18, 1950; "Brant Stood Staunchly By the Anglican Church," *ibid.*, July 13, 1950; "Indians Gave Six Nations Land," *ibid.*, Nov. 23, 1956; and "Replica of Indian Chief Brant's Home Recalls Hospitable Welcome Given All in Early Days." *London Free Press*, June 26, 1954.

Anthony F. C. Wallace. *The Death and Rebirth of the Seneca.* New York, 1970.

Anthony F. C. Wallace. "Origins of Iroquois Neutrality: The Grand Settlement of 1701." *Pennsylvania History* 24, no. 3 (July 1957): 223–35.

Paul A. W. Wallace. *Conrad Weiser, 1696–1760: Friend of Colonist and Mohawk.* Philadelphia and London, 1945.

Paul A. W. Wallace. *Indian Paths of Pennsylvania.* Harrisburg, 1965.

Paul A. W. Wallace. *Indians in Pennsylvania.* Harrisburg, 1961.

Paul A. W. Wallace. *The White Roots of Peace.* Philadelphia, 1946.

Humphry Ward and W. Roberts. *Romney: A Biographical and Critical Essay with a Catalogue Raisonné of his Works.* 2 vols. London and New York, 1904.

Frederick Lewis Weis. *The Colonial Clergy of the Middle Colonies, New York, New Jersey, and Pennsylvania 1628–1776.* Worcester, Mass., 1957.

C. A. Weslager. *The Delaware Indians: A History.* New Brunswick, N.J., 1972.

Arthur Preston Whitaker. *The Spanish-American Frontier: 1783–1795.* Boston and New York, 1927.

Norman B. Wilkinson. "Robert Morris and the Treaty of Big Tree." *The Mississippi Valley Historical Review* 40, no. 1 (June 1953): 257–78.

Frazer Ells Wilson. *Arthur St. Clair, Rugged Ruler of the Old Northwest.* Richmond, 1944.

Louis Aubrey Wood. *The War Chief of the Six Nations.* Toronto, 1915.

George M. Wrong. *Canada and the American Revolution.* New York, 1935.

Also, articles in *Dictionary of American Biography*, the new *Dictionary of Canadian Biography*, and standard biographies, if there are such, of all persons with whom Joseph Brant was associated or had dealings.

SUGGESTED READING IN ANTHROPOLOGY

Though this life of Joseph Brant is meant as a history, it sometimes veers toward the field of anthropology. Articles on this aspect of Indians mentioned in connection with Brant may be found in such journals as the *Bulletins* of the U.S. *Bureau of American Ethnology*, the *Proceedings of the American Philosophical Society*, *American Antiquity*, *Current Anthropology*, *American Anthropologist*, *Ethnohistory*, and similar publications of American states and Canadian provinces as well as of museums and universities in both the United States and Canada. Some writers to look for (though this is by no means a complete list, and almost any article found in these journals would be authoritative) are Frank G. Speck, George S. Snyderman, William N. Fenton, Alexander A. Goldenweiser, Paul A. W. Wallace, Anthony F. C. Wallace, Alexander Spoehr, Bruce G. Trigger, Nancy O. Lurie, William T. Hagan, Francis Jennings, Malcolm Montgomery, John A. Noon, Annemarie A. Shimony, John Witthoft, Elisabeth Tooker, and William A. Ritchie, some of whom have previously been mentioned in this bibliography as authors and editors of books and articles.

Index

JB stands for Joseph Brant; n. means that a note contains additional information.

JOSEPH BRANT

was composed in 11-pt. Mergenthaler Goudy Old Style on a Linotron 202 and leaded one point,
with display type also in Goudy Old Style
by Coghill Book Typesetting Co.;
printed by sheet-fed offset on 50-pound, acid-free Glatfelter Smooth Offset,
Smythe-sewn, and bound over boards in Joanna Arrestox B
by Maple-Vail Book Manufacturing Group, Inc.;
and published by

SYRACUSE UNIVERSITY PRESS
SYRACUSE, NEW YORK 13210